THE HEATH INTRODUCTION TO
LITERATURE

SIXTH EDITION

Alice S. Landy

William Rodney Allen
Louisiana School for Math, Science, and the Arts

HOUGHTON MIFFLIN COMPANY
Boston   New York

Senior Sponsoring Editor: Dean Johnson
Editorial Associate: Bruce Cantley
Project Editor: Aileen Mason
Editorial Assistant: Tezeta Tulloch/Jane Lee
Associate Production/Design Coordinator: Jodi O'Rourke
Director of Manufacturing: Michael O'Dea
Senior Marketing Manager: Nancy Lyman
Senior Cover Design Coordinator: Deborah Azerrad Savona

Cover design: Minko Dimov, minkoimages
Cover art: *Ocean Park No. 70, 1974*, Richard Diebenkorn. Courtesy Des Moines Art Center.

Text credits continue on pages 993–996, which constitute an extension of the copyright page.

Library of Congress Catalog Card Number: 99-71981

ISBN: 0-395-98070-4

1 2 3 4 5 6 7 8 9-DC-03 02 01 00 99

CONTENTS

❦

Character Study and Social Commentary

AN ANTHOLOGY OF SHORT STORIES

POETRY

Elements of Poetry

The Speaker in the Poem

Imagery

Sound

AN ANTHOLOGY OF POEMS

DRAMA

PREFACE

All six editions of *The Heath Introduction to Literature* are products of our consultation with hundreds of teachers of literature and writing from all over the country. Although the text has evolved considerably from its first incarnation, our mission continues to be to provide a rich yet inexpensive collection of literature, organized by genre and divided into useful units that focus upon various literary concepts, techniques, and modes. We hope that students will not only "encounter" literature when using this text, but also learn new ways to experience, interact with, and write critically about fiction, poetry, and drama. The chapter introductions, apparatus, study questions, and composition instruction are designed to help the different selections cohere into both a thorough presentation of the different genres and a thoughtful, challenging, and *complete* course in reading and writing about literature.

In addition to offering over a dozen new literary selections, the sixth edition is enhanced by several new features. The publication date of each story, poem, and play now appears at the end of the selection. To help students orient themselves to the various works, short biographies of each author (which formerly appeared only in the *Instructor's Manual*) now appear in the text. A new discussion of various critical approaches (formalist, reader response, deconstruction, and so forth) bolsters Chapter 2, "Writing about Literature." Finally, we have included a filmography of film adaptations of the plays in the drama section.

Like previous editions, the sixth edition is divided into four parts. The first part supplies a general introduction to the study of literature. Its opening chapter, on reading literature, introduces the student to fundamental components such as plot, character, and theme, and to basic critical concepts such as unity and inevitability. This chapter also introduces the philosophy of the text: that literature is a dialogue between writer and reader, the purpose of which is to develop a complex, enriching vision of humanity and the universe. The second chapter, on writing about literature, reiterates these fundamentals and shows how they underlie the processes of writing about literature. Whereas the first chapter is philosophical in bent, the second is practical. Work plans, lists of questions, and the new survey of critical approaches make the idea of writing both concrete and comprehensible and provide "how-to's" for the assignments in the rest of the book.

Although these introductory chapters precede the structured parts on fiction, poetry, and drama, students need not read them first. The instructor who wishes to begin with short stories or poems can elicit spontaneous student responses, unguided by study questions. The instructor can then apply the questions raised in the introductory chapters to works the students have recently read, thus focusing the course on the reading *of* (rather than *about*) literature.

Fiction is the first genre selection. The chapters in this section are organized in terms of modes of narration, which highlights the interplay between listener and narrator and keeps the basic framework of the text simple. Within this structure, other concepts appear as a natural outgrowth of the subject under discussion and easily become a part of the student's critical vocabulary. The presentation provides a variety of critical concepts within a firmly structured framework—a more satisfying organization than the "grasshopper" approach in which each chapter, or each story, heralds a new topic and leaves students and instructors alike negotiating the jumps between topics as best they can. Seven stories are new to this edition.

Poetry follows fiction, because most instructors prefer this order. Throughout the poetry section we use well-known and highly readable works to introduce the student to the technical aspects of poetry, such as rhythm and verse form, and then to the genre's subtler concerns, among them the voice of the speaker, imagery, and the use of sound. This movement allows the student to begin with a general overview of a poem and then to delve more deeply into the specific characteristics that *make* it a poem. For those instructors who wish to offer their students works free of critical commentary, an anthology of poems completes the section. Eight poems have been added to this edition, appearing in both the introductory chapters and the poetry anthology.

Drama receives strong, chronological coverage in this edition. The chronological organization of this section clearly illustrates the important structural and historical developments of this genre. This final section includes works from tragedy, comedy, realism, and contemporary drama. We are pleased to include G. Blakemore Evans's respected editions of *Hamlet* and *Much Ado About Nothing*. We also feature a new contemporary play, George C. Wolfe's *The Colored Museum*.

Each section includes plentiful study aids: introductory essays, study questions, essay suggestions, and questions for further thought. Objective and subjective responses have their place as answers to our questions; the emphasis is on knowing the difference and on achieving a judicious balance between the two. In general, questions near the beginning of a section offer more guidance than those that come later, thus tacitly encouraging students to greater independence as their skills and familiarity with literature grow. Some sets of questions suggest how to organize an essay; others concentrate on showing how to follow a theme through a story, poem, or play; still others encourage students to look at a work from as many angles as possible.

We believe that a good textbook, like the literature it contains, must offer variety within unity, and we have done our best to achieve that goal. We owe our thanks to the following people who have helped us: Skai Ahern, Borough of

Manhattan Community College; Michael Anzelone, Nassau Community College; Phillip D. Atteberry, University of Pittsburgh at Titusville; Granger Babcock, Louisiana School for Math, Science, and the Arts; Nahla Beier, Louisiana School for Math, Science, and the Arts; Ethel Bonds, Virginia Western Community College; Thomas Brazie, Glendale Community College; Susan Bullard, Cedar Valley College; Robert Burke, Joliet Junior College; Bruce Cantley, Houghton Mifflin; Adele Carpenter, Lewis and Clark Community College; Sean Clark, Joliet Junior College; Thomas Cody, El Camino College; Keith Coplin, Colby Community College; Clayton Delery, Louisiana School for Math, Science, and the Arts; John Driscoll, Phoenix College; Allan Duane, Ulster County Community College; Lou Ellison, Lurleen B. Wallace State Junior College; Craig Etchison, Allegany Community College; Kathy Frederickson, Quinsigamond Community College; Robert F. Fuhrmann, Technical Career Institutes; James F. Gordon Jr., Mississippi Delta Junior College; Michael Greene, Wentworth Institute of Technology; Maria Human, Louisiana Technical University; Julia Jay, San Jacinto College, Central Campus; Jeff Jeske, University of California, Los Angeles; Dean Johnson, Houghton Mifflin; Mary Lund, Henry Ford Community College; Aileen Mason, Houghton Mifflin; J. V. McCrory, William Carey College; Richard McLamore, McMurry University; Vernon Miles, University of Arkansas; Eileen Neville, Mount Marty College; Don Richardson, Phoenix College; Richard M. Salamas, Henry Ford Community College; Margaret Shepherd, Surry Community College; Rebecca Shuttleworth, Mississippi Delta Junior College; Bev Smith, Lurleen B. Wallace State Junior College; Paul Smith, Allyn and Bacon Publishers; Joel Stancliff, Georgia Institute of Technology; Margaret Stein, University of Notre Dame; Jean Anne Strebinger, University of Notre Dame; Margaret Sullivan, University of California, Los Angeles; Sheila Tombe, University of South Carolina, Beaufort; Barry Tomkins, Hudson County Community College; John Tucker, Nassau Community College; Lana Way, Mississippi Delta Community College; Jeannette Webber, Santa Barbara City College; John A. Weldon, Clinton Community College; and Roger Zimmerman, Lewis and Clark Community College.

A special word of thanks goes to Daniel Le, who provided invaluable assistance in preparing this edition of the text.

Finally, we thank you, the users of this book, both long-term and new, who bring to it your own love of literature and skills in teaching. We hope that this edition of *The Heath Introduction to Literature* serves you well.

ALICE S. LANDY
WILLIAM RODNEY ALLEN
Editors

INTRODUCTION:
ON LITERATURE

1

THE BASES OF LITERATURE

Literature has its roots in one of the most basic human desires—the desire for pleasure. Its creators find one source of pleasure in mastering the difficult demands of their craft. If they write well, they then reap a second delight from witnessing the pleasure their work gives to others. Readers, meanwhile, derive pleasure not only from the "escape" value of reading but also from literature's power to imitate life. A truly good book can speak of imaginary people so vividly that they seem more alive than people we meet on the street, and can make us care about its characters as if they were close friends.

We are always curious about each other, and usually curious about ourselves as well. Why do we behave as we do? What are the causes of our actions? Literature is far from having all the answers, but it does offer hints, suggestions, and flashes of insight. Moreover, it offers them in such a way as to refresh and encourage our own thinking, and so leads us to insights of our own. Readers have many standards for judging a writer. But one enduring standard is the writer's power of **interpretation**—to interpret us, as humans, to ourselves. We prize those writers who seem to know people deeply, and to share that knowledge with us openly and honestly. We speak with disdain of shallow or insincere writers; we demand truth and sincerity even in the most fantastic fiction.

Literature, then, exists primarily because it pleases us. And it pleases us by imitating life—or, more precisely, by displaying a vision of life as it is or as the writers think it should be. But how does it contrive its imitation? Its only medium is words; and we know how hard it is to make words say what we want them to say. How do writers handle their words so as to get such powerful effects from them? What guidelines help them make the million-and-one choices that result in a play, a poem, or a story?

The first necessities for any work of literature—and therefore the first things that writers must consider—are **plot** and **character**. These may occur to a writer in either order. That is, a writer may first imagine some characters, and then decide what actions they are to perform; or a writer may envision some action, and then decide on the people who must perform it. Every work of literature, however, must have both **action** and characters. If it lacks either, it cannot please us or hold our interest.

It may seem that poetry is an exception to this rule. Whereas stories and plays tend to present fully developed plots with sequences of actions with discernible beginnings, middles, and ends, poems more often plunge us into the middle of an event, and may tell us neither what came before the event nor what comes after it.

Here, for instance, is a poem with no physical action at all. Yet it shows us one person, at least, and gives us some insight into his actions and feelings.

George Gordon, Lord Byron

(1788–1824)

So We'll Go No More A-Roving

So we'll go no more a-roving
  So late into the night,
Though the heart be still as loving,
  And the moon be still as bright.

5 For the sword outwears its sheath,
  And the soul wears out the breast,
And the heart must pause to breathe,
  And Love itself have rest.

Though the night was made for loving,
10   And the day returns too soon,
Yet we'll go no more a-roving
  By the light of the moon.

1817

We know several things about the speaker of this poem. We know that he has enjoyed "roving," and that he still thinks warmly of it, because he declares that "the night was made for loving,/And the day returns too soon." We know that he feels weary, like a sheath worn out by its sword. We hear him declare that his roving days are done. But we also hear him speak of pausing and resting, verbs that imply an eventual return to action. And so we begin to wonder: is he really finished with love, as he says he is? The action of the poem might thus be described as the act of the lover forswearing love. Its interest arises from our recognition of the complex emotions the renunciation reveals. It is the action, and the emotion, of a moment; but it is none the less real—and none the less action—for its momentary nature.

For now, however, let us return to the more thoroughly developed plots of drama and fiction. These, too, must find some balance between action and **emotion**, some method of telling us both what the characters do and how they feel. A given story may emphasize action or feeling; that choice, like so many others, is up to its writer. But it must contain some of both. We have no interest in unfeeling characters or in characters who do nothing.

In addition to a plot and to characters who act and feel, a work of literature must have **unity** and **coherence**. It should make us believe that its characters really would have performed the actions it says they did, and that the actions could reasonably have taken place. At its best, the movement of a play, a poem, or a story ought to make us feel that the tale could have reached no other end, and that it could have reached it in no other way. When this happens, the story's ending seems inevitable. Its characters and its actions have completely convinced us. A sense of **inevitability** is thus another hallmark of a fine work of literature.

The **language** of a work of literature is also important. Words have so many undercurrents of meaning that the change of one word may change our image of a scene or a character. Consider, for instance, the difference between *a thin, tense man; a thin, nervous man;* and *a thin, harried man*—or the difference between *a plump woman, a well-rounded woman,* and *an overweight woman.* A writer should choose his or her language with care. The language of literature should carry overtones that enrich our sense of the story, thus adding to the pleasure we get from the tale. And it must avoid false tones, for those diminish our pleasure. Again, we demand at least that the words fit the actions and characters of which they tell. And again, we find that the best literary language seems almost inevitable. Reading it, we cannot imagine the author having used any other words.

When we read, we usually don't want to be aware of these choices by the writer of words and acts and characters. We don't want to hear the author muttering behind the scenes: "I need this word, not that one. This character must say this; that description must carry this message." Rather, we want to be able to concentrate on the story itself, accepting everything within it as valid and necessary parts of its world. When we discuss and analyze works of literature, however, we do become aware of the choices the writers made in constructing them. We note who the characters are and how they relate to each other. We observe how the action begins, how it ends, and how it is carried from beginning to ending. We study how the language characterizes people and events and consider the broader or deeper meanings it suggests.

These questions, we may note, are **questions of fact**. Their answers can be searched for, found, and agreed upon. We can count the characters in *Hamlet,* and learn that Hamlet is a prince of Denmark, that Gertrude is his mother and Claudius his stepfather, and that the ghost who appears from time to time is very probably the ghost of Hamlet's murdered father. Similarly, we learn that eight people are killed during the course of the play (one by stabbing, one by drowning, two by beheading, one by poison, and three by some combination of sword, wounds, and poison) and that virtually none of the major characters is still alive when the play ends. There is no question about any of these happenings and no reason to argue about them.

Questions of fact, however, are only a beginning in thinking about a work of literature. They tell us certain choices a writer made, but they rarely tell us why the writer made those particular choices. To learn that, we must go on to **questions of interpretation**, questions that deal with the artistic vision underlying the work and thus with such issues as theme, pattern, message, and meaning.

Message and **meaning** are not universal to literature. They belong to one school of literature, the **didactic**. When writers or critics demand that a story carry a message to its readers, that it "mean something" to them, they are saying that literature should "teach" us something in the moral sense of the word. At its most reductive, this approach ends in pat morals: "Always tell the truth; stop beating up on your fellow humans." On a more sophisticated level, however, didacticism becomes what the critic Matthew Arnold called "**high seriousness**" and produces literature that deals with such complex questions as the value of human life and the sources of human ideals and aspirations.

Not all literature is didactic. Some writers believe that literature does not need to make a moral statement. As Ernest Hemingway once famously remarked, "If you want to send a message, try Western Union." For such writers, a work of literature is important for its own sake, not for any telegram-like message it might carry. As one modern poet put it, "A poem should not mean, but be."[1] In works like these, the concept of message does not apply; to impose one on them is to falsify the intent of the writer.

The questions of **theme** and **pattern**, however, concern all literature. Within any imaginative work that strikes us as unified and complete, we will find some sort of pattern into which its parts fit or through which they are perceived. Didactic tales, for example, present acts and people in terms of a moral order. Hence the tales tend to be built around patterns of good and evil, temptation and response. In contrast, a Romantic poem describing a summer day might have sensory impressions of light and shade, coolness and warmth, as its unifying vision.

There may be many **patterns—of action, characterization, language**, or **metaphor**—within a single work. Sometimes each will work separately; sometimes several will intertwine to bear on a single theme. Sometimes, too, several themes will combine within one work to create a complexity of vision that no single theme could contain. But always there will be that sense of a single, ordered vision embracing and unifying all the patterns or themes.

When we study literature, we first look at each story as an entity in itself, existing on its own terms. We enter the world of the story and speak of its characters and narrator as though they were living people. Eventually, however, we begin to wonder about the writers of the stories. Why did they choose to create these characters, to have them perform these actions, to tell their tales from this particular point of view?

We can never know exactly what writers had in mind when they were writing their stories. The process of writing is too complex, with too much of it hidden even from the writers themselves, to allow any sure or simple answers to that question. In this sense, there are **limits to the author's interpretation**. But we should examine our own ideas on the subject—our sense of what the writers seem to consider important and what values or feelings of ours they seem to be invoking—because our impression of the writers' values and intentions plays an important part in our response to their work.

---

[1]Archibald MacLeish, "Ars Poetica," p. 522.

Here interpretation becomes most individual and most varied. We all read the same words when we read a story. We observe the same characters acting out the same deeds and passions. But we each interpret them a little differently because of our individual views of life, our interests, and our experience. Therefore, when we try to explain how the story works, or decide what themes are important, we read some of our own perceptions into the story.

If we realize that we are interpreting, all is well. Then we can say, "This is how it seems to me." We can look for **patterns of imagery** or language and details of action or characterization to support our view. We can listen to others who have other views and evaluate the support they bring for their arguments; and, in the end, we can probably come to a pretty fair idea of what the story does have to offer and how it is able to offer it.

On the other hand, if we do not recognize the extent to which we are active interpreters of what we read, we may have trouble when we try to deal with such subjective issues as theme or message. For then we may make the error of saying, "I see this. Therefore the author intended it that way, and I have found the only correct interpretation this story can possibly have." Literary critics call this error interpretation the **intentional fallacy**. Because very few works of literature will not admit some variation in interpretation, definitive statements about what an author "intended" are wrong more often than not. It is true that there are limits to the range of interpretations we can apply to a work of literature if we are to read it honestly on its own terms. Nathaniel Hawthorne's *The Scarlet Letter,* for example, is absolutely not about baseball. Within those limits, however, we must be willing to acknowledge various ways of looking at literature.

We must also be willing to allow our perceptions to change. It often happens that what we notice the first time we read a story is not what seems most important to us later on. Nor would it make sense to talk or write about a poem or a story if our perception of it could not be enriched by the discussion. Further, we must be willing to use our full judgment, to read the story carefully and attentively. We must be sure we are trying to discover what it really does say rather than simply assuming that it says what we want it to say. Once we have done this, however, we should be able to feel comfortable with our judgments and our responses. Above all, we must not undervalue ourselves. We are the people for whom these stories, plays, and poems are written. If we cannot trust ourselves, we will have a hard time trusting them.

2

WRITING ABOUT LITERATURE

Literature allows writers to share their ideas and visions with their readers. Their work is not complete until someone has read it and responded to it.

As readers, we too have something to say. At the very least, we have opinions about the work itself, but we also may have other ideas to express. Perhaps we are moved to compare this story with others, or perhaps it has given us some new ideas that we want to explore further. Sometimes we share our ideas directly with others in face-to-face discussions. At other times, we become writers in order to communicate our thoughts and opinions.

The first part of writing about literature, therefore, is thinking about it. This step is perhaps the most vital part of the process, because we need to know not only what we think but why we think as we do. Which of our thoughts come from the work itself? Which have been inspired by it? Which come from our predispositions and preconceptions about literature?

We enjoy stories for many reasons. Some are intrinsic to the story itself: artful language, characters we believe in and care about, actions that carry significant messages for us or give us new insight into ourselves and our society. (Whether the story provides that insight by answering questions for us or by urging us into asking our own questions does not matter here. What *does* matter is that the impetus for question or answer comes from within the story itself.) Other causes of enjoyment are external, coming not from the artistry of the story, but from the fact that the story fits our current notions of what a story should be like or calls forth some pleasant personal memories. In short, the external factors in our response to a story come from things we already think or feel. Intrinsic factors come from the writer's craftsmanship and art.[1]

When we read for pleasure alone, we need not care where our pleasure comes from. Any appeal a story may have will be welcome. When we study literature, however, we want to concentrate on the intrinsic qualities of the works we read, for they can teach us most about the craft and the workings of literature. A story's intrinsic qualities, therefore, and our response to them, are what we focus on when we write about literature.

When we rule out external responses to literature and say that we are only going to talk and write about its intrinsic qualities, we are not denying the individuality of our responses. In fact, only when we escape from our prejudices and

---

[1]What is true for stories is true for plays and poems as well. For the rest of this chapter, therefore, the word *stories* will stand for all types of literature.

9

preconceptions about literature can we respond most freely to the stories we read. Even when we write most directly of the story itself and the art that created it, our writing will contain an emotional component as well as an intellectual one. Emotion and intellect together answer such questions as, "Does the hero's death seem inevitable?" and "How has it been made to seem so?"

All analysis ends in **judgment**. All questions of "How is this done?" begin or end with "Is it a success?" It would be useless to ask "How has the writer characterized his heroine?" if we could not also ask "Has he made me care what happens to her?" Literature appeals to mind and emotions alike: our **response** to it, therefore, must be both **analytic** and **emotional**, **objective** and **subjective**. Concentrating on intrinsic aspects of the story does not deny the subjective component of our response. Rather, it frees us for more truly personal reactions, subjective and objective alike, even while it helps us recognize how and why we are responding.

Before we begin to write about a story, therefore, we should ask ourselves some version of the following questions:

1. Which aspects of the story had the greatest impact on me?
2. What did they seem to be saying? How did they say it? (Or what did they make me think that seemed new to me? How did they make me think it?)
3. How did other aspects of the story support or contribute to my response?
4. How did these particular aspects of the story help create the story's total effect?

We start, that is, with our response to the story; we move from there to an analysis of the art that creates the response; and then we return to the overall impression or effect.

When we write, we follow the same pattern of response, analysis, and final judgment. Unless we have unlimited time and paper, however, we will not be able to write down all that we have thought about the story. We must make choices: What shall I include? What shall I emphasize? To make those choices, we must consider not only the story and our response to it, but the purpose of our paper and the audience for which we are writing it.

Let's look at two extreme examples. Let's imagine, first, that we keep a journal or diary and that we want to record in it the fact that we read and enjoyed a story. In this case, our main interest would be our own reaction to the story; our writing, therefore, would concentrate on our subjective response. We would mention only those incidents or characters that impressed us most strongly; and we could write in whatever style we pleased, for we would be our only audience.

At the other extreme, suppose we were writing a paper for a scholarly journal. In this case, we would write in an objective, balanced style, presenting carefully worked-out analyses of each aspect of the story that related to our topic. We would define our terms carefully and provide adequate illustrations to support our thesis. In fact, we would be writing almost like a debater, trying to make our points as clear, convincing, and firmly based on factual evidence as possible.

Most writing assignments lie somewhere between these extremes. Two we might look at are book reviews and English papers. Let's consider what these types of writing most often say. Then let's look at how they can go about saying it.

Book reviews tend to be frankly subjective, focusing on "what I liked and why I liked it" (or, alternatively, "why you shouldn't waste time or money on this book"). By its very nature, a review commits the reviewer to making judgments: the book may be "one of the year's best," or "not up to this author's usual standards," or simply "a pleasant afternoon's reading." Too, the reviewer may try to judge what type of reader would enjoy the book most: "Readers with a taste for psychological studies will enjoy . . . ," or "Mystery fans will welcome the appearance of. . . ."

A brief review may contain little more than these judgments. A more thorough review will usually provide evidence to support them, by discussing some particularly outstanding character or episode or by quoting a few lines of description or dialogue as a sample of the writer's style. Readers of reviews are presumed to be asking themselves, "Is this a book I want to read?" Through judgments and illustrations supporting the judgments, reviews are designed to help readers answer that question.

A review, therefore, will generally begin in one of two ways. It will either start right out with its broadest judgment to show exactly where the reviewer stands, or it will start out with a "teaser," a quotation or detail from the book that seems striking enough to catch the readers' attention and "tease" them into reading at least the review, if not the book itself.

Then will come the explanation, details, and analyses. What was it that made the experience of reading the book so enjoyable? Why is the teaser a good sample of what the book has to offer? Reviews may focus on one aspect of a book, such as its characters, or they may glance at many aspects in turn. But they must maintain a balance between the personal interest of the reviewers' subjective comments and the objective analyses with which they try to convince us that they are sound judges of books whose opinions should be respected. And they must bring their comments and analyses together again in a final summary, judgment, or call to action: "Rush right out and buy this book; you won't be disappointed."

Reviewers, then, consider their audience (potential readers of the book being reviewed) and their purpose (telling their readers that the book exists and helping them decide whether they want to read it). The **reviewer's role** includes offering judgments, supporting them with relevant evidence, and drawing all together to a logical conclusion.

English papers demand many of the same techniques as reviews and are often written in similar formats. They vary in scope and purpose, however, more than reviews do. The **writing assignments** in this book provide a range of possible types of papers.

Many of the assignments are quite narrowly defined. Their purpose is to make you look closely at some particular technique the writer used—the role of the narrator in a story, for example, or the way a theme is carried through a tale. In this case your writing, too, must be tightly focused, your style almost wholly objective. Your first paragraph will probably work up to your basic thesis; and every sentence that follows, down to your final summation, will bear directly on that thesis. The particular points you discuss, and the order in which you present them, may be suggested by the questions or instructions of the assignment itself. The evidence with which you support your answers will come from within the story. But the finished product will be very much your own: a tight, coherent piece of writing built on your own handling of the material given to you by the story.

Other assignments are broader or ask that you define your own subject (for example, "What do you think is the major theme of this story?" "How would you support your view?"). Now you must express your own judgments more boldly. You must decide which aspects of the story you should emphasize, and which are irrelevant to the question at hand. Your responsibility is not only to provide evidence to support a theory you were told to discuss, but first to set up your theory and then to support it.

Again, you will want to write a tightly focused paper, making full use of detailed evidence. But your opening, conclusion, and whatever general statements control your central discussion will be somewhat broader in their implications than those of the earlier assignment, and they will represent your own judgments as to what is most important to the story and to your essay. This essay, too, will follow the general format of initial response → analysis → rafinal summary. But the analysis will be fuller and more complex than is necessary with a more narrowly defined paper.

As you progress in your studies, you will learn more about various critical approaches to literature and the kinds of writing resulting from their application. Examples of these approaches include the biographical, formalist, mythic, Freudian, Marxist, feminist, reader response, deconstructive, and neo-realist readings of literature. These different lenses through which the literary critic may look at a particular work have the advantage of focusing attention on a particular facet of the story at hand.

Biographical criticism, for example, draws connections between the writer's personal experience and his or her work. It is useful to know, for instance, that the Communist government of Czechoslovakia arrested Vaclav Havel in the 1960s for writing subversive plays like *Protest* (1978). **Formalist criticism** focuses on the internal structure of the work itself, to the exclusion of external factors such as the author's biography or social milieu. The **New Critics** of the 1930s championed formalism—the careful analysis of irony, tension, and paradox in literature. In the 1950s and 1960s, **mythic criticism** proponents like Northrop Frye emphasized universal mythical patterns in literary works—the quest, the encounter with one's dark twin or *doppelganger,* the recurrent idea of the loss of a golden age. **Freudian** and **Marxist criticism** systematically apply the insights of those two important thinkers both to literary works and their authors. Freudians focus on the individual's psyche, with its conflicts between the conscious ego and the unconscious id, while Marxists focus on the historical level, seeing economic forces as the determinants of human interactions and personalities.

Since the 1970s, **feminist criticism** has been a particularly rich literary field, as more and more women scholars have entered the universities, and more and more women writers have become the objects of critical scrutiny. Feminists range from essentialists who believe that women have certain universal character traits to those who reject essentialism in favor of a critique of historically constructed gender roles. **Reader response criticism** focuses on the fact that literary works exist in the fullest sense only in the minds of readers, and that those minds differ from each other; consequently, we can agree on a reading of a work only to the extent that we live in an interpretive community of like-minded readers. Likewise, **deconstructive criticism** tries to decenter the authority of a text to suggest that such traditional ideas as "meaning" or "organic unity" are at best highly problematic. Deconstructionists insist on the indeterminacy and textuality not only of literature but of all of human culture as well. From this critical perspective, humanistic—or even scientific—"truths" are simply social constructions with no real authority behind them.

In the last decade, however, a critical reaction against deconstruction has gained momentum. Critics of deconstruction see that perspective as self-contradictory, even nihilistic. Neo-realists insist that there *is* an objective world outside of language, and that literature, like the sciences, should strive to become an ever more accurate "map" of that world. In **neo-realism**, the science of biology and its unifying idea of evolution provide a more enduring perspective on the activities of producing and reading literature than do the speculations about the "reflexivity of language" of deconstruction.

But whatever your level of critical sophistication, the first step in writing about literature is organizing your thoughts. Usually, when we first think of writing an essay, we think of a number of random ideas. If we are clever, we jot those down. Later, more ideas will arrive—some of them outgrowths of our first ideas, some of them totally new ideas; jot those down, too.

Try following these steps:

1. Write down ideas as you get them. You can write them down as a numbered list on a sheet of paper, or you can write each on a separate card (a real 3″ × 5″or 4″ × 6″card, or a computer-software "card").
2. When you have collected a fair number of ideas, look them over. Look for ideas that fall together into groups, ideas that relate to each other. If you are using cards, create physical groups of cards from these logical connections. If you are using a numbered list, write your groups of numbers down on a new sheet of paper. Note that some ideas may not fit neatly into groups. These will be left over, by themselves.

3. Look at your various groups. What is your main topic for each? You may find your general topic already declared as one of your original ideas, or you may have to create it. In any event, create and mark "major topic" cards or list entries to go at the head of each group.

4. Now look at your major topics, and at your "left over" ideas. Which groups and single ideas fit together well into a paper of the sort you want to write? Are there any "holes" in your paper, now that you see it starting to take shape? If so, fill them in now, creating cards or entries for them. Do some ideas, or groups of ideas, not fit into the paper as you now see it? If so, leave them out. Even professional writers often throw away much of their early work, and this gathering, grouping, and arranging process is one that many professional writers use when working on explanatory books and articles.

5. Arrange your chosen major topics, with the ideas that support them, in the order you think will make the strongest paper. If you need new entries for introductory and closing statements, sketch those out now and put them in place. You now have the outline for the first draft of your paper. In fact, if you wrote out your ideas very fully, your first draft may be half written already!

It is possible that, as you work, you will become dissatisfied with your first outline and will modify it. Ideas you first included may end up omitted; ideas that were rejected early on may come back in. Papers and essays are often dynamic things, changing as they go along. Sometimes, indeed, it's not till you've sketched out your first draft that you realize what it was that you *really* wanted to write—and it's not this at all.

The act of writing about literature, by forcing us to look closely at what we have read and to analyze both the work and our own responses to it, is thus the final step in the act of reading. Now we are not only enjoying the words by which someone else speaks to us but also stretching our own minds to the task of communicating with others. In reading and writing, we take an active role and thus reassert ourselves as active, thinking, feeling beings. The opportunity to make that reassertion may well represent one of the deepest values of literature. It is certainly an opportunity well worth responding to.

FICTION

Fiction as Narrative

3

THE ART OF NARRATION: GIVING MEANING TO ACTION

Fiction is the art of the storyteller. Not only are writers of fiction storytellers themselves, but within every story they create a new storyteller, the narrator of the tale. It is the narrator's voice we hear speaking as we read a novel or short story. The narrator introduces the tale to us, keeps us amused during its telling, and says goodbye to us at its end. The narrator describes scenes and characters, relates events, sets the tone of the tale, and supplies whatever meanings or explanations the author sees fit to provide.

Reader and story are thus brought together by the narrator. For this reason, the study of fiction usually begins with a study of types of narrators and narrations. Let us now look at two very brief stories: first a folktale from one of the oldest traditions of storytelling and then a more modern tale. Notice in each case the simplicity of the action and the sharp contrasts drawn among the few characters. Listen to the voices of the storytellers as they build their tales.

Clever Manka (Czechoslovakia)

Anonymous

There was once a rich farmer who was as grasping and unscrupulous as he was rich. He was always driving a hard bargain and always getting the better of his poor neighbors. One of these neighbors was a humble shepherd who, in return for service, was to receive from the farmer a heifer. When the time of payment came, the farmer refused to give the shepherd the heifer, and the shepherd was forced to lay the matter before the burgomaster.

The burgomaster, who was a young man and as yet not very experienced, listened to both sides, and when he had deliberated, he said:

"Instead of deciding this case, I will put a riddle to you both, and the man who makes the best answer shall have the heifer. Are you agreed?"

The farmer and the shepherd accepted this proposal and the burgomaster said:

"Well, then, here is my riddle: What is the swiftest thing in the world? What is the sweetest thing? What is the richest? Think out your answers and bring them to me at this same hour tomorrow."

The farmer went home in a temper.

"What kind of burgomaster is this young fellow!" he growled. "If he had let me keep the heifer, I'd have sent him a bushel of pears. But now I'm in a fair way of losing the heifer, for I can't think of any answer to his foolish riddle."

"What is the matter, husband?" his wife asked.

"It's that new burgomaster. The old one would have given me the heifer without any argument, but this young man thinks to decide the case by asking us riddles."

When he told his wife what the riddle was, she cheered him greatly by telling him that she knew the answers at once.

"Why, husband," said she, "our gray mare must be the swiftest thing in the world. You know yourself nothing ever passes us on the road. As for the sweetest, did you ever taste honey any sweeter than ours? And I'm sure there's nothing richer than our chest of golden ducats that we've been laying by these forty years."

The farmer was delighted.

"You're right, wife, you're right! That heifer remains ours!"

The shepherd, when he got home, was downcast and sad. He had a daughter, a clever girl named Manka, who met him at the door of his cottage and asked:

"What is it, father? What did the burgomaster say?"

The shepherd sighed.

"I'm afraid I've lost the heifer. The burgomaster set us a riddle, and I know I shall never guess it."

"Perhaps I can help you," Manka said. "What is it?"

The shepherd gave her the riddle, and the next day, as he was setting out for the burgomaster's, Manka told him what answers to make.

When he reached the burgomaster's house, the farmer was already there rubbing his hands and beaming with self-importance.

The burgomaster again propounded the riddle and then asked the farmer his answers.

The farmer cleared his throat and with a pompous air began:

"The swiftest thing in the world? Why, my dear sir, that's my gray mare, of course, for no other horse ever passes us on the road. The sweetest? Honey from my beehives, to be sure. The richest? What can be richer than my chest of golden ducats!"

And the farmer squared his shoulders and smiled triumphantly.

"H'm," said the young burgomaster dryly. Then he asked:

"What answers does the shepherd make?"

The shepherd bowed politely and said:

"The swiftest thing in the world is thought, for thought can run any distance in the twinkling of an eye. The sweetest thing of all is sleep, for when a man is tired and sad, what can be sweeter? The richest thing is the earth, for out of the earth come all the riches of the world."

"Good!" the burgomaster cried. "Good! The heifer goes to the shepherd!"

Later the burgomaster said to the shepherd:

"Tell me now, who gave you those answers? I'm sure they never came out of your own head."

At first the shepherd tried not to tell, but when the burgomaster pressed him, he confessed that they came from his daughter, Manka. The burgomaster, who thought he would like to make another test of Manka's cleverness, sent for ten eggs. He gave them to the shepherd and said:

"Take these eggs to Manka and tell her to have them hatched out by tomorrow and to bring me the chicks."

When the shepherd reached home and gave Manka the burgomaster's message, Manka laughed and said: "Take a handful of millet and go right back to the burgomaster. Say to him: 'My daughter sends you this millet. She says that if you plant it, grow it, and have it harvested by tomorrow, she'll bring you the ten chicks and you can feed them the ripe grain.'"

When the burgomaster heard this, he laughed heartily.

"That's a clever girl of yours," he told the shepherd. "If she's as comely as she is clever, I think I'd like to marry her. Tell her to come to see me, but she must come neither by day nor by night, neither riding nor walking, neither dressed nor undressed."

When Manka received this message, she waited until the next dawn when night was gone and day not yet arrived. Then she wrapped herself in a fish net and, throwing one leg over a goat's back and keeping one foot on the ground, she went to the burgomaster's house.

Now I ask you: did she go dressed? No, she wasn't dressed. A fish net isn't clothing. Did she go undressed? Of course not, for wasn't she covered with a fish net? Did she walk to the burgomaster's? No, she didn't walk, for she went with one leg thrown over a goat. Then did she ride? Of course she didn't ride, for wasn't she walking on one foot?

When she reached the burgomaster's house, she called out:

"Here I am, Mr. Burgomaster, and I've come neither by day nor by night, neither riding nor walking, neither dressed nor undressed."

The young burgomaster was so delighted with Manka's cleverness and so pleased with her comely looks that he proposed to her at once and in a short time married her.

"But understand, my dear Manka," he said, "you are not to use that cleverness of yours at my expense. I won't have you interfering in any of my cases. In fact, if ever you give advice to anyone who comes to me for judgment, I'll turn you out of my house at once and send you home to your father."

All went well for a time. Manka busied herself in her housekeeping and was careful not to interfere in any of the burgomaster's cases.

Then one day two farmers came to the burgomaster to have a dispute settled. One of the farmers owned a mare that had foaled in the marketplace. The colt had run under the wagon of the other farmer, and thereupon the owner of the wagon claimed the colt as his property.

The burgomaster, who was thinking of something else while the case was being presented, said carelessly:

"The man who found the colt under his wagon is, of course, the owner of the colt."

As the owner of the mare was leaving the burgomaster's house, he met Manka and stopped to tell her about the case. Manka was ashamed of her husband for making so foolish a decision, and she said to the farmer:

"Come back this afternoon with a fishing net and stretch it across the dusty road. When the burgomaster sees you, he will come out and ask you what you are doing. Say to him that you're catching fish. When he asks you how you can expect to catch fish in a dusty road, tell him it's just as easy for you to catch fish in a dusty road as it is for a wagon to foal. Then he'll see the injustice of his decision and have the colt returned to you. But remember one thing: you mustn't let him find out that it was I who told you to do this."

That afternoon, when the burgomaster chanced to look out the window, he saw a man stretching a fish net across the dusty road. He went out to him and asked:

"What are you doing?"

"Fishing."

"Fishing in a dusty road? Are you daft?"

"Well," the man said, "it's just as easy for me to catch fish in a dusty road as it is for a wagon to foal."

Then the burgomaster recognized the man as the owner of the mare, and he had to confess that what he said was true.

"Of course the colt belongs to your mare and must be returned to you. But tell me," he said, "who put you up to this? You didn't think of it yourself."

The farmer tried not to tell, but the burgomaster questioned him until he found out that Manka was at the bottom of it. This made him very angry. He went into the house and called his wife.

"Manka," he said, "did you forget what I told you would happen if you went interfering in any of my cases? Home you go this very day. I don't care to hear any excuses. The matter is settled. You may take with you the one thing you like best in my house, for I won't have people saying that I treated you shabbily."

Manka made no outcry.

"Very well, my dear husband, I shall do as you say: I shall go home to my father's cottage and take with me the one thing I like best in your house. But don't make me go until after supper. We have been very happy together and I should like to eat one last meal with you. Let us have no more words but be kind to each other as we've always been and then part as friends."

The burgomaster agreed to this, and Manka prepared a fine supper of all the dishes of which her husband was particularly fond. The burgomaster opened his choicest wine and pledged Manka's health. Then he set to, and the supper was so good that he ate and ate and ate. And the more he ate, the more he drank until at last he grew drowsy and fell sound asleep in his chair. Then without awakening him, Manka had him carried out to the wagon that was waiting to take her home to her father.

The next morning, when the burgomaster opened his eyes, he found himself lying in the shepherd's cottage.

"What does this mean?" he roared out.

"Nothing, dear husband, nothing!" Manka said. "You know you told me I might take with me the one thing I liked best in your house, so of course I took you! That's all."

For a moment the burgomaster rubbed his eyes in amazement. Then he laughed loud and heartily to think how Manka had outwitted him.

"Manka," he said, "you're too clever for me. Come on, my dear, let's go home."

So, they climbed back into the wagon and drove home.

The burgomaster never again scolded his wife, but thereafter whenever a very difficult case came up, he always said:

"I think we had better consult my wife. You know she's a very clever woman."

1920

The Story of an Hour

Kate Chopin (1851–1904)

Since the late 1960s, Kate Chopin has become one of the most written-about American writers. Born in St. Louis into a wealthy Catholic family, she grew up to marry Oscar Chopin, a New Orleans cotton merchant. After business reversals in New Orleans, Oscar and Kate moved to a plantation in rural Cloutierville, Louisiana, where they had six children. When Oscar died of a fever in 1882, Kate was left with the responsibility of running the plantation and raising her large family. She moved back to St. Louis in 1884 and began to write stories about the lively, mixed ethnic culture of Louisiana. Chopin was one of the first writers to explore such subjects as divorce, miscegenation, and the unhappiness of many women over their traditional gender roles. Her masterpiece, *The Awakening* (1899), tells the story of a wealthy woman who walks out on her marriage and children in a doomed attempt to find personal fulfillment in a rigid Victorian world.

Knowing that Mrs. Mallard was afflicted with a heart trouble, great care was taken to break to her as gently as possible the news of her husband's death.

It was her sister Josephine who told her, in broken sentences; veiled hints that revealed in half concealing. Her husband's friend Richards was there, too, near her. It was he who had been in the newspaper office when intelligence of the railroad disaster was received, with Brently Mallard's name leading the list of "killed." He had only taken the time to assure himself of its truth by a second telegram, and had hastened to forestall any less careful, less tender friend in bearing the sad message.

She did not hear the story as many women have heard the same, with a paralyzed inability to accept its significance. She wept at once, with sudden, wild abandonment, in her sister's arms. When the storm of grief had spent itself she went away to her room alone. She would have no one follow her.

There stood, facing the open window, a comfortable, roomy armchair. Into this she sank, pressed down by a physical exhaustion that haunted her body and seemed to reach into her soul.

She could see in the open square before her house the tops of trees that were all aquiver with the new spring life. The delicious breath of rain was in the air. In the street below a peddler was crying his wares. The notes of a distant song which some one was singing reached her faintly, and countless sparrows were twittering in the eaves.

There were patches of blue sky showing here and there through the clouds that had met and piled one above the other in the west facing her window.

She sat with her head thrown back upon the cushion of the chair, quite motionless, except when a sob came up into her throat and shook her, as a child who has cried itself to sleep continues to sob in its dreams.

She was young, with a fair, calm face, whose lines bespoke repression and even a certain strength. But now there was a dull stare in her eyes, whose gaze was fixed away off yonder on one of those patches of blue sky. It was not a glance of reflection, but rather indicated a suspension of intelligent thought.

There was something coming to her and she was waiting for it, fearfully. What was it? She did not know; it was too subtle and elusive to name. But she felt it, creeping out of the sky, reaching toward her through the sounds, the scents, the color that filled the air.

Now her bosom rose and fell tumultuously. She was beginning to recognize this thing that was approaching to possess her, and she was striving to beat it back with her will—as powerless as her two white slender hands would have been.

When she abandoned herself a little whispered word escaped her slightly parted lips. She said it over and over under her breath: "free, free, free!" The vacant stare and the look of terror that had followed it went from her eyes. They stayed keen and bright. Her pulses beat fast, and the coursing blood warmed and relaxed every inch of her body.

She did not stop to ask if it were or were not a monstrous joy that held her. A clear and exalted perception enabled her to dismiss the suggestion as trivial.

She knew that she would weep again when she saw the kind, tender hands folded in death; the face that had never looked save with love upon her, fixed and gray and dead. But she saw beyond that bitter moment a long procession of years to come that would belong to her absolutely. And she opened and spread her arms out to them in welcome.

There would be no one to live for her during those coming years; she would live for herself. There would be no powerful will bending hers in that blind persistence with which men and women believe they have a right to impose a private will upon a fellow-creature. A kind intention or a cruel intention made the act seem no less a crime as she looked upon it in that brief moment of illumination.

And yet she had loved him—sometimes. Often she had not. What did it matter! What could love, the unsolved mystery, count for in face of this possession of self-assertion which she suddenly recognized as the strongest impulse of her being!

"Free! Body and soul free!" she kept whispering.

Josephine was kneeling before the closed door with her lips to the keyhole, imploring for admission. "Louise, open the door! I beg; open the door—you will make yourself ill. What are you doing, Louise? For heaven's sake open the door."

"Go away. I am not making myself ill." No; she was drinking in a very elixir of life through that open window.

Her fancy was running riot along those days ahead of her. Spring days, and summer days, and all sorts of days that would be her own. She breathed a quick prayer that life might be long. It was only yesterday she had thought with a shudder that life might be long.

She arose at length and opened the door to her sister's importunities. There was a feverish triumph in her eyes, and she carried herself unwittingly like a goddess of Victory. She clasped her sister's waist, and together they descended the stairs. Richards stood waiting for them at the bottom.

Some one was opening the front door with a latchkey. It was Brently Mallard who entered, a little travel-stained, composedly carrying his grip-sack and umbrella. He had been far from the scene of accident, and did not even know there had been one. He stood amazed at Josephine's piercing cry; at Richards' quick motion to screen him from the view of his wife.

But Richards was too late.

When the doctors came they said she had died of heart disease—of joy that kills.

1894

THINKING ABOUT WHAT WE'VE READ

How can we compare these two stories we have just read? What can we say about them?

We can begin by noticing some things the two stories have in common. For instance, both are quite short. Both have women as their main characters (or **protagonists**); both women are loved by those who know them, and each one's marriage is an important element in her story.

Next, we can look at the ways in which the two stories differ. Before you read further, make a list—by yourselves or as a group—of the differences you notice between the two stories. Then, as we consider what steps one should take when thinking about a story in order to discuss it (either by itself or in comparison with some other story), and how we can apply these steps to "Clever Manka" and "The Story of an Hour," you can find out how many of the ideas in the essay you discovered.

Let's return now to our questions: What steps should one take when thinking about a story in order to discuss it and write about it? How can we apply these steps to "Clever Manka" and "The Story of an Hour"?

STEP 1.   Begin with your initial impressions.

The first thing to do is to jot down whatever points or features about the story (or stories) strike you as being most noticeable—the ideas that affect you most strongly. For example, the most striking difference I notice between these two stories is that Manka, because of her cleverness, is always triumphant—a victor—while Louise Mallard seems destined to be a victim. Manka's story ends happily, with its heroine and her husband living happily ever after, whereas Mrs. Mallard's tale ends, surprisingly and grimly, with her misunderstood death. I notice, too, that my mood after ending each story varies accordingly. You probably had other "first impressions," or more of them; but these will do for a sample.

STEP 2.   Consider the structure of the story.

The ordering of incidents within a story may be spoken of as its **structure**. Traditionally, a story's structure has been said to consist of four basic parts:

1. The **exposition**—the beginning of the story, which introduces the reader to the tale's setting (time and place) and to some or all of its characters.
2. The **conflict**—Every story centers on a conflict of some sort: one person, or group of people, against another; people against nature; an individual against some rule or custom of society. Generally, the conflict increases in tension or in complexity until it reaches a climax.
3. The **climax**—the point of greatest tension, at which the turning point or breaking point is reached.
4. The **denouement** or **resolution**—the ending, which brings the tale to a close, picking up the pieces of the action and reordering the lives left disordered by the conflict and its climax.

Of these four parts, only 2 and 3, the conflict and the climax, are essential. You don't have to begin with an exposition; your first sentence can show your characters already embroiled in their conflict. You don't have to end with a resolution; you can stop your tale short at its climactic moment. But you must have some sort of conflict in your action, and it must rise to some peak of intensity somewhere between the middle and end of your story.

How can we apply this theory to our two stories? Let's find out.

There was once a rich farmer who was as grasping and unscrupulous as he was rich. He was always driving a hard bargain and always getting the better of his poor neighbors. One of these neighbors was a humble shepherd who, in return for service, was to receive from the farmer a heifer. When the time of payment came, the farmer refused to give the shepherd the heifer, and the shepherd was forced to lay the matter before the burgomaster.

This is obviously an exposition. The opening words, "There was once," tell us immediately that this will be a "tall tale," not a realistic story. The rich farmer—"as grasping and unscrupulous as he was rich"—and the "humble shepherd" in danger of being cheated by the rich man reinforce this idea, and alert us to the coming conflict as well, setting out its themes of rich versus poor and justice versus injustice. The burgomaster—young and inexperienced—does not promise to be much help. What will happen?

The conflict develops as we hear the rich man's wife and the poor man's daughter ponder the burgomaster's riddle. The wife, like her husband, thinks of their property: "our gray mare," "our honey," "our chest of golden ducats." The shepherd's daughter thinks of essential things, in which all humans share: thought, sleep, the earth. And so, of course, the underdogs win in the first round of the conflict.

But it is only the first round. The burgomaster now challenges Manka directly: he "thought he would like to make another test of Manka's cleverness."

Manka wins this round as well. The burgomaster begins to think of marriage, and sets a third riddling test. Manka triumphs again, and is married. But now the burgomaster sets limits to Manka's use of her wits:

> "But understand, my dear Manka," he said, "you are not to use that cleverness of yours at my expense. I won't have you interfering in any of my cases. In fact, if ever you give advice to anyone who comes to me for judgment, I'll turn you out of my house at once and send you home to your father."

Do we hear a husband-wife conflict starting here? We certainly do. Once again, Manka sees an injustice about to happen; once again, she prevents the injustice. But the burgomaster, holding to his warning, exiles her, allowing her only to "take with you the one thing you like best in my house." This, of course, is all Manka needs. As the climax of the story, she kidnaps her own husband, once again asserting the claim of the essential over that of mere property: "You know you told me I might take with me the one thing I liked best in your house, so of course I took you! That's all."

The resolution, of course, is reconciliation, happiness, and the firm establishment of Manka's right to use her cleverness for the general good: "I think we had better consult my wife. You know she's a very clever woman."

"The Story of an Hour" begins even more directly: "Knowing that Mrs. Mallard was afflicted with a heart trouble, great care was taken to break to her as gently as possible the news of her husband's death." We are told that there has been a death, and that the dead man's widow is herself in danger from the strain the bad news may place on her weak heart. No conflict between people here: rather, a conflict of caring people against uncaring nature and disease.

As the story develops, a second conflict grows clear: a conflict between grief and joy, between expected and actual emotions. The marriage, loving though it was, has not been happy for her: in the freedom of her widowhood, Louise expects to find happiness.

At the tale's climax, Louise emerges "like a goddess of Victory" to rejoin her sister and friend, only to die from shock at the sight, not of a dead husband, but of a live one. The kindly plan has backfired; the new shock, with its reversal of already-strong emotion, is deadlier than the originally feared shock would have been.

The tale's last sentence provides its resolution: "When the doctors came they said she had died of heart disease—of joy that kills." Nature and illness have defeated care; and no one is left within the tale who can realize the gap between the expected emotion and the true one. Only we, the readers, know whether it was "joy" that killed Louise Mallard.

STEP 3.   Consider the major aspects of each story.

As Chapter 1, "The Bases of Literature," suggested, each work of fiction involves four key elements: **action**, or **plot**; **character**; **setting**; and **lan-**

guage, or **voice**. When considering a work of fiction, we look at these various aspects; we note how they're presented and what is the balance among them. What do we find in this case?

Action, or plot: We notice substantial differences between the plots of the two tales. The action of "Clever Manka" consists of a number of brief episodes, each of which shows the heroine acting cleverly, so that she moves from triumph to triumph toward the successful climax and resolution. In "The Story of an Hour" we have a single, more fully developed episode, in which the heroine *reacts* first to a piece of news, then to her own emotions, finally to the sight of a man believed dead. The climax of this tale represents a complete reversal of everything expected by characters and readers alike, and thus presents a classic "surprise ending," while the resolution, with its irony, underscores the reversals that distinguish this tale.

Character: Manka is a clever, active, resourceful character; she judges situations correctly and acts decisively. Louise reacts, rather than acts; she is defined by her emotions and her illness rather than by her more active attributes. Manka is worth reading about because she does something praiseworthy; Louise is worth reading about because she is the victim of such a remarkable chain of accidents.

Setting: "Clever Manka" has almost a fairy-tale setting, with its burgomaster who wields absolute power but can yield to a wise peasant girl; "The Story of an Hour" is set in its author's own social setting.

Language, or voice: The language of "Clever Manka" is that of the traditional storyteller. Direct and to the point, it spends little time on description, but concentrates instead on the tale's action. "The Story of an Hour," in contrast, uses much more sophisticated language and takes considerable care to describe and comment upon its characters' thoughts and sensations, as when describing "a physical exhaustion that haunted her body and seemed to reach into her soul" or telling how the heroine "carried herself unwittingly like a goddess of Victory."

STEP 4.   Create a synthesis.

Now we've gathered our data. We've noted our initial reactions, and we've filled those out by checking each of the major aspects and structural elements of the stories under discussion, noting key aspects of each and strengthening our understanding of how the story creates those effects we first noted. Now it's time to put together the information thus gathered to arrive at an overall picture of the stories: a sense of the vision that informs each one, and of your interpretation of that vision. If you write a formal essay on a story, this is the point at which you write it. Even if you write only on a single theme out of the number you've noticed, it's best to have this balanced study behind you so that you're working from a firm foundation.

If I were writing an essay on these two tales, for example, I would probably choose to write on one of my first ideas. I'd call the paper something like "Victors and Victims," and concentrate on the character and fortune of the two protagonists. I'd bring in ideas from my study of action, character, setting, and conflict, to show how Manka uses her cleverness to succeed in a world in which people have only other individuals as adversaries, and individual wisdom and honesty are important and valid weapons in the perpetual combat against injustice; and I'd say that Manka's success leaves me, as a reader, feeling good about the possibility of taking action in my own world to make good things happen. Then I'd show, in contrast, how Kate Chopin's tale depicts people as well-meaning, caring creatures (in contrast to the combative types that people Manka's world), but also as creatures whose power is severely limited by the dangers inherent in living in a "real world" in which physical limitations and accidents can overturn whatever people plan. I'd show how Louise Mallard is victim to all these types of dangers. And I'd admit that—although I enjoyed the story, with its study of hidden feelings—it left me less cheerful than did "Clever Manka," and did nothing to increase my sense of my own potential powers.

In doing such an essay, I'd think that I had covered some of the important points about the two stories, and particularly the key difference between the two. But many other, equally valid essays could be written, stressing other themes and ideas about the stories. Perhaps you have already thought of some such ideas. If you were to write an essay on one or both of these tales, what would you want to write?

4

THE STORYTELLERS

We have said that fiction has its roots in the art of the **storyteller**. It is with the storytellers, therefore, that we shall begin. This chapter provides three tales, from three storytelling traditions.

The first tale, "High Horse's Courting," comes from the **oral storytelling tradition**. It is a Native American tale, handed down from one storyteller to another, until it was written down by a scholar to whom a Sioux holy man, Black Elk, told it. Speaking to the scholar, Black Elk recalled that "[Watanye] liked to tell me stories, mostly funny ones. . . . I still remember one story he told me about a young Lakota called High Horse, and what a hard time he had getting the girl he wanted. Watanye said the story happened just as he told it, and maybe it did. If it did not, it could have, just as well as not. I will tell that story now." The second tale, "Old Boss Wants into Heaven" comes from the rich **African American folktales** tradition. This story about slavery was told to a scholar by John Blackamore in the early 1950s, and it shows how African Americans used the power of narrative to deal with slavery and its aftershocks following the Civil War. "If Not Higher," comes from the **Yiddish storytelling tradition**. This tradition began in the villages and ghettos of Eastern Europe, then migrated, with its tellers, to this country. This particular tale is set in Russia. The three tales thus come from different traditions, and from different times, as well. Yet as you read these stories, you may notice a number of similarities among them. First, they all deal with relatively simple, straightforward characters. The actions of which they tell tend to be straightforward, as well, with clearly defined purposes. All use a conversational style, derived from oral storytelling, that draws the audience into the world of the tale. All are told with verve, with the storyteller enjoying the act of telling the tale. And finally, all deal, to some extent, with extremes or exaggeration. As you read these stories, you should note the differences in narrative style and tone among them, but notice also their similarities; as a foundation for studying fiction, it's good to get a firm sense of the methods used by the first masters of the field, the tellers of tales.

Note: Identical study questions are given for all stories in this chapter to make it easier to compare and contrast the stories.

High Horse's Courting

Black Elk (1863–1950)

Black Elk was an Oglala Sioux holy man. He is most famous for his oration "Black Elk Speaks," although recently controversy has arisen among Native American scholars as to the authenticity of the speech, which was written down secondhand rather than by an eyewitness. As a child, Black Elk had a vision of how he would grow up to lead the Oglala to victory against the white man. He found this dream impossible to realize, however, and fled with the remnants of his tribe into Canada to escape annihilation by the encroaching whites.

You know, in the old days, it was not so very easy to get a girl when you wanted to be married. Sometimes it was hard work for a young man and he had to stand a great deal. Say I am a young man and I have seen a young girl who looks so beautiful to me that I feel all sick when I think about her. I can not just go and tell her about it and then get married if she is willing. I have to be a very sneaky fellow to talk to her at all, and after I have managed to talk to her, that is only the beginning.

Probably for a long time I have been feeling sick about a certain girl because I love her so much, but she will not even look at me, and her parents keep a good watch over her. But I keep feeling worse and worse all the time; so maybe I sneak up to her tepee in the dark and wait until she comes out. Maybe I just wait there all night and don't get any sleep at all and she does not come out. Then I feel sicker than ever about her.

Maybe I hide in the brush by a spring where she sometimes goes to get water, and when she comes by, if nobody is looking, then I jump out and hold her and just make her listen to me. If she likes me too, I can tell that from the way she acts, for she is very bashful and maybe will not say a word or even look at me the first time. So I let her go, and then maybe I sneak around until I can see her father alone, and I tell him how many horses I can give him for his beautiful girl, and by now I am feeling so sick that maybe I would give him all the horses in the world if I had them.

Well, this young man I am telling about was called High Horse, and there was a girl in the village who looked so beautiful to him that he was just sick all over from thinking about her so much and he was getting sicker all the time. The girl was very shy, and her parents thought a great deal of her because they were not young any more and this was the only child they had. So they watched her all day long, and they fixed it so that she would be safe at night too when they were asleep. They thought so much of her that they had made a rawhide bed for her to sleep in, and after they knew that High Horse was sneaking around after her, they took rawhide thongs and tied the girl in bed at night so that nobody could steal her when they were asleep, for they were not sure but that their girl might really want to be stolen.

Well, after High Horse had been sneaking around a good while and hiding and waiting for the girl and getting sicker all the time, he finally caught her alone and made her talk to him. Then he found out that she liked him maybe a little. Of course this did not make him feel well. It made him sicker than ever, but now he felt as brave as a bison bull, and so he went right to her father and said he loved the girl so much that he would give two good horses for her—one of them young and the other one not so very old.

But the old man just waved his hand, meaning for High Horse to go away and quit talking foolishness like that.

High Horse was feeling sicker than ever about it; but there was another young fellow who said he would loan High Horse two ponies and when he got some more horses, why, he could just give them back for the ones he had borrowed.

Then High Horse went back to the old man and said he would give four horses for the girl—two of them young and the other two not hardly old at all. But the old man just waved his hand and would not say anything.

So High Horse sneaked around until he could talk to the girl again, and he asked her to run away with him. He told her he thought he would just fall over and die if she did not. But she said she would not do that; she wanted to be bought like a fine woman. You see she thought a great deal of herself too.

That made High Horse feel so very sick that he could not eat a bite, and he went around with his head hanging down as though he might just fall down and die any time.

Red Deer was another young fellow, and he and High Horse were great comrades, always doing things together. Red Deer saw how High Horse was acting, and he said: "Cousin, what is the matter? Are you sick in the belly? You look as though you were going to die."

Then High Horse told Red Deer how it was, and said he thought he could not stay alive much longer if he could not marry the girl pretty quick.

Red Deer thought awhile about it, and then he said: "Cousin, I have a plan, and if you are man enough to do as I tell you, then everything will be all right. She will not run away with you; her old man will not take four horses; and four horses are all you can get. You must steal her and run away with her. Then afterwhile you can come back and the old man cannot do anything because she will be your woman. Probably she wants you to steal her anyway."

So they planned what High Horse had to do, and he said he loved the girl so much that he was man enough to do anything Red Deer or anybody else could think up.

So this is what they did.

That night late they sneaked up to the girl's tepee and waited until it sounded inside as though the old man and the old woman and the girl were sound asleep. Then High Horse crawled under the tepee with a knife. He had to cut the rawhide thongs first, and then Red Deer, who was pulling up the stakes around that side of the tepee, was going to help drag the girl outside and gag her. After that, High Horse could put her across his pony in front of him and hurry out of there and be happy all the rest of his life.

When High Horse had crawled inside, he felt so nervous that he could hear his heart drumming, and it seemed so loud he felt sure it would 'waken the old folks. But it did not, and afterwhile he began cutting the thongs. Every time he cut one it made a pop and nearly scared him to death. But he was getting along all right and all the thongs were cut down as far as the girl's thighs, when he became so nervous that his knife slipped and stuck the girl. She gave a big, loud yell. Then the old folks jumped up and yelled too. By this time High Horse was outside, and he and Red Deer were running away like antelope. The old man and some other people chased the young men but they got away in the dark and nobody knew who it was.

Well, if you ever wanted a beautiful girl you will know how sick High Horse was now. It was very bad the way he felt, and it looked as though he would starve even if he did not drop over dead sometime.

Red Deer kept thinking about this, and after a few days he went to High Horse and said: "Cousin, take courage! I have another plan, and I am sure, if you are man enough, we can steal her this time." And High Horse said: "I am man enough to do anything anybody can think up, if I can only get that girl."

So this is what they did.

They went away from the village alone, and Red Deer made High Horse strip naked. Then he painted High Horse solid white all over, and after that he painted black stripes all over the white and put black rings around High Horse's eyes. High Horse looked terrible. He looked so terrible that when Red Deer was through painting and took a good look at what he had done, he said it scared even him a little.

"Now," Red Deer said, "if you get caught again, everybody will be so scared they will think you are a bad spirit and will be afraid to chase you."

So when the night was getting old and everybody was sound asleep, they sneaked back to the girl's tepee. High Horse crawled in with his knife, as before, and Red Deer waited outside, ready to drag the girl out and gag her when High Horse had all the thongs cut.

High Horse crept up by the girl's bed and began cutting at the thongs. But he kept thinking, "If they see me they will shoot me because I look so terrible." The girl was restless and kept squirming around in bed, and when a thong was cut, it popped. So High Horse worked very slowly and carefully.

But he must have made some noise, for suddenly the old woman awoke and said to her old man: "Old Man, wake up! There is somebody in this tepee!" But the old man was sleepy and didn't want to be bothered. He said: "Of course there is somebody in this tepee. Go to sleep and don't bother me." Then he snored some more.

But High Horse was so scared by now that he lay very still and as flat to the ground as he could. Now, you see, he had not been sleeping very well for a long time because he was so sick about the girl. And while he was lying there waiting for the old woman to snore, he just forgot everything, even how beautiful the girl was. Red Deer who was lying outside ready to do his part, wondered and wondered what had happened in there, but he did not dare call out to High Horse.

Afterwhile the day began to break and Red Deer had to leave with the two ponies he had staked there for his comrade and girl, or somebody would see him.

So he left.

Now when it was getting light in the tepee, the girl awoke and the first thing she saw was a terrible animal, all white with black stripes on it, lying asleep beside her bed. So she screamed, and then the old woman screamed and the old man yelled. High Horse jumped up, scared almost to death, and he nearly knocked the tepee down getting out of there.

People were coming running from all over the village with guns and bows and axes, and everybody was yelling.

By now High Horse was running so fast that he hardly touched the ground at all, and he looked so terrible that the people fled from him and let him run. Some braves wanted to shoot at him, but the others said he might be some sacred being and it would bring bad trouble to kill him.

High Horse made for the river that was near, and in among the brush he found a hollow tree and dived into it. Afterwhile some braves came there and he could hear them saying that it was some bad spirit that had come out of the water and gone back in again.

That morning the people were ordered to break camp and move away from there. So they did, while High Horse was hiding in his hollow tree.

Now Red Deer had been watching all this from his own tepee and trying to look as though he were as much surprised and scared as all the others. So when the camp moved, he sneaked back to where he had seen his comrade disappear. When he was down there in the brush, he called, and High Horse answered, because he knew his friend's voice. They washed off the paint from High Horse and sat down on the river bank to talk about their troubles.

High Horse said he never would go back to the village as long as he lived and he did not care what happened to him now. He said he was going to go on the war-path all by himself. Red Deer said: "No, cousin, you are not going on the war-path alone, because I am going with you."

So Red Deer got everything ready, and at night they started out on the war-path all alone. After several days they came to a Crow camp just about sundown, and when it was dark they sneaked up to where the Crow horses were grazing, killed the horse guard, who was not thinking about enemies because he thought all the Lakotas were far away, and drove off about a hundred horses.

They got a big start because all the Crow horses stampeded and it was probably morning before the Crow warriors could catch any horses to ride. Red Deer and High Horse fled with their herd three days and nights before they reached the village of their people. Then they drove the whole herd right into the village and up in front of the girl's tepee. The old man was there, and High Horse called out to him and asked if he thought maybe that would be enough horses for his girl. The old man did not wave him away that time. It was not the horses that he wanted. What he wanted was a son who was a real man and good for something.

So High Horse got his girl after all, and I think he deserved her.

1932

STUDY QUESTIONS

1. How does the narrator introduce the story?
2. Describe the main characters in the story. How does the narrator depict these characters? How do you respond to the depictions?
3. What goal does each of these characters have? What conflicts or frustrations does each meet with in trying to attain his goal? How does he respond to these challenges? How do you react to the character's endeavors and setbacks?
4. Discuss the ending of the story. On what does the narrator focus? On your first reading, how did you respond to the ending?

Old Boss Wants into Heaven

John Blackamore (18??–?)

John Blackamore was an African American who lived in the deep South and in the 1950s related several folktales to the scholar Richard M. Dorson, who collected them, along with others, in *American Negro Folktales* (Greenwich, CT: Fawcett, 1967).

Old Boss he was a big plantation owner, but he was paralyzed and he couldn't even walk. So every time he was ready to move he'd call Mac up, to carry him around on his back and push him around in his wheel chair. This was back in slavery times, and Mac was his servant, his slave. Old Boss had a whole lot of slaves working for him, but Mac was the main attraction.

Every time the Boss had Mac carry him on his back, Mac figured he was being done wrong, since Boss had a wheel chair. He got to talking to himself about it out loud: "O Lord, these days ain't going to be much longer; God almighty going to call us all in." Then he wouldn't have to carry Old Boss around no more, 'cause he'd be flying around with angels in heaven, and Old Boss'd be down in hell burning with brimstone. Quite a few times the Boss heard him say it; so finally he asked him what did he mean by that remark.

Mac tells him, "You-all know what the Good Book says?" So the Boss says: "What do you mean by that? If anybody's going to Heaven I'm going, because I got all the money I can use, I got a lot of land, I got all the slaves I want to work the land, so I got everything I need to get to Heaven."

"That's just how come you ain't going to Heaven," Mac answers. "The Good Book says so." But Old Boss he really thought because he had all the land and all the money and all the slaves he was fixed straight, that was all he needed. Mac was kind of afraid to speak up any more, being a slave, you know. He just said, "That's all right Boss, you'll see," and kind of walked off from him.

Old Boss couldn't sleep that night. He tried to brush it off his mind but it kept coming on back to him, what Mac had told him. Finally he decided that Mac didn't know what he was talking about, that he was an ignorant slave and didn't know no more than what he (Old Boss) said: "I'll give you a forty-acre farm and a team of mules, if you accept about what work to do." Finally he went on to sleep. Early next morning Mac gets up and starts about his chores. Boss heard him singing.

Soon I will be up in Heaven with the angels,
Having a good time enjoying eternal life.

So that thought kind of hit Old Boss again—he wanted to know how could a slave go to heaven, and he himself being rich and going to hell. That kind of lay on his mind all day. That was Saturday. Sunday morning Mac gets up singing another song. He got on his clean overalls, and a clean shirt, and he gave himself a shave with one of the Boss's old razors—he was barefooted even on Sunday, but he was still happy; he was going to church. The song he was singing was:

I'm going to the mourning bench this morning,
And praise my master up above.

Boss knew they had a church, but he'd never heard a song like that before; so he got curious. He gets his wheel chair, and kind of sneaks on down to the church where they were having the meeting. So when he got there service had already begun. The preacher is up in the pulpit asking did anybody want anything explained to them. Mac raised his hand to let the preacher know he had a question. So he told him about his discussion with Old Boss. Since he could not read, he asked the preacher to explain it to him. The preacher gets his textbook, and gives Mac the book and the chapter and the verse, and then he read it to him. (Some of them could read and some of 'em could not.) So he read, "It's easier for a camel to go through the eye of a needle than it is for a rich man to go to Heaven." (In the meantime Old Boss is outside the window listening, taking it all in.) So he says, "Sisters and Brothers, there only two places to go after you die, and that is Heaven or Hell. And since Old Boss can't go to Heaven, there's no other place for him to go but to Hell."

Old Boss heard enough then. He wheels his chair on back home, he sets down on the porch, and calls his wife to bring him the Bible. He remembered the book and the chapter and the verse and he wanted to see if they knew what they were talking about. When he turns to the page, he found there in big red letters just what the preacher had read. That kind of worried him; he felt uneasy all day Sunday. Mac was away so he couldn't talk to him. Night came; still no Mac. So he decided to set up and wait for him.

On the way home from church Mac had to pass a graveyard. This being Sunday night, a couple of fellows had gone into Old Boss's cornfield and had stole a sack of corn. They went in to get two sacks of corn, but when they heard Mac coming they thought it might be Old Boss, and jumped over the fence into the graveyard. In getting over the fence they dropped a couple of ears. Mac heard them and that kind of scared him, because he thought they was hants, and so he hid behind a big tombstone.

One of the fellows said, "Well, since we didn't get but one sackful we're going to have to divide it." Mac didn't know what they were talking about, so he sat and listened. The two fellows started counting the corn. They figured they didn't have time to count all the ears together and then separate them; so they started counting off, "One for you and one for me." And they kept that up for quite a while.

Mac said, "O Lord, Judgment Day done come. I better go tell the Boss." So he struck out to running. When he gets to the house Old Boss is sitting on the porch smoking his pipe uneasily. Boss was glad to see Mac, and kind of scared for him too, 'cause he was running so hard. Before he could ask Mac how to get to Heaven, Mac fell upon the porch, almost out of breath. "I told you Judgment Day would be soon here; I sure told you!"

Old Boss says: "Well calm yourself. Tell me what this is all about." Mac tells him, "God and the Devil is down there in the graveyard separating the souls." Old Boss doesn't believe it. "Well, that couldn't be true, you know you're just lying." So Mac tells him, "Well if you think I am lying, I'll take you down there and prove it to you."

So he carries Old Boss down to the graveyard on his back. When Old Boss gets there he hears him counting, "One for you and one for me." So he wants to get a closer look; he wants to see what God and the Devil look like. It was dark out there, and the two fellows had moved around to the other side of the fence, where they'd dropped the corn. But when Old Boss gets around there he can't make out who it was because each of them had a great white cotton sack; that was all he could see, that cotton sack. Mac says, "See Boss, I told you so, they're down there sacking up souls." So one of the guys said, "Well, one for you and one for me." T'other pointed over to the fence where they had dropped the two ears, and he said. "There's two over there by the fence—you can have the big one and I'll take the little one."

Old Boss didn't want to hear no more. Mac was scared too. In fact Mac was too scared to move; he froze there in his tracks for a minute. Since Mac wasn't moving fast enough to carry Old Boss, Old Boss jumped down and run. And Mac looked around to see what had happened to Old Boss. Old Boss was out of sight. He figured 'cause Old Boss couldn't walk they must have sacked him up. So Mac run for Old Boss's house to tell Old Missy what happened. When he gets to the house he falls on the porch again, calling Old Missy.

Old Boss come out, without his wheel chair. Mac went to tell him what had happened to Old Boss. Then he realized it was Old Boss he was talking to. He froze again, so Old Boss asked him, "What happened after you left?" Mac told him, and asked Old Boss what happened to him. Boss said, "Well, you weren't moving fast enough; so I decided I'd come on without you." And he's been walking ever since.

Then Old Boss gave all his slaves an equal share in his kingdom that he had already built. He didn't want to get caught in that predicament no more.

1967

STUDY QUESTIONS

1. How does the narrator introduce the story?
2. Describe the main characters in the story. How does the narrator depict these characters? How do you respond to the depictions?
3. What goal does each of these characters have? What conflicts or frustrations does each meet with in trying to attain his goal? How does he respond to these challenges? How do you react to the character's endeavors and setbacks?
4. Discuss the ending of the story. On what does the narrator focus? On your first reading, how did you respond to the ending?

If Not Higher

I. L. Peretz (1851–1915)

I. L. Peretz lived most of his life in Warsaw, Poland. He wrote in Yiddish. His fiction was instrumental in creating a more aesthetically sophisticated Yiddish literature, as opposed to one aimed primarily at popular entertainment. Peretz questioned Jewish traditions and superstitions in the light of modernity. Educator, supporter of the labor movement, humanist, Peretz looks forward to such fine contemporary Jewish writers as I. B. Singer and Saul Bellow.

Early every Friday morning, at the time of the Penitential Prayers, the Rabbi of Nemirov would vanish.

He was nowhere to be seen—neither in the synagogue nor in the two Houses of Study nor at a *minyan.* And he was certainly not at home. His door stood open; whoever wished could go in and out; no one would steal from the rabbi. But not a living creature was within.

Where could the rabbi be? Where should he be? In heaven, no doubt. A rabbi has plenty of business to take care of just before the Days of Awe. Jews, God bless them, need livelihood, peace, health, and good matches. They want to be pious and good, but our sins are so great, and Satan of the thousand eyes watches the whole earth from one end to the other. What he sees he reports; he denounces, informs. Who can help us if not the rabbi!

That's what the people thought.

But once a Litvak came, and he laughed. You know the Litvaks. They think little of the Holy Books but stuff themselves with Talmud and law. So this Litvak points to a passage in the *Gemarah*—it sticks in your eyes—where it is written that even Moses, our Teacher, did not ascend to heaven during his lifetime but remained suspended two and a half feet below. Go argue with a Litvak!

So where can the rabbi be?

"That's not my business," said the Litvak, shrugging. Yet all the while—what a Litvak can do!—he is scheming to find out.

That same night, right after the evening prayers, the Litvak steals into the rabbi's room, slides under the rabbi's bed, and waits. He'll watch all night and discover where the rabbi vanishes and what he does during the Penitential Prayers.

Someone else might have got drowsy and fallen asleep, but a Litvak is never at a loss; he recites a whole tractate of the Talmud by heart.

At dawn he hears the call to prayers.

The rabbi has already been awake for a long time. The Litvak has heard him groaning for a whole hour.

Whoever has heard the Rabbi of Nemirov groan knows how much sorrow for all Israel, how much suffering, lies in each groan. A man's heart might break, hearing it. But a Litvak is made of iron; he listens and remains where he is. The rabbi, long life to him, lies on the bed, and the Litvak under the bed.

Then the Litvak hears the beds in the house begin to creak; he hears people jumping out of their beds, mumbling a few Jewish words, pouring water on their fingernails, banging doors. Everyone has left. It is again quiet and dark; a bit of light from the moon shines through the shutters.

(Afterward the Litvak admitted that when he found himself alone with the rabbi a great fear took hold of him. Goose pimples spread across his skin, and the roots of his earlocks pricked him like needles. A trifle: to be alone with the rabbi at the time of the Penitential Prayers! But a Litvak is stubborn. So he quivered like a fish in water and remained where he was.)

Finally the rabbi, long life to him, arises. First he does what befits a Jew. Then he goes to the clothes closet and takes out a bundle of peasant clothes:

linen trousers, high boots, a coat, a big felt hat, and a long wide leather belt studded with brass nails. The rabbi gets dressed. From his coat pocket dangles the end of a heavy peasant rope.

The rabbi goes out, and the Litvak follows him.

On the way the rabbi stops in the kitchen, bends down, takes an ax from under the bed, puts it in his belt, and leaves the house. The Litvak trembles but continues to follow.

The hushed dread of the Days of Awe hangs over the dark streets. Every once in a while a cry rises from some *minyan* reciting the Penitential Prayers, or from a sickbed. The rabbi hugs the sides of the streets, keeping to the shade of the houses. He glides from house to house, and the Litvak after him. The Litvak hears the sound of his heartbeats mingling with the sound of the rabbi's heavy steps. But he keeps on going and follows the rabbi to the outskirts of the town.

A small wood stands behind the town.

The rabbi, long life to him, enters the wood. He takes thirty or forty steps and stops by a small tree. The Litvak, overcome with amazement, watches the rabbi take the ax out of his belt and strike the tree. He hears the tree creak and fall. The rabbi chops the tree into logs and the logs into sticks. Then he makes a bundle of the wood and ties it with the rope in his pocket. He puts the bundle of wood on his back, shoves the ax back into his belt, and returns to the town.

He stops at a back street beside a small broken-down shack and knocks at the window.

"Who is there?" asks a frightened voice. The Litvak recognizes it as the voice of a sick Jewish woman.

"I," answers the rabbi in the accent of a peasant.

"Who is I?"

Again the rabbi answers in Russian. "Vassil."

"Who is Vassil, and what do you want?"

"I have wood to sell, very cheap." And, not waiting for the woman's reply, he goes into the house.

The Litvak steals in after him. In the gray light of early morning he sees a poor room with broken, miserable furnishings. A sick woman, wrapped in rags, lies on the bed. She complains bitterly, "Buy? How can I buy? Where will a poor widow get money?"

"I'll lend it to you," answers the supposed Vassil. "It's only six cents."

"And how will I ever pay you back?" said the poor woman, groaning.

"Foolish one," says the rabbi reproachfully. "See, you are a poor sick Jew, and I am ready to trust you with a little wood. I am sure you'll pay. While you, you have such a great and mighty God and you don't trust him for six cents."

"And who will kindle the fire?" said the widow. "Have I the strength to get up? My son is at work."

"I'll kindle the fire," answers the rabbi.

As the rabbi put the wood into the oven he recited, in a groan, the first portion of the Penitential Prayers.

As he kindled the fire and the wood burned brightly, he recited, a bit more joyously, the second portion of the Penitential Prayers. When the fire was set he recited the third portion, and then he shut the stove.

The Litvak who saw all this became a disciple of the rabbi.

And ever after, when another disciple tells how the Rabbi of Nemirov ascends to heaven at the time of the Penitential Prayers, the Litvak does not laugh. He only adds quietly, "If not higher."

1953

"Early every Friday morning . . . the Rabbi of Nemirov would vanish." The statement is blunt and surprising. Rabbis do not usually vanish. We read on, expecting some explanation for the rabbi's behavior. But we find only more mystery. First the narrator tells us where the rabbi isn't. Then he tells us where the townspeople think he is; then he introduces the Litvak who argues that the rabbi can't be there, either. "So where can the rabbi be?" By the time the Litvak sets out to discover the answer, we may be pardoned for being curious ourselves. The narrator has certainly done his best to catch our interest and make us curious.

We notice, meanwhile, that the narrator is not unbiased. Although he takes no direct part in the tale, he does identify himself somewhat with the townspeople, slipping from the statement that "*they* want to be pious and good" to the recognition that "*our* sins are so great. . . . Who can help us if not the rabbi!" He pulls back in the next sentence: "That's what the people thought"; but the identification remains in our minds.

That "our" and "us," in fact, might almost include us, the readers. Certainly the narrator treats us as people who share with him knowledge of rabbis and religious matters and Litvaks—especially Litvaks. "You know the Litvaks. . . . Go argue with a Litvak!" The Litvak has an important role in the story. In contrast to the townspeople, who are ready to spread and believe miraculous rumors, the Litvak is a sceptic. He is a well-read man, so studied in law and religious books that he can keep himself awake all night by reciting biblical commentaries; but he is a sceptic, nonetheless. It is precisely because he is sceptical, however, that the Litvak becomes curious enough to find out the real answer to the mystery; and it is he who has the final word at the end of the tale.

The Litvak is almost a type or symbol of the person with more knowledge than faith. The narrator, in fact, insists on seeing him as a type—"the Litvak" rather than a man with a name. At the same time, his prejudice characterizes the narrator. We feel that he'd like to see the Litvak shown up, the rabbi and townsfolk triumphant; we feel he himself has a stake in the outcome of the tale.

As the tale continues, the suspense builds. The narrator helps it along by his talk of "groaning" and "hushed dread," his relation of how even the Litvak suffers "goose pimples" and "a great fear," how he "trembles" and quivers "like a fish in water."

Finally, the mystery is revealed. Now, for the first time, we hear voices other than the narrator's. We hear the rabbi (the only words we do hear from him) and the sick woman (the only characterization we have of her; and it's enough). We see what the Litvak sees, hear what he hears; and we are not told what to think about any of it. The narrator, who heretofore has been generous with his comments, is now letting actions and characters speak for themselves.

Even the conclusion is restrained. We learn that "the Litvak who saw all this became a disciple of the rabbi," and we learn his new attitude toward the tale that the rabbi ascends to heaven on Fridays. Note that this is the Litvak's attitude; it is he, not the narrator, who says, "If not higher," and so makes the final judgment on the rabbi's actions. Note, too, that we are told nothing else of how the Litvak's life may have changed. What does becoming the rabbi's disciple mean for him? That we must figure out for ourselves.

The tale is rich in interpretive value. There is no need for the narrator to characterize the rabbi's actions; we can all supply our own view of their significance. Similarly, we can all tell what the Litvak means by his comment, "If not higher," though we might each phrase the meaning somewhat differently. At the start of the story, the Litvak was looking for something. At the end, he has found it, and we feel the value to him of the discovery. Yet even this is lightly handled, in keeping with the slightly humorous tone of the story. The narrator continues to focus on his one question, "Where does the rabbi go early Friday mornings?" It is the solution of that mystery, the resolution of that conflict between Litvak and the townspeople, that he presents as the "quietly" triumphant ending of his story. Anything else we choose to read into it is our own affair.

"If Not Higher," then, is a tale (almost a "tall tale") told by a narrator who takes no direct part in the action, but who has some concern that the story come out well. His voice is a speaking voice, sometimes humorous, sometimes emphatic, sometimes exasperated. Clearly, this is a practiced speaker, a man who enjoys telling stories. We sense his enjoyment in every line of the tale.

STUDY QUESTIONS

1. How does the narrator introduce the story?
2. Describe the main characters in the story. How does the narrator depict these characters? How do you respond to the depictions?
3. What goal does each of these characters have? What conflicts or frustrations does each meet with in trying to attain his or her goal? How does he or she respond to these challenges? How do you react to the character's endeavors and setbacks?
4. Discuss the ending of the story. On what does the narrator focus? On your first reading, how did you respond to the ending?

5

THE REPORTERS

The stories we have read so far, and those we will read in this chapter, are all related by **omniscient narrators**. As the term implies, these narrators "know all" about the characters and events of which they tell. Somewhat distanced by their greater knowledge from action and actors alike, omniscient narrators project an air of authority over their material. Their relationship to their readers is also variable.

Storytellers, such as those we met in the last chapter and the teller of "Clever Manka" in the third chapter, treat us as a present and welcome audience. Often they may speak to us directly, either asking us questions ("Now I ask you: did she go dressed?") or by making sure that we understand what we need to know in order to appreciate their stories ("You know, in the old days, it was not so very easy to get a girl when you wanted to be married").

Storytellers often seem to care about their protagonists as well. We sense that Black Elk wants High Horse to win his girl, that Peretz's narrator wants the Litvak to understand the rabbi and be satisfied. All in all, there is frequently a strong push for closure in many of the tales told by storytellers: some triumph of action or learning must be achieved within the tale, and some benefit of entertainment or learning must come to the audience in the process.

Reporters, in contrast, hold themselves more aloof from characters and audience alike. For instance, Chopin's narrator in the third chapter keeps us at the same distance that she keeps her material. She tells us of her protagonist's thoughts and feelings, so that we see the contrast between the private thoughts and the public image; but she does so with the objectivity of a reporter. Her prose carries no awareness of its audience. Whereas the storyteller seems actively interested in sharing some knowledge or enjoyment with us, the **objective narrator's** stance is much more "take it or leave it." "Here is a story: something I have observed, imagined, created; make of it what you will, whoever you are."

This chapter contains four stories told by omniscient reporters. Read each story through once, as you would any story, and note your reactions to its plot, characters, and style. Then read and answer the questions that follow the story, rereading the story as necessary while you consider your answers. Note, throughout, how the narrator's voice helps shape your view of the story's action and characters.

Hills like White Elephants

Ernest Hemingway (1899–1961)

Ernest Hemingway was perhaps one of the two most important novelists in America in this century (the other being William Faulkner) in terms of creating a distinctive style that influenced other writers. His spare, lean, "dramatic" (that is, often consisting only of dialogue and action, with no authorial comment) stories and novels embodied his "iceberg" theory: that just as an iceberg has seven-eighths of its mass below the water, a good story should suggest much more than it actually says. Hemingway also referred to his style as "the art of subtraction," the taking out of all unnecessary elements. In such novels as *The Sun Also Rises* (1926), *For Whom the Bell Tolls* (1940), and *The Old Man and the Sea* (1952), he depicted a "code hero" stoically moving through a morally compromised landscape of European decadence, war, and, in the last novel, Cuban peasant life. In his own life Hemingway traveled around the world, hunting, fishing, and involving himself in wars. In his later years he became an international celebrity. But as his father had done years earlier, he killed himself in 1961.

The hills across the valley of the Ebro were long and white. On this side there was no shade and no trees and the station was between two lines of rails in the sun. Close against the side of the station there was the warm shadow of the building and a curtain, made of strings of bamboo beads, hung across the open door into the bar, to keep out flies. The American and the girl with him sat at a table in the shade, outside the building. It was very hot and the express from Barcelona would come in forty minutes. It stopped at this junction for two minutes and went on to Madrid.[1]

"What should we drink?" the girl asked. She had taken off her hat and put it on the table.

"It's pretty hot," the man said.

"Let's drink beer."

"Dos cervezas," the man said into the curtain.

"Big ones?" a woman asked from the doorway.

"Yes. Two big ones."

The woman brought two glasses of beer and two felt pads. She put the felt pads and the beer glasses on the table and looked at the man and the girl. The girl was looking off at the line of hills. They were white in the sun and the country was brown and dry.

"They look like white elephants," she said.

---

[1]The references to the Ebro River and the cities of Barcelona and Madrid identify the setting as Spain.

"I've never seen one," the man drank his beer.

"No, you wouldn't have."

"I might have," the man said. "Just because you say I wouldn't have doesn't prove anything."

The girl looked at the bead curtain. "They've painted something on it," she said. "What does it say?"

"Anis del Toro. It's a drink."

"Could we try it?"

The man called "Listen" through the curtain. The woman came out from the bar.

"Four reales."[2]

"We want two Anis del Toro."

"With water?"

"Do you want it with water?"

"I don't know," the girl said. "Is it good with water?"

"It's all right."

"You want them with water?" asked the woman.

"Yes, with water."

"It tastes like licorice," the girl said and put the glass down.

"That's the way with everything."

"Yes," said the girl. "Everything tastes of licorice. Especially all the things you've waited so long for, like absinthe."

"Oh, cut it out."

"You started it," the girl said. "I was being amused. I was having a fine time."

"Well, let's try and have a fine time."

"All right. I was trying. I said the mountains looked like white elephants. Wasn't that bright?"

"That was bright."

"I wanted to try this new drink. That's all we do, isn't it—look at things and try new drinks?"

"I guess so."

The girl looked across at the hills.

"They're lovely hills," she said. "They don't really look like white elephants. I just meant the coloring of their skin through the trees."

"Should we have another drink?"

"All right."

The warm wind blew the bead curtain against the table.

"The beer's nice and cool," the man said.

"It's lovely," the girl said.

"It's really an awfully simple operation, Jig," the man said. "It's not really an operation at all."

---

[2]Spanish coins

The girl looked at the ground the table legs rested on.

"I know you wouldn't mind it, Jig. It's really not anything. It's just to let the air in."

The girl did not say anything.

"I'll go with you and I'll stay with you all the time. They just let the air in and then it's all perfectly natural."

"Then what will we do afterward?"

"We'll be fine afterward. Just like we were before."

"What makes you think so?"

"That's the only thing that bothers us. It's the only thing that's made us unhappy."

The girl looked at the bead curtain, put her hand out and took hold of two of the strings of beads.

"And you think then we'll be all right and be happy."

"I know we will. You don't have to be afraid. I've known lots of people that have done it."

"So have I," said the girl. "And afterward they were all so happy."

"Well," the man said, "if you don't want to you don't have to. I wouldn't have you do it if you didn't want to. But I know it's perfectly simple."

"And you really want to?"

"I think it's the best thing to do. But I don't want you to do it if you don't really want to."

"And if I do it you'll be happy and things will be like they were and you'll love me?"

"I love you now. You know I love you."

"I know. But if I do it, then it will be nice again if I say things are like white elephants, and you'll like it?"

"I'll love it. I love it now but I just can't think about it. You know how I get when I worry."

"If I do it you won't ever worry?"

"I won't worry about that because it's perfectly simple."

"Then I'll do it. Because I don't care about me."

"What do you mean?"

"I don't care about me."

"Well, I care about you."

"Oh, yes. But I don't care about me. And I'll do it and then everything will be fine."

"I don't want you to do it if you feel that way."

The girl stood up and walked to the end of the station. Across, on the other side, were fields of grain and trees along the banks of the Ebro. Far away, beyond the river, were mountains. The shadow of a cloud moved across the field of grain and she saw the river through the trees.

"And we could have all this," she said. "And we could have everything and every day we make it more impossible."

"What did you say?"

"I said we could have everything."

"We can have everything."

"No, we can't."

"We can have the whole world."

"No, we can't."

"We can go everywhere."

"No, we can't. It isn't ours any more."

"It's ours."

"No, it isn't. And once they take it away, you never get it back."

"But they haven't taken it away."

"We'll wait and see."

"Come on back in the shade," he said. "You mustn't feel that way."

"I don't feel any way," the girl said. "I just know things."

"I don't want you to do anything that you don't want to do—"

"Nor that isn't good for me," she said. "I know. Could we have another beer?"

"All right. But you've got to realize—"

"I realize," the girl said. "Can't we maybe stop talking?"

They sat down at the table and the girl looked across at the hills on the dry side of the valley and the man looked at her and at the table.

"You've got to realize," he said, "that I don't want you to do it if you don't want to. I'm perfectly willing to go through with it if it means anything to you."

"Doesn't it mean anything to you? We could get along."

"Of course it does. But I don't want anybody but you. I don't want any one else. And I know it's perfectly simple."

"Yes, you know it's perfectly simple."

"It's all right for you to say that, but I do know it."

"Would you do something for me now?"

"I'd do anything for you."

"Would you please please please please please please please stop talking?"

He did not say anything but looked at the bags against the wall of the station. There were labels on them from all the hotels where they had spent nights.

"But I don't want you to," he said. "I don't care anything about it."

"I'll scream," the girl said.

The woman came out through the curtains with two glasses of beer and put them down on the damp felt pads. "The train comes in five minutes," she said.

"What did she say?" asked the girl.

"That the train is coming in five minutes."

The girl smiled brightly at the woman, to thank her.

"I'd better take the bags over to the other side of the station," the man said. She smiled at him.

"All right. Then come back and we'll finish the beer."

He picked up the two heavy bags and carried them around the station to the other tracks. He looked up the tracks but could not see the train. Coming back, he walked through the barroom, where people waiting for the train were drinking. He drank an Anis at the bar and looked at the people. They were all waiting reasonably for the train. He went out through the bead curtain. She was sitting at the table and smiled at him.

"Do you feel better?" he asked.

"I feel fine," she said. "There's nothing wrong with me. I feel fine."

1927

STUDY QUESTIONS

1. In contrast to the vivid action of "High Horse's Courting" and "If Not Higher," "Hills like White Elephants" seems to contain almost no action whatever. Nor do the characters at its end seem to have changed, or been changed, from what they were at its beginning. For many years, in fact, critics questioned whether "static" stories like this one deserved the title of "story" at all. What do you think? "Hills like White Elephants" is generally regarded as an excellent example of twentieth-century fiction. Do you agree that it merits this regard? If it is a fine example of the art of fiction, in what lies its artistry?

2. Discuss the mechanics of the story.

   a. How are the characters created? Do you find them clearly drawn? recognizable? or not?

   b. By what means is the tale's conflict defined? How completely is it defined? Is it resolved by the tale's end? What sense do you have regarding its ultimate resolution? Why?

   c. How is the setting described? Is it important? Why or why not?

   d. What amount of time does the story cover? How does this affect your perception of characters, conflict, and setting?

3. How do the elements listed in question 2 work together to create coherence and vision within the story?

A Pair of Silk Stockings

Kate Chopin (1851–1904)

See page 21 for a biographical note on the author.

Little Mrs. Sommers one day found herself the unexpected possessor of fifteen dollars. It seemed to her a very large amount of money, and the way in which it stuffed and bulged her worn old *porte-monnaie*[1] gave her a feeling of importance such as she had not enjoyed for years.

The question of investment was one that occupied her greatly. For a day or two she walked about apparently in a dreamy state, but really absorbed in speculation and calculation. She did not wish to act hastily, to do anything she might afterward regret. But it was during the still hours of the night when she lay awake revolving plans in her mind that she seemed to see her way clearly toward a proper and judicious use of the money.

A dollar or two should be added to the price usually paid for Janie's shoes, which would insure their lasting an appreciable time longer than they usually did. She would buy so and so many yards of percale for new shirt waists for the boys and Janie and Mag. She had intended to make the old ones do by skilful patching. Mag should have another gown. She had seen some beautiful patterns, veritable bargains in the shop windows. And still there would be left enough for new stockings—two pairs apiece—and what darning that would save for a while! She would get caps for the boys and sailor-hats for the girls. The vision of her little brood looking fresh and dainty and new for once in their lives excited her and made her restless and wakeful with anticipation.

The neighbors sometimes talked of certain "better days" that little Mrs. Sommers had known before she had ever thought of being Mrs. Sommers. She herself indulged in no such morbid retrospection. She had no time—no second of time to devote to the past. The needs of the present absorbed her every faculty. A vision of the future like some dim, gaunt monster sometimes appalled her, but luckily tomorrow never comes.

Mrs. Sommers was one who knew the value of bargains; who could stand for hours making her way inch by inch toward the desired object that was selling below cost. She could elbow her way if need be; she had learned to clutch a piece of goods and hold it and stick to it with persistence and determination till her turn came to be served, no matter when it came.

---

[1]purse

But that day she was a little faint and tired. She had swallowed a light luncheon—no! when she came to think of it, between getting the children fed and the place righted, and preparing herself for the shopping bout, she had actually forgotten to eat any luncheon at all!

She sat herself upon a revolving stool before a counter that was comparatively deserted, trying to gather strength and courage to charge through an eager multitude that was besieging breast-works of shirting and figured lawn. An all-gone limp feeling had come over her and she rested her hand aimlessly upon the counter. She wore no gloves. By degrees she grew aware that her hand had encountered something very soothing, very pleasant to touch. She looked down to see that her hand lay upon a pile of silk stockings. A placard near by announced that they had been reduced in price from two dollars and fifty cents to one dollar and ninety-eight cents; and a young girl who stood behind the counter asked her if she wished to examine their line of silk hosiery. She smiled, just as if she had been asked to inspect a tiara of diamonds with the ultimate view of purchasing it. But she went on feeling the soft, sheeny luxurious things—with both hands now, holding them up to see them glisten, and to feel them glide serpent-like through her fingers.

Two hectic blotches came suddenly into her pale cheeks. She looked up at the girl.

"Do you think there are any eights-and-a-half among these?"

There were any number of eights-and-a-half. In fact, there were more of that size than any other. Here was a light-blue pair; there were some lavender, some all black and various shades of tan and gray. Mrs. Sommers selected a black pair and looked at them very long and closely. She pretended to be examining their texture, which the clerk assured her was excellent.

"A dollar and ninety-eight cents," she mused aloud. "Well, I'll take this pair." She handed the girl a five-dollar bill and waited for her change and for her parcel. What a very small parcel it was! It seemed lost in the depths of her shabby old shopping-bag.

Mrs. Sommers after that did not move in the direction of the bargain counter. She took the elevator, which carried her to an upper floor into the region of the ladies' waiting-rooms. Here, in a retired corner, she exchanged her cotton stockings for the new silk ones which she had just bought. She was not going through any acute mental process or reasoning with herself, nor was she striving to explain to her satisfaction the motive of her action. She was not thinking at all. She seemed for the time to be taking a rest from that laborious and fatiguing function and to have abandoned herself to some mechanical impulse that directed her actions and freed her of responsibility.

How good was the touch of the raw silk to her flesh! She felt like lying back in the cushioned chair and reveling for a while in the luxury of it. She did for a little while. Then she replaced her shoes, rolled the cotton stockings together and thrust them into her bag. After doing this she crossed straight over to the shoe department and took her seat to be fitted.

She was fastidious. The clerk could not make her out; he could not reconcile her shoes with her stockings, and she was not too easily pleased. She held back her skirts and turned her feet one way and her head another way as she glanced down at the polished, pointed-tipped boots. Her foot and ankle looked very pretty. She could not realize that they belonged to her and were a part of herself. She wanted an excellent and stylish fit, she told the young fellow who served her, and she did not mind the difference of a dollar or two more in the price so long as she got what she desired.

It was a long time since Mrs. Sommers had been fitted with gloves. On rare occasions when she had bought a pair they were always "bargains," so cheap that it would have been preposterous and unreasonable to have expected them to be fitted to the hand.

Now she rested her elbow on the cushion of the glove counter, and a pretty, pleasant young creature, delicate and deft of touch, drew a long-wristed "kid" over Mrs. Sommer's hand. She smoothed it down over the wrist and buttoned it neatly, and both lost themselves for a second or two in admiring contemplation of the little symmetrical gloved hand. But there were other places where money might be spent.

There were books and magazines piled up in the window of a stall a few paces down the street. Mrs. Sommers bought two high-priced magazines such as she had been accustomed to read in the days when she had been accustomed to other pleasant things. She carried them without wrapping. As well as she could she lifted her skirts at the crossings. Her stockings and boots and well fitting gloves had worked marvels in her bearing—had given her a feeling of assurance, a sense of belonging to the well-dressed multitude.

She was very hungry. Another time she would have stilled the cravings for food until reaching her own home, where she would have brewed herself a cup of tea and taken a snack of anything that was available. But the impulse that was guiding her would not suffer her to entertain any such thought.

There was a restaurant at the corner. She had never entered its doors; from the outside she had sometimes caught glimpses of spotless damask and shining crystal, and soft-stepping waiters serving people of fashion.

When she entered her appearance created no surprise, no consternation, as she had half feared it might. She seated herself at a small table alone, and an attentive waiter at once approached to take her order. She did not want a profusion; she craved a nice and tasty bite—a half dozen blue-points, a plump chop with cress, a something sweet—a crème-frappée, for instance; a glass of Rhine wine, and after all a small cup of black coffee.

While waiting to be served she removed her gloves very leisurely and laid them beside her. Then she picked up a magazine and glanced through it, cutting the pages with a blunt edge of her knife. It was all very agreeable. The damask was even more spotless than it had seemed through the window, and the crystal more sparkling. There were quiet ladies and gentlemen, who did not notice her, lunching at the small tables like her own. A soft, pleasing strain of music could be heard, and a gentle breeze was blowing through the window. She tasted a bite, and she read a word or two, and she sipped the amber wine and wiggled her toes in the silk stockings. The price of it made no difference. She counted the money out to the waiter and left an extra coin on his tray, whereupon he bowed before her as before a princess of royal blood.

There was still money in her purse, and her next temptation presented itself in the shape of a matinée poster.

It was a little later when she entered the theatre, the play had begun and the house seemed to her to be packed. But there were vacant seats here and there, and into one of them she was ushered, between brilliantly dressed women who had gone there to kill time and eat candy and display their gaudy attire. There were many others who were there solely for the play and acting. It is safe to say there was no one present who bore quite the attitude which Mrs. Sommers did to her surroundings. She gathered in the whole—stage and players and people in one wide impression, and absorbed it and enjoyed it. She laughed at the comedy and wept—she and the gaudy woman next to her wept over the tragedy. And they talked a little together over it. And the gaudy woman wiped her eyes and sniffled on a tiny square of filmy, perfumed lace and passed little Mrs. Sommers her box of candy.

The play was over, the music ceased, the crowd filed out. It was like a dream ended. People scattered in all directions. Mrs. Sommers went to the corner and waited for the cable car.

A man with keen eyes, who sat opposite to her, seemed to like the study of her small, pale face. It puzzled him to decipher what he saw there. In truth, he saw nothing unless he were wizard enough to detect a poignant wish, a powerful longing that the cable car would never stop anywhere, but go on and on with her forever.

1896

STUDY QUESTIONS

1. This is a story with only one main character. Because this is the case, what is the source of conflict in "A Pair of Silk Stockings," an element of fiction that all stories must have?

2. What is the narrator's attitude toward "little Mrs. Sommers" and her shopping spree?

3. Does the narrator have a "feminine" voice? If so, how does this affect the narrator's attitude toward Mrs. Sommers? By way of thinking about this question, consider the narrator's voice in "Hills like White Elephants."

A Worn Path

Eudora Welty (1909–   )

Eudora Welty is one of America's most distinguished living writers. Her novels and short stories have won international acclaim for their quiet humanity, their humor, and their ability to explore the great themes of literature through the observation of everyday details. For many years Welty has lived in Jackson, Mississippi, usually taking her fictional settings, as William Faulkner did, from her local scene. Unlike Faulkner's, however, Welty's world is more often one of ordinary but telling moments rather than of gothic exaggeration and violence.

It was December—a bright frozen day in the early morning. Far out in the country there was an old Negro woman with her head tied in a red rag, coming along a path through the pinewoods. Her name was Phoenix Jackson. She was very old and small and she walked slowly in the dark pine shadows, moving a little from side to side in her steps, with the balanced heaviness and lightness of a pendulum in a grandfather clock. She carried a thin, small cane made from an umbrella, and with this she kept tapping the frozen earth in front of her. This made a grave and persistent noise in the still air, that seemed meditative like the chirping of a solitary little bird.

She wore a dark striped dress reaching down to her shoetops, and an equally long apron of bleached sugar sacks, with a full pocket; all neat and tidy, but every time she took a step she might have fallen over her shoe-laces, which dragged from her unlaced shoes. She looked straight ahead. Her eyes were blue with age. Her skin had a pattern all its own of numberless branching wrinkles and as though a whole little tree stood in the middle of her forehead, but a golden color ran underneath, and the two knobs of her cheeks were illuminated by a yellow burning under the dark. Under the red rag her hair came down on her neck in the frailest of ringlets, still black, and with an odor like copper.

Now and then there was a quivering in the thicket. Old Phoenix said, "Out of my way, all you foxes, owls, beetles, jack rabbits, coons, and wild animals! . . . Keep out from under these feet, little bobwhites. . . . Keep the big wild hogs out of my path. Don't let none of those come running my direction. I got a long way." Under her small black-freckled hand her cane, limber as a buggy whip, would switch at the brush as if to rouse up any hiding things.

On she went. The woods were deep and still. The sun made the pine needles almost too bright to look at, up where the wind rocked. The cones dropped as light as feathers. Down in the hollow was the mourning dove—it was not too late for him.

The path ran up a hill. "Seems like there is chains about my feet, time I get this far," she said, in the voice of argument old people keep to use with themselves. "Something always take a hold on his hill—pleads I should stay."

After she got to the top she turned and gave a full, severe look behind her where she had come. "Up through pines," she said at length. "Now down through oaks."

Her eyes opened their widest and she started down gently. But before she got to the bottom of the hill a bush caught her dress.

Her fingers were busy and intent, but her skirts were full and long, so that before she could pull them free in one place they were caught in another. It was not possible to allow the dress to tear. "I in the thorny bush," she said. "Thorns, you doing your appointed work. Never want to let folks pass—no sir. Old eyes thought you was a pretty little green bush."

Finally, trembling all over, she stood free, and after a moment dared to stoop for her cane.

"Sun so high!" she cried, leaning back and looking, while the thick tears went over her eyes. "The time getting all gone here."

At the foot of this hill was a place where a log was laid across the creek.

"Now comes the trial," said Phoenix.

Putting her right foot out, she mounted the log and shut her eyes. Lifting her skirt, levelling her cane fiercely before her, like a festival figure in some parade, she began to march across. Then she opened her eyes and she was safe on the other side.

"I wasn't as old as I thought," she said.

But she sat down to rest. She spread her skirts on the bank around her and folded her hands over her knees. Up above her was a tree in a pearly cloud of mistletoe. She did not dare to close her eyes, and when a little boy brought her a little plate with a slice of marble-cake on it she spoke to him. "That would be acceptable," she said. But when she went to take it there was just her own hand in the air.

So she left that tree, and had to go through a barbed-wire fence. There she had to creep and crawl, spreading her knees and stretching her fingers like a baby trying to climb the steps. But she talked loudly to herself: she could not let her dress be torn now, so late in the day, and she could not pay for having her arm or her leg sawed off if she got caught fast where she was.

At last she was safe through the fence and risen up out in the clearing. Big dead trees, like black men with one arm, were standing in the purple stalks of the withered cotton field. There sat a buzzard.

"Who you watching?"

In the burrow she made her way along.

"Glad this not the season for bulls," she said, looking sideways, "and the good Lord made his snakes to curl up and sleep in the winter. A pleasure I don't see no two-headed snake coming around that tree, where it come once. It took a while to get by him, back in the summer."

She passed through the old cotton and went into a field of dead corn. It whispered and shook, and was taller than her head. "Through the maze now," she said, for there was no path.

Then there was something tall, black, and skinny there, moving before her.

At first she took it for a man. It could have been a man dancing in the field. But she stood still and listened, and it did not make a sound. It was as silent as a ghost.

"Ghost," she said sharply, "who be you the ghost of? For I have heard of nary death close by."

But there was no answer, only the ragged dancing in the wind.

She shut her eyes, reached out her hand, and touched a sleeve. She found a coat and inside that an emptiness, cold as ice.

"You scarecrow," she said. Her face lighted. "I ought to be shut up for good," she said with laughter. "My senses is gone. I too old. I the oldest people I ever know. Dance, old scarecrow," she said, "while I dancing with you."

She kicked her foot over the furrow, and with mouth drawn down shook her head once or twice in a little strutting way. Some husks blew down and whirled in streamers about her skirts.

Then she went on, parting her way from side to side with the cane, through the whispering field. At last she came to the end, to a wagon track, where the silver grass blew between the red ruts. The quail were walking around like pullets, seeming all dainty and unseen.

"Walk pretty," she said. "This the easy place. This the easy going."

She followed the track, swaying through the quiet bare fields, through the little strings of trees silver in their dead leaves, past cabins silver from weather, with the doors and windows boarded shut, all like old women under a spell sitting there. "I walking in their sleep," she said, nodding her head vigorously.

In a ravine she went where a spring was silently flowing through a hollow log. Old Phoenix bent and drank. "Sweetgum makes the water sweet," she said, and drank more. "Nobody knows who made this well, for it was here when I was born."

The track crossed a swampy part where the moss hung as white as lace from every limb. "Sleep on, alligators, and blow your bubbles." Then the track went into the road.

Deep, deep the road went down between the high green-colored banks. Overhead the live-oaks met, and it was as dark as a cave.

A black dog with a lolling tongue came up out of the weeds by the ditch. She was meditating, and not ready, and when he came at her she only hit him a little with her cane. Over she went in the ditch, like a little puff of milk-weed.

Down there, her senses drifted away. A dream visited her, and she reached her hand up, but nothing reached down and gave her a pull. So she lay there and presently went to talking. "Old woman," she said to herself, "that black dog came up out of the weeds to stall you off, and now there he sitting on his fine tail, smiling at you."

A white man finally came along and found her—a hunter, a young man, with his dog on a chain.

"Well, Granny!" he laughed. "What are you doing there?"

"Lying on my back like a June-bug waiting to be turned over, mister," she said, reaching up her hand.

He lifted her up, gave her a swing in the air, and set her down, "Anything broken, Granny?"

"No sir, them old dead weeds is springy enough," said Phoenix, when she had got her breath. "I thank you for your trouble."

"Where do you live, Granny?" he asked, while the two dogs were growling at each other.

"Away back yonder, sir, behind the ridge. You can't even see it from here."

"On your way home?"

"No, sir, I going to town."

"Why, that's too far! That's as far as I walk when I come out myself, and I get something for my trouble." He patted the stuffed bag he carried, and there hung down a little closed claw. It was one of the bobwhites, with its beak hooked bitterly to show it was dead. "Now you go on home, Granny!"

"I bound to go to town, mister," said Phoenix. "The time come around."

He gave another laugh, filling the whole landscape. "I know you colored people! Wouldn't miss going to town to see Santa Claus!"

But something held Old Phoenix very still. The deep lines in her face went into a fierce and different radiation. Without warning she had seen with her own eyes a flashing nickel fall out of the man's pocket on to the ground.

"How old are you, Granny?" he was saying.

"There is no telling, mister," she said, "no telling."

Then she gave a little cry and clapped her hands, and said, "Git on away from here, dog! Look at that dog!" She laughed as if in admiration. "He ain't scared of nobody. He a big black dog." She whispered, "Sick him!"

"Watch me get rid of that cur," said the man. "Sick him, Pete! Sick him!"

Phoenix heard the dogs fighting and heard the man running and throwing sticks. She even heard a gunshot. But she was slowly bending forward by that time, further and further forward, the lids stretched down over her eyes, as if she were doing this in her sleep. Her chin was lowered almost to her knees. The yellow palm of her hand came out from the fold of her apron. Her fingers slid down and along the ground under the piece of money with the grace and care they would have in lifting an egg from under a sitting hen. Then she slowly straightened up, she stood erect, and the nickel was in her apron pocket. A bird flew by. Her lips moved. "God watching me the whole time. I come to stealing."

The man came back, and his own dog panted about them. "Well, I scared him off that time," he said, and then he laughed and lifted his gun and pointed it at Phoenix.

She stood straight and faced him.

"Doesn't the gun scare you?" he said, still pointing it.

"No, sir, I seen plenty go off closer by, in my day, and for less than what I done," she said, holding utterly still.

He smiled, and shouldered the gun. "Well, Granny," he said, "you must be a hundred years old and scared of nothing. I'd give you a dime if I had any money with me. But you take my advice and stay home, and nothing will happen to you."

"I bound to go on my way, mister," said Phoenix. She inclined her head in the red rag. Then they went in different directions, but she could hear the gun shooting again and again over the hill.

She walked on. The shadows hung from the oak trees to the road like curtains. Then she smelled wood-smoke, and smelled the river, and she saw a steeple and the cabins on their steep steps. Dozens of little black children whirled around her. There ahead was Natchez shining. Bells were ringing. She walked on.

In the paved city it was Christmas time. There were red and green electric lights strung and crisscrossed everywhere, and all turned on in the daytime. Old Phoenix would have been lost if she had not distrusted her eyesight and depended on her feet to know where to take her.

She paused quietly on the sidewalk, where people were passing by. A lady came along in the crowd, carrying an armful of red-, green-, and silver-wrapped presents; she gave off perfume like the red roses in hot summer, and Phoenix stopped her.

"Please, missy, will you lace up my shoe?" She held up her foot.

"What do you want, Grandma?"

"See my shoe," said Phoenix. "Do all right for out in the country, but wouldn't look right to go in a big building."

"Stand still then, Grandma," said the lady. She put her packages down carefully on the sidewalk beside her and laced and tied both shoes tightly.

"Can't lace 'em with a cane," said Phoenix. "Thank you, missy. I doesn't mind asking a nice lady to tie up my shoe when I gets out on the street."

Moving slowly and from side to side, she went into the stone building and into a tower of steps, where she walked up and around and around until her feet knew to stop.

She entered a door, and there she saw nailed up on the wall the document that had been stamped with the gold seal and framed in the gold frame which matched the dream that was hung up in her head.

"Here I be," she said. There was a fixed and ceremonial stiffness over her body.

"A charity case, I suppose," said an attendant who sat at the desk before her.

But Phoenix only looked above her head. There was sweat on her face; the wrinkles shone like a bright net.

"Speak up, Grandma," the woman said. "What's your name? We must have your history, you know. Have you been here before? What seems to be the trouble with you?"

Old Phoenix only gave a twitch to her face as if a fly were bothering her.

"Are you deaf?" cried the attendant.

But then the nurse came in.

"Oh, that's just old Aunt Phoenix," she said. "She doesn't come for herself— she has a little grandson. She makes these trips just as regular as clockwork. She lives away back off the Old Natchez Trace." She bent down. "Well, Aunt Phoenix, why don't you just take a seat? We won't keep you standing after your long trip." She pointed.

The old woman sat down, bolt upright in the chair.

"Now, how is the boy?" asked the nurse.

Old Phoenix did not speak.

"I said, how is the boy?"

But Phoenix only waited and stared straight ahead, her face very solemn and withdrawn into rigidity.

"Is his throat any better?" asked the nurse. "Aunt Phoenix, don't you hear me? Is your grandson's throat any better since the last time you came for the medicine?"

With her hand on her knees, the old woman waited, silent, erect and motionless, just as if she were in armor.

"You mustn't take up our time this way, Aunt Phoenix," the nurse said. "Tell us quickly about your grandson, and get it over. He isn't dead, is he?"

At last there came a flicker and then a flame of comprehension across her face, and she spoke.

"My grandson. It was my memory had left me. There I sat and forgot why I made my long trip."

"Forgot?" The nurse frowned. "After you came so far?"

Then Phoenix was like an old woman begging a dignified forgiveness for waking up frightened in the night. "I never did go to school—I was too old at the Surrender," she said in a soft voice. "I'm an old woman without an education. It was my memory fail me. My little grandson, he is just the same, and I forgot it in the coming."

"Throat never heals, does it?" said the nurse, speaking in a loud, sure voice to Old Phoenix. By now she had a card with something written on it, a little list. "Yes. Swallowed lye. When was it—January—two—three years ago—"

Phoenix spoke unasked now. "No, missy, he not dead, he just the same. Every little while his throat begin to close up again, and he not able to swallow. He not get his breath. He not able to help himself. So the time come around, and I go on another trip for the soothing-medicine."

"All right. The doctor said as long as you came to get it you could have it," said the nurse. "But it's an obstinate case."

"My little grandson, he sit up there in the house all wrapped up, waiting by himself," Phoenix went on. "We is the only two left in the world. He suffer and it don't seem to put him back at all. He got a sweet look. He going to last. He wear a little patch quilt and peep out, holding his mouth open like a little bird. I remembers so plain now. I not going to forget him again, no, the whole enduring time. I could tell him from all the others in creation."

"All right." The nurse was trying to hush her now. She brought her a bottle of medicine. "Charity," she said, making a check mark in a book.

Old Phoenix held the bottle close to her eyes and then carefully put it into her pocket.

"I thank you," she said.

"It's Christmas time, Grandma," said the attendant. "Could I give you a few pennies out of my purse?"

"Five pennies is a nickel," said Phoenix stiffly.

"Here's a nickel," said the attendant.

Phoenix rose carefully and held out her hand. She received the nickel and then fished the other nickel out of her pocket and laid it beside the new one. She stared at her palm closely, with her head on one side.

Then she gave a tap with her cane on the floor.

"This is what come to me to do," she said. "I going to the store and buy my child a little windmill they sells, made out of paper. He going to find it hard to believe there such a thing in the world. I'll march myself back where he waiting, holding it straight up in this hand."

She lifted her free hand, gave a little nod, turned round, and walked out of the doctor's office. Then her slow step began on the stairs, going down.

1941

STUDY QUESTIONS

1. How much of the story takes place with Granny Phoenix as its only character? What happens in this first part of the tale? What effect does it have on you, the reader?
2. Describe Granny's first meeting with another person. What new information do we learn from it?
3. The story's climax is the scene in the clinic. Here we finally learn why Granny has made her long journey. What is your reaction to this scene? How have the story and its narrator brought you to feel as you do?

Where Are You Going, Where Have You Been?

Joyce Carol Oates (1938–   )

Joyce Carol Oates is one of the most versatile, accomplished, and prolific contemporary American writers. A poet, short story writer, critic, novelist, editor, and publisher, Oates has impressed and even intimidated other writers with her amazing productivity. Her fiction covers the American scene from the backwoods to suburbia to the urban jungle, often putting her protagonists into violent situations that cause them to see the inadequacy of their confused core values and identities.

For Bob Dylan

Her name was Connie. She was fifteen and she had a quick, nervous giggling habit of craning her neck to glance into mirrors or checking other people's faces to make sure her own was all right. Her mother, who noticed everything and knew everything and who hadn't much reason any longer to look at her own face, always scolded Connie about it. "Stop gawking at yourself. Who are you? You think you're so pretty?" she would say. Connie would raise her eyebrows at these familiar old complaints and look right through her mother, into a shadowy vision of herself as she was right at that moment: she knew she was pretty and that was everything. Her mother had been pretty once too, if you could believe those old snapshots in the album, but now her looks were gone and that was why she was always after Connie.

"Why don't you keep your room clean like your sister? How've you got your hair fixed—what the hell stinks? Hair spray? You don't see your sister using that junk."

Her sister June was twenty-four and still lived at home. She was a secretary in the high school Connie attended, and if that wasn't bad enough—with her in the same building—she was so plain and chunky and steady that Connie had to hear her praised all the time by her mother and her mother's sisters. June did this, June did that, she saved money and helped clean the house and cooked and Connie couldn't do a thing, her mind was all filled with trashy daydreams. Their father was away at work most of the time and when he came home he wanted supper and he read the newspaper at supper and after supper he went to bed. He didn't bother talking much to them, but around his bent head Connie's mother kept picking at her until Connie wished her mother was dead and she herself was dead and it was all over. "She makes me want to throw up sometimes," she complained to her friends. She had a high, breathless, amused voice that made everything she said sound a little forced, whether it was sincere or not.

There was one good thing: June went places with girl friends of hers, girls who were just as plain and steady as she, and so when Connie wanted to do that her mother had no objections. The father of Connie's best girl friend drove the girls the three miles to town and left them at a shopping plaza so they could walk through the stores or go to a movie, and when he came to pick them up again at eleven he never bothered to ask what they had done.

They must have been familiar sights, walking around the shopping plaza in their shorts and flat ballerina slippers that always scuffed on the sidewalk, with charm bracelets jingling on their thin wrists; they would lean together to whisper and laugh secretly if someone passed who amused or interested them. Connie had long dark blond hair that drew anyone's eye to it, and she wore part of it pulled up on her head and puffed out and the rest of it she let fall down her back. She wore a pull-over jersey blouse that looked one way when she was at home and another way when she was away from home. Everything about her had two sides to it, one for home and one for anywhere that was not home: her walk, which could be childlike and bobbing, or languid enough to make anyone think she was hearing music in her head; her mouth, which was pale and smirking most of the time, but bright and pink on these evenings out; her laugh, which was cynical and drawling at home—"Ha, ha, very funny,"—but highpitched and nervous anywhere else, like the jingling of the charms on her bracelet.

Sometimes they did go shopping or to a movie, but sometimes they went across the highway, ducking fast across the busy road, to a drive-in restaurant where older kids hung out. The restaurant was shaped like a big bottle, though squatter than a real bottle, and on its cap was a revolving figure of a grinning boy holding a hamburger aloft. One night in midsummer they ran across, breathless with daring, and right away someone leaned out a car window and invited them over, but it was just a boy from high school they didn't like. It made them feel good to be able to ignore him. They went up through the maze of parked and cruising cars to the bright-lit, fly-infested restaurant, their faces pleased and expectant as if they were entering a sacred building that loomed up out of the night to give them what haven and blessing they yearned for. They sat at the counter and crossed their legs at the ankles, their thin shoulders rigid with excitement, and listened to the music that made everything so good: the music was always in the background, like music at a church service; it was something to depend upon.

A boy named Eddie came in to talk with them. He sat backwards on his stool, turning himself jerkily around in semicircles and then stopping and turning back again, and after a while he asked Connie if she would like something to eat. She said she would and so she tapped her friend's arm on her way out—her friend pulled her face up into a brave, droll look—and Connie said she would meet her at eleven, across the way. "I just hate to leave her like that," Connie said earnestly, but the boy said that she wouldn't be alone for long. So they went out to his car, and on the way Connie couldn't help but let her eyes wander over the windshields and faces all around her, her face gleaming with a joy that had nothing to do with Eddie or even this place; it might have been the music. She drew her shoulders up and sucked in her breath with the pure pleasure of being alive, and just at that moment she happened to glance at a face just a few feet away from hers. It was a boy with shaggy black hair, in a convertible jalopy painted gold. He stared at her and then his lips widened into a grin. Connie slit her eyes at him and turned away, but she couldn't help glancing back and there he was, still watching her. He wagged a finger and laughed and said, "Gonna get you, baby," and Connie turned away again without Eddie noticing anything.

She spent three hours with him, at the restaurant where they ate hamburgers and drank Cokes in wax cups that were always sweating, and then down an alley a mile or so away, and when he left her off at five to eleven only the movie house was still open at the plaza. Her girl friend was there, talking with a boy. When Connie came up, the two girls smiled at each other and Connie said, "How was the movie?" and the girl said, "*You* should know." They rode off with the girl's father, sleepy and pleased, and Connie couldn't help but look back at the darkened shopping plaza with its big empty parking lot and its signs that were faded and ghostly now, and over at the drive-in restaurant where cars were still circling tirelessly. She couldn't hear the music at this distance.

Next morning June asked her how the movie was and Connie said, "So-so."

She and that girl and occasionally another girl went out several times a week, and the rest of the time Connie spent around the house—it was summer vacation—getting in her mother's way and thinking, dreaming about the boys she met. But all the boys fell back and dissolved into a single face that was not even a face but an idea, a feeling, mixed up with the urgent insistent pounding of the music and the humid night air of July. Connie's mother kept dragging her back to the daylight by finding things for her to do or saying suddenly, "What's this about the Pettinger girl?"

And Connie would say nervously, "Oh, her. That dope." She always drew thick clear lines between herself and such girls, and her mother was simple and kind enough to believe it. Her mother was so simple, Connie thought, that it was maybe cruel to fool her so much. Her mother went scuffling around the house in old bedroom slippers and complained over the telephone to one sister about the other, then the other called up and the two of them complained about the third one. If June's name was mentioned her mother's tone was approving, and if Connie's name was mentioned it was disapproving. This did not really mean she disliked Connie, and actually Connie thought that her mother preferred her to June just because she was prettier, but the two of them kept up a pretense of exasperation, a sense that they were tugging and struggling over something of little value to either of them. Sometimes, over coffee, they were almost friends, but something would come up—some vexation that was like a fly buzzing suddenly around their heads—and their faces went hard with contempt.

One Sunday Connie got up at eleven—none of them bothered with church—and washed her hair so that it could dry all day long in the sun. Her parents and sister were going to a barbecue at an aunt's house and Connie said no, she wasn't interested, rolling her eyes to let her mother know just what she thought of it. "Stay home alone then," her mother said sharply. Connie sat out back in a lawn chair and watched them drive away, her father quiet and bald, hunched around so that he could back the car out, her mother with a look that was still angry and not at all softened through the windshield, and in the back seat poor old June, all dressed up as if she didn't know what a barbecue was, with all the running yelling kids and the flies. Connie sat with her eyes closed in the sun, dreaming and dazed with the warmth about her as if this were a kind of love, the caresses of love, and her mind slipped over onto thoughts of the boy she had been with the night before and how nice he had been, how sweet it always was, not the way someone like June would suppose but sweet, gentle, the way it was in movies and promised in songs; and when she opened her eyes she hardly knew where she was, the back yard ran off into weeds and a fence-like line of trees and behind it the sky was perfectly blue and still. The asbestos "ranch house" that was now three years old startled her—it looked small. She shook her head as if to get awake.

It was too hot. She went inside the house and turned on the radio to drown out the quiet. She sat on the edge of her bed, barefoot, and listened for an hour and a half, to a program called XYZ Sunday Jamboree, record after record of hard, fast, shrieking songs she sang along with, interspersed by exclamations from "Bobby King": "An' look here, you girls at Napoleon's—Son and Charley want you to pay real close attention to this song coming up!"

And Connie paid close attention herself, bathed in a glow of slow-pulsed joy that seemed to rise mysteriously out of the music itself and lay languidly about the airless little room, breathed in and breathed out with each gentle rise and fall of her chest.

After a while she heard a car coming up the drive. She sat up at once, startled, because it couldn't be her father so soon. The gravel kept crunching all the way in from the road—the driveway was long—and Connie ran to the window. It was a car she didn't know. It was an open jalopy, painted a bright gold that caught the sunlight opaquely. Her heart began to pound and her fingers snatched at her hair, checking it, and she whispered, "Christ, Christ," wondering how she looked. The car came to a stop at the side door and the horn sounded four short taps, as if this were a signal Connie knew.

She went into the kitchen and approached the door slowly, then hung out the screen door, her bare toes curling down off the step. There were two boys in the car and now she recognized the driver: he had shaggy, shabby black hair that looked crazy as a wig and he was grinning at her.

"I ain't late, am I?" he said.

"Who the hell do you think you are?" Connie said.

"Toldja I'd be out, didn't I?"

"I don't even know who you are."

She spoke sullenly, careful to show no interest or pleasure, and he spoke in a fast, bright monotone. Connie looked past him to the other boy, taking her time.

He had fair brown hair, with a lock that fell onto his forehead. His sideburns gave him a fierce, embarrassed look, but so far he hadn't even bothered to glance at her. Both boys wore sunglasses. The driver's glasses were metallic and mirrored everything in miniature.

"You wanta come for a ride?" he said.

Connie smirked and let her hair fall loose over one shoulder.

"Don'tcha like my car? New paint job," he said. "Hey."

"What?"

"You're cute."

She pretended to fidget, chasing flies away from the door.

"Don'tcha believe me, or what?" he said.

"Look, I don't even know who you are," Connie said in disgust.

"Hey, Ellie's got a radio, see. Mine broke down." He lifted his friend's arm and showed her the little transistor radio the boy was holding, and now Connie began to hear the music. It was the same program that was playing inside the house.

"Bobby King?" she said.

"I listen to him all the time. I think he's great."

"He's kind of great," Connie said reluctantly.

"Listen, that guy's *great*. He knows where the action is."

Connie blushed a little, because the glasses made it impossible for her to see just what this boy was looking at. She couldn't decide if she liked him or if he was a jerk, and so she dawdled in the doorway and wouldn't come down or go back inside. She said, "What's all that stuff painted on your car?"

"Can'tcha read it?" He opened the door very carefully, as if he were afraid it might fall off. He slid out just as carefully, planting his feet firmly on the ground, the tiny metallic world in his glasses slowing down like gelatine hardening, and in the midst of it Connie's bright green blouse. "This here is my name, to begin with," he said. ARNOLD FRIEND was written in tarlike black letters on the side, with a drawing of a round, grinning face that reminded Connie of a pumpkin, except it wore sunglasses. "I wanta introduce myself. I'm Arnold Friend and that's my real name and I'm gonna be your friend, honey, and inside the car's Ellie Oscar, he's kinda shy." Ellie brought his transistor radio up to his shoulder and balanced it there. "Now, these numbers are a secret code, honey," Arnold Friend explained. He read off the numbers 33, 19, 17 and raised his eyebrows at her to see what she thought of that, but she didn't think much of it. The left rear fender had been smashed and around it was written, on the gleaming gold background: DONE BY CRAZY WOMAN DRIVER. Connie had to laugh at that. Arnold Friend was pleased at her laughter and looked up at her. "Around the other side's a lot more—you wanta come and see them?"

"No."

"Why not?"

"Why should I?"

"Don'tcha wanta see what's on the car? Don'tcha wanta go for a ride?"

"I don't know."

"Why not?"

"I got things to do."

"Like what?"

"Things."

He laughed as if she had said something funny. He slapped his thighs. He was standing in a strange way, leaning back against the car as if he were balancing himself. He wasn't tall, only an inch or so taller than she would be if she came down to him. Connie liked the way he was dressed, which was the way all of them dressed: tight faded jeans stuffed into black, scuffed boots, a belt that pulled his waist in and showed how lean he was, and a white pull-over shirt that was a little soiled and showed the hard small muscles of his arms and shoulders. He looked as if he probably did hard work, lifting and carrying things. Even his neck looked muscular. And his face was a familiar face, somehow; the jaw and chin and cheeks slightly darkened because he hadn't shaved for a day or two, and the nose long and hawklike, sniffing as if she were a treat he was going to gobble up and it was all a joke.

"Connie, you ain't telling the truth. This is your day set aside for a ride with me and you know it," he said, still laughing. The way he straightened and recovered from his fit of laughing showed that it had been all fake.

"How do you know what my name is?" she said suspiciously.

"It's Connie."

"Maybe and maybe not."

"I know my Connie," he said, wagging his finger. Now she remembered him even better, back at the restaurant, and her cheeks warmed at the thought of how she had sucked in her breath just at the moment she passed him—how she must have looked to him. And he had remembered her. "Ellie and I come out here especially for you," he said. "Ellie can sit in back. How about it?"

"Where?"

"Where what?"

"Where're we going?"

He looked at her. He took off the sunglasses and she saw how pale the skin around his eyes was, like holes that were not in shadow but instead in light. His eyes were like chips of broken glass that catch the light in an amiable way. He smiled. It was as if the idea of going for a ride somewhere, to someplace, was a new idea to him.

"Just for a ride, Connie sweetheart."

"I never said my name was Connie," she said.

"But I know what it is. I know your name and all about you, lots of things," Arnold Friend said. He had not moved yet but stood still leaning back against the side of his jalopy. "I took a special interest in you, such a pretty girl, and found out all about you—like I know your parents and sister are gone somewheres and I know where and how long they're going to be gone, and I know who you were with last night, and your best girl friend's name is Betty. Right?"

He spoke in a simple lilting voice, exactly as if he were reciting the words to a song. His smile assured her that everything was fine. In the car Ellie turned up the volume on his radio and did not bother to look around at them.

"Ellie can sit in the back seat," Arnold Friend said. He indicated his friend with a casual jerk of his chin, as if Ellie did not count and she should not bother with him.

"How'd you find out all that stuff?" Connie said.

"Listen: Betty Schultz and Tony Fitch and Jimmy Pettinger and Nancy Pettinger," he said in a chant. "Raymond Stanley and Bob Hutter—"

"Do you know all those kids?"

"I know everybody."

"Look, you're kidding. You're not from around here."

"Sure."

"But—how come we never saw you before?"

"Sure you saw me before," he said. He looked down at his boots, as if he were a little offended. "You just don't remember."

"I guess I'd remember you," Connie said.

"Yeah?" He looked up at this, beaming. He was pleased. He began to mark time with the music from Ellie's radio, tapping his fists lightly together. Connie looked away from his smile to the car, which was painted so bright it almost hurt her eyes to look at. She looked at that name, ARNOLD FRIEND. And up at the front fender was an expression that was familiar—MAN THE FLYING SAUCERS. It was an expression kids had used the year before but didn't use this year. She looked at it for a while as if the words meant something to her that she did not yet know.

"What're you thinking about? Huh?" Arnold Friend demanded. "Not worried about your hair blowing around in the car, are you?"

"No."

"Think I maybe can't drive good?"

"How do I know?"

"You're a hard girl to handle. How come?" he said. "Don't you know I'm your friend? Didn't you see me put my sign in the air when you walked by?"

"What sign?"

"My sign." And he drew an X in the air, leaning out toward her. They were maybe ten feet apart. After his hand fell back to his side the X was still in the air, almost visible. Connie let the screen door close and stood perfectly still inside it, listening to the music from her radio and the boy's blend together. She stared at Arnold Friend. He stood there so stiffly relaxed, pretending to be relaxed, with one hand idly on the door handle as if he were keeping himself up that way and had no intention of ever moving again. She recognized most things about him, the tight jeans that showed his thighs and buttocks and the greasy leather boots and the tight shirt, and even that slippery friendly smile of his, that sleepy dreamy smile that all the boys used to get across ideas they didn't want to put into words. She recognized all this and also the sing-song way he talked, slightly mocking, kidding, but serious and a little melancholy, and she recognized the way he tapped one fist against the other in homage to the perpetual music behind him. But all these things did not come together.

She said suddenly, "Hey, how old are you?"

His smile faded. She could see then that he wasn't a kid, he was much older—thirty, maybe more. At this knowledge her heart began to pound faster.

"That's a crazy thing to ask. Can'tcha see I'm your own age?"

"Like hell you are."

"Or maybe a coupla years older. I'm eighteen."

"Eighteen?" she said doubtfully.

He grinned to reassure her and lines appeared at the corners of his mouth. His teeth were big and white. He grinned so broadly his eyes became slits and she saw how thick the lashes were, thick and black as if painted with a black tarlike material. Then, abruptly, he seemed to become embarrassed and looked over his shoulder at Ellie. "*Him,* he's crazy," he said. "Ain't he a riot? He's a nut, a real character." Ellie was still listening to the music. His sunglasses told nothing about what he was thinking. He wore a bright orange shirt unbuttoned halfway to show his chest, which was a pale, bluish chest and not muscular like Arnold Friend's. His shirt collar was turned up all around and the very tips of the collar pointed out past his chin as if they were protecting him. He was pressing the transistor radio up against his ear and sat there in a kind of daze, right in the sun.

"He's kinda strange," Connie said.

"Hey, she says you're kinda strange! Kinda strange!" Arnold Friend cried. He pounded on the car to get Ellie's attention. Ellie turned for the first time and Connie saw with shock that he wasn't a kid either—he had a fair, hairless face, cheeks reddened slightly as if the veins grew too close to the surface of his skin, the face of a forty-year-old baby. Connie felt a wave of dizziness rise in her at this sight and she stared at him as if waiting for something to change the shock of the moment, make it all right again. Ellie's lips kept shaping words, mumbling along with the words blasting in his ear.

"Maybe you two better go away," Connie said faintly.

"What? How come?" Arnold Friend cried. "We come out here to take you for a ride. It's Sunday." He had the voice of the man on the radio now. It was the same voice, Connie thought. "Don'tcha know it's Sunday all day? And honey, no matter who you were with last night, today you're with Arnold Friend and don't you forget it! Maybe you better step out here," he said, and this last was in a different voice. It was a little flatter, as if the heat was finally getting to him.

"No, I got things to do."

"Hey."

"You two better leave."

"We ain't leaving until you come with us."

"Like hell I am—"

"Connie, don't fool around with me. I mean—I mean, don't fool *around,*" he said, shaking his head. He laughed incredulously. He placed his sunglasses on top of his head, carefully, as if he were indeed wearing a wig, and brought the stems down behind his ears. Connie stared at him, another wave of dizziness and fear rising in her so that for a moment he wasn't even in focus but was just a blur standing there against his gold car, and she had the idea that he had driven up the driveway all right but had come from nowhere before that and belonged nowhere and that everything about him and even about the music that was so familiar to her was only half real.

"If my father comes and sees you—"

"He ain't coming. He's at a barbecue."

"How do you know that?"

"Aunt Tillie's. Right now they're—uh—they're drinking. Sitting around," he said vaguely, squinting as if he were staring all the way to town and over to Aunt Tillie's back yard. Then the vision seemed to get clear and he nodded energetically. "Yeah. Sitting around. There's your sister in a blue dress, huh? And high heels, the poor sad bitch—nothing like you, sweetheart! And your mother's helping some fat woman with the corn, they're cleaning the corn—husking the corn—"

"What fat woman?" Connie cried.

"How do I know what fat woman, I don't know every goddamn fat woman in the world!" Arnold Friend laughed.

"Oh, that's Mrs. Hornsby. . . . Who invited her?" Connie said. She felt a little lightheaded. Her breath was coming quickly.

"She's too fat. I don't like them fat. I like them the way you are, honey," he said, smiling sleepily at her. They stared at each other for a while through the screen door. He said softly, "Now, what you're going to do is this: you're going to come out that door. You're going to sit up front with me and Ellie's going to sit in the back, the hell with Ellie, right? This isn't Ellie's date. You're my date. I'm your lover, honey."

"What? You're crazy—"

"Yes. I'm your lover. You don't know what that is but you will," he said. "I know that too. I know all about you. But look: it's real nice and you couldn't ask for nobody better than me, or more polite. I always keep my word. I'll tell you how it is. I'm always nice at first, the first time. I'll hold you so tight you won't think you have to try to get away or pretend anything because you'll know you can't. And I'll come inside you where it's all secret and you'll give in to me and you'll love me—"

"Shut up! You're crazy!" Connie said. She backed away from the door. She put her hands up against her ears as if she'd heard something terrible, something not meant for her. "People don't talk like that, you're crazy," she muttered. Her heart was almost too big now for her chest and its pumping made sweat break out all over her. She looked out to see Arnold Friend pause and then take a step toward the porch, lurching. He almost fell. But, like a clever drunken man, he managed to catch his balance. He wobbled in his high boots and grabbed hold of one of the porch posts.

"Honey?" he said. "You still listening?"

"Get the hell out of here!"

"Be nice, honey. Listen."

"I'm going to call the police—"

He wobbled again and out of the side of his mouth came a fast spat curse, an aside not meant for her to hear. But even this "Christ!" sounded forced. Then he began to smile again. She watched this smile come, awkward as if he were smiling from inside a mask. His whole face was a mask, she thought wildly, tanned down to his throat but then running out as if he had plastered makeup on his face but had forgotten about his throat.

"Honey—? Listen, here's how it is. I always tell the truth and I promise you this: I ain't coming in that house after you."

"You better not! I'm going to call the police if you—if you don't—"

"Honey," he said, talking right through her voice, "honey. I'm not coming in there but you are coming out here. You know why?"

She was panting. The kitchen looked like a place she had never seen before, some room she had run inside but that wasn't good enough, wasn't going to help her. The kitchen window had never had a curtain, after three years, and there were dishes in the sink for her to do—probably—and if you ran your hand across the table you'd probably feel something stick there.

"You listening, honey? Hey?"

"—going to call the police—"

"Soon as you touch the phone I don't need to keep my promise and can come inside. You won't want that."

She rushed forward and tried to lock the door. Her fingers were shaking. "But why lock it," Arnold Friend said gently, talking right into her face. "It's just a screen door. It's just nothing." One of his boots was at a strange angle, as if his foot wasn't in it. It pointed out to the left, bent at the ankle. "I mean, anybody can break through a screen door and glass and wood and iron or anything else if he needs to, anybody at all, and especially Arnold Friend. If the place got lit up with a fire, honey, you'd come runnin' out into my arms, right into my arms an' safe at home—like you knew I was your lover and'd stopped fooling around. I don't mind a nice shy girl but I don't like no fooling around." Part of those words were spoken with a slight rhythmic lilt, and Connie somehow recognized them—the echo of a song from last year, about a girl rushing into her boy friend's arms and coming home again—

Connie stood barefoot on the linoleum floor, staring at him. "What do you want?" she whispered.

"I want you," he said.

"What?"

"Seen you that night and thought, that's the one, yes sir. I never needed to look anymore."

"But my father's coming back. He's coming to get me. I had to wash my hair first—" She spoke in a dry, rapid voice, hardly raising it for him to hear.

"No, your daddy is not coming and yes, you had to wash your hair and you washed it for me. It's nice and shining and all for me. I thank you sweetheart," he said with a mock bow, but again he almost lost his balance. He had to bend and adjust his boots. Evidently his feet did not go all the way down; the boots must have been stuffed with something so that he would seem taller. Connie stared out at him and behind him at Ellie in the car, who seemed to be looking off toward Connie's right, into nothing. This Ellie said, pulling the words out of the air one after another as if he were just discovering them, "You want me to pull out the phone?"

"Shut your mouth and keep it shut," Arnold Friend said, his face red from bending over or maybe from embarrassment because Connie had seen his boots. "This ain't none of your business."

"What—what are you doing? What do you want?" Connie said. "If I call the police they'll get you, they'll arrest you—"

"Promise was not to come in unless you touch that phone, and I'll keep that promise," he said. He resumed his erect position and tried to force his shoulders back. He sounded like a hero in a movie, declaring something important. But he spoke too loudly and it was as if he were speaking to someone behind Connie. "I ain't made plans for coming in that house where I don't belong but just for you to come out to me, the way you should. Don't you know who I am?"

"You're crazy," she whispered. She backed away from the door but did not want to go into another part of the house, as if this would give him permission to come through the door. "What do you . . . you're crazy, you . . ."

"Huh? What're you saying, honey?"

Her eyes darted everywhere in the kitchen. She could not remember what it was, this room.

"This is how it is, honey: you come out and we'll drive away, have a nice ride. But if you don't come out we're gonna wait till your people come home and then they're all going to get it."

"You want that telephone pulled out?" Ellie said. He held the radio away from his ear and grimaced, as if without the radio the air was too much for him.

"I toldja shut up, Ellie," Arnold Friend said, "you're deaf, get a hearing aid, right? Fix yourself up. This little girl's no trouble and's gonna be nice to me, so Ellie keep to yourself, this ain't your date—right? Don't hem in on me, don't hog, don't crush, don't bird dog, don't trail me," he said in a rapid, meaningless voice, as if he were running through all the expressions he'd learned but was no longer sure which of them was in style, then rushing on to new ones, making them up with his eyes closed. "Don't crawl under my fence, don't squeeze in my chipmunk hole, don't sniff my glue, suck my popsicle, keep your own greasy fingers on yourself!" He shaded his eyes and peered in at Connie, who was backed against the kitchen table. "Don't mind him, honey, he's just a creep. He's a dope. Right? I'm the boy for you and like I said, you come out here nice like a lady and give me your hand, and nobody else gets hurt, I mean, your nice old bald-headed daddy and your mummy and your sister in her high heels. Because listen: why bring them in this?"

"Leave me alone," Connie whispered.

"Hey, you know that old woman down the road, the one with the chickens and stuff—you know her?"

"She's dead!"

"Dead? What? You know her?" Arnold Friend said.

"She's dead—."

"Don't you like her?"

"She's dead—she's—she isn't here any more—"

"But don't you like her, I mean, you got something against her? Some grudge or something?" Then his voice dipped as if he were conscious of a rudeness. He touched the sunglasses perched up on top of his head as if to make sure they were still there. "Now, you be a good girl."

"What are you going to do?"

"Just two things, or maybe three," Arnold Friend said. "But I promise it won't last long and you'll like me the way you get to like people you're close to. You will. It's all over for you here, so come on out. You don't want your people in any trouble, do you?"

She turned and bumped against a chair or something, hurting her leg, but she ran into the back room and picked up the telephone. Something roared in her ear, a tiny roaring, and she was so sick with fear that she could do nothing but listen to it—the telephone was clammy and very heavy and her fingers groped down to the dial but were too weak to touch it. She began to scream into the phone, into the roaring. She cried out, she cried for her mother, she felt her breath start jerking back and forth in her lungs as if it were something Arnold Friend was stabbing her with again and again with no tenderness. A noisy sorrowful wailing rose all about her and she was locked inside it the way she was locked inside this house.

After a while she could hear again. She was sitting on the floor with her wet back against the wall.

Arnold Friend was saying from the door, "That's a good girl. Put the phone back."

She kicked the phone away from her.

"No, honey. Pick it up. Put it back right."

She picked it up and put it back. The dial tone stopped.

"That's a good girl. Now, you come outside."

She was hollow with what had been fear but what was now just an emptiness. All that screaming had blasted it out of her. She sat, one leg cramped under her, and deep inside her brain was something like a pinpoint of light that kept going and would not let her relax. She thought, I'm not going to see my mother again. She thought, I'm not going to sleep in my bed again. Her bright green blouse was all wet.

Arnold Friend said, in a gentle-loud voice that was like a stage voice, "The place where you came from ain't there any more, and where you had in mind to go is cancelled out. This place you are now—inside your daddy's house—is nothing but a cardboard box I can knock down any time. You know that and always did know it. You hear me?"

She thought, I have got to think. I have got to know what to do.

"We'll go out to a nice field, out in the country here where it smells so nice and it's sunny," Arnold Friend said. "I'll have my arms tight around you so you won't need to try to get away and I'll show you what love is like, what it does. The hell with this house! It looks solid all right," he said. He ran his fingernail down the screen and the noise did not make Connie shiver, as it would have the day before. "Now, put your hand on your heart, honey. Feel that? That feels solid too but we know better. Be nice to me, be sweet like you can because what else is there for a girl like you but to be sweet and pretty and give in?—and get away before her people get back?"

She felt her pounding heart. Her hand seemed to enclose it. She thought for the first time in her life that it was nothing that was hers, that belonged to her, but just a pounding, living thing inside this body that wasn't really hers either.

"You don't want them to get hurt," Arnold Friend went on. "Now, get up, honey. Get up all by yourself."

She stood.

"Now, turn this way. That's right. Come over here to me—Ellie, put that away, didn't I tell you? You dope. You miserable creepy dope," Arnold Friend said. His words were not angry but only part of an incantation. The incantation was kindly. "Now, come out through the kitchen to me, honey, and let's see a smile, try it, you're a brave, sweet little girl and now they're eating corn and hot dogs cooked to bursting over an outdoor fire, and they don't know one thing about you and never did and honey, you're better than them because not a one of them would have done this for you."

Connie felt the linoleum under her feet; it was cool. She brushed her hair back out of her eyes. Arnold Friend let go of the post tentatively and opened his arms for her, his elbows pointing in toward each other and his wrists limp, to show that this was an embarrassed embrace and a little mocking, he didn't want to make her self-conscious.

She put out her hand against the screen. She watched herself push the door slowly open as if she were back safe somewhere in the other doorway, watching this body and this head of long hair moving out into the sunlight where Arnold Friend waited.

"My sweet little blue-eyed girl," he said in a half-sung sigh that had nothing to do with her brown eyes but was taken up just the same by the vast sunlit reaches of the land behind him and on all sides of him—so much land that Connie had never seen before and did not recognize except to know that she was going to it.

1970

STUDY QUESTIONS

1. The highly realistic style of this story is built on many mundane details.
   a. List some details that describe Connie. What sense of her do they give you?
   b. List some details that describe Connie's family and friends, home and neighborhood. What sense do these give you of her surroundings, and of the society in which she lives?
   c. List some details that describe Arnold Friend. How does he fit, or *not* fit, into the society you have described above?
2. Consider next the narrator's voice. How would you describe it? Does the narrator give you any hints as to how she feels about Connie? about Connie's family and friends? Can you cite instances in which you think the narrator shows sympathy for the girl? Can you cite any instances in which you think she judges her? In each case, why do you think so?
3. Do the narrator's style and the details of the story as she tells them lead you to feel sympathy for Connie? to judge her? How do you find yourself responding to the characters as the story progresses?
4. Consider the ending of the story. When you first read the story, what was your reaction to the ending?
5. Look again at the story, and at what you have written about it so far. In light of this, to what extent do you think the ending seems inevitable? To what extent is it a surprise or a shock? Has Oates moved from the everyday into the realm of horror, or is she, rather, revealing a horror that can be part of an everyday world?
6. Why do you think Oates ends the story where she does? Do you think the story would be stronger or weaker if Oates continued the tale and told the rest of what happened between Connie and Arnold Friend? Discuss your reasoning.

6

FIRST-PERSON NARRATORS

The **role of the narrator** influences the type of relationship we have not only with him or her but also with the story. **Omniscient narrators** stand somewhat apart from their stories. Having no role in the action themselves, they can interpret its events and characters impartially. Even when an omniscient narrator shows us most of the story through one central character's eyes, he or she can still give us glimpses into minds and actions that the character cannot see, and can still interpret the events from his or her own point of view, even when that point of view conflicts with that of the central character.

First-person narrators, on the other hand, are participants in their own stories. They are telling us of something that happened to them, and are telling their tale from their own point of view. They cannot see into the minds of the other characters; indeed, they may hardly understand their own actions. In contrast to the total knowledge of the omniscient narrator, the first-person narrator's powers of interpretation may be slight indeed.

As the narrator's knowledge shrinks, the reader's role expands. If we cannot trust the narrator as an omniscient, final authority, then our own wisdom and judgment must come into play. We must weigh the narrator's perceptions against our own and so create our own understanding of the actions and characters within the story.

Often, therefore, first-person narratives are rich in **irony**, with the narrators describing what they think they see and the readers interpreting the descriptions to discover what "really" happened. In these stories the relationship between readers and narrators is completely reversed. Now we are the wise ones, the ones with the fullest perception of what's going on. If we could only speak to these narrators, as they seem to be speaking to us, how much we could tell them!

In other stories, however, first-person narrators retain the full authority of the storyteller. Indeed, if the tales they tell are set far enough in their pasts, the narrators may view themselves as nearly omniscient. They know what they were thinking and feeling when the events took place, so they can take us into their major character's mind; they know how events turned out, so they feel that they can interpret the patterns within them. Moreover, they may feel that they have grown considerably wiser since the time of the actions they are relating and can therefore combine past feelings and present understanding to interpret events and emotions as no one else could.

In either case, and in less extreme cases as well, we often feel closer to first-person narrators than we feel either to omniscient narrators or to the characters

75

they describe. The limitations of human knowledge and insight within which the first-person narrators work, the blend of attempted objectivity and personal involvement their voices convey, and their apparent openness in telling their own stories appeal to our sympathy and our sense of fellowship. In telling us, as they often do, of their dreams and desires, first-person narrators speak eloquently of human aspirations; in confessing (consciously or unconsciously) their shortcomings, they speak no less eloquently of human limitations.

The narrators of "The Loudest Voice," "My Man Bovanne," and "Not for Sale" are storytellers in the grand tradition. They catch our attention from the opening sentence, and share with us both facts and feelings as they move from incident to incident toward a well-crafted climax. Their voices, however, are very different. Paley's narrator looks back on her childhood, and in doing so gives us the perspectives of both children and adults. While the theme of the story—the clash between Jewish and Christian cultures—is a serious one, Paley's narrator finds humor in the ambivalent attitudes of her parents and their peers with regard to their Jewish children being in a school Christmas play. She also finds humor in her own spunky self-assertion, which manifests itself in her loud voice. Bambara's narrator seems to be carrying on a conversation with people she already knows. Her tone and opinions are direct, and mix humor with insight and common sense; her pace is relatively rapid, as befits an active woman with a strong sense of her own priorities. In contrast, Cofer's narrator speaks in a clean, unadorned, open style. Her tone is reminiscent but direct.

"The Yellow Wall-Paper" represents a second tradition in first-person narrative: the creation of a tale in the shape of a journal or diary. Unlike the first two stories, which claim clear descent from the oral tradition of tale-telling, this story comes from a purely written tradition. You must have journals—and hence writing—before you can create a story that pretends to be a group of entries from somebody's journal.

Stories written in this "diarylike" tradition share several interesting features. First, they allow their narrators to ponder and reveal things the narrators would shrink from saying aloud. As the narrator of "The Yellow Wall-Paper" says, "I would not say it to a living soul, of course, but this is dead paper and a great relief to my mind." We, however, do read this "dead paper"; and we thus gain a closeness to the narrator that his or her closest friends might not have.

Second, the diarylike tale assumes that each event within it is chronicled on the day it occurs. It thus makes possible an immediacy that few other types of writing allow.

Third, there is little room, however, for hindsight in this sort of writing, little chance for the narrator to fit events into a pattern. We, as readers, must provide the pattern ourselves, just as we must come to our own understanding of the narrator by observing how her feelings and perceptions change during the course of the narrative. Caught up in the flow of events, the narrator may or may not be able to interpret them. We, standing outside those events, are challenged to do so.

Each of these stories is well worth reading for its own sake. Taken together, they remind us, once again, of the range of style and effect available to writers, and of the uniqueness of each voice that we hear speaking to us from literature.

The Yellow Wall-Paper

Charlotte Perkins Gilman (1860–1935)

An influential voice in the women's movement from 1890 to 1920, Charlotte Perkins Gilman wrote sociological and fictional works that explored the exploited status of women as second-class citizens. Her first marriage paralleled the events she described in "The Yellow Wall-Paper," in which a sensitive woman undergoes a mental breakdown because her overprotective husband insists on a "rest cure" for her that prohibits any sort of intellectual or artistic activity. Gilman's most famous work of nonfiction is *Women and Economics* (1898), the thesis of which is that marriage is an inherently debasing institution for women who work inside the home and get their status from their husbands' achievements. Her answer to this problem was to socialize the housekeeping chores, so that women who chose to do housework would be paid for it, whereas women who wished to pursue other vocations would be free to do so.

It is very seldom that mere ordinary people like John and myself secure ancestral halls for the summer.

A colonial mansion, a hereditary estate, I would say a haunted house, and reach the height of romantic felicity—but that would be asking too much of fate!

Still I will proudly declare that there is something queer about it.

Else, why should it be let so cheaply? And why have stood so long untenanted?

John laughs at me, of course, but one expects that in marriage.

John is practical in the extreme. He has no patience with faith, an intense horror of superstition, and he scoffs openly at any talk of things not to be felt and seen and put down in figures.

John is a physician, and *perhaps*—(I would not say it to a living soul, of course, but this is dead paper and a great relief to my mind)—*perhaps* that is one reason I do not get well faster.

You see he does not believe I am sick!

And what can one do?

If a physician of high standing, and one's own husband, assures friends and relatives that there is really nothing the matter with one but temporary nervous depression—a slight hysterical tendency—what is one to do?

My brother is also a physician, and also of high standing, and he says the same thing.

So I take phosphates or phosphites—whichever it is, and tonics, and journeys, and air, and exercise, and am absolutely forbidden to "work" until I am well again.

Personally, I disagree with their ideas.

Personally, I believe that congenial work, with excitement and change, would do me good.

But what is one to do?

I did write for a while in spite of them; but it *does* exhaust me a good deal—having to be so sly about it, or else meet with heavy opposition.

I sometimes fancy that in my condition if I had less opposition and more society and stimulus—but John says the very worst thing I can do is to think about my condition, and I confess it always makes me feel bad.

So I will let it alone and talk about the house.

The most beautiful place! It is quite alone, standing well back from the road, quite three miles from the village. It makes me think of English places that you read about, for there are hedges and walls and gates that lock, and lots of separate little houses for the gardeners and people.

There is a *delicious* garden! I never saw such a garden—large and shady, full of box-bordered paths, and lined with long grape-covered arbors with seats under them.

There were greenhouses, too, but they are all broken now.

There was some legal trouble, I believe, something about the heirs and co-heirs; anyhow, the place has been empty for years.

That spoils my ghostliness, I am afraid, but I don't care—there is something strange about the house—I can feel it.

I even said so to John one moonlight evening, but he said what I felt was a *draught,* and shut the window.

I get unreasonably angry with John sometimes. I'm sure I never used to be so sensitive. I think it is due to this nervous condition.

But John says if I feel so, I shall neglect proper self-control; so I take pains to control myself—before him, at least, and that makes me very tired.

I don't like our room a bit. I wanted one downstairs that opened on the piazza and had roses all over the window, and such pretty old-fashioned chintz hangings! but John would not hear of it.

He said there was only one window and not room for two beds, and no near room for him if he took another.

He is very careful and loving, and hardly lets me stir without special direction.

I have a schedule prescription for each hour in the day; he takes all care from me, and so I feel basely ungrateful not to value it more.

He said we came here solely on my account, that I was to have perfect rest and all the air I could get. "Your exercise depends on your strength, my dear," said he, "and your food somewhat on your appetite; but air you can absorb all the time." So we took the nursery at the top of the house.

It is a big, airy room, the whole floor nearly, with windows that look all ways, and air and sunshine galore. It was nursery first and then playroom and gymnasium, I should judge; for the windows are barred for little children, and there are rings and things in the walls.

The paint and paper look as if a boys' school had used it. It is stripped off— the paper—in great patches all around the head of my bed, about as far as I can reach, and in a great place on the other side of the room low down. I never saw a worse paper in my life.

One of those sprawling flamboyant patterns committing every artistic sin.

It is dull enough to confuse the eye in following, pronounced enough to constantly irritate and provoke study, and when you follow the lame uncertain curves for a little distance they suddenly commit suicide—plunge off at outrageous angles, destroy themselves in unheard of contradictions.

The color is repellent, almost revolting; a smouldering unclean yellow, strangely faded by the slow-turning sunlight.

It is a dull yet lurid orange in some places, a sickly sulphur tint in others.

No wonder the children hated it! I should hate it myself if I had to live in this room long.

There comes John, and I must put this away,—he hates to have me write a word.

We have been here two weeks, and I haven't felt like writing before, since that first day.

I am sitting by the window now, up in this atrocious nursery, and there is nothing to hinder my writing as much as I please, save lack of strength.

John is away all day, and even some nights when his cases are serious.

I am glad my case is not serious!

But these nervous troubles are dreadfully depressing.

John does not know how much I really suffer. He knows there is no *reason* to suffer, and that satisfies him.

Of course it is only nervousness. It does weigh on me so not to do my duty in any way!

I meant to be such a help to John, such a real rest and comfort, and here I am a comparative burden already!

Nobody would believe what an effort it is to do what little I am able,—to dress and entertain, and order things.

It is fortunate Mary is so good with the baby. Such a dear baby!

And yet I *cannot* be with him, it makes me so nervous.

I suppose John never was nervous in his life. He laughs at me so about this wall-paper!

At first he meant to repaper the room, but afterwards he said that I was letting it get the better of me, and that nothing was worse for a nervous patient than to give way to such fancies.

He said that after the wall-paper was changed it would be the heavy bedstead, and then the barred windows, and then that gate at the head of the stairs, and so on.

"You know the place is doing you good," he said, "and really, dear, I don't care to renovate the house just for a three months' rental."

"Then do let us go downstairs," I said, "there are such pretty rooms there."

Then he took me in his arms and called me a blessed little goose, and said he would go down to the cellar, if I wished, and have it whitewashed into the bargain.

But he is right enough about the beds and windows and things.

It is an airy and comfortable room as any one need wish, and, of course, I would not be so silly as to make him uncomfortable just for a whim.

I'm really getting quite fond of the big room, all but that horrid paper.

Out of one window I can see the garden, those mysterious deep-shaded arbors, the riotous old-fashioned flowers, and bushes and gnarly trees.

Out of another I get a lovely view of the bay and a little private wharf belonging to the estate. There is a beautiful shaded lane that runs down there from the house. I always fancy I see people walking in these numerous paths and arbors, but John has cautioned me not to give way to fancy in the least. He says that with my imaginative power and habit of story-making, a nervous weakness like mine is sure to lead to all manner of excited fancies, and that I ought to use my will and good sense to check the tendency. So I try.

I think sometimes that if I were only well enough to write a little it would relieve the press of ideas and rest me.

But I find I get pretty tired when I try.

It is so discouraging not to have any advice and companionship about my work. When I get really well, John says we will ask Cousin Henry and Julia down for a long visit; but he says he would as soon put fireworks in my pillow-case as to let me have those stimulating people about now.

I wish I could get well faster.

But I must not think about that. This paper looks to me as if it *knew* what a vicious influence it had!

There is a recurrent spot where the pattern lolls like a broken neck and two bulbous eyes stare at you upside down.

I get positively angry with the impertinence of it and the everlastingness. Up and down and sideways they crawl, and those absurd, unblinking eyes are everywhere. There is one place where two breadths didn't match, and the eyes go all up and down the line, one a little higher than the other.

I never saw so much expression in an inanimate thing before, and we all know how much expression they have! I used to lie awake as a child and get more entertainment and terror out of blank walls and plain furniture than most children could find in a toy-store.

I remember what a kindly wink the knobs of our big, old bureau used to have, and there was one chair that always seemed like a strong friend.

I used to feel that if any of the other things looked too fierce I could always hop into that chair and be safe.

The furniture in this room is no worse than inharmonious, however, for we had to bring it all from downstairs. I suppose when this was used as a playroom they had to take the nursery things out, and no wonder! I never saw such ravages as the children have made here.

The wall-paper, as I said before, is torn off in spots, and it sticketh closer than a brother—they must have had perseverance as well as hatred.

Then the floor is scratched and gouged and splintered, the plaster itself is dug out here and there, and this great heavy bed which is all we found in the room, looks as if it had been through the wars.

But I don't mind it a bit—only the paper.

There comes John's sister. Such a dear girl as she is, and so careful of me! I must not let her find me writing.

She is a perfect and enthusiastic housekeeper, and hopes for no better profession. I verily believe she thinks it is the writing which made me sick!

But I can write when she is out, and see her a long way off from these windows.

There is one that commands the road, a lovely shaded winding road, and one that just looks off over the country. A lovely country, too, full of great elms and velvet meadows.

This wall-paper has a kind of sub-pattern in a different shade, a particularly irritating one, for you can only see it in certain lights, and not clearly then.

But in the places where it isn't faded and where the sun is just so—I can see a strange, provoking, formless sort of figure, that seems to skulk about behind that silly and conspicuous front design.

There's sister on the stairs!

Well, the Fourth of July is over! The people are all gone and I am tired out. John thought it might do me good to see a little company, so we just had mother and Nellie and the children down for a week.

Of course I didn't do a thing. Jennie sees to everything now.

But it tired me all the same.

John says if I don't pick up faster he shall send me to Weir Mitchell in the fall.

But I don't want to go there at all. I had a friend who was in his hands once, and she says he is just like John and my brother, only more so!

Besides, it is such an undertaking to go so far.

I don't feel as if it was worth while to turn my hand over for anything, and I'm getting dreadfully fretful and querulous.

I cry at nothing, and cry most of the time.

Of course I don't when John is here, or anybody else, but when I am alone.

And I am alone a good deal just now. John is kept in town very often by serious cases, and Jennie is good and lets me alone when I want her to.

So I walk a little in the garden or down that lovely lane, sit on the porch under the roses, and lie down up here a good deal.

I'm getting really fond of the room in spite of the wall-paper. Perhaps *because* of the wall-paper.

It dwells in my mind so!

I lie here on this great immovable bed—it is nailed down, I believe—and follow that pattern about by the hour. It is as good as gymnastics, I assure you. I start, we'll say, at the bottom, down in the corner over there where it has not been touched, and I determine for the thousandth time that I *will* follow that pointless pattern to some sort of a conclusion.

I know a little of the principle of design, and I know this thing was not arranged on any laws of radiation, or alternation, or repetition, or symmetry, or anything else that I ever heard of.

It is repeated, of course, by the breadths, but not otherwise.

Looked at in one way each breadth stands alone, the bloated curves and flourishes—a kind of "debased Romanesque" with *delirium tremens*—go waddling up and down in isolated columns of fatuity.

But, on the other hand, they connect diagonally, and the sprawling outlines run off in great slanting waves of optic horror, like a lot of wallowing seaweeds in full chase.

The whole thing goes horizontally, too, at least it seems so, and I exhaust myself in trying to distinguish the order of its going in that direction.

They have used a horizontal breadth for a frieze, and that adds wonderfully to the confusion.

There is one end of the room where it is almost intact, and there, when the crosslights fade and the low sun shines directly upon it, I can almost fancy radiation after all,—the interminable grotesques seem to form around a common centre and rush off in headlong plunges of equal distraction.

It makes me tired to follow it. I will take a nap I guess.

I don't know why I should write this.

I don't want to.

I don't feel able.

And I know John would think it absurd. But I *must* say what I feel and think in some way—it is such a relief!

But the effort is getting to be greater than the relief.

Half the time now I am awfully lazy, and lie down ever so much.

John says I mustn't lose my strength, and has me take cod liver oil and lots of tonics and things, to say nothing of ale and wine and rare meat.

Dear John! He loves me very dearly, and hates to have me sick. I tried to have a real earnest reasonable talk with him the other day, and tell him how I wish he would let me go and make a visit to Cousin Henry and Julia.

But he said I wasn't able to go, nor able to stand it after I got there; and I did not make out a very good case for myself, for I was crying before I had finished.

It is getting to be a great effort for me to think straight. Just this nervous weakness I suppose.

And dear John gathered me up in his arms, and just carried me upstairs and laid me on the bed, and sat by me and read to me till it tired my head.

He said I was his darling and his comfort and all he had, and that I must take care of myself for his sake, and keep well.

He says no one but myself can help me out of it, that I must use my will and self-control and not let any silly fancies run away with me.

There's one comfort, the baby is well and happy, and does not have to occupy this nursery with the horrid wall-paper.

If we had not used it, that blessed child would have! What a fortunate escape! Why, I wouldn't have a child of mine, an impressionable little thing, live in such a room for worlds.

I never thought of it before, but it is lucky that John kept me here after all, I can stand it so much easier than a baby, you see.

Of course I never mention it to them any more—I am too wise,—but I keep watch of it all the same.

There are things in that paper that nobody knows but me, or ever will.

Behind that outside pattern the dim shapes get clearer every day.

It is always the same shape, only very numerous.

And it is like a woman stooping down and creeping about behind that pattern. I don't like it a bit. I wonder—I begin to think—I wish John would take me away from here!

It is so hard to talk with John about my case, because he is so wise, and because he loves me so.

But I tried it last night.

It was moonlight. The moon shines in all around just as the sun does.

I hate to see it sometimes, it creeps so slowly, and always comes in by one window or another.

John was asleep and I hated to waken him, so I kept still and watched the moonlight on that undulating wall-paper till I felt creepy.

The faint figure behind seemed to shake the pattern, just as if she wanted to get out.

I got up softly and went to feel and see if the paper *did* move, and when I came back John was awake.

"What is it, little girl?" he said. "Don't go walking about like that—you'll get cold."

I thought it was a good time to talk, so I told him that I really was not gaining here, and that I wished he would take me away.

"Why darling!" said he, "our lease will be up in three weeks, and I can't see how to leave before.

"The repairs are not done at home, and I cannot possibly leave town just now. Of course if you were in any danger, I could and would, but you really are better, dear, whether you can see it or not. I am a doctor, dear, and I know. You are gaining flesh and color, your appetite is better, I feel really much easier about you."

"I don't weigh a bit more," said I, "nor as much; and my appetite may be better in the evening when you are here, but it is worse in the morning when you are away!"

"Bless her little heart!" said he with a big hug, "she shall be as sick as she pleases! But now let's improve the shining hours by going to sleep, and talk about it in the morning!"

"And you won't go away?" I asked gloomily.

"Why, how can I, dear? It is only three weeks more and then we will take a nice little trip of a few days while Jennie is getting the house ready. Really dear you are better!"

"Better in body perhaps—" I began, and stopped short, for he sat up straight and looked at me with such a stern, reproachful look that I could not say another word.

"My darling," said he, "I beg of you, for my sake and for our child's sake, as well as for your own, that you will never for one instant let that idea enter your mind! There is nothing so dangerous, so fascinating, to a temperament like yours. It is a false and foolish fancy. Can you not trust me as a physician when I tell you so?"

So of course I said no more on that score, and we went to sleep before long. He thought I was asleep first, but I wasn't, and lay there for hours trying to decide whether that front pattern and the back pattern really did move together or separately.

On a pattern like this, by daylight, there is a lack of sequence, a defiance of law, that is a constant irritant to a normal mind.

The color is hideous enough, and unreliable enough, and infuriating enough, but the pattern is torturing.

You think you have mastered it, but just as you get well underway in following, it turns a back-somersault and there you are. It slaps you in the face, knocks you down, and tramples upon you. It is like a bad dream.

The outside pattern is a florid arabesque, reminding one of a fungus. If you can imagine a toadstool in joints, an interminable string of toadstools, budding and sprouting in endless convolutions—why, that is something like it.

That is, sometimes!

There is one marked peculiarity about this paper, a thing nobody seems to notice but myself, and that is that it changes as the light changes.

When the sun shoots in through the east window—I always watch for that first long, straight ray—it changes so quickly that I never can quite believe it.

That is why I watch it always.

By moonlight—the moon shines in all night when there is a moon—I wouldn't know it was the same paper.

At night in any kind of light, in twilight, candle light, lamplight, and worst of all by moonlight, it becomes bars! The outside pattern I mean, and the woman behind it is as plain as can be.

I didn't realize for a long time what the thing was that showed behind, that dim sub-pattern, but now I am quite sure it is a woman.

By daylight she is subdued, quiet. I fancy it is the pattern that keeps her so still. It is so puzzling. It keeps me quiet by the hour.

I lie down ever so much now. John says it is good for me, and to sleep all I can.

Indeed he started the habit by making me lie down for an hour after each meal.

It is a very bad habit I am convinced, for you see I don't sleep.

And that cultivates deceit, for I don't tell them I'm awake—O no!

The fact is I am getting a little afraid of John.

He seems very queer sometimes, and even Jennie has an inexplicable look.

It strikes me occasionally, just as a scientific hypothesis,—that perhaps it is the paper!

I have watched John when he did not know I was looking, and come into the room suddenly on the most innocent excuses, and I've caught him several times *looking at the paper!* And Jennie too. I caught Jennie with her hand on it once.

She didn't know I was in the room, and when I asked her in a quiet, a very quiet voice, with the most restrained manner possible, what she was doing with the paper—she turned around as if she had been caught stealing, and looked quite angry—asked me why I should frighten her so!

Then she said that the paper stained everything it touched, that she had found yellow smooches on all my clothes and John's, and she wished we would be more careful!

Did not that sound innocent? But I know she was studying that pattern, and I am determined that nobody shall find it out but myself!

Life is very much more exciting now than it used to be. You see I have something more to expect, to look forward to, to watch. I really do eat better, and am more quiet than I was.

John is so pleased to see me improve! He laughed a little the other day, and said I seemed to be flourishing in spite of my wall-paper.

I turned it off with a laugh. I had no intention of telling him it was *because* of the wall-paper—he would make fun of me. He might even want to take me away.

I don't want to leave now until I have found it out. There is a week more, and I think that will be enough.

I'm feeling ever so much better! I don't sleep much at night, for it is so interesting to watch developments; but I sleep a good deal in the daytime.

In the daytime it is tiresome and perplexing.

There are always new shoots on the fungus, and new shades of yellow all over it. I cannot keep count of them, though I have tried conscientiously.

It is the strangest yellow, that wall-paper! It makes me think of all the yellow things I ever saw—not beautiful ones like buttercups, but old foul, bad yellow things.

But there is something else about that paper—the smell! I noticed it the moment we came into the room, but with so much air and sun it was not bad. Now we have had a week of fog and rain, and whether the windows are open or not, the smell is here.

It creeps all over the house.

I find it hovering in the dining-room, skulking in the parlor, hiding in the hall, lying in wait for me on the stairs.

It gets into my hair.

Even when I go to ride, if I turn my head suddenly and surprise it—there is that smell!

Such a peculiar odor, too! I have spent hours in trying to analyze it, to find what it smelled like.

It is not bad—at first, and very gentle, but quite the subtlest, most enduring odor I ever met.

In this damp weather it is awful, I wake up in the night and find it hanging over me.

It used to disturb me at first. I thought seriously of burning the house—to reach the smell.

But now I am used to it. The only thing I can think of that it is like is the *color* of the paper! A yellow smell.

There is a very funny mark on this wall, low down, near the mopboard. A streak that runs round the room. It goes behind every piece of furniture, except the bed, a long, straight, even *smooch,* as if it had been rubbed over and over.

I wonder how it was done and who did it, and what they did it for. Round and round and round—round and round and round—it makes me dizzy!

I really have discovered something at last.

Through watching so much at night, when it changes so, I have finally found out.

The front pattern *does* move—and no wonder! The woman behind shakes it!

Sometimes I think there are a great many women behind, and sometimes only one, and she crawls around fast, and her crawling shakes it all over.

Then in the very bright spots she keeps still, and in the very shady spots she just takes hold of the bars and shakes them hard.

And she is all the time trying to climb through. But nobody could climb through that pattern—it strangles so; I think that is why it has so many heads.

They get through, and then the pattern strangles them off and turns them upside down, and makes their eyes white!

If those heads were covered or taken off it would not be half so bad.

I think that woman gets out in the daytime!

And I'll tell you why—privately—I've seen her!

I can see her out of every one of my windows!

It is the same woman, I know, for she is always creeping, and most women do not creep by daylight.

I see her on that long road under the trees, creeping along, and when a carriage comes she hides under the blackberry vines.

I don't blame her a bit. It must be very humiliating to be caught creeping by daylight!

I always lock the door when I creep by daylight. I can't do it at night, for I know John would suspect something at once.

And John is so queer now, that I don't want to irritate him. I wish he would take another room! Besides, I don't want anybody to get that woman out at night but myself.

I often wonder if I could see her out of all the windows at once.

But, turn as fast as I can, I can only see out of one at one time.

And though I always see her, she *may* be able to creep faster than I can turn!

I have watched her sometimes away off in the open country, creeping as fast as a cloud shadow in a high wind.

If only that top pattern could be gotten off from the under one! I mean to try it, little by little.

I have found out another funny thing, but I shan't tell it this time! It does not do to trust people too much.

There are only two more days to get this paper off, and I believe John is beginning to notice. I don't like the look in his eyes.

And I heard him ask Jennie a lot of professional questions about me. She had a very good report to give.

She said I slept a good deal in the daytime.

John knows I don't sleep very well at night, for all I'm so quiet!

He asked me all sorts of questions, too, and pretended to be very loving and kind.

As if I couldn't see through him!

Still, I don't wonder he acts so, sleeping under this paper for three months.

It only interests me, but I feel sure John and Jennie are secretly affected by it.

Hurrah! This is the last day, but it is enough. John is to stay in town over night, and won't be out until this evening.

Jennie wanted to sleep with me—the sly thing! but I told her I should undoubtedly rest better for a night all alone.

That was clever, for really I wasn't alone a bit! As soon as it was moonlight and that poor thing began to crawl and shake the pattern, I got up and ran to help her.

I pulled and she shook, I shook and she pulled, and before morning we had peeled off yards of that paper.

A strip about as high as my head and half around the room.

And then when the sun came and that awful pattern began to laugh at me, I declared I would finish it to-day!

We go away to-morrow, and they are moving all my furniture down again to leave things as they were before.

Jennie looked at the wall in amazement, but I told her merrily that I did it out of pure spite at the vicious thing.

She laughed and said she wouldn't mind doing it herself, but I must not get tired.

How she betrayed herself that time!

But I am here, and no person touches this paper but me,—not *alive!*

She tried to get me out of the room—it was too patent! But I said it was so quiet and empty and clean now that I believed I would lie down again and sleep all I could; and not to wake me even for dinner—I would call when I woke.

So now she is gone, and the servants are gone, and the things are gone, and there is nothing left but that great bedstead nailed down, with the canvas mattress we found on it.

We shall sleep downstairs to-night, and take the boat home to-morrow.

I quite enjoy the room, now it is bare again.

How those children did tear about here!

This bedstead is fairly gnawed!

But I must get to work.

I have locked the door and thrown the key down into the front path.

I don't want to go out, and I don't want to have anybody come in, till John comes.

I want to astonish him.

I've got a rope up here that even Jennie did not find. If that woman does get out, and tries to get away, I can tie her!

But I forgot I could not reach far without anything to stand on!

This bed will *not* move!

I tried to lift and push it until I was lame, and then I got so angry I bit off a little piece at one corner—but it hurt my teeth.

Then I peeled off all the paper I could reach standing on the floor. It sticks horribly and the pattern just enjoys it! All those strangled heads and bulbous eyes and waddling fungus growths just shriek with derision!

I am getting angry enough to do something desperate. To jump out of the window would be admirable exercise, but the bars are too strong even to try.

Besides I wouldn't do it. Of course not. I know well enough that a step like that is improper and might be misconstrued.

I don't like to *look* out of the windows even—there are so many of those creeping women, and they creep so fast.

I wonder if they all come out of that wall-paper as I did?

But I am securely fastened now by my well-hidden rope—you don't get *me* out in the road there!

I suppose I shall have to get back behind the pattern when it comes night, and that is hard!

It is so pleasant to be out in this great room and creep around as I please!

I don't want to go outside. I won't, even if Jennie asks me to.

For outside you have to creep on the ground, and everything is green instead of yellow.

But here I can creep smoothly on the floor, and my shoulder just fits in that long smooch around the wall, so I cannot lose my way.

Why there's John at the door!

It is no use, young man, you can't open it!

How he does call and pound!

Now he's crying for an axe.

It would be a shame to break down that beautiful door!

"John dear!" said I in the gentlest voice, "the key is down by the front steps, under a plantain leaf!"

That silenced him for a few moments.

Then he said—very quietly indeed, "Open the door, my darling!"

"I can't," said I. "The key is down by the front door under a plantain leaf!"

And then I said it again, several times, very gently and slowly, and said it so often that he had to go and see, and he got it of course, and came in. He stopped short by the door.

"What is the matter?" he cried. "For God's sake, what are you doing!"

I kept on creeping just the same, but I looked at him over my shoulder.

"I've got out at last," said I, "in spite of you and Jane. And I've pulled off most of the paper, so you can't put me back!"

Now why should that man have fainted? But he did, and right across my path by the wall, so that I had to creep over him every time!

1892

STUDY QUESTIONS

1. Obviously, the yellow wallpaper is the central image in the story. One way to analyze the story, therefore, would be to trace the narrator's impressions of the wallpaper throughout the tale. How large a part does the paper play in her narration of each episode? How does her description of the paper itself change from scene to scene? How does she describe the effect the paper has

on her? How do those descriptions change? How do you respond to each change, each new description? How do you use the changing descriptions to interpret the narrator's state of mind? What feelings toward her do you have, and how do they change (or develop) as the story progresses?

2. For a brief paper, you might concentrate on the wallpaper as part of the tale's setting. Notice how the surroundings narrow for the narrator, from her description of the house and its grounds on the first day to her description of her path around the room on the final day. How has this narrowing been accomplished? What does it symbolize?

3. Another approach might be to ask why the wallpaper is in the narrator's room at all. What does her explanation of its presence tell you about her marriage—about her feelings about herself and her husband, and about his feelings about himself and her? How is this theme developed throughout the story? How does it end? (Make sure you take note of the tone of the story's final sentence!)

4. "The Yellow Wall-Paper" is certainly a tale that demands much participation from its readers. The narrator and her husband disagree about her needs and her health; and we feel ourselves called on to decide who is right. The wife also describes herself in solitude (particularly with reference to the wallpaper); and again we must decide how far to believe what she says, or how to reinterpret it. You might write a paper, therefore, discussing the narrative style of the tale, explaining where your sympathies lie at various points and describing the means by which the narrative shifts you from being a listener in the first scene (which is a fairly straightforward description) to being the only person who really understands what is going on in the final scene, the one who could answer the narrator's final question.

The Loudest Voice

Grace Paley (1922–   )

Grace Paley was born to Russian-Jewish immigrant parents who had strong socialist ideals and who encouraged their daughter's intellectual pursuits. Paley married twice and had to find time to write while being a mother and working at marginal jobs to help support her family. Her short stories frequently deal with the harsh but often surprisingly vital lives of the working class. A strong proponent of feminist and antiwar ideals, Paley embodies the idea that the personal and political worlds are inextricable for all of us but especially for the working woman who wants to keep the imaginative part of herself alive.

There is a certain place where dumb-waiters boom, doors slam, dishes crash; every window is a mother's mouth bidding the street shut up, go skate somewhere else, come home. My voice is the loudest.

There, my own mother is still as full of breathing as me and the grocer stands up to speak to her. "Mrs. Abramowitz," he says, "people should not be afraid of their children."

"Ah, Mr. Bialik," my mother replies, "if you say to her or her father 'Ssh,' they say, 'In the grave it will be quiet.'"

"From Coney Island to the cemetery," says my papa. "It's the same subway; it's the same fare."

I am right next to the pickle barrel. My pinky is making tiny whirlpools in the brine. I stop a moment to announce: "Campbell's Tomato Soup. Campbell's Vegetable Beef Soup. Campbell's S-c-otch Broth . . ."

"Be quiet," the grocer says, "the labels are coming off."

"Please, Shirley, be a little quiet," my mother begs me.

In that place the whole street groans: Be quiet! Be quiet! but steals from the happy chorus of my inside self not a tittle or a jot.

There, too, but just around the corner, is a red brick building that has been old for many years. Every morning the children stand before it in double lines which must be straight. They are not insulted. They are waiting anyway.

I am usually among them. I am, in fact, the first, since I begin with "A."

One cold morning the monitor tapped me on the shoulder. "Go to Room 409, Shirley Abramowitz," he said. I did as I was told. I went in a hurry up a down staircase to Room 409, which contained sixth-graders. I had to wait at the desk without wiggling until Mr. Hilton, their teacher, had time to speak.

After five minutes he said, "Shirley?"

"What?" I whispered.

He said, "My! My! Shirley Abramowitz! They told me you had a particularly loud, clear voice and read with lots of expression. Could that be true?"

"Oh yes," I whispered.

"In that case, don't be silly; I might very well be your teacher someday. Speak up, speak up."

"Yes," I shouted.

"More like it," he said. "Now, Shirley, can you put a ribbon in your hair or a bobby pin? It's too messy."

"Yes!" I bawled.

"Now, now, calm down." He turned to the class. "Children, not a sound. Open at page 39. Read till 52. When you finish, start again." He looked me over once more. "Now, Shirley, you know, I suppose, that Christmas is coming. We are preparing a beautiful play. Most of the parts have been given out. But I still need a child with a strong voice, lots of stamina. Do you know what stamina is? You do? Smart kid. You know, I heard you read 'The Lord is my shepherd' in Assembly yesterday. I was very impressed. Wonderful delivery. Mrs. Jordan, your teacher, speaks highly of you. Now listen to me, Shirley Abramowitz, if you want to take the part and be in the play, repeat after me, 'I swear to work harder than I ever did before.'"

I looked to heaven and said at once, "Oh, I swear." I kissed my pinky and looked at God.

"That is an actor's life, my dear," He explained: "Like a soldier's, never tardy or disobedient to his general, the director. Everything," he said, "absolutely everything will depend on you."

That afternoon, all over the building, children scraped and scrubbed the turkeys and the sheaves of corn off the schoolroom windows. Goodbye Thanksgiving. The next morning a monitor brought red paper and green paper from the office. We made new shapes and hung them on the walls and glued them to the doors.

The teachers became happier and happier. Their heads were ringing like the bells of childhood. My best friend Evie was prone to evil, but she did not get a single demerit for whispering. We learned "Holy Night" without an error. "How wonderful!" said Miss Glacé, the student teacher. "To think that some of you don't even speak the language!" We learned "Deck the Halls" and "Hark! The Herald Angels." . . . They weren't ashamed and we weren't embarrassed.

Oh, but when my mother heard about it all, she said to my father: "Misha, you don't know what's going on there. Cramer is the head of the Tickets Committee."

"Who?" asked my father. "Cramer? Oh yes, an active woman."

"Active? Active has to have a reason. Listen," she said sadly, "I'm surprised to see my neighbors making tra-la-la for Christmas."

My father couldn't think of what to say to that. Then he decided: "You're in America! Clara, you wanted to come here. In Palestine the Arabs would be eating you alive. Europe you had pogroms. Argentina is full of Indians. Here you got Christmas. . . . Some joke, ha?"

"Very funny, Misha. What is becoming of you? If we came to a new country a long time ago to run away from tyrants, and instead we fall into a creeping pogrom, that our children learn a lot of lies, so what's the joke? Ach, Misha, your idealism is going away."

"So is your sense of humor."

"That I never had, but idealism you had a lot of."

"I'm the same Misha Abramovitch, I didn't change an iota. Ask anyone."

"Only ask me," says my mama, may she rest in peace. "I got the answer."

Meanwhile the neighbors had to think of what to say too.

Marty's father said: "You know, he has a very important part, my boy."

"Mine also," said Mr. Sauerfeld.

"Not my boy!" said Mrs. Klieg. "I said to him no. The answer is no. When I say no! I mean no!"

The rabbi's wife said, "It's disgusting!" But no one listened to her. Under the narrow sky of God's great wisdom she wore a strawberry-blond wig.

Every day was noisy and full of experience. I was Right-hand Man. Mr. Hilton said: "How could I get along without you, Shirley?"

He said: "Your mother and father ought to get down on their knees every night and thank God for giving them a child like you."

He also said: "You're absolutely a pleasure to work with, my dear, dear child."

Sometimes he said: "For God's sakes, what did I do with the script? Shirley! Shirley! Find it."

Then I answered quietly: "Here it is, Mr. Hilton."

Once in a while, when he was very tired, he would cry out: "Shirley, I'm just tired of screaming at those kids. Will you tell Ira Pushkov not to come in till Lester points to that star the second time?"

Then I roared: "Ira Pushkov, what's the matter with you? Dope! Mr. Hilton told you five times already, don't come in till Lester points to that star the second time."

"Ach, Clara," my father asked, "what does she do there till six o'clock she can't even put the plates on the table?"

"Christmas," said my mother coldly.

"Ho! Ho!" my father said. "Christmas. What's the harm? After all, history teaches everyone. We learn from reading this is a holiday from pagan times also, candles, lights, even Chanukah. So we learn it's not altogether Christian. So if they think it's a private holiday, they're only ignorant, not patriotic. What belongs to history, belongs to all men. You want to go back to the Middle Ages? Is it better to shave your head with a secondhand razor? Does it hurt Shirley to learn to speak up? It does not. So maybe someday she won't live between the kitchen and the shop. She's not a fool."

I thank you, Papa, for your kindness. It is true about me to this day. I am foolish but I am not a fool.

That night my father kissed me and said with great interest in my career, "Shirley, tomorrow's your big day. Congrats."

"Save it," my mother said. Then she shut all the windows in order to prevent tonsillitis.

In the morning it snowed. On the street corner a tree had been decorated for us by a kind city administration. In order to miss its chilly shadow our neighbors walked three blocks east to buy a loaf of bread. The butcher pulled down black window shades to keep the colored lights from shining on his chickens. Oh, not me. On the way to school, with both my hands I tossed it a kiss of tolerance. Poor thing, it was a stranger in Egypt.

I walked straight into the auditorium past the staring children. "Go ahead, Shirley!" said the monitors. Four boys, big for their age, had already started work as propmen and stagehands.

Mr. Hilton was very nervous. He was not even happy. Whatever he started to say ended in a sideward look of sadness. He sat slumped in the middle of the first row and asked me to help Miss Glacé. I did this, although she thought my voice too resonant and said, "Show-off!"

Parents began to arrive long before we were ready. They wanted to make a good impression. From among the yards of drapes I peeked out at the audience. I saw my embarrassed mother.

Ira, Lester, and Meyer were pasted to their beards by Miss Glacé. She almost forgot to thread the star on its wire, but I reminded her. I coughed a few times to clear my throat. Miss Glacé looked around and saw that everyone was in costume and on line waiting to play his part. She whispered, "All right . . ." Then:

Jackie Sauerfeld, the prettiest boy in first grade, parted the curtains with his skinny elbow and in a high voice sang out:

> "Parents dear
> We are here
> To make a Christmas play in time.
> It we give
> In narrative
> And illustrate with pantomime."

He disappeared.

My voice burst immediately from the wings to the great shock of Ira, Lester, and Meyer, who were waiting for it but were surprised all the same.

"I remember, I remember, the house where I was born . . ."

Miss Glacé yanked the curtain open and there it was, the house—an old hayloft, where Celia Kornbluh lay in the straw with Cindy Lou, her favorite doll. Ira, Lester, and Meyer moved slowly from the wings toward her, sometimes pointing to a moving star and sometimes ahead to Cindy Lou.

It was a long story and it was a sad story. I carefully pronounced all the words about my lonesome childhood, while little Eddie Braunstein wandered upstage and down with his shepherd's stick, looking for sheep. I brought up lonesomeness again, and not being understood at all except by some women everybody hated. Eddie was too small for that and Marty Groff took his place, wearing his father's prayer shawl. I announced twelve friends, and half the boys in the fourth grade gathered round Marty, who stood on an orange crate while my voice harangued. Sorrowful and loud, I declaimed about love and God and Man, but because of the terrible deceit of Abie Stock we came suddenly to a famous moment. Marty, whose remembering tongue I was, waited at the foot of the cross. He stared desperately at the audience. I groaned, "My God, my God, why hast thou forsaken me?" The soldiers who were sheiks grabbed poor Marty to pin him up to die, but he wrenched free, turned again to the audience, and spread his arms aloft to show despair and the end. I murmured at the top of my voice, "The rest is silence, but as everyone in this room, in this city—in this world—now knows, I shall have life eternal."

That night Mrs. Kornbluh visited our kitchen for a glass of tea.

"How's the virgin?" asked my father with a look of concern.

"For a man with a daughter, you got a fresh mouth, Abramovitch."

"Here," said my father kindly, "have some lemon, it'll sweeten your disposition."

They debated a little in Yiddish, then fell in a puddle of Russian and Polish. What I understood next was my father, who said, "Still and all, it was certainly a beautiful affair, you have to admit, introducing us to the beliefs of a different culture."

"Well, yes," said Mrs. Kornbluh. "The only thing . . . you know Charlie Turner—that cute boy in Celia's class—a couple others? They got very small parts or no part at all. In very bad taste, it seemed to me. After all, it's their religion."

"Ach," explained my mother, "what could Mr. Hilton do? They got very small voices; after all, why should they holler? The English language they know from the beginning by heart. They're blond like angels. You think it's so important they should get in the play? Christmas . . . the whole piece of goods . . . they own it."

I listened and listened until I couldn't listen any more. Too sleepy, I climbed out of bed and kneeled. I made a little church of my hands and said, "Hear, O Israel . . ." Then I called out in Yiddish, "Please, good night, good night. Ssh." My father said, "Ssh yourself," and slammed the kitchen door.

I was happy. I fell asleep at once. I had prayed for everybody: my talking family, cousins far away, passersby, and all the lonesome Christians. I expected to be heard. My voice was certainly the loudest.

1956

STUDY QUESTIONS

1. "The Loudest Voice," a story about the cultural ambiguities of being Jewish in a predominately Christian society, incorporates a good deal of humor. How does the humor serve to further the story's theme?

2. Two opposing minority attitudes are to pursue assimilation or separatism. Which characters in "The Loudest Voice" embody these attitudes?

My Man Bovanne

Toni Cade Bambara (1939–1996)

Toni Bambara was a well-respected writer, teacher, and editor who lived primarily in her adult life in Atlanta and Philadelphia. Her short stories are collected in *Gorilla My Love* (1972) and *The Sea Birds Are Still Alive: Collected Stories* (1977). She was the editor of several anthologies of black writers and founded the Southern Collective of African American Writers.

Blind people got a hummin jones if you notice. Which is understandable completely once you been around one and notice what no eyes will force you into to see people, and you get past the first time, which seems to come out of nowhere, and it's like you in church again with fat-chest ladies and old gents gruntin a hum low in the throat to whatever the preacher be saying. Shakey Bee bottom lip all swole up with Sweet Peach and me explainin how come the sweet-potato bread was a dollar-quarter this time stead of dollar regular and he say uh hunh he understand, then he break into this *thizzin* kind of hum which is quiet, but fiercesome just the same, if you ain't ready for it. Which I wasn't. But I got used to it and the onliest time I had to say somethin bout it was when he was playin checkers on the stoop one time and he commenst to hummin quite churchy seem to me. So I says, "Look here Shakey Bee, I can't beat you and Jesus too." He stop.

So that's how come I asked My Man Bovanne to dance. He ain't my man mind you, just a nice ole gent from the block that we all know cause he fixes things and the kids like him. Or used to fore Black Power[1] got hold their minds and mess em around till they can't be civil to ole folks. So we at this benefit for my niece's cousin who's runnin for somethin with this Black party somethin or other behind her. And I press up close to dance with Bovanne who blind and I'm hummin and he hummin, chest to chest like talkin. Not jammin my breasts into the man. Wasn't bout tits. Was bout vibrations. And he dug it and asked me what color dress I had on and how my hair was fixed and how I was doin without a man, not nosy but nice-like, and who was at this affair and was the canapés dainty-stingy or healthy enough to get hold of proper. Comfy and cheery is what I'm tryin to get across. Touch talkin like the heel of the hand on the tambourine or on a drum.

But right away Joe Lee come up on us and frown for dancin so close to the man. My own son who knows what kind of warm I am about; and don't grown men call me long distance and in the middle of the night for a little Mama comfort? But he frown. Which ain't right since Bovanne can't see and defend himself. Just a nice old man who fixes toasters and busted irons and bicycles and things and changes the lock on my door when my men friends get messy. Nice man. Which is not why they invited him. Grass roots you see. Me and Sister Taylor and the woman who does heads[2] at Mamies and the man from the barber shop, we all there on account of we grass roots.[3] And I ain't never been souther than Brooklyn Battery[4] and no more country than the window box on my fire escape. And just yesterday my kids tellin me to take them countrified rags off my head and be cool. And now can't get Black enough to suit em. So everybody passin sayin My Man Bovanne. Big deal, keep steppin and don't even stop a minute to

---

[1]Black Power was a slogan of certain Civil Rights groups during the 1960s and 1970s.
[2]hairdresser
[3]"Grass roots" refers to the common people.
[4]Brooklyn Battery is a section of Brooklyn, New York.

get the man a drink or one of them cute sandwiches or tell him what's goin on. And him standin there with a smile ready case someone do speak he want to be ready. So that's how come I pull him on the dance floor and we dance squeezin past the tables and chairs and all them coats and people standin round up in each other face talkin bout this and that but got no use for this blind man who mostly fixed skates and skooters for all these folks when they was just kids. So I'm pressed up close and we touch talkin with the hum. And here come my daughter cuttin her eye at me like she do when she tell me about my "apolitical" self like I got hoof and mouf disease and there ain't no hope at all. And I don't pay her no mind and just look up in Bovanne shadow face and tell him his stomach like a drum and he laugh. Laugh real loud. And here come my youngest, Task, with a tap on my elbow like he the third grade monitor and I'm cuttin up on the line to assembly.

"I was just talkin on the drums," I explained when they hauled me into the kitchen. I figured drums was my best defense. They can get ready for drums what with all this heritage business. And Bovanne stomach just like that drum Task give me when he come back from Africa. You just touch it and it hum thizzm, thizzm. So I stuck to the drum story. "Just drummin that's all."

"Mama, what are you talkin about?"

"She had too much to drink," say Elo to Task cause she don't hardly say nuthin to me direct no more since that ugly argument about my wigs.

"Look here Mama," say Task, the gentle one. "We just tryin to pull your coat. You were makin a spectacle of yourself out there dancing like that."

"Dancin like what?"

Task run a hand over his left ear like his father for the world and his father before that.

"Like a bitch in heat," say Elo.

"Well uhh, I was goin to say like one of them sex-starved ladies gettin on in years and not too discriminating. Know what I mean?"

I don't answer cause I'll cry. Terrible thing when your own children talk to you like that. Pullin me out the party and hustlin me into some stranger's kitchen in the back of a bar just like the damn police. And ain't like I'm old old. I can still wear me some sleeveless dresses without the meat hangin off my arm. And I keep up with some thangs through my kids. Who ain't kids no more. To hear them tell it. So I don't say nuthin.

"Dancin with that tom,"[5] say Elo to Joe Lee, who leanin on the folks' freezer. "His feet can smell a cracker a mile away and go into their shuffle number post haste. And them eyes. He could be a little considerate and put on some shades. Who wants to look into them blown-out fuses that—"

"Is this what they call the generation gap?" I say.

---

[5] "Tom" is short for "Uncle Tom," the central character in Harriet Beecher Stowe's novel *Uncle Tom's Cabin*. Uncle Tom is a term of derision used against African Americans who act in a subservient manner to whites.

"Generation gap," spits Elo, like I suggested castor oil and fricassee possum in the milk-shakes or somethin. "That's a white concept for a white phenomenon. There's no generation gap among Black people. We are a col—"

"Yeh, well never mind," says Joe Lee. "The point is Mama . . . well, it's pride. You embarrass yourself and us too dancin like that."

"I wasn't shame." Then nobody say nuthin. Them standin there in they pretty clothes with drinks in they hands and gangin up on me, and me in the third-degree chair and nary a olive to my name. Felt just like the police got hold to me.

"First of all," Task say, holdin up his hand and tickin off the offenses, "the dress. Now that dress is too short, Mama, and too low-cut for a woman your age. And Tamu's going to make a speech tonight to kick off the campaign and will be introducin you and expecting you to organize the council of elders—"

"Me? Didn nobody ask me nuthin. You mean Nisi? She change her name?"

"Well, Norton was supposed to tell you about it. Nisi wants to introduce you and then encourage the older folks to form a Council of the Elders to act as an advisory—"

"And you going to be standing there with your boobs out and that wig on your head and that hem up to your ass. And people'll say, 'Ain't that the horny bitch that was grindin with the blind dude?' "

"Elo, be cool a minute," say Task, gettin to the next finger. "And then there's the drinkin. Mama, you know you can't drink cause next thing you know you be laughin loud and carryin on," and he grab another finger for the loudness. "And then there's the dancin. You been tattooed on the man for four records straight and slow draggin even on the fast numbers. How you think that look for a woman your age?"

"What's my age?"

"What?"

"I'm axin you all a simple question. You keep talkin bout what's proper for a woman my age. How old am I anyhow?" And Joe Lee slams his eyes shut and squinches up his face to figure. And Task run a hand over his ear and stare into his glass like the ice cubes goin calculate for him. And Elo just starin at the top of my head like she goin rip the wig off any minute now.

"Is your hair braided up under that thing? If so, why don't you take it off? You always did do a neat cornroll."

"Uh huh," cause I'm thinkin how she couldn't undo her hair fast enough talking bout cornroll so countrified. None of which was the subject. "How old, I say?"

"Sixtee-one or—"

"You a damn lie Joe Lee Peoples."

"And that's another thing," say Task on the fingers.

"You know what you all can kiss," I say, gettin up and brushin the wrinkles out my lap.

"Oh, Mama," Elo say, puttin a hand on my shoulder like she hasn't done since she left home and the hand landin light and not sure it supposed to be there. Which hurt me to my heart. Cause this was the child in our happiness fore Mr. Peoples die. And I carried that child strapped to my chest till she was nearly two. We was close is what I'm trying to tell you. Cause it was more me in the child than the others. And even after Task it was the girlchild I covered in the night and wept over for no reason at all less it was she was a chub-chub like me and not very pretty, but a warm child. And how did things get to this, that she can't put a sure hand on me and say Mama we love you and care about you and you entitled to enjoy yourself cause you a good woman?

"And then there's Reverend Trent," say Task, glancin from left to right like they hatchin a plot and just now lettin me in on it. "You were suppose to be talkin with him tonight, Mama, about giving us his basement for campaign headquarters and—"

"Didn nobody tell me nuthin. If grass roots mean you kept in the dark I can't use it. I really can't. And Reven Trent a fool anyway the way he tore into the widow man up there on Edgecomb cause he wouldn't take in three of them foster children and the woman not even comfy in the ground yet and the man's mind messed up and—"

"Look here," say Task. "What we need is a family conference so we can get all this stuff cleared up and laid out on the table. In the meantime I think we better get back into the other room and tend to business. And in the meantime, Mama, see if you can't get to Reverend Trent and—"

"You want me to belly rub with the Reven, that it?"

"Oh damn," Elo say and go through the swingin door.

"We'll talk about all this at dinner. How's tomorrow night, Joe Lee?" While Joe Lee being self-important I'm wonderin who's doin the cookin and how come no body ax me if I'm free and do I get a corsage and things like that. Then Joe nod that it's O.K. and he go through the swingin door and just a little hubbub come through from the other room. Then Task smile his smile, lookin just like his daddy and he leave. And it just me in this stranger's kitchen, which was a mess I wouldn't never let my kitchen look like. Poison you just to look at the pots. Then the door swing the other way and it's My Man Bovanne standin there sayin Miss Hazel but lookin at the deep fry and then at the steam table, and most surprised when I come up on him from the other direction and take him on out of there. Pass the folks pushin up towards the stage where Nisi and some other people settin and ready to talk, and folks gettin to the last of the sandwiches and the booze fore they settle down in one spot and listen serious. And I'm thinkin bout tellin Bovanne what a lovely long dress Nisi got on and the earrings and her hair piled up in a cone and the people bout to hear how we all gettin screwed and gotta form our own party[6]

---

[6]political party

and everybody there listenin and lookin. But instead I just haul the man on out of there, and Joe Lee and his wife look at me like I'm terrible, but they ain't said boo to the man yet. Cause he blind and old and don't nobody there need him since they grown up and don't need they skates fixed no more.

"Where we goin, Miss Hazel?" Him knowin all the time.

"First we gonna buy you some dark sunglasses. Then you comin with me to the supermarket so I can pick up tomorrow's dinner, which is goin to be a grand thing proper and you invited. Then we goin to my house."

"That be fine. I surely would like to rest my feet." Bein cute, but you got to let men play out they little show, blind or not. So he chat on bout how tired he is and how he appreciate me takin him in hand this way. And I'm thinkin I'll have him change the lock on my door first thing. Then I'll give the man a nice warm bath with jasmine leaves in the water and a little Epsom salt on the sponge to do his back. And then a good rubdown with rose water and olive oil. Then a cup of lemon tea with a taste in it. And a little talcum, some of that fancy stuff Nisi mother sent over last Christmas. And then a massage, a good face massage round the forehead which is the worryin part. Cause you gots to take care of the older folks. And let them know they still needed to run the mimeo machine and keep the spark plugs clean and fix the mailboxes for folks who might help us get the breakfast program goin, and the school for the little kids and the campaign and all. Cause old folks is the nation. That what Nisi was sayin and I mean to do my part.

"I imagine you are a very pretty woman, Miss Hazel."

"I surely am," I say just like the hussy my daughter always say I was.

1972

STUDY QUESTIONS

The narrator in "The Yellow Wall-Paper" is a diarist yet she speaks a careful, polished, "literary" English.

In contrast, the narrator of "My Man Bovanne" is a conversationalist. She speaks to us directly—"if you notice," "mind you"—and she speaks with the words and rhythm of her natural, conversational speech. She is not an uneducated woman: she can use phrases like "generation gap" and "apolitical"; and she is, in her "grass roots" way, one of her community's leaders. But, as her story points out, she insists on recognition for her own and others' individuality: and her voice is an important part of that individuality.

It is an important element in the story as well. Consider:

1. How do the narrator's voice and her idiom lend humor to her portrayal of the benefit evening? How does it help to put her children's concerns in perspective?

2. How does Bambara draw a portrait of this woman who "mean[s]to do [her]part" for the "little kids" and the "old folks"? What elements stand out? How are they blended into a coherent portrait?
3. How do the family conflict and the larger social issues illuminate each other? What ideas and emotions does the narrator bring to each?
4. What are your feelings about the narrator at the different stages of the story?
5. If you were to project this story into the future, would you expect things to work out well? Why or why not?

Not for Sale

Judith Ortiz Cofer (1952–   )

Judith Oritz Cofer was born in Puerto Rico to a teenage mother and a father in the U.S. Navy. The family moved often, spending some time in Puerto Rico and some on the mainland. This experience of being caught between two cultures informs all of Cofer's work, both in poetry and prose. She received a scholarship to study at Oxford and also to attend the Bread Loaf Writers' Conference, where she later taught. Her work describes the ambiguities of living and thinking in two languages and in two cultures.

El Árabe was what the Puerto Rican women called him. He sold them beautiful things from his exotic homeland in the afternoons, at that hour when the day's work is done and there is a little time before the evening duties. He did not carry anything men would buy. His merchandise, mostly linens, was impractical but exquisite. The bed covers were gorgeously woven into oriental tales that he narrated to his customers in his halting Spanish. My mother bought the Scheherazade.[1] It was expensive, but she desired it for my bed, since it was the year when I was being denied everything by my father: no dating like other sixteen-year-olds (I was a decent Puerto Rican señorita, not a wild American teenager); no driver's license (the streets of Paterson, New Jersey, were too dangerous for an inexperienced driver—he would take me where I needed to go); no end-of-the-school-year weekend trip with my junior class to Seaside Heights (even though three teachers would be chaperoning us). *No, no, no,* with a short Spanish "o." Final: no lingering vowels in my father's pronouncements.

---

[1] a character in an Arabic story who would not be executed by her captors as long as she could spin out engaging stories

She knew that I could be brought out of my surliness, my seething anger at my father's constant vigilance, by a visit from the storytelling salesman. On the days when I heard the heavy footfall on the staircase announcing his coming, I would emerge from my room, where I kept company only with my English-language books no one else in the house could read. Since I was not allowed to linger at the drugstore with my high school classmates nor to go out socially— unless my father could be persuaded to let me after interrogations and arguments I had come to dread—I had turned to reading in seclusion. Books kept me from going mad. They allowed me to imagine my circumstances as romantic: some days I was an Indian princess living in a *zenana,* a house of women, keeping myself pure, being trained for a brilliant future. Other days I was a prisoner: Papillon, preparing myself for my great flight to freedom. When El Árabe came to our door, bearing his immense stack of bed linens on his shoulder, I ran to let him in. Mother brought him a glass of cold water as he settled into a rocking chair. I sat on the linoleum floor Indian-style while he spread his merchandise in front of us. Sometimes he brought jewelry too. He carried the rings and bracelets in a little red velvet bag he pulled out of his coat pocket. The day he showed us the Scheherazade bedspread, he emptied the glittering contents of the velvet bag on my lap, then he took my hand and fitted a gold ring with an immense green stone on my finger. It was ornate and covered my finger up to the knuckle, scratching the tender skin in between fingers. Feeling nervous, I laughed and tried to take it off. But he shook his head no. He said that he wanted me to keep the ring on while he told me some of the stories woven on the bedspread. It was a magic ring, he said, that would help me understand. My mother gave me a little frown from the doorway behind El Árabe, meaning *Be polite but give it back soon.* El Árabe settled back to tell his stories. Every so often he would unfold another corner of the bedspread to illustrate a scene.

On a gold background with green threads running through it, glossy like the patina on the dome at city hall, the weavers had put the seated figure of the storytelling woman among the characters she had created. She seemed to be invisible to them. In each panel she sat slightly behind the action in the posture of wisdom, which the salesman demonstrated: mouth parted and arms extended toward her audience, like a Buddha or a sacred dancer. While Sinbad wields his sword at a pirate, Scheherazade sits calmly in between them. She can be found on the street corner, where Aladdin trades his new lamps for old. But he does not see her.

El Árabe spoke deliberately, but his Spanish was still difficult to understand. It was as if his tongue had trouble with certain of our sound combinations. But he was patient. When he saw that one of us had lost the thread of the story, he would begin again, sometimes at the beginning.

This usually drove my mother out of the room, but I understood that these tales were one continuous story to him. If broken, the pattern would be ruined. They had to be told all the way through. I looked at him closely as he spoke. He appeared to be about my father's age, but it was hard to tell, because a thick beard covered most of his face. His eyes revealed his fatigue. He was stooped from carrying his bundles from building to building, I assumed. No one seemed to know where he lived or whether he had a family. But on the day of the Scheherazade stories he told me about his son. The subject seemed to arise naturally out of the last tale. The king who beheaded his brides was captivated by the storytelling woman and spared her life. I felt uneasy with this ending, though I had read it before, not trusting the gluttonous King Shahryar to keep his word. And what would happen to Scheherazade when she ran out of stories? It was always the same with these fairy tales: the plot was fascinating, but the ending was unsatisfactory to me. "Happily ever after" was a loose knot tied on a valuable package.

El Árabe took the first payment on the bedspread from my mother who had, I knew, gotten the dollar bills out of her underwear drawer where she kept her "secret" little stash of money in the foot of a nylon stocking. She probably thought that neither my father nor I would have any reason to look there. But in that year of my seclusion, nothing was safe from my curiosity: if I could not go out and explore the world, I would learn what I could from within the four walls. Sometimes I was Anne Frank, and what little there was to discover from my keepers belonged by rights to me.

She counted out ten dollars slowly into his hand. He opened his little notebook with frayed pages. He wrote with a pencil: the full amount at the top, her name, the date, and "10.00" with a flourish. She winced a little as she followed his numbers. It would take her a long time to pay it off. She asked me if I really wanted it—three times. But she knew what it meant to me.

My mother left with the bedspread, explaining that she wanted to see how it would look on my bed. El Árabe seemed reluctant to leave. He lit a slender, aromatic cigarette he took out of a gold case with a little diamond in the middle. Then he repeated the story of Scheherazade's winning over of her husband. Though I was by now weary of the repetition, I listened politely. It was then that he said that he had a son, a handsome young man who wanted very much to come to America to take over the business. There was much money to be made. I nodded, not really understanding why he was telling me all this.

But I fell under the spell of his words as he described a heroic vision of a handsome man who rode thoroughbreds over a golden desert. Without my being aware of it, the afternoon passed quickly. It caught me entirely by surprise when I heard the key turning in the front door lock. I was really chagrined at being found out of my room by my father.

He walked in on us before I had time to rise from my childish position on the floor at El Árabe's feet.

He came in, smelling strongly of sweat and coffee from the factory where he was the watchman. I never understood why sacks of unprocessed coffee beans had to be watched, but that's all I knew about his job. He walked in, looking annoyed and suspicious. He did not like any interruption of his routines: he wanted to find my mother and me in our places when he came home. If she had a friend drop by, Mother had to make sure the visit ended before he arrived. I had stopped inviting my friends over after a while, since his silent hostility made them uncomfortable. Long ago, when I was a little girl, he had spent hours every evening playing with me and reading to me in Spanish. Now, since those activities no longer appealed to me, since I wanted to spend time with other people, he showed no interest in me, except to say no to my requests for permission to go out.

Mother tried to mediate between us by reminding me often of my father's early affection. She explained that teenage girls in Puerto Rico did not go out without chaperons as I wanted to do. They stayed home and helped their mothers and obeyed their fathers. Didn't he give me everything I needed?

I had felt furious at her absurd statements. They did not apply to me, or to the present reality of my life in Paterson, New Jersey. I would work myself into a shouting frenzy. I would scream out my protests that we were not living in some backward country where women were slaves.

"Look," I would point out of the window of our fifth-story apartment in a building at the core of the city. "Do you see palm trees, any sand or blue water? All I see is concrete. We are in the United States. I am an American citizen. I speak English better than Spanish and I am as old as you were when you got married!" The arguments would end with her in tears and the heavy blanket of angry silence falling over both of us. It was no use talking to him either. He had her to comfort him for the unfairness of twelve-hour days in a factory and for being too tired to do anything else but read *La Prensa* in the evenings. I felt like an exile in the foreign country of my parents' house.

My father walked into the living room and immediately focused his eyes on the immense ring on my finger. Without greeting the salesman, without acknowledging my mother who had just returned to the room, he kept pointing at my hand. El Árabe stood up and bowed his head to my father in a strange formal way. Then he said something very odd—something like *I greet you as a kinsman, the ring is a gift to your daughter from my son.* What followed was utter confusion. My father kept asking what? what? what? I struggled to my feet trying to remove the ring from my finger, but it seemed to be stuck. My mother waved me into the kitchen where we worked soap around the swollen finger. In silence we listened to the shouting match in the living room. Both men seemed to be talking at once.

From what I could make out, El Árabe was proposing to my father that I be sold to him—for a fair price—to be his son's bride. This was necessary, since his son could not immigrate quickly unless he married an American citizen. The old salesman was willing to bargain with my father over what I was worth in this transaction. I heard figures, a listing of merchandise, a certain number of cattle and horses his son could sell in their country for cash if that was what my father preferred.

My father seemed to be choking. He could not break through the expert haggler's multilingual stream of offers and descriptions of family wealth. My mother pulled the ring off my finger, scraping away some of the skin along with it. I tried not to cry out, but something broke in me when I heard my father's anguished scream of *Not for sale! Not for sale!* persisting until the salesman fell silent. My mother rushed the ring out to the living room while I tried to regain my self-control. But my father's hoarse voice repeating the one phrase echoed in my ears; even after there was the sound of a door being shut and the dull, heavy footsteps of a burdened man descending the stairs, I heard the pained protest.

Then my father came into the kitchen, where I was standing at the sink, washing the blood off my fingers. The ring had cut me deeply. He stood in silence and, unmoving in the doorway, looked at me as if he had not seen me in a long time or just then for the first time. Then he asked me in a soft voice if I was all right. I nodded, hiding my hand behind my back.

In the months that followed, my mother paid on her account at the door. El Árabe did not come into our apartment again. My father learned the word "yes" in English and practiced saying it occasionally, though "no" remained NO in both languages and easier to say for a nonnative speaker.

On my bed Scheherazade kept telling her stories, which I came to understand would never end—as I had once feared—since it was in my voice that she spoke to me, placing my dreams among hers, weaving them in.

1991

STUDY QUESTIONS

1. The conflicts in this story involve all four characters: the narrator, her father, her mother, and El Árabe. Discuss these conflicts. How do they shape the story? How are they resolved?
2. A small number of symbolic items play important roles in this story: the ring, the bedspread, and the figure of Scheherazade. Discuss how the narrator uses these items to enrich the story, and especially to enrich your sense of the narrator herself.

7

TALES WITHIN TALES

Sometimes a writer wants to spend extra care setting the focus or background of a story, or wants to tie several lightly related stories together. A technique often used in this case is the "**tale within a tale**." In this technique, an initial narrator sets the scene within which one or more other narrators tell their stories.

This technique of using **multiple narrators** dates back at least to the Middle Ages: probably the best-known group of tales within a tale is Chaucer's *Canterbury Tales*. In this lengthy poetic work, the outer tale (or "frame story") concerns a diverse group of people who have met on the road while making a pilgrimage to the shrine of St. Thomas Becket at Canterbury. To pass the time, each tells a story. The stories they tell vary widely in style and subject. The frame story, which describes each of the pilgrims and details their interactions with each other, provides links between the tales, and turns what otherwise might have been a fairly commonplace collection of short verse tales into a masterpiece.

The benefit of using multiple narrators in this manner is the ability to either present material from multiple points of view or reinforce a single philosophy by giving it multiple spokespersons. The two works presented in this chapter show both of these potential benefits. The first work, Joseph Conrad's "Youth: A Narrative," may be called a long story or a short novel (or "**novella**"). In this story, both narrators speak in the first person, and both share a common philosophy as men who have worked on the great nineteenth-century sailing vessels (as indeed Conrad had done). The second work, Mark Twain's short story "The Celebrated Jumping Frog of Calaveras County," presents two narrators with opposing points of view. The narrator of the inner tale represents that downside of storytelling, the unmitigated bore. The narrator of the outer tale represents the innocent victim who falls into the bore's clutches and lives to tell about it. (In the process, of course, he repeats every word the bore says—and we may be forgiven for finding those tales more amusing than the narrator pretends to find them.)

These, then, are two contrasting specimens of a venerable technique. May you enjoy them both!

Youth: A Narrative

Joseph Conrad (1857–1924)

Joseph Conrad was born in Poland, went to sea as a young man on a French merchant ship, and eventually became a sea captain and British citizen. After writing a first novel, *Almayer's Folly* (1895), he gave up the sea and became a full-time novelist. Such works as *Lord Jim* (1900) and *Heart of Darkness* (1902) showed a complexity of point of view that made him one of the most technically interesting and innovative fiction writers of the early twentieth century. His major theme was examining how European men respond under the intense pressures of sailing at sea or encountering foreign cultures—how they break down or stand up to the vastness of the ocean or the mystery and cultural differences of Africa or the Orient.

This could have occurred nowhere but in England, where men and sea interpenetrate, so to speak—the sea entering into the life of most men, and the men knowing something or everything about the sea, in the way of amusement, of travel, or of breadwinning.

We were sitting round a mahogany table that reflected the bottle, the claret glasses, and our faces as we leaned on our elbows. There was a director of companies, an accountant, a lawyer, Marlow, and myself. The director had been a *Conway* boy, the accountant had served four years at sea, the lawyer—a fine crusted Tory, High Churchman, the best of old fellows, the soul of honour—had been chief officer in the P. & O. service in the good old days when mail boats were square-rigged at least on two masts, and used to come down the China Sea before a fair monsoon with stunsails set alow and aloft. We all began life in the merchant service. Between the five of us there was the strong bond of the sea, and also the fellowship of the craft, which no amount of enthusiasm for yachting, cruising, and so on can give, since one is only the amusement of life and the other is life itself.

Marlow (at least I think that is how he spelt his name) told the story, or rather the chronicle, of a voyage:

"Yes, I have seen a little of the Eastern seas; but what I remember best is my first voyage there. You fellows know there are those voyages that seem ordered for the illustration of life, that might stand for a symbol of existence. You fight, work, sweat, nearly kill yourself, sometimes do kill yourself, trying to accomplish something—and you can't. Not from any fault of yours. You simply can do nothing, neither great nor little—not a thing in the world—not even marry an old maid, or get a wretched 600-ton cargo of coal to its port of destination.

"It was altogether a memorable affair. It was my first voyage to the East, and my first voyage as second mate; it was also my skipper's first command. You'll admit it was time. He was sixty if a day; a little man, with a broad, not very straight back, with bowed shoulders and one leg more bandy than the other, he had a queer twisted-about appearance you see so often in men who work in the fields. He had a nutcracker face—chin and nose trying to come together over a sunken mouth—and it was framed in iron-grey fluffy hair, that looked like a chin strap of cotton wool sprinkled with coal dust. And he had blue eyes in that old face of his, which were amazingly like a boy's, with that candid expression some quite common men preserve to the end of their days by a rare internal gift of simplicity of heart and rectitude of soul. What induced him to accept me was a wonder. I had come out of a crack Australian clipper, where I had been third officer, and he seemed to have a prejudice against crack clippers as aristocratic and high-toned. He said to me, 'You know, in this ship you will have to work.' I said I had to work in every ship I had ever been in. 'Ah, but this is different, and you gentlemen out of them big ships; . . . but there! I dare say you will do. Join tomorrow.'

"I joined tomorrow. It was twenty-two years ago; and I was just twenty. How time passes! It was one of the happiest days of my life. Fancy! Second mate for the first time—a really responsible officer! I wouldn't have thrown up my new billet for a fortune. The mate looked me over carefully. He was also an old chap, but of another stamp. He had a Roman nose, a snow-white, long beard, and his name was Mahon, but he insisted that it should be pronounced Mann. He was well connected; yet there was something wrong with his luck, and he had never got on.

"As to the captain, he had been for years in coasters, then in the Mediterranean, and last in the West Indian trade. He had never been round the Capes. He could just write a kind of sketchy hand, and didn't care for writing at all. Both were thorough good seamen of course, and between those two old chaps I felt like a small boy between two grandfathers.

"The ship also was old. Her name was the *Judea*. Queer name, isn't it? She belonged to a man Wilmer, Wilcox—some name like that; but he has been bankrupt and dead these twenty years or more, and his name don't matter. She had been laid up in Shadwell basin for ever so long. You may imagine her state. She was all rust, dust, grime—soot aloft, dirt on deck. To me it was like coming out of a palace into a ruined cottage. She was about 400 tons, had a primitive windlass, wooden latches to the doors, not a bit of brass about her, and a big square stern. There was on it, below her name in big letters, a lot of scrollwork, with the gilt off, and some sort of a coat of arms, with the motto 'Do or Die' underneath. I remember it took my fancy immensely. There was a touch of romance in it, something that made me love the old thing—something that appealed to my youth!

"We left London in ballast—sand ballast—to load a cargo of coal in a northern port for Bankok. Bankok! I thrilled. I had been six years at sea, but had only seen Melbourne and Sydney, very good places, charming places in their way—but Bankok!

"We worked out of the Thames under canvas, with a North Sea pilot on board. His name was Jermyn, and he dodged all day long about the galley drying his handkerchief before the stove. Apparently he never slept. He was a dismal man, with a perpetual tear sparkling at the end of his nose, who either had been in trouble, or was in trouble, or expected to be in trouble—couldn't be happy unless something went wrong. He mistrusted my youth, my common sense, and my seamanship, and made a point of showing it in a hundred little ways. I dare say he was right. It seems to me I knew very little then, and I know not much more now; but I cherish a hate for that Jermyn to this day.

"We were a week working up as far as Yarmouth Roads, and then we got in a gale—the famous October gale of twenty-two years ago. It was wind, lightning, sleet, snow, and a terrific sea. We were flying light, and you may imagine how bad it was when I tell you we had smashed bulwarks and a flooded deck. On the second night she shifted her ballast into the lee bow, and by that time we had been blown off somewhere on the Dogger Bank. There was nothing for it but go below with shovels and try to right her, and there we were in that vast hold, gloomy like a cavern, the tallow dips stuck and flickering on the beams, the gale howling above, the sea tossing about like mad on her side; there we all were, Jermyn, the captain, everyone, hardly able to keep our feet, engaged on that gravedigger's work, and trying to toss shovelfuls of wet sand up to windward. At every tumble of the ship you could see vaguely in the dim light men falling down with a great flourish of shovels. One of the ship's boys (we had two), impressed by the weirdness of the scene, wept as if his heart would break. We could hear him blubbering somewhere in the shadows.

"On the third day the gale died out, and by and by a north-country tug picked us up. We took sixteen days in all to get from London to Tyne! When we got into dock we had lost our turn for loading, and they hauled us off to a tier where we remained for a month. Mrs. Beard (the captain's name was Beard) came from Colchester to see the old man. She lived on board. The crew of runners had left, and there remained only the officers, one boy, and the steward, a mulatto who answered to the name of Abraham. Mrs. Beard was an old woman, with a face all wrinkled and ruddy like a winter apple, and the figure of a young girl. She caught sight of me once, sewing on a button, and insisted on having my shirts to repair. This was something different from the captains' wives I had known on board crack clippers. When I brought her the shirts, she said: 'And the socks? They want mending, I am sure, and John's—Captain Beard's—things are all in order now. I would be glad of something to do.' Bless the old woman. She overhauled my outfit for me, and meantime I read for the first time *Sartor Resartus* and Burnaby's *Ride to Khiva*. I didn't understand much of the first then; but I remember I preferred the soldier to the philosopher at the time; a preference which life has only confirmed. One was a man, and the other was either more— or less. However, they are both dead and Mrs. Beard is dead, and youth, strength, genius, thoughts, achievements, simple hearts—all die. . . . No matter.

"They loaded us at last. We shipped a crew. Eight able seamen and two boys. We hauled off one evening in the buoys at the dock gates, ready to go out, and with a fair prospect of beginning the voyage next day. Mrs. Beard was to start for home by a late train. When the ship was fast we went to tea. We sat rather silent through the meal—Mahon, the old couple, and I. I finished first, and slipped away for a smoke, my cabin being in a deckhouse just against the poop. It was high water, blowing fresh with a drizzle; the double dock gates were opened, and the steam colliers were going in and out in the darkness with their lights burning bright, a great plashing of propellers, rattling of winches, and a lot of hailing on the pierheads. I watched the procession of headlights gliding high and of green lights gliding low in the night, when suddenly a red gleam flashed at me, vanished, came into view again, and remained. The fore end of a steamer loomed up close. I shouted down the cabin, 'Come up, quick!' and then heard a startled voice saying afar in the dark, 'Stop her, sir.' A bell jingled. Another voice cried warning, 'We are going right into that barque, sir.' The answer to this was a gruff 'All right,' and the next thing was a heavy crash as the steamer struck a glancing blow with a bluff of her bow about our forerigging. There was a moment of confusion, yelling, and running about. Steam roared. Then somebody was heard saying, 'All clear, sir.' . . . 'Are you all right?' asked the gruff voice. I had jumped forward to see the damage, and hailed back, 'I think so.' 'Easy astern,' said the gruff voice. A bell jingled. 'What steamer is that?' screamed Mahon. By that time she was no more to us than a bulky shadow manoeuvring a little way off. They shouted at us some name—a woman's name. Miranda or Melissa—or some such thing. 'This means another month in this beastly hole,' said Mahon to me, as we peered with lamps about the splintered bulwarks and broken braces. 'But where's the captain?'

"We had not heard or seen anything of him all that time. We went aft to look. A doleful voice arose hailing somewhere in the middle of the dock, *'Judea* ahoy!' . . . How the devil did he get there? . . . 'Hallo!' we shouted. 'I am adrift in our boat without oars,' he cried. A belated water-man offered his services, and Mahon struck a bargain with him for half a crown to tow our skipper alongside; but it was Mrs. Beard that came up the ladder first. They had been floating about the dock in that mizzly cold rain for nearly an hour. I was never so surprised in my life.

"It appears that when he heard my shout 'Come up' he understood at once what was the matter, caught up his wife, ran on deck, and across, and down into our boat, which was fast to the ladder. Not bad for a sixty-year-old. Just imagine that old fellow saving heroically in his arms that old woman—the woman of his life. He set her down on a thwart, and was ready to climb back on board when the painter came adrift somehow, and away they went together. Of course in the confusion, we did not hear him shouting. He looked abashed. She said cheerfully, 'I suppose it does not matter my losing the train now?' 'No, Jenny—you go below and get warm,' he growled. Then to us: 'A sailor has no business with a wife—I say. There I was, out of the ship. Well, no harm done this time. Let's go and look at what that fool of a steamer smashed.'

"It wasn't much, but it delayed us three weeks. At the end of that time, the captain being engaged with his agents, I carried Mrs. Beard's bag to the railway station and put her all comfy into a third-class carriage. She lowered the window to say, 'You are a good young man. If you see John—Captain Beard—without his muffler at night, just remind him from me to keep his throat well wrapped up.' 'Certainly, Mrs. Beard,' I said. 'You are a good young man; I noticed how attentive you are to John—to Captain—' The train pulled out suddenly; I took my cap off to the old woman: I never saw her again. . . . Pass the bottle.

"We went to sea next day. When we made that start for Bankok we had been already three months out of London. We had expected to be a fortnight or so—at the outside.

"It was January, and the weather was beautiful—the beautiful sunny winter weather that has more charm than in the summertime, because it is unexpected, and crisp, and you know it won't, it can't last long. It's like a windfall, like a godsend, like an unexpected piece of luck.

"It lasted all down the North Sea, all down Channel; and it lasted till we were three hundred miles or so to the westward of the Lizards; then the wind went round to the sou'west and began to pipe up. In two days it blew a gale. The *Judea*, hove to, wallowed on the Atlantic like an old candle box. It blew day after day: it blew with spite, without interval, without mercy, without rest. The world was nothing but an immensity of great foaming waves rushing at us, under a sky low enough to touch with the hand and dirty like a smoked ceiling. In the stormy space surrounding us there was as much flying spray as air. Day after day and night after night there was nothing round the ship but the howl of the wind, the tumult of the sea, the noise of water pouring over her deck. There was no rest for her and no rest for us. She tossed, she pitched, she stood on her head, she sat on her tail, she rolled, she groaned, and we had to hold on while on deck and cling to our bunks when below, in a constant effort of body and worry of mind.

"One night Mahon spoke through the small window of my berth. It opened right into my very bed, and I was lying there sleepless, in my boots, feeling as though I had not slept for years, and could not if I tried. He said excitedly:

" 'You got the sounding rod in here, Marlow? I can't get the pumps to suck. By God! it's no child's play.'

"I gave him the sounding rod and lay down again, trying to think of various things—but I thought only of the pumps. When I came on deck they were still at it, and my watch relieved at the pumps. By the light of the lantern brought on deck to examine the sounding rod I caught a glimpse of their weary, serious faces. We pumped all the four hours. We pumped all night, all day, all the week—watch and watch. She was working herself loose, and leaked badly—not enough to drown us at once, but enough to kill us with the work at the pumps. And while we pumped the ship was going from us piecemeal: the bulwarks went, the stanchions were torn out, the ventilators smashed, the cabin door burst in.

There was not a dry spot in the ship. She was being gutted bit by bit. The long-boat changed, as if by magic, into matchwood where she stood in her gripes. I had lashed her myself, and was rather proud of my handiwork, which had withstood so long the malice of the sea. And we pumped. And there was no break in the weather. The sea was white like a sheet of foam, like a cauldron of boiling milk; there was not a break in the clouds, no—not the size of a man's hand—no, not for so much as ten seconds. There was for us no sky, there were for us no stars, no sun, no universe—nothing but angry clouds and an infuriated sea. We pumped watch and watch, for dear life; and it seemed to last for months, for years, for all eternity, as though we had been dead and gone to a hell for sailors. We forgot the day of the week, the name of the month, what year it was, and whether we had ever been ashore. The sails blew away, she lay broadside on under a weather cloth, the ocean poured over her, and we did not care. We turned those handles, and had the eyes of idiots. As soon as we had crawled on deck I used to take a round turn with a rope about the men, the pumps, and the main-mast, and we turned, we turned incessantly, with the water to our waists, to our necks, over our heads. It was all one. We had forgotten how it felt to be dry.

"And there was somewhere in me the thought: By Jove! this is the deuce of an adventure—something you read about; and it is my first voyage as second mate—and I am only twenty—and here I am lasting it out as well as any of these men, and keeping my chaps up to the mark. I was pleased. I would not have given up the experience for worlds. I had moments of exultation. Whenever the old dismantled craft pitched heavily with her counter high in the air, she seemed to me to throw up, like an appeal, like a defiance, like a cry to the clouds without mercy, the words written on her stern: '*Judea*, London. Do or Die.'

"O youth! The strength of it, the faith of it, the imagination of it! To me she was not an old rattletrap carting about the world a lot of coal for a freight—to me she was the endeavour, the test, the trial of life. I think of her with pleasure, with affection, with regret—as you would think of someone dead you have loved. I shall never forget her. . . . Pass the bottle.

"One night when tied to the mast, as I explained, we were pumping on, deafened with the wind, and without spirit enough in us to wish ourselves dead, a heavy sea crashed aboard and swept clean over us. As soon as I got my breath I shouted, as in duty bound, 'Keep on, boys!' when suddenly I felt something hard floating on deck strike the calf of my leg. I made a grab at it and missed. It was so dark we could not see each other's faces within a foot—you understand.

"After that thump the ship kept quiet for a while, and the thing, whatever it was, struck my leg again. This time I caught it—and it was a saucepan. At first, being stupid with fatigue and thinking of nothing but the pumps, I did not understand what I had in my hand. Suddenly it dawned upon me, and I shouted, 'Boys, the house on deck is gone. Leave this, and let's look for the cook.'

"There was a deckhouse forward, which contained the galley, the cook's berth, and the quarters of the crew. As we had expected for days to see it swept away, the hands had been ordered to sleep in the cabin—the only safe place in the ship. The steward, Abraham, however, persisted in clinging to his berth, stupidly, like a mule—from sheer fright I believe, like an animal that won't leave a stable falling in an earthquake. So we went to look for him. It was chancing death, since once out of our lashings we were as exposed as if on a raft. But we went. The house was shattered as if a shell had exploded inside. Most of it had gone overboard—stove, men's quarters, and their property, all was gone; but two posts, holding a portion of the bulkhead to which Abraham's bunk was attached, remained as if by a miracle. We groped in the ruins and came upon this, and there he was, sitting in his bunk, surrounded by foam and wreckage, jabbering cheerfully to himself. He was out of his mind; completely and forever mad, with this sudden shock coming upon the fag end of his endurance. We snatched him up, lugged him aft, and pitched him headfirst down the cabin companion. You understand there was no time to carry him down with infinite precautions and wait to see how he got on. Those below would pick him up at the bottom of the stairs all right. We were in a hurry to go back to the pumps. That business could not wait. A bad leak is an inhuman thing.

"One would think that the sole purpose of that fiendish gale had been to make a lunatic of that poor devil of a mulatto. It eased before morning, and next day the sky cleared, and as the sea went down the leak took up. When it came to bending a fresh set of sails the crew demanded to put back—and really there was nothing else to do. Boats gone, decks swept clean, cabin gutted, men without a stitch but what they stood in, stores spoiled, ship strained. We put her head for home, and—would you believe it? The wind came east right in our teeth. It blew fresh, it blew continuously. We had to beat up every inch of the way, but she did not leak so badly, the water keeping comparatively smooth. Two hours' pumping in every four is no joke—but it kept her afloat as far as Falmouth.

"The good people there live on casualties of the sea, and no doubt were glad to see us. A hungry crew of shipwrights sharpened their chisels at the sight of that carcass of a ship. And, by Jove! they had pretty pickings off us before they were done. I fancy the owner was already in a tight place. There were delays. Then it was decided to take part of the cargo out and caulk her topsides. This was done, the repairs finished, cargo reshipped; a new crew came on board, and we went out—for Bankok. At the end of a week we were back again. The crew said they weren't going to Bankok—a hundred and fifty days' passage—in a something hooker that wanted pumping eight hours out of the twenty-four; and the nautical papers inserted again that little paragraph: '*Judea.* Barque. Tyne to Bankok; coals; put back to Falmouth leaky and with crew refusing duty.'

"There were more delays—more tinkering. The owner came down for a day, and said she was as right as a little fiddle. Poor old Captain Beard looked like the ghost of a Geordie skipper—through the worry and humiliation of it. Remember he was sixty, and it was his first command. Mahon said it was a foolish business, and would end badly. I loved the ship more than ever, and wanted awfully to get to Bankok. To Bankok! Magic name, blessed name. Mesopotamia wasn't a patch on it. Remember I was twenty, and it was my first second-mate's billet, and the East was waiting for me.

"We went out and anchored in the outer roads with a fresh crew—the third. She leaked worse than ever. It was as if those confounded shipwrights had actually made a hole in her. This time we did not even go outside. The crew simply refused to man the windlass.

"They towed us back to the inner harbour, and we became a fixture, a feature, an institution of the place. People pointed us out to visitors as 'That 'ere barque that's going to Bankok—has been here six months—put back three times.' On holidays the small boys pulling about in boats would hail, '*Judea*, ahoy!' and if a head showed above the rail shouted, 'Where you bound to?—Bankok?' and jeered. We were only three on board. The poor old skipper mooned in the cabin. Mahon undertook the cooking, and unexpectedly developed all a Frenchman's genius for preparing nice little messes. I looked languidly after the rigging. We became citizens of Falmouth. Every shopkeeper knew us. At the barber's or tobacconist's they asked familiarly, 'Do you think you will ever get to Bankok?' Meantime the owner, the underwriters, and the charterers squabbled amongst themselves in London, and our pay went on. . . . Pass the bottle.

"It was horrid. Morally it was worse than pumping for life. It seemed as though we had been forgotten by the world, belonged to nobody, would get nowhere; it seemed that, as if bewitched, we would have to live forever and ever in that inner harbour, a derision and a byword to generations of longshore loafers and dishonest boatmen. I obtained three months' pay and a five days' leave, and made a rush for London. It took me a day to get there and pretty well another to come back—but three months' pay went all the same. I don't know what I did with it. I went to a music hall, I believe, lunched, dined, and supped in a swell place in Regent Street, and was back in time, with nothing but a complete set of Byron's works and a new railway rug to show for three months' work. The boatman who pulled me off to the ship said: 'Hallo! I thought you had left the old thing. *She* will never get to Bankok.' 'That's all *you* know about it,' I said scornfully—but I didn't like that prophecy at all.

"Suddenly a man, some kind of agent to somebody, appeared with full powers. He had grog blossoms all over his face, an indomitable energy, and was a jolly soul. We leaped into life again. A hulk came alongside, took our cargo, and then we went into dry dock to get our copper stripped. No wonder she leaked. The poor thing, strained beyond endurance by the gale, had, as if in disgust, spat out all the oakum of her lower seams. She was recaulked, new coppered, and made as tight as a bottle. We went back to the hulk and reshipped our cargo.

"Then, on a fine moonlight night, all the rats left the ship.

"We had been infested with them. They had destroyed our sails, consumed more stores than the crew, affably shared our beds and our dangers, and now, when the ship was made seaworthy, concluded to clear out. I called Mahon to enjoy the spectacle. Rat after rat appeared on our rail, took a last look over his shoulder, and leaped with a hollow thud into the empty hulk. We tried to count them, but soon lost the tale. Mahon said: 'Well, well! don't talk to me about the intelligence of rats. They ought to have left before, when we had that narrow squeak from foundering. There you have the proof how silly is the superstition about them. They leave a good ship for an old rotten hulk, where there is nothing to eat, too, the fools! . . . I don't believe they know what is safe or what is good for them, any more than you or I.'

"And after some more talk, we agreed that the wisdom of rats had been grossly overrated, being in fact no greater than that of men.

"The story of the ship was known, by this, all up the Channel from Land's End to the Forelands, and we could get no crew on the south coast. They sent us one all complete from Liverpool, and we left once more—for Bankok.

"We had fair breezes, smooth water right into the tropics, and the old *Judea* lumbered along in the sunshine. When she went eight knots everything cracked aloft, and we tied our caps to our heads; but mostly she strolled on at the rate of three miles an hour. What could you expect? She was tired—that old ship. Her youth was where mine is—where yours is—you fellows who listen to this yarn; and what friend would throw your years and your weariness in your face? We didn't grumble at her. To us aft, at least, it seemed as though we had been born in her, reared in her, had lived in her for ages, had never known any other ship. I would just as soon have abused the old village church at home for not being a cathedral.

"And for me there was also my youth to make me patient. There was all the East before me, and all life, and the thought that I had been tried in that ship and had come out pretty well. And I thought of men of old who, centuries ago, went that road in ships that sailed no better, to the land of palms, and spices, and yellow sands, and of brown nations ruled by kings more cruel than Nero the Roman, and more splendid than Solomon the Jew. The old bark lumbered on, heavy with her age and the burden of her cargo, while I lived the life of youth in ignorance and hope. She lumbered on through an interminable procession of days; and the fresh gilding flashed back at the setting sun, seemed to cry out over the darkening sea the words painted on her stern, '*Judea,* London. Do or Die.'

"Then we entered the Indian Ocean and steered northerly for Java Head. The winds were light. Weeks slipped by. She crawled on, do or die, and people at home began to think of posting us as overdue.

"One Saturday evening, I being off duty, the men asked me to give them an extra bucket of water or so—for washing clothes. As I did not wish to screw on the fresh-water pump so late, I went forward whistling, and with a key in my hand to unlock the forepeak scuttle, intending to serve the water out of a spare tank we kept there.

"The smell down below was as unexpected as it was frightful. One would have thought hundreds of paraffin lamps had been flaring and smoking in that hole for days. I was glad to get out. The man with me coughed and said, 'Funny smell, sir.' I answered negligently, 'It's good for the health they say,' and walked aft.

"The first thing I did was to put my head down the square of the midship ventilator. As I lifted the lid a visible breath, something like a thin fog, a puff of faint haze, rose from the opening. The ascending air was hot, and had a heavy, sooty, paraffiny smell. I gave one sniff, and put down the lid gently. It was no use choking myself. The cargo was on fire.

"Next day she began to smoke in earnest. You see it was to be expected, for though the coal was of a safe kind, that cargo had been so handled, so broken up with handling, that it looked more like smithy coal than anything else. Then it had been wetted—more than once. It rained all the time we were taking it back from the hulk, and now with this long passage it got heated, and there was another case of spontaneous combustion.

"The captain called us into the cabin. He had a chart spread on the table, and looked unhappy. He said, 'The coast of West Australia is near, but I mean to proceed to our destination. It is the hurricane month, too; but we will just keep her head for Bankok, and fight the fire. No more putting back anywhere, if we all get roasted. We will try to stifle this 'ere damned combustion by want of air.'

"We tried. We battened down everything, and still she smoked. The smoke kept coming through imperceptible crevices; it forced itself through bulkheads and covers; it oozed here and there and everywhere in slender threads, in an invisible film, in an incomprehensible manner. It made its way into the cabin, into the forecastle; it poisoned the sheltered places on the deck, it could be sniffed as high as the mainyard. It was clear that if the smoke came out the air came in. This was disheartening. This combustion refused to be stifled.

"We resolved to try water, and took the hatches off. Enormous volumes of smoke, whitish, yellowish, thick, greasy, misty, choking, ascended as high as the trucks. All hands cleared out aft. Then the poisonous cloud blew away, and we went back to work in a smoke that was no thicker now than that of an ordinary factory chimney.

"We rigged the force-pump, got the hose along, and by and by it burst. Well, it was as old as the ship—a prehistoric hose, and past repair. Then we pumped with the feeble head pump, drew water with buckets, and in this way managed in time to pour lots of Indian Ocean into the main hatch. The bright stream flashed in sunshine, fell into a layor of white crawling smoke, and vanished on the black surface of coal. Steam ascended mingling with the smoke. We poured salt water as into a barrel without a bottom. It was our fate to pump in that ship, to pump out of her, to pump into her; and after keeping water out of her to save ourselves from being drowned, we frantically poured water into her to save ourselves from being burnt.

"And she crawled on, do or die, in the serene weather. The sky was a miracle of purity, a miracle of azure. The sea was polished, was blue, was pellucid, was sparkling like a precious stone, extending on all sides, all round to the horizon— as if the whole terrestrial globe had been one jewel, one colossal sapphire, a single gem fashioned into a planet. And on the lustre of the great calm waters the *Judea* glided imperceptibly, enveloped in languid and unclean vapours, in a lazy cloud that drifted to leeward, light and slow; a pestiferous cloud defiling the splendour of sea and sky.

"All this time of course we saw no fire. The cargo smouldered at the bottom somewhere. Once Mahon, as we were working side by side, said to me with a queer smile: 'Now, if she only would spring a tidy leak—like that time when we first left the Channel—it would put a stopper on this fire. Wouldn't it?' I remarked irrelevantly, 'Do you remember the rats?'

"We fought the fire and sailed the ship too as carefully as though nothing had been the matter. The steward cooked and attended on us. Of the other twelve men, eight worked while four rested. Everyone took his turn, captain included. There was equality, and if not exactly fraternity, then a deal of good feeling. Sometimes a man, as he dashed a bucketful of water down the hatchway, would yell out, 'Hurrah for Bankok!' and the rest laughed. But generally we were taciturn and serious—and thirsty. Oh! how thirsty! And we had to be careful with the water. Strict allowance. The ship smoked, the sun blazed. . . . Pass the bottle.

"We tried everything. We even made an attempt to dig down to the fire. No good, of course. No man could remain more than a minute below. Mahon, who went first, fainted there, and the man who went to fetch him out did likewise. We lugged them out on deck. Then I leaped down to show how easily it could be done. They had learned wisdom by that time, and contented themselves by fishing for me with a chain-hook tied to a broom-handle, I believe. I did not offer to go and fetch up my shovel, which was left down below.

"Things began to look bad. We put the longboat into the water. The second boat was ready to swing out. We had also another, a 14-foot thing, on davits aft, where it was quite safe.

"Then, behold, the smoke suddenly decreased. We redoubled our efforts to flood the bottom of the ship. In two days there was no smoke at all. Everybody was on the broad grin. This was on a Friday. On Saturday no work, but sailing the ship of course, was done. The men washed their clothes and their faces for the first time in a fortnight, and had a special dinner given them. They spoke of spontaneous combustion with contempt, and implied *they* were the boys to put out combustions. Somehow we all felt as though we each had inherited a large fortune. But a beastly smell of burning hung about the ship. Captain Beard had hollow eyes and sunken cheeks. I had never noticed so much before how twisted and bowed he was. He and Mahon prowled soberly about hatches and ventilators, sniffing. It struck me suddenly poor Mahon was a very, very old chap. As to me, I was as pleased and proud as though I had helped to win a great naval battle. O! Youth!

"The night was fine. In the morning a homeward bound ship passed us hull down—the first we had seen for months; but we were nearing the land at last, Java Head being about 190 miles off, and nearly due north.

"Next day it was my watch on deck from eight to twelve. At breakfast the captain observed, 'It's wonderful how that smell hangs about the cabin.' About ten, the mate being on the poop, I stepped down on the main deck for a moment. The carpenter's bench stood abaft the mainmast: I leaned against it suck-

ing at my pipe, and the carpenter, a young chap, came to talk to me. He remarked, 'I think we have done very well, haven't we?' and then I perceived with
annoyance the fool was trying to tilt the bench. I said curtly, 'Don't, Chips,' and
immediately became aware of a queer sensation, of an absurd delusion—I
seemed somehow to be in the air. I heard all round me like a pent-up breath released—as if a thousand giants simultaneously had said Phoo!—and felt a dull
concussion which made my ribs ache suddenly. No doubt about it—I was in the
air, and my body was describing a short parabola. But short as it was, I had the
time to think several thoughts in, as far as I can remember, the following order:
'This can't be the carpenter—What is it?—Some accident—Submarine volcano?
Coals, gas!—By Jove! We are being blown up—Everybody's dead—I am falling
into the after hatch—I see fire in it.'

"The coal dust suspended in the air of the hold had glowed dull red at the
moment of the explosion. In the twinkling of an eye, in an infinitesimal fraction
of a second since the first tilt of the bench, I was sprawling full length on the
cargo. I picked myself up and scrambled out. It was quick like a rebound. The
deck was a wilderness of smashed timber, lying crosswise like trees in a wood after a hurricane; an immense curtain of soiled rags waved gently before me—it
was the mainsail blown to strips. I thought, The masts will be toppling over directly; and to get out of the way bolted on all fours towards the poop ladder. The
first person I saw was Mahon, with eyes like saucers, his mouth open, and the
long white hair standing straight on end round his head like a silver halo. He was
just about to go down when the sight of the main deck stirring, heaving up, and
changing into splinters before his eyes, petrified him on the top step. I stared at
him in unbelief, and he stared at me with a queer kind of shocked curiosity. I did
not know that I had no hair, no eyebrows, no eyelashes, that my young moustache was burnt off, that my face was black, one cheek laid open, my nose cut,
and my chin bleeding. I had lost my cap, one of my slippers, and my shirt was
torn to rags. Of all this I was not aware. I was amazed to see the ship still afloat,
the poop deck whole—and, most of all, to see anybody alive. Also the peace of
the sky and the serenity of the sea were distinctly surprising. I suppose I expected to see them convulsed with horror. . . . Pass the bottle.

"There was a voice hailing the ship from somewhere—in the air, in the
sky—I couldn't tell. Presently I saw the captain—and he was mad. He asked me
eagerly, 'Where's the cabin table?' and to hear such a question was a frightful
shock. I had just been blown up, you understand, and vibrated with that experience—I wasn't quite sure whether I was alive. Mahon began to stamp with both
feet and yelled at him, 'Good God! don't you see the deck's blown out of her?' I
found my voice, and stammered out as if conscious of some gross neglect of
duty, 'I don't know where the cabin table is.' It was like an absurd dream.

"Do you know what he wanted next? Well, he wanted to trim the yards. Very
placidly, and as if lost in thought, he insisted on having the foreyard squared. 'I
don't know if there's anybody alive,' said Mahon, almost tearfully. 'Surely,' he
said, gently, 'there will be enough left to square the foreyard.'

"The old chap, it seems, was in his own berth winding up the chronometers, when the shock sent him spinning. Immediately it occurred to him—as he said afterwards—that the ship had struck something, and he ran out into the cabin. There, he saw, the cabin table had vanished somewhere. The deck being blown up, it had fallen down into the lazarette of course. Where we had our breakfast that morning he saw only a great hole in the floor. This appeared to him so awfully mysterious, and impressed him so immensely, that what he saw and heard after he got on deck were mere trifles in comparison. And, mark, he noticed directly the wheel deserted and his barque off her course—and his only thought was to get the miserable, stripped, undecked, smouldering shell of a ship back again with her head pointing at her port of destination. Bankok! That's what he was after. I tell you this quiet, bowed, bandy-legged, almost deformed little man was immense in the singleness of his idea and in his placid ignorance of our agitation. He motioned us forward with a commanding gesture, and went to take the wheel himself.

"Yes; that was the first thing we did—trim the yards of that wreck! No one was killed, or even disabled, but everyone was more or less hurt. You should have seen them! Some were in rags, with black faces, like coal-heavers, like sweeps, and had bullet heads that seemed closely cropped, but were in fact singed to the skin. Others, of the watch below, awakened by being shot out from their collapsing bunks, shivered incessantly, and kept on groaning even as we went about our work. But they all worked. That crew of Liverpool hard cases had in them the right stuff. It's my experience they always have. It is the sea that gives it—the vastness, the loneliness surrounding their dark stolid souls. Ah! Well! we stumbled, we crept, we fell, we barked our shins on the wreckage, we hauled. The masts stood, but we did not know how much they might be charred down below. It was nearly calm, but a long swell ran from the west and made her roll. They might go at any moment. We looked at them with apprehension. One could not foresee which way they would fall.

"Then we retreated aft and looked about us. The deck was a tangle of planks on edge, of planks on end, of splinters, of ruined woodwork. The masts rose from that chaos like big trees above a matted undergrowth. The interstices of that mass of wreckage were full of something whitish, sluggish, stirring—of something that was like a greasy fog. The smoke of the invisible fire was coming up again, was trailing, like a poisonous thick mist in some valley choked with deadwood. Already lazy wisps were beginning to curl upwards amongst the mass of splinters. Here and there a piece of timber, stuck upright, resembled a post. Half of a fife rail had been shot through the foresail, and the sky made a patch of glorious blue in the ignobly soiled canvas. A portion of several boards holding together had fallen across the rail, and one end protruded overboard, like a gangway leading upon nothing, like a gangway leading over the deep sea, leading to death—as if inviting us to walk the plank at once and be done with our ridiculous troubles. And still the air, the sky—a ghost, something invisible was hailing the ship.

"Someone had the sense to look over, and there was the helmsman, who had impulsively jumped overboard, anxious to come back. He yelled and swam lustily like a merman, keeping up with the ship. We threw him a rope, and presently he stood amongst us streaming with water and very crestfallen. The captain had surrendered the wheel, and apart, elbow on rail and chin in hand, gazed at the sea wistfully. We asked ourselves, What next? I thought, Now, this is something like. This is great. I wonder what will happen. O youth!

"Suddenly Mahon sighted a steamer far astern. Captain Beard said, 'We may do something with her yet.' We hoisted two flags, which said in the international language of the sea. 'On fire. Want immediate assistance.' The steamer grew bigger rapidly, and by and by spoke with two flags on her foremast, 'I am coming to your assistance.'

"In half an hour she was abreast, to windward, within hail, and rolling slightly, with her engines stopped. We lost our composure, and yelled all together in excitement, 'We've been blown up'. A man in a white helmet, on the bridge cried, 'Yes! All right! All right!' and he nodded his head, and smiled, and made soothing motions with his hand as though at a lot of frightened children. One of the boats dropped in the water, and walked towards us upon the sea with her long oars. Four Calashes pulled a swinging stroke. This was my first sight of Malay seamen. I've known them since, but what struck me then was their unconcern; they came alongside, and even the bowman standing up and holding up to our main chains with the boathook did not deign to lift his head for a glance. I thought people who had been blown up deserved more attention.

"A little man, dry like a chip and agile like a monkey, clambered up. It was the mate of the steamer. He gave one look, and cried, 'O boys—you had better quit.'

"We were silent. He talked apart with the captain for a time—seemed to argue with him. Then they went away together to the steamer.

"When our skipper came back we learned that the steamer was the *Somerville*, Captain Nash, from West Australia to Singapore via Batavia with mails, and that the agreement was she should tow us to Anjer or Batavia, if possible, where we could extinguish the fire by scuttling, and then proceed on our voyage—to Bankok! The old man seemed excited. 'We will do it yet,' he said to Mahon, fiercely. He shook his fist at the sky. Nobody else said a word.

"At noon the steamer began to tow. She went ahead slim and high, and what was left of the *Judea* followed at the end of seventy fathom of tow-rope—followed her swiftly like a cloud of smoke with mastheads protruding above. We went aloft to furl the sails. We coughed on the yards, and were careful about the bunts. Do you see the lot of us there, putting a neat furl on the sails of that ship doomed to arrive nowhere? There was not a man who didn't think that at any moment the masts would topple over. From aloft we could not see the ship for smoke, and they worked carefully, passing the gaskets with even turns. 'Harbour furl—aloft there!' cried Mahon from below.

"You understand this? I don't think one of those chaps expected to get down in the usual way. When we did I heard them saying to each other, 'Well, I thought we would come down overboard, in a lump—sticks and all—blame me if I didn't.' 'That's what I was thinking to myself,' would answer wearily another battered and bandaged scarecrow. And, mind these were men without the drilled-in habit of obedience. To an onlooker they would be a lot of profane scallywags without a redeeming point. What made them do it—what made them obey me when I, thinking consciously how fine it was, made them drop the bunt of the foresail twice to try and do it better? What? They had no professional reputation—no examples, no praise. It wasn't a sense of duty; they all knew well enough how to shirk, and laze, and dodge—when they had a mind to it—and mostly they had. Was it the two pounds ten a month that sent them there? They didn't think their pay half good enough. No; it was something in them, something inborn and subtle and everlasting. I don't say positively that the crew of a French or German merchantman wouldn't have done it, but I doubt whether it would have been done in the same way. There was a completeness in it, something solid like a principle, and masterful like an instinct—a disclosure of something secret—of that hidden something, that gift of good or evil that makes racial difference, that shapes the fate of nations.

"It was that night at ten that, for the first time since we had been fighting it, we saw the fire. The speed of the towing had fanned the smouldering destruction. A blue gleam appeared forward, shining below the wreck of the deck. It wavered in patches, it seemed to stir and creep like the light of a glowworm. I saw it first, and told Mahon. 'Then the game's up,' he said. 'We had better stop this towing, or she will burst out suddenly fore and aft before we can clear out.' We set up a yell; rang bells to attract their attention; they towed on. At last Mahon and I had to crawl forward and cut the rope with an axe. There was no time to cast off the lashings. Red tongues could be seen licking the wilderness of splinters under our feet as we made our way back to the poop.

"Of course they very soon found out in the steamer that the rope was gone. She gave a loud blast of her whistle, her lights were seen sweeping in a wide circle, she came up ranging close alongside, and stopped. We were all in a tight group on the poop looking at her. Every man had saved a little bundle or a bag. Suddenly a conical flame with a twisted top shot up forward and threw upon the black sea a circle of light, with the two vessels side by side and heaving gently in its centre. Captain Beard had been sitting on the gratings still and mute for hours, but now he rose slowly and advanced in front of us, to the mizzen shrouds. Captain Nash hailed: 'Come along! Look sharp. I have mailbags on board. I will take you and your boats to Singapore.'

" 'Thank you! No!' said our skipper. 'We must see the last of the ship.'

" 'I can't stand by any longer,' shouted the other. 'Mails—you know.'

" 'Aye! aye! We are all right.'

" 'Very well! I'll report you in Singapore. . . . Good-bye!'

"He waved his hand. Our men dropped their bundles quietly. The steamer moved ahead, and passing out of the circle of light, vanished at once from our sight, dazzled by the fire which burned fiercely. And then I knew that I would see the East first as commander of a small boat. I thought it fine; and the fidelity to the old ship was fine. We should see the last of her. Oh, the glamour of youth! Oh, the fire of it, more dazzling than the flames of the burning ship, throwing a magic light on the wide earth, leaping audaciously to the sky, presently to be quenched by time, more cruel, more pitiless, more bitter than the sea—and like the flames on the burning ship surrounded by an impenetrable night.

"The old man warned us in his gentle and inflexible way that it was part of our duty to save for the underwriters as much as we could of the ship's gear. Accordingly we went to work aft, while she blazed forward to give us plenty of light. We lugged out a lot of rubbish. What didn't we save? An old barometer fixed with an absurd quantity of screws nearly cost me my life: a sudden rush of smoke came upon me, and I just got away in time. There were various stores, bolts of canvas, coils of rope; the poop looked like a marine bazaar, and the boats were lumbered to the gunwales. One would have thought the old man wanted to take as much as he could of his first command with him. He was very, very quiet, but off his balance evidently. Would you believe it? He wanted to take a length of old stream cable and a kedge anchor with him in the longboat. We said, 'Aye, aye, sir,' deferentially, and on the quiet let the things slip overboard. The heavy medicine chest went that way, two bags of green coffee, tins of paint—fancy, paint!—a whole lot of things. Then I was ordered with two hands into the boats to make a stowage and get them ready against the time it would be proper for us to leave the ship.

"We put everything straight, stepped the longboat's mast for our skipper, who was to take charge of her, and I was not sorry to sit down for a moment. My face felt raw, every limb ached as if broken, I was aware of all my ribs, and would have sworn to a twist in the backbone. The boats, fast astern, lay in a deep shadow, and all around I could see the circle of the sea lighted by the fire. A gigantic flame arose forward straight and clear. It flared fierce, with noises like the whirr of wings, with rumbles as of thunder. There were cracks, detonations, and from the cone of flame the sparks flew upwards, as man is born to trouble, to leaky ships, and to ships that burn.

"What bothered me was that the ship, lying broadside to the swell and to such wind as there was—a mere breath—the boats would not keep astern where they were safe, but persisted, in a pigheaded way boats have, in getting under the counter and then swinging alongside. They were knocking about dangerously and coming near the flame, while the ship rolled on them, and, of course, there was always the danger of the masts going over the side at any moment. I and my two boat keepers kept them off as best we could, with oars and boathooks; but to be constantly at it became exasperating, since there was no reason why we should not leave at once. We could not see those on board, nor could we imagine what caused the delay. The boatkeepers were swearing feebly, and I had not only my share of work but also had to keep at it two men who showed a constant inclination to lay themselves down and let things slide.

"At last I hailed, 'On deck there,' and someone looked over. 'We're ready here,' I said. The head disappeared, and very soon popped up again. 'The captain says, All right, sir, and to keep the boats well clear of the ship.'

"Half an hour passed. Suddenly there was a frightful racket, rattle, clanking of chain, hiss of water, and millions of sparks flew up into the shivering column of smoke that stood leaning slightly above the ship. The catheads had burned away, and the two red-hot anchors had gone to the bottom, tearing out after them two hundred fathom of red-hot chain. The ship trembled, the mass of flame swayed as if ready to collapse, and the fore topgallant mast fell. It darted down like an arrow of fire, shot under, and instantly leaping up within an oar's length of the boats, floated quietly, very black on the luminous sea. I hailed the deck again. After some time a man in an unexpectedly cheerful but also muffled tone, as though he had been trying to speak with his mouth shut, informed me, 'Coming directly, sir,' and vanished. For a long time I heard nothing but the whirr and roar of the fire. There were also whistling sounds. The boats jumped, tugged at the painters, ran at each other playfully, knocked their sides together, or, do what we would, swung in a bunch against the ship's side. I couldn't stand it any longer, and swarming up a rope, clambered aboard over the stern.

"It was as bright as day. Coming up like this, the sheet of fire facing me was a terrifying sight, and the heat seemed hardly bearable at first. On a settee cushion dragged out of the cabin Captain Beard, his legs drawn up and one arm under his head, slept with the light playing on him. Do you know what the rest were busy about? They were sitting on deck right aft, round an open case, eating bread and cheese and drinking bottled stout.

"On the background of flames twisting in fierce tongues above their heads they seemed at home like salamanders, and looked like a band of desperate pirates. The fire sparkled in the whites of their eyes, gleamed on patches of white skin seen through the torn shirts. Each had the marks as of a battle about him— bandaged heads, tied up arms, a strip of dirty rag round a knee—and each man had a bottle between his legs and a chunk of cheese in his hand. Mahon got up. With his handsome and disreputable head, his hooked profile, his long white beard, and with an uncorked bottle in his hand, he resembled one of those reckless sea robbers of old making merry amidst violence and disaster. 'The last meal on board,' he explained solemnly. 'We had nothing to eat all day, and it was no use leaving all this.' He flourished the bottle and indicated the sleeping skipper. 'He said he couldn't swallow anything, so I got him to lie down,' he went on; and as I stared, 'I don't know whether you are aware, young fellow, the man had no sleep to speak of for days—and there will be dam' little sleep in the boats.' 'There will be no boats by and by if you fool about much longer,' I said, indignantly. I walked up to the skipper and shook him by the shoulder. At last he opened his eyes, but did not move. 'Time to leave her, sir,' I said quietly.

"He got up painfully, looked at the flames, at the sea sparkling round the ship, and black, black as ink farther away; he looked at the stars shining dim through a thin veil of smoke in a sky black, black as Erebus.

" 'Youngest first,' he said.

"And the ordinary seaman, wiping his mouth with the back of his hand, got up, clambered over the taffrail, and vanished. Others followed. One, on the point of going over, stopped short to drain his bottle, and with a great swing of his arm flung it at the fire. 'Take this!' he cried.

"The skipper lingered disconsolately, and we left him to commune alone for a while with his first command. Then I went up again and brought him away at last. It was time. The ironwork on the poop was hot to the touch.

"Then the painter of the longboat was cut, and the three boats, tied together, drifted clear of the ship. It was just sixteen hours after the explosion when we abandoned her. Mahon had charge of the second boat, and I had the smallest—the 14-foot thing. The longboat would have taken the lot of us; but the skipper said we must save as much property as we could—for the underwriters—and so I got my first command. I had two men with me, a bag of biscuits, a few tins of meat, and a beaker of water. I was ordered to keep close to the longboat, that in case of bad weather we might be taken into her.

"And do you know what I thought? I thought I would part company as soon as I could. I wanted to have my first command all to myself. I wasn't going to sail in a squadron if there were a chance for independent cruising. I would make land by myself. I would beat the other boats. Youth! All youth! The silly, charming, beautiful youth.

"But we did not make a start at once. We must see the last of the ship. And so the boats drifted about that night, heaving and setting on the swell. The men dozed, waked, sighed, groaned. I looked at the burning ship.

"Between the darkness of earth and heaven she was burning fiercely upon a disc of purple sea shot by the blood-red play of gleams; upon a disc of water glittering and sinister. A high, clear flame, an immense and lonely flame, ascended from the ocean, and from its summit the black smoke poured continuously at the sky. She burned furiously; mournful and imposing like a funeral pile kindled in the night, surrounded by the sea, watched over by the stars. A magnificent death had come like a grace, like a gift, like a reward to that old ship at the end of her laborious days. The surrender of her weary ghost to the keeping of stars and sea was stirring like the sight of a glorious triumph. The masts fell just before daybreak, and for a moment there was a burst and turmoil of sparks that seemed to fill with flying fire the night patient and watchful, the vast night lying silent upon the sea. At daylight she was only a charred shell, floating still under a cloud of smoke and bearing a glowing mass of coal within.

"Then the oars were got out, and the boats forming in a line moved round her remains as if in procession—the longboat leading. As we pulled across her stern a slim dart of fire shot out viciously at us, and suddenly she went down, head first, in a great hiss of steam. The unconsumed stern was the last to sink; but the paint had gone, had cracked, had peeled off, and there were no letters, there was no word, no stubborn device that was like her soul, to flash at the rising sun her creed and her name.

"We made our way north. A breeze sprang up, and about noon all the boats came together for the last time. I had no mast or sail in mine, but I made a mast out of a spare oar and hoisted a boat awning for a sail, with a boathook for a yard. She was certainly overmasted, but I had the satisfaction of knowing that with the wind aft I could beat the other two. I had to wait for them. Then we all had a look at the captain's chart, and, after a sociable meal of hard bread and water, got our last instructions. These were simple: steer north, and keep together as much as possible. 'Be careful with that jury rig, Marlow,' said the captain; and Mahon, as I sailed proudly past his boat, wrinkled his curved nose and hailed, 'You will sail that ship of yours under water, if you don't look out, young fellow.' He was a malicious old man—and may the deep sea where he sleeps now rock him gently, rock him tenderly to the end of time!

"Before sunset a thick rainsquall passed over the two boats, which were far astern, and that was the last I saw of them for a time. Next day I sat steering my cockleshell—my first command—with nothing but water and sky around me. I did sight in the afternoon the upper sails of a ship far away, but said nothing, and my men did not notice her. You see I was afraid she might be homeward bound, and I had no mind to turn back from the portals of the East. I was steering for Java—another blessed name—like Bankok, you know. I steered many days.

"I need not tell you what it is to be knocking about in an open boat. I remember nights and days of calm, when we pulled, we pulled, and the boat seemed to stand still, as if bewitched within the circle of the sea horizon. I remember the heat, the deluge of rainsqualls that kept us bailing for dear life (but filled our water cask), and I remember sixteen hours on end with a mouth dry as a cinder and a steering oar over the stern to keep my first command head on to a breaking sea. I did not know how good a man I was till then. I remember the drawn faces, the dejected figures of my two men, and I remember my youth and the feeling that will never come back any more—the feeling that I could last forever, outlast the sea, the earth, and all men; the deceitful feeling that lures us on to joys, to perils, to love, to vain effort—to death; the triumphant conviction of strength, the heat of life in the handful of dust, the glow in the heart that with every year grows dim, grows cold, grows small, and expires—and expires, too soon, too soon—before life itself.

"And this is how I see the East. I have seen its secret places and have looked into its very soul; but now I see it always from a small boat, a high outline of mountains, blue and afar in the morning; like faint mist at noon; a jagged wall of purple at sunset. I have the feel of the oar in my hand, the vision of a scorching blue sea in my eyes. And I see a bay, a wide bay, smooth as glass and polished like ice, shimmering in the dark. A red light burns far off upon the gloom of the land, and the night is soft and warm. We drag at the oars with aching arms, and suddenly a puff of wind, a puff faint and tepid and laden with strange odours of blossoms, of aromatic wood, comes out of the still night—the first sigh of the East on my face. That I can never forget. It was impalpable and enslaving, like a charm, like a whispered promise of mysterious delight.

"We had been pulling this finishing spell for eleven hours. Two pulled, and he whose turn it was to rest sat at the tiller. We had made out the red light in that bay and steered for it, guessing it must mark some small coasting port. We passed two vessels, outlandish and high sterned, sleeping at anchor, and, approaching the light, now very dim, ran the boat's nose against the end of a jutting wharf. We were blind with fatigue. My men dropped the oars and fell off the thwarts as if dead. I made fast to a pile. A current rippled softly. The scented obscurity of the shore was grouped into vast masses, a density of colossal clumps of vegetation, probably—mute and fantastic shapes. And at their foot the semicircle of a beach gleamed faintly, like an illusion. There was not a light, not a stir, not a sound. The mysterious East faced me, perfumed like a flower, silent like death, dark like a grave.

"And I sat weary beyond expression, exulting like a conqueror, sleepless and entranced as if before a profound, a fateful enigma.

"A splashing of oars, a measured dip reverberating on the level of water, intensified by the silence of the shore into loud claps, made me jump up. A boat, a European boat, was coming in. I invoked the name of the dead: I hailed: *Judea* ahoy! A thin shout answered.

"It was the captain. I had beaten the flagship by three hours, and I was glad to hear the old man's voice again, tremulous and tired. 'Is it you, Marlow?' 'Mind the end of that jetty, sir,' I cried.

"He approached cautiously, and brought up with the deep sea lead line which we had saved—for the underwriters. I eased my painter and fell alongside. He sat, a broken figure at the stern, wet with dew, his hands clasped in his lap. His men were asleep already. 'I had a terrible time of it,' he murmured. 'Mahon is behind—not very far.' We conversed in whispers, in low whispers, as if afraid to wake up the land. Guns, thunder, earthquakes would not have awakened the men just then.

"Looking round as we talked, I saw away at sea a bright light travelling in the night. 'There's a steamer passing the bay,' I said. She was not passing, she was entering, and she even came close and anchored. 'I wish,' said the old man, 'you would find out whether she is English. Perhaps they could give us passage somewhere.' He seemed nervously anxious. So by dint of punching and kicking I started one of my men into a state of somnambulism, and giving him an oar, took another and pulled towards the lights of the steamer.

"There was a murmur of voices in her, metallic hollow clangs of the engine room, footsteps on the deck. Her ports shone, round like dilated eyes. Shapes moved about, and there was a shadowy man high up on the bridge. He heard my oars.

"And then, before I could open my lips, the East spoke to me, but it was in a Western voice. A torrent of words was poured into the enigmatical, the fateful silence; outlandish, angry words, mixed with words and even whole sentences of good English, less strange but even more surprising. The voice swore and cursed violently; it riddled the solemn peace of the bay by a volley of abuse. It began by calling me Pig, and from that went crescendo into unmentionable adjectives—in English. The man up there raged aloud in two languages, and with a sincerity in his fury that almost convinced me I had, in some way, sinned against the harmony of the universe. I could hardly see him, but began to think he would work himself into a fit.

"Suddenly he ceased, and I could hear him snorting and blowing like a porpoise. I said:

" 'What steamer is this, pray?'

" 'Eh? What's this? And who are you?'

" 'Castaway crew of an English barque burnt at sea. We came here tonight. I am the second mate. The captain is in the longboat, and wishes to know if you would give us a passage somewhere.'

" 'Oh, my goodness! I say. . . . This is the *Celestial* from Singapore on her return trip. I'll arrange with your captain in the morning, . . . and . . . I say . . . did you hear me just now?'

" 'I should think the whole bay heard you.'

" 'I thought you were a shoreboat. Now, look here—this infernal lazy scoundrel of a caretaker has gone to sleep again—curse him. The light is out, and I nearly ran foul of the end of this damned jetty. This is the third time he plays me this trick. Now, I ask you, can anybody stand this kind of thing? It's enough to drive a man out of his mind. I'll report him . . . I'll get the Assistant Resident to give him the sack, by . . . ! See—there's no light. It's out, isn't it? I take you to witness the light's out. There should be a light, you know. A red light on the—'

" 'There was a light,' I said, mildly.

" 'But it's out, man! What's the use of talking like this? You can see for yourself it's out—don't you? If you had to take a valuable steamer along this Godforsaken coast you would want a light, too. I'll kick him from end to end of his miserable wharf. You'll see if I don't. I will—'

" 'So I may tell my captain you'll take us?' I broke in.

" 'Yes, I'll take you. Good-night,' he said, brusquely.

"I pulled back, made fast again to the jetty, and then went to sleep at last. I had faced the silence of the East. I had heard some of its language. But when I opened my eyes again the silence was as complete as though it had never been broken. I was lying in a flood of light, and the sky had never looked so far, so high, before. I opened my eyes and lay without moving.

"And then I saw the men of the East—they were looking at me. The whole length of the jetty was full of people. I saw brown, bronze, yellow faces, the black eyes, the glitter, the colour of an Eastern crowd. And all these beings stared without a murmur, without a sigh, without a movement. They stared down at the boats, at the sleeping men who at night had come to them from the sea. Nothing moved. The fronds of palms stood still against the sky. Not a branch stirred along the shore, and the brown roofs of hidden houses peeped through the green foliage, through the big leaves that hung shining and still like leaves forged of heavy metal. This was the East of the ancient navigators, so old, so mysterious, resplendent and sombre, living and unchanged, full of danger and promise. And these were the men. I sat up suddenly. A wave of movement passed through the crowd from end to end, passed along the heads, swayed the bodies, ran along the jetty like a ripple on the water, a breath of wind on a field—and all was still again. I see it now—the wide sweep of the bay, the glittering sands, the wealth of green infinite and varied, the sea blue like the sea of a dream, the crowd of attentive faces, the blaze of vivid colour—the water reflecting it all, the curve of the shore, the jetty, the high-sterned outlandish craft floating still, and the three boats with the tired men from the West sleeping, unconscious of the land and the people and of the violence of sunshine. They slept thrown across the thwarts, curled on bottom boards, in the careless attitudes of death. The head of the old skipper, leaning back in the stern of the longboat, had fallen on his breast, and he looked as though he would never wake. Farther out old Mahon's face was upturned to the sky, with the long white beard spread out on his breast, as though he had been shot where he sat at the tiller; and a man, all in a heap in the bows of the boat, slept with both arms embracing the steamhead and with his cheek laid on the gunwale. The East looked at them without a sound.

"I have known its fascination since; I have seen the mysterious shores, the still water, the lands of brown nations, where a stealthy Nemesis lies in wait, pursues, overtakes so many of the conquering race, who are proud of their wisdom, of their knowledge, of their strength. But for me all the East is contained in that vision of my youth. It is all in that moment when I opened my young eyes on it. I came upon it from a tussle with the sea—and I was young—and I saw it looking at me. And this is all that is left of it! Only a moment; a moment of strength, of romance, of glamour—of youth! . . . A flick of sunshine upon a strange shore, the time to remember, the time for a sigh, and—good-bye!—Night—Good-bye . . . !"

He drank.

"Ah! The good old time—the good old time. Youth and the sea. Glamour and the sea! The good, strong sea, the salt, bitter sea, that could whisper to you and roar at you and knock your breath out of you!"

He drank again.

"By all that's wonderful it is the sea, I believe, the sea itself—or is it youth alone? Who can tell? But you here—you all had something out of life: money, love—whatever one gets on shore—and, tell me, wasn't that the best time, that time when we were young at sea; young and had nothing, on the sea that gives nothing, except hard knocks—and sometimes a chance to feel your strength—that only—what you all regret?"

And we all nodded at him: the man of finance, the man of accounts, the man of law, we all nodded at him over the polished table that like a still sheet of brown water reflected our faces, lined, wrinkled; our faces marked by toil, by deceptions, by success, by love; our weary eyes looking still, looking always, looking anxiously for something out of life, that while it is expected is already gone—has passed unseen, in a sigh, in a flash—together with the youth, with the strength, with the romance of illusions.

1902

STUDY QUESTIONS

1. What does the use of the frame story, with its dual narrators, add to Conrad's treatment of the theme "youth"?
2. Marlow begins his narration on what seems a somber note, declaring that

   . . . there are those voyages that seem ordered for the illustration of life, that might stand for a symbol of existence. You fight, work, sweat, nearly kill yourself, sometimes do kill yourself, trying to accomplish something—and you can't. Not from any fault of yours. You simply can do nothing. . . .

   Yet he ends it with a paean in praise of youth as the best time of life—with the same voyage still serving as example. How does he get from one tone to the other? How does he keep the two outlooks balanced, without letting them contradict each other?

The Celebrated Jumping Frog of Calaveras County

Mark Twain (1835–1910)

Samuel Langhorne Clemens changed his name to Mark Twain when he began to write his humorous stories about the American West. The pseudonym came from his days as a riverboat pilot on the Mississippi: the cry "mark twain!" (literally, "mark two" or two fathoms; each fathom—six feet—was marked on a dragline tossed out periodically from the bow when the boat was in possibly shallow water) meant that the water was deep enough—twelve feet—for a steamboat to pass safely. In such works as *Life on the Mississippi* (1883) and his masterpiece, *Adventures of Huckleberry Finn* (1884), Twain used his early experiences on the river to capture the essence of the American experience—the individual's struggle to maintain his innocence, individuality, and freedom as a frontier culture gave way to civilization. Although he started out as a humorist, Twain deepened his themes to include the immorality of slavery, war, and American imperialism in the Philippines. His later works are dark, pessimistic, even cynical about what Twain called "the damned human race."

In compliance with the request of a friend of mine, who wrote me from the East, I called on good-natured, garrulous old Simon Wheeler, and inquired after my friend's friend, Leonidas W. Smiley, as requested to do, and I hereunto append the result. I have a lurking suspicion that *Leonidas W.* Smiley is a myth; that my friend never knew such a personage; and that he only conjectured that if I asked old Wheeler about him, it would remind him of his infamous *Jim* Smiley, and he would go to work and bore me to death with some exasperating reminiscence of him as long and as tedious as it should be useless to me. If that was the design, it succeeded.

I found Simon Wheeler dozing comfortably by the barroom stove of the dilapidated tavern in the decayed mining camp of Angel's, and I noticed that he was fat and bald-headed, and had an expression of winning gentleness and simplicity upon his tranquil countenance. He roused up, and gave me good-day. I told him a friend of mine had commissioned me to make some inquiries about a cherished companion of his boyhood named *Leonidas W.* Smiley—*Rev. Leonidas W.* Smiley, a young minister of the Gospel, who he had heard was at one time a resident of Angel's Camp. I added that if Mr. Wheeler could tell me anything about this Rev. Leonidas W. Smiley, I would feel under many obligations to him.

Simon Wheeler backed me into a corner and blockaded me there with his chair, and then sat down and reeled off the monotonous narrative which follows this paragraph. He never smiled, he never frowned, he never changed his voice from the gentle-flowing key to which he tuned his initial sentence, he never betrayed the slightest suspicion of enthusiasm; but all through the interminable narrative there ran a vein of impressive earnestness and sincerity, which showed me plainly that, so far from his imagining that there was anything ridiculous or funny about his story, he regarded it as a really important matter, and admired its two heroes as men of transcendent genius in *finesse.* I let him go on in his own way, and never interrupted him once.

"Rev. Leonidas W. H'm, Reverend Le—well, there was a feller here once by the name of *Jim* Smiley, in the winter of '49—or may be it was the spring of '50—I don't recollect exactly, somehow, though what makes me think it was one or the other is because I remember the big flume warn't finished when he first come to the camp; but any way, he was the curiosest man about always betting on anything that turned up you ever see, if he could get anybody to bet on the other side; and if couldn't he'd change sides. Any way that suited the other man would suit *him*—any way just so's he got a bet, *he* was satisfied. But still he was lucky, uncommon lucky; he most always come out winner. He was always ready and laying for a chance; there couldn't be no solit'ry thing mentioned but that feller'd offer to bet on it, and take ary side you please, as I was just telling you. If there was a horse-race, you'd find him flush or you'd find him busted at the end of it; if there was a dog-fight, he'd bet on it; if there was a cat-fight, he'd bet on it; if there was a chicken-fight, he'd bet on it; why, if there was two birds setting on a fence, he would bet you which one would fly first; or if there was a camp-meeting, he would be there reg'lar to bet on Parson Walker, which he judged to be the best exhorter about here, and so he was too, and a good man. If he even see a straddle-bug start to go anywheres, he would bet you how long it would take him to get to—to wherever he was going to, and if you took him up, he would foller that straddle-bug to Mexico but what he would find out where he was bound for and how long he was on the road. Lots of the boys here has seen that Smiley, and can tell you about him. Why, it never made no difference to *him*—he'd bet on *any* thing—the dangest feller. Parson Walker's wife laid very sick once, for a good while, and it seemed as if they warn't going to save her; but one morning he come in, and Smiley up and asked him how she was, and he said she was considerable better—thank the Lord for his inf'nite mercy—and coming on so smart that with the blessing of Prov'dence she'd get well yet; and Smiley, before he thought, says, "Well, I'll resk two-and-a-half she don't anyway."

Thish-yer Smiley had a mare—the boys called her the fifteen-minute nag, but that was only in fun, you know, because of course she was faster than that—and he used to win money on that horse, for all she was so slow and always had the asthma, or the distemper, or the consumption, or something of that kind. They used to give her two or three hundred yards start, and then pass her under way; but always at the fag end of the race she'd get excited and desperate like, and come cavorting and straddling up, and scattering her legs around limber, sometimes in the air, and sometimes out to one side among the fences, and kicking up m-o-r-e dust and raising m-o-r-e racket with her coughing and sneezing and blowing her nose—and *always* fetch up at the stand just about a neck ahead, as near as you could cipher it down.

And he had a little small bull-pup, that to look at him you'd think he warn't worth a cent but to set around and look ornery and lay for a chance to steal something. But as soon as money was up on him he was a different dog; his under-jaw'd begin to stick out like the fo'castle of a steamboat, and his teeth would uncover and shine like the furnaces. And a dog might tackle him and bully-rag him, and bite him, and throw him over his shoulder two or three times, and Andrew Jackson—which was the name of the pup—Andrew Jackson would never let on but what *he* was satisfied, and hadn't expected nothing else—and the bets being doubled and doubled on the other side all the time, till the money was all up; and then all of a sudden he would grab the other dog jest by the j'int of his hind leg and freeze to it—not chaw, you understand, but only just grip and hang on till they throwed up the sponge, if it was a year. Smiley always come out winner on that pup, till he harnessed a dog once that didn't have no hind legs, because they'd been sawed off in a circular saw, and when the thing had gone along far enough, and the money was all up, and he come to make a snatch for his pet holt, he see in a minute how he'd been imposed on, and how the other dog had him in the door, so to speak, and he 'peared surprised, and then he looked sorter discouraged-like, and didn't try no more to win the fight, and so he got shucked out bad. He gave Smiley a look, as much as to say his heart was broke, and it was *his* fault, for putting up a dog that hadn't no hind legs for him to take holt of, which was his main dependence in a fight, and then he limped off a piece and laid down and died. It was a good pup, was that Andrew Jackson, and would have made a name for hisself if he'd lived, for the stuff was in him and he had genius—I know it, because he hadn't no opportunities to speak of, and it don't stand to reason that a dog could make such a fight as he could under them circumstances if he hadn't no talent. It always makes me feel sorry when I think of that last fight of his'n, and the way it turned out.

Well, thish-yer Smiley had rat-tarriers, and chicken cocks, and tomcats and all them kind of things, till you couldn't rest, and you couldn't fetch nothing for him to bet on but he'd match you. He ketched a frog one day, and took him home, and said he cal'lated to educate him; and so he never done nothing for three months but set in his back yard and learn that frog to jump. And you bet you he *did* learn him, too. He'd give him a little pinch behind, and the next minute you'd see that frog whirling in the air like a doughnut—see him turn one summerset, or may be a couple, if he got a good start, and come down flat-footed and all right, like a cat. He got him up so in the matter of ketching flies, and kep' him in practice so constant, that he'd nail a fly every time as fur as he could see him. Smiley said all a frog wanted was education, and he could do 'most anything—and I believe him. Why, I've seen him set Dan'l Webster down here on this floor—Dan'l Webster was the name of the frog—and sing out, "Flies, Dan'l, flies!" and quicker'n you could wink he'd spring straight up and snake a fly off'n the counter there, and flop down on the floor ag'in as solid as a gob of mud, and fall to scratching the side of his head with his hind foot as indifferent as if he hadn't no idea he'd been doin' any more'n any frog might do. You never see a frog so modest and straightfor'ard as he was, for all he was so gifted. And when it come to fair and square jumping on a dead level, he could get over more ground at one straddle than any animal of his breed you ever see. Jumping on a dead level was his strong suit, you understand; and when it come to that, Smiley would ante up money on him as long as he had a red. Smiley was monstrous proud of his frog, and well he might be, for fellers that had traveled and been everywheres all said he laid over any frog that ever *they* see.

Well, Smiley kep' the beast in a little lattice box, and he used to fetch him down town sometimes and lay for a bet. One day a feller—a stranger in the camp, he was—come across him with his box, and says:

"What might it be that you've got in the box?"

And Smiley says, sorter indifferent-like, "It might be a parrot, or it might be a canary, maybe, but it ain't—it's only just a frog."

And the feller took it, and looked at it careful, and turned it round this way and that, and says, "H'm—so 'tis. Well, what's *he* good for?"

"Well," Smiley says, easy and careless, "he's good enough for *one* thing, I should judge—he can outjump any frog in Calaveras county."

The feller took the box again, and took another long, particular look, and give it back to Smiley, and says, very deliberate, "Well," he says, "I don't see no p'ints about that frog that's any better'n any other frog."

"Maybe you don't," Smiley says. "Maybe you understand frogs and maybe you don't understand 'em; maybe you've had experience, and maybe you ain't only a amature, as it were. Anyways, I've got *my* opinion, and I'll resk forty dollars that he can outjump any frog in Calaveras county."

And the feller studied a minute, and then says, kinder sad like, "Well, I'm only a stranger here, and I ain't got no frog; but if I had a frog, I'd bet you."

And then Smiley says, "That's all right—that's all right—if you'll hold my box a minute, I'll go and get you a frog." And so the feller took the box, and put up his forty dollars along with Smiley's, and set down to wait.

So he set there a good while thinking and thinking to hisself, and then he got the frog out and prized his mouth open and took a teaspoon and filled him full of quail shot—filled him pretty near up to his chin—and set him on the floor. Smiley he went to the swamp and slopped around in the mud for a long time, and finally he ketched a frog, and fetched him in, and give him to this feller, and says:

"Now, if you're ready, set him alongside of Dan'l, with his forepaws just even with Dan'l's, and I'll give the word." Then he says, "One—two—three—*git!*" and him and the feller touched up the frogs from behind, and the new frog hopped off lively, but Dan'l give a heave, and hysted up his shoulders—so—like a Frenchman, but it warn't no use—he couldn't budge; he was planted as solid as a church, and he couldn't no more stir than if he was anchored out. Smiley was a good deal surprised, and he was disgusted too, but he didn't have no idea what the matter was, of course.

The feller took the money and started away; and when he was going out at the door, he sorter jerked his thumb over his shoulder—so—at Dan'l, and says again, very deliberate, "Well," he says, "*I* don't see no p'ints about that frog that's any better'n any other frog."

Smiley stood scratching his head and looking down at Dan'l a long time, and at last he says, "I do wonder what in the nation that frog throw'd off for—I wonder if there ain't something the matter with him—he 'pears to look mighty baggy, somehow." And he ketched Dan'l by the nap of the neck, and hefted him, and says, "Why blame my cats if he don't weigh five pound!" and turned him upside down and he belched out a double handful of shot. And then he see how it was, and he was the maddest man—he set the frog down and took out after that feller, but he never ketched him. And—"

Here Simon Wheeler heard his name called from the front yard, and got up to see what was wanted. And turning to me as he moved away, he said: "Just set where you are, stranger, and rest easy—I ain't going to be gone a second."

But, by your leave, I did not think that a continuation of the history of the enterprising vagabond *Jim* Smiley would likely to afford me much information concerning the Rev. *Leonidas W.* Smiley, and so I started away.

At the door I met the sociable Wheeler returning, and he buttonholed me and re-commenced:

"Well, thish-yer Smiley had a yaller one-eyed cow that didn't have no tail, only just a short stump like a bannanner, and—"

However, lacking both time and inclination, I did not wait to hear about the afflicted cow, but took my leave.

1865

STUDY QUESTIONS

1. During Twain's lifetime, this story appeared in various forms and with various titles. Do you think the title used here (the one most often used) is a good one for the story? Why or why not?
2. In your opinion, how important is the use of the "frame story" technique for this tale? What does the initial narrator contribute to the story?
3. What are the sources of humor in this story?
4. Compare and contrast the story's two narrators, in terms of their speech patterns, character, and whatever else you'd like to comment on.

Character Study and Social Commentary

8

LOOKING INWARD
AND OUTWARD

Human beings are both individuals and social beings. Fiction, throughout its history, has concerned itself with that duality. One of fiction's most fascinating characteristics, in fact, is its ability to look in two directions at once. Fictional narrators can look into their **characters**, revealing their minds and feelings to us, exploring their personalities. And they can look out at the society to which the characters belong. Looking inward, they seem to ask, "What sort of people are these?" Looking outward, they seem to ask, "What has made them that way?"

Fiction writers of **realism** have long felt that their form's unique ability to deal with the common reality of everyday life made it an ideal vehicle for examining the interaction of individuals with their society. We find that concern reflected in nearly all forms of fiction, from old and traditional tales such as Joseph Conrad's "Youth: A Narrative" to some of the most experimental contemporary works. Many Americans in the latter half of the twentieth century are deeply concerned with questions of society's influence and power over the individual and of the individual's own power to shape his or her own personality and future. Contemporary fiction reflects these concerns.

The four stories that follow are all works that engage our concern for some central character or characters while forcing upon us some realization of or comment on the society in which these characters live. In these stories, as in others we have read, the **physical settings** often become metaphors for the **social settings**. The influence of society, and the characters' reactions to it, thus form an important part of each tale.

As you read these stories, therefore, take note of their physical and social settings, and of how these settings are used to define the characters' actions and personalities. Take note, too—as always when dealing with fiction—of the narrators' **voices**. What tones of voice do you hear in these stories? What attitudes do they convey? How do the narrators blend their stories' dual focus on individual and society into a concern for the fulfillment or happiness of their central characters? What moods do they leave you in at the stories' ends? How do they get you there?

The Minister's Black Veil: A Parable

Nathaniel Hawthorne (1804–1864)

Nathaniel Hawthorne is the great early master of psychological fiction in American literature. In his cool, learned style he probed several recurrent themes: the tendency of intellectuals—artists or scientists, for example—to separate themselves from the rest of society; the weight of the Puritan past on the present; the need to have a healthy balance between the demands of the head and the heart; the impossibility of ever really knowing the innermost secrets of another human being. Hawthorne's works sometimes seem maddeningly ambiguous, as in the case of *The Scarlet Letter* (1850), which appears to condemn Hester Prynne for her adultery while at the same time creating a great deal of sympathy for her. In *The Blithedale Romance* (1852), Hawthorne created a first-person narrator who alternates between endorsing the utopian community in which he lives for a time and making fun of the whole idea. The careful reader of Hawthorne comes away from his fiction with an increased appreciation for the enormous complexity and richness of human experience.

The sexton stood in the porch of Milford meeting-house, pulling lustily at the bell-rope. The old people of the village came stooping along the street. Children, with bright faces, tript merrily beside their parents, or mimicked a graver gait, in the conscious dignity of their Sunday clothes. Spruce bachelors looked sidelong at the pretty maidens, and fancied that the Sabbath sunshine made them prettier than on week-days. When the throng had mostly streamed into the porch, the sexton began to toll the bell, keeping his eye on the Reverend Mr. Hooper's door. The first glimpse of the clergyman's figure was the signal for the bell to cease its summons.

"But what has good Parson Hooper got upon his face?" cried the sexton in astonishment.

All within hearing immediately turned about, and beheld the semblance of Mr. Hooper, pacing slowly his meditative way towards the meeting-house. With one accord they started, expressing more wonder than if some strange minister were coming to dust the cushions of Mr. Hooper's pulpit.

"Are you sure it is our parson?" inquired Goodman Gray of the sexton.

"Of a certainty it is good Mr. Hooper," replied the sexton. "He was to have exchanged pulpits with Parson Shute of Westbury; but Parson Shute sent to excuse himself yesterday, being to preach a funeral sermon."

The cause of so much amazement may appear sufficiently slight. Mr. Hooper, a gentlemanly person of about thirty, though still a bachelor, was dressed with due clerical neatness, as if a careful wife had starched his band, and

brushed the weekly dust from his Sunday's garb. There was but one thing remarkable in his appearance. Swathed about his forehead, and hanging down
over his face, so low as to be shaken by his breath, Mr. Hooper had on a black
veil. On a nearer view, it seemed to consist of two folds of crape, which entirely
concealed his features, except the mouth and chin, but probably did not inter-
cept his sight, farther than to give a darkened aspect to all living and inanimate
things. With this gloomy shade before him, good Mr. Hooper walked onward, at
a slow and quiet pace, stooping somewhat and looking on the ground, as is customary with abstracted men, yet nodding kindly to those of his parishioners
who still waited on the meeting-house steps. But so wonder-struck were they,
that his greeting hardly met with a return.

"I can't really feel as if good Mr. Hooper's face was behind that piece of
crape," said the sexton.

"I don't like it," muttered an old woman, as she hobbled into the meeting-
house. "He has changed himself into something awful, only by hiding his face."

"Our parson has gone mad!" cried Goodman Gray, following him across the
threshold.

A rumor of some accountable phenomenon had preceded Mr. Hooper into
the meeting-house, and set all the congregation astir. Few could refrain from
twisting their heads towards the door; many stood upright, and turned directly
about; while several little boys clambered upon the seats, and came down again
with a terrible racket. There was a general bustle, a rustling of the women's
gowns and shuffling of the men's feet, greatly at variance with that hushed repose which should attend the entrance of the minister. But Mr. Hooper appeared not to notice the perturbation of his people. He entered with an almost
noiseless step, bent his head mildly to the pews on each side, and bowed as he
passed his oldest parishioner, a white-haired great-grandsire, who occupied an
arm-chair in the centre of the aisle. It was strange to observe, how slowly this
venerable man became conscious of something singular in the appearance of the
pastor. He seemed not fully to partake of the prevailing wonder, till Mr. Hooper
had ascended the stairs, and showed himself in the pulpit, face to face with his
congregation, except for the black veil. That mysterious emblem was never once
withdrawn. It shook with his measured breath as he gave out the psalm; it threw
its obscurity between him and the holy page, as he read the Scriptures; and while
he prayed, the veil lay heavily on his uplifted countenance. Did he seek to hide it
from the dread Being whom he was addressing?

Such was the effect of this simple piece of crape, that more than one woman
of delicate nerves was forced to leave the meeting-house. Yet perhaps the pale-
faced congregation was almost as fearful a sight to the minister, as his black veil
to them.

Mr. Hooper had the reputation of a good preacher, but not an energetic
one: he strove to win his people heavenward, by mild persuasive influences,
rather than to drive them thither, by the thunders of the Word. The sermon
which he now delivered, was marked by the same characteristics of style and

manner, as the general series of his pulpit oratory. But there was something, either in the sentiment of the discourse itself, or in the imagination of the auditors, which made it greatly the most powerful effort that they had ever heard from their pastor's lips. It was tinged, rather more darkly than usual, with the gentle gloom of Mr. Hooper's temperament. The subject had reference to secret sin, and those sad mysteries which we hide from our nearest and dearest, and would fain conceal from our own consciousness, even forgetting that the Omniscient can detect them. A subtle power was breathed into his words. Each member of the congregation, the most innocent girl, and the man of hardened breast, felt as if the preacher had crept upon them, behind his awful veil, and discovered their hoarded iniquity of deed or thought. Many spread their clasped hands on their bosoms. There was nothing terrible in what Mr. Hooper said; at least, no violence; and yet, with every tremor of his melancholy voice, the hearers quaked. An unsought pathos came hand in hand with awe. So sensible were the audience of some unwonted attribute in their minister, that they longed for a breath of wind to blow aside the veil, almost believing that a stranger's visage would be discovered, though the form, gesture, and voice were those of Mr. Hooper.

At the close of the services, the people hurried out with indecorous confusion, eager to communicate their pent-up amazement, and conscious of lighter spirits, the moment they lost sight of the black veil. Some gathered in little circles, huddled closely together, with their mouths all whispering in the centre; some went homeward alone, wrapt in silent meditation; some talked loudly, and profaned the Sabbath-day with ostentatious laughter. A few shook their sagacious heads, intimating that they could penetrate the mystery; while one or two affirmed that there was no mystery at all, but only that Mr. Hooper's eyes were so weakened by the midnight lamp, as to require a shade. After a brief interval, forth came good Mr. Hooper also, in the rear of his flock. Turning his veiled face from one group to another, he paid due reverence to the hoary heads, saluted the middle-aged with kind dignity, as their friend and spiritual guide, greeted the young with mingled authority and love, and laid his hands on the little children's heads to bless them. Such was always his custom on the Sabbath-day. Strange and bewildered looks repaid him for his courtesy. None, as on former occasions, aspired to the honor of walking by their pastor's side. Old Squire Saunders, doubtless by an accidental lapse of memory, neglected to invite Mr. Hooper to his table, where the good clergyman had been wont to bless the food, almost every Sunday since his settlement. He returned, therefore, to the parsonage, and, at the moment of closing the door, was observed to look back upon the people, all of whom had their eyes fixed upon the minister. A sad smile gleamed faintly from beneath the black veil, and flickered about his mouth, glimmering as he disappeared.

"How strange," said a lady, "that a simple black veil, such as any woman might wear on her bonnet, should become such a terrible thing on Mr. Hooper's face!"

"Something must surely be amiss with Mr. Hooper's intellects," observed her husband, the physician of the village. "But the strangest part of the affair is the effect of this vagary, even on a sober-minded man like myself. The black veil, though it covers only our pastor's face, throws its influence over his whole person, and makes him ghost-like from head to foot. Do you not feel it so?"

"Truly do I," replied the lady; "and I would not be alone with him for the world. I wonder he is not afraid to be alone with himself!"

"Men sometimes are so," said her husband.

The afternoon service was attended with similar circumstances. At its conclusion, the bell tolled for the funeral of a young lady. The relatives and friends were assembled in the house, and the more distant acquaintances stood about the door, speaking of the good qualities of the deceased, when their talk was interrupted by the appearance of Mr. Hooper, still covered with his black veil. It was now an appropriate emblem. The clergyman stepped into the room where the corpse was laid, and bent over the coffin, to take a last farewell of his deceased parishioner. As he stooped, the veil hung straight down from his forehead, so that, if her eye-lids had not been closed for ever, the dead maiden might have seen his face. Could Mr. Hooper be fearful of her glance, that he so hastily caught back the black veil? A person, who watched the interview between the dead and living, scrupled not to affirm, that, at the instant when the clergyman's features were disclosed, the corpse had slightly shuddered, rustling the shroud and muslin cap, though the countenance retained the composure of death. A superstitious old woman was the only witness of this prodigy. From the coffin, Mr. Hooper passed into the chamber of the mourners, and thence to the head of the staircase, to make the funeral prayer. It was a tender and heart-dissolving prayer, full of sorrow, yet so imbued with celestial hopes, that the music of a heavenly harp, swept by the fingers of the dead, seemed faintly to be heard among the saddest accents of the minister. The people trembled, though they but darkly understood him, when he prayed that they, and himself, and all of mortal race, might be ready, as he trusted his young maiden had been, for the dreadful hour that should snatch the veil from their faces. The bearers went heavily forth, and the mourners followed, saddening all the street, with the dead before them, and Mr. Hooper in his black veil behind.

"Why do you look back?" said one in the procession to his partner.

"I had a fancy," replied she, "that the minister and the maiden's spirit were walking hand in hand."

"And so had I, at the same moment," said the other.

That night, the handsomest couple in Milford village were to be joined in wedlock. Though reckoned a melancholy man, Mr. Hooper had a placid cheerfulness for such occasions, which often excited a sympathetic smile, where livelier merriment would have been thrown away. There was no quality of his disposition which made him more beloved than this. The company at the wedding awaited his arrival with impatience, trusting that the strange awe, which had gathered over him throughout the day, would now be dispelled. But such was not the result. When Mr. Hooper came, the first thing that their eyes rested on was the same horrible black veil, which had added deeper gloom to the funeral, and could portend nothing but evil to the wedding. Such was its immediate effect on the guests, that a cloud seemed to have rolled duskily from beneath the black crape, and dimmed the light of the candles. The bridal pair stood up before the minister. But the bride's cold fingers quivered in the tremulous hand of the bridegroom, and her deathlike paleness caused a whisper, that the maiden who had been buried a few hours before, was come from her grave to be married. If ever another wedding were so dismal, it was that famous one, where they tolled the wedding-knell. After performing the ceremony, Mr. Hooper raised a glass of wine to his lips, wishing happiness to the new-married couple, in a strain of mild pleasantry that ought to have brightened the features of the guests, like a cheerful gleam from the hearth. At that instant, catching a glimpse of his figure in the looking-glass, the black veil involved his own spirit in the horror with which it overwhelmed all others. His frame shuddered—his lips grew white—he spilt the untasted wine upon the carpet—and rushed forth into the darkness. For the Earth, too, had on her Black Veil.

The next day, the whole village of Milford talked of little else than Parson Hooper's black veil. That, and the mystery concealed behind it, supplied a topic for discussion between acquaintances meeting in the street, and good women gossiping at their open windows. It was the first item of news that the tavern-keeper told to his guests. The children babbled of it on their way to school. One imitative little imp covered his face with an old black handerchief, thereby so affrighting his playmates, that the panic seized himself, and he well nigh lost his wits by his own waggery.

It was remarkable, that, of all the busy-bodies and impertinent people in the parish, not one ventured to put the plain question to Mr. Hooper, wherefore he did this thing. Hitherto, whenever there appeared the slightest call for such interference, he had never lacked advisers, nor shown himself averse to be guided by their judgment. If he erred at all, it was by so painful a degree of self-distrust, that even the mildest censure would lead him to consider an indifferent action as a crime. Yet, though so well acquainted with this amiable weakness, no individual among his parishioners chose to make the black veil a subject of friendly remonstrance. There was a feeling of dread, neither plainly confessed nor carefully concealed, which caused each to shift the responsibility upon another, till at length it was found expedient to send a deputation of the church, in order to deal with Mr. Hooper about the mystery, before it should grow into a scandal. Never did an embassy so ill discharge its duties. The minister received them with friendly courtesy, but became silent, after they were seated, leaving to his visitors the whole burthen of introducing their important business. The topic, it might be supposed, was obvious enough. There was the black veil, swathed round Mr. Hooper's forehead, and concealing every feature above his placid mouth, on which, at times, they could perceive the glimmering of a melancholy smile. But that piece of crape, to their imagination, seemed to hang down before his heart, the symbol of a fearful secret between him and them. Were the veil but cast aside, they might speak freely of it, but not till then. Thus they sat a considerable time, speechless, confused, and shrinking uneasily from Mr. Hooper's eye, which they felt to be fixed upon them with an invisible glance. Finally, the deputies returned abashed to their constituents, pronouncing the matter too weighty to be handled, except by a council of the churches, if, indeed, it might not require a general synod.

But there was one person in the village, unappalled by the awe with which the black veil had impressed all beside herself. When the deputies returned without an explanation, or even venturing to demand one, she, with the calm energy of her character, determined to chase away the strange cloud that appeared to be settling round Mr. Hooper, every moment more darkly than before. As his plighted wife, it should be her privilege to know what the black veil concealed. At the minister's first visit, therefore, she entered upon the subject, with a direct simplicity, which made the task easier both for him and her. After he had seated himself, she fixed her eyes steadfastly upon the veil, but could discern nothing of the dreadful gloom that had so overawed the multitude: it was but a double fold of crape, hanging down from his forehead to his mouth, and slightly stirring with his breath.

"No," said she aloud, and smiling, "there is nothing terrible in this piece of crape, except that it hides a face which I am always glad to look upon. Come, good sir, let the sun shine from behind the cloud. First lay aside your black veil: then tell me why you put it on."

Mr. Hooper's smile glimmered faintly.

"There is an hour to come," said he, "when all of us shall cast aside our veils. Take it not amiss, beloved friend, if I wear this piece of crape till then."

"Your words are a mystery too," returned the young lady. "Take away the veil from them, at least."

"Elizabeth, I will," said he, "so far as my vow may suffer me. Know, then, this veil is a type and a symbol, and I am bound to wear it ever, both in light and darkness, in solitude and before the gaze of multitudes, and as with strangers, so with my familiar friends. No mortal eye will see it withdrawn. This dismal shade must separate me from the world: even you, Elizabeth, can never come behind it!"

"What grievous affliction hath befallen you," she earnestly inquired, "that you should thus darken your eyes for ever?"

"If it be a sign of mourning," replied Mr. Hooper, "I, perhaps, like most other mortals, have sorrows dark enough to be typified by a black veil."

"But what if the world will not believe that it is the type of an innocent sorrow?" urged Elizabeth. "Beloved and respected as you are, there may be whispers, that you hide your face under the consciousness of secret sin. For the sake of your holy office, do away this scandal!"

The color rose into her cheeks, as she intimated the nature of the rumors that were already abroad in the village. But Mr. Hooper's mildness did not forsake him. He even smiled again—that same sad smile, which always appeared like a faint glimmering of light, proceeding from the obscurity beneath the veil.

"If I hide my face for sorrow, there is cause enough," he merely replied; "and if I cover it for secret sin, what mortal might not do the same?"

And with this gentle, but unconquerable obstinacy, did he resist all her entreaties. At length Elizabeth sat silent. For a few moments she appeared lost in thought, considering, probably, what new methods might be tried, to withdraw her lover from so dark a fantasy, which, if it had no other meaning, was perhaps a symptom of mental disease. Though of a firmer character than his own, the tears rolled down her cheeks. But, in an instant, as it were, a new feeling took the place of sorrow: her eyes were fixed insensibly on the black veil, when, like a sudden twilight in the air, its terrors fell around her. She arose, and stood trembling before him.

"And do you feel it then at last?" said he mournfully.

She made no reply, but covered her eyes with her hand, and turned to leave the room. He rushed forward and caught her arm.

"Have patience with me, Elizabeth!" cried he passionately. "Do not desert me, though this veil must be between us here on earth. Be mine, and hereafter there shall be no veil over my face, no darkness between our souls! It is but a mortal veil—it is not for eternity! Oh! you know not how lonely I am, and how frightened to be alone behind my black veil. Do not leave me in this miserable obscurity for ever!"

"Lift the veil but once, and look me in the face," said she.

"Never! It cannot be!" replied Mr. Hooper.

"Then, farewell!" said Elizabeth.

She withdrew her arm from his grasp, and slowly departed, pausing at the door, to give one long, shuddering gaze, that seemed almost to penetrate the mystery of the black veil. But, even amid his grief, Mr. Hooper smiled to think that only a material emblem had separated him from happiness, though the horrors which it shadowed forth, must be drawn darkly between the fondest of lovers.

From that time no attempts were made to remove Mr. Hooper's black veil, or, by a direct appeal, to discover the secret which it was supposed to hide. By persons who claimed a superiority to popular prejudice, it was reckoned merely an eccentric whim, such as often mingles with the sober actions of men otherwise rational, and tinges them all with its own semblance of insanity. But with the multitude, good Mr. Hooper was irreparably a bugbear. He could not walk the streets with any peace of mind, so conscious was he that the gentle and timid would turn aside to avoid him, and that others would make it a point of hardihood to throw themselves in his way. The impertinence of the latter class compelled him to give up his customary walk, at sunset, to the burial ground; for when he leaned pensively over the gate, there would always be faces behind the grave-stones, peeping at his black veil. A fable went the rounds, that the stare of the dead people drove him thence. It grieved him, to the very depth of his kind heart, to observe how the children fled from his approach, breaking up their merriest sports, while his melancholy figure was yet afar off. Their instinctive dread caused him to feel, more strongly than aught else, that a preternatural horror was interwoven with the threads of the black crape. In truth, his own antipathy to the veil was known to be so great, that he never willingly passed before a mirror, nor stooped to drink at a still fountain, lest, in its peaceful bosom, he should be affrighted by himself. This was what gave plausibility to the whispers, that Mr. Hooper's conscience tortured him for some great crime, too horrible to be entirely concealed, or otherwise than so obscurely intimated. Thus, from beneath the black veil, there rolled a cloud into the sunshine, an ambiguity of sin or sorrow, which enveloped the poor minister, so that love or sympathy could never reach him. It was said, that ghost and fiend consorted with him there. With self-shudderings and outward terrors, he walked continually in its shadow, groping darkly within his own soul, or gazing through a medium that saddened the whole world. Even the lawless wind, it was believed, respected his dreadful secret, and never blew aside the veil. But still good Mr. Hooper sadly smiled, at the pale visages of the worldly throng as he passed by.

Among all its bad influences, the black veil had the one desirable effect, of making its wearer a very efficient clergyman. By the aid of his mysterious emblem—for there was no other apparent cause—he became a man of awful power, over souls that were in agony for sin. His converts always regarded him with a dread peculiar to themselves, affirming, though but figuratively, that, before he brought them to celestial light, they had been with him behind the black veil. Its gloom, indeed, enabled him to sympathize with all dark affections. Dying sinners cried aloud for Mr. Hooper, and would not yield their breath till he appeared; though ever, as he stooped to whisper consolation, they shuddered at the veiled face so near their own. Such were the terrors of the black veil, even when Death had bared his visage! Strangers came long distances to attend service at his church, with the mere idle purpose of gazing at his figure, because it was forbidden them to behold his face. But many were made to quake ere they departed! Once, during Governor Belcher's administration, Mr. Hooper was appointed to preach the election sermon. Covered with his black veil, he stood before the chief magistrate, the council, and the representatives, and wrought so deep an impression, that the legislative measures of that year, were characterized by all the gloom and piety of our earliest ancestral sway.

In this manner Mr. Hooper spent a long life, irreproachable in outward act, yet shrouded in dismal suspicions; kind and loving, though unloved, and dimly feared; a man apart from men, shunned in their health and joy, but ever summoned to their aid in mortal anguish. As years wore on, shedding their snows above his sable veil, he acquired a name throughout the New-England churches, and they called him Father Hooper. Nearly all his parishioners, who were of mature age when he was settled, had been borne away by many a funeral: he had one congregation in the church, and a more crowded one in the church-yard; and having wrought so late into the evening, and done his work so well, it was now good Father Hooper's turn to rest.

Several persons were visible by the shaded candlelight, in the death-chamber of the old clergyman. Natural connections he had none. But there was the decorously grave, though unmoved physician, seeking only to mitigate the last pangs of the patient whom he could not save. There were the deacons, and other eminently pious members of his church. There, also, was the Reverend Mr. Clark, of Westbury, a young and zealous divine, who had ridden in haste to pray by the bed-side of the expiring minister. There was the nurse, no hired hand-maiden of death, but one whose calm affection had endured thus long, in secresy, in solitude, amid the chill of age, and would not perish, even at the dying hour. Who, but Elizabeth! And there lay the hoary head of good Father Hooper upon the death-pillow, with the black veil still swathed about his brow and reaching down over his face, so that each more difficult gasp of his faint breath caused it to stir. All through life that piece of crape had hung between him and the world: it had separated him from cheerful brotherhood and woman's love, and kept him in that saddest of all prisons, his own heart; and still it lay upon his face, as if to deepen the gloom of his darksome chamber, and shade him from the sunshine of eternity.

For some time previous, his mind had been confused, wavering doubtfully between the past and the present, and hovering forward, as it were, at intervals, into the indistinctness of the world to come. There had been feverish turns, which tossed him from side to side, and wore away what little strength he had. But in his most convulsive struggles, and in the wildest vagaries of his intellect, when no other thought retained its sober influence, he still showed an awful solicitude lest the black veil should slip aside. Even if his bewildered soul could have forgotten, there was a faithful woman at his pillow, who, with averted eyes, would have covered that aged face, which she had last beheld in the comeliness of manhood. At length the death-stricken old man lay quietly in the torpor of mental and bodily exhaustion, with an imperceptible pulse, and breath that grew fainter and fainter, except when a long, deep, and irregular inspiration seemed to prelude the flight of his spirit.

The minister of Westbury approached the bedside.

"Venerable Father Hooper," said he, "the moment of your release is at hand. Are you ready for the lifting of the veil, that shuts in time from eternity?"

Father Hooper at first replied merely by a feeble motion of his head: then, apprehensive, perhaps, that his meaning might be doubtful, he exerted himself to speak.

"Yea," said he, in faint accents, "my soul hath a patient weariness until that veil be lifted."

"And is it fitting," resumed the Reverend Mr. Clark, "that a man so given to prayer, of such a blameless example, holy in deed and thought, so far as mortal judgment may pronounce; is it fitting that a father in the church should leave a shadow on his memory, that may seem to blacken a life so pure? I pray you, my venerable brother, let not this thing be! Suffer us to be gladdened by your triumphant aspect, as you go to your reward. Before the veil of eternity be lifted, let me cast aside this black veil from your face!"

And thus speaking, the Reverend Mr. Clark bent forward to reveal the mystery of so many years. But, exerting a sudden energy, that made all the beholders stand aghast, Father Hooper snatched both his hands from beneath the bedclothes, and pressed them strongly on the black veil, resolute to struggle, if the minister of Westbury would contend with a dying man.

"Never!" cried the veiled clergyman. "On earth, never!"

"Dark old man!" exclaimed the affrighted minister, "with what horrible crime upon your soul are you now passing to the judgment?"

Father Hooper's breath heaved; it rattled in his throat; but, with a mighty effort, grasping forward with his hands, he caught hold of life, and held it back till he should speak. He even raised himself in bed; and there he sat, shivering with the arms of death around him, while the black veil hung down, awful, at that last moment, in the gathered terrors of a life-time. And yet the faint, sad smile, so often there, now seemed to glimmer from its obscurity, and linger on Father Hooper's lips.

"Why do you tremble at me alone?" cried he, turning his veiled face round the circle of pale spectators. "Tremble also at each other! Have men avoided me, and women shown no pity, and children screamed and fled, only for my black veil? What, but the mystery which it obscurely typifies, has made this piece of crape so awful? When the friend shows his inmost heart to his friend; the lover to his best-beloved; when man does not vainly shrink from the eye of his Creator, loathsomely treasuring up the secret of his sin; then deem me a monster, for the symbol beneath which I have lived, and die! I look around me, and, lo! on every visage a Black Veil!"

While his auditors shrank from one another, in mutual affright, Father Hooper fell back upon his pillow, a veiled corpse, with a faint smile lingering on the lips. Still veiled, they laid him in his coffin, and a veiled corpse they bore him to the grave. The grass of many years has sprung up and withered on that grave, the burial-stone is moss-grown, and good Mr. Hooper's face is dust; but awful is still the thought, that it mouldered beneath the Black Veil!

1836

STUDY QUESTIONS

1. This story explores the conflicts arising from the different demands of public and private life. Discuss how Rev. Hooper's wearing of the veil initially affects his public life as a minister and his private life as an individual.
2. Elizabeth, Hooper's "plighted wife," warns Hooper that his parishioners may believe he is wearing the veil because of some grave, specific sin he has committed. What possible candidate for this sin is suggested by the scene at

which Hooper presides over the funeral of the "young lady?" Is this suggestion borne out by the rest of the story?

3. Because he refuses to lift the veil, even for Elizabeth, Hooper becomes something of an outcast and dies a lonely bachelor. Does the story present
Hooper as a devout man who makes a noble sacrifice for his ministry or as a
fanatic who foolishly throws away the love of a good woman?

A Rose for Emily

William Faulkner (1897–1962)

William Faulkner is perhaps the most distinctive voice in American fiction—polysyllabic,
hypnotic, sometimes willfully obscure, at times heroic, at times mock heroic. Along with
James Joyce, he pioneered the stream-of-consciousness technique that revolutionized
twentieth-century fiction. Through that narrative mode the author could get at the actual
processes of the mind as it mixed memory, sensations of the present, and anticipation of
the future. In such masterpieces as *The Sound and the Fury* (1929), *As I Lay Dying* (1930),
and *Absalom, Absalom!* (1936), he offered multiple points of view in such a way as to do
for fiction what Albert Einstein did for physics—show that one's perspective largely de-
termines what one sees. Faulkner lived his whole life in Mississippi and wrote about his
"little postage stamp of native soil" so powerfully that he was awarded the Nobel Prize for
literature in 1949.

I

When Miss Emily Grierson died, our whole town went to her funeral: the men
through a sort of respectful affection for a fallen monument, the women mostly
out of curiosity to see the inside of her house, which no one save an old man-
servant—a combined gardener and cook—had seen in at least ten years.

It was a big, squarish frame house that had once been white, decorated with
cupolas and spires, and scrolled balconies in the heavily lightsome style of the
seventies, set on what had once been our most select street. But garages and cotton gins had encroached and obliterated even the august names of that neighborhood; only Miss Emily's house was left, lifting its stubborn and coquettish decay
above the cotton wagons and the gasoline pumps—an eyesore among eyesores.
And now Miss Emily had gone to join the representatives of those august names
where they lay in the cedar-bemused cemetery among the ranked and anonymous graves of Union and Confederate soldiers who fell at the battle of Jefferson.

Alive, Miss Emily had been a tradition, a duty, and a care; a sort of hereditary obligation upon the town, dating from that day in 1894 when Colonel Sartoris, the mayor—he who fathered the edict that no Negro woman should appear on the street without an apron—remitted her taxes, the dispensation dating from the death of her father on into perpetuity. Not that Miss Emily would have accepted charity. Colonel Sartoris invented an involved tale to the effect that Miss Emily's father had loaned money to the town, which the town, as a matter of business, preferred this way of repaying. Only a man of Colonel Sartoris' generation and thought could have invented it, and only a woman could have believed it.

When the next generation, with its more modern ideas, became mayors and aldermen, this arrangement created some little dissatisfaction. On the first of the year they mailed her a tax notice. February came, and there was no reply. They wrote her a formal letter, asking her to call at the sheriff's office at her convenience. A week later the mayor wrote her himself, offering to call or to send his car for her, and received in reply a note on paper of an archaic shape, in a thin, flowing calligraphy in faded ink, to the effect that she no longer went out at all. The tax notice was also enclosed, without comment.

They called a special meeting of the Board of Aldermen. A deputation waited upon her, knocked at the door through which no visitor had passed since she ceased giving china-painting lessons eight or ten years earlier. They were admitted by the old Negro into a dim hall from which a stairway mounted into still more shadow. It smelled of dust and disuse—a close, dank smell. The Negro led them into the parlor. It was furnished in heavy, leather-covered furniture. When the Negro opened the blinds of one window, they could see that the leather was cracked; and when they sat down, a faint dust rose sluggishly about their thighs, spinning with slow motes in the single sun-ray. On a tarnished gilt easel before the fireplace stood a crayon portrait of Miss Emily's father.

They rose when she entered—a small, fat woman in black, with a thin gold chain descending to her waist and vanishing into her belt, leaning on an ebony cane with a tarnished gold head. Her skeleton was small and spare; perhaps that was why what would have been merely plumpness in another was obesity in her. She looked bloated, like a body long submerged in motionless water, and of that pallid hue. Her eyes, lost in the fatty ridges of her face, looked like two small pieces of coal pressed into a lump of dough as they moved from one face to another while the visitors stated their errand.

She did not ask them to sit. She just stood in the door and listened quietly until the spokesman came to a stumbling halt. Then they could hear the invisible watch ticking at the end of the gold chain.

Her voice was dry and cold. "I have no taxes in Jefferson. Colonel Sartoris explained it to me. Perhaps one of you can gain access to the city records and satisfy yourselves."

"But we have. We are the city authorities, Miss Emily. Didn't you get a notice from the sheriff, signed by him?"

"I received a paper, yes," Miss Emily said. "Perhaps he considers himself the sheriff . . . I have no taxes in Jefferson."

"But there is nothing on the books to show that, you see. We must go by the—"

"See Colonel Sartoris. I have no taxes in Jefferson."

"But Miss Emily—"

"See Colonel Sartoris." (Colonel Sartoris had been dead almost ten years.) "I have no taxes in Jefferson. Tobe!" The Negro appeared. "Show these gentlemen out."

II

So she vanquished them, horse and foot, just as she had vanquished their fathers thirty years before about the smell. That was two years after her father's death and a short time after her sweetheart—the one we believed would marry her—had deserted her. After her father's death she went out very little; after her sweetheart went away, people hardly saw her at all. A few of the ladies had the temerity to call, but were not received, and the only sign of life about the place was the Negro man—a young man then—going in and out with a market basket.

"Just as if a man—any man—could keep a kitchen properly," the ladies said; so they were not surprised when the smell developed. It was another link between the gross, teeming world and the high and mighty Griersons.

A neighbor, a woman, complained to the mayor, Judge Stevens, eighty years old.

"But what will you have me do about it, madam?" he said.

"Why, send her word to stop it," the woman said. "Isn't there a law?"

"I'm sure that won't be necessary," Judge Stevens said. "It's probably just a snake or a rat that nigger of hers killed in the yard. I'll speak to him about it."

The next day he received two more complaints, one from a man who came in diffident deprecation. "We really must do something about it, Judge. I'd be the last one in the world to bother Miss Emily, but we've got to do something." That night the Board of Aldermen met—three graybeards and one younger man, a member of the rising generation.

"It's simple enough," he said. "Send her word to have her place cleaned up. Give her a certain time do it in, and if she don't . . ."

"Dammit, sir," Judge Stevens said, "will you accuse a lady to her face of smelling bad?"

So the next night, after midnight, four men crossed Miss Emily's lawn and slunk about the house like burglars, sniffing along the base of the brickwork and at the cellar openings while one of them performed a regular sowing motion with his hand out of a sack slung from his shoulder. They broke open the cellar door and sprinkled lime there, and in all the outbuildings. As they recrossed the lawn, a window that had been dark was lighted and Miss Emily sat in it, the light behind her, and her upright torso motionless as that of an idol. They crept quietly across the lawn and into the shadow of the locusts that lined the street. After a week or two the smell went away.

That was when people had begun to feel really sorry for her. People in our town, remembering how old lady Wyatt, her great-aunt, had gone completely crazy at last, believed that the Griersons held themselves a little too high for what they really were. None of the young men were quite good enough for Miss Emily and such. We had long thought of them as a tableau, Miss Emily a slender figure in white in the background, her father a spraddled silhouette in the foreground, his back to her and clutching a horsewhip, the two of them framed by the backflung front door. When she got to be thirty and was still single, we were not pleased exactly, but vindicated; even with insanity in the family she wouldn't have turned down all of her chances if they had really materialized.

When her father died, it got about that the house was all that was left to her; and in a way, people were glad. At last they could pity Miss Emily. Being left alone, and a pauper, she had become humanized. Now she too would know the old thrill and the old despair of a penny more or less.

The day after his death all the ladies prepared to call at the house and offer condolence and aid, as is our custom. Miss Emily met them at the door, dressed as usual and with no trace of grief on her face. She told them that her father was not dead. She did that for three days, with the ministers calling on her, and the doctors, trying to persuade her to let them dispose of the body. Just as they were about to resort to law and force, she broke down, and they buried her father quickly.

We did not say she was crazy then. We believed she had to do that. We remembered all the young men her father had driven away, and we knew that with nothing left, she would have to cling to that which had robbed her, as people will.

III

She was sick for a long time. When we saw her again, her hair was cut short, making her look like a girl, with a vague resemblance to those angels in colored church windows—sort of tragic and serene.

The town had just let the contracts for paving the sidewalks, and in the summer after her father's death they began the work. The construction company came with niggers and mules and machinery, and a foreman named Homer Barron, a Yankee—a big, dark, ready man, with a big voice and eyes lighter than his face. The little boys would follow in groups to hear him cuss the niggers, and the niggers singing in time to the rise and fall of picks. Pretty soon he knew everybody in town. Whenever you heard a lot of laughing anywhere about the square, Homer Barron would be in the center of the group. Presently we began to see him and Miss Emily on Sunday afternoons driving in the yellow-wheeled buggy and the matched team of bays from the livery stable.

At first we were glad that Miss Emily would have an interest, because the ladies all said, "Of course a Grierson would not think seriously of a Northerner, a day laborer." But there were still others, older people, who said that even grief could not cause a real lady to forget *noblesse oblige*—without calling it *noblesse oblige*. They just said, "Poor Emily. Her kinsfolk should come to her." She had some kin in Alabama; but years ago her father had fallen out with them over the estate of old Lady Wyatt, the crazy woman, and there was no communication between the two families. They had not even been represented at the funeral.

And as soon as the old people said, "Poor Emily," the whispering began. "Do you suppose it's really so?" they said to one another. "Of course it is. What else could . . ." This behind their hands; rustling of craned silk and satin behind jalousies closed upon the sun of Sunday afternoon as the thin, swift clop-clop-clop of the matched team passed: "Poor Emily."

She carried her head high enough—even when we believed that she was fallen. It was as if she demanded more than ever the recognition of her dignity as the last Grierson; as if it had wanted that touch of earthiness to reaffirm her imperviousness. Like when she bought the rat poison, the arsenic. That was over a year after they had begun to say "Poor Emily," and while the two female cousins were visiting her.

"I want some poison," she said to the druggist. She was over thirty then, still a slight woman, though thinner than usual, with cold, haughty black eyes in a face the flesh of which was strained across the temples and about the eye-sockets as you imagine a lighthouse-keeper's face ought to look. "I want some poison," she said.

"Yes, Miss Emily. What kind? For rats and such? I'd recom—"

"I want the best you have. I don't care what kind."

The druggist named several. "They'll kill anything up to an elephant. But what you want is—"

"Arsenic," Miss Emily said. "Is that a good one?"

"Is . . . arsenic? Yes, ma'am. But what you want—"

"I want arsenic."

The druggist looked down at her. She looked back at him, erect, her face like a strained flag. "Why, of course," the druggist said. "If that's what you want. But the law requires you to tell what you are going to use it for."

Miss Emily just stared at him, her head tilted back in order to look him eye for eye, until he looked away and went and got the arsenic and wrapped it up. The Negro delivery boy brought her the package; the druggist didn't come back. When she opened the package at home there was written on the box, under the skull and bones: "For rats."

IV

So the next day we all said, "She will kill herself"; and we said it would be the best thing. When she had first begun to be seen with Homer Barron, we had said, "She will marry him." Then we said, "She will persuade him yet," because Homer himself had remarked—he liked men, and it was known that he drank with the younger men in the Elks' Club—that he was not a marrying man. Later we said, "Poor Emily" behind the jalousies as they passed on Sunday afternoon in the glittering buggy, Miss Emily with her head high and Homer Barron with his hat cocked and cigar in his teeth, reins and whip in a yellow glove.

Then some of the ladies began to say that it was a disgrace to the town and a bad example to the young people. The men did not want to interfere, but at last the ladies forced the Baptist minister—Miss Emily's people were Episcopal—to call upon her. He would never divulge what happened during that interview, but he refused to go back again. The next Sunday they again drove about the streets, and the following day the minister's wife wrote to Miss Emily's relations in Alabama.

So she had blood-kin under her roof again and we sat back to watch developments. At first nothing happened. Then we were sure that they were to be married. We learned that Miss Emily had been to the jeweler's and ordered a man's toilet set in silver, with the letters H. B. on each piece. Two days later we learned that she had bought a complete outfit of men's clothing, including a nightshirt, and we said, "They are married." We were really glad. We were glad because the two female cousins were even more Grierson than Miss Emily had ever been.

So we were not surprised when Homer Barron—the streets had been finished some time since—was gone. We were a little disappointed that there was not a public blowing-off, but we believed that he had gone on to prepare for Miss Emily's coming, or to give her a chance to get rid of the cousins. (By that time it was a cabal, and we were all Miss Emily's allies to help circumvent the cousins.) Sure enough, after another week they departed. And, as we had expected all along, within three days Homer Barron was back in town. A neighbor saw the Negro man admit him at the kitchen door at dusk one evening.

And that was the last we saw of Homer Barron. And of Miss Emily for some time. The Negro man went in and out with the market basket, but the front door remained closed. Now and then we would see her at a window for a moment, as the men did that night when they sprinkled the lime, but for almost six months she did not appear on the streets. Then we knew that this was to be expected too; as if that quality of her father which had thwarted her woman's life so many times had been too virulent and too furious to die.

When we next saw Miss Emily, she had grown fat and her hair was turning gray. During the next few years it grew grayer and grayer until it attained an even pepper-and-salt iron-gray, when it ceased turning. Up to the day of her death at seventy-four it was still that vigorous iron-gray, like the hair of an active man.

From that time on her front door remained closed, save for a period of six or seven years, when she was about forty, during which she gave lessons in china-painting. She fitted up a studio in one of the downstairs rooms, where the daughters and granddaughters of Colonel Sartoris' contemporaries were sent to her with the same regularity and in the same spirit that they were sent to church on Sunday with a twenty-five-cent piece for the collection plate. Meanwhile her taxes had been remitted.

Then the newer generation became the backbone and the spirit of the town, and the painting pupils grew up and fell away and did not send their children to her with boxes of color and tedious brushes and pictures cut from the ladies' magazines. The front door closed upon the last one and remained closed for good. When the town got free postal delivery, Miss Emily alone refused to let them fasten the metal numbers above her door and attach a mailbox to it. She would not listen to them.

Daily, monthly, yearly we watched the Negro grow grayer and more stooped, going in and out with the market basket. Each December we sent her a tax notice, which would be returned by the post office a week later, unclaimed. Now and then we would see her in one of the downstairs windows—she had evidently shut up the top floor of the house—like the carven torso of an idol in a niche, looking or not looking at us, we could never tell which. Thus she passed from generation to generation—dear, inescapable, impervious, tranquil, and perverse.

And so she died. Fell ill in the house filled with dust and shadows, with only a doddering Negro man to wait on her. We did not even know she was sick; we had long since given up trying to get any information from the Negro. He talked to no one, probably not even to her, for his voice had grown harsh and rusty, as if from disuse.

She died in one of the downstairs rooms, in a heavy walnut bed with a curtain, her gray head propped on a pillow yellow and moldy with age and lack of sunlight.

V

The Negro met the first of the ladies at the front door and let them in, with their hushed, sibilant voices and their quick, curious glances, and then he disappeared. He walked right through the house and out the back and was not seen again.

The two female cousins came at once. They held the funeral on the second day, with the town coming to look at Miss Emily beneath a mass of bought flowers, with the crayon face of her father musing profoundly above the bier and the ladies sibilant and macabre; and the very old men—some in their brushed Confederate uniforms—on the porch and the lawn, talking of Miss Emily as if she had been a contemporary of theirs, believing that they had danced with her and courted her perhaps, confusing time with its mathematical progression, as the old do, to whom all the past is not a diminishing road but, instead, a huge meadow which no winter ever quite touches, divided from them now by the narrow bottle-neck of the most recent decade of years.

Already we knew that there was one room in that region above stairs which no one had seen in forty years, and which would have to be forced. They waited until Miss Emily was decently in the ground before they opened it.

The violence of breaking down the door seemed to fill this room with pervading dust. A thin, acrid pall of the tomb seemed to lie everywhere upon this room decked and furnished as for a bridal: upon the valance curtains of faded rose color, upon the rose-shaded lights, upon the dressing table, upon the delicate array of crystal and the man's toilet things backed with tarnished silver, silver so tarnished that the monogram was obscured. Among them lay a collar and tie, as if they had just been removed, which, lifted, left upon the surface a pale crescent in the dust. Upon a chair hung the suit, carefully folded; beneath it the two mute shoes and the discarded socks.

The man himself lay in the bed.

For a long while we just stood there, looking down at the profound and fleshless grin. The body had apparently once lain in the attitude of an embrace, but now the long sleep that outlasts love, that conquers even the grimace of love, had cuckolded him. What was left of him, rotted beneath what was left of the nightshirt, had become inextricable from the bed in which he lay; and upon him and upon the pillow beside him lay that even coating of the patient and biding dust.

Then we noticed that in the second pillow was the indentation of a head. One of us lifted something from it, and leaning forward, that faint and invisible dust dry and acrid in the nostrils, we saw a long strand of iron-gray hair.

1930

STUDY QUESTIONS

1. Part of the effectiveness of "A Rose for Emily" comes from its surprise ending. How effective do you find the ending? Why?
2. How do the narrator and the townsfolk view the young Miss Emily? How does Miss Emily change with time? How does the town? How does the narrator's view of Miss Emily change? How does yours?

Anxiety

Grace Paley (1922–   )

See page 90 for a biographical note on the author.

The young fathers are waiting outside the school. What curly heads! Such grace-ful brown mustaches. They're sitting on their haunches eating pizza and ex-changing information. They're waiting for the 3 p.m. bell. It's springtime, the season of first looking out the window. I have a window box of greenhouse marigolds. The young fathers can be seen through the ferny leaves.

The bell rings. The children fall out of school, tumbling through the open door. One of the fathers sees his child. A small girl. Is she Chinese? A little. Up u-u-p, he says, and hoists her to his shoulders. U-u-p, says the second father, and hoists his little boy. The little boy sits on top of his father's head for a couple of seconds before sliding to his shoulders. Very funny, says the father.

They start off down the street, right under and past my window. The two children are still laughing. They try to whisper a secret. The fathers haven't fin-ished their conversation. The frailer father is uncomfortable; his little girl wig-gles too much.

Stop it this minute, he says.

Oink oink, says the little girl.

What'd you say?

Oink oink, she says.

The young father says What! three times. Then he seizes the child, raises her high above his head, and sets her hard on her feet.

What'd I do so bad, she says, rubbing her ankle.

Just hold my hand, screams the frail and angry father.

I lean far out the window. Stop! Stop! I cry.

The young father turns, shading his eyes, but sees. What? he says. His friend says, Hey? Who's that? He probably thinks I'm a family friend, a teacher maybe.

Who're you? he says.

I move the pots of marigold aside. Then I'm able to lean on my elbow way out into unshadowed visibility. Once, not too long ago, the tenements were speckled with women like me in every third window up to the fifth story, calling the children from play to receive orders and instruction. This memory enables me to say strictly, Young man, I am an older person who feels free because of that to ask questions and give advice.

Oh? he says, laughs with a little embarrassment, says to his friend, Shoot if you will that old gray head. But he's joking, I know, because he has established himself, legs apart, hands behind his back, his neck arched to see and hear me out.

How old are you? I call. About thirty or so?

Thirty-three.

First I want to say you're about a generation ahead of your father in your attitude and behavior toward your child.

Really? Well? Anything else, ma'am.

Son, I said, leaning another two, three dangerous inches toward him. Son, I must tell you that madmen intend to destroy this beautifully made planet. That the murder of our children by these men has got to become a terror and a sorrow to you, and starting now, it had better interfere with any daily pleasure.

Speech speech, he called.

I waited a minute, but he continued to look up. So, I said, I can tell by your general appearance and loping walk that you agree with me.

I do, he said, winking at his friend; but turning a serious face to mine, he said again, Yes, yes, I do.

Well then, why did you become so angry at that little girl whose future is like a film which suddenly cuts to white. Why did you nearly slam this little doomed person to the ground in your uncontrollable anger.

Let's not go too far, said the young father. She *was* jumping around on my poor back and hollering oink oink.

When were you angriest—when she wiggled and jumped or when she said oink?

He scratched his wonderful head of dark well-cut hair. I guess when she said oink.

Have you ever said oink oink? Think carefully. Years ago, perhaps?

No. Well maybe. Maybe.

Whom did you refer to in this way?

He laughed. He called to his friend, Hey Ken, this old person's got something. The cops. In a demonstration. Oink oink, he said, remembering, laughing.

The little girl smiled and said, Oink oink.

Shut up, he said.

What do you deduce from this?

That I was angry at Rosie because she was dealing with me as though I was a figure of authority, and it's not my thing, never has been, never will be.

I could see his happiness, his nice grin, as he remembered this.

So, I continued, since those children are such lovely examples of what may well be the last generation of humankind, why don't you start all over again, right from the school door, as though none of this had ever happened.

Thank you, said the young father. Thank you. It would be nice to be a horse, he said, grabbing little Rosie's hand. Come on Rosie, let's go. I don't have all day.

U-up, says the first father. U-up, says the second.

Giddap, shout the children, and the fathers yell neigh neigh, as horses do. The children kick their fathers' horsechests, screaming giddap giddap, and they gallop wildly westward.

I lean way out to cry once more, Be careful! Stop! But they've gone too far. Oh, anyone would love to be a fierce fast horse carrying a beloved beautiful rider, but they are galloping toward one of the most dangerous street corners in the world. And they may live beyond that trisection across other dangerous avenues.

So I must shut the window after patting the April-cooled marigolds with their rusty smell of summer. Then I sit in the nice light and wonder how to make sure that they gallop safely home through the airy scary dreams of scientists and the bulky dreams of automakers. I wish I could see just how they sit down at their kitchen tables for a healthy snack (orange juice or milk and cookies) before going out into the new spring afternoon to play.

1985

STUDY QUESTIONS

1. This is a tale of a sidewalk scene and a brief conversation. How does Paley build a story from such commonplace materials?
2. Why is the narrator so concerned about the children's future? What beliefs do she and the young fathers share? (Note particularly the significance of the phrase "Oink oink.")
3. Given this larger concern, why is the narrator's concern for the affairs of the immediate moment so sharp?
4. Does the conversation strike you as something that might really happen or as something that the narrator is imagining, as she imagines the last part of the story? Discuss your reasoning.

CREATIVE WRITING EXERCISE

Have you ever wanted to give someone advice that would make him or her change his or her actions, as Paley's narrator does? Write a brief story or sketch in which you hold this conversation with that person.

Dream-Vision

Tillie Olsen (1913–)

Born in Nebraska of Russian immigrant parents, Tillie Olsen worked at a variety of jobs to support herself and her family. She was a meat packer, waitress, and domestic worker before the age of twenty. The mother of four children, she eventually married a fellow labor organizer and Communist party member. She and her husband were harassed by the FBI during the McCarthy years for their political activities. In the 1960s she began to be recognized as an important writer whose work connects the concerns about economic equality of the 1930s with the feminist and racial equality movements of the post–World War II period.

In the winter of 1955, in her last weeks of life, my mother—so much of whose waking life had been a nightmare, that common everyday nightmare of hardship, limitation, longing; of baffling struggle to raise six children in a world hostile to human unfolding—my mother, dying of cancer, had beautiful dreamvisions—in color.

Already beyond calendar time, she could not have known that the last dream she had breath to tell came to her on Christmas Eve. Nor, conscious, would she have named it so. As a girl in long ago Czarist Russia, she had sternly broken with all observances of organized religion, associating it with pogroms and wars; "mind forg'd manacles"; a repressive state. We did not observe religious holidays in her house.

Perhaps, in her last consciousness, she *did* know that the year was drawing towards that solstice time of the shortest light, the longest dark, the cruelest cold, when—as she had explained to us as children—poorly sheltered ancient peoples in northern climes had summoned their resources to make out of song, light and food, expressions of human love—festivals of courage, hope, warmth, belief.

It seemed to her that there was a knocking at her door. Even as she rose to open it, she guessed who would be there, for she heard the neighing of camels. (I did not say to her: "Ma, camels don't neigh.") Against the frosty lights of a far city she had never seen, "a city holy to three faiths," she said, the three wise men stood: magnificent in jewelled robes of crimson, of gold, of royal blue.

"Have you lost your way?" she asked, "Else, why do you come to me? I am not religious, I am not a believer."

"To talk with *you*, we came," the wise man whose skin was black and robe crimson assured her, "to talk of whys, of wisdom."

"Come in then, come in and be warm—and welcome. I have starved all my life for such talk."

But as they began to talk, she saw that they were not men, but women;

That they were not dressed in jewelled robes, but in the coarse everyday shifts and shawls of the old country women of her childhood, their feet wrapped round and round with rags for lack of boots; snow now sifting into the room;

That their speech was not highflown, but homilies; their bodies not lordly in bearing, magnificent, but stunted, misshapen—used all their lives as beasts of burden are used;

That the camels were not camels, but farm beasts, such as were kept in the house all winter, their white cow breaths steaming into the cold.

And now it was many women, a babble.

One old woman, seamed and bent, began to sing. Swaying, the others joined her, their faces and voices transfiguring as they sang; my mother, through cracked lips, singing too—a lullaby.

For in the shining cloud of their breaths, a baby lay, breathing the universal sounds every human baby makes, sounds out of which are made all the separate languages of the world.

Singing, one by one the women cradled and sheltered the baby.

"The joy, the reason to believe," my mother said, "the hope for the world, the baby, holy with possibility, that is all of us at birth." And she began to cry, out of the dream and its telling now.

"Still I feel the baby in my arms, the human baby," crying now so I could scarcely make out the words, "the human baby before we are misshapen; crucified into a sex, a color, a walk of life, a nationality . . . and the world yet warrings and winter."

I had seen my mother but three times in my adult life, separated as we were by the continent between, by lack of means, by jobs I had to keep and by the needs of my four children. She could scarcely write English—her only education in this country a few months of night school. When at last I flew to her, it was in the last days she had language at all. Too late to talk with her of what was in our hearts; or of harms and crucifying and strengths as she had known and experienced them; or of whys and knowledge, of wisdom. She died a few weeks later.

She, who had no worldly goods to leave, yet left to me an inexhaustible legacy. Inherent in it, this heritage of summoning resources to make out of song, food and warmth, expressions of human love—courage, hope, resistance, belief;

this vision of universality, before the lessenings, harms, divisions of the world are visited upon it.

She sheltered and carried that belief, that wisdom—as she sheltered and carried us, and others—throughout a lifetime lived in a world whose season was, as yet it is, a time of winter.

1984

STUDY QUESTIONS

1. This story combines a description of a woman, a description of her daughter's relationship with her, and a "dream-vision" experienced by the older woman. How are the three interwoven in narrative style? thematically?
2. Would you call this story a tale within a tale? Or do you think that the inner and outer stories are too tightly interwoven for this term to apply? Discuss your reasoning.
3. Discuss the dream-vision itself. How does it fit the character of the mother as the narrator depicts her?
4. Discuss the significance of the story's final phrase, "a time of winter."

9

BEYOND REALITY

In the last chapter, we studied stories that dealt in character study and social commentary in realistic styles and settings. In this chapter, we will look at stories that examine individuals and society by going beyond reality, into **fantasy** or **science fiction**.

The first story, from a nineteenth-century master of fantasy, takes place in a world that could be our own, were it not populated, in part, by exaggerated, fantastic or perhaps even **supernatural** figures. The setting, too, is exaggerated in this and most other fantasy tales: more crowded than usual, more foreboding, more extreme in one way or another. Poe's language, too, insists on these differences, drawing attention to the strangeness of the worlds his stories build.

In contrast, the second story is set thoroughly (indeed, almost depressingly) in the drab world of all-too-real poverty. Into this world of day-to-day crises García Márquez places a single supernatural figure, "a very old man with enormous wings," and then watches the results unfold. The fantasy is thus brought directly into the midst of everyday life. The style, as if to match the setting, is simple and reportorial. All our attention is focused on the characters and their actions.

The third story is science fiction. Vonnegut sets it not in today's world, but in a possible future world. Such future worlds, in science fiction, usually exaggerate one or two traits of today's society, often showing them in an extreme of development. Alternatively, they may show what happens when one form of thinking replaces another, or when some assumption on which we base our society is overturned. The characters, on the other hand, tend to be normal people: the question is, "How will people react, how will they behave, in this changed world?"

Throughout all three stories we may notice that, regardless of what techniques of romanticization or fantasy or scientific theorizing are being used, the emphasis remains on human behavior. The stories are not simple escapism; rather, they are attempts to apply different techniques to the standard questions, to make us look at ourselves and our societies in a new way. Strange as these tales may be, there is no essence in them that we cannot apply directly to our own society, to people we know, perhaps even to ourselves.

The Man of the Crowd

Edgar Allan Poe (1809–1849)

Edgar Allan Poe, along with being a fine critic, the virtual inventor of the detective story, and a memorable if not truly great poet, was the undisputed master of the macabre. In short stories like "The Pit and the Pendulum," "The Fall of the House of Usher," and "The Tell-Tale Heart" he captured the imaginations of readers with well-wrought studies of evil, madness, and death. Sometimes mistakenly confused with his characters, Poe was in fact highly conscious of what the public wanted, and in general was a hard-working and rational man rather than the deranged sort of character usually at the center of his tales. Precocious, willful, married to his young cousin, constantly in financial trouble, Poe was nevertheless a colorful and tragic figure who made a remarkable contribution to literature in his brief lifetime.

> *Ce grand malheur, de ne pouvoir etre seul.*[1]
> —La Bruyere

It was well said of a certain German book that "*er lasst sich nicht lesen*"—it does not permit itself to be read. There are some secrets which do not permit themselves to be told. Men die nightly in their beds, wringing the hands of ghostly confessors, and looking them piteously in the eyes—die with despair of heart and convulsion of throat, on account of the hideousness of mysteries which will not *suffer themselves* to be revealed. Now and then, alas, the conscience of man takes up a burthen so heavy in horror that it can be thrown down only into the grave. And thus the essence of all crime is undivulged.

Not long ago, about the closing in of an evening in autumn, I sat at the large bow window of the D—— Coffee-House in London. For some months I had been ill in health, but was now convalescent, and, with returning strength, found myself in one of those happy moods which are so precisely the converse of *ennui*[2]—moods of the keenest appetency, when the film from the mental vision departs—the αχλυς ος πζιν επτεν[3]—and the intellect, electrified, surpasses as greatly its every-day condition, as does the vivid, yet candid reason of Combe,[4] the mad and flimsy rhetoric of Gorgias.[5] Merely to breathe was enjoyment; and I

---

[1] "The great misery of being unable to be alone."
[2] boredom
[3] "mist that was on it before" (Homer's *Iliad*)
[4] English novelist of the romantic period
[5] skeptical Greek philosopher of the fourth century B.C.

derived positive pleasure even from many of the legitimate sources of pain. I felt a calm but inquisitive interest in every thing. With a cigar in my mouth and a newspaper in my lap, I had been amusing myself for the greater part of the afternoon, now in poring over advertisements, now in observing the promiscuous company in the room, and now in peering through the smoky panes into the street.

This latter is one of the principal thoroughfares of the city, and had been very much crowded during the whole day. But, as the darkness came on, the throng momently increased; and by the time the lamps were well litten two dense and continuous tides of population were rushing past the door. At this particular period of the evening I had never before been in a similar situation, and the tumultuous sea of human heads filled me, therefore, with a delicious novelty of emotion. I gave up at length all care of things within the hotel, and became absorbed in contemplation of the scene without. At first my observations took an abstract and generalizing turn. I looked at the passengers in masses, and thought of them in their aggregate relations. Soon, however, I descended to details, and regarded with minute interest the innumerable varieties of figure, dress, air, gait, visage, and expression of countenance.

By far the greater number of those who went by had a satisfied business-like demeanor, and seemed to be thinking only of making their way through the press. Their brows were knit, and their eyes rolled quickly, when pushed against by fellow-wayfarers they evinced no symptom of impatience, but adjusted their clothes and hurried on. Others, still a numerous class, were restless in their movements, had flushed faces, and talked and gesticulated to themselves, as if feeling in solitude on account of the very denseness of the company around. When impeded in their progress these people suddenly ceased muttering, but redoubled their gesticulations, and awaited, with an absent and overdone smile upon the lips, the course of the persons impeding them. If jostled, they bowed profusely to the jostlers, and appeared overwhelmed with confusion.—There was nothing very distinctive about these two large classes beyond what I have noted. Their habiliments belonged to that order which is pointedly termed the decent. They were undoubtedly noblemen, merchants, attorneys, tradesmen, stockjobbers—the Eupatrids and the common-places of society—men of leisure and men actively engaged in affairs of their own—conducting business upon their own responsibility. They did not greatly excite my attention.

The tribe of clerks was an obvious one, and here I discerned two remarkable divisions. There were the junior clerks of flash houses—young gentlemen with tight coats, bright boots, well-oiled hair, and supercilious lips. Setting aside a certain dapperness of carriage which may be termed deskism for want of a better word, the manner of these persons seemed to me an exact fac-simile of what had been the perfection of *bon ton*[6] about twelve or eighteen months before. They

---

[6]fashion

wore the cast-off graces of the gentry—and this, I believe, involves the best definition of the class.

The division of the upper clerks of staunch firms, or of the "steady old fellows," it was not possible to mistake. These were known by their coats and pantaloons of black or brown, made to sit comfortably, with white cravats and waistcoats, broad solid-looking shoes, and thick hose, or gaiters.—They had all slightly bald heads, from which the right ears, long used to pen-holding, had an odd habit of standing off on end. I observed that they always removed or settled their hats with both hands, and wore watches, with short, gold chains of a substantial and ancient pattern. Theirs was the affectation of respectability—if indeed there be an affectation so honorable.

There were many individuals of dashing appearance, whom I easily set down as belonging to the race of swell pick-pockets, with which all great cities are infested. I watched these gentry with much inquisitiveness, and found it difficult to imagine how they should ever be mistaken for gentlemen by gentlemen themselves. Their voluminousness of wristband, with an air of excessive frankness, should betray them at once.

The gamblers, of whom I descried not a few, were still more easily recognisable. They wore every variety of dress, from that of the desperate thimble-rig[7] bully, with velvet waistcoat, fancy neckerchief, gilt chains, and fillagreed buttons, to that of the scrupulously inornate clergyman, than which nothing could be less liable to suspicion. Still all were distinguished by a certain sodden swarthiness of complexion, a filmy dimness of eye, and pallor and compression of lip. There were two other traits, moreover, by which I could always detect them—a guarded lowness of tone in conversation, and a more than ordinary extension of the thumb in a direction at right angles with the fingers.—Very often in company with these sharpers I observed an order of men somewhat different in habits, but still birds of kindred feather. They may be defined as the gentlemen who live by their wits. They seem to prey upon the public in two battalions—that of the dandies and that of the military men. Of the first grade the leading features are long locks and smiles; of the second frogged coats and frowns.

Descending in the scale of what is termed gentility, I found darker and deeper themes for speculation. I saw Jew pedlars, with hawk eyes flashing from countenances whose every other feature wore only an expression of abject humility; sturdy professional street beggars scowling upon mendicants of a better stamp, whom despair alone had driven forth into the night for charity; feeble and ghastly invalids, upon whom death had placed a sure hand, and who sidled and tottered through the mob looking every one beseechingly in the face, as if in search of some chance consolation, some lost hope; modest young girls returning from long and late labor to a cheerless home, and shrinking more tearfully than indignantly from the glances of ruffians, whose direct contact even could

---

[7] a con man's shell game

not be avoided; women of the town of all kinds and of all ages—the unequivocal beauty in the prime of her womanhood, putting one in mind of the statue of Lucian, with the surface of Parian marble, and the interior filled with filth—the loathsome and utterly lost leper in rags—the wrinkled, bejewelled and paint-begrimed beldame, making a last effort at youth—the mere child of immature form, yet, from long association, an adept in the dreadful coquetries of her trade, and burning with a rabid ambition to be ranked the equal of her elders in vice; drunkards innumerable and indescribable—some in shreds and patches, reeling, inarticulate, with bruised visage and lack-lustre eyes—some in whole although filthy garments, with a slightly unsteady swagger, thick sensual lips, and hearty-looking rubicund faces—others clothed in materials which had once been good, and which even now were scrupulously well-brushed—men who walked with a more than naturally firm and springy step, but whose countenances were fearfully pale, whose eyes hideously wild and red, and who clutched with quivering fingers, as they strode through the crowd, at every object which came within their reach; beside these, pie-men, porters, coal-heavers, sweeps; organ-grinders, monkey-exhibiters and ballad mongers, those who vended with those who sang; ragged artizans and exhausted laborers of every description, and still all full of a noisy and inordinate vivacity which jarred discordantly upon the ear, and gave an aching sensation to the eye.

As the night deepened, so deepened to me the interest of the scene; for not only did the general character of the crowd materially alter (its gentler features retiring in the gradual withdrawal of the more orderly portion of the people, and its harsher ones coming out into bolder relief as the late hour brought forth every species of infamy from its den,) but the rays of the gas-lamps, feeble at first in their struggle with the dying day, had now at length gained ascendency, and threw over every thing a fitful and garish lustre. All was dark yet splendid—as that ebony to which has been likened the style of Tertullian. The wild effects of the light enchained me to an examination of individual faces; and although the rapidity with which the world of life flitted before the window prevented me from casting more than a glance upon each visage, still it seemed that, in my then peculiar mental state, I could frequently read, even in that brief interval of a glance, the history of long years. With my brow to the glass, I was thus occupied in scrutinising the mob, when suddenly there came into view a countenance (that of a decrepid old man, some sixty-five or seventy years of age,) a countenance which at once arrested and absorbed my whole attention, on account of the absolute idosyncrasy of its expression. Any thing even remotely resembling that expression I had never seen before. I well remember that my first thought, upon beholding it, was that Retzch, had he viewed it, would have greatly preferred it to his own pictural incarnations of the fiend. As I endeavored, during the brief minute of my original survey, to form some analysis of the meaning conveyed, there arose confusedly and paradoxically within my mind the ideas of vast mental power, of caution, of penuriousness, of avarice, of coolness, of malice, of blood-thirstiness, of triumph, of merriment, of excessive terror, of intense, of supreme despair. I felt singularly aroused, startled, fascinated. "How wild a history," I said to myself, "is written within that bosom!" Then came a craving desire to keep the man in view—to know more of him. Hurriedly putting on an overcoat, and seizing my hat and cane, I made my way into the street, and pushed through the crowd in the direction which I had seen him take; for he had already disappeared. With some little difficulty I at length came within sight of him, approached, and followed him closely, yet cautiously, so as not to attract his attention.

I had now a good opportunity of examining his person. He was short in stature, very thin, and apparently very feeble. His clothes, generally, were filthy and ragged; but as he came, now and then, within the strong glare of a lamp, I perceived that his linen, although dirty, was of beautiful texture; and my vision deceived me, or, through a rent in a closely-buttoned, and evidently second-handed roquelaire which enveloped him, I caught a glimpse either of a dia-mond, or of a dagger. These observations heightened my curiosity, and I resolved to follow the stranger whithersoever he should go.

It was now fully night-fall, and a thick humid fog hung over the city, threat-ening to end in a settled and heavy rain. This change of weather had an odd ef-fect upon the crowd, the whole of which was at once put into new commotion, and overshadowed by a world of umbrellas. The waver, the jostle, and the hum increased in a tenfold degree. For my own part I did not much regard the rain—the lurking of an old fever in my system rending the moisture somewhat too dangerously pleasant. Tying a handkerchief about my mouth I kept on. For half an hour the old man held his way with difficulty along the great thoroughfare; and I here walked close at his elbow through fear of losing sight of him. Never once turning his head to look back, he did not observe me. By and bye he passed into a cross street, which, although densely filled with people, was not quite so much thronged as the main one he had quitted. Here a change in his demeanor became evident. He walked more slowly and with less object than before—more hesitatingly. He crossed and re-crossed the street way repeatedly without appar-ent aim; and the press was still so thick that at every such movement I was obliged to follow him closely. The street was a narrow and long one, and his course lay within it for nearly an hour, during which the passengers had gradu-ally diminished to about that number which is ordinarily seen at noon in Broad-way near the Park—so vast a difference is there between a London populace and that of the most frequented American city. A second turn brought us into a square, brilliantly litten, and overflowing with life. The old manner of the stranger reappeared. His chin fell upon his breast, while his eyes rolled wildly from under his knit brows in every direction upon those who hemmed him in. He urged his way steadily and perseveringly. I was surprised, however, to find, upon his having made the circuit of the square, that he turned and retraced his steps.—Still more was I astonished to see him repeat the same walk several times—once nearly detecting me as he came round with a sudden movement.

In this exercise he spent about an hour, at the end of which we met with far less interruption from passengers than at first. The rain fell fast; the air grew cool; and the people were retiring to their homes. With a gesture of what seemed to be petulant impatience, the wanderer passed into a bye-street comparatively deserted. Down this, some quarter of a mile long, he rushed with an activity I could not have dreamed of seeing in one so aged, and which put me to much trouble in pursuit. A few minutes brought us to a large and busy bazaar, with the localities of which the stranger appeared well acquainted, and where his original demeanor again became apparent, as he forced his way to and fro, without aim, among the host of buyers and sellers.

During the hour and a half, or thereabouts, which we passed in this place, it required much caution on my part to keep him within reach without attracting his observation. Luckily I wore a pair of gum over-shoes, and could move about in perfect silence. At no moment did he see that I watched him. He entered shop after shop, priced nothing, spoke no word, and looked at all objects with a wild and vacant stare. I was now utterly amazed at his behavior, and firmly resolved that we should not part until I had satisfied myself in some measure respecting him.

A loud-toned clock struck eleven, and the company were fast deserting the bazaar. A shopkeeper, in putting up a shutter, jostled the old man, and at the instant I saw a strong shudder come over his frame. He hurried into the street, looked anxiously around him for an instant, and then ran with incredible swiftness through many crooked and people-less lanes, until we emerged once more upon the great thoroughfare whence we had started—the street of the D———— Hotel. It no longer wore, however, the same aspect. It was still brilliant with gas; but the rain fell fiercely, and there were few persons to be seen. The stranger grew deadly pale. He walked moodily some paces up the once populous avenue, then, with a heavy sigh, turned in the direction of the river, and, plunging through a great variety of devious ways, came out at length in view of one of the principal theatres. It was about being closed, and the audience were thronging from the doors. I saw the old man gasp as if for breath while he threw himself amid the crowd; but I thought that the intense agony of his countenance had, in some measure, abated. His head again fell upon his breast; he appeared as I had seen him at first. I observed that he now took the course in which had gone the greater number of the audience—but, upon the whole, I was at a loss to comprehend the waywardness of his actions.

As he proceeded, the company grew more scattered, and his old uneasiness and vacillation were resumed. For some time he followed closely a party of some ten or twelve roisterers; but from this number one by one dropped off, until three only remained together in a narrow and gloomy lane little frequented. The stranger paused, and, for a moment, seemed lost in thought; then, with every mark of agitation, pursued rapidly a route which brought us to the verge of the city, amid regions very different from those we had hitherto traversed. It was the most noisome quarter of London, where everything wore the worst impress of the most deplorable poverty, and of the most desperate crime. By the dim light of an accidental lamp, tall, antique, worm-eaten, wooden tenements were seen tottering to their fall in directions so many and capricious that scarce the semblance of a passage was discernible between them. The paving-stones lay at random, displaced from their beds by the rankly-growing grass. Horrible filth festered in the dammed-up gutters. The whole atmosphere teemed with desolation. Yet, as we proceeded, the sounds of human life revived by sure degrees, and at length large bands of the most abandoned of a London populace were seen reeling to and fro. The spirits of the old man again flickered up, as a lamp which is near its death-hour.—Once more he strode onward with elastic tread. Suddenly a corner was turned, a blaze of light burst upon our sight, and we stood before one of the huge suburban temples of Intemperance—one of the palaces of the fiend, Gin.

It was now nearly day-break; but a number of wretched inebriates still pressed in and out of the flaunting entrance. With a half shriek of joy the old man forced a passage within, resumed at once his original bearing, and stalked backward and forward, without apparent object, among the throng. He had not been thus long occupied, however, before a rush to the doors gave token that the host was closing them for the night. It was something even more intense than despair that I then observed upon the countenance of the singular being whom I had watched so pertinaciously. Yet he did not hesitate in his career, but with a mad energy retraced his steps at once, to the heart of the mighty London. Long and swiftly he fled, while I followed him in the wildest amazement, resolute not to abandon a scrutiny in which I now felt an interest all-absorbing. The sun arose while we proceeded, and, when we had once again reached that most thronged mart of the populous town, the street of the D——— Hotel, it presented an appearance of human bustle and activity scarcely inferior to what I had seen on the evening before. And here, long, amid the momently increasing confusion, did I persist in my pursuit of the stranger. But, as usual, he walked to and fro, and during the day did not pass from out the turmoil of that street. And, as the shades of the second evening came on, I grew wearied unto death, and, stopping fully in front of the wanderer, gazed at him steadfastly in the face. He noticed me not, but resumed his solemn walk, while I, ceasing to follow, remained absorbed in contemplation. "This old man," I said at length, "is the type and the genius of deep crime. He refuses to be alone. *He is the man of the crowd.* It will be in vain to follow; for I shall learn no more of him, nor of his deeds. The worst heart of the world is a grosser book than the 'Hortulus Animæ,'[8] and perhaps it is but one of the great mercies of God that 'er lasst sich nicht lesen.'"

1840

---

[8]a German book printed in the sixteenth century that included perverse religious illustrations

STUDY QUESTIONS

1. "The Man of the Crowd" is an unusual story in that it contains no dialogue and little in the way of action. How does Poe maintain the reader's interest despite these self-imposed limitations?
2. Does the story operate on a realistic level, or does it involve the supernatural? In what sense is "The Man of the Crowd" a horror story?
3. The narrator concludes that "the man of the crowd" is like a book that "does not permit itself to be read." How do these two ideas—that a being exists who hates to be alone and who is inscrutable—combine to form the story's central idea? Why does an "unreadable" character so disturb the narrator?

A Very Old Man with Enormous Wings: A Tale for Children

Gabriel García Márquez (1928–   )

Gabriel García Márquez is one of the best known of the Latin American and South American writers practicing the "magical realism" of mixing mythical with everyday events in their fiction. Márquez has enjoyed critical as well as popular success with such novels as *One Hundred Years of Solitude* (1967) and *Love in a Time of Cholera* (1988). In 1982 he was awarded the Nobel Prize for literature.

On the third day of rain they had killed so many crabs inside the house that Pelayo had to cross his drenched courtyard and throw them into the sea, because the newborn child had a temperature all night and they thought it was due to the stench. The world had been sad since Tuesday. Sea and sky were a single ash-gray thing and the sands of the beach, which on March nights glimmered like powdered light, had become a stew of mud and rotten shellfish. The light was so weak at noon that when Pelayo was coming back to the house after throwing away the crabs, it was hard for him to see what it was that was moving and groaning in the rear of the courtyard. He had to go very close to see that it was an old man, a very old man, lying face down in the mud, who, in spite of his tremendous efforts, couldn't get up, impeded by his enormous wings.

Frightened by that nightmare, Pelayo ran to get Elisenda, his wife, who was putting compresses on the sick child, and he took her to the rear of the courtyard. They both looked at the fallen body with mute stupor. He was dressed like a ragpicker. There were only a few faded hairs left on his bald skull and very few teeth in his mouth, and his pitiful condition of a drenched great-grandfather had taken away any sense of grandeur he might have had. His huge buzzard wings, dirty and half-plucked, were forever entangled in the mud. They looked at him so long and so closely that Pelayo and Elisenda very soon overcame their surprise and in the end found him familiar. Then they dared speak to him, and he answered in an incomprehensible dialect with a strong sailor's voice. That was how they skipped over the inconvenience of the wings and quite intelligently concluded that he was a lonely castaway from some foreign ship wrecked by the storm. And yet, they called in a neighbor woman who knew everything about life and death to see him, and all she needed was one look to show them their mistake.

"He's an angel," she told them. "He must have been coming for the child, but the poor fellow is so old that the rain knocked him down."

On the following day everyone knew that a flesh-and-blood angel was held captive in Pelayo's house. Against the judgment of the wise neighbor woman, for whom angels in those times were the fugitive survivors of a celestial conspiracy, they did not have the heart to club him to death. Pelayo watched over him all afternoon from the kitchen, armed with his bailiff's club, and before going to bed dragged him out of the mud and locked him up with the hens in the wire chicken coop. In the middle of the night, when the rain stopped, Pelayo and Elisenda were still killing crabs. A short time afterward the child woke up without a fever and with a desire to eat. Then they felt magnanimous and decided to put the angel on a raft with fresh water and provisions for three days and leave him to his fate on the high seas. But when they went out into the courtyard with the first light of dawn, they found the whole neighborhood in front of the chicken coop having fun with the angel, without the slightest reverence, tossing him things to eat through the openings in the wire as if he weren't a supernatural creature but a circus animal.

Father Gonzaga arrived before seven o'clock, alarmed at the strange news. By that time onlookers less frivolous than those at dawn had already arrived and they were making all kinds of conjectures concerning the captive's future. The simplest among them thought that he should be named mayor of the world. Others of sterner mind felt that he should be promoted to the rank of five-star general in order to win all wars. Some visionaries hoped that he could be put to stud in order to implant on earth a race of winged wise men who could take charge of the universe. But Father Gonzaga, before becoming a priest, had been a robust woodcutter. Standing by the wire, he reviewed his catechism in an instant and asked them to open the door so that he could take a close look at that pitiful man who looked more like a huge decrepit hen among the fascinated chickens. He was lying in a corner drying his open wings in the sunlight among the fruit peels and breakfast leftovers that the early risers had thrown him. Alien to the impertinences of the world, he only lifted his antiquarian eyes and murmured something in his dialect when Father Gonzaga went into the chicken coop and said good morning to him in Latin. The parish priest had his first suspicion of an imposter when he saw that he did not understand the language of God or know how to greet His ministers. Then he noticed that seen close up he was much too human: he had an unbearable smell of outdoors, the back side of his wings was strewn with parasites and his main feathers had been mistreated by terrestrial winds, and nothing about him measured up to the proud dignity of angels. Then he came out of the chicken coop and in a brief sermon warned the curious against the risks of being ingenuous. He reminded them that the devil had the bad habit of making use of carnival tricks in order to confuse the unwary. He argued that if wings were not the essential element in determining the difference between a hawk and an airplane, they were even less so in the recognition of angels. Nevertheless, he promised to write a letter to his bishop so that the latter would write to his primate so that the latter would write to the Supreme Pontiff in order to get the final verdict from the highest courts.

His prudence fell on sterile hearts. The news of the captive angel spread with such rapidity that after a few hours the courtyard had the bustle of a marketplace and they had to call in troops with fixed bayonets to disperse the mob that was about to knock the house down. Elisenda, her spine all twisted from sweeping up so much marketplace trash, then got the idea of fencing in the yard and charging five cents admission to see the angel.

The curious came from far away. A traveling carnival arrived with a flying acrobat who buzzed over the crowd several times, but no one paid any attention to him because his wings were not those of an angel but, rather, those of a sidereal bat. The most unfortunate invalids on earth came in search of health: a poor woman who since childhood had been counting her heartbeats and had run out of numbers; a Portuguese man who couldn't sleep because the noise of the stars disturbed him; a sleepwalker who got up at night to undo the things he had done while awake; and many others with less serious ailments. In the midst of that shipwreck disorder that made the earth tremble, Pelayo and Elisenda were happy with fatigue, for in less than a week they had crammed their rooms with money and the line of pilgrims waiting their turn to enter still reached beyond the horizon.

The angel was the only one who took no part in his own act. He spent his time trying to get comfortable in his borrowed nest, befuddled by the hellish heat of the oil lamps and sacramental candles that had been placed along the wire. At first they tried to make him eat some mothballs, which, according to the wisdom of the wise neighbor woman, were the food prescribed for angels. But he turned them down, just as he turned down the papal lunches that the penitents brought him and they never found out whether it was because he was an angel or because he was an old man that in the end he ate nothing but eggplant mush. His only supernatural virtue seemed to be patience. Especially during the first days, when the hens pecked at him, searching for the stellar parasites that proliferated in his wings, and the cripples pulled out feathers to touch their defective parts with, and even the most merciful threw stones at him, trying to get him to rise so they could see him standing. The only time they succeeded in arousing him was when they burned his side with an iron for branding steers, for he had been motionless for so many hours that they thought he was dead. He awoke with a start, ranting in his hermetic language and with tears in his eyes, and he flapped his wings a couple of times, which brought on a whirlwind of chicken dung and lunar dust and a gale of panic that did not seem to be of this world. Although many thought that his reaction had been one not of rage but of pain, from then on they were careful not to annoy him, because the majority understood that his passivity was not that of a hero taking his ease but that of a cataclysm in repose.

Father Gonzaga held back the crowd's frivolity with formulas of maidservant inspiration while awaiting the arrival of a final judgment on the nature of the captive. But the mail from Rome showed no sense of urgency. They spent their time finding out if the prisoner had a navel, if his dialect had any connection with Aramaic, how many times he could fit on the head of a pin, or whether he wasn't just a Norwegian with wings. Those meager letters might have come and gone until the end of time if a providential event had not put an end to the priest's tribulations.

It so happened that during those days, among so many other carnival attractions, there arrived in town the traveling show of the woman who had been changed into a spider for having disobeyed her parents. The admission to see her was not only less than the admission to see the angel, but people were permitted to ask her all manner of questions about her absurd state and to examine her up and down so that no one would ever doubt the truth of her horror. She was a frightful tarantula the size of a ram and with the head of a sad maiden. What was most heart-rending, however, was not her outlandish shape but the sincere affliction with which she recounted the details of her misfortune. While still practically a child she had sneaked out of her parents' house to go to a dance, and while she was coming back through the woods after having danced all night without permission, a fearful thunderclap rent the sky in two and through the crack came the lightning bolt of brimstone that changed her into a spider. Her only nourishment came from the meatballs that charitable souls chose to toss into her mouth. A spectacle like that, full of so much human truth and with such a fearful lesson, was bound to defeat without even trying that of a haughty angel who scarcely deigned to look at mortals. Besides, the few miracles attributed to the angel showed a certain mental disorder, like the blind man who didn't recover his sight but grew three new teeth, or the paralytic who didn't get to walk but almost won the lottery, and the leper whose sores sprouted sunflowers. Those consolation miracles, which were more like mocking fun, had already ruined the angel's reputation when the woman who had been changed into a spider finally crushed him completely. That was how Father Gonzaga was cured forever of his insomnia and Pelayo's courtyard went back to being as empty as during the time it had rained for three days and crabs walked through the bedrooms.

The owners of the house had no reason to lament. With the money they saved they built a two-story mansion with balconies and gardens and high netting so that crabs wouldn't get in during the winter, and with iron bars on the windows so that angels wouldn't get in. Pelayo also set up a rabbit warren close to town and gave up his job as bailiff for good, and Elisenda bought some satin pumps with high heels and many dresses of iridescent silk, the kind worn on Sunday by the most desirable women in those times. The chicken coop was the only thing that didn't receive any attention. If they washed it down with creolin and burned tears of myrrh inside it every so often, it was not in homage to the angel but to drive away the dungheap stench that still hung everywhere like a ghost and was turning the new house into an old one. At first, when the child learned to walk, they were careful that he not get too close to the chicken coop. But then they began to lose their fears and got used to the smell, and before the child got his second teeth he'd gone inside the chicken coop to play, where the wires were falling apart. The angel was no less standoffish with him than with other mortals, but he tolerated the most ingenious infamies with the patience of a dog who had no illusions. They both came down with chicken pox at the same time. The doctor who took care of the child couldn't resist the temptation to listen to the angel's heart, and he found so much whistling in the heart and so many sounds in his kidneys that it seemed impossible for him to be alive. What surprised him most, however, was the logic of his wings. They seemed so natural on that completely human organism that he couldn't understand why other men didn't have them too.

When the child began school it had been some time since the sun and rain had caused the collapse of the chicken coop. The angel went dragging himself about here and there like a stray dying man. They would drive him out of the bedroom with a broom and a moment later find him in the kitchen. He seemed to be in so many places at the same time that they grew to think that he'd been duplicated, that he was reproducing himself all through the house, and the exasperated and unhinged Elisenda shouted that it was awful living in that hell full of angels. He could scarcely eat and his antiquarian eyes had also become so foggy that he went about bumping into posts. All he had left were the bare cannulae of his last feathers. Pelayo threw a blanket over him and extended him the charity of letting him sleep in the shed, and only then did they notice that he had a temperature at night, and was delirious with the tongue twisters of an Old Norwegian. That was one of the few times they became alarmed, for they thought he was going to die and not even the wise neighbor woman had been able to tell them what to do with dead angels.

And yet he not only survived his worst winter, but seemed improved with the first sunny days. He remained motionless for several days in the farthest corner of the courtyard, where no one would see him, and at the beginning of December some large, stiff feathers began to grow on his wings, the feathers of a scarecrow, which looked more like another misfortune of decrepitude. But he must have known the reason for those changes, for he was quite careful that no one should notice them, that no one should hear the sea chanteys that he sometimes sang under the stars. One morning Elisenda was cutting some bunches of onions for lunch when a wind that seemed to come from the high seas blew into the kitchen. Then she went to the window and caught the angel in his first attempts at flight. They were so clumsy that his fingernails opened a furrow in the vegetable patch and he was on the point of knocking the shed down with the ungainly flapping that slipped on the light and couldn't get a grip on the air. But he did manage to gain altitude. Elisenda let out a sigh of relief, for herself and for him, when she saw him pass over the last houses, holding himself up in some way with the risky flapping of a senile vulture. She kept watching him even when she was through cutting the onions and she kept on watching until it was no longer possible for her to see him, because then he was no longer an annoyance in her life but an imaginary dot on the horizon of the sea.

1955

STUDY QUESTIONS

1. A very old man with enormous wings—quite possibly an angel—arrives in a small seaside village. What would you expect to happen? What does happen?
2. Is there any way in which the angel, or his reception, meets your expectations?
3. We have already noted how many stories are built of the careful presentation and accumulation of details. Note the details in this story: the "stellar parasites," the "eggplant mush," the "three extra teeth." What is their cumulative result?
4. What does the story seem to be saying about the people involved with this supernatural episode in the way they treat the angel? in the comparison between the angel and the girl who turned into a spider?
5. How much time passes during this story? How does the narrator show its passage?
6. Why might the author call this "a tale for children"?

Harrison Bergeron

Kurt Vonnegut (1922–   )

Kurt Vonnegut was the most popular writer in America in the late 1960s and early 1970s. His novel *Slaughterhouse-Five* (1969) and the movie based on it captured the imaginations of critics and legions of readers. The novel was based on Vonnegut's experience of being captured during the Battle of the Bulge in World War II, and his subsequent detention in Dresden as a prisoner of war. Dresden was destroyed by Allied bombers on February 13, 1945. At least 130,000 civilians died, but Vonnegut and some of his fellow prisoners and their guards survived because they were quartered in a meat locker—a slaughterhouse—sixty feet below the ground. Vonnegut began his career as a writer of science fiction stories, but his later work might be called political realism. In such recent novels as *Jailbird* (1979), *Galapagos* (1985), and *Bluebeard* (1987) he deals, respectively, with Watergate, evolution, and the place of the artist in postmodern society.

The year was 2081, and everybody was finally equal. They weren't only equal before God and the law. They were equal every which way. Nobody was smarter than anybody else. Nobody was better looking than anybody else. Nobody was stronger or quicker than anybody else. All this equality was due to the 211th, 212th, and 213th Amendments to the Constitution, and to the unceasing vigilance of agents of the United States Handicapper General.

Some things about living still weren't quite right, though. April, for instance, still drove people crazy by not being springtime. And it was in that clammy month that the H-G men took George and Hazel Bergeron's fourteen-year-old son, Harrison, away.

It was tragic, all right, but George and Hazel couldn't think about it very hard. Hazel had a perfectly average intelligence, which meant she couldn't think about anything except in short bursts. And George, while his intelligence was way above normal, had a little mental handicap radio in his ear. He was required by law to wear it at all times. It was tuned to a government transmitter. Every twenty seconds or so, the transmitter would send out some sharp noise to keep people like George from taking unfair advantage of their brains.

George and Hazel were watching television. There were tears on Hazel's cheeks, but she'd forgotten for the moment what they were about.

On the television screen were ballerinas.

A buzzer sounded in George's head. His thoughts fled in panic, like bandits from a burglar alarm.

"That was a real pretty dance, that dance they just did," said Hazel.

"Huh?" said George.

"That dance—it was nice," said Hazel.

"Yup," said George. He tried to think a little about the ballerinas. They weren't really very good—no better than anybody else would have been, anyway. They were burdened with sashweights and bags of birdshot, and their faces were masked, so that no one, seeing a free and graceful gesture or a pretty face, would feel like something the cat drug in. George was toying with the vague notion that maybe dancers shouldn't be handicapped. But he didn't get very far with it before another noise in his ear radio scattered his thoughts.

George winced. So did two out of the eight ballerinas.

Hazel saw him wince. Having no mental handicap herself, she had to ask George what the latest sound had been.

"Sounded like somebody hitting a milk bottle with a ball peen hammer," said George.

"I'd think it would be real interesting, hearing all the different sounds," said Hazel, a little envious. "All the things they think up."

"Um," said George.

"Only, if I was Handicapper General, you know what I would do?" said Hazel. Hazel, as a matter of fact, bore a strong resemblance to the Handicapper General, a woman name Diana Moon Glampers. "If I was Diana Moon Glampers," said Hazel, "I'd have chimes on Sunday—just chimes. Kind of in honor of religion."

"I could think, if it was just chimes," said George.

"Well—maybe make 'em real loud," said Hazel. "I think I'd made a good Handicapper General."

"Good as anybody else," said George.

"Who knows better'n I do what normal is?" said Hazel.

"Right," said George. He began to think glimmeringly about his abnormal son who was now in jail, about Harrison, but a twenty-one-gun salute in his head stopped that.

"Boy!" said Hazel, "that was a doozy, wasn't it?"

It was such a doozy that George was white and trembling, and tears stood on the rims of his red eyes. Two of the eight ballerinas had collapsed to the studio floor, were holding their temples.

"All of a sudden you look so tired," said Hazel. "Why don't you stretch out on the sofa, so's you can rest your handicap bag on the pillows, honeybunch." She was referring to the forty-seven pounds of birdshot in a canvas bag, which was padlocked around George's neck. "Go on and rest the bag for a little while," she said. "I don't care if you're not equal to me for a while."

George weighed the bag with his hands. "I don't mind it," he said. "I don't notice it any more. It's just a part of me."

"You been so tired lately—kind of wore out," said Hazel. "If there was just some way we could make a little hole in the bottom of the bag, and just take out a few of them lead balls. Just a few."

"Two years in prison and two thousand dollars fine for every ball I took out," said George. "I don't call that a bargain."

"If you could just take a few out when you came home from work," said Hazel. "I mean—you don't compete with anybody around here. You just set around."

"If I tried to get away with it," said George, "then other people'd get away with it—and pretty soon we'd be right back to the dark ages again, with everybody competing against everybody else. You wouldn't like that, would you?"

"I'd hate it," said Hazel.

"There you are," said George. "The minute people start cheating on laws, what do you think happens to society?"

If Hazel hadn't been able to come up with an answer to this question, George couldn't have supplied one. A siren was going off in his head.

"Reckon it'd fall all apart," said Hazel.

"What would?" said George blankly.

"Society," said Hazel uncertainly. "Wasn't that what you just said?"

"Who knows?" said George.

The television program was suddenly interrupted for a news bulletin. It wasn't clear at first as to what the bulletin was about, since the announcer, like all announcers, had a serious speech impediment. For about half a minute, and in a state of high excitement, the announcer tried to say, "Ladies and gentlemen—"

He finally gave up, handed the bulletin to a ballerina to read.

"That's all right—" Hazel said of the announcer, "he tried. That's the big thing. He tried to do the best he could with what God gave him. He should get a nice raise for trying so hard."

"Ladies and gentlemen—" said the ballerina, reading the bulletin. She must have been extraordinarily beautiful, because the mask she wore was hideous. And it was easy to see that she was the strongest and most graceful of all the dancers, for her handicap bags were as big as those worn by two-hundred-pound men.

And she had to apologize at once for her voice, which was a very unfair voice for a woman to use. Her voice was a warm, luminous, timeless melody. "Excuse me—" she said, and she began again, making her voice absolutely un-competitive.

"Harrison Bergeron, age fourteen," she said in a grackle squawk, "has just escaped from jail, where he was held on suspicion of plotting to overthrow the government. He is a genius and an athlete, is underhandicapped, and should be regarded as extremely dangerous."

A police photograph of Harrison Bergeron was flashed on the screen upside down, then sideways, upside down again, then right side up. The picture showed the full length of Harrison against a background calibrated in feet and inches. He was exactly seven feet tall.

The rest of Harrison's appearance was Halloween and hardware. Nobody had ever borne heavier handicaps. He had outgrown hindrances faster than the H-G men could think them up. Instead of a little ear radio for a mental handi-cap, he wore a tremendous pair of earphones, and spectacles with thick wavy lenses. The spectacles were intended to make him not only half blind, but to give him whanging headaches besides.

Scrap metal was hung all over him. Ordinarily, there was a certain symme-try, a military neatness to the handicaps issued to strong people, but Harrison looked like a walking junkyard. In the race of life, Harrison carried three hun-dred pounds.

And to offset his good looks, the H-G men required that he wear at all times a red rubber ball for a nose, keep his eyebrows shaved off, and cover his even white teeth with black caps at snaggle-tooth random.

"If you see this boy," said the ballerina, "do not—I repeat, do not—try to reason with him."

There was the shriek of a door being torn from its hinges.

Screams and barking cries of consternation came from the television set. The photograph of Harrison Bergeron on the screen jumped again and again, as though dancing to the tune of an earthquake.

George Bergeron correctly identified the earthquake, and well he might have—for many was the time his own home had danced to the same crashing tune. "My God—" said George, "that must be Harrison!"

The realization was blasted from his mind instantly by the sound of an automobile collision in his head.

When George could open his eyes again, the photograph of Harrison was gone. A living, breathing Harrison filled the screen.

Clanking, clownish, and huge, Harrison stood in the center of the studio. The knob of the uprooted studio door was still in his hand. Ballerinas, technicians, musicians, and announcers cowered on their knees before him, expecting to die.

"I am the Emperor!" cried Harrison. "Do you hear? I am the Emperor! Everybody must do what I say at once!" He stamped his foot and the studio shook.

"Even as I stand here—" he bellowed, "crippled, hobbled, sickened—I am a greater ruler than any man who ever lived! Now watch me become what I *can* become!"

Harrison tore the straps of his handicap harness like wet tissue paper, tore straps guaranteed to support five thousand pounds.

Harrison's scrap-iron handicaps crashed to the floor.

Harrison thrust his thumbs under the bar of the padlock that secured his head harness. The bar snapped like celery. Harrison smashed his headphones and spectacles against the wall.

He flung away his rubber-ball nose, revealed a man that would have awed Thor, the god of thunder.

"I shall now select my Empress!" he said, looking down on the cowering people. "Let the first woman who dares rise to her feet claim her mate and her throne!"

A moment passed, and then a ballerina arose, swaying like a willow.

Harrison plucked the mental handicap from her ear, snapped off her physical handicaps with marvelous delicacy. Last of all, he removed her mask.

She was blindingly beautiful.

"Now—" said Harrison, taking her hand, "shall we show the people the meaning of the word *dance*? Music!" he commanded.

The musicians scrambled back into their chairs, and Harrison stripped them of their handicaps, too. "Play your best," he told them, "and I'll make you barons and dukes and earls."

The music began. It was normal at first—cheap, silly, false. But Harrison snatched two musicians from their chairs, waved them like batons as he sang the music as he wanted it played. He slammed them back into their chairs.

The music began again and was much improved.

Harrison and his Empress merely listened to the music for a while—listened gravely, as though synchronizing their heartbeats with it.

They shifted their weights to their toes.

Harrison placed his big hands on the girl's tiny waist, letting her sense the weightlessness that would soon be hers.

And then, in an explosion of joy and grace, into the air they sprang!

Not only were the laws of the land abandoned, but the law of gravity and the laws of motion as well.

They reeled, whirled, swiveled, flounced, capered, gamboled, and spun.

They leaped like deer on the moon.

The studio ceiling was thirty feet high, but each leap brought the dancers nearer to it.

It became their obvious intention to kiss the ceiling.

They kissed it.

And then, neutralizing gravity with love and pure will, they remained suspended in air inches below the ceiling, and they kissed each other for a long, long time.

It was then that Diana Moon Glampers, the Handicapper General, came into the studio with a double-barreled ten-gauge shotgun. She fired twice, and the Emperor and the Empress were dead before they hit the floor.

Diana Moon Glampers loaded the gun again. She aimed it at the musicians and told them they had ten seconds to get their handicaps back on.

It was then that the Bergerons' television tube burned out.

Hazel turned to comment about the blackout to George. But George had gone out into the kitchen for a can of beer.

George came back in with the beer, paused while a handicap signal shook him up. And then he sat down again. "You been crying?" he said to Hazel.

"Yup," she said.

"What about?" he said.

"I forget," she said. "Something real sad on television."

"What was it?" he said.

"It's all kind of mixed up in my mind," said Hazel.

"Forget sad things," said George.

"I always do," said Hazel.

1961

STUDY QUESTIONS

1. How is the society depicted in "Harrison Bergeron" comparable to today's society? How does it differ?
2. Do you feel that the differences are true differences, or that they merely make extreme or explicit problems that exist today? Or are both points of view true?

3. Note the story's depiction of two characters' rebellion and escape, and the audience's reaction to it. How does this climactic act fit into your comparison and contrast of this imaginative society to our own society?

4. In both "A Very Old Man with Enormous Wings" and "Harrison Bergeron," something surprising happens, and the onlookers fail to give wholehearted response. In each case, why? What might this suggest about the techniques of the two writers?

10

AUTOBIOGRAPHY

In these chapter introductions, we've talked a great deal about fiction giving us insights into society and individuals. In fact, though, the communities and individuals that we each know best are those with which we grow up and in which we live as adults.

Many authors draw from their own experiences when creating their fiction, disguising it lightly or heavily. Other writers, discarding the masks of fiction, write about their experiences directly, in **autobiographies** or **memoirs**. These writers can "name names" and be as open as they like in describing the communities in which they were brought up, the people who influenced them, and their own thoughts, feelings, and actions throughout the various stages of their development. Such writings can be remarkably important, for they give us, as no other writings can, firsthand looks at communities we cannot visit directly.

As to form, the autobiography promises a relatively complete study of the writer's life, from the beginning to the point where the book ends. For this reason, autobiographies are often written in several volumes, with each volume carrying the story over a further span of years. Memoirs are somewhat less formal. They do not promise completeness in discussing the writer's life. Instead, their technique is often aimed at illuminating the high points and passing quickly over the rest. In compensation, they often include fuller discussions of people whom the writer found influential. Their structure may be looser than that of the autobiography, the focus more inclusive of family or community.

This chapter presents three selections from autobiographical works. The works are far too long to be included here in their entirety, so we have chosen samples from each. The first selection comes from three chapters of Mark Twain's *Old Times on the Mississippi* and tells of Twain's training as a riverboat pilot—a tale he wished to tell before those days vanished into history with the steamboats. The second selection comes from *I Know Why the Caged Bird Sings*, the first volume of Maya Angelou's autobiography. This selection describes the revival meetings that came at intervals to the rural Southern community where she and her brother were being brought up by their grandmother, and how those meetings appeared to the young girl. The final selection might be called "faction" (a blending of fact and fiction) rather than straight autobiography, but Michael Herr's *Dispatches* is clearly the vivid product of his actual experience in Vietnam.

As you read these selections, you will notice that all the techniques available to fiction writers are equally available to writers of autobiographical material. A writer of autobiography cannot construct a fictional climax for an incident but can direct our attention, by skillful writing, to an actual climax that we might otherwise not have recognized. They can use voices creatively: Twain uses his finest "story-telling" voice throughout, but Angelou and Herr both use multiple voices in their work. Both slip easily from first person to third person. (Angelou does this within the selection we read.) To this, Herr adds the use of "stream of consciousness," a twentieth-century technique in which the writer attempts to record someone's thoughts as they occur, with all the illogical shifts of direction that such streams of thought normally contain.

These selections, therefore, are to be enjoyed for their artistry as much as for the illumination they provide. Each shows the writer's ability to focus on sharply remembered moments—on a trick played on one, a new toy, a sermon, a song— and, by brilliantly telling about them, making them illuminate the time, place, and people of which the writers tell.

From Old Times on the Mississippi

Mark Twain (1835–1910)

See page 130 for a biographical note on the author.

From II. A "Cub" Pilot's Experience; or, Learning the River

The *Paul Jones* was now bound for St. Louis. I planned a siege against my pilot, and at the end of three hard days he surrendered. He agreed to teach me the Mississippi River from New Orleans to St. Louis for five hundred dollars, payable out of the first wages I should receive after graduating. I entered upon the small enterprise of "learning" twelve or thirteen hundred miles of the great Mississippi River with the easy confidence of my time of life. If I had really known what I was about to require of my faculties, I should not have had the courage to begin. I supposed that all a pilot had to do was to keep his boat in the river, and I did not consider that that could be much of a trick, since it was so wide.

The boat backed out from New Orleans at four in the afternoon, and it was "our watch" until eight. Mr. Bixby, my chief, "straightened her up," plowed her along past the sterns of the other boats that lay at the Levee, and then said, "Here, take her; shave those steamships as close as you'd peel an apple." I took the wheel and my heart went down into my boots; for it seemed to me that we were about to scrape the side off every ship in the line, we were so close. I held my breath and began to claw the boat away from the danger, and I had my own opinion of the pilot who had known no better than to get us into such peril, but I was too wise to express it. In half a minute I had a wide margin of safety intervening between the *Paul Jones* and the ships, and within ten seconds more I was set aside in disgrace and Mr. Bixby was going into danger again and flaying me alive with abuse of my cowardice. I was stung but I was obliged to admire the easy confidence with which my chief loafed from side to side of his wheel and trimmed the ships so closely that disaster seemed ceaselessly imminent. When he had cooled a little he told me that the easy water was close ashore and the current outside, and therefore we must hug the bank up-stream, to get the benefit of the former, and stay well out down-stream, to take advantage of the latter. In my own mind I resolved to be a down-stream pilot and leave the up-streaming to people dead to prudence.

Now and then Mr. Bixby called my attention to certain things. Said he, "This is Six-Mile Point." I assented. It was pleasant enough information but I could not see the bearing of it. I was not conscious that it was a matter of any interest to me. Another time he said, "This is Nine-Mile Point." Later he said, "This is Twelve-Mile Point." They were all about level with the water's edge; they all looked about alike to me; they were monotonously unpicturesque. I hoped Mr. Bixby would change the subject. But no, he would crowd up around a point, hugging the shore with affection, and then say: "The slack water ends here, abreast this bunch of China trees; now we cross over." So he crossed over. He gave me the wheel once or twice but I had no luck. I either came near chipping off the edge of a sugar-plantation, or I yawed too far from shore and so dropped back into disgrace again and got abused. . . .

It was a rather dingy night, although a fair number of stars were out. The big mate was at the wheel and he had the old tub pointed at a star and was holding her straight up the middle of the river. The shores on either hand were not much more than half a mile apart, but they seemed wonderfully far away and ever so vague and indistinct. The mate said:

"We've got to land at Jones's plantation, sir."

The vengeful spirit in me exulted. I said to myself, "I wish you joy of your job, Mr. Bixby; you'll have a good time finding Mr. Jones's plantation such a night as this, and I hope you never *will* find it as long as you live."

Mr. Bixby said to the mate:

"Upper end of the plantation, or the lower?"

"Upper."

"I can't do it. The stumps there are out of water at this stage. It's no great distance to the lower and you'll have to get along with that."

"All right, sir. If Jones don't like it, he'll have to lump it, I reckon."

And then the mate left. My exultation began to cool and my wonder to come up. Here was a man who not only proposed to find this plantation on such a night but to find either end of it you preferred. I dreadfully wanted to ask a question, but I was carrying about as many short answers as my cargo-room would admit of, so I held my peace. All I desired to ask Mr. Bixby was the simple question whether he was ass enough to really imagine he was going to find that plantation on a night when all plantations were exactly alike and all of the same color. But I held in. I used to have fine inspirations of prudence in those days.

Mr. Bixby made for the shore and soon was scraping it, just the same as if it had been daylight. And not only that but singing:

"Father in heaven, the day is declining," etc.

It seemed to me that I had put my life in the keeping of a peculiarly reckless outcast. Presently he turned on me and said:

"What's the name of the first point above New Orleans?"

I was gratified to be able to answer promptly, and I did. I said I didn't know.

"Don't *know?*"

This manner jolted me. I was down at the foot again, in a moment. But I had to say just what I had said before.

"Well, you're a smart one!" said Mr. Bixby. "What's the name of the *next* point?"

Once more I didn't know.

"Well, this beats anything. Tell me the name of *any* point or place I told you."

I studied awhile and decided that I couldn't.

"Look here! What do you start out from, above Twelve-Mile Point, to cross over?"

"I—I—don't know."

"You—you—don't know?" mimicking my drawling manner of speech. "What *do* you know?"

"I—I—nothing, for certain."

"By the great Caesar's ghost, I believe you! You're the stupidest dunderhead I ever saw or ever heard of, so help me Moses! The idea of *you* being a pilot—*you!* Why, you don't know enough to pilot a cow down a lane."

Oh, but his wrath was up! He was a nervous man, and he shuffled from one side of his wheel to the other as if the floor was hot. He would boil awhile to himself and then overflow and scald me again.

"Look here! What do you suppose I told you the names of those points for?"

I tremblingly considered a moment and then the devil of temptation provoked me to say:

"Well to—to—be entertaining, I thought."

This was a red rag to the bull. He raged and stormed so (he was crossing the river at the time) that I judged it made him blind, because he ran over the steering-oar of a trading-scow. Of course the traders sent up a volley of red-hot profanity. Never was a man so grateful as Mr. Bixby was, because he was brimful and here were subjects who could *talk back*. He threw open a window, thrust his head out, and such an irruption followed as I never had heard before. The fainter and farther away the scowmen's curses drifted, the higher Mr. Bixby lifted his voice and the weightier his adjectives grew. When he closed the window he was empty. You could have drawn a seine through his system and not caught curses enough to disturb your mother with. Presently he said to me in the gentlest way:

"My boy, you must get a little memorandum-book, and every time I tell you a thing, put it down right away. There's only one way to be a pilot and that is to get this entire river by heart. You have to know it just like ABC."

That was a dismal revelation to me, for my memory was never loaded with anything but blank cartridges. However, I did not feel discouraged long. I judged that it was best to make some allowances, for doubtless Mr. Bixby was "stretching." Presently he pulled a rope and struck a few strokes on the big bell. The stars were all gone now and the night was as black as ink. I could hear the wheels churn along the bank but I was not entirely certain that I could see the shore. The voice of the invisible watchman called up from the hurricane-deck:

"What's this, sir?"

"Jones's plantation."

I said to myself, "I wish I might venture to offer a small bet that it isn't." But I did not chirp. I only waited to see. Mr. Bixby handled the engine-bells and in due time the boat's nose came to the land, a torch glowed from the forecastle, a man skipped ashore, a darky's voice on the bank said: "Gimme de k'yarpet-bag, Mass' Jones," and the next moment we were standing up the river again, all serene. I reflected deeply awhile, and then said—but not aloud—"Well, the finding of that plantation was the luckiest accident that ever happened, but it couldn't happen again in a hundred years." And I fully believed it *was* an accident, too.

From iv. Pilot's Education Nearly Completed

I thought I had finished this chapter, but I wish to add a curious thing, while it is in my mind. It is only relevant in that it is connected with piloting. There used to be an excellent pilot on the river, a Mr. X, who was a somnambulist. It was said that if his mind was troubled about a bad piece of river, he was pretty sure to get up and walk in his sleep and do strange things. He was once fellow-pilot for a trip or two with George Ealer, on a great New Orleans passenger-packet. During a considerable part of the first trip George was uneasy but got over it by and by, as X seemed content to stay in his bed when asleep. Late one night the boat was approaching Helena, Ark.; the water was low and the crossing above the town in a very blind and tangled condition. X had seen the crossing since Ealer had and as the night was particularly drizzly, sullen, and dark, Ealer was considering whether he had not better have X called to assist in running the place, when the door opened and X walked in. Now, on very dark nights light is a deadly enemy to piloting; you are aware that if you stand in a lighted room, on such a night, you cannot see things in the street to any purpose, but if you put out the lights and stand in the gloom you can make out objects in the street pretty well. So, on very dark nights pilots do not smoke, they allow no fire in the pilot-house stove if there is a crack which can allow the least ray to escape, they order the furnaces to be curtained with huge tarpaulins and the skylights to be closely blinded.

Then no light whatever issues from the boat. The undefinable shape that now entered the pilot-house had Mr. X's voice. This said:

"Let me take her, George; I've seen this place since you have and it is so crooked that I reckon I can run it myself easier than I could tell you how to do it."

"It is kind of you and I swear *I* am willing. I haven't got another drop of perspiration left in me. I have been spinning around and around the wheel like a squirrel. It is so dark I can't tell which way she is swinging till she is coming around like a whirligig."

So Ealer took a seat on the bench, panting and breathless. The black phantom assumed the wheel without saying anything, steadied the waltzing steamer with a turn or two, and then stood at ease, coaxing her a little to this side and then to that, as gently and as sweetly as if the time had been noonday. When Ealer observed this marvel of steering, he wished he had not confessed! He stared and wondered, and finally said:

"Well, I thought I knew how to steer a steamboat but that was another mistake of mine."

X said nothing but went serenely on with his work. He rang for the leads; he rang to slow down the steam; he worked the boat carefully and neatly into invisible marks, then stood at the center of the wheel and peered blandly out into the blackness, fore and aft, to verify his position, as the leads shoaled more and more he stopped the engines entirely, and the dead silence and suspense of "drifting" followed; when the shoalest water was struck, he cracked on the steam, carried her handsomely over, and then began to work her warily into the next system of shoal-marks; the same patient, heedful use of leads and engines followed, the boat slipped through without touching bottom, and entered upon the third and last intricacy of the crossing; imperceptibly she moved through the gloom, crept by inches into her marks, drifted tediously till the shoalest water was cried, and then, under a tremendous head of steam, went swinging over the reef and away into deep water and safety!

Ealer let his long-pent breath pour in a great relieving sigh, and said:

"That's the sweetest piece of piloting that was ever done on the Mississippi River! I wouldn't believe it could be done, if I hadn't seen it."

There was no reply, and he added:

"Just hold her five minutes longer, partner, and let me run down and get a cup of coffee."

A minute later Ealer was biting into a pie, down in the "texas," and comforting himself with coffee. Just then the night watchman happened in, and was about to happen out again when he noticed Ealer and exclaimed:

"Who is at the wheel, sir?"

"X."

"Dart for the pilot-house, quicker than lightning!"

The next moment both men were flying up the pilot-house companionway, three steps at a jump! Nobody there! The great steamer was whistling down the middle of the river at her own sweet will! The watchman shot out of the place again; Ealer seized the wheel, set an engine back with power, and held his breath while the boat reluctantly swung away from a "towhead" which she was about to knock into the middle of the Gulf of Mexico!

By and by the watchman came back and said:

"Didn't that lunatic tell you he was asleep, when he first came up here?"

"No."

"Well, he was. I found him walking along on top of the railings, just as unconcerned as another man would walk a pavement, and I put him to bed; now just this minute there he was again, away astern, going through that sort of tightrope deviltry the same as before."

"Well, I think I'll stay by next time he has one of those fits. But I hope he'll have them often. You just ought to have seen him take this boat through Helena crossing. *I* never saw anything so gaudy before. And if he can do such gold-leaf, kid-glove, diamond-breastpin piloting when he is sound asleep, what *couldn't* he do if he was dead!"

From v. "Sounding." Faculties Peculiarly Necessary to a Pilot

A pilot must have a memory, but there are two higher qualities which he must also have. He must have good and quick judgment and decision, and a cool, calm courage that no peril can shake. Give a man the merest trifle of pluck to start with and by the time he has become a pilot he cannot be unmanned by any danger a steamboat can get into, but one cannot quite say the same for judgment. Judgment is a matter of brains and a man must *start* with a good stock of that article or he will never succeed as a pilot.

The growth of courage in the pilot-house is steady all the time but it does not reach a high and satisfactory condition until some time after the young pilot has been "standing his own watch" alone and under the staggering weight of all the responsibilities connected with the position. When the apprentice has become pretty thoroughly acquainted with the river, he goes clattering along so fearlessly with his steamboat, night or day, that he presently begins to imagine that it is *his* courage that animates him, but the first time the pilot steps out and leaves him to his own devices he finds out it was the other man's. He discovers that the article has been left out of his own cargo altogether. The whole river is bristling with exigencies in a moment, he is not prepared for them, he does not know how to meet them; all his knowledge forsakes him, and within fifteen minutes he is as white as a sheet and scared almost to death. Therefore pilots wisely train these cubs by various strategic tricks to look danger in the face a little more calmly. A favorite way of theirs is to play a friendly swindle upon the candidate.

Mr. Bixby served me in this fashion once and for years afterward I used to blush, even in my sleep, when I thought of it. I had become a good steersman; so good, indeed, that I had all the work to do on our watch, night and day. Mr. Bixby seldom made a suggestion to me; all he ever did was to take the wheel on particularly bad nights or in particularly bad crossings, land the boat when she needed to be landed, play gentleman of leisure nine-tenths of the watch, and collect the wages. The lower river was about bank-full and if anybody had questioned my ability to run any crossing between Cairo and New Orleans without help or instruction, I should have felt irreparably hurt. The idea of being afraid of any crossing in the lot, in the *daytime,* was a thing too preposterous for contemplation. Well, one matchless summer's day I was bowling down the bend above Island 66, brimful of self-conceit and carrying my nose as high as a giraffe's, when Mr. Bixby said:

"I am going below awhile. I suppose you know the next crossing?"

This was almost an affront. It was about the plainest and simplest crossing in the whole river. One couldn't come to any harm whether he ran it right or not, and as for depth, there never had been any bottom there. I knew all this, perfectly well.

"Know how to *run* it? Why, I can run it with my eyes shut."

"How much water is there in it?"

"Well, that is an odd question. I couldn't get bottom there with a church steeple."

"You think so, do you?"

The very tone of the question shook my confidence. That was what Mr. Bixby was expecting. He left, without saying anything more. I began to imagine all sorts of things. Mr. Bixby, unknown to me, of course, sent somebody down to the forecastle with some mysterious instructions to the leadsmen, another messenger was sent to whisper among the officers, and then Mr. Bixby went into hiding behind a smoke-stack where he could observe results. Presently the captain stepped out on the hurricane-deck; next the chief mate appeared; then a clerk. Every moment or two a straggler was added to my audience, and before I got to the head of the island I had fifteen or twenty people assembled down there under my nose. I began to wonder what the trouble was. As I started across, the captain glanced aloft at me and said, with a sham uneasiness in his voice:

"Where is Mr. Bixby?"

"Gone below, sir."

But that did the business for me. My imagination began to construct dangers out of nothing, and they multiplied faster than I could keep the run of them. All at once I imagined I saw shoal water ahead! The wave of coward agony that surged through me then came near dislocating every joint in me. All my confidence in that crossing vanished. I seized the bell-rope; dropped it, ashamed; seized it again; dropped it once more; clutched it tremblingly once again, and pulled it so feebly that I could hardly hear the stroke myself. Captain and mate sang out instantly, and both together:

"Starboard lead there! and quick about it!"

This was another shock. I began to climb the wheel like a squirrel, but I would hardly get the boat started to port before I would see new dangers on that side and away I would spin to the other, only to find perils accumulating to starboard and be crazy to get to port again. Then came the leadsman's sepulchral cry:

"D-e-e-p four!"

Deep four in a bottomless crossing! The terror of it took my breath away.

"M-a-r-k three! M-a-r-k three! Quarter-less-three! Half twain!"

This was frightful! I seized the bell-ropes and stopped the engines.

"Quarter twain! Quarter twain! *Mark* twain!"

I was helpless. I did not know what in the world to do. I was quaking from head to foot and I could have hung my hat on my eyes, they stuck out so far.

"Quarter-*less*-twain! Nine-and-a-*half!*"

We were *drawing* nine! My hands were in a nerveless flutter. I could not ring a bell intelligibly with them. I flew to the speaking-tube and shouted to the engineer:

"Oh, Ben, if you love me, *back* her! Quick, Ben! Oh, back the immortal *soul* out of her!"

I heard the door close gently. I looked around, and there stood Mr. Bixby, smiling a bland, sweet smile. Then the audience on the hurricane-deck sent up a thundergust of humiliating laughter. I saw it all, now, and I felt meaner than the meanest man in human history. I laid in the lead, set the boat in her marks, came ahead on the engines, and said:

"It was a fine trick to play on an orphan, *wasn't* it? I suppose I'll never hear the last of how I was ass enough to heave the lead at the head of 66."

"Well, no, you won't, maybe. In fact I hope you won't, for I want you to learn something by that experience. Didn't you *know* there was no bottom in that crossing?"

"Yes, sir, I did."

"Very well, then. You shouldn't have allowed me or anybody else to shake your confidence in that knowledge. Try to remember that. And another thing, when you get into a dangerous place, don't turn coward. That isn't going to help matters any."

It was a good enough lesson but pretty hardly learned. Yet about the hardest part of it was that for months I so often had to hear a phrase which I had conceived a particular distaste for. It was, "Oh, Ben, if you love me, back her!"

1883

STUDY QUESTIONS

1. How does Twain balance teaching, entertainment, and self-revelation in these selections from *Old Times on the Mississippi*? Discuss at least one example of each.
2. Why, in a narrative of his own experiences, does Twain include the tale of the sleepwalking Mr. X? What does this tale add to the narrative?

3. Why does Twain tell the tale on himself that ends Chapter V?
4. Twain is considered one of the masters of the southern United States comic tradition. In your opinion, do the selections chosen here bear this out? Discuss.
5. Discuss the narrator's style and voice. Note, for example, such sentences as "You could have drawn a seine through his system and not caught enough curses to disturb your mother with." What do the various elements of style and voice that you have noticed add to your enjoyment of the narrative, or to your perspective on it?
6. How does the narrator's voice in *Old Times on the Mississippi* differ from that of the narrators in "The Celebrated Jumping Frog of Calaveras County"? Why might these differences exist?
7. How does Twain's narrative voice in *Old Times on the Mississippi* compare with other narrative voices you have met in the fiction in Chapters 2 and 5 of this anthology? Discuss some examples of similarities and differences that seem noteworthy to you.

From I Know Why the Caged Bird Sings

Maya Angelou (1928–   )

Maya Angelou is among the best known African American writers. She was asked to read at President Clinton's inauguration, the first time a poet had been so honored since Robert Frost read at President Kennedy's inauguration. Born into poverty in rural Arkansas, an unwed mother at sixteen, Angelou nevertheless became a dancer, singer, actress, poet, and playwright. She is currently the Reynolds Professor of American Studies at Wake Forest University.

18

Another day was over. In the soft dark the cotton truck spilled the pickers out and roared out of the yard with a sound like a giant's fart. The workers stepped around in circles for a few seconds as if they had found themselves unexpectedly in an unfamiliar place. Their minds sagged.

In the Store the men's faces were the most painful to watch, but I seemed to have no choice. When they tried to smile to carry off their tiredness as if it was nothing, the body did nothing to help the mind's attempt at disguise. Their shoulders drooped even as they laughed, and when they put their hands on their hips in a show of jauntiness, the palms slipped the thighs as if the pants were waxed.

"Evening, Sister Henderson. Well, back where we started, huh?"

"Yes, sir, Brother Stewart. Back where you started, bless the Lord." Momma could not take the smallest achievement for granted. People whose history and future were threatened each day by extinction considered that it was only by divine intervention that they were able to live at all. I find it interesting that the meanest life, the poorest existence, is attributed to God's will, but as human beings become more affluent, as their living standard and style begin to ascend the material scale, God descends the scale of responsibility at a commensurate speed.

"That's just who get the credit. Yes, ma'am. The blessed Lord." Their overalls and shirts seemed to be torn on purpose and the cotton lint and dust in their hair gave them the appearance of people who had turned gray in the past few hours.

The women's feet had swollen to fill the discarded men's shoes they wore, and they washed their arms at the well to dislodge dirt and splinters that had accrued to them as part of the day's pickings.

I thought them all hateful to have allowed themselves to be worked like oxen, and even more shameful to try to pretend that things were not as bad as they were. When they leaned too hard on the partly glass candy counter, I wanted to tell them shortly to stand up and "assume the posture of a man," but Momma would have beaten me if I'd opened my mouth. She ignored the creaks of the counter under their weight and moved around filling their orders and keeping up a conversation. "Going to put your dinner on, Sister Williams?" Bailey and I helped Momma, while Uncle Willie sat on the porch and heard the day's account.

"Praise the Lord, no, ma'am. Got enough left over from last night to do us. We going home and get cleaned up to go to the revival meeting."

Go to church in that cloud of weariness? Not go home and lay those tortured bones in a feather bed? The idea came to me that my people may be a race of masochists and that not only was it our fate to live the poorest, roughest life but that we liked it like that.

"I know what you mean, Sister Williams. Got to feed the soul just like you feed the body. I'm taking the children, too, the Lord willing. Good Book say, 'Raise a child in the way he should go and he will not depart from it.'"

"That's what it say. Sure is what it say."

The cloth tent had been set on the flatlands in the middle of a field near the railroad tracks. The earth was carpeted with a silky layer of dried grass and cotton stalks. Collapsible chairs were poked into the still-soft ground and a large wooden cross was hung from the center beam at the rear of the tent. Electric lights had been strung from behind the pulpit to the entrance flap and continued outside on poles made of rough two-by-fours.

Approached in the dark the swaying bulbs looked lonely and purposeless. Not as if they were there to provide light or anything meaningful. And the tent, that blurry bright three-dimensional A, was so foreign to the cotton field, that it might just get up and fly away before my eyes.

People, suddenly visible in the lamplight, streamed toward the temporary church. The adults' voices relayed the serious intent of their mission. Greetings were exchanged, hushed.

"Evening, sister, how you?"

"Bless the Lord, just trying to make it in."

Their minds were concentrated on the coming meeting, soul to soul, with God. This was no time to indulge in human concerns or personal questions.

"The good Lord give me another day, and I'm thankful." Nothing personal in that. The credit was God's, and there was no illusion about the Central Position's shifting or becoming less than Itself.

Teenagers enjoyed revivals as much as adults. They used the night outside meetings to play at courting. The impermanence of a collapsible church added to the frivolity, and their eyes flashed and winked and the girls giggled little silver drops in the dusk while the boys postured and swaggered and pretended not to notice. The nearly grown girls wore skirts as tight as the custom allowed and the young men slicked their hair down with Moroline Hairdressing and water.

To small children, though, the idea of praising God in a tent was confusing, to say the least. It seemed somehow blasphemous. The lights hanging slack overhead, the soft ground underneath and the canvas wall that faintly blew in and out, like cheeks puffed with air, made for the feeling of a country fair. The nudgings and jerks and winks of the bigger children surely didn't belong in a church. But the tension of the elders—their expectation, which weighted like a thick blanket over the crowd—was the most perplexing of all.

Would the gentle Jesus care to enter into that transitory setting? The altar wobbled and threatened to overturn and the collection table sat at a rakish angle. One leg had yielded itself to the loose dirt. Would God the Father allow His only Son to mix with this crowd of cotton pickers and maids, washerwomen and handymen? I knew He sent His spirit on Sundays to the church, but after all that was a church and the people had had all day Saturday to shuffle off the cloak of work and the skin of despair.

Everyone attended the revival meetings. Members of the hoity-toity Mount Zion Baptist Church mingled with the intellectual members of the African Methodist Episcopal and African Methodist Episcopal Zion, and the plain working people of the Christian Methodist Episcopal. These gatherings provided the one time in the year when all of those good village people associated with the followers of the Church of God in Christ. The latter were looked upon with some suspicion because they were so loud and raucous in their services. Their explanation that "the Good Book say, 'Make a joyful noise unto the Lord, and be exceedingly glad'" did not in the least minimize the condescension of their fellow Christians. Their church was far from the others, but they could be heard on

Sunday, a half mile away, singing and dancing until they sometimes fell down in a dead faint. Members of the other churches wondered if the Holy Rollers were going to heaven after all their shouting. The suggestion was that they were having their heaven right here on earth.

This was their annual revival.

Mrs. Duncan, a little woman with a bird face, started the service. "I know I'm a witness for my Lord . . . I know I'm a witness for my Lord, I know I'm a witness . . ."

Her voice, a skinny finger, stabbed high up in the air and the church responded. From somewhere down front came the jangling sound of a tambourine. Two beats on "know," two beats on "I'm a" and two beats on the end of "witness."

Other voices joined the near shriek of Mrs. Duncan. They crowded around and tenderized the tone. Handclaps snapped in the roof and solidified the beat. When the song reached its peak in sound and passion, a tall, thin man who had been kneeling behind the altar all the while stood up and sang with the audience for a few bars. He stretched out his long arms and grasped the platform. It took some time for the singers to come off their level of exaltation, but the minister stood resolute until the song unwound like a child's playtoy and lay quieted in the aisles.

"Amen." He looked at the audience.

"Yes, sir, amen." Nearly everyone seconded him.

"I say, Let the Church say 'Amen.'"

Everyone said, "Amen."

"Thank the Lord. Thank the Lord."

"That's right, thank the Lord. Yes, Lord. Amen."

"We will have prayer, led by Brother Bishop."

Another tall, brown-skinned man wearing square glasses walked up to the altar from the front row. The minister knelt at the right and Brother Bishop at the left.

"Our Father"—he was singing—"You who took my feet out the mire and clay—"

The church moaned, "Amen."

"You who saved my soul. One day. Look, sweet Jesus. Look down, on these your suffering children—"

The church begged, "Look down, Lord."

"Build us up where we're torn down . . . Bless the sick and the afflicted . . ."

It was the usual prayer. Only his voice gave it something new. After every two words he gasped and dragged the air over his vocal chords, making a sound like an inverted grunt. "You who"—grunt—"saved my"—gasp—"soul one"—inhalation—"day"—humph.

Then the congregation, led again by Mrs. Duncan, flew into "Precious Lord, take my hand, lead me on, let me stand." It was sung at a faster clip than the usual one in the C.M.E. Church, but at that tempo it worked. There was a joy about the tune that changed the meaning of its sad lyrics. "When the darkness appears, and the night draweth near and my life is almost gone . . ." There seemed to be an abandon which suggested that with all those things it should be a time for great rejoicing.

The serious shouters had already made themselves known, and their fans (cardboard advertisements from Texarkana's largest Negro funeral home) and lacy white handkerchiefs waved high in the air. In their dark hands they looked like small kites without the wooden frames.

The tall minister stood again at the altar. He waited for the song and the revelry to die.

He said, "Amen. Glory."

The church skidded off the song slowly. "Amen. Glory."

He still waited, as the last notes remained in the air, staircased on top of each other. "At the river I stand—" "I stand, guide my feet—" "Guide my feet, take my hand." Sung like the last circle in a round. Then quiet descended.

The Scripture reading was from Matthew, twenty-fifth chapter, thirtieth verse through the forty-sixth.

His text for the sermon was "The least of these."

After reading the verses to the accompaniment of a few Amens he said, "First Corinthians tells me, 'Even if I have the tongue of men and of angels and have not charity, I am as nothing. Even if I give all my clothes to the poor and have not charity, I am as nothing. Even if I give my body to be burned and have not charity it availeth me nothing. Burned, I say, and have not charity, it availeth nothing.' I have to ask myself, what is this thing called Charity? If good deeds are not charity—"

The church gave in quickly. "That's right, Lord."

"—if giving my flesh and blood is not charity?"

"Yes, Lord."

"I have to ask myself what is this charity they talking so much about."

I had never heard a preacher jump into the muscle of his sermon so quickly. Already the humming pitch had risen in the church, and those who knew had popped their eyes in anticipation of the coming excitement. Momma sat treetrunk still, but she had balled her handkerchief in her hand and only the corner, which I had embroidered, stuck out.

"As I understand it, charity vaunteth not itself. Is not puffed up." He blew himself up with a deep breath to give us the picture of what Charity was not. "Charity don't go around saying 'I give you food and I give you clothes and by rights you ought to thank me.'"

The congregation knew whom he was talking about and voiced agreement with his analysis. "Tell the truth, Lord."

"Charity don't say, 'Because I give you a job, you got to bend your knee to me.'" The church was rocking with each phrase. "It don't say, 'Because I pays you what you due, you got to call me master.' It don't ask me to humble myself and belittle myself. That ain't what Charity is."

Down front to the right, Mr. and Mrs. Stewart, who only a few hours earlier had crumbled in our front yard, defeated by the cotton rows, now sat on the edges of their rickety-rackety chairs. Their faces shone with the delight of their souls. The mean whitefolks was going to get their comeuppance. Wasn't that what the minister said, and wasn't he quoting from the words of God Himself? They had been refreshed with the hope of revenge and the promise of justice.

"Aaagh. Raagh. I said . . . Charity. Woooooo, a Charity. It don't want nothing for itself. It don't want to be bossman . . . Waah . . . It don't want to be headman . . . Waah . . . It don't want to be foreman . . . Waah . . . It . . . I'm talking about Charity . . . It don't want . . . Oh Lord . . . help me tonight . . . It don't want to be bowed to and scraped at . . ."

America's historic bowers and scrapers shifted easily and happily in the makeshift church. Reassured that although they might be the lowest of the low they were at least not uncharitable, and "in that great Gettin' Up Morning, Jesus was going to separate the sheep (them) from the goats (the whitefolks)."

"Charity is simple." The church agreed, vocally.

"Charity is poor." That was us he was talking about.

"Charity is plain." I thought, that's about right. Plain and simple.

"Charity is . . . Oh, Oh, Oh. Cha-ri-ty. Where are you? Wooo . . . Charity . . . Hump."

One chair gave way and the sound of splintering wood split the air in the rear of the church.

"I call you and you don't answer. Woooh, oh Charity."

Another holler went up in front of me, and a large woman flopped over, her arms above her head like a candidate for baptism. The emotional release was contagious. Little screams burst around the room like Fourth of July firecrackers.

The minister's voice was a pendulum. Swinging left and down and right and down and left and—"How can you claim to be my brother, and hate me? Is that Charity? How can you claim to be my sister and despise me? Is that supposed to be Charity? How can you claim to be my friend and misuse and wrongfully abuse me? Is that Charity? Oh, my children, I stopped by here—"

The church swung on the end of his phrases. Punctuating. Confirming. "Stop by here, Lord."

"—to tell you, to open your heart and let Charity reign. Forgive your enemies for His sake. Show the Charity that Jesus was speaking of to this sick old world. It has need of the charitable giver." His voice was falling and the explosions became fewer and quieter.

"And now I repeat the words of the Apostle Paul, and 'now abideth faith, hope and charity, these three; but the greatest of these is charity.'"

The congregation lowed with satisfaction. Even if they were society's pariahs, they were going to be angels in a marble white heaven and sit on the right hand of Jesus, the Son of God. The Lord loved the poor and hated those cast high in the world. Hadn't He Himself said it would be easier for a camel to go through the eye of a needle than for a rich man to enter heaven? They were assured that they were going to be the only inhabitants of that land of milk and honey, except of course a few whitefolks like John Brown who history books said was crazy anyway. All the Negroes had to do generally, and those at the revival especially, was bear up under this life of toil and cares, because a blessed home awaited them in the far-off bye and bye.

"Bye and bye, when the morning come, when all the saints of God's are gathering home, we will tell the story of how we overcome and we'll understand it better bye and bye."

A few people who had fainted were being revived on the side aisles when the evangelist opened the doors of the church. Over the sounds of "Thank you, Jesus," he started a long-meter hymn:

> "I came to Jesus, as I was,
> worried, wounded and sad,
> I found in Him a resting place,
> And He has made me glad."

The old ladies took up the hymn and shared it in tight harmony. The humming crowd began to sound like tired bees, restless and anxious to get home.

"All those under the sound of my voice who have no spiritual home, whose hearts are burdened and heavy-ladened, let them come. Come before it's too late. I don't ask you to join the Church of God in Christ. No. I'm a servant of God, and in this revival, we are out to bring straying souls to Him. So if you join this evening, just say which church you want to be affiliated with, and we will turn you over to a representative of that church body. Will one deacon of the following churches come forward?"

That was revolutionary action. No one had ever heard of a minister taking in members for another church. It was our first look at Charity among preachers. Men from the A.M.E., A.M.E.Z., Baptist and C.M.E. churches went down front and assumed stances a few feet apart. Converted sinners flowed down the aisles to shake hands with the evangelist and stayed at his side or were directed to one of the men in line. Over twenty people were saved that night.

There was nearly as much commotion over the saving of the sinners as there had been during the gratifying melodic sermon.

The Mothers of the Church, old ladies with white lace disks pinned to their thinning hair, had a service all their own. They walked around the new converts singing,

> "Before this time another year,
> I may be gone,
> In some lonesome graveyard,
> Oh, Lord, how long?"

When the collection was taken up and the last hymn given to the praise of God, the evangelist asked that everyone in his presence rededicate his soul to God and his life's work to Charity. Then we were dismissed.

Outside and on the way home, the people played in their magic, as children poke in mud pies, reluctant to tell themselves that the game was over.

"The Lord touched him tonight, didn't He?"

"Surely did. Touched him with a mighty fire."

"Bless the Lord. I'm glad I'm saved."

"That's the truth. It make a whole lot of difference."

"I wish them people I works for could of heard that sermon. They don't know what they letting theyselves in for."

"Bible say, 'He who can hear, let him hear. He who can't, shame on 'em.'"

They basked in the righteousness of the poor and the exclusiveness of the downtrodden. Let the whitefolks have their money and power and segregation and sarcasm and big houses and schools and lawns like carpets, and books, and mostly—mostly—let them have their whiteness. It was better to be meek and lowly, spat upon and abused for this little time than to spend eternity frying in the fires of hell. No one would have admitted that the Christian and charitable people were happy to think of their oppressors' turning forever on the Devil's spit over the flames of fire and brimstone.

But that was what the Bible said and it didn't make mistakes. "Ain't it said somewhere in there that 'before one word of this changes, heaven and earth shall fall away'? Folks going to get what they deserved."

When the main crowd of worshipers reached the short bridge spanning the pond, the ragged sound of honky-tonk music assailed them. A barrelhouse blues was being shouted over the stamping of feet on a wooden floor. Miss Grace, the good-time woman, had her usual Saturday-night customers. The big white house blazed with lights and noise. The people inside had forsaken their own distress for a little while.

Passing near the din, the godly people dropped their heads and conversation ceased. Reality began its tedious crawl back into their reasoning. After all, they were needy and hungry and despised and dispossessed, and sinners the world over were in the driver's seat. How long, merciful Father? How long?

A stranger to the music could not have made a distinction between the songs sung a few minutes before and those being danced to in the gay house by the railroad tracks. All asked the same questions. How long, oh God? How long?

1969

STUDY QUESTIONS

1. Write an essay discussing how Angelou's narrator describes the revival meeting and how she uses it to illuminate various issues in the daily life of the field hands who make up a large segment of her community.

2. Angelou's narrator, though a member of the community she describes, seems ironic about and alienated from it. Pick out several passages that show this alienation.
3. What is the central irony the narrator discerns in the Christianity of the people at the revival?

From Dispatches

Michael Herr (1940–   )

During the late 1960s, Michael Herr spent over a year in Vietnam as a correspondent for *Esquire* magazine. Few of his articles actually appeared while the war was in progress, but in 1977 Herr published *Dispatches*, which continues to be regarded as one of the most powerful treatments of the American experience in Vietnam. His "new journalism" style, which involves the reporter so directly in his story as to do away with any pretense of objectivity, caught the terror, futility, and sheer absurdity of a conflict unlike any other in which the United States had found itself entangled. Herr collaborated on the screenplays for two highly regarded movies on Vietnam, *Apocalypse Now* (1979) and *Full Metal Jacket* (1987).

I

Going out at night the medics gave you pills, Dexedrine breath like dead snakes kept too long in a jar. I never saw the need for them myself, a little contact or anything that even sounded like contact would give me more speed than I could bear. Whenever I heard something outside of our clenched little circle I'd practically flip, hoping to God that I wasn't the only one who'd noticed it. A couple of rounds fired off in the dark a kilometer away and the Elephant would be there kneeling on my chest, sending me down into my boots for a breath. Once I thought I saw a light moving in the jungle and I caught myself just under a whisper saying, "I'm not ready for this, I'm not ready for this." That's when I decided to drop it and do something else with my nights. And I wasn't going out like the night ambushers did, or the Lurps, long-range recon patrollers who did it night after night for weeks and months, creeping up on VC base camps or around moving columns of North Vietnamese. I was living too close to my bones as it was, all I had to do was accept it. Anyway, I'd save the pills for later, for Saigon and the awful depressions I always had there.

I knew one 4th Division Lurp who took his pills by the fistful, downs from the left pocket of his tiger suit and ups from the right, one to cut the trail for him and the other to send him down it. He told me that they cooled things out just right for him, that he could see that old jungle at night like he was looking at it through a starlight scope. "They sure give you the range," he said.

This was his third tour. In 1965 he'd been the only survivor in a platoon of the Cav wiped out going into the Ia Drang Valley. In '66 he'd come back with the Special Forces and one morning after an ambush he'd hidden under the bodies of his team while the VC[1] walked all around them with knives, making sure. They stripped the bodies of their gear, the berets too, and finally went away, laughing. After that, there was nothing left for him in the war except the Lurps.

"I just can't hack it back in the World," he said. He told me that after he'd come back home the last time he would sit in his room all day, and sometimes he'd stick a hunting rifle out the window, leading people and cars as they passed his house until the only feeling he was aware of was all up in the tip of that one finger. "It used to put my folks real uptight," he said. But he put people uptight here too, even here.

"No man, I'm sorry, he's just too crazy for me," one of the men in his team said. "All's you got to do is look in his eyes, that's the whole fucking story right there."

"Yeah, but you better do it quick," someone else said. "I mean, you don't want to let him catch you at it."

But he always seemed to be watching for it, I think he slept with his eyes open, and I was afraid of him anyway. All I ever managed was one quick look in, and that was like looking at the floor of an ocean. He wore a gold earring and a headband torn from a piece of camouflage parachute material, and since nobody was about to tell him to get his hair cut it fell below his shoulders, covering a thick purple scar. Even at division he never went anywhere without at least a .45 and a knife, and he thought I was a freak because I wouldn't carry a weapon.

"Didn't you ever meet a reporter before?" I asked him.

"Tits on a bull," he said. "Nothing personal."

But what a story he told, as one-pointed and resonant as any war story I ever heard, it took me a year to understand it:

"Patrol went up the mountain. One man came back. He died before he could tell us what happened."

I waited for the rest, but it seemed not to be that kind of story; when I asked him what had happened he just looked like he felt sorry for me, fucked if he'd waste time telling stories to anyone dumb as I was.

His face was all painted up for night walking now like a bad hallucination, not like the painted faces I'd seen in San Francisco only a few weeks before, the other extreme of the same theater. In the coming hours he'd stand as faceless and

---

[1]Viet Cong, North Vietnamese troops fighting against American and South Vietnamese troops

quiet in the jungle as a fallen tree, and God help his opposite numbers unless they had at least half a squad along, he was a good killer, one of our best. The rest of his team were gathered outside the tent, set a little apart from the other division units, with its own Lurp-designated latrine and its own exclusive freeze-dry rations, three-star war food, the same chop they sold at Abercrombie & Fitch. The regular division troops would almost shy off the path when they passed the area on their way to and from the mess tent. No matter how toughened up they became in the war, they still looked innocent compared to the Lurps. When the team had grouped they walked in a file down the hill to the lz[2] across the strip to the perimeter and into the treeline.

I never spoke to him again, but I saw him. When they came back in the next morning he had a prisoner with him, blindfolded and with his elbows bound sharply behind him. The Lurp area would definitely be off limits during the interrogation, and anyway, I was already down at the strip waiting for a helicopter to come and take me out of there.

"Hey, what're you guys, with the USO[3]? Aw, we thought you was with the USO 'cause your hair's so long." Page took the kid's picture, I got the words down and Flynn laughed and told him we were the Rolling Stones. The three of us traveled around together for about a month that summer. At one lz the brigade chopper came in with a real foxtail hanging off the aerial, when the commander walked by us he almost took an infarction.

"Don't you men salute officers?"

"We're not men," Page said. "We're correspondents."

When the commander heard that, he wanted to throw a spontaneous operation for us, crank up his whole brigade and get some people killed. We had to get out on the next chopper to keep him from going ahead with it, amazing what some of them would do for a little ink. Page liked to augment his field gear with freak paraphernalia, scarves and beads, plus he was English, guys would stare at him like he'd just come down off a wall on Mars. Sean Flynn could look more incredibly beautiful than even his father, Errol, had thirty years before as Captain Blood, but sometimes he looked more like Artaud coming out of some heavy heart-of-darkness trip, overloaded on the information, the input! The input! He'd give off a bad sweat and sit for hours, combing his mustache through with the saw blade of his Swiss Army knife. We packed grass and tape: Have You Seen Your Mother Baby Standing in the Shadows, Best of the Animals, Strange Days, Purple Haze, Archie Bell and the Drells, "C'mon now everybody, do the Tighten Up...." Once in a while we'd catch a chopper straight into one of the lower hells, but it was a quiet time in the war, mostly it was lz's and camps, grunts hanging around, faces, stories.

"Best way's to just keep moving," one of them told us. "Just keep moving, stay in motion, you know what I'm saying?"

---

[2]landing zone

[3]United Service Organization; its purpose is to entertain troops.

We knew. He was a moving-target-survivor subscriber, a true child of the war, because except for the rare times when you were pinned or stranded the system was geared to keep you mobile, if that was what you thought you wanted. As a technique for staying alive it seemed to make as much sense as anything, given naturally that you were there to begin with and wanted to see it close; it started out sound and straight but it formed a cone as it progressed, because the more you moved the more you saw, the more you saw the more besides death and mutilation you risked, and the more you risked of that the more you would have to let go of one day as a "survivor." Some of us moved around the war like crazy people until we couldn't see which way the run was even taking us anymore, only the war all over its surface was occasional, unexpected penetration. As long as we could have choppers like taxis it took real exhaustion or depression near shock or a dozen pipes of opium to keep us even apparently quiet, we'd still be running around inside our skins like something was after us, ha ha, La Vida Loca.[4]

In the months after I got back the hundreds of helicopters I'd flow in began to draw together until they'd formed a collective meta-chopper, and in my mind it was the sexiest thing going; saver-destroyed, provider-waster, right hand–left hand, nimble, fluent, canny and human; hot steel, grease, jungle-saturated canvas webbing, sweat cooling and warming up again, cassette rock and roll in one ear and door-gun fire in the other, fuel, heat, vitality and death, death itself, hardly an intruder. Men on the crews would say that once you'd carried a dead person he would always be there, riding with you. Like all combat people they were incredibly superstitious and invariably self-dramatic, but it was (I knew) unbearably true that close exposure to the dead sensitized you to the force of their presence and made for long reverberations; long. Some people were so delicate that one look was enough to wipe them away; but even bone-dumb grunts seemed to feel that something weird and extra was happening to them.

Helicopters and people jumping out of helicopters, people so in love they'd run to get on even when there wasn't any pressure. Choppers rising straight out of small cleared jungle spaces, wobbling down onto city rooftops, cartons of rations and ammunition thrown off, dead and wounded loaded on. Sometimes they were so plentiful and loose that you could touch down at five or six places in a day, look around, hear the talk, catch the next one out. There were installations as big as cities with 30,000 citizens, once we dropped in to feed supply to one man. God knows what kind of Lord Jim phoenix numbers he was doing in there, all he said to me was, "You didn't see a thing, right Chief? You weren't even here." There were posh fat air-conditioned camps like comfortable middle-class scenes with the violence tacit, "far away"; camps named for commanders' wives, LZ Thelma, LZ Betty Lou; number-named hilltops in trouble where I didn't want to stay; trail, paddy, swamp, deep hairy bush, scrub, swale, village, even

---

[4]The Crazy Life

city, where the ground couldn't drink up what the action spilled, it made you careful where you walked.

Sometimes the chopper you were riding in would top a hill and all the ground in front of you as far as the next hill would be charred and pitted and still smoking, and something between your chest and your stomach would turn over. Frail gray smoke where they'd phosphorus ("Willy Peter/Make you a buh liever"), deep black smoke from 'palm, they said that if you stood at the base of a column of napalm smoke it would suck the air right out of your lungs. Once we fanned over a little ville that had just been airstruck and the words of a song by Wingy Manone that I'd heard when I was a few years old snapped into my head, "Stop the War, These Cats Is Killing Themselves." Then we dropped, hovered, settled down into purple lz smoke, dozens of children broke from their hootches to run in toward the focus of our landing, the pilot laughing and saying, "Vietnam, man, Bomb 'em and feed 'em, bomb 'em and feed 'em."

Flying over jungle was almost pure pleasure, doing it on foot was nearly all pain. I never belonged in there. Maybe it really was what its people had always called it, Beyond; at the very least it was serious, I gave up things to it I probably never got back. ("Aw, jungle's okay. If you know her you can live in her real good, if you don't she'll take you down in an hour. Under.") Once in some thick jungle corner with some grunts standing around, a correspondent said, "Gee, you must really see some beautiful sunsets in here," and they almost pissed themselves laughing. But you could fly up and into hot tropic sunsets that would change the way you thought about light forever. You could also fly out of places that were so grim they turned to black and white in your head five minutes after you'd gone.

That could be the coldest one in the world, standing at the edge of a clearing watching the chopper you'd just come in on taking off again, leaving you there to think about what it was going to be for you now: if this was a bad place, the wrong place, maybe even the last place, and whether you'd made a terrible mistake this time.

There was a camp at Soc Trang where a man at the lz said, "If you come looking for a story this is your lucky day, we got Condition Red here," and before the sound of the chopper had faded out, I knew I had it too.

"That's affirmative," the camp commander said, "we are *definitely* expecting rain. Glad to see you." He was a young captain, he was laughing and taping a bunch of sixteen clips together bottom to bottom for faster reloading, "grease." Everyone there was busy at it, cracking crates, squirreling away grenades, checking mortar pieces, piling rounds, clicking banana clips into automatic weapons that I'd never even seen before. They were wired into their listening posts out around the camp, into each other, into themselves, and when it got dark it got worse. The moon came up nasty and full, a fat moist piece of decadent fruit. It was soft and saffron-misted when you looked up at it, but its light over the sandbags and into the jungle was harsh and bright. We were all rubbing Army issue nightfighter cosmetic under our eyes to cut the glare and the terrible things it made you see. (Around midnight, just for something to do, I crossed to the other perimeter and looked at the road running engineer-straight toward Route 4 like a yellow frozen ribbon out of sight and I saw it move, the whole road.) There were a few sharp arguments about who the light really favored, attackers or defenders, men were sitting around with Cinema-scope eyes and jaws stuck out like they could shoot bullets, moving and antsing and shifting around inside their fatigues. "No sense us getting too relaxed, Charlie don't relax, just when you get good and comfortable is when he comes over and takes a giant shit on you." That was the level until morning, I smoked a pack an hour all night long, and nothing happened. Ten minutes after daybreak I was down at the lz asking about choppers.

A few days later Sean Flynn and I went up to a big firebase in the American TAOR[5] that took it all the way over to another extreme. National Guard week-end. The colonel in command was so drunk that day that he could barely get his words out, and when he did, it was to say things like, "We aim to make good and goddammit sure that if *those guys* try *anything cute* they won't catch us with our pants down." The main mission there was to fire H&I,[6] but one man told us that their record was the worst in the whole Corps, probably the whole country, they'd harassed and interdicted a lot of sleeping civilians and Korean Marines, even a couple of Americal patrols, but hardly any Viet Cong. (The colonel kept calling it "artillerary." The first time he said it Flynn and I looked away from each other, the second time we blew beer through our noses, but the colonel fell in laughing right away and more than covered us.) No sandbags, exposed shells, dirty pieces, guys going around giving us that look, "We're cool, how come you're not?" At the strip Sean was talking to the operator about it and the man got angry. "Oh *yeah*? Well fuck *you*, how tight do you think you want it? There ain't been any veecees around here in three months."

"So far so good," Sean said. "Hear anything on that chopper yet?"

But sometimes everything stopped, nothing flew, you couldn't even find out why. I got stuck for a chopper once in some lost patrol outpost in the Delta where the sergeant chain-ate candy bars and played country-and-western tapes twenty hours a day until I heard it in my sleep, some sleep, *Up on Wolverton Mountain* and *Lonesome as the bats and the bears in Miller's Cave* and *I fell into a burning ring of fire*, surrounded by strungout rednecks who weren't getting much sleep either because they couldn't trust one of their 400 mercenary troop-ers or their own hand-picked perimeter guards or anybody else except maybe Baby Ruth and Johnny Cash, they'd been waiting for it so long now they were afraid they wouldn't know it when they finally got it, *and it burns burns burns*. . . . Finally on the fourth day a helicopter came in to deliver meat and

---

[5]tactical area of responsibility
[6]high explosives and incendiary bombs

movies to the camp and I went out on it, so happy to get back to Saigon that I didn't crash for two days.

Airmobility, dig it, you weren't going anywhere. It made you feel safe, it made you feel Omni, but it was only a stunt, technology. Mobility was just mobility, it saved lives or took them all the time (saved mine I don't know how many times, maybe dozens, maybe none), what you really needed was a flexibility far greater than anything the technology could provide, some generous, spontaneous gift for accepting surprises, and I didn't have it. I got to hate surprises, control freak at the crossroads, if you were one of those people who always thought they had to know what was coming next, the war could cream you. It was the same with your ongoing attempts at getting used to the jungle or the blow-you-out climate or the saturating strangeness of the place which didn't lessen with exposure so often as it fattened and darkened in accumulating alienation. It was great if you could adapt, you had to try, but it wasn't the same as making a discipline, going into your own reserves and developing a real war metabolism, slow yourself down when your heart tried to punch its way through your chest, get swift when everything went to stop and all you could feel of your whole life was the entropy whipping through it. Unlovable terms.

The ground was always in play, always being swept. Under the ground was his, above it was ours. We had the air, we could get up in it but not disappear in *to* it, we could run but we couldn't hide, and he could do each so well that sometimes it looked like he was doing them both at once, while our finder just went limp. All the same, one place or another it was always going on, rock around the clock, we had the days and he had the nights. You could be in the most protected space in Vietnam and still know that your safety was provisional, that early death, blindness, loss of legs, arms or balls, major and lasting disfigurement— the whole rotten deal—could come in on the freaky-fluky as easily as in the so-called expected ways, you heard so many of those stories it was a wonder anyone was left alive to die in firefights and mortar-rocket attacks. After a few weeks, when the nickel had jarred loose and dropped and I saw that everyone around me was carrying a gun, I also saw that any one of them could go off at any time, putting you where it wouldn't matter whether it had been an accident or not. The roads were mined, the trails booby-trapped, satchel charges and grenades blew up jeeps and movie theaters, the VC got work inside all the camps as shoeshine boys and laundresses and honey-dippers, they'd starch your fatigues and burn your shit and then go home and mortar your area. Saigon and Cholon and Danang held such hostile vibes that you felt you were being dry-sniped every time someone looked at you, and choppers fell out of the sky like fat poisoned birds a hundred times a day. After a while I couldn't get on one without thinking that I must be out of my fucking mind.

Fear and motion, fear and standstill, no preferred cut there, no way even to be clear about which was really worse, the wait or the delivery. Combat spared far more men than it wasted, but everyone suffered the time between contact, especially when they were going out every day looking for it; bad going on foot, terrible in trucks and APC's,[7] awful in helicopters, the worst, traveling so fast toward something so frightening. I can remember times when I went half dead with my fear of the motion, the speed and direction already fixed and pointed one way. It was painful enough just flying "safe" hops between firebases and lz's; if you were ever on a helicopter that had been hit by ground fire your deep, perpetual chopper anxiety was guaranteed. At least actual contact when it was happening would draw long ragged strands of energy out of you, it was juicy, fast and refining, and traveling toward it was hollow, dry, cold and steady, it never let you alone. All you could do was look around at the other people on board and see if they were as scared and numbed out as you were. If it looked like they weren't you thought they were insane, if it looked like they were it made you feel a lot worse.

I went through that thing a number of times and only got a fast return on my fear once, a too classic hot landing with the heat coming from the trees about 300 yards away, sweeping machine-gun fire that sent men head down into swampy water, running on their hands and knees toward the grass where it wasn't blown flat by the rotor blades, not much to be running for but better than nothing. The helicopter pulled up before we'd all gotten out, leaving the last few men to jump twenty feet down between the guns across the paddy and the gun on the chopper door. When we'd all reached the cover of the wall and the captain had made a check, we were amazed to see that no one had even been hurt, except for one man who'd sprained both his ankles jumping. Afterwards, I remembered that I'd been down in the muck worrying about leeches. I guess you could say that I was refusing to accept the situation.

"Boy, you sure get offered some shitty choices," a Marine once said to me, and I couldn't help but feel that what he really meant was that you didn't get offered any at all. Specifically, he was just talking about a couple of C-ration cans, "dinner," but considering his young life you couldn't blame him for thinking that if he knew one thing for sure, it was that there was no one anywhere who cared less about what *he* wanted. There wasn't anybody he wanted to thank for his food, but he was grateful that he was still alive to eat it, that the motherfucker hadn't scarfed him up first. He hadn't been anything but tired and scared for six months and he'd lost a lot, mostly people, and seen far too much, but he was breathing in and breathing out, some kind of choice all by itself.

He had one of those faces, I saw that face at least a thousand times at a hundred bases and camps, all the youth sucked out of the eyes, the color drawn from the skin, cold white lips, you knew he wouldn't wait for any of it to come back. Life had made him old, he'd live it out old. All those faces, sometimes it was like looking into faces at a rock concert, locked in, the event had them; or like students who were very heavily advanced, serious beyond what you'd call their years

---

[7] armored personnel carrier

if you didn't know for yourself what the minutes and hours of those years were made up of. Not just like all the ones you saw who looked like they couldn't drag their asses through another day of it. (How do you feel when a nineteen-year-old kid tells you from the bottom of his heart that he's gotten too old for this kind of shit?) Not like the faces of the dead or wounded either, they could look more released than overtaken. These were the faces of boys whose whole lives seemed to have backed up on them, they'd be a few feet away but they'd be looking back at you over a distance you knew you'd never really cross. We'd talk, sometimes fly together, guys going out on R&R, guys escorting bodies, guys who'd flipped over into extremes of peace or violence. Once I flew with a kid who was going home, he looked back down once at the ground where he'd spent the year and spilled his whole load of tears. Sometimes you even flew with the dead.

Once I jumped on a chopper that was full of them. The kid in the op shack had said that there would be a body on board, but he'd been given some wrong information. "How bad do you want to get to Danang?" he'd asked me, and I'd said, "Bad."

When I saw what was happening I didn't want to get on, but they'd made a divert and a special landing for me, I had to go with the chopper I'd drawn, I was afraid of looking squeamish. (I remember, too, thinking that a chopper full of dead men was far less likely to get shot down than one full of living.) They weren't even in bags. They'd been on a truck near one of the firebases in the DMZ[8] that was firing support for Khe Sanh, and the truck had hit a Command-detonated mine, then they'd been rocketed. The Marines were always running out of things, even food, ammo and medicine, it wasn't so strange that they'd run out of bags too. The men had been wrapped around in ponchos, some of them carelessly fastened with plastic straps, and loaded on board. There was a small space cleared for me between one of them and the door gunner, who looked pale and so tremendously furious that I thought he was angry with me and I couldn't look at him for a while. When we went up the wind blew through the ship and made the ponchos shake and tremble until the one next to me blew back in a fast brutal flap, uncovering the face. They hadn't even closed his eyes for him.

The gunner started hollering as loud as he could, "Fix it! Fix it!," maybe he thought the eyes were looking at him, but there wasn't anything I could do. My hand went there a couple of times and I couldn't, and then I did. I pulled the poncho tight, lifted his head carefully and tucked the poncho under it, and then I couldn't believe that I'd done it. All during the ride the gunner kept trying to smile, and when we landed at Dong Ha he thanked me and ran off to get a detail. The pilots jumped down and walked away without looking back once, like they'd never seen that chopper before in their lives. I flew the rest of the way to Danang in a general's plane.

1977

---

[8]demilitarized zone

STUDY QUESTIONS

1. *Dispatches* has a compelling narrative style that could be characterized as "nonlinear." Discuss the elements of this style and how they are appropriate to presenting the subject of the Vietnam War.
2. Discuss the ambiguities of Herr's position as a correspondent rather than a soldier. How do the regular soldiers react to him? The officers?
3. This passage is largely concerned not so much with the tactics and weaponry of war as it is with the psychological toll the fighting takes on the "grunts." Show how Herr suggests that almost everyone he sees is a psychic casualty of the war.

SUGGESTIONS FOR FURTHER READING AND WRITING

You may wish to read, and write a paper on, an entire book, either an autobiography or a novel, by one of the authors included in this section. You might choose from

1. MAYA ANGELOU, *I Know Why the Caged Bird Sings* (New York: Bantam Classics Spectra, 1983); autobiography.
2. JOHN G. NEIHARDT, ed., *Black Elk Speaks* (Lincoln: U Nebraska P, 1979); autobiography.
3. MARK TWAIN (Samuel Clemens), *Life on the Mississippi* (1883); autobiography.
4. MARK TWAIN (Samuel Clemens), *Adventures of Huckleberry Finn* (1885); fiction.

AN ANTHOLOGY OF
SHORT STORIES

Chickamauga[1]

Ambrose Bierce (1842–1914)

Ambrose Bierce was a writer ahead of his time who experimented with early versions of stream-of-consciousness narration and even surrealism. Born in Ohio to poor parents, he participated in the Civil War as a Union soldier and surveyor. He surveyed many of the war's most significant battlefields, including Chickamauga. After traveling widely after the war, to London and all over America, Bierce married and settled in San Francisco, where he wrote often scathing journalistic pieces attacking the hypocrisy of public figures. He began to gain a reputation for his unsentimental, vivid short stories. At the end of his life, in 1913, he mysteriously disappeared while on a trip to Mexico to meet the revolutionary leader Pancho Villa.

One sunny autumn afternoon a child strayed away from its rude home in a small field and entered a forest unobserved. It was happy in a new sense of freedom from control—happy in the opportunity of exploration and adventure; for this child's spirit, in bodies of its ancestors, had for many thousands of years been trained to memorable feats of discovery and conquest—victories in battles whose critical moments were centuries, whose victors' camps were cities of hewn stone. From the cradle of its race it had conquered its way through two continents, and, passing a great sea, had penetrated a third, there to be born to war and dominance as a heritage.

The child was a boy, aged about six years, the son of a poor planter. In his younger manhood the father had been a soldier, had fought against naked savages, and followed the flag of his country into the capital of a civilized race to the far South. In the peaceful life of a planter the warrior-fire survived; once kindled it is never extinguished. The man loved military books and pictures, and the boy had understood enough to make himself a wooden sword, though even the eye of his father would hardly have known it for what it was. This weapon he now bore bravely, as became the son of an heroic race, and pausing now and again in the sunny spaces of the forest, assumed, with some exaggeration, the postures of aggression and defense that he had been taught by the engraver's art. Made reckless by the ease with which he overcame invisible foes attempting to stay his advance, he committed the common enough military error of pushing the pursuit to a dangerous extreme, until he found himself upon the margin of a wide but shallow brook, whose rapid waters barred his direct advance against the flying foe who had crossed with illogical ease. But the intrepid victor was not to be

---

[1]The Battle of Chickamauga Creek took place in Tennessee on September 19–20, 1863. Casualties in the first four hours of battle ran to over fifty percent on both sides. There were nearly 40,000 casualties in all, making it one of the most confusing and deadly battles of the Civil War.

baffled; the spirit of the race which had passed the great sea burned unconquerable in that small breast and would not be denied. Finding a place where some bowlders in the bed of the stream lay but a step apart, he made his way across and fell again upon the rear guard of his imaginary foe, putting all to the sword.

Now that the battle had been won, prudence required that he withdraw to his base of operations. Alas! like many a mightier conquerer, and like one, the mightiest, he could not

curb the lust for war,
Nor learn that tempted Fate will leave the loftiest star.[2]

Advancing from the bank of the creek, he suddenly found himself confronted with a new and more formidable enemy; in the path that he was following, bolt upright, with ears erect and paws suspended before it, sat a rabbit. With a startled cry the child turned and fled, he knew not in what direction, calling with inarticulate cries for his mother, weeping, stumbling, his tender skin cruelly torn by brambles, his little heart beating hard with terror—breathless, blind with tears—lost in the forest! Then, for more than an hour, he wandered with erring feet through the tangled undergrowth, till at last, overcome with fatigue, he lay down in a narrow space between two rocks, within a few yards of the stream, and, still grasping his toy sword, no longer a weapon but a companion, sobbed himself to sleep. The wood birds sang merrily above his head; the squirrels, whisking their bravery of tail, ran barking from tree to tree, unconscious of the pity of it, and somewhere far away was a strange, muffled thunder, as if the partridges were drumming in celebration of nature's victory over the son of her immemorial enslavers. And back at the little plantation, where white men and black were hastily searching the fields and hedgerows in alarm, a mother's heart was breaking for her missing child.

Hours passed, and then the little sleeper rose to his feet. The chill of the evening was in his limbs, the fear of the gloom in his heart. But he had rested, and he no longer wept. With some blind instinct which impelled to action, he struggled through the undergrowth about him and came to a more open ground—on his right the brook, to the left a gentle acclivity studded with infrequent trees; over all the gathering gloom of twilight. A thin, ghostly mist rose along the water. It frightened and repelled him; instead of recrossing, in the direction whence he had come, he turned his back upon it and went forward toward the dark inclosing wood. Suddenly he saw before him a strange moving object which he took to be some large animal—a dog, a pig—he could not name it; perhaps it was a bear. He had seen pictures of bears, but knew of nothing to their discredit, and had vaguely wished to meet one. But something in form or movement of this object—something in the awkwardness of its approach—told

---

[2]From *Childe Harold's Pilgrimage* by Lord Byron. Byron's "conqueror" is Napoleon.

him that it was not a bear, and curiosity was stayed by fear. He stood still, and as it came slowly on, gained courage every moment, for he saw that at least it had not the long, menacing ears of the rabbit. Possibly his impressionable mind was half conscious of something familiar in its shambling, awkward gait. Before it had approached near enough to resolve his doubts, he saw that it was followed by another and another. To right and to left were many more; the whole open space about him was alive with them—all moving forward toward the brook.

They were men. They crept upon their hands and knees. They used their hands only, dragging their legs. They used their knees only, their arms hanging useless at their sides. They strove to rise to their feet, but fell prone in the attempt. They did nothing naturally, and nothing alike, save only to advance foot by foot in the same direction. Singly, in pairs, and in little groups, they came on through the gloom, some halting now and again while others crept slowly past them, then resuming their movement. They came by dozens and by hundreds; as far on either hand as one could see in the deepening gloom they extended, and the black wood behind them appeared to be inexhaustible. The very ground seemed in motion toward the creek. Occasionally one who had paused did not again go on, but lay motionless. He was dead. Some, pausing, made strange gestures with their hands, erected their arms and lowered them again, clasped their heads; spread their palms upward, as men are sometimes seen to do in public prayer.

Not all of this did the child note; it is what would have been noted by an older observer; he saw little but that these were men, yet crept like babes. Being men, they were not terrible, though some of them were unfamiliarly clad. He moved among them freely, going from one to another and peering into their faces with childish curiosity. All their faces were singularly white and many were streaked and gouted with red. Something in this—something too, perhaps, in their grotesque attitudes and movements—reminded him of the painted clown whom he had seen last summer in the circus, and he laughed as he watched them. But on and ever on they crept, these maimed and bleeding men, as heedless as he of the dramatic contrast between his laughter and their own ghastly gravity. To him it was a merry spectacle. He had seen his father's negroes creep upon their hands and knees for his amusement—had ridden them so, "making believe" they were his horses. He now approached one of these crawling figures from behind and with an agile movement mounted it astride. The man sank upon his breast, recovered, flung the small boy fiercely to the ground as an unbroken colt might have done, then turned upon him a face that lacked a lower jaw—from the upper teeth to the throat was a great red gap fringed with hanging shreds of flesh and splinters of bone. The unnatural prominence of nose, the absence of chin, the fierce eyes, gave this man the appearance of a great bird of prey crimsoned in throat and breast by the blood of its quarry. The man rose to his knees, the child to his feet. The man shook his fist at the child; the child, terrified at last, ran to a tree near by, got upon the farther side of it, and took a more serious view of the situation. And so the uncanny multitude dragged itself slowly and painfully along in hideous pantomime— moved forward down the slope like a swarm of great black beetles, with never a sound of going—in silence profound, absolute.

Instead of darkening, the haunted landscape began to brighten. Through the belt of trees beyond the brook shone a strange red light, the trunks and branches of the trees making a black lacework against it. It struck the creeping figures and gave them monstrous shadows, which caricatured their movements on the lit grass. It fell upon their faces, touching their whiteness with a ruddy tinge, accentuating the stains with which so many of them were freaked and maculated. It sparkled on buttons and bits of metal in their clothing. Instinctively the child turned toward the growing splendor and moved down the slope with his horrible companions; in a few moments had passed the foremost of the throng—not much of a feat, considering his advantages. He placed himself in the lead, his wooden sword still in hand, and solemnly directed the march, conforming his pace to theirs and occasionally turning as if to see that his forces did not straggle. Surely such a leader never before had such a following.

Scattered about upon the ground now slowly narrowing by the encroachment of this awful march to water, were certain articles to which, in the leader's mind, were coupled no significant associations; an occasional blanket, tightly rolled lengthwise, doubled and the ends bound together with a string; a heavy knapsack here, and there a broken musket—such things, in short, as are found in the rear of retreating troops, the "spoor" of men flying from their hunters. Everywhere near the creek, which here had a margin of lowland, the earth was trodden into mud by the feet of men and horses. An observer of better experience in the use of his eyes would have noticed that these footprints pointed in both directions; the ground had been twice passed over—in advance and in retreat. A few hours before, these desperate, stricken men, with their more fortunate and now distant comrades, had penetrated the forest in thousands. Their successive battalions, breaking into swarms and reforming in lines, had passed the child on every side—had almost trodden on him as he slept. The rustle and murmur of their march had not awakened him. Almost within a stone's throw of where he lay they had fought a battle; but all unheard by him were the roar of the musketry, the shock of the cannon, "the thunder of the captains and the shouting."[3] He had slept through it all, grasping his little wooden sword with perhaps a tighter clutch in unconscious sympathy with his martial environment, but as heedless of the grandeur of the struggle as the dead who died to make the glory.

The fire beyond the belt of woods on the farther side of the creek, reflected to earth from the canopy of its own smoke, was now suffusing the whole landscape. It transformed the sinuous line of mist to the vapor of gold. The water gleamed with dashes of red, and red, too, were many of the stones protruding

---

[3]Job 39:25: "He saith among the trumpets, Ha, ha! and he smelleth the battle afar off, the thunder of the captains, and the shouting."

above the surface. But that was blood; the less desperately wounded had stained them in crossing. On them, too, the child now crossed with eager steps; he was going to the fire. As he stood upon the farther bank, he turned about to look at the companions of his march. The advance was arriving at the creek. The stronger had already drawn themselves to the brink and plunged their faces in the flood. Three or four who lay without motion appeared to have no heads. At this the child's eyes expanded with wonder; even his hospitable understanding could not accept a phenomenon implying such vitality as that. After slaking their thirst these men had not the strength to back away from the water, nor to keep their heads above it. They were drowned. In rear of these the open spaces of the forest showed the leader as many formless figures of his grim command as at first; but not nearly so many were in motion. He waved his cap for their encouragement and smilingly pointed with his weapon in the direction of the guiding light—a pillar of fire to this strange exodus.[4]

Confident of the fidelity of his forces, he now entered the belt of woods, passed through it easily in the red illumination, climbed a fence, ran across a field, turning now and again to coquette with his responsive shadow, and so approached the blazing ruin of a dwelling. Desolation everywhere. In all the wide glare not a living thing was visible. He cared nothing for that; the spectacle pleased, and he danced with glee in imitation of the wavering flames. He ran about collecting fuel, but every object that he found was too heavy for him to cast in from the distance to which the heat limited his approach. In despair he flung in his sword—a surrender to the superior forces of nature. His military career was at an end.

Shifting his position, his eyes fell upon some outbuildings which had an oddly familiar appearance, as if he had dreamed of them. He stood considering them with wonder, when suddenly the entire plantation, with its inclosing forest, seemed to turn as if upon a pivot. His little world swung half around; the points of the compass were reversed. He recognized the blazing building as his own home!

For a moment he stood stupefied by the power of the revelation, then ran with stumbling feet, making a half circuit of the ruin. There, conspicuous in the light of the conflagration, lay the dead body of a woman—the white face turned upward, the hands thrown out and clutched full of grass, the clothing deranged, the long dark hair in tangles and full of clotted blood. The greater part of the forehead was torn away, and from the jagged hole the brain protruded, overflowing the temple, a frothy mass of gray, crowned with clusters of crimson bubbles—the work of a shell!

The child moved his little hands, making wild, uncertain gestures. He uttered a series of inarticulate and indescribable cries—something between the

---

[4]Exodus 13:21; during the flight from Egypt, God led the Israelites with a pillar of fire lighting the night.

chattering of an ape and the gobbling of a turkey—a startling, soulless, unholy sound, the language of a devil. The child was a deaf mute.

Then he stood motionless, with quivering lips, looking down upon the wreck.

1889

The Rocking-Horse Winner

D. H. Lawrence (1885–1930)

D. H. Lawrence came from a working-class family in the English Midlands. His father was a miner who drank heavily; his mother was better educated and dreamed of helping her children out of their strained economic circumstances. Lawrence escaped through getting an education and teaching. He married a divorced German woman and got into trouble with the authorities because of his objections to England's participation in World War I. In *Sons and Lovers* (1913), his first important novel, Lawrence gave an autobiographical account of his family life. *The Rainbow* (1915), a sexually frank intergenerational novel of great power, was branded as indecent by many readers. The rest of Lawrence's life and career were troubled by restless travel—to Italy, the American Southwest, Mexico—and by trouble with critics and censors. Lawrence's constant theme was not so much that complete sexual freedom is necessary but that modern man has been tamed and reduced in stature by the dominance of reason over intuition. Lawrence argued passionately for human freedom, for a knowledge of the heart rather than of the head.

There was a woman who was beautiful, who started with all the advantages, yet she had no luck. She married for love, and the love turned to dust. She had bonny children, yet she felt they had been thrust upon her, and she could not love them. They looked at her coldly, as if they were finding fault with her. And hurriedly she felt she must cover up some fault in herself. Yet what it was that she must cover up she never knew. Nevertheless, when her children were present, she always felt the centre of her heart go hard. This troubled her, and in her manner she was all the more gentle and anxious for her children, as if she loved them very much. Only she herself knew that at the centre of her heart was a hard little place that could not feel love, no, not for anybody. Everybody else said of her: "She is such a good mother. She adores her children." Only she herself, and her children themselves, knew it was not so. They read it in each other's eyes.

There were a boy and two little girls. They lived in a pleasant house, with a garden, and they had discreet servants, and felt themselves superior to anyone in the neighbourhood.

Although they lived in style, they felt always an anxiety in the house. There was never enough money. The mother had a small income, and the father had a small income, but not nearly enough for the social position which they had to keep up. The father went into town to some office. But though he had good prospects, these prospects never materialized. There was always the grinding sense of the shortage of money, though the style was always kept up.

At last the mother said: "I will see if I can't make something." But she did not know where to begin. She racked her brains, and tried this thing and the other, but could not find anything successful. The failure made deep lines come into her face. Her children were growing up, they would have to go to school. There must be more money, there must be more money. The father, who was always very handsome and expensive in his tastes, seemed as if he never would be able to do anything worth doing. And the mother, who had a great belief in herself, did not succeed any better, and her tastes were just as expensive.

And so the house came to be haunted by the unspoken phrase: There must be more money! There must be more money! The children could hear it all the time, though nobody said it aloud. They heard it at Christmas, when the expensive and splendid toys filled the nursery. Behind the shining modern rocking horse, behind the smart doll's-house, a voice would start whispering: "There must be more money! There must be more money!" And the children would stop playing, to listen for a moment. They would look into each other's eyes, to see if they had all heard. And each one saw in the eyes of the other two that they too had heard. "There must be more money! There must be more money!"

It came whispering from the springs of the still-swaying rocking horse, and even the horse, bending his wooden, champing head, heard it. The big doll, sitting so pink and smirking in her new pram, could hear it quite plainly, and seemed to be smirking all the more self-consciously because of it. The foolish puppy, too, that took the place of the Teddy bear, he was looking so extraordinarily foolish for no other reason but that he heard the secret whisper all over the house: "There must be more money!"

Yet nobody ever said it aloud. The whisper was everywhere, and therefore no one spoke it. Just as no one ever says: "We are breathing!" in spite of the fact that breath is coming and going all the time.

"Mother," said the boy Paul one day, "why don't we keep a car of our own? Why do we always use uncle's, or else a taxi?"

"Because we're the poor members of the family," said the mother.

"But why are we, mother?"

"Well—I suppose," she said slowly and bitterly, "it's because your father has no luck."

The boy was silent for some time.

"Is luck money, mother?" he asked, rather timidly.

"No, Paul. Not quite. It's what causes you to have money."

"Oh!" said Paul vaguely. "I thought when Uncle Oscar said filthy lucker, it meant money."

"Filthy lucre does mean money," said the mother. "But it's lucre, not luck."

"Oh!" said the boy. "Then what is luck, mother?"

"It's what causes you to have money. If you're lucky you have money. That's why it's better to be born lucky than rich. If you're rich, you may lose your money. But if you're lucky, you will always get more money."

"Oh! Will you? And is father not lucky?"

"Very unlucky, I should say," she said bitterly.

The boy watched her with unsure eyes.

"Why?" he asked.

"I don't know. Nobody ever knows why one person is lucky and another unlucky."

"Don't they? Nobody at all? Does nobody know?"

"Perhaps God. But He never tells."

"He ought to, then. And aren't you lucky either, mother?"

"I can't be, if I married an unlucky husband."

"But by yourself, aren't you?"

"I used to think I was, before I married. Now I think I am very unlucky indeed."

"Why?"

"Well—never mind! Perhaps I'm not really," she said.

The child looked at her, to see if she meant it. But he saw, by the lines of her mouth, that she was only trying to hide something from him.

"Well, anyhow," he said stoutly, "I'm a lucky person."

"Why?" said his mother, with a sudden laugh.

He stared at her. He didn't even know why he had said it.

"God told me," he asserted, brazening it out.

"I hope He did, dear!" she said, again with a laugh, but rather bitter.

"He did, mother!"

"Excellent!" said the mother, using one of her husband's exclamations.

The boy saw she did not believe him; or, rather, that she paid no attention to his assertion. This angered him somewhat, and made him want to compel her attention.

He went off by himself, vaguely, in a childish way, seeking for the clue to "luck." Absorbed, taking no heed of other people, he went about with a sort of stealth, seeking inwardly for luck. He wanted luck, he wanted it, he wanted it. When the two girls were playing dolls in the nursery, he would sit on his big rocking horse, charging madly into space, with a frenzy that made the little girls peer at him uneasily. Wildly the horse careered, the waving dark hair of the boy tossed, his eyes had a strange glare in them. The little girls dared not speak to him.

When he had ridden to the end of his mad little journey, he climbed down and stood in front of his rocking horse, staring fixedly into its lowered face. Its red mouth was slightly open, its big eye was wide and glassy-bright.

"Now!" he would silently command the snorting steed. "Now, take me to where there is luck! Now take me!"

And he would slash the horse on the neck with the little whip he had asked Uncle Oscar for. He knew the horse could take him to where there was luck, if only he forced it. So he would mount again, and start on his furious ride, hoping at last to get there. He knew he could get there.

"You'll break your horse, Paul!" said the nurse.

"He's always riding like that! I wish he'd leave off!" said his elder sister Joan.

But he only glared down on them in silence. Nurse gave him up. She could make nothing of him. Anyhow he was growing beyond her.

One day his mother and his Uncle Oscar came in when he was on one of his furious rides. He did not speak to them.

"Hallo, you young jockey! Riding a winner?" said his uncle.

"Aren't you growing too big for a rocking horse? You're not a very little boy any longer, you know," said his mother.

But Paul only gave a blue glare from his big, rather close-set eyes. He would speak to nobody when he was in full tilt. His mother watched him with an anxious expression on her face.

At last he suddenly stopped forcing his horse into the mechanical gallop, and slid down.

"Well, I got there!" he announced fiercely, his blue eyes still flaring, and his sturdy long legs straddling apart.

"Where did you get to?" asked his mother.

"Where I wanted to go," he flared back at her.

"That's right, son!" said Uncle Oscar. "Don't you stop till you get there. What's the horse's name?"

"He doesn't have a name," said the boy.

"Gets on without all right?" asked the uncle.

"Well, he has different names. He was called Sansovino last week."

"Sansovino, eh? Won the Ascot. How did you know his name?"

"He always talks about horse races with Bassett," said Joan.

The uncle was delighted to find that his small nephew was posted with all the racing news. Bassett, the young gardener, who had been wounded in the left foot in the war and had got his present job through Oscar Cresswell, whose batman he had been, was a perfect blade of the "turf." He lived in the racing events, and the small boy lived with him.

Oscar Cresswell got it all from Bassett.

"Master Paul comes and asks me, so I can't do more than tell him, sir," said Bassett, his face terribly serious, as if he were speaking of religious matters.

"And does he ever put anything on a horse he fancies?"

"Well—I don't want to give him away—he's a young sport, a fine sport, sir. Would you mind asking him yourself? He sort of takes a pleasure in it, and perhaps he'd feel I was giving him away, sir, if you don't mind."

Bassett was serious as a church.

The uncle went back to his nephew, and took him off for a ride in the car.

"Say, Paul, old man, do you ever put anything on a horse?" the uncle asked.

The boy watched the handsome man closely.

"Why, do you think I oughtn't to?" he parried.

"Not a bit of it! I thought perhaps you might give me a tip for the Lincoln."

The car sped on into the country, going down to Uncle Oscar's place in Hampshire.

"Honour bright?" said the nephew.

"Honour bright, son!" said the uncle.

"Well, then, Daffodil."

"Daffodil! I doubt it, sonny. What about Mirza?"

"I only know the winner," said the boy. "That's Daffodil."

"Daffodil, eh?"

There was a pause. Daffodil was an obscure horse comparatively.

"Uncle!"

"Yes, son?"

"You won't let it go any further, will you? I promised Bassett."

"Bassett be damned, old man! What's he got to do with it?"

"We're partners. We've been partners from the first. Uncle, he lent me my first five shillings, which I lost. I promised him, honour bright, it was only between me and him; only you gave me that ten-shilling note I started winning with, so I thought you were lucky. You won't let it go any further, will you?"

The boy gazed at his uncle from those big, hot, blue eyes, set rather close together. The uncle stirred and laughed uneasily.

"Right you are, son! I'll keep your tip private. Daffodil, eh? How much are you putting on him?"

"All except twenty pounds," said the boy. "I keep that in reserve."

The uncle thought it a good joke.

"You keep twenty pounds in reserve, do you, you young romancer? What are you betting, then?"

"I'm betting three hundred," said the boy gravely. "But it's between you and me, Uncle Oscar! Honour bright?"

The uncle burst into a roar of laughter.

"It's between you and me all right, you young Nat Gould," he said, laughing. "But where's your three hundred?"

"Bassett keeps it for me. We're partners."

"You are, are you! And what is Bassett putting on Daffodil?"

"He won't go quite as high as I do, I expect. Perhaps he'll go a hundred and fifty."

"What, pennies?" laughed the uncle.

"Pounds," said the child, with a surprised look at his uncle. "Bassett keeps a bigger reserve than I do."

Between wonder and amusement Uncle Oscar was silent. He pursued the matter no further, but he determined to take his nephew with him to the Lincoln races.

"Now, son," he said, "I'm putting twenty on Mirza, and I'll put five for you on any horse you fancy. What's your pick?"

"Daffodil, uncle."

"No, not the fiver on Daffodil!"

"I should if it was my own fiver," said the child.

"Good! Good! Right you are! A fiver for me and a fiver for you on Daffodil."

The child had never been to a race meeting before, and his eyes were blue fire. He pursed his mouth tight, and watched. A Frenchman just in front had put his money on Lancelot. Wild with excitement, he flayed his arms up and down, yelling "Lancelot! Lancelot!" in his French accent.

Daffodil came in first, Lancelot second, Mirza third. The child, flushed and with eyes blazing, was curiously serene. His uncle brought him four five-pound notes, four to one.

"What am I to do with these?" he cried, waving them before the boy's eyes.

"I suppose we'll talk to Bassett," said the boy. "I expect I have fifteen hundred now; and twenty in reserve; and this twenty."

His uncle studied him for some moments.

"Look here, son!" he said. "You're not serious about Bassett and that fifteen hundred, are you?"

"Yes, I am. But it's between you and me, uncle. Honour bright!"

"Honour bright all right, son! But I must talk to Bassett."

"If you'd like to be a partner, uncle, with Bassett and me, we could all be partners. Only, you'd have to promise, honour bright, uncle, not to let it go beyond us three. Bassett and I are lucky, and you must be lucky, because it was your ten shillings I started winning with . . ."

Uncle Oscar took both Bassett and Paul into Richmond Park for an afternoon, and there they talked.

"It's like this, you see, sir," Bassett said. "Master Paul would get me talking about racing events, spinning yarns, you know, sir. And he was always keen on knowing if I'd made or if I'd lost. It's about a year since, now, that I put five shillings on Blush of Dawn for him—and we lost. Then the luck turned, with that ten shillings he had from you, that we put on Singhalese. And since that time, it's been pretty steady, all things considering. What do you say, Master Paul?"

"We're all right when we're sure," said Paul. "It's when we're not quite sure that we go down."

"Oh, but we're careful then," said Bassett.

"But when are you sure?" smiled Uncle Oscar.

"It's Master Paul, sir," said Bassett, in a secret, religious voice. "It's as if he had it from heaven. Like Daffodil, now, for the Lincoln. That was as sure as eggs."

"Did you put anything on Daffodil?" asked Oscar Cresswell.

"Yes, sir, I made my bit."

"And my nephew?"

Bassett was obstinately silent, looking at Paul.

"I made twelve hundred, didn't I, Bassett? I told uncle I was putting three hundred on Daffodil."

"That's right," said Bassett, nodding.

"But where's the money?" asked the uncle.

"I keep it safe locked up, sir. Master Paul he can have it any minute he likes to ask for it."

"What, fifteen hundred pounds?"

"And twenty! and forty, that is, with the twenty he made on the course."

"It's amazing!" said the uncle.

"If Master Paul offers you to be partners, sir, I would, if I were you; if you'll excuse me," said Bassett.

Oscar Cresswell thought about it.

"I'll see the money," he said.

They drove home again, and sure enough, Bassett came round to the garden-house with fifteen hundred pounds in notes. The twenty pounds reserve was left with Joe Glee, in the Turf Commission deposit.

"You see, it's all right, uncle, when I'm sure! Then we go strong, for all we're worth. Don't we, Bassett?"

"We do that, Master Paul."

"And when are you sure?" said the uncle, laughing.

"Oh, well, sometimes I'm absolutely sure, like about Daffodil," said the boy; "and sometimes I have an idea; and sometimes I haven't even an idea, have I, Bassett? Then we're careful, because we mostly go down."

"You do, do you! And when you're sure, like about Daffodil, what makes you sure, sonny?"

"Oh, well, I don't know," said the boy uneasily. "I'm sure, you know, uncle; that's all."

"It's as if he had it from heaven, sir," Bassett reiterated.

"I should say so!" said the uncle.

But he became a partner. And when the Leger was coming on, Paul was "sure" about Lively Spark, which was a quite inconsiderable horse. The boy insisted on putting a thousand on the horse, Bassett went for five hundred, and Oscar Cresswell two hundred. Lively Spark came in first, and the betting had been ten to one against him. Paul had made ten thousand.

"You see," he said, "I was absolutely sure of him."

Even Oscar Cresswell had cleared two thousand.

"Look here, son," he said, "this sort of thing makes me nervous."

"It needn't, uncle! Perhaps I shan't be sure again for a long time."

"But what are you going to do with your money?" asked the uncle.

"Of course," said the boy, "I started it for mother. She said she had no luck, because father is unlucky, so I thought if I was lucky, it might stop whispering."

"What might stop whispering?"

"Our house. I hate our house for whispering."

"What does it whisper?"

"Why—why"—the boy fidgeted—"why, I don't know. But it's always short of money, you know, uncle."

"I know it, son, I know it."

"You know people send mother writs, don't you, uncle?"

"I'm afraid I do," said the uncle.

"And then the house whispers, like people laughing at you behind your back. It's awful, that is! I thought if I was lucky . . ."

"You might stop it," added the uncle.

The boy watched him with big blue eyes that had an uncanny cold fire in them, and he said never a word.

"Well, then!" said the uncle. "What are we doing?"

"I shouldn't like mother to know I was lucky," said the boy.

"Why not, son?"

"She'd stop me."

"I don't think she would."

"Oh!"—and the boy writhed in an odd way—"I don't want her to know, uncle."

"All right, son! We'll manage it without her knowing."

They managed it very easily. Paul, at the other's suggestion, handed over five thousand pounds to his uncle, who deposited it with the family lawyer, who was then to inform Paul's mother that a relative had put five thousand pounds into his hands, which sum was to be paid out a thousand pounds at a time, on the mother's birthday, for the next five years.

"So she'll have a birthday present of a thousand pounds for five successive years," said Uncle Oscar. "I hope it won't make it all the harder for her later."

Paul's mother had her birthday in November. The house had been "whispering" worse than ever lately, and, even in spite of his luck, Paul could not bear up against it. He was very anxious to see the effect of the birthday letter, telling his mother about the thousand pounds.

When there were no visitors, Paul now took his meals with his parents, as he was beyond the nursery control. His mother went into town nearly every day. She had discovered that she had an odd knack of sketching furs and dress materials, so she worked secretly in the studio of a friend who was the chief "artist" for the leading drapers. She drew the figures of ladies in furs and ladies in silk and sequins for the newspaper advertisements. This young woman artist earned several thousand pounds a year, but Paul's mother only made several hundreds, and she was again dissatisfied. She so wanted to be first in something, and she did not succeed, even in making sketches for drapery advertisements.

She was down to breakfast on the morning of her birthday. Paul watched her face as she read her letters. He knew the lawyer's letter. As his mother read it, her face hardened and became more expressionless. Then a cold, determined look came on her mouth. She hid the letter under the pile of others, and said not a word about it.

"Didn't you have anything nice in the post for your birthday, mother?" said Paul.

"Quite moderately nice," she said, her voice cold and absent.

She went away to town without saying more.

But in the afternoon Uncle Oscar appeared. He said Paul's mother had had a long interview with the lawyer, asking if the whole five thousand could be advanced at once, as she was in debt.

"What do you think, uncle?" said the boy.

"I leave it to you, son."

"Oh, let her have it, then! We can get some more with the other," said the boy.

"A bird in the hand is worth two in the bush, laddie!" said Uncle Oscar.

"But I'm sure to know for the Grand National; or the Lincolnshire; or else the Derby. I'm sure to know for one of them," said Paul.

So Uncle Oscar signed the agreement, and Paul's mother touched the whole five thousand. Then something very curious happened. The voices in the house suddenly went mad, like a chorus of frogs on a spring evening. There were certain new furnishings, and Paul had a tutor. He was really going to Eton, his father's school, in the following autumn. There were flowers in the winter, and a blossoming of the luxury Paul's mother had been used to. And yet the voices in the house, behind the sprays of mimosa and almond blossom, and from under the piles of iridescent cushions, simply trilled and screamed in a sort of ecstasy: "There must be more money! Oh-h-h, there must be more money. Oh, now, now-w! Now-w-w—there must be more money—more than ever! More than ever!"

It frightened Paul terribly. He studied away at his Latin and Greek with his tutors. But his intense hours were spent with Bassett. The Grand National had gone by: he had not "known," and had lost a hundred pounds. Summer was at hand. He was in agony for the Lincoln. But even for the Lincoln he didn't "know" and he lost fifty pounds. He became wild-eyed and strange, as if something were going to explode in him.

"Let it alone, son! Don't you bother about it!" urged Uncle Oscar. But it was as if the boy couldn't really hear what his uncle was saying.

"I've got to know for the Derby! I've got to know for the Derby!" the child reiterated, his big blue eyes blazing with a sort of madness.

His mother noticed how overwrought he was.

"You'd better go to the seaside. Wouldn't you like to go now to the seaside, instead of waiting? I think you'd better," she said, looking down at him anxiously, her heart curiously heavy because of him.

But the child lifted his uncanny blue eyes.

"I couldn't possibly go before the Derby, mother!" he said. "I couldn't possibly!"

"Why not?" she said, her voice becoming heavy when she was opposed. "Why not? You can still go from the seaside to see the Derby with your Uncle Oscar, if that's what you wish. No need for you to wait here. Besides, I think you care too much about these races. It's a bad sign. My family has been a gambling family, and you won't know till you grow up how much damage it has done. But it has done damage. I shall have to send Bassett away, and ask Uncle Oscar not to talk racing to you, unless you promise to be reasonable about it; go away to the seaside and forget it. You're all nerves!"

"I'll do what you like, mother, so long as you don't send me away till after the Derby," the boy said.

"Send you away from where? Just from this house?"

"Yes," he said, gazing at her.

"Why, you curious child, what makes you care about this house so much, suddenly? I never knew you loved it."

He gazed at her without speaking. He had a secret within a secret, something he had not divulged, even to Bassett or to his Uncle Oscar.

But his mother, after standing undecided and a little bit sullen for some moments, said:

"Very well, then! Don't go to the seaside till after the Derby, if you don't wish it. But promise me you won't let your nerves go to pieces. Promise you won't think so much about horse racing and events, as you call them!"

"Oh, no," said the boy casually. "I won't think much about them, mother. You needn't worry. I wouldn't worry, mother, if I were you."

"If you were me and I were you," said his mother, "I wonder what we should do!"

"But you know you needn't worry, mother, don't you?" the boy repeated.

"I should be awfully glad to know it," she said wearily.

"Oh, well, you can, you know. I mean, you ought to know you needn't worry," he insisted.

"Ought I? Then I'll see about it," she said.

Paul's secret of secrets was his wooden horse, that which had no name. Since he was emancipated from a nurse and a nursery-governess, he had had his rocking horse removed to his own bedroom at the top of the house.

"Surely, you're too big for a rocking horse!" his mother had remonstrated.

"Well, you see, mother, till I can have a real horse, I like to have some sort of animal about," had been his quaint answer.

"Do you feel he keeps you company?" she laughed.

"Oh, yes! He's very good, he always keeps me company, when I'm there," said Paul.

So the horse, rather shabby, stood in an arrested prance in the boy's bedroom.

The Derby was drawing near, and the boy grew more and more tense. He hardly heard what was spoken to him, he was very frail, and his eyes were really uncanny. His mother had sudden seizures of uneasiness about him. Sometimes, for half-an-hour, she would feel a sudden anxiety about him that was almost anguish. She wanted to rush to him at once, and know he was safe.

Two nights before the Derby, she was at a big party in town, when one of her rushes of anxiety about her boy, her first-born, gripped her heart till she could hardly speak. She fought with the feeling, might and main, for she believed in common sense. But it was too strong. She had to leave the dance and go downstairs to telephone to the country. The children's nursery-governess was terribly surprised and startled at being rung up in the night.

"Are the children all right, Miss Wilmot?"

"Oh, yes, they are quite all right."

"Master Paul? Is he all right?"

"He went to bed as right as a trivet. Shall I run up and look at him?"

"No," said Paul's mother reluctantly. "No! Don't trouble. It's all right. Don't sit up. We shall be home fairly soon." She did not want her son's privacy intruded upon.

"Very good," said the governess.

It was about one o'clock when Paul's mother and father drove up to their house. All was still. Paul's mother went to her room and slipped off her white fur coat. She had told her maid not to wait up for her. She heard her husband downstairs, mixing a whisky-and-soda.

And then, because of the strange anxiety at her heart, she stole upstairs to her son's room. Noiselessly she went along the upper corridor. Was there a faint noise? What was it?

She stood, with arrested muscles, outside his door, listening. There was a strange, heavy, and yet not loud noise. Her heart stood still. It was a soundless noise, yet rushing and powerful. Something huge, in violent, hushed motion. What was it? What in God's name was it? She ought to know. She felt that she knew the noise. She knew what it was.

Yet she could not place it. She couldn't say what it was. And on and on it went, like a madness.

Softly, frozen with anxiety and fear, she turned the door handle.

The room was dark. Yet in the space near the window, she heard and saw something plunging to and fro. She gazed in fear and amazement.

Then suddenly she switched on the light, and saw her son, in his green pyjamas, madly surging on the rocking horse. The blaze of light suddenly lit him up, as he urged the wooden horse, and lit her up, as she stood, blonde, in her dress of pale green and crystal, in the doorway.

"Paul!" she cried. "Whatever are you doing?"

"It's Malabar!" he screamed, in a powerful, strange voice. "It's Malabar."

His eyes blazed at her for one strange and senseless second, as he ceased urging his wooden horse. Then he fell with a crash to the ground, and she, all her tormented motherhood flooding upon her, rushed to gather him up.

But he was unconscious, and unconscious he remained, with some brain-fever. He talked and tossed, and his mother sat stonily by his side.

"Malabar! It's Malabar! Bassett, Bassett, I know it! It's Malabar!"

So the child cried, trying to get up and urge the rocking horse that gave him his inspiration.

"What does he mean by Malabar?" asked the heart-frozen mother.

"I don't know," said the father stonily.

"What does he mean by Malabar?" she asked her brother Oscar.

"It's one of the horses running for the Derby," was the answer.

And, in spite of himself, Oscar Cresswell spoke to Bassett, and himself put a thousand on Malabar: at fourteen to one.

The third day of the illness was critical: they were waiting for a change. The boy, with his rather long, curly hair, was tossing ceaselessly on the pillow. He neither slept nor regained consciousness, and his eyes were like blue stones. His mother sat, feeling her heart had gone, turned actually into a stone.

In the evening, Oscar Cresswell did not come, but Bassett sent a message, saying could he come up for one moment, just one moment? Paul's mother was very angry at the intrusion, but on second thought she agreed. The boy was the same. Perhaps Bassett might bring him to consciousness.

The gardener, a shortish fellow with a little brown moustache, and sharp little brown eyes, tiptoed into the room, touched his imaginary cap to Paul's mother, and stole to the bedside, staring with glittering, smallish eyes, at the tossing, dying child.

"Master Paul!" he whispered. "Master Paul! Malabar come in first all right, a clean win. I did as you told me. You've made over seventy thousand pounds, you have; you've got over eighty thousand. Malabar came in all right, Master Paul."

"Malabar! Malabar! Did I say Malabar, mother? Did I say Malabar? Do you think I'm lucky, mother? I knew Malabar, didn't I? Over eighty thousand pounds! I call that lucky, don't you, mother? Over eighty thousand pounds! I knew, didn't I know I knew? Malabar came in all right. If I ride my horse till I'm sure, then I tell you, Bassett, you can go as high as you like. Did you go for all you were worth, Bassett?"

"I went a thousand on it, Master Paul."

"I never told you, mother that if I can ride my horse, and get there, then I'm absolutely sure—oh, absolutely! Mother, did I ever tell you? I'm lucky."

"No, you never did," said the mother.

But the boy died in the night.

And even as he lay dead, his mother heard her brother's voice saying to her: "My God, Hester, you're eighty-odd thousand to the good and a poor devil of a son to the bad. But, poor devil, poor devil, he's best gone out of a life where he rides his rocking horse to find a winner."

1933

Sonny's Blues

James Baldwin (1924–1987)

James Baldwin's work is a testament to the difficulty for African Americans of living during the 1950s, 1960s, and even beyond in a society that often treats them as second-class citizens. In such works as *Go Tell It on the Mountain* (1953) and *Going to Meet the Man* (1965), Baldwin poured out his anger, frustration, and sorrow at the racial strife he encountered growing up in Harlem. In the late 1940s Baldwin became an exile from his native country and took up residence in Paris. In such works as *Giovanni's Room* (1956) he began to deal with his homosexuality. But his great strength is as an essayist who demands justice for all citizens of a country that prides itself on seeing all people as equal under the law.

I read about it in the paper, in the subway, on my way to work. I read it, and I couldn't believe it, and I read it again. Then perhaps I just stared at it, at the newsprint spelling out his name, spelling out the story. I stared at it in the swinging lights of the subway car, and in the faces and bodies of the people, and in my own face, trapped in the darkness which roared outside.

It was not to be believed and I kept telling myself that as I walked from the subway station to the high school. And at the same time I couldn't doubt it. I was scared, scared for Sonny. He became real to me again. A great block of ice got settled in my belly and kept melting there slowly all day long, while I taught my classes algebra. It was a special kind of ice. It kept melting, sending trickles of ice water all up and down my veins, but it never got less. Sometimes it hardened and seemed to expand until I felt my guts were going to come spilling out or that I was going to choke or scream. This would always be at a moment when I was remembering some specific thing Sonny had once said or done.

When he was about as old as the boys in my classes his face had been bright and open, there was a lot of copper in it; and he'd had wonderfully direct brown eyes, and great gentleness and privacy. I wondered what he looked like now. He had been picked up, the evening before, in a raid on an apartment downtown, for peddling and using heroin.

I couldn't believe it: but what I mean by that is that I couldn't find any room for it anywhere inside me. I had kept it outside me for a long time. I hadn't wanted to know. I had had suspicions, but I didn't name them, I kept putting them away. I told myself that Sonny was wild, but he wasn't crazy. And he'd always been a good boy, he hadn't ever turned hard or evil or disrespectful, the way kids can, so quick, so quick, especially in Harlem. I didn't want to believe that I'd ever see my brother going down, coming to nothing, all that light in his face gone out, in the condition I'd already seen so many others. Yet it had happened and here I was, talking about algebra to a lot of boys who might, every one of them for all I knew, be popping off needles every time they went to the head. Maybe it did more for them than algebra could.

I was sure that the first time Sonny had ever had horse, he couldn't have been much older than these boys were now. These boys, now, were living as we'd been living then, they were growing up with a rush and their heads bumped abruptly against the low ceiling of their actual possibilities. They were filled with rage. All they really knew were two darknesses, the darkness of their lives, which was now closing in on them, and the darkness of the movies, which had blinded them to that other darkness, and in which they now, vindictively, dreamed, at once more together than they were at any other time, and more alone.

When the last bell rang, the last class ended, I let out my breath. It seemed I'd been holding it for all that time. My clothes were wet—I may have looked as though I'd been sitting in a steam bath, all dressed up, all afternoon. I sat alone in the classroom a long time. I listened to the boys outside, downstairs, shouting and cursing and laughing. Their laughter struck me for perhaps the first time. It was not the joyous laughter which—God knows why—one associates with children. It was mocking and insular, its intent was to denigrate. It was disenchanted, and in this, also, lay the authority of their curses. Perhaps I was listening to them because I was thinking about my brother and in them I heard my brother. And myself.

One boy was whistling a tune, at once very complicated and very simple, it seemed to be pouring out of him as though he were a bird, and it sounded very cool and moving through all that harsh, bright air, only just holding its own through all those other sounds.

I stood up and walked over to the window and looked down into the courtyard. It was the beginning of the spring and the sap was rising in the boys. A teacher passed through them every now and again, quickly, as though he or she couldn't wait to get out of that courtyard, to get those boys out of their sight and off their minds. I started collecting my stuff. I thought I'd better get home and talk to Isabel.

The courtyard was almost deserted by the time I got downstairs. I saw this boy standing in the shadow of a doorway, looking just like Sonny. I almost called his name. Then I saw that it wasn't Sonny, but somebody we used to know, a boy from around our block. He'd been Sonny's friend. He'd never been mine, having been too young for me, and, anyway, I'd never liked him. And now, even though he was a grown-up man, he still hung around that block, still spent hours on the street corner, was always high and raggy. I used to run into him from time to time and he'd often work around to asking me for a quarter or fifty cents. He always had some real good excuse, too, and I always gave it to him, I don't know why.

But now, abruptly, I hated him. I couldn't stand the way he looked at me, partly like a dog, partly like a cunning child. I wanted to ask him what the hell he was doing in the school courtyard.

He sort of shuffled over to me, and he said, "I see you got the papers. So you already know about it."

"You mean about Sonny? Yes, I already know about it. How come they didn't get you?"

He grinned. It made him repulsive and it also brought to mind what he'd looked like as a kid. "I wasn't there. I stay away from them people."

"Good for you." I offered him a cigarette and I watched him through the smoke. "You come all the way down here just to tell me about Sonny?"

"That's right." He was sort of shaking his head and his eyes looked strange, as though they were about to cross. The bright sun deadened his damp dark brown skin and it made his eyes look yellow and showed up the dirt in his conked hair. He smelled funky. I moved a little away from him and I said, "Well, thanks. But I already know about it and I got to get home."

"I'll walk you a little ways," he said. We started walking. There were a couple of kids still loitering in the courtyard and one of them said good night to me and looked strangely at the boy beside me.

"What're you going to do?" he asked me. "I mean, about Sonny?"

"Look. I haven't seen Sonny for over a year, I'm not sure I'm going to do anything. Anyway, what the hell *can* I do?"

"That's right," he said quickly, "ain't nothing you can do. Can't much help old Sonny no more, I guess."

It was what I was thinking and so it seemed to me he had no right to say it.

"I'm surprised at Sonny, though," he went on—he had a funny way of talking, he looked straight ahead as though he were talking to himself—"I thought Sonny was a smart boy, I thought he was too smart to get hung."

"I guess he thought so too," I said sharply, "and that's how he got hung. And how about you? You're pretty goddamn smart, I bet."

Then he looked directly at me, just for a minute. "I ain't smart," he said. "If I was smart, I'd have reached for a pistol a long time ago."

"Look. Don't tell *me* your sad story, if it was up to me, I'd give you one." Then I felt guilty—guilty, probably, for never having supposed that the poor bastard *had* a story of his own, much less a sad one, and I asked, quickly, "What's going to happen to him now?"

He didn't answer this. He was off by himself some place. "Funny thing," he said, and from his tone we might have been discussing the quickest way to get to Brooklyn, "when I saw the papers this morning, the first thing I asked myself was if I had anything to do with it. I felt sort of responsible."

I began to listen more carefully. The subway station was on the corner, just before us, and I stopped. He stopped, too. We were in front of a bar and he ducked slightly, peering in, but whoever he was looking for didn't seem to be there. The juke box was blasting away with something black and bouncy and I half watched the barmaid as she danced her way from the juke box to her place behind the bar. And I watched her face as she laughingly responded to something someone said to her, still keeping time to the music. When she smiled one saw the little girl, one sensed the doomed, still-struggling woman beneath the battered face of the semi-whore.

"I never *give* Sonny nothing," the boy said finally, "but a long time ago I come to school high and Sonny asked me how it felt." He paused, I couldn't bear to watch him, I watched the barmaid, and I listened to the music which seemed to be causing the pavement to shake. "I told him it felt great." The music stopped, the barmaid paused and watched the juke box until the music began again. "It did."

All this was carrying me some place I didn't want to go. I certainly didn't want to know how it felt. It filled everything, the people, the houses, the music, the dark, quicksilver barmaid, with menace; and this menace was their reality.

"What's going to happen to him now?" I asked again.

"They'll send him away some place and they'll try to cure him." He shook his head. "Maybe he'll even think he's kicked the habit. Then they'll let him loose"—he gestured, throwing his cigarette into the gutter. "That's all."

"What do you mean, that's *all?*"

But I knew what he meant.

"I *mean,* that's *all.*" He turned his head and looked at me, pulling down the corners of his mouth. "Don't you know what I mean?" he asked softly.

"How the hell *would* I know what you mean?" I almost whispered it, I don't know why.

"That's right," he said to the air, "how would *he* know what I mean?" He turned toward me again, patient and calm, and yet I somehow felt him shaking, shaking as though he were going to fall apart. I felt that ice in my guts again, the dread I'd felt all afternoon; and again I watched the barmaid, moving about the bar, washing glasses, and singing. "Listen. They'll let him out and then it'll just start all over again. That's what I mean."

"You mean—they'll let him out. And then he'll just start working his way back in again. You mean he'll never kick the habit. Is that what you mean?"

"That's right," he said, cheerfully. "*You* see what I mean."

"Tell me," I said at last, "why does he want to die? He must want to die, he's killing himself, why does he want to die?"

He looked at me in surprise. He licked his lips. "He don't want to die. He wants to live. Don't nobody want to die, ever."

Then I wanted to ask him—too many things. He could not have answered, or if he had, I could not have borne the answers. I started walking. "Well, I guess it's none of my business."

"It's going to be rough on old Sonny," he said. We reached the subway station. "This is your station?" he asked. I nodded. I took one step down. "Damn!" he said, suddenly. I looked up at him. He grinned again. "Damn if I didn't leave all my money home. You ain't got a dollar on you, have you? Just for a couple of days, is all."

All at once something inside gave and threatened to come pouring out of me. I didn't hate him any more. I felt that in another moment I'd start crying like a child.

"Sure," I said. "Don't sweat." I looked in my wallet and didn't have a dollar, I only had a five. "Here," I said. "That hold you?"

He didn't look at it—he didn't want to look at it. A terrible, closed look came over his face, as though he were keeping the number on the bill a secret from him and me. "Thanks," he said, and now he was dying to see me go. "Don't worry about Sonny. Maybe I'll write him or something."

"Sure," I said. "You do that. So long."

"Be seeing you," he said. I went on down the steps.

And I didn't write Sonny or send him anything for a long time. When I finally did, it was just after my little girl died, he wrote me back a letter which made me feel like a bastard.

Here's what he said:

DEAR BROTHER,

You don't know how much I needed to hear from you. I wanted to write you many a time but I dug how much I must have hurt you and so I didn't write. But now I feel like a man who's been trying to climb up out of some deep, real deep and funky hole and just saw the sun up there, outside. I got to get outside.

I can't tell you much about how I got here. I mean I don't know how to tell you. I guess I was afraid of something or I was trying to escape from something and you know I have never been very strong in the head (smile). I'm glad Mama and Daddy are dead and can't see what's happened to their son and I swear if I'd known what I was doing I would never have hurt you so, you and a lot of other fine people who were nice to me and who believed in me.

I don't want you to think it had anything to do with me being a musician. It's more than that. Or maybe less than that. I can't get anything straight in my head down here and I try not to think about what's going to happen to me when I get outside again. Sometime I think I'm going to flip and *never* get outside and sometime I think I'll come straight back. I tell you one thing, though, I'd rather blow my brains out than go through this again. But that's what they all say, so they tell me. If I tell you when I'm coming to New York and if you could meet me, I sure would appreciate it. Give my love to Isabel and the kids and I was sorry to hear about little Gracie. I wish I could be like Mama and say the Lord's will be done, but I don't know it seems to me that trouble is the one thing that never does get stopped and I don't know what good it does to blame it on the Lord. But maybe it does some good if you believe it.

Your brother,
SONNY

Then I kept in constant touch with him and I sent him whatever I could and I went to meet him when he came back to New York. When I saw him many things I thought I had forgotten came flooding back to me. This was because I had begun, finally, to wonder about Sonny, about the life that Sonny lived inside. This life, whatever it was, had made him older and thinner and it had deepened the distant stillness in which he had always moved. He looked very unlike my baby brother. Yet, when he smiled, when we shook hands, the baby brother I'd never known looked out from the depths of his private life, like an animal waiting to be coaxed into the light.

"How you been keeping?" he asked me.

"All right. And you?"

"Just fine." He was smiling all over his face. "It's good to see you again."

"It's good to see you."

The seven years' difference in our ages lay between us like a chasm: I wondered if these years would ever operate between us as a bridge. I was remembering, and it made it hard to catch my breath, that I had been there when he was born; and I had heard the first words he had ever spoken. When he started to walk, he walked from our mother straight to me. I caught him just before he fell when he took the first steps he ever took in this world.

"How's Isabel?"

"Just fine. She's dying to see you."

"And the boys?"

"They're fine, too. They're anxious to see their uncle."

"Oh, come on. You know they don't remember me."

"Are you kidding? Of course they remember you."

He grinned again. We got into a taxi. We had a lot to say to each other, far too much to know how to begin.

As the taxi began to move, I asked, "You still want to go to India?"

He laughed. "You still remember that. Hell, no. This place is Indian enough for me."

"It used to belong to them," I said.

And he laughed again. "They damn sure knew what they were doing when they got rid of it."

Years ago, when he was around fourteen, he'd been all hipped on the idea of going to India. He read books about people sitting on rocks, naked, in all kinds of weather, but mostly bad, naturally, and walking barefoot through hot coals and arriving at wisdom. I used to say that it sounded to me as though they were getting away from wisdom as fast as they could. I think he sort of looked down on me for that.

"Do you mind," he asked, "if we have the driver drive alongside the park? On the west side—I haven't seen the city in so long."

"Of course not," I said. I was afraid that I might sound as though I were humoring him, but I hoped he wouldn't take it that way.

So we drove along, between the green of the park and the stony, lifeless elegance of hotels and apartment buildings, toward the vivid, killing streets of our childhood. These streets hadn't changed, though housing projects jutted up out of them now like rocks in the middle of a boiling sea. Most of the houses in which we had grown up had vanished, as had the stores from which we had stolen, the basements in which we had first tried sex, the rooftops from which we had hurled tin cans and bricks. But houses exactly like the houses of our past yet dominated the landscape, boys exactly like the boys we once had been found themselves smothering in these houses, came down into the streets for light and air and found themselves encircled by disaster. Some escaped the trap, most didn't. Those who got out always left something of themselves behind, as some animals amputate a leg and leave it in the trap. It might be said, perhaps, that I had escaped, after all, I was a school teacher; or that Sonny had, he hadn't lived in Harlem for years. Yet, as the cab moved uptown through streets which seemed, with a rush, to darken with dark people, and as I covertly studied Sonny's face, it came to me that what we both were seeking through our separate cab windows was that part of ourselves which had been left behind. It's always at the hour of trouble and confrontation that the missing member aches.

We hit 110th Street and started rolling up Lenox Avenue. And I'd known this avenue all my life, but it seemed to me again, as it had seemed on the day I'd first heard about Sonny's trouble, filled with a hidden menace which was its very breath of life.

"We almost there," said Sonny.

"Almost." We were both too nervous to say anything more.

We live in a housing project. It hasn't been up long. A few days after it was up it seemed uninhabitably new, now, of course, it's already run-down. It looks like a parody of the good, clean, faceless life—God knows the people who live in it do their best to make it a parody. The beat-looking grass lying around isn't enough to make their lives green, the hedges will never hold out the streets, and they know it. The big windows fool no one, they aren't big enough to make space out of no space. They don't bother with the windows, they watch the TV screen instead. The playground is most popular with the children who don't play at jacks, or skip rope, or roller skate, or swing, and they can be found in it after dark. We moved in partly because it's not too far from where I teach, and partly for the kids; but it's really just like the houses in which Sonny and I grew up. The same things happen, they'll have the same things to remember. The moment Sonny and I started into the house I had the feeling that I was simply bringing him back into the danger he had almost died trying to escape.

Sonny has never been talkative. So I don't know why I was sure he'd be dying to talk to me when supper was over the first night. Everything went fine, the oldest boy remembered him, and the youngest boy liked him, and Sonny had remembered to bring something for each of them; and Isabel, who is really much nicer than I am, more open and giving, had gone to a lot of trouble about dinner and was genuinely glad to see him. And she's always been able to tease Sonny in a way that I haven't. It was nice to see her face so vivid again and to hear her laugh and watch her make Sonny laugh. She wasn't, or, anyway, she didn't seem to be, at all uneasy or embarrassed. She chatted as though there were no subject which had to be avoided and she got Sonny past his first, faint stiffness. And thank God she was there, for I was filled with that icy dread again. Everything I did seemed awkward to me, and everything I said sounded freighted with hidden meaning. I was trying to remember everything I'd heard about dope addiction and I couldn't help watching Sonny for signs. I wasn't doing it out of malice. I was trying to find out something about my brother. I was dying to hear him tell me he was safe.

"Safe!" my father grunted, whenever Mama suggested trying to move to a neighborhood which might be safer for children. "Safe, hell! Ain't no place safe for kids, nor nobody."

He always went on like this, but he wasn't, ever, really as bad as he sounded, not even on weekends, when he got drunk. As a matter of fact, he was always on the lookout for "something a little better," but he died before he found it. He died suddenly, during a drunken weekend in the middle of the war, when Sonny was fifteen. He and Sonny hadn't ever got on too well. And this was partly because Sonny was the apple of his father's eye. It was because he loved Sonny so much and was frightened for him, that he was always fighting with him. It doesn't do any good to fight with Sonny. Sonny just moves back, inside himself, where he can't be reached. But the principal reason that they never hit it off is that they were so much alike. Daddy was big and rough and loud-talking, just the opposite of Sonny, but they both had—that same privacy.

Mama tried to tell me something about this, just after Daddy died. I was home on leave from the army.

This was the last time I ever saw my mother alive. Just the same, this picture gets all mixed up in my mind with pictures I had of her when she was younger. The way I always see her is the way she used to be on a Sunday afternoon, say, when the old folks were talking after the big Sunday dinner. I always see her wearing pale blue. She'd be sitting on the sofa. And my father would be sitting in the easy chair, not far from her. And the living room would be full of church folks and relatives. There they sit, in chairs all around the living room, and the night is creeping up outside, but nobody knows it yet. You can see the darkness growing against the window-panes and you hear the street noises every now and again, or maybe the jangling beat of a tambourine from one of the churches close by, but it's real quiet in the room. For a moment nobody's talking, but every face looks darkening, like the sky outside. And my mother rocks a little from the waist, and my father's eyes are closed. Everyone is looking at something a child can't see. For a minute they've forgotten the children. Maybe a kid is lying on the rug half asleep. Maybe somebody's got a kid on his lap and is absent-mindedly stroking the kid's head. Maybe there's a kid, quiet and big-eyed, curled up in a big chair in the corner. The silence, the darkness coming, and the darkness in the faces frightens the child obscurely. He hopes that the hand which strokes his forehead will never stop—will never die. He hopes that there will never come a time when the old folks won't be sitting around the living room, talking about where they've come from, and what they've seen, and what's happened to them and their kinfolk.

But something deep and watchful in the child knows that this is bound to end, is already ending. In a moment someone will get up and turn on the light. Then the old folks will remember the children and they won't talk any more that day. And when light fills the room, the child is filled with darkness. He knows that every time this happens he's moved just a little closer to that darkness outside. The darkness outside is what the old folks have been talking about. It's what they've come from. It's what they endure. The child knows that they won't talk any more because if he knows too much about what's happened to *them*, he'll know too much too soon, about what's going to happen to *him*.

The last time I talked to my mother, I remember I was restless. I wanted to get out and see Isabel. We weren't married then and we had a lot to straighten out between us.

There Mama sat, in black, by the window. She was humming an old church song, *Lord, you brought me from a long ways off.* Sonny was out somewhere. Mama kept watching the streets.

"I don't know," she said, "if I'll ever see you again, after you go off from here. But I hope you'll remember the things I tried to teach you."

"Don't talk like that," I said, and smiled. "You'll be here a long time yet."

She smiled, too, but she said nothing. She was quiet for a long time. And I said, "Mama, don't you worry about nothing. I'll be writing all the time, and you be getting the checks. . . ."

"I want to talk to you about your brother," she said, suddenly. "If anything happens to me he ain't going to have nobody to look out for him."

"Mama," I said, "ain't nothing going to happen to you *or* Sonny. Sonny's all right. He's a good boy and he's got good sense."

"It ain't a question of his being a good boy," Mama said, "nor of his having good sense. It ain't only the bad ones, nor yet the dumb ones that gets sucked under." She stopped, looking at me. "Your Daddy once had a brother," she said, and she smiled in a way that made me feel she was in pain. "You didn't never know that, did you?"

"No," I said, "I never knew that," and I watched her face.

"Oh, yes," she said, "your Daddy had a brother." She looked out of the window again. "I know you never saw your Daddy cry. But *I* did—many a time, through all these years."

I asked her, "What happened to his brother? How come nobody's ever talked about him?"

This was the first time I ever saw my mother look old.

"His brother got killed," she said, "when he was just a little younger than you are now. I knew him. He was a fine boy. He was maybe a little full of the devil, but he didn't mean nobody no harm."

Then she stopped and the room was silent, exactly as it had sometimes been on those Sunday afternoons. Mama kept looking out into the streets.

"He used to have a job in the mill," she said, "and, like all young folks, he just liked to perform on Saturday nights. Saturday nights, him and your father would drift around to different places, go to dances and things like that, or just sit around with people they knew, and your father's brother would sing, he had a fine voice, and play along with himself on his guitar. Well, this particular Saturday night, him and your father was coming home from some place, and they were both a little drunk and there was a moon that night, it was bright like day. Your father's brother was feeling kind of good, and he was whistling to himself, and he had his guitar slung over his shoulder. They was coming down a hill and beneath them was a road that turned off from the highway. Well, your father's brother, being always kind of frisky, decided to run down this hill, and he did, with that guitar banging and clanging behind him, and he ran across the road, and he was making water behind a tree. And your father was sort of amused at him and he was still coming down the hill, kind of slow. Then he heard a car motor and that same minute his brother stepped from behind the tree, into the road, in the moonlight. And he started to cross the road. And your father started to run down the hill, he says he don't know why. This car was full of white men. They was all drunk, and when they seen your father's brother they let out a great whoop and holler and they aimed the car straight at him. They was having fun, they just wanted to scare him, the way they do sometimes, you know. But they was drunk. And I guess the boy, being drunk, too, and scared, kind of lost his head. By the time he jumped it was too late. Your father says he heard his brother scream when the car rolled over him, and he heard the wood of that guitar when it give, and he heard them strings go flying, and he heard them white men shouting, and the car kept on a-going and it ain't stopped till this day. And, time your father got down the hill, his brother weren't nothing but blood and pulp."

Tears were gleaming on my mother's face. There wasn't anything I could say.

"He never mentioned it," she said, "because I never let him mention it before you children. Your Daddy was like a crazy man that night and for many a night thereafter. He says he never in his life seen anything as dark as that road after the lights of that car had gone away. Weren't nothing, weren't nobody on that road, just your Daddy and his brother and that busted guitar. Oh, yes. Your Daddy never did really get right again. Till the day he died he weren't sure but that every white man he saw was the man that killed his brother."

She stopped and took out her handkerchief and dried her eyes and looked at me.

"I ain't telling you all this," she said, "to make you scared or bitter or to make you hate nobody. I'm telling you this because you got a brother. And the world ain't changed."

I guess I didn't want to believe this. I guess she saw this in my face. She turned away from me, toward the window again, searching those streets.

"But I praise my Redeemer," she said at last, "that He called your Daddy home before me. I ain't saying it to throw no flowers at myself, but, I declare, it keeps me from feeling too cast down to know I helped your father get safely through this world. Your father always acted like he was the roughest, strongest man on earth. And everybody took him to be like that. But if he hadn't had *me* there—to see his tears!"

She was crying again. Still, I couldn't move. I said, "Lord, Lord, Mama, I didn't know it was like that."

"Oh, honey," she said, "there's a lot that you don't know. But you are going to find it out." She stood up from the window and came over to me. "You got to hold on to your brother," she said, "and don't let him fall, no matter what it looks like is happening to him and no matter how evil you gets with him. You going to be evil with him many a time. But don't you forget what I told you, you hear?"

"I won't forget," I said. "Don't you worry, I won't forget. I won't let nothing happen to Sonny."

My mother smiled as though she were amused at something she saw in my face. Then, "You may not be able to stop nothing from happening. But you got to let him know you's *there*."

Two days later I was married, and then I was gone. And I had a lot of things on my mind and I pretty well forgot my promise to Mama until I got shipped home on a special furlough for her funeral.

And, after the funeral, with just Sonny and me alone in the empty kitchen, I tried to find out something about him.

"What do you want to do?" I asked him.

"I'm going to be a musician," he said.

For he had graduated, in the time I had been away, from dancing to the juke box to finding out who was playing what, and what they were doing with it, and he had bought himself a set of drums.

"You mean, you want to be a drummer?" I somehow had the feeling that being a drummer might be all right for other people but not for my brother Sonny.

"I don't think," he said, looking at me very gravely, "that I'll ever be a good drummer. But I think I can play a piano."

I frowned. I'd never played the role of the older brother quite so seriously before, had scarcely ever, in fact, *asked* Sonny a damn thing. I sensed myself in the presence of something I didn't really know how to handle, didn't understand. So I made my frown a little deeper as I asked: "What kind of musician do you want to be?"

He grinned. "How many kinds do you think there are?"

"Be *serious*," I said.

He laughed, throwing his head back, and then looked at me. "I *am* serious."

"Well, then, for Christ's sake, stop kidding around and answer a serious question. I mean, do you want to be a concert pianist, you want to play classical music and all that, or—or what?" Long before I finished he was laughing again. "For Christ's *sake*, Sonny!"

He sobered, but with difficulty. "I'm sorry. But you sound so—*scared!*" and he was off again.

"Well, you may think it's funny now, baby, but it's not going to be so funny when you have to make your living at it, let me tell you *that.*" I was furious because I knew he was laughing at me and I didn't know why.

"No," he said, very sober now, and afraid, perhaps, that he'd hurt me, "I don't want to be a classical pianist. That isn't what interests me. I mean"—he paused, looking hard at me, as though his eyes would help me to understand, and then gestured helplessly, as though perhaps his hand would help—"I mean, I'll have a lot of studying to do, and I'll have to study *everything,* but I mean, I want to play *with*—jazz musicians." He stopped. "I want to play jazz," he said.

Well, the word had never before sounded as heavy, as real, as it sounded that afternoon in Sonny's mouth. I just looked at him and I was probably frowning a real frown by this time. I simply couldn't see why on earth he'd want to spend his time hanging around night clubs, clowning around on bandstands, while people pushed each other around a dance floor. It seemed—beneath him, somehow. I had never thought about it before, had never been forced to, but I suppose I had always put jazz musicians in a class with what Daddy called "good-time people."

"Are you *serious?*"

"Hell, *yes,* I'm serious."

He looked more helpless than ever, and annoyed, and deeply hurt.

I suggested, helpfully: "You mean—like Louis Armstrong?"

His face closed as though I'd struck him. "No. I'm not talking about none of that old-time, down home crap."

"Well, look, Sonny, I'm sorry, don't get mad. I just don't altogether get it, that's all. Name somebody—you know, a jazz musician you admire."

"Bird."

"Who?"

"Bird! Charlie Parker! Don't they teach you nothing in the goddamn army?"

I lit a cigarette. I was surprised and then a little amused to discover that I was trembling. "I've been out of touch," I said. "You'll have to be patient with me. Now. Who's this Parker character?"

"He's just one of the greatest jazz musicians alive," said Sonny, sullenly, his hands in his pockets, his back to me. "Maybe *the* greatest," he added, bitterly, "that's probably why *you* never heard of him."

"All right," I said, "I'm ignorant. I'm sorry. I'll go out and buy all the cat's records right away, all right?"

"It don't," said Sonny, with dignity, "make any difference to me. I don't care what you listen to. Don't do me no favors."

I was beginning to realize that I'd never seen him so upset before. With another part of my mind I was thinking that this would probably turn out to be one of those things kids go through and that I shouldn't make it seem important by pushing it too hard. Still, I didn't think it would do any harm to ask: "Doesn't all this take a lot of time? Can you make a living at it?"

He turned back to me and half leaned, half sat, on the kitchen table. "Everything takes time," he said, "and—well, yes, sure, I can make a living at it. But what I don't seem to be able to make you understand is that it's the only thing I want to do."

"Well Sonny," I said, gently, "you know people can't always do exactly what they *want* to do—"

"*No,* I don't know that," said Sonny, surprising me. "I think people *ought* to do what they want to do, what else are they alive for?"

"You getting to be a big boy," I said desperately, "it's time you started thinking about your future."

"I'm thinking about my future," said Sonny, grimly. "I think about it all the time."

I gave up. I decided, if he didn't change his mind, that we could always talk about it later. "In the meantime," I said, "you got to finish school." We had already decided that he'd have to move in with Isabel and her folks. I knew this wasn't the ideal arrangement because Isabel's folks are inclined to be dicty and they hadn't especially wanted Isabel to marry me. But I didn't know what else to do. "And we have to get you fixed up at Isabel's."

There was a long silence. He moved from the kitchen table to the window. "That's a terrible idea. You know it yourself."

"Do you have a *better* idea?"

He just walked up and down the kitchen for a minute. He was as tall as I was. He had started to shave. I suddenly had the feeling that I didn't know him at all.

He stopped at the kitchen table and picked up my cigarettes. Looking at me with a kind of mocking, amused defiance, he put one between his lips. "You mind?"

"You smoking already?"

He lit the cigarette and nodded, watching me through the smoke. "I just wanted to see if I'd have the courage to smoke in front of you." He grinned and blew a great cloud of smoke to the ceiling. "It was easy." He looked at my face. "Come on, now. I bet you was smoking at my age, tell the truth."

I didn't say anything but the truth was on my face, and he laughed. But now there was something very strained in his laugh. "Sure. And I bet that ain't all you was doing."

He was frightening me a little. "Cut the crap," I said. "We already decided that you was going to go and live at Isabel's. Now what's got into you all of a sudden?"

"*You* decided it," he pointed out. "*I* didn't decide nothing." He stopped in front of me, leaning against the stove, arms loosely folded. "Look, brother. I don't want to stay in Harlem no more, I really don't." He was very earnest. He looked at me, then over toward the kitchen window. There was something in his eyes I'd never seen before, some thoughtfulness, some worry all his own. He rubbed the muscle of one arm. "It's time I was getting out of here."

"Where do you want to *go,* Sonny?"

"I want to join the army. Or the navy, I don't care. If I say I'm old enough they'll believe me."

Then I got mad. It was because I was so scared. "You must be crazy. You goddamn fool, what the hell do you want to go and join the *army* for?"

"I just told you. To get out of Harlem."

"Sonny, you haven't even finished *school*. And if you really want to be a musician, how do you expect to study if you're in the *army?*"

He looked at me, trapped, and in anguish. "There's ways. I might be able to work out some kind of deal. Anyway, I'll have the G.I. Bill when I come out."

"*If* you come out." We stared at each other. "Sonny, please. Be reasonable. I know the setup is far from perfect. But we got to do the best we can."

"I ain't learning nothing in school," he said. "Even when I go." He turned away from me and opened the window and threw his cigarette out into the narrow alley. I watched his back. "At least, I ain't learning nothing you'd want me to learn." He slammed the window so hard I thought the glass would fly out, and turned back to me. "And I'm sick of the stink of these garbage cans!"

"Sonny," I said, "I know how you feel. But if you don't finish school now, you're going to be sorry later that you didn't." I grabbed him by the shoulders. "And you only got another year. It ain't so bad. And I'll come back and I swear I'll help you do *whatever* you want to do. Just try to put up with it till I come back. Will you please do that? For me?"

He didn't answer and he wouldn't look at me.

"Sonny. You hear me?"

He pulled away. "I hear you. But you never hear anything *I* say."

I didn't know what to say to that. He looked out of the window and then back at me. "OK," he said, and sighed. "I'll try."

Then I said, trying to cheer him up a little, "They got a piano at Isabel's. You can practice on it."

And as a matter of fact, it did cheer him up for a minute. "That's right," he said to himself. "I forgot that." His face relaxed a little. But the worry, the thoughtfulness, played on it still, the way shadows play on a face which is staring into the fire.

But I thought I'd never hear the end of that piano. At first, Isabel would write me, saying how nice it was that Sonny was so serious about his music and how, as soon as he came in from school, or wherever he had been when he was supposed to be at school, he went straight to that piano and stayed there until suppertime. And, after supper, he went back to that piano and stayed there until everybody went to bed. He was at the piano all day Saturday and all day Sunday. Then he bought a record player and started playing records. He'd play one record over and over again, all day long sometimes, and he'd improvise along with it on the piano. Or he'd play one section of the record, one chord, one change, one progression, then he'd do it on the piano. Then back to the record. Then back to the piano.

Well, I really don't know how they stood it. Isabel finally confessed that it wasn't like living with a person at all, it was like living with sound. And the sound didn't make any sense to her, didn't make any sense to any of them—naturally. They began, in a way, to be afflicted by this presence that was living in their home. It was as though Sonny were some sort of god, or monster. He moved in an atmosphere which wasn't like theirs at all. They fed him and he ate, he washed himself, he walked in and out of their door; he certainly wasn't nasty or unpleasant or rude, Sonny isn't any of those things; but it was as though he were all wrapped up in some cloud, some fire, some vision all his own; and there wasn't any way to reach him.

At the same time, he wasn't really a man yet, he was still a child, and they had to watch out for him in all kinds of ways. They certainly couldn't throw him out. Neither did they dare to make a great scene about that piano because even they dimly sensed, as I sensed, from so many thousands of miles away, that Sonny was at that piano playing for his life.

But he hadn't been going to school. One day a letter came from the school board and Isabel's mother got it—there had, apparently, been other letters but Sonny had torn them up. This day, when Sonny came in, Isabel's mother showed him the letter and asked where he'd been spending his time. And she finally got it out of him that he'd been down in Greenwich Village, with musicians and other characters, in a white girl's apartment. And this scared her and she started to scream at him and what came up, once she began—though she denies it to this day—was what sacrifices they were making to give Sonny a decent home and how little he appreciated it.

Sonny didn't play the piano that day. By evening, Isabel's mother had calmed down but then there was the old man to deal with, and Isabel herself. Isabel says she did her best to be calm but she broke down and started crying. She says she just watched Sonny's face. She could tell, by watching him, what was happening with him. And what was happening was that they penetrated his cloud, they had reached him. Even if their fingers had been a thousand times more gentle than human fingers ever are, he could hardly help feeling that they had stripped him naked and were spitting on that nakedness. For he also had to see that his presence, that music, which was life or death to him, had been torture for them and that they had endured it, not at all for his sake, but only for mine. And Sonny couldn't take that. He can take it a little better today than he could then but he's still not very good at it and, frankly, I don't know anybody who is.

The silence of the next few days must have been louder than the sound of all the music ever played since time began. One morning, before she went to work, Isabel was in his room for something and she suddenly realized that all of his records were gone. And she knew for certain that he was gone. And he was. He went as far as the navy would carry him. He finally sent me a postcard from some place in Greece and that was the first I knew that Sonny was still alive. I didn't see him any more until we were both back in New York and the war had long been over.

He was a man by then, of course, but I wasn't willing to see it. He came by the house from time to time, but we fought almost every time we met. I didn't like the way he carried himself, loose and dreamlike all the time, and I didn't like his friends, and his music seemed to be merely an excuse for the life he led. It sounded just that weird and disordered.

Then we had a fight, a pretty awful fight, and I didn't see him for months. By and by I looked him up, where he was living, in a furnished room in the Village, and I tried to make it up. But there were lots of other people in the room and Sonny just lay on his bed, and he wouldn't come downstairs with me, and he treated these other people as though they were his family and I weren't. So I got mad and then he got mad, and then I told him that he might just as well be dead as live the way he was living. Then he stood up and he told me not to worry about him any more in life, that he *was* dead as far as I was concerned. Then he pushed me to the door and the other people looked on as though nothing were happening, and he slammed the door behind me. I stood in the hallway, staring at the door. I heard somebody laugh in the room and then the tears came to my eyes. I started down the steps, whistling to keep from crying. I kept whistling to myself, *You going to need me, baby, one of these cold, rainy days.*

I read about Sonny's trouble in the spring. Little Grace died in the fall. She was a beautiful little girl. But she only lived a little over two years. She died of polio and she suffered. She had a slight fever for a couple of days, but it didn't seem like anything and we just kept her in bed. And we would certainly have called the doctor, but the fever dropped, she seemed to be all right. So we thought it had just been a cold. Then, one day, she was up, playing, Isabel was in the kitchen fixing lunch for the two boys when they'd come in from school, and she heard Grace fall down in the living room. When you have a lot of children you don't always start running when one of them falls, unless they start scream-ing or something. And, this time, Grace was quiet. Yet, Isabel says that when she heard that *thump* and then that silence, something happened in her to make her afraid. And she ran to the living room and there was little Grace on the floor, all twisted up and the reason she hadn't screamed was that she couldn't get her breath. And when she did scream, it was the worst sound, Isabel says, that she'd ever heard in all her life, and she still hears it sometimes in her dreams. Isabel will sometimes wake up with a low, moaning, strangled sound and I have to be quick to awaken her and hold her to me and where Isabel is weeping against me seems a mortal wound.

I think I may have written Sonny the very day that little Grace was buried. I was sitting in the living room in the dark, by myself, and I suddenly thought of Sonny. My trouble made his real.

One Saturday afternoon, when Sonny had been living with us, or, anyway, been in our house, for nearly two weeks, I found myself wandering aimlessly about the living room, drinking from a can of beer, and trying to work up the courage to search Sonny's room. He was out, he was usually out whenever I was home, and Isabel had taken the children to see their grandparents. Suddenly I was standing still in front of the living room window, watching Seventh Avenue. The idea of searching Sonny's room made me still. I scarcely dared to admit to myself what I'd be searching for. I didn't know what I'd do if I found it. Or if I didn't.

On the sidewalk across from me, near the entrance to a barbecue joint, some people were holding an old-fashioned revival meeting. The barbecue cook, wearing a dirty white apron, his conked hair reddish and metallic in the pale sun, and a cigarette between his lips, stood in the doorway, watching them. Kids and older people paused in their errands and stood there, along with some older men and a couple of very tough-looking women who watched everything that happened on the avenue, as though they owned it, or were maybe owned by it. Well, they were watching this, too. The revival was being carried on by three sisters in black, and a brother. All they had were their voices and their Bibles and a tambourine. The brother was testifying and while he testified two of the sisters stood together, seeming to say, Amen, and the third sister walked around with the tambourine outstretched and a couple of people dropped coins into it. Then the brother's testimony ended and the sister who had been taking up the collection dumped the coins into her palm and transferred them to the pocket of her long black robe. Then she raised both hands, striking the tambourine against the air, and then against one hand, and she started to sing. And the two other sisters and the brother joined in.

It was strange, suddenly, to watch, though I had been seeing these street meetings all my life. So, of course, had everybody else down there. Yet, they paused and watched and listened and I stood still at the window. *"Tis the old ship of Zion,"* they sang, and the sister with the tambourine kept a steady, jangling beat, *"It has rescued many a thousand!"* Not a soul under the sound of their voices was hearing this song for the first time, not one of them had been rescued. Nor had they seen much in the way of rescue work being done around them. Neither did they especially believe in the holiness of the three sisters and the brother, they knew too much about them, knew where they lived, and how. The woman with the tambourine, whose voice dominated the air, whose face was bright with joy, was divided by very little from the woman who stood watching her, a cigarette between her heavy, chapped lips, her hair a cuckoo's nest, her face scarred and swollen from many beatings, and her black eyes glittering like coal. Perhaps they both knew this, which was why, when, as rarely, they addressed each other, they addressed each other as Sister. As the singing filled the air the watching, listening faces underwent a change, the eyes focusing on something within; the music seemed to soothe a poison out of them; and time seemed, nearly, to fall away from the sullen, belligerent, battered faces, as though they were fleeing back to their first condition, while dreaming of their last. The barbecue cook half shook his head and smiled, and dropped his cigarette and disappeared into his joint. A man fumbled in his pockets for change and stood holding it in his hand impatiently, as though he had just remembered a pressing appointment further up the avenue. He looked furious. Then I saw Sonny, standing on the edge of the crowd. He was carrying a wide, flat notebook with a green cover, and it made him look, from where I was standing, almost like a school-boy. The coppery sun brought out the copper in his skin, he was very faintly smiling, standing very still. Then the singing stopped, the tambourine turned into a collection plate again. The furious man dropped in his coins and vanished, so did a couple of the women, and Sonny dropped some change in the plate, looking directly at the woman with a little smile. He started across the avenue, toward the house. He has a slow, loping walk, something like the way Harlem hipsters walk, only he's imposed on this his own halfbeat. I had never really noticed it before.

I stayed at the window, both relieved and apprehensive. As Sonny disappeared from my sight, they began singing again. And they were still singing when his key turned in the lock.

"Hey," he said.

"Hey, yourself. You want some beer?"

"No. Well, maybe." But he came up to the window and stood beside me, looking out. "What a warm voice," he said.

They were singing *If I could only hear my mother pray again!*

"Yes," I said, "and she can sure beat that tambourine."

"But what a terrible song," he said, and laughed. He dropped his notebook on the sofa and disappeared into the kitchen. "Where's Isabel and the kids?"

"I think they went to see their grandparents. You hungry?"

"No." He came back into the living room with his can of beer. "You want to come some place with me tonight?"

I sensed, I don't know how, that I couldn't possibly say No. "Sure. Where?"

He sat down on the sofa and picked up his notebook and started leafing through it. "I'm going to sit in with some fellows in a joint in the Village."

"You mean, you're going to play, tonight?"

"That's right." He took a swallow of his beer and moved back to the window. He gave me a sidelong look. "If you can stand it."

"I'll try," I said.

He smiled to himself and we both watched as the meeting across the way broke up. The three sisters and the brother, heads bowed, were singing *God be with you till we meet again.* The faces around them were very quiet. Then the song ended. The small crowd dispersed. We watched the three women and the lone man walk slowly up the avenue.

"When she was singing before," said Sonny, abruptly, "her voice reminded me for a minute of what heroin feels like sometimes—when it's in your veins. It makes you feel sort of warm and cool at the same time. And distant. And—and sure." He sipped his beer, very deliberately not looking at me. I watched his face. "It makes you feel—in control. Sometimes you've got to have that feeling."

"Do you?" I sat down slowly in the easy chair.

"Sometimes." He went to the sofa and picked up his notebook again. "Some people do."

"In order," I asked, "to play?" And my voice was very ugly, full of contempt and anger.

"Well"—he looked at me with great, troubled eyes, as though, in fact, he hoped his eyes would tell me things he could never otherwise say—"they *think* so. And *if* they think so—!"

"And what do *you* think?" I asked.

He sat on the sofa and put his can of beer on the floor. "I don't know," he said, and I couldn't be sure if he were answering my question or pursuing his thoughts. His face didn't tell me. "It's not so much to *play*. It's to *stand* it, to be able to make it at all. On any level." He frowned and smiled: "In order to keep from shaking to pieces."

"But these friends of yours," I said, "they seem to shake themselves to pieces pretty goddamn fast."

"Maybe." He played with the notebook. And something told me that I should curb my tongue, that Sonny was doing his best to talk, that I should listen. "But of course you only know the ones that've gone to pieces. Some don't—or at least they haven't *yet* and that's just about all *any* of us can say." He paused. "And then there are some who just live, really, in hell, and they know it and they see what's happening and they go right on. I don't know." He sighed, dropped the notebook, folded his arms. "Some guys, you can tell from the way they play, they on something *all* the time. And you can see that, well, it makes something real for them. But of course," he picked up his beer from the floor and sipped it and put the can down again, "they *want* to, too, you've got to see that. Even some of them that say they don't—*some*, not all."

"And what about you?" I asked—I couldn't help it. "What about you? Do *you* want to?"

He stood up and walked to the window and remained silent for a long time. Then he sighed. "Me," he said. Then: "While I was downstairs before, on my way here, listening to that woman sing, it struck me all of a sudden how much suffering she must have had to go through—to sing like that. It's *repulsive* to think you have to suffer that much."

I said: "But there's no way not to suffer—is there, Sonny?"

"I believe not," he said, and smiled, "but that's never stopped anyone from trying." He looked at me. "Has it?" I realized, with this mocking look, that there stood between us, forever, beyond the power of time or forgiveness, the fact that I had held silence—so long!—when he had needed human speech to help him. He turned back to the window. "No, there's no way not to suffer. But you try all kinds of ways to keep from drowning in it, to keep on top of it, and to make it seem—well, like *you*. Like you did something, all right, and now you're suffering for it. You know?" I said nothing. "Well you know," he said, impatiently, "why *do* people suffer? Maybe it's better to do something to give it a reason, *any* reason."

"But we just agreed," I said, "that there's no way not to suffer. Isn't it better, then, just to—take it?"

"But nobody just takes it," Sonny cried, "that's what I'm telling you! *Everybody* tries not to. You're just hung up on the *way* some people try—it's not *your* way!"

The hair on my face began to itch, my face felt wet. "That's not true," I said, "that's not true. I don't give a damn what other people do, I don't even care how they suffer. I just care how *you* suffer." And he looked at me. "Please believe me," I said, "I don't want to see you—die—trying not to suffer."

"I won't," he said, flatly, "die trying not to suffer. At least, not any faster than anybody else."

"But there's no need," I said, trying to laugh, "is there? in killing yourself."

I wanted to say more, but I couldn't. I wanted to talk about will power and how life could be—well, beautiful. I wanted to say that it was all within; but was it? or, rather, wasn't that exactly the trouble? And I wanted to promise that I would never fail him again. But it would all have sounded—empty words and lies.

So I made the promise to myself and prayed that I would keep it.

"It's terrible sometimes, inside," he said, "that's what's the trouble. You walk these streets, black and funky and cold, and there's not really a living ass to talk to, and there's nothing shaking, and there's no way of getting it out—that storm inside. You can't talk it and you can't make love with it, and when you finally try to get with it and play it, you realize *nobody's* listening. So *you've* got to listen. You got to find a way to listen."

And then he walked away from the window and sat on the sofa again, as though all the wind had suddenly been knocked out of him. "Sometimes you'll do *anything* to play, even cut your mother's throat." He laughed and looked at me. "Or your brother's." Then he sobered. "Or your own." Then: "Don't worry. I'm all right now and I think I'll *be* all right. But I can't forget—where I've been. I don't mean just the physical place I've been, I mean where I've *been*. And *what* I've been."

"What have you been, Sonny?" I asked.

He smiled—but sat sideways on the sofa, his elbow resting on the back, his fingers playing with his mouth and chin, not looking at me. "I've been something I didn't recognize, didn't know I could be. Didn't know anybody could be." He stopped, looking inward, looking helplessly young, looking old. "I'm not talking about it now because I feel *guilty* or anything like that—maybe it would be better if I did, I don't know. Anyway, I can't really talk about it. Not to you, not to anybody," and now he turned and faced me. "Sometimes, you know, and it was actually when I was most *out* of the world, I felt that I was in it, and that I was *with* it, really, and I could play or I didn't really have to *play*, it just came out of me, it was there. And I don't know how I played, thinking about it now, but I know I did awful things, those times, sometimes, to people. Or it wasn't that I *did* anything to them—it was that they weren't real." He picked up the beer can; it was empty; he rolled it between his palms: "And other times—well, I needed a fix, I needed to find a place to lean, I needed to clear a space to *listen*—and I couldn't find it, and I—went crazy, I did terrible things to *me*, I was terrible *for* me." He began pressing the beer can between his hands, I watched the metal begin to give. It glittered, as he played with it, like a knife, and I was afraid he would cut himself, but I said nothing. "Oh well, I can never tell you. I was all by myself at the bottom of something, stinking and sweating and crying and shaking, and I smelled it, you know? *my* stink, and I thought I'd die if I couldn't get away from it and yet, all the same, I knew that everything I was doing was just locking me in with it. And I didn't know," he paused, still flattening the beer can, "I didn't know, I still *don't* know, something kept telling me that maybe it was good to smell your own stink, but I didn't think that *that* was what I'd been trying to do—and—who can stand it?" and he abruptly dropped the ruined beer can, looking at me with a small, still smile, and then rose, walking to the window as though it were the lodestone rock. I watched his face, he watched the avenue. "I couldn't tell you when Mama died—but the reason I wanted to leave Harlem so bad was to get away from drugs. And then, when I ran away, that's what I was running from—really. When I came back, nothing had changed, I hadn't changed, I was just—older." And he stopped, drumming with his fingers on the windowpane. The sun had vanished, soon darkness would fall. I watched his face. "It can come again," he said, almost as though speaking to himself. Then he turned to me. "It can come again," he repeated. "I just want you to know that."

"All right," I said, at last. "So it can come again. All right."

He smiled, but the smile was sorrowful. "I had to try to tell you," he said.

"Yes," I said. "I understand that."

"You're my brother," he said, looking straight at me, and not smiling at all.

"Yes," I repeated, "yes. I understand that."

He turned back to the window, looking out. "All that hatred down there," he said, "all that hatred and misery and love. It's a wonder it doesn't blow the avenue apart."

We went to the only night club on a short, dark street, downtown. We squeezed through the narrow, chattering, jam-packed bar to the entrance of the big room, where the bandstand was. And we stood there for a moment, for the lights were very dim in this room and we couldn't see. Then, "Hello, boy," said a voice and an enormous black man, much older than Sonny or myself, erupted out of all that atmospheric lighting and put an arm around Sonny's shoulder. "I been sitting right here," he said, "waiting for you."

He had a big voice, too, and heads in the darkness turned toward us.

Sonny grinned and pulled a little away, and said, "Creole, this is my brother. I told you about him."

Creole shook my hand. "I'm glad to meet you, son," he said, and it was clear that he was glad to meet me *there*, for Sonny's sake. And he smiled, "You got a real musician in *your* family," and he took his arm from Sonny's shoulder and slapped him, lightly, affectionately, with the back of his hand.

"Well. Now I've heard it all," said a voice behind us. This was another musician, and a friend of Sonny's, a coal-black, cheerful-looking man, built close to the ground. He immediately began confiding to me, at the top of his lungs, the most terrible things about Sonny, his teeth gleaming like a lighthouse and his laugh coming up out of him like the beginning of an earthquake. And it turned out that everyone at the bar knew Sonny, or almost everyone; some were musicians, working there, or nearby, or not working, some were simply hangers-on, and some were there to hear Sonny play. I was introduced to all of them and they were all very polite to me. Yet, it was clear that, for them, I was only Sonny's brother. Here, I was in Sonny's world. Or, rather: his kingdom. Here, it was not even a question that his veins bore royal blood.

They were going to play soon and Creole installed me, by myself, at a table in a dark corner. Then I watched them, Creole, and the little black man, and Sonny, and the others, while they horsed around, standing just below the bandstand. The light from the bandstand spilled just a little short of them and, watching them laughing and gesturing and moving about, I had the feeling that they, nevertheless, were being most careful not to step into that circle of light too suddenly: that if they moved into the light too suddenly, without thinking, they would perish in flame. Then, while I watched, one of them, the small, black man, moved into the light and crossed the bandstand and started fooling around with his drums. Then—being funny and being, also, extremely ceremonious—Creole took Sonny by the arm and led him to the piano. A woman's voice called Sonny's name and a few hands started clapping. And Sonny, also being funny and being ceremonious, and so touched, I think, that he could have cried, but neither hiding it nor showing it, riding it like a man, grinned, and put both hands to his heart and bowed from the waist.

Creole then went to the bass fiddle and a lean, very bright-skinned brown man jumped up on the bandstand and picked up his horn. So there they were, and the atmosphere on the bandstand and in the room began to change and tighten. Someone stepped up to the microphone and announced them. Then there were all kinds of murmurs. Some people at the bar shushed others. The waitress ran around, frantically getting in the last orders, guys and chicks got closer to each other, and the lights on the bandstand, on the quartet, turned to a kind of indigo. Then they all looked different there. Creole looked about him for the last time, as though he were making certain that all his chickens were in the coop, and then he—jumped and struck the fiddle. And there they were.

All I know about music is that not many people ever really hear it. And even then, on the rare occasions when something opens within, and the music enters, what we mainly hear, or hear corroborated, are personal private, vanishing evocations. But the man who creates the music is hearing something else, is dealing with the roar rising from the void and imposing order on it as it hits the air. What is evoked in him, then, is of another order, more terrible because it has no words, and triumphant, too, for that same reason. And his triumph, when he triumphs, is ours. I just watched Sonny's face. His face was troubled, he was working hard, but he wasn't with it. And I had the feeling that, in a way, everyone on the bandstand was waiting for him, both waiting for him and pushing him along. But as I began to watch Creole, I realized that it was Creole who held them all back. He had them on a short rein. Up there, keeping the beat with his whole body, wailing on the fiddle, with his eyes half closed, he was listening to everything, but he was listening to Sonny. He was having a dialogue with Sonny. He wanted Sonny to leave the shore line and strike out for the deep water. He was Sonny's witness that deep water and drowning were not the same thing—he had been there, and he knew. And he wanted Sonny to know. He was waiting for Sonny to do the things on the keys which would let Creole know that Sonny was in the water.

And, while Creole listened, Sonny moved, deep within, exactly like someone in torment. I had never before thought of how awful the relationship must be between the musician and his instrument. He has to fill it, this instrument, with the breath of life, his own. He has to make it do what he wants it to do. And a piano is just a piano. It's made out of so much wood and wires and little hammers and big ones, and ivory. While there's only so much you can do with it, the only way to find this out is to try and make it do everything.

And Sonny hadn't been near a piano for over a year. And he wasn't on much better terms with his life, not the life that stretched before him now. He and the piano stammered, started one way, got scared, stopped; started another way, panicked, marked time, started again; then seemed to have found a direction, panicked again, got stuck. And the face I saw on Sonny I'd never seen before. Everything had been burned out of it, and, at the same time, things usually hidden were being burned in, by the fire and fury of the battle which was occurring in him up there.

Yet, watching Creole's face as they neared the end of the first set, I had the feeling that something had happened, something I hadn't heard. Then they finished, there was scattered applause, and then, without an instant's warning, Creole started into something else, it was almost sardonic, it was *Am I Blue*. And, as though he commanded, Sonny began to play. Something began to happen. And Creole let out the reins. The dry, low, black man said something awful on the drums, Creole answered, and the drums talked back. Then the horn insisted, sweet and high, slightly detached perhaps, and Creole listened, commenting now and then, dry, and driving, beautiful and calm and old. Then they all came together again, and Sonny was part of the family again. I could tell this from his face. He seemed to have found, right there beneath his fingers, a damn brand-new piano. It seemed that he couldn't get over it. Then, for awhile, just being happy with Sonny, they seemed to be agreeing with him that brand-new pianos certainly were a gas.

Then Creole stepped forward to remind them that what they were playing was the blues. He hit something in all of them, he hit something in me, myself, and the music tightened and deepened, apprehension began to beat the air. Creole began to tell us what the blues were all about. They were not about anything very new. He and his boys up there were keeping it new, at the risk of ruin, destruction, madness, and death, in order to find new ways to make us listen. For, while the tale of how we suffer, and how we are delighted, and how we may triumph is never new, it always must be heard. There isn't any other tale to tell, it's the only light we've got in all this darkness.

And this tale, according to that face, that body, those strong hands on those strings, has another aspect in every country, and a new depth in every generation. Listen, Creole seemed to be saying, listen. Now these are Sonny's blues. He made the little black man on the drums know it, and the bright, brown man on the horn. Creole wasn't trying any longer to get Sonny in the water. He was wishing him Godspeed. Then he stepped back, very slowly, filling the air with the immense suggestion that Sonny speak for himself.

Then they all gathered around Sonny and Sonny played. Every now and again one of them seemed to say, Amen. Sonny's fingers filled the air with life, his life. But that life contained so many others. And Sonny went all the way back, he really began with the spare, flat statement of the opening phrase of the song. Then he began to make it his. It was very beautiful because it wasn't hurried and it was no longer a lament. I seemed to hear with what burning he had made it his, with what burning we had yet to make it ours, how we could cease lamenting. Freedom lurked around us and I understood, at last, that he could help us to be free if we would listen, that he would never be free until we did. Yet, there was no battle in his face now. I heard what he had gone through, and would continue to go through until he came to rest in earth. He had made it his: that long line, of which we knew only Mama and Daddy. And he was giving it back, as everything must be given back, so that, passing through death, it can live forever. I saw my mother's face again, and felt, for the first time, how the stones of the road she had walked on must have bruised her feet. I saw the moonlit road where my father's brother died. And it brought something else back to me, and carried me past it, I saw my little girl again and felt Isabel's tears again, and I felt my own tears begin to rise. And I was yet aware that this was only a moment, that the world waited outside, as hungry as a tiger, and that trouble stretched above us, longer than the sky.

Then it was over. Creole and Sonny let out their breath, both soaking wet, and grinning. There was a lot of applause and some of it was real. In the dark, the girl came by and I asked her to take drinks to the bandstand. There was a long pause, while they talked up there in the indigo light and after awhile I saw the girl put a Scotch and milk on top of the piano for Sonny. He didn't seem to notice it, but just before they started playing again, he sipped from it and looked toward me, and nodded. Then he put it back on top of the piano. For me, then, as they began to play again, it glowed and shook above my brother's head like the very cup of trembling.

1957

The Man Who Was Almost a Man

Richard Wright (1908–1960)

Richard Wright grew up in poverty in Mississippi during the 1920s and 1930s. As an African American living in the deep South, in the state usually cited as being the one most troubled by racism, Wright experienced the slights, insults, and outright hatred dealt out as a matter of course to blacks. He worked at menial jobs, and moved with his family many times—to Arkansas, to Tennessee, and finally north to escape the world that would provide the basis for his fiction. His best known novel, *Native Son* (1940), tells the story of a black murderer named Bigger Thomas who rages back at his white oppressors. The novel was considered shocking in 1940 for the intensity with which it expressed "black rage."

Dave struck out across the fields, looking homeward through paling light. Whut's the use talkin wid em niggers in the field? Anyhow, his mother was putting supper on the table. Them niggers can't understan nothing. One of these days he was going to get a gun and practice shooting, then they couldn't talk to him as though he were a little boy. He slowed, looking at the ground. Shucks, Ah ain scareda them even ef they are biggern me! Aw, Ah know whut Ahma do. Ahm going by ol Joe's sto n git that Sears Roebuck catlog n look at them guns. Mebbe Ma will lemme buy one when she gits mah pay from ol man Hawkins. Ahma beg her t gimme some money. Ahm ol ernough to hava gun. Ahm seventeen. Almost a man. He strode, feeling his long loose-jointed limbs. Shucks, a man oughta hava little gun aftah he done worked hard all day.

He came in sight of Joe's store. A yellow lantern glowed on the front porch. He mounted steps and went through the screen door, hearing it bang behind him. There was a strong smell of coal oil and mackerel fish. He felt very confident until he saw fat Joe walk in through the rear door, then his courage began to ooze.

"Howdy, Dave! Whutcha want?"

"How yuh, Mistah Joe? Aw, Ah don wanna buy nothing. Ah jus wanted t see ef yuhd lemme look at tha catlog erwhile."

"Sure! You wanna see it here?"

"Nawsuh. Ah wans t take it home wid me. Ah'll bring it back termorrow when Ah come in from the fiels."

"You plannin on buying something?"

"Yessuh."

"Your ma lettin you have your own money now?"

"Shucks. Mistah Joe, Ahm gittin t be a man like anybody else!"

Joe laughed and wiped his greasy white face with a red bandanna.

"Whut you plannin on buyin?"

Dave looked at the floor, scratched his head, scratched his thigh, and smiled. Then he looked up shyly.

"Ah'll tell yuh, Mistah Joe, ef yuh promise yuh won't tell."

"I promise."

"Waal, Ahma buy a gun."

"A gun? Whut you want with a gun?"

"Ah wanna keep it."

"You ain't nothing but a boy. You don't need a gun."

"Aw, lemme have the catlog, Mistah Joe. Ah'll bring it back."

Joe walked through the rear door. Dave was elated. He looked around at barrels of sugar and flour. He heard Joe coming back. He craned his neck to see if he were bringing the book. Yeah, he's got it. Gawddog, he's got it!

"Here, but be sure you bring it back. It's the only one I got."

"Sho, Mistah Joe."

"Say, if you wanna buy a gun, why don't you buy one from me? I gotta gun to sell."

"Will it shoot?"

"Sure it'll shoot."

"Whut kind is it?"

"Oh, it's kinda old . . . a left-hand Wheeler. A pistol. A big one."

"Is it got bullets in it?"

"It's loaded."

"Kin Ah see it?"

"Where's your money?"

"Whut yuh wan fer it?"

"I'll let you have it for two dollars."

"Just two dollahs? Shucks, Ah could buy tha when Ah git mah pay."

"I'll have it here when you want it."

"Awright, suh. Ah be in fer it."

He went through the door, hearing it slam again behind him. Ahma git some money from Ma n buy me a gun! Only two dollahs! He tucked the thick catalogue under his arm and hurried.

"Where yuh been, boy?" His mother held a steaming dish of black-eyed peas.

"Aw, Ma, Ah jus stopped down the road t talk wid the boys."

"Yuh know bettah t keep suppah waitin."

He sat down, resting the catalogue on the edge of the table.

"Yuh git up from there and git to the well n wash yoself! Ah ain feedin no hogs in mah house!"

She grabbed his shoulder and pushed him. He stumbled out of the room, then came back to get the catalogue.

"Whut this?"

"Aw, Ma, it's jusa catlog."

"Who yuh git it from?"

"From Joe, down at the sto."

"Waal, thas good. We kin use it in the outhouse."

"Naw, Ma." He grabbed for it. "Gimme ma catlog, Ma."

She held onto it and glared at him.

"Quit hollerin at me! Whut's wrong wid yuh? Yuh crazy?"

"But Ma, please. It ain mine! It's Joe's! He tol me t bring it back t im termorrow."

She gave up the book. He stumbled down the back steps, hugging the thick book under his arm. When he had splashed water on his face and hands, he groped back to the kitchen and fumbled in a corner for the towel. He bumped into a chair; it clattered to the floor. The catalogue sprawled at his feet. When he had dried his eyes he snatched up the book and held it again under his arm. His mother stood watching him.

"Now, ef yuh gonna act a fool over that ol book, Ah'll take it n burn it up."

"Naw, Ma, please."

"Waal, set down n be still!"

He sat down and drew the oil lamp close. He thumbed page after page, unaware of the food his mother set on the table. His father came in. Then his small brother.

"Whutcha got there, Dave?" his father asked.

"Jusa catlog," he answered, not looking up.

"Yeah, here they is!" His eyes glowed at blue-and-black revolvers. He glanced up, feeling sudden guilt. His father was watching him. He eased the book under the table and rested it on his knees. After the blessing was asked, he ate. He scooped up peas and swallowed fat meat without chewing. Buttermilk helped to wash it down. He did not want to mention money before his father. He would do much better by cornering his mother when she was alone. He looked at his father uneasily out of the edge of his eye.

"Boy, how come yuh don quit foolin wid tha book n eat yo suppah?"

"Yessuh."

"How you n ol man Hawkins gitten erlong?"

"Suh?"

"Can't yuh hear? Why don yuh lissen? Ah ast yu how wuz yuh n ol man Hawkins gittin erlong?"

"Oh, swell, Pa. Ah plows mo lan than anybody over there."

'Waal, yuh oughta keep yo mind on whut yuh doin."

"Yessuh."

He poured his plate full of molasses and sopped it up slowly with a chunk of cornbread. When his father and brother had left the kitchen, he still sat and looked again at the guns in the catalogue, longing to muster courage enough to present his case to his mother. Lawd, ef Ah only had tha pretty one! He could almost feel the slickness of the weapon with his fingers. If he had a gun like that he would polish it and keep it shining so it would never rust. N Ah'd keep it loaded, by Gawd!

"Ma?" His voice was hesitant.

"Hunh?"

"Ol man Hawkins give yuh mah money yit?"

"Yeah, but ain no usa yuh thinking bout throwin nona it erway. Ahm keepin tha money sos yuh kin have cloes t go to school this winter."

He rose and went to her side with the open catalogue in his palms. She was washing dishes, her head bent low over a pan. Shyly he raised the book. When he spoke, his voice was husky, faint.

"Ma, Gawd knows Ah wans one of these."

"One of whut?" she asked, not raising her eyes.

"One of these," he said again, not daring even to point. She glanced up at the page, then at him with wide eyes.

"Nigger, is yuh gone plumb crazy?"

"Aw, Ma—"

"Git outta here! Don yuh talk t me bout no gun! Yuh a fool!"

"Ma, Ah kin buy one fer two dollahs."

"Not ef Ah knows it, yuh ain!"

"But yuh promised me one—"

"Ah don care whut Ah promised! Yuh ain nothing but a boy yit!"

"Ma, ef yuh lemme buy one Ah'll *never* ast yuh fer nothing no mo."

"Ah tol yuh t git outta here! Yuh ain gonna toucha penny of tha money fer no gun! Thas how come Ah has Mistah Hawkins t pay yo wages t me, cause Ah knows yuh ain got no sense."

"But, Ma, we needa gun. Pa ain got no gun. We needa gun in the house. Yuh kin never tell whut might happen."

"Now don yuh try to maka fool outta me, boy! Ef we did hava gun, yuh wouldn't have it!"

He laid the catalogue down and slipped his arm around her waist.

"Aw, Ma, Ah done worked hard alla summer n ain ast yuh fer nothin, is Ah, now?"

"Thas whut yuh spose t do!"

"But Ma, Ah wans a gun. Yuh kin lemme have two dollahs outta mah money. Please, Ma. I kin give it to Pa . . . Please, Ma! Ah loves yuh, Ma."

When she spoke her voice came soft and low.

"Whut yu wan wida gun, Dave? Yuh don need no gun. You'll git in trouble. N ef yo pa jus thought Ah let yuh have money t buy a gun he'd hava fit."

"Ah'll hide it, Ma. It ain but two dollahs."

"Lawd, chil, whut's wrong wid yuh?"

"Ain nothin wrong, Ma. Ahm almos a man now. Ah wans a gun."

"Who gonna sell yuh a gun?"

"Ol Joe at the sto."

"N it don cos but two dollahs?"

"Thas all, Ma. Jus two dollahs. Please, Ma."

She was stacking the plates away; her hands moved slowly, reflectively. Dave kept an anxious silence. Finally, she turned to him.

"Ah'll let yuh git tha gun ef yuh promise me one thing."

"Whut's tha, Ma?"

"Yuh bring it straight back t me, yuh hear? It be fer Pa."

"Yessum! Lemme go now, Ma."

She stooped, turned slightly to one side, raised the hem of her dress, rolled down the top of her stocking, and came up with a slender wad of bills.

"Here," she said. "Lawd knows yuh don need no gun. But yer pa does. Yuh bring it right back t me, yuh hear? Ahma put it up. Now ef yuh don, Ahma have yuh pa lick yuh so hard yuh won fergit it."

"Yessum."

He took the money, ran down the steps, and across the yard.

"Dave! Yuuuuuh Daaaaave!"

He heard, but he was not going to stop now. "Naw, Lawd!"

The first movement he made the following morning was to reach under his pillow for the gun. In the gray light of dawn he held it loosely, feeling a sense of power. Could kill a man with a gun like this. Kill anybody, black or white. And if he were holding his gun in his hand, nobody could run over him; they would have to respect him. It was a big gun, with a long barrel and a heavy handle. He raised and lowered it in his hand, marveling at its weight.

He had not come straight home with it as his mother had asked; instead he had stayed out in the fields, holding the weapon in his hand, aiming it now and then at some imaginary foe. But he had not fired it; he had been afraid that his father might hear. Also he was not sure he knew how to fire it.

To avoid surrendering the pistol he had not come into the house until he knew that they were all asleep. When his mother had tiptoed to his bedside late that night and demanded the gun, he had first played possum; then he had told her that the gun was hidden outdoors, that he would bring it to her in the morning. Now he lay turning it slowly in his hands. He broke it, took out the cartridges, felt them, and then put them back.

He slid out of bed, got a long strip of old flannel from a trunk, wrapped the gun in it, and tied it to his naked thigh while it was still loaded. He did not go in to breakfast. Even though it was not yet daylight, he started for Jim Hawkins' plantation. Just as the sun was rising he reached the barns where the mules and plows were kept.

"Hey! That you, Dave?"

He turned. Jim Hawkins stood eying him suspiciously.

"What're yuh doing here so early?"

"Ah didn't know Ah wuz gittin up so early, Mistah Hawkins. Ah wuz fixin t hitch up ol Jenny n take her t the fiels."

"Good. Since you're so early, how about plowing that stretch down by the woods?"

"Suits me, Mistah Hawkins."

"O.K. Go to it!"

He hitched Jenny to a plow and started across the fields. Hot dog! This was just what he wanted. If he could get down by the woods, he could shoot his gun and nobody would hear. He walked behind the plow, hearing the traces creaking, feeling the gun tied tight to his thigh.

When he reached the woods, he plowed two whole rows before he decided to take out the gun. Finally, he stopped, looked in all directions, then untied the gun and held it in his hand. He turned to the mule and smiled.

"Know whut this is, Jenny? Naw, yuh wouldn know! Yuhs jusa ol mule! Anyhow, this is a gun, n it kin shoot, by Gawd!"

He held the gun at arm's length. Whut t hell, Ahma shoot this thing! He looked at Jenny again.

"Lissen here, Jenny! When Ah pull this ol trigger, Ah don wan yuh t run n acka fool now!"

Jenny stood with head down, her short ears pricked straight. Dave walked off about twenty feet, held the gun far out from him at arm's length, and turned his head. Hell, he told himself, Ah ain afraid. The gun felt loose in his fingers; he waved it wildly for a moment. Then he shut his eyes and tightened his forefinger. Bloom! A report half deafened him and he thought his right hand was torn from his arm. He heard Jenny whinnying and galloping over the field, and he found himself on his knees squeezing his fingers hard between his legs. His hand was numb; he jammed it into his mouth, trying to warm it, trying to stop the pain. The gun lay at his feet. He did not quite know what had happened. He stood up and stared at the gun as though it were a living thing. He gritted his teeth and kicked the gun. Yuh almos broke mah arm! He turned to look for Jenny; she was far over the fields, tossing her head and kicking wildly.

"Hol on there, ol mule!"

When he caught up with her she stood trembling, walling her big white eyes at him. The plow was far away; the traces had broken. Then Dave stopped short, looking, not believing. Jenny was bleeding. Her left side was red and wet with blood. He went closer. Lawd, have mercy! Wondah did Ah shoot this mule? He grabbed for Jenny's mane. She flinched, snorted, whirled, tossing her head.

"Hol on now! Hol on."

Then he saw the hole in Jenny's side, right between the ribs. It was round, wet, red. A crimson stream streaked down the front leg, flowing fast. Good Gawd! Ah wuzn't shootin at tha mule. He felt panic. He knew he had to stop that blood, or Jenny would bleed to death. He had never seen so much blood in all his life. He chased the mule for half a mile, trying to catch her. Finally she stopped, breathing hard, stumpy tail half arched. He caught her mane and led her back to where the plough and gun lay. Then he stooped and grabbed handfuls of damp black earth and tried to plug the bullet hole. Jenny shuddered, whinnied, and broke from him.

"Hol on! Hol on now!"

He tried to plug it again, but blood came anyhow. His fingers were hot and sticky. He rubbed dirt into his palms, trying to dry them. Then again he attempted to plug the bullet hole, but Jenny shied away, kicking her heels high. He stood helpless. He had to do something. He ran at Jenny; she dodged him. He watched a red stream of blood flow down Jenny's leg and form a bright pool at her feet.

"Jenny . . . Jenny," he called weakly.

His lips trembled. She's bleeding t death! He looked in the direction of home, wanting to go back, wanting to get help. But he saw the pistol lying in the damp black clay. He had a queer feeling that if he only did something, this would not be; Jenny would not be there bleeding to death.

When he went to her this time, she did not move. She stood with sleepy, dreamy eyes; and when he touched her she gave a low-pitched whinny and knelt to the ground, her front knees slopping in blood.

"Jenny . . . Jenny . . ." he whispered.

For a long time she held her neck erect; then her head sank, slowly. Her ribs swelled with a mighty heave and she went over.

Dave's stomach felt empty, very empty. He picked up the gun and held it gingerly between his thumb and forefinger. He buried it at the foot of a tree. He took a stick and tried to cover the pool of blood with dirt—but what was the use? There was Jenny lying with her mouth open and her eyes walled and glassy. He could not tell Jim Hawkins he had shot his mule. But he had to tell something. Yeah, Ah'll tell em Jenny started gittin wil n fell on the joint of the plow. . . . But that would hardly happen to a mule. He walked across the field slowly, head down.

It was sunset. Two of Jim Hawkins' men were over near the edge of the woods digging a hole in which to bury Jenny. Dave was surrounded by a knot of people, all of whom were looking down at the dead mule.

"I don't see how in the world it happened," said Jim Hawkins for the tenth time.

The crowd parted and Dave's mother, father, and small brother pushed into the center.

"Where Dave?" his mother called.

"There he is," said Jim Hawkins.

His mother grabbed him.

"Whut happened, Dave? Whut yuh done?"

"Nothin."

"C mon, boy, talk," his father said.

Dave took a deep breath and told the story he knew nobody believed.

"Waal," he drawled. "Ah brung ol Jenny down here sos Ah could do mah plowin. Ah plowed bout two rows, just like yuh see." He stopped and pointed at the long rows of upturned earth. "Then somethin musta been wrong wid ol Jenny. She wouldn ack right a-tall. She started snortin n kickin her heels. Ah tried t hol her, but she pulled erway, rearin n goin in. Then when the point of the plow was stickin up in the air, she swung erroun n twisted herself back on it . . . She stuck herself n started t bleed. N fo Ah could do anything, she wuz dead."

"Did you ever hear of anything like that in all your life?" asked Jim Hawkins.

There were white and black standing in the crowd. They murmured. Dave's mother came close to him and looked hard into his face. "Tell the truth, Dave," she said.

"Looks like a bullet hole to me," said one man.

"Dave, whut yuh do wid the gun?" his mother asked.

The crowd surged in, looking at him. He jammed his hands into his pockets, shook his head slowly from left to right, and backed away. His eyes were wide and painful.

"Did he hava gun?" asked Jim Hawkins.

"By Gawd, Ah tol him tha wuz a gun wound," said a man, slapping his thigh.

His father caught his shoulders and shook him till his teeth rattled.

"Tell whut happened, yuh rascal! Tell whut . . ."

Dave looked at Jenny's stiff legs and began to cry.

"Whut yuh do wid tha gun?" his mother asked.

"Whut wuz he doin wida gun?" his father asked.

"Come on and tell the truth," said Hawkins. "Ain't nobody going to hurt you . . ."

His mother crowded close to him.

"Did yuh shoot tha mule, Dave?"

Dave cried, seeing blurred white and black faces.

"Ahh ddinn gggo tt sshooot hher . . . Ah ssswear ffo Gawd Ahh ddin . . . Ah wuz a-tryin t sssee ef the old gggun would sshoot—"

"Where yuh git the gun from?" his father asked.

"Ah got it from Joe, at the sto."

"Where yuh git the money?"

"Ma give it t me."

"He kept worryin me, Bob. Ah had t. Ah tol im t bring the gun right back t me . . . It was fer yuh, the gun."

"But how yuh happen to shoot that mule?" asked Jim Hawkins.

"Ah wuzn shootin at the mule, Mistah Hawkins. The gun jumped when Ah pulled the trigger . . . N for Ah knowed anythin Jenny was there a-bleedin."

Somebody in the crowd laughed. Jim Hawkins walked close to Dave and looked into his face.

"Well, looks like you have bought a mule, Dave."

"Ah swear to Gawd, Ah didn go t kill the mule, Mistah Hawkins!"

"But you killed her!"

All the crowd was laughing now. They stood on tiptoe and poked heads over one another's shoulders.

"Well, boy, looks like yuh done bought a dead mule! Hahaha!"

"Ain tha ershame."

"Hohohohoho."

Dave stood, head down, twisting his feet in the dirt.

"Well, you needn't worry about it, Bob," said Jim Hawkins to Dave's father. "Just let the boy keep on working and pay me two dollars a month."

"Whut yuh wan fer yo mule, Mistah Hawkins?"

Jim Hawkins screwed up his eyes.

"Fifty dollars."

"Whut yuh do wid tha gun?" Dave's father demanded.

Dave said nothing.

"Yuh wan me t take a tree n beat yuh till yuh talk!"

"Nawsuh!"

"Whut yuh do wid it?"

"Ah throwed it erway."

"Where?"

"Ah . . . Ah throwed it in the creek."

"Waal, c mon home. N firs thing in the mawnin git to tha creek n fin tha gun."

"Yessuh."

"Whut yuh pay fer it?"

"Two dollahs."

"Take tha gun n git yu money back n carry it t Mistah Hawkins, yuh hear? N don fergit Ahma lam you black bottom good fer this! Now march yosef on home, suh!"

Dave turned and walked slowly. He heard people laughing. Dave glared, his eyes welling with tears. Hot anger bubbled in him. Then he swallowed and stumbled on.

That night Dave did not sleep. He was glad that he had gotten out of killing the mule so easily, but he was hurt. Something hot seemed to turn over inside him each time he remembered how they had laughed. He tossed on his bed, feeling his hard pillow. N Pa says he's gonna beat me . . . He remembered other beatings, and his back quivered. Naw, naw. Ah sho don wan im t beat me tha way no mo. Dam em all! Nobody ever gave him anything. All he did was work. They treat me like a mule, n then they beat me. He gritted his teeth. N Ma had t tell on me.

Well, if he had to, he would take old man Hawkins that two dollars. But that meant selling the gun. And he wanted to keep that gun. Fifty dollars for a dead mule.

He turned over, thinking how he had fired the gun. He had an itch to fire it again. Ef other men kin shoota gun, by Gawd, Ah kin! He was still, listening. Mebbe they all sleepin now. The house was still. He heard the soft breathing of his brother. Yes, now! He would go down and get that gun and see if he could fire it! He eased out of bed and slipped into overalls.

The moon was bright. He ran almost all the way to the edge of the woods. He stumbled over the ground, looking for the spot where he had buried the gun. Yeah, here it is. Like a hungry dog scratching for a bone, he pawed it up. He puffed his black cheeks and blew dirt from the trigger and barrel. He broke it and found four cartridges unshot. He looked around; the fields were filled with silence and moonlight. He clutched the gun stiff and hard in his fingers. But, as soon as he wanted to pull the trigger, he shut his eyes and turned his head. Naw, Ah can't shoot wid mah eyes closed n mah head turned. With effort he held his eyes open; then he squeezed. *Blooooom!* He was stiff, not breathing. The gun was still in his hands. Dammit, he'd done it! He fired again. *Blooooom!* He smiled. *Blooooom! Blooooom! Click, click.* There! It was empty. If anybody could shoot a gun, he could. He put the gun into his hip pocket and started across the fields.

When he reached the top of a ridge he stood straight and proud in the moonlight, looking at Jim Hawkins' big white house, feeling the gun sagging in his pocket. Lawd, ef Ah had just one mo bullet Ah'd taka shot at tha house. Ah'd like t scare ol man Hawkins jusa little . . . Jusa enough t let im know Dave Saunders is a man.

To his left the road curved, running to the tracks of the Illinois Central. He jerked his head, listening. From far off came a faint *hoooof-hoooof; hoooof-hoooof; hoooof-hoooof*. . . . He stood rigid. Two dollahs a mont. Les see now . . . Tha means it'll take bout two years. Shucks! Ah'll be dam!

He started down the road, toward the tracks. Yeah, here she comes! He stood beside the track and held himself stiffly. Here she comes, erroun the ben . . . C mon, yuh slow poke! C mon! He had his hand on his gun; something quivered in his stomach. Then the train thundered past, the gray and brown box cars rumbling and clinking. He gripped the gun tightly; then he jerked his hand out of his pocket. Ah betcha Bill wouldn't do it! Ah-betcha . . . The cars slid past, steel grinding upon steel. Ahm ridin yuh ternight, so hep me Gawd! He was hot all over. He hesitated just a moment; then he grabbed, pulled atop of a car, and lay flat. He felt his pocket; the gun was still there. Ahead the long rails were glinting in the moonlight, stretching away, away to somewhere, somewhere where he could be a man . . .

1939

The Jilting of Granny Weatherall

Katherine Anne Porter (1890–1980)

Katherine Anne Porter had a long, historically rich life of ninety years. Born in 1890 in Texas, she nearly died in Colorado of the influenza epidemic that killed millions just after World War I. In Mexico she was involved in the Obregon Revolution, an experience she recounted in her short story "Flowering Judas." She saw the rise of fascism in Germany in the 1930s, and in the 1960s was a favorite of fellow Texan President Lyndon B. Johnson, who frequently invited her to White House dinners. Her literary output was relatively small—two dozen short stories, a collection of essays, and a single novel, *Ship of Fools* (1962). She was widely respected as a "writer's writer" for her polished style, and she received the Pulitzer Prize in 1966.

She flicked her wrist neatly out of Doctor Harry's pudgy careful fingers and pulled the sheet up to her chin. The brat ought to be in knee breeches. Doctoring around the country with spectacles on his nose! "Get along now, take your schoolbooks and go. There's nothing wrong with me."

Doctor Harry spread a warm paw like a cushion on her forehead where the forked green vein danced and made her eyelids twitch. "Now, now, be a good girl, and we'll have you up in no time."

"That's no way to speak to a woman nearly eighty years old just because she's down. I'd have you respect your elders, young man."

"Well, Missy, excuse me." Doctor Harry patted her cheek. "But I've got to warn you, haven't I? You're a marvel, but you must be careful or you're going to be good and sorry."

"Don't tell me what I'm going to be. I'm on my feet now, morally speaking. It's Cornelia. I had to go to bed to get rid of her."

Her bones felt loose, and floated around in her skin, and Doctor Harry floated like a balloon around the foot of the bed. He floated and pulled down his waistcoat and swung his glasses on a cord. "Well, stay where you are, it certainly can't hurt you."

"Get along and doctor your sick," said Granny Weatherall. "Leave a well woman alone. I'll call for you when I want you . . . . Where were you forty years ago when I pulled through milk-leg[1] and double pneumonia? You weren't even born. Don't let Cornelia lead you on," she shouted, because Doctor Harry appeared to float up to the ceiling and out. "I pay my own bills, and I don't throw my money away on nonsense!"

---

[1] a painful swelling of the legs sometimes occurring in women after childbirth

She meant to wave good-by, but it was too much trouble. Her eyes closed of themselves, it was like a dark curtain drawn around the bed. The pillow rose and floated under her, pleasant as a hammock in a light wind. She listened to the leaves rustling outside the window. No, somebody was swishing newspapers: no, Cornelia and Doctor Harry were whispering together. She leaped broad awake, thinking they whispered in her ear.

"She was never like this, *never* like this!" "Well, what can we expect?" "Yes, eighty years old . . ."

Well, and what if she was? She still had ears. It was like Cornelia to whisper around doors. She always kept things secret in such a public way. She was always being tactful and kind. Cornelia was dutiful; that was the trouble with her. Dutiful and good: "So good and dutiful," said Granny, "that I'd like to spank her." She saw herself spanking Cornelia and making a fine job of it.

"What'd you say, Mother?"

Granny felt her face tying up in hard knots.

"Can't a body think, I'd like to know?"

"I thought you might want something."

"I do. I want a lot of things. First off, go away and don't whisper."

She lay and drowsed, hoping in her sleep that the children would keep out and let her rest a minute. It had been a long day. Not that she was tired. It was always pleasant to snatch a minute now and then. There was always so much to be done, let me see: tomorrow.

Tomorrow was far away and there was nothing to trouble about. Things were finished somehow when the time came; thank God there was always a little margin over for peace: then a person could spread out the plan of life and tuck in the edges orderly. It was good to have everything clean and folded away, with the hair brushes and tonic bottles sitting straight on the white embroidered linen: the day started without fuss and the pantry shelves laid out with rows of jelly glasses and brown jugs and white stone-china jars with blue whirligigs and words painted on them: coffee, tea, sugar, ginger, cinnamon, allspice: and the bronze clock with the lion on top nicely dusted off. The dust that lion could collect in twenty-four hours! The box in the attic with all those letters tied up, well, she'd have to go through that tomorrow. All those letters—George's letters and John's letters and her letters to them both—lying around for the children to find afterwards made her uneasy. Yes, that would be tomorrow's business. No use to let them know how silly she had been once.

While she was rummaging around she found death in her mind and it felt clammy and unfamiliar. She had spent so much time preparing for death there was no need for bringing it up again. Let it take care of itself now. When she was sixty she had felt very old, finished, and went around making farewell trips to see her children and grandchildren, with a secret in her mind: This is the very last of your mother, children! Then she made her will and came down with a long fever. That was all just a notion like a lot of other things, but it was lucky too, for she had once for all got over the idea of dying for a long time. Now she couldn't be worried. She hoped she had better sense now. Her father had lived to be one hundred and two years old and had drunk a noggin[2] of strong hot toddy[3] on his last birthday. He told the reporters it was his daily habit, and he owed his long life to that. He had made quite a scandal and was very pleased about it. She believed she'd just plague Cornelia a little.

"Cornelia! Cornelia!" No footsteps, but a sudden hand on her cheek. "Bless you, where have you been?"

"Here, mother."

"Well, Cornelia, I want a noggin of hot toddy."

"Are you cold, darling?"

"I'm chilly, Cornelia. Lying in bed stops the circulation. I must have told you that a thousand times."

Well, she could just hear Cornelia telling her husband that Mother was getting a little childish and they'd have to humor her. The thing that most annoyed her was that Cornelia thought she was deaf, dumb, and blind. Little hasty glances and tiny gestures tossed around her and over her head saying, "Don't cross her, let her have her way, she's eighty years old," and she sitting there as if she lived in a thin glass cage. Sometimes Granny almost made up her mind to pack up and move back to her own house where nobody could remind her every minute that she was old. Wait, wait, Cornelia, till your own children whisper behind your back!

In her day she had kept a better house and had got more work done. She wasn't too old yet for Lydia to be driving eighty miles for advice when one of the children jumped the track, and Jimmy still dropped in and talked things over: "Now, Mammy, you've a good business head, I want to know what you think of this? . . ." Old. Cornelia couldn't change the furniture around without asking. Little things, little things! They had been so sweet when they were little. Granny wished the old days were back again with the children young and everything to be done over. It had been a hard pull, but not too much for her. When she thought of all the food she had cooked, and all the clothes she had cut and sewed, and all the gardens she had made—well, the children showed it. There they were, made out of her, and they couldn't get away from that. Sometimes she wanted to see John again and point to them and say, Well, I didn't do so badly, did I? But that would have to wait. That was for tomorrow. She used to think of him as a man, but now all the children were older than their father, and he would be a child beside her if she saw him now. It seemed strange and there was something wrong in the idea. Why, he couldn't possibly recognize her. She had fenced in a hundred acres once, digging the post holes herself and clamping the wires with just a Negro boy to help. That changed a woman. John would be looking for a young woman with the peaked Spanish comb in her hair and the painted fan. Digging post holes changed a woman. Riding country roads

---

[2] a small mug
[3] a drink consisting of brandy or other liquor mixed with hot water, lemon, sugar, and spices

in the winter when women had their babies was another thing: sitting up nights with sick horses and sick Negroes and sick children and hardly ever losing one. John, I hardly ever lost one of them! John would see that in a minute, that would be something he could understand, she wouldn't have to explain anything!

It made her feel like rolling up her sleeves and putting the whole place to rights again. No matter if Cornelia was determined to be everywhere at once, there were a great many things left undone on this place. She would start tomorrow and do them. It was good to be strong enough for everything, even if all you made melted and changed and slipped under your hands, so that by the time you finished you almost forgot what you were working for. What was it I set out to do? she asked herself intently, but she could not remember. A fog rose over the valley, she saw it marching across the creek swallowing the trees and moving up the hill like an army of ghosts. Soon it would be at the near edge of the orchard, and then it was time to go in and light the lamps. Come in, children, don't stay out in the night air.

Lighting the lamps had been beautiful. The children huddled up to her and breathed like little calves waiting at the bars in the twilight. Their eyes followed the match and watched the flame rise and settle in a blue curve, then they moved away from her. The lamp was lit, they didn't have to be scared and hang on to mother any more. Never, never, never more. God, for all my life I thank Thee. Without Thee, my God, I could never have done it. Hail, Mary, full of grace.

I want you to pick all the fruit this year and see that nothing is wasted. There's always someone who can use it. Don't let good things rot for want of using. You waste life when you waste good food. Don't let things get lost. It's bitter to lose things. Now, don't let me get to thinking, not when I am tired and taking a little nap before supper. . . .

The pillow rose about her shoulders and pressed against her heart and the memory was being squeezed out of it: oh, push down the pillow, somebody: it would smother her if she tried to hold it. Such a fresh breeze blowing and such a green day with no threats in it. But he had not come, just the same. What does a woman do when she has put on the white veil and set out the white cake for a man and he doesn't come? She tried to remember. No, I swear he never harmed me but in that. He never harmed me but in that . . . and what if he did? There was the day, the day, but a whirl of dark smoke rose and covered it, crept up and over into the bright field where everything was planted so carefully in orderly rows. That was hell, she knew hell when she saw it. For sixty years she had prayed against remembering him and against losing her soul in the deep pit of hell, and now the two things were mingled in one and the thought of him was a smoky cloud from hell that moved and crept in her head when she had just got rid of Doctor Harry and was trying to rest a minute. Wounded vanity, Ellen, said a sharp voice in the top of her mind. Don't let your wounded vanity get the upper hand of you. Plenty of girls get jilted. You were jilted, weren't you? Then stand up to it. Her eyelids wavered and let in streamers of blue-gray light like tissue paper over her eyes. She must get up and pull the shades down or she'd never sleep. She was in bed again and the shades were not down. How could that happen? Better turn over, hide from the light, sleeping in the light gave you nightmares. "Mother, how do you feel now?" and a stinging wetness on her forehead. But I don't like having my face washed in cold water!

Hapsy? George? Lydia? Jimmy? No, Cornelia, and her features were swollen and full of little puddles. "They're coming, darling, they'll all be here soon." Go wash your face, child, you look funny.

Instead of obeying, Cornelia knelt down and put her head on the pillow. She seemed to be talking but there was no sound. "Well, are you tongue-tied? Whose birthday is it? Are you going to give a party?"

Cornelia's mouth moved urgently in strange shapes. "Don't do that, you bother me, daughter."

"Oh, no, Mother. Oh, no. . . ."

Nonsense. It was strange about children. They disputed your every word. "No what, Cornelia?"

"Here's Doctor Harry."

"I won't see that boy again. He just left five minutes ago."

"That was this morning, Mother. It's night now. Here's the nurse."

"This is Doctor Harry, Mrs. Weatherall. I never saw you look so young and happy!"

"Ah, I'll never be young again—but I'd be happy if they'd let me lie in peace and get rested."

She thought she spoke up loudly, but no one answered. A warm weight on her forehead, a warm bracelet on her wrist, and a breeze went on whispering, trying to tell her something. A shuffle of leaves in the everlasting hand of God, He blew on them and they danced and rattled. "Mother, don't mind, we're going to give you a little hypodermic." "Look here, daughter, how do ants get in this bed? I saw sugar ants yesterday." Did you send for Hapsy too?

It was Hapsy she really wanted. She had to go a long way back through a great many rooms to find Hapsy standing with a baby on her arm. She seemed to herself to be Hapsy also, and the baby on Hapsy's arm was Hapsy and himself and herself, all at once, and there was no surprise in the meeting. Then Hapsy melted from within and turned flimsy as gray gauze and the baby was a gauzy shadow, and Hapsy came up close and said, "I thought you'd never come," and looked at her very searchingly and said, "You haven't changed a bit!" They leaned forward to kiss, when Cornelia began whispering from a long way off, "Oh, is there anything you want to tell me? Is there anything I can do for you?"

Yes, she had changed her mind after sixty years and she would like to see George. I want you to find George. Find him and be sure to tell him I forgot him. I want him to know I had my husband just the same and my children and my house like any other woman. A good house too and a good husband that I loved and fine children out of him. Better than I hoped for even. Tell him I was given back everything he took away and more. Oh, no, oh, God, no, there was something else besides the house and the man and the children. Oh, surely they were not all? What was it? Something not given back. . . . Her breath crowded down under her ribs and grew into a monstrous frightening shape with cutting edges; it bored up into her head, and the agony was unbelievable: Yes, John, get the Doctor now, no more talk, my time has come.

When this one was born it should be the last. The last. It should have been born first, for it was the one she had truly wanted. Everything came in good time. Nothing left out, left over. She was strong, in three days she would be as well as ever. Better. A woman needed milk in her to have her full health.

"Mother, do you hear me?"

"I've been telling you—"

"Mother, Father Connolly's here."

"I went to Holy Communion only last week. Tell him I'm not so sinful as all that."

"Father just wants to speak to you."

He could speak as much as he pleased. It was like him to drop in and inquire about her soul as if it were a teething baby, and then stay on for a cup of tea and a round of cards and gossip. He always had a funny story of some sort, usually about an Irishman who made his little mistakes and confessed them, and the point lay in some absurd thing he would blurt out in the confessional showing his struggles between native piety and original sin. Granny felt easy about her soul. Cornelia, where are your manners? Give Father Connolly a chair. She had her secret comfortable understanding with a few favorite saints who cleared a straight road to God for her. All as surely signed and sealed as the papers for the new Forty Acres. Forever . . . heirs and assigns forever. Since the day the wedding cake was not cut, but thrown out and wasted. The whole bottom dropped out of the world, and there she was blind and sweating with nothing under her feet and the walls falling away. His hand had caught her under the breast, she had not fallen, there was the freshly polished floor with the green rug on it, just as before. He had cursed like a sailor's parrot and said, "I'll kill him for you." Don't lay a hand on him, for my sake leave something to God. "Now, Ellen, you must believe what I tell you. . . ."

So there was nothing, nothing to worry about any more, except sometimes in the night one of the children screamed in a nightmare, and they both hustled out shaking and hunting for the matches and calling, "There, wait a minute, here we are!" John, get the doctor now, Hapsy's time has come. But there was Hapsy standing by the bed in a white cap. "Cornelia, tell Hapsy to take off her cap. I can't see her plain."

Her eyes opened very wide and the room stood out like a picture she had seen somewhere. Dark colors with the shadows rising towards the ceiling in long angles. The tall black dresser gleamed with nothing on it but John's picture, enlarged from a little one, with John's eyes very black when they should have been blue. You never saw him, so how do you know how he looked? But the man insisted the copy was perfect, it was very rich and handsome. For a picture, yes, but it's not my husband. The table by the bed had a linen cover and a candle and a crucifix. The light was blue from Cornelia's silk lampshades. No sort of light at all, just frippery. You had to live forty years with kerosene lamps to appreciate honest electricity. She felt very strong and she saw Doctor Harry with a rosy nimbus around him.

"You look like a saint, Doctor Harry, and I vow that's as near as you'll ever come to it."

"She's saying something."

"I heard you, Cornelia. What's all this carrying-on?"

"Father Connolly's saying—"

Cornelia's voice staggered and bumped like a cart in a bad road. It rounded corners and turned back again and arrived nowhere. Granny stepped up in the cart very lightly and reached for the reins, but a man sat beside her and she knew him by his hands, driving the cart. She did not look in his face, for she knew without seeing, but looked instead down the road where the trees leaned over and bowed to each other and a thousand birds were singing a Mass. She felt like singing too, but she put her hand in the bosom of her dress and pulled out a rosary, and Father Connolly murmured Latin in a very solemn voice and tickled her feet. My God, will you stop that nonsense? I'm a married woman. What if he did run away and leave me to face the priest by myself? I found another a whole world better. I wouldn't have exchanged my husband for anybody except St. Michael himself, and you may tell him that for me with a thank you in the bargain.

Light flashed on her closed eyelids, and a deep roaring shook her. Cornelia, is that lightning? I hear thunder. There's going to be a storm. Close all the windows. Call the children in. . . . "Mother, here we are, all of us." "Is that you, Hapsy?" "Oh, no, I'm Lydia. We drove as fast as we could." Their faces drifted above her, drifted away. The rosary fell out of her hands and Lydia put it back. Jimmy tried to help, their hands fumbled together, and Granny closed two fingers around Jimmy's thumb. Beads wouldn't do, it must be something alive. She was so amazed her thoughts ran round and round. So, my dear Lord, this is my death and I wasn't even thinking about it. My children have come to see me die. But I can't, it's not time. Oh, I always hated surprises. I wanted to give Cornelia the amethyst set—Cornelia, you're to have the amethyst set, but Hapsy's to wear it when she wants, and, Doctor Harry, do shut up. Nobody sent for you. Oh, my dear Lord, do wait a minute. I meant to do something about the Forty Acres, Jimmy doesn't need it and Lydia will later on, with that worthless husband of hers. I meant to finish the altar cloth and send six bottles of wine to Sister Borgia for the dyspepsia.[4] I want to send six bottles of wine to Sister Borgia, Father Connolly, now don't let me forget.

Cornelia's voice made short turns and tilted over and crashed.

"Oh, Mother, oh, Mother, oh, Mother. . . ."

"I'm not going, Cornelia. I'm taken by surprise. I can't go."

You'll see Hapsy again. What about her? "I thought you'd never come." Granny made a long journey outward, looking for Hapsy. What if I don't find

---

[4]indigestion

her? What then? Her heart sank down and down, there was no bottom to death, she couldn't come to the end of it. The blue light from Cornelia's lampshade drew into a tiny point in the center of her brain, it flickered and winked like an eye, quietly it fluttered and dwindled. Granny lay curled down within herself, amazed and watchful, staring at the point of light that was herself; her body was now only a deeper mass of shadow in an endless darkness and this darkness would curl around the light and swallow it up. God, give a sign!

For the second time there was no sign. Again no bridegroom and the priest in the house. She could not remember any other sorrow because this grief wiped them all away. Oh, no, there's nothing more cruel than this—I'll never forgive it. She stretched herself with a deep breath and blew out the light.

1930

The Chrysanthemums

John Steinbeck (1902–1968)

John Steinbeck, best known for his Pulitzer Prize-winning novel *The Grapes of Wrath* (1939), which depicts the struggles of a poor family from Oklahoma heading to California during the Depression, was a prolific writer who showed great compassion for the ordinary person caught up in political and economic circumstances beyond his or her control. In such works as *Tortilla Flat* (1935) and *Of Mice and Men* (1937), Steinbeck showed human beings as always being torn between doing what was necessary to survive and obeying a deeper moral impulse. Steinbeck was asked by Presidents Franklin D. Roosevelt and Lyndon B. Johnson to participate in writing their political platforms and to provide ideas for helping the working poor. Steinbeck was a goodwill ambassador for the United Nations. He was awarded the Nobel Prize for literature in 1962.

The high gray-flannel fog of winter closed off the Salinas Valley[1] from the sky and from all the rest of the world. On every side it sat like a lid on the mountains and made of the great valley a closed pot. On the broad, level land floor the gang plows bit deep and left the black earth shining like metal where the shares had cut. On the foothill ranches across the Salinas River, the yellow stubble fields seemed to be bathed in pale cold sunshine, but there was no sunshine in the

---

[1]The Salinas Valley, south of the town of Salinas in central California, is one of the state's richest agricultural areas.

valley now in December. The thick willow scrub along the river flamed with sharp and positive yellow leaves.

It was a time of quiet and of waiting. The air was cold and tender. A light wind blew up from the southwest so that the farmers were mildly hopeful of a good rain before long; but fog and rain do not go together.

Across the river, on Henry Allen's foothill ranch there was little work to be done, for the hay was cut and stored and the orchards were plowed up to receive the rain deeply when it should come. The cattle on the higher slopes were becoming shaggy and rough-coated.

Elisa Allen, working in her flower garden, looked down across the yard and saw Henry, her husband, talking to two men in business suits. The three of them stood by the tractor shed, each man with one foot on the side of the little Fordson.[2] They smoked cigarettes and studied the machine as they talked.

Elisa watched them for a moment and then went back to her work. She was thirty-five. Her face was lean and strong and her eyes were as clear as water. Her figure looked blocked and heavy in her gardening costume, a man's black hat pulled down over her eyes, clodhopper shoes, a figured print dress almost completely covered by a big corduroy apron with four big pockets to hold the snips, the trowel and scratcher, the seeds and the knife she worked with. She wore heavy leather gloves to protect her hands while she worked.

She was cutting down the old year's chrysanthemum stalks with a pair of short and powerful scissors. She looked down toward the men by the tractor shed now and then. Her face was eager and mature and handsome; even her work with the scissors was over-eager, over-powerful. The chrysanthemum stems seemed too small and easy for her energy.

She brushed a cloud of hair out of her eyes with the back of her glove, and left a smudge of earth on her cheek in doing it. Behind her stood the neat white farm house with red geraniums close-banked around it as high as the windows. It was a hard-swept looking little house, with hard-polished windows, and a clean mud-mat on the front steps.

Elisa cast another glance toward the tractor shed. The strangers were getting into their Ford coupe. She took off a glove and put her strong fingers down into the forest of new green chrysanthemum sprouts that were growing around the old roots. She spread the leaves and looked down among the close-growing stems. No aphids were there, no sow-bugs or snails or cutworms. Her terrier fingers[3] destroyed such pests before they could get started.

Elisa started at the sound of her husband's voice. He had come near quietly, and he leaned over the wire fence that protected her flower garden from cattle and dogs and chickens.

"At it again," he said. "You've got a strong new crop coming."

---

[2]two-door Ford car, or coupe
[3]Terriers (which take their name from a word meaning "earth") were originally bred for hunting out animals living under the ground in burrows.

Elisa straightened her back and pulled on the gardening glove again. "Yes. They'll be strong this coming year." In her tone and on her face there was a little smugness.

"You've got a gift with things," Henry observed. "Some of those yellow chrysanthemums you had this year were ten inches across. I wish you'd work out in the orchard and raise some apples that big."

Her eyes sharpened. "Maybe I could do it, too. I've a gift with things, all right. My mother had it. She could stick anything in the ground and make it grow. She said it was having planters' hands that knew how to do it."

"Well, it sure works with flowers," he said.

"Henry, who were those men you were talking to?"

"Why, sure, that's what I came to tell you. They were from the Western Meat Company. I sold them those thirty head of three-year-old steers. Got nearly my own price, too."

"Good," she said. "Good for you."

"And I thought," he continued, "I thought how it's Saturday afternoon, and we might go into Salinas for dinner at a restaurant, and then to a picture show— to celebrate, you see."

"Good," she repeated. "Oh, yes. That will be good."

Henry put on his joking tone. "There's fights tonight. How'd you like to go to the fights?"

"Oh, no," she said breathlessly. "No, I wouldn't like fights."

"Just fooling, Elisa. We'll go to a movie. Let's see. It's two now. I'm going to take Scotty and bring down those steers from the hill. It'll take us maybe two hours. We'll go in town about five and have dinner at the Cominos Hotel. Like that?"

"Of course I'll like it. It's good to eat away from home."

"All right, then, I'll go get up a couple of horses."

She said, "I'll have plenty of time to transplant some of these sets, I guess."

She heard her husband calling Scotty down by the barn. And a little later she saw the two men ride up the pale yellow hillside in search of the steers.

There was a little square sandy bed kept for rooting the chrysanthemums. With her trowel she turned the soil over and over, and smoothed it and patted it firm. Then she dug ten parallel trenches to receive the sets. Back at the chrysanthemum bed she pulled out the little crisp shoots, trimmed off the leaves of each one with her scissors and laid it on a small orderly pile.

A squeak of wheels and plod of hoofs came from the road. Elisa looked up. The country road ran along the dense bank of willows and cottonwoods that bordered the river, and up this road came a curious vehicle, curiously drawn. It was an old spring-wagon, with a round canvas top on it like the cover of a prairie schooner. It was drawn by an old bay horse and a little gray-and-white burro. A big stubble-bearded man sat between the cover flaps and drove the crawling team. Underneath the wagon, between the hind wheels, a lean and rangy mongrel dog walked sedately. Words were painted on the canvas, in clumsy, crooked letters. "Pots, pans, knives, sisors, lawn mores, Fixed." Two rows of articles, and the triumphantly definitive "Fixed" below. The black paint had run down in little sharp points beneath each letter.

Elisa, squatting on the ground, watched to see the crazy, loose-jointed wagon pass by. But it didn't pass. It turned into the farm road in front of her house, crooked old wheels skirling and squeaking. The rangy dog darted from between the wheels and ran ahead. Instantly the two ranch shepherds flew out at him. Then all three stopped and with stiff and quivering tails, with taut straight legs, with ambassadorial dignity, they slowly circled, sniffing daintily. The caravan pulled up to Elisa's wire fence and stopped. Now the newcomer dog, feeling out-numbered, lowered his tail and retired under the wagon with raised hackles and bared teeth.

The man on the wagon seat called out, "That's a bad dog in a fight when he gets started."

Elisa laughed. "I see he is. How soon does he generally get started?"

The man caught up her laughter and echoed it heartily. "Sometimes not for weeks and weeks," he said. He climbed stiffly down, over the wheel. The horse and the donkey drooped like unwatered flowers.

Elisa saw that he was a very big man. Although his hair and beard were graying, he did not look old. His worn black suit was wrinkled and spotted with grease. The laughter had disappeared from his face and eyes the moment his laughing voice ceased. His eyes were dark, and they were full of the brooding that gets in the eyes of teamsters[4] and of sailors. The calloused hands he rested on the wire fence were cracked, and every crack was a black line. He took off his battered hat.

"I'm off my general road, ma'am," he said. "Does this dirt road cut over across the river to the Los Angeles highway?"

Elisa stood up and shoved the thick scissors in her apron pocket. "Well, yes, it does, but it winds around and then fords the river. I don't think your team could pull through the sand."

He replied with some asperity, "It might surprise you what them beasts can pull through."

"When they get started?" she asked.

He smiled for a second. "Yes. When they get started."

"Well," said Elisa, "I think you'll save time if you go back to the Salinas road and pick up the highway there."

He drew a big finger down the chicken wire and made it sing. "I ain't in any hurry, ma'am. I go from Seattle to San Diego and back every year. Takes all my time. About six months each way. I aim to follow nice weather."

Elisa took off her gloves and stuffed them in the apron pocket with the scissors. She touched the under edge of her man's hat, searching for fugitive hairs. "That sounds like a nice kind of way to live," she said.

---

[4]truckdrivers

He leaned confidentially over the fence. "Maybe you noticed the writing on my wagon. I mend pots and sharpen knives and scissors. You got any of them things to do?"

"Oh, no," she said quickly. "Nothing like that." Her eyes hardened with resistance.

"Scissors is the worst thing," he explained. "Most people just ruin scissors trying to sharpen 'em, but I know how. I got a special tool. It's a little bobbit kind of thing, and patented. But it sure does the trick."

"No. My scissors are all sharp."

"All right, then. Take a pot," he continued earnestly, "a bent pot, or a pot with a hole. I can make it like new so you don't have to buy no new ones. That's a saving for you."

"No," she said shortly. "I tell you I have nothing like that for you to do."

His face fell to an exaggerated sadness. His voice took on a whining undertone. "I ain't had a thing to do today. Maybe I won't have no supper tonight. You see I'm off my regular road. I know folks on the highway clear from Seattle to San Diego. They save their things for me to sharpen up because they know I do it so good and save them money."

"I'm sorry," Elisa said irritably. "I haven't anything for you to do."

His eyes left her face and fell to searching the ground. They roamed about until they came to the chrysanthemum bed where she had been working. "What's them plants, ma'am?"

The irritation and resistance melted from Elisa's face. "Oh, those are chrysanthemums, giant whites and yellows. I raise them every year, bigger than anybody around here."

"Kind of a long-stemmed flower? Looks like a quick puff of colored smoke?" he asked.

"That's it. What a nice way to describe them."

"They smell kind of nasty till you get used to them," he said.

"It's a good bitter smell," she retorted, "not nasty at all."

He changed his tone quickly. "I like the smell myself."

"I had ten-inch blooms this year," she said.

The man leaned farther over the fence. "Look. I know a lady down the road a piece, has got the nicest garden you ever seen. Got nearly every kind of flower but no chrysanthemums. Last time I was mending a copper-bottom washtub for her (that's a hard job but I do it good), she said to me, 'If you ever run acrost some nice chrysanthemums I wish you'd try to get me a few seeds.' That's what she told me."

Elisa's eyes grew alert and eager. "She couldn't have known much about chrysanthemums. You *can* raise them from seed, but it's much easier to root the little sprouts you see there."

"Oh," he said, "I s'pose I can't take none to her, then."

"Why yes you can," Elisa cried. "I can put some in damp sand, and you can carry them right along with you. They'll take root in the pot if you keep them damp. And then she can transplant them."

"She'd sure like to have some, ma'am. You say they're nice ones?"

"Beautiful," she said. "Oh, beautiful." Her eyes shone. She tore off the battered hat and shook out her dark pretty hair. "I'll put them in a flower pot, and you can take them right with you. Come into the yard."

While the man came through the picket gate Elisa ran excitedly along the geranium-bordered path to the back of the house. And she returned carrying a big red flower pot. The gloves were forgotten now. She kneeled on the ground by the starting bed and dug up the sandy soil with her fingers and scooped it into the bright new flower pot. Then she picked up the little pile of shoots she had prepared. With her strong fingers she pressed them into the sand and tamped around them with her knuckles. The man stood over her. "I'll tell you what to do," she said. "You remember so you can tell the lady."

"Yes, I'll try to remember."

"Well, look. These will take root in about a month. Then she must set them out, about a foot apart in good rich earth like this, see?" She lifted a handful of dark soil for him to look at. "They'll grow fast and tall. Now remember this: In July tell her to cut them down, about eight inches from the ground."

"Before they bloom?" he asked.

"Yes, before they bloom." Her face was tight with eagerness. "They'll grow right up again. About the last of September the buds will start."

She stopped and seemed perplexed. "It's the budding that takes the most care," she said hesitantly. "I don't know how to tell you." She looked deep into his eyes, searchingly. Her mouth opened a little, and she seemed to be listening. "I'll try to tell you," she said. "Did you ever hear of planting hands?"

"Can't say I have, ma'am."

"Well, I can only tell you what it feels like. It's when you're picking off the buds you don't want. Everything goes right down into your fingertips. You watch your fingers work. They do it themselves. You can feel how it is. They pick and pick the buds. They never make a mistake. They're with the plant. Do you see? Your fingers and the plant. You can feel that, right up your arm. They know. They never make a mistake. You can feel it. When you're like that you can't do anything wrong. Do you see that? Can you understand that?"

She was kneeling on the ground looking up at him. Her breast swelled passionately.

The man's eyes narrowed. He looked away self-consciously. "Maybe I know," he said. "Sometimes in the night in the wagon there—"

Elisa's voice grew husky. She broke in on him, "I've never lived as you do, but I know what you mean. When the night is dark—why, the stars are sharp-pointed, and there's quiet. Why, you rise up and up! Every pointed star gets driven into your body. It's like that. Hot and sharp and—lovely."

Kneeling there, her hand went out toward his legs in the greasy black trousers. Her hesitant fingers almost touched the cloth. Then her hand dropped to the ground. She crouched low like a fawning dog.

He said, "It's nice, just like you say. Only when you don't have no dinner, it ain't."

She stood up then, very straight, and her face was ashamed. She held the flower pot out to him and placed it gently in his arms. "Here. Put it in your wagon, on the seat, where you can watch it. Maybe I can find something for you to do."

At the back of the house she dug in the can pile and found two old and battered aluminum saucepans. She carried them back and gave them to him. "Here, maybe you can fix these."

His manner changed. He became professional. "Good as new I can fix them." At the back of his wagon he set a little anvil, and out of an oily tool box dug a small machine hammer. Elisa came through the gate to watch him while he pounded out the dents in the kettles. His mouth grew sure and knowing. At a difficult part of the work he sucked his underlip.

"You sleep right in the wagon?" Elisa asked.

"Right in the wagon, ma'am. Rain or shine I'm dry as a cow in there."

"It must be nice," she said. "It must be very nice. I wish women could do such things."

"It ain't the right kind of a life for a woman."

Her upper lip raised a little, showing her teeth. "How do you know? How can you tell?" she said.

"I don't know, ma'am," he protested. "Of course I don't know. Now here's your kettles, done. You don't have to buy no new ones."

"How much?"

"Oh, fifty cents'll do. I keep my prices down and my work good. That's why I have all them satisfied customers up and down the highway."

Elisa brought him a fifty-cent piece from the house and dropped it in his hand. "You might be surprised to have a rival some time. I can sharpen scissors, too. And I can beat the dents out of little pots. I could show you what a woman might do."

He put his hammer back in the oily box and shoved the little anvil out of sight. "It would be a lonely life for a woman, ma'am, and a scarey life, too, with animals creeping under the wagon all night." He climbed over the singletree,[5] steadying himself with a hand on the burro's white rump. He settled himself in the seat, picked up the lines. "Thank you kindly, ma'am," he said. "I'll do like you told me; I'll go back and catch the Salinas road."

"Mind," she called, "if you're long in getting there, keep the sand damp."

"Sand, ma'am? . . . Sand? Oh, sure. You mean around the chrysanthemums. Sure I will." He clucked his tongue. The beasts leaned luxuriously into their collars. The mongrel dog took his place between the back wheels. The wagon turned and crawled out the entrance road and back the way it had come, along the river.

Elisa stood in front of her wire fence watching the slow progress of the caravan. Her shoulders were straight, her head thrown back, her eyes half-closed, so

---

[5]the horizontal crossbar on a wagon to which the draft animals are attached

that the scene came vaguely into them. Her lips moved silently, forming the words "Good-bye—good-bye." Then she whispered, "That's a bright direction. There's a glowing there." The sound of her whisper startled her. She shook herself free and looked about to see whether anyone had been listening. Only the dogs had heard. They lifted their heads toward her from their sleeping in the dust, and then stretched out their chins and settled asleep again. Elisa turned and ran hurriedly into the house.

In the kitchen she reached behind the stove and felt the water tank. It was full of hot water from the noonday cooking. In the bathroom she tore off her soiled clothes and flung them into the corner. And then she scrubbed herself with a little block of pumice, legs and thighs, loins and chest and arms, until her skin was scratched and red. When she had dried herself she stood in front of a mirror in her bedroom and looked at her body. She tightened her stomach and threw out her chest. She turned and looked over her shoulder at her back.

After a while she began to dress slowly. She put on her newest underclothing and her nicest stockings and the dress which was the symbol of her prettiness. She worked carefully on her hair, penciled her eyebrows and rouged her lips.

Before she was finished she heard the little thunder of hoofs and the shouts of Henry and his helper as they drove the red steers into the corral. She heard the gate bang shut and set herself for Henry's arrival.

His steps sounded on the porch. He entered the house calling, "Elisa, where are you?"

"In my room dressing. I'm not ready. There's hot water for your bath. Hurry up. It's getting late."

When she heard him splashing in the tub, Elisa laid his dark suit on the bed, and shirt and socks and tie beside it. She stood his polished shoes on the floor beside the bed. Then she went to the porch and sat primly and stiffly down. She looked toward the river road where the willow-line was still yellow with frosted leaves so that under the high gray fog they seemed a thin band of sunshine. This was the only color in the gray afternoon. She sat unmoved for a long time. Her eyes blinked rarely.

Henry came banging out of the door, shoving his tie inside his vest as he came. Elisa stiffened and her face grew tight. Henry stopped short and looked at her. "Why—why, Elisa. You look so nice!"

"Nice? You think I look nice? What do you mean by 'nice'?"

Henry blundered on. "I don't know. I mean you look different, strong and happy."

"I am strong? Yes, strong. What do you mean 'strong'?"

He looked bewildered. "You're playing some kind of a game," he said helplessly. "It's a kind of a play. You look strong enough to break a calf over your knee, happy enough to eat it like a watermelon."

For a second she lost her rigidity. "Henry! Don't talk like that. You didn't know what you said." She grew complete again. "I'm strong," she boasted. "I never knew before how strong."

Henry looked down toward the tractor shed, and when he brought his eyes back to her, they were his own again. "I'll get out the car. You can put on your coat while I'm starting."

Elisa went into the house. She heard him drive to the gate and idle down his motor, and then she took a long time to put on her hat. She pulled it here and pressed it there. When Henry turned the motor off she slipped into her coat and went out.

The little roadster bounced along on the dirt road by the river, raising the birds and driving the rabbits into the brush. Two cranes flapped heavily over the willow-line and dropped into the riverbed.

Far ahead on the road Elisa saw a dark speck. She knew.

She tried not to look as they passed it, but her eyes would not obey. She whispered to herself sadly, "He might have thrown them off the road. That wouldn't have been much trouble, not very much. But he kept the pot," she explained. "He had to keep the pot. That's why he couldn't get them off the road."

The roadster turned a bend and she saw the caravan ahead. She swung full around toward her husband so she could not see the little covered wagon and the mismatched team as the car passed them.

In a moment it was over. The thing was done. She did not look back.

She said loudly, to be heard above the motor, "It will be good, tonight, a good dinner."

"Now you're changed again," Henry complained. He took one hand from the wheel and patted her knee. "I ought to take you in to dinner oftener. It would be good for both of us. We get so heavy out on the ranch."

"Henry," she asked, "could we have wine at dinner?"

"Sure we could. Say! That will be fine."

She was silent for a while; then she said, "Henry, at those prize fights, do the men hurt each other very much?"

"Sometimes a little, not often. Why?"

"Well, I've read how they break noses, and blood runs down their chests. I've read how the fighting gloves get heavy and soggy with blood."

He looked around at her. "What's the matter, Elisa? I didn't know you read things like that." He brought the car to a stop, then turned to the right over the Salinas River bridge.

"Do any women ever go to the fights?" she asked.

"Oh, sure, some. What's the matter, Elisa? Do you want to go? I don't think you'd like it, but I'll take you if you really want to go."

She relaxed limply in the seat. "Oh, no. No. I don't want to go. I'm sure I don't." Her face was turned away from him. "It will be enough if we can have wine. It will be plenty." She turned up her coat collar so he could not see that she was crying weakly—like an old woman.

1938

A Good Man Is Hard to Find

Flannery O'Connor (1925–1964)

Flannery O'Connor grew up in Baptist central Georgia as a Roman Catholic. Her sense of being an outsider, both as a Catholic rather than a Protestant, and as a Christian rather than a secularist, pervaded her fiction. In her black comic stories her usual tactic was to invite the reader to laugh at her simple country folk and to identify with a cynical or even nihilistic intellectual character—a writer or someone who had been to college. Then O'Connor would turn the tables and show the hollowness and self-delusion of the secular intellectual's stance. The grotesqueness of her characters and the violence that often befalls them are distinguishing elements of her fiction. But underlying these effects is O'Connor's intense, unwavering preoccupation with the Christian idea of salvation through grace.

The grandmother didn't want to go to Florida. She wanted to visit some of her connections in east Tennessee and she was seizing at every chance to change Bailey's mind. Bailey was the son she lived with, her only boy. He was sitting on the edge of his chair at the table, bent over the orange sports section of the *Journal*. "Now look here, Bailey," she said, "see here, read this," and she stood with one hand on her thin hip and the other rattling the newspaper at his bald head. "Here this fellow that calls himself The Misfit is aloose from the Federal Pen and headed toward Florida and you read here what it says he did to these people. Just you read it. I wouldn't take my children in any direction with a criminal like that aloose in it. I couldn't answer to my conscience if I did."

Bailey didn't look up from his reading so she wheeled around then and faced the children's mother, a young woman in slacks, whose face was as broad and innocent as a cabbage and was tied round with a green head-kerchief that had two points on the top like rabbit's ears. She was sitting on the sofa, feeding the baby his apricots out of a jar. "The children have been to Florida before," the old lady said. "You all ought to take them somewhere else for a change so they would see different parts of the world and be broad. They never have been to east Tennessee."

The children's mother didn't seem to hear her but the eight-year-old boy, John Wesley, a stocky child with glasses, said, "If you don't want to go to Florida, why dontcha stay at home?" He and the little girl, June Star, were reading the funny papers on the floor.

"She wouldn't stay at home to be queen for a day," June Star said without raising her yellow head.

"Yes and what would you do if this fellow, The Misfit, caught you?" the grandmother asked.

"I'd smack his face," John Wesley said.

"She wouldn't stay at home for a million bucks," June Star said. "Afraid she'd miss something. She has to go everywhere we go."

"All right, Miss," the grandmother said. "Just remember that the next time you want me to curl your hair."

June Star said her hair was naturally curly.

The next morning the grandmother was the first one in the car, ready to go. She had her big black valise that looked like the head of a hippopotamus in one corner, and underneath it she was hiding a basket with Pitty Sing, the cat, in it. She didn't intend for the cat to be left alone in the house for three days because he would miss her too much and she was afraid he might brush against one of the gas burners and accidentally asphyxiate himself. Her son, Bailey, didn't like to arrive at a motel with a cat.

She sat in the middle of the back seat with John Wesley and June Star on either side of her. Bailey and the children's mother and the baby sat in the front and they left Atlanta at eight forty-five with the mileage on the car at 55890. The grandmother wrote this down because she thought it would be interesting to say how many miles they had been when they got back. It took them twenty minutes to reach the outskirts of the city.

The old lady settled herself comfortably, removing her white cotton gloves and putting them up with her purse on the shelf in front of the back window. The children's mother still had on slacks and still had her head tied up in a green kerchief, but the grandmother had on a navy blue straw sailor hat with a bunch of white violets on the brim and a navy blue dress with a small white dot in the print. Her collar and cuffs were white organdy trimmed with lace and at her neckline she had pinned a purple spray of cloth violets containing a sachet. In case of an accident, anyone seeing her dead on the highway would know at once that she was a lady.

She said she thought it was going to be a good day for driving, neither too hot nor too cold, and she cautioned Bailey that the speed limit was fifty-five miles an hour and that the patrolmen hid themselves behind billboards and small clumps of trees and sped out after you before you had a chance to slow down. She pointed out interesting details of the scenery: Stone Mountain; the blue granite that in some places came up to both sides of the highway; the brilliant red clay banks slightly streaked with purple; and the various crops that made rows of green lace-work on the ground. The trees were full of silver-white sunlight and the meanest of them sparkled. The children were reading comic magazines and their mother had gone back to sleep.

"Let's go through Georgia fast so we won't have to look at it much," John Wesley said.

"If I were a little boy," said the grandmother, "I wouldn't talk about my native state that way. Tennessee has the mountains and Georgia has the hills."

"Tennessee is just a hillbilly dumping ground," John Wesley said, "and Georgia is a lousy state too."

"You said it," June Star said.

"In my time," said the grandmother, folding her thin veined fingers, "children were more respectful of their native states and their parents and everything else. People did right then. Oh look at the cute little pickaninny!" she said and pointed to a Negro child standing in the door of a shack. "Wouldn't that make a picture, now?" she asked and they all turned and looked at the little Negro out of the back window. He waved.

"He didn't have any britches on," June said.

"He probably didn't have any," the grandmother explained. "Little niggers in the country don't have things like we do. If I could paint, I'd paint that picture," she said.

The children exchanged comic books.

The grandmother offered to hold the baby and the children's mother passed him over the front seat to her. She set him on her knee and bounced him and told him about the things they were passing. She rolled her eyes and screwed up her mouth and stuck her leathery thin face into his smooth bland one. Occasionally he gave her a faraway smile. They passed a large cotton field with five or six graves fenced in the middle of it, like a small island. "Look at the graveyard!" the grandmother said, pointing it out. "That was the old family burying ground. That belonged to the plantation."

"Where's the plantation?" John Wesley asked.

"Gone With the Wind," said the grandmother. "Ha. Ha."

When the children finished all the comic books they had brought, they opened the lunch and ate it. The grandmother ate a peanut butter sandwich and an olive and would not let the children throw the box and the paper napkins out the window. When there was nothing else to do they played a game by choosing a cloud and making the other two guess what shape it suggested. John Wesley took one the shape of a cow and June Star guessed a cow and John Wesley said, no, an automobile, and June Star said he didn't play fair, and they began to slap each other over the grandmother.

The grandmother said she would tell them a story if they would keep quiet. When she told a story, she rolled her eyes and waved her head and was very dramatic. She said once when she was a maiden lady she had been courted by a Mr. Edgar Atkins Teagarden from Jasper, Georgia. She said he was a very good-looking man and a gentleman and that he brought her a watermelon every Saturday afternoon with his initials cut in it, E. A. T. Well, one Saturday, she said, Mr. Teagarden brought the watermelon and there was nobody at home and he left it on the front porch and returned in his buggy to Jasper, but she never got the watermelon, she said, because a nigger boy ate it when he saw the initials, E. A. T.! This story tickled John Wesley's funny bone and he giggled and giggled but June Star didn't think it was any good. She said she wouldn't marry a man that just brought her a watermelon on Saturday. The grandmother said she would have done well to marry Mr. Teagarden because he was a gentleman and had bought Coca-Cola stock when it first came out and that he had died only a few years ago, a very wealthy man.

They stopped at The Tower for barbecued sandwiches. The Tower was a part stucco and part wood filling station and dance hall set in a clearing outside of Timothy. A fat man named Red Sammy Butts ran it and there were signs stuck here and there on the building and for miles up and down the highway saying, TRY RED SAMMY'S FAMOUS BARBECUE. NONE LIKE FAMOUS RED SAMMY'S! RED SAM! THE FAT BOY WITH THE HAPPY LAUGH. A VETERAN! SAMMY'S YOUR MAN!

Red Sammy was lying on the bare ground outside The Tower with his head under a truck while a gray monkey about a foot high, chained to a small china-berry tree, chattered nearby. The monkey sprang back into the tree and got on the highest limb as soon as he saw the children jump out of the car and run toward him.

Inside, The Tower was a long dark room with a counter at one end and tables at the other and dancing space in the middle. They all sat down at a broad table next to the nickelodeon and Red Sam's wife, a tall burnt-brown woman with hair and eyes lighter than her skin, came and took their order. The children's mother put a dime in the machine and played "The Tennessee Waltz," and the grandmother said that tune always made her want to dance. She asked Bailey if he would like to dance but he only glared at her. He didn't have a naturally sunny disposition like she did and trips made him nervous. The grandmother's brown eyes were very bright. She swayed her head from side to side and pretended she was dancing in her chair. June Star said play something she could tap to so the children's mother put in another dime and played a fast number and June Star stepped out onto the dance floor and did her tap routine.

"Ain't she cute?" Red Sam's wife said, leaning over the counter. "Would you like to come be my little girl?"

"No I certainly wouldn't," June Star said. "I wouldn't live in a broken-down place like this for a million bucks!" and she ran back to the table.

"Ain't she cute?" the woman repeated, stretching her mouth politely.

"Aren't you ashamed?" hissed the grandmother.

Red Sam came in and told his wife to quit lounging on the counter and hurry with these people's order. His khaki trousers reached just to his hip bones and his stomach hung over them like a sack of meal swaying under his shirt. He came over and sat down at a table nearby and let out a combination sigh and yodel. "You can't win," he said. "You can't win," and he wiped his sweating red face off with a gray handkerchief. "These days you don't know who to trust," he said. "Ain't that the truth?"

"People are certainly not nice like they used to be," said the grandmother.

"Two fellers come in here last week," Red Sammy said, "driving a Chrysler. It was a old beat-up car but it was a good one and these boys looked all right to me. Said they worked at the mill and you know I let them fellers charge the gas they bought? Now why did I do that?"

"Because you're a good man!" the grandmother said at once.

"Yes'm, I suppose so," Red Sam said as if he were struck with the answer.

His wife brought the orders, carrying the five plates all at once without a tray, two in each hand and one balanced on her arm. "It isn't a soul in this green world of God's that you can trust," she said. "And I don't count anybody out of that, not nobody," she repeated, looking at Red Sammy.

"Did you read about that criminal, The Misfit, that's escaped?" asked the grandmother.

"I wouldn't be a bit surprised if he didn't attact this place right here," said the woman. "If he hears about it being here, I wouldn't be none surprised to see him. If he hears it's two cent in the cash register, I wouldn't be a tall surprised if he . . ."

"That'll do," Red Sam said. "Go bring these people their Co'Colas," and the woman went off to get the rest of the order.

"A good man is hard to find," Red Sammy said. "Everything is getting terrible. I remember the day you could go off and leave your screen door unlatched. Not no more."

He and the grandmother discussed better times. The old lady said that in her opinion Europe was entirely to blame for the way things were now. She said the way Europe acted you would think we were made of money and Red Sam said it was no use talking about it, she was exactly right. The children ran outside into the white sunlight and looked at the monkey in the lacy chinaberry tree. He was busy catching fleas on himself and biting each one carefully between his teeth as if it were a delicacy.

They drove off again into the hot afternoon. The grandmother took cat naps and woke up every few minutes with her own snoring. Outside of Toombsboro she woke up and recalled an old plantation that she had visited in this neighborhood once when she was a young lady. She said the house had six white columns across the front and that there was an avenue of oaks leading up to it and two little wooden trellis arbors on either side in front where you sat down with your suitor after a stroll in the garden. She recalled exactly which road to turn off to get to it. She knew that Bailey would not be willing to lose any time looking at an old house, but the more she talked about it, the more she wanted to see it once again and find out if the little twin arbors were still standing. "There was a secret panel in this house," she said craftily, not telling the truth but wishing that she were, "and the story went that all the family silver was hidden in it when Sherman came through but it was never found . . ."

"Hey!" John Wesley said. "Let's go see it! We'll find it! We'll poke all the woodwork and find it! Who lives there? Where do you turn off at? Hey Pop, can't we turn off there?"

"We never have seen a house with a secret panel!" June Star shrieked. "Let's go to the house with the secret panel! Hey, Pop, can't we go see the house with the secret panel!"

"It's not far from here, I know," the grandmother said. "It wouldn't take over twenty minutes."

Bailey was looking straight ahead. His jaw was as rigid as a horseshoe. "No," he said.

The children began to yell and scream that they wanted to see the house with the secret panel. John Wesley kicked the back of the front seat and June Star hung over her mother's shoulder and whined desperately into her ear that they never had any fun even on their vacation, and that they could never do what THEY wanted to do. The baby began to scream and John Wesley kicked the back of the seat so hard that his father could feel the blows in his kidney.

"All right!" he shouted, and drew the car to a stop at the side of the road. "Will you all shut up? Will you all just shut up for one second? If you don't shut up, we won't go anywhere."

"It would be very educational for them," the grandmother murmured.

"All right," Bailey said, "but get this: this is the only time we're going to stop for anything like this. This is the one and only time."

"The dirt road that you have to turn down is about a mile back," the grandmother directed. "I marked it when we passed."

"A dirt road," Bailey groaned.

After they had turned around and were headed toward the dirt road, the grandmother recalled other points about the house, the beautiful glass over the front doorway and the candle-lamp in the hall. John Wesley said that the secret panel was probably in the fireplace.

"You can't go inside this house," Bailey said. "You don't know who lives there."

"While you all talk to the people in front, I'll run around behind and get in a window," John Wesley suggested.

"We'll all stay in the car," his mother said.

They turned onto the dirt road and the car raced roughly along in a swirl of pink dust. The grandmother recalled the times when there were no paved roads and thirty miles was a day's journey. The dirt road was hilly and there were sudden washes in it and sharp curves on dangerous embankments. All at once they would be on a hill, looking down over the blue tops of trees for miles around, then the next minute, they would be in a red depression with the dust-coated trees looking down on them.

"This place had better turn up in a minute," Bailey said, "or I'm going to turn around."

The road looked as if no one had traveled on it in months.

"It's not much farther," the grandmother said and just as she said it, a horrible thought came to her. The thought was so embarrassing that she turned red in the face and her eyes dilated and her feet jumped up, upsetting her valise in the corner. The instant the valise moved, the newspaper top she had over the basket under it rose with a snarl and Pitty Sing, the cat, sprang onto Bailey's shoulder.

The children were thrown to the floor and their mother, clutching the baby, was thrown out the door onto the ground, the old lady was thrown into the front seat. The car turned over once and landed right-side-up in a gulch on the side of the road. Bailey remained in the driver's seat with the cat—gray-striped with a broad white face and an orange nose—clinging to his neck like a caterpillar.

As soon as the children saw they could move their arms and legs, they scrambled out of the car, shouting, "We've had an ACCIDENT!" The grandmother was curled up under the dashboard, hoping she was injured so that Bailey's wrath would not come down on her all at once. The horrible thought she had had before the accident was that the house she had remembered so vividly was not in Georgia but in Tennessee.

Bailey removed the cat from his neck with both hands and flung it out the window against the side of a pine tree. Then he got out of the car and started looking for the children's mother. She was sitting against the side of the red gutted ditch, holding the screaming baby, but she only had a cut down her face and a broken shoulder. "We've had an ACCIDENT!" the children screamed in a frenzy of delight.

"But nobody's killed," June Star said with disappointment as the grandmother limped out of the car, her hat still pinned to her head but the broken front brim standing up at a jaunty angle and the violet spray hanging off the side. They all sat down in the ditch, except the children, to recover from the shock. They were all shaking.

"Maybe a car will come along," said the children's mother hoarsely.

"I believe I have injured an organ," said the grandmother, pressing her side, but no one answered her. Bailey's teeth were clattering. He had on a yellow sport shirt with bright blue parrots designed in it and his face was as yellow as the shirt. The grandmother decided that she would not mention that the house was in Tennessee.

The road was about ten feet above and they could see only the tops of the trees on the other side of it. Behind the ditch they were sitting in there were more woods, tall and dark and deep. In a few minutes they saw a car some distance away on top of a hill, coming slowly as if the occupants were watching them. The grandmother stood up and waved both arms dramatically to attract their attention. The car continued to come on slowly, disappeared around a bend and appeared again, moving even slower, on top of the hill they had gone over. It was a big black battered hearse-like automobile. There were three men in it.

It came to a stop just over them and for some minutes, the driver looked down with a steady expressionless gaze to where they were sitting, and didn't speak. Then he turned his head and muttered something to the other two and they got out. One was a fat boy in black trousers and a red sweat shirt with a silver stallion embossed on the front of it. He moved around on the right side of them and stood staring, his mouth partly open in a kind of loose grin. The other had on khaki pants and a blue striped coat and a gray hat pulled down very low, hiding most of his face. He came around slowly on the left side. Neither spoke.

The driver got out of the car and stood by the side of it, looking down at them. He was an older man than the other two. His hair was just beginning to gray and he wore silver-rimmed spectacles that gave him a scholarly look. He had a long creased face and didn't have on any shirt or undershirt. He had on blue jeans that were too tight for him and was holding a black hat and a gun. The two boys also had guns.

"We've had an ACCIDENT!" the children screamed.

The grandmother had the peculiar feeling that the bespectacled man was someone she knew. His face was as familiar to her as if she had known him all her life but she could not recall who he was. He moved away from the car and began to come down the embankment, placing his feet carefully so that he wouldn't slip. He had on tan and white shoes and no socks, and his ankles were red and thin. "Good afternoon," he said. "I see you all had you a little spill."

"We turned over twice!" said the grandmother.

"Oncet," he corrected. "We seen it happen. Try their car and see will it run, Hiram," he said quietly to the boy with the gray hat.

"What you got that gun for?" John Wesley asked. "Whatcha gonna do with that gun?"

"Lady," the man said to the children's mother, "would you mind calling them children to sit down by you? Children make me nervous. I want all you all to sit down right together there where you're at."

"What are you telling us what to do for?" June Star asked.

Behind them the line of woods gaped like a dark open mouth. "Come here," said their mother.

"Look here now," Bailey began suddenly, "we're in a predicament! We're in . . ."

The grandmother shrieked. She scrambled to her feet and stood staring. "You're The Misfit!" she said. "I recognized you at once."

"Yes'm," the man said, smiling slightly as if he were pleased in spite of himself to be known, "but it would have been better for all of you, lady, if you hadn't of reckernized me."

Bailey turned his head sharply and said something to his mother that shocked even the children. The old lady began to cry and The Misfit reddened.

"Lady," he said, "don't you get upset. Sometimes a man says things he don't mean. I don't reckon he meant to talk to you thataway."

"You wouldn't shoot a lady, would you?" the grandmother said and removed a clean handkerchief from her cuff and began to slap at her eyes with it.

The Misfit pointed the toe of his shoe into the ground and made a little hole and then covered it up again. "I would hate to have to," he said.

"Listen," the grandmother almost screamed, "I know you're a good man. You don't look a bit like you have common blood. I know you must come from nice people!"

"Yes mam," he said, "finest people in the world." When he smiled he showed a row of strong white teeth. "God never made a finer woman than my mother and my daddy's heart was pure gold," he said. The boy with the red sweat shirt had come around behind them and was standing with his gun at his hip. The

Misfit squatted down on the ground. "Watch them children, Bobby Lee," he said. "You know they make me nervous." He looked at the six of them huddled together in front of him and he seemed to be embarrassed as if he couldn't think of anything to say. "Ain't a cloud in the sky," he remarked, looking up at it. "Don't see no sun but don't see no cloud neither."

"Yes, it's a beautiful day," said the grandmother. "Listen," she said, "you shouldn't call yourself The Misfit because I know you're a good man at heart. I can just look at you and tell."

"Hush!" Bailey yelled. "Hush! Everybody shut up and let me handle this." He was squatting in the position of a runner about to sprint forward but he didn't move.

"I pre-chate that, lady," The Misfit said and drew a little circle in the ground with the butt of his gun.

"It'll take a half a hour to fix this here car," Hiram called, looking over the raised hood of it.

"Well, first you and Bobby Lee get him and that little boy to step over yonder with you," The Misfit said, pointing to Bailey and John Wesley. "The boys want to ask you something," he said to Bailey. "Would you mind stepping back in them woods there with them?"

"Listen," Bailey began, "we're in a terrible predicament. Nobody realizes what this is," and his voice cracked. His eyes were as blue and intense as the parrots in his shirt and he remained perfectly still.

The grandmother reached up to adjust her hat brim as if she were going to the woods with him but it came off in her hand. She stood staring at it and after a second she let it fall on the ground. Hiram pulled Bailey up by the arm as if he were assisting an old man. John Wesley caught hold of his father's hand and Bobby Lee followed. They went off toward the woods and just as they reached the dark edge, Bailey turned and supporting himself against a gray naked pine trunk, he shouted, "I'll be back in a minute, Mamma, wait on me!"

"Come back this instant!" his mother shrilled but they all disappeared into the woods.

"Bailey Boy!" the grandmother called in a tragic voice but she found she was looking at The Misfit squatting on the ground in front of her. "I just know you're a good man," she said desperately. "You're not a bit common!"

"Nome, I ain't a good man," The Misfit said after a second as if he had considered her statement carefully, "but I ain't the worst in the world neither. My daddy said I was different breed of dog from my brothers and sisters. 'You know,' Daddy said, 'it's some that can live their whole life out without asking about it and it's others has to know why it is, and this boy is one of the latters. He's going to be into everything!'" He put on his black hat and looked up suddenly and then away deep into the woods as if he were embarrassed again. "I'm sorry I don't have on a shirt before you ladies," he said, hunching his shoulders slightly. "We buried our clothes that we had on when we escaped and we're just making do until we can get better. We borrowed these from some folks we met," he explained.

"That's perfectly all right," the grandmother said. "Maybe Bailey has an extra shirt in his suitcase."

"I'll look and see terrectly," The Misfit said.

"Where are they taking him?" the children's mother screamed.

"Daddy was a card himself," The Misfit said. "You couldn't put anything over on him. He never got in trouble with the Authorities though. Just had the knack of handling them."

"You could be honest too if you'd only try," said the grandmother. "Think how wonderful it would be to settle down and live a comfortable life and not have to think about somebody chasing you all the time."

The Misfit kept scratching in the ground with the butt of his gun as if he were thinking about it. "Yes'm, somebody is always after you," he murmured.

The grandmother noticed how thin his shoulder blades were just behind his hat because she was standing up looking down on him. "Do you ever pray?" she asked.

He shook his head. All she saw was the black hat wiggle between his shoulder blades. "Nome," he said.

There was a pistol shot from the woods, followed closely by another. Then silence. The old lady's head jerked around. She could hear the wind move through the tree tops like a long satisfied insuck of breath. "Bailey Boy!" she called.

"I was a gospel singer for a while," The Misfit said. "I been most everything. Been in the arm service, both land and sea, at home and abroad, been twict married, been an undertaker, been with the railroads, plowed Mother Earth, been in a tornado, seen a man burnt alive oncet," and he looked up at the children's mother and the little girl who were sitting close together, their faces white and their eyes glassy; "I even seen a woman flogged," he said.

"Pray, pray," the grandmother began, "pray, pray . . ."

"I never was a bad boy that I remember of," The Misfit said in an almost dreamy voice, "but somewheres along the line I done something wrong and got sent to the penitentiary. I was buried alive," and he looked up and held her attention to him by a steady stare.

"That's when you should have started to pray," she said. "What did you do to get sent to the penitentiary that first time?"

"Turn to the right, it was a wall," The Misfit said, looking up again at the cloudless sky. "Turn to the left, it was a wall. Look up it was a ceiling, look down it was a floor. I forgot what I done, lady. I set there and set there, trying to remember what it was I done and I ain't recalled it to this day. Oncet in a while, I would think it was coming to me, but it never come."

"Maybe they put you in by mistake," the old lady said vaguely.

"Nome," he said. "It wasn't no mistake. They had the papers on me."

"You must have stolen something," she said.

The Misfit sneered slightly. "Nobody had nothing I wanted," he said. "It was a head-doctor at the penitentiary said what I had done was kill my daddy but I know that for a lie. My daddy died in nineteen ought nineteen of the epidemic flu and I never had a thing to do with it. He was buried in the Mount Hopewell Baptist churchyard and you can go there and see for yourself."

"If you would pray," the old lady said, "Jesus would help you."

"That's right," The Misfit said.

"Well then, why don't you pray?" she asked trembling with delight suddenly.

"I don't want no hep," he said. "I'm doing all right by myself."

Bobby Lee and Hiram came ambling back from the woods. Bobby Lee was dragging a yellow shirt with bright blue parrots in it.

"Throw me that shirt, Bobby Lee," The Misfit said. The shirt came flying at him and landed on his shoulder and he put it on. The grandmother couldn't name what the shirt reminded her of. "No, lady," The Misfit said while he was buttoning it up. "I found out the crime don't matter. You can do one thing or you can do another, kill a man or take a tire off his car, because sooner or later you're going to forget what it was you done and just be punished for it."

The children's mother had begun to make heaving noises as if she couldn't get her breath. "Lady," he asked, "would you and that little girl like to step off yonder with Bobby Lee and Hiram and join your husband?"

"Yes, thank you," the mother said faintly. Her left arm dangled helplessly and she was holding the baby, who had gone to sleep, in the other. "Hep that lady up, Hiram," The Misfit said as she struggled to climb out of the ditch, "and Bobby Lee, you hold onto that little girl's hand."

"I don't want to hold hands with him," June Star said. "He reminds me of a pig."

The fat boy blushed and laughed and caught her by the arm and pulled her off into the woods after Hiram and her mother.

Alone with The Misfit, the grandmother found that she had lost her voice. There was not a cloud in the sky nor any sun. There was nothing around her but woods. She wanted to tell him that he must pray. She opened and closed her mouth several times before anything came out. Finally she found herself saying, "Jesus, Jesus," meaning Jesus will help you, but the way she was saying it, it sounded as if she might be cursing.

"Yes'm," The Misfit said as if he agreed. "Jesus thown everything off balance. It was the same case with Him as with me except He hadn't committed any crime and they could prove I had committed one because they had the papers on me. Of course," he said, "they never shown me any papers. That's why I sign myself now. I said long ago, you get you a signature and sign everything you do and keep a copy of it. Then you'll know what you done and you can hold up the crime to the punishment and see do they match and in the end you'll have something to prove you ain't been treated right. I call myself The Misfit," he said, "because I can't make what all I done wrong fit what all I gone through in punishment."

There was a piercing scream from the woods, followed closely by a pistol report. "Does it seem right to you, lady, that one is punished a heap and another ain't punished at all?"

"Jesus!" the old lady cried. "You've got good blood! I know you wouldn't shoot a lady! I know you come from nice people! Pray! Jesus, you ought not to shoot a lady. I'll give you all the money I've got!"

"Lady," The Misfit said, looking beyond her far into the woods, "there never was a body that give the undertaker a tip."

There were two more pistol reports and the grandmother raised her head like a parched old turkey hen crying for water and called, "Bailey Boy, Bailey Boy!" as if her heart would break.

"Jesus was the only One that ever raised the dead," The Misfit continued, "and He shouldn't have done it. He thown everything off balance. If He did what He said, then it's nothing for you to do but thow away everything and follow Him, and if He didn't, then it's nothing for you to do but enjoy the few minutes you got left the best way you can—by killing somebody or burning down his house or doing some other meanness to him. No pleasure but meanness," he said and his voice had become almost a snarl.

"Maybe He didn't raise the dead," the old lady mumbled, not knowing what she was saying and feeling so dizzy that she sank down in the ditch with her legs twisted under her.

"I wasn't there so I can't say He didn't," The Misfit said. "I wisht I had of been there," he said, hitting the ground with his fist. "It ain't right I wasn't there because if I had of been there I would of known. Listen lady," he said in a high voice, "if I had of been there I would of known and I wouldn't be like I am now." His voice seemed about to crack and the grandmother's head cleared for an instant. She saw the man's face twisted close to her own as if he were going to cry and she murmured, "Why you're one of my babies. You're one of my own children!" She reached out and touched him on the shoulder. The Misfit sprang back as if a snake had bitten him and shot her three times through the chest. Then he put his gun down on the ground and took off his glasses and began to clean them.

Hiram and Bobby Lee returned from the woods and stood over the ditch, looking down at the grandmother who half sat and half lay in a puddle of blood with her legs crossed under her like a child's and her face smiling up at the cloudless sky.

Without his glasses, The Misfit's eyes were red-rimmed and pale and defenseless-looking. "Take her off and thow her where you thown the others," he said, picking up the cat that was rubbing itself against his leg.

"She was a talker, wasn't she?" Bobby Lee said, sliding down the ditch with a yodel.

"She would of been a good woman," The Misfit said, "if it had been somebody there to shoot her every minute of her life."

"Some fun!" Bobby Lee said.

"Shut up, Bobby Lee," The Misfit said. "It's no real pleasure in life."

1953

I Stand Here Ironing

Tillie Olsen (1913–   )

See page 159 for a biographical note on the author.

I stand here ironing, and what you asked me moves tormented back and forth with the iron.

"I wish you would manage the time to come in and talk with me about your daughter. I'm sure you can help me understand her. She's a youngster who needs help and whom I'm deeply interested in helping."

"Who needs help." . . . Even if I came, what good would it do? You think because I am her mother I have a key, or that in some way you could use me as a key? She has lived for nineteen years. There is all that life that has happened outside of me, beyond me.

And when is there time to remember, to sift, to weigh, to estimate, to total? I will start and there will be an interruption and I will have to gather it all together again. Or I will become engulfed with all I did or did not do, with what should have been and what cannot be helped.

She was a beautiful baby. The first and only one of our five that was beautiful at birth. You do not guess how new and uneasy her tenancy in her now-loveliness. You did not know her all those years she was thought homely, or see her poring over her baby pictures, making me tell her over and over how beautiful she had been—and would be, I would tell her—and was now, to the seeing eye. But the seeing eyes were few or nonexistent. Including mine.

I nursed her. They feel that's important nowadays. I nursed all the children, but with her, with all the fierce rigidity of first motherhood, I did like the books then said. Though her cries battered me to trembling and my breasts ached with swollenness, I waited till the clock decreed.

Why do I put that first? I do not even know if it matters, or if it explains anything.

She was a beautiful baby. She blew shining bubbles of sound. She loved motion, loved light, loved color and music and textures. She would lie on the floor in her blue overalls patting the surface so hard in ecstasy her hands and feet would blur. She was a miracle to me, but when she was eight months old I had to leave her daytimes with the woman downstairs to whom she was no miracle at all, for I worked or looked for work and for Emily's father, who "could no longer endure" (he wrote in his good-bye note) "sharing want with us."

I was nineteen. It was the pre-relief, pre-WPA[1] world of the depression. I would start running as soon as I got off the streetcar, running up the stairs, the place smelling sour, and awake or asleep to startle awake, when she saw me she would break into a clogged weeping that could not be comforted, a weeping I can hear yet.

After a while I found a job hashing at night so I could be with her days, and it was better. But it came to where I had to bring her to his family and leave her.

It took a long time to raise the money for her fare back. Then she got chicken pox and I had to wait longer. When she finally came, I hardly knew her, walking quick and nervous like her father, looking like her father, thin, and dressed in a shoddy red that yellowed her skin and glared at the pockmarks. All the baby loveliness gone.

She was two. Old enough for nursery school they said, and I did not know then what I know now—the fatigue of the long day, and the lacerations of group life in the kinds of nurseries that are only parking places for children.

Except that it would have made no difference if I had known. It was the only place there was. It was the only way we could be together, the only way I could hold a job.

And even without knowing, I knew. I knew the teacher that was evil because all these years it has curdled into my memory, the little boy hunched in the corner, her rasp, "why aren't you outside, because Alvin hits you? that's no reason, go out, scaredy." I knew Emily hated it even if she did not clutch and implore "don't go Mommy" like the other children, mornings.

She always had a reason why we should stay home. Momma, you look sick. Momma, I feel sick. Momma, the teachers aren't here today, they're sick. Momma, we can't go, there was a fire there last night. Momma, it's a holiday today, no school, they told me.

But never a direct protest, never rebellion. I think of our others in their three-, four-year-oldness—the explosions, tempers, the denunciations, the demands—and I feel suddenly ill. I put the iron down. What in me demanded that goodness in her? And what was the cost, the cost to her of such goodness?

The old man living in the back once said in his gentle way: "You should smile at Emily more when you look at her." What *was* in my face when I looked at her? I loved her. There were all the acts of love.

It was only with the others I remembered what he said, and it was the face of joy, and not of care or tightness or worry I turned to them—too late for Emily. She does not smile easily, let alone almost always as her brothers and sisters do. Her face is closed and sombre, but when she wants, how fluid. You must have

---

[1]Works Progress Administration. This government program provided work to many unemployed people during the Depression.

seen it in her pantomimes, you spoke of her rare gift for comedy on the stage that rouses laughter out of the audience so dear they applaud and applaud and do not want to let her go.

Where does it come from, that comedy? There was none of it in her when she came back to me that second time, after I had to send her away again. She had a new daddy now to learn to love, and I think perhaps it was a better time.

Except when we left her alone nights, telling ourselves she was old enough.

"Can't you go some other time, Mommy, like tomorrow?" she would ask. "Will it be just a little while you'll be gone? Do you promise?"

The time we came back, the front door open, the clock on the floor in the hall. She rigid awake. "It wasn't just a little while. I didn't cry. Three times I called you, just three times, and then I ran downstairs to open the door so you could come faster. The clock talked loud. I threw it away, it scared me what it talked."

She said the clock talked loud again that night I went to the hospital to have Susan. She was delirious with the fever that comes before red measles, but she was fully conscious all the week I was gone and the week after we were home when she could not come near the new baby or me.

She did not get well. She stayed skeleton thin, not wanting to eat, and night after night she had nightmares. She would call for me, and I would rouse from exhaustion to sleepily call back: "You're all right, darling, go to sleep, it's just a dream," and if she still called, in a sterner voice, "now to go sleep, Emily, there's nothing to hurt you." Twice, only twice, when I had to get up for Susan anyhow, I went in to sit with her.

Now when it is too late (as if she would let me hold and comfort her like I do the others) I get up and go to her at once at her moan or restless stirring. "Are you awake, Emily? Can I get you something?" And the answer is always the same: "No, I'm all right, go back to sleep, Mother."

They persuaded me at the clinic to send her away to a convalescent home in the country where "she can have the kind of food and care you can't manage for her, and you'll be free to concentrate on the new baby." They still send children to that place. I see pictures on the society page of sleek young women planning affairs to raise money for it, or dancing at the affairs, or decorating Easter eggs or filling Christmas stockings for the children.

They never have a picture of the children so I do not know if the girls still wear those gigantic red bows and the ravaged looks on the every other Sunday when parents can come to visit "unless otherwise notified"—as we were notified the first six weeks.

Oh it is a handsome place, green lawns and tall trees and fluted flower beds. High up on the balconies of each cottage the children stand, the girls in their red bows and white dresses, the boys in white suits and giant red ties. The parents stand below shrieking up to be heard and the children shriek down to be heard, and between them the invisible wall "Not To Be Contaminated by Parental Germs or Physical Affection."

There was a tiny girl who always stood hand in hand with Emily. Her parents never came. One visit she was gone. "They moved her to Rose Cottage" Emily shouted in explanation. "They don't like you to love anybody here."

She wrote once a week, the labored writing of a seven-year-old. "I am fine. How is the baby. If I write my letter nicely I will have a star. Love." There never was a star. We wrote every other day, letters she could never hold or keep but only hear read—once. "We simply do not have room for children to keep any personal possessions," they patiently explained when we pieced one Sunday's shrieking together to plead how much it would mean to Emily, who loved so to keep things, to be allowed to keep her letters and cards.

Each visit she looked frailer. "She isn't eating," they told us.

(They had runny eggs for breakfast or mush with lumps, Emily said later, I'd hold it in my mouth and not swallow. Nothing ever tasted good, just when they had chicken.)

It took us eight months to get her released home, and only the fact that she gained back so little of her seven lost pounds convinced the social worker.

I used to try to hold and love her after she came back, but her body would stay stiff, and after a while she'd push away. She ate little. Food sickened her, and I think much of life too. Oh she had physical lightness and brightness, twinkling by on skates, bouncing like a ball up and down up and down over the jump rope, skimming over the hill; but these were momentary.

She fretted about her appearance, thin and dark and foreign-looking at a time when every little girl was supposed to look or thought she should look a chubby blonde replica of Shirley Temple. The doorbell sometimes rang for her, but no one seemed to come and play in the house or be a best friend. Maybe because we moved so much.

There was a boy she loved painfully through two school semesters. Months later she told me how she had taken pennies from my purse to buy him candy. "Licorice was his favorite and I brought him some every day, but he still liked Jennifer better'n me. Why, Mommy?" The kind of question for which there is no answer.

School was a worry to her. She was not glib or quick in a world where glibness and quickness were easily confused with ability to learn. To her overworked and exasperated teachers she was an overconscientious "slow learner" who kept trying to catch up and was absent entirely too often.

I let her be absent, though sometimes the illness was imaginary. How different from my now-strictness about attendance with the others. I wasn't working. We had a new baby, I was home anyhow. Sometimes, after Susan grew old enough, I would keep her home from school, too, to have them all together.

Mostly Emily had asthma, and her breathing, harsh and labored, would fill the house with a curiously tranquil sound. I would bring the two old dresser mirrors and her boxes of collections to her bed. She would select beads and single earrings, bottle tops and shells, dried flowers and pebbles, old postcards and scraps, all sorts of oddments; then she and Susan would play Kingdom, setting up landscapes and furniture, peopling them with action.

Those were the only times of peaceful companionship between her and Susan. I have edged away from it, that poisonous feeling between them, that terrible balancing of hurts and needs I had to do between the two, and did so badly, those earlier years.

Oh there are conflicts between the others too, each one human, needing, demanding, hurting, taking—but only between Emily and Susan, no, Emily toward Susan that corroding resentment. It seems so obvious on the surface, yet it is not obvious. Susan, the second child, Susan, golden- and curly-haired and chubby, quick and articulate and assured, everything in appearance and manner Emily was not; Susan, not able to resist Emily's precious things, losing or sometimes clumsily breaking them; Susan telling jokes and riddles to company for applause while Emily sat silent (to say to me later: that was *my* riddle, Mother, I told it to Susan); Susan, who for all the five years' difference in age was just a year behind Emily in developing physically.

I am glad for that slow physical development that widened the difference between her and her contemporaries, though she suffered over it. She was too vulnerable for that terrible world of youthful competition, of preening and parading, of constant measuring of yourself against every other, of envy, "If I had that copper hair," "If I had that skin. . . ." She tormented herself enough about not looking like the others, there was enough of the unsureness, the having to be conscious of words before you speak, the constant caring—what are they thinking of me? without having it all magnified by the merciless physical drives.

Ronnie is calling. He is wet and I change him. It is rare there is such a cry now. That time of motherhood is almost behind me when the ear is not one's own but must always be racked and listening for the child cry, the child call. We sit for a while and I hold him, looking out over the city spread in charcoal with its soft aisles of light. "*Shoogily*," he breathes and curls closer. I carry him back to bed, asleep. *Shoogily*. A funny word, a family word, inherited from Emily, invented by her to say: *comfort*.

In this and other ways she leaves her seal, I say aloud. And startle at my saying it. What do I mean? What did I start to gather together, to try and make coherent? I was at the terrible, growing years. War years. I do not remember them well. I was working, there were four smaller ones now, there was not time for her. She had to help be a mother, and housekeeper, and shopper. She had to set her seal. Mornings of crisis and near hysteria trying to get lunches packed, hair combed, coats and shoes found, everyone to school or Child Care on time, the baby ready for transportation. And always the paper scribbled on by a smaller one, the book looked at by Susan then mislaid, the homework not done. Running out to that huge school where she was one, she was lost, she was a drop; suffering over the unpreparedness, stammering and unsure in her classes.

There was so little time left at night after the kids were bedded down. She would struggle over books, always eating (it was in those years she developed her enormous appetite that is legendary in our family) and I would be ironing, or preparing food for the next day, or writing V-mail to Bill, or tending the baby. Sometimes, to make me laugh, or out of her despair, she would imitate happenings or types at school.

I think I said once: "Why don't you do something like this in the school amateur show?" One morning she phoned me at work, hardly understandable through the weeping: "Mother, I did it. I won, I won; they gave me first prize; they clapped and clapped and wouldn't let me go."

Now suddenly she was Somebody, and as imprisoned in her difference as she had been in anonymity.

She began to be asked to perform at other high schools, even in colleges, then at city and statewide affairs. The first one we went to, I only recognized her that first moment when thin, shy, she almost drowned herself into the curtains. Then: Was this Emily? The control, the command, the convulsing and deadly clowning, the spell, then the roaring, stamping audience, unwilling to let this rare and precious laughter out of their lives.

Afterwards: You ought to do something about her with a gift like that—but without money or knowing how, what does one do? We have left it all to her, and the gift has as often eddied inside, clogged and clotted, as been used and growing.

She is coming. She runs up the stairs two at a time with her light graceful step, and I know she is happy tonight. Whatever it was that occasioned your call did not happen today.

"Aren't you ever going to finish the ironing, Mother? Whistler painted his mother in a rocker. I'd have to paint mine standing over an ironing board." This is one of her communicative nights and she tells me everything and nothing as she fixes herself a plate of food out of the icebox.

She is so lovely. Why did you want me to come in at all? Why were you concerned? She will find her way.

She starts up the stairs to bed. "Don't get me up with the rest in the morning." "But I thought you were having midterms." "Oh, those," she comes back in, kisses me, and says quite lightly, "in a couple of years when we'll all be atom-dead they won't matter a bit."

She has said it before. She *believes* it. But because I have been dredging the past, and all that compounds a human being is so heavy and meaningful in me, I cannot endure it tonight.

I will never total it all. I will never come in to say: She was a child seldom smiled at. Her father left me before she was a year old. I had to work her first six years when there was work, or I sent her home and to his relatives. There were years she had care she hated. She was dark and thin and foreign-looking in a world where the prestige went to blondeness and curly hair and dimples, she was slow where glibness was prized. She was a child of anxious, not proud, love. We were poor and could not afford for her the soil of easy growth. I was a young mother, I was a distracted mother. There were other children pushing up, demanding. Her younger sister seemed all that she was not. There were years she did not want me to touch her. She kept too much in herself, her life was such she had to keep too much in herself. My wisdom came too late. She has much to her and probably little will come of it. She is a child of her age, of depression, of war, of fear.

Let her be. So all that is in her will not bloom—but in how many does it? There is still enough left to live by. Only help her to know—help make it so there is cause for her to know—that she is more than this dress on the ironing board, helpless before the iron.

1961

POETRY

11

READING POETRY

Poetry is the oldest of all literary forms. Certainly, a great deal of the oldest literature of which we have written records is in verse. Yet today poetry is often regarded as the most sophisticated or difficult of literary forms. What has happened to cause the change? Why should something that seems so difficult to us today have seemed so natural to our ancestors? There are two answers to these questions. The first deals with music; the second with memory.

Poetry is musical, or at least rhythmic, speech. It is also usually a harmonious speech, employing words whose sounds echo each other or blend well. It may even be set to music, to be chanted or sung rather than simply spoken.

Because of its musical nature, poetry is easily remembered. Everyone knows how much easier it is to memorize the words to a song than to memorize even a few paragraphs from a newspaper or textbook. Poetry can thus serve as an aid to memory. If you must remember something, and have no written notes to help you, you can make a song of what you need to remember, and your chances of keeping it in your head will improve.

The desire to keep records, remember events, or tell stories preceded the invention of writing. Poetry, being pleasant and memorable, is then the natural first form for histories and tales. Once the art of writing develops, however, poetry is no longer essential. But it is still pleasing and has by now a tradition of use behind it. Prose takes over for record keeping and for transmitting technical information, but poetry keeps its hold on certain important affairs. Songs are still written to celebrate victories and loves, to mourn deaths, and to worship.

The printing of books, which gave so many people access to written words, has been one factor in the promotion of prose in our society. The invention of radio and television—whose announcers universally speak in the blandest, least musical cadences possible—has been another factor. After the age of nursery rhymes, most of us live in a world where the cadences of poetry are no longer part of our everyday life. (The exception is popular music, which employs such poetic devices as the double entendres of country music, the epic [or mock epic] phrases of rock, or the gritty street rhythms and rhymes of rap.) We live in a society where so many written and spoken words bombard us that we learn to skim through them quickly for whatever information they carry. We take no time to look for the beauty of words or for rhythm—neither of which is very likely to be there, anyway.

Poetry, however, cannot be read rapidly. Newspapers can be, and, in fact, are meant to be. Fiction can be. And, again, some of it is meant for the quick, careless reader, though most good fiction improves with slow, thoughtful read-ing. Drama, in general, must be read more slowly, if we are to catch the sound of the individual speeches. But poetry must be read most slowly of all. It requires not only that we read it silently at the same pace that we would read it aloud, but also that we pause after we read it, to think about it for a few moments at least, to savor the mood the poem has created before we go on to something else.

It is no wonder, then, that poetry sometimes seems strange or difficult. Al-most every other influence in our environment is telling us, "Hurry up! Grab the central fact or idea I'm selling and run!" Poetry is saying, "Slow down! Enjoy the music; let yourself become part of the emotion. I have many suggestions to make. Take time to let them unfold for you." In today's rush of prepackaged ideas, the stubborn individualism and refusal to be hurried that poetry repre-sents are indeed unusual.

But anything that lets us think for ourselves, that offers us a chance to find our own feelings, ideas, and emotions, is worth pursuing. And poetry certainly encourages this kind of thinking and reflection. Moreover, once we agree to slow down enough to savor a poem completely, we discover that poetry is very similar to the literature we've been enjoying all along. Like fiction and drama, poetry tells us of people, of what it means to them and to us to be human. And, like the other forms of literature, it relays this information through the sound of human voices.

So closely related are poetry, fiction, and drama, in fact, that it is sometimes hard to tell which is which. Some poetic dramas seem better suited for reading than for performance. Should they be classed as poetry or as plays? Similarly, there are narratives that tell a complete story in verse. Should they be considered fiction as well as poetry? Or shall we simply ignore the classifications and enjoy each work for what we like best in it, whether that be a supposedly "poetic" qual-ity, such as rhythm, or a supposedly "fictional" or "dramatic" one, such as plot, characterization, or dramatic irony?

We must, then, read poetry with the same close attention we give to all our readings in this course. Poetry, too, demands these basic questions:

1. Who is speaking?
2. What kind of person is he or she? in what mood? thinking what thoughts? feeling what emotions?
3. Of whom or what is he or she speaking?
4. How is this person or object being described?
5. What attitudes are being projected?
6. Are we led to share the attitudes and emotions in sympathy, or to rebel against them with feelings of anger or irony?

But, because poetry is both the most structured and the most subjective of liter-ary forms, we may also ask questions about its forms and its sounds, to learn how they contribute to the poem's effect on us. In doing this, we may get some sense of which qualities we want to consider poetic.

Because poetry is a genre of great variety, it cannot easily be defined. Only by reading a variety of poems can we create our knowledge of poetry, enhance our enjoyment of it, and gain a sense of what it has to offer us.

This chapter includes several traditional ballads. **Ballads** are tales told in song. Traditional ballads (or folk ballads) are songs that have been passed from one singer to another, not by having been written down but by having been sung, heard, and resung.[1] Ballads are thus very like **folktales** in their mode of creation and in their sense of the audience. So we may expect that the voices within the ballads will be like the voices of those archetypal storytellers we first met when reading fiction. And yet ballads are sung. Their creators are singers, not speakers. How, then, will these tales sung in verse differ from tales told in prose? How will their stories be told? What will we hear that we have not heard before?

Simon Ortiz

(1941–)

Simon Ortiz, a member of the Acoma Pueblo tribe in New Mexico, attended Indian schools before enrolling at the University of New Mexico, where he came under the influence of N. Scott Momaday, another Native American writer. Ortiz worked for a time in the uranium mines in New Mexico, where he developed a strong sense both that the workers were being endangered by what they were required to do and that the company for which they worked did not care about preserving the environment. Ortiz's poetry is characterized by a strong sense of place, a devotion to Native American concerns, and a commitment to environmentalism.

And there is always one more story

And there is always one more story. My mother was telling this one. It must be an old story but this time she heard a woman telling it at one of those Sunday meetings. The woman was telling about her grandson who was telling the story which was told to him by somebody else. All these voices telling the story, including the voices in the story—yes, it must be an old one.

One time,
(or like Rainy said, "You're sposed to say, 'Onesa ponsa time,' Daddy")

there were some Quail Women grinding corn.
Tsuushki—Coyote Lady—was with them.

---

[1]This oral tradition accounts for the number of variations ballads possess. A singer may repeat a ballad just as he or she first heard it; or he or she may change the ballad slightly, either on purpose or accidentally. A third singer then learns this new version, and either preserves or changes it. Thus a ballad of any great age may exist in many versions, each being sung by a different group of singers.

5   She was
grinding u-uuhshtyah—juniper berries.
I don't know why she wasn't grinding corn too—
that's just in the story.

It was a hot, hot day, very hot,
10 and the Quail Women got thirsty,
and they decided to go get some water to drink.
They said,
           "Let's go for a drink of water,
and let's take along our beloved comadre."
15 So they said, "Comadre, let's all go
and get some water to drink."
                     "Shrow-uh,"
Coyote said.

The water was in a little cistern
20 at the top of a tall rock pinnacle
which stands southeast of Aacqu.
                  They walked
over there but they had to fly to get to the top.
The Quail Women looked at Tsuushki who couldn't fly
25 to the top because she had no feathers,
                       and they felt
very sorry and sad for Tsuushki.

So they decided, "Let us give shracomadre
some of our feathers."
30   The Quail Women said that
and they took some feathers out of themselves
and stuck them on Coyote.
             And then they all flew
to the top of the pinnacle where the water was.
35 They all drank their fill and Coyote
was the last to drink.
           While she was drinking
from the cistern, on her hands and knees,
the Quail Women decided to play a trick, a joke
40 on Coyote Lady.
          They said,
"Let's take the feathers from our comadre
and leave her here."
              "Alright," they all agreed,
45 and they did that, and they all left.

When Tsuushki had drank her fill of water
and was ready to descend the pinnacle,
she found that she could not
because she had no feathers to fly with anymore.
50 She felt very bad,
                    and she sat down,
                                        wondering
what to do.
The rock pinnacle was too high up
55 to jump down from.

But, pretty soon,
                    Kahmaasquu Dya-ow—
Spider Grandmother—came climbing over the edge
of the pinnacle to drink water also.
60 And Coyote thought to herself,
                            Aha,
I will ask my Grandmother to help me off.
She is always a wonderful helpful person.

So Coyote asked,
65 "Dya-ow Kahmaasquu, do you think you could help me
descend this pinnacle? You are always such
a wonderful helpful person."

And Spider Grandmother said,
                        "Why yes,
70 beloved one, I will help you.
Climb into my basket."
                        She pointed at a basket
tied at the end of her rope.
                        And then
75 she said, "But I must ask you one thing.
While I am letting you down,
you must not look up, not once,
not even just a little bit.
                        For if you do,
80 I will drop you.
And that is quite a long ways down."

"Oh, don't worry about that, Dya-ow,
I won't look up. I'm not that kind of person,"
Coyote promised.

85   "Alright then,"
Spider said, "Climb in
and I will let you down."

The basket began to descend,
                          down
90   and
                                              down,
But on the way down,
                      Coyote looked up
(At this point, the voice telling the story
95 is that of the boy who said,
                              "But Tsuushki
looked up and saw her butt!")
and Spider Grandmother dropped the basket
and Coyote went crashing down.

100 Well, at this point, the story ends but,
as you know, it also goes on.
                            Well, sometime later,
the Shuuwimuu Guiguikuutchah—
Skeleton Fixer—came along.
105 He saw a scatter of bones at the foot of the pinnacle.
Skeleton Fixer said,
                      "Oh look,
some poor beloved one must have died.
I wonder who it may be?"
110   The bones
were drying white in the sun, lying around.
And Skeleton Fixer said,
                          "I think I will put
the bones together
115 and find out and he will live again."

And he joined the bones together,
                                    very carefully,
and when he had finished doing that,
he danced around them while he sang,

120 "Shuuwimuu shuuwimuu chuichukuu
Shuuwimuu shuuwimuu chuichukuu
Bah Bah."
          (which is to say)
Skeleton skeleton join together
125 Skeleton skeleton join together
Bah Bah.

And the skeleton bones did,
and the skeleton jumped up,
and it was Coyote.

130 "Ah kumeh, Tsuushkitruda," Skeleton Fixer said.
Oh, it's just you Coyote—I thought
it was someone else.
And as Coyote ran away,
Skeleton Fixer called after her,

135   "Nahkeh-eh,
bah aihatih eyownih trudrai-nah!"
Go ahead and go, may you get crushed
by a falling rock somewhere!

1992

STUDY QUESTIONS

1. Ortiz's "And there is always one more story" is not in traditional ballad form, but it clearly looks back to the oral traditions out of which ballads arise. Identify points in the poem where the narrator acknowledges that many voices from the past echo through the narrative.

2. How are these elements from the past juxtaposed with what appear to be contemporary references? What is the thematic effect of having this seemingly ancient folk story about magical animals being told "at one of those Sunday meetings"?

3. In the poem, the Coyote Lady gets feathers from the Quail Women so that she can fly with them up to the cistern to get water, but then the Quail Women take her feathers away. Then the Coyote falls to her death after looking up at the Spider Grandmother, only to be brought back to life by the Skeleton Fixer. How do you interpret these strange events? Why do the Quail Women at first help, then strand the Coyote Woman? What might the Spider Grandmother represent? Finally, why does the Skeleton Fixer, after bringing the Coyote Woman back to life, yell to her: "may you get crushed/by a falling rock somewhere"?

Leslie Marmon Silko

(1948–   )

Leslie Marmon Silko is of Native American, Mexican, and white American ancestry. She grew up in New Mexico and attended the University of New Mexico. Her novel *Ceremony* (1977) was the first to be published by a Native American writer. She has written about the difficulty for Native Americans of preserving their cultural heritage, about the atomic bomb (which was developed in New Mexico at Los Alamos), and about the way all events in history are repetitions.

The Storyteller's Escape

The storyteller keeps the stories
        all the escape stories
              she says "With these stories of ours
                 we can escape almost anything
5   with these stories we will survive."

The old teller has been on every journey
and she knows all the escape stories
        even stories told before she was born.
She keeps the stories for those who return
10   but more important
        for the dear ones who do not come back
        so that we may remember them
        and cry for them with the stories.

15   "In this way
                 we hold them
                 and keep them with us forever
                 and in this way
                 we continue."

20   This story is remembered
          as her best story
           it is the storyteller's own escape.

In those days
the people would leave the village
25 and hurry into the lava flows
where they waited until the enemy had gone.

               "This time they were close behind us
               and we could not stop to rest.
               On the afternoon of the fourth day
30   I was wearing the sun
             for a hat.

             Always before
             it was me
         turning around
35   for the last look
             at the pregnant woman

the crippled boy
old man Shio'see
slowing up
40   lying down
never getting up again.

Always before
I was the one who looked back
before the humpback hills
45   rose between us
so I could tell where these dear ones stopped."

But sooner or later
even a storyteller knows it will happen.
The only thing was
50   this time
she couldn't be sure
if there would be anyone
to look back
and later tell the others:
55   She stopped on the north side of Dough Mountain
and she said:

"The sun is a shawl on my back
its heat makes tassels that
shimmer down my arms."

60   And then she sat down in the shade
and closed her eyes.

She was thinking
this was how she would want them
to remember her and cry for her
65 If only somebody had looked back
to see her face for the last time

Someone who would know then
and tell the others:

"The black hills rose between us
70   the shady rock was above her head
and she was thinking
There won't be any escape story this time
unless maybe someone tells
how the sweat spilled over the rock
75   making streams in hills
that had no water.

She was thinking
                    I could die peacefully
                    if there was just someone to tell
80   how I finally stopped
                    and where.

    She believed
                    in this kind of situation
                    you have to do the best you can.

85   So I just might as well think of a story
                            while I'm waiting to die:

                                    A'moo'ooh, the child looked back.

                                        "Don't wait!
                                        Go on without me!
90   Tell them I said that—
                                        Tell them I'm too old too tired

                                            I'd rather just die here
                                            in the shade
                                            I'd rather just die
95   than climb these rocky hills
                                            in the hot sun.

        The child turned back for a last look at her
        off in the distance leaning against a cool rock
        the old teller waiting for the enemy to find her.
100   The child knew
                            how she had been on all the escape journeys
                            how she hated the enemy.
        She knew
                        what she was thinking
105   what she was saying to herself:

                                        "I'll fix them good!
                                        I'll fool them!
                                        I'll already be dead
                                        when the enemies come."

110   She laughed out loud.

                                I'll die just to spite them!

She was resting close to the boulder
hoping the child would tell—
otherwise

115   how could they remember her
           how could they cry for her
           without this story?

About this time
           the sun lifted off from her shoulders like a butterfly.

120   Let the enemy wear it now!
                                           Let them see how they like the heat
                                           wrapping them in its blanket!

She laughed sitting there
thinking to herself
125 until it got dark.
                     They would cry when they were told
                     the sun had been her hat
                     until she could walk no more
                     the sun had been a shawl
130   until she had to sit down in the shade.

                                        This one's the best one yet—
                                        too bad nobody may ever hear it.

She waited all night
but at dawn
135 there was still no sign of the enemy.
So she decided
to go back to the village.

What difference would it make
if she ran into the enemy?
140 She had already waited
all night
, for them to come along
and finish her.

                        But she didn't see anyone
145   no enemy.
                 Maybe the sun got to be too much for them too

And it was the best escape story she had come up with yet

> How four days later when the people came back
> from their hide-outs in the lava flow

150   there she was
> > sitting in front of her house
> > waiting for them.

> This is the story she told,
> > the child who looked back,

155   the old teller's escape—
> > the story she was thinking of
> > her getaway story
> > > how they remembered her
> > > and cried for her

160   Because she always had a way with stories
> > even on the last day
> > when she stopped in the shade
> > on the north side of Dough Mountain.

1981

STUDY QUESTIONS

1. What does "The Storyteller's Escape" say about the importance of the story-teller or poet in a preliterate society?
2. What virtues does the storyteller exhibit and celebrate during her ordeal on Dough Mountain?
3. What is the function of the child in the poem?
4. How do simile and metaphor contribute to the poem?

Anonymous

Sir Patrick Spens

The king sits in Dumferling town,
   Drinking the blude-reid wine:
"O whar will I get guid sailor,
   To sail this ship of mine?"

5

Up and spak an eldern knicht,
   Sat at the king's richt knee:
"Sir Patrick Spens is the best sailor
   That sails upon the sea."

The king has written a braid letter
10   And signed it wi' his hand,
And sent it to Sir Patrick Spens,
     Was walking on the sand.

The first line that Sir Patrick read,
     A loud lauch[1] lauched he;
15 The next line that Sir Patrick read,
     The tear blinded his ee.[2]

"O wha is this has done this deed,
     This ill deed done to me,
To send me out this time o' the year,
20   To sail upon the sea?

"Mak haste, mak haste, my mirry men all,
     Our guid ship sails the morn."
"O say na sae, my master dear,
     For I fear a deadly storm.

25 "Late, late yestre'en I saw the new moon
     Wi' the auld moon in hir arm,
And I fear, I fear, my dear master,
     That we will come to harm."

O our Scots nobles were richt laith[3]
30   To weet[4] their cork-heeled shoon,[5]
But lang or[6] a' the play were played
     Their hats they swam aboon.[7]

O lang, lang may their ladies sit,
     Wi' their fans into their hand,
35 Or ere they see Sir Patrick Spens
     Come sailing to the land.

O lang, lang may the ladies stand
     Wi' their gold kems[8] in their hair,
Waiting for their ain dear lords,
40   For they'll see them na mair.

---

[1]laugh
[2]eye
[3]loath
[4]wet
[5]shoes
[6]before
[7]above
[8]combs

Half o'er, half o'er to Aberdour[9]
    It's fifty fadom[10] deep,
And there lies guid Sir Patrick Spens
    Wi' the Scots lords at his feet.

date unknown

Anonymous

The Cherry-Tree Carol

Joseph was an old man,
    and an old man was he,
When he wedded Mary,
    in the land of Galilee.

5 Joseph and Mary walked
    through an orchard good,
Where was cherries and berries,
    so red as any blood.

Joseph and Mary walked
10   through an orchard green,
Where was berries and cherries,
    as thick as might be seen.

O then bespoke Mary,
    so meek and so mild:
15 "Pluck me one cherry, Joseph,
    for I am with child."

O then bespoke Joseph:
    with words most unkind:
"Let him pluck thee a cherry
20   that brought thee with child."

O then bespoke the babe,
    within his mother's womb:
"Bow down then the tallest tree,
    for my mother to have some."

25 Then bowed down the highest tree
    unto his mother's hand;

---

[9]halfway back to Aberdour, on the Firth of Forth
[10]fathoms

Then she cried, "See, Joseph,
    I have cherries at command."

O then bespoke Joseph:
30   "I have done Mary wrong;
But cheer up, my dearest,
    and be not cast down."

Then Mary plucked a cherry,
    as red as the blood,
35 Then Mary went home
    with her heavy load.

Then Mary took her babe,
    and sat him on her knee,
Saying, "My dear son, tell me
40   what this world will be."

"O I shall be as dead, mother,
    as the stones in the wall;
O the stones in the streets, mother,
    shall mourn for me all.

45 "Upon Easter-day, mother,
    my uprising shall be;
O the sun and the moon, mother,
    shall both rise with me."

date unknown

Anonymous

Get Up and Bar the Door

It fell about the Martinmas[1] time,
    And a gay time it was then,
When our good wife got puddings[2] to make,
    And she's boild them in the pan.

5 The wind sae cauld blew south and north,
    And blew into the floor;
Quoth our goodman to our goodwife,
    "Gae out and bar the door."

---

[1]November 11
[2]sausages

"My hands is in my hussyfskap,[3]
10   Goodman, as ye may see;
An it shoud nae be barrd this hundred year,
    It's no be barrd for me."

They made a paction tween them twa,
    They made it firm and sure,
15 That the first word whaeer shoud speak,
    Shoud rise and bar the door.

Then by there came two gentlemen,
    At twelve oclock at night,
And they could neither see house nor hall,
20   Nor coal nor candle-light.

"Now whether is this a rich man's house,
    Or whether is it a poor?"
But neer a word wad ane o them speak,
    For barring of the door.

25 And first they ate the white puddings,
    And then they ate the black;
Tho muckle[4] thought the goodwife to hersel,
    Yet neer a word she spake.

Then said the one unto the other,
30   "Here, man, tak ye my knife;
Do ye tak aff the auld man's beard,
    And I'll kiss the goodwife."

"But there's nae water in the house,
    And what shall we do than?"
35 "What ails ye at the pudding-broo,
    That boils into the pan?"

O up then started our goodman,
    An angry man was he:
"Will ye kiss my wife before my een,
40   And scad me wi pudding-bree?"

Then up and started our goodwife,
    Gied three skips on the floor:
"Goodman, you've spoken the foremost word,
    Get up and bar the door."

date unknown

---

[3]household chores
[4]much

STUDY QUESTIONS

1. Because ballads come out of the oral tradition, it is only natural that they would sound different than more "literary" poems composed by a single author. Comment on the effect of the informal diction and dialect words that characterize "Sir Patrick Spens," "The Cherry-Tree Carol," and "Get Up and Bar the Door."
2. Comment on the different tones of the three ballads. Are ballads limited in the range of moods they can convey?
3. Compare these three anonymous ballads with Dudley Randall's modern "Ballad of Birmingham," which follows. What differences in subject matter and tone do you notice?

Dudley Randall

(1914–   )

Randall grew up in and continues to work in the city of Detroit. He is best known as the founder and publisher of The Broadside Press, which has served as an outlet for many African American poets. The National Endowment for the Arts awarded Randall its Lifetime Achievement Award.

Ballad of Birmingham

(On the bombing of a church in Birmingham, Alabama, 1963)

"Mother dear, may I go downtown
Instead of out to play,
5 And march the streets of Birmingham
In a Freedom March today?"

"No, baby, no, you may not go,
For the dogs are fierce and wild,
And clubs and hoses, guns and jails
10 Aren't good for a little child."

"But, mother, I won't be alone.
Other children will go with me,
And march the streets of Birmingham
To make our country free."

15 "No, baby, no, you may not go,
For I fear those guns will fire.
But you may go to church instead
And sing in the children's choir."

She has combed and brushed her night-dark hair,
And bathed rose petal sweet,
And drawn white gloves on her small brown hands,
20 And white shoes on her feet.

The mother smiled to know her child
Was in the sacred place,
But that smile was the last smile
To come upon her face.

25 For when she heard the explosion,
Her eyes grew wet and wild.
She raced through the streets of Birmingham
Calling for her child.

She clawed through bits of glass and brick,
30 Then lifted out a shoe.
"O, here's the shoe my baby wore,
But, baby, where are you?"

1969

STUDY QUESTION

What is the central irony in "Ballad of Birmingham?" How is the irony made
more intense by the fact that the poem was based on the actual bombing of a
black church?

Edgar Allan Poe

(1809–1849)

See page 164 for a biographical note on the author.

Annabel Lee

It was many and many a year ago,
                    In a kingdom by the sea,
That a maiden there lived whom you may know
                    By the name of Annabel Lee;—
5 And this maiden she lived with no other thought
                    Than to love and be loved by me.

She was a child and *I* was a child,
                    In this kingdom by the sea,

But we loved with a love that was more than love—
10   I and my Annabel Lee—
With a love that the wingèd seraphs of Heaven
         Coveted her and me.

And this was the reason that, long ago,
         In this kingdom by the sea,
15 A wind blew out of a cloud by night
         Chilling my Annabel Lee;
So that her highborn kinsmen came
         And bore her away from me,
To shut her up in a sepulchre
20   In this kingdom by the sea.

The angels, not half so happy in Heaven,
         Went envying her and me—
Yes!—that was the reason (as all men know,
         In this kingdom by the sea)
25 That the wind came out of the cloud chilling
         And killing my Annabel Lee.

But our love it was stronger by far than the love
         Of those who were older than we—
         Of many far wiser than we—
30 And neither the angels in Heaven above,
         Nor the demons down under the sea,
Can ever dissever my soul from the soul
         Of the beautiful Annabel Lee:—

For the moon never beams without bringing me dreams
35   Of the beautiful Annabel Lee;
And the stars never rise but I see the bright eyes
         Of the beautiful Annabel Lee;
And so, all the night-tide, I lie down by the side
Of my darling, my darling, my life and my bride,
40   In her sepulchre there by the sea—
         In her tomb by the side of the sea.

1849

STUDY QUESTIONS

1. How would you characterize the narrator of the poem? Do you find him
   sympathetic? Does he seem reliable in his judgments?

2. Consider the story told by the poem, and the emotions it evokes. Is the story one that fits well into the ballad form? Again, what elements harmonize well with the ballad tradition? Which suggest a more sophisticated speaker and audience?

Sterling Brown

(1901–1989)

Sterling Brown came from an educated family, earned a B.A. degree from Williams College, and did graduate work at Harvard. He taught English in Virginia and began to write poetry, influenced both by highbrow modernist aesthetics and by black folk life. He published anthologies of black writing, scholarly books on black literature, and his own rich collections of poetry.

Slim in Hell

I

Slim Greer went to heaven;
 St. Peter said, "Slim,
You been a right good boy."
 An' he winked at him.

5
  "You been a travelin' rascal
   In yo' day.
  You kin roam once mo';
   Den you comes to stay.

10 "Put dese wings on yo' shoulders,
  An' save yo' feet."
Slim grin, and he speak up
 "Thankye, Pete."

  Den Peter say, "Go
15   To Hell an' see,
  All dat is doing, and
   Report to me.

"Be sure to remember
 How everything go."
20 Slim say, "I be seein' yuh
 On de late watch, bo."

  Slim got to cavortin',
   Swell as you choose,

Like Lindy in de "Spirit
    Of St. Louis Blues!"

25 He flew an' he flew,
    Till at last he hit
A hangar wid de sign readin'
    DIS IS IT.

    Den he parked his wings,
30   An' strolled aroun'
    Gettin' used to his feet
        On de solid ground.

II

Big bloodhound came aroarin'
    Like Niagry Falls,
35 Sicked on by white devils
    In overhalls.

Now Slim warn't scared,
    Cross my heart, it's a fac',
An' de dog went on a bayin'
40   Some po' devil's track.

    Den Slim saw a mansion
        An' walked right in;
    De Devil looked up
        Wid a sickly grin.

45 "Suttinly didn't look
    Fo' you, Mr. Greer,
How it happen you comes
    To visit here?"

    Slim say—"Oh, jes' thought
50   I'd drap by a spell."
    "Feel at home, seh, an' here's
        De keys to Hell."

Den he took Slim around
    An' showed him people
55 Raisin' hell as high as
    De First Church Steeple.

    Lots of folks fightin'
        At de roulette wheel,
    Like old Rampart Street,
60   Or leastwise Beale.

Showed him bawdy houses
   An' cabarets,
Slim thought of New Orleans
   An' Memphis days.

65   Each devil was busy
         Wid a devilish broad,
      An' Slim cried, "Lawdy,
         Lawd, Lawd, Lawd."

Took him in a room
70   Where Slim see
De preacher wid a brownskin
   On each knee.

      Showed him giant stills,
         Going everywhere
75   Wid a passel of devils,
         Stretched dead drunk there.

Den he took him to de furnace
   Dat some devils was firing,
Hot as hell, an' Slim start
80   A mean presspirin';

      White devils wid pitchforks
         Threw black devils on,
      Slim thought he'd better
         Be gittin' along.

85 An' he say—"Dis makes
      Me think of home—
Vicksburg, Little Rock, Jackson,
   Waco, and Rome."

      Den de devil gave Slim
90   De big Ha-Ha;
      An' turned into a cracker,
         Wid a sheriff's star.

Slim ran fo' his wings,
   Lit out from de groun'
95 Hauled it back to St. Peter,
   Safety boun'.

III

St. Peter said, "Well,
   You got back quick.
How's de devil? An' what's
   His latest trick?"

100

An' Slim say, "Peter,
   I really cain't tell,
De place was Dixie
   Dat I took for Hell."

105   Then Peter say, "You must
   Be crazy, I vow,
Where'n hell dja think Hell *was,*
   Anyhow?

"Git on back to de yearth,
110   Cause I got de fear,
You'se a leetle too dumb,
   Fo' to stay up here . . ."

1932

STUDY QUESTIONS

1. "Slim in Hell" is based on a simple joke. How would you state this joke in two or three sentences?
2. How does Brown's use of dialect contribute to the humor of the poem?
3. Does the poem merely criticize whites for racism, or does it also find fault with blacks? If so, why?

Elements of Poetry
12

REPETITION AND RHYTHM

Two prominent elements in ballads are **repetition** and **rhythm**. Sometimes single words or phrases are repeated for emphasis, as in Poe's "Annabel Lee": "She was a child and I was a child/In this kingdom by the sea." Sometimes one or more lines, perhaps with slight variations, appear in nearly every verse as a **refrain**: "I and my Annabel Lee/. . . . In this kingdom by the sea." In each case, the repetition emphasizes both the content and the rhythm of the ballad, calling our attention to the **meter** (that is, to the rhythmic pattern of each line) or to the grouping of lines into stanzas.

Of the ballads or ballad-influenced poems printed in the previous chapter, "Annabel Lee" is the most repetitive. In fact, it is built on a technique known as **incremental repetition**. Many phrases recur throughout the stanzas, creating a melancholy, hypnotic effect. The subtle changes in the repeated lines develop the narrative of the poem and help convey the narrator's sorrow over the death of his beloved.

Repetition is important not only in ballads, but in lyric poetry in general. It is most pronounced in songs, as in the next example. But it appears frequently (and often quite subtly) in spoken lyrics as well. Let us look at some poems in which repetition plays an important role, and let us see what effects are produced by it.

William Shakespeare

(1564–1616)

As well as being the greatest dramatist in world literature, William Shakespeare was also a great lyric poet and sonneteer. Many of his finest lyrics come from his plays. Shakespeare moved from Stratford-on-Avon to London sometime in the early 1590s, where he soon showed himself as a master in the comic and historical modes. His company won the favor of King James, who sponsored them. Around 1600, Shakespeare composed his great tragedies. He retired to Stratford as a rich and well-respected master of his craft.

It Was a Lover and His Lass

It was a lover and his lass,
    With a hey, and a ho, and hey nonino,

That o'er the green corn-field did pass
    In the spring time, the only pretty ring time,
5   When birds do sing, hey ding a ding, ding:
Sweet lovers love the spring.

Between the acres of the rye,
    With a hey, and a ho, and a hey nonino,
These pretty country folk would lie,
10   In the spring time, the only pretty ring time,
When birds do sing, hey ding a ding, ding:
Sweet lovers love the spring.

This carol they began that hour,
    With a hey, and a ho, and a hey nonino,
15   How that a life was but a flower
    In the spring time, the only pretty ring time,
When birds do sing, hey ding a ding, ding:
Sweet lovers love the spring.

And therefore take the present time,
20   With a hey, and a ho, and a hey nonino,
For love is crownèd with the prime
    In the spring time, the only pretty ring time,
When birds do sing, hey ding a ding, ding:
Sweet lovers love the spring.

1600

STUDY QUESTIONS

1. How would you characterize this song? What is its mood?
2. How does the refrain help set the mood of the song?
3. What other repetitions of sounds do you find in the poem? What do they contribute? (Note: Two important categories here are **rhyme**—the use of words that *end* with the same sound, like *rye* and *lie*—and **alliteration,** the use of words that *begin* with the same sound, like *lover* and *lass; hey, ho,* and *hey.*)
4. Discuss the progression of thought and feeling from the first stanza to the final one. What sense of completeness does the progression impart to Shakespeare's song?

Thomas Hardy

(1840–1928)

Thomas Hardy was part of the realist movement in literature during the second half of the nineteenth century. His novels present human beings against the ancient rhythms of the seasons and the harvest, and suggest that individuals are not really in control of their destinies. A deep pessimism underlies Hardy's writing, despite his insistence that he was not really a pessimist. The harsh critical reaction to *Jude the Obscure* (1895) caused him to give up fiction writing in favor of lyric poetry that reflected the elegiac, melancholy, fatalistic, intellectually sophisticated temper of modernist thought.

The Ruined Maid

"O 'Melia, my dear, this does everything crown!
Who could have supposed I should meet you in Town?
And whence such fair garments, such prosperi-ty?"—
"O didn't you know I'd been ruined?" said she.

5 —"You left us in tatters, without shoes or socks,
Tired of digging potatoes, and spudding up docks;[1]
And now you've gay bracelets and bright feathers three!"—
"Yes: that's how we dress when we're ruined," said she.

—"At home in the barton[2] you said 'thee' and 'thou,'
10 And 'thik oon,' and 'theäs oon,' and 't'other'; but now
Your talking quite fits 'ee for high compa-ny!"—
"Some polish is gained with one's ruin," said she.

—"Your hands were like paws then, you face blue and bleak
But now I'm bewitched by your delicate cheek,
15 And your little gloves fit as on any la-dy!"—
"We never do work when we're ruined," said she.

—"You used to call home-life a hag-ridden dream,
And you'd sign, and you'd sock; but at present you seem
To know not of megrims[3] or melancho-ly!"—
20 "True. One's pretty lively when ruined," said she.

---

[1]digging up weeds
[2]farmyard
[3]low spirits

—"I wish I had feathers, a fine sweeping gown,
And a delicate face, and could strut about Town!"—
"My dear—a raw country girl, such as you be,
Cannot quite expect that. You ain't ruined," said she.

1901

STUDY QUESTIONS

1. How does Hardy use question and answer to characterize the two women?
2. What balance exists here between the two sides of the dialogue? What is the effect of the repetitions in the final line of each stanza?
3. What sort of tone or consciousness would you expect to find in a poem about a "ruined maid" that is absent from this poem? What effect does this have on the tone of the poem and on the characterization of the speakers? On the poet's apparent attitude toward them?

E. E. Cummings

(1894–1962)

E. E. Cummings was an innovative and insistently modern artist who exploded the traditional verse forms of the previous century and redefined in free verse what poetry could be. While serving as a volunteer ambulance driver, he was detained in a French prison during World War I. This experience gave him an enduring distrust of bureaucratic institutions and wartime propaganda. His playful, teasing, sometimes aggressively mocking poetry satirized the emotional deadness of people caught up in the pursuit of money, status, and conventional "ideals." Ignoring the conventions of syntax and grammar, he figuratively blew up language and put it back together again in his distinctive style of oddly broken up lines, words prefaced by *not* or *un*, and lines shunning capital letters.

All in green went my love riding

All in green went my love riding
on a great horse of gold
into the silver dawn.

four lean hounds crouched low and smiling
5   the merry deer ran before.

Fleeter be they than dappled dreams
the swift sweet deer
the red rare deer.

Four red roebuck at a white water
10   the cruel bugle sang before.

Horn at hip went my love riding
riding the echo down
into the silver dawn.

four lean hounds crouched low and smiling
15   the level meadows ran before.

Softer be they than slippered sleep
the lean lithe deer
the fleet flown deer.

Four fleet does at a gold valley
20   the famished arrow sang before.

Bow at belt went my love riding
riding the mountain down
into the silver dawn.

four lean hounds crouched low and smiling
25   the sheer peaks ran before.

Paler be they than daunting death
the sleek slim deer
the tall tense deer.

Four tall stags at a green mountain
30   the lucky hunter sang before.

All in green went my love riding
on a great horse of gold
into the silver dawn.

four lean hounds crouched low and smiling
35   my heart fell dead before.

1904

STUDY QUESTIONS

1. Incremental repetition is used in this modern poem for an almost balladlike effect. But how would you describe the way stanzas are linked in this poem?
2. What effects would you say the poem achieves? How would you distinguish between its effects and those of traditional ballads?

N. Scott Momaday

(1934–)

N. Scott Momaday's writing reflects his experience of straddling two cultures: white American and Native American. Momaday attended public as well as reservation schools, and received a Ph.D. from Stanford, where he worked with critic Yvor Winters. He has taught literature at the University of California at Berkeley and the University of Arizona. His work shows his struggle to establish an "Indian" sense of self without falling into posing or sentimentalizing.

The Delight Song of Tsoai-talee

I am a feather in the bright sky.
I am the blue horse that runs in the plain.
I am the fish that rolls, shining, in the water.
I am the shadow that follows a child.
I am the evening light, the lustre of meadows.
5   I am an eagle playing with the wind.
I am a cluster of bright beads.
I am the farthest star.
I am the cold of the dawn.
I am the roaring of the rain.
10   I am the glitter on the crust of the snow.
I am the long track of the moon in a lake.
I am a flame of four colors.
I am a deer standing away in the dusk.
I am a field of sumac and the pomme blanche.
15   I am an angle of geese upon the winter sky.
I am the hunger of a young wolf.
I am the whole dream of these things.

You see, I am alive, I am alive.
I stand in good relation to the earth.
20   I stand in good relation to the gods.
I stand in good relation to all that is beautiful.
I stand in good relation to the daughter of Tsen-tainte.
You see, I am alive, I am alive.

1974

STUDY QUESTIONS

1. Why does Momaday use metaphor rather than simile throughout the poem?

2. Are the metaphors random, or do they form a pattern?
3. How is the line "I am the whole dream of these things" radically different from the lines that precede it?
4. What is the effect of the repetition of "I am . . ." and "I stand . . ." in the poem?

Etheridge Knight

(1931–1991)

Etheridge Knight grew up in Mississippi, fought in the Korean War, became addicted to heroin, and spent time in prison in Indiana for robbery. He was greatly influenced by his prison reading, which included *The Autobiography of Malcom X* (1965). Dudley Randall discovered Knight and helped publish his first volume, aptly called *Poems from Prison* (1968). Knight was a strong voice in contemporary African American poetry, who tempered his characteristic anger and honesty with compassion and hard-won wisdom.

Ilu, the Talking Drum

The deadness was threatening us—15 Nigerians and 1 Mississippi nigger.
It hung heavily, like stones around our necks, pulling us down
to the ground, black arms and legs outflung
on the wide green lawn of the big white house
5 near the wide brown beach by the wide blue sea.
The deadness was threatening us, the day
was dying with the sun, the stillness—
unlike the sweet silence after love/making or
the pulsating quietness of a summer night—
10 the stillness was skinny and brittle and wrinkled
by the precise people sitting on the wide white porch
of the big white house. . . .
The darkness was threatening us, menacing . . .
we twisted, turned, shifted positions, picked our noses,
15 stared at our bare toes, hissed air thru our teeth. . . .
Then Tunji, green robes flowing as he rose,
strapped on *Ilu,* the talking drum,
and began:

kah doom/kah doom-doom/kah doom/kah doom-doom-doom
20 kah doom/kah doom-doom/kah doom/kah doom-doom-doom
kah doom/kah doom-doom/kah doom/kah doom-doom-doom
kah doom/kah doom-doom/kah doom/kah doom-doom-doom

the heart, the heart beats, the heart, the heart beats slow
the heart beats slowly, the heart beats

25 the blood flows slowly, the blood flows
    the blood, the blood flows, the blood, the blood flows slow

    kah doom/kah doom-doom/kah doom/kah doom-doom-doom
    and the day opened to the sound
    kah doom/kah doom-doom/kah doom/kah doom-doom-doom
30 and our feet moved to the sound of life
    kah doom/kah doom-doom/kah doom/kah doom-doom-doom
    and we rode the rhythms as one
    from Nigeria to Mississippi
    and back
35 kah doom/kah doom-doom/kah doom/kah doom-doom-doom

    1980

STUDY QUESTIONS

1. What is the apparent setting in place and time of the poem?
2. Why is the drum called a "talking drum"?
3. Why does Knight increase the amount of repetition as the poem progresses?

13

COMPRESSION AND VERSE FORMS

To write a short story based on the tale told in "Get Up and Bar the Door" would require at least one thousand words. This ballad, however, has less than five hundred words, including refrains and repetitions. And even though ballads are much shorter than a very short story, they seem long and loosely constructed when they are compared with such tightly written lyrics as "It Was a Lover and His Lass."

Verse, then, is a highly compressed form. Eliminating inessentials, it takes us directly to the heart of a situation, to the one or two moments most highly charged with emotion. In the case of "Get Up and Bar the Door," this technique produces a ballad centering on two episodes: the one that begins the quarrel and the one that ends it.

Time becomes flexible in ballads, as one memorable moment is juxtaposed with the next, ignoring all that may have gone between: "Then by there came two gentlemen,/At twelve oclock at night." We can imagine that the lateness of the hour would have made the silent house seem even stranger than it was to the "gentlemen," and we may also suspect that quite a few hours must have passed since the feuding couple made their pact. But all the singer gives us is the crucial hour—"twelve"—and the number of intruders. The time between incidents is not important. The conflict between the couple is.

Similarly, "The Cherry-Tree Carol" moves with almost no consciousness of elapsed time from the wedding of Joseph and Mary to the scene in the orchard to a final scene between Mary and her infant son. In each case, a simple "then" defines the sequence, whether the incidents follow each other instantly, as in "then bespoke the babe," "then bowed down the highest tree," and "O then bespoke Joseph," or whether a gap of several months is indicated: "Then Mary took her babe." The passage of time, which affects everyone, is of no concern to the singer. The unique situation of parents confronted with their child's divinity engrosses all the attention, linking the unusual circumstances of Joseph's marriage, the miracle in the orchard, and Christ's prophecy of his death and resurrection. "The Cherry-Tree Carol" assumes that its hearers are all familiar with the story of Christ's birth and death; it therefore feels free to concentrate on those aspects of the legend that bear on its central theme, leaving us to place them in chronological time if we wish.

Poetic form demands **compression**. A line of eight or ten syllables, a stanza of two, four, or six lines will not allow any wasted words. The poet must pare away all the needless background and inessential details in order to fit the essential ones into those brief stanzas.

Yet this strictness of form also helps the hearer to accept the compression it produces. In a prose account, we would not accept so few details as "Get Up and Bar the Door" gives us. Nor could the information in "The Ruined Maid" stand alone as prose. Ballad and lyric alike need the **cadence** of their verse—the rhyme, the rhythm, the **rounded-off pattern** formed by the stanzas—to give our ear and mind the sense of completeness and satisfaction that allows us to enjoy the brief, tightly focused statements their poetry makes.

Compression, then, is another technique that allows the material presented and the form of its presentation to reinforce each other, providing for the reader not only a satisfying unity, but also one that seems notably poetic. Let us now examine that technique in action by looking at a few types of poetry that have compression as their most notable feature, beginning with the oldest of these forms, the **epigram**.

Epigrams may be serious or humorous, flattering or insulting. But they are usually descriptive of a person, animal, or object; and they are invariably brief. Probably the most popular type today is the **satiric epigram**, a form that can be described as a description with a sting. Here is an example:

Countee Cullen

(1903–1946)

Along with Langston Hughes, Countee Cullen was one of the most influential writers of the Harlem Renaissance in the 1920s.

For a Lady I Know

She even thinks that up in heaven
Her class lies late and snores,
While poor black cherubs rise at seven
To do celestial chores.

1925

STUDY QUESTIONS

1. What single fact do the four lines of this poem tell us about the "Lady" who is their subject?
2. What further facts do they suggest about her?
3. How do words like *her class* and *poor black cherubs* characterize the lady and the attitudes that the poet suggests she holds?

4. What do words like *snores* and *celestial chores* do for the poem? What do they suggest about the poet's attitude?

Not all brief poems with a punch are epigrams, however. The following poem has a sting of its own and is as highly compressed in technique as any poem you will see. Yet its structure is not that of the epigram. How would you define it?

Gwendolyn Brooks

(1917–   )

Gwendolyn Brooks grew up in the rich cultural milieu of Chicago, where her supportive parents encouraged her early interest in poetry. She met and was recognized as talented by Langston Hughes, who became her mentor. In 1950 she became the first African American to receive the Pulitzer Prize for poetry. Guggenheim fellowships and election to the National Institute of Arts and Letters followed. She has been active in promoting the arts and civil rights, both through her poetry and through lectures.

We Real Cool

The Pool Players.
Seven at the Golden Shovel.

We real cool. We
Left school. We

Lurk late. We
Strike straight. We

Sing sin. We
5   Thin gin. We

Jazz June. We
Die soon.

1960

STUDY QUESTIONS

1. What does the subtitle tell us about the speakers of the poem?
2. How do the speakers characterize themselves?
3. Discuss the use of repetition in the poem.

4. Note also the breaks in the pattern. Why has Brooks placed the word *we* at the end of each line rather than letting it come at the beginning as it does in the first line? Is the word *we* stressed more heavily, less heavily, or just as heavily at the end of the line as it would be at the beginning? What happens to the verbs? Does placing them at the beginning of the line give them any extra stress? What happens to the length of the last line? What effect does it produce?
5. What does Brooks seem to be saying in this poem about the "Seven" or about people like them? How does the form of her poem express or emphasize her feelings?

Here are two more brief, pointed poems. How do these poems combine serious and humorous elements? What makes them enjoyable to read?

Arthur Guiterman

(1871–1943)

Like Ogden Nash, Arthur Guiterman wrote poetry satirizing the pretensions of man that often feature intentionally silly rhymes.

On the Vanity of Earthly Greatness

The tusks that clashed in mighty brawls
Of mastodons, are billiard balls.

The sword of Charlemagne the Just
Is ferric oxide, known as rust.

5   The grizzly bear whose potent hug
Was feared by all, is now a rug.

Great Caesar's bust is on the shelf,
And I don't feel so well myself.

1940

Marianne Moore

(1887–1972)

A friend of both William Carlos Williams and Wallace Stevens, Marianne Moore had her early poetry published in *The Dial* magazine, which she later edited. Influenced by the imagists, she wrote carefully observed poems about animals—and people—that won the respect of her peers. Such poets as T. S. Eliot praised her idiosyncratic and elegant style.

I May, I Might, I Must

If you will tell me why the fen
appears impassable, I then
will tell you why I think that I
can get across it if I try.

1959

Another extremely brief form, which was introduced to English and American poetry in the twentieth century, is the **imagist** poem. Imagist poetry grew out of an interest in Oriental poetry, especially in the brief, seventeen-syllable form known as **haiku**. (The poem by Pound that follows is sometimes called haiku.) As the word *imagist* implies, this poetry focuses on a single sensory image—a sight, sound, or feeling—and presents it in as brief and vivid a form as the writer can manage. Read the following two poems, and then ask what image each poem starts from and what further images it uses to reinforce the first one. How are the images combined? How would you contrast the form and effect of these poems with the form and effect of the epigrams you have just read, or with the effect and form of lyrics?

Ezra Pound

(1885–1972)

Ezra Pound was, along with T. S. Eliot, among the most influential of the American expatriate poets of the 1920s. He was a fierce champion of high culture, and he sprinkled his poetry with allusions to many national literatures and historical eras. He was one of the chief proponents of "imagism," and issued, with F. S. Flint, a famous "manifesto" of the movement. After becoming obsessed with economics, he made broadcasts for the fascist Italian government during World War II, and afterwards he was committed to a mental institution in Washington D.C. in lieu of being charged with treason. Robert Frost and others worked to get him released in the 1960s. Pound spent his last days in Italy.

In a Station of the Metro

The apparition of these faces in the crowd;
Petals on a wet, black bough.

1926

Amy Lowell

(1874–1925)

Amy Lowell was one of the imagist poets of the 1920s. She was notable for her love poems, which often conveyed a sort of intellectual wistfulness and longing.

Wind and Silver

Greatly shining,
The Autumn moon floats in the thin sky;
And the fish-ponds shake their backs and flash their
    dragon scales
As she passes over them.

1921

So far, we have looked at poems that achieved effectiveness through spareness, using as few words as possible and choosing very tight verse forms. But compression can also be achieved within other verse forms. Note, for instance, the richness of words and images that William Carlos Williams manages to crowd into "The Dance," so that the poetic form seems almost too small for the magnitude of the sounds and motions it contains. Notice, too, in the poem that follows, the intensity of argument and feeling that William Wordsworth fits gracefully into the fourteen lines of a sonnet.

William Carlos Williams

(1883–1963)

William Carlos Williams worked most of his life as a doctor in Rutherford, New Jersey. He was also one of the most influential poets of the century, despite the fact that he did not frequent the artistic circles of New York. Like Ezra Pound, he favored the lean, spare aesthetic of imagism. He was influenced by modernist painting and worked to achieve collagelike effects in his poetry. "No ideas but in things" became his realistic, concrete, distinctly American poetic credo.

The Dance

In Breughel's[1] great picture, The Kermess,[2]
the dancers go round, they go round and

---

[1]Pieter Breughel, or Brueghel (1525?–1569), a Flemish painter
[2]a carnival or fair

around, the squeal and the blare and the
tweedle of bagpipes, a bugle and fiddles
5 tipping their bellies (round as the thick-
sided glasses whose wash they impound)
their hips and their bellies off balance
to turn them. Kicking and rolling about
the Fair Grounds, swinging their butts, those
10 shanks must be sound to bear up under such
rollicking measures, prance as they dance
in Breughel's great picture, The Kermess.

1944

STUDY QUESTIONS

1. Although you might expect a poem describing a painting to concentrate on color or form, Williams's poem concentrates at least as heavily on motion and sound. What words or phrases describe the sounds of the scene? Which describe shapes or forms? Which describe motion? What sorts of music and dancers does Williams seem to be portraying with these terms?

2. How do the poem's rhythm and shape support the sense of sound and motion? Note particularly the large number of heavily stressed monosyllables. What effect do they provide? How have sentence structure and grammar been reshaped to contribute to the sensation of noise and speed?

3. Note the plays on words within the poem: "bellies" for both fiddles and dancers, legs called "sound" in a poem much concerned with musical sounds. How does such wordplay help unify the scene? Note also the use of repetition: how does it help shape the poem?

4. If you are able to find a print of *The Kermess*, decide how well you think Williams has caught the spirit of the painting. What aspects of the poem stand out for you as being particularly apt?

William Wordsworth

(1770–1850)

William Wordsworth, along with Samuel Taylor Coleridge, changed forever the nature of English poetry with the publication of *Lyrical Ballads* in 1798. Insisting that poets shun "poetic diction" in favor of natural speech; that they treat all subjects, not just "high" ones, with respect; that they see the miraculous in the commonplace and the commonplace in the miraculous, Wordsworth brought an equivalent of the French Revolution to aesthetics. In his great autobiographical work *The Prelude* (1850) he recorded the growth of his imagination with an intimacy never before achieved in poetry.

The World Is Too Much with Us

The world is too much with us; late and soon,
Getting and spending, we lay waste our powers:
Little we see in Nature that is ours;
We have given our hearts away, a sordid boon!
5   This Sea that bares her bosom to the moon;
The winds that will be howling at all hours,
And are up-gathered now like sleeping flowers;
For this, for everything, we are out of tune;
It moves us not.—Great God! I'd rather be
10 A Pagan suckled in a creed outworn;
So might I, standing on this pleasant lea,
Have glimpses that would make me less forlorn;
Have sight of Proteus rising from the sea;
Or hear old Triton blow his wreathèd horn.[1]

1807

STUDY QUESTIONS

1. What is the argument of this poem?
2. How does Wordsworth's invocation of Triton and Proteus fit in with the argument of the poem?
3. What words or images in the poem do you find most striking? How do they support the poem's argument?
4. Note the poem's movement from "us" and "we" in the first lines to "I" at the end. At what line does the change take place? How is it marked or signaled? What changes of tone of voice and of mood go with it? What change of imagery?
5. What qualities in the poem make it suitable as a study in compression? Alternatively, if you disagree with this classification, why do you challenge the poem's placement in this chapter?

Finally, we will look at some poems by Emily Dickinson. No study of compression in poetry would be complete without a consideration of the work of this American poet, who was far ahead of her time in the concentration and spareness of her verse. Description and argument blend in Dickinson's poetry into a remarkable unity of vision and idea. Notice, in the following two poems, how images of light and motion bridge the gap between the physical and spiri-

---

[1]In Greek mythology Proteus was a prophetic sea god who, when seized, changed shape to try to escape prophesying. Triton, the son of the sea god Poseidon, played a trumpet made of a conch shell.

tual worlds and between our own physical and spiritual responses to these worlds.

Emily Dickinson

(1830–1886)

Emily Dickinson was much more complex than her popular persona of the recluse in a white dress would suggest. She was an intellectually demanding, diverse, strangely comic, and utterly bold poet—perhaps the most enduringly important in our literature. She had only a few influences—William Shakespeare, the Bible—but they were profound ones that she had read deeply. Frustrated in her single attempt to publish her works when Thomas Wentworth Higginson tried to make her more "conventional," Dickinson wrote for herself, a few friends, and for posterity. She died early of Bright's disease, but left 1,775 poems neatly bound up in packets. They would not all be published until the famous edition by Thomas H. Johnson appeared in the 1950s.

There's a Certain Slant of Light (#258)[1]

There's a certain Slant of light,
Winter Afternoons—
That oppresses, like the Heft
Of Cathedral Tunes—

5 Heavenly Hurt, it gives us—
We can find no scar,
But internal difference,
Where the Meanings, are—

None may teach it—Any—
10 'Tis the Seal Despair—
An imperial affliction
Sent us of the Air—

When it comes, the Landscape listens—
Shadows—hold their breath—
15 When it goes, 'tis like the Distance
On the look of Death—

1951

---

[1]Dickinson did not title her poems. The first line of each poem conventionally serves as a title. The number in parentheses after the title refers to the order of the poems in Thomas H. Johnson's edition of her complete poems.

Tell All the Truth but Tell It Slant (#1129)

Tell all the Truth but tell it slant—
Success in Circuit lies
Too bright for our infirm Delight
The Truth's superb surprise
5 As Lightning to the Children eased
With explanation kind
The Truth must dazzle gradually
Or every man be blind—

1957

STUDY QUESTIONS

1. Give examples of images of light and motion in these poems. How are the two types of images connected?
2. Give examples of lines or phrases that you think are particularly good examples of compression. How is Dickinson creating this effect? For what purpose is she using it?
3. What does being human seem to mean in these poems? What aspects of our nature are being emphasized? (Note that we as readers are definitely included in these descriptions of what being human entails. How are we brought into them?)

14

WORD CHOICE:
MEANINGS AND SUGGESTIONS

Common Phrases and New Meanings

Our study of ballads gave us insight into the use of repetition and selectivity in poetry, and thus into poetry's balance of **narrative** and **rhythmic patterns**. We saw that poetry is based on the combination of satisfying sounds and sharply focused content. And we saw how the pattern of sounds and words created by the skillful use of rhythm, repetition, and word-sound can heighten the effect of compression or set the **atmosphere**, or **mood**.

But ballads could not tell us a great deal about **word choice** in poetry. For ballads, like other oral poetry, tend to rely on a shared vocabulary of predictable phrases and stock epithets. Hearing ballads, we recognize in them traditional terms, pairings, and comparisons: "my true-love," "my hawks and my hounds," "the sun and the moon," "as red as the blood," and "as dead as the stones." We are not meant to linger on any of them, or on any particular line. Rather, we let each recognized phrase add its bit to mood or situation but reserve our main attention for the pattern made by the story as it unfolds.

In written poetry, on the other hand, word choice is all-important. The **wordplay** by which William Shakespeare blends spring, songs, and rings to create an atmosphere (p. 325) and the indelicate verb *snores* with which Countee Cullen mocks his "lady's" pretensions to gentility (p. 334) testify to the power of the well-chosen word. The words themselves are not unusual ones; but they surprise us when they appear, nonetheless. They call on us to pay attention and reward us for our attention by bringing their overtones of **meaning** and **suggestion** into the poem, enriching our enjoyment and understanding.

The language of poetry, then, is not necessarily composed of strange, unusual, or uniquely "poetic" words. More often, poetry gains its effects through unexpected juxtapositions of **common words and phrases**, bringing new meaning into the ordinary. Look, for instance, at this poem by Emily Dickinson, and consider how the poet gives significance to the simplest language.

The Bustle in a House (#1078)

The Bustle in a House
The Morning after Death
Is solemnest of industries
Enacted upon Earth—

5 The Sweeping up the Heart
And putting Love away
We shall not want to use again
Until Eternity.

1951

The language of the first stanza is almost like prose. A few extra words, and it would be a simple prose statement: The bustle that takes place in a house, the day after someone who lived there has died, represents one of the most solemn tasks on earth. (The word *industries* may seem a bit strange in this context. At the time this poem was written, however, it was used to denote any sort of labor, just as the word *industrious* does today.)

In the second stanza, however, we notice a change. Here the poet is amplifying her first statement. She is explaining that the "bustle" is caused by the housecleaning that takes place between a death and the funeral, and that it is "solemn" because the workers must reconcile themselves to the loss of a loved one. In fact, the workers are coming to grips with their emotions even as they do the chores.

She does not, however, resort to wordy explanations. Rather, she combines housework and emotions in a tightly **compressed pair of images**. The verbs of the second stanza speak of housecleaning matters; the nouns, of love. It is not dust that is swept up, but "the heart"; not blankets to be put away, but "love." The combination conveys the sense of loss. "The sweeping up the heart," in particular, suggests that the heart is broken, is in pieces; and the thought of a broken heart, in turn, suggests grief.

But the poet also says that the grief and loss are not permanent. "Love" is not thrown away, but rather "put away" to be used again on a future occasion. "Until eternity": the phrase suggests a fearfully long wait, but insists, nonetheless, that the waiting will end. "Eternity" thus balances "earth," tempering the present sense of loss with faith in restoration. And in that balance the poem ends and rests.

Here is another poem by Dickinson that is notable for its unusual use of words. How would you analyze it?

Because I Could Not Stop for Death (#712)

Because I could not stop for Death—
He kindly stopped for me—
The Carriage held but just Ourselves—
And Immortality.

5 We slowly drove—He knew no haste
And I had put away
My labor and my leisure too,
For His Civility—

We passed the School, where Children strove
10 At Recess—in the Ring—
We passed the Fields of Gazing Grain—
We passed the Setting Sun—

Or rather—He passed Us—
The Dews drew quivering and chill—
15 For only Gossamer, my Gown—
My Tippet¹—only Tulle²—

We paused before a House that seemed
A Swelling of the Ground—
The Roof was scarcely visible—
20 The Cornice—in the Ground—

Since then—'tis Centuries—and yet
Feels shorter than the Day
I first surmised the Horses' Heads
Were toward Eternity—

1951

Suggestion and Interpretation

In a poem like Dickinson's "There's a Certain Slant of Light," just as in "Because I Could Not Stop for Death," the language is richly suggestive. In the former poem, Dickinson takes a common experience—the melancholy feeling one sometimes gets during the winter—and deepens and intensifies it. She uses **synesthesia,** the mixing up of one sense with another, by comparing the way the light looks to the "heft" of cathedral tunes. Of course neither light nor sound can be "hefted" as one might lift a book to test its weight, yet the word "heft" seems just right to describe the "oppressive" sound of a pipe organ in a cathedral, or the subtle "feel" of winter sunlight. Dickinson also uses **oxymorons** like "Heavenly Hurt" and "imperial affliction" to add to both the suggestiveness and ambiguity of the poem. And because the speaker receives a "Seal" indicating poetic sensitivity, it is difficult to tell whether Dickinson is describing a purely painful experience or one that is in a sense pleasurable. In all these respects, "There's a Certain Slant of Light" always moves toward greater suggestiveness, never toward a narrowing of meaning.

---

¹a shoulder cape
²a stiff, sheer fabric

Sound, sense, and **suggestion** all blend in poetry. Words gain new relevance, new connections. They carry several meanings, suggest several more, and join with other words to suggest yet further meanings. Word choice, the craft of selecting and joining words to enrich their power to communicate, is one of the basic skills of the poet's craft.

Because the rhythms of the following two poems are smoother than those of "The Bustle in the House," and their rhymes are more exactly matched, they have a more traditional sound. Yet their use of language resembles that in Dickinson's poem in that their words and **syntax,** basically simple and straightforward, are highlighted by a few unexpected words or images. Discuss what you think the highlights in these poems are, and how you think they function.

William Wordsworth

(1770–1850)

See page 339 for a biographical note on the author.

She Dwelt Among the Untrodden Ways

She dwelt among the untrodden ways
    Beside the springs of Dove.
A Maid whom there were none to praise
    And very few to love;

5 A violet by a mossy stone
    Half hidden from the eye!
—Fair as a star, when only one
    Is shining in the sky.

She lived unknown, and few could know
10   When Lucy ceased to be;
But she is in her grave, and, oh,
    The difference to me!

1800

Robert Herrick

(1591–1674)

Robert Herrick was born in London, fell under the influence of the great poet Ben Jonson, became a minister in Devonshire, and quietly composed over one thousand poems in his lifetime. Turned out of his position during the English Civil War, he returned to

London and published his secular poems in *Hesperides* (1648) and his religious ones in *Noble Numbers* (1648). Herrick's fine lyric poems went largely unread until he was rediscovered in the nineteenth century. His work, seemingly casual and cheery, is crafted with great precision and reflects Herrick's distinctive Christian–pagan sensibility.

Upon Julia's Clothes

Whenas in silks my Julia goes,
Then, then, methinks, how sweetly flows
That liquefaction of her clothes.

Next, when I cast mine eyes and see
5 That brave vibration each way free,
O how that glittering taketh me!

1648

Again, the following poem presents a straightforward statement. But here the language is slightly richer, the play on words is more pronounced, and the words take on more resonance of meaning. Discuss the poem and its language. How does the choice of words give the poem more impact than its main statement, "Many friends of mine have died," would have?

A. E. Housman

(1859–1936)

A. E. Housman was a noted classical scholar who brought to his poetry the classical qualities of compression, precision of form, and a stoic acceptance of fate. The traditional ballad was an influence on him as well. His typical theme was that of the doomed youth whose life or joy in life is cut short for some reason. Housman's most famous volume of poems is *A Shropshire Lad* (1896).

With Rue My Heart Is Laden

With rue my heart is laden
    For golden friends I had,
For many a rose-lipt maiden
    And many a lightfoot lad.

5 By brooks too broad for leaping
    The lightfoot boys are laid;
The rose-lipt girls are sleeping
    In fields where roses fade.

1939

STUDY QUESTIONS

1. What repetitions do you find in the poem? How does the second stanza develop the images begun in the first stanza?
2. How does the word *golden* in line 2 fit into the mood and imagery?
3. Note the heavy use of "r" and "l" sounds. What effect does the alliteration of these sounds produce? What other examples of alliteration can you find in the poem? How would you summarize your view of Housman's choice of words for sound and sense?

The next poem presents a wish or desire and paints a scene representing the fulfillment of the wish. Note how the poem creates a simple and direct, yet powerful, evocation of scene and mood. Note the use of details, of images that appeal to sight and hearing, touch and motion, and the use of rhyme, rhythm, and alliteration.

Gerard Manley Hopkins

(1844–1889)

Gerard Manley Hopkins was a deeply religious man who felt divided between his loyalty to God and his devotion to poetry. As a Jesuit serving in a number of working-class parishes, including one in Liverpool, Hopkins was greatly affected by the poverty, both physical and spiritual, that he encountered. In 1884 he was appointed to a Classics position at University College in Dublin. Although not sufficiently appreciated during his lifetime, his poetry was among the most influential of the early twentieth century. Hopkins coined words, used imaginative hyphenated words, invented what he called "sprung rhythm"—all as ways to recover "the dearest freshness deep down [in] things." He is usually regarded as a twentieth-century poet born before his time.

Heaven–Haven

A Nun Takes the Veil

> I have desired to go
>   Where springs not fail,
> To fields where flies no sharp and sided hail
>   And a few lilies blow.
>
> 5   And I have asked to be
>   Where no storms come,
> Where the green swell is in the havens dumb,
>   And out of the swing of the sea.

1876

STUDY QUESTIONS

1. Can you explain the poem's title? Is the subtitle necessary for an understanding of the poem?
2. Each stanza in this poem describes a different scene, a different location. What links the two together? How do these scenes develop the subject set out in the poem's title?
3. Notice the differences between the structure of these sentences and that of normal English; notice also the spareness of the form and imagery (even down to the "few lilies" in the fourth line) and the relatively heavy use of alliteration. How do these contribute to the poem's effect?

The next two poems are written in **free verse**, a verse form invented in the early twentieth century. Free verse is marked by uneven line lengths and often by the absence of rhyme, as well. Note how these poems mix repetition and compression to create their very different effects.

Marge Piercy

(1936–   )

Marge Piercy grew up in Detroit, one of only two Jewish girls in her grade school. In the 1960s she began to write seriously and became involved in the civil rights and antiwar movements. She has lived an unconventional life and is known as one who acts out on her feminist and ecological ideals.

The Secretary Chant

My hips are a desk.
From my ears hang
chains of paper clips.
Rubber bands form my hair.
5 My breasts are wells of mimeograph ink.
My feet bear casters.
Buzz. Click.
My head is a badly organized file.
My head is a switchboard
10 where crossed lines crackle.
Press my fingers
and in my eyes appear
credit and debit.
Zing. Tinkle.
15 My navel is a reject button.
From my mouth issue canceled reams.

Swollen, heavy, rectangular
I am about to be delivered
of a baby
20 Xerox machine.
File me under W
because I wonce
was
a woman.

1973

STUDY QUESTIONS

1. In its title, this poem identifies itself as a "chant." In what respect does Piercy's poem sound like a chant? What is the purpose of making it sound this way?
2. What is the tone of this poem? What is the balance in it between humor and serious social commentary about the plight of working women? Does this mixed tone help or hurt the advancement of Piercy's major thematic point?
3. Since the poem was published in the 1970s, the work environment associated with secretaries it describes is in many respects outdated. Try rewriting the poem and bringing it up to date by substituting computers, fax machines, pagers, scanners, and the like for the earlier technology described in "The Secretary Chant."

Ezra Pound

(1885–1972)

See page 337 for a biographical note on the author.

These Fought in Any Case[1]

These fought in any case,
and some believing,
                    pro domo,[2] in any case . . .

Some quick to arm,
5 some for adventure,
some from fear of weakness,

---

[1]Section IV from "E. P. Ode pour L'Election de Son Sépulcre" ("E. P. Ode on the Selection of His Tomb")
[2]"for homeland"

some from fear of censure,
some for love of slaughter, in imagination,
learning later . . .
10 some in fear, learning love of slaughter;

Died some, pro patria,
             non "dulce" non "et decor"[3] . . .
walked eye-deep in hell
believing in old men's lies, then unbelieving
15 came home, home to a lie,
home to many deceits,
home to old lies and new infamy;
usury age-old and age-thick
and liars in public places.

20 Daring as never before, wastage as never before.
Young blood and high blood,
fair cheeks, and fine bodies;

fortitude as never before

frankness as never before,
25 disillusions as never told in the old days,
hysterias, trench confessions,
laughter out of dead bellies.

1926

STUDY QUESTIONS

1. How would you describe the tone of voice in this poem? What do the repetitions contribute to it? the word choice? Give examples to prove your assertions.
2. What attitude does the poem suggest toward the soldiers of which it speaks? Is the attitude simple or complex? How is it suggested?
3. What of the poem's attitude toward war in general?
4. An **ode** is a poem of irregular form. How does Pound use irregularity of form to reinforce the suggestions his poem makes?

    The words in this final poem deserve special notice. Their underlying **tone**—the author's attitude toward the subject matter—and **syntax** are more casual and friendly than any we have met so far. And yet Cummings has taken

---

[3] an ironic allusion to Horace's famous line: "Dulce et decorum est pro patria mori" ("It is sweet and fitting to die for one's country")

enormous liberties with words and syntax alike, even to the point of inventing new words and positioning each word individually on the page. To what new responses does the resulting poem seem to invite you?

E. E. Cummings

(1894–1962)

See page 328 for a biographical note on the author.

in Just-

in Just-
spring   when the world is mud-
luscious the little
lame balloonman

5   whistles   far   and wee

and eddieandbill come
running from marbles and
piracies and it's
spring

10   when the world is puddle-wonderful

the queer
old balloonman whistles
far   and   wee
and bettyandisbel come dancing

15   from hop-scotch and jump-rope and

it's
spring
and
        the

20   goat-footed

balloonMan   whistles
far
and
wee

1920

STUDY QUESTIONS

1. In analyzing this poem, we may begin with its wordplay. How do compound words such as *mud-luscious* and *puddle-wonderful* affect the sound and meaning of the lines in which they occur? How many meanings does the word *wee* have, and what is the effect of using it? The balloon-man is described through incremental repetition, beginning as "lame" and ending as "goat-footed." Why goat-footed?

2. We may then note two unusual rhythmic devices: the breaking of lines in the middle of words or phrases, and the spacing out or running together of words. And we may ask how these affect the sound and mood of the poem, and our sense of the scene it describes.

3. Then we may put this play with words and rhythms together with the poem's use of names and detail, and ask how Cummings creates and enhances his description. What does the intent of the poem seem to be? What message does it seem to carry? How do the sound and word choices create the tone and the message?

The Speaker in the Poem

15

THE SPEAKER'S VOICE

We have said that ballads, being traditional, oral poetry, rely on common words and images rather than on the unique images of written poetry. We may now make one final distinction by remarking that this stylization of ballads leaves these songs lacking uniquely memorable **voices**. A deserted lover in one ballad, for instance, sounds much like a deserted lover in any other ballad. They will speak at least some of the same words in the same **tones** and rhythms. This is not the case in written poetry, where we would take the appearance of a lover who sounds like any other lover as the sign of a second-rate poem. If we read twenty lyrics about love—or even twenty lyrics about lost love—we expect to hear twenty different voices.

This reflection brings us to one of the basic paradoxes of poetry. Because of its use of **rhythm** and **sound patterns**, the language of poetry may be the farthest of all literary languages from everyday speech. Yet the voices within poems are the most intimate of literary voices, speaking to us most vividly and directly and conveying to us most openly the speakers' deepest and most immediate emotions. No other form of literature demands so much care and craft in its writing as poetry; yet no other form can seem to present the spontaneous flow of emotion as convincingly as poetry can.

Because poetry can so thoroughly convince us that in responding to it we are sharing a genuine, strongly felt emotion, it can attract our strongest response. Subjectively, this is good; it represents poetry doing what it should do. Objectively, however, poetry's seeming frankness raises the critical danger that we may mistake the voice within the poem for the voice of the poet. The further danger then arises that we may generalize from a single poem, slipping from the critically acceptable statement ("Dickinson's 'There's a Certain Slant of Light' is a poem about depression") to the unacceptable ("as 'There's a Certain Slant of Light' shows, Dickinson was always depressed.")

We cannot fall into this error so easily in drama or fiction, where the number of characters and the abundance of circumstantial detail continually warn us of the distance between author and work. Poetry, however, often has but one voice in a poem. The voice often speaks in the first person: "Oh, how that glittering taketh me!" And the intensity of emotion that is felt only in the climatic scenes of fiction and drama may illuminate an entire lyric. This combination of single voice, first person, and unflagging intensity of emotion often obliterates the distance between the poet and speaker. If the speaker than gives us the

355

slightest hint that he or she may represent the poet, we become all too willing to make the identification.

But we must not make the identification so simply. We can speak of a poet's voice—can compare Poe's voice to Dickinson's, for example. But when we do this we must compare all the voices from at least a dozen of Poe's poems to all the voices from an equal number of Dickinson's. We can then speak either of a range of voices that seems typical of each poet or of some specific characteristics that remain constant through all their individual voices. Moreover, we may equally well make comparisons between voices belonging to a single poet—comparing the voices of Poe's early poems to those of his later poems, for instance—which we could not do if the voice in each poem were the poet's only voice.

To further emphasize this distance between speaker and poet, we may look again at poems such as "We Real Cool" and "Sir Patrick Spens." They seem to speak to us as directly and to be as immediately felt as any other poems, but we know no author for "Sir Patrick Spens" and are sure that Gwendolyn Brooks is not seven adolescents in a pool hall.

The poem is the poet's vision, nothing more. Its speakers may be inside the action (as in "Upon Julia's Clothes") or outside it (as in "The Cherry-Tree Carol"). They may have elements of the poet's own situation or emotions in them, or they may not. But they are speakers and not writers; they are the poet's creations and not the poet's self.

For discussing speakers who *do* seem to mirror their poets, we have the useful critical term **persona**. The speakers of Browning's "My Last Duchess," of Frost's "Birches," and of Levertov's "At David's Grave" may be called their poets' personae. Personae represent one aspect of their poet's personality or experience, isolated from the rest of the poet's life, dramatized, and re-created through art. Poets—like all human beings—are complex and changeable. Personae are simpler: fixed, changeless, and slightly exaggerated. Unlike their makers, who must respond to the many demands of the everyday world in which they live, personae exist only within their poems and respond only to the thoughts and sensations that gave the poems birth.

Here, for the further study of speakers in poetry, are eleven poems. Most of these poems employ speakers who might well be spoken of as personae, but at least one has a speaker who cannot be so described. Be aware, as you read these poems, of sound and language and total effect. But pay most attention to the characterization of the speakers and to the varying voices with which they speak.

Theodore Roethke

(1908–1963)

Theodore Roethke's early poetry often depicts the world of nature. Personally troubled by alcoholism and mental breakdowns, Roethke was alternately fascinated by and terrified of the natural world, the mysteries of human speech, and the need of the poet to confess his innermost self. He was revered as a great teacher by those young poets who studied with him at the University of Washington. His late love poems are among the most engaging in recent American verse.

My Papa's Waltz

The whiskey on your breath
Could make a small boy dizzy;
But I hung on like death:
Such waltzing was not easy.

5 We romped until the pans
Slid from the kitchen shelf;
My mother's countenance
Could not unfrown itself.

The hand that held my wrist
10 Was battered on one knuckle;
At every step you missed
My right ear scraped a buckle.

You beat time on my head
With a palm caked hard by dirt,
15 Then waltzed me off to bed
Still clinging to your shirt.

1942

I Knew a Woman

I knew a woman, lovely in her bones,
When small birds sighed, she would sigh back at them;
Ah, when she moved, she moved more ways than one:
The shapes a bright container can contain!
5 Of her choice virtues only gods should speak,
Or English poets who grew up on Greek
(I'd have them sing in chorus, cheek to cheek).

How well her wishes went! She stroked my chin,
She taught me Turn, and Counter-turn, and Stand;[1]
10 She taught me Touch, that undulant white skin;
I nibbled meekly from her proffered hand;
She was the sickle; I, poor I, the rake,
Coming behind her for her pretty sake
(But what prodigious mowing we did make).

15 Love likes a gander, and adores a goose:
Her full lips pursed, the errant note to seize;
She played it quick, she played it light and loose;
My eyes, they dazzled at her flowing knees;
Her several parts could keep a pure repose,
20 Or one hip quiver with a mobile nose
(She moved in circles, and those circles moved).

Let seed be grass, and grass turn into hay:
I'm martyr to a motion not my own;
What's freedom for? To know eternity.
25 I swear she cast a shadow white as stone.
But who would count eternity in days?
These old bones live to learn her wanton ways:
(I measure time by how a body sways).

1954

STUDY QUESTIONS

1. What is the subject of each of these poems? What is the emotional state of the speaker?
2. How does the language of the two poems compare? What sort of images does each use? How does the language match the subject and mood in each?
3. How would you characterize the speaker of each poem? What would you have to say to move from a characterization of the speakers to a characterization of the poet?

---

[1]terms for the three parts of a Pindaric ode

Edna St. Vincent Millay

(1892–1950)

Edna St. Vincent Millay achieved early fame in the 1920s as one of the new, modern women who lived a liberated life and wrote candidly about erotic matters in her poetry. Despite her reputation as a bohemian, she was conventional in her aesthetics, favoring established forms like the sonnet. Her reputation declined in the 1930s and 1940s, although she remained politically active in defending individual rights and opposing fascism.

What Lips My Lips Have Kissed, and Where, and Why

What lips my lips have kissed, and where, and why,
I have forgotten, and what arms have lain
Under my head till morning; but the rain
Is full of ghosts tonight, that tap and sigh
5 Upon the glass and listen for reply,
And in my heart there stirs a quiet pain
For unremembered lads that not again
Will turn to me at midnight with a cry.
Thus in the winter stands the lonely tree,
10 Nor knows what birds have vanished one by one,
Yet knows its boughs more silent than before:
I cannot say what loves have come and gone,
I only know that summer sang in me
A little while, that in me sings no more.

1922

Nikki Giovanni

(1943–   )

Nikki Giovanni was born in Knoxville, Tennessee, and published her first work in the 1960s. She was praised as one of the best of the new African American poets in the post–World War II era.

You Are There

i shall save my poems
for the winter of my dreams
i look forward to huddling
in my rocker with my life

5 i wonder what i'll contemplate
lovers—certainly those

i can remember
and knowing my life
you'll be there

10 you'll be there in the cold
like a Siamese on my knee
proud purring when you let me stroke you

you'll be there in the rain
like an umbrella over my head
15 sheltering me from the damp mist

you'll be there in the dark
like a lighthouse in the fog
seeing me through troubled waters

you'll be there in the sun
20 like coconut oil on my back
to keep me from burning

i shall save a special poem
for you to say
you always made me smile
25 and even though i cried sometimes
you said i will not let you
down

my rocker and i on winter's porch
will never be sad if you're gone
30 the winter's cold has been stored
against
you will always be
there

1978

STUDY QUESTIONS

1. "What My Lips Have Kissed, and Where, and Why" and "You Are There"
   concern the same subject: a woman remembering her former lovers. The
   voices of the speakers of the two poems, however, sound decidedly different.

Characterize each voice, paying special attention to the figurative language each speaker employs.

2. Does there seem to be much distance between the poets and the voices of their personae in these poems?

Robert Hayden

(1913–1980)

Robert Hayden was born to poor parents who soon divorced and left him to the care of neighbors. The young boy was shy but a voracious reader. He later worked his way to an M.A. degree and began a lifetime of teaching and writing, at Fisk University and at the University of Michigan. He rejected the idea that African Americans should write only for a black audience, and so tried to use his experience to reach universal truths about human character. He converted to the Baha'i faith in the 1940s, which stresses the unity of all the world's people.

Mourning Poem for the Queen of Sunday

Lord's lost Him His mockingbird,
His fancy warbler;
Satan sweet-talked her,
four bullets hushed her.
5   Who would have thought
she'd end that way?

Four bullets hushed her. And the world a-clang with evil.
Who's going to make old hardened sinner men tremble now
and the righteous rock?
10 Oh who and oh who will sing Jesus down
to help with struggling and doing without and being colored
all through blue Monday?
Till way next Sunday?

All those angels
15   in their cretonne clouds and finery
the true believer saw
when she rared back her head and sang,
all those angels are surely weeping.
Who would have thought
20   she'd end that way?

Four holes in her heart. The gold works wrecked.
But she looks so natural in her big bronze coffin
among the Broken Hearts and Gates-Ajar,

it's as if any moment she'd lift her head
25 from its pillow of chill gardenias
and turn this quiet into shouting Sunday
and make folks forget what she did on Monday.
       Oh, Satan sweet-talked her,
       and four bullets hushed her.
30   Lord's lost Him His diva,
       His fancy warbler's gone.
       Who would have thought,
       who would have thought she'd end that way?

1975

STUDY QUESTIONS

1. Discuss "Mourning Poem for the Queen of Sunday" in terms of situation, irony, paradox, and tone.
2. How does the poem use a balladlike repetition of key phrases and refrain?
3. Speculate on what the Queen of Sunday "did on Monday" to bring about her murder. How do the Queen of Sunday's paradoxical qualities fit into the theology of the poem?

Those Winter Sundays

Sundays too my father got up early
and put his clothes on in the blueblack cold,
then with cracked hands that ached
from labor in the weekday weather made
5 banked fires blaze. No one ever thanked him.

I'd wake and hear the cold splintering, breaking.
When the rooms were warm, he'd call,
and slowly I would rise and dress,
fearing the chronic angers of that house,

10 Speaking indifferently to him,
who had driven out the cold
and polished my good shoes as well.
What did I know, what did I know
of love's austere and lonely offices?

1962

STUDY QUESTIONS

1. Discuss the speaker's ambivalence toward his father.
2. How is that ambivalence a function of the implied lapse of time between the narrator's childhood and the "present," in which the events in the poem are recalled?

Denise Levertov

(1923–1997)

Denise Levertov was born in England, emigrated to the United States after World War II, and taught at various universities while establishing herself as one of the best of America's contemporary poets. One of her principal ideas is that poetry is a necessary outlet for people seeking to keep their imaginative selves alive. Her willingness to use intimate recollections from her personal experience and her belief in the important function of poetry in enhancing the reader's and the writer's spiritual development distinguish her work.

At David's Grave

for B. and H. F.

Yes, he is here in this
open field, in sunlight, among
the few young trees set out
to modify the bare facts—

5 he's here, but only
because we are here.
When we go, he goes with us

to be your hands that never
do violence, your eyes
10 that wonder, your lives

that daily praise life
by living it, by laughter.

He is never alone here,
never cold in the field of graves.

1970

STUDY QUESTIONS

1. Like "Mourning Poem for the Queen of Sunday," "At David's Grave" is an elegy, a lament for one who has died. What compensations for the loss of the loved one does the speaker of the poem find?
2. What is the significance of the phrase "the bare facts"?

William Butler Yeats

(1865–1939)

William Butler Yeats was one of the handful of the most important poets writing in English during the first half of this century. In a long career he went through a whole compendium of poetic styles—late romanticism, the art-for-art's-sake style of the 1890s, an Eliot-like combination of the intellectual and the colloquial into a new "metaphysical" style in the 1920s, and a complex symbolic style derived from the prophetic writings of William Blake in the late 1920s and early 1930s. Irish nationalism was a constant theme in his writing, as were his grand if somewhat obscure ideas about cycles of history. Yeats had a theory about human personality and phases of the moon linked to two-thousand-year "primary" and "antithetical" historical cycles. He set out this scheme in a cryptic prose/poetic work called *A Vision* (1925). One critic archly remarked that Yeats made divine poetry out of divine nonsense.

The Folly of Being Comforted

One that is ever kind said yesterday:
"Your well-belovèd's hair has threads of gray,
And little shadows come about her eyes;
Time can but make it easier to be wise
5 Though now it seem impossible, and so
All that you need is patience."

                               Heart cries, "No,
I have not a crumb of comfort, not a grain.
Time can but make her beauty over again:
Because of that great nobleness of hers
10 The fire that stirs about her, when she stirs,
Burns but more clearly. O she had not these ways
When all the wild summer was in her gaze."

O heart! O heart! if she'd but turn her head,
You'd know the folly of being comforted.

1902

STUDY QUESTIONS

1. To whom does this lover speak?
2. In what situation does he find himself? What is his reaction to the situation? What emotions and thoughts does he express?
3. How do the form and language of the poem, together with the emotion and situation represented, create your picture of each of this lover?

The next poem represents a form known as **dramatic monologue**. After you have read the poem, answer the following questions:

1. Who is the speaker?
2. To whom is he speaking? On what occasion?
3. What does the speaker tell you about his own character? How does he do so?
4. What do you think happened to the "last duchess"?
5. If you were the person being addressed, how would you feel at the end of the monologue?

Robert Browning

(1812–1889)

Robert Browning did not gain the public reputation his wife Elizabeth Barrett Browning had enjoyed until he was in his fifties, but he turned out to be a much more important poet. He had a storybook marriage to Elizabeth Barrett and a happy life with her in Italy for fifteen years, but when she died Browning returned to England. In his "dramatic monologues"—poems featuring a single speaker, as in a dramatic soliloquy—he pioneered the direction twentieth-century poets like T. S. Eliot would take, toward the "interior" of their personae's consciousness.

My Last Duchess

Ferrara

That's my last duchess painted on the wall,
Looking as if she were alive. I call
That piece a wonder, now: Frà Pandolf's[1] hands
Worked busily a day, and there she stands.
5 Will't please you sit and look at her? I said
"Frà Pandolf" by design, for never read
Strangers like you that pictured countenance,

---

[1] a fictitious artist, as is Claus of Innsbruck in the last line

The depth and passion of its earnest glance,
But to myself they turned (since none puts by
10 The curtain I have drawn for you, but I)
And seemed as they would ask me, if they durst,
How such a glance came there; so, not the first
Are you to turn and ask thus. Sir, 'twas not
Her husband's presence only, called that spot
15 Of joy into the Duchess' cheek: perhaps
Frà Pandolf chanced to say "Her mantle laps
"Over my lady's wrist too much," or "Paint
"Must never hope to reproduce the faint
"Half-flush that dies along her throat": such stuff
20 Was courtesy, she thought, and cause enough
For calling up that spot of joy. She had
A heart—how shall I say?—too soon made glad,
Too easily impressed; she liked whate'er
She looked on, and her looks went everywhere.
25 Sir, 'twas all one! My favor at her breast,
The dropping of the daylight in the West,
The bough of cherries some officious fool
Broke in the orchard for her, the white mule
She rode with round the terrace—all and each
30 Would draw from her alike the approving speech,
Or blush, at least. She thanked men—good! but thanked
Somehow—I know not how—as if she ranked
My gift of a nine-hundred-years-old name
With anybody's gift. Who'd stoop to blame
35 This sort of trifling? Even had you skill
In speech—which I have not—to make your will
Quite clear to such an one, and say, "Just this
"Or that in you disgusts me; here you miss,
"Or there exceed the mark"—and if she let
40 Herself be lessoned so, nor plainly set
Her wits to yours, forsooth, and made excuse,
—E'en then would be some stooping; and I choose
Never to stoop. Oh sir, she smiled, no doubt,
Whene'er I passed her; but who passed without
45 Much the same smile? This grew; I gave commands;
Then all smiles stopped together. There she stands
As if alive. Will 't please you rise? We'll meet
The company below, then. I repeat,
The Count your master's known munificence
50 Is ample warrant that no just pretense
Of mine for dowry will be disallowed;

Though his fair daughter's self, as I avowed
At starting, is my object. Nay, we'll go
Together down, sir. Notice Neptune, though,
55 Taming a sea-horse, thought a rarity,
Which Claus of Innsbruck cast in bronze for me!

1842

Robert Frost

(1874–1963)

Robert Frost in a sense did for American poetry what Mark Twain had done for American prose: legitimized the American vernacular. Using the vocabulary and rhythms of ordinary speech, Frost created a persona of the rural New England farmer who was at once down to earth and philosophical, straightforward and "sly," traditional in his forms yet modern in his subject matter. Rather than being the simple "nature poet" he is often described as, Frost was something more: his real concern was the human subject *in* nature, with all the subject's fears, anxieties, and oddities lurking just under the "natural" surface of the poem. Influenced both by Darwin and the new physics of Einstein, Frost was concerned about preserving meaning in an indifferent world of biological competition and cosmic entropy. Ironically celebrated (despite his dark themes) by the public as its "most beloved poet," Frost was invited to read at the inauguration ceremony of President Kennedy.

Birches

When I see birches bend to left and right
Across the lines of straighter darker trees,
I like to think some boy's been swinging them.
But swinging doesn't bend them down to stay
5 As ice-storms do. Often you must have seen them
Loaded with ice a sunny winter morning
After a rain. They click upon themselves
As the breeze rises, and turn many-colored
As the stir cracks and crazes their enamel.
10 Soon the sun's warmth makes them shed crystal shells
Shattering and avalanching on the snowcrust—
Such heaps of broken glass to sweep away
You'd think the inner dome of heaven had fallen.
They are dragged to the withered bracken by the load,
15 And they seem not to break; though once they are bowed
So low for long, they never right themselves:
You may see their trunks arching in the woods

Years afterwards, trailing their leaves on the ground
Like girls on hands and knees that throw their hair
20 Before them over their heads to dry in the sun.
But I was going to say when Truth broke in
With all her matter-of-fact about the ice-storm,
I should prefer to have some boy bend them
As he went out and in to fetch the cows—
25 Some boy too far from town to learn baseball,
Whose only play was what he found himself,
Summer or winter, and could play alone.
One by one he subdued his father's trees
By riding them down over and over again
30 Until he took the stiffness out of them,
And not one but hung limp, not one was left
For him to conquer. He learned all there was
To learn about not launching out too soon
And so not carrying the tree away
35 Clear to the ground. He always kept his poise
To the top branches, climbing carefully
With the same pains you use to fill a cup
Up to the brim, and even above the brim.
Then he flung outward, feet first, with a swish,
40 Kicking his way down through the air to the ground.
So was I once myself a swinger of birches.
And so I dream of going back to be.
It's when I'm weary of considerations,
And life is too much like a pathless wood
45 Where your face burns and tickles with the cobwebs
Broken across it, and one eye is weeping
From a twig's having lashed across it open.
I'd like to get away from earth awhile
And then come back to it and begin over.
50 May no fate willfully misunderstand me
And half grant what I wish and snatch me away
Not to return. Earth's the right place for love:
I don't know where it's likely to go better.
I'd like to go by climbing a birch tree,
55 And climb black branches up a snow-white trunk,
Toward heaven, till the tree could bear no more,
But dipped its top and set me down again.
That would be good both going and coming back.
One could do worse than be a swinger of birches.

1936

STUDY QUESTIONS

1. Frost is famous for creating speakers with apparently simple, plain-spoken, matter-of-fact voices; yet his speakers usually work their way around to thinking about deeply philosophical issues. How is this the case in "Birches"?

2. A clue that Frost hints at an underlying sexual theme in "Birches" is his persona's description of the bent-over trees as looking "Like girls on hands and knees that throw their hair/Before them over their heads to dry in the sun." Discuss how the apparently literal descriptions of the birches take on metaphoric meanings that give the reader a sense of complexity rather than simplicity in the speaker's voice.

Simon Ortiz

(1941–   )

See page 303 for a biographical note on the author.

Notes for My Child

July 5, 1973, when she was born

Wake slow this morning.

Hear Joy moan,
stir around,
and get up sometime after five.

5   Bit of morning light.

Get up and wash,
put on two days-old coffee.

Later,
we walk for you
10   over to University Drug.

Sun slants
through trees,
cool morning.

See two cicadas.
15   One is dead,
the other is buzzing
trying to take off
from the sidewalk.

I want to turn back
20 and help it
to fly again,
but I realize
the inevitable.

Yesterday,
25 while chopping weeds,
I uncovered two chrysalis,
the cicadas within them
curled, soft yet.

We get to the hospital.
30 The taxi driver says, "Good luck."
"Okay, thanks." Smiling nervous.

Hospitals are consistent.
Crummy. We wait
for someone to notice us.

35 I tell Joy
to make herself visible.
She can't be anymore visible
she thinks than now,
her belly sticking out.

40 I ask where my wheelchair is
when Joy gets in hers
and is pushed down the hall
and into an elevator
by a fat unsmiling aide
45 who doesn't think
I am funny at all.

Upstairs and down a hall,
and Joy disappears
behind some doors.

50 I squat on the tile floor,
remember a poem Joy has written
about the story teller.

The aide walks by.
She smiles this time
55 and says, "Okay."
I say, "Okay," too.

Seven other people wait
and make small talk.
A couple of women
60 are rolled by.

I smile at the six women
and one guy.
A couple smile back.

When the women roll by
65 everything becomes somber
and slow.

. . . the Wisconsin Horse
is silent, looks through
the chainlink fence,
70 the construction going on
a mile away. . . .

Finally,
I get to join Joy.
She's getting anxious.
75 Can tell in her eyes,
movements, tremble
about her mouth.

A nurse tells me
to go to Admitting.
80 A girl asks me a question.
"Are you the responsible party?"
I say, "Yes."
She means money, of course.
Who's going to pay?
85 I mean I'm the father
of the child bringing life
and continuance.

I go back upstairs.
A woman on the other side
90 of the room moans a bit,
struggles in her sheets.
An older woman holds her hand.

Joy is pretty relaxed,
takes deep breaths

95 to make it easier.
Amazing how anyone can relax
at the eve of birth—
only a step along the way,
of course.
100 I ask Joy if it hurts,
realize it's a dumb
but important question.

A doctor comes along
and puts a plastic machine
105 upon Joy's belly
and flicks it on.
The doctor calls it
a doptone and says,
"Don't ask me why it's called that.
110 I don't know. It runs on batteries."

I call it
steady, gentle beating noises
called flesh, bones, blood,
runs on mysteries, dreams,
115 the coming child.

I am hungry now
but the hospital atmosphere
prevents any real hunger.
The repressiveness of institutions
120 has trained my stomach.
Tell myself to relax and say,
"When you come out, child,
let's go dance in a while, okay?"

Look out the window
125 and see the sun
and the parking lot.

Remember I wanted to write
something about that old dog,
kind of skinny and pathetic,
130 been hanging around our home
for a while, a week or so,
write a story or poem about it.

And then she was born.

. . . I will tell her
135 about the Wisconsin Horse. . . .

She was born then.

"She's as pretty as a silver dollar,"
said Ed Marlow, a miner
in Eastern Kentucky about Caroline Kennedy.
140 "She's just plain folks."

Albermarle County Sheriff says,
"We found nekkid women
with nekkid pubic hair offensive."

July 5, 1973 is now and soon enough

145 You come forth
the color of a stone cliff
at dawn,
changing colors,
blue to red,
150 to all the colors of the earth.

Grandmother Spider speaks
laughter and growing
and weaving things and threading them
together to make life to wear,
155 all these, all these.

You come out, child,
naked as that cliff at sunrise,
shorn of anything
except spots of your mother's blood.
160 You kept blinking your eyes
and trying to catch your breath.

In five more days,
they will come,
singing, dancing,
165 bringing gifts,
the stones with voices,
the plants with bells.
They will come.

Child, they will come.

1992

STUDY QUESTIONS

1. Why does Ortiz make his poem conversational, even prosaic?
2. What tensions arise in the poem between the personal and public spheres, between different cultures, between people in different economic circumstances?
3. What is the mysterious "Wisconsin Horse"? Does the poem tell us enough to know for sure? If not, why?
4. At the end of the poem the speaker assures the newborn child that "they will come." Who are "they"?

16

THE SPEAKER'S VISION

Like other writers, poets find their **visions** in three basic sources: the world around them, their own experiences, and their inner vision of what is or might be. The speakers of their poems, who are charged with communicating these visions, may therefore be observers, recording scenes and experiences for our mutual pleasure and insight; or they may be visionaries, recasting real or imagined scenes to produce a new vision for our sharing.

We can see the distinction clearly enough in poems we have already read. For instance, we have already seen two types of reporters at work. The speakers in "Get Up and Bar the Door" and "The Cherry-Tree Carol" are most obviously reporters; they simply tell us what occurred and let us draw our own conclusions about it. The speakers of "We Real Cool" and "For a Lady I Know" are also reporters but are less obviously so, because we sense that the poets are not as objective as their speakers. The speakers provide no interpretation and show no emotion. But the poets' attitudes come through, nonetheless. Indeed, much of the effectiveness of these poems comes from the disparity between the speakers' objectivity and the poets' concern, a disparity felt by the reader as **irony**. But we will speak more thoroughly about that subject in the next chapter.

We can also recall poems in which the speaker was primarily a visionary; Emily Dickinson's poems come to mind here. "Tell All the Truth" is pure vision, having no objective scene or experience whatever as its starting point. Another visionary is the speaker of Ezra Pound's "These Fought in Any Case," who draws on visions of so many real or imagined soldiers that we soon lose all sense of individuals in the more compelling vision of the war itself.

These, then, are poems that mark the two extremes of the speaker's stance: the objective extreme and the visionary extreme. Between them come those poems (probably typical of the majority of poems) in which the speaker is both reporter and interpreter. These poems balance what is seen and what is felt, allowing neither to overwhelm the other. Their speakers report on what is happening while explaining or suggesting its implications. Thus "There's a Certain Slant of Light" conveys its atmospheric sensation most vividly by interpreting its spiritual overtones. And poems such as "in Just-," and "I Knew a Woman" blend recollection and response so perfectly that it's hard to say where one stops and the other begins. Through the speaker's emotional response, the vision is made real for us; reporter, responder, and interpreter are one.

The poems we will look at in this chapter blend objective and visionary stances, observation and interpretation. Take careful note of the speaker's character and stance within each poem. Before you answer any of the questions, make sure you know what sort of person is speaking, to what the speaker is responding, and how much of the speaker's response is to things outside himself or herself and how much to inner visions or emotions.

William Wordsworth

(1770–1850)

See page 339 for a biographical note on the author.

I Wandered Lonely as a Cloud

I wandered lonely as a cloud
That floats on high o'er vales and hills,
When all at once I saw a crowd,
A host, of golden daffodils;
5 Beside the lake, beneath the trees,
Fluttering and dancing in the breeze.

Continuous as the stars that shine
And twinkle on the Milky Way,
They stretched in never-ending line
10 Along the margin of a bay:
Ten thousand saw I at a glance,
Tossing their heads in sprightly dance.

The waves beside them danced; but they
Outdid the sparkling waves in glee;
15 A poet could not but be gay,
In such a jocund company;
I gazed—and gazed—but little thought
What wealth the show to me had brought:

For oft, when on my couch I lie
20 In vacant or in pensive mood,
They flash upon that inward eye
Which is the bliss of solitude;
And then my heart with pleasure fills,
And dances with the daffodils.

1807

STUDY QUESTIONS

1. The major presence in this poem is that of the "host of golden daffodils" seen by the poet-speaker. How does the speaker describe and characterize the daffodils? What words and images does he use for them? How many of these words and images would normally be used for people?

    How active a role do the daffodils play in this vision—in the original scene and in their repeated appearances?

2. How does the speaker describe himself? What images does he use? In what activities does he depict himself? How active is his role in his relationship with the daffodils? in relation to the poem itself?

John Keats

(1795–1821)

John Keats started writing poetry at the age of eighteen, and he died just seven years later of tuberculosis. But in that short time he composed many of the most memorable of the major poems of the Romantic period. Encouraged by such writers as Leigh Hunt, Charles Lamb, and Percy Byssche Shelley, Keats shrugged off critical attacks on his 1817 poetic romance *Endymion* and went on to write "The Eve of St. Agnes," "La Belle Dame sans Merci," many fine sonnets, and his great odes. His poetry conveys a striking sensuousness, a strong identification of the observer with the objects of his contemplation, and a sure and memorable sense of phrasing. His awareness of his fatal illness combined with his youth made him acutely aware of a common Romantic theme: the interconnectedness of the erotic and death.

When I Have Fears

When I have fears that I may cease to be
   Before my pen has gleaned my teeming brain,
Before high-piled books, in charactery,[1]
   Hold like rich garners the full ripened grain;
5 When I behold, upon the night's starred face,
   Huge cloudy symbols of a high romance,
And think that I may never live to trace
   Their shadows, with the magic hand of chance;
And when I feel, fair creature of an hour,
10   That I shall never look upon thee more,
Never have relish in the faery power
   Of unreflecting love;—then on the shore

---

[1]characters, writing

Of the wide world I stand alone, and think
Till love and fame to nothingness do sink.

1818

STUDY QUESTIONS

1. Because the whole poem is one sentence, its syntax gets a bit complicated. Let's start, therefore, by examining it clause by clause, beginning with the three "when" clauses that make up the first eleven and a half lines of the poem: What are the first four lines concerned with? the second four? the third? How are the three tied together? (Who is the "fair creature of an hour"? Why might the speaker call her so at this point in the poem?)
2. What overtones do words like *rich, romance, magic,* and *faery* give to the poem? What contrast do they suggest between the poet's wishes and his sense of reality?
3. Then look at the final clause of the sentence—the last two and a half lines. What action does it show the speaker taking? How explicit are his feelings made? What are you left to fill in?

Walt Whitman

(1819–1892)

Walt Whitman was the great American bard whom Ralph Waldo Emerson had anticipated in his essays. Whitman's *Leaves of Grass,* first published in 1855, revolutionized American poetry. In his long, free verse lines, Whitman celebrated the whole "Kosmos" around him: working men and women, New York City, animals, evolution, sexuality. His work was a healthy shock to the tradition of gentlemanly and genteel poetry. When Whitman was advised by Emerson to tone down the sexuality of some of his poems to avoid adverse criticism, Whitman politely refused. During the Civil War he served as a wound dresser, letter writer, and companion to hundreds of seriously injured or dying men. In a political essay entitled "Democratic Vistas, 1871," he attacked the materialism and corruption he saw tainting American democracy after the war. Weakened by strokes during the last years of life, he became an often-photographed icon of the American bard: a handsome old man with sad, knowing eyes and a long, free-flowing beard.

A Noiseless Patient Spider

A noiseless patient spider,
I mark'd where on a little promontory it stood isolated,
Mark'd how to explore the vacant vast surrounding,
It launch'd forth filament, filament, filament, out of itself,
5 Ever unreeling down, ever tirelessly speeding them.

And you O my soul where you stand,
Surrounded, detached, in measureless oceans of space,
Ceaselessly musing, venturing, throwing, seeking the spheres to connect them,
Till the bridge you will need be form'd, till the ductile anchor hold,
10 Till the gossamer thread you fling catch somewhere, O my soul.

1868

STUDY QUESTIONS

1. Note how this poem is balanced between the first stanza, describing the speaker's vision of the spider, and the second stanza, describing his vision of his own soul. What comparison is made between the two? What characteristics and activities do they share?

2. Note that the speaker describes the spider as "isolated" and as needing or wishing "to explore the vacant vast surrounding." How apt is this as a description of an actual spider? How does it prepare the reader for the depiction of the speaker in the second stanza?

   Similarly, how apt or evocative is the description of the spider's activity? How does it complete the picture of the spider and prepare for the speaker's invocation to his soul?

3. With what words, images, and ideas does the speaker extend his vision of the spider so that it becomes a vision of his own soul's needs?

4. The poem's final lines speak of "the bridge you will need" and "the ductile anchor." What do you think these images represent? What is needed? What does the lack of detailed definition here and in the last line's "somewhere" do for your sense of the speaker's vision?

William Butler Yeats

(1865–1939)

See page 364 for a biographical note on the author.

An Irish Airman Foresees His Death[1]

I know that I shall meet my fate
Somewhere among the clouds above;
Those that I fight I do not hate,

---

[1]Major Robert Gregory, son of Yeats's friend and patroness Lady Augusta Gregory, was killed in action in 1918.

Those that I guard I do not love;
5 My country is Kiltartan Cross,[2]
My countrymen Kiltartan's poor,
No likely end could bring them loss
Or leave them happier than before.
Nor law, nor duty bade me fight,
10 Nor public men, nor cheering crowds,
A lonely impulse of delight
Drove to this tumult in the clouds;
I balanced all, brought all to mind,
The years to come seemed waste of breath,
15 A waste of breath the years behind
In balance with this life, this death.

1919

STUDY QUESTIONS

1. Yeats's poem is "visionary" in the sense that it foretells an event that has not yet happened. Comment on how this element of precognition adds an eerie power to the speaker's vision of the world.
2. How does the poem contrast the private motives of the speaker with the usual "public" motives for going to war? How are these motives complicated by the speaker's nationality?

Robert Frost

(1874–1963)

See page 367 for a biographical note on the author.

Two Tramps in Mud Time

Out of the mud two strangers came
And caught me splitting wood in the yard.
And one of them put me off my aim
By hailing cheerily "Hit them hard!"
5 I knew pretty well why he dropped behind
And let the other go on a way.

---

[2]Kiltartan is an Irish village near Coole Park, the estate of the Gregorys.

I knew pretty well what he had in mind:
He wanted to take my job for pay.

Good blocks of oak it was I split,
10 As large around as the chopping block;
And every piece I squarely hit
Fell splinterless as a cloven rock.
The blows that a life of self-control
Spares to strike for the common good,
15 That day, giving a loose to my soul,
I spent on the unimportant wood.

The sun was warm but the wind was chill.
You know how it is with an April day
When the sun is out and the wind is still,
20 You're one month on in the middle of May.
But if you so much as dare to speak,
A cloud comes over the sunlit arch,
A wind comes off a frozen peak,
And you're two months back in the middle of March.

25 A bluebird comes tenderly up to alight
And turns to the wind to unruffle a plume,
His song so pitched as not to excite
A single flower as yet to bloom.
It is snowing a flake: and he half knew
30 Winter was only playing possum.
Except in color he isn't blue,
But he wouldn't advise a thing to blossom.

The water for which we may have to look
In summertime with a witching wand,
35 In every wheelrut's now a brook,
In every print of a hoof a pond.
Be glad of water, but don't forget
The lurking frost in the earth beneath
That will steal forth after the sun is set
40 And show on the water its crystal teeth.

The time when most I loved my task
These two must make me love it more
By coming with what they came to ask.
You'd think I never had felt before
45 The weight of an ax-head poised aloft,
The grip on earth of outspread feet,
The life of muscles rocking soft
And smooth and moist in vernal heat.

Out of the woods two hulking tramps
50   (From sleeping God knows where last night,
But not long since in the lumber camps).
They thought all chopping was theirs of right.
Men of the woods and lumberjacks,
They judged me by their appropriate tool.
55   Except as a fellow handled an ax
They had no way of knowing a fool.

Nothing on either side was said.
They knew they had but to stay their stay
And all their logic would fill my head:
60   As that I had no right to play
With that was another man's work for gain.   .
My right might be love but theirs was need.
And where the two exist in twain
Theirs was the better right—agreed.

65   But yield who will to their separation,
My object in living is to unite
My avocation and my vocation
As my two eyes make one in sight.
Only where love and need are one,
70   And the work is play for mortal stakes,
Is the deed ever really done
For Heaven and the future's sakes.

1936

STUDY QUESTIONS

Frost's poem begins with a detailed description of an incident, and ends with as explicit a vision of the speaker's "goal in living" as we've met yet. How does this final vision grow out of the incident?

1. Consider how the speaker presents the incident: how he describes the physical scene, the tramps, his own emotions and sensations.
2. Notice the particular descriptions of the wood, sun and wind, bluebird, and water, and of the speaker himself in the sixth stanza. How do these create a sense of "love" to buttress the speaker's claim to love in the sixth and final stanzas?
3. Consider the speaker's voice: its rhythms and phrasings, its appeal to common knowledge with its audience, its blend of detailed observation and of interpretation, of seriousness and humor. What role does the voice play in determining your reaction to the poem?

4. Consider the speaker's proclamation in the final verse. How would you paraphrase it? Does it seem a fitting vision to close this poem? Is it a vision with which you yourself might be comfortable? Why or why not?

Garrett Hongo

(1951–   )

Garrett Hongo was born in Hawaii, but his family moved several times, finally settling in the Japanese community in Los Angeles. Hongo graduated from Claremont College and received an M.F.A. from the University of California at Irvine. He is one of the most productive Asian American poets writing today. His work is frequently an exploration of his complex ethnic roots and his anthropological sense of how human beings develop and maintain their identities.

Something Whispered in the *Shakuhachi*[1]

No one knew the secret of my flutes,
and I laugh now
because some said
I was enlightened.
5 But the truth is
I'm only a gardener
who before the War
was a dirt farmer and learned
how to grow the bamboo
10 in ditches next to the fields,
how to leave things alone
and let the silt build up
until it was deep enough to stink
bad as night soil, bad
15 as the long, witch-grey
hair of a ghost.

No secret in that.

My land was no good, rocky,
and so dry I had to sneak
20 water from the whites,
hacksaw the locks off the chutes at night,

---

[1]traditional Japanese bamboo flute

and blame Mexicans, Filipinos,
or else some wicked spirit
of a migrant, murdered in his sleep
25   by sheriffs and wanting revenge.
Even though they never believed me,
it didn't matter—no witnesses,
and my land was never thick with rice,
only the bamboo
30   growing lush as old melodies
and whispering like brush strokes
against the fine scroll of wind.

I found some string in the shed
or else took a few stalks
35   and stripped off their skins,
wove the fibers, the floss,
into cords I could bind
around the feet, ankles, and throats
of only the best bamboos.
40   I used an ice pick for an awl,
a fish knife to carve finger holes,
and a scythe to shape the mouthpiece.

I had my flutes.

When the War came,
45   I told myself I lost nothing.
My land, which was barren,
was not actually mine but leased
(we could not own property)
and the shacks didn't matter.

50   What did were the power lines nearby
and that sabotage was suspected.

What mattered to me
were the flutes I burned
in a small fire
55   by the bath house.

All through Relocation,
in the desert where they put us,

at night when the stars talked
and the sky came down
60 and drummed against the mesas,
I could hear my flutes
wail like fists of wind
whistling through the barracks.
I came out of Camp,
65 a blanket slung over my shoulder,
found land next to this swamp,
planted strawberries and beanplants,
planted the dwarf pines and tended them,
got rich enough to quit
70 and leave things alone,
let the ditches clog with silt again
and the bamboo grow thick as history.

So, when it's bad now,
when I can't remember what's lost
75 and all I have for the world to take
means nothing,
I go out back of the greenhouse
at the far end of my land
where the grasses go wild
80 and the arroyos come up
with cat's-claw and giant dahlias,
where the children of my neighbors
consult with the wise heads
of sunflowers, huge against the sky,
85 where the rivers of weather
and the charred ghosts of old melodies
converge to flood my land
and sustain the one thicket
of memory that calls for me
90 to come and sit
among the tall canes
and shape full-throated songs
out of wind, out of bamboo,
out of a voice
95 that only whispers.

1982

STUDY QUESTIONS

1. Hongo's poem concerns the "relocation" of Japanese Americans to intern-
   ment camps for the duration of World War II when American officials
   feared that Japanese American citizens might commit acts of sabotage in
   support of Japan. Discuss the complex attitude of the speaker of the poem,
   who reflects back on having been in one of the camps.
2. What do his flutes symbolize?
3. What does the poem have to say about the idea of ownership—of one's
   land, one's cultural heritage, of history?

17

PROTEST AND SOCIAL COMMENT

Protest poems do not celebrate the beautiful; they rage at ugliness—at racial hatred, sexual violence, cultural chauvinism, the ultimate hideousness of war. The protest poem is a cry from a wounded heart, an impassioned condemnation of injustices in a particular place and time. The narrator of such a poem is often difficult to distinguish from the author, who usually writes from an openly autobiographical stance. The poet almost always seems to be saying: "I was there. I saw these terrible things with my own eyes—and they must not continue." This sharp location in place and time, combined with the angry passion of the poet and vivid, often disturbing language, gives poems of protest their special power. Wilfred Owen's "Dulce et Decorum Est" and E. E. Cummings's " 'next to of course god america i" are reactions to World War I, whereas the other poems in this chapter reflect contemporary concerns about racial strife, loss of cultural heritage, and violence against women.

Implicit in poems of protest is the idea of being in some sort of minority: Owen and Cummings were individual soldiers trying to sound warnings to their propagandized countrymen about the madness of mechanized slaughter in the trench warfare of World War I. In Audre Lorde's "Power," the speaker is obviously an African American who is outraged by a white policeman's acquittal in court for shooting a ten-year-old black child to death in Queens. Joy Harjo's "Anchorage" speaks to the plight of another American minority: Native Americans who must watch Alaska taken over by corporations and all the social ills of contemporary society. Marge Piercy's "Rape Poem" graphically demonstrates that even members of a majority (women outnumber men) may have to use the protest poem as a weapon of self-defense.

Although protest poems may be open to the charge of being didactic—of subverting aesthetics to get a message across—they insist that aestheticism divorced from social concerns is empty at best. Moreover, although poems of protest typically sound bleak or even desparing, at the core they carry at least the implicit hope that things can get better if enough people are made aware of an injustice and are motivated to eliminate it.

Audre Lorde

(1934–1992)

Audre Lorde attended Hunter College and received an M.L.S. from Columbia University in 1961. She married, had two children, divorced, became the librarian at the City University of New York, "came out" as a lesbian, and finally took posts at Tougaloo College and the City University of New York. Her poetry is assertive, often deliberately abrasive and confrontational. It often celebrates the power of strong black women.

Power

The difference between poetry and rhetoric
is being
ready to kill
yourself
5   instead of your children.

I am trapped on a desert of raw gunshot wounds
and a dead child dragging his shattered black
face off the edge of my sleep
blood from his punctured cheeks and shoulders
10   is the only liquid for miles and my stomach
churns at the imagined taste while
my mouth splits into dry lips
without loyalty or reason
thirsting for the wetness of his blood
15   as it sinks into the whiteness
of the desert where I am lost
without imagery or magic
trying to make power out of hatred and destruction
trying to heal my dying son with kisses
20   only the sun will bleach his bones quicker.

The policeman who shot down a 10-year-old in Queens
stood over the boy with his cop shoes in childish blood
and a voice said "Die you little motherfucker" and
there are tapes to prove that. At his trial
25   this policeman said in his own defense
"I didn't notice the size or nothing else
only the color," and
there are tapes to prove that, too.

Today that 37-year-old white man with 13 years of police forcing
30   has been set free

by 11 white men who said they were satisfied
justice had been done
and one black woman who said
"They convinced me" meaning
35 they had dragged her 4′10″ black woman's frame
over the hot coals of four centuries of white male approval
until she let go the first real power she ever had
and lined her own womb with cement
to make a graveyard for our children.

40 I have not been able to touch the destruction within me.
But unless I learn to use
the difference between poetry and rhetoric
my power too will run corrupt as poisonous mold
or lie limp and useless as an unconnected wire
45 and one day I will take my teenaged plug
and connect it to the nearest socket
raping an 85-year-old white woman
who is somebody's mother
and as I beat her senseless and set a torch to her bed
50 a greek chorus will be singing in 3/4 time
"Poor thing. She never hurt a soul. What beasts they are."

1978

STUDY QUESTIONS

1. What does Lorde mean when she defines the difference between poetry and rhetoric as "being ready to kill/yourself/instead of your children"?
2. How does Lorde use a series of numbers to add power to the poem?
3. What does the conclusion of the poem say about how violence and injustice compound themselves—about how one wrong breeds others?

Joy Harjo

(1951–)

Joy Harjo is a Native American born in the Creek tribe in Tulsa, Oklahoma. She received an M.F.A. degree from the University of Iowa Writers' Workshop. She currently teaches at the University of Colorado. Native American themes of dispossession, pride in the difficult task of preserving culture, and a lyricism of the open spaces of the Southwest characterize her work.

Anchorage

for Audre Lorde

This city is made of stone, of blood, and fish.
There are Chugach Mountains[1] to the east
and whale and seal to the west.
It hasn't always been this way, because glaciers
5 who are ice ghosts create oceans, carve earth
and shape this city here, by the sound.
They swim backwards in time.

Once a storm of boiling earth cracked open
the streets, threw open the town.
10 It's quiet now, but underneath the concrete
is the cooking earth,
                              and above that, air
which is another ocean, where spirits we can't see
are dancing   joking   getting full
15 on roasted caribou, and the praying
goes on, extends out.

Nora and I go walking down 4th Avenue
and know it is all happening.
On a park bench we see someone's Athabascan[2]
20 grandmother, folded up, smelling like 200 years
of blood and piss, her eyes closed against some
unimagined darkness, where she is buried in an ache
in which nothing makes
                              sense.

25 We keep on breathing, walking, but softer now,
the clouds whirling in the air above us.
What can we say that would make us understand
better than we do already?
Except to speak of her home and claim her
30 as our own history, and know that our dreams
don't end here, two blocks away from the ocean
where our hearts still batter away at the muddy shore.

---

[1]A range extending about 280 miles along the coast of south Alaska just above the panhandle;
Chugach Eskimo (Ahtnas) reside there.
[2]Athabascan is a complicated but widespread Indian language, part of the Na-Dene Indian language
superstock of North America. Indians speak Athabascan in the sub-Arctic interior of Alaska, along
the Pacific Northwest Coast (Tlingit of Alaska panhandle, Tolowa of Oregon, and Hupa of California), and in the American Southwest (Apache and Navajo).

And I think of the 6th Avenue jail, of mostly Native
and Black men, where Henry told about being shot at
35 eight times outside a liquor store in L.A., but when
the car sped away he was surprised he was alive,

no bullet holes, man, and eight cartridges strewn
on the sidewalk
            all around him.

40 Everyone laughed at the impossibility of it,
but also the truth. Because who would believe
the fantastic and terrible story of all of our survival
those who were never meant
                to survive?

1983

STUDY QUESTIONS

1. How are Anchorage's past and present contrasted?
2. One line in the poem, "Once a storm of boiling earth cracked open/the streets, threw open the town," refers to the great earthquake that struck Alaska in 1964. Why does Harjo bring in this detail?
3. How does the anecdote about the man who was shot at eight times but not hit by any of the bullets fit into the poem?

Marge Piercy

(1936–   )

See page 349 for a biographical note on the author.

Rape Poem

There is no difference between being raped
and being pushed down a flight of cement steps
except that the wounds also bleed inside.

There is no difference between being raped
5 and being run over by a truck
except that afterward men ask if you enjoyed it.

There is no difference between being raped
and being bit on the ankle by a rattlesnake
except that people ask if your skirt was short
10 and why you were out alone anyhow.

There is no difference between being raped
and going head first through a windshield
except that afterward you are afraid
not of cars
15 but half the human race.

The rapist is your boyfriend's brother.
He sits beside you in the movies eating popcorn.
Rape fattens on the fantasies of the normal male
like a maggot in garbage.

20 Fear of rape is a cold wind blowing
all of the time on a woman's hunched back.
Never to stroll alone on a sand road through pine woods,
never to climb a trail across a bald
without that aluminum in the mouth
25 when I see a man climbing toward me.

Never to open the door to a knock
without that razor just grazing the throat.
The fear of the dark side of hedges,
the back seat of the car, the empty house
30 rattling keys like a snake's warning.
The fear of the smiling man
in whose pocket is a knife.
The fear of the serious man
in whose fist is locked hatred.

35 All it takes to cast a rapist to be able to see your body
as jackhammer, as blowtorch, as adding-machine-gun.
All it takes is hating that body
your own, your self, your muscle that softens to flab.

All it takes is to push what you hate,
40 what you fear onto the soft alien flesh.
To bucket out invincible as a tank
armored with treads without senses
to possess and punish in one act,
to rip up pleasure, to murder those who dare
45 live in the leafy flesh open to love.

1982

STUDY QUESTIONS

1. "Rape Poem" is painfully graphic in its images. Does this seem justified, or is the poet simply being excessive?
2. Identify the metaphors and similes in the poem and discuss how they contribute to its theme.

Wilfred Owen

(1893–1918)

Wilfred Owen wrote war poetry that is all the more compelling because Owen was killed in World War I. Along with his friend Siegfried Sassoon, he responded to the horrors of what he experienced with powerful, ironic, compassionate poems that did not spare the grim details of war—mustard gas attacks, screaming shells, "the stuttering rifles' rapid rattle."

Dulce et Decorum Est

Bent double, like old beggars under sacks,
Knock-kneed, coughing like hags, we cursed through sludge,
Till on the haunting flares we turned our backs
And towards our distant rest began to trudge.
5 Men marched asleep. Many had lost their boots
But limped on, blood-shod. All went lame; all blind;
Drunk with fatigue; deaf even to the hoots
Of tired, outstripped Five-Nines that dropped behind.

Gas! Gas! Quick, boys!—An ecstasy of fumbling,
10 Fitting the clumsy helmets just in time;
But someone still was yelling out and stumbling
And flound'ring like a man in fire or lime . . .
Dim, through the misty panes and thick green light,
As under a green sea, I saw him drowning.
15 In all my dreams, before my helpless sight,
He plunges at me, guttering, choking, drowning.

If in some smothering dreams you too could pace
Behind the wagon that we flung him in,
And watch the white eyes writhing in his face,
20 His hanging face, like a devil's sick of sin;
If you could hear, at every jolt, the blood
Come gargling from the froth-corrupted lungs,
Obscene as cancer, bitter as the cud
Of vile, incurable sores on innocent tongues,—

25 My friend, you would not tell with such high zest
To children ardent for some desperate glory,
The old Lie: Dulce et decorum est
Pro patria mori.

1919

STUDY QUESTIONS

1. How does the poem systematically undercut traditional heroic images of war?
2. Why does Owen directly address the reader as "you" and "my friend" in the poem's last stanza?
3. The Latin passage that concludes the poem translates as: "It is sweet and proper to die for one's country." Why do you think Owen did not translate it for the reader?

E. E. Cummings

(1894–1962)

See page 328 for a biographical note on the author.

"next to of course god america i

"next to of course god america i
love you land of the pilgrims' and so forth oh
say can you see by the dawn's early my
country 'tis of centuries come and go
5 and are no more what of it we should worry
in every language even deafanddumb
thy sons acclaim your glorious name by gorry
by jingo by gee by gosh by gum
why talk of beauty what could be more beaut-
10 iful than these heroic happy dead
who rushed like lions to the roaring slaughter
they did not stop to think they died instead
then shall the voice of liberty be mute?"

He spoke. And drank rapidly a glass of water

1904

STUDY QUESTIONS

1. Collage is a visual art form combing bits of newspaper, photos, and small "found objects." What does Cummings's poem have in common with collage?
2. How might you punctuate the poem to clarify its meaning?

Adrienne Rich

(1929–)

Adrienne Rich, raised in an encouraging and demanding family, won early praise for her poetry. W. H. Auden selected her as the winner of the Yale Younger Poets award, and he wrote a glowing preface for her first collection, *A Change of World* (1951). Rich traveled to Europe on a Guggenheim Fellowship, then returned to America and married. She and her husband, Harvard economist Alfred Conrad, had three sons, whom Rich raised at home in the 1950s. Her frustrations with finding little time for her own work are evident in *Snapshots of a Daughter-in-Law* (1963). Her carefully crafted poems became freer, more political, more angry. In the 1960s her feminism became the overt focus of her poetry. In 1974 she won the National Book Award for her work. Few poets have so effectively combined technical mastery with political passion as Rich has.

Hunger

(For Audre Lorde)

1.

A fogged hill-scene on an enormous continent,
intimacy rigged with terrors,
a sequence of blurs the Chinese painter's ink-stick planned,
a scene of desolation comforted
5　by two human figures recklessly exposed,
leaning together in a sticklike boat
in the foreground. Maybe we look like this,
I don't know. I'm wondering
whether we even have what we think we have—
10　lighted windows signifying shelter,
a film of domesticity
over fragile roofs. I know I'm partly somewhere else—
huts strung across a drought-stretched land
not mine, dried breasts, mine and not mine, a mother
15　watching my children shrink with hunger.
I live in my Western skin,
my Western vision, torn

and flung to what I can't control or even fathom.
Quantify suffering, you could rule the world.

2.

20 They can rule the world while they can persuade us
our pain belongs in some order.
Is death by famine worse than death by suicide,
than a life of famine and suicide, if a black lesbian dies,
if a white prostitute dies, if a woman genius
25 starves herself to feed others,
self-hatred battening on her body?
Something that kills us or leaves us half-alive
is raging under the name of an "act of god"
in Chad, in Niger, in the Upper Volta—
30 yes, that male god that acts on us and on our children,
that male State that acts on us and on our children
till our brains are blunted by malnutrition,
yet sharpened by the passion for survival,
our powers expanded daily on the struggle
35 to hand a kind of life on to our children,
to change reality for our lovers
even in a single trembling drop of water.

3.

We can look at each other through both our lifetimes
like those two figures in the sticklike boat
40 flung together in the Chinese ink-scene;
even our intimacies are rigged with terror.
Quantify suffering? My guilt at least is open,
I stand convicted by all my convictions—
you, too. We shrink from touching
45 our power, we shrink away, we starve ourselves
and each other, we're scared shitless
of what it could be to take and use our love,
hose it on a city, on a world,
to wield and guide its spray, destroying
50 poisons, parasites, rats, viruses—
like the terrible mothers we long and dread to be.

4.

The decision to feed the world
is the real decision. No revolution
has chosen it. For that choice requires
55 that women shall be free.

I choke on the taste of bread in North America
but the taste of hunger in North America
is poisoning me. Yes, I'm alive to write these words,
to leaf through Kollwitz's women
60 huddling the stricken children into their stricken arms
the "mothers" drained of milk, the "survivors" driven
to self-abortion, self-starvation, to a vision
bitter, concrete, and wordless.
I'm alive to want more than life,
65 want it for others starving and unborn,
to name the deprivations boring
into my will, my affections, into the brains
of daughters, sisters, lovers caught in the crossfire
of terrorists of the mind.
70 In the black mirror of the subway window
hangs my own face, hollow with anger and desire.
Swathed in exhaustion, on the trampled newsprint,
a woman shields a dead child from the camera.
The passion to be inscribes her body.
75 Until we find each other, we are alone.

1984

STUDY QUESTIONS

1. How does the Chinese painting the narrator describes in stanza 1 relate to the poem's overall theme?
2. In stanza 2, the narrator identifies at least two enemies of those around the world who are suffering. Who are these enemies? Do you think the narrator is fair to blame them?
3. In stanzas 3 and 4, the poem turns to the narrator's sense of her own guilt. How does she feel she has failed to help her "sisters" around the world? What is the step she must take if she is to bridge the gap between herself and those less fortunate?

Ishmael Reed

(1938–   )

Ishmael Reed is one of the most experimentally daring poet-novelists on the literary scene. He borrows from both high and popular culture in producing a sort of literary jazz fusion of conflicting and usually hilarious forms. While African American themes dominate his work, he often seems just as critical of black attitudes and politics as he is of those of whites.

Al Capone in Alaska

or
hoodoo ecology vs the judeo-
christian tendency to *let em*
have it!

5 The Eskimo hunts
the whale & each year
the whale flowers for the
Eskimo.
This must be love baby!
10 One receiving with respect
from a Giver who was
plenty.
There is no hatred here.
There is One Big Happy
15 Family here.

American & Canadian Christians
submachine gun the whales.
They gallantly sail out &
shoot them as if the Pacific
20 were a Chicago garage on
St. Valentine's day

1973

STUDY QUESTIONS

1. Reed contrasts the native Eskimo culture in Alaska with the very different non-native Western culture of Canada and America, both of which originated in Europe. He obviously favors the Eskimo ways of living in their environment. What choices of diction make this preference obvious?
2. Do you think Reed's depiction of the two cultures is fair, or is it a didactic oversimplification?
3. What is the significance of the poem's title? To what event is it and the events described in the final stanza an allusion?

18

BEYOND THE SPEAKER:
THE DOUBLE VISION OF IRONY

Irony exists whenever we say one thing and mean the opposite. "An exam? What fun!" is an ironic statement. More generally, irony exists whenever we feel a disparity between what someone says or thinks and what we know to be the truth. Irony can be intentional or unintentional, depending on whether the speaker means the statement to be ironic. A student who says, "A test today? What fun!" is almost certainly indulging in deliberate irony: he or she neither thinks of the test as fun nor expects others to think of it in that manner.

Suppose, however, that we are fellow students; suppose that you know (but I don't) that an English test has been scheduled for today; and suppose that I now say something like, "Boy, am I tired! I think I'll sleep through English class today!" This is unintentional irony. I am seriously planning to sleep. You know, however, that I will *not* be sleeping through English class. Instead, I will be cudgeling my tired brain, trying to pass an unexpected exam. In this case, it is your perception (as audience) that creates the irony. You know (as I, the innocent speaker, cannot know) how far from reality my words and expectations are.

The emotions of irony arise from our perceptions of a conflict between intent or ideal and reality. The technique of irony consists of creating a parallel disparity in words, by creating an opposition between the apparent meaning of the words and their ironic significance. Always there is some hint of pain in irony, some overtone of pity or anger. And always the emotion is a shared one: shared between reader and speaker if the irony is intentional, shared between reader and writer if it is not.

In responding to irony, then, we are aligning ourselves with someone whose perceptions we share, having been invited—as one right-thinking person by another—to share both the ironist's view of the subject and the emotions of scorn or pity or rage that go with it. Always, therefore, there will be some hint of argument (implicit or explicit) in an ironic poem. And always, the use of irony will produce some distancing of effect, as we stand back and judge the presented disparity.

Beyond these basic facts, however, we will see that irony is a technique that allows many variations of **meaning**, **tone**, and **effect**. As with most definitions, when we have defined a poem as ironic, we have only begun to talk about its construction, its meaning, and its power to touch us.

When you have read the poems that follow, review them in order to answer the following questions:

1. What disparity is highlighted?
2. What ideals or beliefs that you hold are appealed to? Is the appeal explicit or implicit?
3. Is the speaker conscious or unconscious of the irony of his or her speech?
4. If there is more than one voice in the poem, how are they contrasted? What part does the contrast play in your sense of the poem's irony?
5. What range of feelings does the poem suggest?

Then discuss each poem more fully, making whatever points you think are most helpful in deciding what role the irony plays in your appreciation of the poem as a whole.

Adrienne Rich

(1929–   )

See page 395 for a biographical note on the author.

Aunt Jennifer's Tigers

Aunt Jennifer's tigers prance across a screen,
Bright topaz denizens of a world of green.
They do not fear the men beneath the tree;
They pace in sleek chivalric certainty.

5   Aunt Jennifer's fingers fluttering through her wool
Find even the ivory needle hard to pull.
The massive weight of Uncle's wedding band
Sits heavily upon Aunt Jennifer's hand.

When Aunt is dead, her terrified hands will lie
10 Still ringed with ordeals she was mastered by.
The tigers in the panel that she made
Will go on prancing, proud and unafraid.

1951

A. E. Housman

(1859–1936)

See page 347 for a biographical note on the author.

From **A Shropshire Lad**

When I Was One-and-Twenty

When I was one-and-twenty
    I heard a wise man say,
"Give crowns and pounds and guineas
    But not your heart away;

5 Give pearls away and rubies
    But keep you fancy free."
But I was one-and-twenty,
    No use to talk to me.

When I was one-and-twenty
10   I heard him say again,
"The heart out of the bosom
    Was never given in vain;

'Tis paid with sighs a plenty
    And sold for endless rue."
15 And I am two-and-twenty,
    And oh, 'tis true, 'tis true.

1939

Dorothy Parker

(1893–1967)

Dorothy Parker was a well-known wit in the New York literary circles of the 1940s and 1950s. She wrote poetry, fiction, and journalism and frequently had less-than-flattering but usually perfectly on-target things to say about the writers, movie stars, and aristocrats with whom she wined and dined in the Big Apple.

Résumé

Razors pain you;
Rivers are damp;
Acids stain you;
And drugs cause cramp.
5 Guns aren't lawful;
Nooses give;
Gas smells awful;
You might as well live.

1926

W. H. Auden

(1907–1973)

W. H. Auden, born in England and educated at Oxford, was influenced by such poets as T. S. Eliot and Gerard Manley Hopkins and became one of the most technically impressive and unpredictably innovative poets of the twentieth century. His poems show the intellectual influence of Sigmund Freud and Karl Marx, but, like Eliot's, are always a lively mixture of the intellectual and the colloquial. Auden wrote with feeling about the economic troubles of England, about the "unknown citizens" of his day who struggled to find meaning in a life on the "dole" (what Americans know as welfare). He also chronicled the affluent life in America of the 1950s—a period he dubbed "the age of anxiety." Auden became an American citizen in midlife, though he returned to live at Oxford in his last days.

The Unknown Citizen

(To JS/07/M/378
This Marble Monument
Is Erected by the State)

He was found by the Bureau of Statistics to be
One against whom there was no official complaint,
And all the reports on his conduct agree
That, in the modern sense of an old-fashioned word, he was a saint,
5 For in everything he did he served the Greater Community.
Except for the War till the day he retired
He worked in a factory and never got fired,
But satisfied his employers, Fudge Motors Inc.
Yet he wasn't a scab or odd in his views,
10 For his Union reports that he paid his dues,
(Our report on his Union shows it was sound)
And our Social Psychology workers found
That he was popular with his mates and liked a drink.
The Press are convinced that he bought a paper every day
15 And that his reactions to advertisements were normal in every way.
Policies taken out in his name prove that he was fully insured,
And his Health-card shows he was once in hospital but left it cured.
Both Producers Research and High-Grade Living declare
He was fully sensible to the advantages of the Instalment Plan
20 And had everything necessary to the Modern Man,
A phonograph, a radio, a car, and a frigidaire.
Our researchers into Public Opinion are content
That he held the proper opinions for the time of year;

When there was peace, he was for peace; when there was war, he went.
25 He was married and added five children to the population,
Which our Eugenist says was the right number for a parent of his generation,
And our teachers report that he never interfered with their education.
Was he free? Was he happy? The question is absurd:
Had anything been wrong, we should certainly have heard.

1940

Philip Larkin

(1922–1985)

Philip Larkin was born in Coventry, England, and studied literature at Oxford. For many years he served as a librarian at several universities, among them the University of Hull, where he lived a bachelor's life until his death in 1985. His poems are lean, unsentimental, often melancholy. As one of the leaders of "The Movement," he rejected the neo-Romantic style of such poets as William Butler Yeats and Dylan Thomas in favor of the unsparing realism of his favorite writer, Thomas Hardy. He confirmed his reputation as an important poet in 1964 with the publication of *The Witsun Weddings*, and again in 1974 with *High Windows*.

A Study of Reading Habits

When getting my nose in a book
Cured most things short of school,
It was worth ruining my eyes
5 To know I could still keep cool,
And deal out the old right hook
To dirty dogs twice my size.

Later, with inch-thick specs,
Evil was just my lark:
10 Me and my cloak and fangs
Had ripping times in the dark.
The women I clubbed with sex!
I broke them up like meringues.

Don't read much now: the dude
15 Who lets the girl down before
The hero arrives, the chap
Who's yellow and keeps the store,
Seem far too familiar. Get stewed:
Books are a load of crap.

1964

STUDY QUESTIONS

1. What sort of persona does Larkin create in this poem?
2. Discuss the "tough guy" diction in the poem. How does Larkin's use of it contribute to the poem's theme?
3. What ironies does the poem create?

Denise Levertov

(1923–1997)

See page 363 for a biographical note on the author.

Mid-American Tragedy

They want to be their own old vision
of Mom and Dad. They want their dying son
to be eight years old again, not a gay man,
not ill, not dying. They have accepted him,
5   they would say if asked, unlike some who shut
errant sons out of house and heart,
and this makes them preen a little, secretly;
but enough of that, some voice within them
whispers, even more secretly, *he's our kid,*
10 *Mom and Dad are going to give him*
what all kids long for, a trip to Disney World,
what fun, the best Xmas ever.
And he, his wheelchair strung with bottles and tubes,
glass and metal glittering in winter sun,
15 shivers and sweats and tries to breathe as *Jingle Bells*
pervades the air and his mother, his father,
chatter and still won't talk, won't listen,
will never listen, never give him
the healing silence
20 in which they could have heard
his questions, his answers,
his life at last.

1992

Imagery
19

SIMILES, METAPHORS, AND PERSONIFICATION

The three basic elements of any poem are the vision it embodies, the speaker who gives voice to the vision, and the language that creates voice and vision alike. (By stretching the terminology a bit, we could call them the three V's: vision, voice, and vocabulary.) In the preceding chapters, we examined the ways in which the language of a poem—its vocabulary, its connotations, its sounds—created and characterized the poem's speaker. Now it is time to look at the ways the language creates the vision.

Vision in literature always implies a shared vision. Originating in the writer's mind, the vision is first translated into words and then re-created in our minds, to be felt by us as it was felt by its writer. When we come to the end of a poem, therefore, the feeling we experience is likely to be a blend of recognition and surprise. We will have seen something familiar—perhaps even something of ourselves—as we have never seen it before.

Poets can go about creating this feeling in two ways. The first is to word their vision so precisely that we feel we are seeing things with a new closeness and clearness. This is the method Ezra Pound uses in "In a Station of the Metro" and Emily Dickinson employs in "There's a Certain Slant of Light."

The second method relies on figures of speech or on unexpected comparisons to lead us into making connections we may not have made before. Pound also uses this method in "In a Station of the Metro," where human "faces in the crowd" are seen as "petals on a wet black bough," beauty and impersonality mingling. It is Dickinson's method, too, when she describes her "certain slant of light" as being one that "oppresses, like the weight/Of cathedral tunes."

This trick of mingling appeals to different senses in a single image—of describing a sound in terms of color, or a sight in terms of sound or feel—is called **synaesthesia**. Rather than trying to define a type of light in terms of its appearance, Dickinson compares it to a sound. But she speaks of both in terms of weight that presses down physically or spiritually. The word *cathedral*, meanwhile, not only defines the solemn, religious music that parallels the "slant of light," but also prepares us for the image of "heavenly hurt" introduced in the next line. Thus the poem weaves its pattern of **imagery**.

We have, then, already met poems that make use of both the literal and the figurative **styles of imagery**. To make sure the contrast is clear, however, let's look at two poems on one subject and see how the language works in each.

405

Walt Whitman

(1819–1892)

See page 378 for a biographical note on the author.

The Dalliance of the Eagles

Skirting the river road, (my forenoon walk, my rest,)
Skyward in air a sudden muffled sound, the dalliance of the eagles,
The rushing amorous contact high in space together,
The clinching interlocking claws, a living, fierce, gyrating wheel,
5   Four beating wings, two beaks, a swirling mass tight grappling,
In tumbling turning clustering loops, straight downward falling,
Till o'er the river pois'd, the twain yet one, a moment's lull,
A motionless still balance in the air, then parting, talons loosing,
Upward again on slow-firm pinions slanting, their separate diverse flight,
10 She hers, he his, pursuing.

1880

Alfred, Lord Tennyson

(1809–1892)

Alfred, Lord Tennyson was enormously celebrated during his lifetime but critically de-
rided early in the twentieth century; his reputation has largely recovered in the present
day. Tennyson attended Cambridge, where he met Arthur Hallam, who would later become engaged to Tennyson's sister, then die suddenly in 1833. Tennyson's grief found an
outlet in *In Memoriam* (1850), a long poem not just about the loss of Hallam but about industrialism, evolution, and religion. Tennyson was a master of metrical effects and of the
epic pitch of poetry. *Idylls of the King* (1859; 1885) is perhaps his best-remembered late
work. Looking at once to the epic past and the uncertain technological future, Tennyson
was in many ways the most comprehensive and accomplished poet of the Victorian period.

The Eagle

He clasps the crag with crooked hands;
Close to the sun in lonely lands,
Ringed with the azure world, he stands.

The wrinkled sea beneath him crawls;
5   He watches from his mountain walls,
And like a thunderbolt he falls.

1851

Obviously, these are very dissimilar poems. One, talking of a single eagle that remains still throughout most of the poem, creates an atmosphere of space and solitude. The other, speaking of two eagles, seems a constant rush of motion. In part, it is the sound of the words the poets have chosen that creates these different atmospheres. Tennyson's words, lines, and sentences are all short, and the stop at the end of each line is strongly marked. Whitman uses longer lines, with less pronounced breaks between them; and his sentences are so involved and complex that they keep the reader's mind and voice in almost constant motion as dizzying as that of the eagles themselves. Yet the basic difference in the way these eagles are shown to us lies not in their motion or motionlessness, but rather in the imagery in which they are described.

If we go through each poem, noting carefully each descriptive term, we will discover a marked contrast. Whitman relies heavily on adjectives, particularly on participles (adjectives formed from verbs). *Clinching, interlocking, living, gyrating, beating, swirling, grappling, tumbling, turning, clustering, falling*—from these comes the poem's sense of action, as well as much of its power of description. The poet's stance is primarily one of **observation**. Taking a walk, he has been startled first by the "sudden muffled sound" and then by the sight of the eagles; and he describes sight and sound alike as carefully and vividly as he can:

> The clinching interlocking claws, a living, fierce, gyrating
>   wheel,
> Four beating wings, two beaks, a swirling mass tight
>   grappling,
> In tumbling turning clustering loops, straight downward
>   falling.

Tennyson's fragment, too, is pure description. But its phrasing and its imagery come as much from the poet's imagination as from his powers of observation. Where Whitman uses no words that could not, in sober prose, be applied to an eagle, Tennyson uses almost none that could. His eagle is presented largely in terms that compare it to other things: an old man, grown crooked with age; an explorer in "lonely lands"; a thunderbolt. By calling our attention to these other things, he draws on our feelings about them (respect, for instance, or awe) and uses those feelings to influence our feelings about the eagle itself. Thus, instead of a bird's "clinching . . . claws," Tennyson's eagle has "crooked hands." He "stands"—which, to some readers, may sound more human than birdlike—and "watches," as men and birds both do. Later, he "falls"—an ambiguous verb. The landscape in which he is pictured is similarly humanized. The lands are "lonely," the sea is "wrinkled" and "crawls." There is exaggeration (or **hyperbole**) as well. The eagle's perch is "close to the sun"; the sky against which he is seen is an entire "azure world"; the eagle falls "like a thunderbolt." High and remote, yet somehow in his very remoteness human, Tennyson's eagle presents a striking image of a being in lofty isolation.

By linking disparate things, by forcing us to think of one thing in terms of another, poets make us see those things in new ways, creating new images, calling forth unexpected emotions, fostering new insights. With homely and familiar images, they bring strange things closer to us, while with exotic images they cast new light on everyday things. Concrete images give vivid life to abstract ideas, whereas more abstract imagery suggests new significance for particular items or experiences. Poets can speak of their subjects in the most precise, closely fitting words they can find; or they can seek out unexpected, startling terms that will call our own imaginations and creative impulses into play. Because a poet's choices concerning diction and figurative language determine our sense of that poem—for example, the totally different feelings that Whitman's torrent of precisely denotative adjectives and Tennyson's careful balance of connotations of humanity, space, and isolation provoke—it will be worth our while to examine some of the techniques that poets use in the creation of imagery. Let us look, therefore, at some of the commoner forms of imagery found in poetry. Because comparisons are often the result of figurative speech, we will start with figures that are forms of comparison: the explicit comparisons, the simile and the metaphor; and the implicit ones, implied metaphor and personification.

Simile

A **simile** is a comparison and is always stated as such. You will always find *like, as, so,* or some such word of comparison within it. Usually, the things it compares resemble each other in only one or two ways, differing in all other respects. An eagle and a thunderbolt are not really much alike; yet the fact that both go from the sky to the ground can allow Tennyson to declare that "like a thunderbolt he falls." In the differences between the two lies the simile's power. The fact that a thunderbolt is so much swifter, so much more powerful and dangerous than the eagle, lends a sense of speed and power and danger to the eagle's fall. A simile may be as brief as the traditional "red as blood," or it may be considerably more complicated, as in this example from "Tell All the Truth":

> As Lightning to the Children eased
> With explanation kind
> The Truth must dazzle gradually
> Or every man be blind—

Notice the use of similes in the following poem.

Langston Hughes

(1902–1967)

Langston Hughes was the most influential of the artists of the "Harlem Renaissance" of the 1920s. His first collection of poems, *The Weary Blues* (1926), was a source of inspiration for a whole group of young black writers. Settling in New York, Hughes became the center of a group that included Countee Cullen, Arna Bontemps, and Zora Neal Hurston.

Hughes made use of spirituals, jazz and blues music, and African American speech in his poetry. He wrote fiction, plays, essays, and histories. His character "Jessie B. Simple" entertained black New Yorkers for years as a sly, satiric voice attacking racism and the privileges of the wealthy in the city.

Harlem

What happens to a dream deferred?

Does it dry up
like a raisin in the sun?
Or fester like a sore—
5 And then run?
Does it stink like rotten meat?
Or crust and sugar over—
like a syrupy sweet?

Maybe it just sags
10 like a heavy load.

Or does it explode?

1951

STUDY QUESTIONS

1. What relationship do the various similes have to each other and to the subject of the poem, as defined by the title and first line?
2. What has been done with the last simile? Why?

Metaphor and Implied Metaphor

Like similes, **metaphors** are direct comparisons of one object with another. In metaphors, however, the fusion between the two objects is more complete, for metaphor uses no "as" or "like" to separate the two things being compared. Instead, a metaphor simply declares that *A* "is" *B;* one element of the comparison becomes, for the moment at least, the other.

Some metaphors go even farther and omit the "is." They simply talk about *A* as if it were *B,* using terms appropriate to *B.* They may not even name *B* at all but rather let us guess what it is from the words being used. In this case, the metaphor becomes an **implied metaphor.**

Because a simile merely says that *A* is "like" *B,* it needs to find only one point or moment of similarity between two otherwise dissimilar objects in order to achieve its effect. (For example, the cherry that is "red as the blood" resembles blood in no other way.) Metaphors, in contrast, tend to make more detailed claims for closer likenesses between the subjects of their comparisons. Notice, for instance, how many points of similarity are suggested by the metaphors in the next two poems. Ask yourself, in each case, what points of comparison the metaphor makes openly or explicitly and what further points of comparison it suggests to you.

John Keats

(1795–1821)

See page 377 for a biographical note on the author.

On First Looking into Chapman's Homer

Much have I travelled in the realms of gold,
  And many goodly states and kingdoms seen;
  Round many western islands have I been
Which bards in fealty to Apollo hold.
5 Oft of one wide expanse had I been told
     That deep-browed Homer ruled as his demesne;
     Yet did I never breathe its pure serene
Till I heard Chapman speak out loud and bold:
Then felt I like some watcher of the skies
10   When a new planet swims into his ken;
Or like stout Cortez when with eagle eyes
     He stared at the Pacific—and all his men
  Looked at each other with a wild surmise—
     Silent, upon a peak in Darien.

1816

STUDY QUESTIONS

1. The vocabulary in the first eight lines of this poem is taken mostly from the Middle Ages and its system of feudalism: *realms* for *kingdoms,* for example; *bards* for *poets; fealty* for the system under which a nobleman would rule part of a country, being himself ruled by a king or a greater nobleman; and *demesne* for the nobleman's domain, the part of the country he ruled. *(Oft* for *often, serene* for *air,* and *ken* for *knowledge* are also old words that are no longer in daily use.) Apollo, on the other hand, comes from classical mythology, and is the god of poets. (He's also the god of the sun, but that doesn't particularly enter into this poem.) Homer is an ancient Greek poet and Chapman a sixteenth-century English poet who translated Homer's *Iliad* into English verse. The question therefore arises: why should Keats use

the language of the Middle Ages and the metaphor of traveling to talk about his joy in reading poetry and the great delight he felt when his discovery of Chapman's translation let him feel that he was really hearing Homer for the first time?

2. When Keats does discover Chapman's translation, two new similes occur to him that support the traveler metaphor. What is the first (ll. 9–10)? What sort of progression has been made: how does the new identity the poet feels resemble his earlier identity as traveler? How is it different? What sort of feelings go with each identity? (Note the phrase "a new planet"; why *new?*)

3. In lines 11–14, the second simile is set out. Whom does Keats feel like now? What kinds of feelings go with this third identity? How do they form a climax for the poem? (It was really Balboa, and not Cortez, who was the first European to see the Pacific Ocean. Does this make any difference to your enjoyment of the poem?)

Carl Sandburg

(1878–1967)

Carl Sandburg was a populist poet in the tradition of Walt Whitman. After working many odd jobs as a young man, in 1913 he settled in Chicago, a city undergoing a cultural renaissance featuring such diverse figures as architect Frank Lloyd Wright, novelist Theodore Dreiser, and poet Edgar Lee Masters. Sandburg celebrated in free verse the people on the margins of American life: immigrants, the poor, those with socialist rather than capitalist ideals. He often wrote of the painful dislocation of many workers by industrialization. Sandburg was one of the most widely read poets of the 1920s and 1930s.

Fog

The fog comes
on little cat feet.
It sits looking
over harbor and city
5 on silent haunches
and then moves on.

1916

Personification

Implied metaphors, being more compact and requiring the reader to share in their creation slightly more than regular metaphors do, are frequent in poetry. But one type appears so frequently that it has a name of its own. This is **personification**, the trick of talking about some nonhuman thing as if it were human. We saw personification in the "crooked hands" of Alfred, Lord Tennyson's "Eagle."

The poems in the rest of this chapter are notable for their figures of speech. They can thus serve both as exercises in identifying metaphors, similes, and implied metaphors, and as poems illustrating how these figures of speech can help create **tone** and **meaning** in poetry. Read each of the poems through at least once. Then go through the poem and note the figures of speech you find in it. Identify each one: is it a simile, a metaphor, an implied metaphor, a personification? Decide what elements make up the comparison: what is being compared to what? And jot down your ideas on why the poet might have wanted his or her readers to think about that comparison.

When you have done this, read the poem through once more. Then look again at the figures of speech you have found. Decide how each relates to the subject of the poem, and how each contributes to your sense of the speaker's feelings toward that subject. Decide, too, how many subjects of comparison there are. Is each subject compared to one other thing, or is one subject compared to several things?

If one subject is compared to one other thing, is that comparison developed at any length? If it is, what does its development lend your sense of the poem and its progression?

If one subject is compared to more than one other thing, or if several subjects of comparison exist, how are the different images fitted together? Are unrelated images juxtaposed for you to fit into some total picture, or does the speaker suggest some relationship of similarity or contrast between them? How does the **pattern of images** thus created help create your sense of the speaker's vision, of the poem's meaning or movement?

Finally, read the poem through once again to see whether you are satisfied with the conclusions you have come to, or whether you think there are other things that should be said about the poem or its imagery.

This may sound like a very complicated procedure. But the method of reading through, looking closely, and reading through again allows you to give attention to details of technique without losing your grip on the poem as a whole. When dealing with relatively simple poems, it's a handy practice. When dealing with more complex poetry, it's essential.

William Wordsworth

(1770–1850)

See page 339 for a biographical note on the author.

Composed upon Westminster Bridge, September 3, 1802

Earth has not anything to show more fair:
Dull would he be of soul who could pass by
A sight so touching in its majesty;

This City now doth, like a garment, wear
5   The beauty of the morning; silent, bare,
Ships, towers, domes, theaters, and temples lie
Open unto the fields, and to the sky;
All bright and glittering in the smokeless air.
Never did sun more beautifully steep
10 In his first splendor, valley, rock, or hill;
Ne'er saw I, never felt, a calm so deep!
The river glideth at his own sweet will:
Dear God! the very houses seem asleep;
And all that mighty heart is lying still!

1807

Emily Dickinson

(1830–1886)

See page 341 for a biographical note on the author.

I Like to See It Lap the Miles (#585)

I like to see it lap the Miles—
And lick the Valleys up—
And stop to feed itself at Tanks—
And then—prodigious step

5   Around a Pile of Mountains—
And supercilious peer
In Shanties—by the sides of Roads—
And then a Quarry pare

To fit its sides
10 And crawl between
Complaining all the while
In horrid—hooting stanza—
Then chase itself down Hill—

And neigh like Boanerges[1]—
15 Then—prompter than a Star
Stop—docile and omnipotent
At its own stable door—

1951

---

[1]Jesus' name for his apostles John and James; also used to refer to a loud-voiced preacher or speaker

A Narrow Fellow in the Grass

A narrow Fellow in the Grass
Occasionally rides—
You may have met Him—did you not
His notice sudden is—

5 The Grass divides as with a Comb—
A spotted shaft is seen—
And then it closes at your feet
And opens further on—

He likes a Boggy Acre
10 A floor too cool for Corn—
Yet when a Boy, and Barefoot—
I more than once at Noon
Have passed, I thought, a Whip lash
Unbraiding in the Sun
15 When stooping to secure it
It wrinkled, and was gone—

Several of Nature's People
I know, and they know me—
I feel for them a transport
20 Of cordiality—

But never met this Fellow
Attended, or alone
Without a tighter breathing
And Zero at the Bone—

1910

Nikki Giovanni

(1943–   )

See page 359 for a biographical note on the author.

Woman

she wanted to be a blade
of grass amid the fields
but he wouldn't agree
to be the dandelion

5 she wanted to be a robin singing
through the leaves
but he refused to be
her tree

she spun herself into a web
10 and   looking for a place to rest
turned to him
but he stood straight
declining to be her corner

she tried to be a book
15 but he wouldn't read

she turned herself into a bulb
but he wouldn't let her grow

she decided to become
a woman
20 and though he still refused
to be a man
she decided it was all
right

1978

Sylvia Plath

(1932–1963)

Sylvia Plath is remembered for her suicide, but she was a fine poet who produced many of her best works just before her death. She grew up in an academic family but had a troubled relationship with her father, a professor of German. After he died, Plath went to Smith College and won prizes for her early poems. On a Fulbright fellowship at Cambridge, she met English poet Ted Hughes, whom she married. The couple had two children and lived at times in England and at times in America. Plath struggled with her personal demons, the duties of raising children, and an increasingly unhappy marriage. She wrote all of this down in directly autobiographical poems that epitomized the "Confessional" school of poetry. Her work is raw, often shocking, metaphorically rich. She killed herself in 1963 in London.

Metaphors

I'm a riddle in nine syllables,
An elephant, a ponderous house,
A melon strolling on two tendrils.
O red fruit, ivory, fine timbers!

5 This loaf's big with its yeasty rising.
Money's new-minted in this fat purse.
I'm a means, a stage, a cow in calf.
I've eaten a bag of green apples,
Boarded the train there's no getting off.

1960

Most metaphors and similes have a certain timelessness to them. Wordsworth's vision of London asleep and Hughes's picture of energy turning angry in Harlem are both visions of something real and, therefore, enduring. In the following poem, however, the metaphorical vision is transitory and illusory. Nonetheless, it illuminates the speaker's view of the world. Note the movement of the imagery from metaphorical to literal within the poem. Consider how it expresses and develops the statement made by the poem's title. (Note particularly the "difficult balance" in the last line. What meanings does that phrase have here at the end of the poem?) Then discuss how the metaphor's statement and development create both the specific picture of the waking man and the wider vision that fills the speaker's mind.

Richard Wilbur

(1921–)

Richard Wilbur is an academic poet whose work is intellectual, poised, technically finished. He was educated at Amherst College and Harvard, and taught at Harvard, Wellesley, Wesleyan College, and Smith College. Avoiding the "confessional" route, Wilbur has been criticized by some critics as lacking in passion. But those who appreciate fine ironies and an almost classical sense of restraint will find both technical brilliance and soul in his work. He won the National Book Award in 1957 for *Things of this World*.

Love Calls Us to the Things of This World

The eyes open to a cry of pulleys,
And spirited from sleep, the astounded soul
Hangs for a moment bodiless and simple
As false dawn.
5   Outside the open window
The morning air is all awash with angels.

Some are in bed-sheets, some are in blouses,
Some are in smocks: but truly there they are.
Now they are rising together in calm swells
10 Of halcyon feeling, filling whatever they wear
With the deep joy of their impersonal breathing;

Now they are flying in place, conveying
The terrible speed of their omnipresence, moving
And staying like white water; and now of a sudden
15 They swoon down into so rapt a quiet
That nobody seems to be there.
                                    The soul shrinks

From all that it is about to remember,
From the punctual rape of every blessèd day,
20 And cries,
              "Oh, let there be nothing on earth but laundry,
Nothing but rosy hands in the rising steam
And clear dances done in the sight of heaven."

Yet, as the sun acknowledges
25 With a warm look the world's hunks and colors,
The soul descends once more in bitter love
To accept the waking body, saying now
In a changed voice as the man yawns and rises,

"Bring them down from their ruddy gallows;
30 Let there be clean linen for the backs of thieves;
Let lovers go fresh and sweet to be undone,
And the heaviest nuns walk in a pure floating
Of dark habits,
                keeping their difficult balance."

1956

20

SYMBOL AND ALLEGORY

Similes and metaphors make their comparisons quickly and explicitly. They occupy a line or two; and then they are set, ready for further development, but equally ready to be superseded by another simile or metaphor. How the poet uses them, or how many are used within a poem, is up to the poet. The range of possibilities is wide.

Symbol and allegory, however, tend to dominate the poems in which they appear. Moreover, they usually stand alone: one symbol or allegory is usually the most any given poem can support.

Similes and metaphors make us look more attentively at the poem's subject: at the beauty of an evening or early morning scene, at laundry on a clothesline, at a mirror. They appeal directly to our senses: "a cry of pulleys," a "cowling plated forehead." Often, they illuminate some larger question: "What happens to a dream deferred?" What does it mean to be a woman or a lover? Yet they illuminate the larger question by keeping our attention on the things they describe: the rotten meat and the clean laundry.

Symbols and allegories, on the other hand, urge us to look beyond the literal significance of the poem's statements or action. "The Tyger" does not call our attention to tigers so much as to the awesome qualities suggested.

When we meet with imagery that seems to be calling to us to look beyond the immediate event and its emotional ramifications, we may suspect we are dealing with symbol or allegory. But how are we to distinguish which we are dealing with?

An **allegory** always tells of an action. The events of that action should make sense literally but make more profound sense through a second, allegorical, interpretation. Usually that second interpretation will have a spiritual or a psychological significance; for allegories are particularly good at using physical actions to describe the workings of the human mind and spirit.

In allegory, then, we are given a story that presents a one-to-one correspondence between some physical action (most often an encounter of some kind) and some second action (usually psychological or spiritual), with each step in the literal tale corresponding to a parallel step on the allegorical level. **Symbolism** may likewise present us with a tale or an action. But it may equally well present us with a description of some unchanging being or object. And it is more likely to suggest several possible interpretations than it is to insist on a single one.

Some symbols, however, are conventional; and these will suggest a single interpretation. "The Lamb," relying on the traditional association of the lamb as Christ, is an example of conventional symbolism in poetry. Alternatively, the poet may invent a symbol and provide its interpretation as well. In general, however, symbols in poetry ask the reader to interpret them. The interaction between poet and reader thus admits the greatest possible freedom of suggestion and response.

As you read the following poems, decide whether you think them better interpreted symbolically or allegorically. How would you discuss the poem's language, imagery, and progression to support your interpretation?

George Herbert

(1593–1633)

George Herbert was educated at Cambridge and seemed headed for a political career, but instead he became a minister is Salisbury, distinguishing himself there for his devotion to the poor and the sincerity of his faith. Like John Donne, he is usually classified as a metaphysical poet; unlike Donne, however, Herbert has a sweetness of expression and temper that balance his intellectual fascination with extravagant images. Few poets in English—perhaps only Gerard Manley Hopkins—can match Herbert for the purity and freshness of his religious poems.

Love (III)

Love bade me welcome; yet my soul drew back,
    Guilty of dust and sin.
But quick-eyed Love, observing me grow slack
    From my first entrance in,
5 Drew nearer to me, sweetly questioning
    If I lacked anything.

"A guest," I answered, "worthy to be here."
    Love said, "You shall be he."
"I, the unkind, ungrateful? Ah my dear,
10   I cannot look on Thee."
Love took my hand, and smiling, did reply,
    "Who made the eyes but I?"

"Truth, Lord, but I have marred them; let my shame
    Go where it doth deserve."
15 "And know you not," says Love, "who bore the blame?"
    "My dear, then I will serve."

"You must sit down," says Love, "and taste my meat."
     So I did sit and eat.

1633

Ralph Waldo Emerson

(1803–1882)

Ralph Waldo Emerson was the central figure in the American Literary Renaissance of the 1850s. In his transcendental essays, he set out the forward-looking, highly individualistic, optimistic ethic that inspired Henry David Thoreau, Walt Whitman, and to some extent Emily Dickinson, and against which Nathaniel Hawthorne and Herman Melville defined themselves in their own ways. Influenced by German idealism and oriental religion, Emerson argued that the intuition was a higher faculty than reason, and that through meditation on nature and on their own souls people could connect the divinity within themselves with the cosmic "oversoul." Insisting that "the sun is new each day," Emerson believed it was not necessary to be a slave to the past—that people could strike out in genuinely new directions. Thoreau put into practice what Emerson preached in his experiment in free living on Walden Pond. Emerson's essays are perhaps the most important philosophical statements in American literature.

Days

Daughters of Time, the hypocritic Days,
Muffled and dumb like barefoot dervishes,
And marching single in an endless file,
Bring diadems and fagots in their hands.
5 To each they offer gifts after his will,
Bread, kingdoms, stars, and sky that holds them all.
I, in my pleached garden, watched the pomp,
Forgot my morning wishes, hastily
Took a few herbs and apples, and the Day
10 Turned and departed silent. I, too late,
Under her solemn fillet saw the scorn.

1857

Edna St. Vincent Millay

(1892–1950)

See page 359 for a biographical note on the author.

First Fig

My candle burns at both ends;
    It will not last the night;
But ah, my foes, and oh, my friends—
    It gives a lovely light!

1922

Stephen Crane

(1871–1900)

Stephen Crane died before the age of thirty of tuberculosis, but he nevertheless had a remarkable literary career. Best known as the author of *The Red Badge of Courage* (1895), Crane adopted the aesthetic credo of the realists in depicting not just war but urban life with a gritty honesty designed to puncture windy platitudes. Bohemian in lifestyle, adventurous at heart, Crane won the intense loyalty of those who knew him with his bravery, generosity, and artistic integrity. His short stories are among the most frequently anthologized in American literature. He married a prostitute and lived with her in England in the years just before his death, years in which he enjoyed the friendship of such esteemed writers as Henry James and Joseph Conrad.

The Heart

In the desert
I saw a creature, naked, bestial,
Who, squatting on the ground,
Held his heart in his hands,
5 And ate of it.

I said, "Is it good, friend?"
"It is bitter—bitter," he answered;
"But I like it
Because it is bitter,
10 And because it is my heart."

1895

Allen Ginsberg

(1926–1997)

Allen Ginsberg is usually identified as one of the "Beat Poets" of the 1950s—"beat" as in "beatnik" and as in musical beat. Influenced by William Carlos Williams and Walt Whitman, Ginsberg brought his distinctive jazzy, existential, Zen-influenced style to prominence with poems like "Howl." He moved from his native New Jersey and established himself in San Francisco, befriending Lawrence Ferlinghetti at the famous City Light bookstore. In 1973 he won the National Book Award for *The Fall of America: Poems of These States.* Always the political activist, Ginsberg was often a presence on university campuses, giving lively poetry readings that both critiqued and celebrated America.

In back of the real

railroad yard in San Jose
    I wandered desolate
in front of a tank factory
    and sat on a bench
5 near the switchman's shack.

A flower lay on the hay on
    the asphalt highway
—the dread hay flower
    I thought—It had a
10 brittle black stem and
    corolla of yellowish dirty
spikes like Jesus' inchlong
    crown, and a soiled
dry center cotton tuft
15   like a used shaving brush
that's been lying under
    the garage for a year.

Yellow, yellow flower, and
    flower of industry,
20 tough spikey ugly flower,
    flower nonetheless,
with the form of the great yellow
    Rose in your brain!
This is the flower of the World.

1954

Langston Hughes

(1902–1967)

See page 408 for a biographical note on the author.

Mother to Son

Well, son, I'll tell you:
Life for me ain't been no crystal stair.
It's had tacks in it,
And splinters,
5   And boards torn up,
And places with no carpet on the floor—
Bare.
But all the time
I'se been a-climbin' on,
10   And reachin' landin's,
And turnin' corners,
And sometimes goin' in the dark
Where there ain't been no light.
So boy, don't you turn back
15   Don't you set down on the steps
'Cause you finds it's kinder hard.
Don't you fall now—
For I'se still goin', honey,
I'se still climbin',
20   And life for me ain't been no crystal stair.

1926

John Keats

(1795–1821)

See page 377 for a biographical note on the author.

Ode on a Grecian Urn

1

Thou still unravished bride of quietness,
    Thou foster-child of silence and slow time,

Sylvan historian, who canst thus express
  A flowery tale more sweetly than our rhyme:
5 What leaf-fringed legend haunts about thy shape
  Of deities or mortals, or of both,
    In Tempe or the dales of Arcady?[1]
  What men or gods are these? What maidens loath?
What mad pursuit? What struggle to escape?
10   What pipes and timbrels? What wild ecstasy?

2

Heard melodies are sweet, but those unheard
  Are sweeter; therefore, ye soft pipes, play on;
Not to the sensual ear, but, more endeared,
  Pipe to the spirit ditties of no tone:
15 Fair youth, beneath the trees, thou canst not leave
  Thy song, nor ever can those trees be bare;
    Bold Lover, never, never canst thou kiss,
Though winning near the goal—yet, do not grieve;
    She cannot fade, though thou hast not thy bliss,
20   Forever wilt thou love, and she be fair!

3

Ah, happy, happy boughs! that cannot shed
  Your leaves, nor ever bid the Spring adieu;
And, happy melodist, unwearièd,
  Forever piping songs forever new;
25 More happy love! more happy, happy love!
  Forever warm and still to be enjoyed,
    Forever panting, and forever young;
All breathing human passion far above,
  That leaves a heart high-sorrowful and cloyed,
30   A burning forehead, and a parching tongue.

4

Who are these coming to the sacrifice?
  To what green altar, O mysterious priest,
Lead'st thou that heifer lowing at the skies,
  And all her silken flanks with garlands dressed?
35 What little town by river or sea shore,
  Or mountain-built with peaceful citadel,

---

[1]The vale of Tempe and Arcady (Arcadia) in Greece are symbolic of pastoral beauty.

Is emptied of this folk, this pious morn?
And, little town, thy streets for evermore
   Will silent be; and not a soul to tell
40   Why thou art desolate, can e'er return.

5

O Attic[2] shape! Fair attitude! with brede[3]
   Of marble men and maidens overwrought,
With forest branches and the trodden weed;
   Thou, silent form, dost tease us out of thought
45 As doth eternity: Cold Pastoral!
     When old age shall this generation waste,
       Thou shalt remain, in midst of other woe
     Than ours, a friend to man, to whom thou say'st,
"Beauty is truth, truth beauty,—that is all
50   Ye know on earth, and all ye need to know."

1819

William Blake

(1757–1827)

William Blake was the earliest of the major Romantic writers, and in some ways he was the most radical in his insistence on the importance of imagination over reason for the artist. A champion of the French Revolution, Blake took literal and figurative revolution as his lifelong theme. As much artist as poet, Blake created illustrations of his own work and that of such figures as Geoffrey Chaucer and John Milton that are as memorable as poems like "London" and "The Chimney Sweeper." Proclaiming that all he knew came from the Bible, Blake nevertheless invented his own mythical version of the fall of humanity, and prophesied humanity's reintegration into imaginative "unity." More Emersonian idealist than orthodox Christian, Blake wrote long books of prophetic poetry such as *Milton* (1808) and *Jerusalem* (1820) in which he described how humanity would recover its lost union with God.

From **Songs of Innocence**

The Lamb

Little Lamb, who made thee?
Dost thou know who made thee?

---

[2]Grecian, especially Athenian
[3]embroidery

Gave thee life & bid thee feed,
By the stream & o'er the mead;
5 Gave thee clothing of delight,
Softest clothing wooly bright;
Gave thee such a tender voice,
Making all the vales rejoice!
    Little Lamb who made thee?
10   Dost thou know who made thee?

    Little Lamb I'll tell thee,
    Little Lamb I'll tell thee!
He is callèd by thy name,
For he calls himself a Lamb:
15 He is meek & he is mild,
He became a little child:
I a child & thou a lamb,
We are callèd by his name.
    Little Lamb God bless thee.
20   Little Lamb God bless thee.

1789

From **Songs of Experience**

The Tyger

Tyger! Tyger! burning bright
In the forests of the night,
What immortal hand or eye
Could frame thy fearful symmetry?

5 In what distant deeps or skies
Burnt the fire of thine eyes?
On what wings dare he aspire?
What the hand, dare seize the fire?

And what shoulder, & what art,
10 Could twist the sinews of thy heart?
And when thy heart began to beat,
What dread hand? & what dread feet?

What the hammer? what the chain?
In what furnace was thy brain?
15 What the anvil? what dread grasp
Dare its deadly terrors clasp?

When the stars threw down their spears,
And water'd heaven with their tears,
Did he smile his work to see?
20 Did he who made the Lamb make thee?

Tyger! Tyger! burning bright
In the forests of the night,
What immortal hand or eye
Dare frame thy fearful symmetry?

1794

21

CONCEITS AND ALLUSIONS

Metaphors and similes, because of their instant appeal, are usually the first types of figurative speech to catch our attention. Symbols and allegories, which develop as their poems progress, require more preparation from us if we are to enjoy them fully. They offer themselves only to those who are willing not only to read closely and well, but also to go beyond the poem's literal meaning into a realm of wider suggestion. Conceits and allusions may be brief or extensive in scope; but they are the most demanding figures of all, requiring the reader to be extremely alert and to have some outside knowledge in order to unravel them.

Conceits

A **conceit** could be defined as an outrageous metaphor, but a more traditional definition is a comparison between two highly dissimilar objects. Conceits are often developed at some length, revealing and weighing point after point of comparison or contrast between their two objects. In love poetry, they often grow out of Renaissance traditions that depict the man as a warrior and the woman as a walled town; he attacks, she defends herself or surrenders. Or the man might be a hunter and the woman a wild animal. Or she might be the warrior, wounding him with sharp looks or sharper words. Or, if she were kinder, she might be a treasure mine or a goddess of love. (The list could go on and on.) Some **Renaissance poets** take the conceits seriously; others play with them, making use of the surprise that can come from turning an expected cliché upside down.

In the **metaphysical poetry** of the seventeenth century, the unexpected becomes a key ingredient in the conceit. The metaphysical poets used conceits not only in love poetry, but in religious poetry as well, thereby creating for both types of poetry conceits of unparalleled complexity and ingenuity. Physics, astronomy, navigation—any science, any intellectual endeavor—might yield a conceit that viewed the soul's progress and passions as parallels to the workings of the universe it inhabited. The resulting poetry tends to be remarkably tough intellectually (you read this poetry *very* slowly the first few times), but also remarkably free, self-assured, and optimistic in its visions.

Here is an example of conceits in metaphysical poetry. Note the two main clusters of imagery in the poem. The first turns on maps and voyages, the second on the image of Christ as "the second Adam." And note also that the two are connected by the concept of the soul's journey to salvation as an annihilation of time and space and by the physical image of the sick man, flat on his back in bed and sweating heavily with fever.

John Donne

(1572–1631)

John Donne is always identified as a "metaphysical" poet, a term not used in his lifetime. The metaphysicals included such diverse poets as George Herbert, Andrew Marvell, and Richard Crashaw. Donne's difficult, complex poetry was characterized by the use of extended "conceits" or metaphors, by a rapid association of thought from image to image, by roughness of meter, and by a synthesis of thought and emotion that sometimes seems odd to the modern mind. For example, Donne might describe love in a scientific or mathematical image, as in the famous image from "A Valediction: Forbidding Mourning" in which he describes two lovers as being like the two legs of a geometric compass. Donne wrote passionate erotic poetry as well as religious verse of great conviction and intellectual depth. At the urging of King James, Donne took Anglican orders and became Dean of St. Paul's, where he preached his dramatic, witty sermons to a sophisticated city audience. After his death, Donne's style of poetry fell out of favor during the English Civil War, but his reputation was revived in the early twentieth century. He is now recognized as one of the most important English poets.

Hymn to God My God, in My Sickness

Since I am coming to that holy room,
    Where, with thy choir of Saints for evermore,
I shall be made thy music; as I come
    I tune the instrument here at the door,
5   And what I must do then, think now before.

Whilst my physicians by their love are grown
    Cosmographers, and I their map, who lie
Flat on this bed, that by them may be shown
    That this is my Southwest discovery
10   *Per fretum febris,*[1] by these straits to die,

I joy, that in these straits, I see my west;[2]
    For, though their currents yield return to none,
What shall my west hurt me? As west and east
    In all flat maps (and I am one) are one,
15   So death doth touch the Resurrection.

---

[1]through the straits of fever
[2]my death

Is the Pacific Sea my home? Or are
   The eastern riches? Is Jerusalem?
Anyan,[3] and Magellan, and Gibraltàr,
   All straits, and none but straits, are ways to them,
20   Whether where Japhet dwelt, or Cham, or Shem.[4]

We think that Paradise and Calvary,
   Christ's Cross, and Adam's tree, stood in one place;
Look Lord, and find both Adams met in me;
   As the first Adam's sweat surrounds my face,
25   May the last Adam's blood my soul embrace.

So, in his purple wrapped receive me, Lord,
   By these his thorns give me his other crown;
And as to others' souls I preached thy word,
   Be this my text, my sermon to mine own,
30   Therefore that he may raise, the Lord throws down.

1635

Allusions

Conceits ask that we bring some knowledge to our reading if we are to understand their implications. For example, we must understand the distortions of space involved in making a flat map represent a round world if we are to understand Donne's hymn. An **allusion** likewise asks us to bring some knowledge to our reading, for an allusion may be defined as a reference to some work of art or literature, or to some well-known person, event, or story. If we do not catch the reference, then we will miss the point of the allusion.

Here is a frequently anthologized Middle English poem that celebrates spring. Following that poem is a "celebration" of winter by a twentieth-century poet who, knowing of the earlier poem's popularity, felt free to burlesque it. Note that Ezra Pound's poem can stand on its own, and that it makes no direct reference to the lyric to which it alludes. But note also how much more effective its irascible tone becomes when set off in its reader's mind against the cheerfulness of its medieval model.

---

[3]modern Annam, then thought of as a strait between Asia and America
[4]sons of Noah, said to have settled Europe, Asia, and Africa after the flood

Anonymous—Middle English Lyric

Sumer Is Icumen In[1]

Sumer is icumen in,
   Lhude sing cuccu!
Groweth sed and bloweth med
   And springth the wude nu.
5   Sing cuccu!

Awe bleteth after lomb,
   Lhouth after calve cu,
Bulluc sterteth, bucke verteth;
   Murie sing cuccu!
10   Cuccu! cuccu!
Wel singes thu cuccu.
Ne swik thu naver nu!

Sing cuccu nu, Sing cuccu!
Sing cuccu, Sing cuccu nu!

date unknown

Ezra Pound

(1885–1972)

See page 337 for a biographical note on the author.

Ancient Music

Winter is icumen in,
Lhude sing Goddamm,
Raineth drop and staineth slop,

---

[1] *Translation:*
Spring has come in,
   Loudly sing cuckoo!
Grows seed and blooms mead
   And springs the wood now.
     Sing cuckoo!

Ewe bleats after lamb,
   Lows after calf the cow,

Bullock starts, buck farts;
   Merrily sing cuckoo!
     Cuckoo! cuckoo!
Well sing thou cuckoo.
Cease thou never now!

Sing cuckoo now
   etc.

And how the wind doth ramm!
5   Sing : Goddamm.
Skiddeth bus and sloppeth us,
An ague hath my ham.
Freezeth river, turneth liver,
            Damn you, sing : Goddamm.
10 Goddamm, Goddamm, 'tis why I am, Goddamm,
            So 'gainst the winter's balm.
Sing goddamm, damm, sing Goddamm,
Sing goddamm, sing goddamm, DAMM.

1926

Discuss how the speakers of the following three poems use conceits or allusions to praise the women they love and to enlarge on the benefits of love. (You will want to concentrate on the poems' imagery; but note also the use of **apostrophe**, or direct address, and the different tones and logical progressions within each poem. Use the questions that follow each poem to help you.)

William Shakespeare

(1564–1616)

See page 325 for a biographical note on the author.

Sonnet 18

Shall I compare thee to a summer's day?
Thou art more lovely and more temperate:
Rough winds do shake the darling buds of May,
And summer's lease hath all too short a date:
5 Sometime too hot the eye of heaven shines,
And often is his gold complexion dimmed;
And every fair from fair sometime declines,
By chance or nature's changing course untrimmed:
But thy eternal summer shall not fade
10 Nor lose possession of that fair thou ow'st,[1]
Nor shall Death brag thou wand'rest in his shade,

---

[1]ownest

When in eternal lines to time thou grow'st.
   So long as men can breathe or eyes can see,
   So long lives this, and this gives life to thee.

1609

STUDY QUESTION

This sonnet starts with a question relating to physical qualities—beauty and temperature—and ends up dealing with intangible ones. By what contrasts and what train of logic does it achieve this progression? (Note in particular the "summer's day" of line 1, "the eye of heaven" in line 5, and "eternal summer" in line 9. These phrases mark the starting points of three stages in the argument, with the last two lines marking the final stage. And be warned that "fair" has three meanings. It's a noun meaning "a lovely thing," an adjective meaning "lovely," and a noun meaning "beauty.")

Robert Frost

(1874–1963)

See page 367 for a biographical note on the author.

The Silken Tent

She is as in a field a silken tent
At midday when a sunny summer breeze
Has dried the dew and all its ropes relent,
So that in guys it gently sways at ease,
5 And its supporting central cedar pole,
That is its pinnacle to heavenward
And signifies the sureness of the soul,
Seems to owe naught to any single cord,
But strictly held by none, is loosely bound
10 By countless silken ties of love and thought
To everything on earth the compass round,
And only by one's going slightly taut
In the capriciousness of summer air
Is of the slightest bondage made aware.

1942

John Donne

(1572–1631)

See page 430 for a biographical note on the author.

The Sun Rising

     Busy old fool, unruly sun,
        Why dost thou thus
Through windows and through curtains call on us?
Must to thy motions lovers' seasons run?
5   Saucy, pedantic wretch, go chide
       Late schoolboys and sour 'prentices,
    Go tell court huntsmen that the king will ride,
    Call country ants to harvest offices.
Love, all alike, no season knows nor clime,
10 Nor hours, days, months, which are the rags of time.

     Thy beams, so reverend and strong
        Why shouldst thou think?
I could eclipse and cloud them with a wink,
But that I would not lose her sight so long.
15   If her eyes have not blinded thine,
       Look, and tomorrow late tell me
       Whether both th' Indias of spice and mine
    Be where thou left'st them, or lie here with me;
Ask for those kings whom thou saw'st yesterday,
20 And thou shalt hear: All here in one bed lay.

     She's all states, and all princes I;
        Nothing else is.
Princes do but play us; compared to this,
All honor's mimic, all wealth alchemy.
25   Thou, sun, art half as happy as we,
       In that the world's contracted thus;
    Thine age asks ease, and since thy duties be
To warm the world, that's done in warming us.
Shine here to us, and thou art everywhere;
30 This bed thy center is, these walls thy sphere.

1633

STUDY QUESTIONS

1. This poem falls into the category of **aubades,** or "dawn songs." What dramatic value does this placement in time give it?
2. Note that here again earthly riches are first equated with the woman's beauty and then devalued by it, and that time is forced to yield to timelessness. How does Donne's treatment of these conceits differ from those of Shakespeare and Frost?
3. In general, how would you compare this love poem with those two earlier ones?

The next two poems are spoken by discontented lovers. What could you say about the ways in which they use conceits or allusions to describe their predicaments or to convince themselves or their hearers that some change should be made?

Sir Philip Sidney

(1554–1586)

Sir Philip Sidney was killed in battle in Europe when he was only thirty-two years old, but he had earned a reputation among the Elizabethans as the ideal courtier, poet, and gentleman. His best-remembered work is the pastoral romance *Arcadia* (1590). He also completed a sonnet cycle called *Astrophel and Stella* (1591). In a work of criticism published after his death, *The Defense of Poesy* (1595), he argued for the importance of the poet to teach and delight readers and to offer people an ideal of conduct.

From **Astrophel and Stella**

Sonnet 31

With how sad steps, O moon,[1] thou climb'st the skies!
    How silently, and with how wan a face!
    What! may it be that even in heavenly place
    That busy archer his sharp arrows tries?
Sure, if that long-with-love-acquainted eyes
    Can judge of love, thou feel'st a lover's case;
    I read it in thy looks—thy languished grace
    To me, that feel the like, thy state descries.
Then, even of fellowship, O moon, tell me,

5

---

[1]The technique of having the speaker seem to address someone or something within a poem is called **apostrophe.**

10   Is constant love deemed there but want of wit?
        Are beauties there as proud as here they be?
     Do they above love to be loved, and yet
        Those lovers scorn whom that love doth possess?
        Do they call virtue there ungratefulness?

1591

Andrew Marvell

(1621–1678)

Andrew Marvell was best known in his lifetime as the assistant to John Milton during the
Commonwealth period, when Milton was serving as Latin Secretary. Marvell published a
few satires during the Restoration, but the bulk of his poems appeared only after his
death. Wit, playfulness, metrical versatility, and an underlying intellectual seriousness
characterize his work.

To His Coy Mistress

     Had we but world enough, and time,
     This coyness, lady, were no crime.
     We would sit down, and think which way
     To walk, and pass our long love's day.
5   Thou by the Indian Ganges' side
     Shouldst rubies find; I by the tide
     Of Humber would complain. I would
     Love you ten years before the Flood,
     And you should, if you please, refuse
10   Till the conversion of the Jews.
     My vegetable love should grow
     Vaster than empires, and more slow;
     An hundred years should go to praise
     Thine eyes and on thy forehead gaze,
15   Two hundred to adore each breast,
     But thirty thousand to the rest:
     An age at least to every part,
     And the last age should show your heart.
     For, lady, you deserve this state,
20   Nor would I love at lower rate.
         But at my back I always hear
     Time's wingèd chariot hurrying near;
     And yonder all before us lie

Deserts of vast eternity.
25 Thy beauty shall no more be found,
    Nor in thy marble vault shall sound
    My echoing song; then worms shall try
    That long preserved virginity,
    And your quaint honor turn to dust,
30 And into ashes all my lust.
    The grave's a fine and private place,
    But none, I think, do there embrace.
        Now, therefore, while the youthful hue
    Sits on thy skin like morning dew,
35 And while thy willing soul transpires
    At every pore with instant fires,
    Now let us sport us while we may,
    And now, like am'rous birds of prey,
    Rather at once our time devour
40 Than languish in his slow-chapped power.
    Let us roll all our strength and all
    Our sweetness up into one ball,
    And tear our pleasures with rough strife
    Through the iron gates of life.
45 Thus, though we cannot make our sun
    Stand still, yet we will make him run.

1681

Carolyn Kizer

(1925–   )

Carolyn Kizer, one of the most highly respected of contemporary poets, is known for her technical adeptness. She writes epigrams, sonnets, villanelles, terza rima, all with seeming effortlessness. As the title of one of her collections—*Mermaids in the Basement* (1986)—shows, Emily Dickinson is one of the major influences on Kizer's work. Like Dickinson, Kizer records very precise shades of emotion within her tight formal structures. A winner of the Pulitzer Prize, Kizer recently published *Harping On: Poems 1985–1995* (1996).

Food for Love

Eating is touch carried to the bitter end.
                    —Samuel Butler II

I'm going to murder you with love;
I'm going to suffocate you with embraces;

I'm going to hug you, bone by bone,
Till you're dead all over.
5   Then I will dine on your delectable marrow.

You will become my personal Sahara;
I'll sun myself in you, then with one swallow
Drain your remaining brackish well.
With my female blade I'll carve my name
10   In your most aspiring palm
Before I chop it down.
Then I'll inhale your last oasis whole.

But in the total desert you become
You'll see me stretch, horizon to horizon,
15   Opulent mirage!
Wisteria balconies dripping cyclamen.
Vistas ablaze with crystal, laced in gold.

So you will summon each dry grain of sand
And move towards me in undulating dunes
20   Till you arrive at sudden ultramarine:
A Mediterranean to stroke your dusty shores;
Obstinate verdure, creeping inland, fast renudes
Your barrens; succulents spring up everywhere,
Surprising life! And I will be that green.

25   When you are fed and watered, flourishing
With shoots entwining trellis, dome and spire,
Till you are resurrected field in bloom,
I will devour you, my natural food,
My host, my final supper on the earth,
30   And you'll begin to die again.

1984

STUDY QUESTIONS

1. How does the epigram from Samuel Butler contribute to your understanding of the poem?
2. If this is a love poem, how does that square with all of the poem's violent imagery?

Judith Ortiz Cofer's "The Latin Deli: An Ars Poetica" employs both a conceit and allusions. After you identify the central conceit, discuss the historical allusions that add poignancy to the poem.

Judith Ortiz Cofer

(1952–   )

See page 101 for a biographical note on the author.

The Latin Deli: An Ars Poetica

Presiding over a formica counter,
plastic Mother and Child magnetized
to the top of an ancient register,
the heady mix of smells from the open bins
5   of dried codfish, the green plantains
hanging in stalks like votive offerings,
she is the Patroness of Exiles,
a woman of no-age who was never pretty,
who spends her days selling canned memories
10   while listening to the Puerto Ricans complain
that it would be cheaper to fly to San Juan
than to buy a pound of Bustelo coffee here,
and to Cubans perfecting their speech
of a "glorious return" to Havana—where no one
15   has been allowed to die and nothing to change until then;
to Mexicans who pass through, talking lyrically
of *dólares* to be made in El Norte—
                        all wanting the comfort
of spoken Spanish, to gaze upon the family portrait
20   of her plain wide face, her ample bosom
resting on her plump arms, her look of maternal interest
as they speak to her and each other
of their dreams and their disillusions—
how she smiles understanding,
25   when they walk down the narrow aisles of her store
reading the labels of packages aloud, as if
they were the names of lost lovers: *Suspiros,*
Merengues, the stale candy of everyone's childhood,
                        She spends her days
30   slicing *jamón y queso* and wrapping it in wax paper
tied with string: plain ham and cheese
that would cost less at the A&P, but it would not satisfy
the hunger of the fragile old man lost in the folds
of his winter coat, who brings her lists of items
35   that he reads to her like poetry, or the others,

whose needs she must divine, conjuring up products
from places that now exist only in their hearts—
closed ports she must trade with.

1991

STUDY QUESTIONS

1. Why is the poem subtitled "An Ars Poetica"—an "art of poetry"?
2. How does Ortiz Cofer equate food, language, and memory in the poem?
3. Discuss the poem's theme of exile.

22

PATTERNS OF IMAGERY

So far, we have spoken of different figures of speech in isolation. In practice, however, the various figures almost always appear in combination with each other. "Days," for instance, is an allegory. But the various gifts the days carry are symbolic; and the phrase "morning wishes" is metaphorical. Moreover, just as **form and meaning** reinforce each other, so a poem's figures of speech reinforce each other to create the poem's overall patterns of meaning and imagery. When we discuss a poem, we may start by discussing some particularly striking aspect; and that may mean noting a particular use of imagery. But eventually we will want to talk of the complete poem; and that will mean talking of the patterns it contains.

The poems in the last chapter were heavily patterned. The **Renaissance poems** tended to be static, stating a position and then elaborating on it. The **metaphysical poems** showed more movement, following the speaker's mind through the ramifications of an idea or situation. The poems in this chapter will also display carefully worked-out patterns of imagery. And, as most of them are somewhat longer poems, the patterns will be even more complex. But these poems will also show a freer and more passionate movement, for they come either from the **Romantic poetry** of the nineteenth century or from twentieth-century poetry that was influenced by that movement. In the more melodious rhythms and harmonies of these poems, we find a vivid sense of immediacy, of unfolding memories or emotions, of minds and spirits caught up in vision and experience. Flowing sound and richly suggestive imagery create the sense of intense experience that was a trademark of the Romantic movement and that still provides some overtones of meaning to the common use of the word *romantic*.

As you read the following poems, be prepared for shifts of emotion as much as for shifts of thought. Note how these more modern poets create scenes, moods, and speakers through sound and imagery.

Percy Bysshe Shelley

(1792–1822)

Percy Bysshe Shelley lived out the radically free life that some of the other Romantic writers only wrote about. Expelled from Oxford for writing a pamphlet expressing his atheism, Shelley married Harriet Westbrook (he was eighteen, she sixteen) and eloped with her to Edinburgh. Living off his parents' money, Shelley moved back to London, where he became a disciple of the radical social reformer William Godwin. Shelley also became a disciple of Godwin's beautiful daughter, Mary Wollstonecraft Godwin, and ran away with her to France with her half-sister, Claire Clairmont. Shelley then invited the wife he had abandoned for a time to come live with them. This behavior earned Shelley the scorn of the British public, who saw him as an atheistic libertine. After Harriet drowned herself, Shelley and Mary moved to Italy. In desperate financial circumstances and unhappy domestic ones, Shelley composed his most important poems—*Prometheus Unbound* (1820), "Adonais" (his 1821 elegy on the death of Keats), and *Hellas* (1822). Shelley's poetry calls for the redemption of the fallen world through love and imagination. A brave philosophical and emotional idealism characterizes his work—an idealism tempered by tragic personal experience. Shelley and a friend drowned off the Italian coast in 1822.

Ode to the West Wind

1

O wild West Wind, thou breath of Autumn's being,
Thou, from whose unseen presence the leaves dead
Are driven, like ghosts from an enchanter fleeing,

Yellow, and black, and pale, and hectic red,
5 Pestilence-stricken multitudes: O thou,
Who chariotest to their dark wintry bed

The wingèd seeds, where they lie cold and low,
Each like a corpse within its grave, until
Thine azure sister of the Spring shall blow

10 Her clarion o'er the dreaming earth, and fill
(Driving sweet buds like flocks to feed in air)
With living hues and odors plain and hill:

Wild Spirit, which art moving everywhere;
Destroyer and preserver; hear, oh, hear!

2

15 Thou on whose stream, mid the steep sky's commotion,
Loose clouds like earth's decaying leaves are shed,
Shook from the tangled boughs of Heaven and Ocean,

Angels of rain and lightning: there are spread
On the blue surface of thine aery surge,
20 Like the bright hair uplifted from the head

Of some fierce Maenad,[1] even from the dim verge
Of the horizon to the zenith's height,
The locks of the approaching storm. Thou dirge

Of the dying year, to which this closing night
25 Will be the dome of a vast sepulcher,
Vaulted with all thy congregated might

Of vapors, from whose solid atmosphere
Black rain, and fire, and hail will burst: oh, hear!

3

Thou who didst waken from his summer dreams
30 The blue Mediterranean, where he lay,
Lulled by the coil of his crystàlline streams,

Beside a pumice isle in Baiae's[2] bay,
And saw in sleep old palaces and towers
Quivering within the wave's intenser day,

35 All overgrown with azure moss and flowers
So sweet, the sense faints picturing them! Thou
For whose path the Atlantic's level powers

Cleave themselves into chasms, while far below
The sea-blooms and the oozy woods which wear
40 The sapless foliage of the ocean, know

Thy voice, and suddenly grow gray with fear,
And tremble and despoil themselves: oh, hear!

4

If I were a dead leaf thou mightest bear;
If I were a swift cloud to fly with thee;
45 A wave to pant beneath thy power, and share

The impulse of thy strength, only less free
Than thou, O uncontrollable! If even
I were as in my boyhood, and could be

---

[1] a female attendant of Dionysus
[2] ancient Roman resort whose submerged ruins can be seen north of Naples

The comrade of thy wanderings over Heaven,
50 As then, when to outstrip thy skiey speed
Scarce seem a vision; I would ne'er have striven

As thus with thee in prayer in my sore need.
Oh, lift me as a wave, a leaf, a cloud!
I fall upon the thorns of life! I bleed!

55 A heavy weight of hours has chained and bowed
One too like thee: tameless, and swift, and proud.

5

Make me thy lyre, even as the forest is:
What if my leaves are falling like its own!
The tumult of thy mighty harmonies

60 Will take from both a deep, autumnal tone,
Sweet though in sadness. Be thou, Spirit fierce,
My spirit! be thou me, impetuous one!

Drive my dead thoughts over the universe
Like withered leaves to quicken a new birth!
65 And, by the incantation of this verse,

Scatter, as from an unextinguished hearth
Ashes and sparks, my words among mankind!
Be through my lips to unawakened earth

The trumpet of a prophecy! O Wind,
70 If Winter comes, can Spring be far behind?

1820

John Keats

(1795–1821)

See page 377 for a biographical note on the author.

Ode to a Nightingale

1

My heart aches, and a drowsy numbness pains
    My sense, as though of hemlock I had drunk,

Or emptied some dull opiate to the drains
 One minute past, and Lethe-wards[1] had sunk:
5 'Tis not through envy of thy happy lot,
 But being too happy in thine happiness—
  That thou, light-wingèd Dryad of the trees,
   In some melodious plot
 Of beechen green, and shadows numberless,
10   Singest of summer in full-throated ease.

2

O, for a draught of vintage! that hath been
 Cooled a long age in the deep-delvèd earth,
Tasting of Flora[2] and the country green,
 Dance, and Provençal song, and sunburnt mirth!
15 O for a beaker full of the warm South,
 Full of the true, the blushful Hippocrene,[3]
  With beaded bubbles winking at the brim,
   And purple-stainèd mouth;
 That I might drink, and leave the world unseen,
20   And with thee fade away into the forest dim:

3

Fade far away, dissolve, and quite forget
 What thou among the leaves hast never known,
The weariness, the fever, and the fret
 Here, where men sit and hear each other groan;
25 Where palsy shakes a few, sad, last gray hairs,
 Where youth grows pale, and spectre-thin, and dies,
 Where but to think is to be full of sorrow
  And leaden-eyed despairs,
Where Beauty cannot keep her lustrous eyes,
30 Or new Love pine at them beyond tomorrow.

4

Away! away! for I will fly to thee,
 Not charioted by Bacchus and his pards,[4]
But on the viewless wings of Poesy,
 Though the dull brain perplexes and retards:

---

[1]toward the river Lethe, in the underworld
[2]goddess of flowers
[3]fountain of the Muses on Mt. Helicon
[4]leopards drawing the chariot of Bacchus, god of wine

35 Already with thee! tender is the night,
    And haply the Queen-Moon is on her throne,
        Clustered around by all her starry Fays;
           But here there is no light,
    Save what from heaven is with the breezes blown
40   Through verdurous glooms and winding mossy ways.

5

    I cannot see what flowers are at my feet,
      Nor what soft incense hangs upon the boughs,
    But, in embalmèd darkness, guess each sweet
      Wherewith the seasonable month endows
45 The grass, the thicket, and the fruit-tree wild;
      White hawthorn, and the pastoral eglantine;
        Fast fading violets covered up in leaves;
           And mid-May's eldest child,
    The coming musk-rose, full of dewy wine,
50   The murmurous haunt of flies on summer eves.

6

    Darkling[5] I listen; and for many a time
      I have been half in love with easeful Death,
    Called him soft names in many a musèd rhyme,
      To take into the air my quiet breath;
55 Now more than ever seems it rich to die,
      To cease upon the midnight with no pain,
        While thou art pouring forth thy soul abroad
           In such an ecstasy!
    Still wouldst thou sing, and I have ears in vain—
60   To thy high requiem become a sod.

7

    Thou wast not born for death, immortal Bird!
      No hungry generations tread thee down;
    The voice I hear this passing night was heard
      In ancient days by emperor and clown:
65 Perhaps the selfsame song that found a path
      Through the sad heart of Ruth, when, sick for home,
        She stood in tears amid the alien corn:
           The same that oft-times hath
    Charmed magic casements, opening on the foam
70   Of perilous seas, in faery lands forlorn.

---

[5]in the darkness

8

Forlorn! the very word is like a bell
   To toll me back from thee to my sole self!
Adieu! the fancy cannot cheat so well
   As she is famed to do, deceiving elf.
75 Adieu! adieu! thy plaintive anthem fades
   Past the near meadows, over the still stream,
     Up the hill side; and now 'tis buried deep
      In the next valley-glades:
   Was it a vision, or a waking dream?
80   Fled is that music:—Do I wake or sleep?

1819

Matthew Arnold

(1822–1888)

Matthew Arnold was an influential poet, literary critic, and social commentator on religion and education. Like all the Victorians, he was concerned about the radical changes the industrial revolution brought to England, the country in which it first occurred. Arnold believed in the importance of poetry, especially in an age of religious doubt and confusion. Poetry should exhibit a "high seriousness" about both its subject matter and its mission of helping people live their lives. As a critic, Arnold developed the idea of "touchstones"—classical works of literature that evidence the qualities he admired. Arnold saw his mission as enhancing and conveying "culture," which he famously defined as "the best that has been thought and said."

Dover Beach

The sea is calm tonight.
The tide is full, the moon lies fair
Upon the straits;—on the French coast the light
Gleams and is gone; the cliffs of England stand,
5 Glimmering and vast, out in the tranquil bay.
Come to the window, sweet is the night-air!
Only, from the long line of spray
Where the sea meets the moon-blanched land,
Listen! you hear the grating roar
10 Of pebbles which the waves draw back, and fling,
At their return, up the high strand,
Begin, and cease, and then again begin,
With tremulous cadence slow, and bring
The eternal note of sadness in.

15 Sophocles long ago
   Heard it on the Aegean, and it brought
   Into his mind the turbid ebb and flow
   Of human misery; we
   Find also in the sound a thought,
20 Hearing it by this distant northern sea.

   The Sea of Faith
   Was once, too, at the full, and round earth's shore
   Lay like the folds of a bright girdle furled.
   But now I only hear
25 Its melancholy, long, withdrawing roar,
   Retreating, to the breath
   Of the night-wind, down the vast edges drear
   And naked shingles of the world.

   Ah, love, let us be true
30 To one another! for the world, which seems
   To lie before us like a land of dreams,
   So various, so beautiful, so new,
   Hath really neither joy, nor love, nor light,
   Nor certitude, nor peace, nor help for pain;
35 And we are here as on a darkling plain
   Swept with confused alarms of struggle and flight,
   Where ignorant armies clash by night.

   1867

William Butler Yeats

(1865–1939)

See page 364 for a biographical note on the author.

Sailing to Byzantium

1

That is no country for old men. The young
In one another's arms, birds in the trees
—Those dying generations—at their song,
The salmon-falls, the mackerel-crowded seas,
5 Fish, flesh, or fowl, commend all summer long
Whatever is begotten, born, and dies.
Caught in that sensual music all neglect
Monuments of unageing intellect.

2

An aged man is but a paltry thing,
10 A tattered coat upon a stick, unless
Soul clap its hands and sing, and louder sing
For every tatter in its mortal dress,
Nor is there singing school but studying
Monuments of its own magnificence;
15 And therefore I have sailed the seas and come
To the holy city of Byzantium.

3

O sages standing in God's holy fire
As in the gold mosaic of a wall,
Come from the holy fire, perne in a gyre,
20 And be the singing-masters of my soul.
Consume my heart away; sick with desire
And fastened to a dying animal
It knows not what it is; and gather me
Into the artifice of eternity.

4

25 Once out of nature I shall never take
My bodily form from any natural thing,
But such a form as Grecian goldsmiths make
Of hammered gold and gold enamelling
To keep a drowsy Emperor awake;
30 Or set upon a golden bough to sing
To lords and ladies of Byzantium
Of what is past, or passing, or to come.

1928

Dylan Thomas

(1914–1953)

Dylan Thomas was born in Wales and made his reputation as a wild, if sometimes incomprehensible, Welsh bard. Weaving his images from the Bible, Welsh folklore, and later from his readings of Sigmund Freud, Thomas celebrated the life force flowing through all things—"the force that through the green fuse drives the flower," as he put it in one famous poem. He was a wonderful performer of his own work and created a sensation during all three of his reading tours of America. He drank himself to death before he reached forty, yet he left behind not only his colorful personal legend but also a small but enduring body of lyric poetry.

Fern Hill

Now as I was young and easy under the apple boughs
About the lilting house and happy as the grass was green,
   The night above the dingle starry,
    Time let me hail and climb
5   Golden in the heydays of his eyes,
And honored among wagons I was prince of the apple towns
And once below a time I lordly had the trees and leaves
    Trail with daisies and barley
   Down the rivers of the windfall light.

10 And as I was green and carefree, famous among the barns
About the happy yard and singing as the farm was home,
   In the sun that is young once only,
    Time let me play and be
   Golden in the mercy of his means,
15 And green and golden I was huntsman and herdsman, the calves
Sang to my horn, the foxes on the hills barked clear and cold,
    And the sabbath rang slowly
   In the pebbles of the holy streams.

All the sun long it was running, it was lovely, the hay
20 Fields high as the house, the tunes from the chimneys, it was air
    And playing, lovely and watery
    And fire green as grass.
   And nightly under the simple stars
As I rode to sleep the owls were bearing the farm away,
25 All the moon long I heard, blessed among stables, the night-jars
    Flying with the ricks, and the horses
    Flashing into the dark.

And then to awake, and the farm, like a wanderer white
With the dew, come back, the cock on his shoulder: it was all
30   Shining, it was Adam and maiden,
    The sky gathered again
   And the sun grew round that very day.
So it must have been after the birth of the simple light
In the first, spinning place, the spellbound horses walking warm
35   Out of the whinnying green stable
    On to the fields of praise.

And honored among foxes and pheasants by the gay house
Under the new made clouds and happy as the heart was long,
   In the sun born over and over,
40   I ran my heedless ways,

My wishes raced through the house high hay
And nothing I cared, at my sky blue trades, that time allows
    In all his tuneful turning so few and such morning songs
        Before the children green and golden
45   Follow him out of grace,

Nothing I cared, in the lamb white days, that time would take me
Up to the swallow thronged loft by the shadow of my hand,
        In the moon that is always rising,
            Nor that riding to sleep
50   I should hear him fly with the high fields
And wake to the farm forever fled from the childless land.
Oh as I was young and easy in the mercy of his means,
            Time held me green and dying
        Though I sang in my chains like the sea.

1945

Sound

23

METER AND ITS VARIATIONS

Sound in poetry is a function of two elements: the rhythm of a poem's lines, and the sounds of its words. Throughout our study of poetry, we have been aware of the important part sound and rhythm play in establishing our sense of a poem. But we have been more concerned with recognizing how the sounds of a given poem reinforce its ideas or emotions than with classifying the sounds themselves; and so we have not paused to build up a vocabulary of technical terms for meter and versification. Now it is time to learn that vocabulary, so that we may supplement our discussions of character and language in poetry with more detailed comments on the techniques of sound that reinforce them. Because rhythm is perhaps the most basic element of sound in a poem, and meter the most basic element of rhythm, we will start with meter.

Meter is the term used to describe the underlying rhythm of a poem, based on the number and the placement of stressed syllables in each line. In most poetry, these **stresses** will fall into a pattern and the pattern will have a particular name: **iambic pentameter**, for instance, to name one of the most common. When we learn to **scan** a poem, therefore, to find out the rhythm or meter in which it is written, these stresses and their patterns are what we will be looking at.

What do we mean by a **stress** or a **stressed syllable**? We mean that the word or syllable involved is one to which our voice will give greater emphasis than to its neighbors. Every word of more than one syllable in English has one accented, or stressed, syllable and one or more unaccented, or unstressed, ones. Thus in the word *human* we stress the first syllable: *hú - man;* in the word *humane* we stress the second: *hu - máne.* When we speak a sentence, these natural accents, or stresses, will be heard. Usually they will be joined by a second type of stress, one used for emphasis. If I say, "Is she coming?," for instance, and leave the strongest stress on the first syllable of *coming* ("Is she *coming?*"), there will be nothing startling in the sentence. If, however, I move the accent to the word *is* ("*Is* she coming?"), I sound doubtful or surprised that she'd come; while if I accent the word *she* ("Is *she* coming?") the stressed word suggests that "she" is the last person I would have expected (or perhaps wanted) to come. The emphasis may fall in an expected or an unexpected place. But it is sure to fall somewhere, because English is a heavily accented language; it sounds neither normal nor natural without the contrast of its stressed and unstressed syllables.

The number of stresses in a line of poetry, therefore, is the number of sylla-bles on which our voice naturally tends to put a stronger emphasis. The empha-sis must be natural; it must come either from the sound of the words themselves or from the meaning and emphasis of the lines. Thus we must be able to find the meter by reading naturally; we should not distort either the sense or the natural rhythm of the lines to make them fit some preconceived meter.

So basic is this matter of stresses, in fact, that line lengths receive their names according to the number of stressed syllables they contain. One simply counts up the stressed syllables, translates the resulting number into Greek, and adds the word *meter* to finish out the term, as follows:

Dimeter—two stresses per line:
Díe soón
Trimeter—three stresses:
Dóst thou knów who máde thee?
Tetrameter—four stresses:
Tell aĺl the trúth but téll it slánt
Pentameter—five stresses:
Leáve me, O Lóve, which reáches bút to duśt
Hexameter—six stresses (also known as an **alexandrine**):
Which, líke a wóunded snake, draǵs its slow length alońg

By counting the number of stresses per line, we thus discover the skeleton of a poem's rhythm. The question then becomes how those stresses are linked. In **accentual poetry**, they are linked by **alliteration** or **assonance**. There will be (usually) four stressed syllables per line; and two or three of them will start with the same sound or contain the same vowel. Here is an example, from a poem you will meet again later in the chapter:

> Bitter breást-cares have Í abíded,
> Knowń on my kéel many a caŕe's hoĺd,
> And díŕe seá-suŕge, and there I oft speńt
> Naŕŕow nightwatch niǵh the ship's héad
> While she tośsed close to clíffs. Coldly afflicted,
> My féet weŕe by fróst benuḿbed.

The first line is marked by the alliteration of *bitter* and *breast* and the assonance of *I* and *abided*. The second is similarly linked by the alliteration of the *k* sound in *keel* and *care* and the assonance of the *o* sound in *known* and *hold*. But the other lines are all marked by the alliteration of one sound each: *s* in the third line, *n* in the fourth, *c* in the fifth, and *f* in the sixth. This is the patterning of **Old English poetry**, a patterning used for several hundred years before the Norman Conquest brought French influences and rhymed verse to England. Since that time, accentual poetry has been relatively rare. One nineteenth-century poet, Gerard Manley Hopkins, however, worked out an accentual style of his own, which he called **sprung rhythm**. His style reflects the Old English influence in its irregular placement of stresses and its marked use of alliteration and assonance.

Most English and American verse is **accentual syllabic**. This means that its rhythm depends not only on the number of stressed syllables, but also on the total number of syllables per line, and on the placement of the stresses within that totality. Tetrameter lines, for instance, vary in length from the four stressed syllables of "We real cool. We," to the eight syllables, half of them stressed, of "Tell all the truth but tell it slant," to the eleven or twelve syllables (every third syllable stressed) of "You left us in tatters, without shoes or socks,/Tired of digging potatoes and spudding up docks."

To define its various combinations of stressed and unstressed syllables, therefore, accentual-syllabic meters divide each line of poetry into **feet**, a **foot** consisting of one stressed syllable with its attendant unstressed syllables. Each type of foot—that is, each **pattern of syllables**—is given a name. An unstressed syllable followed by a stressed one, for instance (*the wórd*) is an **iamb**; two unstressed syllables followed by a stressed one (*that she heárd*) make an **anapest**. The meter of the poem thus consists of the *name of the foot* most frequently found in the poem joined to the basic *line length*. "There's a certain slant of light" thus becomes **iambic trimeter**, despite the fact that not all its feet are iambs and not all its lines have three feet.

With this background in mind, let us chart the types of feet most commonly found in English poetry. One of the most common **duple meters** is the **iambic**, which has two syllables, the second stressed:

Tell áll | the trúth | but téll | it slańt

The **trochaic** has two syllables, the first stressed:

Dóst thou | knów who | máde thee?

One of the two most common **triple meters** is the **anapestic**, with three syllables, the last stressed:

And thére | was my Ró- | land to béar | the whole weíght

The **dactylic** has three syllables, the first stressed:

Táking me | báck down the | vísta of | yéars, till I | sée

One should also know the **spondee**, a two-syllable foot with both syllables accented. The spondee is used only to lend particular emphasis or variety to poetry written in other meters; there is no "spondaic meter." The **amphibrach** is a three-syllable foot with the accent on the middle syllable. Unlike the spondee, the amphibrach can be used as a sustained meter; but it's not an easy meter to work with and isn't often used for an entire poem. The **monosyllabic foot** has one syllable, accented; Gwendolyn Brooks's "We Real Cool" is an example of this foot in action. The **paeon** is a four-syllable foot. It may be called first paeon, second paeon, third paeon, or fourth paeon, depending on whether the accented syllable comes first, second, third, or fourth. There may also be a secondary accent within the foot. Traditional ballads are often written in paeonic meters.

Meter, then, will create the basic rhythm of a poem, setting up a pattern to be repeated or varied with each line. Seldom does the pattern remain perfectly regular, because to hold too closely to a meter in spoken verse is to risk monotony and boredom.

A poet can avoid monotony by shifting stresses, so that a poem written in iambic meter will have some feet that are trochees and some that are spondees; by adding syllables, so that an iambic line will contain an occasional dactyl or anapest; or by dropping syllables, substituting a pause for the expected sound, or laying greater stress on the remaining syllables, as when a spondee is substituted for an anapest.

More importantly, poets vary their meters by making the sense of the poem, and the cadence of the speaker's voice, move in counterpoint to the rhythm:

> The sea is calm tonight.
> The tide is full, the moon lies fair
> Upon the straits;—on the French coast the light
> Gleams and is gone; the cliffs of England stand,
> Glimmering and vast, out in the tranquil bay.

The first statement fits the first line perfectly. But the next overlaps the second line, so that your voice cannot stop on "fair" but must continue with "Upon the straits." A pause, then, and the thought continues through that line and half of the next; then pauses more briefly, finishes the line with a slight pause, and comes to rest at the end of the fifth line. Because your voice stops at the end of them, the first and fifth lines are called **end-stopped lines**. Because the movement of thought and phrase forces your voice to continue past their ends, the second, third, and fourth lines are called **run-on lines**. Both end-stopped and run-on lines may contain internal pauses. We find one such pause after "full" in the second line, one after "straits" in the third," one after "gone" in the fourth, and one after "vast" in the fifth. These pauses are called **caesuras**; and their use and placement are vital in breaking the rhythms of poetry to create the sound of a speaking voice.

In contrast to "Dover Beach" (which you might want to reread in its entirety, to notice how flexible the lines are throughout), recall William Blake's poems "The Lamb" and "The Tyger." Notice that many of their lines are end-stopped and that the regularity of the rhythm, with its procession of end-stopped lines and repeated questions, gives these poems almost the sound of incantations, sounds far removed from the wistful accents of Matthew Arnold's speaker. But notice, too, that even here, although each phrase is strongly separated from its fellows and heavily accented, the length of the phrases still varies, and caesuras and occasional run-on lines are still found:

> What the hammer? what the chain?
> In what furnace was thy brain?

What the anvil? what dread grasp
Dare its deadly terrors clasp?

We may notice, too, that Blake restricts himself to seven-syllable lines in "The Tyger," and to a patterned alternation between trimeter and tetrameter lines in "The Lamb," whereas Arnold varies his line lengths in "Dover Beach," the lines growing longer as the speaker warms to his topic. And, finally, we notice that all the lines quoted from Blake and Arnold end with stressed syllables. Your voice rises slightly to the stress at the end of these lines, and they are therefore said to have a **rising rhythm**. In contrast, lines that end on unstressed syllables—"O wild West Wind, thou breath of Autumn's being"—are said to have a **falling rhythm**. It's a small thing, but it can create subtle variations in tone.

These, then, are the basic meters of accentual-syllabic verse and the most common devices used to lend them variety. You will no doubt find many other devices at work as you continue your study of poetry. And you will also find that in much modern verse, such as that of Walt Whitman and E. E. Cummings, the rules of accentual-syllabic verse have been replaced by the uncharted techniques and devices of **free verse**. Pauses and phrasings in free verse tend to be visual devices as well as rhythmic ones; line lengths and stress placement vary at the poet's will. Sounds are still being shaped with care, but the writers of free verse are being equally careful to avoid setting up rules to which critics can then bind them. In free verse, as in all verse, ultimately the total effect is the sole criterion.

Here are a modern translation of an Old English poem and an example of Hopkins's sprung rhythm. How would you compare and contrast the two types of verse?

Anonymous

(eighth century)

The Seafarer (modern version by Ezra Pound)

May I for my own self song's truth reckon,
Journey's jargon, how I in harsh days
Hardship endured oft.
Bitter breast-cares have I abided,
5 Known on my keel many a care's hold,
And dire sea-surge, and there I oft spent
Narrow nightwatch nigh the ship's head
While she tossed close to cliffs. Coldly afflicted,
My feet were by frost benumbed.
10 Chill its chains are; chafing signs
Hew my heart round and hunger begot.
Mere-weary mood. Lest man know not
That he on dry land loveliest liveth,

List how I, care-wretched, on ice-cold sea,
15 Weathered the winter, wretched outcast
Deprived of my kinsmen;
Hung with hard ice-flakes, where hail-scur flew,
There I heard naught save the harsh sea
And ice-cold wave, at whiles the swan cries,
20 Did for my games the gannet's clamor,
Sea-fowls' loudness was for me laughter,
The mews' singing all my mead-drink.
Storms, on the stone-cliffs beaten, fell on the stern
In icy feathers; full oft the eagle screamed
25 With spray on his pinion.
                                    Not any protector
May make merry man faring needy.
This he little believes, who aye in winsome life
Abides 'mid burghers some heavy business,
Wealthy and wine-flushed, how I weary oft
30 Must bide above brine.
Neareth nightshade, snoweth from north,
Frost froze the land, hail fell on earth then,
Corn of the coldest. Nathless there knocketh now
The heart's thought that I on high streams
35 The salt-wavy tumult traverse alone.
Moaneth alway my mind's lust
That I fare forth, that I afar hence
Seek out a foreign fastness.
For this there's no mood-lofty man over earth's midst,
40 Not though he be given his good, but will have in his youth greed;
Nor his deed to the daring, nor his king to the faithful
But shall have his sorrow for sea-fare
Whatever his lord will.
He hath not heart for harping, nor in ring-having
45 Nor winsomeness to wife, nor world's delight
Nor any whit else save the wave's slash,
Yet longing comes upon him to fare forth on the water.
Bosque taketh blossom, cometh beauty of berries,
Fields to fairness, land fares brisker,
50 All this admonisheth man eager of mood,
The heart turns to travel so that he then thinks
On flood-ways to be far departing.
Cuckoo calleth with gloomy crying,
He singeth summerward, bodeth sorrow,
55 The bitter heart's blood. Burgher knows not—
He the prosperous man—what some perform
Where wandering them widest draweth.

So that but now my heart burst from my breastlock,
My mood 'mid the mere-flood,
60 Over the whale's acre, would wander wide.
On earth's shelter cometh oft to me,
Eager and ready, the crying lone-flyer,
Whets for the whale-path the heart irresistibly,
O'er tracks of ocean; seeing that anyhow
65 My lord deems to me this dead life
On loan and on land, I believe not
That any earth-weal eternal standeth
Save there be somewhat calamitous
That, ere a man's tide go, turn it to twain.
70 Disease or oldness or sword-hate
Beats out the breath from doom-gripped body.
And for this, every earl whatever, for those speaking after—
Laud of the living, boasteth some last word,
That he will work ere he pass onward,
75 Frame on the fair earth 'gainst foes his malice,
Daring ado, . . .
So that all men shall honor him after
And his laud beyond them remain 'mid the English,
Aye, for ever, a lasting life's-blast,
80 Delight 'mid the doughty.
                              Days little durable,
And all arrogance of earthen riches,
There come now no kings nor Caesars
Nor gold-giving lords like those gone.
Howe'er in mirth most magnified,
85 Whoe'er lived in life most lordliest,
Drear all this excellence, delights undurable!
Waneth the watch, but the world holdeth.
Tomb hideth trouble. The blade is layed low.
Earthly glory ageth and seareth.
90 No man at all going the earth's gait,
But age fares against him, his face paleth,
Grey-haired he groaneth, knows gone companions,
Lordly men, are to earth o'ergiven,
Nor may he then the flesh-cover, whose life ceaseth,
95 Nor eat the sweet nor feel the sorry,
Nor stir hand nor think in mid heart,
And though he strew the grave with gold,
His born brothers, their buried bodies
Be an unlikely treasure hoard.

1912

STUDY QUESTIONS

Notice the movement of the speaker's mood and thought. How does he characterize himself? What response does he seek from his audience?

Gerard Manley Hopkins

(1844–1889)

See page 348 for a biographical note on the author.

Felix Randal

Felix Randal the farrier, O he is dead then? my duty all ended
Who have watched his mould of man, big-boned and
    hardy-handsome
Pining, pining, till time when reason rambled in it and some
Fatal four disorders, fleshed there, all contended?

5 Sickness broke him. Impatient he cursed at first, but mended
Being anointed and all; though a heavenlier heart began some
Months earlier, since I had our sweet reprieve and ransom
Tendered to him. Ah well, God rest him all road ever he offended!

This seeing the sick endears them to us, us too it endears.
10 My tongue had taught thee comfort, touch had quenched thy tears,
Thy tears that touched my heart, child, Felix, poor Felix Randal;

How far from then forethought of, all thy more boisterous years,
When thou at the random grim forge, powerful amidst peers,
Didst fettle for the great grey drayhorse his bright and
    battering sandal!

1918

STUDY QUESTIONS

1. Again, how does the speaker portray himself? How does he portray the blacksmith, Felix Randal?
2. Note the movement of the poem, from present to past. Why might Hopkins have chosen this organization for this poem?

Now read these two examples of accentual-syllabic verse. Note the metrical techniques that make the first sound like a song. The second is like the voice of a man arguing with himself.

Alfred, Lord Tennyson

(1809–1892)

See page 406 for a biographical note on the author.

The Splendor Falls on Castle Walls

The splendor falls on castle walls
    And snowy summits old in story:
The long light shakes across the lakes,
    And the wild cataract leaps in glory.
5 Blow, bugle, blow, set the wild echoes flying.
Blow, bugle; answer, echoes, dying, dying, dying.

    O hark, O hear! how thin and clear,
        And thinner, clearer, farther going!
    O sweet and far from cliff and scar
10   The horns of Elfland faintly blowing!
Blow, let us hear the purple glens replying:
Blow, bugle; answer, echoes, dying, dying, dying.

    O love, they die in yon rich sky,
        They faint on hill or field or river;
15   Our echoes roll from soul to soul,
        And grow for ever and for ever.
Blow, bugle, blow, set the wild echoes flying,
And answer, echoes, answer, dying, dying, dying.

1850

STUDY QUESTIONS

1. What is the meter of the main part of the poem? What is the meter of the refrain? What has been achieved by combining the two?
2. What does Tennyson mean by the phrase "our echoes" (line 15)? How do these echoes differ from the other "echoes" of which the poem speaks?
3. Fairyland and fairy things are usually depicted in literature as being immortal and unchanging, in contrast to human affairs, which are transitory. Why does Tennyson reverse that contrast in this poem?
4. How do sound and imagery combine in this poem to reinforce the speaker's message?

George Herbert

(1593–1633)

See page 420 for a biographical note on the author.

The Collar[1]

I struck the board[2] and cried, "No more!
      I will abroad!
What, shall I ever sigh and pine?
My lines and life are free: free as the road,
5   Loose as the wind, as large as store.
      Shall I be still in suit?[3]
Have I no harvest but a thorn
To let me blood, and not restore
What I have lost with cordial[4] fruit?
10   Sure there was wine
Before my sighs did dry it; there was corn
     Before my tears did drown it.
   Is the year only lost to me?
    Have I no bays[5] to crown it,
15 No flowers, no garlands gay? all blasted?
      All wasted?
Not so, my heart; but there is fruit,
     And thou hast hands.
Recover all thy sigh-blown age
20 On double pleasures. Leave thy cold dispute
Of what is fit and not. Forsake thy cage,
      Thy rope of sands,
Which petty thoughts have made and made to thee
   Good cable, to enforce and draw,
25   And be thy law,
While thou didst wink and wouldst not see.
      Away! take heed!
      I will abroad!

---

[1]the iron band encircling the neck of a prisoner or slave; also perhaps a pun on "choler" as "rebellious anger"
[2]dining table
[3]always petitioning
[4]restorative
[5]laurels

Call in thy death's-head there! Tie up thy fears!
30   He that forbears
   To suit and serve his need,
       Deserves his load."
But as I raved, and grew more fierce and wild
       At every word,
35   Methought I heard one calling, "Child!"
       And I replied, "My Lord."

1633

STUDY QUESTION

Discuss how the movement of sound in "The Collar" helps create the sound of the speaker arguing with himself. (Note the addition of a second voice near the end of the poem. How do the speech of this second voice and the speaker's response to it bring the poem to its resolution?)

Finally, here are two examples of iambic pentameter by two masters of that meter. Note that even the use of the identical meter does not give these poems identical sounds. The rhythm of William Shakespeare's sonnet, for all its basic regularity, is flexible and almost conversational; the rhythm of John Milton's poem is as firm and regular as the marble tomb he uses as his poem's chief conceit. Read the two poems and then answer the following questions:

1. How does each poet handle his meter? How are phrasing and sentence structure fitted to the pentameter? How is the progression of the speaker's thought emphasized?
2. How does each poem's rhythm enhance or emphasize its imagery? Give examples.

William Shakespeare

(1564–1616)

See page 325 for a biographical note on the author.

Sonnet 29

When, in disgrace with Fortune and men's eyes,
I all alone beweep my outcast state,
And trouble deaf heaven with my bootless cries,
And look upon myself and curse my fate,

5   Wishing me like to one more rich in hope,
    Featured like him, like him with friends possessed,
    Desiring this man's art, and that man's scope,
    With what I most enjoy contented least;
    Yet in these thoughts myself almost despising,
10 Haply I think on thee, and then my state,
    Like to the lark at break of day arising
    From sullen earth, sings hymns at heaven's gate;
        For thy sweet love remembered such wealth brings
        That when I scorn to change my state with kings.

1629

John Milton

(1608–1674)

John Milton was said to have read everything of significance in at least three languages—English, Italian, and Latin. His epic *Paradise Lost* (1667) is usually cited as the most important poem in the English language. Milton was on the Puritan side in the English Civil War, serving in the Commonwealth government as Latin Secretary. He narrowly escaped imprisonment and perhaps even execution during the Restoration. Having lost his high position and having gone blind, he had to employ a secretary to write down *Paradise Lost* as he composed it in his head. In his powerful blank-verse line, he told the whole story of humanity in Christian terms, from creation through the fall to possible redemption through Christ.

On Shakespeare

    What needs my Shakespeare for his honored bones
    The labor of an age in pilèd stones?
    Or that his hallowed reliques should be hid
    Under a star-ypointing[1] pyramid?
5   Dear son of memory, great heir of fame,
    What need'st thou such weak witness of thy name?
    Thou in our wonder and astonishment
    Has built thyself a livelong monument.
    For whilst, to the shame of slow-endeavoring art,
10 Thy easy numbers flow, and that each heart
    Hath from the leaves of thy unvalued[2] book
    Those Delphic[3] lines with deep impression took,

---

[1]Milton added the "y" for the sake of rhythm.
[2]invaluable
[3]inspired—as by the oracle at Delphi

Then thou, our fancy of itself bereaving,
Dost make us marble with too much conceiving,[4]
15 And so sepùlchred in such pomp dost lie
That kings for such a tomb would wish to die.

1632

STUDY QUESTIONS

Look back at the poems you have read in this book. Select several that you especially like. Analyze the meter in each, and consider the techniques by which it is
varied. Then discuss how these metrical techniques enhance your enjoyment of
each poem.

---

[4]thinking

24

RHYME SCHEMES AND
VERSE FORMS

Although rhyme is not found in all poetry written in English, it has been so important in the history of English and American verse that we often first divide poetry into two categories—rhymed and unrhymed—and then divide further from there. Accepting that categorization for the moment, we will note that **unrhymed poems** tend to fall into one of three major divisions: **accentual verse**, which has existed from Old English times and which we met in "The Seafarer" and "Felix Randal"; **blank verse** (unrhymed iambic pentameter), a sixteenth-century invention, of which Hamlet's soliloquies are classic examples; or **free verse**, sometimes called by the French name **vers libre**, a modern (and not always unrhymed) form that we met in the works of such diverse poets as Walt Whitman, E. E. Cummings, Ezra Pound, and Denise Levertov.

Rhymed Verse

Rhymed verse is harder to classify. There are so many ways of combining rhymed lines. Still, one can distinguish between those forms of rhymed verse that have a fixed total length (such as the **limerick**, with five lines; the **sonnet**, with fourteen; and the **villanelle**, with nineteen) and those that do not. Rhymed verse with no fixed length is usually composed of **stanzas**. Each stanza usually has a fixed length; but the number of stanzas, and hence the length of the poem as a whole, remain variable.

Underlying both types of rhymed verse, however, stand the basic combinations of rhyme. These embrace two-, three-, and four-line patterns, called the couplet, triplet, terza rima, and the quatrain. The **couplet** has two consecutive lines that rhyme:

> So long as men can breathe or eyes can see,
> So long lives this, and this gives life to thee.

The **tercet** or **triplet** has three lines that rhyme:

> He clasps the crag with crooked hands;
> Close to the sun in lonely lands,
> Ringed with the azure world, he stands.

The **terza rima** also has three lines, but only the first and last rhyme. When terza rima stanzas are linked together, the middle line of one stanza rhymes with the first and third lines of the stanza that follows.

> O wild West Wind, thou breath of Autumn's being,
> Thou, from whose unseen presence the leaves dead
> Are driven, like ghosts from an enchanter fleeing,
>
> Yellow, and black, and pale, and hectic red,
> Pestilence-stricken multitudes: O thou
> Who chariotest to their dark wintry bed

The **quatrain** has four lines joined by any one of the following rhyme schemes:

- Second and fourth lines rhyming (*abcb*):

> When I was one-and-twenty
>   I heard a wise man say,
> "Give crowns and pounds and guineas
>   But not your heart away;

- First and third, second and fourth lines rhyming (*abab*):

> She even thinks that up in heaven
> Her class lies late and snores,
> While poor black cherubs rise at seven
> To do celestial chores.

- First and fourth, second and third lines rhyming (*abba*):

> Earth hath not anything to show more fair!
> Dull would he be of soul who could pass by
> A sight so touching in its majesty.
> The city now doth, like a garment, wear

- First and second, third and fourth lines rhyming (*aabb*):

> "O 'Melia, my dear, this does everything crown!
> Who could have supposed I should meet you in Town?
> And whence such fair garments, such prosperi-ty?"—
> "O didn't you know I'd been ruined?" said she.

Any of these patterns can stand alone as a stanza, or patterns may be added to or combined to produce more complicated stanzas. For example, the first poem in this chapter, Robert Herrick's "The Night-Piece, To Julia," has two five-line stanzas consisting of two couplets and a final line rhyming with the first two lines. The next poem, Robert Browning's "Home-Thoughts, from Abroad," combines couplets and *abab* quatrains into two stanzas of eight and twelve lines. The third poem, Sir Thomas Wyatt's "They Flee from Me," is written in **rime royale**, a seven-line stanza rhyming *ababbcc*.

Robert Herrick

(1591–1674)

See page 346 for a biographical note on the author.

The Night-Piece, to Julia

Her eyes the glowworm lend thee;
The shooting stars attend thee;
   And the elves also,
   Whose little eyes glow
5 Like the sparks of fire, befriend thee.

No will-o'-the-wisp mislight thee;
Nor snake or slowworm bite thee;
   But on, on thy way,
   Not making a stay,
10 Since ghost there's none to affright thee.

Let not the dark thee cumber;
What though the moon does slumber?
   The stars of the night
   Will lend thee their light,
15 Like tapers clear without number.

Then, Julia, let me woo thee,
Thus, thus to come unto me;
   And when I shall meet
   Thy silvery feet,
20 My soul I'll pour into thee.

1648

Robert Browning

(1812–1889)

See page 365 for a biographical note on the author.

Home-Thoughts, from Abroad

1

Oh, to be in England
Now that April's there,

And whoever wakes in England
Sees, some morning, unaware,
5   That the lowest boughs and the brushwood sheaf
Round the elm-tree bole are in tiny leaf,
While the chaffinch sings on the orchard bough
In England—now!

2

And after April, when May follows,
10   And the whitethroat builds, and all the swallows!
Hark, where my blossomed pear-tree in the hedge
Leans to the field and scatters on the clover
Blossoms and dewdrops—at the bent spray's edge—
That's the wise thrush; he sings each song twice over,
15   Lest you should think he never could recapture
The first fine careless rapture!
And though the fields look rough with hoary dew,
All will be gay when noontide wakes anew
The buttercups, the little children's dower
20   —Far brighter than this gaudy melon-flower!

1845

Sir Thomas Wyatt

(1503–1542)

Sir Thomas Wyatt was a courtier who served Henry VIII and managed to survive two imprisonments under that temperamental monarch. An accomplished lyric poet, Wyatt did not publish in his lifetime, but rather he circulated his work in manuscript form among his friends. He was a master of the sonnet and other short poetic forms.

They Flee from Me

They flee from me that sometime did me seek
    With naked foot stalking in my chamber.
I have seen them gentle tame and meek
    That now are wild and do not remember
5   That sometime they put themselves in danger
To take bread at my hand; and now they range
Busily seeking with a continual change.

Thankèd be Fortune, it hath been otherwise
  Twenty times better; but once in special,
10 In thin array after a pleasant guise,
  When her loose gown from her shoulders did fall,
  And she me caught in her arms long and small;
And therewithall sweetly did me kiss,
And softly said, "Dear heart, how like you this?"

15 It was no dream: I lay broad waking.
  But all is turned thorough my gentleness
Into a strange fashion of forsaking;
  And I have leave to go of her goodness,
  And she also to use newfangleness.
20 But since that I so kindely am served,
I fain would know what she hath deserved.

1557

Limericks and Villanelles

Let us now look at two rhymed forms of fixed length: the limerick and the villanelle. (We will consider a third fixed-length form, the sonnet, in the next chapter.)

Limericks have five lines. The rhyme scheme is *aabba,* with all *a* lines having three feet, and all *b* lines two feet. The meter is usually anapestic.

Limericks are humorous verse, frequently employing puns, off-color humor, or deliberately tortured rhymes or rhythms. As one anonymous writer and critic remarks,

The limerick packs laughs anatomical,
Into space that is quite economical.
  But the good ones I've seen
  So seldom are clean,
And the clean ones so seldom are comical.

More serious, but equally tightly controlled in form, is the **villanelle**. Entire lines, as well as rhyme sounds, are repeated in the villanelle to make up its prescribed pattern. Here is one of the finest twentieth-century villanelles. Analyze its form and discuss what the poet has done with it.

Dylan Thomas

(1914–1953)

See page 451 for a biographical note on the author.

Do Not Go Gentle into That Good Night

Do not go gentle into that good night,
Old age should burn and rave at close of day;
Rage, rage against the dying of the light.

Though wise men at their end know dark is right,
5 Because their words had forked no lightning they
Do not go gentle into that good night.

Good men, the last wave by, crying how bright
Their frail deeds might have danced in a green bay,
Rage, rage against the dying of the light.

10 Wild men who caught and sang the sun in flight,
And learn, too late, they grieved it on its way,
Do not go gentle into that good night.

Grave men, near death, who see with blinding sight
Blind eyes could blaze like meteors and be gay,
15 Rage, rage against the dying of the light.

And you, my father, there on the sad height,
Curse, bless, me now with your fierce tears, I pray.
Do not go gentle into that good night.
Rage, rage against the dying of the light.

1945

Ballades, Ballads, and Odes

Three forms without fixed length are the **ballade, ballad,** and **ode.** The **ballade** was popular during the Middle Ages. It uses seven- or eight-line stanzas, usually in groups of three. Each stanza ends with the same line, the **refrain.** The ballade itself ends with a shorter stanza, the **envoy** or **envoi.** The envoy is addressed directly to the person for whom the ballade is being written. It, too, ends with the refrain.

In contrast to the tightly defined ballade, the term **ballad** (without the final *e*) may be used for poems that are, or can be, sung, and that have regular stanzas. Frequently, like the ballade, they make use of repeated lines or refrains. Note, in this next poem, how effectively the refrain works as its implication shifts a little in each stanza.

Anonymous

Lord Randal

"O where ha you been, Lord Randal, my son?
And where ha you been, my handsome young man?"
"I ha been at the greenwood; mother, mak my bed soon,
For I'm wearied wi hunting, and fain wad lie down."

5 "An wha met ye there, Lord Randal, my son?
An wha met you there, my handsome young man?"
"O I met wi my true-love; mother, mak my bed soon,
For I'm wearied wi huntin, and fain wad lie down."

"And what did she give you, Lord Randal, my son?
10 And what did she give you, my handsome young man?"
"Eels fried in a pan; mother, mak my bed soon,
For I'm wearied wi huntin, and fain wad lie down."

"And wha gat your leavins, Lord Randal, my son?
And wha gat your leavins, my handsome young man?"
15 "My hawks and my hounds; mother, mak my bed soon,
For I'm wearied wi hunting, and fain wad lie down."

"And what becam of them, Lord Randal, my son?
And what becam of them, my handsome young man?"
"They stretched their legs out and died; mother, mak my bed soon,
20 For I'm wearied wi huntin, and fain wad lie down."

"O I fear you are poisoned, Lord Randal, my son!
I fear you are poisoned, my handsome young man!"
"O yes, I am poisoned; mother, mak my bed soon,
For I'm sick at the heart, and I fain wad lie down."

25 "What d'ye leave to your mother, Lord Randal, my son?
What d'ye leave to your mother, my handsome young man?"
"Four and twenty milk kye[1]; mother, mak my bed soon,
For I'm sick at the heart, and I fain wad lie down."

"What d'ye leave to your sister, Lord Randal, my son?
30 What d'ye leave to your sister, my handsome young man?"

---

[1] cows

"My gold and my silver; mother, mak my bed soon,
For I'm sick at the heart, an I fain wad lie down."

"What d'ye leave to your brother, Lord Randal, my son?
What d'ye leave to your brother, my handsome young man?"
35   "My houses and my lands; mother, mak my bed soon,
For I'm sick at the heart, and I fain wad lie down."

"What d'ye leave to your true-love, Lord Randal, my son?
What d'ye leave to your true-love, my handsome young man?"
"I leave her hell and fire; mother, mak my bed soon,
40   For I'm sick at the heart, and I fain wad lie down."

c. 1500s

Among the rhymed poetic forms, the **ode** is unique in leaving both the rhyme scheme and the length of each individual line to the poet's discretion. The one constant feature of odes in English poetry, in fact, is their elevated tone. In John Keats's "Ode on a Grecian Urn" and "Ode to a Nightingale," and in Percy Bysshe Shelley's "Ode to the West Wind," we saw three different stanzaic patterns. Look back at these odes now (on pages 424, 446, and 444) and define their patterns. Note, too, that in each case the stanzaic form is constant throughout the ode. For this reason, these are sometimes called **Horatian odes**.

To conclude this chapter, we will read one further ode, this one of the type called the **irregular ode**. This particular ode, written by the early Romantic poet William Wordsworth, makes skillful use of rhyme and rhythm both. Yet, for all its careful contrivance, it maintains a remarkable freshness of tone, in keeping with its subject of early joys and maturer delights. Because it is an irregular ode, the stanzas in this poem vary among themselves, changing shape to follow the motions of the poet's mind. The basic meter remains iambic throughout, but line lengths and rhyme schemes shift constantly. The result is an unusual blend of patterning and fluidity that sometimes mutes its tone to a thoughtful expression of philosophy and sometimes rises to a hymn of joyful praise.

The ode deals with the relations between the human soul, nature, and immortality. In it, Wordsworth suggests not only that we know immortality after death, but that we know it before birth as well: "trailing clouds of glory do we come,/ From God, who is our home." The ode thus celebrates the heavenlike joy the young child sees in the natural world; and it laments the dulling of that joy that occurs when the child, responding to the novelty of his mundane existence, turns his mind more fully upon earthly things. Yet the final tone is not sorrow but a greater joy, as Wordsworth passes beyond mourning this early loss into celebrating the fully human joys and loves that are the gift of the mature soul.

As you read the ode, pay careful attention to the way Wordsworth develops this train of thought, and notice how the sound and shape of the stanzas convey the changing emotions the speaker feels.

William Wordsworth

(1770–1850)

See page 339 for a biographical note on the author.

Ode

Intimations of Immortality from Recollections of Early Childhood

The Child is father of the Man;
And I could wish my days to be
Bound each to each by natural piety.

1

There was a time when meadow, grove, and stream,
The earth, and every common sight,
    To me did seem
    Apparelled in celestial light,
5 The glory and the freshness of a dream.
It is not now as it hath been of yore;—
    Turn wheresoe'er I may,
      By night or day,
The things which I have seen I now can see no more.

2

10   The Rainbow comes and goes,
    And lovely is the Rose,
    The Moon doth with delight
Look round her when the heavens are bare;
    Waters on a starry night
15   Are beautiful and fair;
    The sunshine is a glorious birth;
    But yet I know, where'er I go,
That there hath past away a glory from the earth.

3

Now, while the birds thus sing a joyous song,
20   And while the young lambs bound
      As to the tabor's sound,
To me alone there came a thought of grief:
A timely utterance gave that thought relief,
      And I again am strong:

25 The cataracts blow their trumpets from the steep;
   No more shall grief of mine the season wrong;
   I hear the Echoes through the mountains throng,
   The Winds come to me from the fields of sleep,
       And all the earth is gay;
30   Land and sea
       Give themselves up to jollity,
           And with the heart of May
       Doth every Beast keep holiday;—
           Thou Child of Joy,
35 Shout round me, let me hear thy shouts, thou happy Shepherd-boy!

                    4

   Ye blessèd Creatures, I have heard the call
       Ye to each other make; I see
   The heavens laugh with you in your jubilee;
       My heart is at your festival,
40   My head hath its coronal,
   The fulness of your bliss, I feel—I feel it all.
           Oh evil day! if I were sullen
           While Earth herself is adorning,
               This sweet May-morning,
45   And the Children are culling
                   On every side,
           In a thousand valleys far and wide,
           Fresh flowers; while the sun shines warm,
   And the Babe leaps up on his Mother's arm:—
50   I hear, I hear, with joy I hear!
           —But there's a Tree, of many, one,
   A single Field which I have looked upon,
   Both of them speak of something that is gone:
           The Pansy at my feet
55   Doth the same tale repeat:
   Whither is fled the visionary gleam?
   Where is it now, the glory and the dream?

                    5

   Our birth is but a sleep and a forgetting:
   The Soul that rises with us, our life's Star,
60   Hath had elsewhere its setting,
               And cometh from afar:
           Not in entire forgetfulness,
           And not in utter nakedness,

But trailing clouds of glory do we come
65   From God, who is our home:
Heaven lies about us in our infancy!
Shades of the prison-house begin to close
     Upon the growing Boy,
          But He
70 Beholds the light, and whence it flows,
     He sees it in his joy;
The Youth, who daily farther from the east
     Must travel, still is Nature's Priest,
     And by the vision splendid
75   Is on his way attended;
At length the Man perceives it die away,
And fade into the light of common day.

6

Earth fills her lap with pleasures of her own;
Yearnings she hath in her own natural kind,
80 And, even with something of a Mother's mind,
     And no unworthy aim,
     The homely Nurse doth all she can
To make her Foster-child, her Inmate Man,
     Forget the glories he hath known,
85 And that imperial palace whence he came.

7

Behold the Child among his new-born blisses,
A six years' Darling of a pigmy size!
See, where 'mid work of his own hand he lies,
Fretted by sallies of his mother's kisses,
90 With light upon him from his father's eyes!
See, at his feet, some little plan or chart,
Some fragment from his dream of human life,
Shaped by himself with newly-learnèd art;
     A wedding or a festival,
95   A mourning or a funeral;
          And this hath now his heart,
     And unto this he frames his song:
          Then will he fit his tongue
To dialogues of business, love, or strife;
100   But it will not be long
     Ere this be thrown aside,
     And with new joy and pride

The little Actor cons another part;
Filling from time to time his "humorous stage"
105 With all the Persons, down to palsied Age,
That Life brings with her in her equipage;
          As if his whole vocation
          Were endless imitation.

8

Thou, whose exterior semblance doth belie
110   Thy Soul's immensity;
Thou best Philosopher, who yet dost keep
Thy heritage, thou Eye among the blind,
That, deaf and silent, read'st the eternal deep,
Haunted for ever by the eternal mind,—
115   Mighty Prophet! Seer blest!
          On whom those truths do rest,
Which we are toiling all our lives to find,
In darkness lost, the darkness of the grave;
Thou, over whom thy Immortality
120 Broods like the Day, a Master o'er a Slave,
A Presence which is not to be put by;
Thou little Child, yet glorious in the might
Of heaven-born freedom on thy being's height,
Why with such earnest pains dost thou provoke
125 The years to bring the inevitable yoke,
Thus blindly with thy blessedness at strife?
Full soon thy Soul shall have her earthly freight,
And custom lie upon thee with a weight,
Heavy as frost, and deep almost as life!

9

130   O joy! that in our embers
          Is something that doth live,
          That nature yet remembers
          What was so fugitive!
The thought of our past years in me doth breed
135 Perpetual benediction: not indeed
For that which is most worthy to be blest;
Delight and liberty, the simple creed
Of Childhood, whether busy or at rest,
With new-fledged hope still fluttering in his breast:—
140   Not for these I raise
          The song of thanks and praise;
     But for those obstinate questionings

Of sense and outward things,
Falling from us, vanishings;
145   Blank misgivings of a Creature
Moving about in worlds not realised,
High instincts before which our mortal Nature
Did tremble like a guilty Thing surprised:
    But for those first affections,
150   Those shadowy recollections,
    Which, be they what they may,
Are yet the fountain-light of all our day,
Are yet a master-light of all our seeing;
    Uphold us, cherish, and have power to make
155 Our noisy years seem moments in the being
Of the eternal Silence: truths that wake,
    To perish never:
Which neither listlessness, nor mad endeavor,
    Nor Man nor Boy,
160 Nor all that is at enmity with joy,
Can utterly abolish or destroy!
    Hence in a season of calm weather
    Though inland far we be,
Our Souls have sight of that immortal sea
165   Which brought us hither,
    Can in a moment travel thither,
And see the Children sport upon the shore,
And hear the mighty waters rolling evermore.

10

Then sing, ye Birds, sing, sing a joyous song!
170   And let the young Lambs bound
    As to the tabor's sound!
We in thought will join your throng,
    Ye that pipe and ye that play,
    Ye that through your hearts to-day
175   Feel the gladness of the May!
What though the radiance which was once so bright
Be now for ever taken from my sight,
    Though nothing can bring back the hour
Of splendor in the grass, of glory in the flower;
180   We will grieve not, rather find
    Strength in what remains behind;
    In the primal sympathy
    Which having been must ever be;
    In the soothing thoughts that spring

185   Out of human suffering;
        In the faith that looks through death,
In years that bring the philosophic mind.

11

And O, ye Fountains, Meadows, Hills, and Groves,
Forebode not any severing of our loves!
190 Yet in my heart of hearts I feel your might;
I only have relinquished one delight
To live beneath your more habitual sway.
I love the Brooks which down their channels fret,
Even more than when I tripped lightly as they;
195 The innocent brightness of a new-born Day
            Is lovely yet;
The Clouds that gather round the setting sun
Do take a sober coloring from an eye
That hath kept watch o'er man's mortality;
200 Another race hath been, and other palms are won.
Thanks to the human heart by which we live,
Thanks to its tenderness, its joys, and fears,
To me the meanest flower that blows can give
Thoughts that do often lie too deep for tears.

1807

25

THE SONNET

Without a doubt, the most popular of the defined forms in English and American poetry is the **sonnet**. Sonnets are always fourteen lines long. Traditionally, they are divided into two main forms. The **Petrarchan sonnet** consists of an octet, rhymed *abba abba*, and a sestet, rhymed either *cdcdcd* or *cdecde;* and the **Shakespearean sonnet**, with three quatrains, usually rhymes *abab cdcd efef,* and a couplet at the end, *gg*. Less standard rhyme forms do, of course, exist. Notice, for example, the rhyme scheme in E. E. Cummings's "the Cambridge ladies who live in furnished souls," at the end of this chapter.

Of the two traditional forms, the Shakespearean usually seems the more emphatic. Because no rhyme needs to appear more than twice, it is also slightly easier to write. It was the favored form during the Renaissance. The Petrarchan sonnet, on the other hand, tends to have a somewhat smoother flow and often seems more graceful. It was therefore preferred by the Romantic poets of the nineteenth century.

The sonnet came into English as a love poem: we have read love sonnets by Shakespeare and Sidney. But the sonnet has proved capable of handling almost any subject and of expressing many moods and tones. Look back, for example, at "Composed upon Westminster Bridge" (p. 412). And look, too, at the following examples of what can be done with the sonnet form.

William Shakespeare

(1564–1616)

See page 325 for a biographical note on the author.

Sonnet 116

Let me not to the marriage of true minds
Admit impediments. Love is not love
Which alters when it alteration finds,
Or bends with the remover to remove.
5 O no! it is an ever-fixèd mark
That looks on tempests and is never shaken;
It is the star to every wand'ring bark,
Whose worth's unknown, although his height be taken.

Love's not Time's fool, though rosy lips and cheeks
10 Within his bending sickle's compass come.
Love alters not with his brief hours and weeks,
But bears it out even to the edge of doom.
    If this be error, and upon me proved,
    I never writ, nor no man ever loved.

1609

John Donne

(1572–1631)

See page 430 for a biographical note on the author.

Sonnet 10

Death, be not proud, though some have callèd thee
Mighty and dreadful, for thou art not so;
For those whom thou think'st thou dost overthrow
Die not, poor Death, nor yet canst thou kill me.
5 From rest and sleep, which but thy pictures be,
Much pleasure; then from thee much more must flow;
And soonest our best men with thee do go,
Rest of their bones and souls' delivery.
Thou'rt slave to fate, chance, kings, and desperate men,
10 And dost with poison, war, and sickness dwell;
And poppy or charms can make us sleep as well
And better than thy stroke. Why swell'st thou then?
One short sleep past, we wake eternally,
And Death shall be no more: Death, thou shalt die.

1633

John Milton

(1608–1674)

See page 466 for a biographical note on the author.

On His Blindness

When I consider how my light is spent,
Ere half my days, in this dark world and wide,

And that one talent which is death to hide
Lodged with me useless, though my soul more bent
5   To serve therewith my Maker, and present
My true account, lest he returning chide,
"Doth God exact day labor, light denied?"
I fondly ask; but Patience, to prevent
That murmur, soon replies: "God doth not need
10   Either man's work or his own gifts; who best
Bear his mild yoke, they serve him best. His state
Is kingly: thousands at his bidding speed
And post o'er land and ocean without rest.
They also serve who only stand and wait."

1651

Gerard Manley Hopkins

(1844–1889)

See page 348 for a biographical note on the author.

God's Grandeur

The world is charged with the grandeur of God.
    It will flame out, like shining from shook foil;[1]
    It gathers to a greatness, like the ooze of oil
Crushed. Why do men then now not reck his rod?[2]
5   Generations have trod, have trod, have trod;
    And all is seared with trade; bleared, smeared with toil;
    And wears man's smudge and shares man's smell: the soil
Is bare now, nor can foot feel, being shod.

And for all this, nature is never spent;
10   There lives the dearest freshness deep down things;
And though the last lights off the black West went
    Oh, morning, at the brown brink eastward, springs—
Because the Holy Ghost over the bent
    World broods with warm breast and with ah! bright wings.

1877

---

[1]tinsel, goldfoil
[2]acknowledge his discipline

Robert Frost

(1874–1963)

See page 367 for a biographical note on the author.

Design

I found a dimpled spider, fat and white,
On a white heal-all, holding up a moth
Like a white piece of rigid satin cloth—
Assorted characters of death and blight
5 Mixed ready to begin the morning right,
Like the ingredients of a witches' broth—
A snow-drop spider, a flower like a froth,
And dead wings carried like a paper kite.

What had that flower to do with being white,
10 The wayside blue and innocent heal-all?
What brought the kindred spider to that height,
Then steered the white moth thither in the night?
What but design of darkness to appall?—
If design govern in a thing so small.

1936

Edna St. Vincent Millay

(1892–1950)

See page 359 for a biographical note on the author.

Love Is Not All: It Is Not Meat nor Drink

Love is not all: it is not meat nor drink
Nor slumber nor a roof against the rain;
Nor yet a floating spar to men that sink
And rise and sink and rise and sink again;
5 Love can not fill the thickened lung with breath,
Nor clean the blood, nor set the fractured bone;
Yet many a man is making friends with death
Even as I speak, for lack of love alone.
It well may be that in a difficult hour,
10 Pinned down by pain and moaning for release,

Or nagged by want past resolution's power,
I might be driven to sell your love for peace,
Or trade the memory of this night for food.
It well may be. I do not think I would.

1922

Wilfred Owen

(1893–1918)

See page 393 for a biographical note on the author.

Anthem for Doomed Youth

What passing-bells for these who die as cattle?
    Only the monstrous anger of the guns.
    Only the stuttering rifles' rapid rattle
Can patter out their hasty orisons.
5 No mockeries now for them; no prayers nor bells,
    Nor any voice of mourning save the choirs—
The shrill, demented choirs of wailing shells;
    And bugles calling for them from sad shires.

What candles may be held to speed them all?
10   Not in the hands of boys, but in their eyes
Shall shine the holy glimmers of good-byes.
    The pallor of girls' brows shall be their pall;
Their flowers the tenderness of patient minds,
And each slow dusk a drawing-down of blinds.

1919

E. E. Cummings

(1894–1962)

See page 328 for a biographical note on the author.

the Cambridge ladies who live in furnished souls

the Cambridge ladies who live in furnished souls
are unbeautiful and have comfortable minds
(also, with the church's protestant blessings

daughters, unscented shapeless spirited)
5   they believe in Christ and Longfellow, both dead,
are invariably interested in so many things—
at the present writing one still finds
delighted fingers knitting for the is it Poles?
perhaps. While permanent faces coyly bandy
10 scandal of Mrs. N and Professor D
. . . . the Cambridge ladies do not care, above
Cambridge if sometimes in its box of
sky lavender and cornerless, the
moon rattles like a fragment of angry candy

1904

AN ANTHOLOGY OF POEMS

Anonymous—Middle English Lyric

Western Wind

Western wind, when will thou blow,
　　The small rain down can rain?
Christ, if my love were in my arms
　　And I in my bed again.

c. 1500

Christopher Marlowe

(1564–1593)

Christopher Marlowe, had his life not been cut short by his murder in a tavern quarrel, could have rivaled William Shakespeare in brilliance as a dramatist. His plays *Tamburlaine* (1587), *The Jew of Malta* (1590), and *Dr. Faustus* (1592) earned him acclaim as expressions of the heroic intellectual spirit of the Renaissance. *Dr. Faustus,* because of its theme of the individual's quest to go beyond all limits, is often called the first expression of the modern consciousness, as opposed to a medieval one.

The Passionate Shepherd to His Love

Come live with me, and be my love,
And we will all the pleasures prove
That hills and valleys, dales and fields,
Woods, or steepy mountain yields.

5　And we will sit upon the rocks,
Seeing the shepherds feed their flocks,
By shallow rivers, to whose falls
Melodious birds sing madrigals.

And I will make thee beds of roses
10　And a thousand fragrant posies,
A cap of flowers, and a kirtle
Embroidered all with leaves of myrtle;

A gown made of the finest wool,
Which from our pretty lambs we pull,
15　Fair linèd slippers, for the cold,
With buckles of the purest gold;

A belt of straw and ivy-buds
With coral clasps and amber studs.
And if these pleasures may thee move,
20　Come live with me, and be my love.

The shepherds' swains shall dance and sing
For thy delight each May morning.
If these delights thy mind may move,
Then live with me, and be my love.

1599

Sir Walter Raleigh

(1552?–1618)

Walter Raleigh was a poet, courtier, historian, explorer, and philosopher. His short lyrics made him almost as famous as the fact that he was the founder of the Virginia colony in the New World. Imprisoned by King James, he was finally executed in 1618, despite his general popularity with the public.

The Nymph's Reply to the Shepherd

If all the world and love were young,
And truth in every shepherd's tongue,
These pretty pleasures might me move
To live with thee and be thy love.

5　Time drives the flocks from field to fold
When rivers rage and rocks grow cold,
And Philomel[1] becometh dumb;
The rest complains of cares to come.

The flowers do fade, and wanton fields
10　To wayward winter reckoning yields;
A honey tongue, a heart of gall,
Is fancy's spring, but sorrow's fall.

Thy gowns, thy shoes, thy beds of roses,
Thy cap, thy kirtle,[2] and thy posies
15　Soon break, soon wither, soon forgotten—
In folly ripe, in reason rotten.

Thy belt of straw and ivy buds,
Thy coral clasps and amber studs,
All these in me no means can move
20　To come to thee and be thy love.

---

[1]nightingale
[2]skirt

But could youth last and love still breed,
Had joys no date nor age no need,
Then these delights my mind might move
To live with thee and be thy love.

1600

William Shakespeare

(1564–1616)

See page 325 for a biographical note on the author.

Sonnet 55

Not marble nor the gilded monuments
Of princes shall outlive this powerful rime;
But you shall shine more bright in these contents
Than unswept stone, besmeared with sluttish time.
5 When wasteful war shall statues overturn,
And broils root out the work of masonry,
Nor Mars his sword nor war's quick fire shall burn
The living record of your memory.
'Gainst death and all oblivious enmity
10 Shall you pace forth; your praise shall still find room
Even in the eyes of all posterity
That wear this world out to the ending doom.
    So, till the Judgment that yourself arise,
        You live in this, and dwell in lovers' eyes.

1609

John Donne

(1572–1631)

See page 430 for a biographical note on the author.

Sonnet 7

At the round earth's imagined corners, blow
Your trumpets, angels, and arise, arise
From death, you numberless infinities

Of souls, and to your scattered bodies go;
5 All whom the flood did, and fire shall o'erthrow;
All whom war, dearth, age, agues, tyrannies,
Despair, law, chance, hath slain, and you whose eyes
Shall behold God, and never taste death's woe.
But let them sleep, Lord, and me mourn a space,
10 For if above all these my sins abound,
'Tis late to ask abundance of thy grace
When we are there; here on this lowly ground
Teach me how to repent; for that's as good
As if thou hadst sealed my pardon with thy blood.

1633

Edmund Waller

(1606–1687)

Edmund Waller was enormously popular in his lifetime as a master of the lyric form. He lacked the intellectual depth of a poet like John Donne, but he often exhibited the technical polish and restraint of a Ben Jonson. During his long life he served in parliament, enjoyed wealth, and contributed to the English lyric tradition.

Go, Lovely Rose

   Go, lovely rose,
Tell her that wastes her time and me
   That now she knows,
When I resemble her to thee,
5 How sweet and fair she seems to be.

   Tell her that's young
And shuns to have her graces spied
   That hadst thou sprung
In deserts where no men abide,
10 Thou must have uncommended died.

   Small is the worth
Of beauty from the light retired;
   Bid her come forth,
Suffer herself to be desired,
15 And not blush so to be admired.

   Then die, that she
The common fate of all things rare

May read in thee:
How small a part of time they share
20   That are so wondrous sweet and fair!

1645

Sir John Suckling

(1609–1642)

John Suckling is perhaps the epitome of the "Cavalier" poets: witty, gallant, fond of gambling, determined to make his poetry look casual and easy. Like his fellow Cavaliers, he supported King Charles Stuart, seeming to relish his bittersweet position of being part of a lost cause.

The Constant Lover

Out upon it! I have loved
   Three whole days together;
And am like to love three more,
   If it prove fair weather!

5 Time shall moult away his wings,
   Ere he shall discover
In the whole wide world again
   Such a constant lover.

But the spite on't is, no praise
10   Is due at all to me:
Love with me had made no stays,
   Had it any been but she.

1646

William Blake

(1757–1827)

See page 426 for a biographical note on the author.

London

I wander thro' each charter'd street,
Near where the charter'd Thames does flow,

And mark in every face I meet
Marks of weakness, marks of woe.

5 In every cry of every Man,
In every Infant's cry of fear,
In every voice, in every ban,
The mind-forg'd manacles I hear.

How the Chimney-sweeper's cry
10 Every blackning Church appalls;
And the hapless Soldier's sigh
Runs in blood down Palace walls.

But most thro' midnight streets I hear
How the youthful Harlot's curse
15 Blasts the new-born Infant's tear,
And blights with plagues the Marriage hearse.

1794

Samuel Taylor Coleridge

(1772–1834)

Samuel Taylor Coleridge reported that he dreamed this surreal poem after having taken opium for a stomach ailment. While he was in the process of writing the poem down after he awakened, he was interrupted by a visitor, and when he returned to his writing desk, he could not remember the rest of the dream. "Kubla Kahn" incorporates many of the standard tropes of romanticism: exotic settings, close observations of nature, supernaturalism. Kubla Kahn has built a "pleasure-dome" by "Alph, the sacred river." This river, which runs into an underground chasm, seems to become an emblem of the romantic imagination. Then the speaker describes a "damsel with a dulcimer" whom he had seen in a vision. He says that if he could revive her song within himself he could build the pleasure dome in the air—he could become the bard whose imagination changes the world. Then, everyone could look at him and realize that he had "drunk the milk of Paradise."

Kubla Khan

In Xanadu did Kubla Khan
A stately pleasure-dome decree:
Where Alph, the sacred river, ran
Through caverns measureless to man
5   Down to a sunless sea.
So twice five miles of fertile ground
With walls and towers were girdled round:
And there were gardens bright with sinuous rills,

Where blossomed many an incense-bearing tree;
10 And here were forests ancient as the hills,
Enfolding sunny spots of greenery.

But oh! that deep romantic chasm which slanted
Down the green hill athwart a cedarn cover!
A savage place! as holy and enchanted
15 As e'er beneath a waning moon was haunted
By woman wailing for her demon-lover!
And from this chasm, with ceaseless turmoil seething,
As if this earth in fast thick pants were breathing,
A mighty fountain momently was forced:
20 Amid whose swift half-intermitted burst
Huge fragments vaulted like rebounding hail,
Or chaffy grain beneath the thresher's flail:
And 'mid these dancing rocks at once and ever
It flung up momently the sacred river.
25 Five miles meandering with a mazy motion
Through wood and dale the sacred river ran,
Then reached the caverns measureless to man,

And sank in tumult to a lifeless ocean:
And 'mid this tumult Kubla heard from far
30 Ancestral voices prophesying war!

The shadow of the dome of pleasure
Floated midway on the waves;
Where was heard the mingled measure
From the fountain and the caves.

35 It was a miracle of rare device,
A sunny pleasure-dome with caves of ice!

A damsel with a dulcimer
In a vision once I saw:
It was an Abyssinian maid,
40 And on her dulcimer she played,
Singing of Mount Abora.
Could I revive within me
Her symphony and song,
To such a deep delight 'twould win me,

45 That with music loud and long,
I would build that dome in air,
That sunny dome! those caves of ice!
And all who heard should see them there,
And all should cry, Beware! Beware!

50 His flashing eyes, his floating hair!
    Weave a circle round him thrice,
    And close your eyes with holy dread,
    For he on honey-dew hath fed,
    And drunk the milk of Paradise.

1798

Alfred, Lord Tennyson

(1809–1892)

See page 406 for a biographical note on the author.

Ulysses

    It little profits that an idle king,
    By this still hearth, among these barren crags,
    Matched with an aged wife, I mete and dole
    Unequal laws unto a savage race,
5   That hoard, and sleep, and feed, and know not me.
    I cannot rest from travel; I will drink
    Life to the lees. All times I have enjoyed
    Greatly, have suffered greatly, both with those
    That loved me, and alone; on shore, and when
10 Through scudding drifts the rainy Hyades[1]
    Vexed the dim sea: I am become a name;
    For always roaming with a hungry heart
    Much have I seen and known—cities of men
    And manners, climates, councils, governments,
15 Myself not least, but honored of them all;
    And drunk delight of battle with my peers,
    Far on the ringing plains of windy Troy.
    I am a part of all that I have met;
    Yet all experience is an arch wherethrough
20 Gleams that untraveled world whose margin fades
    For ever and for ever when I move.
    How dull it is to pause, to make an end,
    To rust unburnished, not to shine in use!
    As though to breathe were life! Life piled on life
25 Were all too little, and of one to me

---

[1]a group of stars in the constellation Taurus, whose rise with the sun heralded the spring rains

Little remains; but every hour is saved
From that eternal silence, something more,
A bringer of new things; and vile it were
For some three suns to store and hoard myself,
30 And this gray spirit yearning in desire
To follow knowledge like a sinking star,
Beyond the utmost bound of human thought.

This is my son, mine own Telemachus,
To whom I leave the scepter and the isle—
35 Well-loved of me, discerning to fulfil
This labor, by slow prudence to make mild
A rugged people, and through soft degrees
Subdue them to the useful and the good.
Most blameless is he, centered in the sphere
40 Of common duties, decent not to fail
In offices of tenderness, and pay
Meet adoration to my household gods,
When I am gone. He works his work, I mine.

There lies the port; the vessel puffs her sail;
45 There gloom the dark, broad seas. My mariners,
Souls that have toiled, and wrought, and thought with me—
That ever with a frolic welcome took
The thunder and the sunshine, and opposed
Free hearts, free foreheads—you and I are old;
50 Old age hath yet his honor and his toil.
Death closes all; but something ere the end,
Some work of noble note, may yet be done,
Not unbecoming men that strove with Gods.
The lights begin to twinkle from the rocks:
55 The long day wanes: the slow moon climbs: the deep
Moans round with many voices. Come, my friends,
'Tis not too late to seek a newer world.
Push off, and sitting well in order smite
The sounding furrows; for my purpose holds
60 To sail beyond the sunset, and the baths
Of all the western stars, until I die.
It may be that the gulfs will wash us down;
It may be we shall touch the Happy Isles,
And see the great Achilles, whom we knew.
65 Though much is taken, much abides; and though

We are not now that strength which in old days
Moved earth and heaven, that which we are, we are;
One equal temper of heroic hearts,
Made weak by time and fate, but strong in will
70 To strive, to seek, to find, and not to yield.

1842

Robert Browning

(1812–1889)

See page 365 for a biographical note on the author.

The Bishop Orders His Tomb at Saint Praxed's Church

Rome, 15—

Vanity, saith the preacher, vanity!
Draw round my bed: is Anselm keeping back?
Nephews[1]—sons mine . . . ah God, I know not! Well—
She, men would have to be your mother once,
5 Old Gandolf envied me, so fair she was!
What's done is done, and she is dead beside,
Dead long ago, and I am Bishop since,
And as she died so must we die ourselves,
And thence ye may perceive the world's a dream.
10 Life, how and what is it? As here I lie
In this state-chamber, dying by degrees,
Hours and long hours in the dead night, I ask
"Do I live, am I dead?" Peace, peace seems all.
Saint Praxed's ever was the church for peace;
15 And so, about this tomb of mine. I fought
With tooth and nail to save my niche, ye know:
—Old Gandolf cozened me, despite my care;
Shrewd was that snatch from out the corner South
He graced his carrion with, God curse the same!
20 Yet still my niche is not so cramped but thence
One sees the pulpit o' the epistle side,[2]
And somewhat of the choir, those silent seats,
And up into the aery dome where live

---

[1]euphemism for illegitimate sons
[2]the right-hand side, as one faces the altar

The angels, and a sunbeam's sure to lurk:
25   And I shall fill my slab of basalt there,
And 'neath my tabernacle take my rest,
With those nine columns round me, two and two,
The odd one at my feet where Anselm stands:
Peach-blossom marble all, the rare, the ripe
30   As fresh-poured red wine of a mighty pulse.
—Old Gandolf with his paltry onion-stone,
Put me where I may look at him! True peach,
Rosy and flawless: how I earned the prize!
Draw close: that conflagration of my church
35   —What then? So much was saved if aught were missed!
My sons, ye would not be my death? Go dig
The white-grape vineyard where the oil-press stood,
Drop water gently till the surface sink,
And if ye find . . . Ah God, I know not, I! . . .
40   Bedded in store of rotten fig-leaves soft,
And corded up in a tight olive-frail,
Some lump, ah God, of *lapis lazuli,*
Big as a Jew's head cut off at the nape,
Blue as a vein o'er the Madonna's breast . . .
45   Sons, all have I bequeathed you, villas, all,
That brave Frascati villa with its bath,
So, let the blue lump poise between my knees,
Like God the Father's globe on both his hands
Ye worship in the Jesu Church so gay,
50   For Gandolf shall not choose but see and burst!
Swift as a weaver's shuttle fleet our years:
Man goeth to the grave, and where is he?
Did I say basalt for my slab, sons? Black—
'Twas ever antique-black I meant! How else
55   Shall ye contrast my frieze to come beneath?
The bas-relief in bronze ye promised me,
Those Pans and Nymphs ye wot of, and perchance
Some tripod,[3] thyrsus,[4] with a vase or so,
The Saviour at his sermon on the mount,
60   Saint Praxed in a glory, and one Pan
Ready to twitch the Nymph's last garment off,
And Moses with the tables . . . but I know
Ye mark me not! What do they whisper thee,
Child of my bowels, Anselm? Ah, ye hope

---

[3]three-legged stool used by the oracle at Delphi
[4]staff carried by Dionysus and his followers

65 To revel down my villas while I gasp
   Bricked o'er with beggar's moldy travertine
   Which Gandolf from his tomb-top chuckles at!
   Nay, boys, ye love me—all of jasper, then!
   'Tis jasper ye stand pledged to, lest I grieve
70 My bath must needs be left behind, alas!
   One block, pure green as a pistachio nut,
   There's plenty jasper somewhere in the world—
   And have I not Saint Praxed's ear to pray
   Horses for ye, and brown Greek manuscripts,
75 And mistresses with great smooth marbly limbs?
   —That's if ye carve my epitaph aright,
   Choice Latin, picked phrase, Tully's[5] every word,
   No gaudy ware like Gandolf's second line—
   Tully, my masters? Ulpian[6] serves his need!
80 And then how I shall lie through centuries,
   And hear the blessed mutter of the mass,
   And see God made and eaten all day long,
   And feel the steady candle-flame, and taste
   Good strong thick stupefying incense-smoke!
85 For as I lie here, hours of the dead night,
   Dying in state and by such slow degrees,
   I fold my arms as if they clasped a crook,
   And stretch my feet forth straight as stone can point,
   And let the bedclothes, for a mortcloth, drop
90 Into great laps and folds of sculptor's-work:
   And as yon tapers dwindle, and strange thoughts
   Grow, with a certain humming in my ears,
   About the life before I lived this life,
   And this life too, popes, cardinals, and priests,
95 Saint Praxed at his sermon on the mount,[7]
   Your tall pale mother with her talking eyes,
   And new-found agate urns as fresh as day,
   And marble's language, Latin pure, discreet
   —Aha, ELUCESCEBAT[8] quoth our friend?
100 No Tully, said I, Ulpian at the best!
   Evil and brief hath been my pilgrimage.
   All *lapis,* all, sons! Else I give the Pope

---

[5]Marcus Tullius Cicero, master of Latin prose style
[6]Domitius Ulpianus, third-century Roman jurist, noted for bad prose
[7]The bishop's failing mind attributes the Sermon on the Mount to Saint Praxed (a woman) instead of Christ.
[8]"He was illustrious," an example of Ulpian Latin

My villas! Will ye ever eat my heart?
Ever your eyes were as a lizard's quick,
105 They glitter like your mother's for my soul,
Or ye would heighten my impoverished frieze,
Piece out its starved design, and fill my vase
With grapes, and add a vizor and a Term,[9]
And to the tripod you would tie a lynx
110 That in his struggle throws the thyrsus down,
To comfort me on my entablature
Whereon I am to lie till I must ask
"Do I live, am I dead?" There, leave me, there!
For ye have stabbed me with ingratitude
115 To death—ye wish it—God, ye wish it! Stone—
Gritstone, a-crumble! Clammy squares which sweat
As if the corpse they keep were oozing through—
And no more *lapis* to delight the world!
Well go! I bless ye. Fewer tapers there,
120 But in a row: and, going, turn your backs
—Aye, like departing altar-ministrants,
And leave me in my church, the church for peace,
That I may watch at leisure if he leers—
Old Gandolf, at me, from his onion-stone,
125 As still he envied me, so fair she was!

1845

Walt Whitman

(1819–1892)

See page 378 for a biographical note on the author.

Out of the Cradle Endlessly Rocking

Out of the cradle endlessly rocking,
Out of the mocking-bird's throat, the musical shuttle,
Out of the Ninth-month midnight,
Over the sterile sands and the fields beyond, where the child leaving his bed
    wander'd alone, bareheaded, barefoot,
5 Down from the shower'd halo
Up from the mystic play of shadows twining and twisting as if they were alive,

---

[9]a mask and bust on a pedestal

Out from the patches of briers and blackberries,
From the memories of the bird that chanted to me,
From your memories sad brother, from the fitful risings and fallings I heard,
10 From under that yellow half-moon late-risen and swollen as if with tears,
From those beginning notes of yearning and love there in the mist,
From the thousand responses of my heart never to cease,
From the myriad thence-arous'd words,
From the word stronger and more delicious than any,
15 From such as now they start the scene revisiting,
As a flock, twittering, rising, or overhead passing,
Borne hither, ere all eludes me, hurriedly,
A man, yet by these tears a little boy again,
Throwing myself on the sand, confronting the waves,
20 I, chanter of pains and joys, uniter of here and hereafter,
Taking all hints to use them, but swiftly leaping beyond them,
A reminiscence sing.

Once Paumanok,[1]
When the lilac-scent was in the air and Fifth-month grass was growing,
25 Up this seashore in some briers,
Two feather'd guests from Alabama, two together,
And their nest, and four light-green eggs spotted with brown,
And every day the he-bird to and fro near at hand,
And every day the she-bird crouch'd on her nest, silent, with bright eyes,
30 And every day I, a curious boy, never too close, never disturbing them,
Cautiously peering, absorbing, translating.

Shine! shine! shine!
Pour down your warmth, great sun!
While we bask, we two together.

35 *Two together!*
Winds blow south, or winds blow north,
Day come white, or night come black,
Home, or rivers and mountains from home,
Singing all time, minding no time,
40 *While we two keep together.*

Till of a sudden,
May-be kill'd, unknown to her mate,
One forenoon, the she-bird crouch'd not on the nest,
Nor return'd that afternoon, nor the next,
45 Nor ever appear'd again.

----
[1] the Indian name for Long Island

And thenceforward all summer in the sound of the sea,
And at night under the full of the moon in calmer weather,
Over the hoarse surging of the sea,
Or flitting from brier to brier by day,
50 I saw, I heard at intervals the remaining one, the he-bird,
The solitary guest from Alabama.

Blow! blow! blow!
Blow up sea-winds along Paumanok's shore;
I wait and I wait till you blow my mate to me.

55 Yes, when the stars glisten'd,
All night long on the prong of a moss-scallop'd stake,
Down almost amid the slapping waves,
Sat the lone singer wonderful causing tears.

He call'd on his mate,
60 He pour'd forth the meanings which I of all men know.

Yes my brother I know,
The rest might not, but I have treasur'd every note,
For more than once dimly down to the beach gliding,
Silent, avoiding the moonbeams, blending myself with the shadows,
65 Recalling now the obscure shapes, the echoes, the sounds and sights
      after their sorts,
The white arms out in the breakers tirelessly tossing,
I, with bare feet, a child, the wind wafting my hair,
Listen'd long and long.

Listen'd to keep, to sing, now translating the notes,
70 Following you my brother.

Soothe! soothe! soothe!
Close on its wave soothes the wave behind,
And again another behind embracing and lapping, every one close,
But my love soothes not me, not me.

75 *Low hangs the moon, it rose late,*
It is lagging—O I think it is heavy with love, with love.

O madly the sea pushes upon the land,
With love, with love.

O night! do I not see my love fluttering out among the breakers?
80 *What is that little black thing I see there in the white?*

Loud! loud! loud!
Loud I call to you, my love!
High and clear I shoot my voice over the waves,

Surely you must know who is here, is here,
85 *You must know who I am, my love.*

Low-hanging moon!
What is that dusky spot in your brown yellow?
O it is the shape, the shape of my mate!
O moon do not keep her from me any longer.

90 *Land! land! O land!*
Whichever way I turn, O I think you could give me my mate back
        again if you only would,
For I am almost sure I see her dimly whichever way I look.

O rising stars!
Perhaps the one I want so much will rise, will rise with some of you.

95 *O throat! O trembling throat!*
Sound clearer through the atmosphere!
Pierce the woods, the earth,
Somewhere listening to catch you must be the one I want.

Shake out carols!
100 *Solitary here, the night's carols!*
Carols of lonesome love! death's carols!
Carols under that lagging, yellow, waning moon!
O under that moon where she droops almost down into the sea!
O reckless despairing carols.

105 *But soft! sink low!*
Soft! let me just murmur,
And do you wait a moment you husky-nois'd sea,
For somewhere I believe I heard my mate responding to me,
So faint, I must be still, be still to listen,
110 *But not altogether still, for then she might not come immediately to me.*

Hither my love!
Here I am! here!
With this just-sustain'd note I announce myself to you,
This gentle call is for you my love, for you.

115 *Do not be decoy'd elsewhere,*
That is the whistle of the wind, it is not my voice,
That is the fluttering, the fluttering of the spray,
Those are the shadows of leaves.

O darkness! O in vain!
120 *O I am very sick and sorrowful.*

O brown halo in the sky near the moon, drooping upon the sea!
O troubled reflection in the sea!

O throat! O throbbing heart!
And I singing uselessly, uselessly all the night.

125 *O past! O happy life! O songs of joy!*
In the air, in the woods, over fields,
Loved! loved! loved! loved! loved!
But my mate no more, no more with me!
We two together no more.

130 The aria sinking,
All else continuing, the stars shining,
The winds blowing, the notes of the bird continuous echoing,
With angry moans the fierce old mother incessantly moaning,
On the sands of Paumanok's shore gray and rustling,
135 The yellow half-moon enlarged, sagging down, drooping, the face of the sea
almost touching,
The boy ecstatic, with his bare feet the waves, with his hair the atmosphere
dallying,
The love in the heart long pent, now loose, now at last tumultuously
bursting,
The aria's meaning, the ears, the soul, swiftly depositing,
The strange tears down the cheeks coursing,
140 The colloquy there, the trio, each uttering,
The undertone, the savage old mother incessantly crying,
To the boy's soul's questions sullenly timing, some drown'd secret
hissing,
To the outsetting bard.

Demon or bird! (said the boy's soul,)
145 Is it indeed toward your mate you sing? or is it really to me?
For I, that was a child, my tongue's use sleeping, now I have heard you,
Now in a moment I know what I am for, I awake,
And already a thousand singers, a thousand songs, clearer, louder and more
sorrowful than yours,
A thousand warbling echoes have started to life within me, never to die.

150 O you singer solitary, singing by yourself, projecting me,
O solitary me listening, never more shall I cease perpetuating you,
Never more shall I escape, never more the reverberations,
Never more the cries of unsatisfied love be absent from me,
Never again leave me to be the peaceful child I was before what there in the
night,
155 By the sea under the yellow and sagging moon,
The messenger there arous'd, the fire, the sweet hell within,
The unknown want, the destiny of me.

O give me the clew! (it lurks in the night here somewhere,)
O if I am to have so much, let me have more!

160 A word then, (for I will conquer it,)
The word final, superior to all,
Subtle, sent up—what is it?—I listen;
Are you whispering it, and have been all the time, you sea-waves?
Is that it from your liquid rims and wet sands?

165 Whereto answering, the sea,
Delaying not, hurrying not,
Whisper'd me through the night, and very plainly before daybreak,
Lisp'd to me the low and delicious word death,
And again death, death, death, death,
170 Hissing melodious, neither like the bird nor like my arous'd child's heart,
But edging near as privately for me rustling at my feet,
Creeping thence steadily up to my ears and laving me softly all over,
Death, death, death, death, death.

Which I do not forget,
175 But fuse the song of my dusky demon and brother,
That he sang to me in the moonlight on Paumanok's gray beach,
With the thousand responsive songs at random,
My own songs awaked from that hour,
And with them the key, the word up from the waves,
180 The word of the sweetest song and all songs,
That strong and delicious word which, creeping to my feet,
(Or like some old crone rocking the cradle, swathed in sweet garments, bending
        aside,)
The sea whisper'd me.

1859

A. E. Housman

(1859–1936)

See page 347 for a biographical note on the author.

"Terence, This Is Stupid Stuff . . ."

"Terence, this is stupid stuff:
You eat your victuals fast enough;
There can't be much amiss, 'tis clear,
To see the rate you drink your beer.

5 But oh, good Lord, the verse you make,
  It gives a chap the belly-ache.
  The cow, the old cow, she is dead;
  It sleeps well, the hornèd head:
  We poor lads, 'tis our turn now
10 To hear such tunes as killed the cow.
  Pretty friendship 'tis to rhyme
  Your friends to death before their time
  Moping melancholy mad:
  Come, pipe a tune to dance to, lad."

15   Why, if 'tis dancing you would be,
  There's brisker pipes than poetry.
  Say, for what were hop-yards meant,
  Or why was Burton built on Trent?[1]
  Oh many a peer of England brews
20 Livelier liquor than the Muse,
  And malt does more than Milton can
  To justify God's ways to man.
  Ale, man, ale's the stuff to drink
  For fellows whom it hurts to think:
25 Look into the pewter pot
  To see the world as the world's not.
  And faith, 'tis pleasant till 'tis past:
  The mischief is that 'twill not last.
  Oh I have been to Ludlow fair
30 And left my necktie God knows where,
  And carried half-way home, or near,
  Pints and quarts of Ludlow beer:
  Then the world seemed none so bad,
  And I myself a sterling lad;
35 And down in lovely muck I've lain,
  Happy till I woke again.
  Then I saw the morning sky:
  Heigho, the tale was all a lie;
  The world, it was the old world yet,
40 I was I, my things were wet,
  And nothing now remained to do
  But begin the game anew.

    Therefore, since the world has still
  Much good, but much less good than ill,
45 And while the sun and moon endure

---

[1] a town noted for its breweries

Luck's a chance, but trouble's sure,
I'd face it as a wise man would,
And train for ill and not for good.
'Tis true, the stuff I bring for sale
50 Is not so brisk a brew as ale:
Out of a stem that scored the hand
I wrung it in a weary land.
But take it: if the smack is sour,
The better for the embittered hour;
55 It should do good to heart and head
When your soul is in my soul's stead;
And I will friend you, if I may,
In the dark and cloudy day.

There was a king reigned in the East:
60 There, when kings will sit to feast,
They get their fill before they think
With poisoned meat and poisoned drink.
He gathered all that springs to birth
From the many-venomed earth;
65 First a little, thence to more,
He sampled all her killing store;
An easy, smiling, seasoned sound,
Sate the king when healths went round.
They put arsenic in his meat
70 And stared aghast to watch him eat;
They poured strychnine in his cup
And shook to see him drink it up:
They shook, they stared as white's their shirt:
Them it was their poison hurt.
75 —I tell the tale that I heard told.
Mithridates,[2] he died old.

1939

To an Athlete Dying Young

The time you won your town the race
We chaired you through the market-place;
Man and boy stood cheering by,
And home we brought you shoulder-high.

---

[2]king of Pontus in the first century B.C., who made himself immune to certain poisons by taking
them frequently in small doses

5 To-day, the road all runners come,
  Shoulder-high we bring you home,
  And set you at your threshold down,
  Townsman of a stiller town.

  Smart lad, to slip betimes away
10 From fields where glory does not stay
  And early though the laurel grows
  It withers quicker than the rose.

  Eyes the shady night has shut
  Cannot see the record cut,
15 And silence sounds no worse than cheers
  After earth has stopped the ears:

  Now you will not swell the rout
  Of lads that wore their honors out,
  Runners whom renown outran
20 And the name died before the man.

  So set, before its echoes fade,
  The fleet foot on the sill of shade,
  And hold to the low lintel up
  The still-defended challenge-cup.

25 And round that early-laurelled head
  Will flock to gaze the strengthless dead,
  And find unwithered on its curls
  The garland briefer than a girl's.

  1939

James Weldon Johnson

(1871–1938)

James Weldon Johnson was a poet, critic, biographer, novelist, and historian of African American culture. Serving at various universities, he encouraged other writers, served in the National Association for the Advancement of Colored People, and founded the *Daily American*, the first black daily newspaper. He is usually considered one of the forerunners of the Harlem Renaissance.

O Black and Unknown Bards

O black and unknown bards of long ago,
How came your lips to touch the sacred fire?
How, in your darkness, did you come to know

The power and beauty of the minstrel's lyre?
5   Who first from midst his bonds lifted his eyes?
Who first from out the still watch, lone and long,
Feeling the ancient faith of prophets rise
Within his dark-kept soul, burst into song?

Heart of what slave poured out such melody
10   As "Steal away to Jesus"? On its strains
His spirit must have nightly floated free,
Though still about his hands he felt his chains.
Who heard great "Jordan roll"? Whose starward eye
Saw chariot "swing low"? And who was he
15   That breathed that comforting, melodic sigh,
"Nobody knows de trouble I see"?

What merely living clod, what captive thing,
Could up toward God through all its darkness grope,
And find within its deadened heart to sing
20   These songs of sorrow, love and faith, and hope?
How did it catch that subtle undertone,
That note in music heard not with the ears?
How sound the elusive reed so seldom blown,
Which stirs the soul or melts the heart to tears?

25   Not that great German master[1] in his dream
Of harmonies that thundered amongst the stars
At the creation, ever heard a theme
Nobler than "Go down, Moses." Mark its bars,
How like a mighty trumpet-call they stir
30   The blood. Such are the notes that men have sung
Going to valorous deeds; such tones there were
That helped make history when Time was young.

There is a wide, wide wonder in it all,
That from degraded rest and servile toil
35   The fiery spirit of the seer should call
These simple children of the sun and soil.
O black slave singers, gone, forgot, unfamed,
You—you alone, of all the long, long line
Of those who've sung untaught, unknown, unnamed,
40   Have stretched out upward, seeking the divine.

You sang not deeds of heroes or of kings;
No chant of bloody war, no exulting paean

---

[1]Beethoven

Of arms-won triumphs; but your humble strings
You touched in chord with music empyrean.
45 You sang far better than you knew; the songs
That for your listeners' hungry hearts sufficed
Still live—but more than this to you belongs:
You sang a race from wood and stone to Christ.

1909

Wallace Stevens

(1879–1955)

Wallace Stevens, along with William Carlos Williams and T. S. Eliot, was one of the most important American poets of the first half of the twentieth century. He worked all his adult life as an insurance executive, however, keeping himself apart from literary circles. From his first collection, *Harmonium*, published in 1923, until his death, Stevens wrote distinctively modern poems characterized by intellectual sophistication, verbal playfulness, and a carefully considered humanist and agnostic philosophy.

Thirteen Ways of Looking at a Blackbird

I

Among the twenty snowy mountains,
The only moving thing
Was the eye of the blackbird.

II

I was of three minds,
5 Like a tree
In which there are three blackbirds.

III

The blackbird whirled in the autumn winds.
It was a small part of the pantomime.

IV

A man and a woman
10 Are one.
A man and a woman and a blackbird
Are one.

V

I do not know which to prefer,
The beauty of inflections,
15 Or the beauty of innuendoes,
The blackbird whistling
Or just after.

VI

Icicles filled the long window
With barbaric glass.
20 The shadow of the blackbird
Crossed it, to and fro.
The mood
Traced in the shadow
An indecipherable cause.

VII

25 O thin men of Haddam[1]
Why do you imagine golden birds?
Do you not see how the blackbird
Walks around the feet
Of the women about you?

VIII

30 I know noble accents
And lucid, inescapable rhythms;
But I know, too,
That the blackbird is involved
In what I know.

IX

35 When the blackbird flew out of sight,
It marked the edge
Of one of many circles.

X

At the sight of blackbirds
Flying in a green light,
40 Even the bawds of euphony
Would cry out sharply.

---

[1] A town in Connecticut; Stevens liked its name.

XI

He rode over Connecticut
In a glass coach.
Once, a fear pierced him,
45 In that he mistook
The shadow of his equipage
For blackbirds.

XII

The river is moving.
The blackbird must be flying.

XIII

50 It was evening all afternoon.
It was snowing
And it was going to snow.
The blackbird sat
In the cedar-limbs.

1923

William Butler Yeats

(1865–1939)

See page 364 for a biographical note on the author.

Leda and the Swan[1]

A sudden blow: the great wings beating still
Above the staggering girl, her thighs caressed
By the dark webs, her nape caught in his bill,
He holds her helpless breast upon his breast.

5 How can those terrified vague fingers push
The feathered glory from her loosening thighs?
And how can body, laid in that white rush,
But feel the strange heart beating where it lies?

---

[1]Zeus, in the form of a swan, violated *Leda,* who gave birth to Helen and Clytemnestra. Helen's flight with Paris to Troy, leaving her husband Menelaus, Agamemnon's brother, caused the war between the Greeks and the Trojans. Clytemnestra murdered her husband Agamemnon on his return from victory at Troy.

A shudder in the loins engenders there
10 The broken wall, the burning roof and tower
And Agamemnon dead.
                          Being so caught up,
So mastered by the brute blood of the air,
Did she put on his knowledge with his power
15 Before the indifferent beak could let her drop?

1928

H. D. (Hilda Doolittle)

(1886–1961)

H. D., along with William Carlos Williams and Ezra Pound, was first recognized as an
imagist poet. Like the other modernists, she tried to find new ways of ordering experience
in the face of technological advances, war, and the alienation of the individual. Although
educated in the classics, she was influenced by James Joyce, Virginia Woolf, and, to some
extent, by William Faulkner in developing her stream-of-consciousness fiction. She was a
strong voice for feminist concerns, both with respect to opposing war and to celebrating
the female artist.

Heat

O wind, rend open the heat,
cut apart the heat,
rend it to tatters.

Fruit cannot drop
5 through this thick air—
fruit cannot fall into heat
that presses up and blunts
the points of pears
and rounds the grapes.

10 Cut the heat—
plough through it,
turning it on either side
of your path.

1912

Marianne Moore

(1887–1972)

See page 336 for a biographical note on the author.

Poetry

I, too, dislike it: there are things that are important beyond all this fiddle.
  Reading it, however, with a perfect contempt for it, one discovers in
  it after all, a place for the genuine.
    Hands that can grasp, eyes
5   that can dilate, hair that can rise
      if it must, these things are important not because a

high-sounding interpretation can be put upon them but because they are
  useful. When they become so derivative as to become unintelligible,
  the same thing may be said for all of us, that we
10   do not admire what
    we cannot understand: the bat
      holding on upside down or in quest of something to

eat, elephants pushing, a wild horse taking a roll, a tireless wolf under
  a tree, the immovable critic twitching his skin like a horse that feels a flea, the
15   base-
  ball fan, the statistician—
    nor is it valid
      to discriminate against "business documents and

school-books"; all these phenomena are important. One must make
      a distinction
  however: when dragged into prominence by half poets, the result
      is not poetry,
20 nor till the poets among us can be
    "literalists of
    the imagination"—above
      insolence and triviality and can present

for inspection, "imaginary gardens with real toads in them," shall we have
25 it. In the meantime, if you demand on the one hand,
  the raw material of poetry in
    all its rawness and
    that which is on the other hand
      genuine, you are interested in poetry.

1959

T. S. Eliot

(1888–1965)

T. S. Eliot was the most influential poet writing in English in the 1920s and 1930s. His poetic output was relatively slight, but it received a vast amount of critical attention. His essays on the metaphysical poets and the nature of literary tradition were enormously influential in defining the modernist aesthetic. Such Eliotic ideas as the "objective correlative," the "dissociation of sensibility," and the "impersonality" of good poetry became part of the standard critical vocabulary of the day. Mixing the learned and the colloquial was a defining element in Eliot's poems, especially in *The Waste Land* (1922), which combined elements of classical myth with modern-day realism. Born in St. Louis, Eliot became one of the American expatriates to Europe, eventually becoming a British citizen. His later poems reflect his conversion to the Anglican Church.

The Love Song of J. Alfred Prufrock

S'io credesse che mia risposta fosse
A persona che mai tornasse al mondo,
Questa fiamma staria senza piu scosse.
Ma perciocche giammai di questo fondo
Non torno vivo alcun, s'i'odo il vero,
Senza tema d'infamia ti rispondo.[1]

Let us go then, you and I,
When the evening is spread out against the sky
Like a patient etherized upon a table;
Let us go, through certain half-deserted streets,
5 The muttering retreats
Of restless nights in one-night cheap hotels
And sawdust restaurants with oyster-shells:
Streets that follow like a tedious argument
Of insidious intent
10 To lead you to an overwhelming question . . .

Oh, do not ask, "What is it?"
Let us go and make our visit.

In the room the women come and go
Talking of Michelangelo.

---

[1]"If I thought that my response were given to one who would ever return to the world, this flame would move no more. But since never from this depth has man returned alive, if what I hear is true, without fear of infamy I answer thee." In Dante's *Inferno* these words are addressed to the poet by the spirit of Guido da Montefeltro.

15 The yellow fog that rubs its back upon the window-panes
The yellow smoke that rubs its muzzle on the window panes
Licked its tongue into the corners of the evening,
Lingered upon the pools that stand in drains,
Let fall upon its back the soot that falls from chimneys,
20 Slipped by the terrace, made a sudden leap,
And seeing that it was a soft October night,
Curled once about the house, and fell asleep.

And indeed there will be time
For the yellow smoke that slides along the street,
25 Rubbing its back upon the window-panes;
There will be time, there will be time
To prepare a face to meet the faces that you meet;
There will be time to murder and create,
And time for all the works and days of hands
30 That lift and drop a question on your plate;
Time for you and time for me,
And time yet for a hundred indecisions,
And for a hundred visions and revisions,
Before the taking of a toast and tea.

35 In the room the women come and go
Talking of Michelangelo.

And indeed there will be time
To wonder, "Do I dare?" and, "Do I dare?"
Time to turn back and descend the stair,
40 With a bald spot in the middle of my hair—
[They will say: "How his hair is growing thin!"]
My morning coat, my collar mounting firmly to the chin,
My necktie rich and modest, but asserted by a simple pin—
[They will say: "But how his arms and legs are thin!"]
45 Do I dare
Disturb the universe?
In a minute there is time
For decisions and revisions which a minute will reverse.

For I have known them all already, known them all:
50 Have known the evenings, mornings, afternoons,
I have measured out my life with coffee spoons;
I know the voices dying with a dying fall
Beneath the music from a farther room.
      So how should I presume?

55 And I have known the eyes already, known them all—
The eyes that fix you in a formulated phrase,
And when I am formulated, sprawling on a pin,
When I am pinned and wriggling on the wall,
Then how should I begin
60 To spit out all the butt-ends of my days and ways?
      And how should I presume?

And I have known the arms already, known them all—
Arms that are braceleted and white and bare
[But in the lamplight, downed with light brown hair!]
65 Is it perfume from a dress
That makes me so digress?
Arms that lie along a table, or wrap about a shawl.
      And should I then presume?
      And how should I begin?

70 Shall I say, I have gone at dusk through narrow streets
And watched the smoke that rises from the pipes
Of lonely men in shirt-sleeves, leaning out of windows? . . .

I should have been a pair of ragged claws
Scuttling across the floors of silent seas.

75 And the afternoon, the evening, sleeps so peacefully!
Smoothed by long fingers,
Asleep . . . tired . . . or it malingers,
Stretched on the floor, here beside you and me.
Should I, after tea and cakes and ices,
80 Have the strength to force the moment to its crisis?
But though I have wept and fasted, wept and prayed,
Though I have seen my head [grown slightly bald] brought in upon a
      platter,
I am no prophet—and here's no great matter;
I have seen the moment of my greatness flicker,
85 And I have seen the eternal Footman hold my coat, and snicker,
And in short, I was afraid.

And would it have been worth it, after all,
After the cups, the marmalade, the tea,
Among the porcelain, among some talk of you and me,
90 Would it have been worth while,

To have bitten off the matter with a smile,
To have squeezed the universe into a ball
To roll it toward some overwhelming question,

To say: "I am Lazarus, come from the dead,
95 Come back to tell you all, I shall tell you all"—
If one, settling a pillow by her head,
      Should say: "That is not what I meant at all.
      That is not it, at all."

And would it have been worth it, after all,
100 Would it have been worth while,
After the sunsets and the dooryards and the sprinkled streets,
After the novels, after the teacups, after the skirts that trail along the floor—
And this, and so much more?—
It is impossible to say just what I mean!
105 But as if a magic lantern threw the nerves in patterns on a screen:
Would it have been worth while
If one, settling a pillow or throwing off a shawl,
And turning toward the window, should say:
      "That is not it at all,
110   That is not what I meant, at all."

No! I am not Prince Hamlet, nor was meant to be;
Am an attendant lord, one that will do
To swell a progress, start a scene or two,
Advise the prince; no doubt, an easy tool,
115 Deferential, glad to be of use,
Politic, cautious, and meticulous;
Full of high sentence, but a bit obtuse;
At times, indeed, almost ridiculous—
Almost, at times, the Fool.

120 I grow old . . . I grow old . . .
I shall wear the bottoms of my trousers rolled.

Shall I part my hair behind? Do I dare to eat a peach?
I shall wear white flannel trousers, and walk upon the beach.
I have heard the mermaids singing, each to each.

125 I do not think that they will sing to me.

I have seen them riding seaward on the waves
Combing the white hair of the waves blown back
When the wind blows the water white and black.

We have lingered in the chambers of the sea
130 By sea-girls wreathed with seaweed red and brown
Till human voices wake us, and we drown.

1909

Archibald MacLeish

(1892–1982)

Archibald MacLeish graduated from Yale, earned a Harvard law degree, served in World War I, and then lived with his wife in Paris while he worked to become a poet. Returning to America, he wrote several works in the 1930s that warned of the rise of fascism. Although influenced by Ezra Pound and T. S. Eliot, he wanted a more public role for the poet than their intellectual, highly allusive aestheticism allowed. He held several public posts, including Librarian of Congress, and he won both the Pulitzer Prize and the National Book Award for his poetry.

Ars Poetica

A poem should be palpable and mute
As a globed fruit,

Dumb
As old medallions to the thumb,

5 Silent as the sleeve-worn stone
Of casement ledges where the moss has grown—

A poem should be wordless
As the flight of birds.

A poem should be motionless in time
10 As the moon climbs,

Leaving, as the moon releases
Twig by twig the night-entangled trees,

Leaving, as the moon behind the winter leaves
Memory by memory the mind—

15 A poem should be motionless in time
As the moon climbs.

A poem should be equal to:
Not true.

For all the history of grief
20 An empty doorway and a maple leaf.

For love
The leaning grasses and two lights above the sea—

A poem should not mean
But be.

1917

W. H. Auden

(1907–1973)

See page 402 for a biographical note on the author.

Musée des Beaux Arts[1]

About suffering they were never wrong,
The Old Masters: how well they understood
Its human position; how it takes place
While someone else is eating or opening a window or just walking dully along;
5   How, when the aged are reverently, passionately waiting
For the miraculous birth, there always must be
Children who did not specially want it to happen, skating
On a pond at the edge of the wood:
They never forgot
10   That even the dreadful martyrdom must run its course
Anyhow in a corner, some untidy spot
Where the dogs go on with their doggy life and the torturer's horse
Scratches its innocent behind on a tree.

In Brueghel's *Icarus*,[2] for instance: how everything turns away
15   Quite leisurely from the disaster; the plowman may
Have heard the splash, the forsaken cry,
But for him it was not an important failure; the sun shone
As it had to on the white legs disappearing into the green
Water; and the expensive delicate ship that must have seen
20   Something amazing, a boy falling out of the sky,
Had somewhere to get to and sailed calmly on.

1940

---

[1]the Museum of Fine Arts in Brussels, where Brueghel's *Landscape with the Fall of Icarus* hangs
[2]In Greek mythology Icarus falls into the sea and drowns when he flies too close to the sun on his
wings of wax. In Brueghel's painting Icarus is an insignificant part of the picture.

Allen Tate

(1899–1979)

Allen Tate, one of the members of the Fugitive Movement at Vanderbilt University, impressed John Crowe Ransom, Robert Penn Warren, and Hart Crane with his poetic talents. He contributed to the manifesto of the agrarians, *I'll Take My Stand* (1930), urging an abandonment of Northern industrialism in favor of the Jeffersonian ideal of the self-sufficient farmer. He was one of the proponents of the New Criticism, urging a close reading of the text rather than concentration on biographical matters. His best-known poem is "Ode to the Confederate Dead," in which he explores the complexity of the Southerner's relationship to the past.

The Wolves

There are wolves in the next room waiting
With heads bent low, thrust out, breathing
At nothing in the dark; between them and me
A white door patched with light from the hall
5 Where it seems never (so still is the house)
A man has walked from the front door to the stair.
It has all been forever. Beasts claw the floor.
I have brooded on angels and archfiends
But no man has ever sat where the next room's
10 Crowded with wolves, and for the honor of man
I affirm that never have I before. Now while
I have looked for the evening star at a cold window
And whistled when Arcturus spilt his light,
I've heard the wolves scuffle, and said: So this
15 Is man; so—what better conclusion is there—
The day will not follow night, and the heart
Of man has a little dignity, but less patience
Than a wolf's, and a duller sense that cannot
Smell its own mortality. (This and other
20 Meditations will be suited to other times
After dog silence howls his epitaph.)
Now remember courage, go to the door,
Open it and see whether coiled on the bed
Or cringing by the wall, a savage beast
25 Maybe with golden hair, with deep eyes
Like a bearded spider on a sunlit floor
Will snarl—and man can never be alone.

1977

James Dickey

(1923–)

James Dickey earned a reputation early in his career as a sort of Ernest Hemingway of poetry, because he celebrated the earthly pleasures of the outdoors, sexuality, and war. He has worked variously as an advertising man and teacher, and he achieved fame for his novel *Deliverance* (1970), which was made into a popular motion picture for which he wrote the screenplay. All of his work, like that of D. H. Lawrence, is concerned with the instinctual side of human beings, which he saw as having been too radically sublimated in the modern world.

The Heaven of Animals

Here they are. The soft eyes open.
If they have lived in a wood
It is a wood.
If they have lived on plains
5 It is grass rolling
Under their feet forever.

Having no souls, they have come,
Anyway, beyond their knowing.
Their instincts wholly bloom
10 And they rise.
The soft eyes open.

To match them, the landscape flowers,
Outdoing, desperately
Outdoing what is required:
15 The richest wood,
The deepest field.

For some of these,
It could not be the place
It is, without blood.
20 These hunt, as they have done
But with claws and teeth grown perfect,

More deadly than they can believe.
They stalk more silently,
And crouch on the limbs of trees,
25 And their descent
Upon the bright backs of their prey

May take years
In a sovereign floating of joy.
And those that are hunted
30 Know this as their life,
Their reward: to walk

Under such trees in full knowledge
Of what is in glory above them,
And to feel no fear,
35 But acceptance, compliance.
Fulfilling themselves without pain

At the cycle's center,
They tremble, they walk
Under the tree,
40 They fall, they are torn,
They rise, they walk again.

1957

Gwendolyn Brooks

(1917–   )

See page 335 for a biographical note on the author.

The Bean Eaters

They eat beans mostly, this old yellow pair.
Dinner is a casual affair.
Plain chipware on a plain and creaking wood,
Tin flatware.

5 Two who are Mostly Good.
Two who have lived their day,
But keep on putting on their clothes
And putting things away.

And remembering . . .
10 Remembering, with twinklings and twinges,
As they lean over the beans in their rented back room that is full of beads and
receipts and dolls and clothes, tobacco crumbs, vases and fringes.

1987

Lawrence Ferlinghetti

(1919–)

Lawrence Ferlinghetti was one of the San Francisco poets associated with the "Beat" movement. His City Lights bookstore was a mecca for all sorts of unconventional artists. When he published Allen Ginsberg's Howl, he was charged with obscenity but later acquitted. Ferlinghetti has been a frequent critic of American foreign policy, especially during the war in Vietnam.

The pennycandystore beyond the El

The pennycandystore beyond the El
is where I first
         fell in love
            with unreality
5 Jellybeans glowed in the semi-gloom
of that september afternoon
A cat upon the counter moved among
              the licorice sticks
       and tootsie rolls
10   and Oh Boy Gum

Outside the leaves were falling as they died

A wind had blown away the sun

A girl ran in
Her hair was rainy
15 Her breasts were breathless in the little room

Outside the leaves were falling
         and they cried
            Too soon! too soon!

1958

Allen Ginsberg

(1926–1997)

See page 423 for a biographical note on the author.

A Supermarket in California

What thoughts I have of you tonight, Walt Whitman, for I walked down the sidestreets under the trees with a headache self-conscious looking at the full moon.

In my hungry fatigue, and shopping for images, I went into the neon fruit
5   supermarket, dreaming of your enumerations!

What peaches and what penumbras! Whole families shopping at night! Aisles full of husbands! Wives in the avocados, babies in the tomatoes!—and you, Garcia Lorca,[1] what were you doing down by the watermelons?

10   I saw you, Walt Whitman, childless, lonely old grubber, poking among the meats in the refrigerator and eyeing the grocery boys.

I heard you asking questions of each: Who killed the pork chops? What price bananas? Are you my Angel?

I wandered in and out of the brilliant stacks of cans following you, and
15   followed in my imagination by the store detective.

We strode down the open corridors together in our solitary fancy tasting artichokes, possessing every frozen delicacy, and never passing the cashier.

Where are we going, Walt Whitman? The doors close in an hour. Which
20   way does your beard point tonight?

(I touch your book and dream of our odyssey in the supermarket and feel absurd.)

Will we walk all night through solitary streets? The trees add shade to shade, lights out in the houses, we'll both be lonely.

25   Will we stroll dreaming of the lost America of love past blue automobiles in driveways, home to our silent cottage?

Ah, dear father, graybeard, lonely old courage-teacher, what America did you have when Charon quit poling his ferry and you got out on a smoking bank and stood watching the boat disappear on the black waters of Lethe?[2]

1955

---

[1]Federico Garciá Lorca (1899–1936), Spanish poet and playwright. He was murdered at the start of the Spanish Civil War, and his works were suppressed by the Franco government.
[2]Charon, in Greek myth, ferried the shades of the dead to Hades across Lethe, River of Forgetfulness.

Anne Sexton

(1928–1974)

Anne Sexton is associated with the "Confessional" school of poetry. She studied with Robert Lowell at Boston University and was a friend of Sylvia Plath. She married, had two children, and during the 1960s, achieved notoriety for her poetry. She wrote with great candor about her emotional distress, which finally resulted in her suicide.

Welcome Morning

There is joy
in all:
in the hair I brush each morning,
in the Cannon towel, newly washed,
5 that I rub my body with each morning,
in the chapel of eggs I cook
each morning,
in the outcry from the kettle
that heats my coffee,
10 each morning,
in the spoon and the chair,
that cry "hello there, Anne"
each morning,
in the godhead of the table
15 that I set my silver, plate, cup upon,
each morning.

All this is God,
right here in my pea green house,
each morning
20 and I mean,
though often forget,
to give thanks,
to faint down by the kitchen table
in a prayer of rejoicing
25 as the holy birds at the kitchen window
peck into their marriage of seeds.

So while I think of it,
let me paint a thank you on my palm
for this God, this laughter of the morning,
30 lest it go unspoken.

The Joy that isn't shared, I've heard,
dies young.

1975

Ted Hughes

(1930–1998)

Ted Hughes was educated at Cambridge, where he met Sylvia Plath, the American poet whom he married. His poems are intense, unsentimental, often startling in their visceral imagery. His attitude toward the natural world is more Darwinian than romantic.

Pike

Pike, three inches long, perfect
Pike in all parts, green tigering the gold.
Killers from the egg: the malevolent aged grin.
They dance on the surface among the flies.

5 Or move, stunned by their own grandeur,
Over a bed of emerald, silhouette
Of submarine delicacy and horror.
A hundred feet long in their world.

In ponds, under the heat-struck lily pads—
10 Gloom of their stillness:
Logged on last year's black leaves, watching upwards.
Or hung in an amber cavern of weeds

The jaw's hooked clamp and fangs
Not to be changed at this date;
15 A life subdued to its instrument;
The gills kneading quietly, and the pectorals.

Three we kept behind glass,
Jungled in weed: three inches, four,
And four and a half: fed fry to them—
20 Suddenly there were two. Finally one

With a sag belly and the grin it was born with.
And indeed they spare nobody.
Two, six pounds each, over two feet long,
High and dry and dead in the willow-herb—

25 One jammed past its gills down the other's gullet:
The outside eye stared: as a vice locks—

The same iron in this eye
Though its film shrank in death.

A pond I fished, fifty yards across,
30 Whose lilies and muscular tench
Had outlasted every visible stone
Of the monastery that planted them—

Stilled legendary depth:
It was as deep as England. It held
35 Pike too immense to stir, so immense and old
That past nightfall I dared not cast

But silently cast and fished
With the hair frozen on my head
For what might move, for what eye might move.
40 The still splashes on the dark pond,

Owls hushing the floating woods
Frail on my ear against the dream
Darkness beneath night's darkness had freed,
That rose slowly towards me, watching.

1970

Amiri Baraka (LeRoi Jones)

(1934–   )

Amiri Baraka, after a stint in the Air Force, moved to Greenwich Village, married, and met such Beat poets as Allen Ginsberg. He visited Cuba in 1960 and returned with a sense that American capitalism exploited people of color. The assassination of Malcolm X further radicalized Jones, and he changed his name in 1966 to Amiri Baraka, a proclamation of his Islamic identity. In the 1970s he joined the faculty at SUNY Stony Brook and continues to be a strong voice of African American concerns.

W. W.

Back home the black women are all beautiful,
and the white ones fall back, cutoff from 1000
years stacked booty, and Charles of the Ritz
where jooshladies turn into billy burke in blueglass
5 kicks. With wings, and jingly bew-teeful things.
The black women in Newark are fine. Even with all that grease
in their heads. I mean even the ones where the wigs
slide around, and they coming at you 75 degrees off course.

I could talk to them. Bring them around. To something.
10 Some kind of quick course, on the sidewalk, like Hey baby
why don't you take that thing off yo' haid. You look like
Miss Muffet in a runaway ugly machine. I mean. Like that.

1969

Garrett Hongo

(1951–   )

See page 383 for a biographical note on the author.

Yellow Light

One arm hooked around the frayed strap
of a tar-black patent-leather purse,
the other cradling something for dinner:
fresh bunches of spinach from a J-Town *yaoya*,
5 sides of split Spanish mackerel from Alviso's,
maybe a loaf of Langendorf; she steps
off the hissing bus at Olympic and Fig,
begins the three-block climb up the hill,
passing gangs of schoolboys playing war,
10 Japs against Japs, Chicanas chalking sidewalks
with the holy double-yoked crosses of hopscotch,
and the Korean grocer's wife out for a stroll
around this neighborhood of Hawaiian apartments
just starting to steam with cooking
15 and the anger of young couples coming home
from work, yelling at kids, flicking on
TV sets for the Wednesday Night Fights.

If it were May, hydrangeas and jacaranda
flowers in the streetside trees would be
20 blooming through the smog of late spring.
Wisteria in Masuda's front yard would be
shaking out the long tresses of its purple hair.
Maybe mosquitoes, moths, a few orange butterflies
settling on the lattice of monkey flowers
25 tangled in chain-link fences by the trash.

But this is October, and Los Angeles
seethes like a billboard under twilight.
From used-car lots and the movie houses uptown,

long silver sticks of light probe the sky.
30 From the Miracle Mile, whole freeways away,
a brilliant fluorescence breaks out
and makes war with the dim squares
of yellow kitchen light winking on
in all the side streets of the Barrio.

35 She climbs up the two flights of flagstone
stairs to 201-B, the spikes of her high heels
clicking like kitchen knives on a cutting board,
props the groceries against the door,
fishes through memo pads, a compact,
40 empty packs of chewing gum, and finds her keys.

The moon then, cruising from behind
a screen of eucalyptus across the street,
covers everything, everything in sight,
in a heavy light like yellow onions.

1982

Sharon Olds

(1942–)

Sharon Olds was born in San Francisco and educated at Stanford and Columbia. In 1984 her collection of poems *The Living and the Dead* won the National Book Critics Circle Award. She has received fellowships from the Guggenheim Foundation and the National Endowment for the Humanities. Her most recent collection of poems is called *The Wellspring* (1996).

Sex without Love

How do they do it, the ones who make love
without love? Beautiful as dancers,
gliding over each other like ice skaters
over the ice, fingers hooked
5 inside each other's bodies, faces
red as steak, wine, wet as the
children at birth whose mothers are going to
give them away. How do they come to the
come to the   come to the   God   come to the
10 still waters, and not love
the one who came there with them, light
rising slowly as steam off their joined

skin? These are the true religious,
the purists, the pros, the ones who will not
15 accept a false Messiah, love the
priest instead of the God. They do not
mistake the lover for their own pleasure,
they are like great runners: they know they are alone
with the road surface, the cold, the wind,
20 the fit of their shoes, their over-all cardio-
vascular health—just factors, like the partner
in the bed, and not the truth, which is the
single body alone in the universe
against its own best time.

1984

DRAMA

26

READING DRAMA

Analyzing Greek drama around 330 B.C., the philosopher Aristotle found each play to be composed of six parts: plot, character, thought, diction, spectacle, and music. Of these, he considered the **plot**—the putting together of diverse happenings to create a complete and unified action—the most important. Without plot, he says, there can be no play, for the chief purpose of drama is the acting-out of an action.

Characters come next in importance for Aristotle. **Thought**—by which he seems to mean not only the ideas expressed by the various speakers, but also their use of speech to sway the emotions of the audience—comes third. **Diction**, the choice of words, is fourth. **Music** and **spectacle**, being pleasant and often impressive, but not essential, come last.

With the exception of music and spectacle, which apply only to plays in performance, Aristotle's categories are essentially the same categories we've been using in discussing fiction. The further we read in Aristotle, the more similarities we find: Aristotle warns would-be authors that their plots, to be complete, must have a natural beginning, middle, and end; that they must provide scope for their heroes to pass from happiness to unhappiness, or from unhappiness to happiness; and that they must be unified, containing nothing that could be taken away without leaving the drama incomplete.

In addition, Aristotle points out that the most important moments in the plot are those concerned with **reversals** and **recognition**. A reversal occurs when an action that is expected to have one result produces the opposite result instead. A recognition occurs when a character suddenly "recognizes" some fact or person, thus moving from a state of ignorance to a state of knowledge. In the best plays, the two events are joined and form the turning point of the play: the hero suddenly learns something of great personal importance, either by being informed of some facts by another character or by coming to a realization or insight himself. In either case, the result of the hero's enlightenment is a reversal, changing the course of the play's action and of the hero's life (from happiness to unhappiness or vice versa).

In discussing characterization, Aristotle reminds us that all characters must be people basically like ourselves, though some may be better and some worse. And again, he insists that consistency and probability are the two most important standards of judgment. The writer must make sure that the characters' actions are consistent with their natures, and that their natures remain consistent throughout the drama.

If we have not already discussed all of these ideas, at least we have no difficulty in applying them to the fiction we've read. To discuss consistency of character, for instance, we need only look at the narrator of "Youth," with his reflective, philosophical, but still sympathetic account of the illusions of adventurous young men, or at the narrator of "My Man Bovanne," with her caring nature and her strong concern for individual dignity. The basic elements of drama, then, are the same as those of fiction. It is the method of presentation that differs.

Fiction is the telling of tales. Its roots go back to the archetypal figure of the storyteller, rehearsing old legends and inventing new marvels for the listeners. The importance of voice in fiction, therefore, can hardly be overemphasized. Indeed, as fiction has become a more silent experience, writers seem to have attached increasing importance to the question of what voice speaks through their works. Listening to stories is still enjoyable. Any good story can be read aloud and enjoyed the better for it. But our society seems to feel that listening to tales is a pleasure most proper for children and for those who cannot read to themselves. For most of us, therefore, fiction is something we read silently and alone. It involves one book, one writer, one reader. We discuss stories in company, but we tend to read them in solitude.

Drama—in performance, at least—is wholly different. It is not written for one voice, but for many. It depends not on storytellers but on actors, men and women who impersonate their tale's characters not only in voice, but also in motion, gesture, and appearance, making them live for our eyes as well as our ears. Moreover, it is written for many viewers, for only in the midst of an audience can we appreciate fully the magic of drama. Laughing alone at a joke in print is enjoyable; being one laughing person among a hundred people can be hilarious.

Actors know this well. They know how fully they must bring their characters alive for their audience. They know, too, how dependent they are on the audience's response if they are to perform well. Many actors have declared that the best performances are those during which the emotions portrayed on stage are caught and sent back by the audience until audience and actors alike are caught up in the atmosphere they have created between them, and the illusion of the play becomes more real than the realities of the world outside. Similarly, many have said that acting in films, where no audience is present to reflect the emotional impact of the scene, is a more difficult and less enjoyable form of acting than acting on the stage. Playgoers and filmgoers, in their turn, agree that the experience of attending a live performance has an electric quality not to be found in viewing a film.

The fervor with which most of us discuss a really good play or film we've just seen, as opposed to the milder delight with which we discuss a really good book, testifies to the power of drama to move and delight us. A knowledge of the origins of drama, about which we will speak in the next chapter, may help explain the intensity of our response. Within this course, however, we are readers rather than viewers of drama. And so the very power of drama in performance is likely to raise questions for us. "Here we are," we say, "with no stage, no actors—nothing but a playscript in front of us. What can we expect from this experience?"

Reading drama is certainly different from reading fiction. Drama generally gives us no narrator to describe scenes and characters, to comment on the significance of the action, to tie scenes together, or to provide a unifying viewpoint. Instead, drama gives us several characters, distinguished in the text only by their names, talking mostly to each other rather than to us, intent on their own affairs, entering and leaving the scene in bewildering succession.

If we were *watching* a play, we would recognize the characters by their appearance, mannerisms, and voices. Knowing the characters, we would then find it easy to follow the action. When we *read* a play, however, we must do without these visual clues—or rather, we must supply them for ourselves. We must use the text as the play's director would, judging from its words and from the actions they describe how the play would look and sound on stage.

Reading plays, in fact, gives our imagination free rein. How would I stage this scene? What sort of actor would I want for this role? What kind of stage setting would I use? What kind of camera work would I use in a film? Which would be my long shots, which my close-ups? What emotions would my filming be trying to capture?

Most of all, perhaps, you will think of the various characters as they are revealed in the text. What characteristics will each one exhibit? How will they carry themselves on stage? What tones of voice will they use in their speeches? How will they act toward each other?[1] The more clearly you can visualize the play's action and characters, the more readily the text will come alive for you.

Don't be afraid to experiment in your thinking. Actors, directors, and scene designers all allow themselves some freedom of interpretation when they put on a play. You can read for days about famous actors who have played Hamlet, each applying a very personal interpretation to emphasize one aspect or another of the prince's complex personality. Why should not we, as readers, enjoy the same freedom to visualize the play, interpreting and fitting together its parts to develop our vision of its conflicts and its meanings?

The text of a play will supply us with plenty of help. Because drama does depend so largely on the art of the actor, dramatists must create characters who can carry the play by their speeches and actions. Everything the actors (and readers) need must be contained in the speeches and stage directions. Here are some of the things we can look for:

We can look for characters who, like **first-person narrators** in fiction, reveal in their speech information about their habits, personalities, and thinking—information they do not always know they are giving us. We can expect to

---

[1]A handy device for keeping track of a play's characters, in fact, is to "cast" the play for yourself with actors you'd enjoy watching in it. Then you can follow those actors through each scene, imagining how they would interpret the roles.

be wiser than most of these characters, because we have the ability to stand apart from the action in which they participate, to see it fully or judge it objectively.

We can look for patterns in characterization and for conflicts between characters. We can look for characters who support each other and characters who oppose each other. We can expect to see strong characters opposed to weak ones, inflexible characters opposed to reasonable ones, good characters opposed to evil ones.

The speeches of the actors, therefore, set down in the play's text, will describe the play's characters for us, develop the action and conflict of the play, and contain the play's themes. The conflict between the ideas expressed in speeches will often be basic to the conflict of the play. Thus, in *Oedipus Rex*, much of the play's conflict centers on the question of whether it is wise or foolish for Oedipus to seek the truth about Laïos's murder. And in *Hamlet*, the conflict between Hamlet and Claudius over who will rule Denmark becomes almost secondary to the mental conflicts between Hamlet and the other characters (and within Hamlet himself) on the moral and practical issues arising from the political conflict.

Patterns of speech, characterization, and **thought**, then, are as important in drama as they are in fiction. **Patterns of language** and **imagery**, too, are important. Some plays, such as *A Doll's House*, try to imitate everyday speech patterns in their language. Other plays, such as *Hamlet* or *Oedipus Rex*, use the full power of poetry in their speeches. Dialogue in these plays can move in a few lines from the accents of everyday speech to those of extreme poetic passion, as the playwrights draw from the rhythms of poetry a capacity for dignity and grandeur and openness of expression that the limits of everyday speech deny them.

Patterns of imagery, too, can be used to great effect in these poetic plays. But imagery, as we have seen already in our work with fiction, is not restricted to poetry. Certainly, *Hamlet* is the richest in imagery of the eight plays presented here. But all make some use of imagery, such as the imagery of physical and mental blindness in *Oedipus Rex*.

Reading drama, therefore, can offer an intensification of the pleasure provided by reading fiction. More richly patterned in action, language, and characterization than most short stories, allowing its readers more scope for interpretation and for the visual imagination, drama offers us a chance to be actors, director, and audience in one.

27

GREEK TRAGEDY

Western drama is often said to have originated in ancient Greece. Certainly its two most outstanding forms, **tragedy** and **comedy**, began there.

About the beginnings of this drama, we know little, for few records have survived. We do know, however, that it began at festivals honoring Dionysus, or Bacchus, a god who was supposed to have taught people to cultivate grapes and make wine. Song and dance were the means by which this god was worshipped. At early festivals, **choruses** of fifty men dressed in tattered garments with wine-smeared faces or disguised as Dionysus's mythical companions, the satyrs, sang hymns praising the god's deeds while they half-danced, half-mimed his exploits. Eventually one man stepped out of the chorus and engaged his fellows in dialogue. Later still, the soloist began impersonating the god, thus dramatizing the events of which he was singing.

Sometime during this process, the content of the songs also shifted. Some still pertained to Dionysus, but some dealt with other, human, heroes. Although worshippers were reportedly shocked at the first introduction of the new tales, asking, "What has this to do with Dionysus?", the novelty soon became the rule. By 530 B.C., the performances were being called tragedies and were competing in Athens for an annual prize.

In the next hundred years, **Greek tragedy** reached what Aristotle considered its full form. A second actor was added, and then a third. Episodes of dialogue among the actors, with the chorus occasionally joining in, became as important as the choric songs and dances with which they alternated. Painted backdrops, stage machinery, and special effects were introduced.

For all its developments, however, Greek drama remained a religious event. Plays were performed only at Dionysus's festivals; actors were considered his servants. Performances took place three times a year: twice at Athens, once at various rural festivals. The older of the Athenian festivals, the *Lenaea*, became the festival for comedy; but the *City Dionysia*, which drew visitors from all over Greece, was the festival for tragedy.

For this festival, three playwrights were chosen by Athenian authorities. Each was given a chorus and actors, who were paid and costumed by some rich citizen as a public service; each was allotted one day of the festival on which to perform. The performance would consist of three tragedies (sometimes on the same subject, sometimes not), followed by a **satyr play**, an obscene or satiric **parody** of some legendary event. At the end of the three days of playing, a jury of ten citizens, chosen by lot, judged the plays and awarded the prizes.[1] Any Athenian was welcome to attend these plays, which were held in a natural amphitheater that seated some 30,000 people. Because the theater was reported to be crowded at every performance, we may assume that virtually everybody who could attend, did.

All in all, drama in ancient Athens seems to have been regarded almost as a public possession. Looked on with a mixture of religious devotion, civic pride, and open enjoyment, it maintained a great and general popularity that seems to have declined only with the decline of Athens itself. And still the plays remained influential, both in themselves and in the theory of drama that Aristotle's comments on them provided. First the Romans copied them. Then, some 1,500 years later, Renaissance playwrights took ideas from both Greek and Roman drama. We will discuss that development in the next chapter.

Tragedy and Comedy

Greek drama segregated its forms carefully. Tragedy dealt with the noble, the heroic, the sacrificial. In performance, three tragedies would be followed by a satyr play, which turned heroic figures into tricksters or clowns and often mocked the very legends that had supplied the day's tragedies. Comedy had its own festival, in which it could deal with the more practical aspirations of everyday people—good food, warm beds, and peaceful households and cities. The heroes of comedy battle such unheroic opponents as thieves, con men, unreasonable parents, and crooked politicians. Often, they must resort to trickery to outwit these unsavory sorts, who may very well be tricksters themselves. A happy ending is guaranteed.

Oedipus Rex and *Antigonê*

Oedipus Rex is, in many ways, the embodiment of Greek tragedy. It deals with a somewhat idealized, larger-than-life **hero**, a man caught in a dilemma between his ideals and his personal safety and fighting his way toward a terrifying knowledge. "Ah," cries the Shepherd in one climactic scene, "I am on the brink of dreadful speech." "And I of dreadful hearing," replies Oedipus. "Yet I must hear." This insistence on following through in a search, an action, the pursuit of an ideal has always attracted readers, perhaps because we all know how difficult that sort of courage is to sustain. It is the one force that is constant in tragedy.

The sad or terrible ending, incidentally, is not essential to tragedy. Some Greek tragedies end happily, in a reconciliation of their opposed forces, new

---

[1]Sophocles, the author of *Oedipus Rex*, held the all-time record of eighteen first prizes and is said never to have won less than second prize. Yet *Oedipus Rex* itself, which was praised by Aristotle and is still considered one of the finest of Greek tragedies, won only second prize when it was first produced.

knowledge having created new peace. The essentials of tragedy are the protagonist's own insistence on action or enlightenment and the ability of the play, however it ends, to arouse a sympathetic "fear and pity" (Aristotle's terms) in the audience as they watch the working-out of the hero's quest. *Oedipus Rex* clearly has these essentials.

Oedipus Rex gains much of its power from the unwavering intensity of its focus on the central character. But this focus, though not uncommon in tragedy, is also not essential to it. Many Greek tragedies have more than one central character. *The Trojan Women,* for example, has as heroines all the famous women who were caught up in the sack of Troy. *Antigonê,* which follows *Oedipus Rex* in this chapter, concentrates not so much on a single character as on the clash of wills between two characters. One of these characters is Kreon, Oedipus's uncle, now the ruler of Thebes; the other is Antigonê, Oedipus's daughter.

The action of *Antigonê* takes place some years after that of *Oedipus Rex.* In the time between the two plays, Oedipus's two sons have quarreled. In fact, just before *Antigonê* opens, one of the brothers (Polyneicês) has gathered a group of supporters and has attacked both his brother (Eteoclês) and the city of Thebes itself. In the battle, the two brothers have killed each other. Kreon, now ruling Thebes, has ordered a hero's funeral for Eteoclês, the defender of Thebes, but has refused burial to Polyneicês, Thebes's attacker. Antigonê's response to this proclamation, and Kreon's reaction to her response, form the action of the tragedy.

Throughout the play, Kreon's concern is for public welfare and order; he speaks most frequently as the voice of public authority, the defender of the public good. Antigonê's concern is for piety and for family ties. She speaks most often from her own conscience, as a private person. When she does speak of public matters, it is generally to contrast social law with divine law. Between these two forces of public and private good lies the play's tension. This is a play in which *thought,* Aristotle's third element of tragedy, is predominant. Yet, as with *Oedipus,* it is the strong-willed, dedicated nature of the antagonists that makes the play a true tragedy, not merely an argument. The issues involved are still argued; their expression here in tragedy is unique.

Oedipus Rex

SOPHOCLES (496–406 B.C.)

An English version by Dudley Fitts and Robert Fitzgerald

Sophocles was born into a rich family and educated in the sciences and arts like other privileged sons of Athens destined for public life. As a sixteen-year-old, however, he witnessed the near destruction of Athens by the Persians under the leadership of the ruthless Xerxes. Only the brilliant fighting of a much smaller Athenian fleet against the massive Persian army saved the Greeks from total annihilation. Though the Persians were defeated, Athens was in ruins, and Sophocles never forgot the sight when he returned from the island of Salamis, where the civilians had retreated. His tragic sense was formed early and powerfully by these events.

Sophocles wrote over a hundred plays (most of which have not survived), and won many prizes at the Dionysian drama festival held twice a year in Athens. His long life almost exactly coincided with the Golden Age of Athens; he died just two years before the city fell to the Spartans. Universally respected as handsome, talented, and lucky, Sophocles nevertheless understood the tenuousness of human existence, the fragility of the new form of government called democracy, and the essentially tragic nature of life. Along with Aeschylus and Euripides, he is considered one of the great Greek playwrights.

CHARACTERS

OEDIPUS, *King of Thebes, supposed son of Polybos and Meropê, King and Queen of Corinth*
IOKASTÊ, *wife of Oedipus and widow of the late King Laïos*
KREON, *brother of Iokastê, a prince of Thebes*
TEIRESIAS, *a blind seer who serves Apollo*
PRIEST
MESSENGER, *from Corinth*
SHEPHERD, *former servant of Laïos*
SECOND MESSENGER, *from the palace*
CHORUS OF THEBAN ELDERS
CHORAGOS, *leader of the Chorus*
ANTIGONÊ *and* ISMENÊ, *young daughters of Oedipus and Iokastê. They appear in the Exodos but do not speak.*
SUPPLIANTS, GUARDS, SERVANTS

THE SCENE. *Before the palace of* OEDIPUS, *King of Thebes. A central door and two lateral doors open onto a platform that runs the length of the façade. On the platform, right and left, are altars; and three steps lead down into the "orchestra" or chorus-ground. At the beginning of the action these steps are crowded by suppliants who have brought branches and chaplets of olive leaves and who sit in various attitudes of despair.* OEDIPUS *enters.*

Prologue

OEDIPUS   My children, generations of the living
In the line of Kadmos,[1] nursed at his ancient hearth:
Why have you strewn yourselves before these altars
In supplication, with your boughs and garlands?
5   The breath of incense rises from the city
With a sound of prayer and lamentation.
                                          Children,
I would not have you speak through messengers,
And therefore I have come myself to hear you—
10   I, Oedipus, who bear the famous name.
(*to a* PRIEST) You, there, since you are eldest in the company,
Speak for them all, tell me what preys upon you,
Whether you come in dread, or crave some blessing:
Tell me, and never doubt that I will help you
15   In every way I can; I should be heartless
Were I not moved to find you suppliant here.
PRIEST   Great Oedipus, O powerful king of Thebes!
You see how all the ages of our people
Cling to your altar steps: here are boys
20   Who can barely stand alone, and here are priests
By weight of age, as I am a priest of God,
And young men chosen from those yet unmarried;
As for the others, all that multitude,
They wait with olive chaplets in the squares,
25   At the two shrines of Pallas, and where Apollo
Speaks in the glowing embers.
                                          Your own eyes
Must tell you: Thebes is tossed on a murdering sea
And can not lift her head from the death surge.
30   A rust consumes the buds and fruits of the earth;
The herds are sick; children die unborn,
And labor is vain. The god of plague and pyre
Raids like detestable lightning through the city,
And all the house of Kadmos is laid waste,
35   All emptied, and all darkened: Death alone
Battens upon the misery of Thebes.

You are not one of the immortal gods, we know;
Yet we have come to you to make our prayer
As to the man surest in mortal ways

---

[1]founder of Thebes

40   And wisest in the ways of God. You saved us
     From the Sphinx, that flinty singer, and the tribute
     We paid to her so long; yet you were never
     Better informed than we, nor could we teach you:
     A god's touch, it seems, enabled you to help us.

45   Therefore, O mighty power, we turn to you:
     Find us our safety, find us a remedy,
     Whether by counsel of the gods or of men.
     A king of wisdom tested in the past
     Can act in a time of troubles, and act well.
50   Noblest of men, restore
     Life to your city! Think how all men call you
     Liberator for your boldness long ago;
     Ah, when your years of kingship are remembered,
     Let them not say *We rose, but later fell*—
55   Keep the State from going down in the storm!
     Once, years ago, with happy augury,
     You brought us fortune; be the same again!
     No man questions your power to rule the land:
     But rule over men, not over a dead city!
60   Ships are only hulls, high walls are nothing,
     When no life moves in the empty passageways.
OEDIPUS   Poor children! You may be sure I know
     All that you longed for in your coming here.
     I know that you are deathly sick; and yet,
65   Sick as you are, not one is as sick as I.
     Each of you suffers in himself alone
     His anguish, not another's; but my spirit
     Groans for the city, for myself, for you.

     I was not sleeping, you are not waking me.
70   No, I have been in tears for a long while
     And in my restless thought walked many ways.
     In all my search I found one remedy,
     And I have adopted it: I have sent Kreon,
     Son of Menoikeus, brother of the queen,
75   To Delphi, Apollo's place of revelation,
     To learn there, if he can,
     What act or pledge of mine may save the city.
     I have counted the days, and now, this very day,
     I am troubled, for he has overstayed his time.
80   What is he doing? He has been gone too long.

Yet whenever he comes back, I should do ill
Not to take any action the god orders.
PRIEST   It is a timely promise. At this instant
They tell me Kreon is here.
85 OEDIPUS   O Lord Apollo!
May his news be fair as his face is radiant!
PRIEST   Good news, I gather! he is crowned with bay,
The chaplet is thick with berries.
OEDIPUS   We shall soon know;
90   He is near enough to hear us now.

(*Enter* KREON.)

                              O prince:
Brother: son of Menoikeus:
What answer do you bring us from the god?
KREON   A strong one. I can tell you, great afflictions
95   Will turn out well, if they are taken well.
OEDIPUS   What was the oracle? These vague words
Leave me still hanging between hope and fear.
KREON   Is it your pleasure to hear me with all these
Gathered around us? I am prepared to speak,
100   But should we not go in?
OEDIPUS   Speak to them all,
It is for them I suffer, more than for myself.
KREON   Then I will tell you what I heard at Delphi.
In plain words
105   The god commands us to expel from the land of Thebes
An old defilement we are sheltering.
It is a deathly thing, beyond cure;
We must not let it feed upon us longer.
OEDIPUS   What defilement? How shall we rid ourselves of it?
110 KREON   By exile or death, blood for blood. It was
Murder that brought the plague-wind on the city.
OEDIPUS   Murder of whom? Surely the god has named him?
KREON   My lord: Laïos once ruled this land,
Before you came to govern us.
115 OEDIPUS   I know;
I learned of him from others; I never saw him.
KREON   He was murdered; and Apollo commands us now
To take revenge upon whoever killed him.
OEDIPUS   Upon whom? Where are they? Where shall we find a clue
120   To solve that crime, after so many years?

KREON   Here in this land, he said. Search reveals
    Things that escape an inattentive man.
OEDIPUS   Tell me: Was Laïos murdered in his house,
    Or in the fields, or in some foreign country?
125 KREON   He said he planned to make a pilgrimage.
    He did not come home again.
OEDIPUS   And was there no one,
    No witness, no companion, to tell what happened?
KREON   They were all killed but one, and he got away
130   So frightened that he could remember one thing only.
OEDIPUS   What was the one thing? One may be the key
    To everything, if we resolve to use it.
KREON   He said that a band of highwaymen attacked them,
    Outnumbered them, and overwhelmed the king.
135 OEDIPUS   Strange, that a highwayman should be so daring—
    Unless some faction here bribed him to do it.
KREON   We thought of that. But after Laïos' death
    New troubles arose and we had no avenger.
OEDIPUS   What troubles could prevent your hunting down
140   the killers?
KREON   The riddling Sphinx's song
    Made us deaf to all mysteries but her own.
OEDIPUS   Then once more I must bring what is dark to light.
    It is most fitting that Apollo shows,
145   As you do, this compunction for the dead.
    You shall see how I stand by you, as I should,
    Avenging this country and the god as well,
    And not as though it were for some distant friend,
    But for my own sake, to be rid of evil.
150   Whoever killed King Laïos might—who knows?—
    Lay violent hands even on me—and soon.
    I act for the murdered king in my own interest.

    Come, then, my children: leave the altar steps,
    Lift up your olive boughs!
155   One of you go
    And summon the people of Kadmos to gather here.
    I will do all that I can; you may tell them that.

(*Exit a* PAGE.)

    So, with the help of God,
    We shall be saved—or else indeed we are lost.

160 PRIEST   Let us rise, children. It was for this we came,
        And now the king has promised it.
        Phoibos[2] has sent us an oracle; may he descend
        Himself to save us and drive out the plague.

(*Exeunt* OEDIPUS *and* KREON *into the palace by the central door. The* PRIEST *and the* SUPPLIANTS *disperse R and L. After a short pause the* CHORUS *enters the* orchestra.)

Párodos[3]

Strophe I

CHORUS   What is God singing in his profound
        Delphi of gold and shadow?
        What oracle for Thebes, the sunwhipped city?
        Fear unjoints me, the roots of my heart tremble.
5   Now I remember, O Healer, your power, and wonder:
        Will you send doom like a sudden cloud, or weave it
        Like nightfall of the past?
        Speak to me, tell me, O
        Child of golden Hope, immortal Voice.

Antistrophe I

10   Let me pray to Athenê, the immortal daughter of Zeus,
        And to Artemis her sister
        Who keeps her famous throne in the market ring,
        And to Apollo, archer from distant heaven—
        O gods, descend! Like three streams leap against
15   The fires of our grief, the fires of darkness;
        Be swift to bring us rest!
        As in the old time from the brilliant house
        Of air you stepped to save us, come again!

---

[2]Apollo
[3]The song or ode chanted by the chorus on its entry. It is accompanied by dancing and music played on a flute. The chorus in this play represents elders of the city of Thebes. Chorus members remain onstage (on a level lower than the principal actors) for the remainder of the play. The choral odes and dances serve to separate one scene from another (there was no curtain in Greek theater) as well as to comment on the action, reinforce the emotion, and interpret the situation. The chorus also performs dance movements during certain portions of the scenes themselves. Strophe and antistrophe are terms denoting the movement and countermovement of the chorus from one side of its playing area to the other. When the chorus participates in dialogue with the other characters, its lines are spoken by the Choragos, its leader.

Strophe 2

Now our afflictions have no end,
20   Now all our stricken host lies down
And no man fights off death with his mind;
The noble plowland bears no grain,
And groaning mothers can not bear—
See, how our lives like birds take wing,
25   Like sparks that fly when a fire soars,
To the shore of the god of evening.

Antistrophe 2

The plague burns on, it is pitiless,
Though pallid children laden with death
Lie unwept in the stony ways,
30   And old gray women by every path
Flock to the strand about the altars
There to strike their breasts and cry
Worship of Phoibos in wailing prayers:
Be kind, God's golden child!

Strophe 3

35   There are no swords in this attack by fire,
No shields, but we are ringed with cries.
Send the besieger plunging from our homes
Into the vast sea-room of the Atlantic
Or into the waves that foam eastward of Thrace—
40   For the day ravages what the night spares—
Destroy our enemy, lord of the thunder!
Let him be riven by lightning from heaven!

Antistrophe 3

Phoibos Apollo, stretch the sun's bowstring,
That golden cord, until it sing for us,
45   Flashing arrows in heaven!
                Artemis, Huntress,
Race with flaring lights upon our mountains!
O scarlet god, O golden-banded brow,
O Theban Bacchos in a storm of Maenads,

(*Enter* OEDIPUS, *C.*)

50   Whirl upon Death, that all the Undying hate!
    Come with blinding torches, come in joy!

Scene I

OEDIPUS   Is this your prayer? It may be answered. Come,
    Listen to me, act as the crisis demands,
    And you shall have relief from all these evils.

    Until now I was a stranger to this tale,
5   As I had been a stranger to the crime.
    Could I track down the murderer without a clue?
    But now, friends,
    As one who became a citizen after the murder,
    I make this proclamation to all Thebans:
10   If any man knows by whose hand Laïos, son of Labdakos,
    Met his death, I direct that man to tell me everything,
    No matter what he fears for having so long withheld it.
    Let it stand as promised that no further trouble
    Will come to him, but he may leave the land in safety.

15   Moreover: If anyone knows the murderer to be foreign,
    Let him not keep silent: he shall have his reward from me.
    However, if he does conceal it; if any man
    Fearing for his friend or for himself disobeys this edict,
    Hear what I propose to do:

20   I solemnly forbid the people of this country,
    Where power and throne are mine, ever to receive that man
    Or speak to him, no matter who he is, or let him
    Join in sacrifice, lustration, or in prayer.
    I decree that he be driven from every house,
25   Being, as he is, corruption itself to us: the Delphic
    Voice of Apollo has pronounced this revelation.
    Thus I associate myself with the oracle
    And take the side of the murdered king.

    As for the criminal, I pray to God—
30   Whether it be a lurking thief, or one of a number—
    I pray that that man's life be consumed in evil and wretchedness.
    And as for me, this curse applies no less
    If it should turn out that the culprit is my guest here,
    Sharing my hearth.
35   You have heard the penalty.

I lay it on you now to attend to this
For my sake, for Apollo's, for the sick
Sterile city that heaven has abandoned.
Suppose the oracle had given you no command:
40   Should this defilement go uncleansed for ever?
You should have found the murderer: your king,
A noble king, had been destroyed!

                                        Now I,
Having the power that he held before me,
45   Having his bed, begetting children there
Upon his wife, as he would have, had he lived—
Their son would have been my children's brother,
If Laïos had had luck in fatherhood!
(And now his bad fortune has struck him down)—
50   I say I take the son's part, just as though
I were his son, to press the fight for him
And see it won! I'll find the hand that brought
Death to Labdakos' and Polydoros' child,
Heir of Kadmos' and Agenor's line.[4]
55   And as for those who fail me,
May the gods deny them the fruit of the earth,
Fruit of the womb, and may they rot utterly!
Let them be wretched as we are wretched, and worse!

For you, for loyal Thebans, and for all
60   Who find my actions right, I pray the favor
Of justice, and of all the immortal gods.
CHORAGOS   Since I am under oath, my lord, I swear
I did not do the murder, I can not name
The murderer. Phoibos ordained the search;
65   Why did he not say who the culprit was?
OEDIPUS   An honest question. But no man in the world
Can make the gods do more than the gods will.
CHORAGOS   There is an alternative, I think—
OEDIPUS   Tell me.
70   Any or all, you must not fail to tell me.
CHORAGOS   A lord clairvoyant to the lord Apollo,
As we all know, is the skilled Teiresias.
One might learn much about this from him, Oedipus.

---

[4]father, grandfather, great-grandfather, and great-great-grandfather of Laïos

OEDIPUS   I am not wasting time:
75   Kreon spoke of this, and I have sent for him—
    Twice, in fact; it is strange that he is not here.
    CHORAGOS   The other matter—that old report—seems useless.
    OEDIPUS   What was that? I am interested in all reports.
    CHORAGOS   The king was said to have been killed by highwaymen.
80 OEDIPUS   I know. But we have no witnesses to that.
    CHORAGOS   If the killer can feel a particle of dread,
        Your curse will bring him out of hiding!
    OEDIPUS   No.
        The man who dared that act will fear no curse.

(*Enter the blind seer* TEIRESIAS, *led by a* PAGE.)

85 CHORAGOS   But there is one man who may detect the criminal.
        This is Teiresias, this is the holy prophet
        In whom, alone of all men, truth was born.
    OEDIPUS   Teiresias: seer: student of mysteries,
        Of all that's taught and all that no man tells,
90   Secrets of Heaven and secrets of the earth:
        Blind though you are, you know the city lies
        Sick with plague; and from this plague, my lord,
        We find that you alone can guard or save us.

        Possibly you did not hear the messengers?
95   Apollo, when we sent to him,
        Sent us back word that this great pestilence
        Would lift, but only if we established clearly
        The identity of those who murdered Laïos.
        They must be killed or exiled.
                                            Can you use
100   Birdflight[5] or any art of divination
        To purify yourself, and Thebes, and me
        From this contagion? We are in your hands.
        There is no fairer duty
        Than that of helping others in distress.
105 TEIRESIAS   How dreadful knowledge of the truth can be
        When there's no help in truth! I knew this well,
        But did not act on it: else I should not have come.
    OEDIPUS   What is troubling you? Why are your eyes so cold?
    TEIRESIAS   Let me go home. Bear your own fate, and I'll
110   Bear mine. It is better so: trust what I say.

---

[5]Prophets predicted the future or divined the unknown by observing the flight of birds.

OEDIPUS   What you say is ungracious and unhelpful
    To your native country. Do not refuse to speak.
TEIRESIAS   When it comes to speech, your own is neither temperate
    Nor opportune. I wish to be more prudent.
115 OEDIPUS   In God's name, we all beg you—
TEIRESIAS   You are all ignorant.
    No; I will never tell you what I know.
    Now it is my misery; then, it would be yours.
OEDIPUS   What! You do know something, and will not tell us?
120   You would betray us all and wreck the State?
TEIRESIAS   I do not intend to torture myself, or you.
    Why persist in asking? You will not persuade me.
OEDIPUS   What a wicked old man you are! You'd try a stone's
    Patience! Out with it! Have you no feeling at all?
125 TEIRESIAS   You call me unfeeling. If you could only see
    The nature of your own feelings . . .
OEDIPUS   Why,
    Who would not feel as I do? Who could endure
    Your arrogance toward the city?
130 TEIRESIAS   What does it matter?
    Whether I speak or not, it is bound to come.
OEDIPUS   Then, if "it" is bound to come, you are bound to tell me.
TEIRESIAS   No, I will not go on. Rage as you please.
OEDIPUS   Rage? Why not!
135   And I'll tell you what I think:
    You planned it, you had it done, you all but
    Killed him with your own hands; if you had eyes,
    I'd say the crime was yours, and yours alone.
TEIRESIAS   So? I charge you, then,
140   Abide by the proclamation you have made:
    From this day forth
    Never speak again to these men or to me;
    You yourself are the pollution of this country.
OEDIPUS   You dare say that! Can you possibly think you have
145   Some way of going free, after such insolence?
TEIRESIAS   I have gone free. It is the truth that sustains me.
OEDIPUS   Who taught you shamelessness? It was not your craft.
TEIRESIAS   You did. You made me speak. I did not want to.
OEDIPUS   Speak what? Let me hear it again more clearly.
150 TEIRESIAS   Was it not clear before? Are you tempting me?
OEDIPUS   I did not understand it. Say it again.
TEIRESIAS   I say that you are the murderer whom you seek.
OEDIPUS   Now twice you have spat out infamy. You'll pay for it!
TEIRESIAS   Would you care for more? Do you wish to be really angry?

155 OEDIPUS   Say what you will. Whatever you say is worthless.
    TEIRESIAS   I say you live in hideous shame with those
        Most dear to you. You can not see the evil.
    OEDIPUS   Can you go on babbling like this for ever?
    TEIRESIAS   I can, if there is power in truth.
160 OEDIPUS   There is:
        But not for you, not for you,
        You sightless, witless, senseless, mad old man!
    TEIRESIAS   You are the madman. There is no one here
        Who will not curse you soon, as you curse me.
165 OEDIPUS   You child of total night! I would not touch you;
        Neither would any man who sees the sun.
    TEIRESIAS   True: it is not from you my fate will come.
        That lies within Apollo's competence,
        As it is his concern.
170 OEDIPUS   Tell me, who made
        These fine discoveries? Kreon? or someone else?
    TEIRESIAS   Kreon is no threat. You weave your own doom.
    OEDIPUS   Wealth, power, craft of statesmanship!
        Kingly position, everywhere admired!
175   What savage envy is stored up against these,
        If Kreon, whom I trusted, Kreon my friend,
        For this great office which the city once
        Put in my hands unsought—if for this power
        Kreon desires in secret to destroy me!

180   He has bought this decrepit fortune-teller, this
        Collector of dirty pennies, this prophet fraud—
        Why, he is no more clairvoyant than I am!
                                        Tell us:
        Has your mystic mummery ever approached the truth?
185   When that hellcat the Sphinx was performing here,
        What help were you to these people?
        Her magic was not for the first man who came along:
        It demanded a real exorcist. Your birds—
        What good were they? or the gods, for the matter of that?
190   But I came by,
        Oedipus, the simple man, who knows nothing—
        I thought it out for myself, no birds helped me!
        And this is the man you think you can destroy,
        That you may be close to Kreon when he's king!
195   Well, you and your friend Kreon, it seems to me,
        Will suffer most. If you were not an old man,
        You would have paid already for your plot.

CHORAGOS   We can not see that his words or yours
　　　　　Have been spoken except in anger, Oedipus,
200　　　And of anger we have no need. How to accomplish
　　　　　The god's will best: that is what most concerns us.
TEIRESIAS   You are a king. But where argument's concerned
　　　　　I am your man, as much a king as you.
　　　　　I am not your servant, but Apollo's.
205　　　I have no need of Kreon or Kreon's name.

　　　　　Listen to me. You mock my blindness, do you?
　　　　　But I say that you, with both your eyes, are blind:
　　　　　You can not see the wretchedness of your life,
　　　　　Nor in whose house you live, no, nor with whom.
210　　　Who are your father and mother? Can you tell me?
　　　　　You do not even know the blind wrongs
　　　　　That you have done them, on earth and in the world below.
　　　　　But the double lash of your parents' curse will whip you
　　　　　Out of this land some day, with only night
215　　　Upon your precious eyes.
　　　　　Your cries then—where will they not be heard?
　　　　　What fastness of Kithairon[6] will not echo them?
　　　　　And that bridal-descant of yours—you'll know it then,
　　　　　The song they sang when you came here to Thebes
220　　　And found your misguided berthing.
　　　　　All this, and more, that you can not guess at now,
　　　　　Will bring you to yourself among your children.

　　　　　Be angry, then. Curse Kreon. Curse my words.
　　　　　I tell you, no man that walks upon the earth
225　　　Shall be rooted out more horribly than you.
OEDIPUS   Am I to bear this from him?—Damnation
　　　　　Take you! Out of this place! Out of my sight!
TEIRESIAS   I would not have come at all if you had not asked me.
OEDIPUS   Could I have told that you'd talk nonsense, that
230　　　You'd come here to make a fool of yourself, and of me?
TEIRESIAS   A fool? Your parents thought me sane enough.
OEDIPUS   My parents again!—Wait: who were my parents?
TEIRESIAS   This day will give you a father, and break your heart.
OEDIPUS   Your infantile riddles! Your damned abracadabra!
235 TEIRESIAS   You were a great man once at solving riddles.
OEDIPUS   Mock me with that if you like; you will find it true.
TEIRESIAS   It was true enough. It brought about your ruin.

----

[6]the mountain where Oedipus was taken to be exposed as an infant

OEDIPUS   But if it saved this town?

TEIRESIAS   (*to the* PAGE)   Boy, give me your hand.

240 OEDIPUS   Yes, boy; lead him away.

—While you are here
We can do nothing. Go; leave us in peace.

TEIRESIAS   I will go when I have said what I have to say.
How can you hurt me? And I tell you again:

245   The man you have been looking for all this time,
The damned man, the murderer of Laïos,
That man is in Thebes. To your mind he is foreign-born,
But it will soon be shown that he is a Theban,
A revelation that will fail to please.

250   A blind man,
Who has his eyes now; a penniless man, who is rich now;
And he will go tapping the strange earth with his staff.
To the children with whom he lives now he will be
Brother and father—the very same; to her

255   Who bore him, son and husband—the very same
Who came to his father's bed, wet with his father's blood.

Enough. Go think that over.
If later you find error in what I have said,
You may say that I have no skill in prophecy.

(*Exit* TEIRESIAS, *led by his* PAGE. OEDIPUS *goes into the palace.*)

Ode I

Strophe I

CHORUS   The Delphic stone of prophecies
Remembers ancient regicide
And a still bloody hand.
That killer's hour of flight has come.

5   He must be stronger than riderless
Coursers of untiring wind,
For the son[7] of Zeus armed with his father's thunder
Leaps in lightning after him;
And the Furies hold his track, the sad Furies.

---

[7]Apollo

Antistrophe 1

10   Holy Parnassos'[8] peak of snow
Flashes and blinds that secret man,
That all shall hunt him down:
Though he may roam the forest shade
Like a bull gone wild from pasture
15   To rage through glooms of stone.
Doom comes down on him; flight will not avail him;
For the world's heart calls him desolate,
And the immortal voices follow, for ever follow.

Strophe 2

But now a wilder thing is heard
20   From the old man skilled at hearing Fate in the wing-beat of a bird.
Bewildered as a blown bird, my soul hovers and can not find
Foothold in this debate, or any reason or rest of mind.
But no man ever brought—none can bring
Proof of strife between Thebes' royal house,
25   Labdakos' line, and the son of Polybos;
And never until now has any man brought word
Of Laïos' dark death staining Oedipus the King.

Antistrophe 2

Divine Zeus and Apollo hold
Perfect intelligence alone of all tales ever told;
30   And well though this diviner works, he works in his own night;
No man can judge that rough unknown or trust in second sight,
For wisdom changes hands among the wise.
Shall I believe my great lord criminal
At a raging word that a blind old man let fall?
35   I saw him, when the carrion woman[9] faced him of old,
Prove his heroic mind. These evil words are lies.

Scene II

KREON   Men of Thebes:
I am told that heavy accusations
Have been brought against me by King Oedipus.

---

[8]mountain sacred to Apollo
[9]the Sphinx

I am not the kind of man to bear this tamely.

5   If in these present difficulties
       He holds me accountable for any harm to him
       Through anything I have said or done—why, then,
       I do not value life in this dishonor.
       It is not as though this rumor touched upon
10   Some private indiscretion. The matter is grave.
       The fact is that I am being called disloyal
       To the State, to my fellow citizens, to my friends.
CHORAGOS   He may have spoken in anger, not from his mind.
KREON   But did you not hear him say I was the one
15   Who seduced the old prophet into lying?
CHORAGOS   The thing was said; I do not know how seriously.
KREON   But you were watching him! Were his eyes steady?
       Did he look like a man in his right mind?
CHORAGOS   I do not know.
20   I can not judge the behavior of great men.
       But here is the king himself.

(*Enter* Oedipus.)

OEDIPUS   So you dared come back.
       Why? How brazen of you to come to my house,
       You murderer!
25   Do you think I do not know
       That you plotted to kill me, plotted to steal my throne?
       Tell me, in God's name: am I coward, a fool,
       That you should dream you could accomplish this?
       A fool who could not see your slippery game?
30   A coward, not to fight back when I saw it?
       You are the fool, Kreon, are you not? hoping
       Without support or friends to get a throne?
       Thrones may be won or bought: you could do neither.
KREON   Now listen to me. You have talked; let me talk, too.
35   You can not judge unless you know the facts.
OEDIPUS   You speak well: there is one fact; but I find it hard
       To learn from the deadliest enemy I have.
KREON   That above all I must dispute with you.
OEDIPUS   That above all I will not hear you deny.
40 KREON   If you think there is anything good in being stubborn
       Against all reason, then I say you are wrong.

OEDIPUS   If you think a man can sin against his own kind
  And not be punished for it, I say you are mad.
 KREON   I agree. But tell me: What have I done to you?
45 OEDIPUS   You advised me to send for that wizard, did you not?
 KREON   I did. I should do it again.
 OEDIPUS   Very well. Now tell me:
  How long has it been since Laïos—
 KREON   What of Laïos?
50 OEDIPUS   Since he vanished in that onset by the road?
 KREON   It was long ago, a long time.
 OEDIPUS   And this prophet,
  Was he practicing here then?
 KREON   He was; and with honor, as now.
55 OEDIPUS   Did he speak of me at that time?
 KREON   He never did,
  At least, not when I was present.
 OEDIPUS   But . . . the enquiry?
  I suppose you held one?
60 KREON   We did, but we learned nothing.
 OEDIPUS   Why did the prophet not speak against me then?
 KREON   I do not know; and I am the kind of man
  Who holds his tongue when he has no facts to go on.
 OEDIPUS   There's one fact that you know, and you could tell it.
65 KREON   What fact is that? If I know it, you shall have it.
 OEDIPUS   If he were not involved with you, he could not say
  That it was I who murdered Laïos.
 KREON   If he says that, you are the one that knows it!—
  But now it is my turn to question you.
70 OEDIPUS   Put your questions. I am no murderer.
 KREON   First, then: You married my sister?
 OEDIPUS   I married your sister.
 KREON   And you rule the kingdom equally with her?
 OEDIPUS   Everything that she wants she has from me.
75 KREON   And I am the third, equal to both of you?
 OEDIPUS   That is why I call you a bad friend.
 KREON   No. Reason it out, as I have done.
  Think of this first: Would any sane man prefer
  Power, with all a king's anxieties,
80 To that same power and the grace of sleep?
  Certainly not I.
  I have never longed for the king's power—only his rights.
  Would any wise man differ from me in this?
  As matters stand, I have my way in everything

85   With your consent, and no responsibilities.
      If I were king, I should be a slave to policy.

      How could I desire a scepter more
      Than what is now mine—untroubled influence?
      No, I have not gone mad; I need no honors,
90   Except those with the perquisites I have now.
      I am welcome everywhere; every man salutes me,
      And those who want your favor seek my ear,
      Since I know how to manage what they ask.
      Should I exchange this ease for that anxiety?
95   Besides, no sober mind is treasonable.
      I hate anarchy
      And never would deal with any man who likes it.
      Test what I have said. Go to the priestess
      At Delphi, ask if I quoted her correctly.
100   And as for this other thing: if I am found
      Guilty of treason with Teiresias,
      Then sentence me to death. You have my word
      It is a sentence I should cast my vote for—
      But not without evidence!
105   You do wrong
      When you take good men for bad, bad men for good.
      A true friend thrown aside—why, life itself
      Is not more precious!
                            In time you will know this well:
110   For time, and time alone, will show the just man,
      Though scoundrels are discovered in a day.
      CHORAGOS   This is well said, and a prudent man would ponder it.
      Judgments too quickly formed are dangerous.
      OEDIPUS   But is he not quick in his duplicity?
115   And shall I not be quick to parry him?
      Would you have me stand still, hold my peace, and let
      This man win everything, through my inaction?
      KREON   And you want—what is it, then? To banish me?
      OEDIPUS   No, not exile. It is your death I want,
120   So that all the world may see what treason means.
      KREON   You will persist, then? You will not believe me?
      OEDIPUS   How can I believe you?
      KREON   Then you are a fool.
      OEDIPUS   To save myself?
125   KREON   In justice, think of me.
      OEDIPUS   You are evil incarnate.

KREON   But suppose that you are wrong?

OEDIPUS   Still I must rule.

KREON   But not if you rule badly.

130   OEDIPUS   O city, city!

KREON   It is my city, too!

CHORAGOS   Now, my lords, be still. I see the queen,
    Iokastê, coming from her palace chambers;
    And it is time she came, for the sake of you both.
135   This dreadful quarrel can be resolved through her.

(*Enter* IOKASTÊ.)

IOKASTÊ   Poor foolish men, what wicked din is this?
    With Thebes sick to death, is it not shameful
    That you should rake some private quarrel up?
    (*to* OEDIPUS) Come into the house.
140   —And you, Kreon, go now:
    Let us have no more of this tumult over nothing.

KREON   Nothing? No, sister: what your husband plans for me
    Is one of two great evils: exile or death.

OEDIPUS   He is right.
145   Why, woman I have caught him squarely
    Plotting against my life.

KREON   No! Let me die
    Accurst if ever I have wished you harm!

IOKASTÊ   Ah, believe it, Oedipus!
150   In the name of the gods, respect this oath of his
    For my sake, for the sake of these people here!

Strophe I

CHORAGOS   Open your mind to her, my lord. Be ruled by her, I beg you!

OEDIPUS   What would you have me do?

CHORAGOS   Respect Kreon's word. He has never spoken like a fool,
155   And now he has sworn an oath.

OEDIPUS   You know what you ask?

CHORAGOS   I do.

OEDIPUS   Speak on, then.

CHORAGOS   A friend so sworn should not be baited so,
160   In blind malice, and without final proof.

OEDIPUS   You are aware, I hope, that what you say
    Means death for me, or exile at the least.

Strophe 2

CHORAGOS   No, I swear by Helios, first in Heaven!
　　　May I die friendless and accurst,
165　　　The worst of deaths, if ever I meant that!
　　　　　　It is the withering fields
　　　　　　　　That hurt my sick heart:
　　　　　　Must we bear all these ills,
　　　　　　　　And now your bad blood as well?
170 OEDIPUS   Then let him go. And let me die, if I must,
　　　Or be driven by him in shame from the land of Thebes.
　　　It is your unhappiness, and not his talk,
　　　That touches me.
　　　　　　As for him—
175　Wherever he goes, hatred will follow him.
　　KREON   Ugly in yielding, as you were ugly in rage!
　　　Natures like yours chiefly torment themselves.
　　OEDIPUS   Can you not go? Can you not leave me?
　　KREON   I can.
180　You do not know me; but the city knows me,
　　　And in its eyes I am just, if not in yours.

(*Exit* KREON.)

Antistrophe 1

CHORAGOS   Lady Iokastê, did you not ask the King to go to his chambers?
IOKASTÊ   First tell me what has happened.
CHORAGOS   There was suspicion without evidence; yet it rankled
185　As even false charges will.
　　IOKASTÊ   On both sides?
　　CHORAGOS   On both.
　　IOKASTÊ   But what was said?
　　CHORAGOS   Oh let it rest, let it be done with!
190　Have we not suffered enough?
　　OEDIPUS   You see to what your decency has brought you:
　　　You have made difficulties where my heart saw none.

Antistrophe 2

CHORAGOS   Oedipus, it is not once only I have told you—
　　　You must know I should count myself unwise
195　To the point of madness, should I now forsake you—

You, under whose hand,
    In the storm of another time,
    Our dear land sailed out free.
    But now stand fast at the helm!

200 IOKASTÊ   In God's name, Oedipus, inform your wife as well:
    Why are you so set in this hard anger?

OEDIPUS   I will tell you, for none of these men deserves
    My confidence as you do. It is Kreon's work,
    His treachery, his plotting against me.

205 IOKASTÊ   Go on, if you can make this clear to me.

OEDIPUS   He charges me with the murder of Laïos.

IOKASTÊ   Has he some knowledge? Or does he speak from hearsay?

OEDIPUS   He would not commit himself to such a charge,
    But he has brought in that damnable soothsayer
210   To tell his story.

IOKASTÊ   Set your mind at rest.
    If it is a question of soothsayers, I tell you
    That you will find no man whose craft gives knowledge
    Of the unknowable.

215   Here is my proof:
    An oracle was reported to Laïos once
    (I will not say from Phoibos himself, but from
    His appointed ministers, at any rate)
    That his doom would be death at the hands of his own son—
220   His son, born of his flesh and of mine!

    Now, you remember the story: Laïos was killed
    By marauding strangers where three highways meet;
    But his child had not been three days in this world
    Before the king had pierced the baby's ankles
225   And left him to die on a lonely mountainside.

    Thus, Apollo never caused that child
    To kill his father, and it was not Laïos' fate
    To die at the hands of his son, as he had feared.
    This is what prophets and prophecies are worth!
230   Have no dread of them.
                    It is God himself
    Who can show us what he wills, in his own way.

OEDIPUS   How strange a shadowy memory crossed my mind,
    Just now while you were speaking; it chilled my heart.

235 IOKASTÊ   What do you mean? What memory do you speak of?

OEDIPUS   If I understand you, Laïos was killed
    At a place where three roads meet.
IOKASTÊ   So it was said;
    We have no later story.
240 OEDIPUS   Where did it happen?
    IOKASTÊ   Phokis, it is called: at a place where the Theban Way
    Divides into the roads toward Delphi and Daulia.
    OEDIPUS   When?
    IOKASTÊ   We had the news not long before you came
245   And proved the right to your succession here.
    OEDIPUS   Ah, what net has God been weaving for me?
    IOKASTÊ   Oedipus! Why does this trouble you?
    OEDIPUS   Do not ask me yet.
    First, tell me how Laïos looked, and tell me
250   How old he was.
    IOKASTÊ   He was tall, his hair just touched
    With white; his form was not unlike your own.
    OEDIPUS   I think that I myself may be accurst
    By my own ignorant edict.
255 IOKASTÊ   You speak strangely.
    It makes me tremble to look at you, my king.
    OEDIPUS   I am not sure that the blind man can not see.
    But I should know better if you were to tell me—
    IOKASTÊ   Anything—though I dread to hear you ask it.
260 OEDIPUS   Was the king lightly escorted, or did he ride
    With a large company, as a ruler should?
    IOKASTÊ   There were five men with him in all: one was a herald.
    And a single chariot, which he was driving.
    OEDIPUS   Alas, that makes it plain enough!
265   But who—
    Who told you how it happened?
    IOKASTÊ   A household servant,
    The only one to escape.
    OEDIPUS   And is he still
270   A servant of ours?
    IOKASTÊ   No; for when he came back at last
    And found you enthroned in the place of the dead king,
    He came to me, touched my hand with his, and begged
    That I would send him away to the frontier district
275   Where only the shepherds go—
    As far away from the city as I could send him.
    I granted his prayer; for although the man was a slave,
    He had earned more than this favor at my hands.
    OEDIPUS   Can he be called back quickly?

280 IOKASTÊ   Easily.
    But why?
  OEDIPUS   I have taken too much upon myself
    Without enquiry; therefore I wish to consult him.
  IOKASTÊ   Then he shall come.
285   But am I not one also
    To whom you might confide these fears of yours?
  OEDIPUS   That is your right; it will not be denied you,
    Now least of all; for I have reached a pitch
    Of wild foreboding. Is there anyone
290   To whom I should sooner speak?

    Polybos of Corinth is my father.
    My mother is a Dorian: Meropê.
    I grew up chief among the men of Corinth
    Until a strange thing happened—
295   Not worth my passion, it may be, but strange.
    At a feast, a drunken man maundering in his cups
    Cries out that I am not my father's son![10]
    I contained myself that night, though I felt anger
    And a sinking heart. The next day I visited
300   My father and mother, and questioned them. They stormed,
    Calling it all the slanderous rant of a fool;
    And this relieved me. Yet the suspicion
    Remained always aching in my mind;
    I knew there was talk; I could not rest;
305   And finally, saying nothing to my parents,
    I went to the shrine at Delphi.

    The god dismissed my question without reply;
    He spoke of other things.
                Some were clear,
310   Full of wretchedness, dreadful, unbearable:
    As, that I should lie with my own mother, breed
    Children from whom all men would turn their eyes;
    And that I should be my father's murderer.

    I heard all this, and fled. And from that day
315   Corinth to me was only in the stars

---

[10]Oedipus perhaps interprets this as an allegation that he is a bastard, the son of Meropê but not of
  Polybos. The implication, at any rate, is that he is not of royal birth, not the legitimate heir to the
  throne of Corinth.

Descending in that quarter of the sky,
As I wandered farther and farther on my way
To a land where I should never see the evil
Sung by the oracle. And I came to this country
320   Where, so you say, King Laïos was killed.

I will tell you all that happened there, my lady.

There were three highways
Coming together at a place I passed;
And there a herald came towards me, and a chariot
325   Drawn by horses, with a man such as you describe
Seated in it. The groom leading the horses
Forced me off the road at his lord's command;
But as this charioteer lurched over towards me
I struck him in my rage. The old man saw me
330   And brought his double goad down upon my head
As I came abreast.

                       He was paid back, and more!
Swinging my club in this right hand I knocked him
Out of his car, and he rolled on the ground.
335   I killed him.
I killed them all.
Now if that stranger and Laïos were—kin,
Where is a man more miserable than I?
More hated by the gods? Citizen and alien alike
340   Must never shelter me or speak to me—
I must be shunned by all.

                     And I myself
Pronounced this malediction upon myself!

Think of it: I have touched you with these hands,
345   These hands that killed your husband. What defilement!

Am I all evil, then? It must be so,
Since I must flee from Thebes, yet never again
See my own countrymen, my own country,
For fear of joining my mother in marriage
350   And killing Polybos, my father.

                             Ah,
If I was created so, born to this fate,
Who could deny the savagery of God?

O holy majesty of heavenly powers!
355   May I never see that day! Never!
    Rather let me vanish from the race of men
    Than know the abomination destined me!
  CHORAGOS   We too, my lord, have felt dismay at this.
    But there is hope: you have yet to hear the shepherd.
360 OEDIPUS   Indeed, I fear no other hope is left me.
  IOKASTÊ   What do you hope from him when he comes?
  OEDIPUS   This much:
    If his account of the murder tallies with yours,
    Then I am cleared.
365 IOKASTÊ   What was it that I said
    Of such importance?
  OEDIPUS   Why, "marauders," you said,
    Killed the king, according to this man's story.
    If he maintains that still, if there were several,
370   Clearly the guilt is not mine: I was alone.
    But if he says one man, singlehanded, did it,
    Then the evidence all points to me.
  IOKASTÊ   You may be sure that he said there were several;
    And can he call back that story now? He can not.
375   The whole city heard it as plainly as I.
    But suppose he alters some detail of it:
    He can not ever show that Laïos's death
    Fulfilled the oracle: for Apollo said
    My child was doomed to kill him; and my child—
380   Poor baby!—it was my child that died first.
    No. From now on, where oracles are concerned,
    I would not waste a second thought on any.
  OEDIPUS   You may be right.
                        But come: let someone go
385   For the shepherd at once. This matter must be settled.
  IOKASTÊ   I will send for him.
    I would not wish to cross you in anything,
    And surely not in this.—Let us go in.

(Exeunt into the palace.)

Ode II

Strophe I

CHORUS   Let me be reverent in the ways of right,
    Lowly the paths I journey on;

Let all my words and actions keep
The laws of the pure universe
From highest Heaven handed down.
For Heaven is their bright nurse,
Those generations of the realms of light;
Ah, never of mortal kind were they begot,
Nor are they slaves of memory, lost in sleep:
Their Father is greater than Time, and ages not.

Antistrophe 1

The tyrant is a child of Pride
Who drinks from his great sickening cup
Recklessness and vanity,
Until from his high crest headlong
He plummets to the dust of hope.
That strong man is not strong.
But let no fair ambition be denied;
May God protect the wrestler for the State
In government, in comely policy,
Who will fear God, and on His ordinance wait.

Strophe 2

Haughtiness and the high hand of disdain
Tempt and outrage God's holy law;
And any mortal who dares hold
No immortal Power in awe
Will be caught up in a net of pain:
The price for which his levity is sold.
Let each man take due earnings, then,
And keep his hands from holy things,
And from blasphemy stand apart—
Else the crackling blast of heaven
Blows on his head, and on his desperate heart.
Though fools will honor impious men,
In their cities no tragic poet sings.

Antistrophe 2

Shall we lose faith in Delphi's obscurities,
We who have heard the world's core
Discredited, and the sacred wood
Of Zeus at Elis praised no more?

The deeds and the strange prophecies
Must make a pattern yet to be understood.
40 Zeus, if indeed you are lord of all,
Throned in light over night and day,
Mirror this in your endless mind:
Our masters call the oracle
Words on the wind, and the Delphic vision blind!
45 Their hearts no longer know Apollo,
And reverence for the gods has died away.

Scene III

(*Enter* IOKASTÊ.)

IOKASTÊ   Princes of Thebes, it has occurred to me
To visit the altars of the gods, bearing
These branches as a suppliant, and this incense.
Our king is not himself: his noble soul
5 Is overwrought with fantasies of dread,
Else he would consider
The new prophecies in the light of the old.
He will listen to any voice that speaks disaster,
And my advice goes for nothing.

(*She approaches the altar, R.*)

10   To you, then, Apollo,
Lycéan lord, since you are nearest, I turn in prayer.
Receive these offerings, and grant us deliverance
From defilement. Our hearts are heavy with fear
When we see our leader distracted, as helpless sailors
15 Are terrified by the confusion of their helmsman.

(*Enter* MESSENGER.)

MESSENGER   Friends, no doubt you can direct me:
Where shall I find the house of Oedipus,
Or, better still, where is the king himself?
CHORAGOS   It is this very place, stranger; he is inside.
20 This is his wife and mother of his children.
MESSENGER   I wish her happiness in a happy house,
Blest in all the fulfillment of her marriage.
IOKASTÊ   I wish as much for you: your courtesy
Deserves a like good fortune. But now, tell me:
25 Why have you come? What have you to say to us?

MESSENGER   Good news, my lady, for your house and your husband.

IOKASTÊ   What news? Who sent you here?

MESSENGER   I am from Corinth.

The news I bring ought to mean joy for you,

30   Though it may be you will find some grief in it.

IOKASTÊ   What is it? How can it touch us in both ways?

MESSENGER   The word is that the people of the Isthmus

Intend to call Oedipus to be their king.

IOKASTÊ   But old King Polybos—is he not reigning still?

35 MESSENGER   No. Death holds him in his sepulchre.

IOKASTÊ   What are you saying? Polybos is dead?

MESSENGER   If I am not telling the truth, may I die myself.

IOKASTÊ (*to a* MAIDSERVANT)   Go in, go quickly; tell this to your master.

O riddlers of God's will, where are you now!

40   This was the man whom Oedipus, long ago,

Feared so, fled so, in dread of destroying him—

But it was another fate by which he died.

(*Enter* OEDIPUS, *C.*)

OEDIPUS   Dearest Iokastê, why have you sent for me?

IOKASTÊ   Listen to what this man says, and then tell me

45   What has become of the solemn prophecies.

OEDIPUS   Who is this man? What is his news for me?

IOKASTÊ   He has come from Corinth to announce your father's death!

OEDIPUS   Is it true, stranger? Tell me in your own words.

MESSENGER   I can not say it more clearly: the king is dead.

50 OEDIPUS   Was it by treason? Or by an attack of illness?

MESSENGER   A little thing brings old men to their rest.

OEDIPUS   It was sickness, then?

MESSENGER   Yes, and his many years.

OEDIPUS   Ah!

55   Why should a man respect the Pythian hearth,[11] or

Give heed to the birds that jangle above his head?

They prophesied that I should kill Polybos,

Kill my own father; but he is dead and buried,

And I am here—I never touched him, never,

60   Unless he died of grief for my departure,

And thus, in a sense, through me. No. Polybos

Has packed the oracles off with him underground.

They are empty words.

---

[11]Delphi

IOKASTÊ		Had I not told you so?

65 OEDIPUS   You had; it was my faint heart that betrayed me.

IOKASTÊ   From now on never think of those things again.

OEDIPUS   And yet—must I not fear my mother's bed?

IOKASTÊ   Why should anyone in this world be afraid,
Since Fate rules us and nothing can be foreseen?
70   A man should live only for the present day.

Have no more fear of sleeping with your mother:
How many men, in dreams, have lain with their mothers!
No reasonable man is troubled by such things.

OEDIPUS   That is true; only—
75   If only my mother were not still alive!
But she is alive. I can not help my dread.

IOKASTÊ   Yet this news of your father's death is wonderful.

OEDIPUS   Wonderful. But I fear the living woman.

MESSENGER   Tell me, who is this woman that you fear?

80 OEDIPUS   It is Meropê, man; the wife of King Polybos.

MESSENGER   Meropê? Why should you be afraid of her?

OEDIPUS   An oracle of the gods, a dreadful saying.

MESSENGER   Can you tell me about it or are you sworn to silence?

OEDIPUS   I can tell you, and I will.
85   Apollo said through his prophet that I was the man
Who should marry his own mother, shed his father's blood
With his own hands. And so, for all these years
I have kept clear of Corinth, and no harm has come—
Though it would have been sweet to see my parents again.

90 MESSENGER   And is this the fear that drove you out of Corinth?

OEDIPUS   Would you have me kill my father?

MESSENGER   As for that
You must be reassured by the news I gave you.

OEDIPUS   If you could reassure me, I would reward you.

95 MESSENGER   I had that in mind, I will confess: I thought
I could count on you when you returned to Corinth.

OEDIPUS   No: I will never go near my parents again.

MESSENGER   Ah, son, you still do not know what you are doing—

OEDIPUS   What do you mean? In the name of God tell me!

100 MESSENGER   —if these are your reasons for not going home.

OEDIPUS   I tell you, I fear the oracle may come true.

MESSENGER   And guilt may come upon you through your parents?

OEDIPUS   That is the dread that is always in my heart.

MESSENGER   Can you not see that all your fears are groundless?

105 OEDIPUS   Groundless? Am I not my parents' son?

MESSENGER   Polybos was not your father.

OEDIPUS   Not my father?

MESSENGER   No more your father than the man speaking to you.

OEDIPUS   But you are nothing to me!

110 MESSENGER   Neither was he.

OEDIPUS   Then why did he call me son?

MESSENGER   I will tell you:
    Long ago he had you from my hands, as a gift.

OEDIPUS   Then how could he love me so, if I was not his?

115 MESSENGER   He had no children, and his heart turned to you.

OEDIPUS   What of you? Did you buy me? Did you find me by chance?

MESSENGER   I came upon you in the woody vales of Kithairon.

OEDIPUS   And what were you doing there?

MESSENGER   Tending my flocks.

120 OEDIPUS   A wandering shepherd?

MESSENGER   But your savior, son, that day.

OEDIPUS   From what did you save me?

MESSENGER   Your ankles should tell you that.

OEDIPUS   Ah, stranger, why do you speak of that childhood pain?

125 MESSENGER   I pulled the skewer that pinned your feet together.

OEDIPUS   I have had the mark as long as I can remember.

MESSENGER   That was why you were given the name you bear.

OEDIPUS   God! Was it my father or my mother who did it?
    Tell me!

130 MESSENGER   I do not know. The man who gave you to me
    Can tell you better than I.

OEDIPUS   It was not you that found me, but another?

MESSENGER   It was another shepherd gave you to me.

OEDIPUS   Who was he? Can you tell me who he was?

135 MESSENGER   I think he was said to be one of Laïos' people.

OEDIPUS   You mean the Laïos who was king here years ago?

MESSENGER   Yes; King Laïos; and the man was one of his herdsmen.

OEDIPUS   Is he still alive? Can I see him?

MESSENGER   These men here
140   Know best about such things.

OEDIPUS   Does anyone here
    Know this shepherd that he is talking about?
    Have you seen him in the fields, or in the town?
    If you have, tell me. It is time things were made plain.

145 CHORAGOS   I think the man he means is that same shepherd
    You have already asked to see. Iokastê perhaps
    Could tell you something.

OEDIPUS   Do you know anything
    About him, Lady? Is he the man we have summoned?
150   Is that the man this shepherd means?

IOKASTÊ   Why think of him?
    Forget this herdsman. Forget it all.
    This talk is a waste of time.
OEDIPUS   How can you say that,
155 When the clues to my true birth are in my hands?
  IOKASTÊ   For God's love, let us have no more questioning!
    Is your life nothing to you?
    My own is pain enough for me to bear.
  OEDIPUS   You need not worry. Suppose my mother a slave,
160 And born of slaves: no baseness can touch you.
  IOKASTÊ   Listen to me, I beg you: do not do this thing!
  OEDIPUS   I will not listen; the truth must be made known.
  IOKASTÊ   Everything that I say is for your own good!
  OEDIPUS   My own good
165 Snaps my patience, then! I want none of it.
  IOKASTÊ   You are fatally wrong! May you never learn who you are!
  OEDIPUS   Go, one of you, and bring the shepherd here.
    Let us leave this woman to brag of her royal name.
  IOKASTÊ   Ah, miserable!
170 That is the only word I have for you now.
    That is the only word I can ever have.

(*Exit into the palace.*)

CHORAGOS   Why has she left us, Oedipus? Why has she gone
    In such a passion of sorrow? I fear this silence:
    Something dreadful may come of it.
175 OEDIPUS   Let it come!
    However base my birth, I must know about it.
    The Queen, like a woman, is perhaps ashamed
    To think of my low origin. But I
    Am a child of Luck; I can not be dishonored.
180 Luck is my mother; the passing months, my brothers,
    Have seen me rich and poor.
                If this is so,
    How could I wish that I were someone else?
    How could I not be glad to know my birth?

Ode III

Strophe

CHORUS   If ever the coming time were known
    To my heart's pondering,
    Kithairon, now by Heaven I see the torches

At the festival of the next full moon,
5   And see the dance, and hear the choir sing
A grace to your gentle shade:
Mountain where Oedipus was found,
O mountain guard of a noble race!
May the god[12] who heals us lend his aid,
10   And let that glory come to pass
For our king's cradling-ground.

Antistrophe

Of the nymphs that flower beyond the years,
Who bore you,[13] royal child,
To Pan of the hills or the timberline Apollo,
15   Cold in delight where the upland clears,
Or Hermês for whom Kyllenê's heights are piled?
Or flushed as evening cloud,
Great Dionysos, roamer of mountains,
He—was it he who found you there,
20   And caught you up in his own proud
Arms from the sweet god-ravisher
Who laughed by the Muses' fountains?

Scene IV

OEDIPUS   Sirs: though I do not know the man,
I think I see him coming, this shepherd we want:
He is old, like our friend here, and the men
Bringing him seem to be servants of my house.
5   But you can tell, if you have ever seen him.

(*Enter* SHEPHERD *escorted by* SERVANTS.)

CHORAGOS   I know him, he was Laïos' man. You can trust him.
OEDIPUS   Tell me first, you from Corinth: is this the shepherd
We were discussing?
MESSENGER   This is the very man.
10 OEDIPUS (*to* SHEPHERD)   Come here. No, look at me. You must answer
Everything I ask.—You belonged to Laïos?
SHEPHERD   Yes: born his slave, brought up in his house.

---

[12]Apollo   [13]The chorus is suggesting that perhaps Oedipus is the son of one of the immortal nymphs and of a god—Pan, Apollo, Hermes, or Dionysos. The "sweet god-ravisher" is the presumed mother.

OEDIPUS   Tell me: what kind of work did you do for him?

SHEPHERD   I was a shepherd of his, most of my life.

15 OEDIPUS   Where mainly did you go for pasturage?

SHEPHERD   Sometimes Kithairon, sometimes the hills near-by.

OEDIPUS   Do you remember ever seeing this man out there?

SHEPHERD   What would he be doing there? This man?

OEDIPUS   This man standing here. Have you ever seen him before?

20 SHEPHERD   No. At least, not to my recollection.

MESSENGER   And that is not strange, my lord. But I'll refresh
 His memory: he must remember when we two
 Spent three whole seasons together, March to September,
 On Kithairon or thereabouts. He had two flocks;

25 I had one. Each autumn I'd drive mine home
 And he would go back with his to Laïos' sheepfold.—
 Is this not true, just as I have described it?

SHEPHERD   True, yes; but it was all so long ago.

MESSENGER   Well, then: do you remember, back in those days,

30 That you gave me a baby boy to bring up as my own?

SHEPHERD   What if I did? What are you trying to say?

MESSENGER   King Oedipus was once that little child.

SHEPHERD   Damn you, hold your tongue!

OEDIPUS   No more of that!

35 It is your tongue needs watching, not this man's.

SHEPHERD   My king, my master, what is it I have done wrong?

OEDIPUS   You have not answered his question about the boy.

SHEPHERD   He does not know . . . He is only making trouble . . .

OEDIPUS   Come, speak plainly, or it will go hard with you.

40 SHEPHERD   In God's name, do not torture an old man!

OEDIPUS   Come here, one of you; bind his arms behind him.

SHEPHERD   Unhappy king! What more do you wish to learn?

OEDIPUS   Did you give this man the child he speaks of?

SHEPHERD   I did.

45 And I would to God I had died that very day.

OEDIPUS   You will die now unless you speak the truth.

SHEPHERD   Yet if I speak the truth, I am worse than dead.

OEDIPUS (*to* ATTENDANT)   He intends to draw it out, apparently—

SHEPHERD   No! I have told you already that I gave him the boy.

50 OEDIPUS   Where did you get him? From your house? From somewhere else?

SHEPHERD   Not from mine, no. A man gave him to me.

OEDIPUS   Is that man here? Whose house did he belong to?

SHEPHERD   For God's love, my king, do not ask me any more!

OEDIPUS   You are a dead man if I have to ask you again.

55 SHEPHERD   Then . . . Then the child was from the palace of Laïos.

OEDIPUS   A slave child? or a child of his own line?

SHEPHERD   Ah, I am on the brink of dreadful speech!
OEDIPUS   And I of dreadful hearing. Yet I must hear.
SHEPHERD   If you must be told, then...

60   They said it was Laïos' child;
But it is your wife who can tell you about that.
OEDIPUS   My wife!—Did she give it to you?
SHEPHERD   My lord, she did.
OEDIPUS   Do you know why?
65 SHEPHERD   I was told to get rid of it.
OEDIPUS   Oh heartless mother!
SHEPHERD   But in dread of prophecies...
OEDIPUS   Tell me.
SHEPHERD   It was said that the boy would kill his own father.
70 OEDIPUS   Then why did you give him over to this old man?
SHEPHERD   I pitied the baby, my king,
And I thought that this man would take him far away
To his own country.
                            He saved him—but for what a fate!
75   For if you are what this man says you are,
No man living is more wretched than Oedipus.
OEDIPUS   Ah God!
It was true!
            All the prophecies!
80   —Now,
O Light, may I look on you for the last time!
I, Oedipus,
Oedipus, damned in his birth, in his marriage damned,
Damned in the blood he shed with his own hand!

(*He rushes into the palace.*)

Ode IV

Strophe I

CHORUS   Alas for the seed of men.
What measure shall I give these generations
That breathe on the void and are void
And exist and do not exist?
5   Who bears more weight of joy
Than mass of sunlight shifting in images,
Or who shall make his thought stay on
That down time drifts away?
Your splendor is all fallen.

10   O naked brow of wrath and tears,
     O change of Oedipus!
     I who saw your days call no man blest—
     Your great days like ghosts gone.

Antistrophe 1

     That mind was a strong bow.
15   Deep, how deep you drew it then, hard archer,
     At a dim fearful range,
     And brought dear glory down!
     You overcame the stranger[14]—
     The virgin with her hooking lion claws—
20   And though death sang, stood like a tower
     To make pale Thebes take heart.
     Fortress against our sorrow!
     True king, giver of laws,
     Majestic Oedipus!
25   No prince in Thebes had ever such renown,
     No prince won such grace of power.

Strophe 2

     And now of all men ever known
     Most pitiful is this man's story:
     His fortunes are most changed, his state
30   Fallen to a low slave's
     Ground under bitter fate.
     O Oedipus, most royal one!
     The great door[15] that expelled you to the light
     Gave at night—ah, gave night to your glory:
35   As to the father, to the fathering son.
     All understood too late.
     How could that queen whom Laïos won,
     The garden that he harrowed at his height,
     Be silent when that act was done?

Antistrophe 2

40   But all eyes fail before time's eye,
     All actions come to justice there.

---

[14]the Sphinx   [15]Iokastê's womb

Though never willed, though far down the deep past,
Your bed, your dread sirings,
Are brought to book at last.

45   Child by Laïos doomed to die,
Then doomed to lose that fortunate little death,
Would God you never took breath in this air
That with my wailing lips I take to cry:
For I weep the world's outcast.

50   I was blind, and now I can tell why:
Asleep, for you had given ease of breath
To Thebes, while the false years went by.

Exodos[16]

(*Enter, from the palace,* SECOND MESSENGER.)

SECOND MESSENGER   Elders of Thebes, most honored in this land,
What horrors are yours to see and hear, what weight
Of sorrow to be endured, if, true to your birth,
You venerate the line of Labdakos!

5   I think neither Istros nor Phasis, those great rivers,
Could purify this place of all the evil
It shelters now, or soon must bring to light—
Evil not done unconsciously, but willed.

The greatest griefs are those we cause ourselves.
10   CHORAGOS   Surely, friend, we have grief enough already;
What new sorrow do you mean?
SECOND MESSENGER   The queen is dead.
CHORAGOS   O miserable queen! But at whose hand?
SECOND MESSENGER   Her own.

15   The full horror of what happened you can not know,
For you did not see it; but I, who did, will tell you
As clearly as I can how she met her death.

When she had left us,
In passionate silence, passing through the court,
20   She ran to her apartment in the house,
Her hair clutched by the fingers of both hands.
She closed the doors behind her; then, by that bed
Where long ago the fatal son was conceived—
That son who should bring about his father's death—
25   We heard her call upon Laïos, dead so many years,

---

[16]final scene

And heard her wail for the double fruit of her marriage,
A husband by her husband, children by her child.

Exactly how she died I do not know:
For Oedipus burst in moaning and would not let us
30 Keep vigil to the end: it was by him
As he stormed about the room that our eyes were caught.
From one to another of us he went, begging a sword,
Hunting the wife who was not his wife, the mother
Whose womb had carried his own children and himself.
35 I do not know: it was none of us aided him,
But surely one of the gods was in control!
For with a dreadful cry
He hurled his weight, as though wrenched out of himself,
At the twin doors: the bolts gave, and he rushed in.
40 And there we saw her hanging, her body swaying
From the cruel cord she had noosed about her neck.
A great sob broke from him, heartbreaking to hear,
As he loosed the rope and lowered her to the ground.

I would blot out from my mind what happened next!
45 For the king ripped from her gown the golden brooches
That were her ornament, and raised them, and plunged them down
Straight into his own eyeballs, crying, "No more,
No more shall you look on the misery about me,
The horrors of my own doing! Too long you have known
50 The faces of those whom I should never have seen,
Too long been blind to those for whom I was searching!
From this hour, go in darkness!" And as he spoke,
He struck at his eyes—not once, but many times;
And the blood spattered his beard,
55 Bursting from his ruined sockets like red hail.

So from the unhappiness of two this evil has sprung,
A curse on the man and woman alike. The old
Happiness of the house of Labdakos
Was happiness enough: where is it today?
60 It is all wailing and ruin, disgrace, death—all
The misery of mankind that has a name—
And it is wholly and for ever theirs.
CHORAGOS   Is he in agony still? Is there no rest for him?
SECOND MESSENGER   He is calling for someone to open the doors wide
65 So that all the children of Kadmos may look upon
His father's murderer, his mother's—no,
I can not say it!

And then he will leave Thebes,
Self-exiled, in order that the curse
70   Which he himself pronounced may depart from the house.
He is weak, and there is none to lead him,
So terrible is his suffering.
                    But you will see:
Look, the doors are opening; in a moment
75   You will see a thing that would crush a heart of stone.

(*The central door is opened;* OEDIPUS, *blinded, is led in.*)

CHORAGOS   Dreadful indeed for men to see.
Never have my own eyes
Looked on a sight so full of fear.

Oedipus!
80   What madness came upon you, what daemon
Leaped on your life with heavier
Punishment than a mortal man can bear?
No: I can not even
Look at you, poor ruined one.
85   And I would speak, question, ponder,
If I were able. No.
You make me shudder.
OEDIPUS   God. God.
Is there a sorrow greater?
90   Where shall I find harbor in this world?
My voice is hurled far on a dark wind.
What has God done to me?
CHORAGOS   Too terrible to think of, or to see.

Strophe I

OEDIPUS   O cloud of night,
95   Never to be turned away: night coming on,
I can not tell how: night like a shroud!
My fair winds brought me here.
                            O God. Again
The pain of the spikes where I had sight,
100   The flooding pain
Of memory, never to be gouged out.
CHORAGOS   This is not strange.
You suffer it all twice over, remorse in pain,
Pain in remorse.

Antistrophe 1

105 OEDIPUS   Ah dear friend
        Are you faithful even yet, you alone?
        Are you still standing near me, will you stay here,
        Patient, to care for the blind?
                              The blind man!
110   Yet even blind I know who it is attends me,
        By the voice's tone—
        Though my new darkness hide the comforter.
    CHORAGOS   Oh fearful act!
        What god was it drove you to rake black
115   Night across your eyes?

Strophe 2

    OEDIPUS   Apollo. Apollo. Dear
        Children, the god was Apollo.
        He brought my sick, sick fate upon me.
        But the blinding hand was my own!
120   How could I bear to see
        When all my sight was horror everywhere?
    CHORAGOS   Everywhere; that is true.
    OEDIPUS   And now what is left?
        Images? Love? A greeting even,
125   Sweet to the senses? Is there anything?
        Ah, no, friends: lead me away.
        Lead me away from Thebes.
                              Lead the great wreck
        And hell of Oedipus, whom the gods hate.
130 CHORAGOS   Your misery, you are not blind to that.
        Would God you had never found it out!

Antistrophe 2

    OEDIPUS   Death take the man who unbound
        My feet on that hillside
        And delivered me from death to life! What life?
135   If only I had died,
        This weight of monstrous doom
        Could not have dragged me and my darlings down.
    CHORAGOS   I would have wished the same.
    OEDIPUS   Oh never to have come here
140   With my father's blood upon me! Never

To have been the man they call his mother's husband!
Oh accurst! Oh child of evil,
To have entered that wretched bed—
                                    the selfsame one!

145   More primal than sin itself, this fell to me.

CHORAGOS   I do not know what words to offer you.
You were better dead than alive and blind.

OEDIPUS   Do not counsel me any more. This punishment
That I have laid upon myself is just.

150   If I had eyes,
I do not know how I could bear the sight
Of my father, when I came to the house of Death,
Or my mother: for I have sinned against them both
So vilely that I could not make my peace

155   By strangling my own life.
                            Or do you think my children,
Born as they were born, would be sweet to my eyes?
Ah never, never! Nor this town with its high walls,
Nor the holy images of the gods.

160   For I,
Thrice miserable!—Oedipus, noblest of all the line
Of Kadmos, have condemned myself to enjoy
These things no more, by my own malediction
Expelling that man whom the gods declared

165   To be a defilement in the house of Laïos.
After exposing the rankness of my own guilt,
How could I look men frankly in the eyes?
No, I swear it,
If I could have stifled my hearing at its source,

170   I would have done it and made all this body
A tight cell of misery, blank to light and sound:
So I should have been safe in my dark mind
Beyond external evil.
                    Ah Kithairon!

175   Why did you shelter me? When I was cast upon you,
Why did I not die? Then I should never
Have shown the world my execrable birth.

Ah Polybos! Corinth, city that I believed
The ancient seat of my ancestors: how fair

180   I seemed, your child! And all the while this evil
Was cancerous within me!
                        For I am sick
In my own being, sick in my origin.

O three roads, dark ravine, woodland and way
185 Where three roads met: you, drinking my father's blood,
My own blood, spilled by my own hand: can you remember
The unspeakable things I did there, and the things
I went on from there to do?

O marriage, marriage!
190 That act that engendered me, and again the act
Performed by the son in the same bed—

Ah, the net
Of incest, mingling fathers, brothers, sons,
With brides, wives, mothers: the last evil
195 That can be known by men: no tongue can say
How evil!

No. For the love of God, conceal me
Somewhere far from Thebes; or kill me; or hurl me
Into the sea, away from men's eyes for ever.

200 Come, lead me. You need not fear to touch me.
Of all men, I alone can bear this guilt.

(*Enter* KREON.)

CHORAGOS   Kreon is here now. As to what you ask,
He may decide the course to take. He only
Is left to protect the city in your place.
205 OEDIPUS   Alas, how can I speak to him? What right have I
To beg his courtesy whom I have deeply wronged?
KREON   I have not come to mock you, Oedipus,
Or to reproach you, either. (*to* ATTENDANTS)
—You, standing there:
210 If you have lost all respect for man's dignity,
At least respect the flame of Lord Helios:
Do not allow this pollution to show itself
Openly here, an affront to the earth
And Heaven's rain and the light of day. No, take him
215 Into the house as quickly as you can.
For it is proper
That only the close kindred see his grief.
OEDIPUS   I pray you in God's name, since your courtesy
Ignores my dark expectation, visiting
220 With mercy this man of all men most execrable:
Give me what I ask—for your good, not for mine.
KREON   And what is it that you turn to me begging for?
OEDIPUS   Drive me out of this country as quickly as may be
To a place where no human voice can ever greet me.

225 KREON   I should have done that before now—only,
God's will had not been wholly revealed to me.
  OEDIPUS   But his command is plain: the parricide
Must be destroyed. I am that evil man.
  KREON   That is the sense of it, yes; but as things are,
230   We had best discover clearly what is to be done.
  OEDIPUS   You would learn more about a man like me?
  KREON   You are ready now to listen to the god.
  OEDIPUS   I will listen. But it is to you
That I must turn for help. I beg you, hear me.

235   The woman in there—
Give her whatever funeral you think proper:
She is your sister.
                        —But let me go, Kreon!
Let me purge my father's Thebes of the pollution
240   Of my living here, and go out to the wild hills,
To Kithairon, that has won such fame with me,
The tomb my mother and father appointed for me,
And let me die there, as they willed I should.
And yet I know
245   Death will not ever come to me through sickness
Or in any natural way: I have been preserved
For some unthinkable fate. But let that be.

As for my sons, you need not care for them.
They are men, they will find some way to live.
250   But my poor daughters, who have shared my table,
Who never before have been parted from their father—
Take care of them, Kreon; do this for me.

And will you let me touch them with my hands
A last time, and let us weep together?
255   Be kind, my lord,
Great prince, be kind!
                        Could I but touch them,
They would be mine again, as when I had my eyes.

(*Enter* ANTIGONÊ *and* ISMENÊ, *attended.*)

Ah, God!
260   Is it my dearest children I hear weeping?
Has Kreon pitied me and sent my daughters?
  KREON   Yes, Oedipus: I knew that they were dear to you
In the old days, and know you must love them still.

OEDIPUS   My God bless you for this—and be a friendlier
265   Guardian to you than he has been to me!

Children, where are you?
Come quickly to my hands: they are your brother's—
Hands that have brought your father's once clear eyes
To this way of seeing—
270   Ah dearest ones,
I had neither sight nor knowledge then, your father
By the woman who was the source of his own life!
And I weep for you—having no strength to see you—,
I weep for you when I think of the bitterness
275   That men will visit upon you all your lives.
What homes, what festivals can you attend
Without being forced to depart again in tears?
And when you come to marriageable age,
Where is the man, my daughters, who would dare
280   Risk the bane that lies on all my children?
Is there any evil wanting? Your father killed
His father; sowed the womb of her who bore him;
Engendered you at the fount of his own existence!
That is what they will say of you.
285   Then, whom
Can you ever marry? There are no bridegrooms for you,
And your lives must wither away in sterile dreaming.

O Kreon, son of Menoikeus!
You are the only father my daughters have,
290   Since we, their parents, are both of us gone for ever.
They are your own blood: you will not let them
Fall into beggary and loneliness;
You will keep them from the miseries that are mine!
Take pity on them; see, they are only children,
295   Friendless except for you. Promise me this,
Great prince, and give me your hand in token of it.

(KREON *clasps his right hand.*)

Children:
I could say much, if you could understand me,
But as it is, I have only this prayer for you:
300   Live where you can, be as happy as you can—
Happier, please God, than God has made your father.
KREON   Enough. You have wept enough. Now go within.

OEDIPUS   I must; but it is hard.

KREON   Time eases all things.

305   OEDIPUS   You know my mind, then?

KREON   Say what you desire.

OEDIPUS   Send me from Thebes!

KREON   God grant that I may!

OEDIPUS   But since God hates me . . .

310   KREON   No, he will grant your wish.

OEDIPUS   You promise?

KREON   I can not speak beyond my knowledge.

OEDIPUS   Then lead me in.

KREON   Come now, and leave your children.

315   OEDIPUS   No! Do not take them from me!

KREON   Think no longer

That you are in command here, but rather think
How, when you were, you served your own destruction.

(*Exeunt into the house all but the* CHORUS; *the* CHORAGOS *chants directly to the audience.*)

CHORAGOS   Men of Thebes: look upon Oedipus.

320   This is the king who solved the famous riddle
And towered up, most powerful of men.
No mortal eyes but looked on him with envy,
Yet in the end ruin swept over him.

Let every man in mankind's frailty
325   Consider his last day; and let none
Presume on his good fortune until he find
Life, at his death, a memory without pain.

c. 430 B.C.

STUDY QUESTIONS

According to Aristotle, tragedies such as *Oedipus Rex* succeed by arousing pity and fear in their audiences—pity for the suffering the plays' heroes endure, fear that we might sometime face similar agonies. How does *Oedipus Rex* call forth these feelings? In thinking out your answer, you might want to consider the following questions:

1. What sort of person is Oedipus? What are his strengths and weaknesses? How is he different from the other characters in the play?

2. What sorts of tensions are built up (for Oedipus, for the other characters, and for the audience) by the gradual unfolding of the truth about Laïos's murder and Oedipus's history?
3. How does your knowledge of the story of Oedipus, and hence your knowledge of how the play will end, affect your reaction to such scenes as those with Teiresias and the shepherds?
4. How are the images of sight and blindness used throughout the play?

Antigonê   SOPHOCLES

An English version by Dudley Fitts and Robert Fitzgerald

See page 545 for a biographical note on the author.

CHARACTERS

ANTIGONÊ
ISMENÊ
EURYDICÊ
KREON
HAIMON
TEIRESIAS
A SENTRY
A MESSENGER
CHORUS

SCENE. *Before the palace of* KREON, *King of Thebes. A central double door, and two lateral doors. A platform extends the length of the façade, and from this platform three steps lead down into the "orchestra," or chorus-ground.*

TIME. *Dawn of the day after the repulse of the Argive army from the assault on Thebes.*

Prologue

(ANTIGONÊ *and* ISMENÊ *enter from the central door of the palace.*)

ANTIGONÊ   Ismenê, dear sister,
    You would think that we had already suffered enough
    For the curse on Oedipus.
    I cannot imagine any grief
5   That you and I have not gone through. And now—
    Have they told you of the new decree of our King Kreon?
ISMENÊ   I have heard nothing: I know
    That two sisters lost two brothers, a double death
    In a single hour; and I know that the Argive army
10   Fled in the night; but beyond this, nothing.
ANTIGONÊ   I thought so. And that is why I wanted you
    To come out here with me. There is something we must do.
ISMENÊ   Why do you speak so strangely?
ANTIGONÊ   Listen, Ismenê:
15   Kreon buried our brother Eteoclês

591

With military honors, gave him a soldier's funeral,
And it was right that he should; but Polyneicês,
Who fought as bravely and died as miserably,—
They say that Kreon has sworn
20   No one shall bury him, no one mourn for him,
But his body must lie in the fields, a sweet treasure
For carrion birds to find as they search for food.
That is what they say, and our good Kreon is coming here
To announce it publicly; and the penalty—
25   Stoning to death in the public square!

                                    There it is,
And now you can prove what you are:
A true sister, or a traitor to your family.

ISMENÊ   Antigonê, you are mad! What could I possibly do?
30 ANTIGONÊ   You must decide whether you will help me or not.
ISMENÊ   I do not understand you. Help you in what?
ANTIGONÊ   Ismenê, I am going to bury him. Will you come?
ISMENÊ   Bury him! You have just said the new law forbids it.
ANTIGONÊ   He is my brother. And he is your brother, too.
35 ISMENÊ   But think of the danger! Think what Kreon will do!
ANTIGONÊ   Kreon is not strong enough to stand in my way.
ISMENÊ   Ah, sister!
Oedipus died, everyone hating him
For what his own search brought to light, his eyes
40   Ripped out by his own hand; and Iokastê died,
His mother and wife at once: she twisted the cords
That strangled her life; and our two brothers died,
Each killed by the other's sword. And we are left:
But oh, Antigonê,
45   Think how much more terrible than these
Our own death would be if we should go against Kreon
And do what he has forbidden! We are only women,
We cannot fight with men, Antigonê!
The law is strong, we must give in to the law
50   In this thing, and in worse. I beg the Dead
To forgive me, but I am helpless: I must yield
To those in authority. And I think it is dangerous business
To be always meddling.

ANTIGONÊ   If that is what you think,
55   I should not want you, even if you asked to come.
You have made your choice, you can be what you want to be.
But I will bury him; and if I must die,
I say that this crime is holy: I shall lie down

With him in death, and I shall be as dear
60   To him as he to me.
                   It is the dead,
Not the living, who make the longest demands:
We die for ever . . .
                You may do as you like,
65   Since apparently the laws of the gods mean nothing to you.
ISMENÊ   They mean a great deal to me; but I have no strength
    To break laws that were made for the public good.
ANTIGONÊ   That must be your excuse, I suppose. But as for me,
    I will bury the brother I love.
70 ISMENÊ   Antigonê,
    I am so afraid for you!
ANTIGONÊ   You need not be:
    You have yourself to consider, after all.
ISMENÊ   But no one must hear of this, you must tell no one!
75   I will keep it a secret, I promise!
ANTIGONÊ   O tell it! Tell everyone!
    Think how they'll hate you when it all comes out
    If they learn that you knew about it all the time!
ISMENÊ   So fiery! You should be cold with fear.
80 ANTIGONÊ   Perhaps. But I am doing only what I must.
ISMENÊ   But can you do it? I say that you cannot.
ANTIGONÊ   Very well: when my strength gives out,
    I shall do no more.
ISMENÊ   Impossible things should not be tried at all.
85 ANTIGONÊ   Go away, Ismenê:
    I shall be hating you soon, and the dead will too,
    For your words are hateful. Leave me my foolish plan:
    I am not afraid of the danger; if it means death,
    It will not be the worst of deaths—death without honor.
90 ISMENÊ   Go then, if you feel that you must.
    You are unwise,
    But a loyal friend indeed to those who love you.

(*Exit into the palace.* ANTIGONÊ *goes off, left. Enter the* CHORUS.)

Párodos

Strophe I

CHORUS   Now the long blade of the sun, lying
    Level east to west, touches with glory

Thebes of the Seven Gates. Open, unlidded
Eye of golden day! O marching light
5   Across the eddy and rush of Dircê's stream,[1]
Striking the white shields of the enemy
Thrown headlong backward from the blaze of morning!
CHORAGOS[2]   Polyneicês their commander
Roused them with windy phrases,
10   He the wild eagle screaming
Insults above our land,
His wings their shields of snow,
His crest their marshalled helms.

Antistrophe 1

CHORUS   Against our seven gates in a yawning ring
15   The famished spears came onward in the night;
But before his jaws were sated with our blood,
Or pinefire took the garland of our towers,
He was thrown back; and as he turned, great Thebes—
No tender victim for his noisy power—
20   Rose like a dragon behind him, shouting war.
CHORAGOS   For God hates utterly
The bray of bragging tongues;
And when he beheld their smiling,
Their swagger of golden helms,
25   The frown of his thunder blasted
Their first man from our walls.

Strophe 2

CHORUS   We heard his shout of triumph high in the air
Turn to a scream; far out in a flaming arc
He fell with his windy torch, and the earth struck him.
30   And others storming in fury no less than his
Found shock of death in the dusty joy of battle.
CHORAGOS   Seven captains at seven gates
Yielded their clanging arms to the god
That bends the battle-line and breaks it.
35   These two only, brothers in blood,
Face to face in matchless rage,
Mirroring each the other's death,
Clashed in long combat.

------

[1] a stream to the west of Thebes   [2] the leader of the Chorus

Antistrophe 2

CHORUS   But now in the beautiful morning of victory
40   Let Thebes of the many chariots sing for joy!
        With hearts for dancing we'll take leave of war:
        Our temples shall be sweet with hymns of praise,
        And the long nights shall echo with our chorus.

Scene 1

CHORAGOS   But now at last our new King is coming:
        Kreon of Thebes, Menoikeus' son.
        In this auspicious dawn of his rein
        What are the new complexities
5   That shifting Fate has woven for him?
        What is his counsel? Why has he summoned
        The old men to hear him?

(*Enter* KREON *from the palace, center. He addresses the* CHORUS *from the top step.*)

KREON   Gentlemen: I have the honor to inform you that our Ship of State,
        which recent storms have threatened to destroy, has come safely to harbor at
10   last, guided by the merciful wisdom of Heaven. I have summoned you here
        this morning because I know that I can depend upon you: your devotion to
        King Laïos was absolute; you never hesitated in your duty to our late ruler
        Oedipus; and when Oedipus died, your loyalty was transferred to his chil-
        dren. Unfortunately, as you know, his two sons, the princes Eteoclês and
15   Polyneicês, have killed each other in battle; and I, as the next in blood, have
        succeeded to the full power of the throne.
                I am aware, of course, that no Ruler can expect complete loyalty from
        his subjects until he has been tested in office. Nevertheless, I say to you at
        the very outset that I have nothing but contempt for the kind of Governor
20   who is afraid, for whatever reason, to follow the course that he knows is best
        for the State; and as for the man who sets private friendship above the pub-
        lic welfare,—I have no use for him, either. I call God to witness that if I saw
        my country headed for ruin, I should not be afraid to speak out plainly; and
        I need hardly remind you that I would never have any dealings with an en-
25   emy of the people. No one values friendship more highly than I; but we
        must remember that friends made at the risk of wrecking our Ship are not
        real friends at all.
                These are my principles, at any rate, and that is why I have made the fol-
        lowing decision concerning the sons of Oedipus: Eteoclês, who died as a
30   man should die, fighting for his country, is to be buried with full military
        honors, with all the ceremony that is usual when the greatest heroes die; but
        his brother Polyneicês, who broke his exile to come back with fire and sword

against his native city and the shrines of his fathers' gods, whose one idea was to spill the blood of his blood and sell his own people into slavery—

35   Polyneicês, I say, is to have no burial: no man is to touch him or say the least prayer for him; he shall lie on the plain, unburied; and the birds and the scavenging dogs can do with him whatever they like.

    This is my command, and you can see the wisdom behind it. As long as I am King, no traitor is going to be honored with the loyal man. But who-

40   ever shows by word and deed that he is on the side of the State,—he shall have my respect while he is living and my reverence when he is dead.

CHORAGOS   If that is your will, Kreon son of Menoikeus,
    You have the right to enforce it: we are yours.
KREON   That is my will. Take care that you do your part.

45 CHORAGOS   We are old men: let the younger ones carry it out.
KREON   I do not mean that: the sentries have been appointed.
CHORAGOS   Then what is it that you would have us do?
KREON   You will give no support to whoever breaks this law.
CHORAGOS   Only a crazy man is in love with death!

50 KREON   And death it is; yet money talks, and the wisest
    Have sometimes been known to count a few coins too many.

(*Enter* SENTRY *from left.*)

SENTRY   I'll not say that I'm out of breath from running, King, because every time I stopped to think about what I have to tell you, I felt like going back. And all the time a voice kept saying, "You fool, don't you know you're walk-

55   ing straight into trouble?"; and then another voice: "Yes, but if you let some-body else get the news to Kreon first, it will be even worse than that for you!" But good sense won out, at least I hope it was good sense, and here I am with a story that makes no sense at all; but I'll tell it anyhow, because, as they say, what's going to happen's going to happen and—

60 KREON   Come to the point. What have you to say?
SENTRY   I did not do it. I did not see who did it. You must not punish me for what someone else has done.
KREON   A comprehensive defense! More effective, perhaps,
    If I knew its purpose. Come: what is it?

65 SENTRY   A dreadful thing . . . I don't know how to put it—
KREON   Out with it!
SENTRY   Well, then;
    The dead man—
             Polyneicês—

(*Pause. The* SENTRY *is overcome, fumbles for words.* KREON *waits impassively.*)

70   out there—
                                          someone,—

New dust on the slimy flesh!

(*Pause. No sign from* KREON.)

Someone has given it burial that way, and
    Gone . . .

(*Long pause.* KREON *finally speaks with deadly control.*)

75 KREON   And the man who dared do this?
SENTRY   I swear I
    Do not know! You must believe me!
                                        Listen:
    The ground was dry, not a sign of digging, no,
80   Not a wheeltrack in the dust, no trace of anyone.
    It was when they relieved us this morning: and one of them,
    The corporal, pointed to it.
                            There it was,
    The strangest—
85   Look:
    The body, just mounded over with light dust: you see?
    Not buried really, but as if they'd covered it
    Just enough for the ghost's peace. And no sign
    Of dogs or any wild animal that had been there.

90   And then what a scene there was! Every man of us
    Accusing the other: we all proved the other man did it,
    We all had proof that we could not have done it.
    We were ready to take hot iron in our hands,
    Walk through fire, swear by all the gods,
95   *It was not I!*
    I do not know who it was, but it was not I!

(KREON'*s rage has been mounting steadily, but the* SENTRY *is too intent upon his
story to notice it.*)

    And then, when this came to nothing, someone said
    A thing that silenced us and made us stare
    Down at the ground: you had to be told the news,
100   And one of us had to do it! We threw the dice,
    And the bad luck fell to me. So here I am,
    No happier to be here than you are to have me:
    Nobody likes the man who brings bad news.
CHORAGOS   I have been wondering, King: can it be that the gods have done
105   this?
KREON (*furiously*)   Stop!
    Must you doddering wrecks
    Go out of your heads entirely? "The gods"!
    Intolerable!

110 The gods favor this corpse? Why? How had he served them?
Tried to loot their temples, burn their images,
Yes, and the whole State, and its laws with it!
Is it your senile opinion that the gods love to honor bad men?
A pious thought!—

115   No, from the very beginning
There have been those who have whispered together,
Stiff-necked anarchists, putting their heads together,
Scheming against me in alleys. These are the men,
And they have bribed my own guard to do this thing.

120 (*sententiously*) Money!
There's nothing in the world so demoralizing as money.
Down go your cities,
Homes gone, men gone, honest hearts corrupted,
Crookedness of all kinds, and all for money!

125 (*to* SENTRY)   But you—!
I swear by God and by the throne of God,
The man who has done this thing shall pay for it!
Find that man, bring him here to me, or your death
Will be the least of your problems: I'll string you up

130 Alive, and there will be certain ways to make you
Discover your employer before you die;
And the process may teach you a lesson you seem to have
    missed:
The dearest profit is sometimes all too dear:

135 That depends on the source. Do you understand me?
A fortune won is often misfortune.

SENTRY   King, may I speak?
KREON   Your very voice distresses me.
SENTRY   Are you sure that it is my voice, and not your conscience?
140 KREON   By God, he wants to analyze me now!
SENTRY   It is not what I say, but what has been done, that hurts you.
KREON   You talk too much.
SENTRY   Maybe; but I've done nothing.
KREON   Sold your soul for some silver: that's all you've done.
145 SENTRY   How dreadful it is when the right judge judges wrong!
KREON   Your figures of speech
May entertain you now; but unless you bring me the man,
You will get little profit from them in the end.

(*Exit* KREON *into the palace.*)

SENTRY   "Bring me the man"—!
150 I'd like nothing better than bringing him the man!

But bring him or not, you have seen the last of me here.
At any rate, I am safe!

(*Exit* SENTRY.)

Ode I

Strophe I

CHORUS Numberless are the world's wonders, but none
More wonderful than man; the stormgray sea
Yields to his prows, the huge crests bear him high;
Earth, holy and inexhaustible, is graven
5   With shining furrows where his plows have gone
Year after year, the timeless labor of stallions.

Antistrophe I

The lightboned birds and beasts that cling to cover,
The lithe fish lighting their reaches of dim water,
All are taken, tamed in the net of his mind;
10   The lion on the hill, the wild horse windy-maned,
Resign to him; and his blunt yoke has broken
The sultry shoulders of the mountain bull.

Strophe 2

Words also, and thought as rapid as air,
He fashions to his good use; statecraft is his,
15   And his the skill that deflects the arrows of snow,
The spears of winter rain: from every wind
He has made himself secure—from all but one:
In the late wind of death he cannot stand.

Antistrophe 2

O clear intelligence, force beyond all measure!
20   O fate of man, working both good and evil!
When the laws are kept, how proudly his city stands!
When the laws are broken, what of his city then?
Never may the anárchic man find rest at my hearth,
Never be it said that my thoughts are his thoughts.

Scene II

(*Reenter* SENTRY *leading* ANTIGONÊ.)

CHORAGOS   What does this mean? Surely this captive woman
　　　Is the Princess, Antigonê. Why should she be taken?
SENTRY   Here is the one who did it! We caught her
　　　In the very act of burying him.—Where is Kreon?
5 CHORAGOS   Just coming from the house.

(*Enter* KREON, *center.*)

KREON　　　　　　　　　　　　　　　What has happened?
　　　Why have you come back so soon?
SENTRY (*expansively*)　　　　　　　　O King,
　　　A man should never be too sure of anything:
10　　　I would have sworn
　　　That you'd not see me here again: your anger
　　　Frightened me so, and the things you threatened me with;
　　　But how could I tell then
　　　That I'd be able to solve the case so soon?
15　　　No dice-throwing this time: I was only too glad to come!
　　　Here is this woman. She is the guilty one:
　　　We found her trying to bury him.
　　　Take her, then; question her; judge her as you will.
　　　I am through with the whole thing now, and glad of it.
20 KREON   But this is Antigonê! Why have you brought her here?
SENTRY   She was burying him, I tell you!
KREON (*severely*)　　　　　　　　　　Is this the truth?
SENTRY   I saw her with my own eyes. Can I say more?
KREON   The details: come, tell me quickly!
25 SENTRY　　　　　　　　　　　　　It was like this:
　　　After those terrible threats of yours, King,
　　　We went back and brushed the dust away from the body.
　　　The flesh was soft by now, and stinking,
　　　So we sat on a hill to windward and kept guard.
30　　　No napping this time! We kept each other awake.
　　　But nothing happened until the white round sun
　　　Whirled in the center of the round sky over us:
　　　Then, suddenly,
　　　A storm of dust roared up from the earth, and the sky
35　　　Went out, the plain vanished with all its trees
　　　In the stinging dark. We closed our eyes and endured it.
　　　The whirlwind lasted a long time, but it passed;
　　　And then we looked, and there was Antigonê!

I have seen
40 A mother bird come back to a stripped nest, heard
Her crying bitterly a broken note or two
For the young ones stolen. Just so, when this girl
Found the bare corpse, and all her love's work wasted,
She wept, and cried on heaven to damn the hands
45 That had done this thing.

                      And then she brought more dust
And sprinkled wine three times for her brother's ghost.

We ran and took her at once. She was not afraid,
Not even when we charged her with what she had done.
50 She denied nothing.

                And this was a comfort to me,
And some uneasiness: for it is a good thing
To escape from death, but it is no great pleasure
To bring death to a friend.
55   Yet I always say
There is nothing so comfortable as your own safe skin!
KREON (*slowly, dangerously*)   And you, Antigonê,
    You with your head hanging,—do you confess this thing?
ANTIGONÊ   I do. I deny nothing.
60 KREON (*to* SENTRY)   You may go.

(*Exit* SENTRY.)

(*to* ANTIGONÊ)   Tell me, tell me briefly:
    Had you heard my proclamation touching this matter?
ANTIGONÊ   It was public. Could I help hearing it?
65 KREON   And yet you dared defy the law.
ANTIGONÊ   I dared.
    It was not God's proclamation. That final Justice
That rules the world below makes no such laws.

Your edict, King, was strong,
70 But all your strength is weakness itself against
The immortal unrecorded laws of God.
They are not merely now: they were, and shall be,
Operative for ever, beyond man utterly.

I knew I must die, even without your decree:
75 I am only mortal. And if I must die
Now, before it is my time to die,
Surely this is no hardship: can anyone
Living, as I live, with evil all about me,
Think Death less than a friend? This death of mine

80   Is of no importance; but if I had left my brother
      Lying in death unburied, I should have suffered.
      Now I do not.
                          You smile at me. Ah Kreon,
      Think me a fool, if you like; but it may well be
85   That a fool convicts me of folly.

CHORAGOS   Like father, like daughter: both headstrong,
          deaf to reason!
      She has never learned to yield:
KREON   She has much to learn.
90   The inflexible heart breaks first, the toughest iron
      Cracks first, and the wildest horses bend their necks
      At the pull of the smallest curb.
                              Pride? In a slave?
      This girl is guilty of a double insolence,
95   Breaking the given laws and boasting of it.
      Who is the man here,
      She or I, if this crime goes unpunished?
      Sister's child, or more than sister's child,
      Or closer yet in blood—she and her sister
100   Win bitter death for this!
      (*to* SERVANTS)   Go, some of you,
      Arrest Ismenê. I accuse her equally.
      Bring her: you will find her sniffling in the house there.

      Her mind's a traitor: crimes kept in the dark
105   Cry for light, and the guardian brain shudders;
      But how much worse than this
      Is brazen boasting of barefaced anarchy!
ANTIGONÊ   Kreon, what more do you want than my death?
KREON   Nothing.
110   That gives me everything.
ANTIGONÊ   Then I beg you: kill me.
      This talking is a great weariness: your words
      Are distasteful to me, and I am sure that mine
      Seem so to you. And yet they should not seem so:
115   I should have praise and honor for what I have done.
      All these men here would praise me
      Were their lips not frozen shut with fear of you.
      (*bitterly*) Ah the good fortune of kings,
      Licensed to say and do whatever they please!
120 KREON   You are alone here in that opinion.
ANTIGONÊ   No, they are with me. But they keep their tongues
          in leash.

KREON   Maybe. But you are guilty, and they are not.

ANTIGONÊ   There is no guilt in reverence for the dead.

125 KREON   But Eteoclês—was he not your brother too?

ANTIGONÊ   My brother too.

KREON   And you insult his memory?

ANTIGONÊ (*softly*)   The dead man would not say that I insult it.

KREON   He would: for you honor a traitor as much as him.

130 ANTIGONÊ   His own brother, traitor or not, and equal in blood.

KREON   He made war on his country. Eteoclês defended it.

ANTIGONÊ   Nevertheless, there are honors due all the dead.

KREON   But not the same for the wicked as for the just.

ANTIGONÊ   Ah Kreon, Kreon,

135   Which of us can say what the gods hold wicked?

KREON   An enemy is an enemy, even dead.

ANTIGONÊ   It is my nature to join in love, not hate.

KREON (*finally losing patience*)   Go join them then; if you must have your love,

140   Find it in hell!

CHORAGOS   But see, Ismenê comes:

(*Enter* ISMENÊ, *guarded.*)

    Those tears are sisterly, the cloud
    That shadows her eyes rains down gentle sorrow.

KREON   You too, Ismenê,

145   Snake in my ordered house, sucking my blood
    Stealthily—and all the time I never knew
    That these two sisters were aiming at my throne!

                                                Ismenê
    Do you confess your share in this crime, or deny it?

150   Answer me.

ISMENÊ   Yes, if she will let me say so. I am guilty.

ANTIGONÊ (*coldly*)   No, Ismenê. You have no right to say so.
    You would not help me, and I will not have you help me.

ISMENÊ   But now I know what you meant; and I am here

155   To join you, to take my share of punishment.

ANTIGONÊ   The dead man and the gods who rule the dead
    Know whose act this was. Words are not friends.

ISMENÊ   Do you refuse me, Antigonê? I want to die with you:
    I too have a duty that I must discharge to the dead.

160 ANTIGONÊ   You shall not lessen my death by sharing it.

ISMENÊ   What do I care for life when you are dead?

ANTIGONÊ   Ask Kreon. You're always hanging on his opinions.

ISMENÊ   You are laughing at me. Why, Antigonê?

ANTIGONÊ   It's a joyless laughter, Ismenê.
165 ISMENÊ   But can I do nothing?
ANTIGONÊ   Yes. Save yourself. I shall not envy you.
    There are those who will praise you; I shall have honor, too.
ISMENÊ   But we are equally guilty!
ANTIGONÊ   No more, Ismenê.
170   You are alive, but I belong to Death.
KREON (*to the* CHORUS)   Gentlemen, I beg you to observe these
    girls:
    One has just now lost her mind; the other,
    It seems, has never had a mind at all.
175 ISMENÊ   Grief teaches the steadiest minds to waver, King.
KREON   Yours certainly did, when you assumed guilt with the guilty!
ISMENÊ   But how could I go on living without her?
KREON   You are.
    She is already dead.
180 ISMENÊ   But your own son's bride!
KREON   There are places enough for him to push his plow.
    I want no wicked women for my sons!
ISMENÊ   O dearest Haimon, how your father wrongs you!
KREON   I've had enough of your childish talk of marriage!
185 CHORAGOS   Do you really intend to steal this girl from your son?
KREON   No; Death will do that for me.
CHORAGOS   Then she must die?
KREON (*ironically*)   You dazzle me.
               —But enough of this talk!
190   (*to* GUARDS) You, there, take them away and guard them well:
    For they are but women, and even brave men run
    When they see Death coming.

(*Exeunt* ISMENÊ, ANTIGONÊ, *and* GUARDS.)

Ode II

Strophe 1

CHORUS   Fortunate is the man who has never tasted God's
    vengeance!
    Where once the anger of heaven has struck, that house is
    shaken
5   For ever: damnation rises behind each child
    Like a wave cresting out of the black northeast,
    When the long darkness under sea roars up
    And bursts drumming death upon the windwhipped sand.

Antistrophe I

I have seen this gathering sorrow from time long past
10 Loom upon Oedipus' children: generation from generation
Takes the compulsive rage of the enemy god.
So lately this last flower of Oedipus' line
Drank the sunlight; but now a passionate word
And a handful of dust have closed up all its beauty.

Strophe 2

15 What mortal arrogance
Transcends the wrath of Zeus?
Sleep cannot lull him nor the effortless long months
Of the timeless gods: but he is young for ever,
And his house is the shining day of high Olympos.
20 All that is and shall be,
And all the past, is his.
No pride on earth is free of the curse of heaven.

Antistrophe 2

The straying dreams of men
May bring them ghosts of joy:
25 But as they drowse, the waking embers burn them;
Or they walk with fixed eyes, as blind men walk.
But the ancient wisdom speaks for our own time:
Fate works most for woe
With Folly's fairest show.
30 Man's little pleasure is the spring of sorrow.

Scene III

CHORAGOS   But here is Haimon, King, the last of all your sons.
Is it grief for Antigonê that brings him here,
And bitterness at being robbed of his bride?

(*Enter* HAIMON.)

KREON   We shall soon see, and no need of diviners.
5   —Son,
You have heard my final judgment on that girl:
Have you come here hating me, or have you come
With deference and with love, whatever I do?

HAIMON   I am your son, father. You are my guide.
10   You make things clear for me, and I obey you.
No marriage means more to me than your continuing
wisdom.

KREON   Good. That is the way to behave: subordinate
Everything else, my son, to your father's will.
15   This is what a man prays for, that he may get
Sons attentive and dutiful in his house,
Each one hating his father's enemies,
Honoring his father's friends. But if his sons
Fail him, if they turn out unprofitably,
20   What has he fathered but trouble for himself
And amusement for the malicious?

                                So you are right
Not to lose your head over this woman.
Your pleasure with her would soon grow cold, Haimon,
25   And then you'd have a hellcat in bed and elsewhere.
Let her find her husband in Hell!
Of all the people in this city, only she
Has had contempt for my law and broken it.

Do you want me to show myself weak before the people?
30   Or to break my sworn word? No, and I will not.
The woman dies.
I suppose she'll plead "family ties." Well, let her.
If I permit my own family to rebel,
How shall I earn the world's obedience?
35   Show me the man who keeps his house in hand,
He's fit for public authority.

                        I'll have no dealings
With lawbreakers, critics of the government:
Whoever is chosen to govern should be obeyed—
40   Must be obeyed, in all things, great and small,
Just and unjust! O Haimon,
The man who knows how to obey, and that man only,
Knows how to give commands when the time comes.
You can depend on him, no matter how fast
45   The spears come: he's a good soldier, he'll stick it out.

Anarchy, anarchy! Show me a greater evil!
This is why cities tumble and the great houses rain down,
This is what scatters armies!
No, no: good lives are made so by discipline.
50   We keep the laws then, and the lawmakers,
And no woman shall seduce us. If we must lose,
Let's lose to a man, at least! Is a woman stronger than we?

CHORAGOS   Unless time has rusted my wits,
    What you say, King, is said with point and dignity.
55 HAIMON (*boyishly earnest*)   Father:
    Reason is God's crowning gift to man, and you are right
    To warn me against losing mine. I cannot say—
    I hope that I shall never want to say!—that you
    Have reasoned badly. Yet there are other men
60 Who can reason, too; and their opinions might be helpful.
    You are not in a position to know everything
    That people say or do, or what they feel:
    Your temper terrifies—everyone
    Will tell you only what you like to hear.
65 But I, at any rate, can listen; and I have heard them
    Muttering and whispering in the dark about this girl.
    They say no woman has ever, so unreasonably,
    Died so shameful a death for a generous act:
    "She covered her brother's body. Is this indecent?
70 She kept him from dogs and vultures. Is this a crime?
    Death?—She should have all the honor that we can give her!"

    This is the way they talk out there in the city.

    You must believe me:
    Nothing is closer to me than your happiness.
75 What could be closer? Must not any son
    Value his father's fortune as his father does his?
    I beg you, do not be unchangeable:
    Do not believe that you alone can be right.
    The man who thinks that,
80 The man who maintains that only he has the power
    To reason correctly, the gift to speak, the soul—
    A man like that, when you know him, turns out empty.

    It is not reason never to yield to reason!

    In flood time you can see how some trees bend,
85 And because they bend, even their twigs are safe,
    While stubborn trees are torn up, roots and all.
    And the same thing happens in sailing:
    Make your sheet fast, never slacken,—and over you go,
    Head over heels and under: and there's your voyage.
90 Forget you are angry! Let yourself be moved!
    I know I am young; but please let me say this:
    The ideal condition
    Would be, I admit, that men should be right by instinct;
    But since we are all too likely to go astray,
95 The reasonable thing is to learn from those who can teach.

CHORAGOS   You will do well to listen to him, King,
    If what he says is sensible. And you, Haimon,
    Must listen to your father.—Both speak well.
KREON   You consider it right for a man of my years
100   and experience
    To go to school to a boy?
HAIMON   It is not right
    If I am wrong. But if I am young, and right,
    What does my age matter?
105 KREON   You think it right to stand up for an anarchist?
HAIMON   Not at all. I pay no respect to criminals.
KREON   Then she is not a criminal?
HAIMON   The City would deny it, to a man.
KREON   And the City proposes to teach me how to rule?
110 HAIMON   Ah. Who is it that's talking like a boy now?
KREON   My voice is the one voice giving orders in this City!
HAIMON   It is no City if it takes orders from one voice.
KREON   The State is the King!
HAIMON   Yes, if the State is a desert.

(*Pause.*)

115 KREON   This boy, it seems, has sold out to a woman.
HAIMON   If you are a woman: my concern is only for you.
KREON   So? Your "concern"! In a public brawl with your
        father!
HAIMON   How about you, in a public brawl with justice?
120 KREON   With justice, when all that I do is within my rights?
HAIMON   You have no right to trample on God's right.
KREON (*completely out of control*)   Fool, adolescent fool! Taken
        in by a woman!
HAIMON   You'll never see me taken in by anything vile.
125 KREON   Every word you say is for her!
HAIMON (*quietly, darkly*)   And for you.
    And for me. And for the gods under the earth.
KREON   You'll never marry her while she lives.
HAIMON   Then she must die.—But her death will cause another.
130 KREON   Another?
    Have you lost your senses? Is this an open threat?
HAIMON   There is no threat in speaking to emptiness.
KREON   I swear you'll regret this superior tone of yours!
    You are the empty one!
135 HAIMON   If you were not my father,
    I'd say you were perverse.

KREON   You girlstruck fool, don't play at words with me!

HAIMON   I am sorry. You prefer silence.

KREON   Now, by God—!

140   I swear, by all the gods in heaven above us,
       You'll watch it, I swear you shall!
       (*to the* SERVANTS)   Bring her out!
       Bring the woman out! Let her die before his eyes!
       Here, this instant, with her bridegroom beside her!

145 HAIMON   Not here, no; she will not die here, King.
       And you will never see my face again.
       Go on raving as long as you've a friend to endure you.

(*Exit* HAIMON.)

CHORAGOS   Gone, gone.
       Kreon, a young man in a rage is dangerous!

150 KREON   Let him do, or dream to do, more than a man can.
       He shall not save these girls from death.

CHORAGOS   These girls?
       You have sentenced them both?

KREON   No, you are right.

155   I will not kill the one whose hands are clean.

CHORAGOS   But Antigonê?

KREON (*somberly*)   I will carry her far away
       Out there in the wilderness, and lock her
       Living in a vault of stone. She shall have food,

160   As the custom is, to absolve the State of her death.
       And there let her pray to the gods of hell:
       They are her only gods:
       Perhaps they will show her an escape from death,
       Or she may learn,

165   though late,
       That piety shown the dead is pity in vain.

(*Exit* KREON.)

Ode III

Strophe

CHORUS   Love, unconquerable
       Waster of rich men, keeper
       Of warm lights and all-night vigil
       In the soft face of a girl:

5   Sea-wanderer, forest-visitor!

Even the pure Immortals cannot escape you,
And mortal man, in his one day's dusk,
Trembles before your glory.

Antistrophe

Surely you swerve upon ruin
10   The just man's consenting heart,
As here you have made bright anger
Strike between father and son—
And none has conquered but Love!
A girl's glance working the will of heaven:
15   Pleasure to her alone who mocks us,
Merciless Aphroditê.[3]

Scene IV

CHORAGOS (*as* ANTIGONÊ *enters guarded*)   But I can no longer
    stand in awe of this,
Nor, seeing what I see, keep back my tears.
Here is Antigonê, passing to that chamber
5   Where all find sleep at last.

Strophe I

ANTIGONÊ   Look upon me, friends, and pity me
Turning back at the night's edge to say
Good-by to the sun that shines for me no longer;
Now sleepy Death
10   Summons me down to Acheron,[4] that cold shore:
There is no bridesong there, nor any music.
CHORUS   Yet not unpraised, not without a kind of honor,
You walk at last into the underworld;
Untouched by sickness, broken by no sword.
15   What woman has ever found your way to death?

Antistrophe I

ANTIGONÊ   How often I have heard the story
    of Niobê,[5]

---

[3]goddess of love   [4]a river in the underworld   [5]Niobê, the daughter of Tantalos, was turned into a stone on Mount Sipylus while bemoaning the destruction of her many children by Leto, the mother of Apollo.

Tantalos' wretched daughter, how the stone
Clung fast about her, ivy-close: and they say
20 The rain falls endlessly
And sifting soft snow; her tears are never done.
I feel the loneliness of her death in mine.
CHORUS   But she was born of heaven, and you
Are woman, woman-born. If her death is yours,
25 A mortal woman's, is this not for you
Glory in our world and in the world beyond?

Strophe 2

ANTIGONÊ   You laugh at me. Ah, friends, friends,
Can you not wait until I am dead? O Thebes,
O men many-charioted, in love with Fortune,
30 Dear springs of Dircê, sacred Theban grove,
Be witnesses for me, denied all pity,
Unjustly judged! and think a word of love
For her whose path turns
Under dark earth, where there are no more tears.
35 CHORUS   You have passed beyond human daring and come at last
Into a place of stone where Justice sits.
I cannot tell
What shape of your father's guilt appears in this.

Antistrophe 2

ANTIGONÊ   You have touched it at last:
40   that bridal bed
Unspeakable, horror of son and mother mingling:
Their crime, infection of all our family!
O Oedipus, father and brother!
Your marriage strikes from the grave to murder mine.
45 I have been a stranger here in my own land:
All my life
The blasphemy of my birth has followed me.
CHORUS   Reverence is a virtue, but strength
Lives in established law: that must prevail.
50 You have made your choice,
Your death is the doing of your conscious hand.

Epode

ANTIGONÊ   Then let me go, since all your words are bitter,
And the very light of the sun is cold to me.

Lead me to my vigil, where I must have
55   Neither love nor lamentation; no song, but silence.

(KREON *interrupts impatiently.*)

KREON   If dirges and planned lamentations could put off death,
Men would be singing for ever.
(*to the* SERVANTS)   Take her, go!
You know your orders: take her to the vault
60   And leave her alone there. And if she lives or dies,
That's her affair, not ours: our hands are clean.

ANTIGONÊ   O tomb, vaulted bride-bed in eternal rock,
Soon I shall be with my own again
Where Persephonê[6] welcomes the thin ghosts
65   underground:
And I shall see my father again, and you, mother,
And dearest Polyneicês—

                    dearest indeed
To me, since it was my hand
70   That washed him clean and poured the ritual wine:
And my reward is death before my time!

And yet, as men's hearts know, I have done no wrong,
I have not sinned before God. Or if I have,
I shall know the truth in death. But if the guilt
75   Lies upon Kreon who judged me, then, I pray,
May his punishment equal my own.
CHORAGOS   O passionate heart,
Unyielding, tormented still by the same winds!
KREON   Her guards shall have good cause to regret their delaying.
80 ANTIGONÊ   Ah! That voice is like the voice of death!
KREON   I can give you no reason to think you are mistaken.
ANTIGONÊ   Thebes, and you my fathers' gods,
And rulers of Thebes, you see me now, the last
Unhappy daughter of a line of kings,
85   Your kings, led away to death. You will remember
What things I suffer, and at what men's hands,
Because I would not transgress the laws of heaven.
(*to the* GUARDS, *simply*) Come: let us wait no longer.

(*Exit* ANTIGONÊ, *left, guarded.*)

---

[6]queen of the underworld

Ode IV

Strophe 1

CHORUS   All Danaê's[7] beauty was locked away
In a brazen cell where the sunlight could not come:
A small room still as any grave, enclosed her.
Yet she was a princess too,
5   And Zeus in a rain of gold poured love upon her.
O child, child,
No power in wealth or war
Or tough sea-blackened ships
Can prevail against untiring Destiny!

Antistrophe 1

10   And Dryas' son[8] also, that furious king,
Bore the god's prisoning anger for his pride:
Sealed up by Dionysos in deaf stone,
His madness died among echoes.
So at the last he learned what dreadful power
15   His tongue had mocked:
For he had profaned the revels,
And fired the wrath of the nine
Implacable Sisters[9] that love the sound of the flute.

Strophe 2

And old men tell a half-remembered tale
20   Of horror where a dark ledge splits the sea
And a double surf beats on the gráy shóres:
How a king's new woman,[10] sick
With hatred for the queen he had imprisoned,
Ripped out his two sons' eyes with her bloody hands
25   While grinning Arês[11] watched the shuttle plunge
Four times: four blind wounds crying for revenge.

Antistrophe 2

Crying, tears and blood mingled.—Piteously born,
Those sons whose mother was of heavenly birth!

---

[7] the mother of Perseus by Zeus, who visited her during her imprisonment in the form of a golden rain   [8] Lycurgus, king of Thrace   [9] the Muses   [10] Eidothea, King Phineus' second wife, blinded her stepsons.   [11] god of war

Her father was the god of the North Wind
30   And she was cradled by gales,
She raced with young colts on the glittering hills
And walked untrammeled in the open light:
But in her marriage deathless Fate found means
To build a tomb like yours for all her joy.

Scene V

(*Enter blind* TEIRESIAS, *led by a boy. The opening speeches of* TEIRESIAS *should be in singsong contrast to the realistic lines of* KREON.)

TEIRESIAS   This is the way the blind man comes, Princes, Princes,
    Lock-step, two heads lit by the eyes of one.
KREON   What new thing have you to tell us, old Teiresias?
TEIRESIAS   I have much to tell you: listen to the prophet, Kreon.
5 KREON   I am not aware that I have ever failed to listen.
TEIRESIAS   Then you have done wisely, King, and ruled well.
KREON   I admit my debt to you. But what have you to say?
TEIRESIAS   This, Kreon: you stand once more on the edge of fate.
KREON   What do you mean? Your words are a kind of dread.
10 TEIRESIAS   Listen, Kreon:
    I was sitting in my chair of augury, at the place
    Where the birds gather about me. They were all a-chatter,
    As is their habit, when suddenly I heard
    A strange note in their jangling, a scream, a
15   Whirring fury; I knew that they were fighting,
    Tearing each other, dying
    In a whirlwind of wings clashing. And I was afraid.
    I began the rites of burnt-offering at the altar,
    But Hephaistos[12] failed me: instead of bright flame,
20   There was only the sputtering slime of the fat thigh-flesh
    Melting: the entrails dissolved in gray smoke,
    The bare bone burst from the welter. And no blaze!

    This was a sign from heaven. My boy described it,
    Seeing for me as I see for others.

25   I tell you, Kreon, you yourself have brought
    This new calamity upon us. Our hearths and altars
    Are stained with the corruption of dogs and carrion birds
    That glut themselves on the corpse of Oedipus' son.
    The gods are deaf when we pray to them, their fire

---

[12]god of fire

30   Recoils from our offering, their birds of omen
Have no cry of comfort, for they are gorged
With the thick blood of the dead.

                       O my son,
These are no trifles! Think: all men make mistakes,
35   But a good man yields when he knows his course is wrong,
And repairs the evil. The only crime is pride.

    Give in to the dead man, then: do not fight with a corpse—
What glory is it to kill a man who is dead?
Think, I beg you:
40   It is for your own good that I speak as I do.
You should be able to yield for your own good.
    KREON   It seems that prophets have made me their especial
       province.
All my life long
45   I have been a kind of butt for the dull arrows
Of doddering fortune-tellers!

                   No, Teiresias:
If your birds—if the great eagles of God himself
Should carry him stinking bit by bit to heaven,
50   I would not yield. I am not afraid of pollution:
No man can defile the gods.

               Do what you will,
Go into business, make money, speculate
In India gold or that synthetic gold from Sardis,
55   Get rich otherwise than by my consent to bury him.
Teiresias, it is a sorry thing when a wise man
Sells his wisdom, lets out his words for hire!
    TEIRESIAS   Ah Kreon! Is there no man left in the world—
    KREON   To do what?—Come, let's have the aphorism!
60 TEIRESIAS   No man who knows that wisdom outweighs any wealth?
    KREON   As surely as bribes are baser than any baseness.
    TEIRESIAS   You are sick, Kreon! You are deathly sick!
    KREON   As you say: it is not my place to challenge a prophet.
    TEIRESIAS   Yet you have said my prophecy is for sale.
65 KREON   The generation of prophets has always loved gold.
    TEIRESIAS   The generation of kings has always loved brass.
    KREON   You forget yourself! You are speaking to your King.
    TEIRESIAS   I know it. You are a king because of me.
    KREON   You have a certain skill; but you have sold out.
70 TEIRESIAS   King, you will drive me to words that—
    KREON   Say them, say them!
    Only remember: I will not pay you for them.

TEIRESIAS   No, you will find them too costly.

KREON   No doubt. Speak:
75   Whatever you say, you will not change my will.

TEIRESIAS   Then take this, and take it to heart!
        The time is not far off when you shall pay back
        Corpse for corpse, flesh of your own flesh.
        You have thrust the child of this world into living night,
80   You have kept from the gods below the child that is theirs:
        The one in a grave before her death, the other,
        Dead, denied the grave. This is your crime:
        And the Furies and the dark gods of Hell
        Are swift with terrible punishment for you.
85   Do you want to buy me now, Kreon?

                                                    Not many days,
        And your house will be full of men and women weeping,
        And curses will be hurled at you from far
        Cities grieving for sons unburied, left to rot
90   Before the walls of Thebes.

        These are my arrows, Kreon: they are all for you.

        (*To* BOY.) But come, child: lead me home.
        Let him waste his fine anger upon younger men.
        Maybe he will learn at last
95   To control a wiser tongue in a better head.

        (*Exit* TEIRESIAS.)

CHORAGOS   The old man has gone, King, but his words
        Remain to plague us. I am old, too,
        But I cannot remember that he was ever false.

KREON   That is true. . . . It troubles me.
100   Oh it is hard to give in! but it is worse
        To risk everything for stubborn pride.

CHORAGOS   Kreon: take my advice.

KREON   What shall I do?

CHORAGOS   Go quickly: free Antigonê from her vault
105   And build a tomb for the body of Polyneicês.

KREON   You would have me do this!

CHORAGOS   Kreon, yes!
        And it must be done at once: God moves
        Swiftly to cancel the folly of stubborn men.

110 KREON   It is hard to deny the heart! But I
        Will do it: I will not fight with destiny.

CHORAGOS   You must go yourself, you cannot leave it to others.
KREON   I will go.
                            —Bring axes, servants:
115   Come with me to the tomb. I buried her, I
Will set her free.
                            Oh quickly!
My mind misgives—
The laws of the gods are mighty, and a man must serve them
120   To the last day of his life!

(*Exit* KREON.)

Paean[13]

Strophe I

CHORAGOS   God of many names
CHORUS   O Iacchos[14]
                                                    son
        of Kadmeian Sémelê[15]
5   O born of the Thunder!
        Guardian of the West
                            Regent
        of Eleusis' plain
                            O Prince of maenad Thebes
10   and the Dragon Field by rippling Ismenós:[16]

Antistrophe I

CHORAGOS   God of many names
CHORUS   the flame of torches
        flares on our hills
                            the nymphs of Iacchos
15   dance at the spring of Castalia:[17]
        from the vine-close mountain
                                        come ah come in ivy:
        Evohé evohé! sings through the streets of Thebes

---

[13]a hymn of praise [14]another name for Dionysos (Bacchus) [15]the daughter of Kadmos, the founder of Thebes [16]a river east of Thebes; the ancestors of the Theban nobility sprang from dragon's teeth sown by the Ismenós. [17]a spring on Mount Parnasos

Strophe 2

CHORAGOS   God of many names
20 CHORUS   Iacchos of Thebes
heavenly Child
of Sémelê bride of the Thunderer!
The shadow of plague is upon us:
come
25   with clement feet
oh come from Parnasos
down the long slopes
across the lamenting water

Antistrophe 2

CHORAGOS   Iô Fire! Chorister of the throbbing stars!
30   O purest among the voices of the night!
Thou son of God, blaze for us!
CHORUS   Come with choric rapture of circling Maenads[18]
Who cry *Iô Iacche!*
God of many names!

Exodos

(*Enter* MESSENGER *from left.*)

MESSENGER   Men of the line of Kadmos, you who live
Near Amphion's citadel,[19]
I cannot say
Of any condition of human life "This is fixed,
5   This is clearly good, or bad." Fate raises up,
And Fate casts down the happy and unhappy alike:
No man can foretell his Fate.
Take the case of Kreon:
Kreon was happy once, as I count happiness:
10   Victorious in battle, sole governor of the land,
Fortunate father of children nobly born.
And now it has all gone from him! Who can say
That a man is still alive when his life's joy fails?
He is a walking dead man. Grant him rich,
15   Let him live like a king in his great house:

---

[18]the worshippers of Dionysos   [19]Amphion used the music of his magic lyre to lure stones to form a wall around Thebes.

If his pleasure is gone, I would not give
So much as the shadow of smoke for all he owns.
CHORAGOS   Your words hint at sorrow: what is your news for us?
MESSENGER   They are dead. The living are guilty of their death.
20 CHORAGOS   Who is guilty? Who is dead? Speak!
MESSENGER   Haimon.
Haimon is dead; and the hand that killed him
Is his own hand.
CHORAGOS   His father's? or his own?
25 MESSENGER   His own, driven mad by the murder his father had
done.
CHORAGOS   Teiresias, Teiresias, how clearly you saw it all!
MESSENGER   This is my news: you must draw what conclusions
you can from it.
30 CHORAGOS   But look: Eurydicê, our Queen:
Has she overheard us?

(*Enter* EURYDICÊ *from the palace, center.*)

EURYDICÊ   I have heard something, friends:
As I was unlocking the gate of Pallas'[20] shrine,
For I needed her help today, I heard a voice
35 Telling of some new sorrow. And I fainted
There at the temple all my maidens about me.
But speak again: whatever it is, I can bear it:
Grief and I are no strangers.
MESSENGER   Dearest Lady,
40 I will tell you plainly all that I have seen.
I shall not try to comfort you: what is the use,
Since comfort could lie only in what is not true?
The truth is always best.
                                        I went with Kreon
45 To the outer plain where Polyneicês was lying,
No friend to pity him, his body shredded by dogs.
We made our prayers in that place to Hecatê
And Pluto,[21] that they would be merciful. And we bathed
The corpse with holy water, and we brought
50 Fresh-broken branches to burn what was left of it,
And upon the urn we heaped up a towering barrow
Of the earth of his own land.
                                        When we were done, we ran
To the vault where Antigonê lay on her couch of stone.

---

[20]Pallas Athena, the goddess of wisdom   [21]*Hecatê . . . Pluto* the ruling deities of the underworld

55   One of the servants had gone ahead,
     And while he was yet far off he heard a voice
     Grieving within the chamber, and he came back
     And told Kreon. And as the King went closer,
     The air was full of wailing, the words lost,
60   And he begged us to make all haste. "Am I a prophet?"
     He said, weeping, "And must I walk this road,
     The saddest of all that I have gone before?
     My son's voice calls me on. Oh quickly, quickly!
     Look through the crevice there, and tell me
65   If it is Haimon, or some deception of the gods!"

     We obeyed; and in the cavern's farthest corner
     We saw her lying:
     She had made a noose of her fine linen veil
     And hanged herself. Haimon lay beside her,
70   His arms about her waist, lamenting her,
     His love lost under ground, crying out
     That his father had stolen her away from him.

     When Kreon saw him the tears rushed to his eyes
     And he called to him: "What have you done, child?
75   Speak to me.
     What are you thinking that makes your eyes so strange?
     O my son, my son, I come to you on my knees!"
     But Haimon spat in his face. He said not a word,
     Staring—
80   And suddenly drew his sword
     And lunged. Kreon shrank back, the blade missed; and the
           boy,
     Desperate against himself, drove it half its length
     Into his own side, and fell. And as he died
85   He gathered Antigonê close in his arms again,
     Choking, his blood bright red on her white cheek.
     And now he lies dead with the dead, and she is his
     At last, his bride in the house of the dead.

     (*Exit* Eurydicê *into the palace.*)

CHORAGOS   She has left us without a word. What can this mean?
90 MESSENGER   It troubles me, too; yet she knows what is best,
        Her grief is too great for public lamentation,
        And doubtless she has gone to her chamber to weep
        For her dead son, leading her maidens in his dirge.

     (*Pause.*)

CHORAGOS   It may be so: but I fear this deep silence.
95 MESSENGER   I will see what she is doing. I will go in.

(*Exit* MESSENGER *into the palace. Enter* KREON *with attendants, bearing* HAI-
MON'S *body.*)

CHORAGOS   But here is the king himself: oh look at him,
    Bearing his own damnation in his arms.
KREON   Nothing you say can touch me any more.
    My own blind heart has brought me
100   From darkness to final darkness. Here you see
    The father murdering, the murdered son—
    And all my civic wisdom!

    Haimon my son, so young, so young to die,
    I was the fool, not you; and you died for me.
105 CHORAGOS   That is the truth; but you were late in learning it.
KREON   This truth is hard to bear. Surely a god
    Has crushed me beneath the hugest weight of heaven,
    And driven me headlong a barbaric way
    To trample out the thing I held most dear.

110   The pains that men will take to come to pain!

(*Enter* MESSENGER *from the palace.*)

MESSENGER   The burden you carry in your hands is heavy,
    But it is not all: you will find more in your house.
KREON   What burden worse than this shall I find there?
MESSENGER   The Queen is dead.
115 KREON   O port of death, deaf world,
    Is there no pity for me? And you, Angel of evil,
    I was dead, and your words are death again.
    Is it true, boy? Can it be true?
    Is my wife dead? Has death bred death?
120 MESSENGER   You can see for yourself.

(*The doors are opened and the body of* EURYDICÊ *is disclosed within.*)

KREON   Oh pity!
    All true, all true, and more than I can bear!
    O my wife, my son!
MESSENGER   She stood before the altar, and her heart
125   Welcomed the knife her own hand guided,
    And a great cry burst from her lips for Megareus[22] dead,

---

[22]Megareus, brother of Haimon, had died in the assault on Thebes.

And for Haimon dead, her sons; and her last breath
Was a curse for their father, the murderer of her sons.
And she fell, and the dark flowed in through her closing eyes.

130 KREON   O God, I am sick with fear.
Are there no swords here? Has no one a blow for me?

MESSENGER   Her curse is upon you for the deaths of both.

KREON   It is right that it should be. I alone am guilty.
I know it, and I say it. Lead me in,

135   Quickly, friends.
I have neither life nor substance. Lead me in.

CHORAGOS   You are right, if there can be right in so much wrong.
The briefest way is best in a world of sorrow.

KREON   Let it come,

140   Let death come quickly, and be kind to me.
I would not ever see the sun again.

CHORAGOS   All that will come when it will; but we, meanwhile,
Have much to do. Leave the future to itself.

KREON   All my heart was in that prayer!

145 CHORAGOS   Then do not pray any more: the sky is deaf.

KREON   Lead me away. I have been rash and foolish.
I have killed my son and my wife.
I look for comfort; my comfort lies here dead.
Whatever my hands have touched has come to nothing.

150   Fate has brought all my pride to a thought of dust.

(*As* KREON *is being led into the house, the* CHORAGOS *advances and speaks directly to the audience.*)

CHORAGOS   There is no happiness where there is no wisdom;
No wisdom but in submission to the gods.
Big words are always punished,
And proud men in old age learn to be wise.

c. 441 B.C.

STUDY QUESTIONS

1. One might argue that in *Antigonê* each of the major characters undergoes his or her own moment of recognition and subsequent reversal of fortune. For instance, one can say that the play opens on Antigonê's recognition of Kreon's edict—both because she has just learned of the edict and because she here expresses her realization of how she must react to it and of what retaliation her reaction is likely to draw.
   a. Arguing along these lines, identify the scenes, events, and speeches that mark Kreon's recognition. What reversal follows from it?

b. Would you also want to argue for recognitions for Haimon, Eurydicê, and Ismenê? If so, where would you place them, and what reversals follow them?

c. Write an essay that (1) discusses each of these recognitions and their significance to the characters involved, and (2) demonstrates how the placement and cumulative effect of these several recognitions and reversals give the play its shape and dramatic impact. (Remember that you must define the structure and movement of the play as you see it, to ensure that you and your reader are working from the same basic understanding.)

2. How would you balance the claims of "thought" and "character" as the more important element in *Antigonê?* (In other words, is it the questions argued or the character and fate of the debaters that you feel provide the strongest source of the play's appeal?) Would either element alone suffice? Why or why not?

3. Antigonê and Kreon are, of course, the major antagonists in *Antigonê.* But each has another opponent as well. Ismenê argues against Antigonê's actions, and Haimon argues against Kreon. What do the presence and actions of these two characters add to the play?

28

HAMLET *AND*
ELIZABETHAN DRAMA

Origins of English Drama

English, or **Elizabethan, drama** can be traced back to two origins, one in tenth-century England and one in ancient Greece. The two beginnings differed greatly in style and content but did have one important thing in common: both formed parts of religious rituals.

Medieval Drama

Medieval European drama seems to have begun as part of the Easter services. At some appropriate point during the Mass or the matins service, one or two men would unobtrusively position themselves near the altar or near some representation of a tomb. There, they would be approached by three other men, whose heads were covered to look like women and who moved slowly, as if seeking something. Singing in the Latin of the church service, the "angel" at the tomb would question the "women," "Whom seek you in the tomb, O followers of Christ?" The women would then sing the answer of the three Marys, "Jesus of Nazareth, who was crucified, O heavenly one." The angel then would sing again, "He is not here; he is risen, just as he foretold. Go, announce that he is risen from the tomb."

The dramatization might stop there, or it might continue with the showing of the empty tomb to the women, their song of joy, and the spreading of the good news to the disciples. In either case, the culmination of the drama would mark a return to the service itself with the singing of the Mass's *Ressurexi* ("I have risen") or the matins' final *Te deum, laudamus* ("We praise thee, Lord").

One medieval manuscript in particular emphasizes the closeness of the connection. It describes the singers of the *Te Deum* as rejoicing with the three women at Christ's triumph over death and commands that all the church bells be rung together as soon as the hymn of praise has begun. Drama and service thus celebrate the same event. The joy expressed by the women at the news of the resurrection is the same joy felt by the worshippers in the congregation.

Latin drama continued to develop within the church services. Manuscripts still survive, not only of **Easter** and **Christmas plays** but of plays dealing with prophets and saints as well. They show the plays growing longer and more elaborate than the early one just described, but they still emphasize the close ties between the plays and the services at which they are performed. Thus one Christmas pageant of the shepherds calls for many boys dressed as angels to sit in the roof of the church and sing in loud voices the angels' song, "Glory to God." But it also directs that, at the end of the pageant, the shepherds must return into the choir and there act as choir leaders for the Mass that follows.

By the fourteenth century, however, drama had also moved outside the church. There it was spoken almost wholly in the vernacular, though some bits of Latin, and a good deal of singing, remained. The plays were acted by laymen (including some professional actors) rather than by clerics, and they were developing modes of performance that might encompass up to three days of playing and involve most of the citizens of the towns where they were performed.

These were the **Corpus Christi** plays, also known as **cycle plays** or the **mystery plays**. Performed in celebration of Corpus Christi day, they comprised a series of pageants beginning with the creation of the world, proceeding through the history of the Old and New Testaments, and ending with the Last Judgment. Each pageant was performed on its own movable stage—its "pageant wagon." Mounted on four or six wheels, two stories high, the wagons provided facilities for some surprisingly complex stage effects and allowed each pageant to be presented several times at several different locations. One after another, the pageants would move through a town, usually stopping at three or four prearranged places to repeat their performances, so that everyone in town might see all of the twenty to fifty plays that made up the cycle.

The presentation of these cycles was undertaken by the towns themselves, with the town authorities ordering the performances. But the individual pageants were produced by the local trade and craft guilds. Ordinarily each guild would present one pageant, but sometimes several small guilds would team up to perform a single pageant or share the cost of a wagon that each could use. It is easy to imagine the competition this could produce, with each guild trying to outdo the next. But the plays were still religious in subject and import. They often spoke directly to the audience and always emphasized how the events they depicted pertained to each viewer's salvation.

Early English Dramatic Forms

As we suggested in the last chapter, Greek drama carefully labeled and segregated its forms. Tragedy dealt with noble persons and heroic actions. Comedy dealt with everyday affairs.

Medieval drama did not so carefully distinguish its forms. It had one central sacrificial subject: the death of Christ for the salvation of mankind. This sacrifice was always treated seriously; neither Christ nor Mary was ever burlesqued. But the world that Christ entered at his birth was the world of thin clothes and bad weather, of thieves and tricksters and con men, with the Devil himself, the arch-trickster, as Christ's opponent. It was, in short, the world of comedy. A drama that dealt with the history of humanity's fall and salvation would thus have to be both comic and tragic. There would be no way of separating the two.

Nor would medieval writers have wanted to separate them. Medieval art always seems to have preferred inclusiveness to exclusiveness. The great Gothic cathedrals themselves, with their profusion of sculpture and stained glass, would give their most prominent and most beautiful art to scenes of Christ, the Virgin, and the saints. But less prominent carvings would be likely to show small boys stealing apples, or people quarreling; while, in other places, comically or frighteningly grotesque demons would round out the portrayals.

A Corpus Christi cycle, therefore, would contain both serious and humorous elements. Some plays would be wholly serious; others would mix the serious with the comic. "The Sacrifice of Isaac," for instance, was always serious. The dilemma of the father, the emotions of the son as he realized what was happening, combined to produce plays that could virtually be described as tragedies with happy endings. "Noah's Flood," on the other hand, was usually given a comic treatment. (What would you do if your husband suddenly started building a giant boat in your front yard?) In some of the plays, Noah's wife thinks her husband has gone crazy. In others, she joins in the building until it is time to get on board, then rebels against leaving the world she knows and loves. In either case, a physical fight ensues before Noah can get her on board, and Noah's prophecies of doom are mixed with his complaints about marriage. Crucifixion plays, meanwhile, generally mixed the solemnity of the highest sacrifice with a certain amount of low comedy centering on the executioners. There was no thought of separating the two. Both were parts of the same event.

In this way, seeking to mirror life and to emphasize its mixture of noble and ignoble, sacred and mundane, the medieval drama provided Elizabethan playwrights a heritage of flexible, all-inclusive drama, capable at its best of seeing both sides of a subject at once, always insistent that both be recognized. By mixing this heritage with the more single-minded Greek tragic tradition, Elizabethan dramatists produced a tragic form of their own as rich and compelling as any that has existed.

In this chapter, we will study one of the most highly praised and frequently acted Elizabethan tragedies, Shakespeare's *Hamlet*, as well as one of his great "mature" comedies, *Much Ado About Nothing*.

Hamlet and *Oedipus Rex*

In many ways, *Hamlet* is similar to *Oedipus Rex*. Both were written at times when tragedy was just coming to its full maturity in their playwrights' cultures. Both were written by the most influential playwrights of their time. Both helped set the shape of tragedy for their own period's drama and for the drama of future ages.

Both plays have heroes who dominate the action, catching the audience's attention early in the play and holding their attention and their sympathy throughout. (Hamlet, in fact, can even address the audience in **soliloquies** and

asides that no one on stage is meant to hear.) Princely in nature and position, both men seem born to rule. The heroes are somewhat alike in their situations, as well. Both must avenge their father's murder and thus remove a pollution from their land. To do so, however, they must first find out who the murderer is; and they must pursue their search among people who want the truth to remain hidden.

Here, however, the situations diverge. Oedipus' companions want to conceal the truth for Oedipus' own sake. Hamlet's opponent, Claudius, wants the truth to remain hidden because he is the murderer. The element of active, willed evil, which is absent from *Oedipus Rex*, is thus present in *Hamlet*. Hamlet must not only destroy his father's murderer but also do so before the murderer destroys him.

Hamlet, as we suggested earlier, is a play derived from both Greek and medieval drama. From Greek tragedy, it has taken the tragic hero—dominant, strong-willed, determined to accomplish his desires. It has also taken from Greek tragedy a certain elevation of tone and insistence on the dignity of human beings. From medieval drama, it has taken the medieval desire for inclusiveness and the medieval love of significant detail. *Hamlet* is much longer than *Oedipus Rex*. It has more characters, a more complex plot, and a generous amount of comedy.

Let us look at each of these elements in turn. Regarding characters, we notice that Oedipus is unique, but that Hamlet sees himself reflected in two other characters: first in Fortinbras, another son of a warrior king whose father has died and whose uncle has seized the throne, leaving him practically powerless; and later in Laertes, another son determined to avenge himself on his father's murderer. The deeds of Laertes and Fortinbras contrast with and comment on the actions of Hamlet himself, thus enriching our view of Hamlet and his dilemma. At the same time, the actions of the three men intertwine to create three of the play's major themes: fathers and sons, honor, and thought versus action.

Regarding plot, we can be sure that the affairs of three families will create a more complex plot than the affairs of one family. Thus critics sometimes speak of the Fortinbras "**overplot**" (which is mostly concerned with war and kingship) and the Laertes "**underplot**" (concerned with private family relationships) and how these two "subplots" complement the "main plot" (which deals with Hamlet's familial and princely concerns). But the English inclusiveness goes even beyond this, adding also a love story between Hamlet and Laertes' sister, Ophelia, a study of true versus false friendship in the persons of Horatio and Rosencrantz and Guildenstern, and a few comments on the contemporary theater by a troupe of strolling players. There are also glimpses of three purely comic characters: two gravediggers and one intolerably affected courtier. Again, all these themes and characters are interwoven to illuminate Hamlet's character and dilemma. (The gravediggers, for instance, who seem at first wildly irrelevant, ultimately serve to bring Hamlet to a new understanding of mortality, an understanding that is crucial to his ability to face his own death.)

In *Hamlet,* comedy is not separate from tragedy. Rather, it is used as a means to create a fuller awareness of tragedy. Hamlet himself is a master of comic wordplay. His first speech turns on a pun; and puns and bitter quips mark his speech to Claudius and his courtiers throughout the play. Many of these quips are spoken under the guise of pretended madness; and here the audience shares secrets with Hamlet. We know he is not really mad. But those on stage think he is. (The exception is Claudius, who suspects that Hamlet is not mad but who cannot reveal Hamlet's sanity without revealing his own crimes.) Pretending madness, therefore, Hamlet makes speeches that sound like nonsense to the courtiers but that we recognize as referring to his father's murder and his recognition of treachery in those around him. We are thus let into Hamlet's secrets and feelings as no single character in the play is let into them. Hamlet's use of jesting speech thus becomes not merely a weapon in his fight against Claudius but also a means of winning the sympathetic partnership of the audience. In comic speech and tragic soliloquy alike, Hamlet reveals himself to us. By the play's end, we know Hamlet as we know few other stage characters.

Adding to our sense of knowledge is the fact that Hamlet is a complex and changing character. In this he differs markedly from Oedipus, whose character remains firm and fixed until it changes so drastically in his final scene. The essentially fixed character is typical of Greek drama, which seems to have been more interested in the clash of character against character (or of character against fate) than it was in the changes within or the development of a single character. It is far less typical of Elizabethan tragedy.

This emphasis on Hamlet's developing character is an indication of the influence of medieval Christian drama, with its concern for salvation and the dangers and triumphs of the soul. English drama was secular drama by Shakespeare's time, being performed regularly by professional troupes for paying audiences. Concern for the soul, however, remained one of its major concerns. When Elizabethan dramatists wrote tragedies, therefore, they tended to make the hero's inner concerns—his passions, his temptations, his spiritual triumphs or defeats—the central focus of their plays. Even the ghost in *Hamlet,* coming to call for revenge, warns Hamlet to "taint not thy mind, nor let thy soul contrive/Against thy mother aught." Hamlet must avenge his father and free Denmark from the polluting rule of Claudius, but he must do so in a manner that will imperil neither his own nor his mother's salvation.

When the play opens, Hamlet is a bitter man. So far from being at peace with himself or his surroundings is he that he seems to have little chance of fulfilling the ghost's demands. So close does he come to flinging away his own soul in pursuit of Claudius, in fact, that some critics have refused to believe that Hamlet's speeches in Act III, Scene 3, mean what they say. In fact, they mean exactly what they say. Hamlet in this scene is on the brink of disaster.

In the next scene, the "closet scene," the unexpected happens. Hamlet is caught in the wrong, realizes it, and begins the painful process of returning from his bitterness and hatreds to a reconciliation with himself, his mother, and humanity in general. Throughout the rest of the play, we watch Hamlet's speeches on human nature become gentler, his attitude more compassionate; we hear a new acceptance of his fate, a new trust in providence, revealed. By the play's end, when Hamlet gets his one chance at Claudius, he is fully ready for the task and its consequences. And so the play ends in mingled loss and triumph: loss to Denmark and to us in the death of Hamlet, triumph that Hamlet has nobly achieved his purpose.

One final word must be said about the language of *Hamlet,* which is like the language of no other play we will read in this book. Seeking some meter in English that would match the beauty and dignity of the meters in which classical tragedy had been written, the sixteenth-century dramatists had created **blank verse**. Blank verse does not rhyme. It usually has ten syllables to a line (though lines may be shorter or longer by a few syllables), and the second, fourth, sixth, eighth, and tenth syllables are generally accented more strongly than the rest. This meter was easily spoken. It was dignified and flexible. And it could slip neatly into prose (for comic scenes) or into **rhymed couplets** to mark a scene's end.

Blank verse was fairly new when Shakespeare began writing. In some of his early plays, it still sounds stiff and awkward. By the time he wrote *Hamlet,* however, Shakespeare was entering into a mastery of blank verse that no one has ever surpassed. The rhythms and imagery of Hamlet's language warn us of every change in his moods, from pretended madness to honest friendship to bitter passion. By the modulation of Hamlet's language, as well as by his actions, Shakespeare shows us the battle within Hamlet's soul.

If you can see *Hamlet*—live or on film—or if you can hear recordings of it, do so. If not, read as much of it aloud as you can. For readers unfamiliar with Shakespearean language, *Hamlet* is not an easy play to read. Nearly every word of it counts; so every word must be attended to. But the play is well worth the effort it takes, for it is truly one of the finest plays of all time.

Comedy and *Much Ado About Nothing*

In a typical tragedy, a thriving prince or king undergoes a "tragic fall" into the world of sorrow, suffering, and death. This reversal of fortune occurs partly because of fate, partly because of the ambitious schemes of evil men, and partly because of the protagonist's own character flaws. The protagonist, who had been integrated into his society, suddenly finds himself estranged from it. The only compensation for his suffering is the tragic knowledge he gains from his experience, and the resignation he usually displays before he dies.

In comedy, on the other hand, a different process takes place. Although the protagonists may have a high social standing at the beginning of the play, they are often blocked from full integration into their culture because they are experiencing difficulties in finding or wooing a mate. If death by murder or suicide is the distinguishing feature of tragedy, marriage is the unmistakable generic marker of comedy. Tragedy deals with the loneliness of being a morally sensitive being in a fallen world; comedy celebrates the universal pleasures of friendship, erotic love, and community—the bonds that constantly renew and sustain individuals even through their troubles.

Much Ado About Nothing fits this pattern perfectly. Its double wedding in Act V between Hero and Claudio and Beatrice and Benedick is a joyous celebration reconciling all the frustrations, tensions, and confusions of identity that make up its plot. But just as Shakespeare mixed comic elements into *Hamlet*, he darkened *Much Ado* with an Iago-like villain who threatens to turn the play into tragedy. Don Juan, Don Pedro's bastard brother, out of jealousy over Claudio's friendship with Don Pedro, temporarily sets Claudio against Hero, Hero's father Leonato against both his daughter and Claudio, and Benedick against Claudio as well. These tensions are so extreme that even so great a dramatist as Shakespeare had trouble wrestling the tone of his play back toward comedy in Act V. Unlike the "happy" early comedies, such as *Two Gentlemen of Verona* or *The Taming of the Shrew,* such late comedies as *The Merchant of Venice, Much Ado,* and *Twelfth Night* reveal a more philosophical, even melancholic, comic imagination at work.

The two contrasting tonal elements in *Much Ado* are reflected in the contrasting love plots. Claudio and Hero's story is Italianate, both in its style and probable sources. It is driven by plot rather than by character, because the two lovers behave more like Petrarchan stereotypes than well-rounded protagonists. The sensational reversals in Claudio's attitude toward Hero—his passionate love; his instant belief in, despite little evidence of, her infidelity, his profession of grief when he finds he had falsely accused Hero, his strange willingness to marry the "dead" Hero's nonexistent cousin as a substitute—all seem designed to provide melodramatic scenes rather than to depict a realistic and consistent characterization. Leonato's hysterics at both Hero and Claudio, as well as Don Pedro's and Claudio's taunting of the old man when Leonato challenges them to a fight, are in the same dramatic vein. The real magic of the play, however, is in the rich and more realistic love-battle between Beatrice and Benedick. Their story is clearly in the English comic tradition of the war between the sexes. As wooden and "ideal" in the negative sense as are Hero and Claudio, Beatrice and Benedick are natural and earthy in their independence, their humor, their insecurity about committing themselves to each other. Their wordplay is some of the most delightful in all of Shakespeare. Their hard-won marriage—not Hero and Claudio's—is the great comic achievement and real cause for celebration of the play.

But we must not forget the other "English" aspect of this fine comedy—Constable Dogberry and his hapless band of Watchmen. Like the "rude mechanicals" who put on the unintentionally hilarious play for the king in *A Midsummer Night's Dream,* Dogberry and his men are delightful bumpkins who mangle their syntax, make fools of themselves in trying to impress their betters, and in the end bungle their way to success. Always the master of mixing the high and the low, Shakespeare makes us laugh at both Beatrice's and Benedick's learned puns and allusions and Dogberry's ironic, repeated insistence that the town clerk's record show "that I am an ass."

The Tragedy of Hamlet, Prince of Denmark

WILLIAM SHAKESPEARE

See page 325 for a biographical note on the author.

CHARACTERS

CLAUDIUS, *King of Denmark*
HAMLET, *son to the late King Hamlet, and nephew to the present King*
POLONIUS, *Lord Chamberlain*
HORATIO, *friend to Hamlet*
LAERTES, *son to Polonius*
VOLTEMAND ⎫
CORNELIUS ⎪
ROSENCRANTZ ⎬ *courtiers*
GUILDENSTERN ⎪
OSRIC ⎪
GENTLEMAN ⎭
MARCELLUS ⎫
BARNARDO ⎭ *officers*
FRANCISCO, *a soldier*
REYNALDO, *servant to Polonius*
FORTINBRAS, *Prince of Norway*
NORWEGIAN CAPTAIN
DOCTOR OF DIVINITY
PLAYERS
Two CLOWNS, *grave-diggers*
ENGLISH AMBASSADORS
GERTRUDE, *Queen of Denmark, and mother to Hamlet*
OPHELIA, *daughter to Polonius*
GHOST *of Hamlet's Father*
LORDS, LADIES, OFFICERS, SOLDIERS, SAILORS, MESSENGERS, *and* ATTENDANTS

SCENE: *Denmark*

Act I

Scene I

(*Enter* BARNARDO *and* FRANCISCO, *two sentinels* [*meeting*].)

Words and passages enclosed in square brackets in the text are either emendations of the copy-text or additions to it.
I.i. Location: Elsinore; a guard-platform of the castle

BARNARDO	Who's there?
FRANCISCO	Nay, answer me. Stand and unfold yourself.
BARNARDO	Long live the King!
FRANCISCO	Barnardo.

5 BARNARDO   He.

FRANCISCO   You come most carefully upon your hour.

BARNARDO   'Tis now strook twelf. Get thee to bed, Francisco.

FRANCISCO   For this relief much thanks. 'Tis bitter cold,
    And I am sick at heart.

10 BARNARDO   Have you had quiet guard?

FRANCISCO   Not a mouse stirring.

BARNARDO   Well, good night.
    If you do meet Horatio and Marcellus,
    The rivals of my watch, bid them make haste.

(*Enter* HORATIO *and* MARCELLUS.)

15 FRANCISCO   I think I hear them. Stand ho! Who is there?

HORATIO   Friends to this ground.

MARCELLUS   And liegemen to the Dane.

FRANCISCO   Give you good night.

MARCELLUS   O, farewell, honest [soldier].

20   Who hath reliev'd you?

FRANCISCO   Barnardo hath my place.
    Give you good night.   (*Exit* FRANCISCO.)

MARCELLUS   Holla, Barnardo!

BARNARDO   Say—

25   What, is Horatio there?

HORATIO   A piece of him.

BARNARDO   Welcome, Horatio, welcome, good Marcellus.

HORATIO   What, has this thing appear'd again to-night?

BARNARDO   I have seen nothing.

30 MARCELLUS   Horatio says 'tis but our fantasy,
    And will not let belief take hold of him
    Touching this dreaded sight twice seen of us;
    Therefore I have entreated him along,
    With us to watch the minutes of this night,
35   That if again this apparition come,
    He may approve our eyes and speak to it.

---

2. **answer me:** *You* answer *me.* Francisco is on watch; Barnardo has come to relieve him.   **unfold yourself:** Make known who you are.   3. **Long . . . King:** perhaps a password, perhaps simply an utterance to allow the voice to be recognized   7. **strook twelf:** struck twelve   9. **sick at heart:** in low spirits   14. **rivals:** partners   17. **liegemen . . . Dane:** loyal subjects to the king of Denmark   18. **Give:** God give   30. **fantasy:** imagination   36. **approve:** corroborate

HORATIO   Tush, tush, 'twill not appear.

BARNARDO   Sit down a while,
      And let us once again assail your ears,
40   That are so fortified against our story,
      What we have two nights seen.

HORATIO   Well, sit we down,
      And let us hear Barnardo speak of this.

BARNARDO   Last night of all,
45   When yond same star that's westward from the pole
      Had made his course t' illume that part of heaven
      Where now it burns, Marcellus and myself,
      The bell then beating one—

(*Enter* GHOST.)

MARCELLUS   Peace, break thee off! Look where it comes again!
50 BARNARDO   In the same figure like the King that's dead.

MARCELLUS   Thou art a scholar, speak to it, Horatio.

BARNARDO   Looks 'a not like the King? Mark it, Horatio.

HORATIO   Most like; it [harrows] me with fear and wonder.

BARNARDO   It would be spoke to.
55 MARCELLUS   Speak to it, Horatio.

HORATIO   What art thou that usurp'st this time of night,
      Together with that fair and warlike form
      In which the majesty of buried Denmark
      Did sometimes march? By heaven I charge thee speak!
60 MARCELLUS   It is offended.

BARNARDO   See, it stalks away!

HORATIO   Stay! Speak, speak, I charge thee speak!

(*Exit* GHOST.)

MARCELLUS   'Tis gone, and will not answer.

BARNARDO   How now, Horatio? you tremble and look pale.
65   Is not this something more than fantasy?
      What think you on't?

HORATIO   Before my God, I might not this believe
      Without the sensible and true avouch
      Of mine own eyes.

---

45. **pole:** pole star   46. **his:** its (the commonest form of the neuter possessive singular in Shake-speare's day)   50. **like:** in the likeness of   51. **a scholar:** one who knows how best to address it   52. **'a:** he   54. **It . . . to:** A ghost had to be spoken to before it could speak.   56. **usurp'st:** The ghost, a supernatural being, has invaded the realm of nature.   58. **majesty . . . Denmark:** late king of Denmark   59. **sometimes:** formerly   68. **sensible:** relating to the senses   **avouch:** guarantee

70 MARCELLUS   Is it not like the King?
  HORATIO   As thou art to thyself.
        Such was the very armor he had on
        When he the ambitious Norway combated.
        So frown'd he once when in an angry parle
75   He smote the sledded [Polacks] on the ice.
        'Tis strange.
  MARCELLUS   Thus twice before, and jump at this dead hour,
        With martial stalk hath he gone by our watch.
  HORATIO   In what particular thought to work I know not,
80   But in the gross and scope of mine opinion,
        This bodes some strange eruption to our state.
  MARCELLUS   Good row, sit down, and tell me, he that knows,
        Why this same strict and most observant watch
        So nightly toils the subject of the land,
85   And [why] such daily [cast] of brazen cannon,
        And foreign mart for implements of war,
        Why such impress of shipwrights, whose sore task
        Does not divide the Sunday from the week,
        What might be toward, that this sweaty haste
90   Doth make the night joint-laborer with the day:
        Who is't that can inform me?
  HORATIO   That can I,
        At least the whisper goes so: our last king,
        Whose image even but now appear'd to us,
95   Was, as you know, by Fortinbras of Norway,
        Thereto prick'd on by a most emulate pride,
        Dar'd to the combat; in which our valiant Hamlet
        (For so this side of our known world esteem'd him)
        Did slay this Fortinbras, who, by a seal'd compact
100   Well ratified by law and heraldy,
        Did forfeit (with his life) all [those] his lands
        Which he stood seiz'd of, to the conqueror;
        Against the which a moi'ty competent
        Was gaged by our king, which had [return'd]
105   To the inheritance of Fortinbras,

---

73. **Norway:** king of Norway   74. **parle:** parley   75. **sledded:** using sleds or sledges   **Polacks:**
Poles   77. **jump:** precisely   79–80. **In . . . opinion:** while I have no precise theory about it, my general feeling is that; *gross* =wholeness, totality; *scope* = range   81. **eruption:** upheaval   84. **toils:**
causes to work   **subject:** subjects   86. **foreign mart:** dealing with foreign markets   87. **impress:**
forced service   89. **toward:** in preparation   96. **emulate:** emulous, proceeding from rivalry
100. **law and heraldy:** heraldic law (governing combat)   *Heraldy* is a variant of *heraldry.*
102. **seiz'd of:** possessed of   103. **moi'ty:** portion   **competent:** adequate, equivalent
104. **gaged:** pledged   **had:** would have   105. **inheritance:** possession

Had he been vanquisher; as by the same comart
And carriage of the article [design'd],
His fell to Hamlet. Now, sir, young Fortinbras,
Of unimproved mettle hot and full,
110   Hath in the skirts of Norway here and there
Shark'd up a list of lawless resolutes
For food and diet to some enterprise
That hath a stomach in't, which is no other,
As it doth well appear unto our state,
115   But to recover of us, by strong hand
And terms compulsatory, those foresaid lands
So by his father lost; and this, I take it,
Is the main motive of our preparations,
The source of this our watch, and the chief head
120   Of this post-haste and romage in the land.
BARNARDO   I think it be no other but e'en so.
Well may it sort that this portentous figure
Comes armed through our watch so like the King
That was and is the question of these wars.
125 HORATIO   A mote it is to trouble the mind's eye.
In the most high and palmy state of Rome,
A little ere the mightiest Julius fell,
The graves stood [tenantless] and the sheeted dead
Did squeak and gibber in the Roman streets.
130   As stars with trains of fire, and dews of blood,
Disasters in the sun; and the moist star
Upon whose influence Neptune's empire stands
Was sick almost to doomsday with eclipse.
And even the like precurse of [fear'd] events,
135   As harbingers preceding still the fates
And prologue to the omen coming on,
Have heaven and earth together demonstrated
Unto our climatures and countrymen.

(*Enter* GHOST.)

---

106. **comart:** bargain   107. **carriage:** tenor   **design'd:** drawn up   109. **unimproved:** untried (?) or
not directed to any useful end (?)   110. **skirts:** outlying territories   111. **Shark'd up:** gathered up
hastily and indiscriminately   113. **stomach:** relish of danger (?) or demand for courage (?)
119. **head:** source   120. **romage:** rummage, bustling activity   122. **sort:** fit   **portentous:** ominous
129. One or more lines may have been lost between this line and the next.   131. **Disasters:** ominous
signs   **moist star:** moon   132. **Neptune's empire stands:** the seas are dependent   133. **sick . . .
doomsday:** almost totally darkened. When the Day of Judgment is imminent, says Matthew 24:29, "the
moon shall not give her light."   **eclipse:** There were a solar and two total lunar eclipses visible in England in 1598; they caused gloomy speculation.   134. **precurse:** foreshadowing   135. **harbingers:** advance messengers   **still:** always   136. **omen:** the events portended   138. **climatures:** regions

But soft, behold! lo where it comes again!

(*It spreads his arms.*)

140   I'll cross it though it blast me. Stay, illusion!
    If thou hast any sound or use of voice,
    Speak to me.
    If there be any good thing to be done
    That may to thee do ease, and grace to me,
145   Speak to me.
    If thou art privy to thy country's fate,
    Which happily foreknowing may avoid,
    O speak!
    Or if thou hast uphoarded in thy life
150   Extorted treasure in the womb of earth,
    For which, they say, your spirits oft walk in death,
    Speak of it, stay and speak!   (*The cock crows.*)   Stop it, Marcellus.

MARCELLUS   Shall I strike it with my partisan?

HORATIO   Do, if it will not stand.

155 BARNARDO   'Tis here!

HORATIO   'Tis here!

[*Exit* GHOST.]

MARCELLUS   'Tis gone!
    We do it wrong, being so majestical,
    To offer it the show of violence,
160   For it is as the air, invulnerable,
    And our vain blows malicious mockery.

BARNARDO   It was about to speak when the cock crew.

HORATIO   And then it started like a guilty thing
    Upon a fearful summons. I have heard
165   The cock, that is the trumpet to the morn,
    Doth with his lofty and shrill-sounding throat
    Awake the god of day, and at his warning,
    Whether in sea or fire, in earth or air,
    Th' extravagant and erring spirit hies
170   To his confine; and of the truth herein
    This present object made probation.

---

139 s.d. (stage direction) **his:** its   140. **cross it:** cross its path, confront it directly   **blast:** wither (by supernatural means)   147. **happily:** haply, perhaps   151. **your:** Colloquial and impersonal; cf. I.v.186, IV.iii.23–25. Most editors adopt *you* from F1.   153. **partisan:** long-handled spear 161. **malicious mockery:** mockery of malice, empty pretenses of harming it.   165. **trumpet:** trumpeter   169. **extravagant:** wandering outside its proper bounds   **erring:** wandering abroad   **hies:** hastens   171. **object:** sight   **probation:** proof

MARCELLUS   It faded on the crowing of the cock.
Some say that ever 'gainst that season comes
Wherein our Saviour's birth is celebrated,
175   This bird of dawning singeth all night long,
And then they say no spirit dare stir abroad,
The nights are wholesome, then no planets strike,
No fairy takes, nor witch hath power to charm,
So hallowed, and so gracious, is that time.
180   HORATIO   So have I heard and do in part believe it.
But look, the morn in russet mantle clad
Walks o'er the dew of yon high eastward hill.
Break we our watch up, and by my advice
Let us impart what we have seen to-night
185   Unto young Hamlet, for, upon my life,
This spirit, dumb to us, will speak to him.
Do you consent we shall acquaint him with it,
As needful in our loves, fitting our duty?
MARCELLUS   Let's do't, I pray, and I this morning know
190   Where we shall find him most convenient.

(*Exeunt.*)

[Scene II]

(*Flourish. Enter* CLAUDIUS, KING OF DENMARK, GERTRUDE THE QUEEN, COUNCIL: *as* POLONIUS; *and his son* LAERTES, HAMLET, *cum aliis* [*including* VOLTEMAND *and* CORNELIUS].)

KING   Though yet of Hamlet our dear brother's death
The memory be green, and that it us befitted
To bear our hearts in grief, and our whole kingdom
To be contracted in one brow of woe,
5   Yet so far hath discretion fought with nature
That we with wisest sorrow think on him
Together with remembrance of ourselves.
Therefore our sometime sister, now our queen,
Th' imperial jointress to this warlike state,
10   Have we, as 'twere with a defeated joy,

---

173. **'gainst:** just before   177. **strike:** exert malevolent influence   178. **takes:** bewitches, charms   179. **gracious:** blessed   181. **russet:** coarse greyish-brown cloth

I.ii. Location: the castle
o.s.d. (opening stage direction) **Flourish:** trumpet fanfare   **cum aliis:** with others   2. **befitted:** would befit   4. **contracted in:** (1) reduced to; (2) knit or wrinkled in   **brow of woe:** mournful brow   9. **jointress:** joint holder   10. **defeated:** impaired

With an auspicious, and a dropping eye,
With mirth in funeral, and with dirge in marriage,
In equal scale weighing delight and dole,
Taken to wife; nor have we herein barr'd
15   Your better wisdoms, which have freely gone
With this affair along. For all, our thanks.
Now follows that you know young Fortinbras,
Holding a weak supposal of our worth,
Or thinking by our late dear brother's death
20   Our state to be disjoint and out of frame,
Co-leagued with this dream of his advantage,
He hath not fail'd to pester us with message
Importing the surrender of those lands
Lost by his father, with all bands of law,
25   To our most valiant brother. So much for him.
Now for ourself, and for this time of meeting,
Thus much the business is: we have here writ
To Norway, uncle of young Fortinbras—
Who, impotent and bedred, scarcely hears
30   Of this his nephew's purpose—to suppress
His further gait herein, in that the levies,
The lists, and full proportions are all made
Out of his subject; and we here dispatch
You, good Cornelius, and you, Voltemand,
35   For bearers of this greeting to old Norway,
Giving to you no further personal power
To business with the King, more than the scope
Of these delated articles allow.   [*Giving a paper.*]
Farewell, and let your haste commend your duty.
40 CORNELIUS, VOLTEMAND   In that, and all things, will we show our duty.
KING   We doubt it nothing; heartily farewell.

[*Exeunt* VOLTEMAND *and* CORNELIUS.]

And now, Laertes, what's the news with you?
You told us of some suit, what is't, Laertes?
You cannot speak of reason to the Dane
45   And lose your voice. What wouldst thou beg, Laertes,

---

11. **auspicious . . . dropping:** cheerful . . . weeping   15. **freely:** fully, without reservation
17. **know:** be informed, learn   18. **supposal:** conjecture, estimate   21. **Co-leagued:** joined
22. **pester . . . message:** trouble me with persistent messages (the original sense of *pester* is "over-crowd")   23. **Importing:** having as import   24. **bands:** bonds, binding terms   29. **impotent and bedred:** feeble and bedridden   31. **gait:** proceeding   31–33. **in . . . subject:** since the troops are all drawn from his subjects   38. **delated:** extended, detailed (a variant of *dilated*)   41. **nothing:** not at all   45. **lose:** waste

That shall not be my offer, not thy asking?
The head is not more native to the heart,
The hand more instrumental to the mouth,
Than is the throne of Denmark to thy father.
50 What wouldst thou have, Laertes?
LAERTES   My dread lord,
Your leave and favor to return to France,
From whence though willingly I came to Denmark
To show my duty in your coronation,
55 Yet now I must confess, that duty done,
My thoughts and wishes bend again toward France,
And bow them to your gracious leave and pardon.
KING   Have you your father's leave? What says Polonius?
POLONIUS   H'ath, my lord, wrung from me my slow leave
60 By laborsome petition, and at last
Upon his will I seal'd my hard consent.
I do beseech you give him leave to go.
KING   Take thy fair hour, Laertes, time be thine,
And thy best graces spend it at thy will!
65 But now, my cousin Hamlet, and my son—
HAMLET [*Aside.*]   A little more than kin, and less than kind.
KING   How is it that the clouds still hang on you?
HAMLET   Not so, my lord, I am too much in the sun.
QUEEN   Good Hamlet, cast thy nighted color off,
70 And let thine eye look like a friend on Denmark.
Do not for ever with thy vailed lids
Seek for thy noble father in the dust.
Thou know'st 'tis common, all that lives must die,
Passing through nature to eternity.
75 HAMLET   Ay, madam, it is common.
QUEEN   If it be,
Why seems it so particular with thee?
HAMLET   Seems, madam? nay, it is, I know not "seems."
'Tis not alone my inky cloak, [good] mother,
80 Nor customary suits of solemn black,
Nor windy suspiration of forc'd breath,
No, nor the fruitful river in the eye,
Nor the dejected havior of the visage,

---

47. **native:** closely related   48. **instrumental:** serviceable   52. **leave and favor:** gracious permission
57. **pardon:** permission to depart   59. **H'ath:** he hath   61. **hard:** reluctant   65. **cousin:** kinsman (used in familiar address to any collateral relative more distant than a brother or sister; here to a nephew)
66. **A little . . . kind:** closer than a nephew, since you are my mother's husband; yet more distant than a son, too (and not well disposed to you)   68. **sun:** with obvious quibble on *son*
71. **vailed:** downcast   73. **common:** general, universal   77. **particular:** individual, personal
82. **fruitful:** copious

Together with all forms, moods, [shapes] of grief,
85 That can [denote] me truly. These indeed seem,
For they are actions that a man might play,
But I have that within which passes show,
These but the trappings and the suits of woe.

KING 'Tis sweet and commendable in your nature, Hamlet,
90 To give these mourning duties to your father.
But you must know your father lost a father,
That father lost, lost his, and the survivor bound
In filial obligation for some term
To do obsequious sorrow. But to persever
95 In obstinate condolement is a course
Of impious stubbornness, 'tis unmanly grief,
It shows a will most incorrect to heaven,
A heart unfortified, or mind impatient,
An understanding simple and unschool'd:
100 For what we know must be, and is as common
As any the most vulgar thing to sense,
Why should we in our peevish opposition
Take it to heart? Fie, 'tis a fault to heaven,
A fault against the dead, a fault to nature,
105 To reason most absurd, whose common theme
Is death of fathers, and who still hath cried,
From the first corse till he that died to-day,
"This must be so." We pray you throw to earth
This unprevailing woe, and think of us
110 As of a father, for let the world take note
You are the most immediate to our throne,
And with no less nobility of love
Than that which dearest father bears his son
Do I impart toward you. For your intent
115 In going back to school in Wittenberg,
It is most retrograde to our desire,
And we beseech you bend you to remain
Here in the cheer and comfort of our eye,
Our chiefest courtier, cousin, and our son.
120 QUEEN Let not thy mother lose her prayers, Hamlet,
I pray thee stay with us, go not to Wittenberg.
HAMLET I shall in all my best obey you, madam.
KING Why, 'tis a loving and a fair reply.
Be as ourself in Denmark. Madam, come.

---

94. **obsequious:** proper to obsequies 95. **condolement:** grief 97. **incorrect:** unsubmissive
101. **any . . . sense:** what is perceived to be commonest 103. **to:** against 105. **absurd:** contrary
109. **unprevailing:** unavailing 113. **dearest:** most loving 114. **impart:** impart love

125 This gentle and unforc'd accord of Hamlet
Sits smiling to my heart, in grace whereof,
No jocund health that Denmark drinks to-day,
But the great cannon to the clouds shall tell,
And the King's rouse the heaven shall bruit again,
130 Respeaking earthly thunder. Come away.

(*Flourish. Exeunt all but* HAMLET.)

HAMLET   O that this too too sallied flesh would melt,
Thaw, and resolve itself into a dew!
Or that the Everlasting had not fix'd
His canon 'gainst [self-]slaughter! O God, God,
135 How [weary], stale, flat, and unprofitable
Seem to me all the uses of this world!
Fie on't, ah fie! 'tis an unweeded garden
That grows to seed, things rank and gross in nature
Possess it merely. That it should come [to this]!
140 But two months dead, nay, not so much, not two.
So excellent a king, that was to this
Hyperion to a satyr, so loving to my mother
That he might not beteem the winds of heaven
Visit her face too roughly. Heaven and earth,
145 Must I remember? Why, she should hang on him
As if increase of appetite had grown
By what it fed on, and yet, within a month—
Let me not think on't! Frailty, thy name is woman!—
A little month, or ere those shoes were old
150 With which she followed my poor father's body,
Like Niobe, all tears—why, she, [even she]—
O God, a beast that wants discourse of reason
Would have mourn'd longer—married with my uncle,
My father's brother, but no more like my father
155 Than I to Hercules. Within a month,
Ere yet the salt of most unrighteous tears
Had left the flushing in her galled eyes,
She married—O most wicked speed: to post
With such dexterity to incestious sheets,

---

129. **rouse:** bumper, drink   **bruit:** loudly declare   131. **sallied:** sullied.   Many editors prefer the
F1 reading, *solid.*   134. **canon:** law   136. **uses:** customs   139. **merely:** utterly   141. **to:** in comparison with   142. **Hyperion:** the sun-god   143. **beteem:** allow   149. **or ere:** before   151. **Niobe:** She
wept endlessly for her children, whom Apollo and Artemis had killed.   152. **wants . . . reason:** lacks the
power of reason (which distinguishes men from beasts)   156. **unrighteous:** hypocritical   157. **flushing:** redness   **galled:** inflamed   159. **incestious:** incestuous. The marriage of a man to his brother's
widow was so regarded until long after Shakespeare's day.

160 It is not, nor it cannot come to good,
     But break my heart, for I must hold my tongue.

(*Enter* HORATIO, MARCELLUS *and* BARNARDO.)

HORATIO   Hail to your lordship!
HAMLET   I am glad to see you well.
     Horatio—or I do forget myself.
165 HORATIO   The same, my lord, and your poor servant ever.
HAMLET   Sir, my good friend—I'll change that name with you.
     And what make you from Wittenberg, Horatio?
     Marcellus.
MARCELLUS   My good lord.
170 HAMLET   I am very glad to see you.   [*to* BARNARDO]   Good even, sir.—
     But what, in faith, make you from Wittenberg?
HORATIO   A truant disposition, good my lord.
HAMLET   I would not hear your enemy say so,
     Nor shall you do my ear that violence
175   To make it truster of your own report
     Against yourself. I know you are no truant.
     But what is your affair in Elsinore?
     We'll teach you to drink [deep] ere you depart.
HORATIO   My lord, I came to see your father's funeral.
180 HAMLET   I prithee do not mock me, fellow student,
     I think it was to [see] my mother's wedding.
HORATIO   Indeed, my lord, it followed hard upon.
HAMLET   Thrift, thrift, Horatio, the funeral bak'd-meats
     Did coldly furnish forth the marriage tables.
185   Would I had met my dearest foe in heaven
     Or ever I had seen that day, Horatio!
     My father—methinks I see my father.
HORATIO   Where, my lord?
HAMLET   In my mind's eye, Horatio.
190 HORATIO   I saw him once, 'a was a goodly king.
HAMLET   'A was a man, take him for all in all,
     I shall not look upon his like again.
HORATIO   My lord, I think I saw him yesternight.
HAMLET   Saw, who?
195 HORATIO   My lord, the King your father.
HAMLET   The King my father?

---

166. **change:** exchange   167. **what . . . from:** what are you doing away from   172. **truant disposi-**
tion: inclination to play truant   180. **student:** student   184. **coldly:** when cold
185. **dearest:** most intensely hated   186. **Or:** ere, before

HORATIO   Season your admiration for a while
    With an attent ear, till I may deliver,
    Upon the witness of these gentlemen,
200   This marvel to you.
HAMLET   For God's love let me hear!
HORATIO   Two nights together had these gentlemen,
    Marcellus and Barnardo, on their watch,
    In the dead waste and middle of the night,
205   Been thus encount'red: a figure like your father,
    Armed at point exactly, cap-a-pe,
    Appears before them, and with solemn march
    Goes slow and stately by them; thrice he walk'd
    By their oppress'd and fear-surprised eyes
210   Within his truncheon's length, whilst they, distill'd
    Almost to jelly with the act of fear,
    Stand dumb and speak not to him. This to me
    In dreadful secrecy impart they did,
    And I with them the third night kept the watch,
215   Where, as they had delivered, both in time,
    Form of the thing, each word made true and good,
    The apparition comes. I knew your father,
    These hands are not more like.
HAMLET   But where was this?
220 MARCELLUS   My lord, upon the platform where we watch.
HAMLET   Did you not speak to it?
HORATIO   My lord, I did,
    But answer made it none. Yet once methought
    It lifted up it head and did address
225   Itself to motion like as it would speak;
    But even then the morning cock crew loud,
    And at the sound it shrunk in haste away
    And vanish'd from our sight.
HAMLET   'Tis very strange.
230 HORATIO   As I do live, my honor'd lord, 'tis true,
    And we did think it writ down in our duty
    To let you know of it.
HAMLET   Indeed, [indeed,] sirs. But this troubles me.
    Hold you the watch to-night?

---

197. **Season:** temper   **admiration:** wonder   198. **deliver:** report   204. **waste:** empty expanse
206. **at point exactly:** in every particular   **cap-a-pe:** from head to foot   209. **fear-surprised:** overwhelmed by fear   210. **truncheon:** short staff carried as a symbol of military command
211. **act:** action, operation   213. **dreadful:** held in awe, solemnly sworn   218. **are . . . like:** do not resemble each other more closely than the apparition resembled him   224. **it:** its
224–225. **address . . . motion:** begin to make a gesture

235 [MARCELLUS, BARNARDO]   We do, my lord.
    HAMLET   Arm'd, say you?
    [MARCELLUS, BARNARDO]   Arm'd, my lord.
    HAMLET   From top to toe?
    [MARCELLUS, BARNARDO]   My lord, from head to foot.
240 HAMLET   Then saw you not his face.
    HORATIO   O yes, my lord, he wore his beaver up.
    HAMLET   What, look'd he frowningly?
    HORATIO   A countenance more
        In sorrow than in anger.
245 HAMLET   Pale, or red?
    HORATIO   Nay, very pale.
    HAMLET   And fix'd his eyes upon you?
    HORATIO   Most constantly.
    HAMLET   I would I had been there.
250 HORATIO   It would have much amaz'd you.
    HAMLET   Very like, [very like]. Stay'd it long?
    HORATIO   While one with moderate haste might tell a hundredth.
    BOTH [MARCELLUS, BARNARDO]   Longer, longer.
    HORATIO   Not when I saw't.
255 HAMLET   His beard was grisl'd, no?
    HORATIO   It was, as I have seen it in his life,
        A sable silver'd.
    HAMLET   I will watch to-night,
        Perchance 'twill walk again.
260 HORATIO   I warr'nt it will.
    HAMLET   If it assume my noble father's person,
        I'll speak to it though hell itself should gape
        And bid me hold my peace. I pray you all,
        If you have hitherto conceal'd this sight,
265   Let it be tenable in your silence still,
        And whatsomever else shall hap to-night,
        Give it an understanding but no tongue.
        I will requite your loves. So fare you well.
        Upon the platform 'twixt aleven and twelf
270   I'll visit you.
    ALL   Our duty to your honor.
    HAMLET   Your loves, as mine to you; farewell.

(*Exeunt [all but* HAMLET].)

---

241. **beaver:** visor   252. **tell a hundreth:** count a hundred   255. **grisl'd:** grizzled, mixed with grey   265. **tenable:** held close   269. **aleven:** eleven

My father's spirit—in arms! All is not well,
I doubt some foul play. Would the night were come!
275   Till then sit still, my soul. [Foul] deeds will rise,
Though all the earth o'erwhelm them, to men's eyes.

(*Exit.*)

[Scene III]

(*Enter* LAERTES *and* OPHELIA, *his sister.*)

LAERTES   My necessaries are inbark'd. Farewell.
And, sister, as the winds give benefit
And convey [is] assistant, do not sleep,
But let me hear from you.
5 OPHELIA   Do you doubt that?
LAERTES   For Hamlet, and the trifling of his favor,
Hold it a fashion and a toy in blood,
A violet in the youth of primy nature,
Forward, not permanent, sweet, not lasting,
10   The perfume and suppliance of a minute—
No more.
OPHELIA   No more but so?
LAERTES   Think it no more:
For nature crescent does not grow alone
15   In thews and [bulk], but as this temple waxes,
The inward service of the mind and soul
Grows wide withal. Perhaps he loves you now,
And now no soil nor cautel doth besmirch
The virtue of his will, but you must fear,
20   His greatness weigh'd, his will is not his own,
[For he himself is subject to his birth:]
He may not, as unvalued persons do,
Carve for himself, for on his choice depends
The safety and health of this whole state,
25   And therefore must his choice be circumscrib'd
Unto the voice and yielding of that body

---

274. **doubt:** suspect   I.iii. Location: Polonius's quarters in the castle   1. **inbark'd:** embarked, abroad   3. **convey is assistant:** means of transport is available   7. **a fashion:** standard behavior for a young man   **toy in blood:** idle fancy of youthful passion   8. **primy:** springlike   9. **Forward:** early of growth   10. **suppliance:** pastime   14. **crescent:** growing, increasing   15. **thews:** muscles, sinews   15–17. **as . . . withal:** as the body develops, the powers of mind and spirit grow along with it   18. **soil:** stain   **cautel:** deceit   19. **will:** desire   20. **His greatness weigh'd:** considering his princely status   22. **unvalued:** of low rank   23. **Carve for himself:** indulge his own wishes   26. **voice:** vote, approval   **yielding:** consent   **that body:** the state

Whereof he is the head. Then if he says he loves you,
It fits your wisdom so far to believe it
As he in his particular act and place
30   May give his saying deed, which is no further
Than the main voice of Denmark goes withal.
Then weigh what loss your honor may sustain
If with too credent ear you list his songs,
Or lose your heart, or your chaste treasure open
35   To his unmast'red importunity.
Fear it, Ophelia, fear it, my dear sister,
And keep you in the rear of your affection,
Out of the shot and danger of desire.
The chariest maid is prodigal enough
40   If she unmask her beauty to the moon.
Virtue itself scapes not calumnious strokes.
The canker galls the infants of the spring
Too oft before their buttons be disclos'd,
And in the morn and liquid dew of youth
45   Contagious blastments are most imminent.
Be wary then, best safety lies in fear:
Youth to itself rebels, though none else near.
OPHELIA   I shall the effect of this good lesson keep
As watchman to my heart. But, good my brother,
50   Do not, as some ungracious pastors do,
Show me the steep and thorny way to heaven,
Whiles, [like] a puff'd and reckless libertine,
Himself the primrose path of dalliance treads,
And reaks not his own rede.
55 LAERTES   O, fear me not.

(*Enter* POLONIUS.)

I stay too long—but here my father comes.
A double blessing is a double grace,
Occasion smiles upon a second leave.
POLONIUS   Yet here, Laertes? Aboard, aboard, for shame!
60   The wind sits in the shoulder of your sail,
And you are stay'd for. There—[*laying his hand on* LAERTES' *head*] my
blessing with thee!

---

29. **in . . . place:** acting as he must act in the position he occupies   31. **main:** general
goes withal: accord with   33. **credent:** credulous   38. **shot:** range   42. **canker:** canker-worm
43. **buttons:** buds   **disclos'd:** opened   45. **blastments:** withering blights   49. **to:** of
50. **ungracious:** graceless   52. **puff'd:** bloated   54. **reaks:** recks, heeds   **rede:** advice
55. **fear me not:** don't worry about me   58. **Occasion:** opportunity (here personified, as
often)   **smiles upon:** graciously bestows

And these few precepts in thy memory
Look thou character. Give thy thoughts no tongue,
65   Nor any unproportion'd thought his act.
Be thou familiar, but by no means vulgar:
Those friends thou hast, and their adoption tried,
Grapple them unto thy soul with hoops of steel,
But do not dull thy palm with entertainment
70   Of each new-hatch'd, unfledg'd courage. Beware
Of entrance to a quarrel, but being in,
Bear't that th' opposed may beware of thee.
Give every man thy ear, but few thy voice,
Take each man's censure, but reserve thy judgment.
75   Costly thy habit as thy purse can buy,
But not express'd in fancy, rich, not gaudy,
For the apparel oft proclaims the man,
And they in France of the best rank and station
[Are] of a most select and generous chief in that.
80   Neither a borrower nor a lender [be],
For [loan] oft loses both itself and friend,
And borrowing dulleth [th'] edge of husbandry.
This above all: to thine own self be true,
And it must follow, as the night the day,
85   Thou canst not then be false to any man.
Farewell, my blessing season this in thee!

LAERTES   Most humbly do I take my leave, my lord.
POLONIUS   The time invests you, go, your servants tend.
LAERTES   Farewell, Ophelia, and remember well
90   What I have said to you.
OPHELIA   'Tis in my memory lock'd,
And you yourself shall keep the key of it.
LAERTES   Farewell.   (*Exit* LAERTES.)
POLONIUS   What is't, Ophelia, he hath said to you?
95 OPHELIA   So please you, something touching the Lord Hamlet.
POLONIUS   Marry, well bethought.
'Tis told me, he hath very oft of late
Given private time to you, and you yourself
Have of your audience been most free and bounteous.

---

64. **character:** inscribe   65. **unproportion'd:** unfitting   66. **familiar:** affable, sociable   **vulgar:** friendly with everybody   67. **their adoption tried:** their association with you tested and proved   70. **courage:** spirited, young blood   72. **Bear't that:** manage it in such a way that   74. **Take:** listen to   **censure:** opinion   79. **generous:** noble   **chief:** eminence (?) But the line is probably corrupt. Perhaps *of a* is intrusive, in which case *chief* = chiefly.   82. **husbandry:** thrift   86. **season:** preserve (?) or ripen, make fruitful (?)   88. **invests:** besieges   **tend:** wait   96. **Marry:** indeed (originally the name of the Virgin Mary used as an oath)

100   If it be so—as so 'tis put on me,
      And that in way of caution—I must tell you,
      You do not understand yourself so clearly
      As it behooves my daughter and your honor.
      What is between you? Give me up the truth.
105 OPHELIA   He hath, my lord, of late made many tenders
      Of his affection to me.
   POLONIUS   Affection, puh! You speak like a green girl,
      Unsifted in such perilous circumstance.
      Do you believe his tenders, as you call them?
110 OPHELIA   I do not know, my lord, what I should think.
   POLONIUS   Marry, I will teach you: think yourself a baby
      That you have ta'en these tenders for true pay,
      Which are not sterling. Tender yourself more dearly,
      Or (not to crack the wind of the poor phrase,
115   [Wringing] it thus) you'll tender me a fool.
   OPHELIA   My lord, he hath importun'd me with love
      In honorable fashion.
   POLONIUS   Ay, fashion you may call it. Go to, go to.
   OPHELIA   And hath given countenance to his speech, my lord,
120   With almost all the holy vows of heaven.
   POLONIUS   Ay, springes to catch woodcocks. I do know,
      When the blood burns, how prodigal the soul
      Lends the tongue vows. These blazes, daughter,
      Giving more light than heat, extinct in both
125   Even in their promise, as it is a-making,
      You must not take for fire. From this time
      Be something scanter of your maiden presence,
      Set your entreatments at a higher rate
      Than a command to parle. For Lord Hamlet,
130   Believe so much in him, that he is young,
      And with a larger teder may he walk
      Than may be given you. In few, Ophelia,
      Do not believe his vows, for they are brokers,

---

100. **put on:** told to   105. **tenders:** offers   108. **Unsifted:** untried   112. **tenders:** with play on the sense "money offered in payment" (as in *legal tender*)   113. **Tender:** hold, value   115. **Wringing:** straining, forcing to the limit   **tender . . . fool:** (1) show me that you are a fool; (2) make me look like a fool; (3) present me with a (bastard) grandchild   118. **fashion:** See note on line 7.
119. **countenance:** authority   121. **springes:** snares   **woodcocks:** proverbially gullible birds
128–29. **Set . . . parle:** Place a higher value on your favors; do not grant interviews simply because he asks for them. Polonius uses a military figure: *entreatments* = negotiations for surrender; *parle* = parley, discuss terms.   130. **so . . . him:** no more than this with respect to him   131. **larger teder:** longer tether   133. **brokers:** procurers

135   Not of that dye which their investments show,
      But mere [implorators] of unholy suits,
      Breathing like sanctified and pious bonds,
      The better to [beguile]. This is for all:
      I would not, in plain terms, from this time forth
      Have you so slander any moment leisure
140   As to give words or talk with the Lord Hamlet.
      Look to't, I charge you. Come your ways.
OPHELIA   I shall obey, my lord.

(*Exeunt.*)

[Scene IV]

(*Enter* HAMLET, HORATIO, *and* MARCELLUS.)

HAMLET   The air bites shrowdly, it is very cold.
HORATIO   It is [a] nipping and an eager air.
HAMLET   What hour now?
HORATIO   I think it lacks of twelf.
5 MARCELLUS   No, it is strook.
HORATIO   Indeed? I heard it not. It then draws near the season
      Wherein the spirit held his wont to walk.

(*A flourish of trumpets, and two pieces goes off* [*within*].)

      What does this mean, my lord?
HAMLET   The King doth wake to-night and takes his rouse,
10   Keeps wassail, and the swagg'ring up-spring reels;
      And as he drains his draughts of Rhenish down,
      The kettle-drum and trumpet thus bray out
      The triumph of his pledge.
HORATIO   Is it a custom?
15 HAMLET   Ay, marry, is't,
      But to my mind, though I am native here
      And to the manner born, it is a custom

---

134. **Not . . . show:** not of the color that their garments (*investments*) exhibit; not what they
seem   135. **mere:** out-and-out   136. **bonds:** (lover's) vows or assurances. Many editors follow
Theobald in reading *bawds.*   139. **slander:** disgrace   **moment:** momentary   141. **Come your
ways:** come along

I.iv. Location: the guard-platform of the castle   1. **shrowdly:** shrewdly, wickedly   2. **eager:** sharp
7. s.d. **pieces:** cannon   9. **doth . . . rouse:** holds revels far into the night   10. **wassail:** carousal
up-spring: wild dance   11. **Rhenish:** Rhine wine   13. **triumph . . . pledge:** accomplishment of his
toast (by draining his cup at a single draught)   17. **manner:** custom (of carousing)

More honor'd in the breach than the observance.
This heavy-headed revel east and west

20   Makes us traduc'd and tax'd of other nations.
They clip us drunkards, and with swinish phrase
Soil our addition, and indeed it takes
From our achievements, though perform'd at height,
The pith and marrow of our attribute.

25   So, oft it chances in particular men,
That for some vicious mole of nature in them,
As in their birth, wherein they are not guilty
(Since nature cannot choose his origin),
By their o'ergrowth of some complexion

30   Oft breaking down the pales and forts of reason,
Or by some habit, that too much o'er-leavens
The form of plausive manners—that these men,
Carrying, I say, the stamp of one defect,
Being nature's livery, or fortune's star,

35   His virtues else, be they as pure as grace,
As infinite as man may undergo,
Shall in the general censure take corruption
From that particular fault: the dram of [ev'l]
Doth all the noble substance of a doubt

40   To his own scandal.

(*Enter* GHOST.)

HORATIO   Look, my lord, it comes!
HAMLET   Angels and ministers of grace defend us!
Be thou a spirit of health, or goblin damn'd,
Bring with thee airs from heaven, or blasts from hell,

45   Be thy intents wicked, or charitable,
Thou com'st in such a questionable shape
That I will speak to thee. I'll call thee Hamlet,
King, father, royal Dane. O, answer me!

---

18. **More . . . observance:** which it is more honorable to break than to observe   20. **tax'd of:** censured by   21. **clip:** clepe, call   22. **addition:** titles of honor   23. **at height:** most excellently   24. **attribute:** reputation   25. **particular:** individual   26. **vicious . . . nature:** small natural blemish   28. **his:** its   29. **By . . . complexion:** by the excess of some one of the humors (which were thought to govern the disposition)   30. **pales:** fences   31. **o'er-leavens:** makes itself felt throughout (as leaven works in the whole mass of dough)   32. **plausive:** pleasing   34. **Being . . . star:** whether they were born with it, or got it by misfortune. *Star* means "blemish."   36. **undergo:** carry the weight of, sustain   37. **general censure:** popular opinion   38. **dram:** minute amount   **ev'l:** evil, with a pun on *eale*, "yeast" (cf. *o'er-leavens* in line 31)   39. **of a doubt:** a famous crux, for which many emendations have been suggested, the most widely accepted being Steevens' *often dout* (extinguish)   40. **To . . . scandal:** so that it all shares in the disgrace   43. **of health:** wholesome, good   46. **questionable:** inviting talk

Let me not burst in ignorance, but tell
50 Why thy canoniz'd bones, hearsed in death,
Have burst their cerements; why the sepulchre,
Wherein we saw thee quietly [inurn'd,]
Hath op'd his ponderous and marble jaws
To cast thee up again. What may this mean,
55 That thou, dead corse, again in complete steel
Revisits thus the glimpses of the moon,
Making night hideous, and we fools of nature
So horridly to shake our disposition
With thoughts beyond the reaches of our souls?
60 Say why is this? wherefore? what should we do?

([Ghost] *beckons* [Hamlet].)

HORATIO   It beckons you to go away with it,
As if it some impartment did desire
To you alone.
MARCELLUS   Look with what courteous action
65 It waves you to a more removed ground,
But do not go with it.
HORATIO   No, by no means.
HAMLET   It will not speak, then I will follow it.
HORATIO   Do not, my lord.
70 HAMLET   Why, what should be the fear?
I do not set my life at a pin's fee,
And for my soul, what can it do to that,
Being a thing immortal as itself?
It waves me forth again, I'll follow it.
75 HORATIO   What if it tempt you toward the flood, my lord,
Or to the dreadful summit of the cliff
That beetles o'er his base into the sea,
And there assume some other horrible form
Which might deprive your sovereignty of reason,
80 And draw you into madness? Think of it.
The very place puts toys of desperation,
Without more motive, into every brain
That looks so many fadoms to the sea
And hears it roar beneath.

---

50. **canoniz'd:** buried with the prescribed rites   51. **cerements:** grave-clothes   55. **complete steel:** full armor   56. **Revisits:** The -*s* ending in the second-person singular is common.   57. **fools of nature:** the children (or the dupes) of a purely natural order, baffled by the supernatural   58. **disposition:** nature   62. **impartment:** communication   71. **fee:** worth   79. **deprive . . . reason:** unseat reason from the rule of your mind   81. **toys of desperation:** fancies of desperate action, inclinations to jump off   83. **fadoms:** fathoms

85 HAMLET   It waves me still.—
    Go on, I'll follow thee.
    MARCELLUS   You shall not go, my lord.
    HAMLET   Hold off your hands.
    HORATIO   Be rul'd, you shall not go.
90 HAMLET   My fate cries out,
    And makes each petty artere in this body
    As hardy as the Nemean lion's nerve.
    Still am I call'd. Unhand me, gentlemen.
    By heaven, I'll make a ghost of him that lets me!
95   I say away!—Go on, I'll follow thee.

(*Exeunt* GHOST *and* HAMLET.)

    HORATIO   He waxes desperate with [imagination].
    MARCELLUS   Let's follow. 'Tis not fit thus to obey him.
    HORATIO   Have after. To what issue will this come?
    MARCELLUS   Something is rotten in the state of Denmark.
100 HORATIO   Heaven will direct it.
    MARCELLUS   Nay, let's follow him.

(*Exeunt.*)

[Scene V]

(*Enter* GHOST *and* HAMLET.)

    HAMLET   Whither wilt thou lead me? Speak, I'll go no further.
    GHOST   Mark me.
    HAMLET   I will.
    GHOST   My hour is almost come
5   When I to sulph'rous and tormenting flames
        Must render up myself.
    HAMLET   Alas, poor ghost!
    GHOST   Pity me not, but lend thy serious hearing
        To what I shall unfold.
10 HAMLET   Speak, I am bound to hear.
    GHOST   So art thou to revenge, when thou shalt hear.
    HAMLET   What?
    GHOST   I am thy father's spirit,
        Doom'd for a certain term to walk the night,

---

91. **artere:** variant spelling of *artery;* here, ligament, sinew   92. **Nemean lion:** slain by Hercules as one of his twelve labors   **nerve:** sinew   94. **lets:** hinders   100. **it:** the issue

I.v. Location: on the battlements of the castle

15   And for the day confin'd to fast in fires,
Till the foul crimes done in my days of nature
Are burnt and purg'd away. But that I am forbid
To tell the secrets of my prison-house,
I could a tale unfold whose lightest word
20   Would harrow up thy soul, freeze thy young blood,
Make thy two eyes like stars start from their spheres,
Thy knotted and combined locks to part,
And each particular hair to stand an end,
Like quills upon the fearful porpentine.
25   But this eternal blazon must not be
To ears of flesh and blood. List, list, O, list!
If thou didst ever thy dear father love—

HAMLET   O God!

GHOST   Revenge his foul and most unnatural murther.

30 HAMLET   Murther!

GHOST   Murther most foul, as in the best it is,
But this most foul, strange, and unnatural.

HAMLET   Haste me to know't, that I with wings as swift
As meditation, or the thoughts of love,
35   May sweep to my revenge.

GHOST   I find thee apt,
And duller shouldst thou be than the fat weed
That roots itself in ease on Lethe wharf,
Wouldst thou not stir in this. Now, Hamlet, hear:
40   'Tis given out that, sleeping in my orchard,
A serpent stung me, so the whole ear of Denmark
Is by a forged process of my death
Rankly abus'd; but know, thou noble youth,
The serpent that did sting thy father's life
45   Now wears his crown.

HAMLET   O my prophetic soul!
My uncle?

GHOST   Ay, that incestuous, that adulterate beast,
With witchcraft of his wits, with traitorous gifts—
50   O wicked wit and gifts that have the power
So to seduce!—won to his shameful lust
The will of my most seeming virtuous queen.

---

15. **fast:** do penance   16. **crimes:** sins   21. **spheres:** eye-sockets; with allusion to the revolving spheres in which, according to the Ptolemaic astronomy, the stars were fixed   23. **an end:** on end   24. **fearful porpentine:** frightened porcupine   25. **eternal blazon:** revelation of eternal things 34. **meditation:** thought   38. **Lethe:** river of Hades, the water of which made the drinker forget the past   **wharf:** bank   40. **orchard:** garden   42. **forged process:** false account   43. **abus'd:** deceived 48. **adulterate:** adulterous

O Hamlet, what [a] falling-off was there
From me, whose love was of that dignity
55   That it went hand in hand even with the vow
I made to her in marriage, and to decline
Upon a wretch whose natural gifts were poor
To those of mine!
But virtue, as it never will be moved,
60   Though lewdness court it in a shape of heaven,
So [lust], though to a radiant angel link'd,
Will [sate] itself in a celestial bed
And prey on garbage.
But soft, methinks I scent the morning air,
65   Brief let me be. Sleeping within my orchard,
My custom always of the afternoon,
Upon my secure hour thy uncle stole,
With juice of cursed hebona in a vial,
And in the porches of my ears did pour
70   The leprous distillment, whose effect
Holds such an enmity with blood of man
That swift as quicksilver it courses through
The natural gates and alleys of the body,
And with a sudden vigor it doth [posset]
75   And curd, like eager droppings into milk,
The thin and wholesome blood. So did it mine,
And a most instant tetter bark'd about,
Most lazar-like, with vile and loathsome crust
All my smooth body.
80   Thus was I, sleeping, by a brother's hand
Of life, of crown, of queen, at once dispatch'd,
Cut off even in the blossoms of my sin,
Unhous'led, disappointed, unanel'd,
No reck'ning made, but sent to my account
85   With all my imperfections on my head.
O, horrible, O, horrible, most horrible!
If thou hast nature in thee, bear it not,
Let not the royal bed of Denmark be
A couch for luxury and damned incest.

---

60. **shape of heaven:** angelic form   67. **secure:** carefree   68. **hebona:** ebony (which Shakespeare, following a literary tradition, and perhaps also associating the word with *henbane,* thought the name of a poison)   74. **posset:** curdle   75. **eager:** sour   77. **tetter:** scabby eruption   **bark'd:** formed a hard covering, like bark on a tree   78. **lazar-like:** leperlike   81. **at once:** all at the same time   **dispatch'd:** deprived   83. **Unhous'led:** without the Eucharist   **disappointed:** without (spiritual) preparation   **unanel'd:** unanointed, without extreme unction   87. **nature:** natural feeling   89. **luxury:** lust

90   But howsomever thou pursues this act,
        Taint not thy mind, nor let thy soul contrive
        Against thy mother aught. Leave her to heaven,
        And to those thorns that in her bosom lodge
        To prick and sting her. Fare thee well at once!
95   The glow-worm shows the matin to be near,
        And gins to pale his uneffectual fire.
        Adieu, adieu, adieu! remember me.

[*Exit.*]

HAMLET   O all you host of heaven! O earth! What else?
        And shall I couple hell? O fie, hold, hold, my heart,
100   And you, my sinows, grow not instant old,
        But bear me [stiffly] up. Remember thee!
        Ay, thou poor ghost, whiles memory holds a seat
        In this distracted globe. Remember thee!
        Yea, from the table of my memory
105   I'll wipe away all trivial fond records,
        All saws of books, all forms, all pressures past
        That youth and observation copied there,
        And thy commandement all alone shall live
        Within the book and volume of my brain,
110   Unmix'd with baser matter. Yes, by heaven!
        O most pernicious woman!
        O villain, villain, smiling, damned villain!
        My tables—meet it is I set it down
        That one may smile, and smile, and be a villain!
115   At least I am sure it may be so in Denmark.   [*He writes.*]
        So, uncle, there you are. Now to my word:
        It is "Adieu, adieu! remember me."
        I have sworn't.
HORATIO [*Within.*]   My lord, my lord!
120 MARCELLUS [*Within.*]   Lord Hamlet!

(*Enter* HORATIO *and* MARCELLUS.)

HORATIO   Heavens secure him!
HAMLET   So be it!
MARCELLUS   Illo, ho, ho, my lord!

---

95. **matin:** morning 96. **gins:** begins 100. **sinows:** sinews 103. **globe:** head 104. **table:** writing tablet 105. **fond:** foolish 106. **saws:** wise sayings **forms:** shapes, images **pressures:** impressions 116. **word:** word of command from the Ghost

HAMLET   Hillo, ho, ho, boy! Come, [bird,] come.

125 MARCELLUS   How is't, my noble lord?

HORATIO   What news, my lord?

HAMLET   O, wonderful!

HORATIO   Good my lord, tell it.

HAMLET   No, you will reveal it.

130 HORATIO   Not I, my lord, by heaven.

MARCELLUS   Nor I, my lord.

HAMLET   How say you then, would heart of man once think it?—
     But you'll be secret?

BOTH [HORATIO, MARCELLUS]   Ay, by heaven, [my lord].

135 HAMLET   There's never a villain dwelling in all Denmark
     But he's an arrant knave.

HORATIO   There needs no ghost, my lord, come from the grave
     To tell us this.

HAMLET   Why, right, you are in the right,
140   And so, without more circumstance at all,
     I hold it fit that we shake hands and part,
     You, as your business and desire shall point you,
     For every man hath business and desire,
     Such as it is, and for my own poor part,
145   I will go pray.

HORATIO   These are but wild and whirling words, my lord.

HAMLET   I am sorry they offend you, heartily,
     Yes, faith, heartily.

HORATIO   There's no offense, my lord.

150 HAMLET   Yes, by Saint Patrick, but there is, Horatio,
     And much offense too. Touching this vision here,
     It is an honest ghost, that let me tell you.
     For your desire to know what is between us,
     O'ermaster't as you may. And now, good friends,
155   As you are friends, scholars, and soldiers,
     Give me one poor request.

HORATIO   What is't, my lord, we will.

HAMLET   Never make known what you have seen tonight.

BOTH [HORATIO, MARCELLUS]   My lord, we will not.

160 HAMLET   Nay, but swear't.

HORATIO   In faith,
     My lord, not I.

MARCELLUS   Nor I, my lord, in faith.

HAMLET   Upon my sword.

---

124. **Hillo . . . come:** Hamlet answers Marcellus' halloo with a falconer's cry   140. **circumstance:** ceremony   152. **honest:** true, genuine   157. **What is't:** whatever it is   164. **Upon my sword:** on the cross formed by the hilt

165 MARCELLUS   We have sworn, my lord, already.
    HAMLET   Indeed, upon my sword, indeed.

(GHOST *cries under the stage.*)

    GHOST   Swear.
    HAMLET   Ha, ha, boy, say'st thou so? Art thou there, truepenny?
    Come on, you hear this fellow in the cellarage,
170   Consent to swear.
    HORATIO   Propose the oath, my lord.
    HAMLET   Never to speak of this that you have seen,
    Swear by my sword.
    GHOST [*beneath*]   Swear.
175 HAMLET   *Hic et ubique?* Then we'll shift our ground.
    Come hither, gentlemen,
    And lay your hands again upon my sword.
    Swear by my sword
    Never to speak of this that you have heard.
180 GHOST [*beneath*]   Swear by his sword.
    HAMLET   Well said, old mole, canst work i' th' earth so fast?
    A worthy pioner! Once more remove, good friends.
    HORATIO   O day and night, but this is wondrous strange!
    HAMLET   And therefore as a stranger give it welcome.
185   There are more things in heaven and earth, Horatio,
    Than are dreamt of in your philosophy.
    But come—
    Here, as before, never, so help you mercy,
    How strange or odd some'er I bear myself—
190   As I perchance hereafter shall think meet
    To put an antic disposition on—
    That you, at such times seeing me, never shall,
    With arms encumb'red thus, or this headshake,
    Or by pronouncing of some doubtful phrase,
195   As "Well, well, we know," or "We could, and if we would,"
    Or "If we list to speak," or "There be, and if they might,"
    Or such ambiguous giving out, to note
    That you know aught of me—this do swear,
    So grace and mercy at your most need help you.
200 GHOST [*beneath*]   Swear.   [*They swear.*]

---

168. **truepenny:** trusty fellow   175. **Hic et ubique:** here and everywhere   182. **pioner:** digger,
miner (variant of *pioneer*)   184. **as . . . welcome:** give it the welcome due in courtesy to strangers
186. **your:** See note on I.i.151.   **philosophy:** natural philosophy, science   191. **put . . . on:** behave in
some fantastic manner, act like a madman   193. **encumb'red:** folded   195. **and if:** if
196. **list:** cared, had a mind   197. **note:** indicate

HAMLET   Rest, rest, perturbed spirit! So, gentlemen,
　　With all my love I do commend me to you,
　　And what so poor a man as Hamlet is
　　May do t' express his love and friending to you,
205　God willing, shall not lack. Let us go in together,
　　And still your fingers on your lips, I pray.
　　The time is out of joint—O cursed spite,
　　That ever I was born to set it right!
　　Nay, come, let's go together.

(*Exeunt.*)

Act II

Scene I

(*Enter old* POLONIUS *with his man* [REYNALDO].)

POLONIUS   Give him this money and these notes, Reynaldo.
REYNALDO   I will, my lord.
POLONIUS   You shall do marvell's wisely, good Reynaldo,
　　Before you visit him, to make inquire
5　Of his behavior.
REYNALDO　　　　　　My lord, I did intend it.
POLONIUS   Marry, well said, very well said. Look you, sir,
　　Inquire me first what Danskers are in Paris,
　　And how, and who, what means, and where they keep,
10　What company, at what expense; and finding
　　By this encompassment and drift of question
　　That they do know my son, come you more nearer
　　Than your particular demands will touch it.
　　Take you as 'twere some distant knowledge of him,
15　As thus, "I know his father and his friends,
　　And in part him." Do you mark this, Reynaldo?
REYNALDO   Ay, very well, my lord.
POLONIUS   "And in part him—but," you may say, "not well.
　　But if't be he I mean, he's very wild,
20　Addicted so and so," and there put on him
　　What forgeries you please: marry, none so rank

---

206. **still:** always   209. **Nay . . . together:** They are holding back to let him go first.

II.i. Location: Polonius's quarters in the castle   3. **marvell's:** marvellous(ly)   8. **Danskers:** Danes
9. **keep:** lodge   11. **encompassment:** circuitousness   **drift of question:** directing of the conversation   13. **particular demands:** direct questions   21. **forgeries:** invented charges

As may dishonor him, take heed of that,
But, sir, such wanton, wild, and usual slips
As are companions and most known
25   To youth and liberty.
REYNALDO   As gaming, my lord.
POLONIUS   Ay, or drinking, fencing, swearing, quarreling,
    Drabbing—you may go so far.
REYNALDO   My lord, that would dishonor him.
30 POLONIUS   Faith, as you may season it in the charge:
    You must not put another scandal on him,
    That he is open to incontinency—
    That's not my meaning. But breathe his faults so quaintly
    That they may seem the taints of liberty,
35   The flash and outbreak of a fiery mind,
    A savageness in unreclaimed blood,
    Of general assault.
REYNALDO   But, my good lord—
POLONIUS   Wherefore should you do this?
40 REYNALDO   Ay, my lord,
    I would know that.
POLONIUS   Marry, sir, here's my drift,
    And I believe it is a fetch of wit:
    You laying these slight sallies on my son,
45   As 'twere a thing a little soil'd [wi' th'] working,
    Mark you,
    Your party in converse, him you would sound,
    Having ever seen in the prenominate crimes
    The youth you breathe of guilty, be assur'd
50   He closes with you in this consequence:
    "Good sir," or so, or "friend," or "gentleman,"
    According to the phrase or the addition
    Of man and country.
REYNALDO   Very good, my lord.
55 POLONIUS   And then, sir, does 'a this—'a does—what was I about to say?
    By the mass, I was about to say something.
    Where did I leave?
REYNALDO   At "closes in the consequence."

---

23. **wanton:** sportive   28. **Drabbing:** whoring   30. **Faith:** Most editors read *Faith, no,* following
F1; this makes easier sense.   **season:** qualify, temper   32. **open to incontinency:** habitually profli-
gate   33. **quaintly:** artfully   36. **unreclaimed:** untamed   37. **Of general assault:** to which young
men are generally subject   43. **fetch of wit:** ingenious device   44. **sallies:** sullies, blemishes
45. **soil'd . . . working:** shopworn   48. **Having:** if he has   **prenominate crimes:** aforementioned
faults   50. **closes:** falls in   **in this consequence:** as follows   52. **addition:** style of address

POLONIUS   At "closes in the consequence," ay, marry.

60   He closes thus: "I know the gentleman.
        I saw him yesterday, or th' other day,
        Or then, or then, with such or such, and as you say,
        There was 'a gaming, there o'ertook in 's rouse,
        There falling out at tennis"; or, perchance,
65   "I saw him enter such a house of sale,"
        Videlicet, a brothel, or so forth. See you now,
        Your bait of falsehood take this carp of truth,
        And thus do we of wisdom and of reach,
        With windlasses and with assays of bias,
70   By indirections find directions out;
        So by my former lecture and advice
        Shall you my son. You have me, have you not?
REYNALDO   My lord, I have.
POLONIUS   God buy ye, fare ye well.
75 REYNALDO   Good my lord.
POLONIUS   Observe his inclination in yourself.
REYNALDO   I shall, my lord.
POLONIUS   And let him ply his music.
REYNALDO   Well, my lord.
80 POLONIUS   Farewell.

(*Exit* REYNALDO.)

(*Enter* OPHELIA.)

        How now, Ophelia, what's the matter?
OPHELIA   O my lord, my lord, I have been so affrighted!
POLONIUS   With what, i' th' name of God?
OPHELIA   My lord, as I was sewing in my closet,
85   Lord Hamlet, with his doublet all unbrac'd,
        No hat upon his head, his stockins fouled,
        Ungart'red, and down-gyved to his ankle,
        Pale as his shirt, his knees knocking each other,
        And with a look so piteous in purport
90   As if he had been loosed out of hell
        To speak of horrors—he comes before me.

---

63. **o'ertook in 's rouse:** overcome by drink   68. **reach:** capacity, understanding   69. **windlasses:** roundabout methods   **assays of bias:** indirect attempts (a figure from the game of bowls, in which the player must make allowance for the curving course his bowl will take toward its mark)   70. **directions:** the way things are going   72. **have me:** understand me   74. **God buy ye:** good-bye (a contraction of *God be with you*)   76. **in:** by. Polonius asks him to observe Laertes directly, as well as making inquiries.   78. **let him ply:** see that he goes on with   84. **closet:** private room   85. **unbrac'd:** unlaced   86. **stockins fouled:** stockings dirty   87. **down-gyved:** hanging down like fetters on a prisoner's legs

POLONIUS   Mad for thy love?

OPHELIA   My lord, I do not know,
But truly I do fear it.

95 POLONIUS   What said he?

OPHELIA   He took me by the wrist, and held me hard,
Then goes he to the length of all his arm,
And with his other hand thus o'er his brow,
He falls to such perusal of my face

100 As 'a would draw it. Long stay'd he so.
At last, a little shaking of mine arm,
And thrice his head thus waving up and down,
He rais'd a sigh so piteous and profound
As it did seem to shatter all his bulk

105 And end his being. That done, he lets me go,
And with his head over his shoulder turn'd,
He seem'd to find his way without his eyes,
For out a' doors he went without their helps,
And to the last bended their light on me.

110 POLONIUS   Come, go with me. I will go seek the King.
This is the very ecstasy of love,
Whose violent property fordoes itself,
And leads the will to desperate undertakings
As oft as any passions under heaven

115 That does afflict our natures. I am sorry—
What, have you given him any hard words of late?

OPHELIA   No, my good lord, but as you did command
I did repel his letters, and denied
His access to me.

120 POLONIUS   That hath made him mad.
I am sorry that with better heed and judgment
I had not coted him. I fear'd he did but trifle
And meant to wrack thee, but beshrow my jealousy!
By heaven, it is as proper to our age

125 To cast beyond ourselves in our opinions,
As it is common for the younger sort
To lack discretion. Come, go we to the King.
This must be known, which, being kept close, might move
More grief to hide, than hate to utter love.

130 Come.

---

104. **bulk:** body   111. **ecstasy:** madness   112. **property:** quality   **fordoes:** destroys   122. **coted:** observed   123. **beshrow:** beshrew, plague take   **jealousy:** suspicious mind   124. **proper . . . age:** characteristic of men of my age   125. **cast beyond ourselves:** overshoot, go too far (by way of caution)   128. **close:** secret   128–129. **move . . . love:** cause more grievous consequences by its concealment than we shall incur displeasure by making it known

(*Exeunt.*)

[Scene II]

(*Flourish. Enter* KING *and* QUEEN, ROSENCRANTZ *and* GUILDENSTERN [*cum aliis*].)

KING   Welcome, dear Rosencrantz and Guildenstern!
    Moreover that we much did long to see you,
    The need we have to use you did provoke
    Our hasty sending. Something have you heard
5   Of Hamlet's transformation; so call it,
    Sith nor th' exterior nor the inward man
    Resembles that it was. What it should be,
    More than his father's death, that thus hath put him
    So much from th' understanding of himself,
10   I cannot dream of. I entreat you both
    That, being of so young days brought up with him,
    And sith so neighbored to his youth and havior,
    That you voutsafe your rest here in our court
    Some little time, so by your companies
15   To draw him on to pleasures, and to gather
    So much as from occasion you may glean,
    Whether aught to us unknown afflicts him thus,
    That, open'd, lies within our remedy.
QUEEN   Good gentlemen, he hath much talk'd of you,
20   And sure I am two men there is not living
    To whom he more adheres. If it will please you
    To show us so much gentry and good will
    As to expend your time with us a while
    For the supply and profit of our hope,
25   Your visitation shall receive such thanks
    As fits a king's remembrance.
ROSENCRANTZ   Both your Majesties
    Might, by the sovereign power you have of us,
    Put your dread pleasures more into command
30   Than to entreaty.
GUILDENSTERN   But we both obey,
    And here give up ourselves, in the full bent,
    To lay our service freely at your feet,
    To be commanded.

II.ii. Location: the castle   2. **Moreover . . . you:** besides the fact that we wanted to see you for your own sakes   6. **Sith:** since   11. **of:** from   13. **voutsafe your rest:** vouchsafe to remain   21. **more adheres:** is more attached   22. **gentry:** courtesy   24. **supply and profit:** support and advancement   32. **in . . . bent:** to our utmost

35 KING   Thanks, Rosencrantz and gentle Guildenstern.

QUEEN   Thanks, Guildenstern and gentle Rosencrantz.
   And I beseech you instantly to visit
   My too much changed son. Go some of you
   And bring these gentlemen where Hamlet is.

40 GUILDENSTERN   Heavens make our presence and our practices
   Pleasant and helpful to him!

QUEEN   Ay, amen!

(*Exeunt* ROSENCRANTZ *and* GUILDENSTERN [*with some* ATTENDANTS].)

(*Enter* POLONIUS.)

POLONIUS   Th' embassadors from Norway, my good lord,
   Are joyfully return'd.

45 KING   Thou still hast been the father of good news.

POLONIUS   Have I, my lord? I assure my good liege
   I hold my duty as I hold my soul,
   Both to my God and to my gracious king;
   And I do think, or else this brain of mine

50   Hunts not the trail of policy so sure
   As it hath us'd to do, that I have found
   The very cause of Hamlet's lunacy.

KING   O, speak of that, that do I long to hear.

POLONIUS   Give first admittance to th' embassadors;

55   My news shall be the fruit to that great feast.

KING   Thyself do grace to them, and bring them in.   [*Exit* POLONIUS.]
   He tells me, my dear Gertrude, he hath found
   The head and source of all your son's distemper.

QUEEN   I doubt it is no other but the main,

60   His father's death and our [o'erhasty] marriage.

(*Enter* [POLONIUS *with* VOLTEMAND *and* CORNELIUS, *the*] EMBASSADORS.)

KING   Well, we shall sift him.—Welcome, my good friends!
   Say, Voltemand, what from our brother Norway?

VOLTEMAND   Most fair return of greetings and desires.
   Upon our first, he sent out to suppress

65   His nephew's levies, which to him appear'd
   To be a preparation 'gainst the Polack;
   But better look'd into, he truly found
   It was against your Highness. Whereat griev'd,

---

43. **embassadors:** ambassadors   45. **still:** always   46. **liege:** sovereign   50. **policy:** statecraft
55. **fruit:** dessert   58. **head:** synonymous with *source*   **distemper:** (mental) illness   59. **doubt:** suspect   **main:** main cause   64. **Upon our first:** at our first representation   68. **griev'd:** aggrieved,
offended

That so his sickness, age, and impotence
70 Was falsely borne in hand, sends out arrests
On Fortinbras, which he, in brief, obeys,
Receives rebuke from Norway, and in fine,
Makes vow before his uncle never more
To give th' assay of arms against your Majesty.
75 Whereon old Norway, overcome with joy,
Gives him threescore thousand crowns in annual fee,
And his commission to employ those soldiers,
So levied, as before, against the Polack,
With an entreaty, herein further shown,   [*giving a paper*]
80 That it might please you to give quiet pass
Through your dominions for this enterprise,
On such regards of safety and allowance
As therein are set down.
KING   It likes us well,
85 And at our more considered time we'll read,
Answer, and think upon this business.
Mean time, we thank you for your well-took labor.
Go to your rest, at night we'll feast together.
Most welcome home!

(*Exeunt* EMBASSADORS [*and* ATTENDANTS].)
90 POLONIUS   This business is well ended.
My liege, and madam, to expostulate
What majesty should be, what duty is,
Why day is day, night night, and time is time,
Were nothing but to waste night, day, and time;
95 Therefore, [since] brevity is the soul of wit,
And tediousness the limbs and outward flourishes,
I will be brief. Your noble son is mad:
Mad call I it, for to define true madness,
What is't but to be nothing else but mad?
100 But let that go.
QUEEN   More matter with less art.
POLONIUS   Madam, I swear I use no art at all.
That he's mad, 'tis true, 'tis true 'tis pity,
And pity 'tis 'tis true—a foolish figure,
105 But farewell it, for I will use no art.

---

70. **borne in hand:** taken advantage of   72. **in fine:** in the end   74. **assay:** trial   82. **On . . . al-**
lowance: with such safeguards and provisos   84. **likes:** pleases   85. **consider'd:** suitable for consideration   91. **expostulate:** expound   95. **wit:** understanding, wisdom   101. **art:** rhetorical art
104. **figure:** figure of speech

Mad let us grant him then, and now remains
That we find out the cause of this effect,
Or rather say, the cause of this defect,
For this effect defective comes by cause:

110 Thus it remains, and the remainder thus.
Perpend.
I have a daughter—have while she is mine—
Who in her duty and obedience, mark,
Hath given me this. Now gather, and surmise.

[*reads the salutation of the letter*]

115 "To the celestial and my soul's idol, the most beautified Ophelia"—
That's an ill phrase, a vile phrase, "beautified" is a vile phrase. But you shall
hear. Thus:
"In her excellent white bosom, these, etc."
QUEEN   Came this from Hamlet to her?
120 POLONIUS   Good madam, stay awhile. I will be faithful.

([*reads the*] *letter*)

"Doubt thou the stars are fire,
Doubt that the sun doth move,
Doubt truth to be a liar,
But never doubt I love.

125 O dear Ophelia, I am ill at these numbers. I have not art to reckon my
groans, but that I love thee best, O most best, believe it. Adieu.
Thine evermore, most dear lady,
whilst this machine is to him, Hamlet."
This in obedience hath my daughter shown me,

130 And more [above], hath his solicitings,
As they fell out by time, by means, and place,
All given to mine ear.
KING   But how hath she
Receiv'd his love?

135 POLONIUS   What do you think of me?
KING   As of a man faithful and honorable.
POLONIUS   I would fain prove so. But what might you think,
When I had seen this hot love on the wing—
As I perceiv'd it (I must tell you that)

---

109. **For . . . cause:** for this effect (which shows as a defect in Hamlet's reason) is not merely accidental, and has a cause we may trace   111. **Perpend:** consider   115. **beautified:** beautiful (not an
uncommon usage)   124. **Doubt:** suspect   125. **ill . . . numbers:** bad at versifying   **reckon:** count
(with a quibble on *numbers*)   128. **machine:** body   130. **more above:** furthermore
137. **fain:** willingly, gladly

140   Before my daughter told me—what might you,
       Or my dear Majesty your queen here, think,
       If I had play'd the desk or table-book,
       Or given my heart a [winking,] mute and dumb,
       Or look'd upon this love with idle sight,
145   What might you think? No, I went round to work,
       And my young mistress thus I did bespeak:
       "Lord Hamlet is a prince out of thy star;
       This must not be"; and then I prescripts gave her,
       That she should lock herself from [his] resort,
150   Admit no messengers, receive no tokens.
       Which done, she took the fruits of my advice;
       And he repell'd, a short tale to make,
       Fell into a sadness, then into a fast,
       Thence to a watch, thence into a weakness,
155   Thence to [a] lightness, and by this declension,
       Into the madness wherein now he raves,
       And all we mourn for.

KING   Do you think ['tis] this?

QUEEN   It may be, very like.

160 POLONIUS   Hath there been such a time—I would fain know that—
       That I have positively said, " 'Tis so,"
       When it prov'd otherwise?

KING   Not that I know.

POLONIUS [*points to his head and shoulder*]   Take this from this, if this be
165   otherwise.
       If circumstances lead me, I will find
       Where truth is hid, though it were hid indeed
       Within the centre.

KING   How may we try it further?

170 POLONIUS   You know sometimes he walks four hours together
       Here in the lobby.

QUEEN   So he does indeed.

POLONIUS   At such a time I'll loose my daughter to him.
       Be you and I behind an arras then,
175   Mark the encounter: if he love her not,
       And be not from his reason fall'n thereon,
       Let me be no assistant for a state,
       But keep a farm and carters.

---

142. **play'd . . . table-book**: noted the matter secretly   143. **winking**: closing of the eyes
144. **idle sight**: noncomprehending eyes   145. **round**: straightforwardly   146. **bespeak**: address
147. **star**: sphere, lot in life   151. **took . . . of**: profited by, carried out   152. **repell'd**: repulsed
154. **watch**: sleeplessness   155. **lightness**: lightheadedness   168. **centre**: of the earth (which in the
Ptolemaic system is also the centre of the universe)   174. **arras**: hanging tapestry   176. **thereon**:
because of that

KING   We will try it.

(*Enter* HAMLET [*reading on a book*].)

180 QUEEN   But look where sadly the poor wretch comes reading.
POLONIUS   Away, I do beseech you, both away.
    I'll board him presently.

(*Exeunt* KING *and* QUEEN.)

                               O, give me leave,
    How does my good Lord Hamlet?
185 HAMLET   Well, God-a-mercy.
POLONIUS   Do you know me, my lord?
HAMLET   Excellent well, you are a fishmonger.
POLONIUS   Not I, my lord.
HAMLET   Then I would you were so honest a man.
190 POLONIUS   Honest, my lord?
HAMLET   Ay, sir, to be honest, as this world goes, is to be one man pick'd out of
    ten thousand.
POLONIUS   That's very true, my lord.
HAMLET   For if the sun breed maggots in a dead dog, being a good kissing car-
195   rion—Have you a daughter?
POLONIUS   I have, my lord.
HAMLET   Let her not walk i' th' sun. Conception is a blessing, but as your
    daughter may conceive, friend, look to't.
POLONIUS [*aside*]   How say you by that? still harping on my daughter. Yet he
200   knew me not at first, 'a said I was a fishmonger. 'A is far gone. And truly in
    my youth I suff'red much extremity for love—very near this. I'll speak to
    him again.—What do you read, my lord?
HAMLET   Words, words, words.
POLONIUS   What is the matter, my lord?
205 HAMLET   Between who?
POLONIUS   I mean, the matter that you read, my lord.
HAMLET   Slanders, sir; for the satirical rogue says here that old men have grey
    beards, that their faces are wrinkled, their eyes purging thick amber and
    plumtree gum, and that they have a plentiful lack of wit, together with most
210   weak hams; all which, sir, though I most powerfully and potently believe, yet
    I hold it not honesty to have it thus set down, for yourself, sir, shall grow old
    as I am, if like a crab you could go backward.

---

182. **board:** accost   **presently:** at once   185. **God-a-mercy:** thank you   187. **fishmonger:** Usually
explained as slang for "bawd," but no evidence has been produced for such a usage in Shakespeare's
day.   194–95. **good kissing carrion:** flesh good enough for the sun to kiss   197. **Conception:** understanding (with following play on the sense "conceiving a child")   204. **matter:** subject; but
Hamlet replies as if he had understood Polonius to mean "cause for a quarrel."   211. **honesty:** a fitting thing

POLONIUS [*aside*]   Though this be madness, yet there is method in't.—Will you walk out of the air, my lord?

215 HAMLET   Into my grave.

POLONIUS   Indeed that's out of the air. [*aside*] How pregnant sometimes his replies are! a happiness that often madness hits on, which reason and [sanity] could not so prosperously be deliver'd of. I will leave him, [and suddenly contrive the means of meeting between him] and my daughter.—My
220   lord, I will take my leave of you.

HAMLET   You cannot take from me any thing that I will not more willingly part withal—except my life, except my life, except my life.

POLONIUS   Fare you well, my lord.

HAMLET   These tedious old fools!

(*Enter* GUILDENSTERN *and* ROSENCRANTZ.)

225 POLONIUS   You go to seek the Lord Hamlet, there he is.

ROSENCRANTZ [*to* POLONIUS]   God save you, sir!

[*Exit* POLONIUS.]

GUILDENSTERN   My honor'd lord!

ROSENCRANTZ   My most dear lord!

HAMLET   My [excellent] good friends! How dost thou, Guildenstern? Ah,
230   Rosencrantz! Good lads, how do you both?

ROSENCRANTZ   As the indifferent children of the earth.

GUILDENSTERN   Happy, in that we are not [over-]happy, on Fortune's [cap] we are not the very button.

HAMLET   Nor the soles of her shoe?

235 ROSENCRANTZ   Neither, my lord.

HAMLET   Then you live about her waist, or in the middle of her favors?

GUILDENSTERN   Faith, her privates we.

HAMLET   In the secret parts of Fortune? O, most true, she is a strumpet. What news?

240 ROSENCRANTZ   None, my lord, but the world's grown honest.

HAMLET   Then is doomsday near. But your news is not true. [Let me question more in particular. What have you, my good friends, deserv'd at the hands of Fortune, that she sends you to prison hither?

GUILDENSTERN   Prison, my lord?

245 HAMLET   Denmark's a prison.

ROSENCRANTZ   Then is the world one.

---

213. **method:** orderly arrangement, sequence of ideas   214. **out . . . air:** Outdoor air was thought to be bad for invalids.   216. **pregnant:** apt   218–19. **suddenly:** at once   231. **indifferent:** average   237. **privates:** (1) intimate friends; (2) genitalia   238. **strumpet:** a common epithet for Fortune, because she grants favors to all men

HAMLET   A goodly one, in which there are many confines, wards, and dungeons, Denmark being one o' th' worst.

ROSENCRANTZ   We think not so, my lord.

250 HAMLET   Why then 'tis none to you; for there is nothing either good or bad, but thinking makes it so. To me it is a prison.

ROSENCRANTZ   Why then your ambition makes it one. 'Tis too narrow for your mind.

HAMLET   O God, I could be bounded in a nutshell, and count myself a king of 255   infinite space—were it not that I have bad dreams.

GUILDENSTERN   Which dreams indeed are ambition, for the very substance of the ambitious is merely the shadow of a dream.

HAMLET   A dream itself is but a shadow.

ROSENCRANTZ   Truly, and I hold ambition of so airy and light a quality that it is 260   but a shadow's shadow.

HAMLET   Then are our beggars bodies, and our monarchs and outstretch'd heroes the beggars' shadows. Shall we to th' court? for, by my fay, I cannot reason.

BOTH [ROSENCRANTZ, GUILDENSTERN]   We'll wait upon you.

265 HAMLET   No such matter. I will not sort you with the rest of my servants; for to speak to you like an honest man, I am most dreadfully attended.] But in the beaten way of friendship, what make you at Elsinore?

ROSENCRANTZ   To visit you, my lord, no other occasion.

HAMLET   Beggar that I am, I am [even] poor in thanks—but I thank you, and 270   sure, dear friends, my thanks are too dear a halfpenny. Were you not sent for? is it your own inclining? is it a free visitation? Come, come, deal justly with me. Come, come—nay, speak.

GUILDENSTERN   What should we say, my lord?

HAMLET   Any thing but to th' purpose. You were sent for, and there is a kind of 275   confession in your looks, which your modesties have not craft enough to color. I know the good King and Queen have sent for you.

ROSENCRANTZ   To what end, my lord?

HAMLET   That you must teach me. But let me conjure you, by the rights of our fellowship, by the consonancy of our youth, by the obligation of our ever-280   preserv'd love, and by what more dear a better proposer can charge you withal, be even and direct with me, whether you were sent for or no!

ROSENCRANTZ [*aside to* GUILDENSTERN]   What say you?

---

247. **wards:** cells   261. **bodies:** not shadows (since they lack ambition)   **outstretch'd:** with their ambition extended to the utmost (and hence producing stretched-out or elongated shadows)
262. **fay:** faith   264. **wait upon you:** attend you thither   265. **sort:** associate   266. **dreadfully:** execrably   270. **too . . . halfpenny:** too expensive priced at a halfpenny; not worth much
271. **justly:** honestly   274. **but:** Ordinarily punctuated with a comma preceding, to give the sense "provided that it is"; but Q2 has no comma, and Hamlet may intend, or include, the sense "except."
275. **modesties:** sense of shame   279. **consonancy . . . youth:** similarity of our ages   280. **charge:** urge, adjure   **even:** frank, honest (cf. modern "level with me")

HAMLET [*aside*]　Nay then I have an eye of you!—If you love me, hold not off.

GUILDENSTERN　My lord, we were sent for.

285　HAMLET　I will tell you why, so shall my anticipation prevent your discovery, and your secrecy to the King and Queen moult no feather. I have of late—but wherefore I know not—lost all my mirth, forgone all custom of exercises; and indeed it goes so heavily with my disposition, that this goodly frame, the earth, seems to me a sterile promontory; this most excellent

290　canopy, the air, look you, this brave o'erhanging firmament, this majestical roof fretted with golden fire, why, it appeareth nothing to me but a foul and pestilent congregation of vapors. What [a] piece of work is a man, how noble in reason, how infinite in faculties, in form and moving, how express and admirable in action, how like an angel in apprehension, how like a god!

295　the beauty of the world; the paragon of animals; and yet to me what is this quintessence of dust? Man delights not me—nor women neither, though by your smiling you seem to say so.

ROSENCRANTZ　My lord, there was no such stuff in my thoughts.

HAMLET　Why did ye laugh then, when I said, "Man delights not me"?

300　ROSENCRANTZ　To think, my lord, if you delight not in man, what lenten entertainment the players shall receive from you. We coted them on the way, and hither are they coming to offer you service.

HAMLET　He that plays the king shall be welcome—his Majesty shall have tribute on me, the adventerous knight shall use his foil and target, the lover

305　shall not sigh gratis, the humorous man shall end his part in peace, [the clown shall make those laugh whose lungs are [tickle] a' th' sere,] and the lady shall say her mind freely, or the [blank] verse shall halt for't. What players are they?

ROSENCRANTZ　Even those you were wont to take such delight in, the tragedi-

310　ans of the city.

HAMLET　How chances it they travel? Their residence, both in reputation and profit, was better both ways.

---

283. **of:** on　285. **prevent your discovery:** forestall your disclosure (of what the king and queen have said to you in confidence)　286. **moult no feather:** not be impaired in the least
287–88. **custom of exercises:** my usual athletic activities　290. **brave:** splendid　291. **fretted:** ornamented as with fretwork　292. **piece of work:** masterpiece　293–94. **how infinite . . . god:** See the Textual Notes for the different punctuation in F1.　293. **express:** exact　296. **quintessence:** finest and purest extract　300–301. **lenten entertainment:** meagre reception　301. **coted:** outstripped　304. **on:** of, from　**adventerous:** adventurous, wandering in search of adventure　**foil and target:** light fencing sword and small shield　305. **gratis:** without reward　**humorous:** dominated by some eccentric trait (like the melancholy Jaques in *As You Like It*)　306. **tickle . . . sere:** easily made to laugh (literally, describing a gun that goes off easily; *sere* = a catch in the gunlock; *tickle* = easily affected, highly sensitive to stimulus)　307. **halt:** limp, come off lamely (the verse will not scan if she omits indecent words)

ROSENCRANTZ   I think their inhibition comes by the means of the late innovation.

315 HAMLET   Do they hold the same estimation they did when I was in the city? Are
they so follow'd?

ROSENCRANTZ   No indeed are they not.

[HAMLET   How comes it? do they grow rusty?

ROSENCRANTZ   Nay, their endeavor keeps in the wonted pace; but there is, sir,
320   an aery of children, little eyases, that cry out on the top of question, and are
most tyrannically clapp'd for't. These are now the fashion, and so [berattle]
the common stages—so they call them—that many wearing rapiers are
afraid of goose-quills and dare scarce come thither.

HAMLET   What, are they children? Who maintains 'em? How are they escoted?
325   Will they pursue the quality no longer than they can sing? Will they not say
afterwards, if they should grow themselves to common players (as it is
[most like], if their means are [no] better), their writers do them wrong, to
make them exclaim against their own succession?

ROSENCRANTZ   Faith, there has been much to do on both sides, and the nation
330   holds it no sin to tarre them to controversy. There was for a while no money
bid for argument, unless the poet and the player went to cuffs in the question.

HAMLET   Is't possible?

GUILDENSTERN   O, there has been much throwing about of brains.

335 HAMLET   Do the boys carry it away?

ROSENCRANTZ   Ay, that they do, my lord—Hercules and his load too.]

---

313. **inhibition:** hindrance (to playing in the city). The word could be used of an official prohibi-
tion. See next note.   313–314. **innovation:** Shakespeare elsewhere uses this word of a political up-
rising or revolt, and lines 313–314 are often explained as meaning that the company had been forbidden to play in the city as the result of some disturbance. It is commonly conjectured that the
allusion is to the Essex rebellion of 1601, but it is known that Shakespeare's company, though to
some extent involved on account of the special performance of *Richard II* they were commissioned
to give on the eve of the rising, were not in fact punished by inhibition. A second interpretation explains *innovation* as referring to the new theatrical vogue described in lines 320 ff., and conjectures
that *inhibition* may allude to a Privy Council order of 1600 restricting the number of London playhouses to two and the number of performances to two a week.   318–336. **How . . . too:** This passage refers topically to the "War of the Theatres" between the child actors and their poet Jonson on
the one side, and on the other the adults, with Dekker, Marston, and possibly Shakespeare as
spokesmen, in 1600–1601.   320. **aery:** nest   **eyases:** unfledged hawks   **cry . . . question:** cry
shrilly above others in controversy   321. **tyrannically:** outrageously   **berattle:** cry down, satirize
322. **common stages:** public theatres (the children played at the Blackfriars, a private theatre)
323. **goose-quills:** pens (of satirical playwrights)   324. **escoted:** supported   325. **quality:** profession (of acting)   **no . . . sing:** only until their voices change   328. **succession:** future   329. **to do:**
ado   330. **tarre:** incite   331. **argument:** plot of a play   331–32. **in the question:** as part of the
script   335. **carry it away:** win   336. **Hercules . . . too:** Hercules in the course of one of his twelve
labors supported the world for Atlas; the children do better, for they carry away the world and Hercules as well. There is an allusion to the Globe playhouse, which reportedly had for its sign the figure of Hercules upholding the world.

HAMLET   It is not very strange, for my uncle is King of Denmark, and those that
would make mouths at him while my father liv'd, give twenty, forty, fifty, a
hundred ducats a-piece for his picture in little. 'Sblood, there is something
340   in this more than natural, if philosophy could find it out. (*a flourish* [*for the*
PLAYERS])
GUILDENSTERN   There are the players.
HAMLET   Gentlemen, you are welcome to Elsinore. Your hands, come then: th'
appurtenance of welcome is fashion and ceremony. Let me comply with you
345   in this garb, [lest my] extent to the players, which, I tell you, must show
fairly outwards, should more appear like entertainment than yours. You are
welcome; but my uncle-father and aunt-mother are deceiv'd.
GUILDENSTERN   In what, my dear lord?
HAMLET   I am but mad north-north-west. When the wind is southerly I know a
350   hawk from a hand-saw.

(*Enter* POLONIUS.)

POLONIUS   Well be with you, gentlemen!
HAMLET [*aside to them*]   Hark you, Guildenstern, and you too—at each ear a
hearer—that great baby you see there is not yet out of his swaddling-clouts.
ROSENCRANTZ   Happily he is the second time come to them, for they say an old
355   man is twice a child.
HAMLET   I will prophesy, he comes to tell me of the players, mark it. [*aloud*]
You say right, sir, a' Monday morning, 'twas then indeed.
POLONIUS   My lord, I have news to tell you.
HAMLET   My lord, I have news to tell you. When Roscius was an actor in
360   Rome—
POLONIUS   The actors are come hither, my lord.
HAMLET   Buzz, buzz!
POLONIUS   Upon my honor—
HAMLET   "Then came each actor on his ass"—
365 POLONIUS   The best actors in the world, either for tragedy, comedy, history,
pastoral, pastoral-comical, historical-pastoral, [tragical-historical, tragical-
comical-historical-pastoral,] scene individable, or poem unlimited; Seneca

---

338. **mouths:** derisive faces   339. **'Sblood:** by God's (Christ's) blood   344. **comply:** observe the
formalities   345. **garb:** fashion, manner   **my extent:** the degree of courtesy I show   346. **more . . .
yours:** seem to be a warmer reception than I have given you   350. **hawk, hand-saw:** both cutting
tools; but also both birds, if *hand-saw* quibbles on *hernshaw,* "heron," a bird preyed upon by the
hawk   353. **swaddling-clouts:** swaddling clothes   354. **Happily:** haply, perhaps   355. **twice:** for
the second time   359. **Roscius:** the most famous of Roman actors (died 62 B.C.). News about him
would be stale news indeed.   362. **Buzz:** exclamation of impatience at someone who tells news already known   367. **scene individable:** play observing the unity of place   **poem unlimited:** play ignoring rules such as the three unities   **Seneca:** Roman writer of tragedies

cannot be too heavy, nor Plautus too light, for the law of writ and the liberty: these are the only men.

370   HAMLET   O Jephthah, judge of Israel, what a treasure hadst thou!

POLONIUS   What a treasure had he, my lord?

HAMLET   Why—

> "One fair daughter, and no more,
>   The which he loved passing well."

375   POLONIUS [*aside*]   Still on my daughter.

HAMLET   Am I not i' th' right, old Jephthah?

POLONIUS   If you call me Jephthah, my lord, I have a daughter that I love passing well.

HAMLET   Nay, that follows not.

380   POLONIUS   What follows then, my lord?

HAMLET   Why—

> "As by lot, God wot,"

and then, you know,

> "It came to pass, as most like it was"—

385   the first row of the pious chanson will show you more, for look where my abridgment comes.

(*Enter the* PLAYERS, [*four or five*].)

You are welcome, masters, welcome all. I am glad to see thee well. Welcome, good friends. O, old friend! why, thy face is valanc'd since I saw thee last; com'st thou to beard me in Denmark? What, my young lady and mistress!
390   by' lady, your ladyship is nearer to heaven than when I saw you last, by the altitude of a chopine. Pray God your voice, like a piece of uncurrent gold, be not crack'd within the ring. Masters, you are all welcome. We'll e'en to't like [French] falc'ners—fly at any thing we see; we'll have a speech straight. Come give us a taste of your quality, come, a passionate speech.

395   [1.] PLAYER   What speech, my good lord?

HAMLET   I heard thee speak me a speech once, but it was never acted, or if it was, not above once; for the play, I remember, pleas'd not the million, 'twas

---

368. **Plautus:** Roman writer of comedies   368–69. **for . . . liberty:** for strict observance of the rules, or for freedom from them (with possible allusion to the location of playhouses, which were not built in properties under city jurisdiction, but in the "liberties"—land once monastic and now outside the jurisdiction of the city authorities)   369. **only:** very best (a frequent use)   370. **Jephthah . . . Israel:** title of a ballad, from which Hamlet goes on to quote. For the story of Jephthah and his daughter, see Judges 11.   385. **row:** stanza   **chanson:** song, ballad   386. **abridgment:** (1) interruption; (2) pastime   388. **valanc'd:** fringed, bearded   389. **beard:** confront boldly (with obvious pun)   390. **by' lady:** by Our Lady   391. **chopine:** thick-soled shoe   392. **crack'd . . . ring:** broken to the point where you can no longer play female roles. A coin with a crack extending far enough in from the edge to cross the circle surrounding the stamp of the sovereign's head was unacceptable in exchange (*uncurrent*).   393. **straight:** straightway   394. **quality:** professional skill

caviary to the general, but it was—as I receiv'd it, and others, whose judgments in such matters cried in the top of mine—an excellent play, well di-
gested in the scenes, set down with as much modesty as cunning. I remember one said there were no sallets in the lines to make the matter savory, nor
no matter in the phrase that might indict the author of affection, but call'd
it an honest method, as wholesome as sweet, and by very much more handsome than fine. One speech in't I chiefly lov'd, 'twas Aeneas' [tale] to Dido,
and thereabout of it especially when he speaks of Priam's slaughter. If it live
in your memory, begin at this line—let me see, let me see:
"The rugged Pyrrhus, like th' Hyrcanian beast—"
'Tis not so, it begins with Pyrrhus:
"The rugged Pyrrhus, he whose sable arms,
Black as his purpose, did the night resemble
When he lay couched in th' ominous horse,
Hath now this dread and black complexion smear'd
With heraldy more dismal: head to foot
Now is he total gules, horridly trick'd
With blood of fathers, mothers, daughters, sons,
Bak'd and impasted with the parching streets,
That lend a tyrannous and a damned light
To their lord's murther. Roasted in wrath and fire,
And thus o'er-sized with coagulate gore,
With eyes like carbuncles, the hellish Pyrrhus
Old grandsire Priam seeks."
So proceed you.
POLONIUS 'Fore God, my lord, well spoken, with good accent and good
discretion.
[1.] PLAYER   "Anon he finds him
Striking too short at Greeks. His antique sword,
Rebellious to his arm, lies where it falls,
Repugnant to command. Unequal match'd,
Pyrrhus at Priam drives, in rage strikes wide,
But with the whiff and wind of his fell sword

398. **caviary . . . general:** caviare to the common people, too choice for the multitude   399. **cried
. . . of:** were louder than, carried more authority than   401. **sallets:** salads, spicy jokes   **savory:**
zesty   402. **affection:** affectation   404. **fine:** showily dressed (in language)   405. **Priam's slaughter:** the slaying of Priam (at the fall of Troy)   407. **Pyrrhus:** another name for Neoptolemus,
Achilles' son   **Hyrcanian beast:** Hyrcania in the Caucasus was notorious for its tigers.   409. **sable
arms:** The Greeks within the Trojan horse had blackened their skin so as to be inconspicuous when
they emerged at night.   413. **heraldy:** heraldry   **dismal:** ill-boding   414. **gules:** red (heraldic
term)   **trick'd:** adorned   416. **Bak'd:** caked   **impasted:** crusted   **with . . . streets:** by the heat
from the burning streets   419. **o'er-sized:** covered over as with a coat of sizing   420. **carbuncles:** jewels believed to shine in the dark   428. **Repugnant:** resistant, hostile   430. **fell:** cruel

Th' unnerved father falls. [Then senseless Ilium,]
Seeming to feel this blow, with flaming top
Stoops to his base, and with a hideous crash
Takes prisoner Pyrrhus' ear; for lo his sword,
435   Which was declining on the milky head
Of reverent Priam, seem'd i' th' air to stick.
So as a painted tyrant Pyrrhus stood
[And,] like a neutral to his will and matter,
Did nothing.
440   But as we often see, against some storm,
A silence in the heavens, the rack stand still,
The bold winds speechless, and the orb below
As hush as death, anon the dreadful thunder
Doth rend the region; so after Pyrrhus' pause,
445   A roused vengeance sets him new a-work,
And never did the Cyclops' hammers fall
On Mars's armor forg'd for proof eterne
With less remorse than Pyrrhus' bleeding sword
Now falls on Priam.
450   Out, out, thou strumpet Fortune! All you gods,
In general synod take away her power!
Break all the spokes and [fellies] from her wheel,
And bowl the round nave down the hill of heaven
As low as to the fiends!"
455 POLONIUS   This is too long.
HAMLET   It shall to the barber's with your beard. Prithee say on, he's for a jig
or a tale of bawdry, or he sleeps. Say on, come to Hecuba.
[1.] PLAYER   "But who, ah woe, had seen the mobled queen"—
HAMLET   "The mobled queen"?
460 POLONIUS   That's good, ["[mobled] queen" is good] .
[1.] PLAYER   "Run barefoot up and down, threat'ning the flames
With bisson rheum, a clout upon that head
Where late the diadem stood, and for a robe,
About her lank and all o'er-teemed loins,
465   A blanket, in the alarm of fear caught up—
Who this had seen, with tongue in venom steep'd,

---

431. **unnerved:** drained of strength   **senseless:** insensible   **Ilium:** the citadel of Troy   436. **rever-**
ent: reverend, aged   438. **like . . . matter:** poised midway between intention and performance   440. **against:** just before   441. **rack:** cloud-mass   444. **region:** air   446. **Cyclops:** giants
who worked in Vulcan's smithy, where armor was made for the gods   447. **proof eterne:** eternal endurance   448. **remorse:** pity   452. **fellies:** rims   453. **nave:** hub   456. **jig:** song-and-dance entertainment performed after the main play   460. **mobled:** muffled   462. **bisson rheum:** blinding
tears   **clout:** cloth   464. **o'er-teemed:** worn out by childbearing

'Gainst Fortune's state would treason have pronounc'd.
But if the gods themselves did see her then,
When she saw Pyrrhus make malicious sport
470   In mincing with his sword her [husband's] limbs,
The instant burst of clamor that she made,
Unless things mortal move them not at all,
Would have made milch the burning eyes of heaven,
And passion in the gods."

475   POLONIUS   Look whe'er he has not turn'd his color and has tears in 's eyes.
Prithee no more.

HAMLET   'Tis well, I'll have thee speak out the rest of this soon. Good my lord,
will you see the players well bestow'd? Do you hear, let them be well us'd, for
they are the abstract and brief chronicles of the time. After your death you
480   were better have a bad epitaph than their ill report while you live.

POLONIUS   My lord, I will use them according to their desert.

HAMLET   God's bodkin, man, much better: use every man after his desert, and
who shall scape whipping? Use them after your own honor and dignity—
the less they deserve, the more merit is in your bounty. Take them in.

485   POLONIUS   Come, sirs.

[*Exit.*]

HAMLET   Follow him, friends, we'll hear a play tomorrow.

[*Exeunt all the* PLAYERS *but the* FIRST.]

Dost thou hear me, old friend? Can you play "The Murther of Gonzago"?

[1.] PLAYER   Ay, my lord.

HAMLET   We'll ha't to-morrow night. You could for need study a speech of
490   some dozen lines, or sixteen lines, which I would set down and insert in't,
could you not?

[1.] PLAYER   Ay, my lord.

HAMLET   Very well. Follow that lord, and look you mock him not.

[*Exit* FIRST PLAYER.]

My good friends, I'll leave you [till] night. You are welcome to Elsinore.

495   ROSENCRANTZ   Good my lord!

HAMLET   Ay so, God buy to you.

(*Exeunt* [ROSENCRANTZ *and* GUILDENSTERN].)

---

467. **state:** rule, government   473. **milch:** moist (literally, milky)   474. **passion:** grief
475. **Look . . . not:** note how he has   478. **bestow'd:** lodged   **us'd:** treated   482. **God's bodkin:** by
God's (Christ's) little body   489. **for need:** if necessary

Now I am alone.
O, what a rogue and peasant slave am I!
Is it not monstrous that this player here,
500   But in a fiction, in a dream of passion,
Could force his soul so to his own conceit
That from her working all the visage wann'd,
Tears in his eyes, distraction in his aspect,
A broken voice, an' his whole function suiting
505   With forms to his conceit? And all for nothing,
For Hecuba!
What's Hecuba to him, or he to [Hecuba],
That he should weep for her? What would he do
Had he the motive and [the cue] for passion
510   That I have? He would drown the stage with tears,
And cleave the general ear with horrid speech,
Make mad the guilty, and appall the free,
Confound the ignorant, and amaze indeed
The very faculties of eyes and ears. Yet I,
515   A dull and muddy-mettled rascal, peak
Like John-a-dreams, unpregnant of my cause,
And can say nothing; no, not for a king,
Upon whose property and most dear life
A damn'd defeat was made. Am I a coward?
520   Who calls me villain, breaks my pate across,
Plucks off my beard and blows it in my face,
Tweaks me by the nose, gives me the lie i' th' throat
As deep as to the lungs? Who does me this?
Hah, 'swounds, I should take it; for it cannot be
525   But I am pigeon-liver'd, and lack gall
To make oppression bitter, or ere this
I should 'a' fatted all the region kites
With this slave's offal. Bloody, bawdy villain!
Remorseless, treacherous, lecherous, kindless villain!
530   Why, what an ass am I! This is most brave,
That I, the son of a dear [father] murthered,
Prompted to my revenge by heaven and hell,

---

501. **conceit:** imaginative conception   504. **his whole function:** the operation of his whole body
505. **forms:** actions, expressions   512. **free:** innocent   513. **amaze:** confound   515. **muddy-
mettled:** dull-spirited   **peak:** mope   516. **John-a-dreams:** a sleepy fellow   **unpregnant of:** un-
quickened by   519. **defeat:** destruction   522–23. **gives . . . lungs:** calls me a liar in the extremest
degree   524. **'swounds:** by God's (Christ's) wounds   **should:** would certainly   525. **am . . . gall:**
am constitutionally incapable of resentment. That doves were mild because they had no gall was a
popular belief.   528. **offal:** entrails   529. **kindless:** unnatural

Must like a whore unpack my heart with words,
And fall a-cursing like a very drab,

535   A stallion. Fie upon't, foh!
About, my brains! Hum—I have heard
That guilty creatures sitting at a play
Have by the very cunning of the scene
Been strook so to the soul, that presently

540   They have proclaim'd their malefactions:
For murther, though it have no tongue, will speak
With most miraculous organ. I'll have these players
Play something like the murther of my father
Before mine uncle. I'll observe his looks,

545   I'll tent him to the quick. If 'a do blench,
I know my course. The spirit that I have seen
May be a [dev'l], and the [dev'l] hath power
T' assume a pleasing shape, yea, and perhaps,
Out of my weakness and my melancholy,

550   As he is very potent with such spirits,
Abuses me to damn me. I'll have grounds
More relative than this—the play's the thing
Wherein I'll catch the conscience of the King.

(*Exit.*)

Act III

Scene I

(*Enter* King, Queen, Polonius, Ophelia, Rosencrantz, Guildenstern, Lords.)

KING   An' can you by no drift of conference
Get from him why he puts on this confusion,
Grating so harshly all his days of quiet
With turbulent and dangerous lunacy?

5 ROSENCRANTZ   He does confess he feels himself distracted,
But from what cause 'a will by no means speak.

---

535. **stallion:** male whore. Most editors adopt the F1 reading *scullion*, "kitchen menial."
536. **About:** to work   539. **presently:** at once, then and there   545. **tent:** probe   **blench:** flinch
550. **spirits:** states of temperament   551. **Abuses:** deludes   552. **relative:** closely related (to fact), conclusive

III.i. Location: the castle   1. **An':** and   **drift of conference:** leading on of conversation

GUILDENSTERN   Nor do we find him forward to be sounded,
But with a crafty madness keeps aloof
When we would bring him on to some confession
10   Of his true state.
QUEEN   Did he receive you well?
ROSENCRANTZ   Most like a gentleman.
GUILDENSTERN   But with much forcing of his disposition.
ROSENCRANTZ   Niggard of question, but of our demands
15   Most free in his reply.
QUEEN   Did you assay him
To any pastime?
ROSENCRANTZ   Madam, it so fell out that certain players
We o'erraught on the way; of these we told him,
20   And there did seem in him a kind of joy
To hear of it. They are here about the court,
And as I think, they have already order
This night to play before him.
POLONIUS   'Tis most true,
25   And he beseech'd me to entreat your Majesties
To hear and see the matter.
KING   With all my heart, and it doth much content me
To hear him so inclin'd.
Good gentlemen, give him a further edge,
30   And drive his purpose into these delights.
ROSENCRANTZ   We shall, my lord.

(*Exeunt* ROSENCRANTZ *and* GUILDENSTERN.)

KING   Sweet Gertrude, leave us two,
For we have closely sent for Hamlet hither,
That he, as 'twere by accident, may here
35   Affront Ophelia. Her father and myself,
We'll so bestow ourselves that, seeing unseen,
We may of their encounter frankly judge,
And gather by him, as he is behav'd,
If't be th' affliction of his love or no
40   That thus he suffers for.
QUEEN   I shall obey you.
And for your part, Ophelia, I do wish

---

7. **forward:** readily willing   **sounded:** plumbed, probed   8. **crafty madness:** mad craftiness, the shrewdness that mad people sometimes exhibit   13. **disposition:** inclination   14. **question:** conversation   **demands:** questions   16. **assay:** attempt to win   19. **o'erraught:** passed (literally, overreached)   29. **edge:** stimulus   30. **into:** on to   33. **closely:** privately   35. **Affront:** meet   37. **frankly:** freely

That your good beauties be the happy cause
Of Hamlet's wildness. So shall I hope your virtues
45   Will bring him to his wonted way again,
To both your honors.

OPHELIA   Madam, I wish it may.   [*Exit* QUEEN.]

POLONIUS   Ophelia, walk you here.—Gracious, so please you,
We will bestow ourselves.   [*to* OPHELIA]   Read on this book,
50   That show of such an exercise may color
Your [loneliness]. We are oft to blame in this—
'Tis too much prov'd—that with devotion's visage
And pious action we do sugar o'er
The devil himself.

55 KING   [*aside*]   O, 'tis too true!
How smart a lash that speech doth give my conscience!
The harlot's cheek, beautied with plast'ring art,
Is not more ugly to the thing that helps it
Than is my deed to my most painted word.
60   O heavy burthen!

POLONIUS   I hear him coming. Withdraw, my lord.

[*Exeunt* KING *and* POLONIUS.]

(*Enter* HAMLET.)

HAMLET   To be, or not to be, that is the question:
Whether 'tis nobler in the mind to suffer
The slings and arrows of outrageous fortune,
65   Or to take arms against a sea of troubles,
And by opposing, end them. To die, to sleep—
No more, and by a sleep to say we end
The heart-ache and the thousand natural shocks
That flesh is heir to; 'tis a consummation
70   Devoutly to be wish'd. To die, to sleep—
To sleep, perchance to dream—ay, there's the rub,
For in that sleep of death what dreams may come,
When we have shuffled off this mortal coil,
Must give us pause; there's the respect
75   That makes calamity of so long life:
For who would bear the whips and scorns of time,

---

50. **exercise:** religious exercise (as the next sentence makes clear)   50–51. **color Your loneliness:**
make your solitude seem natural   52. **too much prov'd:** too often proved true   53. **action:** demeanor   58. **to . . . it:** in comparison with the paint that makes it look beautiful   63. **suffer:** submit to, endure patiently   69. **consummation:** completion, end   71. **rub:** obstacle (a term from the
game of bowls)   73. **shuffled off:** freed ourselves from   **this mortal coil:** the turmoil of this mortal life   74. **respect:** consideration   75. **of . . . life:** so long-lived   76. **time:** the world

Th' oppressor's wrong, the proud man's contumely,
The pangs of despis'd love, the law's delay,
The insolence of office, and the spurns
80   That patient merit of th' unworthy takes,
When he himself might his quietus make
With a bare bodkin; who would fardels bear,
To grunt and sweat under a weary life,
But that the dread of something after death,
85   The undiscover'd country, from whose bourn
No traveller returns, puzzles the will,
And makes us rather bear those ills we have,
Than fly to others that we know not of?
Thus conscience does make cowards [of us all],
90   And thus the native hue of resolution
Is sicklied o'er with the pale cast of thought,
And enterprises of great pitch and moment
With this regard their currents turn awry,
And lose the name of action.—Soft you now,
95   The fair Ophelia. Nymph, in thy orisons
Be all my sins rememb'red.

OPHELIA   Good my lord,
How does your honor for this many a day?

HAMLET   I humbly thank you, well, [well, well].

100 OPHELIA   My lord, I have remembrances of yours
That I have longed long to redeliver.
I pray you now receive them.

HAMLET   No, not I,
I never gave you aught.

105 OPHELIA   My honor'd lord, you know right well you did,
And with them words of so sweet breath compos'd
As made these things more rich. Their perfume lost,
Take these again, for to the noble mind
Rich gifts wax poor when givers prove unkind.
110   There, my lord.

HAMLET   Ha, ha! are you honest?

OPHELIA   My lord?

HAMLET   Are you fair?

OPHELIA   What means your lordship?

---

81. **his quietus make:** write paid to his account   82. **bare bodkin:** mere dagger   **fardels:** burdens
85. **undiscover'd:** not disclosed to knowledge; about which men have no information   **bourn:**
boundary, region   86. **puzzles:** paralyzes   89. **conscience:** reflection (but with some of the modern sense, too)   90. **native hue:** natural (ruddy) complexion   91. **pale cast:** pallor   **thought:**
melancholy thought, brooding   92. **pitch:** loftiness (a term from falconry, signifying the highest
point of a hawk's flight   95. **orisons:** prayers   111. **honest:** chaste

115 HAMLET   That if you be honest and fair, [your honesty] should admit no discourse to your beauty.

OPHELIA   Could beauty, my lord, have better commerce than with honesty?

HAMLET   Ay, truly, for the power of beauty will sooner transform honesty from what it is to a bawd than the force of honesty can translate beauty into his
120   likeness. This was sometime a paradox, but now the time gives it proof. I did love you once.

OPHELIA   Indeed, my lord, you made me believe so.

HAMLET   You should not have believ'd me, for virtue cannot so [inoculate] our old stock but we shall relish of it. I lov'd you not.

125 OPHELIA   I was the more deceiv'd.

HAMLET   Get thee [to] a nunn'ry, why wouldst thou be a breeder of sinners? I am myself indifferent honest, but yet I could accuse me of such things that it were better my mother had not borne me: I am very proud, revengeful, ambitious, with more offenses at my beck than I have thoughts to put them
130   in, imagination to give them shape, or time to act them in. What should such fellows as I do crawling between earth and heaven? We are arrant knaves, believe none of us. Go thy ways to a nunn'ry. Where's your father?

OPHELIA   At home, my lord.

HAMLET   Let the doors be shut upon him, that he may play the fool no where
135   but in 's own house. Farewell.

OPHELIA   O, help him, you sweet heavens!

HAMLET   If thou dost marry, I'll give thee this plague for thy dowry: be thou as chaste as ice, as pure as snow, thou shalt not escape calumny. Get thee to a nunn'ry, farewell. Or if thou wilt needs marry, marry a fool, for wise men
140   know well enough what monsters you make of them. To a nunn'ry, go, and quickly too. Farewell.

OPHELIA   Heavenly powers, restore him!

HAMLET   I have heard of your paintings, well enough. God hath given you one face, and you make yourselves another. You jig and amble, and you [lisp,]
145   you nickname God's creatures and make your wantonness [your] ignorance. Go to, I'll no more on't, it hath made me mad. I say we will have no moe marriage. Those that are married already (all but one) shall live, the rest shall keep as they are. To a nunn'ry, go.

(*Exit.*)

---

120. **sometime:** formerly   **paradox:** tenet contrary to accepted belief   123–124. **virtue . . . it:** Virtue, engrafted on our old stock (of viciousness), cannot so change the nature of the plant that no trace of the original will remain.   127. **indifferent honest:** tolerably virtuous   140. **monsters:** alluding to the notion that the husbands of unfaithful wives grew horns   **you:** you women
144–45. **You . . . creatures:** you walk and talk affectedly   145–46. **make . . . ignorance:** excuse your affectation as ignorance   147. **moe:** more

OPHELIA   O, what a noble mind is here o'erthrown!
150   The courtier's, soldier's, scholar's, eye, tongue, sword,
           Th' expectation and rose of the fair state,
           The glass of fashion and the mould of form,
           Th' observ'd of all observers, quite, quite down!
           And I, of ladies most deject and wretched,
155   That suck'd the honey of his [music] vows,
           Now see [that] noble and most sovereign reason
           Like sweet bells jangled out of time, and harsh;
           That unmatch'd form and stature of blown youth
           Blasted with ecstasy. O, woe is me
160   T' have seen what I have seen, see what I see!

[OPHELIA *withdraws.*]

(*Enter* KING *and* POLONIUS.)

KING   Love? his affections do not that way tend,
       Nor what he spake, though it lack'd form a little,
       Was not like madness. There's something in his soul
       O'er which his melancholy sits on brood,
165   And I do doubt the hatch and the disclose
       Will be some danger; which for to prevent,
       I have in quick determination
       Thus set it down: he shall with speed to England
       For the demand of our neglected tribute.
170   Haply the seas, and countries different,
       With variable objects, shall expel
       This something-settled matter in his heart,
       Whereon his brains still beating puts him thus
       From fashion of himself. What think you on't?
175 POLONIUS   It shall do well; but yet do I believe
       The origin and commencement of his grief
       Sprung from neglected love.   [OPHELIA *comes forward.*]
              How now, Ophelia?
       You need not tell us what Lord Hamlet said,
180   We heard it all. My lord, do as you please,
       But if you hold it fit, after the play

---

151. **expectation:** hope   **rose:** ornament   **fair:** probably proleptic: "(the kingdom) made fair by his presence"   152. **glass:** mirror   **mould of form:** pattern of (courtly) behavior   153. **observ'd ... observers:** Shakespeare uses *observe* to mean not only "behold, mark attentively" but also "pay honor to".   158. **blown:** in full bloom   159. **Blasted:** withered   **ecstasy:** madness   161. **affections:** inclinations, feelings   165. **doubt:** fear   **disclose:** Synonymous with *hatch;* see also V.i.247. 177. **neglected:** unrequited

Let his queen-mother all alone entreat him
To show his grief. Let her be round with him,
And I'll be plac'd (so please you) in the ear
185   Of all their conference. If she find him not,
To England send him, or confine him where
Your wisdom best shall think.

KING   It shall be so.
Madness in great ones must not [unwatch'd] go.

(*Exeunt.*)

[Scene II]

(*Enter* HAMLET *and three of the* PLAYERS.)

HAMLET   Speak the speech, I pray you, as I pronounc'd it to you, trippingly on
the tongue, but if you mouth it, as many of our players do, I had as live the
town-crier spoke my lines. Nor do not saw the air too much with your hand,
thus, but use all gently, for in the very torrent, tempest, and, as I may say,
5   whirlwind of your passion, you must acquire and beget a temperance that
may give it smoothness. O, it offends me to the soul to hear a robustious
periwig-pated fellow tear a passion to totters, to very rags, to spleet the ears
of the groundlings, who for the most part are capable of nothing but inexplicable dumb shows and noise. I would have such a fellow whipt for o'er-
10   doing Termagant, it out-Herods Herod, pray you avoid it.
[1.] PLAYER   I warrant your honor.
HAMLET   Be not too tame neither, but let your own discretion be your
tutor. Suit the action to the word, the word to the action, with this special
observance, that you o'erstep not the modesty of nature: for any thing so
15   o'erdone is from the purpose of playing, whose end, both at the first and
now, was and is, to hold as 'twere the mirror up to nature: to show virtue her
feature, scorn her own image, and the very age and body of the time his
form and pressure. Now this overdone, or come tardy off, though it makes
the unskillful laugh, cannot but make the judicious grieve; the censure of

---

183. **his grief:** what is troubling him   **round:** blunt, outspoken   185. **find him:** learn the truth
about him.

III.ii. Location: the castle   2. **mouth:** pronounce with exaggerated distinctness or declamatory effect   **live:** lief, willingly   7. **totters:** tatters   **spleet:** split   8. **groundlings:** those who paid the
lowest admission price and stood on the ground in the "yard" or pit of the theatre   **capable of:** able
to take in   10. **Termagant:** a supposed god of the Saracens, whose role in medieval drama, like that
of Herod (line 10), was noisy and violent   14. **modesty:** moderation   15. **from:** contrary to
17. **scorn:** that which is worthy of scorn   18. **pressure:** impression (as of a seal), exact image
tardy: inadequately   19. **censure:** judgment

20   which one must in your allowance o'erweigh a whole theatre of others. O,
there be players that I have seen play—and heard others [praise], and that
highly—not to speak it profanely, that, neither having th' accent of Christians nor the gait of Christian, pagan, nor man, have so strutted and bellow'd that I have thought some of Nature's journeymen had made men, and
25   not made them well, they imitated humanity so abominably.

[1.] PLAYER   I hope we have reform'd that indifferently with us, [sir].

HAMLET   O, reform it altogether. And let those that play your clowns speak no
more than is set down for them, for there be of them that will themselves
laugh to set on some quantity of barren spectators to laugh too, though in
30   the mean time some necessary question of the play be then to be consider'd.
That's villainous, and shows a most pitiful ambition in the fool that uses it.
Go make you ready.

[*Exeunt* PLAYERS.]

(*Enter* POLONIUS, GUILDENSTERN, *and* ROSENCRANTZ.)

How now, my lord? Will the King hear this piece of work?

POLONIUS   And the Queen too, and that presently.

35   HAMLET   Bid the players make haste.   [*Exit* POLONIUS.]
Will you two help to hasten them?

ROSENCRANTZ   Ay, my lord.   (*Exeunt they two.*)

HAMLET   What ho, Horatio!

(*Enter* HORATIO.)

HORATIO   Here, sweet lord, at your service.

40   HAMLET   Horatio, thou art e'en as just a man
As e'er my conversation cop'd withal.

HORATIO   O my dear lord—

HAMLET   Nay, do not think I flatter,
For what advancement may I hope from thee
45   That no revenue hast but thy good spirits
To feed and clothe thee? Why should the poor be flatter'd?
No, let the candied tongue lick absurd pomp,
And crook the pregnant hinges of the knee

---

20. **which one:** (even) one of whom   **allowance:** estimation   22. **profanely:** irreverently
24–25. **some . . . abominably:** They were so unlike men that it seemed Nature had not made them
herself, but had delegated the task to mediocre assistants.   26. **indifferently:** pretty well
28. **of them:** some of them   31. **fool:** (1) stupid person; (2) actor playing a fool's role   33. **piece of
work:** masterpiece (said jocularly)   34. **presently:** at once   40. **thou . . . man:** you come as close to
being what a man should be (*just* = exact, precise)   41. **my . . . withal:** my association with people
has brought me into contact with   47. **candied:** sugared, flattering   **absurd:** tasteless (Latin sense)
48. **pregnant:** moving readily

Where thrift may follow fawning. Dost thou hear?
50   Since my dear soul was mistress of her choice
And could of men distinguish her election,
Sh' hath seal'd thee for herself, for thou hast been
As one in suff'ring all that suffers nothing,
A man that Fortune's buffets and rewards
55   Hast ta'en with equal thanks; and blest are those
Whose blood and judgment are so well co-meddled,
That they are not a pipe for Fortune's finger
To sound what stop she please. Give me that man
That is not passion's slave, and I will wear him
60   In my heart's core, ay, in my heart of heart,
As I do thee. Something too much of this.
There is a play to-night before the King,
One scene of it comes near the circumstance
Which I have told thee of my father's death.
65   I prithee, when thou seest that act afoot,
Even with the very comment of thy soul
Observe my uncle. If his occulted guilt
Do not itself unkennel in one speech,
It is a damned ghost that we have seen,
70   And my imaginations are as foul
As Vulcan's stithy. Give him heedful note,
For I mine eyes will rivet to his face,
And after we will both our judgments join
In censure of his seeming.
75   HORATIO   Well, my lord.
If'a steal aught the whilst this play is playing,
And scape [detecting], I will pay the theft.

([*Sound a flourish. Danish march.*] *Enter Trumpets and Kettle-drums,* KING,
QUEEN, POLONIUS, OPHELIA, [ROSENCRANTZ, GUILDENSTERN, *and other* LORDS
attendant, with his GUARD *carrying torches*].)

HAMLET   They are coming to the play. I must be idle; Get you a place.
KING   How fares our cousin Hamlet?

---

49. **thrift:** thriving, profit   56. **blood:** passions   **co-meddled:** mixed, blended   60. **my heart of
heart:** the heart of my heart   66. **very . . . soul:** your most intense critical observation
67. **occulted:** hidden   68. **unkennel:** bring into the open   69. **damned ghost:** evil spirit, devil
71. **stithy:** forge   74. **censure . . . seeming:** reaching a verdict on his behavior   78. **be idle:** act
foolish, pretend to be crazy   79. **fares:** Hamlet takes up this word in another sense.

80 HAMLET   Excellent, i' faith, of the chameleon's dish: I eat the air, promise-
cramm'd—you cannot feed capons so.

KING   I have nothing with this answer, Hamlet, these words are not mine.

HAMLET   No, nor mine now. [*to* POLONIUS] My lord, you play'd once i' th' university, you say?

85 POLONIUS   That did I, my lord, and was accounted a good actor.

HAMLET   What did you enact?

POLONIUS   I did enact Julius Caesar. I was kill'd i' th' Capitol; Brutus kill'd me.

HAMLET   It was a brute part of him to kill so capital a calf there. Be the players
ready?

90 ROSENCRANTZ   Ay, my lord, they stay upon your patience.

QUEEN   Come hither, my dear Hamlet, sit by me.

HAMLET   No, good mother, here's metal more attractive.   [*lying down at*
OPHELIA's *feet*]

POLONIUS [*to the* KING]   O ho, do you mark that?

95 HAMLET   Lady, shall I lie in your lap?

OPHELIA   No, my lord.

[HAMLET   I mean, my head upon your lap?

OPHELIA   Ay, my lord.]

HAMLET   Do you think I meant country matters?

100 OPHELIA   I think nothing, my lord.

HAMLET   That's a fair thought to lie between maids' legs.

OPHELIA   What is, my lord?

HAMLET   Nothing.

OPHELIA   You are merry, my lord.

105 HAMLET   Who, I?

OPHELIA   Ay, my lord.

HAMLET   O God, your only jig-maker. What should a man do but be merry, for
look you how cheerfully my mother looks, and my father died within 's two
hours.

110 OPHELIA   Nay, 'tis twice two months, my lord.

HAMLET   So long? Nay then let the dev'l wear black, for I'll have a suit of sables.
O heavens, die two months ago, and not forgotten yet? Then there's hope a
great man's memory may outlive his life half a year, but, by'r lady, 'a must

---

80. **chameleon's dish:** Chameleons were thought to feed on air. Hamlet says that he subsists on
an equally nourishing diet, the promise of succession. There is probably a pun on *air/heir*.
82. **have nothing with:** do not understand   **mine:** an answer to my question   88. **part:** action
99. **country matters:** indecency   107. **only:** very best   **jig-maker:** one who composed or played
in the farcical song-and-dance entertainments that followed plays   108. **'s:** this   111. **let . . .
sables:** To the devil with my garments; after so long a time I am ready for the old man's garb of
sables (fine fur).

115 build churches then, or else shall 'a suffer not thinking on, with the hobby-horse, whose epitaph is, "For O, for O, the hobby-horse is forgot."

(*The trumpets sounds. Dumb show follows.*)

(*Enter a King and a Queen* [*very lovingly*], *the Queen embracing him and he her.* [*She kneels and makes show of protestation unto him.*] *He takes her up and declines his head upon her neck. He lies him down upon a bank of flowers. She, seeing him asleep, leaves him. Anon come in another man, takes off his crown, kisses it, pours poison in the sleeper's ears, and leaves him. The Queen returns, finds the King dead, makes passionate action. The pois'ner with some three or four* [*mutes*] *come in again, seem to condole with her. The dead body is carried away. The pois'ner woos the Queen with gifts; she seems harsh* [*and unwilling*] *awhile, but in the end accepts love.* [*Exeunt.*])

OPHELIA   What means this, my lord?
HAMLET   Marry, this' [miching] mallecho, it means mischief.
OPHELIA   Belike this show imports the argument of the play.

(*Enter* PROLOGUE.)

HAMLET   We shall know by this fellow. The players cannot keep [counsel],
120   they'll tell all.
OPHELIA   Will 'a tell us what this show meant?
HAMLET   Ay, or any show that you will show him. Be not you asham'd to show, he'll not shame to tell you what it means.
OPHELIA   You are naught, you are naught. I'll mark the play.
125 PROLOGUE   For us, and for our tragedy,
            Here stooping to your clemency,
            We beg your hearing patiently.   [*Exit.*]
HAMLET   Is this a prologue, or the posy of a ring?
OPHELIA   'Tis brief, my lord.
130 HAMLET   As woman's love.

(*Enter* [*two* PLAYERS,] KING *and* QUEEN.)

[P.] KING   Full thirty times hath Phoebus' cart gone round
            Neptune's salt wash and Tellus' orbed ground,
            And thirty dozen moons with borrowed sheen
            About the world have times twelve thirties been,

---

114. **not thinking on**: not being thought of, being forgotten   115. **For . . . forgot**: line from a popular ballad lamenting puritanical suppression of such country sports as the May-games, in which the hobby-horse, a character costumed to resemble a horse, traditionally appeared   117. **this' miching mallecho**: this is sneaking mischief   118. **argument**: subject, plot   119. **counsel**: secrets   122. **Be not you**: if you are not   124. **naught**: wicked   128. **posy . . . ring**: verse motto inscribed in a ring (necessarily short)   131. **Phoebus' cart**: the sun-god's chariot   132. **Tellus**: goddess of the earth

135   Since love our hearts and Hymen did our hands
    Unite comutual in most sacred bands.
   [P.] QUEEN   So many journeys may the sun and moon
    Make us again count o'er ere love be done!
    But woe is me, you are so sick of late,
140   So far from cheer and from [your] former state,
    That I distrust you. Yet though I distrust,
    Discomfort you, my lord, it nothing must,
    [For] women's fear and love hold quantity,
    In neither aught, or in extremity.
145   Now what my [love] is, proof hath made you know,
    And as my love is siz'd, my fear is so.
    Where love is great, the littlest doubts are fear;
    Where little fears grow great, great love grows there.
   [P.] KING   Faith, I must leave thee, love, and shortly too;
150   My operant powers their functions leave to do,
    And thou shalt live in this fair world behind,
    Honor'd, belov'd, and haply one as kind
    For husband shalt thou—
   [P.] QUEEN   O, confound the rest!
155   Such love must needs be treason in my breast.
    In second husband let me be accurs'd!
    None wed the second but who kill'd the first.
   HAMLET [*aside*]   That's wormwood!
   [P.] QUEEN   The instances that second marriage move
160   Are base respects of thrift, but none of love.
    A second time I kill my husband dead,
    When second husband kisses me in bed.
   [P.] KING   I do believe you think what now you speak,
    But what we do determine, oft we break.
165   Purpose is but the slave to memory,
    Of violent birth, but poor validity,
    Which now, the fruit unripe, sticks on the tree,
    But fall unshaken when they mellow be.
    Most necessary 'tis that we forget
170   To pay ourselves what to ourselves is debt.

---

135. **Hymen:** god of marriage   136. **bands:** bonds   141. **distrust:** fear for   143. **hold quantity:** are related in direct proportion   145. **proof:** experience   150. **operant:** active, vital   **leave to do:** cease to perform   154. **confound the rest:** May destruction befall what you are about to speak of— a second marriage on my part.   159. **instances:** motives   **move:** give rise to   160. **respects of thrift:** considerations of advantage   166. **validity:** strength, power to last   169–70. **Most . . . debt:** Such resolutions are debts we owe to ourselves, and it would be foolish to pay such debts.

What to ourselves in passion we propose,
The passion ending, doth the purpose lose.
The violence of either grief or joy
Their own enactures with themselves destroy.
175   Where joy most revels, grief doth most lament;
Grief [joys], joy grieves, on slender accident.
This world is not for aye, nor 'tis not strange
That even our loves should with our fortunes change:
For 'tis a question left us yet to prove,
180   Whether love lead fortune, or else fortune love.
The great man down, you mark his favorite flies,
The poor advanc'd makes friends of enemies.
And hitherto doth love on fortune tend,
For who not needs shall never lack a friend,
185   And who in want a hollow friend doth try,
Directly seasons him his enemy.
But orderly to end where I begun,
Our wills and fates do so contrary run
That our devices still are overthrown,
190   Our thoughts are ours, their ends none of our own:
So think thou wilt no second husband wed,
But die thy thoughts when thy first lord is dead.
[P.] QUEEN   Nor earth to me give food, nor heaven light,
Sport and repose lock from me day and night,
195   To desperation turn my trust and hope,
[An] anchor's cheer in prison be my scope!
Each opposite that blanks the face of joy
Meet what I would have well and it destroy!
Both here and hence pursue me lasting strife,
200   If once I be a widow, ever I be a wife!
HAMLET   If she should break it now!
[P.] KING   'Tis deeply sworn. Sweet, leave me here a while,
My spirits grow dull, and fain I would beguile
The tedious day with sleep.   [*sleeps*]
205 [P.] QUEEN   Sleep rock thy brain,
And never come mischance between us twain!   (*Exit.*)
HAMLET   Madam, how like you this play?
QUEEN   The lady doth protest too much, methinks.

---

171. **passion:** violent emotion   173–74. **The violence . . . destroy:** Both violent grief and violent
joy fail of their intended acts because they destroy themselves by their very violence.   176. **slender
accident:** slight occasion   186. **seasons:** ripens, converts into   189. **devices:** devisings,
intentions   **still:** always   196. **anchor's cheer:** hermit's fare   **my scope:** the extent of my comforts
197. **blanks:** blanches, makes pale (a symptom of grief)

HAMLET   O but she'll keep her word.

210 KING   Have you heard the argument? is there no offense in't?

HAMLET   No, no, they do but jest, poison in jest—no offense i' th' world.

KING   What do you call the play?

HAMLET   "The Mouse-trap." Marry, how? tropically: this play is the image of a murther done in Vienna; Gonzago is the duke's name, his wife, Baptista. You

215   shall see anon. 'Tis a knavish piece of work, but what of that? Your Majesty, and we that have free souls, it touches us not. Let the gall'd jade winch, our withers are unwrung.

(*Enter* LUCIANUS.)

This is one Lucianus, nephew to the king.

OPHELIA   You are as good as a chorus, my lord.

220 HAMLET   I could interpret between you and your love, if I could see the puppets dallying.

OPHELIA   You are keen, my lord, you are keen.

HAMLET   It would cost you a groaning to take off mine edge.

OPHELIA   Still better, and worse.

225 HAMLET   So you mistake your husbands. Begin, murtherer, leave thy damnable faces and begin. Come, the croaking raven doth bellow for revenge.

LUCIANUS   Thoughts black, hands apt, drugs fit, and time agreeing,
    [Confederate] season, else no creature seeing,
    Thou mixture rank, of midnight weeds collected,

230   With Hecat's ban thrice blasted, thrice [infected],
    Thy natural magic and dire property
    On wholesome life usurps immediately.

[*pours the poison in his ears*]

HAMLET   'A poisons him i' th' garden for his estate. His name's Gonzago, the story is extant, and written in very choice Italian. You shall see anon how the

235   murtherer gets the love of Gonzago's wife.

---

210. **offense:** offensive matter (but Hamlet quibbles on the sense "crime")   211. **jest:** pretend
213. **tropically:** figuratively (with play on *tropically*—which is the reading of Q1—and probably with allusion to the children's saying *marry trap*, meaning "now you're caught")   **image:** representation   216. **free souls:** clear consciences   **gall'd jade:** chafed horse   **winch:** wince   217. **withers:** ridge between a horse's shoulders.   **unwrung:** not rubbed sore   219. **chorus:** one who explains the forthcoming action   220–21. **I . . . dallying:** I could speak the dialogue between you and your lover like a puppet-master (with an indecent jest).   222. **keen:** bitter, sharp   224. **better, and worse:** more pointed and less decent   225. **So:** "for better, for worse," in the words of the marriage service   **mistake:** mis-take, take wrongfully. Their vows, Hamlet suggests, prove false.   226. **faces:** facial expressions   **the croaking . . . revenge:** misquoted from an old play, *The True Tragedy of Richard III*   228. **Confederate season:** the time being my ally   230. **Hecat's ban:** the curse of Hecate, goddess of witchcraft

OPHELIA   The King rises.

[HAMLET   What, frighted with false fire?]

QUEEN   How fares my lord?

POLONIUS   Give o'er the play.

240 KING   Give me some light. Away!

POLONIUS   Lights, lights, lights!

(*Exeunt all but* HAMLET *and* HORATIO.)

HAMLET   "Why, let the strooken deer go weep,
　　　　　The hart ungalled play,
　　　　For some must watch while some
245　　　　　　must sleep,
　　　　　Thus runs the world away."
　　　　Would not this, sir, and a forest of feathers—if the rest of my fortunes turn
　　　　Turk with me—with [two] Provincial roses on my raz'd shoes, get me a
　　　　fellowship in a cry of players?

250 HORATIO   Half a share.

HAMLET   A whole one, I.
　　　　　"For thou dost know, O Damon dear,
　　　　　　This realm dismantled was
　　　　　Of Jove himself, and now reigns here
255　　　　　　A very, very"—pajock.

HORATIO   You might have rhym'd.

HAMLET   O good Horatio, I'll take the ghost's word for a thousand pound.
　　　　Didst perceive?

HORATIO   Very well, my lord.

260 HAMLET   Upon the talk of the pois'ning?

HORATIO   I did very well note him.

HAMLET   Ah, ha! Come, some music! Come, the recorders!
　　　　　For if the King like not the comedy,
　　　　　Why then belike he likes it not, perdy.
265　　　　Come, some music!

(*Enter* ROSENCRANTZ *and* GUILDENSTERN.)

GUILDENSTERN   Good my lord, voutsafe me a word with you.

HAMLET   Sir, a whole history.

---

237. **false fire:** a blank cartridge   242. **strooken:** struck, wounded   243. **ungalled:** un-
wounded   244. **watch:** stay awake   247. **feathers:** the plumes worn by tragic actors   248. **turn
Turk:** go to the bad   **Provincial roses:** rosettes designed to look like a variety of French rose
raz'd: with decorating slashing   249. **fellowship:** partnership **cry:** company   253. **dismantled:**
divested, deprived   255. **pajock:** peacock (substituting for the rhyme-word *ass*). The natural history of the time attributed many vicious qualities to the peacock.   264. **perdy:** assuredly (French
pardieu, "by God")

GUILDENSTERN   The King, sir—

HAMLET   Ay, sir, what of him?

270 GUILDENSTERN   Is in his retirement marvellous distemp'red.

HAMLET   With drink, sir?

GUILDENSTERN   No, my lord, with choler.

HAMLET   Your wisdom should show itself more richer to signify this to the doctor, for for me to put him to his purgation would perhaps plunge him

275   into more choler.

GUILDENSTERN   Good my lord, put your discourse into some frame, and [start] not so wildly from my affair.

HAMLET   I am tame, sir. Pronounce.

GUILDENSTERN   The Queen, your mother, in most great affliction of spirit,

280   hath sent me to you.

HAMLET   You are welcome.

GUILDENSTERN   Nay, good my lord, this courtesy is not of the right breed. If it shall please you to make me a wholesome answer, I will do your mother's commandement; if not, your pardon and my return shall be the end of [my]

285   business.

HAMLET   Sir, I cannot.

ROSENCRANTZ   What, my lord?

HAMLET   Make you a wholesome answer—my wit's diseas'd. But, sir, such answer as I can make, you shall command, or rather, as you say, my mother.

290   Therefore no more, but to the matter: my mother, you say—

ROSENCRANTZ   Then thus she says: your behavior hath strook her into amazement and admiration.

HAMLET   O wonderful son, that can so stonish a mother! But is there no sequel at the heels of this mother's admiration? Impart.

295 ROSENCRANTZ   She desires to speak with you in her closet ere you go to bed.

HAMLET   We shall obey, were she ten times our mother. Have you any further trade with us?

ROSENCRANTZ   My lord, you once did love me.

HAMLET   And do still, by these pickers and stealers.

300 ROSENCRANTZ   Good my lord, what is your cause of distemper? You do surely bar the door upon your own liberty if you deny your griefs to your friend.

HAMLET   Sir, I lack advancement.

ROSENCRANTZ   How can that be, when you have the voice of the King himself for your succession in Denmark?

---

272. **choler:** anger (but Hamlet willfully takes up the word in the sense "biliousness")
274. **put . . . purgation:** prescribe for what's wrong with him   276. **frame:** logical structure
283. **wholesome:** sensible, rational   284. **pardon:** permission for departure
291–92. **amazement and admiration:** bewilderment and wonder   293. **stonish:** astound
295. **closet:** private room   299. **pickers and stealers:** hands, which, as the Catechism says, we must keep "from picking and stealing"

305 HAMLET   Ay, sir, but "While the grass grows"—the proverb is something
      musty.

(*Enter the* PLAYERS *with recorders.*)

      O, the recorders! Let me see one.—To withdraw with you—why do you go
      about to recover the wind of me, as if you would drive me into a toil?
      GUILDENSTERN   O my lord, if my duty be too bold, my love is too unmannerly.
310 HAMLET   I do not well understand that. Will you play upon this pipe?
      GUILDENSTERN   My lord, I cannot.
      HAMLET   I pray you.
      GUILDENSTERN   Believe me, I cannot.
      HAMLET   I do beseech you.
315 GUILDENSTERN   I know no touch of it, my lord.
      HAMLET   It is as easy as lying. Govern these ventages with your fingers and
      [thumbs], give it breath with your mouth, and it will discourse most elo-
      quent music. Look you, these are the stops.
      GUILDENSTERN   But these cannot I command to any utt'rance of harmony. I
320   have not the skill.
      HAMLET   Why, look you now, how unworthy a thing you make of me! You
      would play upon me, you would seem to know my stops, you would pluck
      out the heart of my mystery, you would sound me from my lowest note to
      [the top of] my compass; and there is much music, excellent voice, in this
325   little organ, yet cannot you make it speak. 'Sblood, do you think I am easier
      to be play'd on than a pipe? Call me what instrument you will, though you
      fret me, [yet] you cannot play upon me.

(*Enter* POLONIUS.)

      God bless you, sir.
      POLONIUS   My lord, the Queen would speak with you, and presently.
330 HAMLET   Do you see yonder cloud that's almost in shape of a camel?
      POLONIUS   By th' mass and 'tis, like a camel indeed.
      HAMLET   Methinks it is like a weasel.
      POLONIUS   It is back'd like a weasel.
      HAMLET   Or like a whale.
335 POLONIUS   Very like a whale.
      HAMLET   Then I will come to my mother by and by. [*aside*] They fool me to
      the top of my bent.—I will come by and by.
      POLONIUS   I will say so.   [*Exit.*]

---

305. proverb: "While the grass grows, the steed starves."   305–306. something musty: somewhat
stale 308. recover the wind: get to windward toil: snare 316. ventages: stops 325. organ: instrument 327. fret: (1) finger (an instrument); (2) vex 329. presently: at once 336–337. They
. . . bent: They make me play the fool to the limit of my ability. 337. by and by: at once

HAMLET "By and by" is easily said. Leave me, friends. [*Exeunt all but*
340   HAMLET.]
       'Tis now the very witching time of night,
       When churchyards yawn and hell itself [breathes] out
       Contagion to this world. Now could I drink hot blood,
       And do such [bitter business as the] day
345   Would quake to look on. Soft, now to my mother.
       O heart, lose not thy nature! let not ever
       The soul of Nero enter this firm bosom,
       Let me be cruel, not unnatural;
       I will speak [daggers] to her, but use none.
350   My tongue and soul in this be hypocrites—
       How in my words somever she be shent,
       To give them seals never my soul consent!

(*Exit.*)

[Scene III]

(*Enter* KING, ROSENCRANTZ, *and* GUILDENSTERN.)

KING   I like him not, nor stands it safe with us
        To let his madness range. Therefore prepare you.
        I your commission will forthwith dispatch,
        And he to England shall along with you.
5   The terms of our estate may not endure
        Hazard so near 's as doth hourly grow
        Out of his brows.
GUILDENSTERN   We will ourselves provide.
        Most holy and religious fear it is
10   To keep those many many bodies safe
        That live and feed upon your Majesty.
ROSENCRANTZ   The single and peculiar life is bound
        With all the strength and armor of the mind
        To keep itself from noyance, but much more
15   That spirit upon whose weal depends and rests
        The lives of many. The cess of majesty
        Dies not alone, but like a gulf doth draw

---

341. **witching:** when the powers of evil are at large   346. **nature:** natural affection, filial feeling
347. **Nero:** murderer of his mother   351. **shent:** rebuked   352. **give them seals:** confirm them by
deeds

III.iii. Location: the castle   1. **him:** his state of mind, his behavior   3. **dispatch:** have drawn up
5. **terms:** conditions, nature   **our estate:** my position (as king)   7. **his brows:** the madness visible
in his face (?)   9. **fear:** concern   12. **single and peculiar:** individual and private   14. **noyance:** injury   16. **cess:** cessation, death   17. **gulf:** whirlpool

What's near it with it. Or it is a massy wheel
Fix'd on the summit of the highest mount,
20   To whose [huge] spokes ten thousand lesser things
Are mortis'd and adjoin'd, which when it falls,
Each small annexment, petty consequence,
Attends the boist'rous [ruin]. Never alone
Did the King sigh, but [with] a general groan.
25 KING   Arm you, I pray you, to this speedy viage,
For we will fetters put about this fear,
Which now goes too free-footed.
ROSENCRANTZ   We will haste us.

(*Exeunt* GENTLEMEN [ROSENCRANTZ *and* GUILDENSTERN].)

(*Enter* POLONIUS.)

POLONIUS   My lord, he's going to his mother's closet.
30   Behind the arras I'll convey myself
To hear the process. I'll warrant she'll tax him home,
And as you said, and wisely was it said,
'Tis meet that some more audience than a mother,
Since nature makes them partial, should o'erhear
35   The speech, of vantage. Fare you well, my liege,
I'll call upon you ere you go to bed,
And tell you what I know.
KING   Thanks, dear my lord.

(*Exit* [POLONIUS].)

O, my offense is rank, it smells to heaven,
40   It hath the primal eldest curse upon't,
A brother's murther. Pray can I not,
Though inclination be as sharp as will.
My stronger guilt defeats my strong intent,
And, like a man to double business bound,
45   I stand in pause where I shall first begin,
And both neglect. What if this cursed hand
Were thicker than itself with brother's blood,
Is there not rain enough in the sweet heavens

---

21. **mortis'd:** fixed   23. **Attends:** accompanies   **ruin:** fall   25. **Arm:** prepare   **viage:** voyage
26. **fear:** object of fear   31. **process:** course of the talk   **tax him home:** take him severely to task
35. **of vantage:** from an advantageous position (?) or in addition (?)   40. **primal eldest curse:**
God's curse on Cain, who also slew his brother   42. **Though . . . will:** though my desire is as strong
as my resolve to do so   44. **bound:** committed   46. **neglect:** omit

To wash it white as snow? Whereto serves mercy
50 But to confront the visage of offense?
And what's in prayer but this twofold force,
To be forestalled ere we come to fall,
Or [pardon'd] being down? then I'll look up.
My fault is past, but, O, what form of prayer
55 Can serve my turn? "Forgive me my foul murther"?
That cannot be, since I am still possess'd
Of those effects for which I did the murther:
My crown, mine own ambition, and my queen.
May one be pardon'd and retain th' offense?
60 In the corrupted currents of this world
Offense's gilded hand may [shove] by justice,
And oft 'tis seen the wicked prize itself
Buys out the law, but 'tis not so above:
There is no shuffling, there the action lies
65 In his true nature, and we ourselves compell'd,
Even to the teeth and forehead of our faults,
To give in evidence. What then? What rests?
Try what repentance can. What can it not?
Yet what can it, when one can not repent?
70 O wretched state! O bosom black as death!
O limed soul, that struggling to be free
Art more engag'd! Help, angels! Make assay,
Bow, stubborn knees, and heart, with strings of steel,
Be soft as sinews of the new-born babe!
75 All may be well.   [*He kneels.*]

(*Enter* HAMLET.)

HAMLET   Now might I do it [pat], now 'a is a-praying;
And now I'll do't—and so 'a goes to heaven,
And so am I [reveng'd]. That would be scann'd:
A villain kills my father, and for that
80 I, his sole son, do this same villain send
To heaven.
Why, this is [hire and salary], not revenge.

49–50. **Whereto . . . offense:** what function has mercy except when there has been sin   59. **th' offense:** the "effects" or fruits of the offense   60. **currents:** courses   61. **gilded:** bribing   62. **wicked
prize:** rewards of vice   64. **shuffling:** evasion   **the action lies:** the charge comes for legal consideration   66. **Even . . . forehead:** fully recognizing their features, extenuating nothing   67. **rests:** remains   71. **limed:** caught (as in birdlime, a sticky substance used for catching birds)   72. **engag'd:**
entangled   78. **would be scann'd:** must be carefully considered

'A took my father grossly, full of bread,
With all his crimes broad blown, as flush as May,
85 And how his audit stands who knows save heaven?
But in our circumstance and course of thought
'Tis heavy with him. And am I then revenged,
To take him in the purging of his soul,
When he is fit and season'd for his passage?
90 No!
Up, sword, and know thou a more horrid hent:
When he is drunk asleep, or in his rage,
Or in th' incestious pleasure of his bed,
At game a-swearing, or about some act
95 That has no relish of salvation in't—
Then trip him, that his heels may kick at heaven,
And that his soul may be as damn'd and black
As hell, whereto it goes. My mother stays,
This physic but prolongs thy sickly days.   (*Exit.*)
100 KING [*rising*]   My words fly up, my thoughts remain below:
Words without thoughts never to heaven go.

(*Exit.*)

[Scene IV]

(*Enter* [QUEEN] GERTRUDE *and* POLONIUS.)

POLONIUS   'A will come straight. Look you lay home to him.
Tell him his pranks have been too broad to bear with,
And that your Grace hath screen'd and stood between
Much heat and him. I'll silence me even here;
5 Pray you be round [with him].
QUEEN   I'll [warr'nt] you, fear me not. Withdraw,
I hear him coming.   [POLONIUS *hides behind the arras.*]

(*Enter* HAMLET.)

HAMLET   Now, mother, what's the matter?
QUEEN   Hamlet, thou hast thy father much offended.

---

83. **grossly:** in a gross state; not spiritually prepared   84. **crimes:** sins   **broad blown:** in full bloom   **flush:** lusty, vigorous   85. **audit:** account   86. **in . . . thought:** to the best of our knowledge and belief   91. **Up:** into the sheath   **know . . . hent:** be grasped at a more dreadful time   95. **relish:** trace   99. **physic:** (attempted) remedy, prayer.

III.iv. Location: the queen's closet in the castle   1. **lay . . . him:** reprove him severely   2. **broad:** unrestrained   5. **round:** plain-spoken   6. **fear me not:** have no fears about my handling of the situation

10   HAMLET   Mother, you have my father much offended.

QUEEN   Come, come, you answer with an idle tongue.

HAMLET   Go, go, you question with a wicked tongue.

QUEEN   Why, how now, Hamlet?

HAMLET   What's the matter now?

15   QUEEN   Have you forgot me?

HAMLET   No, by the rood, not so:
You are the Queen, your husband's brother's wife,
And would it were not so, you are my mother.

QUEEN   Nay, then I'll set those to you that can speak.

20   HAMLET   Come, come, and sit you down, you shall not boudge;
You go not till I set you up a glass
Where you may see the [inmost] part of you.

QUEEN   What wilt thou do? Thou wilt not murther me?
Help ho!

25   POLONIUS [*behind*]   What ho, help!

HAMLET [*drawing*]   How now? A rat? Dead, for a ducat, dead!   [*Kills* POLO-
NIUS *through the arras.*]

POLONIUS [*behind*]   O, I am slain.

QUEEN   O me, what hast thou done?

30   HAMLET   Nay, I know not, is it the King?

QUEEN   O, what a rash and bloody deed is this!

HAMLET   A bloody deed! almost as bad, good mother,
As kill a king, and marry with his brother.

QUEEN   As kill a king!

35   HAMLET   Ay, lady, it was my word.

[*parts the arras and discovers* POLONIUS]

Thou wretched, rash, intruding fool, farewell!
I took thee for thy better. Take thy fortune;
Thou find'st to be too busy is some danger.—
Leave wringing of your hands. Peace, sit you down,
40   And let me wring your heart, for so I shall
If it be made of penetrable stuff,
If damned custom have not brass'd it so
That it be proof and bulwark against sense.

QUEEN   What have I done, that thou dar'st wag thy tongue
45   In noise so rude against me?

HAMLET   Such an act
That blurs the grace and blush of modesty,

---

11. **idle:** foolish   16. **rood:** cross   20. **boudge:** budge   26. **for a ducat:** I'll wager a ducat
38. **busy:** officious, meddlesome   42. **damned custom:** the habit of ill-doing   **brass'd:** hardened,
literally, plated with brass   43. **proof:** armor   **sense:** feeling

Calls virtue hypocrite, takes off the rose
From the fair forehead of an innocent love
50 And sets a blister there, makes marriage vows
As false as dicers' oaths, O, such a deed
As from the body of contraction plucks
The very soul, and sweet religion makes
A rhapsody of words. Heaven's face does glow
55 O'er this solidity and compound mass
With heated visage, as against the doom;
Is thought-sick at the act.
QUEEN   Ay me, what act,
That roars so loud and thunders in the index?
60 HAMLET   Look here upon this picture, and on this,
The counterfeit presentment of two brothers.
See what a grace was seated on this brow:
Hyperion's curls, the front of Jove himself,
An eye like Mars, to threaten and command,
65 A station like the herald Mercury
New lighted on a [heaven-]kissing hill,
A combination and a form indeed,
Where every god did seem to set his seal
To give the world assurance of a man.
70 This was your husband. Look you now what follows:
Here is your husband, like a mildewed ear,
Blasting his wholesome brother. Have you eyes?
Could you not on this fair mountain leave to feed,
And batten on this moor? ha, have you eyes?
75 You cannot call it love, for at your age
The heyday in the blood is tame, it's humble,
And waits upon the judgment, and what judgment
Would step from this to this? Sense sure you have,
Else could you not have motion, but sure that sense
80 Is apoplex'd, for madness would not err,
Nor sense to ecstasy was ne'er so thrall'd
But it reserv'd some quantity of choice
To serve in such a difference. What devil was't

---

50. **blister:** brand of shame   52. **contraction:** the making of contracts, the assuming of solemn obligation   53. **religion:** sacred vows   54. **rhapsody:** miscellaneous collection, jumble   **glow:** with anger   55. **this . . . mass:** the earth; *compound* = compounded of the four elements   56. **as . . . doom:** as if for Judgment Day   59. **index:** table of contents. The index was formerly placed at the beginning of a book.   61. **counterfeit presentment:** painted likenesses   63. **Hyperion's:** the sun-god's   **front:** forehead   65. **station:** bearing   71. **ear:** of grain   74. **batten:** gorge   76. **heyday:** excitement   78. **Sense:** sense perception, the five senses   80. **apoplex'd:** paralyzed   80–83. **madness . . . difference:** Madness itself could not go so far astray, nor were the senses ever so enslaved by lunacy that they did not retain the power to make so obvious a distinction.

That thus hath cozen'd you at hoodman-blind?
85   Eyes without feeling, feeling without sight,
Ears without hands or eyes, smelling sans all,
Or but a sickly part of one true sense
Could not so mope. O shame, where is thy blush?
Rebellious hell,
90   If thou canst mutine in a matron's bones,
To flaming youth let virtue be as wax
And melt in her own fire. Proclaim no shame
When the compulsive ardure gives the charge,
Since frost itself as actively doth burn,
95   And reason [panders] will.

QUEEN   O Hamlet, speak no more!
Thou turn'st my [eyes into my very] soul,
And there I see such black and [grained] spots
As will [not] leave their tinct.

100   HAMLET   Nay, but to live
In the rank sweat of an enseamed bed,
Stew'd in corruption, honeying and making love
Over the nasty sty!

QUEEN   O, speak to me no more!
105   These words like daggers enter in my ears.
No more, sweet Hamlet!

HAMLET   A murtherer and a villain!
A slave that is not twentith part the [tithe]
Of your precedent lord, a Vice of kings,
110   A cutpurse of the empire and the rule,
That from a shelf the precious diadem stole,
And put it in his pocket—

QUEEN   No more!

(*Enter* GHOST [*in his night-gown*].)

HAMLET   A king of shreds and patches—
115   Save me, and hover o'er me with your wings,
You heavenly guards! What would your gracious figure?

QUEEN   Alas, he's mad!

---

84. **cozen'd:** cheated   **hoodman-blind:** blindman's bluff   86. **sans:** without   88. **mope:** be dazed
90. **mutine:** rebel   92–95. **Proclaim . . . will:** Do not call it sin when the hot blood of youth is responsible for lechery, since here we see people of calmer age on fire for it; and reason acts as procurer for desire, instead of restraining it. *Ardure* = ardor   98. **grained:** fast-dyed, indelible   99. **leave their tinct:** lose their color   101. **enseamed:** greasy   108. **twentith:** twentieth   109. **precedent:** former   **Vice:** buffoon (like the Vice of the morality plays)   s.d. **night-gown:** dressing gown
114. **of . . . patches:** clownish (alluding to the motley worn by jesters) (?) or patched-up, beggarly (?)

HAMLET   Do you not come your tardy son to chide,
 That, laps'd in time and passion, lets go by
120 Th' important acting of your dread command?
 O, say!
GHOST   Do not forget! This visitation
 Is but to whet thy almost blunted purpose.
 But look, amazement on thy mother sits,
125 O, step between her and her fighting soul.
 Conceit in weakest bodies strongest works,
 Speak to her, Hamlet.
HAMLET   How is it with you, lady?
QUEEN   Alas, how is't with you,
130 That you do bend your eye on vacancy,
 And with th' incorporal air do hold discourse?
 Forth at your eyes your spirits wildly peep,
 And as the sleeping soldiers in th' alarm,
 Your bedded hair, like life in excrements,
135 Start up and stand an end. O gentle son,
 Upon the heat and flame of thy distemper
 Sprinkle cool patience. Whereon do you look?
HAMLET   On him, on him! look you how pale he glares!
 His form and cause conjoin'd, preaching to stones,
140 Would make them capable.—Do not look upon me,
 Lest with this piteous action you convert
 My stern effects, then what I have to do
 Will want true color—tears perchance for blood.
QUEEN   To whom do you speak this?
145 HAMLET   Do you see nothing there?
QUEEN   Nothing at all, yet all that is I see.
HAMLET   Nor did you nothing hear?
QUEEN   No, nothing but ourselves.
HAMLET   Why, look you there, look how it steals away!
150 My father, in his habit as he lived!
 Look where he goes, even now, out at the portal!

(*Exit* GHOST.)

---

119. **laps'd . . . passion:** "having suffered time to slip and passion to cool" (Johnson) 120. **important:** urgent 124. **amazement:** utter bewilderment 126. **Conceit:** imagination 133. **in th'
alarm:** when the call to arms is sounded 134. **excrements:** outgrowths; here, hair (also used of
nails) 135. **an end:** on end 137. **patience:** self-control 139. **His . . . cause:** his appearance and
what he has to say 140. **capable:** sensitive, receptive 141. **convert:** alter 142. **effects:** (pur-
posed) actions 143. **want true color:** lack its proper appearance 150. **habit:** dress

QUEEN   This is the very coinage of your brain,
This bodiless creation ecstasy
Is very cunning in.
155   HAMLET   [Ecstasy?]
My pulse as yours doth temperately keep time,
And makes as healthful music. It is not madness
That I have utt'red. Bring me to the test,
And [I] the matter will reword, which madness
160   Would gambol from. Mother, for love of grace,
Lay not that flattering unction to your soul,
That not your trespass but my madness speaks;
It will but skin and film the ulcerous place,
Whiles rank corruption, mining all within,
165   Infects unseen. Confess yourself to heaven,
Repent what's past, avoid what is to come,
And do not spread the compost on the weeds
To make them ranker. Forgive me this my virtue,
For in the fatness of these pursy times
170   Virtue itself of vice must pardon beg,
Yea, curb and woo for leave to do him good.
QUEEN   O Hamlet, thou hast cleft my heart in twain.
HAMLET   O, throw away the worser part of it,
And [live] the purer with the other half.
175   Good night, but go not to my uncle's bed—
Assume a virtue, if you have it not.
That monster custom, who all sense doth eat,
Of habits devil, is angel yet in this,
That to the use of actions fair and good
180   He likewise gives a frock or livery
That aptly is put on. Refrain [to-]night,
And that shall lend a kind of easiness
To the next abstinence, the next more easy;
For use almost can change the stamp of nature,
185   And either [. . . .] the devil or throw him out
With wondrous potency. Once more good night,

---

153. **ecstasy:** madness   160. **gambol:** start, jerk away   161. **flattering unction:** soothing ointment
167. **compost:** manure   169. **pursy:** puffy, out of condition   171. **curb and woo:** bow and entreat
177. **all . . . eat:** wears away all natural feeling   178. **Of habits devil:** though it acts like a devil in establishing bad habits. Most editors read (in lines 171–178) *eat / Of habits evil,* following Theobald.
180–81. **frock . . . on:** a "habit" or customary garment, readily put on without need of any
decision   184. **use:** habit   185. A word seems to be wanting after *either.*

And when you are desirous to be blest,
I'll blessing beg of you. For this same lord,

[*pointing to* POLONIUS]

190   I do repent; but heaven hath pleas'd it so
To punish me with this, and this with me,
That I must be their scourge and minister.
I will bestow him, and will answer well
The death I gave him. So again good night.
I must be cruel only to be kind.
195   This bad begins and worse remains behind.
One word more, good lady.

QUEEN   What shall I do?

HAMLET   Not this, by no means, that I bid you do:
Let the bloat king tempt you again to bed,
200   Pinch wanton on your cheek, call you his mouse,
And let him, for a pair of reechy kisses,
Or paddling in your neck with his damn'd fingers,
Make you to ravel all this matter out,
That I essentially am not in madness,
205   But mad in craft. 'Twere good you let him know,
For who that's but a queen, fair, sober, wise,
Would from a paddock, from a bat, a gib,
Such dear concernings hide? Who would do so?
No, in despite of sense and secrecy,
210   Unpeg the basket on the house's top,
Let the birds fly, and like the famous ape,
To try conclusions in the basket creep,
And break your own neck down.

QUEEN   Be thou assur'd, if words be made of breath,
215   And breath of life, I have no life to breathe
What thou hast said to me.

HAMLET   I must to England, you know that?

QUEEN   Alack,
I had forgot. 'Tis so concluded on.

---

187. **desirous . . . blest:** repentant   191. **scourge and minister:** the agent of heavenly justice against human crime. *Scourge* suggests a permissive cruelty (Tamburlaine was the "scourge of God"), but "woe to him by whom the offense cometh"; the scourge must suffer for the evil it performs.
192. **bestow:** dispose of **answer:** answer for   195. **behind:** to come   201. **reechy:** filthy
207. **paddock:** toad **gib:** tom-cat 208. **dear concernings:** matters of intense concern
210. **Unpeg the basket:** open the door of the cage 211. **famous ape:** The actual story has been lost.
212. **conclusions:** experiments (to see whether he too can fly if he enters the cage and then leaps out) 213. **down:** by the fall

220 HAMLET   There's letters seal'd, and my two schoolfellows,
     Whom I will trust as I will adders fang'd,
     They bear the mandate, they must sweep my way
     And marshal me to knavery. Let it work,
     For 'tis the sport to have the enginer
225   Hoist with his own petar, an't shall go hard
     But I will delve one yard below their mines,
     And blow them at the moon. O, 'tis most sweet
     When in one line two crafts directly meet.
     This man shall set me packing;
230   I'll lug the guts into the neighbor room.
     Mother, good night indeed. This counsellor
     Is now most still, most secret, and most grave,
     Who was in life a foolish prating knave.
     Come, sir, to draw toward an end with you.
235   Good night, mother.

(*Exeunt* [*severally,* HAMLET *tugging in* POLONIUS].)

Act IV

Scene I

(*Enter* KING *and* QUEEN *with* ROSENCRANTZ *and* GUILDENSTERN.)

KING   There's matter in these sighs, these profound heaves—
     You must translate, 'tis fit we understand them.
     Where is your son?
QUEEN   Bestow this place on us a little while.

[*Exeunt* ROSENCRANTZ *and* GUILDENSTERN.]

5   Ah, mine own lord, what have I seen to-night!
KING   What, Gertrude? How does Hamlet?
QUEEN   Mad as the sea and wind when both contend
     Which is the mightier. In his lawless fit,
     Behind the arras hearing something stir,
10   Whips out his rapier, cries, "A rat, a rat!"
     And in this brainish apprehension kills
     The unseen good old man.

---

223. **knavery:** some knavish scheme against me.   224. **enginer:** deviser of military "engines" or contrivances   225. **Hoist with:** blown up by   **petar:** petard, bomb   228. **crafts:** plots   229. **packing:** (1) taking on a load; (2) leaving in a hurry   234. **draw...end:** finish my conversation

IV.i. Location: the castle   11. **brainish apprehension:** crazy notion

KING　　　　　　　　　　　　　O heavy deed!
　　　　It had been so with us had we been there.
15　　　His liberty is full of threats to all,
　　　　To you yourself, to us, to every one.
　　　　Alas, how shall this bloody deed be answer'd?
　　　　It will be laid to us, whose providence
　　　　Should have kept short, restrain'd, and out of haunt
20　　　This mad young man; but so much was our love,
　　　　We would not understand what was most fit,
　　　　But like the owner of a foul disease,
　　　　To keep it from divulging, let it feed
　　　　Even on the pith of life. Where is he gone?
25　QUEEN　To draw apart the body he hath kill'd,
　　　　O'er whom his very madness, like some ore
　　　　Among a mineral of metals base,
　　　　Shows itself pure: 'a weeps for what is done.
　　KING　O Gertrude, come away!
30　　　The sun no sooner shall the mountains touch,
　　　　But we will ship him hence, and this vile deed
　　　　We must with all our majesty and skill
　　　　Both countenance and excuse. Ho, Guildenstern!

(*Enter* ROSENCRANTZ *and* GUILDENSTERN.)

　　　　Friends both, go join you with some further aid:
35　　　Hamlet in madness hath Polonius slain,
　　　　And from his mother's closet hath he dragg'd him.
　　　　Go seek him out, speak fair, and bring the body
　　　　Into the chapel. I pray you haste in this.

[*Exeunt* ROSENCRANTZ *and* GUILDENSTERN.]

　　　　Come, Gertrude, we'll call up our wisest friends
40　　　And let them know both what we mean to do
　　　　And what's untimely done, [. . . .]
　　　　Whose whisper o'er the world's diameter,
　　　　As level as the cannon to his blank,
　　　　Transports his pois'ned shot, may miss our name,
45　　　And hit the woundless air. O, come away!
　　　　My soul is full of discord and dismay.

---

17. **answer'd:** satisfactorily accounted for to the public　18. **providence:** foresight　19. **short:** on a short leash　**out of haunt:** away from other people　23. **divulging:** being revealed　26. **ore:** vein of gold　27. **mineral:** mine　41. Some words are wanting at the end of the line. Capell's conjecture, *so, haply, slander,* probably indicates the intended sense of the passage.　43. **As level:** with aim as good　**blank:** target　45. **woundless:** incapable of being hurt

(*Exeunt.*)

[Scene II]

(*Enter* HAMLET.)

HAMLET   Safely stow'd.
[GENTLEMEN. (*Within.*)   Hamlet! Lord Hamlet!]
[HAMLET]   But soft, what noise? Who calls on Hamlet? O, here they come.

(*Enter* ROSENCRANTZ *and* [GUILDENSTERN].)

ROSENCRANTZ   What have you done, my lord, with the dead body?
5 HAMLET   [Compounded] it with dust, whereto 'tis kin.
ROSENCRANTZ   Tell us where 'tis, that we may take it thence,
    And bear it to the chapel.
HAMLET   Do not believe it.
ROSENCRANTZ   Believe what?
10 HAMLET   That I can keep your counsel and not mine own. Besides, to be de-
    manded of a spunge, what replication should be made by the son of a king?
ROSENCRANTZ   Take you me for a spunge, my lord?
HAMLET   Ay, sir, that soaks up the King's countenance, his rewards, his authori-
    ties. But such officers do the King best service in the end: he keeps them, like
15 [an ape] an apple, in the corner of his jaw, first mouth'd, to be last swal-
    low'd. When he needs what you have glean'd, it is but squeezing you, and,
    spunge, you shall be dry again.
ROSENCRANTZ   I understand you not, my lord.
HAMLET   I am glad of it, a knavish speech sleeps in a foolish ear.
20 ROSENCRANTZ   My lord, you must tell us where the body is, and go with us to
    the King.
HAMLET   The body is with the King, but the King is not with the body. The
    King is a thing—
GUILDENSTERN   A thing, my lord?
25 HAMLET   Of nothing, bring me to him. [Hide fox, and all after.]

(*Exeunt.*)

IV.ii. Location: the castle   10–11. **demanded of:** questioned by   11. **spunge:** sponge   **replica-
tion:** reply 13. **countenance:** favor   19. **sleeps:** is meaningless   22. **The body . . . the body:**
possibly alluding to the legal fiction that the king's dignity is separate from his mortal body
25. **Of nothing:** of no account Cf. "Man is like a thing of nought, his time passeth away like a
shadow" (Psalm 144:4 in the Prayer Book version). "Hamlet at once insults the King and hints
that his days are numbered" (Dover Wilson).   **Hide . . . after:** probably a cry in some game resembling hide-and-seek

[Scene III]

(*Enter* KING *and two or three.*)

KING   I have sent to seek him, and to find the body.
How dangerous is it that this man goes loose!
Yet must not we put the strong law on him.
He's lov'd of the distracted multitude,
5   Who like not in their judgment, but their eyes,
And where 'tis so, th' offender's scourge is weigh'd,
But never the offense. To bear all smooth and even,
This sudden sending him away must seem
Deliberate pause. Diseases desperate grown
10   By desperate appliance are reliev'd,
Or not at all.

(*Enter* ROSENCRANTZ.)

How now, what hath befall'n?
ROSENCRANTZ   Where the dead body is bestow'd, my lord,
We cannot get from him.
15 KING   But where is he?
ROSENCRANTZ   Without, my lord, guarded, to know your pleasure.
KING   Bring him before us.
ROSENCRANTZ   Ho, bring in the lord.

(*They* [HAMLET *and* GUILDENSTERN] *enter.*)

KING   Now, Hamlet, where's Polonius?
20 HAMLET   At supper.
KING   At supper? where?
HAMLET   Not where he eats, but where 'a is eaten; a certain convocation of
politic worms are e'en at him. Your worm is your only emperor for diet: we
fat all creatures else to fat us, and we fat ourselves for maggots; your fat king
25   and your lean beggar is but variable service, two dishes, but to one table—
that's the end.
KING   Alas, alas!
HAMLET   A man may fish with the worm that hath eat of a king, and eat of the
fish that hath fed of that worm.
30 KING   What dost thou mean by this?

IV.iii. Location: the castle   4. **distracted:** unstable   6. **scourge:** punishment   7. **bear:** manage
8–9. **must . . . pause:** must be represented as a maturely considered decision   23. **politic:** crafty,
prying; "such worms as might breed in a politician's corpse" (Dowden)   **e'en:** even now   **for diet:**
with respect to what it eats   25. **variable service:** different courses of a meal

HAMLET   Nothing but to show you how a king may go a progress through the
    guts of a beggar.
KING   Where is Polonius?
HAMLET   In heaven, send thither to see; if your messenger find him not there,
35   seek him i' th' other place yourself. But if indeed you find him not within
    this month, you shall nose him as you go up the stairs into the lobby.
KING [*to* ATTENDANTS]   Go seek him there.
HAMLET   'A will stay till you come.

[*Exeunt* ATTENDANTS.]

KING   Hamlet, this deed, for thine especial safety—
40   Which we do tender, as we dearly grieve
    For that which thou hast done—must send thee hence
    [With fiery quickness]; therefore prepare thyself,
    The bark is ready, and the wind at help,
    Th' associates tend, and every thing is bent
45   For England.
HAMLET   For England.
KING   Ay, Hamlet.
HAMLET   Good.
KING   So is it, if thou knew'st our purposes.
50 HAMLET   I see a cherub that sees them. But come, for England! Farewell, dear
    mother.
KING   Thy loving father, Hamlet.
HAMLET   My mother: father and mother is man and wife, man and wife is one
    flesh—so, my mother. Come, for England!   (*Exit.*)
55 KING   Follow him at foot, tempt him with speed aboard.
    Delay it not, I'll have him hence to-night.
    Away, for every thing is seal'd and done
    That else leans on th' affair. Pray you make haste.

[*Exeunt* ROSENCRANTZ *and* GUILDENSTERN.]

    And, England, if my love thou hold'st at aught—
60   As my great power thereof may give thee sense,
    Since yet thy cicatrice looks raw and red
    After the Danish sword, and thy free awe
    Pays homage to us—thou mayst not coldly set

---

31. **progress:** royal journey of state   40. **tender:** regard with tenderness, hold dear **dearly:** with
intense feeling   43. **at help:** favorable   44. **Th':** thy   **tend:** await **bent:** made ready
50. **I . . . them:** heaven sees them   55. **at foot:** at his heels, close behind   58. **leans on:** relates to
59. **England:** king of England   61. **cicatrice:** scar   62–63. **thy . . . Pays:** your fear makes you pay
voluntarily   63. **coldly set:** undervalue, disregard

Our sovereign process, which imports at full,
65   By letters congruing to that effect,
The present death of Hamlet. Do it, England,
For like the hectic in my blood he rages,
And thou must cure me. Till I know 'tis done,
How e'er my haps, my joys [were] ne'er [begun].

(*Exit.*)

[Scene IV]

(*Enter* Fortinbras *with his army over the stage.*)

FORTINBRAS   Go, captain, from me greet the Danish king.
Tell him that by his license Fortinbras
Craves the conveyance of a promis'd march
Over his kingdom. You know the rendezvous.
5   If that his Majesty would aught with us,
We shall express our duty in his eye,
And let him know so.
CAPTAIN   I will do't, my lord.
FORTINBRAS   Go softly on.   [*Exeunt all but the* CAPTAIN.]

(*Enter* HAMLET, ROSENCRANTZ, [GUILDENSTERN,] *etc.*)

10   HAMLET   Good sir, whose powers are these?
   CAPTAIN   They are of Norway, sir.
   HAMLET   How purpos'd, sir, I pray you?
   CAPTAIN   Against some part of Poland.
   HAMLET   Who commands them, sir?
15   CAPTAIN   The nephew to old Norway, Fortinbras.
   HAMLET   Goes it against the main of Poland, sir,
Or for some frontier?
   CAPTAIN   Truly to speak, and with no addition,
We go to gain a little patch of ground
20   That hath in it no profit but the name.
To pay five ducats, five, I would not farm it;
Nor will it yield to Norway or the Pole
A ranker rate, should it be sold in fee.

---

64. **process:** command   65. **congruing to:** in accord with   66. **present:** immediate   67. **hectic:** continuous fever   69. **haps:** fortunes

IV.iv. Location: the Danish coast, near the castle   3. **conveyance of:** escort for   6. **eye:** presence
9. **softly:** slowly   10. **powers:** forces   16. **main:** main territory   21. **To pay:** for an annual rent
of **farm:** lease   23. **ranker:** higher   **in fee:** outright

HAMLET   Why then the Polack never will defend it.
25 CAPTAIN   Yes, it is already garrison'd.
HAMLET   Two thousand souls and twenty thousand ducats
   Will not debate the question of this straw.
   This is th' imposthume of much wealth and peace,
   That inward breaks, and shows no cause without
30   Why the man dies. I humbly thank you, sir.
CAPTAIN   God buy you, sir.   [*Exit.*]
ROSENCRANTZ   Will't please you go, my lord?
HAMLET   I'll be with you straight—go a little before.

[*Exeunt all but* HAMLET.]

   How all occasions do inform against me,
35   And spur my dull revenge! What is a man,
   If his chief good and market of his time
   Be but to sleep and feed? a beast, no more.
   Sure He that made us with such large discourse,
   Looking before and after, gave us not
40   That capability and godlike reason
   To fust in us unus'd. Now whether it be
   Bestial oblivion, or some craven scruple
   Of thinking too precisely on th' event—
   A thought which quarter'd hath but one part wisdom
45   And ever three parts coward—I do not know
   Why yet I live to say, "This thing's to do,"
   Sith I have cause, and will, and strength, and means
   To do't. Examples gross as earth exhort me:
   Witness this army of such mass and charge,
50   Led by a delicate and tender prince,
   Whose spirit with divine ambition puff'd
   Makes mouths at the invisible event,
   Exposing what is mortal and unsure
   To all that fortune, death, and danger dare,
55   Even for an egg-shell. Rightly to be great
   Is not to stir without great argument,
   But greatly to find quarrel in a straw
   When honor's at the stake. How stand I then,
   That have a father kill'd, a mother stain'd,

---

27. **Will not debate:** will scarcely be enough to fight out   28. **imposthume:** abscess   34. **inform against:** denounce, accuse   36. **market:** purchase, profit   38. **discourse:** reasoning power   41. **fust:** grow mouldy   42. **oblivion:** forgetfulness   43. **event:** outcome   48. **gross:** large, obvious   49. **mass and charge:** size and expense   52. **Makes mouths at:** treats scornfully   **invisible:** unforeseeable   56. **Is not to:** is *not* not to   **argument:** cause   57. **greatly:** nobly

60   Excitements of my reason and my blood,
     And let all sleep, while to my shame I see
     The imminent death of twenty thousand men,
     That for a fantasy and trick of fame
     Go to their graves like beds, fight for a plot
65   Whereon the numbers cannot try the cause,
     Which is not tomb enough and continent
     To hide the slain? O, from this time forth,
     My thoughts be bloody, or be nothing worth!

(*Exit.*)

[Scene V]

(*Enter* HORATIO, [QUEEN] GERTRUDE, *and a* GENTLEMAN.)

QUEEN   I will not speak with her.
GENTLEMAN   She is importunate, indeed distract.
     Her mood will needs be pitied.
QUEEN   What would she have?
5 GENTLEMAN   She speaks much of her father, says she hears
     There's tricks i' th' world, and hems, and beats her heart,
     Spurns enviously at straws, speaks things in doubt
     That carry but half sense. Her speech is nothing,
     Yet the unshaped use of it doth move
10   The hearers to collection; they yawn at it,
     And botch the words up fit to their own thoughts,
     Which as her winks and nods and gestures yield them,
     Indeed would make one think there might be thought,
     Though nothing sure, yet much unhappily.
15 HORATIO   'Twere good she were spoken with, for she may strew
     Dangerous conjectures in ill-breeding minds.
     [QUEEN]   Let her come in.   [*Exit* GENTLEMAN.]
     [*aside*] To my sick soul, as sin's true nature is,
     Each toy seems prologue to some great amiss,

---

60. **Excitements of:** urgings by   63. **fantasy:** caprice   **trick:** trifle   65. **Whereon . . . cause:** which isn't large enough to let the opposing armies engage upon it   66. **continent:** container

IV.v. Location: the castle   7. **Spurns . . . straws:** spitefully takes offense at trifles   **in doubt:** obscurely
8. **Her speech:** what she says   9. **unshaped use:** distracted manner   10. **collection:** attempts to
gather the meaning   **yawn at:** gape eagerly (as if to swallow). Most editors adopt the F1 reading *aim at.*   11. **botch:** patch   12. **Which:** the words   13. **thought:** inferred, conjectured   16. **ill-breeding:** conceiving ill thoughts, prone to think the worst   19. **toy:** trifle   **amiss:** calamity

20   So full of artless jealousy is guilt,
        It spills itself in fearing to be spilt.

(*Enter* OPHELIA [*distracted, with her hair down, playing on a lute*].)

OPHELIA   Where is the beauteous majesty of Denmark?
QUEEN   How now, Ophelia?
OPHELIA   "How should I your true-love   (*She sings.*)
25   know
                From another one?
            By his cockle hat and staff,
            And his sandal shoon."
QUEEN   Alas, sweet lady, what imports this song?
30 OPHELIA   Say you? Nay, pray you mark.
                "He is dead and gone, lady,   (*Song.*)
                He is dead and gone,
            At his head a grass-green turf,
            At his heels a stone."
35   O ho!
QUEEN   Nay, but, Ophelia—
OPHELIA   Pray you mark.   [*Sings.*]
            "White his shroud as the mountain snow"—

(*Enter* KING.)

QUEEN   Alas, look here, my lord.
40 OPHELIA   "Larded all with sweet flowers,   (*Song.*)
                Which bewept to the ground did not go
                With true-love showers."
KING   How do you, pretty lady?
OPHELIA   Well, God dild you! They say the owl was a baker's daughter. Lord,
45   we know what we are, but know not what we may be. God be at your table!
KING   Conceit upon her father.
OPHELIA   Pray let's have no words of this, but when they ask you what it
        means, say you this:

---

20. **artless jealousy:** uncontrolled suspicion   21. **spills:** destroys   24–25. These lines resemble a passage in an earlier ballad beginning "As you came from the holy land / Of Walsingham." Probably all the song fragments sung by Ophelia were familiar to the Globe audience, but only one other line (187) is from a ballad still extant.   27. **cockle hat:** hat bearing a cockle shell, the badge of a pilgrim to the shrine of St. James of Compostela in Spain **staff:** another mark of a pilgrim   28. **shoon:** shoes (already an archaic form in Shakespeare's day)   40. **Larded:** adorned   41. **not:** contrary to the expected sense, and unmetrical; explained as Ophelia's alteration of the line to accord with the facts of Polonius' burial (see line 83)   44. **dild:** yield, reward **owl:** alluding to the legend of a baker's daughter whom Jesus turned into an owl because she did not respond generously to his request for bread   46. **Conceit:** fanciful brooding

"To-morrow is Saint Valentine's   (*Song.*)
50   day,
        All in the morning betime,
        And I a maid at your window,
              To be your Valentine.

    "Then up he rose and donn'd his clo'es,
55   And dupp'd the chamber-door,
        Let in the maid, that out a maid
              Never departed more."

KING   Pretty Ophelia!
OPHELIA   Indeed without an oath I'll make an end on't.   [*Sings.*]
60   "By Gis, and by Saint Charity,
              Alack, and fie for shame!
        Young men will do't if they come to't,
              By Cock, they are to blame.

        "Quoth she, 'Before you tumbled me,
65   You promis'd me to wed.'"
                                                  (He answers.)
        " 'So would I 'a' done, by yonder sun,
              And thou hadst not come to my bed.'"

KING   How long hath she been thus?
OPHELIA   I hope all will be well. We must be patient, but I cannot choose but
70   weep to think they would lay him i' th' cold ground. My brother shall know
       of it, and so I thank you for your good counsel. Come, my coach! Good
       night, ladies, good night. Sweet ladies, good night, good night.   [*Exit.*]
KING   Follow her close, give her good watch, I pray you.   [*Exit* HORATIO.]
       O, this is the poison of deep grief, it springs
75   All from her father's death—and now behold!
       O Gertrude, Gertrude,
       When sorrows come, they come not single spies,
       But in battalions: first, her father slain;
       Next, your son gone, and he most violent author
80   Of his own just remove; the people muddied,
       Thick and unwholesome in [their] thoughts and whispers
       For good Polonius' death; and we have done but greenly
       In hugger-mugger to inter him; poor Ophelia
       Divided from herself and her fair judgment,
85   Without the which we are pictures, or mere beasts;
       Last, and as much containing as all these,

---

55. **dupp'd:** opened   60. **Gis:** contraction of *Jesus*   63. **Cock:** corruption of *God*   67. **And:** if
77. **spies:** soldiers sent ahead of the main force to reconnoiter; scouts.   80. **muddied:** confused
82. **greenly:** unwisely   83. **In hugger-mugger:** secretly and hastily

Her brother is in secret come from France,
Feeds on this wonder, keeps himself in clouds,
And wants not buzzers to infect his ear
90   With pestilent speeches of his father's death,
Wherein necessity, of matter beggar'd,
Will nothing stick our person to arraign
In ear and ear. O my dear Gertrude, this,
Like to a murd'ring-piece, in many places
95   Gives me superfluous death.   (*a noise within*)
[QUEEN   Alack, what noise is this?]
KING   Attend!
Where is my Swissers? Let them guard the door.

(*Enter a* MESSENGER.)

What is the matter?
100 MESSENGER   Save yourself, my lord!
The ocean, overpeering of his list,
Eats not the flats with more impiteous haste
Than young Laertes, in a riotous head,
O'erbears your officers. The rabble call him lord,
105   And as the world were now but to begin,
Antiquity forgot, custom not known,
The ratifiers and props of every word,
[They] cry, "Choose we, Laertes shall be king!"
Caps, hands, and tongues applaud it to the clouds,
110   "Laertes shall be king, Laertes king!"   (*a noise within*)
QUEEN   How cheerfully on the false trail they cry!
O, this is counter, you false Danish dogs!

(*Enter* LAERTES *with others.*)

KING   The doors are broke.
LAERTES   Where is this king? Sirs, stand you all without.
115 ALL   No, let's come in.
LAERTES   I pray you give me leave.
ALL   We will, we will.

---

88. **in clouds:** in cloudy surmise and suspicion (rather than the light of fact)   89. **wants:** lacks   **buzzers:** whispering informers   91. **of matter beggar'd:** destitute of facts   92. **nothing . . . arraign:** scruple not at all to charge me with the crime   94. **murd'ring-piece:** cannon firing a scattering charge   98. **Swissers:** Swiss guards   101. **overpeering . . . list:** rising higher than its shores   103. **in . . . head:** with a rebellious force   105. **as:** as if   107. **word:** pledge, promise   112. **counter:** on the wrong scent (literally, following the scent backward)

LAERTES   I thank you, keep the door.   [*Exeunt* LAERTES' *followers.*]   O thou
 vile king,
120 Give me my father!
QUEEN   Calmly, good Laertes.
LAERTES   That drop of blood that's calm proclaims me bastard,
 Cries cuckold to my father, brands the harlot
 Even here between the chaste unsmirched brow
125 Of my true mother.
KING   What is the cause, Laertes,
 That thy rebellion looks so giant-like?
 Let him go, Gertrude, do not fear our person:
 There's such divinity doth hedge a king
130 That treason can but peep to what it would,
 Acts little of his will. Tell me, Laertes,
 Why thou art thus incens'd. Let him go, Gertrude.
 Speak, man.
LAERTES   Where is my father?
135 KING   Dead.
QUEEN   But not by him.
KING   Let him demand his fill.
LAERTES   How came he dead? I'll not be juggled with.
 To hell, allegiance! vows, to the blackest devil!
140 Conscience and grace, to the profoundest pit!
 I dare damnation. To this point I stand,
 That both the worlds I give to negligence,
 Let come what comes, only I'll be reveng'd
 Most throughly for my father.
145 KING   Who shall stay you?
LAERTES   My will, not all the world's:
 And for my means, I'll husband them so well,
 They shall go far with little.
KING   Good Laertes,
150 If you desire to know the certainty
 Of your dear father, is't writ in your revenge
 That, swoopstake, you will draw both friend and foe,
 Winner and loser?
LAERTES   None but his enemies.
155 KING   Will you know them then?

---

128. **fear:** fear for   130. **would:** would like to do   142. **both . . . negligence:** I don't care what the
consequences are in this world or in the next.   144. **throughly:** thoroughly   146. **world's:** world's
will   152. **swoopstake:** sweeping up everything without discrimination (modern *sweepstake*)

LAERTES To his good friends thus wide I'll ope my arms,
And like the kind life-rend'ring pelican,
Repast them with my blood.

KING   Why, now you speak

160   Like a good child and a true gentleman.
That I am guiltless of your father's death,
And am most sensibly in grief for it,
It shall as level to your judgment 'pear
As day does to your eye.

165   (*a noise within:*)   "Let her come in!"

LAERTES How now, what noise is that?

(*Enter* OPHELIA.)

O heat, dry up my brains! tears seven times salt
Burn out the sense and virtue of mine eye!
By heaven, thy madness shall be paid with weight

170   [Till] our scale turn the beam. O rose of May!
Dear maid, kind sister, sweet Ophelia!
O heavens, is't possible a young maid's wits
Should be as mortal as [an old] man's life?
[Nature is fine in love, and where 'tis fine,

175   It sends some precious instance of itself
After the thing it loves.]

OPHELIA   "They bore him barefac'd on the   (*Song.*)
                bier,
           [Hey non nonny, nonny, hey nonny,]

180   And in his grave rain'd many a tear"—
Fare you well, my dove!

LAERTES Hadst thou thy wits and didst persuade revenge,
It could not move thus.

OPHELIA You must sing, "A-down, a-down," and you call him a-down-a.

185   O how the wheel becomes it! It is the false steward, that stole his master's
daughter.

LAERTES This nothing's more than matter.

OPHELIA There's rosemary, that's for remembrance; pray you, love, remember.
And there is pansies, that's for thoughts.

---

157. **pelican:** The female pelican was believed to draw blood from her own breast to nourish her
young.   160. **good child:** faithful son   162. **sensibly:** feelingly   163. **level:** plain   168. **virtue:** faculty
174. **fine in:** refined or spiritualized by   175. **instance:** proof, token. So delicate is Ophelia's love for
her father that her sanity has pursued him into the grave.   182. **persuade:** argue logically for
184. **and . . . a-down-a:** "if he indeed agrees that Polonius is 'a-down,' fallen low" (Dover Wilson)
185. **wheel:** refrain (?) or spinning-wheel, at which women sang ballads (?)   187. **matter:**
lucid speech

190 LAERTES   A document in madness, thoughts and remembrance fitted.

OPHELIA [*to* CLAUDIUS]   There's fennel for you, and columbines. [*to*
GERTRUDE]   There's rue for you, and here's some for me; we may call it
herb of grace a' Sundays. You may wear your rue with a difference. There's a
daisy. I would give you some violets, but they wither'd all when my father

195   died. They say 'a made a good end—   [*sings*]
                    "For bonny sweet Robin is all my joy."

LAERTES   Thought and afflictions, passion, hell itself,
She turns to favor and to prettiness.

OPHELIA   "And will 'a not come again?   (*Song.*)
200   And will 'a not come again?
                        No, no, he is dead,
                        Go to thy death-bed,
                    He never will come again.

                    "His beard was as white as snow,
205   [All] flaxen was his pole,
                        He is gone, he is gone,
                        And we cast away moan,
                    God 'a' mercy on his soul!"

And of all Christians' souls, [I pray God]. God buy you.   [*Exit.*]

210 LAERTES   Do you [see] this, O God?

KING   Laertes, I must commune with your grief,
Or you deny me right. Go but apart,
Make choice of whom your wisest friends you will,
And they shall hear and judge 'twixt you and me.

215   If by direct or by collateral hand
They find us touch'd, we will our kingdom give,
Our crown, our life, and all that we call ours,
To you in satisfaction; but if not,
Be you content to lend your patience to us,

220   And we shall jointly labor with your soul
To give it due content.

LAERTES   Let this be so.
His means of death, his obscure funeral—

---

190. **A document in madness:** a lesson contained in mad talk   191. **fennel, columbines:** symbols
respectively of flattery and ingratitude   192. **rue:** symbolic of sorrow and repentance   193. **with a
difference:** to represent a different cause of sorrow. *Difference* is a term from heraldry, meaning a
variation in a coat of arms made to distinguish different members of a family.   194. **daisy, violets:**
symbolic respectively of dissembling and faithfulness. It is not clear who are the recipients of these.
197. **Thought:** melancholy   198. **favor:** grace, charm   205. **flaxen:** white   **pole:** poll, head
215. **collateral:** indirect   216. **touch'd:** guilty

No trophy, sword, nor hatchment o'er his bones,
225   No noble rite nor formal ostentation—
Cry to be heard, as 'twere from heaven to earth,
That I must call't in question.
KING   So you shall,
And where th' offense is, let the great axe fall.
230   I pray you go with me.

(*Exeunt.*)

[Scene VI]

(*Enter* HORATIO *and others.*)

HORATIO   What are they that would speak with me?
GENTLEMAN   Sea-faring men, sir. They say they have letters for you.
HORATIO   Let them come in.   [*Exit* GENTLEMAN.]
I do not know from what part of the world
5   I should be greeted, if not from Lord Hamlet.

(*Enter* SAILORS.)

[1.] SAILOR   God bless you, sir.
HORATIO   Let him bless thee too.
[1.] SAILOR   'A shall, sir, and['t] please him. There's a letter for you, sir—it
came from th' embassador that was bound for England—if your name be
10   Horatio, as I am let to know it is.
HORATIO [*reads*]   "Horatio, when thou shalt have overlook'd this, give these
fellows some means to the King, they have letters for him. Ere we were two
days old at sea, a pirate of very warlike appointment gave us chase. Finding
ourselves too slow of sail, we put on a compell'd valor, and in the grapple I
15   boarded them. On the instant they got clear of our ship, so I alone became
their prisoner. They have dealt with me like thieves of mercy, but they knew
what they did: I am to do a [good] turn for them. Let the King have the letters I have sent, and repair thou to me with as much speed as thou wouldest
fly death. I have words to speak in thine ear will make thee dumb, yet are
20   they much too light for the [bore] of the matter. These good fellows will

---

224. **trophy:** memorial   **hatchment:** heraldic memorial tablet   225. **formal ostentation:** fitting and customary ceremony   227. **That:** so that

IV.vi. Location: the castle   16. **thieves of mercy:** merciful thieves   20. **bore:** calibre, size (gunnery term)

bring thee where I am. Rosencrantz and Guildenstern hold their course for
England, of them I have much to tell thee. Farewell.

[He] that thou knowest thine,

Hamlet."

25   Come, I will [give] you way for these your letters,
And do't the speedier that you may direct me
To him from whom you brought them.

(*Exeunt.*)

[Scene VII]

(*Enter* KING *and* LAERTES.)

KING   Now must your conscience my acquittance seal,
And you must put me in your heart for friend,
Sith you have heard, and with a knowing ear,
That he which hath your noble father slain
5   Pursued my life.

LAERTES   It well appears. But tell me
Why you [proceeded] not against these feats
So criminal and so capital in nature,
As by your safety, greatness, wisdom, all things else
10   You mainly were stirr'd up.

KING   O, for two special reasons,
Which may to you perhaps seem much unsinow'd,
But yet to me th' are strong. The Queen his mother
Lives almost by his looks, and for myself—
15   My virtue or my plague, be it either which—
She is so [conjunctive] to my life and soul,
That, as the star moves not but in his sphere,
I could not but by her. The other motive,
Why to a public count I might not go,
20   Is the great love the general gender bear him,
Who, dipping all his faults in their affection,
Work like the spring that turneth wood to stone,
Convert his gyves to graces, so that my arrows,
Too slightly timber'd for so [loud a wind],

IV.vii. Location: the castle   1. **my acquittance seal:** ratify my acquittal; i.e., acknowledge my innocence in Polonius's death.   7. **feats:** acts   9. **safety:** regard for your own safety   10. **mainly:**
powerfully   12. **unsinow'd:** unsinewed, weak   15. **either which:** one or the other   16. **conjunc-
tive:** closely joined   17. **in his sphere:** by the movement of the sphere in which it is fixed (as the
Ptolemaic astronomy taught)   19. **count:** reckoning   20. **the general gender:** everybody
23. **gyves:** fetters

25   Would have reverted to my bow again,
     But not where I have aim'd them.
  LAERTES   And so have I a noble father lost,
     A sister driven into desp'rate terms,
     Whose worth, if praises may go back again,
30   Stood challenger on mount of all the age
     For her perfections—but my revenge will come.
  KING   Break not your sleeps for that. You must not think
     That we are made of stuff so flat and dull
     That we can let our beard be shook with danger
35   And think it pastime. You shortly shall hear more.
     I lov'd your father, and we love ourself,
     And that, I hope, will teach you to imagine—

(Enter a MESSENGER *with letters.)*

     [How now? What news?
  MESSENGER   Letters, my lord, from Hamlet:]
40   These to your Majesty, this to the Queen.
  KING   From Hamlet? Who brought them?
  MESSENGER   Sailors, my lord, they say, I saw them not.
     They were given me by Claudio. He receiv'd them
     Of him that brought them.
45 KING   Laertes, you shall hear them.
     —Leave us.   [*Exit* MESSENGER.]
     [*reads*] "High and mighty, You shall know I am set naked on your kingdom.
     To-morrow shall I beg leave to see your kingly eyes, when I shall, first asking
     you pardon thereunto, recount the occasion of my sudden [and more
50   strange] return.

                                          [Hamlet.] "

     What should this mean? Are all the rest come back?
     Or is it some abuse, and no such thing?
  LAERTES   Know you the hand?
55 KING   'Tis Hamlet's character. "Naked"!
     And in a postscript here he says "alone."
     Can you devise me?
  LAERTES   I am lost in it, my lord. But let him come,
     It warms the very sickness in my heart
60   That I [shall] live and tell him to his teeth,
     "Thus didst thou."

---

28. **terms:** condition   29. **go back again:** refer to what she was before she went mad   30. **on mount:** preeminent   32. **for that:** for fear of losing your revenge   33. **flat:** spiritless   34. **let . . . shook:** To ruffle or tweak a man's beard was an act of insolent defiance that he could not disregard without loss of honor. Cf. II.ii.521.   **with:** by   47. **naked:** destitute   49. **pardon thereunto:** permission to do so   52. **abuse:** deceit   54. **character:** handwriting   57. **devise me:** explain it to me

KING   If it be so, Laertes—
As how should it be so? how otherwise?—
Will you be rul'd by me?

65 LAERTES   Ay, my lord,
So you will not o'errule me to a peace.

KING   To thine own peace. If he be now returned
As [checking] at his voyage, and that he means
No more to undertake it, I will work him
70   To an exploit, now ripe in my device,
Under the which he shall not choose but fall;
And for his death no wind of blame shall breathe,
But even his mother shall uncharge the practice,
And call it accident.

75 LAERTES   My lord, I will be rul'd,
The rather if you could devise it so
That I might be the organ.

KING   It falls right.
You have been talk'd of since your travel much,
80   And that in Hamlet's hearing, for a quality
Wherein they say you shine. Your sum of parts
Did not together pluck such envy from him
As did that one, and that, in my regard,
Of the unworthiest siege.

85 LAERTES   What part is that, my lord?

KING   A very riband in the cap of youth,
Yet needful too, for youth no less becomes
The light and careless livery that it wears
Than settled age his sables and his weeds,
90   Importing health and graveness. Two months since
Here was a gentleman of Normandy:
I have seen myself, and serv'd against, the French,
And they can well on horseback, but this gallant
Had witchcraft in't, he grew unto his seat,
95   And to such wondrous doing brought his horse,
As had he been incorps'd and demi-natur'd
With the brave beast. So far he topp'd [my] thought,

---

63. **As . . . otherwise:** How can he have come back? Yet he obviously has.   66. **So:** provided that
68. **checking at:** turning from (like a falcon diverted from its quarry by other prey)   73. **uncharge
the practice:** adjudge the plot no plot, fail to see the plot   77. **organ:** instrument, agent   80. **quality:** skill   81. **Your . . . parts:** all your (other) accomplishments put together   84. **unworthiest:**
least important (with no implication of unsuitableness)   **siege:** status, position   89. **weeds:** (characteristic) garb   90. **Importing . . . graveness:** signifying prosperity and dignity   93. **can . . .
horseback:** are excellent riders   96. **incorps'd:** made one body   **demi-natur'd:** become half of a
composite animal

That I in forgery of shapes and tricks
Come short of what he did.

100 LAERTES   A Norman was't?

KING   A Norman.

LAERTES   Upon my life, Lamord.

KING   The very same.

LAERTES   I know him well. He is the brooch indeed
105   And gem of all the nation.

KING   He made confession of you,
And gave you such a masterly report
For art and exercise in your defense,
And for your rapier most especial,
110   That he cried out 'twould be a sight indeed
If one could match you. The scrimers of their nation
He swore had neither motion, guard, nor eye,
If you oppos'd them. Sir, this report of his
Did Hamlet so envenom with his envy
115   That he could nothing do but wish and beg
Your sudden coming o'er to play with you.
Now, out of this—

LAERTES   What out of this, my lord?

KING   Laertes, was your father dear to you?
120   Or are you like the painting of a sorrow,
A face without a heart?

LAERTES   Why ask you this?

KING   Not that I think you did not love your father,
But that I know love is begun by time,
125   And that I see, in passages of proof,
Time qualifies the spark and fire of it.
There lives within the very flame of love
A kind of week or snuff that will abate it,
And nothing is at a like goodness still,
130   For goodness, growing to a plurisy,
Dies in his own too much. That we would do,
We should do when we would; for this "would" changes,
And hath abatements and delays as many
As there are tongues, are hands, are accidents,

---

98. **forgery:** mere imagining   104. **brooch:** ornament (worn in the hat)   106. **made . . . you:** acknowledged your excellence   111. **scrimers:** fencers   116. **sudden:** speedy   124. **time:** a particular set of circumstances   125. **in . . . proof:** by the test of experience, by actual examples
126. **qualifies:** moderates   128. **week:** wick   129. **nothing . . . still:** nothing remains forever at the same pitch of perfection   130. **plurisy:** plethora (a variant spelling of *pleurisy,* which was erroneously related to *plus,* stem *plur,* "more, overmuch"   131. **too much:** excess

135 And then this "should" is like a spendthrift's sigh,
That hurts by easing. But to the quick of th' ulcer:
Hamlet comes back. What would you undertake
To show yourself indeed your father's son
More than in words?

140 LAERTES   To cut his throat i' th' church.
KING   No place indeed should murther sanctuarize,
Revenge should have no bounds. But, good Laertes,
Will you do this, keep close within your chamber.
Hamlet return'd shall know you are come home.

145 We'll put on those shall praise your excellence,
And set a double varnish on the fame
The Frenchman gave you, bring you in fine together,
And wager o'er your heads. He, being remiss,
Most generous, and free from all contriving,

150 Will not peruse the foils, so that with ease,
Or with a little shuffling, you may choose
A sword unbated, and in a [pass] of practice
Requite him for your father.

LAERTES   I will do't,

155 And for [that] purpose I'll anoint my sword.
I bought an unction of a mountebank,
So mortal that, but dip a knife in it,
Where it draws blood, no cataplasm so rare,
Collected from all simples that have virtue

160 Under the moon, can save the thing from death
That is but scratch'd withal. I'll touch my point
With this contagion, that if I gall him slightly,
It may be death.

KING   Let's further think of this,

165 Weigh what convenience both of time and means
May fit us to our shape. If this should fail,
And that our drift look through our bad performance,
'Twere better not assay'd; therefore this project
Should have a back or second, that might hold

---

135. **spendthrift's sigh:** A sigh was supposed to draw blood from the heart.   136. **hurts by easing:** injures us at the same time that it gives us relief   141. **sanctuarize:** offer asylum to
143. **Will . . . this:** if you want to undertake this   145. **put on those:** incite those who
146. **double varnish:** second coat of varnish   147. **in fine:** finally   148. **remiss:** careless, over-trustful   149. **generous:** noble-minded   **free . . . contriving:** innocent of sharp practices
150. **peruse:** examine   151. **shuffling:** cunning exchange   152. **unbated:** not blunted   **pass of practice:** tricky thrust   156. **unction:** ointment   **mountebank:** traveling quack-doctor
157. **mortal:** deadly   158. **cataplasm:** poultice   159. **simples:** medicinal herbs   **virtue:** curative power   162. **gall:** graze   166. **fit . . . shape:** suit our purposes best   167. **drift:** purpose   **look through:** become visible, be detected   169. **back or second:** a second plot in reserve for emergency

170   If this did blast in proof. Soft, let me see.
         We'll make a solemn wager on your cunnings—
         I ha't!
         When in your motion you are hot and dry—
         As make your bouts more violent to that end—
175   And that he calls for drink, I'll have preferr'd him
         A chalice for the nonce, whereon but sipping,
         If he by chance escape your venom'd stuck,
         Our purpose may hold there. But stay, what noise?

(*Enter* QUEEN.)

QUEEN   One woe doth tread upon another's heel,
180   So fast they follow. Your sister's drown'd, Laertes.
LAERTES   Drown'd! O, where?
QUEEN   There is a willow grows askaunt the brook,
            That shows his hoary leaves in the glassy stream,
            Therewith fantastic garlands did she make
185   Of crow-flowers, nettles, daisies, and long purples
            That liberal shepherds give a grosser name,
            But our cull-cold maids do dead men's fingers call them.
            There on the pendant boughs her crownet weeds
            Clamb'ring to hang, an envious sliver broke,
190   When down her weedy trophies and herself
            Fell in the weeping brook. Her clothes spread wide,
            And mermaid-like awhile they bore her up,
            Which time she chaunted snatches of old lauds,
            As one incapable of her own distress,
195   Or like a creature native and indued
            Unto that element. But long it could not be
            Till that her garments, heavy with their drink,
            Pull'd the poor wretch from her melodious lay
            To muddy death.
200 LAERTES   Alas, then she is drown'd?
QUEEN   Drown'd, drown'd.
LAERTES   Too much of water hast thou, poor Ophelia,
            And therefore I forbid my tears; but yet
            It is our trick, Nature her custom holds,

---

170. **blast in proof:** blow up while being tried (an image from gunnery)   174. **As:** and you should
175. **preferr'd:** offered to. Most editors adopt the F1 reading *prepar'd*.   176. **nonce:** occasion
177. **stuck:** thrust (from *stoccado,* a fencing term)   182. **askaunt:** sideways over   183. **hoary:** grey-
white   184. **Therewith:** with willow branches   185. **long purples:** wild orchids   186. **liberal:** free-
spoken   187. **cull-cold:** chaste   188. **crownet:** made into coronets   189. **envious sliver:** malicious
branch   193. **lauds:** hymns   194. **incapable:** insensible   195. **indued:** habituated   204. **It:** weeping   **trick:** natural way

205 Let shame say what it will; when these are gone,
The woman will be out. Adieu, my lord,
I have a speech a' fire that fain would blaze,
But that this folly drowns it.   (*Exit.*)

KING   Let's follow, Gertrude.

210 How much I had to do to calm his rage!
Now fear I this will give it start again,
Therefore let's follow.

(*Exeunt.*)

Act V

Scene I

(*Enter two* CLOWNS [*with spades and mattocks*].)

1. CLOWN   Is she to be buried in Christian burial when she willfully seeks her
own salvation?

2. CLOWN   I tell thee she is, therefore make her grave straight. The crowner hath
sate on her, and finds it Christian burial.

5 1. CLOWN   How can that be, unless she drown'd herself in her own defense?

2. CLOWN   Why, 'tis found so.

1. CLOWN   It must be [*se offendendo*], it cannot be else. For here lies the point: if
I drown myself wittingly, it argues an act, and an act hath three branches—
it is to act, to do, to perform; [argal], she drown'd herself wittingly.

10 2. CLOWN   Nay, but hear you, goodman delver—

1. CLOWN   Give me leave. Here lies the water; good. Here stands the man; good.
If the man go to this water and drown himself, it is, will he, nill he, he goes,
mark you that. But if the water come to him and drown him, he drowns not
himself; argal, he that is not guilty of his own death shortens not his own

15 life.

2. CLOWN   But is this law?

1. CLOWN   Ay, marry, is't—crowner's quest law.

2. CLOWN   Will you ha' the truth an't? If this had not been a gentlewoman, she
should have been buried out a' Christian burial.

20 1. CLOWN   Why, there thou say'st, and the more pity that great folk should
have count'nance in this world to drown or hang themselves, more than
their even-Christen. Come, my spade. There is no ancient gentlemen but

---

205. **these:** these tears   206. **The woman . . . out:** My womanish traits will be gone for good.

V.i. Location: a churchyard   o.s.d. **Clowns:** rustics   3. **straight:** immediately   **crowner:** coroner
7. **se offendendo:** blunder for *se defendendo,* "in self-defense"   9. **argal:** blunder for *ergo,* "therefore"   11–15. **Here . . . life:** Alluding to a very famous suicide case, that of Sir James Hales, a judge
who drowned himself in 1554; it was long cited in the courts. The clown gives a garbled account of
the defense summing-up and the verdict.   12. **nill he:** will he not   17. **quest:** inquest   22. **even-
Christen:** fellow-Christians

gard'ners, ditchers, and grave-makers; they hold up Adam's profession.

2. CLOWN   Was he a gentleman?

25 1. CLOWN   'A was the first that ever bore arms.

[2. CLOWN   Why, he had none.

1. CLOWN   What, art a heathen? How dost thou understand the Scripture? The Scripture says Adam digg'd; could he dig without arms?] I'll put another question to thee. If thou answerest me not to the purpose, confess thyself—

30 2. CLOWN   Go to.

1. CLOWN   What is he that builds stronger than either the mason, the shipwright, or the carpenter?

2. CLOWN   The gallows-maker, for that outlives a thousand tenants.

1. CLOWN   I like thy wit well, in good faith. The gallows does well; but how does
35   it well? It does well to those that do ill. Now thou dost ill to say the gallows is built stronger than the church; argal, the gallows may do well to thee. To't again, come.

2. CLOWN   Who builds stronger than a mason, a shipwright, or a carpenter?

1. CLOWN   Ay, tell me that, and unyoke.

40 2. CLOWN   Marry, now I can tell.

1. CLOWN   To't.

2. CLOWN   Mass, I cannot tell.

(*Enter* HAMLET *and* HORATIO [*afar off*].)

1. CLOWN   Cudgel thy brains no more about it, for your dull ass will not mend his pace with beating, and when you are ask'd this question next, say "a
45   grave-maker": the houses he makes lasts till doomsday. Go get thee in, and fetch me a sup of liquor.

[*Exit* SECOND CLOWN. FIRST CLOWN *digs*.]

> "In youth when I did love, did love,   (*song*)
> Methought it was very sweet,
> To contract—O—the time for—a—my behove,
50 >   O, methought there—a—was nothing—a—meet."

HAMLET   Has this fellow no feeling of his business? 'a sings in grave-making.

HORATIO   Custom hath made it in him a property of easiness.

HAMLET   'Tis e'en so, the hand of little employment hath the daintier sense.

1. CLOWN   "But age with his stealing steps   (*song*)
55 >   Hath clawed me in his clutch,
>   And hath shipped me into the land,
>   As if I had never been such."

---

26. **none:** no coat of arms   39. **unyoke:** cease to labor, call it a day   42. **Mass:** by the mass
49. **contract . . . behove:** shorten, spend agreeably . . . advantage. The song, punctuated by the grunts of the clown as he digs, is a garbled version of a poem by Thomas Lord Vaux, entitled "The Aged Lover Renounceth Love."   52. **Custom:** habit   **a property of easiness:** a thing he can do with complete ease of mind   53. **daintier sense:** more delicate sensitivity

[*throws up a shovelful of earth with a skull in it*]

HAMLET   That skull had a tongue in it, and could sing once. How the knave
jowls it to the ground, as if 'twere Cain's jaw-bone, that did the first murder!
60   This might be the pate of a politician, which this ass now o'erreaches, one
that would circumvent God, might it not?

HORATIO   It might, my lord.

HAMLET   Or of a courtier, which could say, "Good morrow, sweet lord! How
dost thou, sweet lord?" This might be my Lord Such-a-one, that prais'd my
65   Lord Such-a-one's horse when 'a [meant] to beg it, might it not?

HORATIO   Ay, my lord.

HAMLET   Why, e'en so, and now my Lady Worm's, chopless, and knock'd about
the [mazzard] with a sexton's spade. Here's fine revolution, and we had the
trick to see't. Did these bones cost no more the breeding, but to play at log-
70   gats with them? Mine ache to think on't.

1. CLOWN   "A pickaxe and a spade, a spade,   (*song*)
                    For and a shrouding sheet:
                    O, a pit of clay for to be made
                    For such a guest is meet."

[*throws up another skull*]

75   HAMLET   There's another. Why may not that be the skull of a lawyer? Where be
his quiddities now, his quillities, his cases, his tenures, and his tricks? Why
does he suffer this mad knave now to knock him about the sconce with a
dirty shovel, and will not tell him of his action of battery? Hum! This fellow
might be in 's time a great buyer of land, with his statutes, his recognizances,
80   his fines, his double vouchers, his recoveries. [Is this the fine of his fines,
and the recovery of his recoveries,] to have his fine pate full of fine dirt? Will
[his] 'vouchers vouch him no more of his purchases, and [double ones too],
than the length and breadth of a pair of indentures? The very conveyances
of his lands will scarcely lie in this box, and must th' inheritor himself have
85   no more, ha?

HORATIO   Not a jot more, my lord.

HAMLET   Is not parchment made of sheep-skins?

---

59. **jowls:** dashes   60. **politician:** schemer, intriguer   **o'erreaches:** gets the better of (with play
on the literal sense)   61. **circumvent God:** bypass God's law   67. **chopless:** lacking the lower
jaw   68. **mazzard:** head   **revolution:** change   **and:** if   69. **trick:** knack, ability   **Did...cost:**
were...worth   69–70. **loggats:** a game in which blocks of wood were thrown at a stake
76. **quiddities:** subtleties, quibbles   **quillities:** fine distinctions   **tenures:** titles to real estate
77. **sconce:** head   79. **statutes, recognizances:** bonds securing debts by attaching land and property   80. **fines, recoveries:** procedures for converting an entailed estate to freehold   **double
vouchers:** documents guaranteeing title to real estate, signed by two persons   **fine:** end   83. **pair
of indentures:** legal document cut into two parts which fitted together on a serrated edge. Perhaps
Hamlet thus refers to the two rows of teeth in the skull, or to the bone sutures.   **conveyances:** documents relating to transfer of property   84. **this box:** the skull itself   **inheritor:** owner

HORATIO   Ay, my lord, and of calves'-skins too.

HAMLET   They are sheep and calves which seek out assurance in that. I will
90   speak to this fellow. Whose grave's this, sirrah?

1. CLOWN   Mine, sir.   [*sings*]
                    "[O], a pit of clay for to be made
                     [For such a guest is meet]."

HAMLET   I think it be thine indeed, for thou liest in't.

95 1. CLOWN   You lie out on't, sir, and therefore 'tis not yours; for my part, I do not
        lie in't, yet it is mine.

HAMLET   Thou dost lie in't, to be in't and say it is thine. 'Tis for the dead, not
        for the quick; therefore thou liest.

1. CLOWN   'Tis a quick lie, sir, 'twill away again from me to you.

100 HAMLET   What man dost thou dig it for?

1. CLOWN   For no man, sir.

HAMLET   What woman then?

1. CLOWN   For none neither.

HAMLET   Who is to be buried in't?

105 1. CLOWN   One that was a woman, sir, but, rest her soul, she's dead.

HAMLET   How absolute the knave is! we must speak by the card, or equivoca-
        tion will undo us. By the Lord, Horatio, this three years I have took note of
        it: the age is grown so pick'd that the toe of the peasant comes so near the
        heel of the courtier, he galls his kibe. How long hast thou been grave-maker?

110 1. CLOWN   Of [all] the days i' th' year, I came to't that day that our last king
        Hamlet overcame Fortinbras.

HAMLET   How long is that since?

1. CLOWN   Cannot you tell that? Every fool can tell that. It was that very day
        that young Hamlet was born—he that is mad, and sent into England.

115 HAMLET   Ay, marry, why was he sent into England?

1. CLOWN   Why, because 'a was mad. 'A shall recover his wits there, or if 'a do
        not, 'tis no great matter there.

HAMLET   Why?

1. CLOWN   'Twill not be seen in him there, there the men are as mad as he.

120 HAMLET   How came he mad?

1. CLOWN   Very strangely, they say.

HAMLET   How strangely?

1. CLOWN   Faith, e'en with losing his wits.

HAMLET   Upon what ground?

125 1. CLOWN   Why, here in Denmark. I have been sexton here, man and boy, thirty
        years.

HAMLET   How long will a man lie i' th' earth ere he rot?

---

90. **sirrah:** term of address to inferiors   106. **absolute:** positive   **by the card:** by the compass,
punctiliously   106–107. **equivocation:** ambiguity   108. **pick'd:** refined   109. **galls his kibe:** rubs
the courtier's chilblain

1. CLOWN   Faith, if 'a be not rotten before 'a die—as we have many pocky
corses, that will scarce hold the laying in—'a will last you some eight year or
nine year. A tanner will last you nine year.

HAMLET   Why he more than another?

1. CLOWN   Why, sir, his hide is so tann'd with his trade that 'a will keep out water a great while, and your water is a sore decayer of your whoreson dead
body. Here's a skull now hath lien you i' th' earth three and twenty years.

HAMLET   Whose was it?

1. CLOWN   A whoreson mad fellow's it was. Whose do you think it was?

HAMLET   Nay, I know not.

1. CLOWN   A pestilence on him for a mad rogue! 'a pour'd a flagon of Rhenish
on my head once. This same skull, sir, was, sir, Yorick's skull, the King's
jester.

HAMLET   This? [*takes the skull*]

1. CLOWN   E'en that.

HAMLET   Alas, poor Yorick! I knew him, Horatio, a fellow of infinite jest, of
most excellent fancy. He hath bore me on his back a thousand times, and
now how abhorr'd in my imagination it is! my gorge rises at it. Here hung
those lips that I have kiss'd I know not how oft. Where be your gibes now,
your gambols, your songs, your flashes of merriment, that were wont to set
the table on a roar? Not one now to mock your own grinning—quite chop-
fall'n. Now get you to my lady's [chamber], and tell her, let her paint an inch
thick, to this favor she must come; make her laugh at that. Prithee, Horatio,
tell me one thing.

HORATIO   What's that, my lord?

HAMLET   Dost thou think Alexander look'd a' this fashion i' th' earth?

HORATIO   E'en so.

HAMLET   And smelt so? pah!   [*puts down the skull*]

HORATIO   E'en so, my lord.

HAMLET   To what base uses we may return, Horatio! Why may not imagination
trace the noble dust of Alexander, till 'a find it stopping a bunghole?

HORATIO   'Twere to consider too curiously, to consider so.

HAMLET   No, faith, not a jot, but to follow him thither with modesty enough
and likelihood to lead it: Alexander died, Alexander was buried, Alexander
returneth to dust, the dust is earth, of earth we make loam, and why of that
loam whereto he was converted might they not stop a beer-barrel?
Imperious Caesar, dead and turn'd to clay,
Might stop a hole to keep the wind away.
O that that earth which kept the world in awe

---

128. **pocky:** rotten with venereal disease   129. **hold . . . in:** last out the burial   148–49. **chop-
fall'n:** (1) lacking the lower jaw; (2) downcast   150. **favor:** appearance   159. **curiously:** closely,
minutely   160. **modesty:** moderation   162. **loam:** a mixture of moistened clay with sand, straw,
etc.   164. **Imperious:** imperial

Should patch a wall t' expel the [winter's] flaw!
But soft, but soft awhile, here comes the King,

(*Enter* KING, QUEEN, LAERTES, *and* [*a* DOCTOR OF DIVINITY, *following*] *the corse,*
[*with* LORDS *attendant*].)

The Queen, the courtiers. Who is this they follow?
170   And with such maimed rites? This doth betoken
The corse they follow did with desp'rate hand
Foredo it own life. 'Twas of some estate.
Couch we a while and mark.   [*retiring with* HORATIO]
LAERTES   What ceremony else?
175 HAMLET   That is Laertes, a very noble youth. Mark.
LAERTES   What ceremony else?
DOCTOR   Her obsequies have been as far enlarg'd
As we have warranty. Her death was doubtful,
And but that great command o'ersways the order,
180   She should in ground unsanctified been lodg'd
Till the last trumpet; for charitable prayers,
[Shards,] flints, and pebbles should be thrown on her.
Yet here she is allow'd her virgin crants,
Her maiden strewments, and the bringing home
185   Of bell and burial.
LAERTES   Must there no more be done?
DOCTOR   No more be done:
We should profane the service of the dead
To sing a requiem and such rest to her
190   As to peace-parted souls.
LAERTES   Lay her i' th' earth,
And from her fair and unpolluted flesh
May violets spring! I tell thee, churlish priest,
A minist'ring angel shall my sister be
195   When thou liest howling.
HAMLET   What, the fair Ophelia!
QUEEN [*scattering flowers*]   Sweets to the sweet, farewell!
I hop'd thou shouldst have been my Hamlet's wife.
I thought thy bride-bed to have deck'd, sweet maid,
200   And not have strew'd thy grave.

---

167. **flaw:** gust   170. **maimed rites:** lack of customary ceremony   172. **Foredo:** fordo, destroy
it: its   **estate:** rank   173. **Couch we:** let us conceal ourselves   178. **doubtful:** the subject of an
"open verdict"   179. **order:** customary procedure   180. **should:** would certainly   181. **for:** instead of   183. **crants:** garland   184. **maiden strewments:** flowers scattered on the grave of an unmarried girl   184–85. **bringing . . . burial:** burial in consecrated ground, with the bell tolling
189. **requiem:** dirge   197. **Sweets:** flowers

LAERTES   O, treble woe
     Fall ten times [treble] on that cursed head
     Whose wicked deed thy most ingenious sense
     Depriv'd thee of! Hold off the earth a while,
205   Till I have caught her once more in mine arms.

[leaps in the grave]

     Now pile your dust upon the quick and dead,
     Till of this flat a mountain you have made
     T' o'ertop old Pelion, or the skyish head
     Of blue Olympus.
210 HAMLET *[coming forward]*   What is he whose grief
     Bears such an emphasis, whose phrase of sorrow
     Conjures the wand'ring stars and makes them stand
     Like wonder-wounded hearers? This is I,
     Hamlet the Dane!

*[*HAMLET *leaps in after* LAERTES.]*

215 LAERTES   The devil take thy soul!   *[grappling with him]*
     HAMLET   Thou pray'st not well.
     I prithee take thy fingers from my throat.
     For though I am not splenitive [and] rash,
     Yet have I in me something dangerous,
220   Which let thy wisdom fear. Hold off thy hand!
     KING   Pluck them asunder.
     QUEEN   Hamlet, Hamlet!
     ALL   Gentlemen!
     HORATIO   Good my lord, be quiet.

[The ATTENDANTS *part them, and they come out of the grave.]*

225 HAMLET   Why, I will fight with him upon this theme
     Until my eyelids will no longer wag.
     QUEEN   O my son, what theme?
     HAMLET   I lov'd Ophelia. Forty thousand brothers
     Could not with all their quantity of love
230   Make up my sum. What wilt thou do for her?
     KING   O, he is mad, Laertes.
     QUEEN   For love of God, forbear him.

---

203. **ingenious:** intelligent   208, 209. **Pelion, Olympus:** mountains in northeastern Greece
211. **emphasis, phrase:** rhetorical terms, here used in disparaging reference to Laertes' inflated language   212. **Conjures:** puts a spell upon   **wand'ring stars:** planets   214. **the Dane:** This title normally signifies the king   218. **splenitive:** impetuous

HAMLET   'Swounds, show me what thou't do.
　　　　Woo't weep, woo't fight, woo't fast, woo't tear thyself?
235　　Woo't drink up eisel, eat a crocadile?
　　　　I'll do't. Dost [thou] come here to whine?
　　　　To outface me with leaping in her grave?
　　　　Be buried quick with her, and so will I.
　　　　And if thou prate of mountains, let them throw
240　　Millions of acres on us, till our ground,
　　　　Singeing his pate against the burning zone,
　　　　Make Ossa like a wart! Nay, and thou'lt mouth,
　　　　I'll rant as well as thou.

QUEEN　　　　　　　　　　　　This is mere madness,
245　　And [thus] a while the fit will work on him;
　　　　Anon, as patient as the female dove,
　　　　When that her golden couplets are disclosed,
　　　　His silence will sit drooping.

HAMLET　　　　　　　　　　　Hear you, sir,
250　　What is the reason that you use me thus?
　　　　I lov'd you ever. But it is no matter.
　　　　Let Hercules himself do what he may,
　　　　The cat will mew, and dog will have his day.

(*Exit* HAMLET.)

KING   I pray thee, good Horatio, wait upon him.

([*Exit*] HORATIO.)

255　　[*to* LAERTES] Strengthen your patience in our last night's speech,
　　　　We'll put the matter to the present push.—
　　　　Good Gertrude, set some watch over your son.
　　　　This grave shall have a living monument.
　　　　An hour of quiet [shortly] shall we see,
260　　Till then in patience our proceeding be.

(*Exeunt.*)

---

233. **thou't:** thou wilt   234-35. **Woo't:** wilt thou   235. **eisel:** vinegar   **crocadile:** crocodile
239. **if . . . mountains:** referring to lines 206–209   241. **burning zone:** sphere of the sun
242. **Ossa:** another mountain in Greece, near Pelion and Olympus   **mouth:** talk bombast (synonymous with *rant* in the next line)   244. **mere:** utter   246. **patient:** calm   247. **golden couplets:** pair
of baby birds, covered with yellow down   **disclosed:** hatched   252–53. **Let . . . day:** nobody can
prevent another from making the scenes he feels he has a right to   255. **in:** by recalling
256. **present push:** immediate test   258. **living:** enduring (?) or in the form of a lifelike effigy (?)

[Scene II]

(*Enter* HAMLET *and* HORATIO.)

HAMLET   So much for this, sir, now shall you see the other—
  You do remember all the circumstance?

HORATIO   Remember it, my lord!

HAMLET   Sir, in my heart there was a kind of fighting
5   That would not let me sleep. [Methought] I lay
  Worse than the mutines in the [bilboes]. Rashly—
  And prais'd be rashness for it—let us know
  Our indiscretion sometime serves us well
  When our deep plots do pall, and that should learn us
10   There's a divinity that shapes our ends,
  Rough-hew them how we will—

HORATIO   That is most certain.

HAMLET   Up from my cabin,
  My sea-grown scarf'd about me, in the dark
15   Grop'd I to find out them, had my desire,
  Finger'd their packet, and in fine withdrew
  To mine own room again, making so bold,
  My fears forgetting manners, to [unseal]
  Their grand commission; where I found, Horatio—
20   Ah, royal knavery!—an exact command,
  Larded with many several sorts of reasons,
  Importing Denmark's health and England's too,
  With, ho, such bugs and goblins in my life,
  That, on the supervise, no leisure bated,
25   No, not to stay the grinding of the axe,
  My head should be strook off.

HORATIO .   Is't possible?

HAMLET   Here's the commission, read it at more leisure.
  But wilt thou hear now how I did proceed?

30 HORATIO   I beseech you.

HAMLET   Being thus benetted round with [villainies],
  Or I could make a prologue to my brains,

V.ii. Location: the castle   1. **see the other:** hear the other news I have to tell you (hinted at in the letter to Horatio, IV.vi.19–20)   6. **mutines:** mutineers (but the term *mutiny* was in Shakespeare's day used of almost any act of rebellion against authority)   **bilboes:** fetters attached to a heavy iron bar   **Rashly:** on impulse   7. **know:** recognize, acknowledge   9. **pall:** lose force, come to nothing   **learn:** teach   10. **shapes our ends:** gives final shape to our designs   11. **Rough-hew them:** block them out in initial form   16. **Finger'd:** filched, "pinched"   21. **Larded:** garnished   22. **Importing:** relating to   23. **bugs . . . life:** terrifying things in prospect if I were permitted to remain alive; *bugs* = bugaboos   24. **supervise:** perusal   **bated:** deducted (from the stipulated speediness)   25. **stay:** wait for   32. **Or:** before

They had begun the play. I sat me down,
Devis'd a new commission, wrote it fair.

35   I once did hold it, as our statists do,
A baseness to write fair, and labor'd much
How to forget that learning, but, sir, now
I did me yeman's service. Wilt thou know
Th' effect of what I wrote?

40 HORATIO   Ay, good my lord.

HAMLET   An earnest conjuration from the King,
As England was his faithful tributary,
As love between them like the palm might flourish,
As peace should still her wheaten garland wear

45   And stand a comma 'tween their amities,
And many such-like [as's] of great charge,
That on the view and knowing of these contents,
Without debatement further, more or less,
He should those bearers put to sudden death,

50   Not shriving time allow'd.

HORATIO   How was this seal'd?

HAMLET   Why, even in that was heaven ordinant.
I had my father's signet in my purse,
Which was the model of that Danish seal;

55   Folded the writ up in the form of th' other,
[Subscrib'd] it, gave't th' impression, plac'd it safely,
The changeling never known. Now the next day
Was our sea-fight, and what to this was sequent
Thou knowest already.

60 HORATIO   So Guildenstern and Rosencrantz go to't.

HAMLET   [Why, man, they did make love to this employment,]
They are not near my conscience. Their defeat
Does by their own insinuation grow.
'Tis dangerous when the baser nature comes

65   Between the pass and fell incensed points
Of mighty opposites.

HORATIO   Why, what a king is this!

---

34. **fair:** in a beautiful hand (such as a professional scribe would use)   35. **statists:** statesmen, public officials   36. **A baseness:** a skill befitting men of low rank   38. **yeman's:** yeoman's; solid, substantial   39. **effect:** purport, gist   45. **comma:** connective, link   46. **as's . . . charge:** (1) weighty clauses beginning with *as;* (2) asses with heavy loads   50. **shriving time:** time for confession and absolution   52. **ordinant:** in charge, guiding   54. **model:** small copy   56. **Subscrib'd:** signed   57. **changeling:** Hamlet's letter, substituted secretly for the genuine letter, as fairies substituted their children for human children   **never known:** never recognized as a substitution (unlike the fairies' changelings)   60. **go to't:** are going to their death   62. **defeat:** ruin, overthrow   63. **insinuation:** winding their way into the affair   64. **baser:** inferior   65. **pass:** thrust   **fell:** fierce

HAMLET   Does it not, think thee, stand me now upon—
    He that hath kill'd my king and whor'd my mother,
70   Popp'd in between th' election and my hopes,
    Thrown out his angle for my proper life,
    And with such coz'nage—is't not perfect conscience
    [To quit him with this arm? And is't not to be damn'd,
    To let this canker of our nature come
75   In further evil?
HORATIO   It must be shortly known to him from England
    What is the issue of the business there.
HAMLET   It will be short; the interim's mine,
    And a man's life's no more than to say "one."
80   But I am very sorry, good Horatio,
    That to Laertes I forgot myself,
    For by the image of my cause I see
    The portraiture of his. I'll [court] his favors.
    But sure the bravery of his grief did put me
85   Into a tow'ring passion.
HORATIO   Peace, who comes here?]

(*Enter* [*young* OSRIC,] *a courtier.*)

OSRIC   Your lordship is right welcome back to Denmark.
HAMLET   I [humbly] thank you, sir.—Dost know this water-fly?
HORATIO   No, my good lord.
90 HAMLET   Thy state is the more gracious, for 'tis a vice to know him. He hath
    much land, and fertile; let a beast be lord of beasts, and his crib shall stand
    at the King's mess. 'Tis a chough, but, as I say, spacious in the possession of
    dirt.
OSRIC   Sweet lord, if your lordship were at leisure, I should impart a thing to
95   you from his Majesty.
HAMLET   I will receive it, sir, with all diligence of spirit. [Put] your bonnet to
    his right use, 'tis for the head.
OSRIC   I thank your lordship, it is very hot.
HAMLET   No, believe me, 'tis very cold, the wind is northerly.
100 OSRIC   It is indifferent cold, my lord, indeed.
HAMLET   But yet methinks it is very [sultry] and hot [for] my complexion.

---

68. **stand . . . upon:** rest upon me as a duty   70. **election:** as king of Denmark   71. **angle:** hook
and line   **proper:** very   72. **coz'nage:** trickery   73. **quit him:** pay him back   74. **canker:** cancerous sore   74–75. **come In:** grow into   79. **a man's . . . more:** to kill a man takes no more time   **say**
"one." Perhaps this is equivalent to "deliver one sword thrust"; see line 259 below, where Hamlet
says "One" as he makes the first hit.   82. **image:** likeness   84. **bravery:** ostentatious expression
88. **water-fly:** tiny, vainly agitated creature   90. **gracious:** virtuous   91–92. **let . . . mess:** If a beast
owned as many cattle as Osric, he could feast with the King.   92. **chough:** jackdaw, a bird that
could be taught to speak   96. **bonnet:** hat   100. **indifferent:** somewhat   101. **complexion:**
temperament

OSRIC   Exceedingly, my lord, it is very sultry—as 'twere—I cannot tell how. My
lord, his Majesty bade me signify to you that 'a has laid a great wager on
your head. Sir, this is the matter—

105 HAMLET   I beseech you remember.

[HAMLET *moves him to put on his hat.*]

OSRIC   Nay, good my lord, for my ease, in good faith. Sir, here is newly come to
court Laertes, believe me, an absolute [gentleman], full of most excellent
differences, of very soft society, and great showing; indeed, to speak sellingly
of him, he is the card or calendar of gentry; for you shall find in him the
110   continent of what part a gentleman would see.

HAMLET   Sir, his definement suffers no perdition in you, though I know to divide him inventorially would dozy th' arithmetic of memory, and yet but
yaw neither in respect of his quick sail; but in the verity of extolment, I take
him to be a soul of great article, and his infusion of such dearth and
115   rareness as, to make true diction of him, his semblable is his mirror, and
who else would trace him, his umbrage, nothing more.

OSRIC   Your lordship speaks most infallibly of him.

HAMLET   The concernancy, sir? Why do we wrap the gentleman in our more
rawer breath?

120 OSRIC   Sir?

HORATIO   Is't not possible to understand in another tongue? You will to't, sir,
really.

HAMLET   What imports the nomination of this gentleman?

OSRIC   Of Laertes?

125 HORATIO   His purse is empty already: all 's golden words are spent.

HAMLET   Of him, sir.

OSRIC   I know you are not ignorant—

HAMLET   I would you did, sir, yet, in faith, if you did, it would not much approve me. Well, sir?

130 OSRIC   You are not ignorant of what excellence Laertes is—

---

106. **for my ease:** I am really more comfortable with my hat off (a polite insistence on maintaining
ceremony).   107. **absolute:** complete, possessing every quality a gentleman should have
108. **differences:** distinguishing characteristics, personal qualities   **soft:** agreeable   **great showing:** splendid appearance   **sellingly:** like a seller to a prospective buyer; in a fashion to do full justice. Most editors follow Q3 in reading *feelingly* = with exactitude, as he deserves.   109. **card or
calendar:** chart or register, compendious guide   **gentry:** gentlemanly behavior   109–110. **the continent . . . part:** one who contains every quality   111. **perdition:** loss   112. **dozy:** make dizzy
113. **yaw:** keep deviating erratically from its course (said of a ship)   **neither:** for all that   **in respect of:** compared with   **in . . . extolment:** to praise him truly   114. **article:** scope (?) or importance (?)   **infusion:** essence, quality   **dearth:** scarceness   115. **make true diction:** speak
truly   **his semblable:** his only likeness or equal   116. **who . . . him:** anyone else who tries to follow
him   **umbrage:** shadow   118. **concernancy:** relevance   118–19. **more rawer breath:** words too
crude to describe him properly   121. **in another tongue:** when someone else is the speaker
121–22. **You . . . really:** you can do it if you try   123. **nomination:** naming, mention
128–29. **approve:** commend

HAMLET   I dare not confess that, lest I should compare with him in excellence, but to know a man well were to know himself.

OSRIC   I mean, sir, for [his] weapon, but in the imputation laid on him by them, in his meed he's unfellow'd.

135 HAMLET   What's his weapon?

OSRIC   Rapier and dagger.

HAMLET   That's two of his weapons—but well.

OSRIC   The King, sir, hath wager'd with him six Barbary horses, against the which he has impawn'd, as I take it, six French rapiers and poniards, with 140 their assigns, as girdle, [hangers], and so. Three of the carriages, in faith, are very dear to fancy, very responsive to the hilts, most delicate carriages, and of very liberal conceit.

HAMLET   What call you the carriages?

HORATIO   I knew you must be edified by the margent ere you had done.

145 OSRIC   The [carriages], sir, are the hangers.

HAMLET   The phrase would be more germane to the matter if we could carry a cannon by our sides; I would it [might be] hangers till then. But on: six Barb'ry horses against six French swords, their assigns, and three liberal-conceited carriages; that's the French bet against the Danish. Why is this all 150 [impawn'd, as] you call it?

OSRIC   The King, sir, hath laid, sir, that in a dozen passes between yourself and him, he shall not exceed you three hits; he hath laid on twelve for nine; and it would come to immediate trial, if your lordship would vouchsafe the answer.

155 HAMLET   How if I answer no?

OSRIC   I mean, my lord, the opposition of your person in trial.

HAMLET   Sir, I will walk here in the hall. If it please his Majesty, it is the breathing time of day with me. Let the foils be brought, the gentleman willing, and the King hold his purpose, I will win for him and I can; if not, I will gain 160 nothing but my shame and the odd hits.

OSRIC   Shall I deliver you so?

HAMLET   To this effect, sir—after what flourish your nature will.

---

131. **compare . . . excellence:** seem to claim the same degree of excellence for myself
132. **but:** The sense seems to require *for*.   **himself:** oneself   133–34. **in . . . them:** in popular estimation   134. **meed:** merit   139. **impawn'd:** staked   140. **assigns:** appurtenances **hangers:** straps on which the swords hang from the girdle   **carriages:** properly, gun-carriages; here used affectedly in place of *hangers*   141. **fancy:** taste   **very responsive to:** matching well 142. **liberal conceit:** elegant design   144. **must . . . margent:** would require enlightenment from a marginal note   151. **laid:** wagered   152. **he . . . hits:** Laertes must win by at least eight to four (if none of the "passes" or bouts are draws), since at seven to five he would be only two up. **he . . . nine:** Not satisfactorily explained despite much discussion. One suggestion is that Laertes has raised the odds against himself by wagering that out of twelve bouts he will win nine. 154. **answer:** encounter (as Hamlet's following quibble forces Osric to explain in his next speech) 157–58. **breathing . . . me:** my usual hour for exercise   162. **after what flourish:** with whatever embellishment of language

OSRIC   I commend my duty to your lordship.

HAMLET   Yours. [*Exit* OSRIC.] ['A] does well to commend it himself,
165   there are no tongues else for 's turn.

HORATIO   This lapwing runs away with the shell on his head.

HAMLET   'A did [comply], sir, with his dug before 'a suck'd it. Thus has he, and
     many more of the same breed that I know the drossy age dotes on, only got
     the tune of the time, and out of an habit of encounter, a kind of [yesty] col-
170   lection, which carries them through and through the most [profound] and
     [winnow'd] opinions, and do but blow them to their trial, the bubbles are
     out.

(*Enter a* LORD.)

LORD   My lord, his Majesty commended him to you by young Osric, who
     brings back to him that you attend him in the hall. He sends to know if your
175   pleasure hold to play with Laertes, or that you will take longer time.

HAMLET   I am constant to my purposes, they follow the King's pleasure. If his
     fitness speaks, mine is ready; now or whensoever, provided I be so able as
     now.

LORD   The King and Queen and all are coming down.

180 HAMLET   In happy time.

LORD   The Queen desires you to use some gentle entertainment to Laertes be-
     fore you fall to play.

HAMLET   She well instructs me. [*Exit* LORD.]

HORATIO   You will lose, my lord.

185 HAMLET   I do not think so; since he went into France I have been in continual
     practice. I shall win at the odds. Thou wouldst not think how ill all's here
     about my heart—but it is no matter.

HORATIO   Nay, good my lord—

HAMLET   It is but foolery, but it is such a kind of [gain-]giving, as would per-
190   haps trouble a woman.

HORATIO   If your mind dislike any thing, obey it. I will forestall their repair
     hither, and say you are not fit.

HAMLET   Not a whit, we defy augury. There is special providence in the fall of a
     sparrow. If it be [now], 'tis not to come; if it be not to come, it will be now; if

---

163. **commend my duty:** offer my dutiful respects (but Hamlet picks up the phrase in the sense
"praise my manner of bowing")   166. **lapwing:** a foolish bird which upon hatching was
supposed to run with part of the eggshell still over its head. (Osric has put his hat on
at last.)   167. **comply . . . dug:** bow politely to his mother's nipple   168. **drossy:** worthless
169. **tune . . . time:** fashionable ways of talk   **habit of encounter:** mode of social intercourse
yesty: yeasty, frothy   169–70. **collection:** anthology of fine phrases   171. **winnow'd:** sifted, choice
opinions: judgments   **blow . . . trial:** test them by blowing on them; make even the least demanding trial of them   172. **out:** blown away (?) or at an end, done for (?)   176–77. **If . . . ready:** If this
is a good moment for him, it is for me also.   181. **gentle entertainment:** courteous greeting
189. **gain-giving:** misgiving   193–94. **special . . . sparrow:** See Matthew 10:29.

195   it be not now, yet it [will] come—the readiness is all. Since no man, of aught
he leaves, knows what is't to leave betimes, let be.

(*A table prepar'd, [and flagons of wine on it. Enter] Trumpets, Drums, and Officers
with cushions, foils, daggers;* KING, QUEEN, LAERTES, [OSRIC,] *and all the State.*)

KING   Come, Hamlet, come, and take this hand from me.

[*The* KING *puts* LAERTES' *hand into* HAMLET'S.]

HAMLET   Give me your pardon, sir. I have done you wrong,
But pardon't as you are a gentleman.
200   This presence knows,
And you must needs have heard, how I am punish'd
With a sore distraction. What I have done
That might your nature, honor, and exception
Roughly awake, I here proclaim was madness.
205   Was't Hamlet wrong'd Laertes? Never Hamlet!
If Hamlet from himself be ta'en away,
And when he's not himself does wrong Laertes,
Then Hamlet does it not, Hamlet denies it.
Who does it then? His madness. If't be so,
210   Hamlet is of the faction that is wronged,
His madness is poor Hamlet's enemy.
[Sir, in this audience,]
Let my disclaiming from a purpos'd evil
Free me so far in your most generous thoughts,
215   That I have shot my arrow o'er the house
And hurt my brother.
LAERTES   I am satisfied in nature,
Whose motive in this case should stir me most
To my revenge, but in my terms of honor
I stand aloof, and will no reconcilement
220   Till by some elder masters of known honor
I have a voice and president of peace
To [keep] my name ungor'd. But [till] that time
I do receive your offer'd love like love,
225   And will not wrong it.

---

195. **of aught:** whatever   196. **knows . . . betimes:** knows what is the best time to leave it
s.d. **State:** nobles   200. **presence:** assembled court   201. **punish'd:** afflicted   203. **exception:**
objection   213. **my . . . evil:** my declaration that I intended no harm   214. **Free:** absolve
217. **in nature:** so far as my personal feelings are concerned   219. **in . . . honor:** as a man governed
by an established code of honor   222–23. **have . . . ungor'd:** can secure an opinion backed by
precedent that I can make peace with you without injury to my reputation

HAMLET   I embrace it freely,
    And will this brothers' wager frankly play.
    Give us the foils. [Come on.]
LAERTES   Come, one for me.
230 HAMLET   I'll be your foil, Laertes; in mine ignorance
    Your skill shall like a star i' th' darkest night
    Stick fiery off indeed.
LAERTES   You mock me, sir.
HAMLET   No, by this hand.
235 KING   Give them the foils, young Osric. Cousin Hamlet,
    You know the wager?
HAMLET   Very well, my lord.
    Your Grace has laid the odds a' th' weaker side.
KING   I do not fear it, I have seen you both;
240   But since he is [better'd], we have therefore odds.
LAERTES   This is too heavy; let me see another.
HAMLET   This likes me well. These foils have all a length?   [*Prepare to play.*]
OSRIC   Ay, my good lord.
KING   Set me the stoups of wine upon that table.
245   If Hamlet give the first or second hit,
    Or quit in answer of the third exchange,
    Let all the battlements their ord'nance fire.
    The King shall drink to Hamlet's better breath,
    And in the cup an [union] shall he throw,
250   Richer than that which four successive kings
    In Denmark's crown have worn. Give me the cups,
    And let the kettle to the trumpet speak,
    The trumpet to the cannoneer without,
    The cannons to the heavens, the heaven to earth,
255   "Now the King drinks to Hamlet." Come begin;

(*trumpets the while*)

    And you, the judges, bear a wary eye.
HAMLET   Come on, sir.
LAERTES   Come, my lord.

[*They play and* HAMLET *scores a hit.*]

---

227. **brothers':** amicable, as if between brothers   **frankly:** freely, without constraint
230. **foil:** thin sheet of metal placed behind a jewel to set it off   232. **Stick . . . off:** blaze out in contrast   238. **laid the odds:** wagered a higher stake (horses to rapiers)   240. **is better'd:** has perfected
his skill   **odds:** the arrangement that Laertes must take more bouts than Hamlet to win
242. **likes:** pleases   **a length:** the same length   244. **stoups:** tankards   246. **quit . . . exchange:**
pays back wins by Laertes in the first and second bouts by taking the third   249. **union:** an especially fine pearl   252. **kettle:** kettle-drum

HAMLET   One.
260 LAERTES   No.
HAMLET   Judgment.
OSRIC   A hit, a very palpable hit.
LAERTES   Well, again.
KING   Stay, give me drink. Hamlet, this pearl is thine,
265   Here's to thy health! Give him the cup.

(*Drum, trumpets* [*sound*] *flourish. A piece goes off* [*within*].)

HAMLET   I'll play this bout first, set it by a while.
    Come.   [*They play again.*]   Another hit; what say you?
LAERTES   [A touch, a touch,] 'I do confess't.
KING   Our son shall win.
270 QUEEN   He's fat, and scant of breath.
    Here, Hamlet, take my napkin, rub thy brows.
    The Queen carouses to thy fortune, Hamlet.
HAMLET   Good madam!
KING   Gertrude, do not drink.
275 QUEEN   I will, my lord, I pray you pardon me.
KING [*aside*]   It is the pois'ned cup, it is too late.
HAMLET   I dare not drink yet, madam; by and by.
QUEEN   Come, let me wipe thy face.
LAERTES   My lord, I'll hit him now.
280 KING   I do not think't.
LAERTES [*aside*]   And yet it is almost against my conscience.
HAMLET   Come, for the third, Laertes, you do but dally.
    I pray you pass with your best violence;
    I am sure you make a wanton of me.
285 LAERTES   Say you so? Come on.   [*They play.*]
OSRIC   Nothing, neither way.
LAERTES   Have at you now!

[LAERTES *wounds* HAMLET; *then, in scuffling, they change rapiers.*]

KING   Part them, they are incens'd.
HAMLET   Nay, come again.

[HAMLET *wounds* LAERTES. *The* QUEEN *falls.*]

290 OSRIC   Look to the Queen there ho!
HORATIO   They bleed on both sides. How is it, my lord?
OSRIC   How is't, Laertes?
LAERTES   Why, as a woodcock to mine own springe, Osric:
    I am justly kill'd with mine own treachery.

---

270. **fat:** sweaty   272. **carouses:** drinks a toast   284. **make . . . me:** are holding back in order to let
me win, as one does with a spoiled child (*wanton*)   293. **springe:** snare

295 HAMLET   How does the Queen?

KING   She sounds to see them bleed.

QUEEN   No, no, the drink, the drink—O my dear Hamlet—
　　　The drink, the drink! I am pois'ned.   [*Dies.*]

HAMLET   O villainy! Ho, let the door be lock'd!
300　　Treachery! Seek it out.

LAERTES   It is here, Hamlet. [Hamlet,] thou art slain.
　　　No med'cine in the world can do thee good;
　　　In thee there is not half an hour's life.
　　　The treacherous instrument is in [thy] hand,
305　　Unbated and envenom'd. The foul practice
　　　Hath turn'd itself on me. Lo here I lie,
　　　Never to rise again. Thy mother's pois'ned.
　　　I can no more—the King, the King's to blame.

HAMLET   The point envenom'd too!
310　　Then, venom, to thy work.   [*hurts the* KING]

ALL   Treason! treason!

KING   O, yet defend me, friends, I am but hurt.

HAMLET   Here, thou incestious, [murd'rous], damned Dane,
　　　Drink [off] this potion! Is [thy union] here?
315　　Follow my mother!   [KING *dies.*]

LAERTES   He is justly served,
　　　It is a poison temper'd by himself.
　　　Exchange forgiveness with me, noble Hamlet.
　　　Mine and my father's death come not upon thee,
320　　Nor thine on me!   [*dies*]

HAMLET   Heaven make thee free of it! I follow thee.
　　　I am dead, Horatio. Wretched queen, adieu!
　　　You that look pale, and tremble at this chance,
　　　That are but mutes or audience to this act,
325　　Had I but time—as this fell sergeant, Death,
　　　Is strict in his arrest—O, I could tell you—
　　　But let it be. Horatio, I am dead,
　　　Thou livest. Report me and my cause aright
　　　To the unsatisfied.

330 HORATIO   Never believe it;
　　　I am more an antique Roman than a Dane.
　　　Here's yet some liquor left.

HAMLET   As th' art a man,
　　　Give me the cup. Let go! By heaven, I'll ha't!

---

296. **sounds:** swoons   305. **Unbated:** not blunted   **foul practice:** vile plot   s.d. **hurts:**
wounds   317. **temper'd:** mixed   321. **make thee free:** absolve you   324. **mutes or audience:** silent
spectators   325. **fell:** cruel   **sergeant:** sheriff's officer   331. **antique Roman:** one who will commit suicide on such an occasion

335 O God, Horatio, what a wounded name,
Things standing thus unknown, shall I leave behind me!
If thou didst ever hold me in thy heart,
Absent thee from felicity a while,
And in this harsh world draw thy breath in pain
340 To tell my story.   (*a march afar off* [*and a shot within*])
What warlike noise is this?

[OSRIC *goes to the door and returns.*]

OSRIC   Young Fortinbras, with conquest come from Poland,
To th' embassadors of England gives
This warlike volley.
345 HAMLET   O, I die, Horatio,
The potent poison quite o'er-crows my spirit.
I cannot live to hear the news from England,
But I do prophesy th' election lights
On Fortinbras, he has my dying voice.
350 So tell him, with th' occurrents more and less
Which have solicited—the rest is silence.   [*dies*]
HORATIO   Now cracks a noble heart. Good night, sweet prince,
And flights of angels sing thee to thy rest!

[*march within*]

Why does the drum come hither?

(*Enter* FORTINBRAS *with the* [ENGLISH] EMBASSADORS, [*with Drum, Colors, and* ATTENDANTS].)

355 FORTINBRAS   Where is this sight?
HORATIO   What is it you would see?
If aught of woe or wonder, cease your search.
FORTINBRAS   This quarry cries on havoc. O proud death,
What feast is toward in thine eternal cell,
360 That thou so many princes at a shot
So bloodily hast strook?
[1.] EMBASSADOR   The sight is dismal,
And our affairs from England come too late.
The ears are senseless that should give us hearing,
365 To tell him his commandment is fulfill'd,
That Rosencrantz and Guildenstern are dead.
Where should we have our thanks?

---

346. **o'er-crows:** triumphs over (a term derived from cockfighting)   **spirit:** vital
energy   349. **voice:** vote   350. **occurrents:** occurrences   351. **solicited:** instigated
358. **This . . . havoc:** this heap of corpses proclaims a massacre   359. **toward:** in preparation

HORATIO   Not from his mouth,
    Had it th' ability of life to thank you.
370   He never gave commandement for their death.
    But since so jump upon this bloody question,
    You from the Polack wars, and you from England,
    Are here arrived, give order that these bodies
    High on a stage be placed to the view,
375   And let me speak to [th'] yet unknowing world
    How these things came about. So shall you hear
    Of carnal, bloody, and unnatural acts,
    Of accidental judgments, casual slaughters,
    Of deaths put on by cunning and [forc'd] cause,
380   And in this upshot, purposes mistook
    Fall'n on th' inventors' heads: all this can I
    Truly deliver.
FORTINBRAS   Let us haste to hear it,
    And call the noblest to the audience.
385   For me, with sorrow I embrace my fortune.
    I have some rights, of memory in this kingdom,
    Which now to claim my vantage doth invite me.
HORATIO   Of that I shall have also cause to speak,
    And from his mouth whose voice will draw [on] more.
390   But let this same be presently perform'd
    Even while men's minds are wild, lest more mischance
    On plots and errors happen.
FORTINBRAS   Let four captains
    Bear Hamlet like a soldier to the stage,
395   For he was likely, had he been put on,
    To have prov'd most royal; and for his passage,
    The soldiers' music and the rite of war
    Speak loudly for him.
    Take up the bodies. Such a sight as this
400   Becomes the field, but here shows much amiss.
    Go bid the soldiers shoot.

c. 1600

(*Exeunt* [*marching; after the which a peal of ordinance are shot off*].)

---

368. **his:** the king's   371. **jump:** precisely, pat   **question:** matter   374. **stage:** platform
378. **judgments:** retributions   **casual:** happening by chance   379. **put on:** instigated
386. **of memory:** unforgotten   387. **my vantage:** my opportune presence at a moment when the throne is empty   389. **his . . . more:** the mouth of one (Hamlet) whose vote will induce others to support your claim   390. **presently:** at once   391. **wild:** distraught   395. **put on:** put to the test (by becoming king)   396. **passage:** death   400. **Becomes . . . amiss:** befits the battlefield, but appears very much out of place here

STUDY QUESTIONS

1. The climax in *Hamlet* extends over several scenes. Which ones are they?
2. What states does Hamlet pass through within these scenes?
3. How do his actions after the climax contrast with his actions before it?
4. What changes in Hamlet's outlook, or in your reaction to him, begin during these climactic scenes and develop during the latter part of the play?
5. Choose some topic that shows how the climax functions as a turning point in *Hamlet* and develop it as fully as possible, making use of specific examples not only from the climactic scenes but from earlier and later scenes as well.

Much Ado About Nothing

WILLIAM SHAKESPEARE

See page 325 for a biographical note on the author.

CHARACTERS

DON PEDRO, *Prince of Arragon*
DON JOHN, *his bastard brother*
CLAUDIO, *a young lord of Florence*
BENEDICK, *a young lord of Padua*
LEONATO, *governor of Messina*
ANTONIO, *his brother*
BALTHASAR, *attendant on Don Pedro*
CONRADE ⎫
BORACHIO ⎭ *followers of Don John*
FRIAR FRANCIS
DOGBERRY, *a constable*
VERGES, *a headborough*
SEXTON
BOY
HERO, *daughter to Leonato*
BEATRICE, *niece to Leonato*
MARGARET ⎫
URSULA ⎭ *gentlewomen attending on Hero*
MESSENGERS, WATCH, LORD, ATTENDANTS, *etc.*

SCENE: *Messina*

Act I

Scene I

(*Enter* LEONATO, *governor of Messina,* HERO *his daughter, and* BEATRICE *his niece, with a* MESSENGER.)

LEONATO   I learn in this letter that Don [Pedro] of Arragon comes this night to Messina.

Words and passages enclosed in square brackets in the text above are either emendations of the copytext or additions to it. The numbers in the footnotes are line numbers.
I.i. Location: Messina, before Leonato's house

MESSENGER   He is very near by this, he was not three leagues off when I left him.

5 LEONATO   How many gentlemen have you lost in this action?

MESSENGER   But few of any sort, and none of name.

LEONATO   A victory is twice itself when the achiever brings home full numbers. I find here that Don [Pedro] hath bestow'd much honor on a young Florentine call'd Claudio.

10 MESSENGER   Much deserv'd on his part, and equally rememb'red by Don Pedro. He hath borne himself beyond the promise of his age, doing in the figure of a lamb the feats of a lion. He hath indeed better bett'red expectation than you must expect of me to tell you how.

LEONATO   He hath an uncle here in Messina will be very much glad of it.

15 MESSENGER   I have already deliver'd him letters, and there appears much joy in him, even so much that joy could not show itself modest enough without a badge of bitterness.

LEONATO   Did he break out into tears?

MESSENGER   In great measure.

20 LEONATO   A kind overflow of kindness. There are no faces truer than those that are so wash'd. How much better is it to weep at joy than to joy at weeping!

BEATRICE   I pray you, is Signior Mountanto return'd from the wars or no?

MESSENGER   I know none of that name, lady. There was none such in the army of any sort.

25 LEONATO   What is he that you ask for, niece?

HERO   My cousin means Signior Benedick of Padua.

MESSENGER   O, he's return'd, and as pleasant as ever he was.

BEATRICE   He set up his bills here in Messina, and challeng'd Cupid at the flight, and my uncle's fool, reading the challenge, subscrib'd for Cupid, and

30   challeng'd him at the burbolt. I pray you, how many hath he kill'd and eaten in these wars? But how many hath he kill'd? for indeed I promis'd to eat all of his killing.

LEONATO   Faith, niece, you tax Signior Benedick too much, but he'll be meet with you, I doubt it not.

---

5. **action:** battle   6. **sort:** rank (so also in line 24)   **name:** reputation, prominence   12. **figure:** appearance   **bett'red:** surpassed   14. **will:** who will (a frequent construction)   16. **modest:** moderate   17. **badge of bitterness:** sign of sorrow. Leonato's next question translates these words into literal terms.   20. **kind:** natural   22. **Mountanto:** from Italian *montanto*, a fencing term meaning an upward blow or thrust   27. **pleasant:** jocular   28. **bills:** public notices   28–29. **at the flight:** to an archery contest. Perhaps she means that Benedick proclaimed himself immune to love.   29. **fool:** jester. It has been suggested that perhaps Beatrice means herself, and is referring obliquely to an earlier romantic encounter with Benedick. See lines 44–46 and II.i.200–202.   **subscrib'd for:** made an undertaking on behalf of   30. **burbolt:** bird-bolt, a blunt-headed arrow for shooting birds at short distance. The bird-bolt was allowed to fools and children as being less dangerous than the barbed long-distance arrow, and was frequently assigned to Cupid, perhaps because he was represented as a child.   31–32. **promis'd . . . killing:** predicted that he wouldn't kill anyone   33. **tax:** take to task, censure   **meet:** even, quits

35 MESSENGER   He hath done good service, lady, in these wars.

BEATRICE   You had musty victual, and he hath holp to eat it. He is a very valiant trencherman, he hath an excellent stomach.

MESSENGER   And a good soldier too, lady.

BEATRICE   And a good soldier to a lady, but what is he to a lord?

40 MESSENGER   A lord to a lord, a man to a man, stuff'd with all honorable virtues.

BEATRICE   It is so indeed, he is no less than a stuff'd man. But for the stuffing— well, we are all mortal.

LEONATO   You must not, sir, mistake my niece. There is a kind of merry war be-
45   twixt Signior Benedick and her; they never meet but there's a skirmish of wit between them.

BEATRICE   Alas, he gets nothing by that. In our last conflict four of his five wits went halting off, and now is the whole man govern'd with one; so that if he have wit enough to keep himself warm, let him bear it for a difference be-
50   tween himself and his horse, for it is all the wealth that he hath left to be known a reasonable creature. Who is his companion now? he hath every month a new sworn brother.

MESSENGER   Is't possible?

BEATRICE   Very easily possible. He wears his faith but as the fashion of his hat:
55   it ever changes with the next block.

MESSENGER   I see, lady, the gentleman is not in your books.

BEATRICE   No, and he were, I would burn my study. But I pray you, who is his companion? Is there no young squarer now that will make a voyage with him to the devil?

60 MESSENGER   He is most in the company of the right noble Claudio.

BEATRICE   O Lord, he will hang upon him like a disease; he is sooner caught than the pestilence, and the taker runs presently mad. God help the noble Claudio! If he have caught the Benedick, it will cost him a thousand pound ere 'a be cur'd.

65 MESSENGER   I will hold friends with you, lady.

BEATRICE   Do, good friend.

LEONATO   You will never run mad, niece.

BEATRICE   No, not till a hot January.

MESSENGER   Don Pedro is approach'd.

---

36. **musty:** stale   **holp:** helped   37. **trencherman:** good eater   **stomach:** appetite   39. **to:** in comparison with   42. **stuff'd man:** a dummy, not a real man   42–43. **for . . . mortal:** as for his character—well, we all have our faults   47. **five wits:** usually listed as memory, fantasy, judgment, imagination, and common wit   48. **halting:** limping   49. **wit . . . warm:** proverbial for minimal intelligence   **difference:** a variation in a coat of arms to distinguish a junior member or branch of a family from the chief line.   51. **known:** recognized as   52. **sworn brother:** friend with whom he has exchanged vows of lifelong fidelity   54. **faith:** loyalty   55. **block:** wooden mould for shaping hats; hence, fashion   56. **books:** good books, favor   57. **and:** if   58. **squarer:** quarreller   62. **presently:** immediately   64. **'a:** he   65. **hold friends:** keep on friendly terms (so as not to incur your wrath)   67. **run mad:** "catch the Benedick"

(*Enter* Don Pedro, Claudio, Benedick, Balthasar, *and* [Don] John *the Bastard.*)

70 DON PEDRO   Good Signior Leonato, are you come to meet your trouble? The fashion of the world is to avoid cost, and you encounter it.

LEONATO   Never came trouble to my house in the likeness of your Grace, for trouble being gone, comfort should remain; but when you depart from me, sorrow abides and happiness takes his leave.

75 DON PEDRO   You embrace your charge too willingly. I think this is your daughter.

LEONATO   Her mother hath many times told me so.

BENEDICK   Were you in doubt, sir, that you ask'd her?

LEONATO   Signior Benedick, no, for then were you a child.

80 DON PEDRO   You have it full, Benedick. We may guess by this what you are, being a man. Truly the lady fathers herself. Be happy, lady, for you are like an honorable father.

BENEDICK   If Signior Leonato be her father, she would not have his head on her shoulders for all Messina, as like him as she is.

85 BEATRICE   I wonder that you will still be talking, Signior Benedick, nobody marks you.

BENEDICK   What, my dear Lady Disdain! are you yet living?

BEATRICE   Is it possible disdain should die while she hath such meet food to feed it as Signior Benedick? Courtesy itself must convert to disdain, if you
90   come in her presence.

BENEDICK   Then is courtesy a turncoat. But it is certain I am lov'd of all ladies, only you excepted; and I would I could find in my heart that I had not a hard heart, for truly I love none.

BEATRICE   A dear happiness to women, they would else have been troubled
95   with a pernicious suitor. I thank God and my cold blood, I am of your humor for that: I had rather hear my dog bark at a crow than a man swear he loves me.

BENEDICK   God keep your ladyship still in that mind! so some gentleman or other shall scape a predestinate scratch'd face.

100 BEATRICE   Scratching could not make it worse, and 'twere such a face as yours were.

BENEDICK   Well, you are a rare parrot-teacher.

BEATRICE   A bird of my tongue is better than a beast of yours.

---

71. **cost:** expense   **encounter:** go to meet   75. **embrace your charge:** welcome your burden
80. **have it full:** are well answered, have got back as good as you gave   81. **fathers herself:** shows who her father is (by her resemblance to him)   83. **his head:** with its marks of age   85. **still:** always   89. **convert:** change   94. **dear happiness:** great stroke of good fortune   96. **humor for that:** inclination in that respect   99. **scape:** escape   **predestinate:** foreordained, inevitable (for anyone who marries Beatrice)   101. **were:** is (the verb has been attracted into the subjunctive by the preceding *'twere*)   102. **rare:** excellent   **parrot-teacher:** one who says the same thing over and over
103. **A bird . . . yours:** A bird taught to speak like me would be better than an animal taught to speak like you, for he would say nothing.

BENEDICK   I would my horse had the speed of your tongue, and so good a con-
105   tinuer. But keep your way a' God's name, I have done.

BEATRICE   You always end with a jade's trick, I know you of old.

DON PEDRO   That is the sum of all: Leonato—Signior Claudio and Signior
    Benedick—my dear friend Leonato hath invited you all. I tell him we shall
    stay here at the least a month, and he heartily prays some occasion may de-
110   tain us longer. I dare swear he is no hypocrite, but prays from his heart.

LEONATO   If you swear, my lord, you shall not be forsworn.   [*to* DON JOHN]
    Let me bid you welcome, my lord, being reconcil'd to the Prince your
    brother: I owe you all duty.

DON JOHN   I thank you. I am not of many words, but I thank you.

115 LEONATO   Please it your Grace lead on?

DON PEDRO   Your hand, Leonato, we will go together.

(*Exeunt. Manent* BENEDICK *and* CLAUDIO.)

CLAUDIO   Benedick, didst thou note the daughter of Signior Leonato?

BENEDICK   I noted her not, but I look'd on her.

CLAUDIO   Is she not a modest young lady?

120 BENEDICK   Do you question me, as an honest man should do, for my simple
    true judgment? or would you have me speak after my custom, as being a
    profess'd tyrant to their sex?

CLAUDIO   No, I pray thee speak in sober judgment.

BENEDICK   Why, i' faith, methinks she's too low for a high praise, too brown for
125   a fair praise, and too little for a great praise; only this commendation I can
    afford her, that were she other than she is, she were unhandsome, and being
    no other but as she is, I do not like her.

CLAUDIO   Thou thinkest I am in sport. I pray thee tell me truly how thou lik'st
    her.

130 BENEDICK   Would you buy her, that you inquire after her?

CLAUDIO   Can the world buy such a jewel?

BENEDICK   Yea, and a case to put it into. But speak you this with a sad brow? or
    do you play the flouting Jack, to tell us Cupid is a good hare-finder and Vul-
    can a rare carpenter? Come, in what key shall a man take you to go in the
135   song?

CLAUDIO   In mine eye, she is the sweetest lady that ever I look'd on.

BENEDICK   I can see yet without spectacles, and I see no such matter. There's
    her cousin, and she were not possess'd with a fury, exceeds her as much in

---

104–105. **so . . . continuer:** (were) so tireless   106. **jade's trick:** A jade is an ill-conditioned horse,
likely to drop out of a race before the end, as Benedick here lamely drops out of the contest of wits.
107. **That . . . all:** Don Pedro and Leonato have been conversing aside.   112. **being:** since you are
118. **noted her not:** didn't observe her in particular   122. **tyrant:** one pitiless and cruel   124. **low:**
short   132. **sad:** serious   133. **flouting Jack:** mocking fellow   133–34. **to . . . carpenter:** by saying
something as obviously wide of the truth as that Cupid has sharp eyes, or calling Vulcan a carpenter
(Cupid was blind, Vulcan the blacksmith of the gods).   134–35. **go . . . song:** sing in harmony with you

beauty as the first of May doth the last of December. But I hope you have no
140   intent to turn husband, have you?

CLAUDIO   I would scarce trust myself, though I had sworn the contrary, if Hero
would be my wife.

BENEDICK   Is't come to this? In faith, hath not the world one man but he will
wear his cap with suspicion? Shall I never see a bachelor of threescore again?
145   Go to, i' faith, and thou wilt needs thrust thy neck into a yoke, wear the print
of it, and sigh away Sundays. Look, Don Pedro is return'd to seek you.

(*Enter* DON PEDRO.)

DON PEDRO   What secret hath held you here, that you follow'd not to
Leonato's?

BENEDICK   I would your Grace would constrain me to tell.

150 DON PEDRO   I charge thee on thy allegiance.

BENEDICK   You hear, Count Claudio, I can be secret as a dumb man; I would
have you think so; but on my allegiance, mark you this, on my allegiance, he
is in love. With who? Now that is your Grace's part. Mark how short his answer is: with Hero, Leonato's short daughter.

155 CLAUDIO   If this were so, so were it utt'red.

BENEDICK   Like the old tale, my lord: "It is not so, nor 'twas not so, but indeed,
God forbid it should be so."

CLAUDIO   If my passion change not shortly, God forbid it should be otherwise.

DON PEDRO   Amen, if you love her, for the lady is very well worthy.

160 CLAUDIO   You speak this to fetch me in, my lord.

DON PEDRO   By my troth, I speak my thought.

CLAUDIO   And in faith, my lord, I spoke mine.

BENEDICK   And by my two faiths and troths, my lord, I spoke mine.

CLAUDIO   That I love her, I feel.

165 DON PEDRO   That she is worthy, I know.

BENEDICK   That I neither feel how she should be lov'd, nor know how she
should be worthy, is the opinion that fire cannot melt out of me; I will die in
it at the stake.

DON PEDRO   Thou wast ever an obstinate heretic in the despite of beauty.

170 CLAUDIO   And never could maintain his part but in the force of his will.

---

144. **wear . . . suspicion:** an allusion to the popular jest that a cuckold (husband of an unfaithful
wife) grew horns   146. **Sundays:** the day a husband would be expected to spend with his wife
153. **part:** speaking part (namely, to ask "With who?")   155. **If . . . utt'red:** If it were true and I had
told him so in confidence, he would have violated my confidence in just this manner.   156. **old
tale:** Apparently some form of the Bluebeard story. In an eighteenth-century version cited by Fur-
ness, a lady who has discovered the bodies of the victims describes her experience, under the fiction
that she is recalling a dream, and at intervals the murderer, who is among the listeners, interjects the
words here quoted.   160. **fetch me in:** trick me, take me in   169. **despite:** despising, contempt
170. **in . . . will:** by willful obstinacy (not by rational argument). Willful adherence to heterodox
opinion was the essential element of heresy.

BENEDICK   That a woman conceiv'd me, I thank her; that she brought me up, I
likewise give her most humble thanks; but that I will have a rechate winded
in my forehead, or hang my bugle in an invisible baldrick, all women shall
pardon me. Because I will not do them the wrong to mistrust any, I will do
175   myself the right to trust none; and the fine is (for the which I may go the
finer), I will live a bachelor.

DON PEDRO   I shall see thee, ere I die, look pale with love.

BENEDICK   With anger, with sickness, or with hunger, my lord, not with love.
Prove that ever I lose more blood with love than I will get again with drink-
180   ing, pick out mine eyes with a ballad-maker's pen, and hang me up at the
door of a brothel-house for the sign of blind Cupid.

DON PEDRO   Well, if ever thou dost fall from this faith, thou wilt prove a notable argument.

BENEDICK   If I do, hang me in a bottle like a cat, and shoot at me, and he that
185   hits me, let him be clapp'd on the shoulder, and call'd Adam.

DON PEDRO   Well, as time shall try: "In time the savage bull doth bear the yoke."

BENEDICK   The savage bull may, but if ever the sensible Benedick bear it, pluck
off the bull's horns, and set them in my forehead, and let me be vildly
painted, and in such great letters as they write "Here is good horse to hire,"
190   let them signify under my sign, "Here you may see Benedick the married
man."

CLAUDIO   If this should ever happen, thou wouldst be horn-mad.

DON PEDRO   Nay, if Cupid have not spent all his quiver in Venice, thou wilt
quake for this shortly.

195 BENEDICK   I look for an earthquake too then.

DON PEDRO   Well, you will temporize with the hours. In the mean time, good
Signior Benedick, repair to Leonato's, commend me to him, and tell him I
will not fail him at supper, for indeed he hath made great preparation.

BENEDICK   I have almost matter enough in me for such an embassage, and so I
200   commit you—

172–73. **that . . . forehead:** that I should wear a cuckold's horns. A rechate (or recheat) is a series of
notes sounded (*winded*) on the horn for calling the hounds together.   173. **hang . . . baldrick:** carry
my horn not in the usual place on the usual strap (*baldrick*) but where no strap is seen (because none
is present)—on my forehead   173–74. **shall pardon me:** must excuse me from   175. **fine:** end
179. **Prove:** if you can show   179–80. **I . . . drinking:** It was a common belief that sighing (characteristic of lovers) consumed the blood, but that wine generated fresh blood.   180. **a ballad-maker's
pen:** an instrument of satire   181. **sign:** Inns, shops, etc., were identified by painted signs.
182–83. **notable argument:** outstanding example in discussions of the topic   184. **bottle:** wicker
case. Sometimes a cat was suspended in such a container as a target for archers.   185. **Adam:** probably an allusion to Adam Bell, an archer celebrated in ballads for his skill   186. **try:** test, show   **In
. . . yoke:** inaccurately quoted from Kyd's *The Spanish Tragedy*, II.i.3   187. **sensible:** rational.   188.
vildly: vilely, wretchedly   192. **horn-mad:** mad as a horned beast, stark mad (with the common allusion to cuckold's horns)   193. **spent . . . quiver:** used up all his arrows (with play following on *quiver*
= tremble)   **Venice:** noted at the time for its licentiousness   195. **I . . . too:** it will take an earthquake
as well   196. **temporize:** come to terms, compromise   197. **commend me:** present my compliments
199. **matter:** substance, intelligence   199–200. **and . . . you:** a conventional form of words which
Claudio and Don Pedro jeer at by extending it into a stock complimentary closing for a letter

CLAUDIO   To the tuition of God. From my house—if I had it—

DON PEDRO   The sixt of July. Your loving friend, Benedick.

BENEDICK   Nay, mock not, mock not. The body of your discourse is sometime
guarded with fragments, and the guards are but slightly basted on neither.
205   Ere you flout old ends any further, examine your conscience, and so I leave
you.

[*Exit.*]

CLAUDIO   My liege, your Highness now may do me good.

DON PEDRO   My love is thine to teach; teach it but how,
And thou shalt see how apt it is to learn
210   Any hard lesson that may do thee good.

CLAUDIO   Hath Leonato any son, my lord?

DON PEDRO   No child but Hero, she's his only heir.
Dost thou affect her, Claudio?

CLAUDIO   O my lord,
215   When you went onward on this ended action,
I look'd upon her with a soldier's eye,
That lik'd, but had a rougher task in hand
Than to drive liking to the name of love.
But now I am return'd, and that war-thoughts
220   Have left their places vacant, in their rooms
Come thronging soft and delicate desires,
All prompting me how fair young Hero is,
Saying I lik'd her ere I went to wars.

DON PEDRO   Thou wilt be like a lover presently,
225   And tire the hearer with a book of words.
If thou dost love fair Hero, cherish it,
And I will break with her, and with her father,
And thou shalt have her. Was't not to this end
That thou began'st to twist so fine a story?

230   CLAUDIO   How sweetly you do minister to love,
That know love's grief by his complexion!

---

201. **tuition:** protection   202. **sixt:** sixth   204. **guarded with fragments:** trimmed with odds and
ends (a metaphor from dressmaking, looking back to *body* in the sense "bodice," and continued in
basted on; but suggesting also that Don Pedro can guard his serious concerns from exposure by talking inanities when it suits him)   **the guards . . . neither:** the trimmings are very insecurely stitched
on too (they have little connection with what is being said)   205. **flout:** mock, jeer at   **old ends:**
(1) old tags (= the *fragments* of line 286); (2) conventional closings (of letters)   **examine your conscience:** consider whether you have ever been guilty of the same thing   213. **affect:** love
215. **ended action:** campaign now ended   219. **now I:** now that I   224. **presently:** any moment
now   225. **book of words:** whole book of lover's set speeches   227. **break with:** broach the subject
to   229. **twist:** spin   231. **his complexion:** its outward appearance

But lest my liking might too sudden seem,
I would have salv'd it with a longer treatise.

DON PEDRO   What need the bridge much broader than the flood?
235   The fairest grant is the necessity.
Look what will serve is fit: 'tis once, thou lovest,
And I will fit thee with the remedy.
I know we shall have revelling to-night;
I will assume thy part in some disguise,
240   And tell fair Hero I am Claudio,
And in her bosom I'll unclasp my heart,
And take her hearing prisoner with the force
And strong encounter of my amorous tale;
Then after to her father will I break,
245   And the conclusion is, she shall be thine.
In practice let us put it presently.

(*Exeunt.*)

[Scene II]

(*Enter* LEONATO *and an old man* [ANTONIO], *brother to* LEONATO, [*meeting*].)

LEONATO   How now, brother, where is my cousin, your son? Hath he provided
this music?

ANTONIO   He is very busy about it. But, brother, I can tell you strange news that
you yet dreamt not of.

5 LEONATO   Are they good?

ANTONIO   As the [event] stamps them, but they have a good cover; they show
well outward. The Prince and Count Claudio, walking in a thick-pleach'd
alley in mine orchard, were thus much overheard by a man of mine. The
Prince discover'd to Claudio that he lov'd my niece your daughter, and
10   meant to acknowledge it this night in a dance; and if he found her accordant, he meant to take the present time by the top, and instantly break with
you of it.

LEONATO   Hath the fellow any wit that told you this?

ANTONIO   A good sharp fellow. I will send for him, and question him yourself.

---

233. **salv'd:** smoothed, put a better face on   **treatise:** discourse   235. **The fairest . . . necessity:** The
best gift is the one that fills the need of the occasion.   236. **Look what:** whatever   **'tis once:** the simple
fact is   241. **in . . . unclasp:** to her private hearing I'll disclose the contents (*unclasp* = open the book)
of.

I.ii. Location: Leonato's house
1. **cousin:** used of aunt, uncle, niece, or nephew, as well as of cousin in the modern sense   6. **event:**
outcome   **stamps . . . cover:** Antonio uses the figure of news printed and bound in a book.
7–8. **thick-pleach'd alley:** walk bordered with bushes or small trees and overarched with their
densely entwined boughs   8. **orchard:** garden   9. **discover'd:** revealed   10–11. **accordant:** consenting   11. **top:** forelock   13. **wit:** intelligence

15 LEONATO   No, no, we will hold it as a dream till it appear itself; but I will acquaint my daughter withal, that she may be the better prepar'd for an answer, if peradventure this be true. Go you and tell her of it.   [*Several persons cross the stage.*]   Cousins, you know what you have to do. O, I cry you
mercy, friend, go you with me, and I will use your skill. Good cousin, have a
20   care this busy time.

(*Exeunt.*)

[Scene III]

(*Enter* [DON] JOHN *the Bastard and* CONRADE, *his companion.*)

CONRADE   What the good-year, my lord, why are you thus out of measure sad?
DON JOHN   There is no measure in the occasion that breeds, therefore the sadness is without limit.
CONRADE   You should hear reason.
5 DON JOHN   And when I have heard it, what blessing brings it?
CONRADE   If not a present remedy, at least a patient sufferance.
DON JOHN   I wonder that thou (being, as thou say'st thou art, born under Saturn) goest about to apply a moral medicine to a mortifying mischief. I cannot hide what I am: I must be sad when I have cause, and smile at no man's
10   jests; eat when I have stomach, and wait for no man's leisure; sleep when I
am drowsy, and tend on no man's business; laugh when I am merry, and
claw no man in his humor. ·
CONRADE   Yea, but you must not make the full show of this till you may do it
without controlment. You have of late stood out against your brother, and
15   he hath ta'en you newly into his grace, where it is impossible you should
take true root but by the fair weather that you make yourself. It is needful
that you frame the season for your own harvest.
DON JOHN   I had rather be a canker in a hedge than a rose in his grace, and it
better fits my blood to be disdain'd of all than to fashion a carriage to rob
20   love from any. In this (though I cannot be said to be a flattering honest

---

15. **appear itself:** make itself evident (as a face)   16. **withal:** with it   18–19. **cry you mercy:** beg
your pardon

I.iii. Location: Leonato's house
1. **What the good-year:** an unexplained expletive   **out of measure:** immoderately
2. **breeds:** causes it   4. **hear:** listen to   6. **present:** immediate   **sufferance:** endurance
7–8. **born under Saturn:** born when the planet Saturn was predominant, hence supposedly
morose (cf. *saturnine*)   8. **goest . . . mischief:** dost endeavor to cure a deadly ill by means of
moralizing platitudes   11. **tend on:** attend to   12. **claw:** flatter, humor   **humor:** whims
14. **controlment:** restraint   **stood out:** rebelled   15. **grace:** favor   17. **frame:** create
18. **canker:** wild rose (considered a weed)   19. **blood:** mood, temper   **fashion a carriage:**
counterfeit a behavior

man) it must not be denied but I am a plain-dealing villain. I am trusted
with a muzzle, and enfranchis'd with a clog, therefore I have decreed not to
sing in my cage. If I had my mouth, I would bite; if I had my liberty, I would
do my liking. In the mean time let me be that I am, and seek not to alter me.

25 CONRADE Can you make no use of your discontent?

DON JOHN I make all use of it, for I use it only. Who comes here?

(*Enter* BORACHIO.)

What news Borachio?

BORACHIO I came yonder from a great supper. The Prince your brother is roy-
ally entertain'd by Leonato, and I can give you intelligence of an intended
30   marriage.

DON JOHN Will it serve for any model to build mischief on? What is he for a
fool that betroths himself to unquietness?

BORACHIO Marry, it is your brother's right hand.

DON JOHN Who, the most exquisite Claudio?

35 BORACHIO Even he.

DON JOHN A proper squire! And who, and who? which way looks he?

BORACHIO Marry, one Hero, the daughter and heir of Leonato.

DON JOHN A very forward March-chick! How came you to this?

BORACHIO Being entertain'd for a perfumer, as I was smoking a musty room,
40   comes me the Prince and Claudio, hand in hand in sad conference. I whipt
me behind the arras, and there heard it agreed upon that the Prince should
woo Hero for himself, and having obtain'd her, give her to Count Claudio.

DON JOHN Come, come, let us thither, this may prove food to my displeasure.
That young start-up hath all the glory of my overthrow. If I can cross him
45   any way, I bless myself every way. You are both sure, and will assist me?

CONRADE To the death, my lord.

DON JOHN Let us to the great supper, their cheer is the greater that I am sub-
du'd. Would the cook were a' my mind! Shall we go prove what's to be done?

BORACHIO We'll wait upon your lordship.

(*Exeunt.*)

21–22. **trusted . . . muzzle:** trusted as a muzzled dog is trusted, not trusted at all
22. **enfranchis'd:** given my freedom   **clog:** a heavy block of wood attached to an animal to restrict
its movement   **decreed:** made up my mind   s.d. **Borachio:** Spanish *borracho* means "drunkard."
31–32. **What . . . fool:** what kind of fool is he   33. **Marry:** indeed (originally the name of the Virgin
Mary used as an oath)   36. **proper squire:** handsome young fellow (spoken sneeringly)
38. **forward:** precocious   **March-chick:** chick which has hatched prematurely   39. **entertain'd for:**
hired as   **smoking:** refreshing the air of (by burning some aromatic substance)   40. **sad:**
serious   41. **arras:** tapestry wall-hanging   43. **displeasure:** anger, hatred   44. **start-up:** upstart
cross: thwart (with following quibble on the sense "make the sign of the cross")   45. **sure:** loyal, to
be counted on   48. **prove:** try, discover   49. **wait upon:** attend

Act II

Scene I

(*Enter* LEONATO, [ANTONIO] *his brother,* HERO *his daughter, and* BEATRICE *his niece,* [MARGARET, URSULA,] *and a* KINSMAN.)

LEONATO   Was not Count John here at supper?

ANTONIO   I saw him not.

BEATRICE   How tartly that gentleman looks! I never can see him but I am heart-burn'd an hour after.

5   HERO   He is of a very melancholy disposition.

BEATRICE   He were an excellent man that were made just in the midway be-tween him and Benedick: the one is too like an image and says nothing, and the other too like my lady's eldest son, evermore tattling.

LEONATO   Then half Signior Benedick's tongue in Count John's mouth, and
10   half Count John's melancholy in Signior Benedick's face—

BEATRICE   With a good leg and a good foot, uncle, and money enough in his purse, such a man would win any woman in the world, if 'a could get her good will.

LEONATO   By my troth, niece, thou wilt never get thee a husband, if thou be so
15   shrewd of thy tongue.

ANTONIO   In faith, she's too curst.

BEATRICE   Too curst is more than curst. I shall lessen God's sending that way, for it is said, "God sends a curst cow short horns"—but to a cow too curst he sends none.

20   LEONATO   So, by being too curst, God will send you no horns.

BEATRICE   Just, if he send me no husband, for the which blessing I am at him upon my knees every morning and evening. Lord, I could not endure a hus-band with a beard on his face, I had rather lie in the woollen!

LEONATO   You may light on a husband that hath no beard.

25   BEATRICE   What should I do with him? dress him in my apparel and make him my waiting-gentlewoman? He that hath a beard is more than a youth, and he that hath no beard is less than a man; and he that is more than a youth is not for me, and he that is less than a man, I am not for him; therefore I will even take sixpence in earnest of the berrord, and lead his apes into hell.

30   LEONATO   Well then, go you into hell.

II.i. Location: Leonato's house

3. **tartly:** Modern idiom would require the adjectival form.   3–4. **am heart-burn'd:** suffer from heartburn (caused by Don John's sour looks)   8. **my ... son:** a spoiled child   15. **shrewd:** sharp, satirical   16. **curst:** ill-tempered; here, sharp-tongued; in line 18, vicious, savage   21. **Just:** pre-cisely, just so   **if ... husband:** She implies that God, in sending her a husband, would also send horns—that her husband would certainly be a cuckold.   23. **in the woollen:** between woollen blan-kets, without sheets   29. **in earnest:** as advance payment   **berrord:** bear-ward, one who keeps and trains bears (and sometimes apes)   **lead ... hell:** the proverbial fate of old maids

BEATRICE   No, but to the gate, and there will the devil meet me like an old
cuckold with horns on his head, and say, "Get you to heaven, Beatrice, get
you to heaven, here's no place for you maids." So deliver I up my apes, and
away to Saint Peter. For the heavens, he shows me where the bachelors sit,
35   and there live we as merry as the day is long.

ANTONIO [*to* HERO]   Well, niece, I trust you will be rul'd by your father.

BEATRICE   Yes, faith, it is my cousin's duty to make cur'sy and say, "Father, as it
please you." But yet for all that, cousin, let him be a handsome fellow, or else
make another cur'sy and say, "Father, as it please me."

40 LEONATO   Well, niece, I hope to see you one day fitted with a husband.

BEATRICE   Not till God make men of some other mettle than earth. Would it
not grieve a woman to be overmaster'd with a piece of valiant dust? to make
an account of her life to a clod of wayward marl? No, uncle, I'll none.
Adam's sons are my brethren, and truly I hold it a sin to match in my kinred.

45 LEONATO   Daughter, remember what I told you. If the Prince do solicit you in
that kind, you know your answer.

BEATRICE   The fault will be in the music, cousin, if you be not woo'd in good
time. If the Prince be too important, tell him there is measure in every
thing, and so dance out the answer. For hear me, Hero: wooing, wedding,
50   and repenting, is as a Scotch jig, a measure, and a cinquepace; the first suit
is hot and hasty, like a Scotch jib, and full as fantastical; the wedding,
mannerly-modest, as a measure, full of state and ancientry; and then comes
repentance, and with his bad legs falls into the cinquepace faster and faster,
till he sink into his grave.

55 LEONATO   Cousin, you apprehend passing shrewdly.

BEATRICE   I have a good eye, uncle, I can see a church by daylight.

LEONATO   The revellers are ent'ring, brother, make good room.   [*They put on
their masks.*]

(*Enter Prince* [DON] PEDRO, CLAUDIO, *and* BENEDICK, *and* [DON] JOHN, [*and*
BORACHIO *as maskers, with a Drum*].)

DON PEDRO   Lady, will you walk about with your friend?

HERO   So you walk softly, and look sweetly, and say nothing. I am yours for the
60   walk, and especially when I walk away.

DON PEDRO   With me in your company?

HERO   I may say so when I please.

---

34. **For the heavens:** so far as heaven is concerned   **bachelors:** unmarried persons of either
sex 37. **cur'sy:** curtsy 41. **mettle:** substance 43. **marl:** clay 44. **match . . . kinred:** marry
within the forbidden degrees of relationship; *kinred* = kindred   47–48. **in good time:** with propri-
ety (with obvious pun) 48. **important:** importunate, pressing   **measure:** (1) moderation; (2)
slow, stately dance 50. **cinquepace:** lively dance (trisyllabic) 51. **full:** fully, quite 52. **mannerly-
modest:** becomingly moderate in tempo   **state and ancientry:** traditional stateliness 55. **apprehend passing shrewdly:** perceive with unusual sharpness   s.d. **Drum:** drummer 58. **friend:** often
used in the sense "lover," and perhaps so here 59. **softly:** gently

DON PEDRO   And when please you to say so?

HERO   When I like your favor, for God defend the lute should be like the case!

65   DON PEDRO   My visor is Philemon's roof, within the house is Jove.

HERO   Why then your visor should be thatch'd.

DON PEDRO   Speak low if you speak love.

[They move aside.]

[BORACHIO]   Well, I would you did like me.

MARGARET   So would not I for your own sake, for I have many ill qualities.

70   [BORACHIO]   Which is one?

MARGARET   I say my prayers aloud.

[BORACHIO]   I love you the better; the hearers may cry amen.

MARGARET   God match me with a good dancer!

[BORACHIO]   Amen.

75   MARGARET   And God keep him out of my sight when the dance is done! Answer, clerk.

[BORACHIO]   No more words; the clerk is answer'd.

[They move aside.]

URSULA   I know you well enough, you are Signior Antonio.

ANTONIO   At a word, I am not.

80   URSULA   I know you by the waggling of your head.

ANTONIO   To tell you true, I counterfeit him.

URSULA   You could never do him so ill-well, unless you were the very man. Here's his dry hand up and down. You are he, you are he.

ANTONIO   At a word, I am not.

85   URSULA   Come, come, do you think I do not know you by your excellent wit? Can virtue hide itself? Go to, mum, you are he. Graces will appear, and there's an end.

[They move aside.]

BEATRICE   Will you not tell me who told you so?

BENEDICK   No, you shall pardon me.

90   BEATRICE   Nor will you not tell me who you are?

BENEDICK   Not now.

---

64. **favor:** face   **God . . . case:** God forbid that your face should not be handsomer than your mask.
65. **visor:** mask   **Philemon's roof:** Philemon and his wife Baucis entertained Jove in their peasant cottage, unaware of his identity (Ovid, *Metamorphoses,* viii).   66. **thatch'd:** (1) roofed with thatch (as peasant cottages generally were); (2) bearded   69. **ill:** bad   75–76. **Answer, clerk:** say amen (= so be it) again. It was the duty of the parish clerk to say the responses at church services.
79. **At:** in   82. **do . . . ill-well:** imitate his imperfections so perfectly   83. **dry hand:** a sign of age   **up and down:** exactly   86. **virtue:** excellence (of any kind)   **mum:** silence   87. **an end:** no more to be said

BEATRICE   That I was disdainful, and that I had my good wit out of the "Hundred Merry Tales"—well, this was Signior Benedick that said so.

BENEDICK   What's he?

95 BEATRICE   I am sure you know him well enough.

BENEDICK   Not I, believe me.

BEATRICE   Did he never make you laugh?

BENEDICK   I pray you, what is he?

BEATRICE   Why, he is the Prince's jester, a very dull fool; only his gift is in devis-
100   ing impossible slanders. None but libertines delight in him, and the commendation is not in his wit, but in his villainy, for he both pleases men and
angers them, and then they laugh at him and beat him. I am sure he is in the
fleet; I would he had boarded me.

BENEDICK   When I know the gentleman, I'll tell him what you say.

105 BEATRICE   Do, do, he'll but break a comparison or two on me, which peradventure, not mark'd, or not laugh'd at, strikes him into melancholy, and then
there's a partridge wing sav'd, for the fool will eat no supper that night.
[*Music for the dance begins.*]   We must follow the leaders.

BENEDICK   In every good thing.

110 BEATRICE   Nay, if they lead to any ill, I will leave them at the next turning.

(*Dance. [Then] exeunt [all but* DON JOHN, BORACHIO, *and* CLAUDIO].)

DON JOHN   Sure my brother is amorous on Hero, and hath withdrawn her father to break with him about it. The ladies follow her, and but one visor remains.

BORACHIO   And that is Claudio. I know him by his bearing.

115 DON JOHN   Are not you Signior Benedick?

CLAUDIO   You know me well, I am he.

DON JOHN   Signior, you are very near my brother in his love. He is enamor'd on
Hero. I pray you dissuade him from her, she is no equal for his birth. You
may do the part of an honest man in it.

120 CLAUDIO   How know you he loves her?

DON JOHN   I heard him swear his affection.

BORACHIO   So did I too, and he swore he would marry her to-night.

DON JOHN   Come let us to the banquet.

(*Exeunt. Manet* CLAUDIO.)

92–93. **Hundred Merry Tales:** a popular collection of jests and tales, first published in 1526
99. **dull:** stupid   **only his gift:** his only talent   100. **impossible:** incredible   **libertines:** those who
reject the customary restraints upon thought and behavior   101. **villainy:** satiric rudeness
103. **fleet:** company drifting about the room   **boarded:** come alongside (a ship) to attempt an attack on it; here, tried his wit on   105. **break a comparison:** crack a joke   108. **leaders:** of the
dance   117. **very...love:** a very close friend of my brother's   123. **banquet:** light repast of sweets,
fruit, and wine

CLAUDIO   Thus answer I in name of Benedick,
125   But hear these ill news with the ears of Claudio.
'Tis certain so, the Prince woos for himself.
Friendship is constant in all other things
Save in the office and affairs of love;
Therefore all hearts in love use their own tongues.
130   Let every eye negotiate for itself,
And trust no agent; for beauty is a witch
Against whose charms faith melteth into blood.
This is an accident of hourly proof,
Which I mistrusted not. Farewell therefore Hero!

(*Enter* BENEDICK.)

135   BENEDICK   Count Claudio?
CLAUDIO   Yea, the same.
BENEDICK   Come, will you go with me?
CLAUDIO   Whither?
BENEDICK   Even to the next willow, about your own business, County. What
140   fashion will you wear the garland of? about your neck, like an usurer's
chain? or under your arm, like a lieutenant's scarf? You must wear it one
way, for the Prince hath got your Hero.
CLAUDIO   I wish him joy of her.
BENEDICK   Why, that's spoken like an honest drovier; so they sell bullocks. But
145   did you think the Prince would have serv'd you thus?
CLAUDIO   I pray you leave me.
BENEDICK   Ho, now you strike like the blind man. 'Twas the boy that stole your
meat, and you'll beat the post.
CLAUDIO   If it will not be, I'll leave you.

(*Exit.*)

150   BENEDICK   Alas, poor hurt fowl, now will he creep into sedges. But that my
Lady Beatrice should know me, and not know me! The Prince's fool! hah, it
may be I go under that title because I am merry. Yea, but so I am apt to do
myself wrong. I am not so reputed. It is the base (though bitter) disposition

128. **office:** business   129. **all:** let all   132. **Against whose charms:** in the face of whose
spells   **blood:** passion   133. **accident ... proof:** occurrence of a sort that takes place every
hour   134. **mistrusted:** suspected   139. **next:** nearest   **willow:** the emblem of unrequited love
County: count   140. **garland:** of willow   141–42. **one way:** one way or another   144. **drovier:**
drover, cattle dealer   147. **blind man:** The particular story has not been identified. In the Spanish
romance *Lazarillo de Tormes,* the hero steals a sausage from his master, a blind beggar, and is so severely punished by him that, in revenge, he causes the blind man to jump against a stone pillar.
148. **post:** pillar (but with a quibble on the sense "messenger")   150. **creep into sedges:** find
himself a hiding-place, as an injured bird seeks refuge in the rushes along a river bank
153. **base (though bitter):** low, yet capable of stinging its victim (?). The locution is not very natural, and Johnson emended it to *base, the bitter.*

of Beatrice that puts the world into her person, and so gives me out. Well,
155   I'll be reveng'd as I may.

(*Enter the Prince* [DON PEDRO].)

DON PEDRO   Now, signior, where's the Count? Did you see him?
BENEDICK   Troth, my lord, I have play'd the part of Lady Fame. I found him
here as melancholy as a lodge in a warren. I told him, and I think I told him
true, that your Grace had got the good will of this young lady, and I off'red
160   him my company to a willow-tree, either to make him a garland, as being
forsaken, or to bind him up a rod, as being worthy to be whipt.
DON PEDRO   To be whipt? What's his fault?
BENEDICK   The flat transgression of a schoolboy, who being overjoy'd with
finding a bird's nest, shows it his companion, and he steals it.
165   DON PEDRO   Wilt thou make a trust a transgression? The transgression is in the
stealer.
BENEDICK   Yet it had not been amiss the rod had been made, and the garland
too, for the garland he might have worn himself, and the rod he might have
bestow'd on you, who (as I take it) have stol'n his bird's nest.
170   DON PEDRO   I will but teach them to sing, and restore them to the owner.
BENEDICK   If their singing answer your saying, by my faith you say honestly.
DON PEDRO   The Lady Beatrice hath a quarrel to you. The gentleman that
danc'd with her told her she is much wrong'd by you.
BENEDICK   O, she misus'd me past the endurance of a block; an oak but with
175   one green leaf on it would have answer'd her. My very visor began to assume
life, and scold with her. She told me, not thinking I had been myself, that I
was the Prince's jester, that I was duller than a great thaw, huddling jest
upon jest with such impossible conveyance upon me that I stood like a man
at a mark, with a whole army shooting at me. She speaks poniards, and
180   every word stabs. If her breath were as terrible as her terminations, there
were no living near her, she would infect to the north star. I would not
marry her, though she were endow'd with all that Adam had left him before
he transgress'd. She would have made Hercules have turn'd spit, yea, and
have cleft his club to make the fire too. Come, talk not of her; you shall find

---

154. **puts . . . person:** assumes that everyone is of her opinion   **gives me out:** represents me
157. **Troth:** in truth   **Lady Fame:** Dame Rumor   158. **lodge . . . warren:** burrow in a rabbit warren. Rabbits were proverbially melancholy.   163. **flat:** simple, silly   165. **a trust:** the placing of
one's trust in a person   169. **bestow'd:** used   170. **them:** the nestlings   171. **answer:** correspond
to   172. **to:** with   174. **misus'd:** abused   174–75. **but . . . it:** with the slightest vestige of life in it
177. **a great thaw:** when impassable roads would prevent the usual activities and pastimes
huddling: piling up   178. **impossible conveyance:** incredible adeptness   179. **at a mark:** set up as
a target   180. **terminations:** terms, words   181. **north star:** supposedly the remotest star
182. **left:** bestowed upon   183. **Hercules . . . spit:** Omphale forced the captive Hercules to put on
women's clothes and spin among her maids. Turning the spit was work of a far more menial order.

185   her the infernal Ate in good apparel. I would to God some scholar would
conjure her, for certainly, while she is here, a man may live as quiet in hell as
in a sanctuary, and people sin upon purpose, because they would go thither;
so indeed all disquiet, horror, and perturbation follows her.

(*Enter* CLAUDIO *and* BEATRICE, [LEONATO *and* HERO].)

DON PEDRO   Look here she comes.
190   BENEDICK   Will your Grace command me any service to the world's end? I will
go on the slightest arrand now to the Antipodes that you can devise to send
me on; I will fetch you a toothpicker now from the furthest inch of Asia,
bring you the length of Prester John's foot, fetch you a hair off the great
Cham's beard, do you any embassage to the Pigmies, rather than hold three
195   words' conference with this harpy. You have no employment for me?
DON PEDRO   None, but to desire your good company.
BENEDICK   O God, sir, here's a dish I love not, I cannot endure my Lady
Tongue.

(*Exit.*)

DON PEDRO   Come, lady, come, you have lost the heart of Signior Benedick.
200   BEATRICE   Indeed, my lord, he lent it me awhile, and I gave him use for it, a
double heart for his single one. Marry, once before he won it of me with
false dice, therefore your Grace may well say I have lost it.
DON PEDRO   You have put him down, lady, you have put him down.
BEATRICE   So I would not he should do me, my lord, lest I should prove the
205   mother of fools. I have brought Count Claudio, whom you sent me to seek.
DON PEDRO   Why, how now, Count, wherefore are you sad?
CLAUDIO   Not sad, my lord.
DON PEDRO   How then? sick?
CLAUDIO   Neither, my lord.
210   BEATRICE   The Count is neither sad, nor sick, nor merry, nor well; but civil
count, civil as an orange, and something of that jealous complexion.
DON PEDRO   I' faith, lady, I think your blazon to be true, though I'll be sworn, if
he be so, his conceit is false. Here, Claudio, I have woo'd in thy name, and

---

185. **Ate:** goddess of mischief and discord   **scholar:** one familiar with the Latin formulas for exor-
cising evil spirits   191. **arrand:** errand   193. **Prester John:** a legendary Far Eastern ruler who was
both emperor and Christian priest (*Prester* is a shortened form of *Presbyter,* priest)   194. **Cham:**
Khan of Tartary, ruler of the Mongols   **Pigmies:** supposed to inhabit the mountains of India
195. **harpy:** creature of prey; literally, a mythical monster with the face and trunk of a woman and
the wings and claws of a bird. In heraldry the harpy was assigned to one who had committed
manslaughter (= Beatrice's crime!).   200. **use:** usury, interest   202. **false:** loaded   203. **put him
down:** got the better of him (with following quibble by Beatrice)   210. **civil:** (1) grave, serious;
(2) Seville (a homophone); oranges of Seville are bitter   211. **something:** somewhat, to some degree   **jealous complexion:** yellow, the color associated with jealousy   212. **blazon:** description   213. **so:** jealous   **conceit:** idea

fair Hero is won. I have broke with her father, and his good will obtain'd.
215 Name the day of marriage, and God give thee joy!

LEONATO Count, take of me my daughter, and with her my fortunes. His Grace
hath made the match, and all grace say amen to it.

BEATRICE Speak, Count, 'tis your cue.

CLAUDIO Silence is the perfectest heralt of joy; I were but little happy, if I could
220 say how much! Lady, as you are mine, I am yours. I give away myself for you,
and dote upon the exchange.

BEATRICE Speak, cousin, or (if you cannot) stop his mouth with a kiss, and let
not him speak neither.

DON PEDRO In faith, lady, you have a merry heart.

225 BEATRICE Yea, my lord, I thank it—poor fool, it keeps on the windy side of
care. My cousin tells him in his ear that he is in her heart.

CLAUDIO And so she doth, cousin.

BEATRICE Good Lord, for alliance! Thus goes every one to the world but I, and
I am sunburnt. I may sit in a corner and cry "Heigh-ho for a husband!"

230 DON PEDRO Lady Beatrice, I will get you one.

BEATRICE I would rather have one of your father's getting. Hath your Grace
ne'er a brother like you? Your father got excellent husbands, if a maid could
come by them.

DON PEDRO Will you have me, lady?

235 BEATRICE No, my lord, unless I might have another for working-days. Your
Grace is too costly to wear every day. But I beseech your Grace pardon me, I
was born to speak all mirth and no matter.

DON PEDRO Your silence most offends me, and to be merry best becomes you,
for out a' question, you were born in a merry hour.

240 BEATRICE No, sure, my lord, my mother cried, but then there was a star danc'd,
and under that was I born. Cousins, God give you joy!

LEONATO Niece, will you look to those things I told you of?

BEATRICE I cry you mercy, uncle. By your Grace's pardon.

(*Exit* BEATRICE.)

DON PEDRO By my troth, a pleasant-spirited lady.

245 LEONATO There's little of the melancholy element in her, my lord. She is never
sad but when she sleeps, and not ever sad then, for I have heard my daughter
say, she hath often dreamt of unhappiness, and wak'd herself with laughing.

DON PEDRO She cannot endure to hear tell of a husband.

LEONATO O, by no means, she mocks all her wooers out of suit.

250 DON PEDRO She were an excellent wife for Benedick.

---

217. **all grace:** the grace of God   219. **heralt:** herald   225. **windy:** windward, safe   228. **goes . . .
world:** everyone gets married   229. **sunburnt:** unattractive   **Heigh-ho . . . husband:** the title of a
ballad   231. **getting:** begetting   237. **matter:** substance, sense   246. **ever:** always   247. **unhappiness:** "some amusing roguery or other" (Kittredge)   249. **suit:** courtship

LEONATO   O Lord, my lord, if they were but a week married, they would talk
  themselves mad.

DON PEDRO   County Claudio, when mean you to go to church?

CLAUDIO   To-morrow, my lord. Time goes on crutches till love have all his rites.

255 LEONATO   Not till Monday, my dear son, which is hence a just sevennight, and a
  time too brief too, to have all things answer my mind.

DON PEDRO   Come, you shake the head at so long a breathing, but I warrant
  thee, Claudio, the time shall not go dully by us. I will in the interim undertake one of Hercules' labors, which is, to bring Signior Benedick and the
260   Lady Beatrice into a mountain of affection th' one with th' other. I would
  fain have it a match, and I doubt not but to fashion it, if you three will but
  minister such assistance as I shall give you direction.

LEONATO   My lord, I am for you, though it cost me ten nights' watchings.

CLAUDIO   And I, my lord.

265 DON PEDRO   And you too, gentle Hero?

HERO   I will do any modest office, my lord, to help my cousin to a good husband.

DON PEDRO   And Benedick is not the unhopefullest husband that I know. Thus
  far can I praise him: he is of a noble strain, of approv'd valor, and confirm'd
270   honesty. I will teach you how to humor your cousin, that she shall fall in
  love with Benedick, and I, with your two helps, will so practice on Benedick
  that, in despite of his quick wit and his queasy stomach, he shall fall in love
  with Beatrice. If we can do this, Cupid is no longer an archer; his glory shall
  be ours, for we are the only love-gods. Go in with me, and I will tell you my
275   drift.

(*Exeunt.*)

[Scene II]

(*Enter* [DON] JOHN *and* BORACHIO.)

DON JOHN   It is so, the Count Claudio shall marry the daughter of Leonato.

BORACHIO   Yea, my lord, but I can cross it.

DON JOHN   Any bar, any cross, any impediment will be med'cinable to me. I am
  sick in displeasure to him, and whatsoever comes athwart his affection
5   ranges evenly with mine. How canst thou cross this marriage?

---

253. **go to church:** marry   255. **a just sevennight:** exactly a week   256. **answer my mind:** correspond with my wishes   257. **breathing:** interval, delay   262. **minister:** furnish, supply
263. **watchings:** lying awake   269. **approv'd:** tested   271. **practice on:** scheme against
272. **in despite of:** notwithstanding   **his queasy stomach:** his squeamishness about partaking of
love   275. **drift:** intent

II.ii. Location: Leonato's house
1. **shall:** is going to   2. **cross:** thwart   3. **med'cinable:** medicinal, healing   4. **displeasure
to:** anger against   **comes . . . affection:** goes contrary to his desires   5. **ranges evenly:** runs parallel

BORACHIO   Not honestly, my lord, but so covertly that no dishonesty shall appear in me.

DON JOHN   Show me briefly how.

BORACHIO   I think I told your lordship a year since, how much I am in the favor
10   of Margaret, the waiting-gentlewoman to Hero.

DON JOHN   I remember.

BORACHIO   I can, at any unseasonable instant of the night, appoint her to look out at her lady's chamber-window.

DON JOHN   What life is in that, to be the death of this marriage?

15 BORACHIO   The poison of that lies in you to temper. Go you to the Prince your brother; spare not to tell him that he hath wrong'd his honor in marrying the renown'd Claudio—whose estimation do you mightily hold up—to a contaminated stale, such a one as Hero.

DON JOHN   What proof shall I make of that?

20 BORACHIO   Proof enough to misuse the Prince, to vex Claudio, to undo Hero, and kill Leonato. Look you for any other issue?

DON JOHN   Only to despite them, I will endeavor any thing.

BORACHIO   Go then, find me a meet hour to draw Don Pedro and the Count Claudio alone, tell them that you know that Hero loves me, intend a kind of
25   zeal both to the Prince and Claudio—as in love of your brother's honor, who hath made this match, and his friend's reputation, who is thus like to be cozen'd with the semblance of a maid—that you have discover'd thus. They will scarcely believe this without trial. Offer them instances, which shall bear no less likelihood than to see me at her chamber-window, hear me
30   call Margaret Hero, hear Margaret term me Claudio; and bring them to see this the very night before the intended wedding—for in the mean time I will so fashion the matter that Hero shall be absent—and there shall appear such seeming truth of Hero's disloyalty, that jealousy shall be call'd assurance, and all the preparation overthrown.

35 DON JOHN   Grow this to what adverse issue it can, I will put it in practice. Be cunning in the working this, and thy fee is a thousand ducats.

BORACHIO   Be you constant in the accusation, and my cunning shall not shame me.

DON JOHN   I will presently go learn their day of marriage.

(*Exeunt.*)

---

8. **briefly:** quickly   15. **lies in:** depends upon   **temper:** mix   17. **estimation:** worth
18. **contaminated stale:** common prostitute   20. **misuse:** deceive   **vex:** torment   24. **intend:**
pretend   27. **cozen'd:** deceived   **semblance:** outward appearance   28. **instances:** proofs
30. **term me Claudio:** apparently a slip. Many editors emend to *Borachio* (following Theobald).
33. **jealousy:** suspicion   33–34. **assurance:** certainty   34. **preparation:** for the wedding
36. **ducats:** continental gold coins, variously valued (but Borachio's reward is clearly to be a large
one)   39. **presently:** at once

[Scene III]

(*Enter* BENEDICK *alone.*)

BENEDICK   Boy!

[*Enter* BOY.]

BOY   Signior?

BENEDICK   In my chamber-window lies a book, bring it hither to me in the orchard.

5   BOY   I am here already, sir.

(*Exit.*)

BENEDICK   I know that, but I would have thee hence, and here again. I do much wonder that one man, seeing how much another man is a fool when he dedicates his behaviors to love, will, after he hath laugh'd at such shallow follies in others, become the argument of his own scorn by falling in love—and
10   such a man is Claudio. I have known when there was no music with him but the drum and the fife, and now had he rather hear the tabor and the pipe; I have known when he would have walk'd ten mile afoot to see a good armor, and now will he lie ten nights awake carving the fashion of a new doublet; he was wont to speak plain and to the purpose (like an honest man and a
15   soldier), and now is he turn'd ortography—his words are a very fantastical banquet, just so many strange dishes. May I be so converted and see with these eyes? I cannot tell; I think not. I will not be sworn but love may transform me to an oyster, but I'll take my oath on it, till he have made [an] oyster of me, he shall never make me such a fool. One woman is fair, yet I am
20   well; another is wise, yet I am well; another virtuous, yet I am well; but till all graces be in one woman, one woman shall not come in my grace. Rich she shall be, that's certain; wise, or I'll none; virtuous, or I'll never cheapen her; fair, or I'll never look on her; mild, or come not near me; noble, or not I for an angel; of good discourse, an excellent musician, and her hair shall be
25   of what color it please God. Hah! the Prince and Monsieur Love. I will hide me in the arbor.

[*Withdraws.*]

II.iii. Location: Leonato's garden
4. **orchard:** garden   5. **I . . . already:** I'll be back before you know I've gone.   9. **argument:** subject
11. **tabor:** small drum. The tabor and pipe were used for social merriment, in contrast to the martial drum and fife.   12. **armor:** suit of armor   13. **carving:** planning   **doublet:** close-fitting jacket
15. **turn'd ortography:** become a faddist in language   22. **I'll none:** I'll have none of
her   **cheapen:** bargain for   24. **for an angel:** (1) though she be an angel; (2) for ten shillings (involving a play on *noble* as the name of another coin, worth two thirds as much as an angel)
24–25. **hair . . . God:** if she satisfies all these requirements, I won't stipulate what color her hair
must be.

(*Enter Prince* [DON PEDRO], LEONATO, CLAUDIO. *Music* [*within*].)

DON PEDRO   Come, shall we hear this music?

CLAUDIO   Yea, my good lord. How still the evening is,
As hush'd on purpose to grace harmony!

30   DON PEDRO   See you where Benedick hath hid himself?

CLAUDIO   O, very well, my lord. The music ended,
We'll fit the [hid]-fox with a pennyworth.

(*Enter* BALTHASAR *with Music.*)

DON PEDRO   Come, Balthasar, we'll hear that song again.

BALTHASAR   O good my lord, tax not so bad a voice
35   To slander music any more than once.

DON PEDRO   It is the witness still of excellency
To put a strange face on his own perfection.
I pray thee sing, and let me woo no more.

BALTHASAR   Because you talk of wooing, I will sing;
40   Since many a wooer doth commence his suit
To her he thinks not worthy, yet he woos,
Yet he will swear he loves.

DON PEDRO   Nay, pray thee come,
Or if thou wilt hold longer argument,
45   Do it in notes.

BALTHASAR   Note this before my notes:
There's not a note of mine that's worth the noting.

DON PEDRO   Why, these are very crotchets that he speaks—
Note notes, forsooth, and nothing.   [*Air.*]

50   BENEDICK   Now, divine air! now is his soul ravish'd! It is not strange that
sheep's guts should hale souls out of men's bodies? Well, a horn for my
money when all's done.

The Song

[BALTHASAR]   Sigh no more; ladies, sigh no more,
                                   Men were deceivers ever,
55   One foot in sea, and one on shore,
                                   To one thing constant never.

---

29. **grace harmony:** do honor to music   32. **hid-fox:** an allusion to a children's game; cf. *Hamlet,*
IV.ii.25: "Hide fox, and all after."   **pennyworth:** a good bargain, more than he bargained for
34. **tax:** task   37. **To . . . on:** not to admit   38. **woo:** entreat   45. **notes:** musical notes
48. **crotchets:** (1) whims; (2) quarter notes in music   49. **nothing:** with homophonic pun on *not-ing*   51. **sheep's guts:** violin or lute strings   **hale:** draw, drag   **horn:** hunting horn (but an audience always alive to the cuckold jest would have found the remark comically incongruous in Benedick's mouth)

Then sigh not so, but let them go,
   And be you blithe and bonny,
Converting all your sounds of woe
60   Into hey nonny nonny.
Sing no more ditties, sing no moe,
   Of dumps so dull and heavy;
The fraud of men was ever so,
   Since summer first was leavy.
65   Then sigh not so, etc.

DON PEDRO   By my troth, a good song.

BALTHASAR   And an ill singer, my lord.

DON PEDRO   Ha, no, no, faith, thou sing'st well enough for a shift.

BENEDICK   And he had been a dog that should have howl'd thus, they would
70   have hang'd him, and so I pray God his bad voice bode no mischief. I had as
live have heard the night-raven, come what plague could have come after it.

DON PEDRO   Yea, marry, dost thou hear, Balthasar? I pray thee get us some excellent music; for to-morrow night we would have it at the Lady Hero's
chamber-window.

75 BALTHASAR   The best I can, my lord.

(*Exit* BALTHASAR.)

DON PEDRO   Do so, farewell. Come hither, Leonato. What was it you told me of
to-day, that your niece Beatrice was in love with Signior Benedick?

CLAUDIO [*aside*]   O ay, stalk on, stalk on, the fowl sits.—I did never think that
lady would have lov'd any man.

80 LEONATO   No, nor I neither, but most wonderful that she should so dote on
Signior Benedick, whom she hath in all outward behaviors seem'd ever to
abhor.

BENEDICK   Is't possible? Sits the wind in that corner?

LEONATO   By my troth, my lord, I cannot tell what to think of it but that she
85   loves him with an enrag'd affection; it is past the infinite of thought.

DON PEDRO   May be she doth but counterfeit.

CLAUDIO   Faith, like enough.

LEONATO   O God! counterfeit? There was never counterfeit of passion came so
near the life of passion as she discovers it.

---

61. **moe:** more (in number) 62. **dumps:** mournful tunes 64. **leavy:** leafy 68. **for a shift:** to
make do 71. **live:** lief **night-raven:** a bird, variously identified, whose cry presaged disaster
78. **stalk . . . sits:** walk stealthily, the bird has settled (in a bush) 83. **Sits . . . corner:** is that how the
wind blows 85. **enrag'd:** mad with passion **infinite:** infinity, boundlessness
89. **discovers:** reveals

90 DON PEDRO   Why, what effects of passion shows she?

CLAUDIO [*aside*]   Bait the hook well, this fish will bite.

LEONATO   What effects, my lord? She will sit you—you heard my daughter tell you how.

CLAUDIO   She did indeed.

95 DON PEDRO   How, how, I pray you? You amaze me, I would have thought her spirit had been invincible against all assaults of affection.

LEONATO   I would have sworn it had, my lord, especially against Benedick.

BENEDICK   I should think this a gull, but that the white-bearded fellow speaks it. Knavery cannot sure hide himself in such reverence.

100 CLAUDIO [*aside*]   He hath ta'en th' infection. Hold it up.

DON PEDRO   Hath she made her affection known to Benedick?

LEONATO   No, and swears she never will. That's her torment.

CLAUDIO   'Tis true indeed, so your daughter says. "Shall I," says she, "that have so oft encount'red him with scorn, write to him that I love him?"

105 LEONATO   This says she now when she is beginning to write to him, for she'll be up twenty times a night, and there will she sit in her smock till she have writ a sheet of paper. My daughter tells us all.

CLAUDIO   Now you talk of a sheet of paper. I remember a pretty jest your daughter told [us of].

110 LEONATO   O, when she had writ it, and was reading it over, she found "Benedick" and "Beatrice" between the sheet?

CLAUDIO   That.

LEONATO   O, she tore the letter into a thousand halfpence; rail'd at herself, that she should be so immodest to write to one that she knew would flout her. "I

115 measure him," says she, "by my own spirit, for I should flout him, if he writ to me, yea, though I love him, I should."

CLAUDIO   Then down upon her knees she falls, weeps, sobs, beats her heart, tears her hair, prays, curses: "O sweet Benedick! God give me patience!"

LEONATO   She doth indeed, my daughter says so; and the ecstasy hath so much

120 overborne her that my daughter is sometime afeard she will do a desperate outrage to herself. It is very true.

DON PEDRO   It were good that Benedick knew of it by some other, if she will not discover it.

CLAUDIO   To what end? he would make but a sport of it, and torment the poor

125 lady worse.

DON PEDRO   And he should, it were an alms to hang him. She's an excellent sweet lady, and (out of all suspicion) she is virtuous.

---

92. **effects:** manifestations   **sit you:** sit (a colloquialism)   98. **gull:** trick   100. **Hold it up:** keep it up   106. **smock:** undergarment   113. **halfpence:** very small bits   119. **ecstasy:** madness 121. **outrage:** act of violence   126. **alms:** good deed   127. **out of:** beyond

CLAUDIO   And she is exceeding wise.

DON PEDRO   In every thing but in loving Benedick.

130   LEONATO   O my lord, wisdom and blood combating in so tender a body, we
have ten proofs to one that blood hath the victory. I am sorry for her, as I
have just cause, being her uncle and her guardian.

DON PEDRO   I would she had bestow'd this dotage on me, I would have daff'd
all other respects, and made her half myself. I pray you tell Benedick of it,
135   and hear what 'a will say.

LEONATO   Were it good, think you?

CLAUDIO   Hero thinks surely she will die, for she says she will die if he love her
not, and she will die ere she make her love known, and she will die if he woo
her, rather than she will bate one breath of her accustom'd crossness.

140   DON PEDRO   She doth well. If she should make tender of her love, 'tis very possible he'll scorn it, for the man (as you know all) hath a contemptible spirit.

CLAUDIO   He is a very proper man.

DON PEDRO   He hath indeed a good outward happiness.

CLAUDIO   Before God, and in my mind, very wise.

145   DON PEDRO   He doth indeed show some sparks that are like wit.

CLAUDIO   And I take him to be valiant.

DON PEDRO   As Hector, I assure you, and in the managing of quarrels you may
say he is wise, for either he avoids them with great discretion, or undertakes
them with a most Christian-like fear.

150   LEONATO   If he do fear God, 'a must necessarily keep peace; if he break the
peace, he ought to enter into a quarrel with fear and trembling.

DON PEDRO   And so will he do, for the man doth fear God, howsoever it seems
not in him by some large jests he will make. Well, I am sorry for your niece.
Shall we go seek Benedick, and tell him of her love?

155   CLAUDIO   Never tell him, my lord. Let her wear it out with good counsel.

LEONATO   Nay, that's impossible, she may wear her heart out first.

DON PEDRO   Well, we will hear further of it by your daughter, let it cool the
while. I love Benedick well, and I could wish he would modestly examine
himself, to see how much he is unworthy so good a lady.

160   LEONATO   My lord, will you walk? Dinner is ready.

CLAUDIO   [*aside*]   If he do not dote on her upon this, I will never trust my expectation.

DON PEDRO   [*aside*]   Let there be the same net spread for her, and that must
your daughter and her gentlewomen carry. The sport will be, when they
165   hold one an opinion of another's dotage, and no such matter; that's the

---

130. **blood:** natural feeling   133. **dotage:** doting   **daff'd:** doffed, put aside   134. **respects:** considerations   **half myself:** my wife   139. **bate:** abate   **crossness:** perversity   140. **tender:** offer
141. **contemptible:** contemptuous   142. **proper:** handsome   143. **hath . . . happiness:** is fortunate
in his appearance   147. **Hector:** the greatest of the Trojan warriors   153. **large:** broad, indelicate
155. **good counsel:** giving herself good advice   160. **walk:** go   164. **carry:** undertake
165. **no such matter:** nothing of the kind exists

scene that I would see, which will be merely a dumb show. Let us send her to call him in to dinner.

[*Exeunt* Don Pedro, Claudio, *and* Leonato.]

BENEDICK [*coming forward*] This can be no trick: the conference was sadly borne; they have the truth of this from Hero; they seem to pity the lady. It
170   seems her affections have their full bent. Love me? why, it must be requited. I hear how I am censur'd; they say I will bear myself proudly, if I perceive the love come from her; they say too that she will rather die than give any sign of affection. I did never think to marry. I must not seem proud; happy are they that hear their detractions, and can put them to mending. They say
175   the lady is fair; 'tis a truth, I can bear them witness; and virtuous; 'tis so, I cannot reprove it; and wise, but for loving me; by my troth, it is no addition to her wit, nor no great argument of her folly, for I will be horribly in love with her. I may chance have some odd quirks and remnants of wit broken on me, because I have rail'd so long against marriage; but doth not the ap-
180   petite alter? A man loves the meat in his youth that he cannot endure in his age. Shall quips and sentences and these paper bullets of the brain awe a man from the career of his humor? No, the world must be peopled. When I said I would die a bachelor, I did not think I should live till I were married. Here comes Beatrice. By this day, she's a fair lady. I do spy some marks of
185   love in her.

(*Enter* Beatrice.)

BEATRICE   Against my will I am sent to bid you come in to dinner.
BENEDICK   Fair Beatrice, I thank you for your pains.
BEATRICE   I took no more pains for those thanks than you take pains to thank me. If it had been painful, I would not have come.
190 BENEDICK   You take pleasure in the message?
BEATRICE   Yea, just so much as you may take upon a knive's point, and choke a daw withal. You have no stomach, signior, fare you well.

(*Exit.*)

BENEDICK   Ha! "Against my will I am sent to bid you come in to dinner"— there's a double meaning in that. "I took no more pains for those thanks
195   than you took pains to thank me"—that's as much as to say, "Any pains that

---

166. **merely . . . show:** entirely pantomime (because with no occasion for satiric exchange they will have nothing to say) 168–169. **sadly borne:** seriously conducted 170. **have . . . bent:** are at full stretch 174. **their detractions:** unfavorable criticisms of themselves **put . . . mending:** i.e., apply themselves to correcting their faults 176. **reprove:** disprove, deny 178. **quirks:** jests
181. **sentences:** maxims **paper . . . brain:** verbal ammunition 182. **career . . . humor:** course of his inclination 192. **daw:** jackdaw **stomach:** appetite

I take for you is as easy as thanks." If I do not take pity of her, I am a villain; if I do not love her, I am a Jew. I will go get her picture.

(*Exit.*)

Act III

Scene I

(*Enter* HERO *and two gentlewomen,* MARGARET *and* URSULA.)

HERO   Good Margaret, run thee to the parlor,
    There shalt thou find my cousin Beatrice
    Proposing with the Prince and Claudio.
    Whisper her ear, and tell her I and Ursley
5   Walk in the orchard, and our whole discourse
    Is all of her. Say that thou overheardst us,
    And bid her steal into the pleached bower,
    Where honeysuckles, ripened by the sun,
    Forbid the sun to enter, like favorites
10   Made proud by princes, that advance their pride
    Against that power that bred it. There will she hide her,
    To listen our propose. This is thy office;
    Bear thee well in it, and leave us alone.
MARGARET   I'll make her come, I warrant you, presently.

[*Exit.*]

15 HERO   Now, Ursula, when Beatrice doth come,
    As we do trace this alley up and down,
    Our talk must only be of Benedick.
    When I do name him, let it be thy part
    To praise him more than ever man did merit.
20   My talk to thee must be how Benedick
    Is sick in love with Beatrice. Of this matter
    Is little Cupid's crafty arrow made,
    That only wounds by hearsay.

(*Enter* BEATRICE [*behind*].)

                    Now begin,
25   For look where Beatrice like a lapwing runs
    Close by the ground, to hear our conference.

III.i. Location: Leonato's garden
o.s.d. **Ursley:** variant form of *Ursula*   3. **Proposing:** talking   12. **listen our propose:** listen to our
conversation   23. **only . . . hearsay:** wounds by hearsay only

URSULA   The pleasant'st angling is to see the fish
    Cut with her golden oars the silver stream,
    And greedily devour the treacherous bait;
30   So angle we for Beatrice, who even now
    Is couched in the woodbine coverture.
    Fear you not my part of the dialogue.
HERO   Then go we near her, that her ear lose nothing
    Of the false sweet bait that we lay for it.

[*They advance to the bower.*]

35   No, truly, Ursula, she is too disdainful,
    I know her spirits are as coy and wild
    As haggards of the rock.
URSULA   But are you sure
    That Benedick loves Beatrice so entirely?
40 HERO   So says the Prince and my new-trothed lord.
URSULA   And did they bid you tell her of it, madam?
HERO   They did entreat me to acquaint her of it,
    But I persuaded them, if they lov'd Benedick,
    To wish him wrastle with affection,
45   And never to let Beatrice know of it.
URSULA   Why did you so? Doth not the gentleman
    Deserve as full as fortunate a bed
    As ever Beatrice shall couch upon?
HERO   O god of love! I know he doth deserve
50   As much as may be yielded to a man;
    But nature never fram'd a woman's heart
    Of prouder stuff than that of Beatrice.
    Disdain and scorn ride sparkling in her eyes,
    Misprising what they look on, and her wit
55   Values itself so highly that to her
    All matter else seems weak. She cannot love,
    Nor take no shape nor project of affection,
    She is so self-endeared.
URSULA   Sure I think so,
60   And therefore certainly it were not good
    She knew his love, lest she'll make sport at it.
HERO   Why, you speak truth. I never yet saw man,
    How wise, how noble, young, how rarely featur'd,

---

31. **woodbine coverture:** honeysuckle bower   36. **coy:** shy   37. **haggards . . . rock:** mature female hawks snared in their mountain habitats, hence very difficult to tame   44. **wish him wrastle:** advise him to wrestle   47. **as full as:** fully as   54. **Misprising:** undervaluing, despising   56. **All matter else:** what anyone else has to say   57. **take . . . affection:** formulate any mental image or idea of what love is   58. **self-endeared:** full of self-love   63. **How:** however   **rarely featur'd:** excellent in face and form

But she would spell him backward. If fair-fac'd,
65   She would swear the gentleman should be her sister;
If black, why, Nature, drawing of an antic,
Made a foul blot; if tall, a lance ill-headed;
If low, an agot very vilely cut;
If speaking, why, a vane blown with all winds;
70   If silent, why, a block moved with none.
So turns she every man the wrong side out,
And never gives to truth and virtue that
Which simpleness and merit purchaseth.
URSULA   Sure, sure, such carping is not commendable.
75 HERO   No, not to be so odd, and from all fashions,
As Beatrice is, cannot be commendable.
But who dare tell her so? If I should speak,
She would mock me into air; O, she would laugh me
Out of myself, press me to death with wit.
80   Therefore let Benedick, like cover'd fire,
Consume away in sighs, waste inwardly.
It were a better death than die with mocks,
Which is as bad as die with tickling.
URSULA   Yet tell her of it, hear what she will say.
85 HERO   No, rather I will go to Benedick,
And counsel him to fight against his passion,
And truly I'll devise some honest slanders
To stain my cousin with. One doth not know
How much an ill word may empoison liking.
90 URSULA   O, do not do your cousin such a wrong.
She cannot be so much without true judgment—
Having so swift and excellent a wit
As she is priz'd to have—as to refuse
So rare a gentleman as Signior Benedick.
95 HERO   He is the only man of Italy,
Always excepted my dear Claudio.
URSULA   I pray you be not angry with me, madam,
Speaking my fancy: Signior Benedick,
For shape, for bearing, argument, and valor,
100   Goes foremost in report through Italy.

---

64. **spell him backward:** say the reverse of him, turn his merits into faults   66. **black:** dark
antic: grotesque figure   68. **agot:** agate; here, a small figure incised in agate for a seal or a ring
73. **simpleness:** sincerity   **purchaseth:** deserve   75. **from all fashions:** contrary to all accepted behavior   79. **press...death:** Accused felons who refused to plead either guilty or not guilty were
pressed to death by heavy weights.   81. **Consume...sighs:** an allusion to the belief that each sigh
cost the heart one drop of blood   87. **honest:** harmless   93. **priz'd:** esteemed   95. **only:** very best
99. **argument:** skills in conversation   100. **report:** reputation (so also *name,* line 101)

HERO   Indeed he hath an excellent good name.
URSULA   His excellence did earn it, ere he had it.
　　　When are you married, madam?
HERO   Why, every day to-morrow. Come go in,
105　　I'll show thee some attires, and have thy counsel
　　　Which is the best to furnish me to-morrow.
URSULA [*aside*]   She's limed, I warrant you. We have caught her, madam.
HERO [*aside*]   If it prove so, then loving goes by haps:
　　　Some Cupid kills with arrows, some with traps.

[*Exeunt* HERO *and* URSULA.]

110 BEATRICE [*coming forward*]   What fire is in mine ears? Can this be true?
　　　Stand I condemn'd for pride and scorn so much?
　　　Contempt, farewell, and maiden pride, adieu!
　　　No glory lives behind the back of such.
　　　And, Benedick, love on, I will requite thee,
115　　Taming my wild heart to thy loving hand.
　　　If thou dost love, my kindness shall incite thee
　　　To bind our loves up in a holy band;
　　　For others say thou dost deserve, and I
　　　Believe it better than reportingly.

(*Exit.*)

[Scene II]

(*Enter Prince* [DON PEDRO], CLAUDIO, BENEDICK, *and* LEONATO.)

DON PEDRO   I do but stay till your marriage be consummate, and then go I to-
　　　ward Arragon.
CLAUDIO   I'll bring you thither, my lord, if you'll vouchsafe me.
DON PEDRO   Nay, that would be as great a soil in the new gloss of your mar-
5　　riage as to show a child his new coat and forbid him to wear it. I will only

---

104. **every day to-morrow:** Tomorrow I shall be able to say that I am married every day.
107. **limed:** caught, like a bird entangled in birdlime   108. **haps:** chance   110. **What . . . ears:** alluding to the folk belief that being talked about in one's absence causes one's ears to burn
113. **No . . . such:** nothing good is said about such a person when his back is turned
115. **Taming . . . hand:** Beatrice has been termed a "haggard" and now acknowledges the justness of
the epithet by her use of another image from falconry.   117. **band:** bond   119. **better than reportingly:** on better evidence than mere rumor

III.ii. Location: Leonato's house
3. **bring:** escort   **vouchsafe:** allow

be bold with Benedick for his company, for from the crown of his head to
the sole of his foot, he is all mirth. He hath twice or thrice cut Cupid's bowstring, and the little hangman dare not shoot at him. He hath a heart as
sound as a bell, and his tongue is the clapper, for what his heart thinks, his
10   tongue speaks.

BENEDICK   Gallants, I am not as I have been.

LEONATO   So say I, methinks you are sadder.

CLAUDIO   I hope he be in love.

DON PEDRO   Hang him, truant, there's no true drop of blood in him to be truly
15   touch'd with love. If he be sad, he wants money.

BENEDICK   I have the toothache.

DON PEDRO   Draw it.

BENEDICK   Hang it!

CLAUDIO   You must hang it first, and draw it afterwards.

20 DON PEDRO   What? sigh for the toothache?

LEONATO   Where is but a humor or a worm.

BENEDICK   Well, every one [can] master a grief but he that has it.

CLAUDIO   Yet say I, he is in love.

DON PEDRO   There is no appearance of fancy in him, unless it be a fancy that he
25   hath to strange disguises—as to be a Dutchman to-day, a Frenchman tomorrow, or in the shape of two countries at once, as a German from the
waist downward, all slops, and a Spaniard from the hip upward, no doublet.
Unless he have a fancy to this foolery, as it appears he hath, he is no fool for
fancy, as you would have it appear he is.

30 CLAUDIO   If he be not in love with some woman, there is no believing old signs.
'A brushes his hat a' mornings; what should that bode?

DON PEDRO   Hath any man seen him at the barber's?

CLAUDIO   No, but the barber's man hath been seen with him, and the old ornament of his cheek hath already stuff'd tennis-balls.

35 LEONATO   Indeed he looks younger than he did, by the loss of a beard.

DON PEDRO   Nay, 'a rubs himself with civet. Can you smell him out by that?

CLAUDIO   That's as much as to say, the sweet youth's in love.

[DON PEDRO]   The greatest note of it is his melancholy.

---

6. **be bold with:** take the liberty of asking   8. **hangman:** rogue (with play on Cupid as torturer, a
role played also by the public hangman)   12. **sadder:** more serious   14. **there's . . . him:** he hasn't
enough natural feeling   15. **wants:** lacks   16. **toothache:** Lovers were commonly supposed to suffer from toothaches, but Benedick may only be inventing an excuse for his changed appearance
18. **Hang it:** confound it   19. **hang . . . afterwards:** alluding to the execution of traitors, who were
hanged, cut down while still alive, drawn (disembowelled), and quartered   21. **humor . . . worm:**
Toothaches were supposedly caused by abnormal secretions or by actual worms in the teeth
24. **fancy:** love (with following quibble)   27. **slops:** loose breeches   **no doublet:** with his doublet
completely covered by a cloak   33–34. **old . . . cheek:** his beard   36. **civet:** perfume derived from
the civet cat   **smell him out:** discover his true nature (with obvious play on the literal sense)
37. **sweet:** with quibble on the sense "perfumed"   38. **greatest note:** most conspicuous mark

CLAUDIO   And when was he wont to wash his face?

40   DON PEDRO   Yea, or to paint himself? for the which I hear what they say of him.

CLAUDIO   Nay, but his jesting spirit, which is now crept into a lute-string, and now govern'd by stops.

DON PEDRO   Indeed that tells a heavy tale for him. Conclude, conclude, he is in love.

45   CLAUDIO   Nay, but I know who loves him.

DON PEDRO   That would I know too. I warrant one that knows him not.

CLAUDIO   Yes, and his ill conditions, and in despite of all, dies for him.

DON PEDRO   She shall be buried with her face upwards.

BENEDICK   Yet is this no charm for the toothache. Old signior, walk aside with

50   me, I have studied eight or nine wise words to speak to you, which these hobby-horses must not hear.

[*Exeunt* BENEDICK *and* LEONATO.]

DON PEDRO   For my life, to break with him about Beatrice.

CLAUDIO   'Tis even so. Hero and Margaret have by this play'd their parts with Beatrice, and then the two bears will not bite one another when they meet.

(*Enter* [DON] JOHN *the Bastard.*)

55   DON JOHN   My lord and brother, God save you!

DON PEDRO   Good den, brother.

DON JOHN   If your leisure serv'd, I would speak with you.

DON PEDRO   In private?

DON JOHN   If it please you, yet Count Claudio may hear, for what I would speak

60   of concerns him.

DON PEDRO   What's the matter?

DON JOHN [*to* CLAUDIO]   Means your lordship to be married to-morrow?

DON PEDRO   You know he does.

DON JOHN   I know not that, when he knows what I know.

65   CLAUDIO   If there be any impediment, I pray you discover it.

DON JOHN   You may think I love you not; let that appear hereafter, and aim better at me by that I now will manifest. For my brother, I think he holds you well, and in dearness of heart hath holp to effect your ensuing marriage— surely suit ill spent and labor ill bestow'd.

39, 40. **wash, paint:** with cosmetics   41. **now crept:** Some editors emend to *new-crept* (following Boas) in view of the second *now* in the sentence.   **lute-string:** the lute commonly provided the accompaniment for love songs   42. **govern'd by stops:** regulated by frets (on the fingerboard of the lute), subjected to restraints   47. **Yes:** she does know him   **ill conditions:** bad characteristics   48. **She . . . upwards:** sexual double-entendre, taking off from a quibble on Claudio's *dies* in the sense "experiences sexual climax"   51. **hobby-horses:** buffoons (from the name of a performer in the morris-dance whose costume and antics suggested a horse)   52. **For:** upon   56. **Good den:** good evening   65. **discover:** reveal   66–67. **aim better at:** judge better of   68. **well:** in high esteem   **dearness:** affection

70 DON PEDRO   Why, what's the matter?

DON JOHN   I came hither to tell you, and circumstances short'ned (for she has been too long a-talking of), the lady is disloyal.

CLAUDIO   Who, Hero?

DON JOHN   Even she—Leonato's Hero, your Hero, every man's Hero.

75 CLAUDIO   Disloyal?

DON JOHN   The word is too good to paint out her wickedness. I could say she were worse; think you of a worse title, and I will fit her to it. Wonder not till further warrant. Go but with me to-night, you shall see her chamber-window ent'red, even the night before her wedding-day. If you love her 80 then, to-morrow wed her; but it would better fit your honor to change your mind.

CLAUDIO   May this be so?

DON PEDRO   I will not think it.

DON JOHN   If you dare not trust that you see, confess not that you know. If you 85 will follow me, I will show you enough, and when you have seen more, and heard more, proceed accordingly.

CLAUDIO   If I see any thing to-night why I should not marry her, to-morrow in the congregation, where I should wed, there will I shame her.

DON PEDRO   And as I woo'd for thee to obtain her, I will join with thee to dis-90 grace her.

DON JOHN   I will disparage her no farther till you are my witnesses. Bear it coldly but till midnight, and let the issue show itself.

DON PEDRO   O day untowardly turn'd!

CLAUDIO   O mischief strangely thwarting!

95 DON JOHN   O plague right well prevented! So, will you say when you have seen the sequel.

[*Exeunt.*]

[Scene III]

(*Enter* DOGBERRY *and his compartner* [VERGES] *with the* WATCH.)

DOGBERRY   Are you good men and true?

VERGES   Yea, or else it were pity but they should suffer salvation, body and soul.

---

71. **circumstances short'ned:** without unnecessary details   71–72. **has . . . of:** is not worth even the short time we have spent in mentioning her   77. **paint out:** depict   78. **warrant:** proof (is shown)   84. **that:** what   92. **coldly:** calmly   93. **untowardly turn'd:** perversely altered

III.iii. Location: a street
1. **true:** loyal   2. **salvation:** blunder for *damnation.* Dogberry's and Verges' words frequently mean precisely the opposite of what the speaker intends; witness *allegiance* (line 4), *desartless* (line 6), *senseless* (line 15).

DOGBERRY   Nay, that were a punishment too good for them, if they should have any allegiance in them, being chosen for the Prince's watch.

5 VERGES   Well, give them their charge, neighbor Dogberry.

DOGBERRY   First, who think you the most desartless man to be constable?

1. WATCH   Hugh Oatcake, sir, or George Seacole, for they can write and read.

DOGBERRY   Come hither, neighbor Seacole. God hath blest you with a good name. To be a well-favor'd man is the gift of fortune, but to write and read

10   comes by nature.

2. WATCH   Both which, Master Constable—

DOGBERRY   You have: I knew it would be your answer. Well, for your favor, sir, why, give God thanks, and make no boast of it, and for your writing and reading, let that appear when there is no need of such vanity. You are

15   thought here to be the most senseless and fit man for the constable of the watch; therefore bear you the lanthorn. This is your charge: you shall comprehend all vagrom men; you are to bid any man stand, in the Prince's name.

2. WATCH   How if 'a will not stand?

20 DOGBERRY   Why then take no note of him, but let him go, and presently call the rest of the watch together, and thank God you are rid of a knave.

VERGES   If he will not stand when he is bidden, he is none of the Prince's subjects.

DOGBERRY   True, and they are to meddle with none but the Prince's subjects. You shall also make no noise in the streets; for, for the watch to babble and

25   to talk, is most tolerable, and not to be endur'd.

[2.] WATCH   We will rather sleep than talk, we know what belongs to a watch.

DOGBERRY   Why, you speak like an ancient and most quiet watchman, for I cannot see how sleeping should offend; only have a care that your bills be

30   not stol'n. Well, you are to call at all the alehouses, and bid those that are drunk get them to bed.

[2.] WATCH   How if they will not?

DOGBERRY   Why then let them alone till they are sober. If they make you not then the better answer, you may say they are not the men you took them for.

35 [2.] WATCH   Well, sir.

DOGBERRY   If you meet a thief, you may suspect him, by virtue of your office, to be no true man; and for such kind of men, the less you meddle or make with them, why, the more is for your honesty.

[2.] WATCH   If we know him to be a thief, shall we not lay hands on him?

---

9. **well-favor'd:** good-looking   12. **favor:** appearance   16. **lanthorn:** variant form of *lantern* (by popular etymology from the fact that lanterns often had sides made of transparent sheets of horn) 16–17. **comprehend:** apprehend   17. **vagrom:** vagrant   **stand:** stop   24. **meddle:** have to do 26. **tolerable:** *intolerable*   27. **belongs to:** are the duties of   29. **bills:** hooked blades fastened on long poles   33–34. **make . . . answer:** . . . don't then agree to go home   37. **true:** honest   38. **is:** it is

40 DOGBERRY   Truly by your office you may, but I think they that touch pitch will
be defil'd. The most peaceable way for you, if you do take a thief, is to let
him show himself what he is, and steal out of your company.
VERGES   You have been always call'd a merciful man, partner.
DOGBERRY   Truly, I would not hang a dog by my will, much more a man who
45   hath any honesty in him.
VERGES   If you hear a child cry in the night, you must call to the nurse and bid
her still it.
[2.] WATCH   How if the nurse be asleep and will not hear us?
DOGBERRY   Why then depart in peace, and let the child wake her with crying,
50   for the ewe that will not hear her lamb when it baes will never answer a calf
when he bleats.
VERGES   'Tis very true.
DOGBERRY   This is the end of the charge: you, constable, are to present the
Prince's own person. If you meet the Prince in the night, you may stay him.
55 VERGES   Nay, by'r lady, that I think 'a cannot.
DOGBERRY   Five shillings to one on't, with any man that knows the [statues], he
may stay him; marry, not without the Prince be willing, for indeed the
watch ought to offend no man, and it is an offense to stay a man against his
will.
60 VERGES   By'r lady, I think it be so.
DOGBERRY   Ha, ah ha! Well, masters, good night. And there be any matter of
weight chances, call up me. Keep your fellows' counsels and your own, and
good night. Come, neighbor.
[2.] WATCH   Well, masters, we hear our charge. Let us go sit here upon the
65   church-bench till two, and then all to bed.
DOGBERRY   One word more, honest neighbors. I pray you watch about Signior
Leonato's door, for the wedding being there to-morrow, there is a great coil
to-night. Adieu! Be vigitant, I beseech you.

(*Exeunt* [DOGBERRY *and* VERGES].)

(*Enter* BORACHIO *and* CONRADE.)

BORACHIO   What, Conrade!
70 [2.] WATCH [*aside*]   Peace, stir not.
BORACHIO   Conrade, I say!
CONRADE   Here, man, I am at thy elbow.
BORACHIO   Mass, and my elbow itch'd; I thought there would a scab follow.
CONRADE   I will owe thee an answer for that, and now forward with thy tale.

40–41. **they . . . defil'd:** a commonplace, derived from the Apocryphal book Ecclesiasticus (13:1)
44. **more:** for *less*   47. **still:** quiet   53. **present:** represent   56. **statues:** statutes   57. **without:** unless   67. **coil:** fuss, to-do   68. **vigitant:** vigilant   73. **Mass:** by the Mass   **scab:** scurvy fellow

75 BORACHIO   Stand thee close then under this penthouse, for it drizzles rain, and
   I will, like a true drunkard, utter all to thee.

[2.] WATCH [*aside*]   Some treason, masters, yet stand close.

BORACHIO   Therefore know I have earn'd of Don John a thousand ducats.

CONRADE   Is it possible that any villainy should be so dear?

80 BORACHIO   Thou shouldst rather ask if it were possible any villainy should be
   so rich; for when rich villains have need of poor ones, poor ones may make
   what price they will.

CONRADE   I wonder at it.

BORACHIO   That shows thou art unconfirm'd. Thou knowest that the fashion of
85   a doublet, or a hat, or a cloak, is nothing to a man.

CONRADE   Yes, it is apparel.

BORACHIO   I mean the fashion.

CONRADE   Yes, the fashion is the fashion.

BORACHIO   Tush, I may as well say the fool's the fool. But seest thou not what a
90   deformed thief this fashion is?

[2.] WATCH [*aside*]   I know that Deformed; 'a has been a vile thief this seven
   year; 'a goes up and down like a gentleman. I remember his name.

BORACHIO   Didst thou not hear somebody?

CONRADE   No, 'twas the vane on the house.

95 BORACHIO   Seest thou not, I say, what a deformed thief this fashion is, how gid-
   dily 'a turns about all the hot-bloods between fourteen and five-and-thirty,
   sometimes fashioning them like Pharaoh's soldiers in the reechy painting,
   sometime like god Bel's priests in the old church-window, sometime like the
   shaven Hercules in the smirch'd worm-eaten tapestry, where his codpiece
100   seems as massy as his club?

CONRADE   All this I see, and I see that the fashion wears out more apparel than
   the man. But art not thou thyself giddy with the fashion too, that thou hast
   shifted out of thy tale into telling me of the fashion?

BORACHIO   Not so neither, but know that I have to-night woo'd Margaret, the
105   Lady Hero's gentlewoman, by the name of Hero. She leans me out at her
   mistress' chamber-window, bids me a thousand times good night—I tell
   this tale vildly, I should first tell thee how the Prince, Claudio, and my

---

75. **penthouse:** a kind of porch structure, projecting from the main building   76. **like . . . all:** referring to the Latin tag "In vino veritas"   77. **stand close:** keep concealed   79. **dear:** costly
80. **villainy:** one wanting villainy to be committed   84. **unconfirm'd:** inexperienced
85. **is . . . man:** does not make the man   90. **deformed thief:** ill-formed thief (because fashion
assumes such fantastic shapes [lines 97–100] and robs men of their money by changing so
often)   97. **reechy:** smoky, dirty   98. **Bel's priests:** an allusion to the Apocryphal story of Bel
(Baal) and the Dragon   99. **shaven Hercules:** This allusion has not been identified; probably
the reference is to the Omphale episode (see note to II.i.183).   **codpiece:** the bag-like flap at the
front of men's breeches   101–102. **fashion . . . man:** clothes are more often discarded because the
fashion has changed than because they are worn out   103. **shifted:** with a quibble on the meaning
"changed (clothing)"

master, planted and plac'd and possess'd by my master Don John, saw afar off in the orchard this amiable encounter.

110 CONRADE   And thought they Margaret was Hero?

BORACHIO   Two of them did, the Prince and Claudio, but the devil my master knew she was Margaret; and partly by his oaths, which first possess'd them, partly by the dark night, which did deceive them, but chiefly by my villainy, which did confirm any slander that Don John had made, away went Claudio
115   enrag'd; swore he would meet her as he was appointed next morning at the temple, and there, before the whole congregation, shame her with what he saw o'ernight, and send her home again without a husband.

[2.] WATCH   We charge you, in the Prince's name, stand!

[1.] WATCH   Call up the right Master Constable. We have here recover'd the
120   most dangerous piece of lechery that ever was known in the commonwealth.

[2.] WATCH   And one Deformed is one of them; I know him, 'a wears a lock.

CONRADE   Masters, masters—

[2.] WATCH   You'll be made bring Deformed forth, I warrant you.

125 CONRADE   Masters—

[2.] WATCH   Never speak, we charge you; let us obey you to go with us.

BORACHIO   We are like to prove a goodly commodity, being taken up of these men's bills.

CONRADE   A commodity in question, I warrant you. Come, we'll obey you.

(*Exeunt.*)

[Scene IV]

(*Enter* HERO *and* MARGARET *and* URSULA.)

HERO   Good Ursula, wake my cousin Beatrice, and desire her to rise.

URSULA   I will, lady.

HERO   And bid her come hither.

URSULA   Well.

[*Exit.*]

5 MARGARET   Troth, I think your other rebato were better.

HERO   No, pray thee, good Meg, I'll wear this.

---

108. **possess'd:** informed   109. **amiable:** loving   119. **right Master:** by mistaken analogy with such honorifics as "right honorable" and "right worshipful"   **recover'd:** for *discovered*   120. **lechery:** for *treachery* (?)   122. **lock:** a love-lock of hair   126. **obey:** He means *command*
127. **commodity:** goods   **taken up:** (1) taken on credit; (2) arrested   128. **bills:** (1) bonds; (2) pikes   129. **in question:** (1) questionable; (2) about to be tried at law

III.iv. Location: Hero's apartment in Leonato's house
4. **Well:** very well   5. **rebato:** stiff collar supporting a ruff

MARGARET   By my troth 's not so good, and I warrant your cousin will say so.

HERO   My cousin's a fool, and thou art another. I'll wear none but this.

MARGARET   I like the new tire within excellently, if the hair were a thought
10   browner; and your gown's a most rare fashion, i' faith. I saw the Duchess of
Milan's gown that they praise so.

HERO   O, that exceeds, they say.

MARGARET   By my troth 's but a night-gown [in] respect of yours: cloth a' gold
and cuts, and lac'd with silver, set with pearls, down sleeves, side sleeves, and
15   skirts, round underborne with a bluish tinsel; but for a fine, quaint, graceful, and excellent fashion, yours is worth ten on't.

HERO   God give me joy to wear it, for my heart is exceeding heavy.

MARGARET   'Twill be heavier soon by the weight of a man.

HERO   Fie upon thee, art not asham'd?

20   MARGARET   Of what, lady? of speaking honorably? Is not marriage honorable
in a beggar? Is not your lord honorable without marriage? I think you
would have me say, "saving your reverence, a husband." And bad thinking
do not wrest true speaking, I'll offend nobody. Is there any harm in "the
heavier for a husband"? None, I think, and it be the right husband and the
25   right wife; otherwise 'tis light, and not heavy. Ask my Lady Beatrice else,
here she comes.

(*Enter* BEATRICE.)

HERO   Good morrow, coz.

BEATRICE   Good morrow, sweet Hero.

HERO   Why, how now? Do you speak in the sick tune?

30   BEATRICE   I am out of all other tune, methinks.

MARGARET   Clap 's into "Light a' love"; that goes without a burden. Do you sing
it, and I'll dance it.

BEATRICE   Ye light a' love with your heels! then if your husband have stables
enough, you'll see he shall lack no barns.

35   MARGARET   O illegitimate construction! I scorn that with my heels.

BEATRICE   'Tis almost five a' clock, cousin, 'tis time you were ready. By my
troth, I am exceeding ill. Heigh-ho!

MARGARET   For a hawk, a horse, or a husband?

---

7. **'s:** it is   9. **tire:** headdress   **within:** in the inner room   12. **exceeds:** is beyond comparison
13. **night-gown:** dressing gown   **in respect of:** compared with   14. **cuts:** slashed openings, showing the fabric underneath   **lac'd:** trimmed   **down sleeves:** long tight sleeves   **side sleeves:** wide
ornamental sleeves hanging open from the shoulder   15. **round underborne:** lined around the
bottom of the skirt   **quaint:** elegant   21. **in:** even in   22. **saving your reverence:** a phrase of apology before an improper expression   **And bad:** if bawdy   23. **wrest:** twist, misinterpret   25. **light:**
punning on the meaning "wanton"   **else:** if this isn't true   29. **sick tune:** voice of a sick person
31. **Clap 's:** let's shift   **Light a' love:** a popular song   **burden:** bass undersong (but with punning
reference to "weight of a man")   33. **Ye . . . heels:** you are light-heeled (slang for "unchaste")
34. **barns:** with pun on *bairns,* "children"   35. **with my heels:** contemptuously

BEATRICE   For the letter that begins them all, H.

40 MARGARET   Well, and you be not turn'd Turk, there's no more sailing by the star.

BEATRICE   What means the fool, trow?

MARGARET   Nothing I, but God send every one their heart's desire!

HERO   These gloves the Count sent me, they are an excellent perfume.

45 BEATRICE   I am stuff'd, cousin, I cannot smell.

MARGARET   A maid, and stuff'd! There's goodly catching of cold.

BEATRICE   O, God help me, God help me, how long have your profess'd apprehension?

MARGARET   Ever since you left it. Doth not my wit become me rarely?

50 BEATRICE   It is not seen enough, you should wear it in your cap. By my troth, I am sick.

MARGARET   Get you some of this distill'd *carduus benedictus,* and lay it to your heart; it is the only thing for a qualm.

HERO   There thou prick'st her with a thistle.

55 BEATRICE   *Benedictus!* why *benedictus?* You have some moral in this *benedictus.*

MARGARET   Moral? no, by my troth I have no moral meaning. I meant plain holy-thistle. You may think perchance that I think you are in love. Nay, by'r lady, I am not such a fool to think what I list, nor I list not to think what I can, nor indeed I cannot think, if I would think my heart out of thinking,

60 that you are in love, or that you will be in love, or that you can be in love. Yet Benedick was such another, and now is he become a man. He swore he would never marry, and yet now in despite of his heart he eats his meat without grudging; and how you may be converted I know not, but methinks you look with your eyes as other women do.

65 BEATRICE   What pace is this that thy tongue keeps?

MARGARET   Not a false gallop.

(*Enter* URSULA.)

URSULA   Madam, withdraw, the Prince, the Count, Signior Benedick, Don John, and all the gallants of the town are come to fetch you to church.

HERO   Help to dress me, good coz, good Meg, good Ursula.

[*Exeunt.*]

---

39. **H:** with pun on *ache,* which was pronounced *aitch* in Shakespeare's day   40. **turn'd Turk:** abandoned your faith (which was that you would never fall in love)   40–41. **no . . . star:** no more navigating by the north star, no more trusting to anything   42. **trow:** I wonder   45. **I am stuff'd:** I have a cold (with bawdy pun by Margaret following)   47–48. **profess'd apprehension:** made wit your profession   50. **wear . . . cap:** as a fool does his coxcomb   52. **carduus benedictus:** blessed (or holy) thistle, a medicinal herb   55. **moral:** hidden meaning   58. **list:** please   61. **a man:** like other men   62–63. **eats . . . grudging:** has an appetite like any other man   66. **a false gallop:** (1) a canter; (2) running on untruthfully

[Scene V]

(*Enter* LEONATO *and the Constable* [DOGBERRY] *and the Headborough* [VERGES].)

LEONATO What would you with me, honest neighbor?

DOGBERRY Marry, sir, I would have some confidence with you that decerns you nearly.

LEONATO Brief, I pray you, for you see it is a busy time with me.

5 DOGBERRY Marry, this it is, sir.

VERGES Yes, in truth it is, sir.

LEONATO What is it, my good friends?

DOGBERRY Goodman Verges, sir, speaks a little [off] the matter; an old man, sir, and his wits are not so blunt as, God help, I would desire they were, but
10 in faith, honest as the skin between his brows.

VERGES Yes, I thank God I am as honest as any man living, that is an old man, and no honester than I.

DOGBERRY Comparisons are odorous—*palabras,* neighbor Verges.

LEONATO Neighbors, you are tedious.

15 DOGBERRY It pleases your worship to say so, but we are the poor Duke's officers; but truly, for mine own part, if I were as tedious as a king, I could find in my heart to bestow it all of your worship.

LEONATO All thy tediousness on me, ah?

DOGBERRY Yea, and 'twere a thousand pound more than 'tis, for I hear as good
20 exclamation on your worship as of any man in the city, and though I be but a poor man, I am glad to hear it.

VERGES And so am I.

LEONATO I would fain know what you have to say.

VERGES Marry, sir, our watch to-night, excepting your worship's presence, ha'
25 ta'en a couple of as arrant knaves as any in Messina.

DOGBERRY A good old man, sir, he will be talking; as they say, "When the age is in, the wit is out." God help us, it is a world to see! Well said, i' faith, neighbor Verges. Well, God's a good man; and two men ride of a horse, one must ride behind. An honest soul, i' faith, sir, by my troth he is, as

---

III.v. Location: Leonato's house

o.s.d. **Headborough:** petty constable

2. **confidence:** for *conference* **decerns:** for *concerns* 3. **nearly:** intimately 8. **Goodman:** regular title for one just below the rank of gentleman 10. **honest . . . brows:** a proverbial comparison

13. **odorous:** for *odious* **palabras:** a shortening of Spanish *pocas palabras,* "few words"

15. **poor Duke's:** He intends *Duke's poor.* 17. **of:** on 19. **and:** even if 20. **exclamation:** *acclamation* (?). Dogberry's word is an unfortunate choice, since it normally meant "accusation" or "reproach." 24. **to-night:** last night **excepting:** for *respecting.* Dogberry here intends a polite phrase meaning "If I may speak of such things without offending your worship," but he says something far different. 26–27. **When . . . out:** an adaptation of the proverb "When ale is in, wit is out"

27. **it . . . see:** a proverbial phrase equivalent to "It is wonderful to behold"; but Dogberry seems to mean "What a world we live in" 28. **God's . . . man:** God is good (proverbial) **of a horse:** on one horse

30 ever broke bread; but God is to be worshipp'd; all men are not alike, alas, good neighbor!

LEONATO   Indeed, neighbor, he comes too short of you.

DOGBERRY   Gifts that God gives.

LEONATO   I must leave you.

35 DOGBERRY   One word, sir. Our watch, sir, have indeed comprehended two aspicious persons, and we would have them this morning examin'd before your worship.

LEONATO   Take their examination yourself, and bring it me. I am now in great haste, as it may appear unto you.

40 DOGBERRY   It shall be suffigance.

LEONATO   Drink some wine ere you go; fare you well.

[*Enter a* MESSENGER.]

MESSENGER   My lord, they stay for you to give your daughter to her husband.

LEONATO   I'll wait upon them, I am ready.

[*Exeunt* LEONATO *and* MESSENGER.]

DOGBERRY   Go, good partner, go, get you to Francis Seacole, bid him bring his
45 pen and inkhorn to the jail. We are now to examination these men.

VERGES   And we must do it wisely.

DOGBERRY   We will spare for no wit, I warrant you. Here's that shall drive some of them to a non-come; only get the learned writer to set down our excommunication, and meet me at the jail.

[*Exeunt.*]

Act IV

Scene I

(*Enter Prince* [DON PEDRO, DON JOHN *the*] *Bastard,* LEONATO, FRIAR [FRANCIS], CLAUDIO, BENEDICK, HERO, *and* BEATRICE [*with* ATTENDANTS].)

LEONATO   Come, Friar Francis, be brief—only to the plain form of marriage, and you shall recount their particular duties afterwards.

FRIAR FRANCIS   You come hither, my lord, to marry this lady.

CLAUDIO   No.

5 LEONATO   To be married to her. Friar, you come to marry her.

---

30. **God . . . worshipp'd:** We must praise God for whatever he sees fit to bestow (?).   35. **comprehended:** for *apprehended*   **aspicious:** for *suspicious*   40. **suffigance:** for *sufficient*   43. **wait upon:** attend   48. **non-come:** shortened form of *non compos mentis,* "not of sound mind," but Dogberry seems to intend *nonplus*   48–49. **excommunication:** *examination,* or (perhaps) *communication*

IV.i. Location: a church

FRIAR FRANCIS Lady, you come hither to be married to this count.

HERO I do.

FRIAR FRANCIS If either of you know any inward impediment why you should
    not be conjoin'd, I charge you on your souls to utter it.

10 CLAUDIO Know you any, Hero?

HERO None, my lord.

FRIAR FRANCIS Know you any, Count?

LEONATO I dare make his answer, none.

CLAUDIO O, what men dare do! What men may do! What men daily do, not

15   knowing what they do!

BENEDICK How now! interjections? Why then, some be of laughing, as, ah, ha,
    he!

CLAUDIO Stand thee by, friar. Father, be your leave,
    Will you with free and unconstrained soul

20   Give me this maid, your daughter?

LEONATO As freely, son, as God did give her me.

CLAUDIO And what have I to give you back whose worth
    May counterpoise this rich and precious gift?

DON PEDRO Nothing, unless you render her again.

25 CLAUDIO Sweet Prince, you learn me noble thankfulness.
    There, Leonato, take her back again.
    Give not this rotten orange to your friend,
    She's but the sign and semblance of her honor.
    Behold how like a maid she blushes here!

30   O, what authority and show of truth
    Can cunning sin cover itself withal!
    Comes not that blood as modest evidence
    To witness simple virtue? Would you not swear,
    All you that see her, that she were a maid,

35   By these exterior shows? But she is none:
    She knows the heat of a luxurious bed;
    Her blush is guiltiness, not modesty.

LEONATO What do you mean, my lord?

CLAUDIO   Not to be married,

40   Not to knit my soul to an approved wanton.

LEONATO Dear my lord, if you, in your own proof,
    Have vanquish'd the resistance of her youth,
    And made defeat of her virginity—

---

8. **inward:** secret, private   16–17. **some . . . he:** Grammars classified the interjections according to
the emotions they expressed; Benedick's sample is quoted from Lily's Latin grammar.
23. **counterpoise:** balance, be equivalent to   25. **learn:** teach   30. **authority:** authenticity
32. **modest evidence:** evidence of modesty   36. **luxurious:** lustful   40. **approved:** proved
41. **proof:** test or trial of her

CLAUDIO   I know what you would say. If I have known her,
45   You will say, she did embrace me as a husband,
     And so extenuate the 'forehand sin.
     No, Leonato,
     I never tempted her with word too large,
     But as a brother to his sister, show'd
50   Bashful sincerity and comely love.
  HERO   And seem'd I ever otherwise to you?
  CLAUDIO   Out on thee seeming! I will write against it:
     You seem to me as Dian in her orb,
     As chaste as is the bud ere it be blown;
55   But you are more intemperate in your blood
     Than Venus, or those pamp'red animals
     That rage in savage sensuality.
  HERO   Is my lord well, that he doth speak so wide?
  LEONATO   Sweet Prince, why speak not you?
60 DON PEDRO   What should I speak?
     I stand dishonor'd, that have gone about
     To link my dear friend to a common stale.
  LEONATO   Are these things spoken, or do I but dream?
  DON JOHN   Sir, they are spoken, and these things are true.
65 BENEDICK   This looks not like a nuptial.
  HERO   "True"! O God!
  CLAUDIO   Leonato, stand I here?
     Is this the Prince? is this the Prince's brother?
     Is this face Hero's? are our eyes our own?
70 LEONATO   All this is so, but what of this, my lord?
  CLAUDIO   Let me but move one question to your daughter,
     And by that fatherly and kindly power
     That you have in her, bid her answer truly.
  LEONATO   I charge thee do so, as thou art my child.
75 HERO   O God defend me, how am I beset!
     What kind of catechizing call you this?
  CLAUDIO   To make you answer truly to your name.
  HERO   Is it not Hero? Who can blot that name
     With any just reproach?

---

46. **extenuate:** lesson, excuse   **'forehand sin:** premarital sexual relations   48. **large:** broad, immodest   52. **thee seeming:** you in your mere appearance (of good)   53. **Dian:** Diana, emblematic of virginity   **orb:** sphere. Diana, in one of her aspects, was the moon-goddess.   54. **be blown:** open   58. **wide:** wide of the mark, far from the truth   61. **gone about:** endeavored   62. **stale:** whore   71. **move:** propose   72. **kindly:** natural   77. **answer . . . name:** tell truthfully by what name you should be called (?) or acknowledge that the name you have been called ("common stale") belongs to you (?)

80 CLAUDIO   Marry, that can Hero,
    Hero itself can blot out Hero's virtue.
    What man was he talk'd with you yesternight
    Out at your window betwixt twelve and one?
    Now if you are a maid, answer to this.
85 HERO   I talk'd with no man at that hour, my lord.
    DON PEDRO   Why then are you no maiden. Leonato,
    I am sorry you must hear. Upon mine honor,
    Myself, my brother, and this grieved count
    Did see her, hear her, at that hour last night
90   Talk with a ruffian at her chamber-window,
    Who hath indeed, most like a liberal villain,
    Confess'd the vile encounters they have had
    A thousand times in secret.
    DON JOHN   Fie, fie, they are not to be named, my lord,
95   Not to be spoke of;
    There is not chastity enough in language
    Without offense to utter them. Thus, pretty lady,
    I am sorry for thy much misgovernment.
    CLAUDIO   O Hero! what a Hero hadst thou been,
100   If half thy outward graces had been placed
    About thy thoughts and counsels of thy heart!
    But fare thee well, most foul, most fair! Farewell,
    Thou pure impiety and impious purity!
    For thee I'll lock up all the gates of love,
105   And on my eyelids shall conjecture hang,
    To turn all beauty into thoughts of harm,
    And never shall it more be gracious.
    LEONATO   Hath no man's dagger here a point for me?

[HERO *swoons.*]

    BEATRICE   Why, how now, cousin, wherefore sink you down?
110 DON JOHN   Come, let us go. These things, come thus to light,
    Smother her spirits up.

[*Exeunt* DON PEDRO, DON JOHN, *and* CLAUDIO.]
    BENEDICK   How doth the lady?

---

81. **Hero itself:** the name Hero (now the name of an unchaste woman)   88. **grieved:** aggrieved,
wronged   91. **liberal:** gross, licentious   98. **much misgovernment:** great misconduct
101. **thoughts and counsels:** secret thoughts (hendiadys)   104. **For thee:** because of my experience
with you   105. **conjecture:** suspicion   107. **be gracious:** seem beautiful   111. **spirits:** vital
forces

BEATRICE   Dead, I think. Help, uncle!
    Hero, why, Hero! Uncle! Signior Benedick! Friar!
115 LEONATO   O Fate! take not away thy heavy hand,
    Death is the fairest cover for her shame
    That may be wish'd for.
BEATRICE   How now, cousin Hero?
FRIAR FRANCIS   Have comfort, lady.
120 LEONATO   Dost thou look up?
FRIAR FRANCIS   Yea, wherefore should she not?
LEONATO   Wherefore? why, doth not every earthly thing
    Cry shame upon her? could she here deny
    The story that is printed in her blood?
125   Do not live, Hero, do not ope thine eyes;
    For did I think thou wouldst not quickly die,
    Thought I thy spirits were stronger than thy shames,
    Myself would, on the rearward of reproaches,
    Strike at thy life. Griev'd I, I had but one?
130   Chid I for that at frugal nature's frame?
    O, one too much by thee! Why had I one?
    Why ever wast thou lovely in my eyes?
    Why had I not with charitable hand
    Took up a beggar's issue at my gates,
135   Who smirched thus and mir'd with infamy,
    I might have said, "No part of it is mine;
    This shame derives itself from unknown loins"?
    But mine, and mine I lov'd, and mine I prais'd,
    And mine that I was proud on, mine so much
140   That I myself was to myself not mine,
    Valuing of her—why, she, O she is fall'n
    Into a pit of ink, that the wide sea
    Hath drops too few to wash her clean again,
    And salt too little which may season give
145   To her foul tainted flesh!
BENEDICK   Sir, sir, be patient.
    For my part I am so attir'd in wonder,
    I know not what to say.
BEATRICE   O, on my soul, my cousin is belied!
150 BENEDICK   Lady, were you her bedfellow last night?
BEATRICE   No, truly, not, although until last night,
    I have this twelvemonth been her bedfellow.

---

124. **blood:** blushes   127. **shames:** feelings of shame   128. **on . . . reproaches:** after reproaching you   130. **frame:** design (with respect to the number of my offspring)   140. **I . . . mine:** that I was nothing to myself   141. **Valuing of her:** since I valued her so exclusively   144. **season give:** act as a preservative, as a restorative   147. **attir'd:** wrapped

LEONATO   Confirm'd, confirm'd! O, that is stronger made
    Which was before barr'd up with ribs of iron!
155   Would the two princes lie, and Claudio lie,
    Who lov'd her so, that speaking of her foulness,
    Wash'd it with tears? Hence from her, let her die.
FRIAR FRANCIS   Hear me a little,
    For I have only been silent so long,
160   And given way unto this course of fortune,
    By noting of the lady. I have mark'd
    A thousand blushing apparitions
    To start into her face, a thousand innocent shames
    In angel whiteness beat away those blushes,
165   And in her eye there hath appear'd a fire
    To burn the errors that these princes hold
    Against her maiden truth. Call me a fool,
    Trust not my reading, nor my observations,
    Which with experimental seal doth warrant
170   The tenure of my book; trust not my age,
    My reverence, calling, nor divinity,
    If this sweet lady lie not guiltless here
    Under some biting error.
LEONATO   Friar, it cannot be.
175   Thou seest that all the grace that she hath left
    Is that she will not add to her damnation
    A sin of perjury; she not denies it.
    Why seek'st thou then to cover with excuse
    That which appears in proper nakedness?
180 FRIAR FRANCIS   Lady, what man is he you are accus'd of?
HERO   They know that do accuse me, I know none.
    If I know more of any man alive
    Than that which maiden modesty doth warrant,
    Let all my sins lack mercy! O my father,
185   Prove you that any man with me convers'd
    At hours unmeet, or that I yesternight
    Maintain'd the change of words with any creature,
    Refuse me, hate me, torture me to death!
FRIAR FRANCIS   There is some strange misprision in the princes.

159–61. **I . . . lady:** I have kept silence so long, allowing these events to take their free course, only because I have been occupied in observing the lady (?). The passage has difficulties and may be textually corrupt.   169–70. **experimental . . . book:** The seal of experience guarantees as genuine the conclusions I have drawn from my reading (of her face). *Tenure* = tenor, import   179. **proper:** its own   186. **unmeet:** improper   187. **change:** exchange   188. **Refuse:** renounce, cast off   189. **misprision:** misapprehension

190 BENEDICK   Two of them have the very bent of honor,
   And if their wisdoms be misled in this,
   The practice of it lives in John the Bastard,
   Whose spirits toil in frame of villainies.
  LEONATO   I know not. If they speak but truth of her,
195 These hands shall tear her; if they wrong her honor,
   The proudest of them shall well hear of it.
   Time hath not yet so dried this blood of mine,
   Nor age so eat up my invention,
   Nor fortune made such havoc of my means,
200 Nor my bad life reft me so much of friends,
   But they shall find, awak'd in such a kind,
   Both strength of limb, and policy of mind,
   Ability in means, and choice of friends,
   To quit me of them throughly.
205 FRIAR FRANCIS   Pause awhile,
   And let my counsel sway you in this case.
   Your daughter here the [princes] left for dead,
   Let her awhile be secretly kept in,
   And publish it that she is dead indeed.
210 Maintain a mourning ostentation,
   And on your family's old monument
   Hang mournful epitaphs, and do all rites
   That appertain unto a burial.
  LEONATO   What shall become of this? what will this do?
215 FRIAR FRANCIS   Marry, this well carried shall on her behalf
   Change slander to remorse; that is some good.
   But not for that dream I on this strange course,
   But on this travail look for greater birth:
   She dying, as it must be so maintain'd,
220 Upon the instant that she was accus'd,
   Shall be lamented, pitied, and excus'd
   Of every hearer; for it so falls out
   That what we have we prize not to the worth
   Whiles we enjoy it, but being lack'd and lost,
225 Why then we rack the value; then we find
   The virtue that possession would not show us
   Whiles it was ours. So will it fare with Claudio:

---

190. **the very bent of:** a perfect inclination toward   192. **practice:** plotting   193. **frame:** contriving
198. **eat:** eaten   **invention:** power of devising (retaliation); cf. *policy of mind,* line 202   201. **kind:**
manner, degree   202. **policy of mind:** shrewdness in contriving   204. **quit . . . throughly:** settle
my account with them thoroughly   210. **mourning ostentation:** show of mourning   214. **become
of:** result from   215. **carried:** managed   218. **travail:** labor (in the double sense of "effort" and
"pain of childbirth")   225. **rack:** stretch

When he shall hear she died upon his words,
Th' idea of her life shall sweetly creep
230　Into his study of imagination,
And every lovely organ of her life
Shall come apparell'd in more precious habit,
More moving, delicate, and full of life,
Into the eye and prospect of his soul,
235　Than when she liv'd indeed. Then shall he mourn,
If ever love had interest in his liver,
And wish he had not so accused her;
No, though he thought his accusation true.
Let this be so, and doubt not but success
240　Will fashion the event in better shape
Than I can lay it down in likelihood.
But if all aim but this be levell'd false,
The supposition of the lady's death
Will quench the wonder of her infamy.
245　And if it sort not well, you may conceal her,
As best befits her wounded reputation,
In some reclusive and religious life,
Out of all eyes, tongues, minds, and injuries.
BENEDICK　Signior Leonato, let the friar advise you,
250　And though you know my inwardness and love
Is very much unto the Prince and Claudio,
Yet, by mine honor, I will deal in this
As secretly and justly as your soul
Should with your body.
255　LEONATO　　　　　　　　Being that I flow in grief,
The smallest twine may lead me.
FRIAR FRANCIS　'Tis well consented; presently away,
For to strange sores strangely they strain the cure.
Come, lady, die to live; this wedding-day
260　Perhaps is but prolong'd, have patience and endure.

(*Exit* [*with all but* BENEDICK *and* BEATRICE].)

---

228. **upon:** as a result of　230. **study of imagination:** imaginative study—i.e., musing, reverie
231. **organ . . . life:** aspect of her as she was when she lived　234. **prospect:** view　236. **interest in:**
any claim upon (a legal term)　**liver:** the supposed seat of the passion of love　239. **success:** the
happy working out (of my plan)　240. **event:** outcome　241. **lay . . . likelihood:** suggest its probable consequences　242. **if . . . false:** if we miss our aim in every other respect　245. **sort:** turn out
247. **reclusive:** retired, secluded (as a religious recluse)　248. **injuries:** insults　250. **inwardness**
and love: close friendship (hendiadys)　255. **Being that:** since　**flow in:** am dissolved in (?) or am
afloat on (?)　258. **For . . . cure:** strange diseases require strange and desperate cures
260. **prolong'd:** postponed

BENEDICK   Lady Beatrice, have you wept all this while?

BEATRICE   Yea, and I will weep a while longer.

BENEDICK   I will not desire that.

BEATRICE   You have no reason, I do it freely.

265 BENEDICK   Surely I do believe your fair cousin is wrong'd.

BEATRICE   Ah, how much might the man deserve of me that would right her!

BENEDICK   Is there any way to show such friendship?

BEATRICE   A very even way, but no such friend.

BENEDICK   May a man do it?

270 BEATRICE   It is a man's office, but not yours.

BENEDICK   I do love nothing in the world so well as you—is not that strange?

BEATRICE   As strange as the thing I know not. It were as possible for me to say I lov'd nothing so well as you, but believe me not; and yet I lie not: I confess nothing, nor I deny nothing. I am sorry for my cousin.

275 BENEDICK   By my sword, Beatrice, thou lovest me.

BEATRICE   Do not swear and eat it.

BENEDICK   I will swear by it that you love me, and I will make him eat it that says I love not you.

BEATRICE   Will you not eat your word?

280 BENEDICK   With no sauce that can be devis'd to it. I protest I love thee.

BEATRICE   Why then God forgive me!

BENEDICK   What offense, sweet Beatrice?

BEATRICE   You have stay'd me in a happy hour, I was about to protest I lov'd you.

285 BENEDICK   And do it with all thy heart.

BEATRICE   I love you with so much of my heart that none is left to protest.

BENEDICK   Come, bid me do any thing for thee.

BEATRICE   Kill Claudio.

BENEDICK   Ha, not for the wide world.

290 BEATRICE   You kill me to deny it. Farewell.

BENEDICK   Tarry, sweet Beatrice.

BEATRICE   I am gone, though I am here; there is no love in you. Nay, I pray you let me go.

BENEDICK   Beatrice—

295 BEATRICE   In faith, I will go.

BENEDICK   We'll be friends first.

BEATRICE   You dare easier be friends with me than fight with mine enemy.

BENEDICK   Is Claudio thine enemy?

---

268. **even:** level, easy   272. **As strange:** as much a stranger (playing on Benedick's use of *strange*)   276. **eat it:** go back on your oath   280. **protest:** declare (but Beatrice pretends to take it in the sense of "object," as she uses it herself in line 286)   283. **in . . . hour:** at just the right moment, opportunely   290. **deny:** refuse   292. **am gone:** have left you (in spirit)

BEATRICE   Is 'a not approv'd in the height a villain, that hath slander'd, scorn'd,
300   dishonor'd my kinswoman? O that I were a man! What, bear her in hand
until they come to take hands, and then with public accusation, uncover'd
slander, unmitigated rancor—O God, that I were a man! I would eat his
heart in the market-place.

BENEDICK   Hear me, Beatrice—

305 BEATRICE   Talk with a man out at a window! a proper saying!

BENEDICK   Nay, but, Beatrice—

BEATRICE   Sweet Hero, she is wrong'd, she is sland'red, she is undone.

BENEDICK   Beat—

BEATRICE   Princes and counties! Surely a princely testimony, a goodly count,
310   Count Comfect, a sweet gallant surely! O that I were a man for his sake! or
that I had any friend would be a man for my sake! But manhood is melted
into cur'sies, valor into compliment, and men are only turn'd into tongue,
and trim ones too. He is now as valiant as Hercules that only tells a lie, and
swears it. I cannot be a man with wishing, therefore I will die a woman with
315   grieving.

BENEDICK   Tarry, good Beatrice. By this hand, I love thee.

BEATRICE   Use it for my love some other way than swearing by it.

BENEDICK   Think you in your soul the Count Claudio hath wrong'd Hero?

BEATRICE   Yea, as sure as I have a thought or a soul.

320 BENEDICK   Enough, I am engag'd, I will challenge him. I will kiss your hand,
and so I leave you. By this hand, Claudio shall render me a dear account. As
you hear of me, so think of me. Go comfort your cousin. I must say she is
dead; and so farewell.

[*Exeunt.*]

[Scene II]

(*Enter the Constables* [DOGBERRY *and* VERGES] *and the Town Clerk* [*or* SEXTON] *in gowns,* [*and the* WATCH *with* CONRADE *and*] BORACHIO.)

DOGBERRY   Is our whole dissembly appear'd?

VERGES   O, a stool and a cushion for the sexton.

SEXTON   Which be the malefactors?

---

299. **approv'd:** proved   **height:** highest degree   300. **bear . . . hand:** deceive her with false hopes
301. **uncover'd:** unconcealed, open   309. **counties:** counts   **count:** (1) the title; (2) legal indict-
ment; (3) story   310. **Comfect:** comfit, sweetmeat   **for his sake:** to deal with him
313. **trim:** fine   320. **engag'd:** bound by a pledge   321. **render . . . account:** make a very costly settlement with me

IV.ii. Location: a prison
o.s.d. **gowns:** robes of office   1. **dissembly:** for *assembly*

DOGBERRY   Marry, that am I and my partner.

5   VERGES   Nay, that's certain, we have the exhibition to examine.

SEXTON   But which are the offenders that are to be examin'd? Let them come before Master Constable.

DOGBERRY   Yea, marry, let them come before me. What is your name, friend?

BORACHIO   Borachio.

10   DOGBERRY   Pray write down Borachio. Yours, sirrah?

CONRADE   I am a gentleman, sir, and my name is Conrade.

DOGBERRY   Write down Master Gentleman Conrade. Masters, do you serve God?

BOTH [CONRADE, BORACHIO]   Yea, sir, we hope.

15   DOGBERRY   Write down, that they hope they serve God; and write God first, for God defend but God should go before such villains! Masters, it is prov'd already that you are little better than false knaves, and it will go near to be thought so shortly. How answer you for yourselves?

CONRADE   Marry, sir, we say we are none.

20   DOGBERRY   A marvellous witty fellow, I assure you, but I will go about with him. Come you hither, sirrah; a word in your ear, sir. I say to you, it is thought you are false knaves.

BORACHIO   Sir, I say to you, we are none.

DOGBERRY   Well, stand aside. 'Fore God, they are both in a tale. Have you writ

25   down, that they are none?

SEXTON   Master Constable, you go not the way to examine; you must call forth the watch that are their accusers.

DOGBERRY   Yea, marry, that's the eftest way; let the watch come forth. Masters, I charge you in the Prince's name accuse these men.

30   [1.] WATCH   This man said, sir, that Don John, the Prince's brother, was a villain.

DOGBERRY   Write down Prince John a villain. Why, this is flat perjury, to call a prince's brother villain.

BORACHIO   Master Constable—

DOGBERRY   Pray thee, fellow, peace. I do not like thy look, I promise thee.

35   SEXTON   What heard you him say else?

[2.] WATCH   Marry, that he had receiv'd a thousand ducats of Don John for accusing the Lady Hero wrongfully.

DOGBERRY   Flat burglary as ever was committed.

VERGES   Yea, by mass, that it is.

40   SEXTON   What else, fellow?

[1.] WATCH   And that Count Claudio did mean, upon his words, to disgrace Hero before the whole assembly, and not marry her.

---

5. **exhibition:** possibly for *commission,* but *exhibition* could mean "an allowance of money"; in either case, Verges blunders.   10. **sirrah:** form of address to inferiors   16. **defend:** forbid
20. **witty:** clever, cunning   **go about with:** outmaneuver   24. **in a tale:** agreed on the same lie
28. **eftest:** It is clear that he means something like "easiest" or "quickest" but not what word he may be mangling   41. **upon his words:** on the basis of his accusation

DOGBERRY   O villain! thou wilt be condemn'd into everlasting redemption for
this.
45 SEXTON   What else?
[1. AND 2.] WATCH   This is all.
SEXTON   And this is more, masters, than you can deny. Prince John is this
morning secretly stol'n away. Hero was in this manner accus'd, in this very
manner refus'd, and upon the grief of this suddenly died. Master Constable,
50 let these men be bound, and brought to Leonato's. I will go before and show
him their examination.

[*Exit.*]

[DOGBERRY]   Come let them be opinion'd.
VERGES   Let them be in the hands—
[CONRADE]   [Off,] coxcomb!
55 DOGBERRY   God's my life, where's the sexton? Let him write down the Prince's
officer coxcomb. Come, bind them. Thou naughty varlet!
[CONRADE]   Away, you are an ass, you are an ass.
DOGBERRY   Dost thou not suspect my place? Dost thou not suspect my years?
O that he were here to write me down as ass! But, masters, remember that I
60 am an ass; though it be not written down, yet forget not that I am an ass.
No, thou villain, thou art full of piety, as shall be prov'd upon thee by good
witness. I am a wise fellow, and which is more, an officer, and which is more,
a householder, and which is more, as pretty a piece of flesh as any is in
Messina, and one that knows the law, go to, and a rich fellow enough, go to,
65 and a fellow that hath had losses, and one that hath two gowns, and every
thing handsome about him. Bring him away. O that I had been writ down
an ass!

(*Exeunt.*)

Act V

Scene I

(*Enter* LEONATO *and his brother* [ANTONIO].)

ANTONIO   If you go on thus, you will kill yourself,
And 'tis not wisdom thus to second grief
Against yourself.

---

43. **redemption:** He means the opposite.   49. **refus'd:** renounced   52. **opinion'd:** for *pinioned*
55. **God's:** God save   56. **naughty:** wicked   58. **suspect:** for *respect*   61. **piety:** for *impiety*
63. **as . . . flesh:** as fine a fellow

V.i. Location: near Leonato's house
2. **second:** aid

LEONATO   I pray thee cease thy counsel,
5   Which falls into mine ears as profitless
       As water in a sieve. Give not me counsel,
       Nor let no comforter delight mine ear
       But such a one whose wrongs do suit with mine.
       Bring me a father that so lov'd his child,
10   Whose joy of her is overwhelm'd like mine,
       And bid him speak of patience;
       Measure his woe the length and breadth of mine,
       And let it answer every strain for strain,
       As thus for thus, and such a grief for such,
15   In every lineament, branch, shape, and form;
       If such a one will smile and stroke his beard,
       And, sorrow wag, cry "hem!" when he should groan,
       Patch grief with proverbs, make misfortune drunk
       With candle-wasters, bring him yet to me,
20   And I of him will gather patience.
       But there is no such man, for, brother, men
       Can counsel and speak comfort to that grief
       Which they themselves not feel, but tasting it,
       Their counsel turns to passion, which before
25   Would give preceptial med'cine to rage,
       Fetter strong madness in a silken thread,
       Charm ache with air, and agony with words.
       No, no, 'tis all men's office to speak patience
       To those that wring under the load of sorrow,
30   But no man's virtue nor sufficiency
       To be so moral when he shall endure
       The like himself. Therefore give me no counsel,
       My griefs cry louder than advertisement.
ANTONIO   Therein do men from children nothing differ.
35 LEONATO   I pray thee peace. I will be flesh and blood,
       For there was never yet philosopher
       That could endure the toothache patiently,
       However they have writ the style of gods,
       And made a push at chance and sufferance.

---

7. **delight:** try to please   8. **suit with:** match   12. **Measure his woe:** let his woe equal in its dimen-
sions   13. **strain:** strong feeling   17. **And, sorrow wag:** and, letting sorrow go hang. Many editors
emend to *Bid sorrow wag* (after Capell)—i.e., bid sorrow be off.   18. **drunk:** insensible
19. **candle-wasters:** those who sit up late over books; here, those who write moral treatises, and by
extension, their good advice itself   25. **preceptial:** comprised of precepts   27. **air:** breath, words
29. **wring:** writhe   30. **sufficiency:** ability   31. **moral:** full of moral sentiments
33. **advertisement:** counsel   38. **style of gods:** language worthy of gods (who are above human suffering)   39. **a push at:** an onslaught against (?), or an expression of contempt toward (*push* being a
common form of *pish*) (?), (an expression of contempt)   **sufferance:** suffering

40　ANTONIO　Yet bend not all the harm upon yourself;
　　　　Make those that do offend you suffer too.
　　LEONATO　There thou speak'st reason; nay, I will do so.
　　　　My soul doth tell me Hero is belied,
　　　　And that shall Claudio know; so shall the Prince,
45　　　And all of them that thus dishonor her.

(*Enter Prince* [DON PEDRO] *and* CLAUDIO.)

　　ANTONIO　Here comes the Prince and Claudio hastily.
　　DON PEDRO　Good den, good den.
　　CLAUDIO　　　　　　　　　　　Good day to both of you.
　　LEONATO　Hear you, my lords—
50　DON PEDRO　　　　　　　　We have some haste, Leonato.
　　LEONATO　Some haste, my lord! Well, fare you well, my lord.
　　　　Are you so hasty now? well, all is one.
　　DON PEDRO　Nay, do not quarrel with us, good old man.
　　ANTONIO　If he could right himself with quarrelling,
55　　　Some of us would lie low.
　　CLAUDIO　　　　　　　　　　Who wrongs him?
　　LEONATO　Marry, thou dost wrong me, thou dissembler, thou—
　　　　Nay, never lay thy hand upon thy sword,
　　　　I fear thee not.
60　CLAUDIO　　　　　　　Marry, beshrew my hand,
　　　　If it should give your age such cause of fear.
　　　　In faith, my hand meant nothing to my sword.
　　LEONATO　Tush, tush, man, never fleer and jest at me;
　　　　I speak not like a dotard nor a fool,
65　　　As under privilege of age to brag
　　　　What I have done being young, or what would do
　　　　Were I not old. Know, Claudio, to thy head,
　　　　Thou hast so wrong'd mine innocent child and me
　　　　That I am forc'd to lay my reverence by,
70　　　And with grey hairs and bruise of many days,
　　　　Do challenge thee to trial of a man.
　　　　I say thou hast belied mine innocent child!
　　　　Thy slander hath gone through and through her heart,
　　　　And she lies buried with her ancestors—
75　　　O, in a tomb where never scandal slept,
　　　　Save this of hers, fram'd by thy villainy!
　　CLAUDIO　My villainy?
　　LEONATO　　　　　　　Thine, Claudio, thine, I say.

---

52. **all is one:** It does not matter.　55. **Some of us:** He means Don Pedro and Claudio.
60. **beshrew:** curse　62. **to:** in grasping　63. **fleer:** jeer　67. **head:** face　71. **trial . . . man:** text (or combat) worthy of a man

DON PEDRO　You say not right, old man.

80　LEONATO　　　　　　　　　　　　　　My lord, my lord,
　　　I'll prove it on his body, if he dare,
　　　Despite his nice fence and his active practice,
　　　His May of youth and bloom of lustihood.

CLAUDIO　Away, I will not have to do with you.

85　LEONATO　Canst thou so daff me? Thou hast kill'd my child.
　　　If thou kill'st me, boy, thou shalt kill a man.

ANTONIO　He shall kill two of us, and men indeed;
　　　But that's no matter, let him kill one first.
　　　Win me and wear me, let him answer me.

90　　　Come follow me, boy; come, sir boy, come follow me.
　　　Sir boy, I'll whip you from your foining fence,
　　　Nay, as I am a gentleman, I will.

LEONATO　Brother—

ANTONIO　Content yourself. God knows I lov'd my niece,

95　　　And she is dead, slander'd to death by villains,
　　　That dare as well answer a man indeed
　　　As I dare take a serpent by the tongue.
　　　Boys, apes, braggarts, Jacks, milksops!

LEONATO　　　　　　　　　　　　　　Brother Anthony—

100　ANTONIO　Hold you content. What, man! I know them, yea,
　　　And what they weigh, even to the utmost scruple—
　　　Scambling, outfacing, fashion-monging boys,
　　　That lie and cog and flout, deprave and slander,
　　　Go anticly, and show outward hideousness,

105　　　And speak [off] half a dozen dang'rous words,
　　　How they might hurt their enemies—if they durst—
　　　And this is all.

LEONATO　But, brother Anthony—

ANTONIO　　　　　　　　　　　　　　Come, 'tis no matter;

110　　　Do not you meddle, let me deal in this.

DON PEDRO　Gentlemen both, we will not wake your patience.
　　　My heart is sorry for your daughter's death;

---

82. **nice fence:** dextrous fencing (probably with a sneer in *nice* at the new Italian fashion of duelling with rapier and dagger in place of the older native half-sword and dagger; cf. line 91)
83. **lustihood:** bodily vigor　85. **daff:** doff, thrust aside　87. **men indeed:** true men (cf. line 96)
89. **Win . . . wear me:** If he wants to have me, he'll have to overcome me first (a proverbial phrase used as a summons to action).　**answer me:** meet me in response to my challenge
91. **foining:** thrusting　94. **Content yourself:** don't try to stop me　102. **Scambling:** contentious　**outfacing:** insolent　**fashion-monging:** following the fashions, foppish
103. **cog:** cheat　**deprave:** vilify　104. **Go anticly:** go about fantastically dressed　**outward hideousness:** a threatening appearance　105. **dang'rous:** arrogant, threatening　111. **wake your patience:** test your patience further, add to your troubles

But on my honor she was charg'd with nothing
But what was true, and very full of proof.
115 LEONATO   My lord, my lord—
DON PEDRO   I will not hear you.
LEONATO   No? Come, brother, away! I will be heard.
ANTONIO   And shall, or some of us will smart for it.

(*Exeunt ambo* [LEONATO *and* ANTONIO].)

(*Enter* BENEDICK.)

DON PEDRO   See, see, here comes the man we went to seek.
120 CLAUDIO   Now, signior, what news?
BENEDICK   Good day, my lord.
DON PEDRO   Welcome, signior, you are almost come to part almost a fray.
CLAUDIO   We had lik'd to have had our two noses snapp'd off with two old men
without teeth.
125 DON PEDRO   Leonato and his brother. What think'st thou? Had we fought, I
doubt we should have been too young for them.
BENEDICK   In a false quarrel there is no true valor. I came to seek you both.
CLAUDIO   We have been up and down to seek thee, for we are high-proof
melancholy, and would fain have it beaten away. Wilt thou use thy wit?
130 BENEDICK   It is in my scabbard, shall I draw it?
DON PEDRO   Dost thou wear thy wit by thy side?
CLAUDIO   Never any did so, though very many have been beside their wit. I will
bid thee draw, as we do the minstrels, draw to pleasure us.
DON PEDRO   As I am an honest man, he looks pale. Art thou sick, or angry?
135 CLAUDIO   What, courage, man! What though care kill'd a cat, thou hast mettle
enough in thee to kill care.
BENEDICK   Sir, I shall meet your wit in the career, and you charge it against me.
I pray you choose another subject.
CLAUDIO   Nay then give him another staff, this last was broke cross.
140 DON PEDRO   By this light, he changes more and more. I think he be angry in-
deed.
CLAUDIO   If he be, he knows how to turn his girdle.
BENEDICK   Shall I speak a word in your ear?
CLAUDIO   God bless me from a challenge!

---

s.d. **ambo:** both   126. **doubt:** fear   128. **high-proof:** at a high level of   132. **beside their wit:** out
of their minds   133. **minstrels:** who are bidden to draw their bows across the strings of their in-
struments   137. **in the career:** at full speed (an expression from jousting)   **charge:** direct, level
139. **staff:** lance   **broke cross:** broken crosswise, athwart his opponent's shield. Claudio means that
Benedick has performed wretchedly in this first exchange.   142. **he knows . . . girdle:** Proverbial,
but of uncertain meaning; generally explained as meaning "it's up to him to get himself into a better
frame of mind; I shall make no effort to placate him" (*girdle* = belt).

145 BENEDICK [*aside to* CLAUDIO]   You are a villain. I jest not; I will make it good
how you dare, with what you dare, and when you dare. Do me right, or I will
protest your cowardice. You have kill'd a sweet lady, and her death shall fall
heavy on you. Let me hear from you.

CLAUDIO   Well, I will meet you, so I may have good cheer.

150 DON PEDRO   What, a feast, a feast?

CLAUDIO   I' faith, I thank him, he hath bid me to a calve's-head and a capon, the
which if I do not carve most curiously, say my knife's naught. Shall I not
find a woodcock too?

BENEDICK   Sir, your wit ambles well, it goes easily.

155 DON PEDRO   I'll tell thee how Beatrice prais'd thy wit the other day. I said thou
hadst a fine wit. "True," said she, "a fine little one." "No," said I, "a great wit."
"Right," says she, "a great gross one." "Nay," said I, "a good wit." "Just," said
she, "it hurts nobody." "Nay," said I, "the gentleman is wise." "Certain," said
she, "a wise gentleman." "Nay," said I, "he hath the tongues." "That I believe,"
160 said she, "for he swore a thing to me on Monday night, which he forswore
on Tuesday morning. There's a double tongue, there's two tongues." Thus
did she an hour together trans-shape thy particular virtues, yet at last she
concluded with a sigh, thou wast the proper'st man in Italy.

CLAUDIO   For the which she wept heartily and said she car'd not.

165 DON PEDRO   Yea, that she did, but yet for all that, and if she did not hate him
deadly, she would love him dearly. The old man's daughter told us all.

CLAUDIO   All, all, and, moreover, God saw him when he was hid in the garden.

DON PEDRO   But when shall we set the savage bull's horns on the sensible
Benedick's head?

170 CLAUDIO   Yea, and text underneath, "Here dwells Benedick the married man"?

BENEDICK   Fare you well, boy, you know my mind. I will leave you now to your
gossip-like humor. You break jests as braggards do their blades, which, God
be thank'd, hurt not. My lord, for your many courtesies I thank you. I must
discontinue your company. Your brother the bastard is fled from Messina.
175 You have among you kill'd a sweet and innocent lady. For my Lord Lack-
beard there, he and I shall meet, and till then peace be with him.

[*Exit.*]

---

146. **Do me right:** give me satisfaction   147. **protest:** proclaim   149. **so . . . cheer:** so long
as I may have good cheer   151. **calve's-head, capon, woodcock:** types of stupidity
152. **curiously:** daintily   **naught:** worthless   154. **your . . . easily:** your wit moves smoothly like an
ambling horse (it shows no mettle or fire like a horse at the gallop).   157. **gross:** coarse
158. **hurts nobody:** has no bite   159. **a wise gentleman:** One of the established uses of this phrase
was in an ironic sense   **hath the tongues:** is a master of languages   162. **trans-shape:** distort
163. **proper'st:** handsomest   165. **and if:** if   166. **deadly:** mortally   167. **God . . . garden:** This
reference to the action of III.i contains also an echo of Genesis 3:8.   168–70. **But . . . man:**
Benedick is put on notice that his lordly assertion at I.i.187–191 has not been forgotten.
172. **braggards:** braggarts, those better at boasting of their prowess than of demonstrating it

DON PEDRO　He is in earnest.

CLAUDIO　In most profound earnest, and I'll warrant you, for the love of Beatrice.

180　DON PEDRO　And hath challeng'd thee?

CLAUDIO　Most sincerely.

DON PEDRO　What a pretty thing man is when he goes in his doublet and hose and leaves off his wit!

(*Enter Constables* [DOGBERRY *and* VERGES, *and the* WATCH *with*] CONRADE *and* BORACHIO.)

CLAUDIO　He is then a giant to an ape, but then is an ape a doctor to such a
185　man.

DON PEDRO　But soft you, let me be. Pluck up, my heart, and be sad. Did he not say my brother was fled?

DOGBERRY　Come you, sir. If justice cannot tame you, she shall ne'er weigh more reasons in her balance. Nay, and you be a cursing hypocrite once, you
190　must be look'd to.

DON PEDRO　How now? two of my brother's men bound? Borachio one!

CLAUDIO　Hearken after their offense, my lord.

DON PEDRO　Officers, what offense have these men done?

DOGBERRY　Marry, sir, they have committed false report; moreover they have
195　spoken untruths; secondarily, they are slanders; sixt and lastly, they have belied a lady; thirdly, they have verified unjust things; and to conclude, they are lying knaves.

DON PEDRO　First, I ask thee what they have done; thirdly, I ask thee what's their offense; sixt and lastly, why they are committed; and to conclude, what you
200　lay to their charge.

CLAUDIO　Rightly reason'd, and in his own division, and by my troth there's one meaning well suited.

DON PEDRO　Who have you offended, masters, that you are thus bound to your answer? This learned constable is too cunning to be understood. What's
205　your offense?

BORACHIO　Sweet Prince, let me go no farther to mine answer: do you hear me, and let this count kill me. I have deceiv'd even your very eyes. What your wisdoms could not discover, these shallow fools have brought to light, who in the night overheard me confessing to this man how Don John your

---

182–183. **goes . . . wit:** forgets to put on his good sense along with his clothes　184. **a giant to:** much larger than (*to* = in comparison with)　**doctor:** scholar, learned man　186. **soft you:** wait a minute　**Pluck . . . heart:** collect yourself, my mind　**sad:** serious　189. **reasons:** legal cases (Dogberry seems to have confused *reasons* and *causes*). Perhaps *reasons* quibbles on *raisins,* which it closely resembled in pronunciation.　**balance:** scale　192. **Hearken after:** inquire into　195. **slanders:** slanderers　196. **verified:** affirmed as true (but perhaps a blunder for *testified*)　202. **well suited:** in several garbs　203–204. **bound . . . answer:** bound over for trial (perhaps with puns on *bound* in the senses "pinioned" and "on the way")

210 brother incens'd me to slander the Lady Hero, how you were brought into the orchard, and saw me court Margaret in Hero's garments, how you disgrac'd her when you should marry her. My villainy they have upon record, which I had rather seal with my death than repeat over to my shame. The lady is dead upon mine and my master's false accusation; and briefly, I de-
215 sire nothing but the reward of a villain.

DON PEDRO   Runs not this speech like iron through your blood?

CLAUDIO   I have drunk poison whiles he utter'd it.

DON PEDRO   But did my brother set thee on to this?

BORACHIO   Yea, and paid me richly for the practice of it.

220 DON PEDRO   He is compos'd and fram'd of treachery,
And fled he is upon this villainy.

CLAUDIO   Sweet Hero, now thy image doth appear
In the rare semblance that I lov'd it first.

DOGBERRY   Come, bring away the plaintiffs. By this time our sexton hath re-
225 form'd Signior Leonato of the matter; and, masters, do not forget to specify,
when time and place shall serve, that I am an ass.

VERGES   Here, here comes Master Signior Leonato, and the sexton too.

(*Enter* LEONATO, *his brother* [ANTONIO], *and the* SEXTON.)

LEONATO   Which is the villain? Let me see his eyes,
That when I note another man like him
230 I may avoid him. Which of these is he?

BORACHIO   If you would know your wronger, look on me.

LEONATO   Art thou the slave that with thy breath hast kill'd
Mine innocent child?

BORACHIO   Yea, even I alone.

235 LEONATO   No, not so, villain, thou beliest thyself.
Here stand a pair of honorable men,
A third is fled, that had a hand in it.
I thank you, princes, for my daughter's death;
Record it with your high and worthy deeds.
240 'Twas bravely done, if you bethink you of it.

CLAUDIO   I know not how to pray your patience,
Yet I must speak. Choose your revenge yourself,
Impose me to what penance your invention
Can lay upon my sin; yet sinn'd I not,
245 But in mistaking.

---

210. **incens'd:** incited   212. **upon:** as a result of   219. **practice:** execution   224. **plaintiffs:** blunder for *defendants*   224–25. **reform'd:** for *informed*   225. **specify:** for *testify* (?)   236. **honorable:** of distinguished rank   243. **Impose:** subject

DON PEDRO   By my soul, nor I,
    And yet, to satisfy this good old man,
    I would bend under any heavy weight
    That he'll enjoin me to.
250 LEONATO   I cannot bid you bid my daughter live—
    That were impossible—but I pray you both,
    Possess the people in Messina here
    How innocent she died, and if your love
    Can labor aught in sad invention,
255   Hang her an epitaph upon her tomb,
    And sing it to her bones, sing it to-night.
    To-morrow morning come you to my house,
    And since you could not be my son-in-law,
    Be yet my nephew. My brother hath a daughter,
260   Almost the copy of my child that's dead,
    And she alone is heir to both of us.
    Give her the right you should have giv'n her cousin,
    And so dies my revenge.
CLAUDIO   O noble sir!
265   Your overkindness doth wring tears from me.
    I do embrace your offer, and dispose
    For henceforth of poor Claudio.
LEONATO   To-morrow then I will expect your coming,
    To-night I take my leave. This naughty man
270   Shall face to face be brought to Margaret,
    Who I believe was pack'd in all this wrong,
    Hir'd to it by your brother.
BORACHIO   No, by my soul she was not,
    Nor knew not what she did when she spoke to me,
275   But always hath been just and virtuous
    In any thing that I do know by her.
DOGBERRY   Moreover, sir, which indeed is not under white and black, this
    plaintiff here, the offender, did call me ass. I beseech you let it be remem-
    b'red in his punishment. And also, the watch heard them talk of one De-
280   formed. They say he wears a key in his ear and a lock hanging by it, and bor-
    rows money in God's name, the which he hath us'd so long and never paid
    that now men grow hard-hearted and will lend nothing for God's sake. Pray
    you examine him upon that point.

---

252. **Possess:** inform   261. **heir to both:** Antonio's son (mentioned in I.ii.1–2) has apparently been forgotten.   262. **should:** were to   269. **naughty:** wicked   271. **pack'd:** involved as a conspirator 276. **by:** concerning   277. **under . . . black:** in writing   280. **key . . . it:** Dogberry's transmutation of the *lock* of III.iii.122   281. **in God's name:** like a professional beggar (who commonly used this phrase) **us'd:** made a practice

LEONATO   I thank thee for thy care and honest pains.

285 DOGBERRY   Your worship speaks like a most thankful and reverent youth, and I praise God for you.

LEONATO   There's for thy pains.

DOGBERRY   God save the foundation!

LEONATO   Go, I discharge thee of thy prisoner, and I thank thee.

290 DOGBERRY   I leave an arrant knave with your worship, which I beseech your worship to correct yourself, for the example of others. God keep you worship! I wish your worship well. God restore you to health! I humbly give you leave to depart, and if a merry meeting may be wish'd, God prohibit it! Come, neighbor.

[*Exeunt* DOGBERRY *and* VERGES.]

295 LEONATO   Until to-morrow morning, lords, farewell.

ANTONIO   Farewell, my lords, we look for you to-morrow.

DON PEDRO   We will not fail.

CLAUDIO   To-night I'll mourn with Hero.

LEONATO [*to the* WATCH]   Bring you these fellows on.

300   —We'll talk with Margaret,
           How her acquaintance grew with this lewd fellow.

(*Exeunt* [*severally*].)

[Scene II]

(*Enter* BENEDICK *and* MARGARET, [*meeting*].)

BENEDICK   Pray thee, sweet Mistress Margaret, deserve well at my hands by helping me to the speech of Beatrice.

MARGARET   Will you then write me a sonnet in praise of my beauty?

BENEDICK   In so high a style, Margaret, that no man living shall come over it,

5   for in most comely truth thou deservest it.

MARGARET   To have no man come over me? Why, shall I always keep below stairs?

---

285. **reverent:** Perhaps another blunder, but *reverent* was commonly used in the sense "reverend" (see V.iv.119).   288. **God . . . foundation:** a phrase used by those who received alms from a charitable foundation   290–91. **I . . . yourself:** Dogberry here makes use of locutions which, contrary to his intention, permit the interpretation that he is calling Leonato a knave and urging him to reform. 293. **prohibit:** one last example of Dogberry saying precisely the opposite of what he means 301. **lewd:** low, worthless

V.ii. Location: Leonato's orchard
4. **come over:** (1) exceed; (2) get across (pointing to a quibble on *style / stile* in line 6). Margaret then plays on a third sense, with characteristic ribaldry.   5. **in . . . comely truth:** (1) in good truth; (2) by virtue of your beauty   6. **keep:** dwell, stay   6–7. **below stairs:** in the servants' quarters

BENEDICK   Thy wit is as quick as the greyhound's mouth, it catches.

MARGARET   And yours as blunt as the fencer's foils, which hit, but hurt not.

10 BENEDICK   A most manly wit, Margaret, it will not hurt a woman. And so I pray thee call Beatrice; I give thee the bucklers.

MARGARET   Give us the swords, we have bucklers of our own.

BENEDICK   If you use them, Margaret, you must put in the pikes with a vice, and they are dangerous weapons for maids.

15 MARGARET   Well, I will call Beatrice to you, who I think hath legs.   (*Exit* MARGARET.)

BENEDICK   And therefore will come.   [*sings*]
                                        "The god of love,
                                    That sits above,
20   And knows me, and knows me,
                                        How pitiful I deserve"—

I mean in singing; but in loving, Leander the good swimmer, Troilus the first employer of pandars, and a whole bookful of these quondam carpet-mongers, whose names yet run smoothly in the even road of a blank verse,

25 why, they were never so truly turn'd over and over as my poor self in love. Marry, I cannot show it in rhyme; I have tried. I can find out no rhyme to "lady" but "baby," an innocent rhyme; for "scorn," "horn," a hard rhyme; for "school," "fool," a babbling rhyme: very ominous endings. No, I was not born under a rhyming planet, nor I cannot woo in festival terms.

(*Enter* BEATRICE.)

30   Sweet Beatrice, wouldst thou come when I call'd thee?

BEATRICE   Yea, signior, and depart when you bid me.

BENEDICK   O, stay but till then!

BEATRICE   "Then" is spoken; fare you well now. And yet ere I go, let me go with that I came, which is, with knowing what hath pass'd between you and

35   Claudio.

BENEDICK   Only foul words—and thereupon I will kiss thee.

BEATRICE   Foul words is but foul wind, and foul wind is but foul breath, and foul breath is noisome; therefore I will depart unkiss'd.

---

11. **give . . . bucklers:** give up (*buckler* = a kind of shield)   13. **pikes:** spikes in the centre of a shield   **vice:** screw   18–20. The first lines of a contemporary song   21. **How . . . deserve:** how much I deserve pity (but Benedick twists the meaning to "how pitifully small my deserts are").
22. **Leander:** who swam the Hellespont nightly to see his love Hero   **Troilus:** whose union with Cressida was arranged by her uncle Pandarus   23. **quondam:** of former days   23–24. **carpet-mongers:** Knights who avoided military service were contemptuously called carpet knights. Benedick's use of the term for storied lovers of old implies that they were contemptible performers compared with himself.   27. **innocent:** childish   **hard:** (1) harsh, unpleasant (because associated with the idea of the cuckold's horn); (2) solid   29. **festival terms:** elevated language suitable for a special occasion   34. **that I came:** what I came for   38. **noisome:** ill-smelling

BENEDICK   Thou hast frighted the word out of his right sense, so forcible is thy
40   wit. But I must tell thee plainly, Claudio undergoes my challenge, and either
        I must shortly hear from him, or I will subscribe him a coward. And I pray
        thee now tell me, for which of my bad parts didst thou first fall in love with
        me?

BEATRICE   For them all together, which maintain'd so politic a state of evil that
45   they will not admit any good part to intermingle with them. But for which
        of my good parts did you first suffer love for me?

BENEDICK   Suffer love! a good epithite! I do suffer love indeed, for I love thee
        against my will.

BEATRICE   In spite of your heart, I think. Alas, poor heart, if you spite it for my
50   sake, I will spite it for yours, for I will never love that which my friend hates.

BENEDICK   Thou and I are too wise to woo peaceably.

BEATRICE   It appears not in this confession; there's not one wise man among
        twenty that will praise himself.

BENEDICK   An old, an old instance, Beatrice, that liv'd in the time of good
55   neighbors. If a man do not erect in this age his own tomb ere he dies, he
        shall live no longer in monument than the bell rings and the widow weeps.

BEATRICE   And how long is that, think you?

BENEDICK   Question: why, an hour in clamor and a quarter in rheum; therefore
        is it most expedient for the wise, if Don Worm (his conscience) find no im-
60   pediment to the contrary, to be the trumpet of his own virtues, as I am to
        myself. So much for praising myself, who I myself will bear witness is
        praiseworthy. And now tell me, how doth your cousin?

BEATRICE   Very ill.

BENEDICK   And how do you?

65 BEATRICE   Very ill too.

BENEDICK   Serve God, love me, and mend. There will I leave you too, for here
        comes one in haste.

(*Enter* URSULA.)

URSULA   Madam, you must come to your uncle, yonder's old coil at home. It is
        prov'd my Lady Hero hath been falsely accus'd, the Prince and Claudio
70   mightily abus'd, and Don John is the author of all, who is fled and gone.
        Will you come presently?

---

39. **his right sense:** (1) its senses, its right mind; (2) its correct meaning   40. **undergoes:** is subject
to   41. **subscribe:** formally proclaim   44. **politic:** shrewdly managed   46. **suffer:** (1) experience;
(2) suffer from   47. **epithite:** epithet, expression   52. **It . . . confession:** Your wisdom is not shown
by this declaration that you are wise.   54. **instance:** proverb, maxim (that a wise man does not
praise himself)   54–55. **time . . . neighbors:** good old days when neighbors were willing to speak
well of one another   58. **Question:** that is the question   **clamor:** sound (of the bell)   **rheum:**
tears (of the widow)   59. **Don . . . conscience:** It was a commonplace to describe the conscience as
a gnawing worm.   60. **trumpet:** trumpeter   68. **old coil:** great confusion, much ado
70. **abus'd:** deceived   71. **presently:** immediately

BEATRICE   Will you go hear this news, signior?

BENEDICK   I will live in thy heart, die in thy lap, and be buried in thy eyes, and moreover I will go with thee to thy uncle's.

(*Exeunt.*)

[Scene III]

(*Enter* CLAUDIO, *Prince* [DON PEDRO], *and three or four with tapers.*)

CLAUDIO   Is this the monument of Leonato?

[A] LORD   It is, my lord.

[CLAUDIO, *reading out of a scroll:*]

Epitaph

"Done to death by slanderous tongues
Was the Hero that here lies.
5   Death, in guerdon of her wrongs,
Gives her fame which never dies.
So the life that died with shame
Lives in death with glorious fame."
Hang thou there upon the tomb,

[*hangs up the scroll*]

10   Praising her when I am [dumb].
Now, music, sound, and sing your solemn hymn.

Song

Pardon, goddess of the night,
Those that slew thy virgin knight,
For the which, with songs of woe,
15   Round about her tomb they go.
Midnight, assist our moan,
Help us to sigh and groan,
Heavily, heavily.
Graves, yawn and yield your dead,

---

73. **die:** used with the common sexual implication

V.iii. Location: a churchyard
5. **guerdon:** recompense   12. **goddess . . . night:** See note to IV.i.53.   18. **Heavily:** mournfully
19. **yield your dead:** so that they too may "assist our moan"

20   Till death be uttered,
                          Heavily, heavily.

[CLAUDIO]   Now, unto thy bones good night!
                    Yearly will I do this rite.
     DON PEDRO   Good morrow, masters, put your torches out.
25   The wolves have preyed, and look, the gentle day,
         Before the wheels of Phoebus, round about
         Dapples the drowsy east with spots of grey.
         Thanks to you all, and leave us. Fare you well.
     CLAUDIO   Good morrow, masters—each his several way.
30   DON PEDRO   Come let us hence, and put on other weeds,
         And then to Leonato's we will go.
     CLAUDIO   And Hymen now with luckier issue speed's
         Than this for whom we rend'red up this woe.

(*Exeunt.*)

[Scene IV]

(*Enter* LEONATO, BENEDICK, [BEATRICE,] MARGARET, URSULA, *old man*
[ANTONIO], FRIAR [FRANCIS], HERO.)

FRIAR FRANCIS   Did I not tell you she was innocent?
LEONATO   So are the Prince and Claudio, who accus'd her
         Upon the error that you heard debated.
         But Margaret was in some fault for this,
5   Although against her will, as it appears
         In the true course of all the question.
     ANTONIO   Well, I am glad that all things sorts so well.
     BENEDICK   And so am I, being else by faith enforc'd
         To call young Claudio to a reckoning for it.
10   LEONATO   Well, daughter, and you gentlewoman all,
         Withdraw into a chamber by yourselves,
         And when I send for you, come hither masked.
         The Prince and Claudio promis'd by this hour
         To visit me. You know your office, brother:

---

20. **uttered:** fully expressed, adequately lamented   25. **have preyed:** have finished their night's
preying   26. **Before . . . Phoebus:** preceding the chariot of the sun   30. **weeds:** clothes
32. **Hymen:** the god of marriage   **with . . . speed 's:** favor us with better fortune

V.iv. Location: Leonato's house
3. **Upon:** because of   **debated:** publicly discussed   5. **against her will:** unintentionally
6. **question:** judicial examination   7. **sorts:** turn out   8. **faith:** his pledge to Beatrice   14. **office:**
function, role

15   You must be father to your brother's daughter,
       And give her to young Claudio.

(Exeunt LADIES.)

ANTONIO   Which I will do with confirm'd countenance.
BENEDICK   Friar, I must entreat your pains, I think.
FRIAR FRANCIS   To do what, signior?
20 BENEDICK   To bind me, or undo me—one of them.
       Signior Leonato, truth it is, good signior,
       Your niece regards me with an eye of favor.
LEONATO   That eye my daughter lent her, 'tis most true.
BENEDICK   And I do with an eye of love requite her.
25 LEONATO   The sight whereof I think you had from me,
       From Claudio, and the Prince. But what's your will?
BENEDICK   Your answer, sir, is enigmatical,
       But for my will, my will is your good will
       May stand with ours, this day to be conjoin'd
30   In the state of honorable marriage,
       In which, good friar, I shall desire your help.
LEONATO   My heart is with your liking.
FRIAR FRANCIS   And my help.
       Here comes the Prince and Claudio.

(Enter Prince [DON PEDRO] *and* CLAUDIO *and two or three others.*)

35 DON PEDRO   Good morrow to this fair assembly.
LEONATO   Good morrow, Prince; good morrow, Claudio;
       We here attend you. Are you yet determined
       To-day to marry with my brother's daughter?
CLAUDIO   I'll hold my mind were she an Ethiope.
40 LEONATO   Call her forth, brother, here's the friar ready.   [*Exit* ANTONIO.]
DON PEDRO   Good morrow, Benedick. Why, what's the matter,
       That you have such a February face,
       So full of frost, of storm, and cloudiness?
CLAUDIO   I think he thinks upon the savage bull.
45   Tush, fear not, man, we'll tip thy horns with gold,
       And all Europa shall rejoice at thee,
       As once Europa did at lusty Jove,
       When he would play the noble beast in love.

---

17. **confirm'd:** steadfast, serious   **countenance:** demeanor   20. **undo:** (1) ruin; (2) unbind
37. **yet:** still   44. **savage bull:** another reference to Benedick's complacent statement at I.i.187–191
46. **Europa:** Europe   47. **Europa:** a Phoenician princess whom Jove, in the form of a white bull,
carried off from her native land

BENEDICK   Bull Jove, sir, had an amiable low,

50   And some such strange bull leapt your father's cow,
        And got a calf in that same noble feat
        Much like to you, for you have just his bleat.

        (*Enter Brother* [ANTONIO], HERO, BEATRICE, MARGARET, URSULA, [*the ladies
        masked*].)

CLAUDIO   For this I owe you: here comes other reck'nings.
        Which is the lady I must seize upon?

55 [ANTONIO]   This same is she, and I do give you her.
CLAUDIO   Why then she's mine. Sweet, let me see your face.
LEONATO   No, that you shall not till you take her hand,
        Before this friar, and swear to marry her.
CLAUDIO   Give me your hand before this holy friar—

60   I am your husband if you like of me.
HERO [*unmasking*]   And when I liv'd, I was your other wife,
        And when you lov'd, you were my other husband.
CLAUDIO   Another Hero!
HERO   Nothing certainer:

65   One Hero died defil'd, but I do live,
        And surely as I live, I am a maid.
DON PEDRO   The former Hero! Hero that is dead!
LEONATO   She died, my lord, but whiles her slander liv'd.
FRIAR FRANCIS   All this amazement can I qualify,

70   When after that the holy rites are ended,
        I'll tell you largely of fair Hero's death.
        Mean time let wonder seem familiar,
        And to the chapel let us presently.
BENEDICK   Soft and fair, friar. Which is Beatrice?

75 BEATRICE [*unmasking*]   I answer to that name. What is your will?
BENEDICK   Do not you love me?
BEATRICE   Why, no, no more than reason.
BENEDICK   Why then your uncle and the Prince and Claudio
        Have been deceived. They swore you did.

80 BEATRICE   Do not you love me?
BENEDICK   Troth, no, no more than reason.
BEATRICE   Why then my cousin, Margaret, and Ursula
        Are much deceiv'd, for they did swear you did.

---

49. **amiable low:** winning voice   53. **owe you:** will repay you later   **other reck'nings:** other
accounts (that I must settle first)   60. **like of:** like, are willing to take   65. **defil'd:** disgraced, slan-
dered   69. **qualify:** moderate   71. **largely:** fully, in detail   72. **let . . . familiar:** accept these amazing events as natural

BENEDICK   They swore that you were almost sick for me.

85 BEATRICE   They swore that you were well-nigh dead for me.

BENEDICK   'Tis no such matter. Then you do not love me?

BEATRICE   No, truly, but in friendly recompense.

LEONATO   Come, cousin, I am sure you love the gentleman.

CLAUDIO   And I'll be sworn upon't that he loves her,

90   For here's a paper written in his hand,
      A halting sonnet of his own pure brain,
      Fashion'd to Beatrice.

HERO   And here's another
      Writ in my cousin's hand, stol'n from her pocket,

95   Containing her affection unto Benedick.

BENEDICK   A miracle! here's our own hands against our hearts. Come, I will
      have thee, but by this light, I take thee for pity.

BEATRICE   I would not deny you, but by this good day, I yield upon great per-
      suasion, and partly to save your life, for I was told you were in a consump-

100   tion.

[BENEDICK]   Peace, I will stop your mouth.   [*kissing her*]

DON PEDRO   How dost thou, Benedick the married man?

BENEDICK   I'll tell thee what, Prince: a college of wit-crackers cannot flout me
      out of my humor. Dost thou think I care for a satire or an epigram? No, if a

105   man will be beaten with brains, 'a shall wear nothing handsome about him.
      In brief, since I do purpose to marry, I will think nothing to any purpose
      that the world can say against it, and therefore never flout at me for what I
      have said against it; for man is a giddy thing, and this is my conclusion. For
      thy part, Claudio, I did think to have beaten thee, but in that thou art like to

110   be my kinsman, live unbruis'd, and love my cousin.

CLAUDIO   I had well hop'd thou wouldst have denied Beatrice, that I might have
      cudgell'd thee out of thy single life, to make thee a double-dealer, which out
      of question thou wilt be, if my cousin do not look exceeding narrowly to
      thee.

115 BENEDICK   Come, come, we are friends. Let's have a dance ere we are married,
      that we may lighten our own hearts and our wives' heels.

LEONATO   We'll have dancing afterward.

---

96. **our . . . hearts:** our own written testimony to prove our hearts guilty as charged
102. **How . . man:** Cf. I.i.190–191   103. **college:** company, assemblage   **wit-crackers:** jokesters (cf.
crack a joke)   104–105. **if . . . him:** If a man is going to allow himself to be beaten up by wit, he will
never dare wear good clothes; i.e., if a man allows ridicule to dictate his actions, he will deprive
himself of many desirable things.   108. **giddy:** fickle, changeable   **my conclusion:** the position I
have finally come to   112. **double-dealer:** (1) married man (cf. *single man*); (2) unfaithful
husband   112–13. **out of question:** without doubt   113. **narrowly:** closely

BENEDICK   First, of my word; therefore play, music. Prince, thou art sad, get
    thee a wife, get thee a wife. There is no staff more reverent than one tipp'd
120   with horn.

(*Enter* MESSENGER.)

MESSENGER   My lord, your brother John is ta'en in flight,
    And brought with armed men back to Messina.
BENEDICK   Think not on him till to-morrow. I'll devise thee brave punish-
    ments for him. Strike up, pipers.

(*Dance.* [*Exeunt.*])

c. 1598

STUDY QUESTIONS

1. One of the prevailing verbal motifs in the play is that of the mask. How do
   the masks and mistaken identities contribute to the themes of *Much Ado
   About Nothing?*
2. What are the two essential complications of the play? Is one more believable
   than the other?
3. Discuss the role of Friar Francis, who comes up with the idea of pretending
   Hero has died after she faints upon being humiliated by Claudio at their
   aborted wedding ceremony. Is the Friar's counsel wise, or does it seem con-
   trived so that Shakespeare can have his climactic "recognition" scene between Hero and Claudio in Act V?
4. Do you sense any problems in tone early in Act 5 between the play's poten-
   tially tragic and comic elements?
5. How does Benedick's final speech, in which he concludes that "man is a
   giddy thing," serve to reconcile the play's darker elements with its essentially
   comic vision?

---

118. **of:** on   119. **reverent:** reverend, honorable   120. **horn:** The cuckold joke once more
123. **brave:** capital, fine

29

REALISM

The late nineteenth and early twentieth centuries mark another period of notable theatrical growth and development throughout Europe—the age of **realism**. Realism was an international style, popular from Norway and Russia through England, Ireland, and America.

Realism was, of course, a literary style; but it was a style of production as well. Look, for instance, at the opening of *A Doll's House*. Not only does Henrik Ibsen carefully list the placement of the four doors and the furniture used in the action; he even details the "copperplate etchings on the walls" and the "deluxe editions" that are to fill the "small bookcase."

Note, too, that Ibsen speaks of the "rear wall," "left wall," and "right wall" of the room. To most of us, this seems quite natural. Of course a room has four walls. Of course three of them are shown onstage and the fourth is imagined to be at the front of the stage. Of course characters enter and exit through doors in these walls; how else does one enter or leave a room? In fact, however, this form of stage setting, known as the "box set," was a new form of stage setting. The box set was far more realistic than the older "wings"; but it was more cumbersome as well, requiring long intermissions between acts to allow for scene changes. Thus it may have helped to promote the popularity not only of realistic drama but also of the one-act play, which is often set in one scene and thus requires no change of scenery.

Realism in production, then, meant sets and costumes as like those of everyday life as possible. In playwriting, it meant plots, characters, and language drawn from everyday life, as well. (Comedy, as usual, retained the right of exaggeration in all these areas.)

In addition, realism implied a new approach to drama. The realistic play hoped to make two impacts on its audience. First, of course, it sought to make the audience sympathize with the plight of its characters. But it also strove to raise in the minds of its audience questions as to the rightness of some aspect of social order, and the desire to change what the dramatist perceived as evil or wrong; it sought to make a **social comment**.

From these goals came a new form of play known as the **realistic drama**: a serious play, usually on a domestic or semidomestic theme, featuring middle-class (or sometimes lower-class) characters, a contemporary setting, and a plot that questions some aspect or dictate of society.

Take, for example, *A Doll's House* by Henrik Ibsen, a Norwegian playwright who was one of the earliest and most admired of the realists. We see in *A Doll's*

House, one of Ibsen's most popular plays, the mixture of elements described above. The scene is unrelievedly domestic. Money and marriage (normally the concerns of comedy) are both major concerns in this play. Yet the movement within the play is more like that of tragedy, being, in general, "from happiness to unhappiness." Comedy usually ends in the making of a marriage. *A Doll's House* details the breakup of one. In line with the domesticity of the scene, we notice a new concern with detail: the clothes Nora wears, the ornaments she puts on her Christmas tree, the macaroons she eats or does not eat, all reflect her struggle for self-identity. We see, too, her concern with upbringing: what effect has Nora's father had on her? What effect is she having on her own children? Finally, we observe how the domestic nature of the realistic drama heightens the disparity between what the play's main characters perceive and feel and what is perceived of them by those around them. The onlookers in *Oedipus Rex* and *Antigonê* recognize the magnitude of the struggles they are watching. The onlookers in *A Doll's House* see only a peaceful, prosperous, well-ordered household.

Today, *A Doll's House* is most frequently read as a complaint against the undervaluation and suppression of women. But strong arguments can be made for the theory that Ibsen is showing men and women as equal victims of society's insistence on "respectability." Notice, as you read this play, how the characters are grouped in this regard, how each sins and is sinned against. Consider, too, the ending, which is of a type impossible for both tragedy and comedy. What effect does it have on your response to the play?

Realism and Comedy

Comedy was a favorite form in the nineteenth century, both before and during the age of realism, if only because nineteenth-century theater and comedy are both strongly oriented toward middle-class characters and dilemmas. Nineteenth-century drama, following the theory that people are creatures of their society, saw its role as portraying and commenting on that society. Comedy, too, sees people in their roles as social beings, and has, since the ancient Greeks, been willing to comment on individuals and society alike.

Sometimes, comedy sets the folly of an individual against the good sense of society at large. At other times, a rebellious hero or heroine fights on the side of love and nature, against the follies of society. In either case, society is usually the victor. No matter how hard comic characters may struggle to escape the bonds of society—no matter what unusual methods they may use to outwit other characters or to solve some particular conflict between society's dictates and their own desires—at the play's end they return to the very society they've been fighting. The conflict has been solved, the goal or the marriage won; and society promises to go on exactly as it did before.

As we observed in *Much Ado About Nothing,* William Shakespeare employs the comedy of setting an individual against the good sense of society by having Benedick proclaim himself a lifelong bachelor early in the play. There can be little doubt that in the world of comedy he will soon have to eat his words: in fact, much of our enjoyment comes from our anticipation of seeing this comic formula proceed to its inevitable conclusion, in which Benedick laughs at himself for having been wrong about love and happily marries Beatrice despite the teasing he gets from his friends.

All comedy is in a sense "realistic," because it deals with ordinary human folly, but there are degrees of comic realism. In *Much Ado,* Hero and Claudio are unrealistic stereotypes out of the Petrarchan tradition; Beatrice and Benedick, however, in their more complex and more believable characterization, look forward to the realistic comedy typical of modern drama.

Realism and Tragedy

Tragedy did not fare well during the nineteenth century, for several reasons. First, tragedy took kings and princes for its heroes, not members of the middle class. Second, it tended to insist that these kings and princes speak poetry, a speech form not well suited to discussion of everyday matters. Third, tragedy traditionally portrayed its heroes as people who have power over their societies: Oedipus, Hamlet, and Claudius are directly responsible for the physical and moral health of Thebes and of Denmark. And this characteristic of tragedy did not fit well with the trend of nineteenth-century drama to depict people as beings shaped by the society in which they had been born and reared. The thrust toward realism was thus antithetical to the grand tragedies of the classic and Renaissance styles; and attempts by nineteenth-century playwrights to reproduce some of that grandeur were generally failures.

Once realism was firmly established, however, the twentieth century could try variations on its theme; and some of these variations recreated tragedy as a newly effective form. Some of these new tragedies were written in poetry, but most were in prose—though in some few cases the prose is so artfully handled that it almost becomes poetry.

A Doll's House   HENRIK IBSEN (1828–1906)

A translation by Otto Reinert

Henrik Ibsen grew up in a small town in Norway. He was poor and went to work early as an apprentice to a pharmacist. When a series of revolutions swept Europe in 1848—revolutions during which Karl Marx wrote *The Communist Manifesto* (1848)—Ibsen responded to these events with great passion and hope for political change. The revolutions failed, however, and were followed by even more repression of working people by their governments. Ibsen was frustrated by the hypocrisy and triviality of both politics and small-town life in Norway, and he began to write about them. Having some early successes with plays, he was able to travel to Denmark and Germany to learn his craft.

In the 1850s, he perfected the so-called well-made play then in vogue in France: tightly plotted, suspenseful dramas that closely held the attention of the audience. In 1863, he wrote *The Pretenders*, an overtly political play calling for Scandinavian unity against imperialist Prussia. One of his masterpieces was *Peter Gynt* (1867), the story of a Faustlike Norwegian protagonist who shows the gap between human aspiration and accomplishment. The play looks forward to the expressionist style of August Strindburg. The final phase of Ibsen's work is in the mode of social realism: *A Doll's House* (1879), *Ghosts* (1881), and *An Enemy of the People* (1882) are the high points of this realist phase. Important late plays are *The Wild Duck* (1884) and *Hedda Gabler* (1890). Because of the technical innovations in his plays, their haunting poetic qualities, and their psychologically astute study of character, Ibsen is universally recognized as the founder of modern drama.

CHARACTERS

TORVALD HELMER, *a lawyer*
NORA, *his wife*
DR. RANK
MRS. LINDE
KROGSTAD
THE HELMERS' THREE SMALL CHILDREN
ANNE-MARIE, *the children's nurse*
A HOUSEMAID
A PORTER

SCENE. *The Helmers' living room.*

Act I

A pleasant, tastefully but not expensively furnished, living room. A door on the rear wall, right, leads to the front hall, another door, left, to HELMER's *study. Between the two doors a piano. A third door in the middle of the left wall; further front a window. Near the window a round table and a small couch. Towards the rear of the right wall a fourth door; further front a tile stove with a rocking chair and a couple of armchairs in front of it. Between the stove and the door a small table. Copperplate etchings on the walls. A whatnot with porcelain figurines and other small objects. A small bookcase with de luxe editions. A rug on the floor; fire in the stove. Winter day.*

The doorbell rings, then the sound of the front door opening. NORA, *dressed for outdoors, enters, humming cheerfully. She carries several packages, which she puts down on the table, right. She leaves the door to the front hall open; there a* PORTER *is seen holding a Christmas tree and a basket. He gives them to the* MAID *who has let them in.*

NORA   Be sure to hide the Christmas tree, Helene. The children mustn't see it before tonight when we've trimmed it. (*opens her purse; to the* PORTER:) How much?

PORTER   Fifty ore.

NORA   Here's a crown. No, keep the change. (*The* PORTER *thanks her, leaves.* NORA *closes the door. She keeps laughing quietly to herself as she takes off her coat, etc. She takes a bag of macaroons from her pocket and eats a couple. She walks cautiously over to the door to the study and listens.*) Yes, he's home. (*resumes her humming, walks over to the table, right*)

HELMER (*in his study*)   Is that my little lark twittering out there?

NORA (*opening some packages*)   That's right.

HELMER   My squirrel bustling about?

NORA   Yes.

HELMER   When did squirrel come home?

NORA   Just now. (*puts the bag of macaroons back in her pocket, wipes her mouth*) Come out here, Torvald. I want to show you what I've bought.

HELMER   I'm busy! (*After a little while he opens the door and looks in, pen in hand.*) Bought, eh? All that? So little wastrel has been throwing money around again?

NORA   Oh but Torvald, this Christmas we can be a little extravagant, can't we? It's the first Christmas we don't have to scrimp.

HELMER   I don't know about that. We certainly don't have money to waste.

NORA   Yes, Torvald, we do. A little, anyway. Just a tiny little bit? Now that you're going to get that big salary and make lots and lots of money.

HELMER   Starting at New Year's, yes. But payday isn't till the end of the quarter.

NORA   That doesn't matter. We can always borrow.

HELMER   Nora! (*goes over to her and playfully pulls her ear*) There you go being irresponsible again. Suppose I borrowed a thousand crowns today and you spent it all for Christmas and on New Year's Eve a tile hit me in the head and laid me out cold.

NORA (*putting her hand over his mouth*)   I won't have you say such horrid things.

HELMER   But suppose it happened. Then what?

NORA   If it did, I wouldn't care whether we owed money or not.

HELMER   But what about the people I borrowed from?

NORA   Who cares about them! They are strangers.

HELMER   Nora, Nora, you *are* a woman! No, really! You know how I feel about that. No debts! A home in debt isn't a free home, and if it isn't free it isn't beautiful. We've managed nicely so far, you and I, and that's the way we'll go on. It won't be for much longer.

NORA (*walks over toward the stove*)   All right, Torvald. Whatever you say.

HELMER (*follows her*)   Come, come, my little songbird mustn't droop her wings. What's this? Can't have a pouty squirrel in the house, you know. (*takes out his wallet*) Nora, what do you think I have here?

NORA (*turns around quickly*)   Money!

HELMER   Here. (*gives her some bills*) Don't you think I know Christmas is expensive?

NORA (*counting*)   Ten—twenty—thirty—forty. Thank you, thank you, Torvald. This helps a lot.

HELMER   I certainly hope so.

NORA   It does, it does. But I want to show you what I got. It was cheap, too. Look. New clothes for Ivar. And a sword. And a horse and trumpet for Bob. And a doll and a little bed for Emmy. It isn't any good, but it wouldn't last, anyway. And here's some dress material and scarves for the maids. I feel bad about old Anne-Marie, though. She really should be getting much more.

HELMER   And what's in here?

NORA (*cries*)   Not till tonight!

HELMER   I see. But now what does my little prodigal have in mind for herself?

NORA   Oh, nothing. I really don't care.

HELMER   Of course you do. Tell me what you'd like. Within reason.

NORA   Oh, I don't know. Really, I don't. The only thing—

HELMER   Well?

NORA (*fiddling with his buttons, without looking at him*)   If you really want to give me something, you might—you could—

HELMER   All right, let's have it.

NORA (*quickly*)   Some money, Torvald. Just as much as you think you can spare. Then I'll buy myself something one of these days.

HELMER   No, really Nora—

NORA   Oh yes, please, Torvald. Please? I'll wrap the money in pretty gold paper and hang it on the tree. Won't that be nice?

HELMER   What's the name for little birds that are always spending money?

NORA   Wastrels, I know. But please let's do it my way, Torvald. Then I'll have time to decide what I need most. Now that's sensible, isn't it?

HELMER (*smiling*)   Oh, very sensible. That is, if you really bought yourself something you could use. But it all disappears in the household expenses or you buy things you don't need. And then you come back to me for more.

NORA   Oh, but Torvald—

HELMER   That's the truth, dear little Nora, and you know it. (*puts his arm around her*) My wastrel is a little sweetheart, but she *does* go through an awful lot of money awfully fast. You've no idea how expensive it is for a man to keep a wastrel.

NORA   That's not fair, Torvald. I really save all I can.

HELMER (*laughs*)   Oh, I believe that. All you can. Meaning, exactly nothing!

NORA (*hums, smiles mysteriously*)   You don't know all the things we songbirds and squirrels need money for, Torvald.

HELMER   You know, you're funny. Just like your father. You're always looking for ways to get money, but as soon as you do it runs through your fingers and you can never say what you spent it for. Well, I guess I'll just have to take you the way you are. It's in your blood. Yes, that sort of thing is hereditary, Nora.

NORA   In that case, I wish I had inherited many of Daddy's qualities.

HELMER   And I don't want you any different from just what you are—my own sweet little songbird. Hey!—I think I just noticed something. Aren't you looking—what's the word?—a little—sly—?

NORA   I am?

HELMER   You definitely are. Look at me.

NORA (*looks at him*)   Well?

HELMER (*wagging a finger*)   Little sweet-tooth hasn't by any chance been on a rampage today, has she?

NORA   Of course not. Whatever makes you think that?

HELMER   A little detour by the pastryshop maybe?

NORA   No, I assure you, Torvald—

HELMER   Nibbled a little jam?

NORA   Certainly not!

HELMER   Munched a macaroon or two?

NORA   No, really, Torvald, I honestly—

HELMER   All right. Of course I was only joking.

NORA (*walks toward the table, right*)   You know I wouldn't do anything to displease you.

HELMER   I know. And I have your promise. (*over to her*) All right, keep your little Christmas secrets to yourself, Nora darling. They'll all come out tonight, I suppose, when we light the tree.

NORA   Did you remember to invite Rank?

HELMER   No, but there's no need to. He knows he'll have dinner with us. Anyway, I'll see him later this morning. I'll ask him then. I did order some good wine. Oh Nora, you've no idea how much I'm looking forward to tonight!

NORA   Me, too. And the children Torvald! They'll have such a good time!

HELMER   You know, it *is* nice to have a good, safe job and a comfortable income. Feels good just thinking about it. Don't you agree?

NORA   Oh, it's wonderful!

HELMER   Remember last Christmas? For three whole weeks you shut yourself up every evening till long after midnight making ornaments for the Christmas tree and I don't know what else. Some big surprise for all of us, anyway. I'll be damned if I've ever been so bored in my whole life!

NORA   I wasn't bored at all!

HELMER (*smiling*)   But you've got to admit you didn't have much to show for it in the end.

NORA   Oh, don't tease me again about that! Could I help it that the cat got in and tore up everything?

HELMER   Of course you couldn't, my poor little Nora. You just wanted to please the rest of us, and that's the important thing. But I *am* glad the hard times are behind us. Aren't you?

NORA   Oh yes. I think it's just wonderful.

HELMER   This year, I won't be bored and lonely. And you won't have to strain your dear eyes and your delicate little hands—

NORA (*claps her hands*)   No I won't, will I Torvald? Oh, how wonderful, how lovely, to hear you say that! (*puts her arm under his*) Let me tell you how I think we should arrange things, Torvald. Soon as Christmas is over—(*The doorbell rings.*) Someone's at the door. (*straightens things up a bit*) A caller, I suppose. Bother!

HELMER   Remember, I'm not home for visitors.

THE MAID (*in the door to the front hall*)   Ma'am, there's a lady here—

NORA   All right. Ask her to come in.

THE MAID (*to* HELMER)   And the Doctor just arrived.

HELMER   Is he in the study?

THE MAID   Yes, sir.

(HELMER *exits into his study.* THE MAID *shows* MRS. LINDE *in and closes the door behind her as she leaves.* MRS. LINDE *is in travel dress.*)

MRS. LINDE (*timid and a little hesitant*)   Good morning, Nora.

NORA (*uncertainly*)   Good morning.

MRS. LINDE   I don't believe you know who I am.

NORA   No—I'm not sure—Though I know I should—Of course! Kristine! It's you!

MRS. LINDE   Yes, it's me.

NORA   And I didn't even recognize you! I had no idea. (*in a lower voice*) You've changed, Kristine.

MRS. LINDE   I'm sure I have. It's been nine or ten long years.

NORA   Has it really been that long? Yes, you're right. I've been so happy these last eight years. And now you're here. Such a long trip in the middle of winter. How brave!

MRS. LINDE   I got in on the steamer this morning.

NORA   To have some fun over the holidays, of course. That's lovely. For we are going to have fun. But take off your coat! You aren't cold, are you? (*helps her*) There, now! Let's sit down here by the fire and just relax and talk. No, you sit there. I want the rocking chair. (*takes her hands*) And now you've got your old face back. It was just for a minute, right at first—Though you are a little more pale, Kristine. And maybe a little thinner.

MRS. LINDE   And much, much older, Nora.

NORA   Maybe a little older. Just a teeny-weeny bit, not much. (*interrupts herself, serious*) Oh, but how thoughtless of me, chatting away like this! Sweet, good Kristine, can you forgive me?

MRS. LINDE   Forgive you what, Nora?

NORA (*in a low voice*)   You poor dear, you lost your husband, didn't you?

MRS. LINDE   Three years ago, yes.

NORA   I know. I saw it in the paper. Oh please believe me, Kristine. I really meant to write you, but I never got around to it. Something was always coming up.

MRS. LINDE   Of course, Nora. I understand.

NORA   No, that wasn't very nice of me. You poor thing, all you must have been through. And he didn't leave you much, either, did he?

MRS. LINDE   No.

NORA   And no children?

MRS. LINDE   No.

NORA   Nothing at all, in other words?

MRS. LINDE   Not so much as a sense of loss—a grief to live on—

NORA (*incredulous*)   But Kristine, how can that *be?*

MRS. LINDE (*with a sad smile, strokes* NORA's *hair*)   That's the way it sometimes is, Nora.

NORA   All alone. How awful for you. I have three darling children. You can't see them right now, though; they're out with their nurse. But now you must tell me everything—

MRS. LINDE   No, no; I'd rather listen to you.

NORA   No, you begin. Today I won't be selfish. Today I'll think only of you. Except there's one thing I've just got to tell you first. Something marvelous that's happened to us just these last few days. You haven't heard, have you?

MRS. LINDE   No; tell me.

NORA   Just think. My husband's been made manager of the Mutual Bank.

MRS. LINDE   Your husband—! Oh, I'm so glad!

NORA   Yes, isn't that great? You see, private law practice is so uncertain, especially when you won't have anything to do with cases that aren't—you know—quite nice. And of course Torvald won't do that and I quite agree with him. Oh, you've no idea how delighted we are! He takes over at New Year's, and he'll be getting a big salary and all sorts of extras. From now on we'll be able to live in quite a different way—exactly as we like. Oh, Kristine! I feel so carefree and happy! It's lovely to have lots and lots of money and not have to worry about a thing! Don't you agree?

MRS. LINDE   It would be nice to have enough at any rate.

NORA   No, I don't mean just enough. I mean lots and lots!

MRS. LINDE (*smiles*)   Nora, Nora, when are you going to be sensible? In school you spent a great deal of money.

NORA (*quietly laughing*)   Yes, and Torvald says I still do. (*raises her finger at* MRS. LINDE) But "Nora, Nora" isn't so crazy as you all think. Believe me, we've had nothing to be extravagant with. We've both had to work.

MRS. LINDE   You too?

NORA   Yes. Oh, it's been little things, mostly—sewing, crocheting, embroidery— that sort of thing. (*casually*) And other things too. You know, of course, that Torvald left government service when we got married? There was no chance of promotion in his department, and of course he had to make more money than he had been making. So for the first few years he worked altogether too hard. He had to take jobs on the side and work night and day. It turned out to be too much for him. He became seriously ill. The doctors told him he needed to go south.

MRS. LINDE   That's right; you spent a year in Italy, didn't you?

NORA   Yes, we did. But you won't believe how hard it was to get away. Ivar had just been born. But of course we had to go. Oh, it was a wonderful trip. And it saved Torvald's life. But it took a lot of money, Kristine.

MRS. LINDE   I'm sure it did.

NORA   Twelve hundred specie dollars. Four thousand eight hundred crowns. That's a lot of money.

MRS. LINDE   Yes. So it's lucky you have it when something like that happens.

NORA   Well, actually we got the money from Daddy.

MRS. LINDE   I see. That was about the time your father died, I believe.

NORA   Yes, just about then. And I couldn't even go and take care of him. I was expecting little Ivar any day. And I had poor Torvald to look after, desperately sick and all. My dear, good Daddy! I never saw him again, Kristine. That's the saddest thing that's happened to me since I got married.

MRS. LINDE   I know you were very fond of him. But then you went to Italy?

NORA   Yes, for now we had the money, and the doctors urged us to go. So we left about a month later.

MRS. LINDE   And when you came back your husband was well again?

NORA   Healthy as a horse!

MRS. LINDE   But—the doctor?

NORA   What do you mean?

MRS. LINDE   I thought the maid said it was the doctor, that gentleman who came the same time I did.

NORA   Oh, that's Dr. Rank. He doesn't come as a doctor. He's our closest friend. He looks in at least once every day. No, Torvald hasn't been sick once since then. And the children are strong and healthy, too, and so am I. (*jumps up and claps her hands*) Oh God, Kristine! Isn't it wonderful to be alive and happy! Isn't it just lovely!—But now I'm being mean again, talking only about myself and my things. (*sits down on a footstool close to* MRS. LINDE *and puts her arm on her lap*) Please don't be angry with me! Tell me, is it really true that you didn't care for your husband? Then why did you marry him?

MRS. LINDE   Mother was still alive then, but she was bedridden and helpless. And I had my two younger brothers to look after. I didn't think I had the right to turn him down.

NORA   No, I suppose not. So he had money then?

MRS. LINDE   He was quite well off, I think. But it was an uncertain business, Nora. When he died, the whole thing collapsed and there was nothing left.

NORA   And then—?

MRS. LINDE   Well, I had to manage as best I could. With a little store and a little school and anything else I could think of. The last three years have been one long work day for me, Nora, without any rest. But now it's over. My poor mother doesn't need me any more. She's passed away. And the boys are on their own too. They've both got jobs and support themselves.

NORA   What a relief for you—

MRS. LINDE   No, not relief. Just a great emptiness. Nobody to live for any more. (*gets up restlessly*) That's why I couldn't stand it any longer in that little hole. Here in town it has to be easier to find something to keep me busy and occupy my thoughts. With a little luck I should be able to find a permanent job, something in an office—

NORA   Oh but Kristine, that's exhausting work, and you look worn out already. It would be much better for you to go to a resort.

MRS. LINDE (*walks over to the window*)   I don't have a Daddy who can give me the money, Nora.

NORA (*getting up*)   Oh, don't be angry with me.

MRS. LINDE (*over to her*)   Dear Nora, don't *you* be angry with *me*. That's the worst thing about my kind of situation: you become so bitter. You've nobody to work for, and yet you have to look out for yourself, somehow. You've got to keep on living, and so you become selfish. Do you know— when you told me about your husband's new position I was delighted not so much for your sake as for my own.

NORA   Why was that? Oh, I see. You think maybe Torvald can give you a job?

MRS. LINDE   That's what I had in mind.

NORA   And he will too, Kristine. Just leave it to me. I'll be ever so subtle about it. I'll think of something nice to tell him, something he'll like. Oh I so much want to help you.

MRS. LINDE   That's very good of you, Nora—making an effort like that for me. Especially since you've known so little trouble and hardship in your own life.

NORA   I—?—have known so little—?

MRS. LINDE (*smiling*)   Oh well, a little sewing or whatever it was. You're still a child, Nora.

NORA (*with a toss of her head, walks away*)   You shouldn't sound so superior.

MRS. LINDE   I shouldn't?

NORA   You're just like all the others. None of you think I'm good for anything really serious.

MRS. LINDE   Well, now—

NORA   That I've never been through anything difficult.

MRS. LINDE   But Nora! You just told me all your troubles!

NORA   That's nothing! (*lowers her voice*) I haven't told you about *it*.

MRS. LINDE   It? What's that? What do you mean?

NORA   You patronize me, Kristine, and that's not fair. You're proud that you worked so long and so hard for your mother.

MRS. LINDE   I don't think I patronize anyone. But it *is* true that I'm both proud and happy that I could make mother's last years comparatively easy.

NORA   And you're proud of all you did for your brothers.

MRS. LINDE   I think I have the right to be.

NORA   And so do I. But now I want to tell you something, Kristine. I have something to be proud and happy about too.

MRS. LINDE   I don't doubt that for a moment. But what exactly do you mean?

NORA   Not so loud! Torvald mustn't hear—not for anything in the world. Nobody must know about this, Kristine. Nobody but you.

MRS. LINDE   But what is it?

NORA   Come here. (*pulls her down on the couch beside her*) You see, I *do* have something to be proud and happy about. I've saved Torvald's life.

MRS. LINDE   Saved—? how do you mean—"saved"?

NORA   I told you about our trip to Italy. Torvald would have died if he hadn't gone.

MRS. LINDE   I understand that. And so your father gave you the money you needed.

NORA (*smiles*)   Yes, that's what Torvald and all the others think. But—

MRS. LINDE   But what?

NORA   Daddy didn't give us a penny. *I* raised that money.

MRS. LINDE   *You* did? That whole big amount?

NORA   Twelve hundred specie dollars. Four thousand eight hundred crowns. *Now* what do you say?

MRS. LINDE   But Nora, how could you? Did you win in the state lottery?

NORA (*contemptuously*)   State lottery! (*snorts*) What is so great about that?

MRS. LINDE   Where did it come from then?

NORA (*humming and smiling, enjoying her secret*)   Hmmm. Tra-la-la-la-la!

MRS. LINDE   You certainly couldn't have borrowed it.

NORA   Oh? And why not?

MRS. LINDE   A wife can't borrow money without her husband's consent.

NORA (*with a toss of her head*)   Oh, I don't know—take a wife with a little bit of a head for business—a wife who knows how to manage things—

MRS. LINDE   But Nora, I don't understand at all—

NORA   You don't have to. I didn't say I borrowed the money, did I? I could have gotten it some other way. (*leans back*) An admirer may have given it to me. When you're as tolerably good-looking as I am—

MRS. LINDE   Oh, you're crazy.

NORA   I think you're dying from curiosity, Kristine.

MRS. LINDE   I'm beginning to think you've done something very foolish, Nora.

NORA (*sits up*)   Is it foolish to save your husband's life?

MRS. LINDE   I say it's foolish to act behind his back.

NORA   But don't you see: he couldn't be told! You're missing the whole point, Kristine. We couldn't even let him know how seriously ill he was. The doctors came to *me* and told me his life was in danger, that nothing could save him but a stay in the south. Don't you think I tried to work on him? I told him how lovely it would be if I could go abroad like other young wives. I cried and begged. I said he'd better remember what condition I was in, that he had to be nice to me and do what I wanted. I even hinted he could borrow the money. But that almost made him angry with me. He told me I was being irresponsible and that it was his duty as my husband not to give in to my moods and whims—I think that's what he called it. All right, I said to myself, you've got to be saved somehow, and so I found a way—

MRS. LINDE   And your husband never learned from your father that the money didn't come from him?

NORA   Never. Daddy died that same week. I thought of telling him all about it and ask him not to say anything. But since he was so sick—It turned out I didn't have to—

MRS. LINDE   And you've never told your husband?

NORA   Of course not! Good heavens, how could I? He, with his strict principles! Besides, you know how men are. Torvald would find it embarrassing and humiliating to learn that he owed me anything. It would upset our whole relationship. Our happy, beautiful home would no longer be what it is.

MRS. LINDE   Aren't you ever going to tell him?

NORA   (*reflectively, half smiling*)   Yes—one day, maybe. Many, many years from now, when I'm no longer young and pretty. Don't laugh! I mean when Torvald no longer feels about me the way he does now, when he no longer thinks it's fun when I dance for him and put on costumes and recite for him. Then it will be good to have something in reserve—(*interrupts herself*) Oh, I'm just being silly! That day will never come.—Well, now, Kristine, what do you think of my great secret? Don't you think I'm good for something too?—By the way, you wouldn't believe all the worry I've had because of it. It's been very hard to meet my obligations on schedule. You see, in business there's something called quarterly interest and something called installments on the principal, and those are terribly hard to come up with. I've had to save a little here and a little there, whenever I could. I couldn't use much of the housekeeping money, for Torvald has to eat well. And I couldn't use what I got for clothes for the children. They have to look nice, and I didn't think it would be right to spend less than I got—the sweet little things!

MRS. LINDE   Poor Nora! So you had to take it from your own allowance!

NORA   Yes, of course. After all, it was my affair. Every time Torvald gave me money for a new dress and things like that, I never used more than half of it. I always bought the cheapest, simplest things for myself. Thank God, everything looks good on me, so Torvald never noticed. But it was hard many times, Kristine, for it's fun to have pretty clothes. Don't you think?

MRS. LINDE   Certainly.

NORA   Anyway, I had other ways of making money too. Last winter I was lucky enough to get some copying work. So I locked the door and sat up writing every night till quite late. God! I often got so tired—! But it was great fun, too, working and making money. It was almost like being a man.

MRS. LINDE   But how much have you been able to pay off this way?

NORA   I couldn't tell you exactly. You see, it's very difficult to keep track of business like that. All I know is I have been paying off as much as I've been able to scrape together. Many times I just didn't know what to do. (*smiles*) Then I used to imagine a rich old gentleman had fallen in love with me—

MRS. LINDE   What! What old gentleman?

NORA   Phooey! And now he was dead and they were reading his will, and there it said in big letters, "All my money is to be paid in cash immediately to the charming Mrs. Nora Helmer."

MRS. LINDE   But dearest Nora—who *was* this old gentleman?

NORA   For heaven's sake, Kristine, don't you see? There *was* no old gentleman. He was just somebody I made up when I couldn't think of any way to raise the money. But never mind him. The old bore can be anyone he likes to for all I care. I have no use for him or his last will, for now I don't have a single worry in the world. (*jumps up*) Dear God, what a lovely thought this is! To be able to play and have fun with the children, to have everything nice and pretty in the house, just the way Torvald likes it! Not a care! And soon spring will be here, and the air will be blue and high. Maybe we can travel again. Maybe I'll see the ocean again! Oh, yes, yes!—it's wonderful to be alive and happy!

(*The doorbell rings.*)

MRS. LINDE (*getting up*)   There's the doorbell. Maybe I better be going.

NORA   No, please stay. I'm sure it's just someone for Torvald—

THE MAID (*in the hall door*)   Excuse me, ma'am. There's a gentleman here who'd like to see Mr. Helmer.

NORA   You mean the bank manager.

THE MAID   Sorry, ma'am; the bank manager. But I didn't know—since the Doctor is with him—

NORA   Who is the gentleman?

KROGSTAD (*appearing in the door*)   It's just me, Mrs. Helmer.

(MRS. LINDE *starts, looks, turns away toward the window.*)

NORA (*takes a step toward him, tense, in a low voice*)   You? What do you want? What do you want with my husband?

KROGSTAD   Bank business—in a way. I have a small job in the Mutual, and I understand your husband is going to be our new boss—

NORA   So, it's just—

KROGSTAD   Just routine business, ma'am. Nothing else.

NORA   All right. In that case, why don't you go through the door to the office.

(*Dismisses him casually as she closes the door. Walks over to the stove and tends the fire.*)

MRS. LINDE   Nora—who was that man?

NORA   His name's Krogstad. He's a lawyer.

MRS. LINDE   So it *was* him.

NORA   Do you know him?

MRS. LINDE   I used to—many years ago. For a while he clerked in our part of the country.

NORA   Right. He did.

MRS. LINDE   He has changed a great deal.

NORA   I believe he had a very unhappy marriage.

MRS. LINDE   And now he's a widower, isn't he?

NORA   With many children. There now; it's burning nicely again. (*closes the stove and moves the rocking chair a little to the side*)

MRS. LINDE   They say he's into all sorts of business.

NORA   Really? Maybe so. I wouldn't know. But let's not think about business. It's such a bore.

DR. RANK (*appears in the door to* HELMER'*s study*)   No. I don't want to be in the way. I'd rather talk to your wife a bit. (*closes the door and notices* MRS. LINDE) Oh, I beg your pardon. I believe I'm in the way here too.

NORA   No, not at all. (*introduces them*) Dr. Rank. Mrs. Linde.

RANK   Aha. A name often heard in this house. I believe I passed you on the stairs coming up.

MRS. LINDE   Yes. I'm afraid I climb stairs very slowly. They aren't good for me.

RANK   I see. A slight case of inner decay, perhaps?

MRS. LINDE   Overwork, rather.

RANK   Oh, is that all? And now you've come to town to relax at all the parties?

MRS. LINDE   I have come to look for a job.

RANK   A proven cure for overwork, I take it?

MRS. LINDE   One has to live, Doctor.

RANK   Yes, that seems to be the common opinion.

NORA   Come on, Dr. Rank—you want to live just as much as the rest of us.

RANK   Of course I do. Miserable as I am, I prefer to go on being tortured as long as possible. All my patients feel the same way. And that's true of the moral invalids too. Helmer is talking with a specimen right this minute.

MRS. LINDE (*in a low voice*)   Ah!

NORA   What do you mean?

RANK   Oh, this lawyer, Krogstad. You don't know him. The roots of his character are decayed. But even he began by saying something about having *to live*—as if it were a matter of the highest importance.

NORA   Oh? What did he want with Torvald?

RANK   I don't really know. All I heard was something about the bank.

NORA   I didn't know that Krog—that this Krogstad had anything to do with the Mutual Bank.

RANK   Yes, he seems to have some kind of job there. (*to* MRS. LINDE) I don't know if you are familiar in your part of the country with the kind of person who is always running around trying to sniff out cases of moral decrepitude and as soon as he finds one puts the individual under observation in some excellent position or other. All the healthy ones are left out in the cold.

MRS. LINDE   I should think it's the sick who need looking after the most.

RANK (*shrugs his shoulders*)   There we are. That's the attitude that turns society into a hospital.

(NORA, *absorbed in her own thoughts, suddenly starts giggling and clapping her hands.*)

RANK   What's so funny about that? Do you even know what society is?

NORA   What do I care about your stupid society! I laughed at something entirely different—something terribly amusing. Tell me, Dr. Rank—all the employees in the Mutual Bank, from now on they'll all be dependent on Torvald, right?

RANK   Is that what you find so enormously amusing?

NORA (*smiles and hums*)   That's my business, that's my business! (*walks around*) Yes, I do think it's fun that we—that Torvald is going to have so much influence on so many people's lives. (*brings out the bag of macaroons*) Have a macaroon, Dr. Rank.

RANK   Well, well—macaroons. I thought they were banned around here.

NORA   Yes, but these were some that Kristine gave me.

MRS. LINDE   What! I?

NORA   That's all right. Don't look so scared. You couldn't know that Torvald won't let me have them. He's afraid they'll ruin my teeth. But who cares! Just once in a while—! Right, Dr. Rank? Have one! (*puts a macaroon into his mouth*) You too, Kristine. And one for me. A very small one. Or at most two. (*walks around again*) Yes, I really feel very, very happy. Now there's just one thing I'm dying to do.

RANK   Oh, and what's that?

NORA   Something I'm dying to say so Torvald could hear.

RANK   And why can't you?

NORA   I don't dare to, for it's not nice.

MRS. LINDE   Not nice?

RANK   In that case, I guess you'd better not. But surely to the two of us—? What is it you'd like to say for Helmer to hear?

NORA   I want to say, "Goddammit!"

RANK   Are you out of your mind!

MRS. LINDE   For heaven's sake, Nora!

RANK   Say it. Here he comes.

NORA (*hiding the macaroons*)   Shhh!

(HELMER *enters from his study, carrying his hat and overcoat.*)

NORA (*going to him*)   Well, dear, did you get rid of him?

HELMER   Yes, he just left.

NORA   Torvald, I want you to meet Kristine. She's just come to town.

HELMER   Kristine—? I'm sorry; I don't think—

NORA   Mrs. Linde, Torvald dear. Mrs. Kristine Linde.

HELMER   Ah, yes. A childhood friend of my wife's, I suppose.

MRS. LINDE   Yes, we've known each other for a long time.

NORA   Just think; she has come all this way just to see you.

HELMER   I'm not sure I understand—

MRS. LINDE   Well, not really—

NORA   You see, Kristine is an absolutely fantastic secretary, and she would so much like to work for a competent executive and learn more than she knows already—

HELMER   Very sensible, I'm sure, Mrs. Linde.

NORA   So when she heard about your appointment—there was a wire—she came here as fast as she could. How about it, Torvald? Couldn't you do something for Kristine? For my sake. Please?

HELMER   Quite possibly. I take it you're a widow, Mrs. Linde?

MRS. LINDE   Yes.

HELMER   And you've had office experience?

MRS. LINDE   Some—yes.

HELMER   In that case I think it's quite likely that I'll be able to find you a position.

NORA (*claps her hands*)   I knew it! I knew it!

HELMER   You've arrived at a most opportune time, Mrs. Linde.

MRS. LINDE   Oh, how can I ever thank you—

HELMER   Not at all, not at all. (*puts his coat on*) But today you'll have to excuse me—

RANK   Wait a minute; I'll come with you. (*gets his fur coat from the front hall, warms it by the stove*)

NORA   Don't be long, Torvald.

HELMER   An hour or so; no more.

NORA   Are you leaving, too, Kristine?

MRS. LINDE (*putting on her things*)   Yes, I'd better go and find a place to stay.

HELMER   Good. Then we'll be going the same way.

NORA (*helping her*)   I'm sorry this place is so small, but I don't think we very well could—

MRS. LINDE   Of course! Don't be silly, Nora. Goodbye, and thank you for everything.

NORA   Goodbye. We'll see you soon. You'll be back this evening, of course. And you too, Dr. Rank; right? If you feel well enough? Of course you will. Just wrap yourself up.

(*General small talk as all exit into the hall. Children's voices are heard on the stairs.*)

NORA   There they are! There they are! (*She runs and opens the door. The nurse* ANNE-MARIE *enters with the children.*)

NORA   Come in! Come in! (*bends over and kisses them*) Oh, you sweet, sweet darlings! Look at them, Kristine! Aren't they beautiful?

RANK   No standing around in the draft!

HELMER   Come along, Mrs. Linde. This place isn't fit for anyone but mothers right now.

(DR. RANK, HELMER, *and* MRS. LINDE *go down the stairs. The* NURSE *enters the living room with the children.* NORA *follows, closing the door behind her.*)

NORA   My, how nice you all look! Such red cheeks! Like apples and roses. (*The children all talk at the same time.*) You've had so much fun? I bet you have. Oh, isn't that nice! You pulled both Emmy and Bob on your sleigh? Both at the same time? That's very good, Ivar. Oh, let me hold her for a minute, Anne-Marie. My sweet little doll baby! (*takes the smallest of the children from the* NURSE *and dances with her*) Yes, yes, of course; Mama'll dance with you too, Bob. What? You threw snowballs? Oh, I wish I'd been there! No, no; *I* want to take their clothes off, Anne-Marie. Please let me; I think it's so much fun. You go on in. You look frozen. There's hot coffee on the stove.

(*The* NURSE *exits into the room to the left.* NORA *takes the children's wraps off and throws them all around. They all keep telling her things at the same time.*)

NORA   Oh, really? A big dog ran after you? But it didn't bite you. Of course not. Dogs don't bite sweet little doll babies. Don't peek at the packages, Ivar! What's in them? Wouldn't you like to know! No, no; that's something terrible! Play? You want to play? What do you want to play? Okay, let's play hide-and-seek. Bob hides first. You want *me* to? All right. I'll go first.

(*Laughing and shouting,* NORA *and the children play in the living room and in the adjacent room, right. Finally,* NORA *hides herself under the table; the children rush in, look for her, can't find her. They hear her low giggle, run to the table, lift the rug that covers it, see her. General hilarity. She crawls out, pretends to scare them. New delight. In the meantime there has been a knock on the door between the living room and the front hall, but nobody has noticed. Now the door is opened halfway.* KROGSTAD *appears. He waits a little. The play goes on.*)

KROGSTAD   Pardon me, Mrs. Helmer—

NORA (*with a muted cry turns around, jumps up*)   Ah! What do you want?

KROGSTAD   I'm sorry. The front door was open. Somebody must have forgotten to close it—

NORA (*standing up*)   My husband isn't here, Mr. Krogstad.

KROGSTAD   I know.

NORA   So what do you want?

KROGSTAD   I'd like a word with you.

NORA   With—? (*to the children*) Go in to Anne-Marie. What? No, the strange man won't do anything bad to Mama. When he's gone we'll play some more.

(*She takes the children into the room to the left and closes the door.*)

NORA (*tense, troubled*)   You want to speak with me?

KROGSTAD   Yes I do.

NORA   Today—? It isn't the first of the month yet.

KROGSTAD   No, it's Christmas Eve. It's up to you what kind of holiday you'll have.

NORA   What do you want? I can't possibly—

KROGSTAD   Let's not talk about that just yet. There's something else. You do have a few minutes, don't you?

NORA   Yes. Yes, of course. That is,—

KROGSTAD   Good. I was sitting in Olsen's restaurant when I saw your husband go by.

NORA   Yes—?

KROGSTAD   —with a lady.

NORA   What of it?

KROGSTAD   May I be so free as to ask: wasn't that lady Mrs. Linde?

NORA   Yes.

KROGSTAD   Just arrived in town?

NORA   Yes, today.

KROGSTAD   She's a good friend of yours, I understand?

NORA   Yes, she is. But I fail to see—

KROGSTAD   I used to know her myself.

NORA   I know that.

KROGSTAD   So you know about that. I thought as much. In that case, let me ask you a simple question. Is Mrs. Linde going to be employed in the bank?

NORA   What makes you think you have the right to cross-examine me like this, Mr. Krogstad—you, one of my husband's employees? But since you ask, I'll tell you. Yes, Mrs. Linde is going to be working in the bank. And it was I who recommended her, Mr. Krogstad. Now you know.

KROGSTAD   So I was right.

NORA (*walks up and down*)   After all, one does have a little influence, you know. Just because you're a woman, it doesn't mean that—Really, Mr. Krogstad, people in a subordinate position should be careful not to offend someone who—oh well—

KROGSTAD   —has influence?

NORA   Exactly.

KROGSTAD (*changing his tone*)   Mrs. Helmer, I must ask you to be good enough to use your influence on my behalf.

NORA   What do you mean?

KROGSTAD   I want you to make sure that I am going to keep my subordinate position in the bank.

NORA   I don't understand. Who is going to take your position away from you?

KROGSTAD   There's no point in playing ignorant with me, Mrs. Helmer. I can very well appreciate that your friend would find it unpleasant to run into me. So now I know who I can thank for my dismissal.

NORA   But I assure you—

KROGSTAD   Never mind. Just want to say you still have time. I advise you to use your influence to prevent it.

NORA   But Mr. Krogstad, I don't have any influence—none at all.

KROGSTAD   No? I thought you just said—

NORA   Of course I didn't mean it that way. I! Whatever makes you think that I have any influence of that kind on my husband?

KROGSTAD   I went to law school with your husband. I have no reason to think that the bank manager is less susceptible than other husbands.

NORA   If you're going to insult my husband, I'll ask you to leave.

KROGSTAD   You're brave, Mrs. Helmer.

NORA   I'm not afraid of you any more. After New Year's I'll be out of this thing with you.

KROGSTAD (*more controlled*)   Listen, Mrs. Helmer. If necessary I'll fight as for my life to keep my little job in the bank.

NORA   So it seems.

KROGSTAD   It isn't just the money; that's really the smallest part of it. There is something else—Well, I guess I might as well tell you. It's like this. I'm sure you know, like everybody else, that some years ago I committed—an impropriety.

NORA   I believe I've heard it mentioned.

KROGSTAD   The case never came to court, but from that moment all doors were closed to me. So I took up the kind of business you know about. I had to do something, and I think I can say about myself that I have not been among the worst. But now I want to get out of all that. My sons are growing up. For their sake I must get back as much of my good name as I can. This job in the bank was like the first rung on the ladder. And now your husband wants to kick me down and leave me back in the mud again.

NORA   But I swear to you, Mr. Krogstad; it's not at all in my power to help you.

KROGSTAD   That's because you don't want to. But I have the means to force you.

NORA   You don't mean you're going to tell my husband I owe you money?

KROGSTAD   And if I did?

NORA   That would be a mean thing to do. (*almost crying*) That secret, which is my joy and my pride—for him to learn about it in such a coarse and ugly manner—to learn it from *you*—! It would be terribly unpleasant for me.

KROGSTAD   Just unpleasant?

NORA   (*heatedly*)   But go ahead! Do it! It will be worse for you than for me. When my husband realizes what a bad person you are, you'll be sure to lose your job.

KROGSTAD   I asked you if it was just domestic unpleasantness you were afraid of?

NORA   When my husband finds out, of course he'll pay off the loan, and then we won't have anything more to do with you.

KROGSTAD   (*stepping closer*)   Listen, Mrs. Helmer—either you have a very bad memory, or you don't know much about business. I think I had better straighten you out on a few things.

NORA   What do you mean?

KROGSTAD   When your husband was ill, you came to me to borrow twelve hundred dollars.

NORA   I knew nobody else.

KROGSTAD   I promised to get you the money—

NORA   And you did.

KROGSTAD   I promised to get you the money on certain conditions. At the time you were so anxious about your husband's health and so set on getting him away that I doubt very much that you paid much attention to the details of our transaction. That's why I remind you of them now. Anyway, I promised to get you the money if you would sign an I.O.U., which I drafted.

NORA   And which I signed.

KROGSTAD   Good. But below your signature I added a few lines, making your father security for the loan. Your father was supposed to put his signature to those lines.

NORA   Supposed to—? He did.

KROGSTAD   I had left the date blank. That is, your father was to date his own signature. You recall that, don't you, Mrs. Helmer?

NORA   I guess so—

KROGSTAD   I gave the note to you. You were to mail it to your father. Am I correct?

NORA   Yes.

KROGSTAD   And of course you did so right away, for no more than five or six days later you brought the paper back to me, signed by your father. Then I paid you the money.

NORA   Well? And haven't I been keeping up with the payments?

KROGSTAD   Fairly well, yes. But to get back to what we were talking about— those were difficult days for you, weren't they, Mrs. Helmer?

NORA   Yes, they were.

KROGSTAD   Your father was quite ill, I believe.

NORA   He was dying.

KROGSTAD   And died shortly afterwards?

NORA   That's right.

KROGSTAD   Tell me, Mrs. Helmer; do you happen to remember the date of your father's death? I mean the exact day of the month?

NORA   Daddy died on September 29.

KROGSTAD   Quite correct. I have ascertained that fact. That's why there is something peculiar about this (*takes out a piece of paper*), which I can't account for.

NORA   Peculiar? How? I don't understand—

KROGSTAD   It seems very peculiar, Mrs. Helmer, that your father signed this promissory note three days after his death.

NORA   How so? I don't see what—

KROGSTAD   Your father died on September 29. Now look. He has dated his signature October 2. Isn't that odd?

(NORA *remains silent.*)

KROGSTAD   Can you explain it?

(NORA *is still silent.*)

KROGSTAD   I also find it striking that the date and the month and the year are not in your father's handwriting but in a hand I think I recognize. Well, that might be explained. Your father may have forgotten to date his signature and somebody else may have done it here, guessing at the date before he had learned of your father's death. That's all right. It's only the signature itself that matters. And that is genuine, isn't it, Mrs. Helmer? Your father *did* put his name to this note?

NORA   (*after a brief silence tosses her head back and looks defiantly at him*)   No, he didn't. *I* wrote Daddy's name.

KROGSTAD   Mrs. Helmer—do you realize what a dangerous admission you just made?

NORA   Why? You'll get your money soon.

KROGSTAD   Let me ask you something. Why didn't you mail this note to your father?

NORA   Because it was impossible. Daddy was sick—you know that. If I had asked him to sign it, I would have had to tell him what the money was for. But I couldn't tell him, as sick as he was, that my husband's life was in danger. That was impossible. Surely you can see that.

KROGSTAD   Then it would have been better for you if you had given up your trip abroad.

NORA   No, that was impossible! That trip was to save my husband's life. I couldn't give it up.

KROGSTAD   But didn't you realize that what you did amounted to fraud against me?

NORA   I couldn't let that make any difference. I didn't care about you at all. I hated the way you made all those difficulties for me, even though you knew the danger my husband was in. I thought you were cold and unfeeling.

KROGSTAD   Mrs. Helmer, obviously you have no clear idea of what you have done. Let me tell you that what I did that time was no more and no worse. And it ruined my name and reputation.

NORA   You! Are you trying to tell me that you did something brave once in order to save your wife's life?

KROGSTAD   The law doesn't ask about motives.

NORA   Then it's a bad law.

KROGSTAD   Bad or not—if I produce this note in court you'll be judged according to the law.

NORA   I refuse to believe you. A daughter shouldn't have the right to spare her dying old father worry and anxiety? A wife shouldn't have the right to save her husband's life? I don't know the laws very well, but I'm sure that somewhere they make allowance for cases like that. And you, a lawyer, don't know that? I think you must be a bad lawyer, Mr. Krogstad.

KROGSTAD   That may be. But business—the kind of business you and I have with one another—don't you think I know something about that? Very well. Do what you like. But let me tell you this: if I'm going to be kicked out again, you'll keep me company. (*He bows and exits through the front hall.*)

NORA   (*pauses thoughtfully; then, with a defiant toss of her head*)   Oh, nonsense! Trying to scare me like that! I'm not all that silly. (*starts picking up the children's clothes; soon stops*) But—? No! That's impossible! I did it for love!

THE CHILDREN   (*in the door to the left*)   Mama, the strange man just left. We saw him.

NORA   Yes, yes; I know. But don't tell anybody about the strange man. Do you hear? Not even Daddy.

THE CHILDREN   We won't. But now you'll play with us again, won't you, Mama?

NORA   No, not right now.

THE CHILDREN   But Mama—you promised.

NORA   I know, but I can't just now. Go to your own room. I've so much to do. Be nice now, my little darlings. Do as I say. (*She nudges them gently into the other room and closes the door. She sits down on the couch, picks up a piece of embroidery, makes a few stitches, then stops.*) No! (*throws the embroidery down, goes to the hall door and calls out*) Helene! Bring the Christmas tree in here, please! (*goes to the table, left, opens the drawer, halts*) No—that's impossible!

THE MAID   (*with the Christmas tree*)   Where do you want it, ma'am?

NORA   There. The middle of the floor.

THE MAID   You want anything else?

NORA   No, thanks. I have everything I need. (THE MAID *goes out.* NORA *starts trimming the tree.*) I want candles—and flowers—That awful man! Oh, nonsense! There's nothing wrong. This will be a lovely tree. I'll do everything you want me to, Torvald. I'll sing for you—dance for you—

(HELMER, *a bundle of papers under his arm, enters from outside.*)

NORA   Ah—you're back already?

HELMER   Yes. Has anybody been here?

NORA   Here? No.

HELMER   That's funny. I saw Krogstad leaving just now.

NORA   Oh? Oh yes, that's right. Krogstad was here for just a moment.

HELMER   I can tell from your face that he came to ask you to put in a word for him.

NORA   Yes.

HELMER   And it was supposed to be your own idea, wasn't it? You were not to tell me he'd been here. He asked you that too, didn't he?

NORA   Yes, Torvald, but—

NORA   Nora, Nora, how could you! Talk to a man like that and make him promises! And lying to me about it afterwards—!

NORA   Lying—?

HELMER   Didn't you say nobody had been here? (*shakes his finger at her*) My little songbird must never do that again. Songbirds are supposed to have clean beaks to chirp with—no false notes. (*puts his arms around her waist*) Isn't that so? Of course it is. (*lets her go*) And that's enough about that. (*sits down in front of the fireplace*) Ah, it's nice and warm in here. (*begins to leaf through his papers*)

NORA (*busy with the tree; after a brief pause*)   Torvald.

HELMER   Yes.

NORA   I'm looking forward so much to the Stenborgs' costume party day after tomorrow.

HELMER   And I can't wait to find out what you're going to surprise me with.

NORA   Oh, that silly idea!

HELMER   Oh?

NORA   I can't think of anything. It all seems so foolish and pointless.

HELMER   Ah, my little Nora admits that?

NORA (*behind his chair, her arms on the back of the chair*)   Are you very busy, Torvald?

HELMER   Well—

NORA   What are all those papers?

HELMER   Bank business.

NORA   Already?

HELMER   I've asked the board to give me the authority to make certain changes in organization and personnel. That's what I'll be doing over the holidays. I want it all settled before New Year's.

NORA   So that's why this poor Krogstad—

HELMER   Hm.

NORA (*leisurely playing with the hair on his neck*)   If you weren't so busy, Torvald, I'd ask you for a great big favor.

HELMER   Let's hear it, anyway.

NORA   I don't know anyone with better taste than you, and I want so much to look nice at the party. Couldn't you sort of take charge of me, Torvald, and decide what I'll wear—Help me with my costume?

HELMER   Aha! Little Lady Obstinate is looking for someone to rescue her?

NORA   Yes, Torvald. I won't get anywhere without your help.

HELMER   All right. I'll think about it. We'll come up with something.

NORA   Oh, you *are* nice! (*goes back to the Christmas tree; a pause*) Those red flowers look so pretty.—Tell me, was it really all that bad what this Krogstad fellow did?

HELMER   He forged signatures. Do you have any idea what that means?

NORA   Couldn't it have been because he felt he had to?

HELMER   Yes, or like so many others he may simply have been thoughtless. I'm not so heartless as to condemn a man absolutely because of a single imprudent act.

NORA   Of course not, Torvald!

HELMER   People like him can redeem themselves morally by openly confessing their crime and taking their punishment.

NORA   Punishment—?

HELMER   But that was not the way Krogstad chose. He got out of it with tricks and evasions. That's what has corrupted him.

NORA   So you think that if—?

HELMER   Can't you imagine how a guilty person like that has to lie and fake and dissemble wherever he goes—putting on a mask before everybody he's close to, even his own wife and children. It's this thing with the children that's the worst part of it, Nora.

NORA   Why is that?

HELMER   Because when a man lives inside such a circle of stinking lies he brings infection into his own home and contaminates his whole family. With every breath of air his children inhale the germs of something ugly.

NORA (*moving closer behind him*)   Are you so sure of that?

HELMER   Of course I am. I have seen enough examples of that in my work. Nearly all young criminals have had mothers who lied.

NORA   Why mothers—particularly?

HELMER   Most often mothers. But of course fathers tend to have the same influence. Every lawyer knows that. And yet, for years this Krogstad has been poisoning his own children in an atmosphere of lies and deceit. That's why I call him a lost soul morally. (*reaches out for her hands*) And that's why my sweet little Nora must promise me never to take his side again. Let's shake on that.—What? What's this? Give me your hand.

There! Now that's settled. I assure you, I would find it impossible to work in the same room with that man. I feel literally sick when I'm around people like that.

NORA (*withdraws her hand and goes to the other side of the Christmas tree*)   It's so hot in here. And I have so much to do.

HELMER (*gets up and collects his papers*)   Yes, and I really should try to get some of this reading done before dinner. I must think about your costume too. And maybe just possibly I'll have something to wrap in gilt paper and hang on the Christmas tree. (*puts his hand on her head*) Oh my adorable little songbird! (*enters his study and closes the door*)

NORA (*after a pause, in a low voice*)   It's all a lot of nonsense. It's not that way at all. It's impossible. It has to be impossible.

THE NURSE (*in the door, left*)   The little ones are asking ever so nicely if they can't come in and be with their mama.

NORA   No, no no! Don't let them in here! You stay with them, Anne-Marie.

THE NURSE   If you say so, ma'am. (*closes the door*)

NORA (*pale with terror*)   Corrupt my little children—! Poison my home—? (*Brief pause; she lifts her head.*) That's not true. Never. Never in a million years.

Act II

The same room. The Christmas tree is in the corner by the piano, stripped, shabby-looking, with burnt-down candles. NORA's outside clothes are on the couch. NORA is alone. She walks around restlessly. She stops by the couch and picks up her coat.

NORA (*drops the coat again*)   There's somebody now! (*goes to the door, listens*) No. Nobody. Of course not—not on Christmas. And not tomorrow either.[1]—But perhaps—(*opens the door and looks*) No, nothing in the mailbox. All empty. (*comes forward*) How silly I am! Of course he isn't serious. Nothing like that could happen. After all, I have three small children.

(*The NURSE enters from the room, left, carrying a big carton.*)

THE NURSE   Well, at last I found it—the box with your costume.

NORA   Thanks. Just put it on the table.

NURSE (*does so*)   But it's all a big mess, I'm afraid.

NORA   Oh, I wish I could tear the whole thing to little pieces!

NURSE   Heavens! It's not as bad as all that. It can be fixed all right. All it takes is a little patience.

NORA   I'll go over and get Mrs. Linde to help me.

NURSE   Going out again? In this awful weather? You'll catch a cold.

NORA   That might not be such a bad thing. How are the children?

---

[1]In Norway both December 25 and 26 are legal holidays.

NURSE   The poor little dears are playing with their presents, but—

NORA   Do they keep asking for me?

NURSE   Well, you know, they're used to being with their mamma.

NORA   I know. But Anne-Marie, from now on I can't be with them as much as before.

NURSE   Oh well. Little children get used to everything.

NORA   You think so? Do you think they'll forget their mamma if I were gone altogether?

NURSE   Goodness me—gone altogether?

NORA   Listen, Anne-Marie—something I've wondered about. How could you bring yourself to leave your children with strangers?

NURSE   But I had to, if I were to nurse you.

NORA   Yes, but how could you *want* to?

NURSE   When I could get such a nice place? When something like that happens to a poor young girl, she'd better be grateful for whatever she gets. For *he* didn't do a thing for me—the louse!

NORA   But your daughter has forgotten all about you, hasn't she?

NURSE   Oh no! Not at all! She wrote to me both when she was confirmed and when she got married.

NORA (*putting her arms around her neck*)   You dear old thing—you were a good mother to me when I was little.

NURSE   Poor little Nora had no one else, you know.

NORA   And if my little ones didn't, I know you'd—oh, I'm being silly! (*opens the carton*) Go in to them, please. I really should—. Tomorrow you'll see how pretty I'll be.

NURSE   I know. There won't be anybody at that party half as pretty as you, ma'am. (*goes out, left*)

NORA (*begins to take clothes out of the carton; in a moment she throws it all down*)   If only I dared to go out. If only I knew nobody would come. That nothing would happen while I was gone.—How silly! Nobody'll come. Just don't think about it. Brush the muff. Beautiful gloves. Beautiful gloves. Forget it. Forget it. One, two, three, four, five, six—(*cries out*) There they are! (*moves toward the door, stops irresolutely*)

(MRS. LINDE *enters from the hall. She has already taken off her coat.*)

NORA   Oh, it's you, Kristine. There's no one else out there, is there? I'm so glad you're here.

MRS. LINDE   They told me you'd asked for me.

NORA   I just happened to walk by. I need your help with something—badly. Let's sit here on the couch. Look. Torvald and I are going to a costume party tomorrow night—at Consul Stenborg's upstairs—and Torvald wants me to go as a Neapolitan fisher girl and dance the tarantella. I learned it when we were on Capri.

MRS. LINDE   Well, well! So you'll be putting on a whole show?

NORA   Yes, Torvald thinks I should. Look, here's the costume. Torvald had it made for me while we were there. But it's all so torn and everything. I just don't know—

MRS. LINDE   Oh, that can be fixed. It's not that much. The trimmings have come loose in a few places. Do you have needle and thread? Ah, here we are. All set.

NORA   I really appreciate it, Kristine.

MRS. LINDE (*sewing*)   So you'll be in disguise tomorrow night, eh? You know—I may come by for just a moment, just to look at you.—Oh dear. I haven't even thanked you for the nice evening last night.

NORA (*gets up, moves around*)   Oh, I don't know. I don't think last night was as nice as it usually is.—You should have come to town a little earlier, Kristine.—Yes, Torvald knows how to make it nice and pretty around here.

MRS. LINDE   You too, I should think. After all, you're your father's daughter. By the way, is Dr. Rank always as depressed as he was last night?

NORA   No, last night was unusual. He's a very sick man, you know—very sick. Poor Rank, his spine is rotting away. Tuberculosis, I think. You see, his father was a nasty old man with mistresses and all that sort of thing. Rank has been sickly ever since he was a little boy.

MRS. LINDE (*dropping her sewing to her lap*)   But dearest, Nora, where have you learned about things like that?

NORA (*still walking about*)   Oh, you know—with three children you sometimes get to talk with—other wives. Some of them know quite a bit about medicine. So you pick up a few things.

MRS. LINDE (*resumes her sewing; after a brief pause*)   Does Dr. Rank come here every day?

NORA   Every single day. He's Torvald's oldest and best friend, after all. And my friend too, for that matter. He's part of the family, almost.

MRS. LINDE   But tell me, is he quite sincere? I mean, isn't he the kind of man who likes to say nice things to people?

NORA   No, not at all. Rather the opposite, in fact. What makes you say that?

MRS. LINDE   When you introduced us yesterday, he told me he'd often heard my name mentioned in this house. But later on it was quite obvious that your husband really had no idea who I was. So how could Dr. Rank—?

NORA   You're right, Kristine, but I can explain that. You see, Torvald loves me so very much that he wants me all to himself. That's what he says. When we were first married he got almost jealous when I as much as mentioned anybody from back home that I was fond of. So of course I soon stopped doing that. But with Dr. Rank I often talk about home. You see, he likes to listen to me.

MRS. LINDE   Look here, Nora. In many ways you're still a child. After all, I'm quite a bit older than you and have had more experience. I want to give you a piece of advice. I think you should get out of this thing with Dr. Rank.

NORA   Get out of what thing?

MRS. LINDE   Several things in fact, if you want my opinion. Yesterday you said something about a rich admirer who was going to give you money—

NORA   One who doesn't exist, unfortunately. What of it?

MRS. LINDE   Does Dr. Rank have money?

NORA   Yes, he does.

MRS. LINDE   And no dependents?

MRS. LINDE   No. But—?

MRS. LINDE   And he comes here every day?

NORA   Yes, I told you that already.

MRS. LINDE   But how can that sensitive man be so tactless?

NORA   I haven't the slightest idea what you're talking about.

MRS. LINDE   Don't play games with me, Nora. Don't you think I know who you borrowed the twelve hundred dollars from?

NORA   Are you out of your mind! The very idea—! A friend of both of us who sees us every day—! What a dreadfully uncomfortable position that would be!

MRS. LINDE   So it really isn't Dr. Rank?

NORA   Most certainly not! I would never have dreamed of asking him—not for a moment. Anyway, he didn't have any money then. He inherited it afterwards.

MRS. LINDE   Well, I still think it may have been lucky for you, Nora dear.

NORA   The idea! It would never have occurred to me to ask Dr. Rank—. Though I'm sure that if I *did* ask him—

MRS. LINDE   But of course you wouldn't.

NORA   Of course not. I can't imagine that that would ever be necessary. But I am quite sure that if I told Dr. Rank—

MRS. LINDE   Behind your husband's back?

NORA   I must get out of—this other thing. That's also behind his back. I *must* get out of it.

MRS. LINDE   That's what I told you yesterday. But—

NORA (*walking up and down*)   A man manages these things so much better than a woman—

MRS. LINDE   One's husband, yes.

NORA   Silly, silly! (*stops*) When you've paid off all you owe, you get your I.O.U. back; right?

MRS. LINDE   Yes, of course.

NORA   And you can tear it into a hundred thousand little pieces and burn it—that dirty, filthy, paper!

MRS. LINDE (*looks hard at her, puts down her sewing, rises slowly*)   Nora—you're hiding something from me.

NORA   Can you tell?

MRS. LINDE   Something's happened to you, Nora, since yesterday morning. What is it?

NORA (*going to her*)   Kristine! (*listens*) Shhh. Torvald just came back. Listen. Why don't you go in to the children for a while. Torvald can't stand having sewing around. Get Anne-Marie to help you.

MRS. LINDE (*gathers some of the sewing things together*)   All right, but I'm not leaving here till you and I have talked.

(*She goes out left, as* HELMER *enters from the front hall.*)

NORA (*toward him*)   I have been waiting and waiting for you, Torvald.

HELMER   Was that the dressmaker?

NORA   No, it was Kristine. She's helping me with my costume. Oh Torvald, just wait till you see how nice I'll look!

HELMER   I told you. Pretty good idea I had, wasn't it?

NORA   Lovely! And wasn't it nice of me to go along with it?

HELMER (*his hands under her chin*)   Nice? To do what your husband tells you? All right, you little rascal; I know you didn't mean it that way. But don't let me interrupt you. I suppose you want to try it on.

NORA   And you'll be working?

HELMER   Yes. (*shows her a pile of papers*) Look. I've been down to the bank. (*is about to enter his study*)

NORA   Torvald.

HELMER (*halts*)   Yes?

NORA   What if your little squirrel asked you ever so nicely—

HELMER   For what?

NORA   Would you do it?

HELMER   Depends on what it is.

NORA   Squirrel would run around and do all sorts of fun tricks if you'd be nice and agreeable.

HELMER   All right. What is it?

NORA   Lark would chirp and twitter in all the rooms, up and down—

HELMER   So what? Lark does that anyway.

NORA   I'll be your elfmaid and dance for you in the moonlight, Torvald.

HELMER   Nora, don't tell me it's the same thing you mentioned this morning?

NORA (*closer to him*)   Yes, Torvald. I beg you!

HELMER   You really have the nerve to bring that up again?

NORA   Yes. You've just got to do as I say. You *must* let Krogstad keep his job.

HELMER   My dear Nora. It's his job I intend to give to Mrs. Linde.

NORA   I know. And that's ever so nice of you. But can't you just fire somebody else?

HELMER   This is incredible! You just don't give up do you? Because you make some foolish promise, *I* am supposed to—!

NORA   That's not the reason, Torvald. It's for your own sake. That man writes for the worst newspapers. You've said so yourself. There's no telling what he may do to you. I'm scared to death of him.

HELMER   Ah, I understand. You're afraid because of what happened before.

NORA   What do you mean?

HELMER   You're thinking of your father, of course.

NORA   Yes. Yes, you're right. Remember the awful things they wrote about Daddy in the newspapers. I really think they might have forced him to resign if the ministry hadn't sent you to look into the charges and if you hadn't been so helpful and understanding.

HELMER   My dear little Nora, there is a world of difference between your father and me. Your father's official conduct was not above reproach. Mine is, and I intend for it to remain that way as long as I hold my position.

NORA   Oh, but you don't know what vicious people like that may think of. Oh, Torvald! Now all of us could be so happy together here in our own home, peaceful and carefree. Such a good life, Torvald, for you and me and the children! That's why I implore you—

HELMER   And it's exactly because you plead for him that you make it impossible for me to keep him. It's already common knowledge in the bank that I intend to let Krogstad go. If it gets out that the new manager has changed his mind because of his wife—

NORA   Yes? What then?

HELMER   No, of course, that wouldn't matter at all as long as little Mrs. Pighead here got her way! Do you want me to make myself look ridiculous before my whole staff—make people think I can be swayed by just anybody—by outsiders? Believe me, I would soon enough find out what the consequences would be! Besides, there's another thing that makes it absolutely impossible for Krogstad to stay on in the bank now that I'm in charge.

NORA   What's that?

HELMER   I suppose in a pinch I could overlook his moral shortcomings—

NORA   Yes, you could; couldn't you, Torvald?

HELMER   And I understand he's quite a good worker, too. But we've known each other for a long time. It's one of those imprudent relationships you get into when you're young that embarrass you for the rest of your life. I guess I might as well be frank with you: he and I are on a first name basis. And that tactless fellow never hides the fact even when other people are around. Rather, he seems to think it entitles him to be familiar with me. Every chance he gets he comes out with his damn "Torvald, Torvald." I'm telling you, I find it most awkward. He would make my position in the bank intolerable.

NORA   You don't really mean any of this, Torvald.

HELMER   Oh? I don't? And why not?

NORA   No, for it's all so petty.

HELMER   What! Petty? You think I'm being petty!

NORA   No, I *don't* think you are petty, Torvald dear. That's exactly why I—

HELMER   Never mind. You think my reasons are petty, so it follows that I must be petty too. Petty! Indeed! By God, I'll put an end to this right now! (*opens the door to the front hall and calls out*) Helene!

NORA   What are you doing?

HELMER (*searching among his papers*)   Making a decision. (THE MAID *enters.*) Here. Take this letter. Go out with it right away. Find somebody to deliver it. But quick. The address is on the envelope. Wait. Here's money.

THE MAID   Very good sir. (*She takes the letter and goes out.*)

HELMER (*collecting his papers*)   There now, little Mrs Obstinate!

NORA (*breathless*)   Torvald—what was that letter?

HELMER   Krogstad's dismissal.

NORA   Call it back, Torvald! There's still time! Oh Torvald, please—call it back! For my sake, for your own sake, for the sake of the children! Listen to me, Torvald! Do it! You don't know what you're doing to all of us!

HELMER   Too late.

NORA   Yes. Too late.

HELMER   Dear Nora, I forgive you this fear you're in, although it really is an insult to me. Yes, it is! It's an insult to think that I am scared of a shabby scrivener's revenge. But I forgive you, for it's such a beautiful proof how much you love me. (*takes her in his arms*) And that's the way it should be, my sweet darling. Whatever happens, you'll see that when things get really rough I have both strength and courage. You'll find out that I am man enough to shoulder the whole burden.

NORA (*terrified*)   What do you mean by that?

HELMER   All of it, I tell you—

NORA (*composed*)   You'll never have to do that.

HELMER   Good. Then we'll share the burden, Nora—like husband and wife, the way it ought to be. (*caresses her*) Now are you satisfied? There, there, there. Not that look in your eyes—like a frightened dove. It's all your own foolish imagination.—Why don't you practice the tarantella—and your tambourine, too. I'll be in the inner office and close both doors, so I won't hear you. You can make as much noise as you like. (*turning in the doorway*) And when Rank comes, tell him where to find me. (*He nods to her, enters his study carrying his papers, and closes the door.*)

NORA (*transfixed by terror, whispers*)   He would do it. He'll do it. He'll do it in spite of the whole world.—No, this mustn't happen. Anything rather than that! There must be a way!—(*The doorbell rings.*) Dr. Rank! Anything rather than that! Anything—anything at all.

(*She passes her hand over her face, pulls herself together, and opens the door to the hall. DR. RANK is out there, hanging up his coat. Darkness begins to fall during the following scene.*)

NORA   Hello there, Dr. Rank. I recognized your ringing. Don't go in to Torvald yet. I think he's busy.

RANK   And you?

NORA (*as he enters and she closes the door behind him*)   You know I always have time for you.

RANK   Thanks. I'll make use of that as long as I can.

NORA   What do you mean by that—As long as you can?

RANK   Does that frighten you?

NORA   Well, it's a funny expression. As if something was going to happen.

RANK   Something is going to happen that I've long been expecting. But I admit I hadn't thought it would come quite so soon.

NORA (*seizes his arm*)   What is it you've found out? Dr. Rank—tell me!

RANK (*sits down by the stove*)   I'm going downhill fast. There's nothing to do about that.

NORA (*with audible relief*)   So it's *you*—

RANK   Who else? No point in lying to myself. I'm in worse shape than any of my other patients, Mrs. Helmer. These last few days I've been making up my inner status. Bankrupt. Chances are that within a month I'll be rotting up in the cemetery.

NORA   Shame on you! Talking that horrid way!

RANK   The thing itself is horrid—damn horrid. The worst of it, though, is all that other horror that comes first. There is only one more test I need to make. After that I'll have a pretty good idea when I'll start coming apart. There is something I want to say to you. Helmer's refined nature can't stand anything hideous. I don't want him in my sick room.

NORA   Oh, but Dr. Rank—

RANK   I don't want him there. Under no circumstances. I'll close my door to him. As soon as I have full certainty that the worst is about to begin I'll give you my card with a black cross on it. Then you'll know the last horror of destruction has started.

NORA   Today you're really quite impossible. And I had hoped you'd be in a particularly good mood.

RANK   With death on my hands? Paying for someone else's sins? Is there justice in that? And yet there isn't a single family that isn't ruled by the same law of ruthless retribution, in one way or another.

NORA (*puts her hands over her ears*)   Poppycock! Be fun! Be fun!

RANK   Well, yes. You may just as well laugh at the whole thing. My poor, innocent spine is suffering from my father's frolics as a young lieutenant.

NORA (*over by the table, left*)   Right. He was addicted to asparagus and good liver paté, wasn't he?

RANK   And truffles.

NORA   Of course. Truffles. And oysters too, I think.

RANK   And oysters. Obviously.

NORA   And all the port and champagne that go with it. It's really too bad that goodies like that ruin your backbone.

RANK   Particularly an unfortunate backbone that never enjoyed any of it.

NORA   Ah yes, that's the saddest part of it all.

RANK (*looks searchingly at her*)   Hm—

NORA (*after a brief pause*)   Why did you smile just then?

RANK   No, it was you that laughed.

NORA   No, it was you that smiled, Dr. Rank!

RANK (*gets up*)   You're more of a mischief-maker than I thought.

NORA   I feel in the mood for mischief today.

RANK   So it seems.

NORA (*with both her hands on his shoulders*)   Dear, dear Dr. Rank, don't you go and die and leave Torvald and me.

RANK   Oh, you won't miss me for very long. Those who go away are soon forgotten.

NORA (*with an anxious look*)   Do you believe that?

RANK   You'll make new friends, and then—

NORA   Who'll make new friends?

RANK   Both you and Helmer, once I'm gone. You yourself seem to have made a good start already. What was this Mrs. Linde doing here last night?

NORA   Aha—Don't tell me you're jealous of poor Kristine?

RANK   Yes, I am. She'll be my successor in this house. As soon as I have made my excuses, that woman is likely to—

NORA   Shh—not so loud. She's in there.

RANK   Today too? There you are!

NORA   She's mending my costume. My God, you really *are* unreasonable. (*sits down on the couch*) Now be nice, Dr. Rank. Tomorrow you'll see how beautifully I'll dance, and then you are to pretend I'm dancing just for you—and for Torvald too, of course. (*takes several items out of the carton*) Sit down, Dr. Rank; I want to show you something.

RANK (*sitting down*)   What?

NORA   Look.

RANK   Silk stockings.

NORA   Flesh-colored. Aren't they lovely? Now it's getting dark in here, but tomorrow—No, no. You only get to see the foot. Oh well, you might as well see all of it.

RANK   Hmm.

NORA   Why do you look so critical? Don't you think they'll fit?

RANK   That's something I can't possibly have a reasoned opinion about.

NORA (*looks at him for a moment*)   Shame on you. (*slaps his ear lightly with the stocking*) That's what you get. (*puts the things back in the carton*)

RANK   And what other treasures are you going to show me?

NORA   Nothing at all, because you're naughty. (*She hums a little and rummages in the carton.*)

RANK (*after a brief silence*)   When I sit here like this, talking confidently with you, I can't imagine—I can't possibly imagine what would have become of me if I hadn't had you and Helmer.

NORA (*smiles*)   Well, yes—I do believe you like being with us.

RANK (*in a lower voice, lost in thought*)   And then to have to go away from it all—

NORA   Nonsense. You are not going anywhere.

RANK (*as before*)   —and not to leave behind as much as a poor little token of gratitude, hardly a brief memory of someone missed, nothing but a vacant place that anyone can fill.

NORA   And what if I were to ask you—? No—

RANK   Ask me what?

NORA   For a great proof of your friendship—

RANK   Yes, yes—?

NORA   No, I mean—for an enormous favor—

RANK   Would you really for once make me as happy as all that?

NORA   But you don't even know what it is.

RANK   Well, then; tell me.

NORA   Oh, but I can't, Dr. Rank. It's altogether too much to ask—It's advice and help and a favor—

RANK   So much the better. I can't even begin to guess what it is you have in mind. So for heaven's sake tell me! Don't you trust me?

NORA   Yes, I trust you more than anyone else I know. You are my best and most faithful friend. I know that. So I will tell you. All right, Dr. Rank. There is something you can help me prevent. You know how much Torvald loves me—beyond all words. Never for a moment would he hesitate to give his life for me.

RANK (*leaning over to her*)   Nora—do you really think he's the only one—?

NORA (*with a slight start*)   Who—?

RANK   —would gladly give his life for you.

NORA (*heavily*)   I see.

RANK   I have sworn an oath to myself to tell you before I go. I'll never find a better occasion.—All right, Nora; now you know. And now you also know that you can confide in me more than in anyone else.

NORA (*gets up; in a calm, steady voice*)   Let me get by.

RANK (*makes room for her but remains seated*)   Nora—

NORA (*in the door to the front hall*)   Helene, bring the lamp in here, please. (*walks over to the stove*) Oh, dear Dr. Rank. That really wasn't very nice of you.

RANK (*gets up*)   That I have loved you as much as anybody—was that not nice?

NORA   No; not that. But that you told me. There was no need for that.

RANK   What do you mean? Have you known—?

(*The* MAID *enters with the lamp, puts it on the table, and goes out.*)

RANK   Nora—Mrs. Helmer—I'm asking you: did you know?

NORA   Oh, how can I tell what I knew and didn't know! I really can't say—But that you could be so awkward, Dr. Rank! Just when everything was so comfortable.

RANK   Well, anyway, now you know that I'm at your service with my life and soul. And now you must speak.

NORA (*looks at him*)   After what just happened?

RANK   I beg of you—let me know what it is.

NORA   There is nothing I can tell you now.

RANK   Yes, yes. You mustn't punish me this way. Please let me do for you whatever anyone *can* do.

NORA   Now there is nothing you can do. Besides, I don't think I really need any help, anyway. It's probably just my imagination. Of course that's all it is. I'm sure of it! (*sits down in the rocking chair, looks at him, smiles*) Well, well, well, Dr. Rank! What a fine gentleman you turned out to be! Aren't you ashamed of yourself, now that we have light?

RANK   No, not really. But perhaps I ought to leave—and not come back?

NORA   Don't be silly; of course not! You'll come here exactly as you have been doing. You know perfectly well that Torvald can't do without you.

RANK   Yes, but what about you?

NORA   Oh, I always think it's perfectly delightful when you come.

RANK   That's the very thing that misled me. You are a riddle to me. It has often seemed to me that you'd just as soon be with me as with Helmer.

NORA   Well, you see, there are people you love, and then there are other people you'd almost rather be with.

RANK   Yes, there is something in that.

NORA   When I lived at home with Daddy, of course I loved him most. But I always thought it was so much fun to sneak off down to the maids' room, for they never gave me good advice and they always talked about such fun things.

RANK   Aha! So it's *their* place I have taken.

NORA (*jumps up and goes over to him*)   Oh dear, kind Dr. Rank, you know very well I didn't mean it that way. Can't you see that with Torvald it is the way it used to be with Daddy?

(*The* MAID *enters from the front hall.*)

THE MAID   Ma'am! (*whispers to her and gives her a caller's card*)

NORA (*glances at the card*)   Ah! (*puts it in her pocket*)

RANK   Anything wrong?

NORA   No, no; not at all. It's nothing—just my new costume—

RANK   But your costume is lying right there!

NORA   Oh yes, that one. But this is another one. I ordered it. Torvald mustn't know—

RANK   Aha. So that's the great secret.

NORA   That's it. Why don't you go in to him, please. He's in the inner office. And keep him there for a while—

RANK   Don't worry. He won't get away. (*enters* HELMER'*s study*)

NORA (*to the* MAID)   You say he's waiting in the kitchen?

THE MAID   Yes. He came up the back stairs.

NORA   But didn't you tell him there was somebody with me?

THE MAID   Yes, but he wouldn't listen.

NORA   He won't leave?

THE MAID   No, not till he's had a word with you, ma'am.

NORA   All right. But try not to make any noise. And, Helene—don't tell anyone he's here. It's supposed to be a surprise for my husband.

THE MAID   I understand, ma'am—(*She leaves.*)

NORA   The terrible is happening. It's happening, after all. No, no, no. It can't happen. It won't happen. (*She bolts the study door.*)

(*The* MAID *opens the front hall door for* KROGSTAD *and closes the door behind him. He wears a fur coat for traveling, boots, and a fur hat.*)

NORA (*toward him*)   Keep your voice down. My husband's home.

KROGSTAD   That's all right.

NORA   What do you want?

KROGSTAD   To find out something.

NORA   Be quick, then. What is it?

KROGSTAD   I expect you know I've been fired.

NORA   I couldn't prevent it, Mr. Krogstad. I fought for you as long and as hard as I could but it didn't do any good.

KROGSTAD   Your husband doesn't love you any more than that? He knows what I can do to you, and yet he runs the risk—

NORA   Surely you didn't think I'd tell him?

KROGSTAD   No, I really didn't. It wouldn't be like Torvald Helmer to show that kind of guts—

NORA   Mr. Krogstad, I insist that you show respect for my husband.

KROGSTAD   By all means. All due respect. But since you're so anxious to keep this a secret, may I assume that you are a little better informed than yesterday about exactly what you have done?

NORA   Better than *you* could ever teach me.

KROGSTAD   Of course. Such a bad lawyer as I am—

NORA   What do you want of me?

KROGSTAD   I just wanted to find out how you are, Mrs. Helmer. I've been thinking about you all day. You see, even a bill collector, a pen pusher, a—anyway, someone like me—even he has a little of what they call a heart.

NORA   Then show it. Think of my little children.

KROGSTAD   Have you and your husband thought of mine? Never mind. All I want to tell you is that you don't need to take this business too seriously. I have no intention of bringing charges right away.

NORA   Oh no, you wouldn't; would you? I knew you wouldn't.

KROGSTAD   The whole thing can be settled quite amiably. Nobody else needs to know anything. It will be between the three of us.

NORA My husband must never find out about this.

KROGSTAD How are you going to prevent that? Maybe you can pay me the balance on the loan?

NORA No, not right now.

KROGSTAD Or do you have a way of raising the money one of these next few days?

NORA None I intend to make use of.

KROGSTAD It wouldn't do you any good, anyway. Even if you had the cash in your hand right this minute, I wouldn't give you your note back. It wouldn't make any difference *how* much money you offered me.

NORA Then you'll have to tell me what you plan to use the note *for.*

KROGSTAD Just keep it; that's all. Have it on hand, so to speak. I won't say a word to anybody else. So if you've been thinking about doing something desperate—

NORA I have.

KROGSTAD —like leaving house and home—

NORA I have!

KROGSTAD —or even something worse—

NORA How did you know?

KROGSTAD —then: don't.

NORA How did you know I was thinking of *that?*

KROGSTAD Most of us do, right at first. I did, too, but when it came down to it I didn't have the courage—

NORA (*tonelessly*) Nor do I.

KROGSTAD (*relieved*) See what I mean? I thought so. You don't either.

NORA I don't. I don't.

KROGSTAD Besides, it would be very silly of you. Once that first domestic blowup is behind you—. Here in my pocket is a letter for your husband.

NORA Telling him everything?

KROGSTAD As delicately as possible.

NORA (*quickly*) He mustn't get that letter. Tear it up. I'll get you the money somehow.

KROGSTAD Excuse me, Mrs. Helmer, I thought I just told you—

NORA I'm not talking about the money I owe you. Just let me know how much money you want from my husband, and I'll get it for you.

KROGSTAD I want no money from your husband.

NORA Then, what *do* you want?

KROGSTAD I'll tell you, Mrs. Helmer. I want to rehabilitate myself; I want to get up in the world; and your husband is going to help me. For a year and a half I haven't done anything disreputable. All that time I have been struggling with the most miserable circumstances. I was content to work my way up step by step. Now I've been kicked out, and I'm no longer satisfied just getting my old job back. I want more than that; I want to get to the top. I'm being quite serious. I want the bank to take me back but in a higher position. I want your husband to create a new job for me—

NORA   He'll never do that!

KROGSTAD   He will. I know him. He won't dare not to. And once I'm back inside and he and I are working together, you'll see! Within a year I'll be the manager's right hand. It will be Nils Krogstad and not Torvald Helmer who'll be running the Mutual Bank!

NORA   You'll never see that happen!

KROGSTAD   Are you thinking of—?

NORA   Now I *do* have the courage.

KROGSTAD   You can't scare me. A fine, spoiled lady like you—

NORA   You'll see, you'll see!

KROGSTAD   Under the ice, perhaps? Down into that cold, black water? Then spring comes, and you float up again—hideous, can't be identified, hair all gone—

NORA   You don't frighten me.

KROGSTAD   Nor you me. One doesn't do that sort of thing, Mrs. Helmer. Besides, what good would it do? He'd still be in my power.

NORA   Afterwards? When I'm no longer—?

KROGSTAD   Aren't you forgetting that your reputation would be in my hands?

(NORA *stares at him, speechless.*)

KROGSTAD   All right; now I've told you what to expect. So don't do anything foolish. When Helmer gets my letter I expect to hear from him. And don't you forget that it's your husband himself who forces me to use such means again. That I'll never forgive him. Goodbye, Mrs. Helmer. (*goes out through the hall*)

NORA (*at the door, opens it a little, listens*)   He's going. And no letter. Of course not! That would be impossible. (*opens the door more*) What's he doing? He's still there. Doesn't go down. Having second thoughts—? Will he—?

(*The sound of a letter dropping into the mailbox. Then* KROGSTAD's *steps are heard going down the stairs, gradually dying away.*)

NORA (*with a muted cry runs forward to the table by the couch; brief pause*)   In the mailbox. (*tiptoes back to the door to the front hall*) There it is. Torvald, Torvald—now we're lost!

MRS. LINDE (*enters from the left, carrying* NORA's *Capri costume*)   There now. I think it's all fixed. Why don't we try it on you—

NORA (*in a low, hoarse voice*)   Kristine, come here.

MRS. LINDE   What's wrong with you? You look quite beside yourself.

NORA   Come over here. Do you see that letter? There, look—through the glass in the mailbox.

MRS. LINDE   Yes, yes; I see it.

NORA   That letter is from Krogstad.

MRS. LINDE   Nora—it was Krogstad who lent you the money!

NORA   Yes, and now Torvald will find out about it.

MRS. LINDE   Oh believe me, Nora. That's the best thing for both of you.

NORA   There's more to it than you know. I forged a signature—

MRS. LINDE   Oh my God—!

NORA   I just want to tell you this, Kristine, that you must be my witness.

MRS. LINDE   Witness? How? Witness to what?

NORA   If I lose my mind—and that could very well happen—

MRS. LINDE   Nora!

NORA   —or if something were to happen to me—something that made it impossible for me to be here—

MRS. LINDE   Nora, Nora! You're not yourself!

NORA   —and if someone were to take all the blame, assume the whole responsibility—Do you understand—?

MRS. LINDE   Yes, yes; but how can you think—!

NORA   Then you are to witness that that's not so, Kristine. I am not beside myself. I am perfectly rational, and what I'm telling you is that nobody else has known about this. I've done it all by myself, the whole thing. Just remember that.

MRS. LINDE   I will. But I don't understand any of it.

NORA   Oh, how could you! For it's the wonderful that's about to happen.

MRS. LINDE   The wonderful?

NORA   Yes, the wonderful. But it's so terrible, Kristine. It mustn't happen for anything in the whole world!

MRS. LINDE   I'm going over to talk to Krogstad right now.

NORA   No, don't. Don't go to him. He'll do something bad to you.

MRS. LINDE   There was a time when he would have done anything for me.

NORA   He!

MRS. LINDE   Where does he live?

NORA   Oh, I don't know—Yes, wait a minute—(*reaches into her pocket*)—here's his card.—But the letter, the letter—!

HELMER   (*in his study, knocks on the door*)   Nora!

NORA   (*cries out in fear*)   Oh, what is it? What do you want?

HELMER   That's all right. Nothing to be scared about. We're not coming in. For one thing, you've bolted the door, you know. Are you modeling your costume?

NORA   Yes, yes; I am. I'm going to be so pretty, Torvald.

MRS. LINDE   (*having looked at the card*)   He lives just around the corner.

NORA   Yes, but it's no use. Nothing can save us now. The letter is in the mailbox.

MRS. LINDE   And your husband has the key?

NORA   Yes. He always keeps it with him.

MRS. LINDE Krogstad must ask for his letter back, unread. He's got to think up some pretext or other—

NORA But this is just the time of day when Torvald—

MRS. LINDE Delay him. Go in to him. I'll be back as soon as I can. (*She hurries out through the hall door.*)

NORA (*walks over to* HELMER'*s door, opens it, and peeks in*) Torvald.

HELMER (*still offstage*) Well, well! So now one's allowed in one's own living room again. Come on, Rank. Now we'll see—(*in the doorway*) But what's this?

NORA What, Torvald dear?

HELMER Rank prepared me for a splendid metamorphosis.

RANK (*in the doorway*) That's how I understood it. Evidently I was mistaken.

NORA Nobody gets to admire me in my costume before tomorrow.

HELMER But, dearest Nora—you look all done in. Have you been practicing too hard?

NORA No, I haven't practiced at all.

HELMER But you'll have to, you know.

NORA I know it, Torvald. I simply must. But I can't do a thing unless you help me. I have forgotten everything.

HELMER Oh it will all come back. We'll work on it.

NORA Oh yes, please, Torvald. You just have to help me. Promise? I am so nervous. That big party—. You mustn't do anything else tonight. Not a bit of business. Don't even touch a pen. Will you promise, Torvald?

HELMER I promise. Tonight I'll be entirely at your service—you helpless little thing.—Just a moment, though. First I want to—(*goes to the door to the front hall*)

NORA What are you doing out there?

HELMER Just looking to see if there's any mail.

NORA No, no! Don't, Torvald!

HELMER Why not?

NORA Torvald, I beg you. There is no mail.

HELMER Let me just look, anyway. (*is about to go out*)

(NORA *by the piano, plays the first bars of the tarantella dance.*)

HELMER (*halts at the door*) Aha!

NORA I won't be able to dance tomorrow if I don't get to practice with you.

HELMER (*goes to her*) Are you really all that scared, Nora dear?

NORA Yes, so terribly scared. Let's try it right now. There's still time before we eat. Oh please, sit down and play for me, Torvald. Teach me, coach me, the way you always do.

HELMER Of course I will, my darling, if that's what you want. (*sits down at the piano*)

(NORA *takes the tambourine out of the carton, as well as a long, many-colored shawl. She quickly drapes the shawl around herself, then leaps into the middle of the floor.*)

NORA   Play for me! I want to dance!

(HELMER *plays and* NORA *dances.* DR. RANK *stands by the piano behind* HELMER *and watches.*)

HELMER (*playing*)   Slow down, slow down!

NORA   Can't!

HELMER   Not so violent, Nora!

NORA   It has to be this way.

HELMER (*stops playing*)   No, no. This won't do at all.

NORA (*laughing, swinging her tambourine*)   What did I tell you?

RANK   Why don't you let me play?

HELMER (*getting up*)   Good idea. Then I can direct her better.

(RANK *sits down at the piano and starts playing.* NORA *dances more and more wildly.* HELMER *stands over by the stove, repeatedly correcting her. She doesn't seem to hear. Her hair comes loose and falls down over her shoulders. She doesn't notice but keeps on dancing.* MRS. LINDE *enters.*)

MRS. LINDE (*stops by the door, dumbfounded*)   Ah—!

NORA (*dancing*)   We're having such fun, Kristine!

HELMER   My dearest Nora, you're dancing as if it were a matter of life and death!

NORA   It is! It is!

HELMER   Rank, stop. This is sheer madness. Stop, I say!

(RANK *stops playing;* NORA *suddenly stops dancing.*)

HELMER (*goes over to her*)   If I hadn't seen it I wouldn't have believed it. You've forgotten every single thing I ever taught you.

NORA (*tosses away the tambourine*)   See? I told you.

HELMER   Well! You certainly need coaching.

NORA   Didn't I tell you I did? Now you've seen for yourself. I'll need your help till the very minute we're leaving for the party. Will you promise, Torvald?

HELMER   You can count on it.

NORA   You're not to think of anything except me—not tonight and not tomorrow. You're not to read any letters—not to look in the mailbox—

HELMER   Ah, I see. You're still afraid of that man.

NORA   Yes—yes, that too.

HELMER   Nora, I can tell from looking at you. There's a letter from him out there.

NORA   I don't know. I think so. But you're not to read it now. I don't want anything ugly to come between us before it's all over.

RANK (*to* HELMER *in a low voice*)   Better not argue with her.

HELMER (*throws his arm around her*)   The child shall have her way. But tomorrow night, when you've done your dance—

NORA   Then you'll be free.

THE MAID (*in the door, right*)   Dinner can be served any time, ma'am.

NORA   We want champagne, Helene.

THE MAID   Very good, ma'am. (*goes out*)

HELMER   Aha! Having a party, eh?

NORA   Champagne from now till sunrise! (*calls out*) And some macaroons, Helene. Lots!—just this once.

HELMER (*taking her hands*)   There, there—I don't like this wild—frenzy—Be my own sweet little lark again, the way you always are.

NORA   Oh, I will. But you go on in. You too, Dr. Rank. Kristine, please help me put up my hair.

RANK (*in a low voice to* HELMER *as they go out*)   You don't think she is—you know—expecting—?

HELMER   Oh no. Nothing like that. It's just this childish fear I was telling you about. (*They go out, right.*)

NORA   Well?

MRS. LINDE   Left town.

NORA   I saw it in your face.

MRS. LINDE   He'll be back tomorrow night. I left him a note.

NORA   You shouldn't have. I don't want you to try to stop anything. You see, it's a kind of ecstasy, too, this waiting for the wonderful.

MRS. LINDE   But what is it you're waiting *for*?

NORA   You wouldn't understand. Why don't you go in to the others. I'll be there in a minute.

(MRS. LINDE *enters the dining room, right.*)

NORA (*stands still for a little while, as if collecting herself; she looks at her watch*)   Five o'clock. Seven hours till midnight. Twenty-four more hours till next midnight. Then the tarantella is over. Twenty-four plus seven—thirty-one more hours to live.

HELMER (*in the door, right*)   What's happening to my little lark?

NORA (*to him, with open arms*)   Here's your lark!

Act III

The same room. The table by the couch and the chairs around it have been moved to the middle of the floor. A lighted lamp is on the table. The door to the front hall is open. Dance music is heard from upstairs.

   MRS. LINDE *is seated by the table, idly leafing through the pages of a book. She tries to read but seems unable to concentrate. Once or twice she turns her head in the direction of the door, anxiously listening.*

MRS. LINDE (*looks at her watch*)   Not yet. It's almost too late. If only he hasn't— (*listens again*) Ah! There he is. (*She goes to the hall and opens the front door*

carefully. Quiet footsteps on the stairs. She whispers.) Come in. There's nobody here.

KROGSTAD (*in the door*)   I found your note when I got home. What's this all about?

MRS. LINDE   I've got to talk to you.

KROGSTAD   Oh? And it has to be here?

MRS. LINDE   It couldn't be at my place. My room doesn't have a separate entrance. Come in. We're quite alone. The maid is asleep and the Helmers are
at a party upstairs.

KROGSTAD (*entering*)   Really? The Helmers are dancing tonight, are they?

MRS. LINDE   And why not?

KROGSTAD   You're right. Why not, indeed.

MRS. LINDE   All right, Krogstad. Let's talk, you and I.

KROGSTAD   I didn't know we had anything to talk about.

MRS. LINDE   We have much to talk about.

KROGSTAD   I didn't think so.

MRS. LINDE   No, because you've never really understood me.

KROGSTAD   What was there to understand? What happened was perfectly commonplace. A heartless woman jilts a man when she gets a more attractive
offer.

MRS. LINDE   Do you think I'm all that heartless? And do you think it was easy
for me to break with you?

KROGSTAD   No?

MRS. LINDE   You really thought it was?

KROGSTAD   If it wasn't, why did you write the way you did that time?

MRS. LINDE   What else could I do? If I had to make a break, I also had the duty
to destroy whatever feelings you had for me.

KROGSTAD (*clenching his hands*)   So that's the way it was. And you did—
that—just for money!

MRS. LINDE   Don't forget I had a helpless mother and two small brothers. We
couldn't wait for you, Krogstad. You know yourself how uncertain your
prospects were then.

KROGSTAD   All right. But you still didn't have the right to throw me over for
somebody else.

MRS. LINDE   I don't know. I have asked myself that question many times. Did I
have that right?

KROGSTAD (*in a lower voice*)   When I lost you I lost my footing. Look at me
now. A shipwrecked man on a raft.

MRS. LINDE   Rescue may be near.

KROGSTAD   It *was* near. Then you came between.

MRS. LINDE   I didn't know that, Krogstad. Only today did I find out it's your job
I'm taking over in the bank.

KROGSTAD   I believe you when you say so. But now that you *do* know, aren't you
going to step aside?

MRS. LINDE   No, for it wouldn't do you any good.

KROGSTAD   Whether it would or not—*I* would do it.

MRS. LINDE   I have learned common sense. Life and hard necessity have taught me that.

KROGSTAD   And life has taught me not to believe in pretty speeches.

MRS. LINDE   Then life has taught you a very sensible thing. But you do believe in actions, don't you?

KROGSTAD   How do you mean?

MRS. LINDE   You referred to yourself just now as a shipwrecked man.

KROGSTAD   It seems to me I had every reason to do so.

MRS. LINDE   And I am a shipwrecked woman. No one to grieve for, no one to care for.

KROGSTAD   You made your choice.

MRS. LINDE   I had no other choice that time.

KROGSTAD   Let's say you didn't. What then?

MRS. LINDE   Krogstad, how would it be if we two shipwrecked people got together?

KROGSTAD   What's this!

MRS. LINDE   Two on one wreck are better off than each on his own.

KROGSTAD   Kristine!

MRS. LINDE   Why do you think I came to town?

KROGSTAD   Surely not because of me?

MRS. LINDE   If I'm going to live at all I must work. All my life, for as long as I can remember, I have worked. That's been my one and only pleasure. But now that I'm all alone in the world I feel nothing but this terrible emptiness and desolation. There is no joy in working just for yourself. Krogstad—give me someone and something to work for.

KROGSTAD   I don't believe this. Only hysterical females go in for that kind of high-minded self-sacrifice.

MRS. LINDE   Did you ever know me to be hysterical?

KROGSTAD   You really could do this? Listen—do you know about my past? All of it?

MRS. LINDE   Yes, I do.

KROGSTAD   Do you also know what people think of me around here?

MRS. LINDE   A little while ago you sounded as if you thought that together with me you might have become a different person.

KROGSTAD   I'm sure of it.

MRS. LINDE   Couldn't that still be?

KROGSTAD   Kristine—do you know what you are doing? Yes, I see you do. And you think you have the courage—?

MRS. LINDE   I need someone to be a mother to, and your children need a mother. You and I need one another. Nils, I believe in you—in the real you. Together with you I dare to do anything.

KROGSTAD (*seizes her hands*)   Thanks, thanks, Kristine—Now I know I'll raise myself in the eyes of others—Ah, but I forget—!

MRS. LINDE (*listening*)   Shh!—there's the tarantella. You must go; hurry!

KROGSTAD   Why? What is it?

MRS. LINDE   Do you hear what they're playing up there? When that dance is over they'll be down.

KROGSTAD   All right. I'm leaving. The whole thing is pointless, anyway. Of course you don't know what I'm doing to the Helmers.

MRS. LINDE   Yes, Krogstad; I do know.

KROGSTAD   Still, you're brave enough—?

MRS. LINDE   I very well understand to what extremes despair can drive a man like you.

KROGSTAD   If only it could be undone!

MRS. LINDE   It could, for your letter is still out there in the mailbox.

KROGSTAD   Are you sure?

MRS. LINDE   Quite sure. But—

KROGSTAD (*looks searchingly at her*)   Maybe I'm beginning to understand. You want to save your friend at any cost. Be honest with me. That's it, isn't it?

MRS. LINDE   Krogstad, you may sell yourself once for somebody else's sake, but you don't do it twice.

KROGSTAD   I'll demand my letter back.

MRS. LINDE   No, no.

KROGSTAD   Yes, of course. I'll wait here till Helmer comes down. Then I'll ask him for my letter. I'll tell him it's just about my dismissal—that he shouldn't read it.

MRS. LINDE   No, Krogstad. You are not to ask for that letter back.

KROGSTAD   But tell me—wasn't that the real reason you wanted to meet me here?

MRS. LINDE   At first it was, because I was so frightened. But that was yesterday. Since then I have seen the most incredible things going on in this house. Helmer must learn the whole truth. This miserable secret must come out in the open; those two must come to a full understanding. They simply can't continue with all this concealment and evasion.

KROGSTAD   All right; if you want to take that chance. But there is one thing I *can* do, and I'll do that right now.

MRS. LINDE (*listening*)   But hurry! Go! The dance is over. We aren't safe another minute.

KROGSTAD   I'll be waiting for you downstairs.

MRS. LINDE   Yes, do. You must see me home.

KROGSTAD   I've never been so happy in my whole life. (*He leaves through the front door. The door between the living room and the front hall remains open.*)

MRS. LINDE (*straightens up the room a little and gets her things ready*)   What a change! Oh yes!—what a change! People to work for—to live for—a home to bring happiness to. I can't wait to get to work—! If only they'd come soon—(*listens*) Ah, there they are. Get my coat on—(*puts on her coat and hat*)

(HELMER's *and* NORA's *voices are heard outside. A key is turned in the lock, and* HELMER *almost forces* NORA *into the hall. She is dressed in her Italian costume, with a big black shawl over her shoulders. He is in evening dress under an open black cloak.*)

NORA (*in the door, still resisting*)   No, no, no! I don't want to! I want to go back upstairs. I don't want to leave so early.

HELMER   But dearest Nora—

NORA   Oh please, Torvald—please! I'm asking you as nicely as I can—just another hour!

HELMER   Not another minute, sweet. You know we agreed. There now. Get inside. You'll catch a cold out here. (*She still resists, but he guides her gently into the room.*)

MRS. LINDE   Good evening.

NORA   Kristine!

HELMER   Ah, Mrs. Linde. Still here?

MRS. LINDE   I know. I really should apologize, but I so much wanted to see Nora in her costume.

NORA   You've been waiting up for me?

MRS. LINDE   Yes, unfortunately I didn't get here in time. You were already upstairs, but I just didn't feel like leaving till I had seen you.

HELMER (*removing* NORA's *shawl*)   Yes, do take a good look at her, Mrs. Linde. I think I may say she's worth looking at. Isn't she lovely?

MRS. LINDE   She certainly is—

HELMER   Isn't she a miracle of loveliness, though? That was the general opinion at the party, too. But dreadfully obstinate—that she is, the sweet little thing. What can we do about that? Will you believe it—I practically had to use force to get her away.

NORA   Oh Torvald, you're going to be sorry you didn't give me even half an hour more.

HELMER   See what I mean, Mrs. Linde? She dances the tarantella—she is a tremendous success—quite deservedly so, though perhaps her performance was a little too natural—I mean, more than could be reconciled with the rules of art. But all right! The point is: she's a success, a tremendous success. So should I let her stay after that? Weaken the effect? Of course not. So I take my lovely little Capri girl—I might say, my capricious little Capri girl— under my arm—a quick turn around the room—a graceful bow in all directions, and—as they say in the novels—the beautiful apparition is gone. A finale should always be done for effect, Mrs. Linde, but there doesn't seem to be any way of getting that into Nora's head. Poooh—! It's hot in here. (*throws his cloak down on a chair and opens the door to his room*) Why, it's dark in here! Of course. Excuse me—(*goes inside and lights a couple of candles*)

NORA (*in a hurried, breathless whisper*)   Well?

MRS. LINDE (*in a low voice*)   I have talked to him.

NORA   And—?

MRS. LINDE   Nora—you've got to tell your husband everything.

NORA (*no expression in her voice*)   I knew it.

MRS. LINDE   You have nothing to fear from Krogstad. But you must speak.

NORA   I'll say nothing.

MRS. LINDE   Then the letter will.

NORA   Thank you, Kristine. Now I know what I have to do. Shh!

HELMER (*returning*)   Well, Mrs. Linde, have you looked your fill?

MRS. LINDE   Yes. And now I'll say goodnight.

HELMER   So soon? Is that your knitting?

MRS. LINDE (*takes it*)   Yes, thank you. I almost forgot.

HELMER   So you knit, do you?

MRS. LINDE   Oh yes.

HELMER   You know—you ought to take up embroidery instead.

MRS. LINDE   Oh? Why?

HELMER   Because it's so much more beautiful. Look. You hold the embroidery so—in your left hand. Than with your right you move the needle—like this—in an easy, elongated arc—you see?

MRS. LINDE   Maybe you're right—

HELMER   Knitting, on the other hand, can never be anything but ugly. Look here: arms pressed close to the sides—the needles going up and down—there's something Chinese about it somehow—. That really was an excellent champagne they served us tonight.

MRS. LINDE   Well, goodnight! Nora. And don't be obstinate any more.

HELMER   Well said, Mrs. Linde!

MRS. LINDE   Goodnight, sir.

HELMER (*sees her to the front door*)   Goodnight, goodnight. I hope you'll get home all right? I'd be very glad to—but of course you don't have far to walk, do you? Goodnight, goodnight. (*She leaves. He closes the door behind her and returns to the living room.*) There! At last we got rid of her. She really is an incredible bore, that woman.

NORA   Aren't you very tired, Torvald?

HELMER   No, not in the least.

NORA   Not sleepy either?

HELMER   Not at all. Quite the opposite. I feel enormously—animated. How about you? Yes, you do look tired and sleepy.

NORA   Yes, I am very tired. Soon I'll be asleep.

HELMER   What did I tell you? I was right, wasn't I? Good thing I didn't let you stay any longer.

NORA   Everything you do is right.

HELMER (*kissing her forehead*)   Now my little lark is talking like a human being. But did you notice what splendid spirits Rank was in tonight?

NORA   Was he? I didn't notice. I didn't get to talk with him.

HELMER   Nor did I—hardly. But I haven't seen him in such a good mood for a long time. (*looks at her, comes closer to her*) Ah! It does feel good to be back in our own home again, to be quite alone with you—my young, lovely, ravishing woman!

NORA   Don't look at me like that, Torvald!

HELMER   Am I not to look at my most precious possession? All that loveliness that is mine, nobody's but mine, all of it mine.

NORA (*walks to the other side of the table*)   I won't have you talk to me like that tonight.

HELMER (*follows her*)   The Tarantella is still in your blood. I can tell. That only makes you all the more alluring. Listen! The guests are beginning to leave. (*softly*) Nora—soon the whole house will be quiet.

NORA   Yes, I hope so.

HELMER   Yes, don't you, my darling? Do you know—when I'm at a party with you, like tonight—do you know why I hardly ever talk to you, why I keep away from you, only look at you once in a while—a few stolen glances—do you know why I do that? It's because I pretend that you are my secret love, my young, secret bride-to-be, and nobody has the slightest suspicion that there is anything between us.

NORA   Yes, I know. All your thoughts are with me.

HELMER   Then when we're leaving and I lay your shawl around your delicate young shoulders—around that wonderful curve of your neck—then I imagine you're my young bride, that we're coming away from the wedding, that I am taking you to my home for the first time—that I am alone with you for the first time—quite alone with you, you young, trembling beauty! I have desired you all evening—there hasn't been a longing in me that hasn't been for you. When you were dancing the tarantella, chasing, inviting—my blood was on fire; I couldn't stand it any longer—that's why I brought you down so early—

NORA   Leave me now, Torvald. Please! I don't want all this.

HELMER   What do you mean? You're only playing your little teasing bird game with me; aren't you, Nora? Don't want to? I'm your husband, aren't I?

(*There is a knock on the front door.*)

NORA (*with a start*)   Did you hear that—?

HELMER (*on his way to the hall*)   Who is it?

RANK (*outside*)   It's me. May I come in for a moment?

HELMER (*in a low voice, annoyed*)   Oh, what does he want now? (*aloud*) Just a minute. (*opens the door*) Well! How good of you not to pass by our door.

RANK   I thought I heard your voice, so I felt like saying hello. (*looks around*) Ah yes—this dear, familiar room. What a cozy, comfortable place you have here, you two.

HELMER   Looked to me as if you were quite comfortable upstairs too.
RANK   I certainly was. Why not? Why not enjoy all you can in this world? As much as you can for as long as you can, anyway. Excellent wine.
HELMER   The champagne, particularly.
RANK   You noticed that too? Incredible how much I managed to put away.
NORA   Torvald drank a lot of champagne tonight, too.
RANK   Did he?
NORA   Yes, he did, and then he's always so much fun afterwards.
RANK   Well, why not have some fun in the evening after a well spent day?
HELMER   Well spent? I'm afraid I can't claim that.
RANK (*slapping him lightly on the shoulder*)   But you see, I can!
NORA   Dr. Rank, I believe you must have been conducting a scientific test today.
RANK   Exactly.
HELMER   What do you know—little Nora talking about scientific tests!
NORA   May I congratulate you on the result?
RANK   You may indeed.
NORA   It was a good one?
RANK   The best possible for both doctor and patient—certainty.
NORA (*a quick query*)   Certainty?
RANK   Absolute certainty. So why shouldn't I have myself an enjoyable evening afterwards?
NORA   I quite agree with you, Dr. Rank. You should.
HELMER   And so do I. If only you don't pay for it tomorrow.
RANK   Oh well—you get nothing for nothing in this world.
NORA   Dr. Rank—you are fond of costume parties, aren't you?
RANK   Yes, particularly when there is a reasonable number of amusing disguises.
NORA   Listen—what are the two of us going to be the next time?
HELMER   You frivolous little thing! Already thinking about the next party!
RANK   You and I? That's easy. You'll be Fortune's Child.
HELMER   Yes, but what is a fitting costume for that?
RANK   Let your wife appear just the way she always is.
HELMER   Beautiful. Very good indeed. But how about yourself? Don't you know what you'll go as?
RANK   Yes, my friend. I know precisely what I'll be.
HELMER   Yes?
RANK   At the next masquerade I'll be invisible.
HELMER   That's a funny idea.
RANK   There's a certain black hat—you've heard about the hat that makes you invisible, haven't you? You put that on, and nobody can see you.
HELMER (*suppressing a smile*)   I guess that's right.
RANK   But I'm forgetting what I came for. Helmer, give me a cigar—one of your dark Havanas.

HELMER   With the greatest pleasure. (*offers him his case*)

RANK (*takes one and cuts off the tip*)   Thanks.

NORA (*striking a match*)   Let me give you a light.

RANK   Thanks. (*She holds the match; he lights his cigar.*) And now goodbye!

HELMER   Goodbye, goodbye, my friend.

NORA   Sleep well, Dr. Rank.

RANK   I thank you.

NORA   Wish me the same.

RANK   You? Well, if you really want me to—. Sleep well. And thanks for the light. (*He nods to both of them and goes out.*)

HELMER (*in a low voice*)   He had had quite a bit to drink.

NORA (*absently*)   Maybe so.

(HELMER *takes out his keys and goes out into the hall.*)

NORA   Torvald—what are you doing out there?

HELMER   Emptying the mailbox. It is quite full. There wouldn't be room for the newspapers in the morning—

NORA   Are you going to work tonight?

HELMER   You know very well I won't.—Say! What's this? Somebody's been at the lock.

NORA   The lock—?

HELMER   Yes. Why, I wonder. I hate to think that any of the maids—. Here's a broken hairpin. It's one of yours. Nora.

NORA (*quickly*)   Then it must be one of the children.

HELMER   You better make damn sure they stop that. Hm, hm.—There! I got it open, finally. (*gathers up the mail, calls out to the kitchen*) Helene?—Oh Helene—turn out the light here in the hall, will you? (*He comes back into the living room and closes the door.*) Look how it's been piling up. (*shows her the bundle of letters, starts leafing through it*) What's this?

NORA (*by the window*)   The letter! Oh no, no, Torvald!

HELMER   Two calling cards—from Rank.

NORA   From Dr. Rank?

HELMER (*looking at them*)   "Doctor medicinae Rank." They were on top. He must have put them there when he left just now.

NORA   Anything written on them?

HELMER   A black cross above the name. What a macabre idea. Like announcing his own death.

NORA   That's what it is.

HELMER   Hm? You know about this? Has he said anything to you?

NORA   That card means he has said goodbye to us. He'll lock himself up to die.

HELMER   My poor friend. I knew of course he wouldn't be with me very long. But so soon—. And hiding himself away like a wounded animal—

NORA   When it has to be, it's better it happens without words. Don't you think so, Torvald?

HELMER (*walking up and down*)   He'd grown so close to us. I find it hard to think of him as gone. With his suffering and loneliness he was like a clouded background for our happy sunshine. Well, it may be better this way. For him, at any rate. (*stops*) And perhaps for us, too, Nora. For now we have no-body but each other. (*embraces her*) Oh you—my beloved wife! I feel I just can't hold you close enough. Do you know, Nora—many times I have wished some great danger threatened you, so I could risk my life and blood and everything—everything, for your sake.

NORA (*frees herself and says in a strong and firm voice*)   I think you should go and read your letters now, Torvald.

HELMER   No, no—not tonight. I want to be with you, my darling.

NORA   With the thought of your dying friend—?

HELMER   You are right. This has shaken both of us. Something not beautiful has come between us. Thoughts of death and dissolution. We must try to get over it—out of it. Till then—we'll each go to our own room.

NORA (*her arms around his neck*)   Torvald—goodnight! Goodnight!

HELMER (*kisses her forehead*)   Goodnight, my little songbird. Sleep well, Nora. Now I'll read my letters. (*He goes into his room, carrying the mail; closes the door.*)

NORA (*her eyes desperate, her hands groping, finds Helmer's black cloak and throws it around her; she whispers, quickly, brokenly, hoarsely*)   Never see him again. Never. Never. Never. (*puts her shawl over her head*) And never see the children again, either. Never; never.—The black, icy water—fathomless—this—! If only it was all over.—Now he has it. Now he's reading it. No, no; not yet. Torvald—goodbye—you—the children—

(*She is about to hurry through the hall, when* HELMER *flings open the door to his room and stands there with an open letter in his hand.*)

HELMER   Nora!

NORA (*cries out*)   Ah—!

HELMER   What is it? You know what's in this letter?

NORA   Yes, I do! Let me go! Let me out!

HELMER (*holds her back*)   Where do you think you're going?

NORA (*trying to tear herself loose from him*)   I won't let you save me, Torvald!

HELMER (*tumbles back*)   True! Is it true what he writes? Oh my God! No, no—this can't possibly be true.

NORA   It is true. I have loved you more than anything else in the whole world.

HELMER   Oh, don't give me any silly excuses.

NORA (*taking a step toward him*)   Torvald—!

HELMER   You wretch! What have you done!

NORA   Let me go. You are not to sacrifice yourself for me. You are not to take the blame.

HELMER   No more playacting. (*locks the door to the front hall*) You'll stay here and answer me. Do you understand what you have done? Answer me! Do you understand?

NORA (*gazes steadily at him with an increasingly frozen expression*)   Yes. Now I'm beginning to understand.

HELMER (*walking up and down*)   What a dreadful awakening. All these years—all these eight years—she, my pride and my joy—a hypocrite, a liar—oh worse! worse!—a criminal! Oh, the bottomless ugliness in all this! Damn! Damn! Damn!

(NORA, *silent, keeps gazing at him.*)

HELMER (*stops in front of her*)   I ought to have guessed that something like this would happen. I should have expected it. All your father's loose principles—Silence! You have inherited every one of your father's loose principles. No religion, no morals, no sense of duty—. Now I am being punished for my leniency with him. I did it for your sake, and this is how you pay me back.

NORA   Yes. This is how.

HELMER   You have ruined all my happiness. My whole future—that's what you have destroyed. Oh, it's terrible to think about. I am at the mercy of an unscrupulous man. He can do with me whatever he likes, demand anything of me, command me and dispose of me just as he pleases—I dare not say a word! To go down so miserably, to be destroyed—all because of an irresponsible woman!

NORA   When I am gone from the world, you'll be free.

HELMER   No noble gestures, please. Your father was always full of such phrases too. What good would it do me if you were gone from the world, as you put it? Not the slightest good at all. He could still make the whole thing public, and if he did, people would be likely to think I had been your accomplice. They might even think it was my idea—that it was I who urged you to do it! And for all this I have you to thank—you, whom I've borne on my hands through all the years of our marriage. *Now* do you understand what you've done to me?

NORA (*with cold calm*)   Yes.

HELMER   I just can't get it into my head that this is happening; it's all so incredible. But we have to come to terms with it somehow. Take your shawl off. Take it off, I say! I have to satisfy him one way or another. The whole affair must be kept quiet at whatever cost.—And as far as you and I are concerned, nothing must seem to have changed. I'm talking about appearances, of course. You'll go on living here; that goes without saying. But I won't let you bring up the children; I dare not trust you with them.—Oh! Having to say this to one I have loved so much, and whom I still—! But all that is past. It's not a question of happiness any more but of hanging on to what can be salvaged—pieces, appearances—(*The doorbell rings.*)

HELMER (*jumps*)   What's that? So late. Is the worst—? Has he—! Hide, Nora! Say you're sick.

(NORA *doesn't move.* HELMER *opens the door to the hall.*)

THE MAID (*half dressed, out in the hall*)   A letter for your wife, sir.

HELMER   Give it to me. (*takes the letter and closes the door*) Yes, it's from him. But I won't let you have it. I'll read it myself.

NORA   Yes—you read it.

HELMER (*by the lamp*)   I hardly dare. Perhaps we're lost, both you and I. No; I've got to know. (*tears the letter open, glances through it, looks at an enclosure; a cry of joy*) Nora!

(NORA *looks at him with a question in her eyes.*)

HELMER   Nora!—No, I must read it again.—Yes, yes; it is so! I'm saved! Nora, I'm saved!

NORA   And I?

HELMER   You too, of course; we're both saved, both you and I. Look! He's returning your note. He writes that he's sorry, he regrets, a happy turn in his life—oh, it doesn't matter what he writes. We're saved, Nora! Nobody can do anything to you now. Oh Nora, Nora—. No, I want to get rid of this disgusting thing first. Let me see—(*looks at the signature*) No, I don't want to see it. I don't want it to be more than a bad dream, the whole thing. (*tears up the note and both letters, throws the pieces in the stove, and watches them burn*) There! Now it's gone.—He wrote that ever since Christmas Eve—. Good God, Nora, these must have been three terrible days for you.

NORA   I have fought a hard fight these last three days.

HELMER   And been in agony and seen no other way out than—. No, we won't think of all that ugliness. We'll just rejoice and tell ourselves it's over, it's all over! Oh, listen to me, Nora. You don't seem to understand. It's over. What *is* it? Why do you look like that—that frozen expression on your face? Oh my poor little Nora, don't you think I know what it is? You can't make yourself believe that I have forgiven you. But I have, Nora; I swear to you, I have forgiven you for everything. Of course I know that what you did was for love of me.

NORA   That is true.

HELMER   You have loved me the way a wife ought to love her husband. You just didn't have the wisdom to judge the means. But do you think I love you any less because you don't know how to act on your own? Of course not. Just lean on me. I'll advise you; I'll guide you. I wouldn't be a man if I didn't find you twice as attractive because of your womanly helplessness. You mustn't pay any attention to the hard words I said to you right at first. It was just that first shock when I thought everything was collapsing all around me. I have forgiven you, Nora. I swear to you—I really have forgiven you.

NORA I thank you for your forgiveness. (*She goes out through the door, right.*)

HELMER No, stay—(*looks into the room she entered*) What are you doing in there?

NORA (*within*) Getting out of my costume.

HELMER (*by the open door*) Good, good. Try to calm down and compose yourself, my poor little frightened songbird. Rest safely; I have broad wings to cover you with. (*walks around near the door*) What a nice and cozy home we have, Nora. Here's shelter for you. Here I'll keep you safe like a hunted dove I have rescued from the hawk's talons. Believe me: I'll know how to quiet your beating heart. It will happen by and by, Nora; you'll see. Why, tomorrow you'll look at all this in quite a different light. And soon everything will be just the way it was before. I won't need to keep reassuring you that I have forgiven you; you'll feel it yourself. Did you really think I could have abandoned you, or even reproached you? Oh, you don't know a real man's heart, Nora. There is something unspeakably sweet and satisfactory for a man to know deep in himself that he has forgiven his wife—forgiven her in all the fullness of his honest heart. You see, that way she becomes his very own all over again—in a double sense, you might say. He has, so to speak, given her a second birth; it is as if she had become his wife and his child, both. From now on that's what you'll be to me, you lost and helpless creature. Don't worry about a thing, Nora. Only be frank with me, and I'll be your will and your conscience.—What's this? You're not in bed? You've changed your dress—!

NORA (*in an everyday dress*) Yes, Torvald. I have changed my dress.

HELMER But why—now—this late—?

NORA I'm not going to sleep tonight.

HELMER But my dear Nora—

NORA (*looks at her watch*) It isn't all that late. Sit down here with me, Torvald. You and I have much to talk about. (*sits down at the table*)

HELMER Nora—what is this all about? That rigid face—

NORA Sit down. This will take a while. I have much to say to you.

HELMER (*sits down, facing her across the table*) You worry me, Nora. I don't understand you.

NORA No, that's just it. You don't understand me. And I have never understood you—not till tonight. No, don't interrupt me. Just listen to what I have to say.—This is a settling of accounts, Torvald.

HELMER What do you mean by that?

NORA (*after a brief silence*) Doesn't one thing strike you, now that we are sitting together like this?

HELMER What would that be?

NORA We have been married for eight years. Doesn't it occur to you that this is the first time that you and I, husband and wife, are having a serious talk?

HELMER Well—serious—. What do you mean by that?

NORA For eight whole years—longer, in fact—ever since we first met, we have never talked seriously to each other about a single serious thing.

HELMER   You mean I should forever have been telling you about worries you couldn't have helped me with anyway?

NORA   I am not talking about worries. I'm saying we have never tried seriously to get to the bottom of anything together.

HELMER   But dearest Nora, I hardly think that would have been something *you*—

NORA   That's the whole point. You have never understood me. Great wrong has been done to me, Torvald. First by Daddy and then by you.

HELMER   What! By us two? We who have loved you more deeply than anyone else?

NORA (*shakes her head*)   You never loved me—neither Daddy nor you. You only thought it was fun to be in love with me.

HELMER   But, Nora—what an expression to use!

NORA   That's the way it has been, Torvald. When I was home with Daddy, he told me all his opinions, and so they became my opinions too. If I disagreed with him I kept it to myself, for he wouldn't have liked that. He called me his little doll baby, and he played with me the way I played with my dolls. Then I came to your house—

HELMER   What a way to talk about our marriage!

NORA (*imperturbably*)   I mean that I passed from Daddy's hands into yours. You arranged everything according to your taste, and so I came to share it—or I pretended to; I'm not sure which. I think it was a little of both, now one and now the other. When I look back on it now, it seems to me I've been living here like a pauper—just a hand-to-mouth kind of existence. I have earned my keep by doing tricks for you, Torvald. But that's the way you wanted it. You have great sins against me to answer for, Daddy and you. It's your fault that nothing has become of me.

HELMER   Nora, you're being both unreasonable and ungrateful. Haven't you been happy here?

NORA   No, never. I thought I was, but I wasn't.

HELMER   Not—not happy!

NORA   No; just having fun. And you have always been very good to me. But our home has never been more than a playroom. I have been your doll wife here, just the way I used to be Daddy's doll child. And the children have been my dolls. I thought it was fun when you played with me, just as they thought it was fun when I played with them. That's been our marriage, Torvald.

HELMER   There is something in what you are saying—exaggerated and hysterical though it is. But from now on things will be different. Playtime is over; it's time for growing up.

NORA   Whose growing up—mine or the children's?

HELMER   Both yours and the children's, Nora darling.

NORA   Oh Torvald, you're not the man to bring me up to be the right kind of wife for you.

HELMER   How can you say that?

NORA   And I—? What qualifications do I have for bringing up the children?

HELMER   Nora!

NORA   You said so yourself a minute ago—that you didn't dare to trust me with them.

HELMER   In the first flush of anger, yes. Surely, you're not going to count that.

NORA   But you were quite right. I am *not* qualified. Something else has to come first. Somehow I have to grow up myself. And you are not the man to help me do that. That's a job I have to do by myself. And that's why I'm leaving you.

HELMER (*jumps up*)   What did you say!

NORA   I have to be by myself if I am to find out about myself and about all the other things too. So I can't stay here with you any longer.

HELMER   Nora, Nora!

NORA   I'm leaving now. I'm sure Kristine will put me up for tonight.

HELMER   You're out of your mind! I won't let you! I forbid you!

NORA   You can't forbid me anything any more; it won't do any good. I'm taking my own things with me. I won't accept anything from you, either now or later.

HELMER   But this is madness!

NORA   Tomorrow I'm going home—I mean back to my old home town. It will be easier for me to find some kind of job there.

HELMER   Oh, you blind, inexperienced creature—!

NORA   I must see to it that I get experience, Torvald.

HELMER   Leaving your home, your husband, your children! Not a thought of what people will say!

NORA   I can't worry about that. All I know is that I have to leave.

HELMER   Oh, this is shocking! Betraying your most sacred duties like this!

NORA   And what do you consider my most sacred duties?

HELMER   Do I need to tell you that? They are your duties to your husband and your children.

NORA   I have other duties equally sacred.

HELMER   You do not. What duties would they be?

NORA   My duties to myself.

HELMER   You are a wife and a mother before you are anything else.

NORA   I don't believe that any more. I believe I am first of all a human being, just as much as you—or at any rate that I must try to become one. Oh, I know very well that most people agree with you, Torvald, and that it says something like that in all the books. But what people say and what the books say is no longer enough for me. I have to think about these things myself and see if I can't find the answers.

HELMER   You mean to tell me you don't know what your proper place in your own home is? Don't you have a reliable guide in such matters? Don't you have religion?

NORA   Oh but Torvald—I don't really know what religion is.

HELMER   What are you saying!

NORA   All I know is what the Reverend Hansen told me when he prepared me for confirmation. He said that religion was *this* and it was *that*. When I get by myself, away from here, I'll have to look into that, too. I have to decide if what the Reverend Hansen said was right, or anyway if it is right for *me*.

HELMER   Oh, this is unheard of in a young woman! If religion can't guide you, let me appeal to your conscience. For surely you have moral feelings? Or—answer me—maybe you don't?

NORA   Well, you see, Torvald, I don't really know what to say. I just don't know. I am confused about these things. All I know is that my ideas are quite different from yours. I have just found out that the laws are different from what I thought they were, but in no way can I get it into my head that those laws are right. A woman shouldn't have the right to spare her dying old father or save her husband's life! I just can't believe that.

HELMER   You speak like a child. You don't understand the society you live in.

NORA   No, I don't. But I want to find out about it. I have to make up my mind who is right, society or I.

HELMER   You are sick, Nora; you have a fever. I really don't think you are in your right mind.

NORA   I have never felt so clearheaded and sure of myself as I do tonight.

HELMER   And clearheaded and sure of yourself you're leaving your husband and children?

NORA   Yes.

HELMER   Then there is only one possible explanation.

NORA   What?

HELMER   You don't love me any more.

NORA   No, that's just it.

HELMER   Nora! Can you say that?

NORA   I am sorry, Torvald, for you have always been so good to me. But I can't help it. I don't love you any more.

HELMER   (*with forced composure*)   And this too is a clear and sure conviction?

NORA   Completely clear and sure. That's why I don't want to stay here any more.

HELMER   And are you ready to explain to me how I came to forfeit your love?

NORA   Certainly I am. It was tonight, when the wonderful didn't happen. That was when I realized you were not the man I thought you were.

HELMER   You have to explain. I don't understand.

NORA   I have waited patiently for eight years, for I wasn't such a fool that I thought the wonderful is something that happens any old day. Then this—thing—came crashing in on me, and then there wasn't a doubt in my mind that now—now comes the wonderful. When Krogstad's letter was in that mailbox, never for a moment did it even occur to me that you would submit to his conditions. I was so absolutely certain that you would say to him: make the whole thing public—tell everybody. And when that had happened—

HELMER Yes, then what? When I had surrendered my wife to shame and disgrace—!

NORA When that had happened, I was absolutely certain that you would stand up and take the blame and say, "I'm the guilty one."

HELMER Nora!

NORA You mean I never would have accepted such a sacrifice from you? Of course not. But what would my protests have counted against yours. *That* was the wonderful I was hoping for in terror. And to prevent that I was going to kill myself.

HELMER I'd gladly work nights and days for you, Nora—endure sorrow and want for your sake. But nobody sacrifices his *honor* for his love.

NORA A hundred thousand women have done so.

HELMER Oh, you think and talk like a silly child.

NORA All right. But you don't think and talk like the man I can live with. When you had gotten over your fright—not because of what threatened *me* but because of the risk to *you*—and the whole danger was past, then you acted as if nothing at all had happened. Once again I was your little songbird, your doll, just as before, only now you had to handle her even more carefully, because she was so frail and weak. (*rises*) Torvald—that moment I realized that I had been living here for eight years with a stranger and had borne him three children—Oh, I can't stand thinking about it! I feel like tearing myself to pieces!

HELMER (*heavily*) I see it, I see it. An abyss has opened up between us.—Oh but Nora—surely it can be filled?

NORA The way I am now I am no wife for you.

HELMER I have it in me to change.

NORA Perhaps—if your doll is taken from you.

HELMER To part—to part from you! No, no, Nora! I can't grasp that thought!

NORA (*goes out, right*) All the more reason why it has to be. (*She returns with her outdoor clothes and a small bag, which she sets down on the chair by the table.*)

HELMER Nora, Nora! Not now! Wait till tomorrow.

NORA (*putting on her coat*) I can't spend the night in a stranger's rooms.

HELMER But couldn't we live here together like brother and sister—?

NORA (*tying on her hat*) You know very well that wouldn't last long—. (*wraps her shawl around her*) Goodbye, Torvald. I don't want to see the children. I know I leave them in better hands than mine. The way I am now I can't be anything to them.

HELMER But some day, Nora—some day—?

NORA How can I tell? I have no idea what's going to become of me.

HELMER But you're still my wife, both as you are now and as you will be.

NORA Listen, Torvald—when a wife leaves her husband's house, the way I am doing now, I have heard he has no more legal responsibilities for her. At any rate, I now release you from all responsibility. You are not to feel yourself obliged to me for anything, and I have no obligations to you. There has to be full freedom on both sides. Here is your ring back. Now give me mine.

HELMER   Even this?

NORA   Even this.

HELMER   Here it is.

NORA   There. So now it's over. I'm putting the keys here. The maids know everything about the house—better than I. Tomorrow, after I'm gone, Kristine will
come over and pack my things from home. I want them sent after me.

HELMER   Over! It's all over! Nora, will you never think of me?

NORA   I'm sure I'll often think of you and the children and this house.

HELMER   May I write to you, Nora?

NORA   No—never. I won't have that.

HELMER   But send you things—? You must let me.

NORA   Nothing, nothing.

HELMER   —help you, when you need help—?

NORA   I told you, no; I won't have it. I'll accept nothing from strangers.

HELMER   Nora—can I never again be more to you than a stranger?

NORA (*picks up her bag*)   Oh Torvald—then the most wonderful of all would
have to happen—

HELMER   Tell me what that would be—!

NORA   For that to happen, both you and I would have to change so that—Oh
Torvald, I no longer believe in the wonderful.

HELMER   But I *will* believe. Tell me! Change, so that—?

NORA   So that our living together would become a true marriage. Goodbye.
(*She goes out through the hall.*)

HELMER (*sinks down on a chair near the door and covers his face with his
hands*)   Nora! Nora! (*looks around him and gets up*) All empty. She's gone.
(*with sudden hope*) The most wonderful—?!

(*From downstairs comes the sound of a heavy door slamming shut.*)

1879

STUDY QUESTIONS

1. The action of *A Doll's House* centers on the development and the alterations
of the relationships among Nora, Helmer, Krogstad, and Mrs. Linde. How
does Ibsen portray these characters? How do their relationships illuminate
their personalities and their actions? How do they emphasize the themes
and social comments of the play?

2. Both Nora and Antigonê are women who place moral principles above legal
values. What happens to each character in consequence, in terms of her
play's plot? other characters' reactions to her action? her view of their reaction, and of herself?

3. Discuss the play's ending. Do you find it successful? What is its effect? What
do you think is "the most wonderful of all"?

30

CONTEMPORARY DRAMA

By the middle of the twentieth century, new trends in drama were noticeable. Comedies, tragedies, and the hard-to-classify "dramas" alike often moved beyond realism into **surrealism**, beyond social comment to **psychological portraiture**. In stage settings, language, and refusal to follow a straightforward course of time, twentieth-century playwrights and the **contemporary drama** they wrote often pushed toward new forms of expression, hoping to evoke fresh responses from their audiences.

The study of humans as social beings, and of the way social pressures shape people, similarly modulates into the study of individual beings isolated in the midst of (often overwhelming) social demands. Thus spiritual (and sometimes physical) **isolation** remains an important theme in the three plays we study in this chapter: *The Glass Menagerie, Protest,* and *The Colored Museum.* Yet, as we will see, these plays study isolation in no cold or clinical sense. Rather, they use the drama's traditional role as social critic to call for a more caring society, a society that can accommodate dreams and dreamers as well as the realistic and practical.

Isolation, depicted and set off by failed tenderness, is a notable theme in Tennessee Williams's *The Glass Menagerie.* Amanda lives half in a semiillusory past, half in a present of unpalatable truths that she ignores whenever possible; Laura is isolated by her physical disability and by her great shyness; and Tom has isolated himself from everything except his memories.

The play is performed as a series of remembered scenes, with Tom sometimes narrator and sometimes actor. This device allows for great differences in stagecraft between this play and the realistic plays against which it rebels. The episodic structure; the lyrical, beautifully modulated language that defines each character and differentiates each from his or her companions; the unrealistic stage setting, with its use of lighting and music to set moods and scenes; and the symbolic value of props such as the glass unicorn—all work together to create, in the narrator's words, "truth in the pleasant disguise of illusion."

Whereas *The Glass Menagerie* and *The Colored Museum* are American plays presenting concerns familiar to an American audience, Václav Havel's *The Protest* is set in Communist Czechoslovakia before the disintegration of the Soviet Union and the subsequent establishment of democracies in eastern Europe. In 1968, after a "Prague Spring" of somewhat less oppressive government, Soviet troops took over the city and reinstituted a hard-line Communist government and the practice of firing dissidents from their jobs or putting them in jail. Havel was imprisoned for writing subversive plays. After Communism collapsed in 1989, Havel was elected president of Czechoslovakia. In 1993, however, his country split into its two ethnic components, the Czech Republic and Slovakia.

The Protest explores the moral complexities of living under a repressive government that controls the arts, the media, and most, if not all, significant jobs. What should the artist do under such circumstances? become an outright opponent of the government like Vanek in Havel's play and risk losing opportunities for publication of his work, or even risk going to jail? Or should the artist do as Stanek does, and keep just quiet enough to hold onto his job, all the while chipping away at totalitarianism as best he can from inside the system? Vanek's moral dilemma is whether to sign a letter of protest in support of his daughter's lover, who has been imprisoned as a subversive. His long, at times idealistic, at times self-serving, analysis of whether he should sign the protest letter is the thematic center of this technically conventional but intellectually fascinating one-act play.

The Colored Museum differs from *The Glass Menagerie* and *The Protest* in several ways. Rather than following an essentially realistic plot line, this play is a surreal journey through eleven brief episodes, which the author calls "exhibits." In contrast to Williams or Havel, George C. Wolfe deals not only with a family's financial and psychological problems or with political repression but with the decidedly dramatic but intractable problem of racism. Himself an African American, Wolfe, like Havel in *The Protest*, knows his subject from the inside out from having lived it. Finally, unlike the other two plays in this section, *The Colored Museum* makes its comments on society and its shortcomings primarily through the medium of comedy—dark, bitter, and subversive, but comedy nevertheless.

The striking thing about *The Colored Museum* is that in it Wolfe is able to use laughter as a means of probing the painful wound of racism in America without trivializing the issue, demonizing white Americans, or making saints of all his black characters. One of the chief satiric targets of the play, in fact, is the tradition of African American drama exemplified by *A Raisin in the Sun*—one of many post–World War II plays didactically and humorlessly depicting the trials of long-suffering black urban families. Wolfe skewers this sort of heavy-handed drama throughout *The Colored Museum*, but perhaps most brilliantly in the vignette "The Last Moma-on-the-Couch Play." In this hilarious exhibit, the God-fearing matriarch, the angry young man, and the college-educated young black "princess" are all on display, but as parodies of these familiar types. Near the end of this exhibit the narrator gives the female characters an award for their performances, but convicts the angry young son of overacting in presenting his conflicts with the omnipresent "Man."

Because most of the exhibits are so funny, the more painful ones are all the more poignant because of the juxtaposition. "A Soldier with a Secret" powerfully recounts a black soldier's horrific experience in Vietnam, and in "Permutations" an unmarried young black girl gives birth to an enormous egg. Even the funniest characters in each of the episodes have dark currents of sadness running beneath their mocking poses and furious partying.

In other episodes of the play, a black stewardess welcomes people aboard "Celebrity Slaveship" and encourages them to buckle their shackles, two black wigs (an Afro and a conservative professional style) argue with each other, and a Diana Ross-like diva parades her narcissism in a surreal cabaret. *The Colored Museum* is a raucous, rapid-fire play that suggests the energy, technical experimentalism, and irreverence of the best of contemporary drama.

The Glass Menagerie

Thomas Lanier ("Tennessee") Williams is usually considered, with the possible exception of Eugene O'Neill, the most important American playwright. Born in Columbus, Mississippi, Williams moved with his family to St. Louis when he was eight years old. The differences between Southern culture and that of the urban North would form one of the central tensions in his work. His family was of modest means, and Williams had to take various odd jobs, including one in a shoe factory, to support himself. He had a beloved sister, Rose, who was schizophrenic and served as the model for Laura in *The Glass Menagerie* (1945).

Many of Williams's plays feature lost, lonely people seeking refuge from the harsh realities of the world through fantasy, sex, drinking, or simply running away. In such plays as *A Streetcar Named Desire* (1947), *Suddenly Last Summer* (1958), *Sweet Bird of Youth* (1959), and *The Night of the Iguana* (1961), Williams deals with a few central themes: a denunciation of guilt about sexual matters (Williams's homosexuality was one of the most important forces driving his art), a special concern for thwarted, lonely souls crushed by an unthinking world, and an awareness that time always destroys the sweet bird of youth.

Williams was a two-time winner of the Pulitzer Prize. He gave many candid interviews in his last years and continued to write until his death.

CHARACTERS

AMANDA WINGFIELD, *the mother.*
> *A little woman of great but confused vitality clinging frantically to another time and place. Her characterization must be carefully created, not copied from type. She is not paranoiac, but her life is paranoia. There is much to admire in* **AMANDA**, *and as much to love and pity as there is to laugh at. Certainly she has endurance and a kind of heroism, and though her foolishness makes her unwittingly cruel at times, there is tenderness in her slight person.*

LAURA WINGFIELD, *her daughter.*
> **AMANDA**, *having failed to establish contact with reality, continues to live vitally in her illusions, but* **LAURA'S** *situation is even graver. A childhood illness has left her crippled, one leg slightly shorter than the other, and held in a brace. This defect need not be more than suggested on the stage. Stemming from this,* **LAURA'S** *separation increases till she is like a piece of her own glass collection, too exquisitely fragile to move from the shelf.*

TOM WINGFIELD, *her son, and the narrator of the play.*
> *A poet with a job in a warehouse. His nature is not remorseless, but to escape from a trap he has to act without pity.*

JIM O'CONNOR, *the gentleman caller.*
> *A nice, ordinary, young man.*

SCENE: *An alley in St. Louis.*
PART I: *Preparation for a Gentleman Caller.*
PART II: *The Gentleman Calls.*
TIME: *Now and the Past.*

Scene I

The Wingfield apartment is in the rear of the building, one of those vast hive-like conglomerations of cellular living-units that flower as warty growths in overcrowded urban centers of lower middle-class population and are symptomatic of the impulse of this largest and fundamentally enslaved section of American society to avoid fluidity and differentiation and to exist and function as one interfused mass of automatism.

The apartment faces an alley and is entered by a fire-escape, a structure whose name is a touch of accidental poetic truth, for all of these huge buildings are always burning with the slow and implacable fires of human desperation. The fire-escape is included in the set—that is, the landing of it and steps descending from it.

The scene is memory and is therefore nonrealistic. Memory takes a lot of poetic license. It omits some details; others are exaggerated, according to the emotional value of the articles it touches, for memory is seated predominantly in the heart. The interior is therefore rather dim and poetic.

At the rise of the curtain, the audience is faced with the dark, grim rear wall of the Wingfield tenement. This building, which runs parallel to the footlights, is flanked on both sides by dark, narrow alleys which run into murky canyons of tangled clotheslines, garbage cans and the sinister latticework of neighboring fire-escapes. It is up and down these side alleys that exterior entrances and exits are made, during the play. At the end of TOM's *opening commentary, the dark tenement wall slowly reveals (by means of a transparency) the interior of the ground floor Wingfield apartment.*

Downstage is the living room, which also serves as a sleeping room for LAURA, *the sofa unfolding to make her bed. Upstage, center, and divided by a wide arch or second proscenium with transparent faded portieres (or second curtain), is the dining room. In an old-fashioned what-not in the living room are seen scores of transparent glass animals. A blown-up photograph of the father hangs on the wall of the living room, facing the audience, to the left of the archway. It is the face of a very handsome young man in a doughboy's First World War cap. He is gallantly smiling, ineluctably smiling, as if to say, "I will be smiling forever."*

The audience hears and sees the opening scene in the dining room through both the transparent fourth wall of the building and the transparent gauze portieres of the dining-room arch. It is during this revealing scene that the fourth wall slowly ascends, out of sight. This transparent exterior wall is not brought down again until the very end of the play, during TOM's *final speech.*

The narrator is an undisguised convention of the play. He takes whatever license with dramatic convention as is convenient to his purposes.

TOM *enters dressed as a merchant sailor from alley, stage left, and strolls across the front of the stage to the fire-escape. There he stops and lights a cigarette. He addresses the audience.*

TOM   Yes, I have tricks in my pocket, I have things up my sleeve. But I am the opposite of a stage magician. He gives you illusion that has the appearance of truth. I give you truth in the pleasant disguise of illusion. To begin with, I turn back time. I reverse it to that quaint period, the thirties, when the huge middle class of America was matriculating in a school for the blind. Their eyes had failed them, or they had failed their eyes, and so they were having their fingers pressed forcibly down by the fiery Braille alphabet of a dissolving economy. In Spain there was revolution. Here there was only shouting and confusion. In Spain there was Guernica. Here there were disturbances of labor, sometimes pretty violent, in otherwise peaceful cities such as Chicago, Cleveland, Saint Louis. . . . This is the social background of the play.

(Music.)

The play is memory. Being a memory play, it is dimly lighted, it is sentimental, it is not realistic. In memory everything seems to happen to music. That explains the fiddle in the wings. I am the narrator of the play, and also a character in it. The other characters are my mother, Amanda, my sister, Laura, and a gentleman caller who appears in the final scenes. He is the most realistic character in the play, being an emissary from a world of reality that we were somehow set apart from. But since I have a poet's weakness for symbols, I am using this character also as a symbol; he is the long delayed but always expected something that we live for. There is a fifth character in the play who doesn't appear except in this larger-than-life photograph over the mantel. This is our father who left us a long time ago. He was a telephone man who fell in love with long distances; he gave up his job with the telephone company and skipped the light fantastic out of town . . . The last we heard of him was a picture post-card from Mazatlan, on the Pacific coast of Mexico, containing a message of two words—"Hello—Goodbye!" and an address. I think the rest of the play will explain itself. . . .

(Amanda's voice becomes audible through the portieres.)

(Legend on screen: "Où sont les neiges.")

(He divides the portieres and enters the upstage area.
　　Amanda *and* Laura *are seated at a drop-leaf table. Eating is indicated by gestures without food or utensils.* Amanda *faces the audience.* Tom *and* Laura *are seated in profile.*
　　The interior has lit up softly and through the scrim we see Amanda *and* Laura *seated at the table in the upstage area.)*

Amanda *(calling)*　Tom?

Tom　Yes, Mother.

Amanda　We can't say grace until you come to the table!

Tom　Coming, Mother. *(He bows slightly and withdraws, reappearing a few moments later in his place at the table.)*

Amanda *(to her son)*　Honey, don't *push* with your *fingers.* If you have to push with something, the thing to push with is a crust of bread. And chew—

chew! Animals have sections in their stomachs which enable them to digest food without mastication, but human beings are supposed to chew their food before they swallow it down. Eat food leisurely, son, and really enjoy it. A well-cooked meal has lots of delicate flavors that have to be held in the mouth for appreciation. So chew your food and give your salivary glands a chance to function!

(Tom *deliberately lays his imaginary fork down and pushes his chair back from the table.*)

TOM   I haven't enjoyed one bite of this dinner because of your constant directions on how to eat it. It's you that makes me rush through meals with your hawk-like attention to every bite I take. Sickening—spoils my appetite—all this discussion of animals' secretion—salivary glands—mastication!

AMANDA (*lightly*)   Temperament like a Metropolitan star! (*He rises and crosses downstage.*) You're not excused from the table.

TOM   I am getting a cigarette.

AMANDA   You smoke too much.

(LAURA *rises.*)

LAURA   I'll bring in the blanc mange.

(*He remains standing with his cigarette by the portieres during the following.*)

AMANDA (*rising*)   No, sister, no, sister—you be the lady this time and I'll be the darky.

LAURA   I'm already up.

AMANDA   Resume your seat, little sister—I want you to stay fresh and pretty—for gentlemen callers!

LAURA   I'm not expecting any gentlemen callers.

AMANDA (*crossing out to kitchenette; airily*)   Sometimes they come when they are least expected! Why, I remember one Sunday afternoon in Blue Mountain—(*enters kitchenette*)

TOM   I know what's coming!

LAURA   Yes. But let her tell it.

TOM   Again?

LAURA   She loves to tell it.

(AMANDA *returns with bowl of dessert.*)

AMANDA   One Sunday afternoon in Blue Mountain—your mother received—
seventeen!—gentlemen callers! Why, sometimes there weren't chairs enough to accommodate them all. We had to send the nigger over to bring in folding chairs from the parish house.

TOM (*remaining at portieres*)   How did you entertain those gentlemen callers?

AMANDA   I understood the art of conversation!

TOM   I bet you could talk.

AMANDA   Girls in those days *knew* how to talk, I can tell you.

TOM   Yes?

(Image: Amanda as a girl on a porch greeting callers.)

AMANDA   They knew how to entertain their gentlemen callers. It wasn't enough for a girl to be possessed of a pretty face and a graceful figure—although I wasn't slighted in either respect. She also needed to have a nimble wit and a tongue to meet all occasions.

TOM   What did you talk about?

AMANDA   Things of importance going on in the world! Never anything coarse or common or vulgar. (*She addresses* TOM *as though he were seated in the vacant chair at the table though he remains by portieres. He plays this scene as though he held the book.*) My callers were gentlemen—all! Among my callers were some of the most prominent young planters of the Mississippi Delta—planters and sons of planters!

(TOM *motions for music and a spot of light on* AMANDA. *Her eyes lift, her face glows, her voice becomes rich and elegiac.*)

(Screen legend: "Où sont les neiges.")

There was young Champ Laughlin who later became vice-president of the Delta Planters Bank. Hadley Stevenson who was drowned in Moon Lake and left his widow one hundred and fifty thousand in Government bonds. There were the Cutrere brothers, Wesley and Bates. Bates was one of my bright particular beaux! He got in a quarrel with that wild Wainright boy. They shot it out on the floor of Moon Lake Casino. Bates was shot through the stomach. Died in the ambulance on his way to Memphis. His widow was also well-provided for, came into eight or ten thousand acres, that's all. She married him on the rebound—never loved her—carried my picture on him the night he died! And there was that boy that every girl in the Delta had set her cap for! That beautiful, brilliant young Fitzhugh boy from Green County!

TOM   What did he leave his widow?

AMANDA   He never married! Gracious, you talk as though all of my old admirers had turned up their toes to the daisies!

TOM   Isn't this the first you mentioned that still survives?

AMANDA   That Fitzhugh boy went North and made a fortune—came to be known as the Wolf of Wall Street! He had the Midas touch, whatever he touched turned to gold! And I could have been Mrs. Duncan J. Fitzhugh, mind you! But—I picked your *father!*

LAURA (*rising*)   Mother, let me clear the table.

AMANDA   No, dear, you go in front and study your typewriter chart. Or practice your shorthand a little. Stay fresh and pretty—It's almost time for our gentlemen callers to start arriving. (*She flounces girlishly toward the kitchenette.*) How many do you suppose we're going to entertain this afternoon?

(TOM *throws down the paper and jumps up with a groan.*)

LAURA (*alone in the dining room*)   I don't believe we're going to receive any, Mother.

AMANDA (*reappearing, airily*)   What? No one—not one? You must be joking! (LAURA *nervously echoes her laugh. She slips in a fugitive manner through the half-open portieres and draws them gently behind her. A shaft of very clear light is thrown on her face against the faded tapestry of the curtains. Music: "The Glass Menagerie" under faintly; lightly.*) Not one gentleman caller? It can't be true! There must be a flood, there must have been a tornado!

LAURA   It isn't a flood, it's not a tornado, Mother. I'm just not popular like you were in Blue Mountain. . . . (TOM *utters another groan.* LAURA *glances at him with a faint, apologetic smile; her voice catching a little.*) Mother's afraid I'm going to be an old maid.

(*The scene dims out with "Glass Menagerie" music.*)

Scene II

("*Laura, Haven't You Ever Liked Some Boy?*")

On the dark stage the screen is lighted with the image of blue roses.

   Gradually LAURA*'s figure becomes apparent and the screen goes out.*

   The music subsides.

   LAURA *is seated in the delicate ivory chair at the small clawfoot table.*

   She wears a dress of soft violet material for a kimono—her hair tied back from her forehead with a ribbon.

   She is washing and polishing her collection of glass.

   AMANDA *appears on the fire-escape steps. At the sound of her ascent,* LAURA *catches her breath, thrusts the bowl of ornaments away and seats herself stiffly before the diagram of the typewriter keyboard as though it held her spellbound. Something has happened to* AMANDA. *It is written in her face as she climbs to the landing: a look that is grim and hopeless and a little absurd.*

   She has on one of those cheap or imitation velvety-looking cloth coats with imitation fur collar. Her hat is five or six years old, one of those dreadful cloche hats that were worn in the late twenties and she is clasping an enormous black patent-leather pocket-book with nickel clasp and initials. This is her full-dress outfit, the one she usually wears to the D.A.R.

   Before entering she looks through the door.

   She purses her lips, opens her eyes wide, rolls them upward, and shakes her head.

Then she slowly lets herself in the door. Seeing her mother's expression LAURA *touches her lips with a nervous gesture.*

LAURA   Hello, Mother, I was—(*She makes a nervous gesture toward the chart on the wall.* AMANDA *leans against the shut door and stares at* LAURA *with a martyred look.*)

AMANDA   Deception? Deception? (*She slowly removes her hat and gloves, continuing the swift suffering stare. She lets the hat and gloves fall on the floor—a bit of acting.*)

LAURA (*shakily*)   How was the D.A.R. meeting? (AMANDA *slowly opens her purse and removes a dainty white handkerchief which she shakes out delicately and delicately touches to her lips and nostrils.*) Didn't you go to the D.A.R. meeting, Mother?

AMANDA (*faintly, almost inaudibly*)   —No.—No. (*then more forcibly*) I did not have the strength—to go to the D.A.R. In fact, I did not have the courage! I wanted to find a hole in the ground and hide myself in it forever! (*She crosses slowly to the wall and removes the diagram of the typewriter keyboard. She holds it in front of her for a second, staring at it sweetly and sorrowfully—then bites her lips and tears it in two pieces.*)

LAURA (*faintly*)   Why did you do that, Mother? (AMANDA *repeats the same procedure with the chart of the Gregg Alphabet.*) Why are you—

AMANDA   Why? Why? How old are you, Laura?

LAURA   Mother, you know my age.

AMANDA   I thought that you were an adult; it seems that I was mistaken. (*She crosses slowly to the sofa and sinks down and stares at* LAURA.)

LAURA   Please don't stare at me, Mother.

(AMANDA *closes her eyes and lowers her head. Count ten.*)

AMANDA   What are we going to do, what is going to become of us, what is the future?

(*Count ten.*)

LAURA   Has something happened, Mother? (AMANDA *draws a long breath and takes out the handkerchief again; dabbing process.*) Mother, has—something happened?

AMANDA   I'll be all right in a minute. I'm just bewildered—(*Count five.*)—by life. . . .

LAURA   Mother, I wish that you would tell me what's happened.

AMANDA   As you know, I was supposed to be inducted into my office at the D.A.R. this afternoon. (IMAGE: A SWARM OF TYPEWRITERS.) But I stopped off at Rubicam's Business College to speak to your teachers about your having a cold and ask them what progress they thought you were making down there.

LAURA   Oh. . . .

AMANDA   I went to the typing instructor and introduced myself as your mother. She didn't know who you were. Wingfield, she said. We don't have any such student enrolled at the school! I assured her she did, that you had been going to classes since early in January. "I wonder," she said, "if you could be talking about that terribly shy little girl who dropped out of school after only a few days' attendance?" "No," I said, "Laura, my daughter, has been going to school every day for the past six weeks!" "Excuse me," she said. She took the attendance book out and there was your name, unmistakably printed, and all the dates you were absent until they decided that you had dropped out of school. I still said, "No, there must have been some mistake! There must have been some mix-up in the records!" And she said, "No—I remember her perfectly now. Her hand shook so that she couldn't hit the right keys! The first time we gave a speed-test, she broke down completely—was sick at the stomach and almost had to be carried into the wash-room! After that morning she never showed up any more. We phoned the house but never got any answer"—while I was working at Famous and Barr, I suppose, demonstrating those—Oh!" I felt so weak I could barely keep on my feet! I had to sit down while they got me a glass of water! Fifty dollars' tuition, all of our plans—my hopes and ambitions for you—just gone up the spout, just gone up the spout like that. (LAURA *draws a long breath and gets awkwardly to her feet. She crosses to the victrola and winds it up.*) What are you doing?

LAURA   Oh! (*She releases the handle and returns to her seat.*)

AMANDA   Laura, where have you been going when you've gone out pretending that you were going to business college?

LAURA   I've just been going out walking.

AMANDA   That's not true.

LAURA   It is. I just went walking.

AMANDA   Walking? Walking? In winter? Deliberately courting pneumonia in that light coat? Where did you walk to, Laura?

LAURA   All sorts of places—mostly in the park.

AMANDA   Even after you'd started catching that cold?

LAURA   It was the lesser of two evils, Mother. (IMAGE: WINTER SCENE IN PARK.) I couldn't go back up. I—threw up—on the floor!

AMANDA   From half past seven till after five every day you mean to tell me you walked around in the park, because you wanted to make me think that you were still going to Rubicam's Business College?

LAURA   It wasn't as bad as it sounds. I went inside places to get warmed up.

AMANDA   Inside where?

LAURA   I went in the art museum and the bird-houses at the Zoo. I visited the penguins every day! Sometimes I did without lunch and went to the movies. Lately I've been spending most of my afternoons in the Jewel-box, that big glass house where they raise the tropical flowers.

AMANDA   You did all this to deceive me, just for the deception? (LAURA *looks down.*) Why?

LAURA   Mother, when you're disappointed, you get that awful suffering look on
your face, like the picture of Jesus' mother in the museum!
AMANDA   Hush!
LAURA   I couldn't face it.

(*Pause. A whisper of strings.*)

(*Legend: "The crust of humility."*)

AMANDA (*hopelessly fingering the huge pocketbook*)   So what are we going to do
the rest of our lives? Stay home and watch the parades go by? Amuse ourselves with the glass menagerie, darling? Eternally play those worn-out
phonograph records your father left as a painful reminder of him? We won't
have a business career—we've given that up because it gave us nervous indigestion! (*laughs wearily*) What is there left but dependency all our lives? I
know so well what becomes of unmarried women who aren't prepared to
occupy a position. I've seen such pitiful cases in the South—barely tolerated
spinsters living upon the grudging patronage of sister's husband or
brother's wife!—stuck away in some little mouse-trap of a room—encouraged by one in-law to visit another—little birdlike women without any
nest—eating the crust of humility all their life! Is that the future that we've
mapped out for ourselves? I swear it's the only alternative I can think of! It
isn't a very pleasant alternative, is it? Of course—some girls *do marry.*
(LAURA *twists her hands nervously.*) Haven't you ever liked some boy?
LAURA   Yes. I liked one once. (*rises*) I came across his picture a while ago.
AMANDA (*with some interest*)   He gave you his picture?
LAURA   No, it's in the year-book.
AMANDA (*disappointed*)   Oh—a high-school boy.

(*Screen image: Jim as a high-school hero bearing a silver cup.*)

LAURA   Yes. His name was Jim. (LAURA *lifts the heavy annual from the claw-foot
table.*) Here he is in *The Pirates of Penzance.*
AMANDA (*absently*)   The what?
LAURA   The operetta the senior class put on. He had a wonderful voice and we
sat across the aisle from each other Mondays, Wednesdays and Fridays in
the Aud. Here he is with the silver cup for debating! See his grin?
AMANDA (*absently*)   He must have had a jolly disposition.
LAURA   He used to call me—Blue Roses.

(*Image: Blue roses.*)

AMANDA   Why did he call you such a name as that?
AMANDA   When I had that attack of pleurosis—he asked me what was the matter when I came back. I said pleurosis—he thought that I said Blue Roses!
So that's what he always called me after that. Whenever he saw me, he'd
holler, "Hello, Blue Roses!" I didn't care for the girl that he went out with.

Emily Meisenbach. Emily was the best-dressed girl at Soldan. She never struck me, though, as being sincere ... It says in the Personal Section— they're engaged. That's—six years ago! They must be married by now.

AMANDA   Girls that aren't cut out for business careers usually wind up married to some nice man. (*gets up with a spark of revival*) Sister, that's what you'll do!

(LAURA *utters a startled, doubtful laugh. She reaches quickly for a piece of glass.*)

LAURA   But, Mother—

AMANDA   Yes? (*crossing to photograph*)

LAURA (*in a tone of frightened apology*)   I'm—crippled!

(*Image: Screen.*)

AMANDA   Nonsense! Laura, I've told you never, never to use that word. Why, you're not crippled, you just have a little defect—hardly noticeable, even! When people have some slight disadvantage like that, they cultivate other things to make up for it—develop charm—and vivacity—and—charm! That's all you have to do! (*She turns again to the photograph.*) One thing your father had *plenty of*—was *charm!*

(TOM *motions to the fiddle in the wings.*)

(*The scene fades out with music.*)

Scene III

(*Legend on screen: "After the fiasco—"*)

TOM *speaks from the fire-escape landing.*

TOM   After the fiasco at Rubicam's Business College, the idea of getting a gentleman caller for Laura began to play a more important part in Mother's calculations. It became an obsession. Like some archetype of the universal unconscious, the image of the gentleman caller haunted our small apartment. ... (IMAGE: YOUNG MAN AT DOOR WITH FLOWERS.) An evening at home rarely passed without some allusion to this image, this spectre, this hope. ... Even when he wasn't mentioned, his presence hung in Mother's preoccupied look and in my sister's frightened, apologetic manner—hung like a sentence passed upon the Wingfields! Mother was a woman of action as well as words. She began to take logical steps in the planned direction. Late that winter and in the early spring—realizing that extra money would be needed to properly feather the nest and plume the bird—she conducted a vigorous campaign on the telephone, roping in subscribers to one of those magazines for matrons called *The Home-maker's Companion,* the type of journal that features the serialized sublimations of ladies of letters who think in terms of delicate cup-like breasts, slim, tapering waists, rich, creamy thighs, eyes like wood-smoke in autumn, fingers that soothe and caress like strains of music, bodies as powerful as Etruscan sculpture.

(Screen image: Glamor magazine cover.)

(AMANDA *enters with phone on long extension cord. She is spotted in the dim stage.*)

AMANDA   Ida Scott? This is Amanda Wingfield! We *missed* you at the D.A.R. last Monday! I said to myself: She's probably suffering with that sinus condition! How is that sinus condition? Horrors! Heaven have mercy!—You're a Christian martyr, yes, that's what you are, a Christian martyr! Well, I just now happened to notice that your subscription to the *Companion*'s about to expire! Yes, it expires with the next issue, honey!—just when that wonderful new serial by Bessie Mae Hopper is getting off to such an exciting start. Oh, honey, it's something that you can't miss! You remember how *Gone With the Wind* took everybody by storm? You simply couldn't go out if you hadn't read it. All everybody *talked* was Scarlett O'Hara. Well, this is a book that critics already compare to *Gone With the Wind*. It's the *Gone With the Wind* of the post-World War generation!—What?—Burning?—Oh, honey, don't let them burn, go take a look in the oven and I'll hold the wire! Heavens—I think she's hung up!

(Dim out.)

(Legend on screen: "You think I'm in love with Continental Shoemakers?")

(*Before the stage is lighted, the violent voices of* TOM *and* AMANDA *are heard.*
    They are quarreling behind the portieres. In front of them stands LAURA *with clenched hands and panicky expression.*
    A clear pool of light on her figure throughout this scene.)

TOM   What in Christ's name am I—

AMANDA *(shrilly)*   Don't you use that—

TOM   Supposed to do!

AMANDA   Expression! Not in my—

TOM   Ohhh!

AMANDA   Presence! Have you gone out of your senses?

TOM   I have, that's true, *driven* out!

AMANDA   What is the matter with you, you—big—big—IDIOT!

TOM   Look—I've got *no thing,* no single thing—

AMANDA   Lower your voice!

TOM   In my life here that I can call my own! Everything is—

AMANDA   Stop that shouting!

TOM   Yesterday you confiscated my books! You had the nerve to—

AMANDA   I took that horrible novel back to the library—yes! That hideous
book by that insane Mr. Lawrence. (Tom *laughs wildly.*) I cannot control the
output of diseased minds or people who cater to them—(Tom *laughs still
more wildly.*) BUT I WON'T ALLOW SUCH FILTH BROUGHT INTO MY HOUSE!
No, no, no, no, no!

TOM   House, house! Who pays rent on it, who makes a slave of himself to—

AMANDA (*fairly screeching*)   Don't you DARE to—

TOM   No, no, I mustn't say things! *I've* got to just—

AMANDA   Let me tell you—

TOM   I don't want to hear any more! (*He tears the portieres open. The upstage
area is lit with a turgid smoky red glow.*)

(AMANDA's *hair is in metal curlers and she wears a very old bathrobe, much too
large for her slight figure, a relic of the faithless Mr. Wingfield.*

*An upright typewriter and a wild disarray of manuscripts is on the dropleaf
table. The quarrel was probably precipitated by* AMANDA's *interruption of his creative labor. A chair lying overthrown on the floor.*

Their gesticulating shadows are cast on the ceiling by the fiery glow.)

AMANDA   You *will* hear more, you—

TOM   No, I won't hear more, I'm going out!

AMANDA   You come right back in—

TOM   Out, out out! Because I'm—

AMANDA   Come back here, Tom Wingfield! I'm not through talking to you!

TOM   Oh, go—

LAURA (*desperately*)   —Tom!

AMANDA   You're going to listen, and no more insolence from you! I'm at the
end of my patience! (*He comes back toward her.*)

TOM   What do you think I'm at? Aren't I supposed to have any patience to reach
the end of, Mother? I know, I know. It seems unimportant to you, what I'm
doing—what I *want* to do—having a little *difference* between them! You
don't think that—

AMANDA   I think you've been doing things that you're ashamed of. That's why
you act like this. I don't believe that you go every night to the movies. Nobody goes to the movies night after night. Nobody in their right minds goes
to the movies as often as you pretend to. People don't go to the movies at
nearly midnight, and movies don't let out at two A.M. Come in stumbling.
Muttering to yourself like a maniac! You get three hours sleep and then go
to work. Oh, I can picture the way you're doing down there. Moping, dop-
ing, because you're in no condition.

TOM (*wildly*)   No, I'm in no condition!

AMANDA   What right have you got to jeopardize your job? Jeopardize the security of us all? How do you think we'd manage if you were—

TOM   Listen! You think I'm crazy *about* the *warehouse*? (*He bends fiercely toward
her slight figure.*) You think I'm in love with the Continental Shoemakers?

You think I want to spend fifty-five *years* down there in that—*celotex interior!* with—*fluorescent*—*tubes!* Look! I'd rather somebody picked up a crowbar and battered out my brains—than go back mornings! I *go!* Every time you come in yelling that God damn "*Rise and Shine!*" "*Rise and Shine!*" I say to myself "How *lucky dead* people are!" But I get up. I *go!* For sixty-five dollars a month I give up all that I dream of doing and being *ever!* And you say self—*self's* all I ever think of. Why, listen, if self is what I thought of, Mother, I'd be where he is—GONE! (*pointing to father's picture*) As far as the system of transportation reaches! (*He starts past her. She grabs his arm.*) Don't grab me, Mother!

AMANDA   Where are you going?

TOM   I'm going to the *movies!*

AMANDA   I don't believe that lie!

TOM (*crouching toward her, overtowering her tiny figure. She backs away, gasping.*) I'm going to opium dens! Yes, opium dens, dens of vice and criminals' hangouts, Mother. I've joined the Hogan gang, I'm a hired assassin, I carry a tommy-gun in a violin case! I run a string of cat-houses in the Valley! They call me Killer, Killer Wingfield, I'm leading a double-life, a simple, honest warehouse worker by day, by night, a dynamic *czar* of the *underworld*, Mother. I go to gambling casinos, I spin away fortunes on the roulette table! I wear a patch over one eye and a false mustache, sometimes I put on green whiskers. On those occasions they call me—*El Diablo!* Oh, I could tell you things to make you sleepless! My enemies plan to dynamite this place. They're going to blow us all sky-high some night! I'll be glad, very happy, and so will you! You'll go up, up on a broomstick, over Blue Mountain with seventeen gentlemen callers! You ugly—babbling old—*witch.* . . . (*He goes through a series of violent, clumsy movements, seizing his overcoat, lunging to the door, pulling it fiercely open. The women watch him, aghast. His arm catches in the sleeve of the coat as he struggles to pull it on. For a moment he is pinioned by the bulky garment. With an outraged groan he tears the coat off again, splitting the shoulders of it, and hurls it across the room. It strikes against the shelf of* LAURA*'s glass collection, there is a tinkle of shattering glass.* LAURA *cries out as if wounded.*)

(*Music legend: "The Glass Menagerie."*)

LAURA (*shrilly*)   My glass!—menagerie. . . . (*She covers her face and turns away.*)

(*But* AMANDA *is still stunned and stupefied by the "ugly witch" so that she barely notices this occurrence. Now she recovers her speech.*)

AMANDA (*in an awful voice*)   I won't speak to you—until you apologize! (*She crosses through portieres and draws them together behind her.* TOM *is left with* LAURA. LAURA *clings weakly to the mantel with her face averted.* TOM *stares at her stupidly for a moment. Then he crosses to shelf. Drops awkwardly to his knees to collect the fallen glass, glancing at* LAURA *as if he would speak but couldn't.*)

"The Glass Menagerie" steals in as

(*The scene dims out.*)

Scene IV

The interior is dark. Faint light in the alley.

　　A deep-voiced bell in a church is tolling the hour of five as the scene commences.

　　TOM *appears at the top of the alley. After each solemn boom of the bell in the tower, he shakes a little noise-maker or rattle as if to express the tiny spasm of man in contrast to the sustained power and dignity of the Almighty. This and the unsteadiness of his advance make it evident that he has been drinking.*

　　As he climbs the few steps to the fire-escape landing light steals up inside. LAURA *appears in night-dress, observing* TOM*'s empty bed in the front room.*

　　TOM *fishes in his pockets for the door-key, removing a motley assortment of articles in the search, including a perfect shower of movie-ticket stubs and an empty bottle. At last he finds the key, but just as he is about to insert it, it slips from his fingers. He strikes a match and crouches below the door.*

TOM (*bitterly*)　One crack—and it falls through!

(LAURA *opens the door.*)

LAURA　Tom! Tom, what are you doing?

TOM　Looking for a door-key.

LAURA　Where have you been all this time?

TOM　I have been to the movies.

LAURA　All this time at the movies?

TOM　There was a very long program. There was a Garbo picture and a Mickey Mouse and a travelogue and a newsreel and a preview of coming attractions. And there was an organ solo and a collection for the milk-fund—simultaneously—which ended up in a terrible fight between a fat lady and an usher!

LAURA (*innocently*)　Did you have to stay through everything?

TOM　Of course! And, oh, I forgot! There was a big stage show! The headliner on this stage show was Malvolio the Magician. He performed wonderful tricks, many of them, such as pouring water back and forth between pitchers. First it turned to wine and then it turned to beer and then it turned to whiskey. I know it was whiskey it finally turned into because he needed somebody to come up out of the audience to help him, and I came up—both shows! It was Kentucky Straight Bourbon. A very generous fellow, he gave souvenirs. (*He pulls from his back pocket a shimmering rainbow-colored scarf.*) He gave me this. This is his magic scarf. You can have it,

Laura. You wave it over a canary cage and you get a bowl of gold-fish. You wave it over the gold-fish bowl and they fly away canaries. . . . But the wonderfullest trick of all was the coffin trick. We nailed him into a coffin and he got out of the coffin without removing one nail. (*He has come inside.*) There is a trick that would come in handy for me—get me out of this 2 by 4 situation! (*flops onto bed and starts removing shoes*)

LAURA   Tom—Shhh!

TOM   What you shushing me for?

LAURA   You'll wake up Mother.

TOM   Goody, goody! Pay 'er back for all those "Rise an' Shines." (*lies down, groaning*) You know it don't take much intelligence to get yourself into a nailed-up coffin, Laura. But who in hell ever got himself out of one without removing one nail?

(*As if in answer, the father's grinning photograph lights up.*)

(*Scene dims out.*)

(*Immediately following: The church bell is heard striking six. At the sixth stroke the alarm clock goes off in* AMANDA'*s room, and after a few moments we hear her calling: "Rise and Shine! Rise and Shine! Laura, go tell your brother to rise and shine!"*)

TOM (*sitting up slowly*)   I'll rise—but I won't shine.

(*The light increases.*)

AMANDA   Laura, tell your brother his coffee is ready.

(LAURA *slips into front room.*)

LAURA   Tom! it's nearly seven. Don't make Mother nervous. (*He stares at her stupidly, beseechingly.*) Tom, speak to Mother this morning. Make up with her, apologize, speak to her!

TOM   She won't to me. It's her that started not speaking.

LAURA   If you just say you're sorry she'll start speaking.

TOM   Her not speaking—is that such a tragedy?

LAURA   Please—please!

AMANDA (*calling from kitchenette*)   Laura, are you going to do what I asked you to do, or do I have to get dressed and go out myself?

LAURA   Going, going—soon as I get on my coat! (*She pulls on a shapeless felt hat with nervous, jerky movement, pleadingly glancing at* TOM. *Rushes awkwardly for coat. The coat is one of* AMANDA'*s, inaccurately made-over, the sleeves too short for* LAURA.) Butter and what else?

AMANDA (*entering upstage*)   Just butter. Tell them to charge it.

LAURA   Mother, they make such faces when I do that.

AMANDA   Sticks and stones may break my bones, but the expression on Mr. Garfinkel's face won't harm us! Tell your brother his coffee is getting cold.

LAURA (*at door*)   Do what I asked you, will you, will you, Tom?

(*He looks sullenly away.*)

AMANDA   Laura, go now or just don't go at all!

LAURA (*rushing out*)   Going—going! (*A second later she cries out.* TOMS *springs up and crosses to the door.* AMANDA *rushes anxiously in.* TOM *opens the door.*)

TOM   Laura?

LAURA   I'm all right. I slipped, but I'm all right.

AMANDA (*peering anxiously after her*)   If anyone breaks a leg on those fire-escape steps, the landlord ought to be sued for every cent he possesses! (*She shuts door, remembers she isn't speaking, and returns to other room.*)

(*As* TOM *enters listlessly for his coffee, she turns her back to him and stands rigidly facing the window on the gloomy gray vault of the areaway. Its light on her face with its aged but childish features is cruelly sharp, satirical as a Daumier print.*)

(*Music under: "Ave Maria."*)

(TOM *glances sheepishly but sullenly at her averted figure and slumps at the table. The coffee is scalding hot; he sips it and gasps and spits it back in the cup. At his gasp,* AMANDA *catches her breath and half turns. Then catches herself and turns back to window.*

TOM *blows on his coffee, glancing sidewise at his mother. She clears her throat.* TOM *clears his. He starts to rise. Sinks back down again, scratches his head, clears his throat again.* AMANDA *coughs.* TOM *raises his cup in both hands to blow on it, his eyes staring over the rim of it at his mother for several moments. Then he slowly sets the cup down and awkwardly and hesitantly rises from the chair.*)

TOM (*hoarsely*)   Mother. I—I apologize. Mother. (AMANDA *draws a quick, shuddering breath. Her face works grotesquely. She breaks into childlike tears.*) I'm sorry for what I said, for everything that I said, I didn't mean it.

AMANDA (*sobbingly*)   My devotion has made me a witch and so I make myself hateful to my children!

TOM   No, you *don't.*

AMANDA   I worry so much, don't sleep, it makes me nervous!

TOM (*gently*)   I understand that.

AMANDA   I've had to put up a solitary battle all these years. But you're my right-hand bower! Don't fall down, don't fail!

TOM (*gently*)   I try, Mother.

AMANDA (*with great enthusiasm*)   Try and you will SUCCEED! (*The notion makes her breathless.*) Why, you—you're just *full* of natural endowments! Both of my children—they're *unusual* children! Don't you think I know it? I'm so—*proud!* Happy and—feel I've—so much to be thankful for but— Promise me one thing, son!

TOM   What, Mother?

AMANDA   Promise, son, you'll—never be a drunkard!

TOM (*turns to her grinning*)   I will never be a drunkard, Mother.

AMANDA   That's what frightened me so, that you'd be drinking! Eat a bowl of Purina!

TOM   Just coffee, Mother.

AMANDA   Shredded wheat biscuit?

TOM   No. No, Mother, just coffee.

AMANDA   You can't put in a day's work on an empty stomach. You've got ten minutes—don't gulp! Drinking too-hot liquids makes cancer of the stomach. . . . Put cream in.

TOM   No, thank you.

AMANDA   To cool it.

TOM   No! No, thank you, I want it black.

AMANDA   I know, but it's not good for you. We have to do all that we can to build ourselves up. In these trying times we live in, all that we have to cling to is—each other. . . . That's why it's so important to—Tom, I—I sent out your sister so I could discuss something with you. If you hadn't spoken I would have spoken to you. (*sits down*)

TOM (*gently*)   What is it, Mother, that you want to discuss?

AMANDA   Laura!

(TOM *puts his cup down slowly.*)

(*Legend on screen: "Laura."*)

(*Music: "The Glass Menagerie."*)

TOM   —Oh.—Laura . . .

AMANDA (*touching his sleeve*)   You know how Laura is. So quiet but—still water runs deep! She notices things and I think she—broods about them. (TOM *looks up.*) A few days ago I came in and she was crying.

TOM   What about?

AMANDA   You.

TOM   Me?

AMANDA   She has an idea that you're not happy here.

TOM   What gave her that idea?

AMANDA   What gives her any idea? However, you do act strangely. I—I'm not criticizing, understand *that!* I know your ambitions do not lie in the warehouse, that like everybody in the whole wide world—you've had to—make sacrifices, but—Tom—Tom—life's not easy, it calls for—Spartan endurance! There's so many things in my heart that I cannot describe to you! I've never told you but I—*loved* your father. . . .

TOM (*gently*)   I know that, Mother.

AMANDA   And you—when I see you taking after his ways! Staying out late—and—well, you *had* been drinking the night you were in that—terrifying condition! Laura says that you hate the apartment and that you go out nights to get away from it! Is that true, Tom?

TOM   No. You say there's so much in your heart that you can't describe to me. That's true of me, too. There's so much in my heart that I can't describe to *you!* So let's respect each other's—

AMANDA   But, why—*why,* Tom—are you always so *restless?* Where do you go to, nights?

TOM   I—go to the movies.

AMANDA   Why do you go to the movies so much, Tom?

TOM   I go to the movies because—I like adventure. Adventure is something I don't have much of at work, so I go to the movies.

AMANDA   But, Tom, you go to the movies *entirely* too *much!*

TOM   I like a lot of adventure.

(AMANDA *looks baffled, then hurt. As the familiar inquisition resumes he becomes hard and impatient again.* AMANDA *slips back into her querulous attitude toward him.*)

(*Image on screen: Sailing vessel with Jolly Roger.*)

AMANDA   Most young men find adventure in their careers.

TOM   Then most young men are not employed in a warehouse.

AMANDA   The world is full of young men employed in warehouses and offices and factories.

TOM   Do all of them find adventure in their careers?

AMANDA   They do or they do without it! Not everybody has a craze for adventure.

TOM   Man is by instinct a lover, a hunter, a fighter, and none of those instincts are given much play at the warehouse!

AMANDA   Man is by instinct! Don't quote instinct to me! Instinct is something that people have got away from! It belongs to animals! Christian adults don't want it!

TOM   What do Christian adults want, then, Mother?

AMANDA   Superior things! Things of the mind and the spirit! Only animals have to satisfy instincts! Surely your aims are somewhat higher than theirs! Than monkeys—pigs—

TOM   I reckon they're not.

AMANDA   You're joking. However, that isn't what I wanted to discuss.

TOM (*rising*)   I haven't much time.

AMANDA (*pushing his shoulders*)   Sit down.

TOM   You want me to punch in red at the warehouse, Mother?

AMANDA   You have five minutes. I want to talk about Laura.

(*Legend: "Plans and provisions."*)

TOM   All right! What about Laura?

AMANDA   We have to be making plans and provisions for her. She's older than you, two years, and nothing has happened. She just drifts along doing nothing. It frightens me terribly how she just drifts along.

TOM   I guess she's the type that people call home girls.

AMANDA   There's no such type, and if there is, it's a pity! That is unless the home is hers, with a husband!

TOM   What?

AMANDA   Oh, I can see the handwriting on the wall as plain as I see the nose in front of my face! It's terrifying! More and more you remind me of your father! He was out all hours without explanation—Then *left! Goodbye!* And me with a bag to hold. I saw that letter you got from the Merchant Marine. I know what you're dreaming of. I'm not standing here blindfolded. Very well, then. Then *do* it! But not till there's somebody to take your place.

TOM   What do you mean?

AMANDA   I mean that as soon as Laura has got somebody to take care of her, married, a home of her own, independent—why, then you'll be free to go wherever you please, on land, on sea, whichever way the wind blows! But until that time you've got to look out for your sister. I don't say me because I'm old and don't matter! I say for your sister because she's young and dependent. I put her in business college—a dismal failure! Frightened her so it made her sick to her stomach. I took her over to the Young People's League at the church. Another fiasco. She spoke to nobody, nobody spoke to her. Now all she does is fool with those pieces of glass and play those worn-out records. What kind of life is that for a girl to lead?

TOM   What can I do about it?

AMANDA   Overcome selfishness! Self, self, self is all that you ever think of! (TOM *springs up and crosses to get his coat. It is ugly and bulky. He pulls on a cap with earmuffs.*) Where is your muffler? Put your wool muffler on! (*He snatches it angrily from the closet and tosses it around his neck and pulls both ends tight.*) Tom! I haven't said what I had in mind to ask you.

TOM   I'm too late to—

AMANDA   (*catching his arm—very importunately; then shyly:*)   Down at the warehouse, aren't there some—nice young men?

TOM   No!

AMANDA   There *must* be—*some* . . .

TOM   Mother—

(*Gesture.*)

AMANDA   Find out one that's clean-living—doesn't drink and—ask him out for sister!

TOM   What?

AMANDA   For *sister!* To *meet!* Get *acquainted!*

TOM (*stamping to door*)   Oh, my *go-osh!*

AMANDA   Will you? (*He opens door; imploringly:*) Will you? (*He starts down.*)
Will you? *Will* you, dear?
TOM (*calling back*)   YES!

(AMANDA *closes the door hesitantly and with a troubled but faintly hopeful expression.*)

(*Screen image: Glamor magazine cover.*)

(*Spot* AMANDA *at phone.*)

AMANDA   Ella Cartwright? This is Amanda Wingfield! How are you, honey?
How is that kidney condition? (*Count five.*) Horrors! (*Count five.*) You're
a Christian martyr, yes, honey, that's what you are, a Christian martyr! Well, I
just happened to notice in my little red book that your subscription to the
Companion has just run out! I knew that you wouldn't want to miss out on
the wonderful serial starting in this new issue. It's by Bessie Mae Hopper, the
first thing she's written since *Honeymoon for Three.* Wasn't that a strange and
interesting story? Well, this one is even lovelier, I believe. It has a sophisticated society background. It's all about the horsey set on Long Island!

(*Fade out.*)

Scene V

(*Legend on screen: "Annunciation."*)

Fade with music.

It is early dusk of a spring evening. Supper has just been finished in the Wingfield apartment.
AMANDA *and* LAURA *in light colored dresses are removing dishes from the table, in the upstage area, which is shadowy, their movements formalized almost as a dance or ritual, their
moving forms as pale and silent as moths.*
    Tom, in white shirt and trousers, rises from the table and crosses toward the fire escape.

AMANDA (*as he passes her*)   Son, will you do me a favor?
TOM   What?
AMANDA   Comb your hair! You look so pretty when your hair is combed! (TOM
slouches on sofa with evening paper; enormous caption "Franco Triumphs.")
There is only one respect in which I would like you to emulate your father.
TOM   What respect is that?
AMANDA   The care he always took of his appearance. He never allowed himself
to look untidy. (*He throws down the paper and crosses to fire escape.*) Where
are you going?
TOM   I'm going out to smoke.
AMANDA   You smoke too much. A pack a day at fifteen cents a pack. How much
would that amount to in a month? Thirty times fifteen is how much, Tom?

Figure it out and you will be astounded at what you could save. Enough to give you a night-school course in accounting at Washington U! Just think what a wonderful thing that would be for you, son!

(TOM *is unmoved by the thought.*)

TOM   I'd rather smoke. (*He steps out on landing, letting the screen door slam.*)

AMANDA (*sharply*)   I know! That's the tragedy of it. . . . (*Alone, she turns to look at her husband's picture.*)

(*Dance music: "All the world is waiting for the sunrise!"*)

TOM (*to the audience*)   Across the alley from us was the Paradise Dance Hall. On evenings in spring the windows and doors were open and the music came outdoors. Sometimes the lights were turned out except for a large glass sphere that hung from the ceiling. It would turn slowly about and filter the dusk with delicate rainbow colors. Then the orchestra played a waltz or a tango, something that had a slow and sensuous rhythm. Couples would come outside, to the relative privacy of the alley. You could see them kissing behind ash-pits and telephone poles. This was the compensation for lives that passed like mine, without any change or adventure. Adventure and change were imminent in this year. They were waiting around the corner for all these kids. Suspended in the mist over Berchtesgaden, caught in the folds of Chamberlain's umbrella—In Spain there was Guernica! But here there was only hot swing music and liquor, dance halls, bars, and movies, and sex that hung in the gloom like a chandelier and flooded the world with brief, deceptive rainbows. . . . All the world was waiting for bombardments!

(AMANDA *turns from the picture and comes outside.*)

AMANDA (*sighing*)   A fire-escape landing's a poor excuse for a porch. (*She spreads a newspaper on a step and sits down, gracefully and demurely as if she were settling into a swing on a Mississippi veranda.*) What are you looking at?

TOM   The moon.

AMANDA   Is there a moon this evening?

TOM   It's rising over Garfinkel's Delicatessen.

AMANDA   So it is! A little silver slipper of a moon. Have you made a wish on it yet?

TOM   Um-hum.

AMANDA   What did you wish for?

TOM   That's a secret.

AMANDA   A secret, huh? Well, I won't tell mine either. I will be just as mysterious as you.

TOM   I bet I can guess what yours is.

AMANDA   Is my head so transparent?

TOM   You're not a sphinx.

AMANDA   No, I don't have secrets. I'll tell you what I wished for on the moon. Success and happiness for my precious children! I wish for that whenever there's a moon, and when there isn't a moon, I wish for it, too.

TOM   I thought perhaps you wished for a gentleman caller.

AMANDA   Why do you say that?

TOM   Don't you remember asking me to fetch one?

AMANDA   I remember suggesting that it would be nice for your sister if you brought home some nice young man from the warehouse. I think I've made that suggestion more than once.

TOM   Yes, you have made it repeatedly.

AMANDA   Well?

TOM   We are going to have one.

AMANDA   *What?*

TOM   A gentleman caller!

(The annunciation is celebrated with music.)

(AMANDA *rises.*)

(Image on screen: Caller with bouquet.)

AMANDA   You mean you have asked some nice young man to come over?

TOM   Yep. I've asked him to dinner.

AMANDA   You really did?

TOM   I did!

AMANDA   You did, and did he—*accept?*

TOM   He did!

AMANDA   Well, well—well, well! That's—lovely!

TOM   I thought that you would be pleased.

AMANDA   It's definite, then?

TOM   Very definite.

AMANDA   Soon?

TOM   Very soon.

AMANDA   For heaven's sake, stop putting on and tell me some things, will you?

TOM   What things do you want me to tell you?

AMANDA   *Naturally* I would like to know when he's *coming!*

TOM   He's coming tomorrow.

AMANDA   *Tomorrow?*

TOM   Yep. Tomorrow.

AMANDA   But, Tom!

TOM   Yes, Mother?

AMANDA   Tomorrow gives me no time!

TOM   Time for what?

AMANDA Preparations! Why didn't you phone me at once, as soon as you asked him, the minute that he accepted? Then, don't you see, I could have been getting ready!

TOM You don't have to make any fuss.

AMANDA Oh, Tom, Tom, Tom, of course I have to make a fuss! I want things nice, not sloppy! Not thrown together. I'll certainly have to do some fast thinking, won't I?

TOM I don't see why you have to think at all.

AMANDA You just don't know. We can't have a gentleman caller in a pig-sty! All my wedding silver has to be polished, the monogrammed table linen ought to be laundered! The windows have to be washed and fresh curtains put up. And how about clothes? We have to *wear* something, don't we?

TOM Mother, this boy is no one to make a fuss over!

AMANDA Do you realize he's the first young man we've introduced to your sister? It's terrible, dreadful, disgraceful that poor little sister has never received a single gentleman caller! Tom, come inside! (*She opens the screen door.*)

TOM What for?

AMANDA I want to ask you some things.

TOM If you're going to make such a fuss, I'll call it off, I'll tell him not to come.

AMANDA You certainly won't do anything of the kind. Nothing offends people worse than broken engagements. It simply means I'll have to work like a Turk! We won't be brilliant, but we'll pass inspection. Come on inside. (TOM *follows, groaning.*) Sit down.

TOM Any particular place you would like me to sit?

AMANDA Thank heavens I've got that new sofa! I'm also making payments on a floor lamp I'll have sent out! And put the chintz covers on, they'll brighten things up! Of course I'd hoped to have these walls re-papered. . . . What is the young man's name?

TOM His name is O'Connor.

AMANDA That, of course, means fish—tomorrow is Friday! I'll have that salmon loaf—with Durkee's dressing! What does he do? He works at the warehouse?

TOM Of course! How else would I—

AMANDA Tom, he—doesn't drink?

TOM Why do you ask me that?

AMANDA Your father *did!*

TOM Don't get started on that!

AMANDA He *does* drink, then?

TOM Not that I know of!

AMANDA Make sure, be certain! The last thing I want for my daughter's a boy who drinks!

TOM Aren't you being a little premature? Mr. O'Connor has not yet appeared on the scene!

AMANDA   But will tomorrow. To meet your sister, and what do I know about this character? Nothing! Old maids are better off than wives of drunkards!

TOM   Oh, my God!

AMANDA   Be still!

TOM   (*leaning forward to whisper*)   Lots of fellows meet girls whom they don't marry!

AMANDA   Oh, talk sensibly, Tom—and don't be sarcastic! (*She has gotten a hairbrush.*)

TOM   What are you doing?

AMANDA   I'm brushing that cow-lick down! What is this young man's position at the warehouse?

TOM   (*submitting grimly to the brush and the interrogation*)   This young man's position is that of a shipping clerk, Mother.

AMANDA   Sounds to me like a fairly responsible job, the sort of a job *you* would be in if you just had more *get-up*. What is his salary? Have you got any idea?

TOM   I would judge it to be approximately eighty-five dollars a month.

AMANDA   Well—not princely, but—

TOM   Twenty more than I make.

AMANDA   Yes, how well I know! But for a family man, eighty-five dollars a month is not much more than you can just get by on. . . .

TOM   Yes, but Mr. O'Connor is not a family man.

AMANDA   He might be, mightn't he? Some time in the future?

TOM   I see. Plans and provisions.

AMANDA   You are the only young man that I know of who ignores the fact that the future becomes the present, the present the past, and the past turns into everlasting regret if you don't plan for it!

TOM   I will think that over and see what I can make of it.

AMANDA   Don't be supercilious with your mother! Tell me some more about this—what do you call him?

TOM   James D. O'Connor. The D. is for Delaney.

AMANDA   Irish on *both* sides! *Gracious!* And doesn't drink?

TOM   Shall I call him up and ask him right this minute?

AMANDA   The only way to find out about those things is to make discreet inquiries at the proper moment. When I was a girl in Blue Mountain and it was suspected that a young man drank, the girl whose attentions he had been receiving, if any girl *was,* would sometimes speak to the minister of his church, or rather her father would if her father was living, and sort of feel him out on the young man's character. That is the way such things are discreetly handled to keep a young woman from making a tragic mistake!

TOM   Then how did you happen to make a tragic mistake?

AMANDA   That innocent look of your father's had everyone fooled! He *smiled*—the world was *enchanted!* No girl can do worse than put herself at the mercy of a handsome appearance! I hope that Mr. O'Connor is not too good-looking.

TOM   No, he's not too good-looking. He's covered with freckles and hasn't too much of a nose.

AMANDA   He's not right-down homely, though?

TOM   Not right-down homely. Just medium homely. I'd say.

AMANDA   Character's what to look for in a man.

TOM   That's what I've always said, Mother.

AMANDA   You've never said anything of the kind and I suspect you would never give it a thought.

TOM   Don't be suspicious of me.

AMANDA   At least I hope he's the type that's up and coming.

TOM   I think he really goes in for self-improvement.

AMANDA   What reason have you to think so?

TOM   He goes to night school.

AMANDA (*beaming*)   Splendid! What does he do, I mean study?

TOM   Radio engineering and public speaking!

AMANDA   Then he has visions of being advanced in the world! Any young man who studies public speaking is aiming to have an executive job some day! And radio engineering? A thing for the future! Both of these facts are very illuminating. Those are the sort of things that a mother should know concerning any young man who comes to call on her daughter. Seriously or—not.

TOM   One little warning. He doesn't know about Laura. I didn't let on that we had dark ulterior motives. I just said, why don't you come have dinner with us? He said okay and that was the whole conversation.

AMANDA   I bet it was! You're eloquent as an oyster. However, he'll know about Laura when he gets here. When he sees how lovely and sweet and pretty she is, he'll thank his lucky stars he was asked to dinner.

TOM   Mother, you mustn't expect too much of Laura.

AMANDA   What do you mean?

TOM   Laura seems all those things to you and me because she's ours and we love her. We don't even notice she's crippled any more.

AMANDA   Don't say crippled! You know that I never allow that word to be used!

TOM   But face facts, Mother. She is and—that's not all—

AMANDA   What do you mean "not all"?

TOM   Laura is very different from other girls.

AMANDA   I think the difference is all to her advantage.

TOM   Not quite all—in the eyes of others—strangers—she's terribly shy and lives in a world of her own and those things make her seem a little peculiar to people outside the house.

AMANDA   Don't say peculiar.

TOM   Face the facts. She is.

(The dance-hall music changes to a tango that has a minor and somewhat ominous tone.)

AMANDA   In what was is she peculiar—may I ask?

TOM *(gently)*   She lives in a world of her own—a world of—little glass ornaments, Mother. . . . (*Gets up.* AMANDA *remains holding brush, looking at him, troubled.*) She plays old phonograph records and—that's about all—(*He glances at himself in the mirror and crosses to door.*)

AMANDA *(sharply)*   Where are you going?

TOM   I'm going to the movies. (*out screen door*)

AMANDA   Not to the movies, every night to the movies! (*follows quickly to screen door*) I don't believe you always go to the movies! (*He is gone.* AMANDA *looks worriedly after him for a moment. Then vitality and optimism return and she turns from the door, crossing to portieres.*) Laura! Laura! (LAURA *answers from kitchenette.*)

LAURA   Yes, Mother.

AMANDA   Let those dishes go and come in front! (LAURA *appears with dish towel; gaily:*) Laura, come here and make a wish on the moon!

LAURA *(entering)*   Moon—moon?

AMANDA   A little silver slipper of a moon. Look over your left shoulder, Laura, and make a wish! (LAURA *looks faintly puzzled as if called out of sleep.* AMANDA *seizes her shoulders and turns her at an angle by the door.*) No! Now, darling, wish!

LAURA   What shall I wish for, Mother?

AMANDA *(her voice trembling and her eyes suddenly filling with tears)*   Happiness! Good Fortune!

(The violin rises and the stage dims out.)

Scene VI

(Image: High school hero.)

TOM   And so the following evening I brought Jim home to dinner. I had known Jim slightly in high school. In high school Jim was a hero. He had tremendous Irish good nature and vitality with the scrubbed and polished look of white chinaware. He seemed to move in a continual spotlight. He was a star in basketball, captain of the debating club, president of the senior class and the glee club and he sang the male lead in the annual light operas. He was always running or bounding, never just walking. He seemed always at the point of defeating the law of gravity. He was shooting with such velocity through his adolescence that you would logically expect him to arrive at nothing short of the White House by the time he was thirty. But Jim apparently ran into more interference after his graduation from Soldan. His speed had definitely slowed. Six years after he left high school he was holding a job that wasn't much better than mine.

(Image: Clerk.)

He was the only one at the warehouse with whom I was on friendly terms. I was valuable to him as someone who could remember his former glory, who had seen him win basketball games and the silver cup in debating. He knew of my secret practice of retiring to a cabinet of the washroom to work on poems when business was slack in the warehouse. He called me Shakespeare. And while the other boys in the warehouse regarded me with suspicious hostility, Jim took a humorous attitude toward me. Gradually his attitude affected the others, their hostility wore off and they also began to smile at me as people smile at an oddly fashioned dog who trots across their path at some distance.

I knew that Jim and Laura had known each other at Soldan, and I had heard Laura speak admiringly of his voice. I didn't know if Jim remembered her or not. In high school Laura had been as unobtrusive as Jim had been astonishing. If he did remember Laura, it was not as my sister, for when I asked him to dinner, he grinned and said, "You know, Shakespeare, I never thought of you as having folks!"

He was about to discover that I did. . . .

(Light up stage.)

(Legend on screen: "The accent of a coming foot.")

Friday evening. It is about five o'clock of a late spring evening which comes "scattering poems in the sky."

A delicate lemony light is in the Wingfield apartment.

AMANDA *has worked like a Turk in preparation for the gentleman caller. The results are astonishing. The new floor lamp with its rose-silk shade is in place, a colored paper lantern conceals the broken light fixture in the ceiling, new billowing white curtains are at the windows, chintz covers are on chairs and sofa, a pair of new sofa pillows make their initial appearance.*

Open boxes and tissue paper are scattered on the floor.

LAURA *stands in the middle with lifted arms while* AMANDA *crouches before her, adjusting the hem of the new dress, devout and ritualistic. The dress is colored and designed by memory. The arrangement of* LAURA's *hair is changed; it is softer and more becoming. A fragile, unearthly prettiness has come out in* LAURA: *she is like a piece of translucent glass touched by light, given a momentary radiance, not actual, not lasting.*

AMANDA *(impatiently)*   Why are you trembling?

LAURA   Mother, you've made me so nervous!

AMANDA   How have I made you nervous?

LAURA   By all this fuss! You make it seem so important!

AMANDA   I don't understand you, Laura. You couldn't be satisfied with just sitting home, and yet whenever I try to arrange something for you, you seem to resist it. *(She gets up.)* Now take a look at yourself. No, wait! Wait just a moment—I have an idea!

LAURA   What is it now?

(AMANDA *produces two powder puffs which she wraps in handkerchiefs and stuffs in* LAURA's *bosom.*)

LAURA   Mother, what are you doing?

AMANDA   They call them "Gay Deceivers"!

LAURA   I won't wear them!

AMANDA   You will!

LAURA   Why should I?

AMANDA   Because, to be painfully honest, your chest is flat.

LAURA   You make it seem like we were setting a trap.

AMANDA   All pretty girls are a trap, a pretty trap, and men expect them to be. (*Legend: "A pretty trap."*) Now look at yourself, young lady. This is the prettiest you will ever be! I've got to fix myself now! You're going to be surprised by your mother's appearance! (*She crosses through portieres, humming gaily.*)

(LAURA *moves slowly to the long mirror and stares solemnly at herself.*
    A wind blows the white curtains inward in a slow, graceful motion and with a faint, sorrowful sighing.)

AMANDA (*off stage*)   It isn't dark enough yet. (*She turns slowly before the mirror with a troubled look.*)

    (*Legend on screen: "This is my sister: celebrate her with strings!" Music.*)

AMANDA (*laughing, off*)   I'm going to show you something. I'm going to make a spectacular appearance!

LAURA   What is it, mother?

AMANDA   Possess your soul in patience—you will see! Something I've resurrected from that old trunk! Styles haven't changed so terribly much after all. . . . (*She parts the portieres.*) Now just look at your mother! (*She wears a girlish frock of yellowed voile with a blue silk sash. She carries a bunch of jonquils—the legend of her youth is nearly revived; feverishly:*) This is the dress in which I led the cotillion. Won the cakewalk twice at Sunset Hill, wore one spring to the Governor's ball in Jackson! See how I sashayed around the ballroom, Laura? (*She raises her skirt and does a mincing step around the room.*) I wore it on Sundays for my gentlemen callers! I had it on the day I met your father—I had malaria fever all that spring. The change of climate from East Tennessee to the Delta—weakened resistance—I had a little temperature all the time—not enough to be serious—just enough to make me restless and giddy! Invitations poured in—parties all over the Delta!—"Stay in bed," said Mother, "you have fever!"—but I just wouldn't.—I took quinine but kept on going, going!—Evenings, dances!—Afternoons, long, long, rides! Picnics—lovely!—So lovely, that country in May.—All lacy with dogwood, literally flooded with jonquils!—That was the spring I had the craze for jonquils. Jonquils became an absolute obsession. Mother said, "Honey, there's no more room for jonquils." And still I kept bringing in more jonquils. Whenever, wherever I saw them, I'd say, "Stop! Stop! I see jonquils!" I made the young men help me gather the jonquils! It was a joke, Amanda and her jonquils! Finally there were no more vases to hold them, every available space was filled with jonquils. No vases to hold them? All right, I'll hold them myself! And then I—(*She stops in front of the picture. Music.*) met your father! Malaria fever and jonquils and then—this—boy. . . . (*She switches on the rose-colored lamp.*) I hope they get here before it starts to rain. (*She crosses upstage and places the jonquils in bowl on table.*) I gave your brother a little extra change so he and Mr. O'Connor could take the service car home.

LAURA (*with altered look*) What did you say his name was?
AMANDA O'Connor.
LAURA What is his first name?
AMANDA I don't remember. Oh, yes, I do. It was—Jim!

(LAURA *sways slightly and catches hold of a chair.*)

(*Legend on screen: "Not Jim!"*)

LAURA (*faintly*) Not—Jim!
AMANDA Yes, that was it, it was Jim! I've never known a Jim that wasn't nice!

(*Music: Ominous.*)

LAURA Are you sure his name is Jim O'Connor?
AMANDA Yes. Why?
LAURA Is he the one that Tom used to know in high school?
AMANDA He didn't say so. I think he just got to know him at the warehouse.
LAURA There was a Jim O'Connor we both knew in high school—(*then, with effort:*) If that is the one that Tom is bringing to dinner—you'll have to excuse me, I won't come to the table.
AMANDA What sort of nonsense is this?
LAURA You asked me once if I'd ever liked a boy. Don't you remember I showed you this boy's picture?
AMANDA You mean the boy you showed me in the year book?
LAURA Yes, that boy.
AMANDA Laura, Laura, were you in love with that boy?
LAURA I don't know, Mother. All I know is I couldn't sit at the table if it was him!
AMANDA It won't be him! It isn't the least bit likely. But whether it is or not, you will come to the table. You will not be excused.
LAURA I'll have to be, Mother.

AMANDA   I don't intend to humor your silliness, Laura. I've had too much from you and your brother, both! So just sit down and compose yourself till they come. Tom has forgotten his key so you'll have to let them in, when they arrive.

LAURA (*panicky*)   Oh, Mother—*you* answer the door!

AMANDA (*lightly*)   I'll be in the kitchen—busy!

LAURA   Oh, Mother, please answer the door, don't make me do it!

AMANDA (*crossing into kitchenette*)   I've got to fix the dressing for the salmon. Fuss, fuss—silliness!—over a gentleman caller!

(*Door swings shut.* LAURA *is left alone.*)

(*Legend: "Terror!"*)

(*She utters a low moan and turns off the lamp—sits stiffly on the edge of the sofa, knotting her fingers together.*)

(*Legend on screen: "The opening of a door!"*)

(TOM *and* JIM *appear on the fire-escape steps and climb to landing. Hearing their approach,* LAURA *rises with a panicky gesture. She retreats to the portieres.*
    The doorbell. LAURA *catches her breath and touches her throat. Low drums.*)

AMANDA (*calling*)   Laura, sweetheart! The door!

(LAURA *stares at it without moving.*)

JIM   I think we just beat the rain.

TOM   Uh-huh. (*He rings again, nervously.* JIM *whistles and fishes for a cigarette.*)

AMANDA (*very, very gaily*)   Laura, that is your brother and Mr. O'Connor! Will you let them in, darling?

(LAURA *crosses toward kitchenette door.*)

LAURA (*breathlessly*)   Mother—you go to the door!

(AMANDA *steps out of kitchenette and stares furiously at* LAURA. *She points imperiously at the door.*)

LAURA   Please, please!

AMANDA (*in a fierce whisper*)   What is the matter with you, you silly thing?

LAURA (*desperately*)   Please, you answer it, *please!*

AMANDA   I told you I wasn't going to humor you, Laura. Why have you chosen this moment to lose your mind?

LAURA   Please, please, please, you go!

AMANDA   You'll have to go to the door because I can't!

LAURA (*despairingly*)   I can't either!

AMANDA   Why?

LAURA   I'm *sick!*

AMANDA   I'm sick, too—of your nonsense! Why can't you and your brother be normal people? Fantastic whims and behavior! (Tom *gives a long ring.*) Preposterous goings on! Can you give me one reason—(*calls out lyrically*) COMING! JUST ONE SECOND!—why should you be afraid to open a door? Now you answer it, Laura!

LAURA   Oh, oh, oh . . . (*She returns through the portieres. Darts to the victrola and winds it frantically and turns it on.*)

AMANDA   Laura Wingfield, you march right to that door!

LAURA   Yes—yes, Mother!

(*A faraway, scratchy rendition of "Dardanella" softens the air and gives her strength to move through it. She slips to the door and draws it cautiously open. Tom enters with the caller, JIM O'CONNOR.*)

TOM   Laura, this is Jim. Jim, this is my sister, Laura.

JIM (*stepping inside*)   I didn't know that Shakespeare had a sister!

LAURA (*retreating stiff and trembling from the door*)   How—how do you do?

JIM (*heartily extending his hand*)   Okay!

(LAURA *touches it hesitantly with hers.*)

JIM   Your hand's *cold*, Laura!

LAURA   Yes, well—I've been playing the victrola. . . .

JIM   Must have been playing classical music on it! You ought to play a little hot swing music to warm you up!

LAURA   Excuse me—I haven't finished playing the victrola. . . .

(*She turns awkwardly and hurries into the front room. She pauses a second by the victrola. Then catches her breath and darts through the portieres like a frightened deer.*)

JIM (*grinning*)   What was the matter?

TOM   Oh—with Laura? Laura is—terribly shy.

JIM   Shy, huh? It's unusual to meet a shy girl nowadays. I don't believe you ever mentioned you had a sister.

TOM   Well, now you know. I have one. Here is the *Post Dispatch*. You want a piece of it?

JIM   Uh-huh.

TOM   What piece? The comics?

JIM   Sports! (*glances at it*) Ole Dizzy Dean is on his bad behavior.

TOM (*disinterest*)   Yeah? (*lights cigarette and crosses back to fire-escape door*)

JIM   Where are *you* going?

TOM   I'm going out on the terrace.

JIM (*goes after him*)   You know, Shakespeare—I'm going to sell you a bill of goods!

TOM   What goods?

JIM   A course I'm taking.

TOM   Huh?

JIM   In public speaking! You and me, we're not the warehouse type.

TOM   Thanks—that's good news. But what has public speaking got to do with it?

JIM   It fits you for—executive positions!

TOM   Awww.

JIM   I tell you it's done a helluva lot for me.

(*Image: Executive at desk.*)

TOM   In what respect?

JIM   In every! Ask yourself what is the difference between you an' me and men in the office down front? Brains?—No!—Ability?—No! Then what? Just one little thing—

TOM   What is that one little thing?

JIM   Primarily it amounts to—social poise! Being able to square up to people and hold your own on any social level!

AMANDA (*off stage*)   Tom?

TOM   Yes, Mother?

AMANDA   Is that you and Mr. O'Connor?

TOM   Yes, Mother.

AMANDA   Well, you just make yourselves comfortable in there.

TOM   Yes, Mother.

AMANDA   Ask Mr. O'Connor if he would like to wash his hands.

JIM   Aw—no—no—thank you—I took care of that at the warehouse. Tom—

TOM   Yes?

JIM   Mr. Mendoza was speaking to me about you.

TOM   Favorably?

JIM   What do you think?

TOM   Well—

JIM   You're going to be out of a job if you don't wake up.

TOM   I am waking up—

JIM   You show no signs.

TOM   The signs are interior.

(*Image on screen: The sailing vessel with Jolly Roger again.*)

TOM   I'm planning to change. (*He leans over the rail speaking with quiet exhilaration. The incandescent marquees and signs of the first-run movie houses light his face from across the alley. He looks like a voyager.*) I'm right at the point of committing myself to a future that doesn't include the warehouse and Mr. Mendoza or even a night-school course in public speaking.

JIM   What are you gassing about?

TOM   I'm tired of the movies.

JIM   Movies!

TOM   Yes, movies! Look at them—(*a wave toward the marvels of Grand Avenue*) All of those glamorous people—having adventures—hogging it all, gobbling the whole thing up! You know what happens? People go to the *movies* instead of *moving!* Hollywood characters are supposed to have all the adventures for everybody in America, while everybody in America sits in a dark room and watches them have them! Yes, until there's a war. That's when adventure becomes available to the masses! *Everyone's* dish, not only Gable's! Then the people in the dark room come out of the dark room to have some adventures themselves—Goody, goody!—It's our turn now, to go to the South Sea Island—to make a safari—to be exotic, far-off!—But I'm not patient. I don't want to wait till then. I'm tired of the *movies* and I am *about* to move!

JIM (*incredulously*)   Move?

TOM   Yes.

JIM   When?

TOM   Soon!

JIM   Where? Where?

(*Theme three music seems to answer the question, while Tom thinks it over. He searches among his pockets.*)

TOM   I'm starting to boil inside. I know I seem dreamy, but inside—well, I'm boiling! Whenever I pick up a shoe, I shudder a little thinking how short life is and what I am doing!—Whatever that means. I know it doesn't mean shoes—except as something to wear on a traveler's feet! (*finds paper*) Look—

JIM   What?

TOM   I'm a member.

JIM (*reading*)   The Union of Merchant Seamen.

TOM   I paid my dues this month, instead of the light bill.

JIM   You will regret it when they turn the lights off.

TOM   I won't be here.

JIM   How about your mother?

TOM   I'm like my father. The bastard son of a bastard! See how he grins? And he's been absent going on sixteen years!

JIM   You're just talking, you drip. How does your mother feel about it?

TOM   Shhh!—Here comes Mother! Mother is not acquainted with my plans!

AMANDA (*enters portieres*)   Where are you all?

TOM   On the terrace, Mother.

(*They start inside. She advances to them.* TOM *is distinctly shocked at her appearance. Even* JIM *blinks a little. He is making his first contact with girlish Southern vi-*

vacity and in spite of the night-school course in public speaking is somewhat thrown off the beam by the unexpected outlay of social charm.

Certain responses are attempted by JIM *but are swept aside by* AMANDA'S *gay laughter and chatter.* TOM *is embarrassed but after the first shock* JIM *reacts very warmly. Grins and chuckles, is altogether won over.*)

(*Image: Amanda as a girl.*)

AMANDA (*coyly smiling, shaking her girlish ringlets*) Well, well, well, so this is Mr. O'Connor. Introductions entirely unnecessary. I've heard so much about you from my boy. I finally said to him, Tom—good gracious!—why don't you bring this paragon to supper? I'd like to meet this nice young man at the warehouse!—Instead of just hearing him sing your praises so much! I don't know why my son is so stand-offish—that's not Southern behavior! Let's sit down and—I think we could stand a little more air in here! Tom, leave the door open. I felt a nice fresh breeze a moment ago. Where has it gone? Mmm, so warm already! And not quite summer, even. We're going to burn up when summer really gets started. However, we're having—we're having a very light supper. I think light things are better fo' this time of year. The same as light clothes are. Light clothes an' light food are what warm weather calls fo'. You know our blood gets so thick during th' winter—it takes a while fo' us to *adjust* ou'selves!—when the season changes . . . It's come so quick this year. I wasn't prepared. All of a sudden—heavens! Already summer!—I ran to the trunk an' pulled out this light dress—Terribly old! Historical almost! But feels so good—so good an' co-ol, y'know. . . .

TOM   Mother—

AMANDA   Yes, honey?

TOM   How about—supper?

AMANDA   Honey, you go ask Sister if supper is ready! You know that Sister is in full charge of supper! Tell her you hungry boys are waiting for it. (*to* JIM) Have you met Laura?

JIM   She—

AMANDA   Let you in? Oh, good, you've met already! It's rare for a girl as sweet an' pretty as Laura to be domestic! But Laura is, thank heavens, not only pretty but also very domestic. I'm not at all. I never was a bit. I never could make a thing but angel-food cake. Well, in the South we had so many servants. Gone, gone, gone. All vestige of gracious living! Gone completely! I wasn't prepared for what the future brought me. All of my gentlemen callers were sons of planters and so of course I assumed that I would be married to one and raise my family on a large piece of land with plenty of servants. But man proposes—and woman accepts the proposal!—To vary that old, old saying a little bit—I married no planter! I married a man who worked for the telephone company!—That gallantly smiling gentleman over there! (*points to the picture*) A telephone man who—fell in love with long-distance!—Now he travels and I don't even know where!—But what am I going on for about my—tribulations? Tell me yours—I hope you don't have any! Tom?

TOM (*returning*)   Yes, Mother?

AMANDA   Is supper nearly ready?

TOM   It looks to me like supper is on the table.

AMANDA   Let me look—(*She rises prettily and looks through portieres.*) Oh, lovely!—But where is Sister?

TOM   Laura is not feeling well and she says that she thinks she'd better not come to the table.

AMANDA   What?—Nonsense!—Laura? Oh, Laura!

LAURA (*off stage, faintly*)   Yes, Mother.

AMANDA   You really must come to the table. We won't be seated until you come to the table! Come in, Mr. O'Connor. You sit over there and I'll—Laura? Laura Wingfield! You're keeping us waiting, honey! We can't say grace until you come to the table!

(*The back door is pushed weakly open and* LAURA *comes in. She is obviously quite faint, her lips trembling, her eyes wide and staring. She moves unsteadily toward the table.*)

(*Legend: "Terror!"*)

(*Outside a summer storm is coming abruptly. The white curtains billow inward at the windows and there is a sorrowful murmur and deep blue dusk.*
   LAURA *suddenly stumbles; she catches at a chair with a faint moan.*)

TOM   Laura!

AMANDA   Laura! (*There is a clap of thunder.*) (*Legend: "Ah!"*) (*despairingly:*) Why, Laura, you *are* sick, darling! Tom, help your sister into the living room, dear! Sit in the living room, Laura—rest on the sofa. Well! (*to the gentleman caller:*) Standing over the hot stove made her ill!—I told her that it was just too warm this evening, but—(TOM *comes back in.* LAURA *is on the sofa.*) Is Laura all right now?

TOM   Yes.

AMANDA   What *is* that? Rain? A nice cool rain has come up! (*She gives the gentleman caller a frightened look.*) I think we may—have grace—now . . . (TOM *looks at her stupidly.*) Tom, honey—you say grace!

TOM   Oh . . . "For these and all thy mercies—" (*They bow their heads,* AMANDA *stealing a nervous glance at* JIM. *In the living room* LAURA, *stretched on the sofa, clenches her hand to her lips, to hold back a shuddering sob.*) God's Holy Name be praised—

(*The scene dims out.*)

Scene VII

(Legend: "A souvenir.")

Half an hour later. Dinner is just being finished in the upstage area which is concealed by the drawn portieres.

As the curtain rises LAURA *is still huddled upon the sofa, her feet drawn under her, her head resting on a pale blue pillow, her eyes wide and mysteriously watchful. The new floor lamp with its shade of rose-colored silk gives a soft, becoming light to her face, bringing out the fragile, unearthly prettiness which usually escapes attention. There is a steady murmur of rain, but it is slackening and stops soon after the scene begins; the air outside becomes pale and luminous as the moon breaks out.*

A moment after the curtain rises, the lights in both rooms flicker and go out.

JIM   Hey, there, Mr. Light Bulb!

(AMANDA *laughs nervously.*)

(Legend: "Suspension of a public service.")

AMANDA   Where was Moses when the lights went out? Ha-ha. Do you know the answer to that one, Mr. O'Connor?

JIM   No, Ma'am, what's the answer?

AMANDA   In the dark! (JIM *laughs appreciably.*) Everybody sit still. I'll light the candles. Isn't it lucky we have them on the table? Where's a match? Which of you gentlemen can provide a match?

JIM   Here.

AMANDA   Thank you, sir.

JIM   Not at all, Ma'am!

AMANDA   I guess the fuse has burnt out. Mr. O'Connor, can you tell a burnt-out fuse? I know I can't and Tom is a total loss when it comes to mechanics. (*Sound: Getting up: voices recede a little to kitchenette.*) Oh, be careful you don't bump into something. We don't want our gentleman caller to break his neck. Now wouldn't that be a fine howdy-do?

JIM   Ha-ha! Where is the fuse-box?

AMANDA   Right here next to the stove. Can you see anything?

JIM   Just a minute.

AMANDA   Isn't electricity a mysterious thing? Wasn't it Benjamin Franklin who tied a key to a kite? We live in such a mysterious universe, don't we? Some people say that science clears up all mysteries for us. In my opinion it only creates more! Have you found it yet?

JIM   No, Ma'am. All these fuses look okay to me.

AMANDA   Tom!

TOM   Yes, Mother?

AMANDA   That light bill I gave you several days ago. The one I told you we got the notices about?

TOM   Oh.—Yeah.

(Legend: "Ha!")

AMANDA   You didn't neglect to pay it by any chance?

TOM   Why, I—

AMANDA   Didn't! I might have known it!

JIM   Shakespeare probably wrote a poem on that light bill, Mrs. Wingfield.

AMANDA   I might have known better than to trust him with it! There's such a high price for negligence in this world!

JIM   Maybe the poem will win a ten-dollar prize.

AMANDA   We'll just have to spend the remainder of the evening in the nineteenth century, before Mr. Edison made the Mazda lamp!

JIM   Candlelight is my favorite kind of light.

AMANDA   That shows you're romantic! But that's no excuse for Tom. Well, we got through dinner. Very considerate of them to let us get through dinner before they plunged us into everlasting darkness, wasn't it, Mr. O'Connor?

JIM   Ha-ha!

AMANDA   Tom, as a penalty for your carelessness you can help me with the dishes.

JIM   Let me give you a hand.

AMANDA   Indeed you will not!

JIM   I ought to be good for something.

AMANDA   Good for something? *(Her tone is rhapsodic.) You?* Why, Mr. O'Connor, nobody, *nobody's* given me this much entertainment in years—as you have!

JIM   Aw, now, Mrs. Wingfield!

AMANDA   I'm not exaggerating, not one bit! But Sister is all by her lonesome. You go keep her company in the parlor! I'll give you this lovely old candelabrum that used to be on the altar at the church of the Heavenly Rest. It was melted a little out of shape when the church burnt down. Lightning struck it one spring. Gypsy Jones was holding a revival at the time and he intimated that the church was destroyed because the Episcopalians gave card parties.

JIM   Ha-ha.

AMANDA   And how about coaxing Sister to drink a little wine? I think it would be good for her! Can you carry both at once?

JIM   Sure. I'm Superman!

AMANDA   Now, Thomas, get into this apron!

(The door of kitchenette swings closed on AMANDA'*s gay laughter; the flickering light approaches the portieres.*

LAURA sits up nervously as he enters. Her speech at first is low and breathless from the almost intolerable strain of being alone with a stranger.)

(The legend: "I don't suppose you remember me at all!")

(In her first speeches in his scene, before JIM's *warmth overcomes her paralyzing shyness,* LAURA's *voice is thin and breathless as though she has just run up a steep flight of stairs.*

JIM's attitude is gently humorous. In playing this scene it should be stressed that while the incident is apparently unimportant, it is to LAURA *the climax of her secret life.)*

JIM   Hello, there, Laura.

LAURA *(faintly)*   Hello. *(She clears her throat.)*

JIM   How are you feeling now? Better?

LAURA   Yes. Yes, thank you.

JIM   This is for you. A little dandelion wine. *(He extends it toward her with extravagant gallantry.)*

LAURA   Thank you.

JIM   Drink it—but don't get drunk! *(He laughs heartily.* LAURA *takes the glass uncertainly, laughs shyly.)* Where shall I set the candles?

LAURA   Oh—oh, anywhere . . .

JIM   How about here on the floor? Any objections?

LAURA   No.

JIM   I'll spread a newspaper under to catch the drippings. I like to sit on the floor. Mind if I do?

LAURA   Oh, no.

JIM   Give me a pillow?

LAURA   What?

JIM   A pillow!

LAURA   Oh . . . *(hands him one quickly)*

JIM   How about you? Don't you like to sit on the floor?

LAURA   Oh—yes.

JIM   Why don't you, then?

LAURA   I—will.

JIM   Take a pillow! *(*LAURA *does. Sits on the other side of the candelabrum.* JIM *crosses his legs and smiles engagingly at her.)* I can't hardly see you sitting way over there.

LAURA   I can—see you.

JIM   I know, but that's not fair, I'm in the limelight. *(*LAURA *moves her pillow closer.)* Good! Now I can see you! Comfortable?

LAURA   Yes.

JIM   So am I. Comfortable as a cow. Will you have some gum?

LAURA   No, thank you.

JIM   I think that I will indulge, with your permission. *(musingly unwraps it and holds it up)* Think of the fortune made by the guy that invented the first piece of chewing gum. Amazing, huh? The Wrigley Building is one of the sights of Chicago.—I saw it summer before last when I went up to the Century of Progress. Did you take in the Century of Progress?

LAURA   No, I didn't.

JIM   Well, it was quite a wonderful exposition. What impressed me most was the Hall of Science. Gives you an idea of what the future will be in America, even more wonderful than the present time is! (*pause; smiling at her:*) Your brother tells me you're shy. Is that right, Laura?

LAURA   I—don't know.

JIM   I judge you to be an old-fashioned type of girl. Well, I think that's a pretty good type to be. Hope you don't think I'm being too personal—do you?

LAURA   (*hastily, out of embarrassment*)   I believe I *will* take a piece of gum, if you—don't mind. (*clearing her throat*) Mr. O'Connor, have you—kept up with your singing?

JIM   Singing? Me?

LAURA   Yes, I remember what a beautiful voice you had.

JIM   When did you hear me sing?

(*Voice off stage in the pause.*)

VOICE (*off stage*)

> O blow, ye winds, heigh-ho,
> A-roving I will go!
> I'm off to my love
> With a boxing glove—
> Ten thousand miles away!

JIM   You say you've heard me sing?

LAURA   Oh, yes! Yes, very often . . . I—don't suppose you remember me—at all?

JIM   (*smiling doubtfully*)   You know I have an idea I've seen you before. I had that idea soon as you opened the door. It seemed almost like I was about to remember your name. But the name that I started to call you—wasn't a name! And so I stopped myself before I said it.

LAURA   Wasn't it—Blue Roses?

JIM   (*springs up, grinning*)   Blue Roses! My gosh, yes—Blue Roses! That's what I had on my tongue when you opened the door! Isn't it funny what tricks your memory plays? I didn't connect you with the high school somehow or other. But that's where it was; it was high school. I didn't even know you were Shakespeare's sister! Gosh, I'm sorry.

LAURA   I didn't expect you to. You—barely knew me!

JIM   But we did have a speaking acquaintance, huh?

LAURA   Yes, we—spoke to each other.

JIM   When did you recognize me?

LAURA   Oh, right away!

JIM   Soon as I came in the door?

LAURA   When I heard your name I thought it was probably you. I knew that Tom used to know you a little in high school. So when you came in the door—Well, then I was—sure.

JIM   Why didn't you *say* something, then?

LAURA   (*breathlessly*)   I didn't know what to say, I was—too surprised!

JIM   For goodness' sakes! You know, this sure is funny!

LAURA   Yes! Yes, isn't it, though . . .

JIM   Didn't we have a class in something together?

LAURA   Yes, we did.

JIM   What class was that?

LAURA   It was—singing—Chorus!

JIM   Aw!

LAURA   I sat across the aisle from you in the Aud.

JIM   Aw.

LAURA   Mondays, Wednesdays and Fridays.

JIM   Now I remember—you always came in late.

LAURA   Yes, it was so hard for me, getting upstairs. I had that brace on my leg—it clumped so loud!

JIM   I never heard any clumping.

LAURA   (*wincing at the recollection*)   To me it sounded like—thunder!

JIM   Well, well, well. I never even noticed.

LAURA   And everybody was seated before I came in. I had to walk in front of all those people. My seat was in the back row. I had to go clumping all the way up the aisle with everyone watching!

JIM   You shouldn't have been self-conscious.

LAURA   I know, but I was. It was always such a relief when the singing started.

JIM   Aw, yes. I've placed you now! I used to call you Blue Roses. How was it that I got started calling you that?

LAURA   I was out of school a little while with pleurosis. When I came back you asked me what was the matter. I said I had pleurosis—you thought I said Blue Roses. That's what you always called me after that!

JIM   I hope you didn't mind.

LAURA   Oh, no—I liked it. You see, I wasn't acquainted with many—people. . . .

JIM   As I remember you sort of stuck by yourself.

LAURA   I—I—never had much luck at—making friends.

JIM   I don't see why you wouldn't.

LAURA   Well, I—started out badly.

JIM   You mean being—

LAURA   Yes, it sort of—stood between me—

JIM   You shouldn't have let it!

LAURA   I know, but it did, and—

JIM   You were shy with people!

LAURA   I tried not to be but never could—

JIM   Overcome it?

LAURA   No, I—I never could!

JIM   I guess being shy is something you have to work out of kind of gradually.

LAURA (*sorrowfully*)   Yes—I guess it—

JIM   Takes time!

LAURA   Yes—

JIM   People are not so dreadful when you know them. That's what you have to remember! And everybody has problems, not just you, but practically everybody has got some problems. You think of yourself as having the only problems, as being the only one who is disappointed. But just look around you and you will see lots of people as disappointed as you are. For instance, I hoped when I was going to high school that I would be further along at this time, six years later, than I am now—You remember that wonderful write-up I had in *The Torch*?

LAURA   Yes! (*She rises and crosses to table.*)

JIM   It said I was bound to succeed in anything I went into! (LAURA *returns with the annual.*) Holy Jeez! *The Torch!* (*He accepts it reverently. They smile across it with mutual wonder.* LAURA *crouches beside him and they begin to turn through it.* LAURA's *shyness is dissolving in his warmth.*)

LAURA   Here you are in *Pirates of Penzance!*

JIM (*wistfully*)   I sang the baritone lead in that operetta.

LAURA (*rapidly*)   So—*beautifully!*

JIM (*protesting*)   Aw—

LAURA   Yes, yes—beautifully—beautifully!

JIM   You heard me?

LAURA   All three times!

JIM   No!

LAURA   Yes!

JIM   All three performances?

LAURA (*looking down*)   Yes.

JIM   Why?

LAURA   I—wanted to ask you to—autograph my program.

JIM   Why didn't you ask me to?

LAURA   You were always surrounded by your own friends so much that I never had a chance to.

JIM   You should have just—

LAURA   Well, I—thought you might think I was—

JIM   Thought I might think you was—what?

LAURA   Oh—

JIM (*with reflective relish*)   I was beleaguered by females in those days.

LAURA   You were terribly popular!

JIM   Yeah—

LAURA   You had such a—friendly way—

JIM   I was spoiled in high school.

LAURA   Everybody—liked you!

JIM   Including you?

LAURA   I—yes, I—I did, too—(*She gently closes the book in her lap.*)

JIM   Well, well, well!—Give me that program, Laura. (*She hands it to him. He signs it with a flourish.*) There you are—better late than never!

LAURA   Oh, I—what a—surprise!

JIM   My signature isn't worth very much right now. But some day—maybe—it will increase in value! Being disappointed is one thing and being discouraged is something else. I am disappointed but I am not discouraged. I'm twenty-three years old. How old are you?

LAURA   I'll be twenty-four in June.

JIM   That's not old age!

LAURA   No, but—

JIM   You finished high school?

LAURA (*with difficulty*)   I didn't go back.

JIM   You mean you dropped out?

LAURA   I made bad grades in my final examinations. (*She rises and replaces the book and the program; her voice strained:*) How is—Emily Meisenbach getting along?

JIM   Oh, that kraut-head!

LAURA   Why do you call her that?

JIM   That's what she was.

LAURA   You're not still—going with her?

JIM   I never see her.

LAURA   It said in the Personal Section that you were—engaged!

JIM   I know, but I wasn't impressed by that—propaganda!

LAURA   It wasn't—the truth?

JIM   Only in Emily's optimistic opinion!

LAURA   Oh—

(*Legend: "What have you done since high school?"*)

(JIM *lights a cigarette and leans indolently back on his elbows smiling at* LAURA *with a warmth and charm which lights her inwardly with altar candles. She remains by the table and turns in her hands a piece of glass to cover her tumult.*)

JIM (*after several reflective puffs on a cigarette*)   What have you done since high school? (*She seems not to hear him.*) Huh? (LAURA *looks up.*) I said what have you done since high school, Laura?

LAURA   Nothing much.

JIM   You must have been doing something these six long years.

LAURA   Yes.

JIM   Well, then, such as what?

LAURA   I took a business course at business college—

JIM   How did that work out?

LAURA   Well, not very—well—I had to drop out, it gave me—indigestion—

(JIM *laughs gently.*)

JIM   What are you doing now?

LAURA   I don't do anything—much. Oh, please don't think I sit around doing nothing! My glass collection takes up a good deal of my time. Glass is something you have to take good care of.

JIM   What did you say—about glass?

LAURA   Collection I said—I have one—(*She clears her throat and turns away again, acutely shy.*)

JIM   (*abruptly*)   You know what I judge to be the trouble with you? Inferiority complex! Know what that is? That's what they call it when someone low-rates himself! I understand it because I had it, too. Although my case was not so aggravated as yours seems to be. I had it until I took up public speaking, developed my voice, and learned that I had an aptitude for science. Before that time I never thought of myself as being outstanding in any way whatsoever! Now I've never made a regular study of it, but I have a friend who says I can analyze people better than doctors that make a profession of it. I don't claim that to be necessarily true, but I can sure guess a person's psychology, Laura! (*takes out his gum*) Excuse me, Laura. I always take it out when the flavor is gone. I'll use this scrap of paper to wrap it in. I know how it is to get it stuck on a shoe. Yep—that's what I judge to be your principal trouble. A lack of confidence in yourself as a person. You don't have the proper amount of faith in yourself. I'm basing that fact on a number of your remarks and also on certain observations I've made. For instance that clumping you thought was so awful in high school. You say that you even dreaded to walk into class. You see what you did? You dropped out of school, you gave up an education because of a clump, which as far as I know was practically non-existent! A little physical defect is what you have. Hardly noticeable even! Magnified thousands of times by imagination! You know what my strong advice to you is? Think of yourself as *superior* in some way!

LAURA   In what way would I think?

JIM   Why, man alive, Laura! Just look about you a little. What do you see? A world full of common people! All of 'em born and all of 'em going to die! Which of them has one-tenth of your good points! Or mine! Or anyone else's, as far as that goes—Gosh! Everybody excels in some one thing. Some in many! (*unconsciously glances at himself in the mirror*) All you've got to do is discover in *what*! Take me, for instance. (*He adjusts his tie at the mirror.*) My interest happens to lie in electro-dynamics. I'm taking a course in radio engineering at night school, Laura, on top of a fairly responsible job at the warehouse. I'm taking that course and studying public speaking.

LAURA   Ohhhh.

JIM   Because I believe in the future of television! (*turning back to her*) I wish to be ready to go up right along with it. Therefore I'm planning to get in on the ground floor. In fact, I've already made the right connections and all that remains is for the industry itself to get under way! Full steam—(*His eyes are starry.*) *Knowledge*—Zzzzzp! *Money*—Zzzzzzp!—*Power!* That's the cycle democracy is built on! (*His attitude is convincingly dynamic.* LAURA *stares at him, even her shyness eclipsed in her absolute wonder. He suddenly grins.*) I guess you think I think a lot of myself!

LAURA   No—o-o-o, I—

JIM   Now how about you? Isn't there something you take more interest in than anything else?

LAURA   Well, I do—as I said—have my—glass collection—

(*A peal of girlish laughter from the kitchen.*)

JIM   I'm not right sure I know what you're talking about. What kind of glass is it?

LAURA   Little articles of it, they're ornaments mostly! Most of them are little animals made out of glass, the tiniest little animals in the world. Mother calls them a glass menagerie! Here's an example of one, if you'd like to see it! This one is one of the oldest. It's nearly thirteen. (*He stretches out his hand.*) (*Music: "The Glass Menagerie."*) Oh, be careful—if you breathe, it breaks!

JIM   I'd better not take it. I'm pretty clumsy with things.

LAURA   Go on, I trust you with him! (*places it in his palm*) There now—you're holding him gently! Hold him over the light, he loves the light! You see how the light shines through him?

JIM   It sure does shine!

LAURA   I shouldn't be partial, but he is my favorite one.

JIM   What kind of thing is this one supposed to be?

LAURA   Haven't you noticed the single horn on his forehead?

JIM   A unicorn, huh?

LAURA   Mmm-hmmm!

JIM   Unicorns, aren't they extinct in the modern world?

LAURA   I know!

JIM   Poor little fellow, he must feel sort of lonesome.

LAURA (*smiling*)   Well, if he does he doesn't complain about it. He stays on a shelf with some horses that don't have horns and all of them seem to get along nicely together.

JIM   How do you know?

LAURA (*lightly*)   I haven't heard any arguments among them!

JIM (*grinning*)   No arguments, huh? Well, that's a pretty good sign! Where shall I set him?

LAURA   Put him on the table. They all like a change of scenery once in a while!

JIM (*stretching*)   Well, well, well, well—Look how big my shadow is when I stretch!

LAURA   Oh, oh, yes—it stretches across the ceiling!

JIM (*crossing to the door*)   I think it's stopped raining. (*opens fire-escape door*) Where does the music come from?

LAURA   From the Paradise Dance Hall across the alley.

JIM   How about cutting the rug a little, Miss Wingfield?

AMANDA   Oh, I—

JIM   Or is your program filled up? Let me have a look at it. (*grasps imaginary card*) Why, every dance is taken! I'll just have to scratch some out. (*Waltz music: "La Golondrina."*) Ahhh, a waltz! (*He executes some sweeping turns by himself, then holds his arms toward LAURA.*)

LAURA (*breathlessly*)   I—can't dance!

JIM   There you go, that inferiority stuff.

LAURA   I've never danced in my life!

JIM   Come on, try!

LAURA   Oh, but I'd step on you!

JIM   I'm not made out of glass.

LAURA   How—how—how do we start?

JIM   Just leave it to me. You hold your arms out a little.

LAURA   Like this?

JIM   A little big higher. Right. Now don't tighten up, that's the main thing about it—relax.

LAURA (*laughing breathlessly*)   It's hard not to.

JIM   Okay.

LAURA   I'm afraid you can't budge me.

JIM   What do you bet I can't? (*He swings her into motion.*)

LAURA   Goodness, yes, you can!

JIM   Let yourself go, now, Laura, just let yourself go.

LAURA   I'm—

JIM   Come on!

LAURA   Trying!

JIM   Not so stiff—Easy does it!

LAURA   I know but I'm—

JIM   Loosen th' backbone! There now, that's a lot better.

LAURA   Am I?

JIM   Lots, lots better! (*He moves her about the room in a clumsy waltz.*)

LAURA   Oh, my!

JIM   Ha-ha!

LAURA   Goodness, yes you can!

JIM   Ha-ha-ha! (*They suddenly bump into the table. JIM stops.*) What did we hit on?

LAURA   Table.

JIM   Did something fall off it? I think—

LAURA   Yes.

JIM   I hope that it wasn't the little glass horse with the horn!

LAURA   Yes.

JIM   Aw, aw, aw. Is it broken?

LAURA   Now it is just like all the other horses.

JIM   It's lost its—

LAURA   Horn! It doesn't matter. Maybe it's a blessing in disguise.

JIM   You'll never forgive me. I bet that that was your favorite piece of glass.

LAURA   I don't have favorites much. It's no tragedy, Freckles. Glass breaks so easily. No matter how careful you are. The traffic jars the shelves and things fall off them.

JIM   Still I'm awfully sorry that I was the cause.

LAURA   (*smiling*)   I'll just imagine he had an operation. The horn was removed to make him feel less—freakish! (*They both laugh.*) Now he will feel more at home with the other horses, the ones that don't have horns . . .

JIM   Ha-ha, that's very funny! (*suddenly serious:*) I'm glad to see that you have a sense of humor. You know—you're—well—very different! Surprisingly different from anyone else I know! (*His voice becomes soft and hesitant with a genuine feeling.*) Do you mind me telling you that? (LAURA *is abashed beyond speech.*) You make me feel sort of—I don't know how to put it! I'm usually pretty good at expressing things, but—This is something that I don't know how to say! (LAURA *touches her throat and clears it—turns the broken unicorn in her hands.*) (*even softer:*) Has anyone ever told you that you were pretty? (*Pause: Music*) (LAURA *looks up slowly, with wonder, and shakes her head.*) Well, you are! In a very different way from anyone else. And all the nicer because of the difference, too. (*His voice becomes low and husky.* LAURA *turns away, nearly faint with the novelty of her emotions.*) I wish that you were my sister. I'd teach you to have some confidence in yourself. The different people are not like other people, but being different is nothing to be ashamed of. Because other people are not such wonderful people. They're one hundred times one thousand. You're one times one! They walk all over the earth. You just stay here. They're common as—weeds, but—you—well, you're—*Blue Roses!*

(*Image on screen: Blue roses.*)

(*Music changes.*)

LAURA   But blue is wrong for—roses . . .

JIM   It's right for you—You're—pretty!

LAURA   In what respect am I pretty?

JIM   In all respects—believe me! Your eyes—your hair—are pretty! Your hands are pretty! (*He catches hold of her hand.*) You think I'm making this up because I'm invited to dinner and have to be nice. Oh, I could do that! I could put on an act for you, Laura, and say lots of things without being very sincere. But this time I am. I'm talking to you sincerely. I happened to notice you had this inferiority complex that keeps you from feeling comfortable with people. Somebody needs to build your confidence up and make you proud instead of shy and turning away and—blushing—Somebody ought to—Ought to—*kiss* you, Laura! (*His hand slips slowly up her arm to her shoulder.*) (*Music swells tumultuously.*) (*He suddenly turns her about and kisses her on the lips. When he releases her* LAURA *sinks on the sofa with a bright, dazed look.* JIM *backs away and fishes in his pocket for a cigarette.*) (*Legend on screen: "Souvenir."*) Stumble-john! (*He lights the cigarette, avoiding her look. There is a peal of girlish laughter from* AMANDA *in the kitchen.* LAURA *slowly raises and opens her hand. It still contains the little broken glass animal. She looks at it with a tender, bewildered expression.*) Stumble-john! I shouldn't have done that—That was way off the beam. You don't smoke, do you? (*She looks up, smiling, not hearing the question. He sits beside her a little gingerly. She looks at him speechlessly—waiting. He coughs decorously and moves a little farther aside as he considers the situation and senses her feelings, dimly, with perturbation; gently:*) Would you—care for a—mint? (*She doesn't seem to hear him but her look grows brighter even.*) Peppermint—Life Saver? My pocket's a regular drug store—wherever I go . . . (*He pops a mint in his mouth. Then gulps and decides to make a clean breast of it. He speaks slowly and gingerly.*) Laura, you know, if I had a sister like you, I'd do the same thing as Tom. I'd bring out fellows—introduce her to them. The right type of boys of a type to—appreciate her. Only—well—he made a mistake about me. Maybe I've got no call to be saying this. That may not have been the idea in having me over. But what if it was? There's nothing wrong about that. The only trouble is that in my case—I'm not in a situation to—do the right thing. I can't take down your number and say I'll phone. I can't call up next week and—ask for a date. I thought I had better explain the situation in case you misunderstood it and—hurt your feelings. . . . (*Pause. Slowly, very slowly,* LAURA's *look changes, her eyes returning slowly from his to the ornament in her palm.*)

(AMANDA *utters another gay laugh in the kitchen.*)

LAURA (*faintly*) You—won't—call again?

JIM No, Laura, I can't. (*He rises from the sofa.*) As I was just explaining, I've—got strings on me, Laura, I've—been going steady! I go out all the time with a girl named Betty. She's a home-girl like you, and Catholic, and Irish, and in a great many ways we—get along fine. I met her last summer on a moonlight boat trip up the river to Alton, on the *Majestic*. Well—right away from the start it was—love! (*Legend: Love!*) (LAURA *sways slightly for-*

ward and grips the arm of the sofa. He fails to notice, now enrapt in his own comfortable being.) Being in love has made a new man of me! (*Leaning stiffly forward, clutching the arm of the sofa,* LAURA *struggles visibly with her storm. But* JIM *is oblivious; she is a long way off.*) The power of love is really pretty tremendous! Love is something that—changes the whole world, Laura! (*The storm abates a little and* LAURA *leans back. He notices her again.*) It happened that Betty's aunt took sick, she got a wire and had to go to Centralia. So Tom—when he asked me to dinner—I naturally just accepted the invitation, not knowing that you—that he—that I—(*He stops awkwardly.*) Huh—I'm a stumble-john! (*He flops back on the sofa. The holy candles in the altar of* LAURA'S *face have been snuffed out! There is a look of almost infinite desolation.* JIM *glances at her uneasily.*) I wish that you would—say something. (*She bites her lip which was trembling and then bravely smiles. She opens her hand again on the broken glass ornament. Then she gently takes his hand and raises it level with her own. She carefully places the unicorn in the palm of his hand, then pushes his fingers closed upon it.*) What are you—doing that for? You want me to have him?—Laura? (*She nods.*) What for?

LAURA   A—souvenir . . .

(*She rises unsteadily and crouches beside the victrola to wind it up.*)

(*Legend on screen: "Things have a way of turning out so badly."*)

(*Or image: "Gentleman caller waving goodbye!—gaily."*)

(*At this moment* AMANDA *rushes brightly back in the front room. She bears a pitcher of fruit punch in an old-fashioned cut-glass pitcher and a plate of macaroons. The plate has a gold border and poppies painted on it.*)

AMANDA   Well, well, well! Isn't the air delightful after the shower? I've made you children a little liquid refreshment. (*turns gaily to the gentleman caller*) Jim, do you know that song about lemonade?

> "Lemonade, lemonade
> Made in the shade and stirred with a spade—
> Good enough for any old maid!"

JIM (*uneasily*)   Ha-ha! No—I never heard it.
AMANDA   Why, Laura! You look so serious!
JIM   We were having a serious conversation.
AMANDA   Good! Now you're better acquainted!
JIM (*uncertainly*)   Ha-ha! Yes.
AMANDA   You modern young people are much more serious-minded than my generation. I was so gay as a girl!
JIM   You haven't changed, Mrs. Wingfield.

AMANDA   Tonight I'm rejuvenated! The gaiety of the occasion, Mr. O'Connor! (*She tosses her head with a peal of laughter, spills lemonade.*) Oooo! I'm baptizing myself!

JIM   Here—let me—

AMANDA   (*setting the pitcher down*)   There now. I discovered we had some maraschino cherries. I dumped them in, juice and all!

JIM   You shouldn't have gone to that trouble, Mrs. Wingfield.

AMANDA   Trouble, trouble? Why it was loads of fun! Didn't you hear me cutting up in the kitchen? I bet your ears were burning! I told Tom how outdone with him I was for keeping you to himself so long a time! He should have brought you over much, much sooner! Well, now that you've found your way, I want you to be a very frequent caller! Not just occasional but all the time. Oh, we're going to have a lot of gay times together! I see them coming! Mmm, just breathe that air! So fresh, and the moon's so pretty! I'll skip back out—I know where my place is when young folks are having a—serious conversation!

JIM   Oh, don't go out, Mrs. Wingfield. The fact of the matter is I've got to be going.

AMANDA   Going, now? You're joking! Why, it's only the shank of the evening, Mr. O'Connor!

JIM   Well, you know how it is.

AMANDA   You mean you're a young workingman and have to keep workingmen's hours. We'll let you off early tonight. But only on the condition that next time you stay later. What's the best night for you? Isn't Saturday night the best night for you workingmen?

JIM   I have a couple of time-clocks to punch, Mrs. Wingfield. One at morning, another one at night!

AMANDA   My, but you *are* ambitious! You work at night, too?

JIM   No, Ma'am, not work but—Betty! (*He crosses deliberately to pick up his hat. The band at the Paradise Dance Hall goes into a tender waltz.*)

AMANDA   Betty? Betty? Who's—Betty! (*There is an ominous cracking sound in the sky.*)

JIM   Oh, just a girl. The girl I go steady with! (*He smiles charmingly. The sky falls.*)

(*Legend: "The sky falls."*)

AMANDA   (*a long-drawn exhalation*)   Ohhhh . . . Is it a serious romance, Mr. O'Connor?

JIM   We're going to be married the second Sunday in June.

AMANDA   Ohhhh—how nice! Tom didn't mention that you were engaged to be married.

JIM   The cat's not out of the bag at the warehouse yet. You know how they are. They call you Romeo and stuff like that. (*He stops at the oval mirror to put on his hat. He carefully shapes the brim and the crown to give a discreetly dashing effect.*) It's been a wonderful evening, Mrs. Wingfield. I guess this is what they mean by Southern hospitality.

AMANDA   It really wasn't anything at all.

JIM   I hope it don't seem like I'm rushing off. But I promised Betty I'd pick her up at the Wabash depot, an' by the time I get my jalopy down there her train'll be in. Some women are pretty upset if you keep 'em waiting.

AMANDA   Yes, I know—The tyranny of women! (*extends her hand*) Goodbye, Mr. O'Connor. I wish you luck—and happiness—and success! All three of them, and so does Laura!—Don't you, Laura?

LAURA   Yes!

JIM   (*taking her hand*)   Good-bye, Laura. I'm certainly going to treasure that souvenir. And don't you forget the good advice I gave you. (*raises his voice to a cheery shout*) So long, Shakespeare! Thanks again, ladies—Good night!

(*He grins and ducks jauntily out.*

Still bravely grimacing, AMANDA *closes the door on the gentleman caller. Then she turns back to the room with a puzzled expression. She and* LAURA *don't dare to face each other.* LAURA *crouches beside the victrola to wind it.*)

AMANDA   (*faintly*)   Things have a way of turning out so badly. I don't believe that I would play the victrola. Well, well—well—Our gentleman caller was engaged to be married! Tom!

TOM   (*from back*)   Yes, Mother?

AMANDA   Come in here a minute. I want to tell you something awfully funny.

TOM   (*enters with a macaroon and a glass of the lemonade*)   Has the gentleman caller gotten away already?

AMANDA   The gentleman caller has made an early departure. What a wonderful joke you played on us!

TOM   How do you mean?

AMANDA   You didn't mention that he was engaged to be married.

TOM   Jim? Engaged?

AMANDA   That's what he just informed us.

TOM   I'll be jiggered! I didn't know about that.

AMANDA   That seems very peculiar.

TOM   What's peculiar about it?

AMANDA   Didn't you call him your best friend down at the warehouse?

TOM   He is, but how did I know?

AMANDA   It seems extremely peculiar that you wouldn't know your best friend was going to be married!

TOM   The warehouse is where I work, not where I know things about people!

AMANDA   You don't know things anywhere! You live in a dream; you manufacture illusions! (*He crosses to door.*) Where are you going?

TOM   I'm going to the movies.

AMANDA   That's right, now that you've had us make such fools of ourselves. The effort, the preparations, all the expense! The new floor lamp, the rug, the clothes for Laura! All for what? To entertain some other girl's fiancé! Go to the movies, go! Don't think about us, a mother deserted, an unmarried sister who's crippled and has no job! Don't let anything interfere with your selfish pleasure! Just go, go, go—to the movies!

TOM   All right, I will! The more you shout about my selfishness to me the quicker I'll go, and I won't go to the movies!

AMANDA   Go, then! Then go to the moon—you selfish dreamer!

(TOM *smashes his glass on the floor. He plunges out on the fire-escape, slamming the door,* LAURA *screams—cut off by the door.*

Dance-hall music up. TOM *goes to the rail and grips it desperately, lifting his face in the chill white moonlight penetrating the narrow abyss of the alley.*)

(*Legend on screen: "And so good-bye . . ."*)

(TOM'*s closing speech is timed with the interior pantomime. The interior scene is played as though viewed through soundproof glass.* AMANDA *appears to be making a comforting speech to* LAURA *who is huddled upon the sofa. Now that we cannot hear the mother's speech, her silliness is gone and she has dignity and tragic beauty.* LAURA'*s dark hair hides her face until at the end of the speech she lifts it to smile at her mother.* AMANDA'*s gestures are slow and graceful, almost dancelike, as she comforts the daughter. At the end of her speech she glances a moment at the father's picture—then withdraws through the portieres. At close of* TOM'*s speech,* LAURA *blows out the candles, ending the play.*)

TOM   I didn't go to the moon, I went much further—for time is the longest distance between two places—Not long after that I was fired for writing a poem on the lid of a shoe-box. I left Saint Louis. I descended the steps of this fire-escape for a last time and followed, from then on, in my father's footsteps, attempting to find in motion what was lost in space—I traveled around a great deal. The cities swept about me like dead leaves, leaves that were brightly colored but torn away from the branches. I would have stopped, but I was pursued by something. It always came upon me unawares, taking me altogether by surprise. Perhaps it was a familiar bit of music. Perhaps it was only a piece of transparent glass—Perhaps I am walking along a street at night, in some strange city, before I have found companions. I pass the lighted window of a shop where perfume is sold. The window is filled with pieces of colored glass, tiny transparent bottles in delicate colors, like bits of a shattered rainbow. Then all at once my sister touches my shoulder. I turn around and look into her eyes . . . Oh, Laura, Laura, I tried to leave you behind me, but I am more faithful than I intended to be! I reach for a cigarette, I cross the street, I run into the movies or a bar, I buy a drink, I speak to the nearest stranger—anything that can blow your candles out! (LAURA *bends over the candles.*)—for nowadays the world is lit by lightning! Blow out your candles, Laura—and so good-bye. . . .

(*She blows the candles out.*)

(*The scene dissolves.*)

1945

STUDY QUESTIONS

1. What elements of plot and characterization do you see in *The Glass Menagerie* that remind you of tragedy? of comedy? of realism? What elements will not fit into any of these categories?
2. Consider the play's characters. What strengths and weaknesses does each have? what illusions? What themes are associated with each? What development (if any) does each demonstrate in the play? How do the characterizations reinforce or contrast with each other?
3. Discuss the use Williams makes of the glass menagerie, and especially of the glass unicorn.
4. Discuss the use of candles as a symbol in the play.
5. Discuss the language of the play. How does it differ from the language of other plays you've read?
6. Discuss the device of having the play presented as a set of remembered scenes. How, in particular, does this affect the play's ending and our sense of any future the characters might have beyond the end of the play?

POSSIBLE ESSAY TOPIC

Discuss the relative importance of plot, character, and thought (both in terms of language and of symbolism) within *The Glass Menagerie.*

Protest   VÁCLAV HAVEL (1936–   )

Translated and adapted by Vera Blackwell

Václav Havel grew up in a well-off family that had most of its property confiscated after World War II by the new Communist government in Czechoslovakia. He became fascinated with language as a child, writing poems and plays at an early age. He has said in interviews that he always had a sense of being an outsider—both as a boy, because of his family's position, and as an adult, because he opposed the Communists. After the "Prague Spring" of 1968, a period of relative freedom in Czechoslovakia, Russian troops invaded and took over Prague. Havel was imprisoned for having written subversive literature. After Communism collapsed in 1989, however, Havel was elected president of Czechoslovakia. However, in 1993 the country split apart into its two ethnic parts, the Czech Republic and Slovakia. Havel remains a powerful voice for intellectual freedom, and for a form of government that—unlike either socialism or capitalism in their present manifestations around the world—recognizes human relationships as the ultimate value.

Stanek's ground-floor study in his house on the outskirts of Prague. The house is surrounded by a garden.

(*Doorbell. The front door is opened.*)

STANEK (*loud, cordial*)   Vanek!—Hello!

(*The front door is closed.*)

VANEK (*noncommittal*)   Hello, Mr. Stanek—

STANEK   Come in, come in! (*pause; sudden outburst of emotion*) Vanek! My dear fellow! (*pause; conversationally*) Did you have trouble finding it?

VANEK   Not really—

STANEK   Forgot to mention the flowering magnolias. That's how you know it's my house. Superb, aren't they?

VANEK   Yes—

STANEK   I managed to double their blossoms in less than three years, compared to the previous owner. Have you magnolias in your garden?

VANEK   No—

STANEK   You must have them! I'm going to find you two quality saplings and I'll come and plant them for you personally. (*crosses to the bar*) How about some brandy?

VANEK   I'd rather not, Mr. Stanek, if you don't mind—

STANEK   Come on, Vanek! Just a token one. Eh?

(*Two drinks are poured.*)

VANEK (*sighs*)

935

STANEK   Here we are. Well—here's to our reunion!

VANEK   Cheers—

(*Both drink.*)

VANEK (*shudders slightly, emits a soft groan*)

STANEK   I was afraid you weren't going to come.

VANEK   Why?

STANEK   Well, I mean, things got mixed up in an odd sort of way—What?—
   Won't you sit down?

VANEK (*sits down in an armchair, placing his briefcase on the floor beside
   him*)   Thanks—

STANEK (*sinks into an armchair opposite Vanek with a sigh*)   That's more like it!
   Peanuts?

VANEK   No, thanks—

STANEK (*helps himself; munching*)   You haven't changed much in all these years,
   you know?

VANEK   Neither have you—

STANEK   Me? Come on! Getting on for fifty, going gray, aches and pains setting
   in—Not as we used to be, eh? And the present times don't make one feel any
   better either, what? When did we see each other last, actually?

VANEK   I don't know—

STANEK   Wasn't it at your last opening night?

VANEK   Could be—

STANEK   Seems like another age! We had a bit of an argument—

VANEK   Did we?

STANEK   You took me to task for my illusions and my over-optimism. Good Lord!
   How often since then I've had to admit to myself you were right! Of course, in
   those days I still believed that in spite of everything some of the ideals of my
   youth could be salvaged and I took you for an incorrigible pessimist.

VANEK   But I'm not a pessimist—

STANEK   You see, everything's turned around! (*short pause*) Are you—alone?

VANEK   How do you mean, alone?

STANEK   Well, isn't there somebody—you know—

VANEK   Following me?

STANEK   Not that I care! After all, it was me who rang you up, right?

VANEK   I haven't noticed anybody—

STANEK   By the way, suppose you want to shake them off one of these days, you
   know the best place to do it?

VANEK   No—

STANEK   A department store. You mingle with the crowd, then at a moment
   when they aren't looking you sneak into the loo and wait there for about
   two hours. They become convinced you managed to slip out through a side
   entrance and they give up. You must try it out sometime!

VANEK (*pause*)　Seems very peaceful here—

STANEK　That's why we moved here. It was simply impossible to go on writing near that railway station! We've been here three years, you know. Of course, my greatest joy is the garden. I'll show you around later—I'm afraid I'm going to boast a little—

VANEK　You do the gardening yourself?

STANEK　It's become my greatest private passion these days. Keep puttering about out there almost every day. Just now I've been rejuvenating the apricots. Developed my own method, you see, based on a mixture of natural and artificial fertilizers plus a special way of waxless grafting. You won't believe the results I get! I'll find some cuttings for you later on— (*opens a large silver box on coffee table between them*) Would you like a cigarette?

VANEK　Thanks—

(*clicking of lighter*)

VANEK (*exhales*)

STANEK (*sips his brandy.*)　Well now, Ferdinand, tell me—How *are* you?

VANEK　All right, thanks—

STANEK　Do they leave you alone—at least now and then?

VANEK　It depends—

STANEK (*short pause*)　And how was it in there?

VANEK　Where?

STANEK　Can our sort bear it at all?

VANEK　You mean prison? What else can one do?

STANEK　As far as I recall you used to be bothered by hemorrhoids. Must have been terrible, considering the hygiene in there.

VANEK　They gave me suppositories—

STANEK　You ought to have them operated on, you know. It so happens a friend of mine is our greatest hemorrhoids specialist. Works real miracles. I'll arrange it for you.

VANEK　Thanks—

STANEK (*short pause*)　You know, sometimes it all seems like a beautiful dream—all the exciting opening nights, private views, lectures, meetings— the endless discussions about literature and art! All the energy, the hopes, plans, activities, ideas—the wine-bars crowded with friends, the wild booze-ups, the madcap affrays in the small hours, the jolly girls dancing attendance on us! And the mountains of work we managed to get done, regardless!—That's all over now. It'll never come back!

(*Pause. They both drink.*)

STANEK　Did they beat you?

VANEK　No—

STANEK　Do they beat people up in there?

VANEK   Sometimes. But not the politicals—

STANEK   I thought about you a great deal!

VANEK   Thank you—

STANEK (*short pause*)   I bet in those days it never even occurred to you—

VANEK   What?

STANEK   How it'll all end up! I bet not even you had guessed that!

VANEK   Mmnn—

STANEK   It's disgusting, old boy, disgusting! The nation is governed by scum! And the people? Can this really be the same nation which not very long ago behaved so magnificently? All that horrible cringing, bowing and scraping! The selfishness, corruption and fear wherever you turn! Good Lord! What have they made of us, old boy? Can this really be us? Is this still ourselves at all?

VANEK   I don't believe things are as black as all that—

STANEK   Forgive me, Ferdinand, but you don't happen to live in a normal environment. All you know are people who manage to resist this rot. You just keep on supporting and encouraging each other. You've no idea the sort of environment I've got to put up with! Makes you sick at your stomach!

VANEK   You mean television?

STANEK   In television, in the film studios—you name it.

VANEK   There was a piece by you on the box the other day—

STANEK   You can't imagine what an ordeal that was! First they kept blocking it for over a year, then they started changing it around—changed my whole opening and the entire closing sequence! You wouldn't believe the trifles they find objectionable these days! Nothing but sterility and intrigues, intrigues and sterility! How often I tell myself—wrap it up, chum, forget it, go hide somewhere—grow apricots—

VANEK   I know what you mean—

STANEK   The thing is though, one can't help wondering whether one's got the right to this sort of escape. Supposing even the little one might be able to accomplish today can, in spite of everything, help someone in some way, at least give him a bit of encouragement, uplift him a little—Let me bring you a pair of slippers.

VANEK   Slippers? Why?

STANEK   You can't be comfortable in those boots.

VANEK   I'm all right—

STANEK   Are you sure?

VANEK   Yes. Really—

(*They both drink.*)

STANEK (*pause*)   How about drugs? Did they give you any?

VANEK   No—

STANEK   No dubious injections?

VANEK Only some vitamin ones—

STANEK I bet there's some funny stuff in the food!

VANEK Just bromine against sex—

STANEK But surely they tried to break you down somehow!

VANEK Well—

STANEK If you'd rather not talk about it, it's all right with me.

VANEK Well, in a way, that's the whole point of pre-trial interrogations, isn't it? To take one down a peg or two—

STANEK And to make one talk!

VANEK Mmnn—

STANEK If they should haul me in for questioning—which sooner or later is bound to happen—you know what I'm going to do?

VANEK What?

STANEK Simply not answer any of their questions! Refuse to talk to them at all! That's by far the best way. Least one can be quite sure one didn't say anything one ought not to have said!

VANEK Mmnn—

STANEK Anyway, you must have steel nerves to be able to bear it all and in addition to keep doing the things you do.

VANEK Like what?

STANEK Well, I mean all the protests, petitions, letters—the whole fight for human rights! I mean the things you and your friends keep on doing—

VANEK I'm not doing so much—

STANEK Now don't be too modest, Ferdinand! I follow everything that's going on! I know! If everybody did what you do the situation would be quite different! And that's a fact. It's extremely important there should be at least a few people here who aren't afraid to speak the truth aloud, to defend others, to call a spade a spade! What I'm going to say might sound a bit solemn perhaps, but frankly, the way I see it, you and your friends have taken on an almost superhuman task: to preserve and to carry the remains, the remnant of moral conscience through the present quagmire! The thread you're spinning may be thin, but—who knows—perhaps the hope of a moral rebirth of the nation hangs on it.

VANEK You exaggerate—

STANEK Well, that's how I see it, anyway.

VANEK Surely our hope lies in all the decent people—

STANEK But how many are there still around? How many?

VANEK Enough—

STANEK Are there? Even so, it's you and your friends who are the most exposed to view.

VANEK And isn't that precisely what makes it easier for us?

STANEK I wouldn't say so. The more you're exposed, the more responsibility you have towards all those who know about you, trust you, rely on you and look up to you, because to some extent you keep upholding their honor, too! (*gets up*) I'll get you those slippers!

VANEK   Please don't bother—

STANEK   I insist. I feel uncomfortable just looking at your boots.

(*Pause.* STANEK *returns with slippers.*)

VANEK (*sighs*)

STANEK   Here you are. Do take those ugly things off, I beg you. Let me— (*tries to take off* VANEK's *boots*) Won't you let me—Hold still—

VANEK (*embarrassed*)   No—please don't—no—I'll do it— (*struggles out of his boots, slips on slippers*) There—Nice, aren't they? Thank you very much.

STANEK   Good gracious, Ferdinand, what for?— (*hovering over* VANEK) Some more brandy?

VANEK   No more for me, thanks—

STANEK   Oh, come on. Give me your glass!

VANEK   I'm sorry, I'm not feeling too well—

STANEK   Lost the habit inside, is that it?

VANEK   Could be—But the point is—last night, you see—

STANEK   Ah, that's what it is. Had a drop too many, eh?

VANEK   Mmnn—

STANEK   I understand. (*returns to his chair*) By the way, you know the new wine-bar, "The Shaggy Dog"?

VANEK   No—

STANEK   You don't? Listen, the wine there comes straight from the cask, it's not expensive and usually it isn't crowded. Really charming spot, you know, thanks to a handful of fairly good artists who were permitted—believe it or not—to do the interior decoration. I can warmly recommend it to you. Lovely place. Where did you go, then?

VANEK   Well, we did a little pub-crawling, my friend Landovský and I—

STANEK   Oh, I see! You were with Landovský, were you? Well! In that case, I'm not at all surprised you came to a sticky end! He's a first class actor, but once he starts drinking—that's it! Surely you can take one more brandy! Right?

VANEK (*Sighs.*)

(*Drinks poured. They both drink.*)

VANEK (*shudders, emits a soft groan*)

STANEK (*back in his armchair; short pause*)   Well, how are things otherwise? You do any writing?

VANEK   Trying to—

STANEK   A play?

VANEK   A one-actor—

STANEK   Another autobiographical one?

VANEK   More or less—

STANEK   My wife and I read the one about the brewery the other day. We thought it was very amusing.

VANEK   I'm glad—

STANEK   Unfortunately we were given a rather bad copy. Somewhat illegible.

VANEK   I'm sorry—

STANEK   It's a really brilliant little piece! I mean it! Only the ending seemed to me a bit muddy. The whole thing wants to be brought to a more straightforward conclusion, that's all. No problem. You can do it.

(*Pause. Both drink.* VANEK *shudders.*)

STANEK   Well, how are things? How about Pavel? Do you see him?

VANEK   Yes—

STANEK   Does he do any writing?

VANEK   Just now he's finishing a one-actor, as well. It's supposed to be performed together with mine—

STANEK   Wait a minute. You don't mean to tell me you two have teamed up also as authors!

VANEK   More or less—

STANEK   Well, well!—Frankly, Ferdinand, try as I may, I don't get it. I don't. I simply can't understand this alliance of yours. Is it quite genuine on your part? Is it?—Good heavens! Pavel! I don't know! Just remember the way he started! We both belong to the same generation, Pavel and I, we've both—so to speak—spanned a similar arc of development, but I don't mind telling you that what he did in those days—Well! It was a bit too strong even for me!—Still, I suppose it's your business. You know best what you're doing.

VANEK   That's right—

(*Pause. Both drink.*)

STANEK   Is your wife fond of gladioli?

VANEK   I don't know. I think so—

STANEK   You won't find many places with such a large selection as mine. I've got thirty-two shades, whereas at a common or garden nursery you'll be lucky to find six. Do you think your wife would like me to send her some bulbs?

VANEK   I'm sure she would—

STANEK   There's still time to plant them, you know. (*Pause.*) Ferdinand—

VANEK   Yes?

STANEK   Weren't you surprised when I suddenly rang you up?

VANEK   A bit—

STANEK   I thought so. After all, I happen to be among those who've still managed to keep their heads above water and I quite understand that—because of this—you might want to keep a certain distance from me.

VANEK   No, not I—

STANEK   Perhaps not you yourself, but I realize that some of your friends believe that anyone who's still got some chance today has either abdicated
morally, or is unforgivably fooling himself.

VANEK   I don't think so—

STANEK   I wouldn't blame you if you did, because I know only too well the
grounds from which such prejudice could grow. (*An embarrassed pause.*)
Ferdinand—

VANEK   Yes?

STANEK   I realize what a high price you have to pay for what you're doing. But
please don't think it's all that easy for a man who's either so lucky, or so unfortunate as to be still tolerated by the official apparatus, and who—at the
same time—wishes to live at peace with his conscience.

VANEK   I know what you mean—

STANEK   In some respects it may be even harder for him.

VANEK   I understand.

STANEK   Naturally, I didn't call you in order to justify myself! I don't really
think there's any need. I called you, because I like you and I'd be sorry to see
you sharing the prejudice which I assume exists among your friends.

VANEK   As far as I know nobody has ever said a bad word about you—

STANEK   Not even Pavel?

VANEK   No—

STANEK (*embarrassed pause*)   Ferdinand—

VANEK   Yes?

STANEK   Excuse me— (*gets up; crosses to the tape recorder; switches it on; soft,
nondescript background music under the following dialogue.* STANEK *returns
to his chair.*) Ferdinand, does the name Javurek mean anything to you?

VANEK   Our pop bard? I know him very well—

STANEK   So I expect you know what happened to him.

VANEK   Of course. They locked him up for telling a story during one of his performances. The story about the copper who meets a penguin in the street—

STANEK   Ridiculous, isn't it? It was just an excuse, that's all. The fact is, they
hate his guts because he sings the way he does. Good Lord! The whole thing
is so cruel, so ludicrous, so base!

VANEK   And cowardly—

STANEK   Right! And cowardly! Look, I've been trying to do something for the
lad. I mean, I know a few chaps at the town council and at the prosecutor's
office, but you know how it is. Promises, promises! They all say they're going to look into it, but the moment your back is turned they drop it like a
hot potato, so they don't get their fingers burnt! Sickening, the way everybody looks out for number one!

VANEK   Still, I think it's nice of you to have tried to do something—

STANEK   My dear Ferdinand, I'm really not the sort of man your friends obviously take me for! Peanuts?

VANEK   No, thanks—

STANEK (*short pause*)   About Javurek—

VANEK   Yes?

STANEK Since I didn't manage to accomplish anything through private intervention, it occurred to me perhaps it ought to be handled in a somewhat
different way. You know what I mean. Simply write something—a protest or
a petition? In fact, this is the main thing I wanted to discuss with you. Naturally, you're far more experienced in these matters than I. If this document
contains a few fairly well-known signatures—like yours, for example—it's
bound to be published somewhere abroad which might create some political pressure. Right? I mean, these things don't seem to impress them all that
much, actually—but honestly, I don't see any other way to help the lad. Not
to mention Annie—

VANEK   Annie?

STANEK My daughter.

VANEK   Oh? Is that your daughter?

STANEK That's right.

VANEK   Well, what about her?

STANEK I thought you knew.

VANEK   Knew what?

STANEK She's expecting. By Javurek—

VANEK   Oh, I see. That's why—

STANEK Wait a minute! If you mean the case interests me merely because of
family matters—

VANEK   I didn't mean that—

STANEK But you just said—

VANEK   I only wanted to say, that's how you know about the case at all; you
were explaining to me how you got to know about it. Frankly, I wouldn't
have expected you to be familiar with the present pop scene. I'm sorry if it
sounded as though I meant—

STANEK I'd get involved in this case even if it was someone else expecting his
child! No matter who—

VANEK   I know—

STANEK (*embarrassed pause*)   Well, what do you think about my idea of writing
some sort of protest?

VANEK   Where did I leave my briefcase?

STANEK (*puzzled*)   By your chair—

VANEK   Oh, yes, of course— (*opens his briefcase, rummages inside, finds what he
was looking for, hands the document to* STANEK) I guess this is the sort of
thing you had in mind—

STANEK What?

VANEK   Here—

STANEK (*grabs the document*)   What is it?

VANEK   Have a look—

STANEK (*glances at it*)   Good Lord! (*reads carefully, clearly surprised, getting excited; mumbles as he reads; finishes his reading, flabbergasted*) Well! Well, well! (*jumps up, begins to pace about in some agitation, the document in his hand*) Now isn't it marvelous! Marvelous!—That's a laugh, isn't it? Eh?— Good Lord! Here I was cudgeling my brains how to go about it, finally I take the plunge and consult you—and all this time you've had the whole thing wrapped up and ready! Isn't it marvelous? I knew I was doing the right thing when I turned to you! No question about it! (*sits down, glances at the document, slams it with his hand*) There! Precisely what I had in mind! Brief, to the point, fair, and yet emphatic. Manifestly the work of a professional! I'd be sweating over it for a whole day and I'd never come up with anything remotely like this!

VANEK (*mumbles in shy appreciation at the compliment*)

STANEK   Listen, just a small point—here at the end—do you think "wilfulness" is the right word to use? Couldn't one find a milder synonym, perhaps? Somehow seems a bit misplaced, you know. I mean, the whole text is composed in very measured, factual terms—and this word here suddenly sticks out, sounds much too emotional, wouldn't you agree? Otherwise it's absolutely perfect. Maybe the second paragraph is somewhat superfluous, in fact it's just a rehash of the first one. Except for the reference here to Javurek's impact on nonconformist youth. Excellent! Well done! This must stay. How about putting it at the end instead of your "wilfulness"? Wouldn't that do the trick?—But these are just my personal impressions. Good heavens! Why should you listen to what I have to say! On the whole the text is excellent and no doubt it's going to hit the mark. Let me say again, Ferdinand, how much I admire you. Your knack for expressing the fundamental points of an issue, while avoiding all needless abuse, is indeed rare in these parts!

VANEK   Come on—you don't really mean that—

STANEK   Great piece of work! Thank you for letting me see it. Here— (*hands the document back to* VANEK) You better put it back in your briefcase. (*drinks; short pause*) Anyway, it's good to know there's somebody around whom one can always turn to and rely on in a case like this.

VANEK   Good gracious, it's only natural, isn't it?

STANEK   It may seem so to you. But in the circles where I've to move such things aren't in the least natural! The natural response is much more likely to be the exact opposite. When a man gets into trouble everybody drops him as soon as possible, the lot of them. And out of fear for their own positions they try to convince all and sundry they've never had anything to do with him; on the contrary, they sized him up right away, they wouldn't have ever touched him with a barge pole! But why am I telling you all this, you know best the sort of thing that happens! Right? When you were in prison your long-time theatre pals held forth against you on the box. It was revolting!

VANEK   I'm not angry with them—

STANEK   But I am! And what's more I told them so. In no uncertain terms! You know, a man in my position learns to put up with a lot of things, but—if you'll forgive me—there are limits! I appreciate it might be awkward for you to blame the lads, as you happen to be the injured party. But listen to me, old boy. You've got to distance yourself from the affair, that's all! Just think! Once we, too, begin to tolerate this sort of muck—we're *de facto* assuming co-responsibility for the entire moral marasmus and indirectly contributing to its deeper penetration. Am I right?

VANEK   Mmnn—

STANEK   (*short pause*)   Have you sent it off yet?

VANEK   We're still collecting signatures—

STANEK   How many have you got so far?

VANEK   About fifty—

STANEK   Fifty? Not bad! (*short pause*) Well, never mind, I've just missed the boat, that's all.

VANEK   You haven't—

STANEK   But the thing's already in hand, isn't it?

VANEK   Yes, but it's still open—I mean—

STANEK   All right, but now it's sure to be sent off and published, right? By the way, I wouldn't give it to any of the agencies, if I were you. They'll only print a measly little news item which is bound to be overlooked. Better hand it over directly to one of the big European papers, so the whole text gets published, including all the signatures!

VANEK   I know—

STANEK   (*short pause*)   Do they already know about it?

VANEK   You mean the police?

STANEK   Yes.

VANEK   I don't think so. I suppose not—

STANEK   Look here, I don't want to give you any advice, but it seems to me you ought to wrap it up as soon as possible, else they'll get wind of what's going on and they'll find a way to stop it. Fifty signatures should be enough! Besides, what counts is not the number of signatures, but their significance.

VANEK   Each signature has its own significance!

STANEK   Absolutely, but as far as publicity abroad is concerned, it is essential that some well-known names are represented, right? Has Pavel signed?

VANEK   Yes—

STANEK   Good. His name—no matter what one may think of him personally—does mean something in the world today!

VANEK   No question—

STANEK   (*short pause*)   Listen, Ferdinand—

VANEK   Yes?

STANEK   There's one more thing I wanted to discuss with you. It's a bit delicate, though–

VANEK   Oh?

STANEK   Look here, I'm no millionaire, you know, but so far I've been able to manage—

VANEK   Good for you—

STANEK   Well, I was thinking—I mean—I'd like to—Look, a lot of your friends have lost their jobs. I was thinking—Would you be prepared to accept from me a certain sum of money?

VANEK   That's very nice of you! Some of my friends indeed find themselves in a bit of a spot. But there are problems, you know. I mean, one is never quite sure how to go about it. Those who most need help are often the most reluctant to accept—

STANEK   You won't be able to work miracles with what I can afford, but I expect there are situations when every penny counts. (*takes out his wallet, removes two banknotes, hesitates, adds a third, hands them to* VANEK) Here—please—a small offering.

VANEK   Thank you very much. Let me thank you for all my friends—

STANEK   Gracious, we've got to help each other out, don't we? Peanuts?

VANEK   Not for me—

STANEK   (*helps himself; munching*)   Incidentally, there's no need for you to mention this little contribution comes from me. I don't wish to erect a monument to myself. I'm sure you've gathered that much by now, eh?

VANEK   Yes. Again many thanks—

STANEK   Well now, how about having a look at the garden?

VANEK   Mr. Stanek—

STANEK   Yes?

VANEK   We'd like to send it off tomorrow—

STANEK   What?

VANEK   The protest—

STANEK   Excellent! The sooner the better!

VANEK   So that today there's still—

STANEK   Today you should think about getting some sleep! That's the main thing! Don't forget you've a bit of a hangover after last night and tomorrow is going to be a hard day for you!

VANEK   I know. All I was going to say—

STANEK   Better go straight home and unplug the phone. Else Landovský rings you up again and heaven knows how you'll end up!

VANEK   Yes, I know. There're only a few signatures I've still got to collect—it won't take long. All I was going to say—I hope you'll agree with me—I mean, don't you think it would be helpful—As a matter of fact it would be sensational! After all, practically everybody's read your *Crash!*

STANEK   Oh, come on, Ferdinand! That was fifteen years ago!

VANEK   But it's never been forgotten!

STANEK   What do you mean—sensational?

VANEK   I'm sorry, I had the impression you'd actually like to—

STANEK   What?

VANEK   Participate—

STANEK   Participate? Wait a minute. Are you talking about the signatures? Is that what you're talking about?

VANEK   Yes—

STANEK   You mean I should—

VANEK   I'm sorry, but I had the impression—

STANEK   Good Lord! I'm going to have some more brandy. How about you?

VANEK   No, thanks—

STANEK   Suit yourself— (*crosses to bar, pours himself a drink; returns to his chair; drinks; pause*) Now that's a laugh, isn't it?

VANEK   What's a laugh?

STANEK   For heaven's sake, can't you see how absurd it is? Eh? I ask you over hoping you might write something about Javurek's case, you come here and produce a finished text and what's more, one furnished with fifty signatures! I'm bowled over like a little child, can't believe my eyes and ears, I worry about ways to stop them from ruining your project—and all this time it hasn't occurred to me to do the one simple, natural thing which I should have done in the first place! I mean, at once sign the document myself! Well, you must admit it's absurd!

VANEK   Mmnn—

STANEK   Listen, Ferdinand, isn't this a really terrifying testimony to the situation into which we've been brought? Isn't it? Just think: even I, though I know it's rubbish, even I've got used to the idea that the signing of protests is the business of local specialists, professionals in solidarity, dissidents! While the rest of us—when we want to do something for the sake of ordinary human decency—automatically turn to you, as though you were a sort of service establishment for moral matters. In other words, we're here simply to keep our mouths shut and to be rewarded by the relative peace and quiet, whereas you're here to speak up for us and to be rewarded by kicks on earth and glory in the heavens! Perverse, isn't it?

VANEK   Mmnn—

STANEK   Of course it is! And they've managed to bring things to such a point that even a fairly intelligent and decent fellow—which, with your permission, I still think I am—is more or less ready to take this situation for granted! As though it was quite normal, perfectly natural! Sickening, isn't it? Sickening the depths we've reached! What do you say? Makes one puke, eh?

VANEK   Well—

STANEK   You think the nation can ever recover from all this?

VANEK   Hard to say—

STANEK   What can one do? What can one do? Well, seems clear, doesn't it? In theory, that is. Everybody should start with himself. What? However! Is this country inhabited only by Vaneks? It really doesn't seem that everybody can become a fighter for human rights.

VANEK   Not everybody, no—

STANEK   Where is it?

VANEK   What?

STANEK   The list of signatures, of course.

VANEK (*embarrassed pause*)   Mr. Stanek—

STANEK   Yes?

VANEK   Forgive me, but—I'm sorry, I've suddenly a funny feeling that perhaps—

STANEK   What funny feeling?

VANEK   I don't know—I feel very embarrassed—Well, it seems to me perhaps I
wasn't being quite fair—

STANEK   In what way?

VANEK   Well, what I did—was a bit of a con trick—in a way—

STANEK   What are you talking about?

VANEK   I mean, first I let you talk, and only then I ask for your signature—I
mean, after you're already sort of committed by what you've said before, you
see—

STANEK   Are you suggesting that if I'd known you were collecting signatures for
Javurek, I would never have started talking about him?

VANEK   No, that's not what I mean—

STANEK   Well, what do you mean?

VANEK   How shall I put it—

STANEK   Oh, come on! You mind I didn't organize the whole thing myself, is
that it?

VANEK   No, that's not it—

STANEK   What is it then?

VANEK   Well, it seems to me it would've been a quite different matter if I'd
come to you right away and asked for your signature. That way you
would've had an option—

STANEK   And why didn't you come to me right away, actually? Was it because
you'd simply written me off in advance?

VANEK   Well, I was thinking that in your position—

STANEK   Ah! There you are! You see? Now it's becoming clear what you really
think of me, isn't it? You think that because now and then one of my pieces
happens to be shown on the box, I'm no longer capable of the simplest act
of solidarity!

VANEK   You misunderstand me—What I meant was—

STANEK   Let me tell you something, Ferdinand. (*drinks; short pause*) Look here,
if I've—willy-nilly—got used to the perverse idea that common decency
and morality are the exclusive domain of the dissidents—then you've—
willy-nilly—got used to the idea as well! That's why it never crossed your
mind that certain values might be more important to me than my present
position. But suppose even I wanted to be finally a free man, suppose even I
wished to renew my inner integrity and shake off the yoke of humiliation

and shame? It never entered your head that I might've been actually waiting for this very moment for years, what? You simply placed me once and for all among those hopeless cases, among those whom it would be pointless to count on in any way. Right? And now that you found I'm not entirely indifferent to the fate of others—you made that slip about my signature! But you saw at once what happened, and so you began to apologize to me. Good God! Don't you realize how you humiliate me? What if all this time I'd been hoping for an opportunity to act, to do something that would again make a man of me, help me to be once more at peace with myself, help me to find again the free play of my imagination and my lost sense of humor, rid me of the need to escape my traumas by minding the apricots and the blooming magnolias! Suppose even I prefer to live in truth! What if I want to return from the world of custom-made literature and the proto-culture of the box to the world of art which isn't geared to serve anyone at all?

VANEK   I'm sorry—forgive me! I didn't mean to hurt your feelings—Wait a minute, I'll—Just a moment— (*rummages in his briefcase, extracts the list of signatures from among his papers, and hands it to* STANEK) Here you are, Mr. Stanek—

STANEK   What is it? The signatures?

VANEK   Yes—

STANEK   Ah! Good. (*peruses the list, mumbles, nods, gets up, begins to pace around*) Let me think aloud. May I?

VANEK   By all means—

STANEK (*halts, drinks, begins to pace again as he talks*)   I believe I've already covered the main points concerning the subjective side of the matter. If I sign the document, I'm going to regain—after years of being continually sick at my stomach—my self-esteem, my lost freedom, my honor, and perhaps even some regard among those close to me. I'll leave behind the insoluble dilemmas, forced on me by the conflict between my concern for my position and my conscience. I'll be able to face with equanimity Annie, myself, and even that lad when he comes back. It'll cost me my job. Though my job brings me no satisfaction—on the contrary, it brings me shame—nevertheless, it does support me and my family a great deal better than if I were to become a night watchman. It's more than likely that my son won't be permitted to continue his studies. On the other hand, I'm sure he's going to have more respect for me that way, than if his permission to study was bought by my refusal to sign the protest for Javurek. He happens to worship Javurek, as a matter of fact. He's crazy about him! (*sighs with some exasperation*) —Well then. This is the subjective side of the matter. Now how about the objective side? What happens when—among the signatures of a few well-known dissidents and a handful of Javurek's teenage friends—there suddenly crops up—to everybody's surprise and against all expectation— my signature? The signature of a man who hasn't been heard from regarding civic affairs for years! Well? What? Let's think about it. My co-signatories—as well as many of those who don't sign documents of this sort, but who nonetheless deep down side with those who do—are naturally going to welcome my signature with pleasure. The closed circle of habitual signers— whose signatures, by the way, are already beginning to lose their clout, because they cost practically nothing. I mean, the people in question have long since lost all ways and means by which they could actually pay for their signatures. Right? Well, this circle will be broken. A new name will appear, a name the value of which depends precisely on its previous absence. And of course, I may add, on the high price paid for its appearance! So much for the objective "plus" of my prospective signature. Now what about the authorities? My signature is going to surprise, annoy and upset them for the very reasons which will bring joy to the other signatories. I mean, because it'll make a breach in the barrier the authorities have been building around your lot for so long and with such effort. All right. Let's see about Javurek. Concerning his case, I very much doubt my participation would significantly influence its outcome. And if so, I'm afraid it's more than likely going to have a negative effect. The authorities will be anxious to prove they haven't been panicked. They'll want to show that a surprise of this sort can't make them lose their cool. Which brings us to the consideration of what they're going to do to me. Surely, my signature is bound to have a much more significant influence on what happens in my case. No doubt, they're going to punish me far more cruelly than you'd expect. The point being that my punishment will serve them as a warning signal to all those who might be tempted to follow my example in the future, choose freedom, and thus swell the ranks of the dissidents. You may be sure they'll want to teach them a lesson! Show them what the score is! Right? The thing is—well, let's face it—they're no longer worried all that much about dissident activities within the confines of the established ghetto. In some respects they even seem to prod them on here and there. But! What they're really afraid of is any semblance of a crack in the fence around the ghetto! That's what really scares them! So they'll want to exorcize the bogey of a prospective epidemic of dissent by an exemplary punishment of myself. They'll want to nip it in the bud, that's all. (*drinks; pause*) The last question I've got to ask myself is this: what sort of reaction to my signature can one expect among those who, in one way or another, have followed what you might call "the path of accommodation." I mean people who are, or ought to be, our main concern, because—I'm sure you'll agree—our hope for the future depends above all on whether or not it will be possible to awake them from their slumbers and to enlist them to take an active part in civic affairs. This is what really matters, isn't it? Well, I'm afraid that my signature is going to be received with absolute resentment by this crucial section of the populace. You know why? Because, as a matter of fact, these people secretly hate the dissidents. They've become their bad conscience, their living reproach! That's how they see the dissidents. And at the same time, they envy them their honor and their inner freedom, values which they themselves were denied by fate. This is why they never miss an opportunity to smear the dissidents. And precisely this opportunity is going to be offered to them by my signature. They're going to spread nasty rumors about you and your friends. They're going to say that you who have nothing more to lose—you who have long since landed at the bottom of the heap and, what's more, managed to make yourselves quite at home in there—are now trying to drag down to your own level an unfortunate man, a man who's so far been able to stay above the salt line. You're dragging him down—irresponsible as you are—without the slightest compunction, just for your own whim, just because you wish to irritate the authorities by creating a false impression that your ranks are being swelled! What do you care about losing him his job! Doesn't matter, does it? Or do you mean to suggest you'll find him a job down in the dump in which you yourselves exist? What? No—Ferdinand! I'm sorry. I'm afraid, I'm much too familiar with the way these people think! After all, I've got to live among them, day in day out. I know precisely what they're going to say. They'll say I'm your victim, shamelessly abused, misguided, led astray by your cynical appeal to my humanity! They'll say that in your ruthlessness you didn't shrink even from making use of my personal relationship to Javurek! And you know what? They're going to say that all the humane ideals you're constantly proclaiming have been tarnished by your treatment of me. That's the sort of reasoning one can expect from them! And I'm sure I don't have to tell you that the authorities are bound to support this interpretation, and to fan the coals as hard as they can! There are others, of course, somewhat more intelligent perhaps. These people might say that the extraordinary appearance of my signature among yours is actually counterproductive, in that it concentrates everybody's attention on my signature and away from the main issue concerning Javurek. They'll say it puts the whole protest in jeopardy, because one can't help asking oneself what was the purpose of the exercise: was it to help Javurek, or to parade a new-born dissident? I wouldn't be at all surprised if someone were to say that, as a matter of fact, Javurek was victimized by you and your friends. It might be suggested his personal tragedy only served you to further your ends—which are far removed from the fate of the unfortunate man. Furthermore, it'll be pointed out that by getting my signature you managed to dislodge me from the one area of operation—namely, backstage diplomacy, private intervention—where I've been so far able to maneuver and where I might have proved infinitely more helpful to Javurek in the end! I do hope you understand me, Ferdinand. I don't wish to exaggerate the importance of these opinions, nor am I prepared to become their slave. On the other hand, it seems to be in the interests of our case for me to take them into account. After all, it's a matter of a political decision and a good politician must consider all the issues which are likely to influence the end result of his action. Right? In these circumstances the question one must resolve is as follows:

what do I prefer? Do I prefer the inner liberation which my signature is going to bring me, a liberation paid for—as it now turns out—by a basically negative objective impact—or do I choose the other alternative. I mean, the more beneficial effect which the protest would have without my signature, yet paid for by my bitter awareness that I've again—who knows, perhaps for the last time—missed a chance to shake off the bonds of shameful compromises in which I've been choking for years? In other words, if I'm to act indeed ethically—and I hope by now you've no doubt I want to do just that—which course should I take? Should I be guided by ruthless objective considerations, or by subjective inner feelings?

VANEK   Seems perfectly clear to me—

STANEK   And to me—

VANEK   So that you're going to—

STANEK   Unfortunately—

VANEK   Unfortunately?

STANEK   You thought I was—

VANEK   Forgive me, perhaps I didn't quite understand—

STANEK   I'm sorry if I've—

VANEK   Never mind—

STANEK   But I really believe—

VANEK   I know—

(STANEK *hands* VANEK *the list of signatures, crosses to the tape recorder, switches it off, returns to his chair, sits down.*)

VANEK (*puts papers back in his briefcase*)

(*Both drink.*)

VANEK (*shudders, emits a soft groan*)

STANEK (*embarrassed pause*)   Are you angry?

VANEK   No—

STANEK   You don't agree, though—

VANEK   I respect your reasoning—

STANEK   But what do you think?

VANEK   What should I think?

STANEK   That's obvious, isn't it?

VANEK   Is it?

STANEK   You think that when I saw all the signatures, I did, after all, get the wind up!

VANEK   I don't—

STANEK   I can see you do!

VANEK   I assure you—

STANEK   Why don't you level with me? Don't you realize that your benevolent hypocrisy is actually far more insulting than if you gave it to me straight?! Or do you mean I'm not even worthy of your comment?!

VANEK But I told you, didn't I, I respect your reasoning—

STANEK I'm not an idiot, Vanek!

VANEK Of course not—

STANEK I know precisely what's behind your "respect"!

VANEK What is?

STANEK A feeling of moral superiority!

VANEK You're wrong—

STANEK Only, I'm not quite sure if you—you of all people—have any right to feel so superior!

VANEK What do you mean?

STANEK You know very well what I mean!

VANEK I don't—

STANEK Shall I tell you?

VANEK Please do—

STANEK (*emphatic*) Well! As far as I know, in prison you talked more than you should have!

VANEK (*gasps, jumps up, wildly staring at* STANEK)

STANEK (*stares back in triumph*) Right? (*short, tense pause*)

VANEK (*almost inaudible*) What??

(*The telephone rings.*)

VANEK (*broken, sinks back in his chair*)

STANEK (*crosses to the phone, lifts the receiver*) Hello—Yes—What?—Good Lord! You mean—Wait a minute—I see—I see—Where are you?—Yes, yes, of course—Absolutely!—Good!—You bet!—Sure—I'll be here waiting for you! Bye bye. (*replaces the receiver; pauses; returns to his chair, to* VANEK) You can go and burn it downstairs in the furnace!

VANEK What?

STANEK He's just walked into the canteen! To see Annie.

VANEK Who did?

STANEK Javurek! Who else?

VANEK (*jumps up*) Javurek? You mean he was released? But that's wonderful! So your private intervention did work, after all! Just as well we didn't send off the protest a few days earlier! I'm sure they would've got their backs up and kept him inside!

STANEK (*pause. stares at* VANEK. *then suddenly cordial*) My dear fellow, you mustn't fret! There's always the risk that you can do more harm than good by your activities! Right? Heavens, if you should worry about this sort of thing, you'd never be able to do anything at all! Come, let me get you those saplings—

End

1978

STUDY QUESTIONS

1. What is the significance of all the small comforts, refreshments, and gifts—the slippers, the brandy, the money—that Stanek offers to Vanek?
2. What does Stanek's garden symbolize?
3. Discuss how the personal and the political are intertwined in the play.
4. How does Havel develop the theme of the great moral divide between simply talking about evil and actually doing something to oppose it?

The Colored Museum

George C. Wolfe earned a B.A. in theater at Pomona College, and an M.F.A. in Dramatic Writing and Musical Theater from New York University. He is best known as the Tony Award-winning author of two acclaimed plays, *The Colored Museum* (1987) and *Jelly's Last Jam* (1992). He directed the acclaimed play *Angels in America* (1993). He has received grants from the Rockefeller Foundation and The National Endowment for the Arts. In 1996, Pomona College awarded him an honorary doctorate.

THE CAST

An ensemble of five, two men and three women, all black, who perform all the characters that inhabit the exhibits.[1]

THE STAGE

White walls and recessed lighting. A starkness befitting a museum where the myths and madness of black/Negro/colored Americans are stored.

Built into the walls are a series of small panels, doors, revolving walls, and compartments from which actors can retrieve key props and make quick entrances.

A revolve is used, which allows for quick transitions from one exhibit to the next.

MUSIC

All of the music for the show should be pre-recorded. Only the drummer, who is used in Git on Board, *and then later in* Permutations *and* The Party, *is live.*

THERE IS NO INTERMISSION

THE EXHIBITS

Git on Board
Cookin' with Aunt Ethel
The Photo Session
Soldier with a Secret

---

[1]A Little Girl, seven to twelve years old, is needed for a walk-on part in *Lala's Opening*.

The Gospel According to Miss Roj
The Hairpiece
The Last Mama-on-the-Couch Play
Symbiosis
Lala's Opening
Permutations
The Party

CHARACTERS

Git on Board
   Miss Pat

Cookin' with Aunt Ethel
   Aunt Ethel

The Photo Session
   Girl
   Guy

Soldier with a Secret
   Junie Robinson

The Gospel According to Miss Roj
   Miss Roj
   Waiter

The Hairpiece
   The Woman
   Janine
   La Wanda

The Last Mama-on-the-Couch Play
   Narrator
   Mama
   Walter-Lee-Beau-Willie-Jones
   Lady in Plaid
   Medea Jones

Symbiosis
   The Man
   The Kid

Lala's Opening
   Lala Lamazing Grace
   Admonia
   Flo'rance
   The Little Girl

Permutations
   Normal Jean Reynolds

The Party
   Topsy Washington
   Miss Pat
   Miss Roj
   Lala Lamazing Grace
   The Man *(from Symbiosis)*

Git on Board

(Blackness. Cut by drums pounding. Then slides, rapidly flashing before us. Images we've all seen before, of African slaves being captured, loaded onto ships, tortured. The images flash, flash, flash. The drums crescendo. Blackout. And then lights reveal Miss Pat, *frozen. She is black, pert, and cute. She has a flip to her hair and wears a hot pink mini-skirt stewardess uniform.)*
   (She stands in front of a curtain which separates her from an offstage cockpit.)

(An electronic bell goes "ding" and Miss Pat *comes to life, presenting herself in a friendly but rehearsed manner, smiling and speaking as she had done so many times before.)*

miss pat   Welcome aboard Celebrity Slaveship, departing the Gold Coast and making short stops at Bahia, Port Au Prince, and Havana, before our final destination of Savannah.
   Hi. I'm Miss Pat and I'll be serving you here in Cabin A. We will be crossing the Atlantic at an altitude that's pretty high, so you must wear your shackles at all times.

(She removes a shackle from the overhead compartment and demonstrates.)

To put on your shackle, take the right hand and close the metal ring around your left hand like so. Repeat the action using your left hand to secure the right. If you have any trouble bonding yourself, I'd be more than glad to assist.
   Once we reach the desired altitude, the Captain will turn off the "Fasten Your Shackle" sign ... *(She efficiently points out the "FASTEN YOUR SHACKLE" signs on either side of her, which light up.)* ... allowing you a chance to stretch and dance in the aisles a bit. But otherwise, shackles must be worn at all times.

(The "Fasten Your Shackles" signs go off.)

miss pat   Also, we ask that you please refrain from call-and-response singing between cabins as that sort of thing can lead to rebellion. And, of course, no drums are allowed on board. Can you repeat after me, "No drums." *(She gets the audience to repeat.)* With a little more enthusiasm, please. "No drums." *(After the audience repeats it.)* That was great!
   Once we're airborn, I'll be by with magazines, and earphones can be purchased for the price of your first-born male.

If there's anything I can do to make this middle passage more pleasant, press the little button overhead and I'll be with you faster than you can say, "Go down, Moses." *(She laughs at her "little joke.")* Thanks for flying Celebrity and here's hoping you have a pleasant takeoff.

(The engines surge, the "Fasten Your Shackle" signs go on, and over-articulate Muzak voices are heard singing as Miss Pat *pulls down a bucket seat and "shackles-up" for takeoff.)*

VOICES
GET ON BOARD CELEBRITY SLAVESHIP
GET ON BOARD CELEBRITY SLAVESHIP
GET ON BOARD CELEBRITY SLAVESHIP
THERE'S ROOM FOR MANY A MORE

(The engines reach an even, steady hum. Just as Miss Pat *rises and replaces the shackles in the overhead compartment, the faint sound of African drumming is heard.)*

MISS PAT   Hi. Miss Pat again. I'm sorry to disturb you, but someone is playing drums. And what did we just say . . . "No drums." It must be someone in Coach. But we here in Cabin A are not going to respond to those drums. As a matter of fact, we don't even hear them. Repeat after me. "I don't hear any drums." *(The audience repeats.)* And "I will not rebel."

(The audience repeats. The drumming grows.)

MISS PAT   *(Placating)* OK, now I realize some of us are a bit edgy after hearing about the tragedy on board The Laughing Mary, but let me assure you Celebrity has no intention of throwing you overboard and collecting the insurance. We value you!

(She proceeds to single out individual passengers/audience members.)

Why the songs *you* are going to sing in the cotton fields, under the burning heat and stinging lash, will metamorphose and give birth to the likes of James Brown and the Fabulous Flames. And you, yes *you*, are going to come up with some of the best dances. The best dances! The Watusi! The Funky Chicken! And just think of what *you* are going to mean to William Faulkner.

All right, so you're gonna have to suffer for a few hundred years, but from your pain will come a culture so complex. *And*, with this little item here . . . *(She removes a basketball from the overhead compartment.)* . . . you'll become millionares!

(There is a roar of thunder. The lights quiver and the "Fasten Your Shackle" signs begin to flash. Miss Pat *quickly replaces the basketball in the overhead compartment and speaks very reassuringly.)*

MISS PAT   No, don't panic. We're just caught in a little thunder storm. Now the only way you're going to make it through is if you abandon your God and worship a new one. So, on the count of three, let's all sing. One, two, three . . .

NOBODY KNOWS DE TROUBLE I SEEN

Oh, I forgot to mention, when singing, omit the T-H sound. "The" becomes "de." "They" becomes "dey." Got it? Good!

NOBODY KNOWS . . .
NOBODY KNOWS . . .

Oh, so you don't like that one? Well then let's try another—

SUMMER TIME
AND DE LIVIN' IS EASY

Gershwin. He comes from another oppressed people so he understands.

FISH ARE JUMPIN' . . . come on.
AND DE COTTON IS HIGH.
AND DE COTTON IS . . . Sing, damn*it!*

(Lights begin to flash, the engines surge, and there is wild drumming. MISS PAT sticks her head through the curtain and speaks with an offstage CAPTAIN.)

MISS PAT   What?

VOICE OF CAPTAIN *(O.S.)*   Time warp!

MISS PAT   Time warp! *(She turns to the audience and puts on a pleasant face.)* The Captain has assured me everything is fine. We're just caught in a little time warp. *(Trying to fight her growing hysteria.)* On your right you will see the American Revolution, which will give the U.S. of A. exclusive rights to your life. And on your left, the Civil War, which means you will vote Republican until F.D.R. comes along. And now we're passing over the Great Depression, which means everybody gets to live the way you've been living. *(There is a blinding flash of light, and an explosion. She screams.)* Ahhhhhhhhhh! That was World War I, which is not to be confused with World War II . . . *(There is a larger flash of light, and another explosion.)* . . . Ahhhhh! Which is not to be confused with the Korean War or the Vietnam War, all of which you will play a major role in.

Oh, look, now we're passing over the sixties. Martha and the Vandellas . . . "Julia" with Miss Diahann Carroll . . . Malcolm X . . . those five little girls in Alabama . . . Martin Luther King . . . Oh no! The Supremes broke up! *(The drumming intensifies.)* Stop playing those drums! Those drums will be confiscated once we reach Savannah. You can't change history! You can't turn back the clock! *(To the audience.)* Repeat after me, I don't hear any drums! I will not rebel! I will not rebel! I will not re—

(The lights go out, she screams, and the sound of a plane landing and screeching to a halt is heard. After a beat, lights reveal a wasted, disheveled MISS PAT, but perky nonetheless.)

MISS PAT   Hi. Miss Pat here. Things got a bit jumpy back there, but the Captain has just informed me we have safely landed in Savannah. Please check the overhead before exiting as any baggage you don't claim, we trash.

It's been fun, and we hope the next time you consider travel, it's with Celebrity.

(Luggage begins to revolve onstage from offstage left, going past MISS PAT *and revolving offstage right. Mixed in with the luggage are two male slaves and a woman slave, complete with luggage and I.D. tags around their necks.)*

MISS PAT   *(With routine, rehearsed pleasantness.)*
Have a nice day. Bye bye.
Button up that coat, it's kind of chilly.
Have a nice day. Bye bye.
You take care now.
See you.
Have a nice day.
Have a nice day.
Have a nice day.

Cookin' with Aunt Ethel

(As the slaves begin to revolve off, a low-down gut-bucket blues is heard. AUNT ETHEL, *a down-home black woman with a bandana on her head, revolves to center stage. She stands behind a big black pot and wears a reassuring grin.)*

AUNT ETHEL   Welcome to "Aunt Ethel's Down-Home Cookin' Show," where we explores the magic and mysteries of colored cuisine.

Today, we gonna be servin' ourselves up some . . . *(She laughs.)* I'm not gonna tell you. That's right! I'm not gonna tell you what it is till after you done cooked it. Child, on "The Aunt Ethel Show" we loves to have ourselves some fun. Well, are you ready? Here goes.

(She belts out a hard-driven' blues and throws invisible ingredients into the big, black pot.)

FIRST YA ADD A PINCH OF STYLE
AND THEN A DASH OF FLAIR
NOW YA STIR IN SOME PREOCCUPATION
WITH THE TEXTURE OF YOUR HAIR

NEXT YA ADD ALL KINDS OF RHYTHMS
LOTS OF FEELINGS AND PIZAZZ
THEN HUNNY THROW IN SOME RAGE
TILL IT CONGEALS AND TURNS TO JAZZ

NOW YOU COOKIN'
COOKIN' WITH AUNT ETHEL
YOU REALLY COOKIN'
COOKIN' WITH AUNT ETHEL, OH YEAH

NOW YA ADD A HEAP OF SURVIVAL
AND HUMILITY, JUST A TOUCH
ADD SOME ATTITUDE
OOPS! I PUT TOO MUCH

AND NOW A WHOLE LOT OF HUMOR
SALTY LANGUAGE, MIXED WITH SADNESS
THEN THROW IN A BOX OF BLUES
AND SIMMER TO MADNESS

NOW YOU COOKIN'
COOKIN' WITH AUNT ETHEL, OH YEAH!

NOW YOU BEAT IT—REALLY WORK IT
DISCARD AND DISOWN
AND IN A FEW HUNDRED YEARS
ONCE IT'S AGED AND FULLY GROWN
YA PUT IT IN THE OVEN
TILL IT'S BLACK
AND HAS A SHEEN
OR TILL IT'S NICE AND YELLA
OR ANY SHADE IN BETWEEN

NEXT YA TAKE 'EM OUT AND COOL 'EM
'CAUSE THEY NO FUN WHEN THEY HOT
AND WON'T YOU BE SURPRISED
AT THE CONCOCTION YOU GOT

YOU HAVE BAKED
BAKED YOURSELF A BATCH OF NEGROES
YES YOU HAVE BAKED YOURSELF
BAKED YOURSELF A BATCH OF NEGROES

(She pulls from the pot a handful of Negroes, black dolls.)

But don't ask me what to do with 'em now that you got 'em, 'cause child, that's your problem. *(She throws the dolls back into the pot.)* But in any case, yaw be sure to join Aunt Ethel next week, when we gonna be servin' ourselves up some chitlin quiche . . . some grits-under-glass,

AND A SWEET POTATO PIE
AND YOU'LL BE COOKIN'
COOKIN' WITH AUNT ETHEL
OH YEAH!

(On **AUNT ETHEL***'s final riff, lights reveal . . .)*

The Photo Session

(. . . a very glamorous, gorgeous, black couple, wearing the best of everything and perfect smiles. The stage is bathed in color and bright white light. Disco music with the chant: "We're fabulous" plays in the background. As they pose, larger-than-life images of their perfection are projected on the museum walls. The music quiets and the images fade away as they begin to speak and pose.)

GIRL   The world was becoming too much for us.

GUY   We couldn't resolve the contradictions of our existence.

GIRL   And we couldn't resolve yesterday's pain.

GUY   So we gave away our life and we now live inside *Ebony Magazine.*

GIRL   Yes, we live inside a world where everyone is beautiful, and wears fabulous clothes.

GUY   And no one says anything profound.

GIRL   Or meaningful.

GUY   Or contradictory.

GIRL   Because no one talks. Everyone just smiles and shows off their cheekbones.

(They adopt a profile pose.)

GUY   Last month I was black and fabulous while holding up a bottle of vodka.

GIRL   This month we get to be black and fabulous together.

(They dance/pose. The "We're fabulous" chant builds and then fades as they start to speak again.)

GIRL   There are of course setbacks.

GUY   We have to smile like this for a whole month.

GIRL   And we have no social life.

GUY   And no sex.

GIRL   And at times it feels like we're suffocating, like we're not human anymore.

GUY   And everything is rehearsed, including this other kind of pain we're starting to feel.

GIRL   The kind of pain that comes from feeling no pain at all.

(They then speak and pose with a sudden burst of energy.)

GUY But one can't have everything.

GIRL Can one?

GUY So if the world is becoming too much for you, do like we did.

GIRL Give away your life and come be beautiful with us.

GUY We guarantee, no contradictions.

GIRL/GUY Smile/click, smile/click, smile/click.

GIRL And no pain.

(They adopt a final pose and revolve off as the "We're fabulous" chant plays and fades into the background.)

A Soldier with a Secret

(Projected onto the museum walls are the faces of black soldiers—from the Spanish-American thru to the Vietnam War. Lights slowly reveal JUNIE ROBINSON, *a black combat soldier, posed on an onyx plinth. He comes to life and smiles at the audience. Somewhat dim-witted, he has an easy-going charm about him.)*

JUNIE Pst. Pst. Guess what? I know the secret. The secret to your pain. 'Course, I didn't always know. First I had to die, then come back to life, 'fore I had the gift.

Ya see the Cappin sent me off up ahead to scout for screamin' yella bastards. 'Course, for the life of me I couldn't understand why they'd be screamin', seein' as how we was tryin' to kill them and they us.

But anyway, I'm off lookin', when all of a sudden I find myself caught smack dead in the middle of this explosion. This blindin', burnin', scaldin' explosion. Musta been a booby trap or something, 'cause all around me is fire. Hell, I'm on fire. Like a piece of chicken dropped in a skillet of cracklin' grease. Why, my flesh was justa peelin' off of my bones.

But then I says to myself, "Junie, if yo' flesh is on fire, how come you don't feel no pain!" And I didn't. I swear as I'm standin' here, I felt nuthin'. That's when I sort of put two and two together and realized I didn't feel no whole lot of hurtin' cause I done died.

Well I just picked myself up and walked right on out of that explosion. Hell, once you know you dead, why keep on dyin', ya know?

So, like I say, I walk right outta that explosion, fully expectin' to see white clouds, Jesus, and my Mama, only all I saw was more war. Shootin' goin' on way off in this direction and that direction. And there, standin' around, was all the guys. Hubert, J. F., the Cappin. I guess the sound of the explosion must of attracted 'em, and they all starin' at me like I'm some kind of ghost.

So I yells to 'em, "Hey there Hubert! Hey there Cappin!" But they just stare. So I tells 'em how I'd died and how I guess it wasn't my time 'cause here I am, "Fully in the flesh and not a scratch to my bones." And they still just stare. So I took to starin' back.

(The expression on JUNIE's face slowly turns to horror and disbelief.)

Only what I saw . . . well I can't exactly to this day describe it. But I swear, as sure as they was wearin' green and holdin' guns, they was each wearin' a piece of the future on their faces.

Yeah. All the hurt that was gonna get done to them and they was gonna do to folks was right there clear as day.

I saw how J. F., once he got back to Chicago, was gonna get shot dead by this po-lice, and I saw how Hubert was gonna start beatin' up on his old lady which I didn't understand, 'cause all he could do was talk on and on about how much he loved her. Each and every one of 'em had pain in his future and blood on his path. And God or the Devil one spoke to me and said, "Junie, these colored boys ain't gonna be the same after this war. They ain't gonna have no kind of happiness."

Well right then and there it come to me. The secret to their pain.

Late that night, after the medics done checked me over and found me fit for fightin', after everybody done settle down for the night, I sneaked over to where Hubert was sleepin', and with a needle I stole from the medics . . . pst, pst . . . I shot a little air into his veins. The second he died, all the hurtin-to-come just left his face.

Two weeks later I got J. F. and after that Woodrow . . . Jimmy Joe . . . I even spent all night waitin' by the latrine 'cause I knew the Cappin always made a late night visit and pst . . . pst . . . I got him.

(Smiling, quite proud of himself.) That's how come I died and come back to life. 'Cause just like Jesus went around healin' the sick, I'm supposed to go around healin' the hurtin' all these colored boys wearin' from the war.

Pst, pst. I know the secret. The secret to your pain. The secret to yours, and yours. Pst. Pst. Pst. Pst.

(The lights slowly fade.)

The Gospel According to Miss Roj

(The darkness is cut by electronic music. Cold, pounding, unrelenting. A neon sign which spells out THE BOTTOMLESS PIT clicks on. There is a lone bar stool. Lights flash on and off, pulsating to the beat. There is a blast of smoke and, from the haze, MISS ROJ appears. He is dressed in striped patio pants, white go-go boots, a halter, and cat-shaped sunglasses. What would seem ridiculous on anyone else, MISS ROJ wears as if it were high fashion. He carries himself with total elegance and absolute arrogance.)

MISS ROJ   God created black people and black people created style. The name's Miss Roj . . . that's R.O.J. thank you and you can find me every Wednesday, Friday and Saturday nights at "The Bottomless Pit," the watering hole for the wild and weary which asks the question, "Is there life after Jherri-curl?"

(A waiter enters, hands MISS ROJ *a drink, and then exits.)*

Thanks, doll. *Yes,* if they be black and swish, the B. P. has seen them, which is not to suggest the Pit is lacking in cultural diversity. Oh no. There are your dinge queens, white men who like their chicken legs dark. *(He winks/flirts with a man in the audience.)* And let's not forget, "Los Muchachos de la Neighborhood." But the speciality of the house is The Snap Queens. *(He snaps his fingers.)* We are a rare breed.

For, you see, when something strikes our fancy, when the truth comes piercing through the dark, well you just can't let it pass unnoticed. No darling. You must pronounce it with a snap. *(He snaps.)*

Snapping comes from another galaxy, as do all snap queens. That's right. I ain't just your regular oppressed American Negro. No-no-no! I am an extraterrestrial. And I ain't talkin' none of that shit you seen in the movies! I have real power.

(The waiter enters. MISS ROJ *stops him.)*

Speaking of no power, will you please tell Miss Stingy-with-the-rum, that if Miss Roj had wanted to remain sober, she could have stayed home and drank Kool-aid. *(He snaps.)* Thank you.

(The waiter exits. MISS ROJ *crosses and sits on bar stool.)*

Yes, I was placed here on Earth to study the life habits of a deteriorating society, and child when we talkin' New York City, we are discussing the Queen of Deterioration. Miss New York is doing a slow dance with death, and I am here to warn you all, but before I do, I must know . . . don't you just love my patio pants? Annette Funicello immortalized them in "Beach Blanket Bingo," and I have continued the legacy. And my go-gos? I realize white after Labor Day is very gauche, but as the saying goes, if you've got it flaunt it, if you don't, front it and snap to death any bastard who dares to defy you. *(Laughing)* Oh ho! My demons are showing. Yes, my demons live at the bottom of my Bacardi and Coke.

Let's just hope for all concerned I dance my demons out before I drink them out 'cause child, dancing demons take you on a ride, but those drinkin' demons just take you, and you find yourself doing the strangest things. Like the time I locked my father in the broom closet. Seems the liquor made his tongue real liberal and he decided he was gonna baptize me with the word "faggot" over and over. Well, he's just going on and on with "faggot this" and "faggot that," all the while walking toward the broom closet to piss. So the demons just took hold of my wedges and forced me to kick the drunk son-of-a-bitch into the closet and lock the door. *(Laughter)* Three days later I remembered he was there. *(He snaps.)*

(The waiter enters. **Miss Roj** *takes a drink and downs it.)*

Another!

(The waiter exits.)

(Dancing about.) Oh yes-yes-yes! Miss Roj is quintessential style. I corn row the hairs on my legs so that they spell out M.I.S.S. R.O.J. And I dare any bastard to fuck with me because I will snap your ass into oblivion.

I have the power, you know. Everytime I snap, I steal one beat of your heart. So if you find yourself gasping for air in the middle of the night, chances are you fucked with Miss Roj and she didn't like it.

Like the time this asshole at Jones Beach decided to take issue with my coulotte-sailor ensemble. This child, this muscle-bound Brooklyn thug in a skin-tight bikini, very skin-tight so the whole world can see that instead of a brain, God gave him an extra thick piece of sausage. You know the kind who beat up on their wives for breakfast. Snap your fingers if you know what I'm talking about . . . Come on and snap, child. *(He gets the audience to snap.)* Well, he decided to blurt out when I walked by, "Hey look at da monkey coon in da faggit suit." Well, I walked up to the poor dear, very calmly lifted my hand, and. . . . *(He snaps in rapid succession.)* A heart attack, right there on the beach. *(He singles out someone in the audience.)* You don't believe it? Cross me! Come on! Come on!

(The waiter enters, hands **Miss Roj** *a drink.* **Miss Roj** *downs it. The waiter exits.)*

(Looking around.) If this place is the answer, we're asking all the wrong questions. The only reason I come here is to communicate with my origins. The flashing lights are signals from my planet way out there. Yes, girl, even further than Flatbush. We're talking another galaxy. The flashing lights tell me how much time is left before the end.

(Very drunk and loud by now.) I hate the people here. I hate the drinks. But most of all I hate this goddamn music. That ain't music. Give me Aretha Franklin any day. *(Singing)* "Just a little respect. R.E.S.P.E.C.T." Yeah! Yeah!

Come on and dance your last dance with Miss Roj. Last call is but a drink away and each snap puts you one step closer to the end.

A high-rise goes up. You can't get no job. Come on everybody and dance. A whole race of people gets trashed and debased. Snap those fingers and dance. Some sick bitch throws her baby out the window 'cause she thinks it's the Devil. Everybody snap! *The New York Post.* Snap!

Snap for every time you walk past someone lying in the street, smelling like frozen piss and shit and you don't see it. Snap for every crazed bastard who kills himself so as to get the jump on being killed. And snap for every sick muthafucker who, bored with carrying around his fear, takes to shooting up other people.

Yeah, snap your fingers and dance with Miss Roj. But don't be fooled by the banners and balloons 'cause, child, this ain't no party going on. Hell no! It's a wake. And the casket's made out of stone, steel, and glass and the people are racing all over the pavement like maggots on a dead piece of meat.

Yeah, dance! But don't be surprised if there ain't no beat holding you together 'cause we traded in our drums for respectability. So now it's just words. Words rappin'. Words screechin'. Words flowin' instead of blood 'cause you know that don't work. Words cracklin' instead of fire 'cause by the time a match is struck on 125th Street and you run to midtown, the flame has been blown away.

So come on and dance with Miss Roj and her demons. We don't ask for acceptance. We don't ask for approval. We know who we are and we move on it!

I guarantee you will never hear two fingers put together in a snap and not think of Miss Roj. That's power, baby. Patio pants and all.

(The lights begin to flash in rapid succession.)

So let's dance! And snap! And dance! And snap!

*(**Miss Roj** begins to dance as if driven by his demons. There is a blast of smoke and when the haze settles, **Miss Roj** has revolved off and in place of him is a recording of Aretha Franklin singing "Respect.")*

The Hairpiece

*(As "Respect" fades into the background, a vanity revolves to center stage. On this vanity are two wigs, an Afro wig, circa 1968, and a long, flowing wig, both resting on wig stands. A black **WOMAN** enters, her head and body wrapped in towels. She picks up a framed picture and after a few moments of hesitation, throws it into a small trash can. She then removes one of her towels to reveal a totally bald head. Looking into a mirror on the "fourth wall," she begins applying makeup.)*

*(The wig stand holding the Afro wig opens her eyes. Her name is **JANINE**. She stares in disbelief at the bald woman.)*

JANINE   *(Calling to the other wig stand.)* LaWanda. LaWanda girl, wake up.

(The other wig stand, the one with the long, flowing wig, opens her eyes. Her name is LaWanda.*)*

LAWANDA   What? What is it?

JANINE   Check out girlfriend.

LAWANDA   Oh, girl, I don't believe it.

JANINE *(Laughing)*   Just look at the poor thing, trying to paint some life onto that face of hers. You'd think by now she'd realize it's the hair. It's all about the hair.

LAWANDA   What hair! She ain't go no hair! She done fried, dyed, de-chemical-ized her shit to death.

JANINE   And all that's left is that buck-naked scalp of hers, sittin' up there apol-ogizin' for being odd-shaped and ugly.

LAWANDA   *(Laughing with* JANINE.*)* Girl, stop!

JANINE   I ain't sayin' nuthin' but the truth.

LAWANDA/JANINE   The bitch is bald! *(They laugh.)*

JANINE   And all over some man.

LAWANDA   I tell ya, girl, I just don't understand it. I mean, look at her. She's got a right nice face, a good head on her shoulders. A good job even. And she's got to go fall in love with that fool.

JANINE   That political quick-change artist. Everytime the nigga went and changed his ideology, she went and changed her hair to fit the occasion.

LAWANDA   Well at least she's breaking up with him.

JANINE   Hunny, no!

LAWANDA   Yes child.

JANINE   Oh, girl, dish me the dirt!

LAWANDA   Well, you see, I heard her on the phone, talking to one of her girl-friends, and she's meeting him for lunch today to give him the ax.

JANINE   Well it's about time.

LAWANDA   I hear ya. But don't you worry 'bout a thing, girlfriend. I'm gonna tell you all about it.

JANINE   Hunny, you won't have to tell me a damn thing 'cause I'm gonna be there, front row, center.

LAWANDA   You?

JANINE   Yes, child, she's wearing me to lunch.

LAWANDA *(Outraged)*   I don't think so!

JANINE *(With an attitude)*   What do you mean, you don't think so?

LAWANDA   Exactly what I said, "I don't think so." Damn, Janine, get real. How the hell she gonna wear both of us?

JANINE   She ain't wearing both of us. She's wearing me.

LAWANDA   Says who?

JANINE   Says me! Says her! Ain't that right, girlfriend?

(The WOMAN *stops putting on makeup, looks around, sees no one, and goes back to her makeup.)*

JANINE   I said, ain't that right!

(The WOMAN *picks up the phone.)*

WOMAN   Hello . . . hello . . .

JANINE   Did you hear the damn phone ring?

WOMAN   No.

JANINE   Then put the damn phone down and talk to me.

WOMAN   I ah . . . don't understand.

JANINE   It ain't deep so don't panic. Now, you're having lunch with your boyfriend, right?

WOMAN   *(Breaking into tears.)*   I think I'm having a nervous breakdown.

JANINE   *(Impatient)*   I said you're having lunch with your boyfriend, right!

WOMAN   *(Scared, pulling herself together.)*   Yes, right . . . right.

JANINE   To break up with him.

WOMAN   How did you know that?

LAWANDA   I told her.

WOMAN   *(Stands and screams.)*   Help! Help!

JANINE   Sit down. I said sit your ass down!

(The WOMAN *does.)*

JANINE   Now set her straight and tell her you're wearing me.

LAWANDA   She's the one that needs to be set straight, so go on and tell her you're wearing me.

JANINE   No, tell her you're wearing me.

(There is a pause.)

LAWANDA   Well?

JANINE   Well?

WOMAN   I ah . . . actually hadn't made up my mind.

JANINE   *(Going off)*   What do you mean you ain't made up you mind! After all that fool has put you through, you gonna need all the attitude you can get and there is nothing like attitude and a healthy head of kinks to make his shit shrivel like it should!

That's right! When you wearin' me, you lettin' him know he ain't gonna get no sweet-talkin' comb through your love without some serious resistance. No-no! The kink of my head is like the kink of your heart and neither is about to be hot-pressed into surrender.

LAWANDA   That shit is so tired. The last time attitude worked on anybody was 1968. Janine girl, you need to get over it and get on with it. *(To the* WOMAN.*)* And you need to give the nigga a goodbye he will never forget.

I say give him hysteria! Give him emotion! Give him rage! And there is nothing like a toss of the tresses to make your emotional outburst shine with emotional flair.

You can toss me back, shake me from side to side, all the while screaming, "I want you out of my life forever!!!" And not only will I come bouncing
back for more, but you just might win an Academy Award for best performance by a head of hair in a dramatic role.

JANINE   Miss hunny, please! She don't need no Barbie doll dipped in chocolate
telling her what to do. She needs a head of hair that's coming from a fo' real
place.

LAWANDA   Don't you dare talk about nobody coming from a "fo' real place,"
Miss Made-in-Taiwan!

JANINE   Hey! I ain't ashamed of where I come from. Besides, it don't matter
where you come from as long as you end up in the right place.

LAWANDA   And it don't matter the grade as long as the point gets made. So go
on and tell her you're wearing me.

JANINE   No, tell her you're wearing me.

(The WOMAN, *unable to take it, begins to bite off her fake nails, as* LaWANDA *and*
JANINE *go at each other.)*

LAWANDA	JANINE
Set the bitch straight. Let her know there is no way she could even begin to compete with me. I am quality. She is kink. I am exotic. She is common. I am class and she is trash. That's right. T.R.A.S.H. We're talking three strikes and you're out. So go on and tell her you're wearing me. Go on, tell her! Tell her! Tell her!	Who you callin' a bitch? Why, if I had hands I'd knock you clear into next week. You think you cute. She thinks she's cute just 'cause that synthetic mop of hers blows in the wind. She looks like a fool and you look like an even bigger fool when you wear her, so go on and tell her you're wearing me. Go on, tell her! Tell her! Tell her!

(The WOMAN *screams and pulls the two wigs off the wig stands as the lights go to*
black on three bald heads.)

The Last Mama-on-the-Couch Play

(A NARRATOR, *dressed in a black tuxedo, enters through the audience and stands*
center stage. He is totally solemn.)

NARRATOR   We are pleased to bring you yet another Mama-on-the-Couch play.
A searing domestic drama that tears at the very fabric of racist America. *(He*
crosses upstage center and sits on a stool and reads from a playscript.) Act One.
Scene One.

*(*MAMA *revolves on stage left, sitting on a couch reading a large, oversized Bible. A*
window is placed stage right. MAMA's *dress, the couch, and drapes are made from*
the same material. A doormat lays down center.)

NARRATOR   Lights up on a dreary, depressing, but with middle-class aspirations tenement slum. There is a couch, with a Mama on it. Both are well worn. There is a picture of Jesus on the wall . . . *(A picture of Jesus is instantly revealed.)* . . . and a window which looks onto an abandoned tenement. It is late spring.

Enter Walter-Lee-Beau-Willie-Jones (SON *enters through the audience.)* He is Mama's thirty-year-old son. His brow is heavy from three hundred years of oppression.

MAMA *(Looking up from her Bible, speaking in a slow manner.)*   Son, did you wipe your feet?

SON *(An ever-erupting volcano.)*   No, Mama, I didn't wipe me feet! Out there, every day, Mama is the Man. The Man Mama. Mr. Charlie! Mr. Bossman! And he's wipin' his feet on me. On me, Mama, every damn day of my life. Ain't that enough for me to deal with? Ain't that enough?

MAMA   Son, wipe your feet.

SON   I wanna dream. I wanna be somebody. I wanna take charge of my life.

MAMA   You can do all of that, but first you got to wipe your feet.

SON *(As he crosses to the mat, mumbling and wiping his feet.)*   Wipe my feet . . . wipe my feet . . . wipe my feet . . .

MAMA   That's a good boy.

SON *(Exploding)*   Boy! Boy! I don't wanna be nobody's good boy, Mama. I wanna be my own man!

MAMA   I know son, I know. God will show the way.

SON   God, Mama! Since when did your God ever do a damn thing for the black man. Huh, Mama, huh? You tell me. When did your God ever help me?

MAMA *(Removing her wire-rim glasses.)*   Son, come here.

(SON *crosses to* MAMA, *who slowly stands and in an exaggerated stage slap, backhands* SON *clear across the stage. The* NARRATOR *claps his hands to create the sound for the slap.* MAMA *then lifts her clinched fists to the heavens.)*

MAMA   Not in my house, my house, will you ever talk that way again!

(The NARRATOR, *so moved by her performance, erupts in applause and encourages the audience to do so.)*

NARRATOR   Beautiful. Just stunning.

(He reaches into one of the secret compartments of the set and gets an award which he ceremoniously gives to MAMA *for her performance. She bows and then returns to the couch.)*

NARRATOR   Enter Walter-Lee-Beau-Willie's wife, The Lady in Plaid.

(Music from nowhere is heard, a jazzy pseudo-abstract intro as the LADY IN PLAID *dances in through the audience, wipes her feet, and then twirls about.)*

LADY
> She was a creature of regal beauty
> who in ancient time graced the temples of the Nile
> with her womanliness
> But here she was, stuck being colored
> and a woman in a world that valued neither.

SON   You cooked my dinner?

LADY   *(Oblivious to* SON.*)*
> Feet flat, back broke,
> she looked at the man who, though he be thirty,
> still ain't got his own apartment.
> Yeah, he's still livin' with his Mama!
> And she asked herself, was this the life
> for a Princess Colored, who by the
> translucence of her skin, knew the
> universe was her sister.

(The LADY IN PLAID *twirls and dances.)*

SON   *(Becoming irate.)*   I've had a hard day of dealin' with the Man. Where's my damn dinner? Woman, stand still when I'm talkin' to you!

LADY   And she cried for her sisters in Detroit
> Who knew, as she, that their souls belonged
> in ancient temples on the Nile.
> And she cried for her sisters in Chicago
> who, like her, their life has become
> one colored hell.

SON   There's only one thing gonna get through to you.

LADY   And she cried for her sisters in New Orleans
> And her sisters in Trenton and Birmingham,
> and
> Poughkeepsie and Orlando and Miami Beach
> and
> Las Vegas, Palm Springs.

(As she continues to call out cities, he crosses offstage and returns with two black dolls and then crosses to the window.)

SON   Now are you gonna cook me dinner?

LADY   Walter-Lee-Beau-Willie-Jones, no! Not my babies.

*(*SON *throws them out the window. The* LADY IN PLAID *then lets out a primal scream.)*

LADY   He dropped them!!!!

(*The* **Narrator** *breaks into applause.*)

narrator   Just splendid. Shattering.

(*He then crosses and after an intense struggle with* **Mama**, *he takes the award from her and gives it to the* **Lady in Plaid**, *who is still suffering primal pain.*)

lady   Not my babies . . . not my . . . (*Upon receiving the award, she instantly recovers.*) Help me up, sugar. (*She then bows and crosses and stands behind the couch.*)

narrator   Enter Medea Jones, Walter-Lee-Beau-Willie's sister.

(**Medea** *moves very ceremoniously, wiping her feet and then speaking and gesturing as if she just escaped from a Greek tragedy.*)

medea
>   Ah, see how the sun kneels to speak
>   her evening vespers, exaulting all
>   in her vision, even lowly tenement
>   long abandoned.
>
>   Mother, wife of brother, I trust
>   the approaching darkness finds you
>   safe in Hestia's busom.
>
>   Brother, why wear the face of a man
>   in anguish. Can the garment of thine
>   feelings cause the shape of your
>   countenance to disfigure so?

son (*At the end of his rope.*)   Leave me alone, Medea.

medea   (*To* **Mama**)
>   Is good brother still going on and on and on
>   about He and The Man.

mama/lady   What else?

medea   Ah brother, if with our thoughts and
>   words we could cast thine oppressors
>   into the lowest bowels of wretched
>   hell, would that make us more like the
>   gods or more like our oppressors.
>
>   No, brother, no, do not let thy rage
>   choke the blood which anoints thy
>   heart with love. Forgo thine darkened
>   humor and let love shine on your
>   soul, like a jewel on a young maiden's hand.

(*Dropping to her knees.*)
>   I beseech thee, forgo thine
>   anger and leave wrath to the gods!

SON   Girl, what has gotten into you.

MEDEA   Julliard, good brother. For I am no
longer bound by rhythms of race or
region. Oh, no. My speech, like my
pain and suffering, have become
classical and therefore universal.

LADY   I didn't understand a damn thing she said, but girl you usin' them words.

(LADY IN PLAID crosses and gives MEDEA the award and everyone applauds.)

SON   *(Trying to stop the applause.)*   Wait one damn minute! This my play. It's
about me and the Man. It ain't got nuthin' to do with no ancient temples on
the Nile and it ain't got nuthin' to do with Hestia's busom. And it ain't got
nuthin' to do with you slappin' me across no room. *(His gut-wrenching
best.)* It's about me. Me and my pain! My pain!

THE VOICE OF THE MAN   Walter-Lee-Beau-Willie, this is the Man. You have
been convicted of overacting. Come out with your hands up.

(SON starts to cross to the window.)

SON   Well now that does it.

MAMA   Son, no, don't go near the window. Son, no!

(Gun shots ring out and SON falls dead.)

MAMA *(Crossing to the body, too emotional for words.)*   My son, he was a good
boy. Confused. Angry. Just like his father. And his father's father. And his father's father's father. And now he's dead.

*(Seeing she's about to drop to her knees, the NARRATOR rushes and places
a pillow underneath her just in time.)*

If only he had been born into a world better than this. A world where there
are no well-worn couches and no well-worn Mamas and nobody over-
emotes.

If only he had been born into an all-black musical.

(A song intro begins.)

Nobody ever dies in an all-black musical.

(MEDEA and LADY IN PLAID pull out church fans and begin to fan themselves.)

MAMA *(Singing a soul-stirring gospel.)*
OH WHY COULDN'T HE
BE BORN
INTO A SHOW WITH LOTS OF SINGING
AND DANCING

I SAY WHY
COULDN'T HE
BE BORN

LADY   Go ahead hunny. Take your time.

MAMA

INTO A SHOW WHERE EVERYBODY
IS HAPPY

NARRATOR/MEDEA   Preach! Preach!

MAMA

OH WHY COULDN'T HE BE BORN WITH THE CHANCE
TO SMILE A LOT AND SING AND DANCE
OH WHY
OH WHY

OH WHY
COULDN'T HE
BE BORN
INTO AN ALL-BLACK SHOW
WOAH-WOAH

(The CAST *joins in, singing do-wop gospel background to* MAMA's *lament.)*

OH WHY
COULDN'T HE
BE BORN
(HE BE BORN)
INTO A SHOW WHERE EVERYBODY
IS HAPPY

WHY COULDN'T HE BE BORN WITH THE CHANCE
TO SMILE A LOT AND SING AND DANCE
WANNA KNOW WHY
WANNA KNOW WHY

OH WHY
COULDN'T HE
BE BORN
INTO AN ALL-BLACK SHOW
A-MEN

(A singing/dancing, spirit-raising revival begins.)

OH, SON, GET UP
GET UP AND DANCE
WE SAY GET UP
THIS IS YOUR SECOND CHANCE

DON'T SHAKE A FIST
JUST SHAKE A LEG
AND DO THE TWIST
DON'T SCREAM AND BEG
SON SON SON
GET UP AND DANCE

GET
GET UP
GET UP AND
GET UP AND DANCE—ALL RIGHT!
GET UP AND DANCE—ALL RIGHT!
GET UP AND DANCE!

(WALTER-LEE-BEAU-WILLIE *springs to life and joins in the dancing. A foot-stomping, hand-clapping production number takes off, which encompasses a myriad of black-Broadwayesque dancing styles—shifting speeds and styles with exuberant abandonment.*)

MAMA *(Bluesy)*
    WHY COULDN'T HE BE BORN INTO AN ALL-BLACK SHOW
CAST
    WITH SINGING AND DANCING
MAMA   BLACK SHOW

(MAMA *scats and the dancing becomes manic and just a little too desperate to please.*)

CAST
    WE GOTTA DANCE
    WE GOTTA DANCE
    GET UP GET UP GET UP AND DANCE
    WE GOTTA DANCE
    WE GOTTA DANCE
    GOTTA DANCE!

(*Just at the point the dancing is about to become violent, the cast freezes and pointedly, simply sings:*)

    IF WE WANT TO LIVE
    WE HAVE GOT TO
    WE HAVE GOT TO
    DANCE . . . AND DANCE . . . AND DANCE . . .

(*As they continue to dance with zombie-like frozen smiles and faces, around them images of coon performers flash as the lights slowly fade.*)

Symbiosis

(The Temptations singing "My Girl" are heard as lights reveal a BLACK MAN *in corporate dress standing before a large trash can throwing objects from a Saks Fifth Avenue bag into it. Circling around him with his every emotion on his face is* THE KID, *who is dressed in a late-sixties street style. His moves are slightly heightened. As the scene begins the music fades.)*

MAN *(With contained emotions.)*
My first pair of Converse All-stars. Gone.
My first Afro-comb. Gone.
My first dashiki. Gone.
My autographed pictures of Stokley Carmichael, Jomo Kenyatta and Donna Summer. Gone.

KID *(Near tears, totally upset.)*   This shit's not fair man. Damn! Hell! Shit! Shit! It's not fair!

MAN
My first jar of Murray's Pomade.
My first can of Afro-sheen.
My first box of curl relaxer. Gone! Gone! Gone!
Eldridge Cleaver's *Soul on Ice.*

KID   Not *Soul on Ice!*

MAN   It's been replaced on my bookshelf by *The Color Purple.*

KID *(Horrified)* No!

MAN   Gone!

KID   But—

MAN
Jimi Hendrix's "Purple Haze." Gone.
Sly Stone's "There's A Riot Goin' On." Gone.
The Jackson Five's "I Want You Back."

KID   Man, you can't throw that away. It's living proof Michael had a black nose.

MAN   It's all going. Anything and everything that connects me to you, to who I was, to what we were, is out of my life.

KID   You've got to give me another chance.

MAN   *Fingertips Part 2.*

KID   Man, how can you do that? That's vintage Stevie Wonder.

MAN   You want to know how, Kid? You want to know how? Because my survival depends on it. Whether you know it or not, the Ice Age is upon us.

KID *(Jokingly)*   Man, what the hell you talkin' about. It's 95 damn degrees.

MAN   The climate is changing, Kid, and either you adjust or you end up extinct. A sociological dinosaur. Do you understand what I'm trying to tell you? King Kong would have made it to the top if only he had taken the elevator. Instead he brought attention to his struggle and ended up dead.

KID *(Pleading)*   I'll change. I swear I'll change. I'll maintain a low profile. You won't even know I'm around.

MAN   If I'm to become what I'm to become then you've got to go. . . . I have no history. I have no past.

KID   Just like that?

MAN   *(Throwing away a series of buttons.)*   Free Angela! Free Bobby! Free Huey, Duey, and Louie! U.S. out of Viet Nam. U.S. out of Cambodia. U.S. out of Harlem, Detroit, and Newark. Gone! . . . The Temptations Greatest Hits!

KID   *(Grabbing the album.)*   No!!!

MAN   Give it back, Kid.

KID   No.

MAN   I said give it back!

KID   No. I can't let you trash this. Johnny man, it contains fourteen classic cuts by the tempting Temptations. We're talking, "Ain't Too Proud to Beg," "Papa Was a Rolling Stone," "My Girl."

MAN   *(Warning)*   I don't have all day.

KID   For God's sake, Johnny man, "My Girl" is the jam to end all jams. It's what we are. Who we are. It's a way of life. Come on, man, for old times sake. *(Singing)*

I GOT SUNSHINE ON A CLOUDY DAY
BUM-DA-DUM-DA-DUM-DA-BUM
AND WHEN IT'S COLD OUTSIDE

Come on, Johnny man, you ain't "bummin'," man.

I GOT THE MONTH OF MAY

Here comes your favorite part. Come on, Johnny man, sing.

I GUESS YOU SAY
WHAT CAN MAKE ME FEEL THIS WAY
MY GIRL, MY GIRL, MY GIRL
TALKIN' 'BOUT

MAN   *(Exploding)*   I said give it back!

KID   *(Angry)*   I ain't givin' you a muthafuckin' thing!

MAN   Now you listen to me!

KID   No, you listen to me. This is the kid you're dealin' with, so don't fuck with me!

(He hits his fist into his hand, and THE MAN *grabs for his heart.* THE KID *repeats with two more hits, which causes the man to drop to the ground, grabbing his heart.)*

KID   Jai! Jai! Jai!

MAN   Kid, please.

KID   Yeah. Yeah. Now who's begging who. . . . Well, well, well, look at Mr. Cream-of-the-Crop, Mr. Colored-Man-on-Top. Now that he's making it, he no longer wants anything to do with the Kid. Well, you may put all kinds of silk ties 'round your neck and white lines up your nose, but the Kid is here to stay. You may change your women as often as you change your underwear, but the Kid is here to stay. And regardless of how much of your past that you trash, I ain't goin' no damn where. Is that clear? Is that clear?

MAN *(Regaining his strength, beginning to stand.)*   Yeah.

KID   Good. *(After a beat.)* You all right man? You all right? I don't want to hurt you, but when you start all that talk about getting rid of me, well, it gets me kind of crazy. We need each other. We are one . . .

(Before THE KID *can complete his sentence,* THE MAN *grabs him around his neck and starts to choke him violently.)*

MAN *(As he strangles him.)* The . . . Ice . . . Age . . . is . . . upon us . . . and either we adjust . . . or we end up . . . extinct.

*(*THE KID *hangs limp in* THE MAN's *arms.)*

MAN *(Laughing)*   Man kills his own rage. Film at eleven. *(He then dumps* THE KID *into the trash can, and closes the lid. He speaks in a contained voice.)* I have no history. I have no past. I can't. It's too much. It's much too much. I must be able to smile on cue. And watch the news with an impersonal eye. I have no stake in the madness.

Being black is too emotionally taxing; therefore I will be black only on weekends and holidays.

(He then turns to go, but sees the Temptations album lying on the ground. He picks it up and sings quietly to himself.)

I GUESS YOU SAY
WHAT CAN MAKE ME FEEL THIS WAY

(He pauses, but then crosses to the trash can, lifts the lid, and just as he is about to toss the album in, a hand reaches from inside the can and grabs hold of THE MAN's *arm.* THE KID *then emerges from the can with a death grip on* THE MAN's *arm.)*

KID *(Smiling)*   What's happenin'?

BLACKOUT

Lala's Opening

(Roving follow spots. A timpani drum roll. As we hear the voice of the ANNOUNCER, *outrageously glamorous images of* LALA *are projected onto the museum walls.)*

VOICE OF ANNOUNCER: From Rome to Rangoon! Paris to Prague! We are pleased to present the American debut of the one! The only! The breathtaking! The astounding! The stupendous! The incredible! The magnificent! Lala Lamazing Grace!

(Thunderous applause as LALA *struts on, the definitive black diva. She has long, flowing hair, an outrageous lamé dress, and an affected French accent which she loses when she's upset.)*

LALA

  EVERYBODY LOVES LALA
  EVERYBODY LOVES ME
  PARIS! BERLIN! LONDON! ROME!
  NO MATTER WHERE I GO
  I ALWAYS FEEL AT HOME

  OHHHH
  EVERYBODY LOVES LALA
  EVERYBODY LOVES ME
  I'M TRES MAGNIFIQUE
  AND OH SO UNIQUE
  AND WHEN IT COMES TO GLAMOUR
  I'M CHIC-ER THAN CHIC

(She giggles.)

  THAT'S WHY EVERYBODY
  EVERYBODY
  EVERYBODY-EVERYBODY-EVERYBODY
  LOVES ME

(She begins to vocally reach for higher and higher notes, until she has to point to her final note. She ends the number with a grand flourish and bows to thunderous applause.)

LALA   Yes, it's me! Lala Lamazing Grace and I have come home. Home to the home I never knew as home. Home to you, my people, my blood, my guts.

   My story is a simple one, full of fire, passion, magique. You may ask how did I, a humble girl from the backwoods of Mississippi, come to be the ninth wonder of the modern world. Well, I can't take all of the credit. Part of it goes to him. *(She points toward the heavens.)*

   No, not the light man, darling, but God. For, you see, Lala is a star. A very big star. Let us not mince words, I'm a fucking meteorite. *(She laughs.)* But He is the universe and just like my sister, Aretha la Franklin, Lala's roots are in the black church. *(She sings in a showy gospel style:)*

  THAT'S WHY EVERYBODY LOVES
  SWING LOW SWEET CHARIOT
  THAT'S WHY EVERYBODY LOVES
  GO DOWN MOSES WAY DOWN IN EGYPT LAND
  THAT'S WHY EVERYBODY EVERYBODY LOVES
  ME!!!

(Once again she points to her final note and then basks in applause.)

I love that note. I just can't hit it.

Now, before I dazzle you with more of my limitless talent, tell me something, America. *(Musical underscoring)* Why has it taken you so long to recognize my artistry? Mother France opened her loving arms and Lala came running. All over the world Lala was embraced. But here, ha! You spat at Lala. Was I too exotic? Too much woman, or what?

Diana Ross you embrace. A two-bit nobody from Detroit, of all places. Now, I'm not knocking la Ross. She does the best she can with the little she has. *(She laughs.)* But the Paul la Robesons, the James la Baldwins, the Josephine la Baker's, who was my godmother you know. The Lala Lamazing Grace's you kick out. You drive . . .

AWAY
I AM GOING AWAY
HOPING TO FIND A BETTER DAY
WHAT DO YOU SAY
HEY HEY
I AM GOING AWAY
AWAY

*(**Lala**, caught up in the drama of the song, doesn't see **Admonia**, her maid, stick her head out from offstage.)*

*(Once she is sure **Lala** isn't looking, she wheels onto stage right **Flo'rance**, **Lala**'s lover, who wears a white mask/blonde hair. He is gagged and tied to a chair. **Admonia** places him on stage and then quickly exits.)*

LALA

AU REVOIR—JE VAIS PARTIR MAINTENANT
JE VEUX DIRE MAINTENANT
AU REVOIR
AU REVOIR
AU REVOIR
AU REVOIR
A-MA-VIE

*(On her last note, she see **Flo'rance** and, in total shock, crosses to him.)*

LALA   Flo'rance, what the hell are you doing out here, looking like that. I haven't seen you for three days and you decide to show up now?

(He mumbles.)

I don't want to hear it!

(He mumbles.)

I said shut up!

(ADMONIA enters from stage right and has a letter opener on a silver tray.)

ADMONIA   Pst!

(LALA, embarrassed by the presence of ADMONIA on-stage, smiles apologetically at the audience.)

LALA   Un momento.

(She then pulls ADMONIA to the side.)

LALA   Darling, have you lost your mind coming on-stage while I'm perform-ing. And what have you done to Flo'rance? When I asked you to keep him tied up, I didn't mean to tie him up.

(ADMONIA gives her the letter opener.)

LALA   Why are you giving me this? I have no letters to open. I'm in the middle of my American debut. Admonia, take Flo'rance off this stage with you! Ad-monia!

(ADMONIA is gone. LALA turns to the audience and tries to make the best of it.)

LALA   That was Admonia, my slightly overweight black maid, and this is Flo'rance, my amour. I remember how we met, don't you Flo'rance. I was sitting in a café on the Left Bank, when I looked up and saw the most beau-tiful man staring down at me.

"Who are you," he asked. I told him my name . . . whatever my name was back then. And he said, "No, that cannot be your name. Your name should fly, like Lala." And the rest is la history.

Flo'rance molded me into the woman I am today. He is my Svengali, my reality, my all. And I thought I was all to him, until we came here to Amer-ica, and he fucked that bitch. Yeah, you fucked 'em all. Anything black and breathing. And all this time, I thought you loved me for being me. *(She holds the letter opener to his neck.)*

You may think you made me, but I'll have you know I was who I was, whoever that was, long before you made me what I am. So there! *(She stabs him and breaks into song.)*

OH, LOVE CAN DRIVE A WOMAN TO MADNESS
TO PAIN AND SADNESS
I KNOW
BELIEVE ME I KNOW
I KNOW
I KNOW

(**LALA** *sees what she's done and is about to scream but catches herself and tries to play it off.*)

LALA   Moving right along.

(**ADMONIA** *enters with a telegram on a tray.*)

ADMONIA   Pst.
LALA *(Anxious/hostile)*   What is it now?

(**ADMONIA** *hands* **LALA** *a telegram.*)

LALA *(Excited)*   Oh, la telegram from one of my fans and the concert isn't even over yet. Get me the letter opener. It's in Flo'rance.

(**ADMONIA** *hands* **LALA** *the letter opener.*)

LALA   Next I am going to do for you my immortal hit song, "The Girl Inside." But first we open the telegram. *(She quickly reads it and is outraged.)* What! Which pig in la audience wrote this trash? *(Reading)* "Dear Sadie, I'm so proud. The show's wonderful, but talk less and sing more. Love, Mama."
      First off, no one calls me Sadie. Sadie died the day Lala was born. And secondly, my Mama's dead.
      Anyone who knows anything about Lala Lamazing Grace knows that my mother and Josephine Baker were French patriots together. They infiltrated a carnival rumored to be the center of Nazi intelligence, disguised as Hottentot Siamese twins. You may laugh but it's true. Mama died a heroine. It's all in my autobiography, "Voilá Lala!" So whoever sent this telegram is a liar!

(**ADMONIA** *promptly presents her with another telegram.*)

LALA   This had better be an apology. (*To* **ADMONIA.**) Back up, darling. *(Reading)* "Dear Sadie, I'm not dead. P.S. Your child misses you." What? *(She squares off at the audience.)* Well, now, that does it! If you are my mother, which you are not. And this alleged child is my child, then that would mean I am a mother and I have never given birth. I don't know nothin' 'bout birthin' no babies! *(She laughs.)* Lala made a funny.
      So whoever sent this, show me the child! Show me!

(**ADMONIA** *offers another telegram.*)

LALA *(To* **ADMONIA***)*   You know you're gonna get fired! *(She reluctantly opens it.)* "The child is in the closet." What closet?
ADMONIA   Pst.

(**ADMONIA** *pushes a button and the center wall unit revolves around to reveal a large black door.* **ADMONIA** *exits, taking* **FLO'RANCE** *with her, leaving* **LALA** *alone.*)

LALA *(Laughing)*   I get it. It's a plot, isn't it. A nasty little CIA, FBI kind of plot. Well let me tell you muthafuckers one thing, there is nothing in that closet, real or manufactured, that will be a dimmer to the glimmer of Lamé the star. You may have gotten Billie and Bessie and a little piece of everyone else who's come along since, but you won't get Lala. My clothes are too fabulous! My hair is too long! My accent too french. That's why I came home to America. To prove you ain't got nothing on me!

(The music for her next song starts, but LALA *is caught up in her tirade, and talks/screams over the music.)*

My mother and Josephine Baker were French patriots together! I've had brunch with the Pope! I've dined with the Queen! Everywhere I go I cause riots! Hunny, I am a star! I have transcended pain! So there! *(Yelling)* Stop the music! Stop that goddamn music.

(The music stops. LALA *slowly walks downstage and singles out someone in the audience.)*

Darling, you're not looking at me. You're staring at that damn door. Did you pay to stare at some fucking door or be mesmerized by my talent?

(To the whole audience:)

Very well! I guess I am going to have to go to the closet door, fling it open, in order to dispel all the nasty little thoughts these nasty little telegrams have planted in your nasty little minds. *(Speaking directly to someone in the audience.)* Do you want me to open the closet door? Speak up, darling, this is live. *(Once she gets the person to say "yes.")* I will open the door, but before I do, let me tell you bastards one last thing. To hell with coming home and to hell with lies and insinuations!

*(*LALA *goes into the closet and after a short pause comes running out, ready to scream, and slams the door. Traumatized to the point of no return, she tells the following story as if it were a jazz solo of rushing, shifting emotions.)*

LALA   I must tell you this dream I had last night. Simply magnifique. In this dream, I'm running naked in Sammy Davis Junior's hair. *(Crazed laughter)*

Yes! I'm caught in this larger than life, deep, dark forest of savage, nappy-nappy hair. The kinky-kinks are choking me, wrapped around my naked arms, thighs, breast, face. I can't breath. And there was nothing in that closet!

And I'm thinking if only I had a machete, I could cut away the kinks. Remove once and for all the roughness. But then I look up and it's coming toward me. Flowing like lava. It's pomade! Ohhh, Sammy!

Yes, cakes and cakes of pomade. Making everything nice and white and smooth and shiny, like my black/white/black/white/black behiney.

Mama no!

And then spikes start cutting through the pomade. Combing the coated kink. Cutting through the kink, into me. There are bloodlines on my back. On my thighs.

It's all over. All over . . . all over me. All over for me.

(LALA *accidentially pulls off her wig to reveal her real hair. Stripped of her "disguise" she recoils like a scared little girl and sings.*)

MOMMY AND DADDY
MEET AND MATE
THE CHILD THAT'S BORN
IS TORN WITH LOVE AND WITH HATE
SHE RUNS AWAY TO FIND HER OWN
AND TRIES TO DENY
WHAT SHE'S ALWAYS KNOWN
THE GIRL INSIDE

(*The closet door opens.* LALA *runs away, and a* LITTLE BLACK GIRL *emerges from the closet. Standing behind her is* ADMONIA.)

(*The* LITTLE GIRL *and* LALA *are in two isolated pools of light, and mirror each other's moves until* LALA *reaches past her reflection and the* LITTLE GIRL *comes to* LALA *and they hug.* ADMONIA *then joins them as* LALA *sings. Music underscored.*)

LALA

WHAT'S LEFT IS THE GIRL INSIDE
THE GIRL WHO DIED
SO A NEW GIRL COULD BE BORN

SLOW FADE TO BLACK

Permutations

(*Lights up on* NORMAL JEAN REYNOLDS. *She is very Southern/country and very young. She wears a simple faded print dress and her hair, slightly mussed, is in plaits. She sits, her dress covering a large oval object.*)

NORMAL My mama used to say, God made the exceptional, then God made the special and when God got bored, he made me. 'Course she don't say too much of nuthin' no more, not since I lay me this egg.

(*She lifts her dress to uncover a large, white egg laying between her legs.*)

Ya see it all got started when I had me sexual relations with the garbage man. Ooowee, did he smell.

No, not bad. No! He smelled of all the good things folks never shoulda thrown away. His sweat was like cantaloupe juice. His neck was like a ripe-red strawberry. And the water that fell from his eyes was like a deep, dark, juicy-juicy grape. I tell ya, it was like fuckin' a fruit salad, only I didn't spit out the seeds. I kept them here, deep inside. And three days later, my belly commence to swell, real big like.

Well my mama locked me off in some dark room, refusin' to let me see light of day 'cause, "What would the neighbors think." At first I cried a lot, but then I grew used to livin' my days in the dark, and my nights in the dark. . . . *(She hums.)* And then it wasn't but a week or so later, my mama off at church, that I got this hurtin' feelin' down here. Worse than anything I'd ever known. And then I started bleedin', real bad. I mean there was blood everywhere. And the pain had me howlin' like a near-dead dog. I tell ya, I was yellin' so loud, I couldn't even hear myself. Noooooooooo! Noooooo! Carrying on something like that.

And I guess it was just too much for the body to take, 'cause the next thing I remember . . . is me coming to and there's this big white egg layin' 'tween my legs. First I thought somebody musta put it there as some kind of joke. But then I noticed that all 'round this egg were thin lines of blood that I could trace to back between my legs.

(Laughing) Well, when my mama come home from church she just about died. "Normal Jean, what's that thing 'tween your legs? Normal Jean, you answer me, girl!" It's not a thing, Mama. It's an egg. And I laid it.

She tried separatin' me from it, but I wasn't havin' it. I stayed in that dark room, huggin', holdin' onto it.

And then I heard it. It wasn't anything that coulda been heard 'round the world, or even in the next room. It was kinda like layin' back in the bath tub, ya know, the water just coverin' your ears . . . and if you lay real still and listen real close, you can hear the sound of your heart movin' the water. You ever done that? Well that's what it sounded like. A heart movin' water. And it was happenin' inside here.

Why, I'm the only person I know who ever lay themselves an egg before so that makes me special. You hear that, Mama? I'm special and so's my egg! And special things supposed to be treated like they matter. That's why every night I count to it, so it knows nuthin' never really ends. And I sing it every song I know so that when it comes out, it's full of all kinds of feelings. And I tell it secrets and laugh with it and . . .

(She suddenly stops and puts her ear to the egg and listens intently.)

Oh! I don't believe it! I thought I heard . . . yes! *(Excited)* Can you hear it? Instead of one heart, there's two. Two little hearts just pattering away. Boom-boom-boom. Boom-boom-boom. Talkin' to each other like old friends. Racin' toward the beginnin' of their lives.

(*Listening*) Oh, no, now there's three . . . four . . . five, six. More hearts than I can count. And they're all alive, beatin' out life inside my egg.

(*We begin to hear the heartbeats, drums, alive inside* NORMAL'S *egg.*)

Any day now, this egg is gonna crack open and what's gonna come out a be the likes of which nobody has ever seen. My babies! And their skin is gonna turn all kinds of shades in the sun and their hair a be growin' every which-a-way. And it won't matter and they won't care 'cause they know they are so rare and so special 'cause it's not everyday a bunch of babies break outta a white egg and start to live.

And nobody better not try and hurt my babies 'cause if they do, they gonna have to deal with me.

Yes, any day now, this shell's gonna crack and my babies are gonna fly. Fly! Fly!

(*She laughs at the thought, but then stops and says the word as if it's the most natural thing in the world.*)

Fly.

BLACKOUT

The Party

(*Before we know what's hit us, a hurricane of energy comes bounding into the space. It is* TOPSY WASHINGTON. *Her hair and dress are a series of stylistic contradictions which are hip, black, and unencumbered.*)

(*Music, spiritual and funky, underscores.*)

TOPSY (*Dancing about.*)   Yoho! Party! Party! Turn up the music! Turn up the music!

Have yaw ever been to a party where there was one fool in the middle of the room, dancing harder and yelling louder than everybody in the entire place? Well, hunny, that fool was me!

Yes, child! The name is Topsy Washington and I love to party. As a matter of fact, when God created the world, on the seventh day, he didn't rest. No child, he P-A-R-T-I-E-D. Partied!

But now let me tell you 'bout this function I went to the other night, way uptown. And baby when I say way uptown, I mean way-way-way-way-way-way-way-way uptown. Somewhere's between 125th Street and infinity.

Inside was the largest gathering of black/Negro/colored Americans you'd ever want to see. Over in one corner you got Nat Turner sippin' champagne out of Eartha Kitt's slipper. And over in another corner, Bert Williams and Malcolm X was discussing existentialism as it relates to the shuffle-ball-change. Girl, Aunt Jemima and Angela Davis was in the kitchen sharing a plate of greens and just goin' off about South Africa.

And then Fats sat down and started to work them eighty-eights. And then Stevie joined in. And then Miles and Duke and Ella and Jimi and Charlie and Sly and Lightin' and Count and Louie!

And then everybody joined in. I tell you all the children was just all up in there, dancing to the rhythm of one beat. Dancing to the rhythm of their own definition. Celebrating in their cultural madness.

And then the floor started to shake. And the walls started to move. And before anybody knew what was happening, the entire room lifted up off the ground. The whole place just took off and went flying through space—defying logic and limitations. Just a spinning and a spinning and a spinning until it disappeared inside of my head.

(Topsy stops dancing and regains her balance and begins to listen to the music in her head. Slowly we begin to hear it, too.)

That's right, girl, there's a party goin' on inside of here. That's why when I walk down the street my hips just sashay all over the place. 'Cause I'm dancing to the music of the madness in me.

And whereas I used to jump into a rage anytime anybody tried to deny who I was, now all I got to do is give attitude, quicker than light, and then go on about the business of being me. 'Cause I'm dancing to the music of the madness in me.

(As Topsy continues to speak, Miss Roj, Lala, Miss Pat, and The Man from SYMBIOSIS revolve on, frozen like soft sculptures.)

TOPSY   And here, all this time I been thinking we gave up our drums. But, naw, we still got 'em. I know I got mine. They're here, in my speech, my walk, my hair, my God, my style, my smile, and my eyes. And everything I need to get over in this world, is inside here, connecting me to everybody and everything that's ever been.

So, hunny, don't waste your time trying to label or define me.

(The sculptures slowly begin to come to "life" and they mirror/echo Topsy's words.)

TOPSY/EVERYBODY   . . . 'cause I'm not what I was ten years ago or ten minutes ago. I'm all of that and then some. And whereas I can't live inside yesterday's pain, I can't live without it.

(All of a sudden, madness erupts on the stage. The sculptures begin to speak all at once. Images of black/Negro/colored Americans begin to flash—images of them dancing past the madness, caught up in the madness, being lynched, rioting, partying, surviving. Mixed in with these images are all the characters from the exhibits.

Through all of this TOPSY *sings. It is a vocal and visual cacophony which builds and builds.)*

LALA

I must tell you about this dream I had last night. Simply magnifique. In this dream I'm running naked in Sammy Davis Junior's hair. Yes. I'm caught in this larger-than-life, deep, dark tangled forest of savage, nappy-nappy hair. Yes, the kinky kinks are choking me, are wrapped around my naked arms, my naked thighs, breast, and face, and I can't breath and there was nothing in that closet.

MISS ROJ

Snap for every time you walk past someone lying in the street smelling like frozen piss and shit and you don't see it. Snap for every crazed bastard who kills himself so as to get the jump on being killed. And snap for every sick muthafucker who, bored with carrying about his fear, takes to shooting up other people.

THE MAN

I have no history. I have no past. I can't. It's too much. It's much too much. I must be able to smile on cue and watch the news with an impersonal eye. I have no stake in the madness. Being black is too emotionally taxing, therefore I will be black only on weekends and holidays.

MISS PAT

Stop playing those drums. I said stop playing those damn drums. You can't stop history. You can't stop time. Those drums will be confiscated once we reach Savannah, so give them up now. Repeat after me: I don't hear any drums and I will not rebel. I will not rebel!

TOPSY *(Singing)*

> THERE'S MADNESS IN ME
> AND THAT MADNESS SETS ME FREE
> THERE'S MADNESS IN ME
> AND THAT MADNESS SETS ME FREE
> THERE'S MADNESS IN ME
> AND THAT MADNESS SETS ME FREE
> THERE'S MADNESS IN ME
> AND THAT MADNESS SETS ME FREE
> THERE'S MADNESS IN ME
> AND THAT MADNESS SETS ME FREE

TOPSY   My power is in my . . .

EVERYBODY   *Madness!*

TOPSY   And my colored contradictions.

(The sculptures freeze with a smile on their faces as we hear the voice of MISS PAT.)*

VOICE OF MISS PAT   Before exiting, check the overhead as any baggage you don't claim, we trash.

BLACKOUT

1987

STUDY QUESTIONS

1. How would your sense of *The Colored Museum* change if it were by a white author?
2. While some plays ask us to "suspend our disbelief" for a couple of hours and to look at the events on stage as if they were real, *The Colored Museum* calls attention to its unreality. Note points in the play where this happens and try to explain why Wolfe engages in this sort of "metafictional" drama.
3. Discuss the "tragicomic" nature of this play. How are the tragedy and comedy intertwined?
4. What are the advantages of having eleven short "plays" rather than one continuous action comprise *The Colored Museum*? What, if any, are the disadvantages?
5. At times the language in the play is graphic—even, some might argue, obscene. Is the explicit language justified, or would the play be better off without it?

POSSIBLE ESSAY TOPICS

1. Explore similarities between Stanek in *Protest* and Hamlet in Shakespeare's play.
2. Compare *The Colored Museum* and *Protest* as plays about the psychological effects of living under various kinds of oppression.
3. Discuss Havel's idea of the paradoxical positive effects that may come out of living in a totalitarian state.
4. Discuss the significance of the title of *The Colored Museum*.

SELECTED FILMOGRAPHY OF MOVIE ADAPTATIONS OF PLAYS

The following is a list of major cinematic adaptations of the plays in the drama section.

PLAY	DATE	DIRECTOR	STARS
Antigonê	1962	Dinos Katsourides	Irene Papas, Manos Katrakis
	1991	Amy Greenfield	Janet Eilber, Amy Greenfield
Oedipus Rex	1957	Tyrone Guthrie	Douglas Campbell
	1967	Pier Palol Pasilini	Franco Citti, Carmelo Bene
	1970	Bernard Haitink	Neil Rosenhein
	1993	Julie Taymor	Philip Langridge, Seiji Ozawa
Hamlet	1948	Laurence Olivier	Laurence Olivier
	1969	Tony Richardson	Nichol Williamson, Judy Parfitt
	1970	Peter Wood	Richard Chamberlain, John Gielgud
	1990	Franco Zeffierelli	Mel Gibson, Glenn Close
	1996	Kenneth Branagh	Kenneth Branagh, Kate Winslet
Much Ado About Nothing	1967	Al Cooke	Robert Stephens, Maggie Smith
	1984	Stuart Burge	Robert Linsay, Cherie Lunghi
	1993	Kenneth Branagh	Kenneth Branagh, Emma Thompson
A Doll's House	1959	George Schaefer	Julie Harris, Christopher Plummer
	1989	Patrick Garland	Claire Bloom, Anthony Hopkins
The Glass Menagerie	1950	Irving Rapper	Arthur Kennedy, Gertrude Lawrence
	1973	Anthony Harvey	Katherine Hepburn, Sam Waterston
	1987	Paul Newman	John Malkovich, Joanne Woodward

TEXT CREDITS

INDEX OF TERMS

INDEX OF AUTHORS AND TITLES

INDEX OF FIRST LINES OF POEMS

1007